Lecture Notes in Computer Science 3757

Commenced Publication in 1973
Founding and Former Series Editors:
Gerhard Goos, Juris Hartmanis, and Jan van Leeuwen

Anand Rangarajan   Baba Vemuri
Alan L. Yuille (Eds.)

Energy Minimization Methods in Computer Vision and Pattern Recognition

5th International Workshop, EMMCVPR 2005
St. Augustine, FL, USA, November 9-11, 2005
Proceedings

 Springer

Volume Editors

Anand Rangarajan
Baba Vemuri
University of Florida
Department of Computer and Information Science and Engineering
Room E301, CSE Building, Gainesville, FL 32611-6120, USA
E-mail: {anand, vemuri}@cise.ufl.edu

Alan L. Yuille
University of California at Los Angeles, Departments of Statistics and Psychology
7461D Franz Hall, Los Angeles, CA 90095-1563, USA
E-mail: yuille@stat.ucla.edu

Library of Congress Control Number: 2005935532

CR Subject Classification (1998): I.5, I.4, I.2.10, I.3.5, F.2.2, F.1.1

ISSN   0302-9743
ISBN-10   3-540-30287-5 Springer Berlin Heidelberg New York
ISBN-13   978-3-540-30287-2 Springer Berlin Heidelberg New York

Springer is a part of Springer Science+Business Media

springeronline.com

© Springer-Verlag Berlin Heidelberg 2005
Printed in Germany

Typesetting: Camera-ready by author, data conversion by Scientific Publishing Services, Chennai, India
Printed on acid-free paper   SPIN: 11585978   06/3142   5 4 3 2 1 0

Preface

This volume consists of the 42 papers presented at the International Workshop on Energy Minimization Methods in Computer Vision and Pattern Recognition (EMMCVPR 2005), which was held at the Hilton St. Augustine Historic Bayfront, St. Augustine, Florida, USA, during November 9–11, 2005. This workshop is the fifth in a series which began with EMMCVPR 1997 held in Venice, Italy, in May 1997 and continued with EMMCVPR 1999 held in York, UK, in July 1999, EMMCVPR 2001 held in Sophia-Antipolis, France, in September 2001 and EMMCVPR 2003 held in Lisbon, Portugal, in July 2003.

Many problems in computer vision and pattern recognition (CVPR) are couched in the framework of optimization. The minimization of a global quantity, often referred to as the energy, forms the bulwark of most approaches in CVPR. Disparate approaches such as discrete and probabilistic formulations on the one hand and continuous, deterministic strategies on the other often have optimization or energy minimization as a common theme. Instances of energy minimization arise in Gibbs/Markov modeling, Bayesian decision theory, geometric and variational approaches and in areas in CVPR such as object recognition and retrieval, image segmentation, registration, reconstruction, classification and data mining.

The aim of this workshop was to bring together researchers with interests in these disparate areas of CVPR but with an underlying commitment to some form of not only energy minimization but global optimization in general. Although the subject is traditionally well represented in major international conferences on CVPR, recent advances—information geometry, Bayesian networks and graphical models, Markov chain Monte Carlo, graph algorithms, implicit methods in variational approaches and PDEs—deserve an informal and focused hearing in a workshop setting.

We received 120 submissions each of which was reviewed by three members of the Program Committee and the Co-chairs. Based on the reviews, 24 papers were accepted for oral presentation and 18 for poster presentation. In this volume, no distinction is made between papers that were presented orally or as posters. EMMCVPR from its inception has focused on complementary (but sometimes adversarial) optimization approaches to image analysis—both in problem formulation and in solution methodologies. This "coopetition" is depicted as a mandala in Fig. 1.

The book is organized into four sections with the section titles being *Probabilistic and Informational Approaches*, *Combinatorial Approaches*, *Variational Approaches* and *Other Approaches and Applications*. The section titles follow the basic categories depicted in Figure 1 with the title "Other Approaches" used to lump together methodologies that do not easily fit into the above opponent-quadrant format.

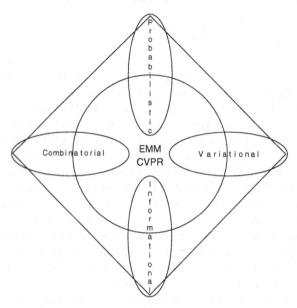

Fig. 1. The four dominant approaches to EMMCVPR arranged in an opponent-quadrant format

EMMCVPR 2005 also included keynote talks by three distinguished scientists: David Mumford (Brown University, USA), Christopher Small (University of Waterloo, Canada), and Demetri Terzopoulos (New York University, USA). The invited talks spanned the areas of differential geometry, shape analysis and deformable models. These three researchers have played leading roles in the fields of algebraic geometry, shape theory and image analysis, respectively.

We would like to thank Marcello Pelillo and Edwin Hancock for their pioneering efforts in launching this series of successful workshops with EMMCVPR 1997 and for much subsequent advice, organizational tips and encouragement. We also thank Anil Jain (Co-chair of EMMCVPR 2001), Josiane Zerubia (Co-chair of EMMCVPR 2001 and EMMCVPR 2003) and Mário Figueiredo (Co-chair of EMMCVPR 2001 and EMMCVPR 2003) for their support. We thank the Program Committee (and numerous un-named graduate students and postdocs who were drafted as reviewers in the 11th hour) for careful and timely reviews which made our task easier.

We acknowledge and thank the University of Florida for providing organizational and financial support to EMMCVPR 2005, the International Association of Pattern Recognition (IAPR) for sponsoring the workshop and providing publicity, and finally Springer for including EMMCVPR under the LNCS rubric.

August 2005   Anand Rangarajan
                                                   Baba Vemuri
                                                   Alan Yuille

Organization

Program Co-chairs

Anand Rangarajan — University of Florida, Gainesville, USA
Baba Vemuri — University of Florida, Gainesville, USA
Alan Yuille — University of California, Los Angeles (UCLA), USA

Program Committee

Arunava Banerjee — University of Florida, USA
Ronen Basri — Weizmann Institute, Israel
Yuri Boykov — University of Western Ontario, Canada
Joachim Buhmann — Eidgenössische Technische Hochschule (ETH) Zürich, Switzerland
Yunmei Chen — University of Florida, USA
Laurent Cohen — Université Paris Dauphine, France
Tim Cootes — University of Manchester, UK
Christos Davatzikos — University of Pennsylvania, USA
Rachid Deriche — INRIA Sophia-Antipolis, France
Mário Figueiredo — Instituto Superior Técnico (IST), Portugal
Daniel Freedman — Rensselaer Polytechnic Institute (RPI), USA
Georgy Gimel'farb — University of Auckland, New Zealand
Edwin Hancock — University of York, UK
Jeffrey Ho — University of Florida, USA
Benjamin Kimia — Brown University, USA
Ron Kimmel — Technion, Israel
Shang-Hong Lai — National Tsing Hua University, Taiwan
Xiuwen Liu — Florida State University, USA
Ravikanth Malladi — GE India Technology Center, India
Jose Marroquin — Centro de Investigación en Matemáticas (CIMAT), Mexico
Stephen Maybank — Birkbeck College, UK
Dimitris Metaxas — Rutgers University, USA
Washington Mio — Florida State University, USA
Nikos Paragios — École Nationale des Ponts et Chaussées (ENPC), France
Marcello Pelillo — University of Venice, Italy
Karl Rohr — University of Heidelberg, Germany
Guillermo Sapiro — University of Minnesota, USA
Sudeep Sarkar — University of South Florida, USA
Mubarak Shah — University of Central Florida, USA
Kaleem Siddiqi — McGill University, Canada

Anuj Srivastava   Florida State University, USA
Lawrence Staib   Yale University, USA
Hemant Tagare   Yale University, USA
Alain Trouvé   Université Paris 13, France
Joachim Weickert   Saarland University, Germany
Richard Wilson   University of York, UK
Anthony Yezzi   Georgia Tech., USA
Laurent Younes   Johns Hopkins University, USA
Ramin Zabih   Cornell University, USA
Josiane Zerubia   INRIA Sophia-Antipolis, France
Song-Chun Zhu   University of California, Los Angeles (UCLA), USA

Additional Reviewers

Lishui Cheng   Shanghai Jiao Tong University (SJTU), China
Bing Jian   University of Florida, USA
Santosh Kodipaka   University of Florida, USA
Adrian Peter   Harris Corporation, USA
Ajit Rajwade   University of Florida, USA
Fei Wang   University of Florida, USA

Sponsoring Institutions

University of Florida, USA
International Association for Pattern Recognition (IAPR)

Table of Contents

I Probabilistic and Informational Approaches

II   Combinatorial Approaches

III   Variational Approaches

IV   Other Approaches and Applications

Part I

Probabilistic and Informational Approaches

Adaptive Simulated Annealing for Energy Minimization Problem in a Marked Point Process Application

Guillaume Perrin[1,2], Xavier Descombes[2], and Josiane Zerubia[2]

[1] Mas Laboratory, Ecole Centrale Paris, Grande Voie des Vignes,
92290 Chatenay-Malabry, France
[2] Ariana, joint research group INRIA/I3S,
INRIA Sophia Antipolis, 2004, route des Lucioles, BP 93,
06902 Sophia Antipolis Cedex, France
Tel : +33 4 9238 7857, Fax : +33 4 9238 7643
Firstname.Lastname@inria.fr
http://www.inria.fr/ariana

Abstract. We use marked point processes to detect an unknown number of trees from high resolution aerial images. This is in fact an energy minimization problem, where the energy contains a prior term which takes into account the geometrical properties of the objects, and a data term to match these objects to the image. This stochastic process is simulated via a Reversible Jump Markov Chain Monte Carlo procedure, which embeds a Simulated Annealing scheme to extract the best configuration of objects.

We compare here different cooling schedules of the Simulated Annealing algorithm which could provide some good minimization in a short time. We also study some adaptive proposition kernels.

1 Introduction

We aim at extracting tree crowns from remotely sensed images in order to assess some useful parameters such as the number of trees, their diameter, and the density of the stem. This problem has been widely tackled in the literature over the past years. In the case of color infrared images, some methods use a pixel based approach and give the delineation of the tree crowns [11], other ones use an object based approach by modelling a synthetic tree crown template to find the tree top positions [18].

In [22], we proposed to use a marked point process approach which can embed most of the geometric properties in the distribution of the trees, especially in plantations where we obtained good results. Indeed, marked point processes enable to model complex geometrical objects in a scene and have been exploited for different applications in image processing [6]. The context is stochastic, and our goal is to minimize an energy on the state space of all possible configurations of objects, using some Markov Chain Monte Carlo (MCMC) algorithms

A. Rangarajan et al. (Eds.): EMMCVPR 2005, LNCS 3757, pp. 3–17, 2005.

and Simulated Annealing (SA). In this paper, we will focus on the optimization problem.

The first section is dedicated to recall some definitions about marked point processes. Then, we present our model adapted to tree crown extraction, and the SA algorithm. In the last section, we perform a range of tests in order to study acceleration techniques of the SA that can be used to get good results in a faster way.

2 Definitions and Notations

For more details about marked point processes we refer to [31], and for their applications to image processing to [6].

2.1 Marked Point Process

Let S be a set of interest, called the state space, typically a subset of $\mathbb{R}^n$. A configuration of objects in S is an unordered list of objects :

$$\mathbf{x} = \{x_1, \ldots, x_n\} \in \Psi_n, x_i \in S, i = 1, \ldots, n \tag{1}$$

A point process X in S is a measurable mapping from a probability space $(\Omega, \mathcal{A}, \mathbb{P})$ to configurations of points of S, in other words a random variable whose realizations are random configurations of points. These configurations $\mathbf{x}$ belong to

$$\Psi = \bigcup_n \Psi_n \tag{2}$$

where Ψ_n contains all configurations of a finite number n of points of S.

A marked point process living in $S = \mathcal{P} \times \mathcal{K}$ is a point process where some marks in $\mathcal{K}$ are added to the positions of the points in $\mathcal{P}$. A configuration of objects $\mathbf{x} = \{(p_1, k_1), \ldots, (p_n, k_n)\}$ is also a finite set of marked points. The marks are some parameters that fully describe the object. For example, ellipses are described by the position of their center, their major and minor axis, and their orientation.

The most obvious example of point processes is the homogeneous Poisson process of intensity measure $\nu(.)$, proportional to the Lebesgue measure on S. It induces a complete spatial randomness, given the fact that the positions are uniformly and independently distributed.

2.2 Application to Object Extraction

The marked point process framework has been successfully applied in different image analysis problems [3, 6, 21, 22], the main issue being that we do not know a priori the number of objects to be extracted. The approach consists of modelling an observed image $\mathcal{I}$ (see Fig. (2), lefthandside) as a realization of a marked point process of geometrical objects. The position state space $\mathcal{P}$ will be given by the image size, and the mark state space $\mathcal{K}$ will be some compact set of $\mathbb{R}^d$.

2.3 Energy Minimization Problem

We consider the probability distribution $\mu(.)$ of an homogeneous Poisson process living in S with intensity measure $\nu(.)$, which gives us a probability measure on Ψ (see [31]). Then, if the probability distribution $\mathcal{P}_X(.)$ of a marked point process X is uniformly continuous with respect to $\mu(.)$, the Radon Nikodym theorem (for more details see [15] for example) defines its unnormalized density $f(.)$ with respect to this dominating reference measure as :

$$\mathcal{P}_X(d\mathbf{x}) = \frac{1}{Z}f(\mathbf{x})\mu(d\mathbf{x}) = \frac{1}{Z}\exp(-U(\mathbf{x}))\mu(d\mathbf{x}) \tag{3}$$

where Z is a normalizing constant, and $U(\mathbf{x})$ the energy of the configuration $\mathbf{x}$.

Within the Bayesian framework, given the data $\mathcal{I}$, the posterior distribution $f(\mathbf{x}|\mathcal{I})$ can be written as :

$$f(\mathbf{x}|\mathcal{I}) \propto f_p(\mathbf{x})\mathcal{L}(\mathcal{I}|\mathbf{x}) \tag{4}$$

From now on we will write $f(\mathbf{x}) = f(\mathbf{x}|\mathcal{I})$. We aim at finding the Maximum A Posteriori estimator $\mathbf{x}_{MAP}$ of this density, which is also the minimum of the Gibbs energy $U(\mathbf{x})$. As for many energy minimization problems, the prior term $f_p(\mathbf{x})$ can be seen as a regularization or a penalization term, while the likelihood $\mathcal{L}(\mathcal{I}|\mathbf{x})$ can be seen as a data term. We note Ψ_{min} the set of all global minima of $U(\mathbf{x})$, of energy $U_{min} > -\infty$. By analogy, $U_{max} \leq +\infty$ is the maximum of $U(\mathbf{x})$.

The landscape of $U(\mathbf{x})$ in the problem of tree crown extraction is very elaborate. $U(\mathbf{x})$ contains a lot of local minima [22], the classical SA scheme should be adapted in order to give a good estimation of $\mathbf{x}_{MAP}$ in a reasonable time.

2.4 Simulation of Marked Point Processes

A marked point process X is fully defined by its unnormalized density $f(\mathbf{x})$ under a reference measure, which is often in practice the homogeneous Poisson measure. Sampling a realization of this process is not obvious, this requires some MCMC algorithms, with $\mathcal{P}_X(d\mathbf{x})$ as equilibrium distribution.

In particular, the Reversible Jump MCMC (RJMCMC) algorithm [12] allows us to build a Markov Chain (X_n) which jumps between the different dimensions of Ψ. At each step, the transition of this chain is managed by a set of proposition kernels $\{Q_m(\mathbf{x}, .)\}_{m \in M}$ which propose the transformation of the current configuration $\mathbf{x}$ into a new configuration $\mathbf{y}$. This move is accepted with a probability $\alpha = \min\{1, R(\mathbf{x}, \mathbf{y})\}$, where :

$$R(\mathbf{x}, \mathbf{y}) = \frac{\mathcal{P}_X(d\mathbf{y})Q_m(\mathbf{y}, d\mathbf{x})}{\mathcal{P}_X(d\mathbf{x})Q_m(\mathbf{x}, d\mathbf{y})} \tag{5}$$

is called the Green ratio. (X_n) converges ergodically to the distribution $\mathcal{P}_X$ under some stability condition on the Papangelou conditional intensity [31] which must be bounded (see [10], with a kernel containing uniform birth and death).

Model optimization is achieved by this RJMCMC algorithm embedded in a SA scheme. This consists of sampling $f^{\frac{1}{T_n}}(.)$ instead of $f(.)$, where T_n is a temperature parameter which tends to zero as $n \to \infty$. The Markov chain (X_n) is now nonhomogeneous, and the convergence properties detailed in [10] do not apply anymore.

3   Our Model for Tree Crown Extraction

We aim at extracting tree crowns from remotely sensed images of forests. Our data contain infrared information, which enhances the chlorophyllean matter of the trees. To perform this object extraction, we use a marked point process of ellipses. The associated state space S is therefore a bounded set of $\mathbb{R}^5$:

$$S = \mathcal{P} \times \mathcal{K} = [0, X_M] \times [0, Y_M] \times [a_m, a_M] \times [b_m, b_M] \times [0, \pi[\qquad (6)$$

where X_M and Y_M are respectively the width and the length of the image $\mathfrak{I}$, (a_m, a_M) and (b_m, b_M) respectively the minimum and the maximum of the major and the minor axes, and $\theta \in [0, \pi[$ the orientation of our objects.

As explained in Section (2.3), we work in the Bayesian framework : the density $f(\mathbf{x})$ of one configuration is split into a prior term and a likelihood term.

3.1   Prior Energy $U_p(\mathbf{x})$

As we are working on plantations of poplars, we model the periodic pattern of the alignments in the prior term, by adding some constraints to the configurations (see [22] for more details) :

- a repulsive term between two overlapping objects $x_i \sim_r x_j$ in order to avoid over-detection. We introduce an overlapping coefficient $\mathcal{A}(x_1, x_2) \in [0, 1]$ which penalizes more or less $x_1 \sim_r x_2$ depending on the way they overlap :

$$U_r(\mathbf{x}) = \gamma_r \sum_{x_i \sim_r x_j} \mathcal{A}(x_i, x_j), \ \gamma_r \in \mathbb{R}^+ \qquad (7)$$

- an attractive term that favours regular alignments in the configuration. The quality of the alignment of two objects $x_1 \sim_a x_2$, with respect to two pre-defined vectors of alignments, is assessed via a quality function $\mathcal{Q}(x_1, x_2) \in [0, 1]$:

$$U_a(\mathbf{x}) = \gamma_a \sum_{x_i \sim_a x_j} \mathcal{Q}(x_i, x_j), \ \gamma_a \in \mathbb{R}^- \qquad (8)$$

- for stability reasons and because of the attractive term, we have to avoid extreme closeness of objects. This can be done by adding a hard core constraint in our prior process :

$$U_h(\mathbf{x}) = \begin{cases} +\infty & \text{if } \exists (x_i, x_j) \in \mathbf{x} \mid d(x_i, x_j) < 1 \\ 0 & \text{otherwise} \end{cases} \qquad (9)$$

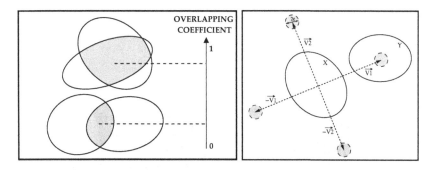

Fig. 1. Lefthandside : two overlapping objects and the quality of this interaction. Righthandside : The four regions around one object where some alignments are favoured.

The first two relationships are shown in Fig. (1). The prior energy is :

$$U_p(\mathbf{x}) = U_r(\mathbf{x}) + U_a(\mathbf{x}) + U_h(\mathbf{x}) \tag{10}$$

3.2 Likelihood $\mathcal{L}(\mathcal{I}|\mathbf{x})$

The likelihood of the data $\mathcal{I}$ given a configuration $\mathbf{x}$ is a statistical model of the image. We consider that the data can be represented by some Gaussian mixture of two classes (the trees with some high grey value and the background with low grey value), where each pixel is associated to one of these two classes :

- $\mathcal{C}_i = \mathcal{N}(m_i, \sigma_i)$ for the pixels inside at least one of the objects of the configuration,
- $\mathcal{C}_o = \mathcal{N}(m_o, \sigma_o)$ for the pixels outside.

Other models to define the likelihood are studied in [22].

3.3 RJMCMC Algorithm

As explained in Section (2.4), we use a RJMCMC dynamics to sample our marked point process. The proposition kernel contains uniform birth and death, translation, dilation, split and merge, and birth and death in a neighbourhood. More details about this kernel can be found in [22].

3.4 Data and Results

Here we present one extraction result obtained on an aerial image of forests provided by the French Forest Inventory (IFN). The parameters of the model can be found in [22]. To compare this result to those obtained in the next sections, a very slow plateau cooling schedule was chosen in order to have a good estimation of U_{min}. Tab. (1) presents some statistics related to the simulation, and Fig. (2)

Table 1. Statistics about the extraction after a slow decrease of the temperature ($N = 30$ millions iterations)

Final energy	$U_N = 134662$
Number of objects	$n(X_N) = 292$

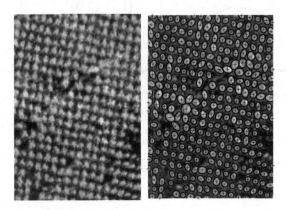

Fig. 2. Lefthandside : some data provided by IFN (resolution 50cm/pixel). Righthand-side : the poplar extraction result, after 30 millions iterations (45 minutes on a Red Hat Linux 3GHz machine).

shows the image and the extraction result. In the following, each scenario will be simulated 10 times, and the statistics will represent the mean values of the statistics observed during these simulations.

4   Simulated Annealing

The SA algorithm is a stochastic global optimization procedure which exploits an analogy between the search of the minima $\mathbf{x} \in \Psi_{min}$ and a statistical thermo-dynamic problem. As explained in [29], the thermal mobility of molecules is lost when the temperature is slowly decreased, going from a liquid state to a pure crystal which is a stable state of minimum energy. Cerny [5] and Kirpatrick [17] simultaneously applied this analogy and proposed an algorithm using a Metropo-lis Monte Carlo method and some temperature parameters, in order to find the global minima of an energy function $U(x)$. Ever since it has been widely used in many optimization problems including applications in image analysis [34]. In this section, we present this algorithm, its convergence properties and some ideas to accelerate it.

4.1   The Algorithm

At each iteration of the SA algorithm, a candidate point y is generated from the current position x using the distribution $Q(x, .)$, and accepted or refused via an acceptance ratio $\alpha(x, y)$. This acceptance ratio is controlled by a parameter T called the temperature [5, 17], which slowly decreases to 0 during the algorithm:

$$\alpha(x, y) = \min \left\{ 1, \exp \left(-\frac{U(y) - U(x)}{T} \right) \right\} \tag{11}$$

The principle of SA is also to accept some random ascent moves since the temperature parameter is high, in order to escape local minima of the energy. When $T \to \infty$, the algorithm tends to sample a uniform distribution on S, while for $T \to 0$ it tends to a Dirac distribution on Ψ_{min}. The evolution of the temperature parameter T_n during the optimization process is called a cooling schedule. SA also samples a nonhomogeneous Markov chain (X_n) which obliges to attain the states of minimum energy Ψ_{min} with an appropriate cooling schedule. A schedule is said to be asymptotically good [2] if it satisfies :

$$\lim_{n \to \infty} P(X_n \in \Psi_{min}) = 1 \tag{12}$$

4.2 Convergence Results

Originally, SA algorithm was introduced for combinatorial problems (especially the Traveling Salesman Problem and Graph Partitioning) on some large finite solution set S. Thus, most of the convergence proofs have been obtained in the case of $\sharp(S) < \infty$.

Geman and Geman [9] showed that some logarithmic decrease of the temperature

$$\lim_{n \to \infty} T_n \log(n) \geq K > 0 \tag{13}$$

with K large enough, depending on $\Delta = U_{max} - U_{min}$, was sufficient to guarantee the convergence (12). Then, Hajek [14] proved that K could be the maximum of the depths d_{x_m} of local minima x_m. He also linked the constant K with the energy landscape, we will see how crucial it is to adapt SA to the energy of the problem at hand. Details about this theorem, and speed of convergence can be found in [29].

More recently, some results have been established in the case of general state spaces for continuous global optimization. Most of the time, the case of compact sets was studied [19], while in [1, 13] more general state spaces were taken. The logarithmic schedule $T_n \geq \frac{K}{\log(n+2)}$ was proven to be asymptotically good for some constant K depending on the energy landscape. This cooling schedule can be accelerated with some restrictions on the proposal distribution $Q(x, .)$.

Finally, point process theory and SA have been linked in [30] and [24], where some convergence proofs of inhomogeneous Markov chain were established respectively in the case of a birth and death process and a RJMCMC scheme.

4.3 Acceleration Methods

In the previous subsection, we noticed that a logarithmic decrease was needed to ensure the convergence of SA. However, these schedules require too much computation time and are not achievable in practice. Even if we are bound to lose the convergence conditions, we prefer implementing some faster cooling schedules. Many methods have been proposed in that prospect (see [2, 7, 23, 32] for instance), and we will test some of them in our application.

The first family of methods consists in adapting the cooling schedule itself [7, 29, 32]. Most of the cooling schedules in the literature rely on exponential, also called geometrical, cooling schedules of the form :

$$T_n = T_0 * a^n \tag{14}$$

with $a < 1$ and very close to 1 (see [29] for more details). A slight adaptation of this schedule brings us to the fixed length plateau cooling schedule, where the temperature parameter is decreased every $k * n$ iterations of the algorithm (k fixed, $n \in \mathbb{N}$). This enables the Markov chain to have more time, at a given temperature, to reach its equilibrium distribution $\mathcal{P}_X^{T_n}(dx) = f(x)^{\frac{1}{T_n}} \mu(dx)$.

Another family of methods consists in adapting the candidate distribution at each step [8, 13, 16]. In the Fast SA [26] or in the Adaptive SA (ASA) [16] for instance, the convergence relies on the asumption that we globally explore at each step the feasible region, i.e. that each state is reachable from the current position X_k, though the probability of sampling points far from X_k decreases to 0 when $n \to \infty$. An additional temperature parameter t_n is added in the proposition density of the next candidate, which can decrease to 0 much faster than logarithmically (exponentially for the ASA), while the cooling schedule of the temperature parameter $T_n \to 0$ without any speed constraint.

In practice, we will run some finite schedules, starting from a temperature T_0 and ending with a temperature T_N. Some papers tackle this problem of optimal schedules in some finite time in combinatorial optimization problems [4, 25]. The goal is to find the optimal temperature schedule for a given number of iterations N, i.e. the schedule that gives the lowest expected value of energy. This leads to the "Best So Far" for instance, which consists in taking the minimum value of the energy $U(X_n)$ encountered during the simulation, instead of the "Where You Are" (last) value $U(X_N)$.

However, finite schedules lead all to what is called broken ergodicity [23], especially in applications with a continuous state space of varying dimension. The Markov chain is no longer ergodic because the state space is too big to be explored and would require a huge number of iterations at each temperature, even if there is a nonzero probability of reaching any state from any other state. This phenomenon have been studied in [20], and a new adaptive annealing schedule which takes into account the convergence delay has been proposed. This one was inspired by [7, 27], where the authors proposed to decrease the temperature in a plateau cooling schedule only if the mean of the energy during the current plateau was bigger than the former one :

$$T_{n+1} = \begin{cases} T_n \text{ if } E[U(X)]_n \leq E[U(X)]_{n-1} \\ a * T_n \text{ otherwise} \end{cases} \tag{15}$$

where $E[U(X)]_n = \frac{1}{k}\sum_{i=kn}^{i=(k+1)n} U(X_i)$. In practice this schedule is very long, that is why Ortner [20] proposed to accept the decrease with less constraints. Moreover, he remarked that the selection of the minimum was done during a specific period of the cooling schedule, called the critical temperature. He also constructed an heuristic that enables the cooling schedule to decrease faster when the region is not interesting, and to go slower, or even to warm the temperature, when the temperature is critical. This adaptive schedule is very interesting because it fits the energy landscape of the problem.

To conclude, in complex optimization problems in a finite time like the problem we have to solve, the adaptability of the algorithm is of high interest, in order to avoid too much computation. We compare in the next section a few results obtained with some of these schedules.

5   Comparative Results

Different experiments were carried out in order to compare some cooling schedules of the SA in our energy minimization problem. As explained above, we simulated 10 times each experiment to avoid too much imprecision.

5.1   Initial and Final Temperature

We still have not discussed the choice of the two bounds T_0 and T_N. In the literature, it is often suggested to link T_0 with the standard deviation of the energy $U(x)$ of random objects $x \in S$, typically twice as large (see [33]). We can, for example, calculate this value by sampling at infinite temperature. For the stopping temperature T_N, it is more difficult to estimate a good value in continuous problems, while in discrete problems [33] suggests taking it of the order of the smallest energy scale. Generally speaking, the cooling schedule should always take into account the energy to be optimized, its scale, its landscape, the number and the size of local minima (see [23]).

First, we would like to assess the influence of the initial temperature T_0 in our problem. To that prospect, we use Fig. (3) and take twice the standard deviation as a first initialization of the temperature : $T_0 \simeq 25000$. Then, we compare this value with a bigger value $T_0 = 1000000$ and some smaller ones $T_0 = 100$ and $T_0 = 1$, in a plateau cooling schedule of fixed length $k = 5000$. Only a is varying in order to end the cooling schedule at the same final temperature : $T_N = 10^{-9}$. Some statistics are presented in Tab. (2), and compare the mean value of the last energy $U(X_N)$ (Where-You-Are), the standard deviation of this energy, and the mean value of the total number of extracted objects. What can be deduced from these results is that the estimation of the initial temperature with the standard deviation is not the best one, considering the final value of the energy. With $T_0 = 100$, we obtain better results. One can suppose that at higher temperature, we lose some time and that the selection of the minimum begins around $T = 100$ (critical temperature). When the cooling starts with $T_0 = 1 < 100$, it is 'too late'.

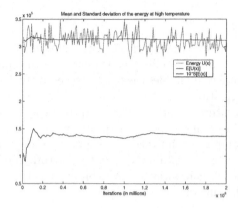

Fig. 3. Estimation of the standard deviation of the energy during an infinite temperature simulation

Table 2. Different starting temperatures T_0, with the same number of iterations ($N = 2000000$) and the same final temperature $T_N = 10^{-9}$

	$T_0 = 1000000$	$T_0 = 25000$	$T_0 = 100$	$T_0 = 1$
Iterations ($*10^6$)	2	2	2	2
Plateau length k	500	500	500	500
Cooling parameter a	0.9914	0.9923	0.9937	0.9948
Mean $E[U(X_N)]$	136317	136200	**136002**	136713
Standard deviation $\sigma[U(X_N)]$	216.12	222.05	139.07	314.65
Mean $E[n(X_N)]$	282.0	283.6	284.3	285.3

Then, we could try to change the final temperature, starting from $T_0 = 100$. The results are presented in Tab. (3). It is interesting to note that it is less important to end with a very low temperature than it is to spend more time around the critical temperature. It seems that $T_N = 10^{-4}$ is a good final temperature. We also deduce that the interesting part of the schedule is $100 > T > 10^{-4}$. The best schedule would be perhaps the one which decreases quickly to this critical temperature, then waits, and then goes fast to a very low temperature for a quasi-ICM schedule.

Table 3. Different ending temperatures T_N, with the same number of iterations ($N = 2000000$) and the same starting temperature $T_0 = 100$

	$T_N = 10^{-3}$	$T_N = 10^{-4}$	$T_N = 10^{-5}$	$T_N = 10^{-7}$	$T_N = 10^{-9}$	$T_N = 10^{-13}$
Iter. ($*10^6$)	2	2	2	2	2	2
k	500	500	500	500	500	500
a	0.9971	0.9966	0.996	0.9948	0.9937	0.9914
$E[U(X_N)]$	135914	**135843**	135848	135961	136002	136713
$\sigma[U(X_N)]$	113.43	239.11	140.88	187.77	139.07	96.70
$E[n(X_N)]$	284.1	284.7	285.0	284.9	284.3	284.6

5.2   Parameters a and k of the Plateau Cooling Schedule

The problem in this cooling schedule is also to determine the two parameters a and k. During how many iterations should the Markov chain X_n stay at a given temperature ? Some tests have been performed in order to see the influence of these parameters. The results are shown in Tab. (4). It appears that the parameters a and k (keeping the same number of iterations) do not have a big impact on the results. This makes sense, because whatever they are, the Markov chain will spend the same time in the critical zone of the temperature.

Table 4. Different fixed length plateau schedules, with the same number of iterations ($N = 2000000$), initial temperature $T_0 = 100$ and stopping temperature $T_N = 10^{-9}$

	$k = 10$	$k = 100$	$k = 500$	$k = 1000$
Iter. ($*10^6$)	2	2	2	2
a	0.99987	0.99874	0.9937	0.9874
$E[U(X_N)]$	135944	136054	136002	135876
$\sigma[U(X_N)]$	151.24	266.65	139.07	226.07
$E[n(X_N)]$	286.1	285.1	284.3	286.4

5.3   Adaptive Cooling Schedule

In the previous results, we noticed that some better values for T_0 and T_N could be found. Unfortunately, we cannot afford doing so many simulations for every image for which we want to use our model. That is why the cooling schedule proposed in [20, 21] is interesting, because it adapts the cooling speed to the energy landscape.

We still set $k = 500$, and $k' = 50$ the length of the 10 sub-plateaus. We note $E[U(X)]_n^i = \frac{1}{k'} \sum_{j=kn+ik'}^{j=kn+(i+1)k'} U(X_j)$ the mean of the energy on the ith sub-plateau. We have $E[U(X)]_n = \frac{1}{10} \sum_{i=0}^{i=9} E[U(X)]_n^i$. A decrease of the temperature would be accepted if at least one sub-plateau has a mean energy $E[U(X)]_n^i$ lower than the global former energy $E[U(X)]_{n-1}$. Moreover, the cooling parameter a_n now depends on n, and we can accelerate or even warm the temperature (if the ergodicity is broken) according to :

$$T_{n+1} = \begin{cases} \frac{1}{a_n} * T_n \text{ if } \sharp\left\{E[U(X)]_n^i \leq E[U(X)]_{n-1}\right\} = 0 \text{ and } a_n = a_n^{\frac{1}{r}} \\ a_n * T_n \text{ if } \sharp\left\{E[U(X)]_n^i \leq E[U(X)]_{n-1}\right\} \in [1,4] \\ a_n * T_n \text{ if } \sharp\left\{E[U(X)]_n^i \leq E[U(X)]_{n-1}\right\} \geq 5 \text{ and } a_n = a_n^r \end{cases} \quad (16)$$

We use $r = 0.9$, and threshold the parameter a_n in order that $0.96 < a_n < 0.996$. Obviously, starting from a temperature T_0 and ending at a temperature T_N, we cannot predict the number of iterations it will take.

In Tab. (5), we compare the results of different adaptive schedules with $T_0 = 25000$ and $T_N = 10^{-9}$. S1 is the simple plateau schedule with a constant speed studied before ($a = 0.9923$). Then, S2 and S3 are some adaptive plateau

Table 5. Comparison of different schedules with $T_0 = 25000$ and $T_N = 10^{-9}$

	S1	S2 : 80%	S3 : 90%	S4 : 100%	S5
Iter. ($*10^6$)	2	2	2	2	$E[N] = 2.03$
Plateau length k	500	500	500	500	500
Cooling parameters	$a = 0.9923$	$a_1 = 0.9789$ $a_2 = 0.9957$	$a_1 = 0.9583$ $a_2 = 0.9962$	$a = 0.9966$	$0.96 < a < 0.996$
$E[U(X_N)]$	136200	136048	135952	135843	**135805**
$\sigma[U(X_N)]$	222.05	218.65	193.58	239.11	132.84
Mean $E[n(X_N)]$	283.6	283.5	284.5	284.7	285

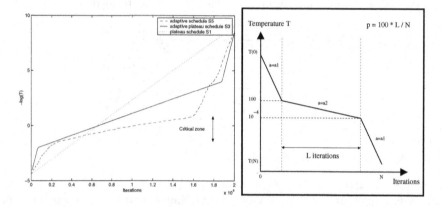

Fig. 4. Lefthandside : Comparison of the adaptive plateau schedule and the adaptive schedule. Righthandside : Cooling schedule of an adaptive plateau schedule, p being the percentage of iterations spent in the critical zone. For $T_0 > T > 100$ and $10^{-4} > T > T_N$, $a_n = a_1$. For $100 > T > 10^{-4}$, $a_n = a_2$. In order to spend more time in the critical zone, $1 > a_2 > a_1$.

schedules for which the speed changes during the simulation in accordance with the previous observations (see Fig. (4), lefthandside). S2 and S3 spend respectively $p = 80\%$ and $p = 90\%$ of the time in the critical zone $100 > T > 10^{-4}$. S4 is the limit adaptive geometric schedule ($p = 100\%$ studied before) where $T_0 = 100$ and $T_N = 10^{-4}$. Finally, S5 is the adaptive schedule presented above, which accelerates or warm the temperature.

As expected, the adaptive schedule makes the most of the N iterations and spend much more time in the interesting part of the temperature (see Fig. (4)). We see that our estimation (around $T = 100$) of the beginning of the critical zone is quite good.

5.4   Adapting the Proposition Kernel to the Temperature

A last optimization can be performed on the proposition kernel $Q(x, y)$. Indeed, this influences the global optimum of the SA, considering that at low tempera-

Table 6. Comparison between a classical kernel and an adaptive proposition kernel

	classical kernel	adaptive kernel
Iterations $(*10^6)$	2	2
Plateau length k	500	500
Cooling parameter a	0.9923	0.9923
$E[U(X_N)]$	136200	**135669**
$\sigma[U(X_N)]$	222.05	78.8
$E[n(X_N)]$	283.6	284.1

ture, the system is looking preferably for small perturbations. We also decrease along with the temperature our parameters in the translation, the rotation, and the dilation moves in order to propose smaller perturbations. Results are shown in Tab. (6). We can see that the results are much better with an adaptive proposition kernel. This can be understood because whatever the temperature is, the energy of the configuration should vary at the same order on the scale of one transition [23]. At a very low temperature for example, many costly energy evaluations will be required to reach any improvement of the objective function if we propose big moves to some of the objects of the configuration. It seems that keeping a good acceptance ratio even for low temperatures is crucial.

6   Conclusion

In this paper, we have performed some optimization tests on a marked point process algorithm applied to tree crown extraction. It is in fact an energy minimization, which can be studied using a SA scheme embedded in RJMCMC procedure.

First, it appears that the adaptive cooling schedule proposed in [20] gives better results that any geometric schedule, knowing the starting and the ending temperatures of the schedule. It fits well the energy landscape, and accelerates or warms the temperature in order to minimize the broken ergodicity phenomenon, which always occurs in finite schedules. Then, adapting the proposition kernel itself is also interesting. It increases the acceptance ratio of the proposition kernel for low temperatures, and also finds better local minima of the energy.

Future work could involve the implementation of another optimization algorithm, such as genetic algorithms. Moreover, other techniques which could improve the Markov chain speed will be studied. Among all, Data Driven Markov Chain Monte Carlo [28] achieves high acceleration by using the data (clustering or edge detection in the image segmentation problem for instance) to compute importance proposal probabilities which drive the Markov chain.

Acknowledgement

The authors wish to thank the anonymous referees who reviewed this paper for their constructive remarks, and the French Forest Inventory (IFN) for providing the data and for interesting discussions. The work of the first author has been partly supported by a grant from the MAS Laboratory of Ecole Centrale Paris. Part of this work has been conducted within the INRIA ARC "Mode de Vie" joint research program.

References

1. C. Andrieu, L.A. Breyer, and A. Doucet. Convergence of Simulated Annealing using Foster-Lyapunov Criteria. *Journal of Applied Probability*, 38(4):975–994, 2001.
2. R. Azencott, editor. *Simulated Annealing. Parallelization Techniques.* John Wiley and Sons, 1992.
3. A. Baddeley and M.N.M. Van Lieshout. Stochastic Geometry Models in High-level Vision. In K.V. Mardia, editor, *Statistics and Images*, volume 1, pages 231–256. 1993.
4. K.D. Boese and A.B. Kahng. Best-so-far vs Where-you-are : Implications for Optimal Finite Time Annealing. *System and Control Letters*, 22:71–78, 1994.
5. V. Cerny. Thermodynamical Approach to the Traveling Salesman Problem: an Efficient Simulation Algorithm. *Journal of Optimization Theory and Applications*, 45(1):41–51, 1985.
6. X. Descombes, F. Kruggel, C. Lacoste, M. Ortner, G. Perrin, and J. Zerubia. Marked Point Process in Image Analysis : from Context to Geometry. In *SPPA Conference*, Castellon, Spain, April 2004. invited paper.
7. A. Fachat. *A Comparison of Random Walks with Different Types of Acceptance Probabilities.* PhD thesis, University of Chemnitz, Germany, May 2000.
8. S.B. Gelfand and S.K. Mitter. Metropolis-type Annealing Algorithms for Global Optimization in R^d. *SIAM Journal of Control and Optimization*, 31(1):111–131, 1993.
9. S. Geman and D. Geman. Stochastic Relaxation, Gibbs Distributions and Bayesian Restoration of Images. *IEEE PAMI*, 6:721–741, 1984.
10. C.J. Geyer and J. Moller. Likelihood Inference for Spatial Point Processes. In O.E. Barndoff Nielsen, W.S. Kendall, and M.N.M. van Lieshout, editors, *Stochastic Geometry, Likelihood and Computation.* Chapmann and Hall, London, 1998.
11. F.A. Gougeon. Automatic Individual Tree Crown Delineation using a Valley-following Algorithm and Rule-based System. In D.A. Hill and D.G. Leckie, editors, *Proc. of the International Forum on Automated Interpretation of High Spatial Resolution Digital Imagery for Forestry*, pages 11–23, Victoria, British Columbia, Canada, February 1998.
12. P.J. Green. Reversible Jump Markov Chain Monte Carlo Computation and Bayesian Model Determination. *Biometrika 82*, pages 711–7320, 1995.
13. H. Haario and E. Saksman. Simulated Annealing Process in General State Space. *Advances Applied Probability*, 23:866–893, 1991.
14. B. Hajek. Cooling Schedules for Optimal Annealing. *Mathematics of Operations Research*, 13(2):311–329, 1985.
15. P.R. Halmos. *Measure Theory.* Springer-Verlag, 1950.
16. L. Ingber. Adaptive Simulated Annealing : Lessons Learned. *Control and Cybernetics*, 25(1):33–54, 1996.
17. S. Kirkpatrick, C. D. Gelatt, and M. P. Vecchi. Optimization by Simulated Annealing. *Science, Number 4598*, 220:671–680, May 1983.

18. M. Larsen. Individual Tree Top Position Estimation by Template Voting. In *Proc. of the Fourth International Airborne Remote Sensing Conference and Exhibition / 21st Canadian Symposium on Remote Sensing*, volume 2, pages 83–90, Ottawa, Ontario, June 1999.

19. M. Locatelli. Simulated Annealing Algorithms for Continuous Global Optimization : Convergence Conditions. *Journal of Optimization Theory and Applications*, 104:121–133, 2000.

20. M. Ortner. *Processus Ponctuels Marqués pour l'Extraction Automatique de Caricatures de Bâtiments à partir de Modèles Numériques d'Élévation*. PhD thesis, University of Nice-Sophia Antipolis, France, October 2004. (in French).

21. M. Ortner, X. Descombes, and J. Zerubia. A Reversible Jump MCMC Sampler for Object Detection in Image Processing. In *MC2QMC Conference*, Antibes Juan Les Pins, France, 2004. to be published in LNS-Springer Verlag.

22. G. Perrin, X. Descombes, and J. Zerubia. Point Processes in Forestry : an Application to Tree Crown Detection. Research Report 5544, INRIA, April 2005.

23. P. Salamon, P. Sibani, and R. Frost. *Facts, Conjectures, and Improvements for Simulated Annealing*. SIAM Monographs on Mathematical Modeling and Computation. Society for Industrial and Applied Mathematics, Philadelphia, PA, 2002.

24. R. Stoica, P. Gregori, and J. Mateu. Simulated Annealing and Object Point Processes : Tools for Analysis of Spatial Patterns. Technical Report 69, University Jaume I, Castellon, Spain, 2004.

25. P.N. Strenski and S. Kirkpatrick. Analysis of Finite Length Annealing Schedules. *Algorithmica*, 6:346–366, 1991.

26. H. Szu and R. Hartley. Fast Simulated Annealing. *Physics Letters A*, 122(3-4):157–162, 1987.

27. R. Tafelmayer and K.H. Hoffmann. Scaling Features in Complex Optimization Problems. *Computer Physics Communications*, 86:81–90, 1995.

28. Z.W. Tu and S.C. Zhu. Image Segmentation by Data-Driven Markov Chain Monte Carlo. *IEEE PAMI*, 24(5), 2002.

29. P.J.M. van Laarhoven and E.H.L. Aarts. *Simulated Annealing : Theory and Applications*. D. Reidel, Boston, 1987.

30. M.N.M. van Lieshout. Stochastic Annealing for Nearest Neighbour Point Process with Application to Object Recognition. Technical Report BS-R9306, Centruum vor Wiskunde en Informatica, Amsterdam, 1993.

31. M.N.M. van Lieshout. *Markov Point Processes and their Applications*. Imperial College Press, London, 2000.

32. J.M. Varanelli. *On the Acceleration of Simulated Annealing*. PhD thesis, University of Virginia, Charlottesville, USA, May 1996.

33. S.R. White. Concepts of Scale in Simulated Annealing. In *IEEE Proc. of the 1984 International Conference on Computer Design*, pages 646–651, 1984.

34. G. Winkler. *Image Analysis, Random Fields and Markov Chain Monte Carlo Methods*. Springer-Verlag, 2^{d} edition, 2003.

A Computational Approach to Fisher Information Geometry with Applications to Image Analysis

Washington Mio[1], Dennis Badlyans[2], and Xiuwen Liu[3]

[1] Department of Mathematics, Florida State University,
Tallahassee, FL 32306-4510, USA
mio@math.fsu.edu

[2] Department of Mathematics, Florida State University,
Tallahassee, FL 32306-4510, USA
dbadlyan@math.fsu.edu

[3] Department of Computer Science, Florida State University,
Tallahassee, FL 32306-4530, USA
liux@cs.fsu.edu

Abstract. We develop a computational approach to non-parametric Fisher information geometry and algorithms to calculate geodesic paths in this geometry. Geodesics are used to quantify divergence of probability density functions and to develop tools of data analysis in information manifolds. The methodology developed is applied to several image analysis problems using a representation of textures based on the statistics of multiple spectral components. Histograms of filter responses are viewed as elements of a non-parametric statistical manifold, and local texture patterns are compared using information geometry. Appearance-based object recognition experiments, as well as region-based image segmentation experiments are carried out to test both the representation and metric. The proposed representation of textures is also applied to the development of a *spectral cartoon model* of images.

1   Introduction

Large ensembles of data are often modeled as random samples of probability distributions. As such, the algorithmic analysis of complex data sets naturally leads to the investigation of families of probability density functions (PDFs). Of particular interest is the development of metrics to quantify divergence of PDFs and to model similarities and variations observed within a family of PDFs.

Information geometry studies differential geometric structures on *manifolds of probability distributions* and provides important tools for the statistical analysis of families of probability density functions. While this area has experienced a vigorous growth on the theoretical front in recent decades (see e.g. [1, 2, 18]), the development of corresponding computational tools for data analysis is still somewhat incipient. In this paper, we develop novel computational methods and

A. Rangarajan et al. (Eds.): EMMCVPR 2005, LNCS 3757, pp. 18–33, 2005.

strategies for the algorithmic study of non-parametric Fisher information geometry and investigate applications to problems in image analysis.

As geodesics are natural interpolators in Riemannian manifolds, a key element developed in this paper is an algorithm to calculate geodesics and geodesic distances in the geometry associated with Fisher information. This basic tool will allow us to devise computational approaches to problems such as: (i) quantifying similarity and divergence of PDFs; (ii) interpolating and extrapolating PDFs; (iii) clustering probability density functions; (iv) dimensionality reduction in the representation of families of PDFs; (v) development of statistical models that account for variability observed within a class of density functions. For simplicty, we shall focus our investigation on PDFs defined on a finite interval, which will be normalized to be $I = [0, 1]$, with respect to the Lebesgue measure. However, the techniques apply to more general settings.

Since the introduction of the discrete *cartoon model* of images by Geman and Geman [8] and Blake and Zisserman [3], and its continuous analogue by Mumford and Shah [17], many variants followed and have been applied to a wide range of image processing tasks [4]. In these models, an image is typically viewed as composed of two basic elements: (i) a *cartoon* formed by regions bounded by sharp edges, within which the variation of pixel values is fairly smooth; (ii) a *texture pattern* within each region, which is frequently modeled as white noise. A drawback in such approaches is the texture model adopted; the view that texture is not noise, but some form of *structured appearance* is becoming prevalent. To address this problem, models such as the *spectrogram model* [15, 24] have been proposed (see also [9]). A common strategy in texture analysis has been to decompose images into their spectral components using bandpass filters and utilize histograms of filter responses to represent textures. Zhu et al. [23] have shown that marginal distributions of spectral components are sufficient to characterize homogeneous textures; other studies of the statistics of spectral components include [19, 6, 22]. Experiments reported in [14] offer empirical evidence that the same applies to non-homogeneous textures if adequate boundary conditions are available; that is, enough pixel values near the boundary of the image domain are known.

In this paper, we model local and global texture patterns using histograms of spectral components viewed as elements of a non-parametric information manifold. Geodesic distances in this manifold are used to quantify texture similarity and divergence. Multi-scale texture representation and analysis can be carried out within this framework by restricting spectral components to sub-windows of the image domain of varying sizes. Several experiments involving appearance-based object classification and recognition, as well as region-based image segmentation are carried out to test the proposed representation and methodology. We also introduce a multi-scale *spectral cartoon model* of images based on this information theoretical representation of textures.

The paper is organized as follows. In Sec. 2, we briefly review basic facts about Fisher information geometry for parametric families of PDFs. Secs. 3 and 4 are devoted to a computational treatment of non-parametric Fisher information and to the development of an algorithm to calculate geodesics in information manifolds. Secs. 5.1, 5.2 address the calculation of basic statistics of collections of PDFs such as means and tangent-space covariance; this is followed by a discussion of clustering techniques in Sec. 5.3. In the remaining sections, the techniques developed are applied to various problems in image analysis including appearance-based recognition and segmentation of images. In the last section, we propose a new *spectral cartoon model* of images, which is a modified version of the well-known Mumford-Shah model that includes a novel representation of textures using histograms of spectral components viewed as elements of a non-parametric information manifold.

2   Fisher Information

Let $I = [0,1]$ and $p: I \times \mathbb{R}^k \to \mathbb{R}^+$, $(x, \theta) \mapsto p(x; \theta)$, a k-dimensional family of positive probability density functions parameterized by $\theta \in \mathbb{R}^k$. In classical information geometry, the Riemannian structure on the parameter space $\mathbb{R}^k$ defined by the *Fisher information matrix* g, whose (i,j)-entry is

$$g_{ij}(\theta) = \int_0^1 \left(\frac{\partial}{\partial \theta_i} \log p(x; \theta) \right) \left(\frac{\partial}{\partial \theta_j} \log p(x; \theta) \right) p(x; \theta) \, dx \,,$$

is regarded as the most natural Riemannian structure on the family from the viewpoint of information theory (see e.g. [2]). Recall that if $p_1, p_2 : I \to \mathbb{R}$ are positive PDFs, the *Kullback-Leibler (KL) divergence* is defined by

$$KL(p_1, p_2) = \int_0^1 \log \left(\frac{p_1(x)}{p_2(x)} \right) p_1(x) \, dx.$$

If restricted to the family $p(x; \theta)$, the KL divergence may be viewed as a function of parameters, with domain $\mathbb{R}^k \times \mathbb{R}^k$. If $\theta, \xi \in \mathbb{R}^k$, we use the notation $KL(\theta, \xi)$ for $KL(p(\cdot, \theta), p(\cdot, \xi))$. Infinitesimally, the double of the KL divergence is known to coincide with the quadratic form

$$ds^2 = \sum_{i,j=1}^k g_{ij}(\theta) \, d\theta_i d\theta_j$$

associated with the Fisher information matrix g. That is, if $E_\theta : \mathbb{R}^k \to \mathbb{R}$ is the energy functional $E_\theta(\xi) = KL(\theta, \xi)$, the Hessian of E_θ at the point $\xi = \theta$ is given by $g(\theta)$. This fact is often expressed as

$$KL(\theta, \theta + d\theta) = \frac{1}{2} \, ds^2.$$

In [5], Dawid suggested the investigation of non-parametric analogues of this geometry and such model was developed by Pistone and Sempi in [18]. This extension to non-parametric families of a.e. positive density functions involves the study of infinite-dimensional manifolds. For technical reasons, the geometry that generalizes Fisher information falls in the realm of infinite-dimensional Banach manifolds, spaces whose geometries are more difficult to analyze. One of our main goals is to develop computational approaches to discrete versions of non-parametric Fisher information obtained by sampling density functions $p \colon I \to \mathbb{R}$ at a finite set of points.

3   Non-parametric Information Manifolds

We investigate a non-parametric statistical manifold $\mathcal{P}$ whose elements represent the log-likelihood of positive probability density functions $p \colon I \to \mathbb{R}^+$. The manifold $\mathcal{P}$ will be endowed with an information-theoretic geometric structure which, among other things, will allow us to quantify variations and dissimilarities of PDFs.

Each tangent space $T_\varphi \mathcal{P}$ will be equipped with a natural inner product $\langle\,,\,\rangle_\varphi$. Although a Hilbert-Riemannian structure might seem to be the natural geometric structure on $\mathcal{P}$ to expect, one is led to a manifold locally modeled on Banach spaces [18]. Since, in this paper, we are primarily interested in computational aspects of information geometry, we construct finite-dimensional analogues of $\mathcal{P}$ by sampling probability density functions uniformly at a finite set of points under the assumption that they are continuous. Then, arguing heuristically, we derive an expression for the inner product on the tangent space $T_\varphi \mathcal{P}$, which induces a Riemannian structure on finite-dimensional, non-parametric analogues of $\mathcal{P}$. From the viewpoint of information theory, the geodesic distance between two PDFs can be interpreted as a measurement of the *uncertainty* or *unpredictability* in a density function relative to the other. Throughout the paper, we abuse notation and refer to both continuous and discrete models with the same symbols; however, the difference should be clear from the context.

Positive PDFs will be represented via their log-likelihood $\varphi(x) = \log p(x)$. Thus, a function $\varphi \colon I \to \mathbb{R}$ represents an element of $\mathcal{P}$ if and only if it satisfies

$$\int_I e^{\varphi(x)} \, dx = 1 . \tag{1}$$

Remark. In the discrete formulation, φ denotes the vector $(\varphi(x_1), \dots, \varphi(x_n))$, where $0 = x_1 < x_2 < \dots < x_n = 1$ are n uniformly spaced points on the unit interval I.

Tangent vectors f to the manifold $\mathcal{P}$ at φ represent infinitesimal (first-order) deformations of φ. Using a "time" parameter t, write such variation as $\varphi(x, t)$, $x \in I$ and $t \in (-\epsilon, \epsilon)$, where

$$\varphi(x, 0) = \varphi(x) \quad \text{and} \quad f(x) = \frac{d}{dt} \varphi(x, 0).$$

Differentiating constraint (1) with respect to t at $t = 0$, it follows that $f \colon I \to \mathbb{R}$ represents a tangent vector at φ if and only if

$$\int_I f(x) e^{\varphi(x)} \, dx = 0. \tag{2}$$

This simply means that $f(x)$ has null expectation with respect to $e^{\varphi(x)}\, dx$. Thus, the tangent space $T_\varphi \mathcal{P}$ to the manifold $\mathcal{P}$ at φ can be described as

$$T_\varphi \mathcal{P} = \{ f \colon I \to \mathbb{R} \mid \int_0^1 f(x) e^{\varphi(x)}\, dx = 0 \}.$$

What is the natural inner product on $T_\varphi \mathcal{P}$ that generalizes Fisher information? In Sec. 2, we remarked that the Fisher information matrix can be viewed as the Hessian of an energy functional associated with the *KL* divergence. In the non-parametric setting, for $\varphi \in \mathcal{P}$, the corresponding energy is given by

$$E_\varphi(\psi) = KL(e^\varphi, e^\psi) = \int_0^1 (\varphi(x) - \psi(x))\, e^{\varphi(x)}\, dx.$$

Calculating the Hessian of E_φ at $\psi = \varphi$, it follows that the inner product induced on $T_\varphi \mathcal{P}$ is given by

$$\langle v, w \rangle_\varphi = \int_I v(x) w(x) e^{\varphi(x)}\, dx, \tag{3}$$

which agrees with Fisher information on parametric submanifolds. A similar calculation with the *Jensen-Shannon (JS) entropy divergence*, which is a symmetrization of *KL*, leads to the same inner product, up to a multiplicative factor independent of φ. This means that both *KL* and *JS* essentially yield the same infinitesimal measure of relative uncertainty or lack of information.

Continuing with this informal argument, Eq. 2 can be rewritten as $\langle f, 1 \rangle_\varphi = 0$, where 1 denotes the constant function 1. Thus, f is tangent to $\mathcal{P}$ if and only if it is orthogonal to 1.

To discretize this model, let $0 = x_1 < x_2 < \ldots < x_{n-1} < x_n = 1$ be n uniformly spaced points on the interval I. Heretoforth, all functions $\psi \colon I \to \mathbb{R}$ will be viewed as n-vectors obtained by sampling the function at these points; that is, $\psi = (\psi_1, \ldots, \psi_n) \in \mathbb{R}^n$, with $\psi_i = \psi(x_i)$. Eqn. 3 suggests that, at each $\varphi \in \mathbb{R}^n$, we consider the inner product

$$\langle f, g \rangle_\varphi = \sum_{i=1}^n f_i g_i\, e^{\varphi_i}, \tag{4}$$

where $f, g \in \mathbb{R}^n$. From (1), it follows that $\varphi \in \mathbb{R}^n$ represents a (discretized) PDF if and only if $\sum_{i=1}^n e^{\varphi_i} = 1$. More formally, consider the function $F \colon \mathbb{R}^n \to \mathbb{R}$ given by

$$F(\varphi) = \sum_{i=1}^n e^{\varphi_i}. \tag{5}$$

The differential of F at φ evaluated at a vector $f \in \mathbb{R}^n$ is

$$dF_\varphi(f) = \sum_{i=1}^n f_i e^{\varphi_i} = \langle f, 1 \rangle_\varphi,$$

which shows that the gradient of F at φ with respect to the inner product $\langle\,,\,\rangle_\varphi$ is $\nabla F(\varphi) = (1,\ldots,1)$, for any φ. This implies that the level sets of F are $(n-1)$-dimensional submanifolds of $\mathbb{R}^n$. Of particular interest, is the manifold

$$\mathcal{P}_n = F^{-1}(1),$$

which is our finite-dimensional analogue of $\mathcal{P}$. As in (2), the tangent space $T_\varphi\mathcal{P}_n$ consists of all vectors $f \in \mathbb{R}^n$ satisfying $\langle f,1\rangle_\varphi = 0$; that is, vectors $f \in \mathbb{R}^n$ orthogonal to $(1,\ldots,1)$ with respect to the inner product $\langle\,,\,\rangle_\varphi$. The *geodesic distance* between $\varphi,\psi \in \mathcal{P}_n$ will be denoted $d(\varphi,\psi)$.

4   Geodesics in $\mathcal{P}_n$

We are interested in developing an algorithm to calculate geodesics in $\mathcal{P}_n$ (with respect to the Levi-Civita connection) with prescribed boundary conditions; that is, with given initial and terminal points φ and ψ, respectively. Following a strategy similar to that adopted in [13] for planar shapes, we propose to construct geodesics in two stages. First, we describe a numerical strategy to calculate geodesics in $\mathcal{P}_n$ with prescribed initial position φ_0 and initial velocity f_0.

4.1   Geodesics with Prescribed Initial Conditions

Recall that $\mathcal{P}_n$ is a submanifold of the Riemannian manifold $(\mathbb{R}^n, \langle\,,\,\rangle_\varphi)$. From (4), $\mathbb{R}^n$ with this metric can be expressed as the n-fold Cartesian product of the real line $\mathbb{R}$ equipped with the Riemannian metric

$$\langle u,v\rangle_x = uve^x,$$

$x \in \mathbb{R}$. This allows us to easily calculate the differential equation that governs geodesics in $\mathbb{R}^n$ with this non-standard (flat) metric and derive explicit expressions for geodesics with initial conditions prescribed to first order. To solve the corresponding initial value problem in $\mathcal{P}_n$, we adopt the following strategy:

(i) Infinitesimally, follow the geodesic path α_0 in $\mathbb{R}^n$ satisfying the given initial conditions.

(ii) The end point $\tilde{\varphi}_1$ of this small geodesic arc in $(\mathbb{R}^n, \langle\,,\,\rangle_\varphi)$ will typically fall slightly off of $\mathcal{P}_n$; to place it back on the level set $\mathcal{P}_n = F^{-1}(1)$ (i.e., to have equation $F(\tilde{\varphi}_1) - 1 = 0$ satisfied), we use Newton's method. Since the gradient of F is $1 = (1,\ldots,1)$ at any point, this projection can be accomplished in a single step since it is equivalent to simply adding a constant to $\tilde{\varphi}_1$ so that $\int_0^1 e^{\tilde{\varphi}_1(x)}\,dx = 1$. This gives $\varphi_1 \in \mathcal{P}_n$.

(iii) To iterate the construction, we need to parallel transport the velocity vector f_0 to the new point φ_1 along the estimated geodesic arc. As an approximation to the parallel transport, from the velocity vector of α_0 at the end point $\tilde{\varphi}_1$, subtract the component normal to $\mathcal{P}_n$ at φ_1 and rescale it to have the same magnitude as f_0 to obtain the velocity vector f_1 at φ_1. This is done because geodesics have constant speed. One can show that this approximation of the parallel transport is a mild variant of Euler's method applied to the differential equation of geodesics in $\mathcal{P}_n$.

(iv) Iterate the construction.

We denote this geodesic by $\Psi(t; \varphi_0, f_0)$, where t is the time parameter. The position $\Psi(1; \varphi_0, f_0)$ of the geodesic at time $t = 1$ is known as the exponential of f_0 and denoted

$$\exp_{\varphi_0}(f_0) = \Psi(1; \varphi_0, f_0).$$

One often refers to f_0 as a logarithm of $\varphi_1 = \Psi(1; \varphi_0, f_0)$, denoted $f_0 = \log_{\varphi_0} \varphi_1$. The procedure just described can be interpreted as a first-order numerical integration of the differential equation that governs geodesics in $\mathcal{P}_n$. Higher-order methods can be adapted similarly.

4.2 Geodesics with Boundary Conditions

Given two points $\varphi, \psi \in \mathcal{P}_n$, how to find a geodesic in $\mathcal{P}_n$ connecting them? Similar to the strategy for computing geodesics in shape manifolds developed in [13], we propose to use a *shooting method*. If we solve the equation

$$\Psi(1; \varphi, f) = \psi \tag{6}$$

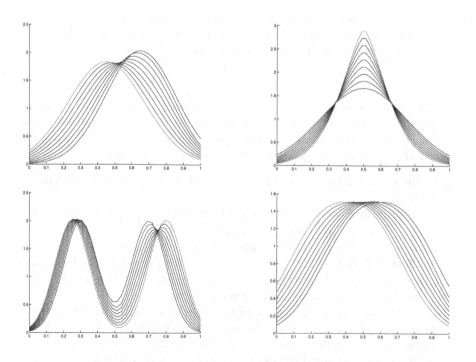

Fig. 1. Examples of geodesics in $\mathcal{P}_n$

for $f \in T_\varphi \mathcal{P}_n$ (i.e., if we find the correct direction f_0 to shoot a geodesic to reach ψ in unit time), then $\Psi(t; \varphi, f_0)$, $0 \leq t \leq 1$, gives the desired geodesic. Solving Eqn. 6 is equivalent to finding the zeros of the *miss function*

$$E(f) = \|\Psi(1; \varphi, f) - \psi\|^2$$

on the tangent space $T_\varphi \mathcal{P}_n$, where $\|.\|$ denotes the standard Euclidean norm. This problem can be approached numerically via Newton's method.

Fig. 1 shows some examples of geodesics in $\mathcal{P}_n$ computed with the algorithmic procedure described above. The examples involve probability density functions obtained by truncating Gaussians, generalized Laplacians and mixtures of Gaussians.

5   Data Analysis

Probability density functions are often used to model large ensembles of data viewed as random samples of the model. To compare different ensembles, it is desirable to adapt existing data analysis tools to the framework of Fisher information. In this section, we consider the problem of defining and computing means and covariance of families of PDFs, as well as extending clustering techniques to the manifold $\mathcal{P}_n$. Note that each PDF will be treated as a point on an information manifold.

5.1   Fréchet Means

We begin with the problem of defining and finding the mean of a family of PDFs on the interval $I = [0, 1]$.

Let $S = \{\varphi_1, \ldots, \varphi_\ell\} \subset \mathcal{P}_n$ be a collection of ℓ probability distributions over I represented by their discretized log-likelihood functions. We are interested in defining and computing sample statistics such as mean and covariance of S. We propose to use the intrinsic notion of *Fréchet mean* [12], which is defined as a (local) minimum of the *total variance function*

$$V(\varphi) = \frac{1}{2} \sum_{i=1}^{\ell} d^2 (\varphi, \varphi_i),$$

where d denotes geodesic distance in $\mathcal{P}_n$. It can be shown [12] that if f_i is the initial velocity of the geodesic that connects φ to φ_i in unit time, then

$$\nabla V(\varphi) = - \sum_{i=1}^{\ell} f_i.$$

Thus, if we compute the velocity vectors f_i, $1 \leq i \leq \ell$, using the algorithmic procedure described in Sec. 4, the calculation of Fréchet means can be approached with gradient methods. Fig. 2 shows examples of Fréchet means computed with the techniques just described.

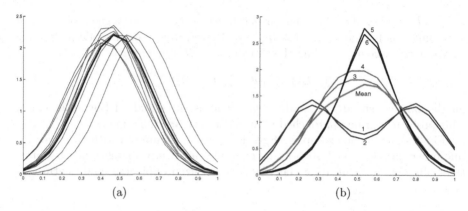

Fig. 2. Examples of Fréchet means of PDFs

5.2   Covariance, Dimension Reduction and Learning

Given $S = \{\varphi_1, \ldots, \varphi_\ell\} \subset \mathcal{P}_n$, let $\hat{\varphi} \in \mathcal{P}_n$ be a Fréchet mean of the collection S, and let $f_i = \log_{\hat{\varphi}} \varphi_i$ be the initial velocity of the geodesic that connects $\hat{\varphi}$ to φ_i in unit time, which can be calculated with the techniques of Sec. 4.

The vectors f_i, $1 \leq i \leq \ell$, yield an alternative *tangent-space representation* of the elements of S as vectors in $T_{\hat{\varphi}}\mathcal{P}_n$. This type of representation of data on Riemannian manifolds via the inverse exponential map was introduced in the context of shape analysis using landmark representations of shapes (see e.g. [7]). Note that the original data point φ_i can be recovered from f_i via the exponential map. The advantage of this representation is that each f_i lies in the inner-product space $(T_{\hat{\varphi}}\mathcal{P}_n, \langle\,,\,\rangle_{\hat{\varphi}})$, where classical data analysis techniques such as Component Analysis can be used. This tangent-space representation may, in principle, distort the geometry of the data somewhat. However, the distortion is small if the data

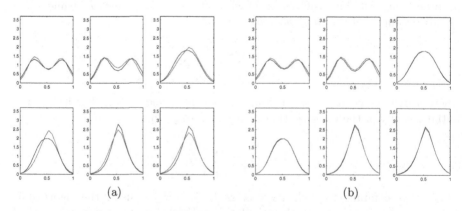

Fig. 3. Reconstructing the data shown in Fig. 2(b) with tangent-space Principal Component Analysis using (a) one and (b) three principal components, respectively

does not exhibit very large spread. This is often the case, in practice, if we assume that the data has been pre-clustered and we are analyzing individual clusters separately.

Once the data has been lifted to $(T_{\hat{\varphi}}\mathcal{P}_n, \langle \, , \, \rangle_{\hat{\varphi}})$, covariance can be defined as usual. One can learn probability models for the family $\{f_i, 1 \leq i \leq \ell\}$ using standard techniques (see e.g. [7, 21]). For example, *Principal Component Analysis* (PCA) can be applied to the tangent-space representation of S to derive a Gaussian model. Fig. 2(b) shows a set of six PDFs and their mean. Figs. 3 (a) and (b) show tangent-space PCA reconstructions of the data using projections over one and three principal directions, respectively. Other well-known data analysis methods such as *Independent Component Analysis* and *Kernel PCA* (see e.g. [11, 20, 10]) can be applied to tangent-space representations, as well.

5.3   Clustering

Classical clustering algorithms can be adapted to the present setting to group large collections of PDFs into smaller subclasses. For example, starting with single-element clusters formed by each element in a dataset, one can use hierarchical clustering techniques to successively combine clusters using the geodesic distance between clusters in $\mathcal{P}_n$ as a merging criterion. Fig. 4 shows the clustering dendrogram obtained for a family twelve PDFs using the nearest-neighbor merging criterion. The techniques for calculating Fréchet means described in Sec. 5.1 allow us to adapt the classical *k-Means Clustering Algorithm* to families of PDFs using the geodesic distance, as well.

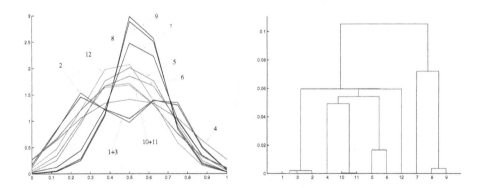

Fig. 4. Twelve PDFs and a "nearest-neighbor" hierarchical clustering dendrogram

6   Spectral Representation and Clustering of Texture

In this section, we employ histograms of spectral components to represent texture patterns in images at different scales. We carry out appearance-based object recognition experiments to test the representation, geodesic metric, and geodesic interpolation. We also use the geodesic metric and a variant of the clustering techniques discussed in Sec. 5.3 to identify regions of similar appearance in images.

6.1   Texture Representation

Given a bank of filters $\mathcal{F} = \{F^j, 1 \leq j \leq K\}$ and an image I, let I^j be the associated spectral components obtained by applying filter F^j to the image. Assume that the histogram of the jth spectral component is modeled on a PDF with log-likelihood $\varphi_j \in \mathcal{P}$. The (texture of) image I will be represented by the K-tuple $\Phi = (\varphi^1, \ldots, \varphi^K) \in \mathcal{P} \times \ldots \times \mathcal{P} = \mathcal{P}^K$. We should point out that this is a global representation of the image I, but the same construction applied to local windows leads to *multi-scale representations* of texture patterns. If $\Phi_A, \Phi_B \in \mathcal{P}^K$ represent images I_A and I_B, respectively, let d_T be the root-mean-square geodesic distance

$$d_T\left(\Phi_A, \Phi_B\right) = \left(\frac{1}{K} \sum_{j=1}^{K} d^2(\varphi_A^j, \varphi_B^j)\right)^{1/2}, \tag{7}$$

which defines a metric on the space $\mathcal{P}^K$ of texture representations.

Remark. In specific applications, one may wish to attribute different weights to the various summands of $d_T\left(\Phi_A, \Phi_B\right)$ in order to emphasize particular filters.

6.2   Region-Based Segmentation

In this section, we present results obtained in image segmentation experiments with the ideas discussed above. To illustrate the ability of the metric d_T to discern and classify local texture patterns, we grouped the pixels of some images into two clusters. We used local histograms associated with five distinct spectral components and the metric d_T as measure of dissimilarity; a hierarchical "centroid" clustering was adopted.

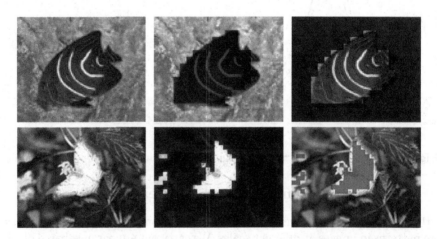

Fig. 5. In each row, the leftmost panel displays a test image. On the other panels, the regions obtained by clustering the pixels into two clusters using histograms of local responses to 5 filters are highlighted in two different ways.

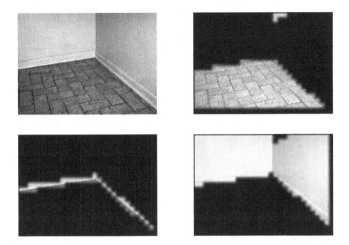

Fig. 6. A low-resolution segmentation of an image into three regions by clustering pixels using 5 spectral components and the geodesic metric derived from Fisher information

On each row of Fig. 5, the leftmost panel shows the original images. The other two panels display the two clusters obtained highlighted in different ways; observe that clusters may be disconnected as in the image with a butterfly. Since clustering was performed at a low resolution, the boundaries of the regions are somewhat irregular. Note that because of the resolution and the local window size utilized in the spectral analysis, the relatively thin white stripes on the fish are clustered with the rest of the fish, not with the background. Fig. 6 shows the results of a similar experiment, where the image was decomposed into three regions.

6.3   Appearance-Based Recognition

As an illustration of possible uses of the proposed spectral representation of textures using information manifolds, we carried out a small object recognition experiment using 10 objects from the COIL-100 database. Each object in the database is represented by 72 images taken at successive views that differ by 5-degree angles. We used histograms of 39 spectral components, as well as the histograms of the original images, so that each image is represented as an element of $\mathcal{P}^{40}$.

In the first recognition experiment, the training set consisted of 4 images corresponding to 90-degree rotations of the objects, with the 68 remaining images used as test images. Table 1 compares the recognition rates achieved with 4 training images for each object to those obtained by estimating four additional views using geodesic interpolations. Similar results are shown for a training set of 8 images. Examples of histograms of intermediate views estimated using geodesic interpolations are shown in Fig. 7. On the first row, we display histograms of images of an object from angles differing by 90° and the corresponding interpolation. A similar illustration for a spectral component of the image is shown on the second row.

Table 1. Recognition rates in an experiment with 10 objects from the COIL-100 database

# of Training Images	# of Test Images	Performance with no Interpolations	Performance with Interpolations
4	68	93%	95%
8	64	97%	100%

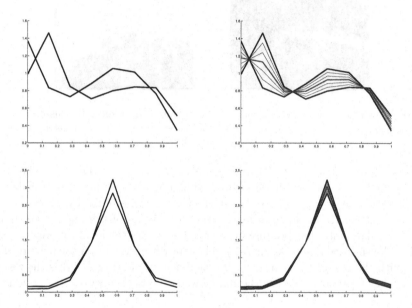

Fig. 7. First row: the left panel shows histograms of images of an object taken from different views and the right panel displays histograms of intermediate views estimated using geodesic interpolations. Second row: similar illustration for a spectral component.

7   The Spectral Cartoon Model

To model texture patterns using *multi-resolution* spectral components of images, we localize the notion of appearance, as follows. Given a bank of filters $\mathcal{F} = \{F_1, \ldots, F_K\}$ and an image I, let I^j, $1 \le j \le K$ be the associated spectral components. For a pixel p, consider a window of fixed size (this determines the scale) centered at p and let h_p^j be the histogram of I^j restricted to this window. The histograms h_p^j yield an s-tuple $\Phi_p = \left(\varphi_p^1, \ldots, \varphi_p^K\right) \in \mathcal{P}^K$, which encodes the local texture pattern near the pixel p. If p, q are two pixels, we use the distance $d_T(\Phi_p, \Phi_q)$ defined in (7) to quantify texture divergence.

To simplify the discussion, we consider a binary model and assume that the image consists of two main regions: a background and a single foreground element, which are separated by a closed contour C. The proposed model can be modified to allow more complex configurations as in [17]. A key difference to be noted is that unlike the classical Ising image model, where a binary cartoon is adopted (see e.g. [15]), we make a similar assumption at the level of spectral representations, so that even cartoons can be non-trivially textured. Thus, variations of pixel values, often treated as white noise, will be modeled on random fluctuations of more richly structured texture patterns.

Let $I: D \to \mathbb{R}$ be an image, where D is the image domain, typically a rectangle in $\mathbb{R}^2$. Consider triples $(\Phi_{in}, \Phi_{out}, C)$, where C is a closed contour in D, and $\Phi_{in}, \Phi_{out} \in \mathcal{P}^K$ represent cartoon models for the local texture patterns in the regions inside and outside C, respectively. We adopt a Bayesian model, with a prior that assumes that C is not "unnecessarily" long, so that the prior energy will be a multiple of the length $\ell(C)$. This can be easily modified to accommodate other commonly used priors such as the elastic energy; a probabilistic interpretation of the elastic energy is given in [16]. The proposed data likelihood energy is of the form

$$
\begin{aligned}
E_d(I|\Phi_{in}, \Phi_{out}, C) = \alpha & \int_{D_{in}} d_T^2(\Phi_p, \Phi_{in}) \, dp \\
+ \beta & \int_{D_{out}} d_T^2(\Phi_p, \Phi_{out}) \, dp \,,
\end{aligned}
\tag{8}
$$

where $\alpha, \beta > 0$, and D_{in}, D_{out} are the regions inside and outside C, respectively. The idea is that E_d will measure the compatibility of local texture patterns in an image I with the texture of a proposed cartoon. The *spectral cartoon* of I is represented by the triple $(\Phi_{in}, \Phi_{out}, C)$ that minimizes the posterior energy

$$
\begin{aligned}
E(\Phi_{in}, \Phi_{out}, C|I) = \alpha & \int_{D_{in}} d_T^2(\Phi_p, \Phi_{in}) \, dp \\
+ \beta & \int_{D_{out}} d_T^2(\Phi_p, \Phi_{out}) \, dp + \gamma \, \ell(C) \,,
\end{aligned}
\tag{9}
$$

$\gamma > 0$.

Since the estimation of the triple $(\Phi_{in}, \Phi_{out}, C)$ may be a costly task, one may modify the model, as follows. For a given curve C, the optimal Φ_{in} can be interpreted as the average value of Φ_p in the region D_{in}, and the integral $\int_{D_{in}} d_T^2(\Phi_p, \Phi_{in}) \, dp$ as the total variance of Φ_p in the region. We propose to replace $d^2(\Phi_p, \Phi_{in})$, the distance square to the mean, with the average distance square from Φ_p to Φ_q, for $q \in D_{in}, q \neq p$, which is given by

$$
\frac{1}{P_{in} - 1} \sum_{\substack{q \in D_{in} \\ q \neq p}} d^2(\Phi_p, \Phi_q) \,.
$$

Here, P_{in} is the number of pixels in D_{in}. Proceeding similarly for the region outside, the task is reduced to the simpler *maximum-a-posteriori* estimation of the curve C; that is, the curve that minimizes the energy functional

$$E(C|I) = \frac{\alpha}{P_{in} - 1} \sum_{\substack{p,\, q\, \in D_{in} \\ q \neq p}} d^2(\Phi_p, \Phi_q)$$

$$+ \frac{\beta}{P_{out} - 1} \sum_{\substack{p,\, q\, \in D_{out} \\ q \neq p}} d^2(\Phi_p, \Phi_q) + \gamma\, \ell(C).$$

8   Summary and Comments

We introduced new computational methods and strategies in non-parametric Fisher information geometry. A basic tool developed is an algorithm to calculate geodesics in information manifolds that allows us to address computational problems arising in the analysis of families of probability density functions such as clustering PDFs and the calculation of means and covariance of families of PDFs. To demonstrate its usefulness, the methodology developed was applied to various image analysis problems such as appearance-based recognition of imaged objects and image segmentation based on local texture patterns. A *spectral cartoon model* of images was proposed using a new representation of local texture patterns. More extensive testing of the methodos introduced in the context of image analysis will be carried out in future work.

Acknowledgment. This work was supported in part by NSF grants CCF-0514743 and IIS-0307998, and ARO grant W911NF-04-01-0268.

References

1. S. Amari, *Differential-geometrical methods of statistics*, Lecture Notes in Statistics, vol. 28, Springer, Berlin, 1985.
2. S. Amari and H. Nagaoka, *Methods of information geometry*, AMS and Oxford University Press, New York, 2000.
3. A. Blake and A. Zisserman, *Visual reconstruction*, The MIT Press, 1987.
4. T. Chan, J. Shen, and L. Vese, *Variational PDE models in image processing*, Notices Amer. Math. Soc. **50** (2003), 14–26.
5. A. P. Dawid, *Discussion of "defining a curvature of a statistical problem (with applications to second-order efficiency)" by B. Efron*, The Annals of Statistics **3** (1975), 1231–1234.
6. D. L. Donoho and A. G. Flesia, *Can recent innovations in harmonic analysis 'explain' key findings in natural image statistics?*, Network: Computation in Neural Systems **12** (2001), no. 3, 371–393.
7. I. L. Dryden and K. V. Mardia, *Statistical shape analysis*, John Wiley & Son, 1998.
8. S. Geman and D. Geman, *Stochastic relaxation, Gibbs distributions, and the Bayesian restoration of images*, IEEE Transactions on Pattern Analysis and Machine Intelligence **6** (1984), no. 6, 721–741.
9. T. Hoffmann and J. M. Buhmann, *Pairwise data clustering by deterministic annealing*, IEEE Trans. on Pattern Analysis and Machine Intelligence **19** (1997), 1–14.

10. A. Hyvarinen, *Survey on independent component analysis*, Neural Computing Surveys **2** (1999), 94–128.

11. I. T. Jolliffe, *Principal component analysis*, Springer-Verlag, New York, 1986.

12. H. Karcher, *Riemann center of mass and mollifier smoothing*, Comm. Pure Appl. Math. **30** (1977), 509–541.

13. E. Klassen, A. Srivastava, W. Mio, and S. Joshi, *Analysis of planar shapes using geodesic paths on shape manifolds*, IEEE Trans. on Pattern Analysis and Machine Intelligence **26** (2004), 372–383.

14. X. Liu and L. Cheng, *Independent spectral representations of images for recognition*, J. Optical Soc. of America **20** (2003), no. 7.

15. D. Mumford, *The Bayesian rationale for energy functionals*, Geometry-Driven Diffusion in Computer Vision (B. Romeny, ed.), Kluwer Academic, 1994, pp. 141–153.

16. ———, *Elastica and computer vision*, pp. 491–506, Springer, New York, 1994.

17. D. Mumford and J. Shah, *Optimal approximations by piecewise smooth functions and associated variational problems*, Comm. Pure Appl. Math. **42** (1989), 577–685.

18. B. Pistone and C. Sempi, *An infinite-dimensional geometric structure on the space of all probability measures equivalent to a given one*, The Annals of Statistics **23** (1995), no. 5, 1543–1561.

19. J. Portilla and E. P. Simoncelli, *A parametric texture model based on join statistics of complex wavelet coeeficients*, International Journal of Computer Vision **40** (2000), no. 1, 49–70.

20. B. Schölkopf, A. Smola, and K. R. Müller, *Nonlinear component analysis as a kernel eigenvalue problem*, Neural Computation **10** (1998), 1299–1319.

21. A. Srivastava, S. Joshi, W. Mio, and X. Liu, *Statistical shape analysis: Clustering, learning and testing*, IEEE Trans. on Pattern Analysis and Machine Intelligence **27** (2005), 590–602.

22. A. Srivastava, X. Liu, and U. Grenander, *Universal analytical forms for modeling image probability*, IEEE Transactions on Pattern Analysis and Machine Intelligence **28** (2002), no. 9, 1200–1214.

23. Y. N. Wu, S. C. Zhu, and X. Liu, *Equivalence of Julesz ensembles and FRAME models*, International Journal of Computer Vision **38** (2000), no. 3, 247–265.

24. S. C. Zhu, Y. Wu, and D. Mumford, *Filters, random fields and maximum entropy (FRAME)*, International Journal of Computer Vision **27** (1998), 1–20.

Optimizing the Cauchy-Schwarz PDF Distance for Information Theoretic, Non-parametric Clustering[*]

Robert Jenssen[1], Deniz Erdogmus[2], Kenneth E. Hild[3], Jose C. Principe[4], and Torbjørn Eltoft[1]

[1] Department of Physics, University of Tromsø, N - 9037 Tromsø, Norway
Phone: (+47) 776 46493, Fax: (+47) 776 45580
robertj@phys.uit.no
[2] Department of Computer Science and Engineering,
Oregon Graduate Institute, OHSU, Portland, OR. 97006, USA
[3] Department of Radiology, University of California,
San Francisco, CA. 94143, USA
[4] Department of Electrical and Computer Engineering,
University of Florida, Gainesville FL. 32611, USA

Abstract. This paper addresses the problem of efficient information theoretic, non-parametric data clustering. We develop a procedure for adapting the cluster memberships of the data patterns, in order to maximize the recent Cauchy-Schwarz (CS) probability density function (pdf) distance measure. Each pdf corresponds to a cluster. The CS distance is estimated analytically and non-parametrically by means of the Parzen window technique for density estimation. The resulting form of the cost function makes it possible to develop an efficient adaption procedure based on constrained gradient descent, using stochastic approximation of the gradients. The computational complexity of the algorithm is $O(MN)$, $M \ll N$, where N is the total number of data patterns and M is the number of data patterns used in the stochastic approximation. We show that the new algorithm is capable of performing well on several odd-shaped and irregular data sets.

1 Introduction

In data analysis, it is often desirable to partition, or cluster, a data set into subsets, such that members within subsets are more similar to each other according to some criterion, than to members of other subsets. Clustering has many important applications in computer vision and pattern recognition. See for example ref. [1] for a review.

Most of the traditional algorithms, such as fuzzy K-means [2] and the expectation-maximization algorithm for a Gaussian mixture model (EMGMM) [3], work well for hyper-spherical and hyper-elliptical clusters, since they are

---

[*] This work was partially supported by NSF grants ECS-9900394 and EIA-0135946.

A. Rangarajan et al. (Eds.): EMMCVPR 2005, LNCS 3757, pp. 34–45, 2005.

often optimized based on a second order statistics criterion. Therefore, in recent years, the main thrust in clustering has been towards developing efficient algorithms capable of handling odd-shaped and highly irregular clusters.

Information theoretic methods appear as particularly appealing alternatives as clustering cost functions when it comes to capturing all the structure in a data set. The reason is that pdf distance measures in theory do capture all the information contained in the data distributions in question. Several information theoretic approaches to clustering have been proposed in recent years, see for example refs. [4, 5, 6, 7]. The problem with many such methods is often that the information theoretic measure can be difficult to estimate. Analytical estimation most often requires the user to choose a parametric model for the data distributions. Hence, the clustering algorithm will only perform well if the parametric model matches the actual densities. Also, the optimization of the cost function is often computationally demanding.

In this paper, we address the problem of efficient information theoretic, non-parametric data clustering. We develop a procedure for adjusting the cluster memberships of the data points, which seeks to maximize the CS pdf distance measure. Since the estimated pdfs, at each iteration cycle, are based on the current clusters, the approach is to assign the memberships of the data such that the CS distance between the obtained clusters is maximized. The CS distance can be estimated analytically and non-parametrically by means of the Parzen window technique for density estimation. Hence, the cost function captures all the statistical information contained in the data.

By estimating the cluster pdfs using the Parzen window technique, the CS distance can be expressed in terms of cluster memberships with respect to a predetermined number of clusters. Of course, in clustering, the memberships are not known beforehand, and have to be initialized randomly. The adaption procedure for these memberships, maximizing the CS cost function, is carried out by means of the Lagrange multiplier formalism. The procedure can be considered a constrained gradient descent search, with built in variable step-sizes for each coordinate direction.

The resulting algorithm has a complexity of order $O(N^2)$, where N is the number of data patterns. In practical clustering problems, the data sets may be very large. Thus, it is of crucial importance to reduce the complexity of the algorithm. To achieve this goal, we derive a stochastic approximation approach to estimating the gradients used in the clustering rule. Instead of calculating the gradients based on information from the memberships corresponding to all the data points, we stochastically sample the membership space, using only $M \ll N$ randomly selected membership functions and their corresponding data points, to calculate the gradients. As a result, we obtain an efficient information theoretic clustering algorithm of only $O(MN)$ complexity.

The Parzen window size will also be used to avoid a pitfall of gradient descent learning in non-convex cost functions, i.e., the convergence to a local optimum of the cost function. We show that in our algorithm, this problem can to a high degree be avoided, by allowing the size of the Parzen kernel to be annealed over a range of values around the optimally estimated value. The effect of using a large kernel compared to the optimal kernel size, is to obtain an over-smoothed version of the CS cost function, such that many local optima are eliminated. As the algorithm converges toward the optimum of the smoothed CS distance, the kernel size is continuously decreased, leading the algorithm toward the true global optimum. We propose a method to select a suitable annealing scheme based on the optimal Parzen kernel, which is, however, rather heuristic at this point.

The organization of this paper is as follows. In section 2, we review the Cauchy-Schwarz pdf distance measure. In section 3, we develop the Lagrange multiplier optimization procedure, and show how the gradients can be stochastically approximated to obtain an efficient clustering algorithm. We present some clustering experiments in section 4, and make our concluding remarks in section 5.

2   Cauchy-Schwarz PDF Distance

Based on the Cauchy-Schwarz inequality; $||\mathbf{x}||^2 \, ||\mathbf{y}||^2 \geq (\mathbf{x}^T\mathbf{y})^2$, the following holds;

$$- \log \frac{\mathbf{x}^T\mathbf{y}}{\sqrt{||\mathbf{x}||^2 \, ||\mathbf{y}||^2}} \geq 0. \tag{1}$$

By replacing inner products between vectors in (1), by inner products between pdfs, i.e. $\langle p, q \rangle = \int p(\mathbf{x})q(\mathbf{x})d\mathbf{x}$, we define the following distance measure [8]

$$D(p, q) = - \log \frac{\int p(\mathbf{x})q(\mathbf{x})d\mathbf{x}}{\sqrt{\int p^2(\mathbf{x})d\mathbf{x} \, \int q^2(\mathbf{x})d\mathbf{x}}} \geq 0. \tag{2}$$

We refer to $D(p, q)$ as the Cauchy-Schwarz pdf distance measure. It can be seen that $D(p, q)$ is always non-negative, it obeys the identity property, and it is also symmetric. The $D(p, q)$ goes to infinity when the overlap between the two pdfs goes to zero. The measure does however not obey the triangle inequality, such that it does not satisfy the strictly mathematical definition of a distance measure.

Since the logarithm is a monotonic function, maximization of $D(p, q)$ is equivalent to minimization of the argument of the log in (2). In this paper, we refer to this quantity as $J(p, q)$, and the goal is to develop an efficient minimization scheme for this quantity.

Assume that we estimate $p(\mathbf{x})$ based on the data points in cluster $C_1 = \{\mathbf{x}_i\}$, $i = 1, \ldots, N_1$, and $q(\mathbf{x})$ based on $C_2 = \{\mathbf{x}_j\}$, $j = 1, \ldots, N_2$. By the Parzen [9] method

$$\hat{p}(\mathbf{x}) = \frac{1}{N_1} \sum_{i=1}^{N_1} G(\mathbf{x} - \mathbf{x}_i, \sigma^2\mathbf{I}),$$

$$\hat{q}(\mathbf{x}) = \frac{1}{N_2} \sum_{j=1}^{N_2} G(\mathbf{x} - \mathbf{x}_j, \sigma^2\mathbf{I}), \tag{3}$$

where we have used symmetric Gaussian kernels, $G(\mathbf{x}, \mathbf{\Sigma})$, where $\mathbf{\Sigma} = \sigma^2 \mathbf{I}$. According to the convolution theorem for Gaussians, the following relation holds

$$\int G(\mathbf{x} - \mathbf{x}_i, \sigma^2 \mathbf{I}) G(\mathbf{x} - \mathbf{x}_j, \sigma^2 \mathbf{I}) d\mathbf{x} = G_{ij, 2\sigma^2 \mathbf{I}}, \tag{4}$$

where $G_{ij, 2\sigma^2 \mathbf{I}} = G(\mathbf{x}_i - \mathbf{x}_j, 2\sigma^2 \mathbf{I})$.

Thus, when we plug the Parzen pdf estimates of (3) into (2), and utilize (4), we obtain

$$\int p(\mathbf{x}) q(\mathbf{x}) d\mathbf{x} \approx \frac{1}{N_1 N_2} \sum_{i,j=1}^{N_1, N_2} G_{ij, 2\sigma^2 \mathbf{I}}, \tag{5}$$

$$\int p^2(\mathbf{x}) d\mathbf{x} \approx \frac{1}{N_1^2} \sum_{i,i'=1}^{N_1, N_1} G_{ii', 2\sigma^2 \mathbf{I}}, \tag{6}$$

and likewise for $\int q^2(\mathbf{x}) d\mathbf{x}$, such that

$$J(p, q) = \frac{\frac{1}{N_1 N_2} \sum_{i,j=1}^{N_1, N_2} G_{ij, 2\sigma^2 \mathbf{I}}}{\sqrt{\frac{1}{N_1^2} \sum_{i,i'=1}^{N_1, N_1} G_{ii', 2\sigma^2 \mathbf{I}} \frac{1}{N_2^2} \sum_{j,j'=1}^{N_2, N_2} G_{jj', 2\sigma^2 \mathbf{I}}}}. \tag{7}$$

For each data pattern $\mathbf{x}_i$, $i = 1, \ldots, N$, $N = N_1 + N_2$, we now define a membership vector $\mathbf{m}_i$. If $\mathbf{x}_i$ belongs to cluster C_1 (C_2), the corresponding crisp membership vector equals $\mathbf{m}_i = [1, 0]^T$ ($[0, 1]^T$). This allows us to rewrite (7) as a function of the memberships, obtaining;

$$J(p, q) = \frac{\frac{1}{2} \sum_{i,j=1}^{N,N} \left(1 - \mathbf{m}_i^T \mathbf{m}_j\right) G_{ij, 2\sigma^2 \mathbf{I}}}{\sqrt{\prod_{k=1}^{2} \sum_{i,j=1}^{N,N} m_{ik} m_{jk} G_{ij, 2\sigma^2 \mathbf{I}}}}, \tag{8}$$

where m_{ik} (m_{jk}), $k = 1, 2$, denotes element number k of $\mathbf{m}_i$ ($\mathbf{m}_j$). In the sequel we will make explicit that the variable quantities in (8) are the membership vectors, thus, we will use the notation $J(\mathbf{m}_1, \ldots, \mathbf{m}_N)$ instead of $J(p, q)$.

In the case of multiple clusters, C_k, $k = 1, \ldots, K$, we extend the previous definition as follows

$$J(\mathbf{m}_1, \ldots, \mathbf{m}_N) = \frac{\frac{1}{2} \sum_{i,j=1}^{N,N} \left(1 - \mathbf{m}_i^T \mathbf{m}_j\right) G_{ij, 2\sigma^2 \mathbf{I}}}{\sqrt{\prod_{k=1}^{K} \sum_{i,j=1}^{N,N} m_{ik} m_{jk} G_{ij, 2\sigma^2 \mathbf{I}}}}, \tag{9}$$

where each $\mathbf{m}_i$, $i = 1, \ldots, N$, is a binary K dimensional vector. Only the k'th element of any $\mathbf{m}_i$ equals one, meaning that the corresponding data pattern $\mathbf{x}_i$ is assigned to cluster k.

The cost function $J(\mathbf{m}_1, \ldots, \mathbf{m}_N)$ is related to the cluster evaluation function used by Gokcay and Principe [10]. They basically clustered based on the numerator of (9), which can be considered equivalent to a "between-cluster" Renyi entropy measure. Their clustering technique was based on calculating the cluster evaluation function for all clustering possibilities, hence impractical for anything but very small data sets. We incorporate the "within-cluster" Renyi entropies in the cost function, which are equivalent to the quantities in the denominator of (9). This helps balance the cost function, and avoids problems such as obtaining a minimum of the cost function when only one data point is isolated in a cluster, and all the other data points in the remaining cluster. In addition, in the following we will derive an efficient optimization technique for minimizing $J(\mathbf{m}_1, \ldots, \mathbf{m}_N)$.

We assume a-priori knowledge about the number, K, of clusters inherit in the data set. This may seem to be a strict assumption, and in some cases it probably is. However, much research has been conducted with regard to estimating the number of clusters present in a data set. See e.g. [11] for an overview of different cluster indicies.

3   Lagrange Optimization

In order to minimize (9) using differential calculus techniques, we need to fuzzify the membership vectors such that $\mathbf{m}_i \in [0, 1]$, $i = 1, \ldots, N$. Accordingly, we suggest to solve the following constrained optimization problem

$$\min_{\mathbf{m}_1, \ldots, \mathbf{m}_N} J(\mathbf{m}_1, \ldots, \mathbf{m}_N), \tag{10}$$

subject to $\mathbf{m}_j^T \mathbf{1} - 1 = 0$, $j = 1, \ldots, N$, where $\mathbf{1}$ is a K-dimensional ones-vector. Now we make a convenient change of variables. Let $m_{ik} = v_{ik}^2$, $k = 1, \ldots, K$. Consider

$$\min_{\mathbf{v}_1, \ldots, \mathbf{v}_N} J(\mathbf{v}_1, \ldots, \mathbf{v}_N), \tag{11}$$

subject to $\mathbf{v}_j^T \mathbf{v}_j - 1 = 0$, $j = 1, \ldots, N$. The constraints for the problem stated in (11) are equivalent to the constraints for (10). The optimization problem, (11), amounts to adjusting the vectors $\mathbf{v}_i$, $i = 1, \ldots, N$, such that

$$\frac{\partial J}{\partial \mathbf{v}_i} = \left(\frac{\partial J}{\partial \mathbf{m}_i}^T \frac{\partial \mathbf{m}_i}{\partial \mathbf{v}_i} \right)^T = \mathbf{\Gamma} \frac{\partial J}{\partial \mathbf{m}_i} \to \mathbf{0}, \tag{12}$$

where $\mathbf{\Gamma} = \mathrm{diag}(2\sqrt{m_{i1}}, \ldots, 2\sqrt{m_{iK}})$. We force all elements $2\sqrt{m_{ik}}$, $k = 1, \ldots, K$, to always be positive by adding a small positive constant ϵ during each membership update. Hence, $\frac{\partial J}{\partial \mathbf{v}_i} \to 0$ implies $\frac{\partial J}{\partial \mathbf{m}_i} \to 0$. Thus, these scalars can be interpreted as variable step-sizes built into the gradient descent search process, as a consequence of the change of variables that we made. We will return to the derivation of $\frac{\partial J}{\partial \mathbf{m}_i}$ in subsection 3.2, and to the stochastic approximation of this quantity.

The necessary conditions for the solution of (11) are commonly generated by constructing the Lagrange function, given by

$$L = J(\mathbf{v}_1, \ldots, \mathbf{v}_N) + \sum_{j=1}^{N} \lambda_j \left(\mathbf{v}_j^T \mathbf{v}_j - 1 \right), \tag{13}$$

where λ_j, $j = 1, \ldots, N$, are the *Lagrange multipliers*. The necessary conditions for the extremum of L are given by

$$\frac{\partial L}{\partial \mathbf{v}_i} = \frac{\partial J}{\partial \mathbf{v}_i} + \sum_{k=1}^{N} \lambda_k \frac{\partial}{\partial \mathbf{v}_i} \left(\mathbf{v}_k^T \mathbf{v}_k - 1 \right) = \mathbf{0}, \tag{14}$$

$$\frac{\partial L}{\partial \lambda_j} = \mathbf{v}_j^T \mathbf{v}_j - 1 = 0, \tag{15}$$

for $i, j = 1, \ldots, N$. From (14) we derive the following *fixed-point adaption rule* for the vector $\mathbf{v}_i$ as follows

$$\frac{\partial J}{\partial \mathbf{v}_i} + 2\lambda_i \mathbf{v}_i = \mathbf{0} \Rightarrow \mathbf{v}_i^+ = -\frac{1}{2\lambda_i} \frac{\partial J}{\partial \mathbf{v}_i}, \tag{16}$$

$i = 1, \ldots, N$, and where $\mathbf{v}_i^+$ denotes the updated vector.

We solve for the Lagrange multipliers, λ_i, $i = 1, \ldots, N$, by evaluating (15), yielding

$$\lambda_i = \frac{1}{2} \sqrt{\frac{\partial J}{\partial \mathbf{v}_i}^T \frac{\partial J}{\partial \mathbf{v}_i}}. \tag{17}$$

After convergence of the algorithm, or after a predetermined number of iterations, we designate the maximum value of the elements of each $\mathbf{m}_i$, $i = 1, \ldots, N$, to one, and the rest to zero.

We initialize the membership vectors randomly according to a uniform distribution. That way $\mathbf{m}_i \in [0, 1]$ $\forall i$, even though the constraint of (10) is not obeyed. We have observed that after the first iteration through the algorithm, the constraint is always obeyed. Better initialization schemes may be used, although in our experiments, the algorithm is very little affected by the actual initialization used.

3.1   Kernel Size and Annealing Scheme

In section 2, the same kernel size, σ, was used in the Parzen estimate of both (all) the pdfs of the clusters. Obviously, to obtain a perfect pdf estimate for each cluster, this assumption may not be valid. But since we don't know which data points belong to which cluster (since this is exactly what we are trying to determine) it is impossible to obtain a separate kernel size for each cluster. Given an input data set, the best we can do is to estimate the optimal kernel size σ based on the whole data set. In section 4, we show that for the purpose of clustering, using a single kernel size for each cluster gives promising results, even though the underlying densities are not necessarily optimally estimated.

We will use Silverman's rule-of-thumb to determine the optimal kernel size with respect to a mean integrated square error criterion between the estimated and the actual pdf. It is given by [12]

$$\sigma_{\text{opt}} = \sigma_X \left\{ 4N^{-1}(2d+1)^{-1} \right\}^{\frac{1}{d+4}}, \tag{18}$$

where d is the dimensionality of the data and $\sigma_X^2 = d^{-1} \sum_i \Sigma_{X_{ii}}$ and $\Sigma_{X_{ii}}$ are the diagonal elements of the sample covariance matrix.

The new CS-clustering algorithm that we propose can be operated in a fully automatic mode by selecting the kernel size using (18), assuming that the correct number of clusters, K, has been estimated beforehand. Hence no user-specified parameters are needed. However, since the CS-cost function is non-convex, it may exhibit more than one optimum. For many data sets, the algorithm may always converge to the correct solution, but for other data sets, it may in some cases converge to a local non-optimal solution.

The Parzen windowing makes it possible to incorporate a learning strategy into the algorithm to help avoid local minima. The kernel size is allowed to be annealed over a range of values around the optimal value. We start out with a relatively large kernel size, which has the effect of smoothing out local minima of the cost function. As the algorithm converges toward the global minimum of the smoothed cost function, which is biased wrt. the location of the true minimum, the kernel size is continuously annealed, such that the minimum of the smoothed cost function gets more and more aligned with the true minimum. By incorporating the annealing into the algorithm, we can be more certain that the solution obtained is close to the desired solution.

3.2   Stochastic Approximation

In this subsection we examine the stochastic approximation approach for calculating the gradient $\frac{\partial J}{\partial \mathbf{m}_i}$.

Let $J = \frac{U}{V}$, where

$$U = \frac{1}{2} \sum_{i,j=1}^{N,N} \left(1 - \mathbf{m}_i^T \mathbf{m}_j\right) G_{ij,2\sigma^2 \mathbf{I}},$$

$$V = \sqrt{\prod_{k=1}^{K} v_k} \text{ and } v_k = \sum_{i,j=1}^{N,N} m_{ik} m_{jk} G_{ij,2\sigma^2 \mathbf{I}}. \tag{19}$$

Hence

$$\frac{\partial J}{\partial \mathbf{m}_i} = \frac{V \frac{\partial U}{\partial \mathbf{m}_i} - U \frac{\partial V}{\partial \mathbf{m}_i}}{V^2}, \tag{20}$$

$$\frac{\partial U}{\partial \mathbf{m}_i} = - \sum_{j=1}^{N} \mathbf{m}_j G_{ij,2\sigma^2 \mathbf{I}}, \tag{21}$$

$$\frac{\partial V}{\partial \mathbf{m}_i} = \frac{1}{2} \sum_{k'=1}^{K} \sqrt{\frac{\prod_{\substack{k=1 \\ k \neq k'}}^{K} v_k}{v_{k'}}} \frac{\partial v_{k'}}{\partial \mathbf{m}_i}, \tag{22}$$

where $\frac{\partial v_{k'}}{\partial \mathbf{m}_i} = \begin{bmatrix} 0 & \cdots & 2 \sum_{j=1}^{N} m_{jk'} G_{ij,2\sigma^2 \mathbf{I}} & \cdots & 0 \end{bmatrix}^T$. Thus, only element number k' of this vector is nonzero.

The key point to note, is that we can calculate all quantities of interest in (20), by determining (21), for $\forall i$. Since (21) is a sum over N elements, calculating all these quantities is an $O(N^2)$ procedure. An $O(N^2)$ algorithm may become intractable for large data sets. To reduce complexity, we estimate (21) by *stochastically sampling* the membership space, and utilize M randomly selected membership vectors, and corresponding data points, to compute

$$-\sum_{m=1}^{M} \mathbf{m}_m G_{im,2\sigma^2 \mathbf{I}}, \tag{23}$$

as an approximation to (21). Hence, the overall complexity of the algorithm is reduced to $O(MN)$ for each iteration. We will show that we obtain very good clustering results, even selecting M to be as small as 15% of N.

4   Clustering Experiments

In this section we report clustering results on two artificially created data sets, and one real. In all experiments, we use (18) to estimate the kernel size with respect to Parzen pdf estimation. The upper limit of the kernel size, which we start out with in the annealing procedure, is chosen to be $\sigma_{\text{upper}} = 2\sigma_{\text{opt}}$, and the lower limit is selected as $\sigma_{\text{lower}} = 0.5\sigma_{\text{opt}}$. The kernel size is linearly decreased using a step size $\Delta_\sigma = (\sigma_{\text{upper}} - \sigma_{\text{lower}})/100$. If convergence is not obtained when reaching σ_{lower}, the algorithm continues using σ_{lower} as the kernel size. These values are selected based on our experimental experience. It should be said that the algorithm is quite robust with regard to these values. Also, the value of M is always selected as 15% of the value of N (rounded to the nearest integer). Our experiments show that even thought we only use a few randomly chosen points to estimate the gradients, the results are as good as utilizing the whole data set. The memberships are initialized as proposed in section 3, and the constant $\epsilon = 0.05$. In order to stop the algorithm, we examine the crisp memberships every tenth iteration. If there is no change in crisp memberships over these ten iterations, it is assumed that the algorithm has either converged to a reasonable solution, or that the algorithm is trapped in a local minimum from which it cannot escape. Hence, when the algorithm terminates, it has in practice converged at least ten iterations earlier.

In our first experiment, we consider the data set shown in Fig. 1 (a). A human can observe that it contains two "half-moon"-shaped clusters with a highly non-linear cluster boundary. There are totally $N = 419$ data patterns. The data set is clustered 20 times using the CS-clustering algorithm. In absolutely all trials, a result similar to that shown in Fig. 1 (b) is produced, after on average about 100 iterations. It can be seen that the clustering reveals the structure of the data set. It should be said that a similar result is also obtained in 80% of the trials using the fixed kernel mode, that is, the kernel is not annealed. Hence, in fixed kernel mode, the algorithm converges to a local optimum in 20% of the trials. For comparison, a typical result using the EMGMM algorithm is shown in Fig. 1 (c).

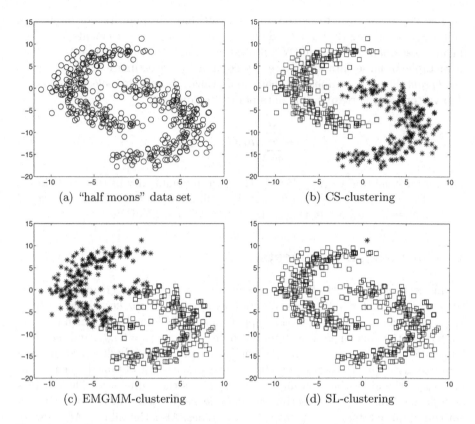

(a) "half moons" data set   (b) CS-clustering

(c) EMGMM-clustering   (d) SL-clustering

Fig. 1. The CS-clustering algorithm performs very well on this two-cluster data set, where the boundary between the clusters is highly non-linear, and there are some overlap

The EMGMM algorithm never obtains the desired result, but always produces a near-linear cluster boundary. The same is the case for the Fuzzy K-means algorithm, which produces a result similar to the EMGMM (not shown). Also, the result using the single-link clustering algorithm [1] is shown in Fig. 1 (d). It can be seen that it isolates a single point in one cluster, and links together all the rest. This behavior is typical for the single-link algorithm when the clusters have some overlap. Fortunately, the CS-clustering algorithm shows no such tendency. Note that all the clustering methods we compare with are popular and often used in practice.

In the second experiment, we cluster the data set shown in Fig. 2 (a). It contains $N = 819$ data patterns. As can be observed, there seems to be three clusters, but the boundaries are not very clear. Consistently, the CS-algorithm produces a clustering result as shown in Fig. 2 (b), after on average about 120 iterations. The result clearly seems to be reasonable, considering the structure of the data set. For comparison, the result obtained using fuzzy K-means is shown in Fig. 2 (c). The linear cluster boundaries this method produces are shown by the straight lines,

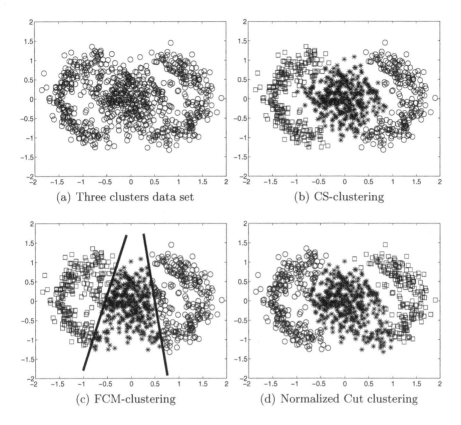

(a) Three clusters data set

(b) CS-clustering

(c) FCM-clustering

(d) Normalized Cut clustering

Fig. 2. Data set consisting of three clusters used in second clustering experiment

obviously not capturing the non-linear nature of the data. The result obtained using the EMGMM algorithm is quite similar, and is not shown. The single-link algorithm fails completely on this kind of data, because the data is noisy. We also include a comparison to a recent graph-based clustering algorithm known as the Normalized Cut method [13]. The scale parameter used in this method to define graph edge-weights was recommended by the authors to be in the range $10 - 20\%$ of the total range of the Euclidean feature vector distances. We use 15%. The resulting clustering is shown in Fig. 2 (d). It is clearly an improvement over fuzzy K-means, but seems not to capture the cluster structure to the same degree as our proposed method.

As a final experiment, the Wisconsin breast-cancer (WBC) data set [14] is clustered. It consists of 683 data points (444 benign and 239 malignant). WBC is a nine-dimensional dataset with features related to clump thickness, uniformity of cell size, shape, and so forth. See [14] for details. On average, we obtained a correct classification rate of 94.5%, which is comparable to the best results reported for other clustering schemes on this data set.

5 Conclusions

In this paper, we have developed a clustering algorithm that is based on optimizing the Cauchy-Schwarz information theoretic distance measure between densities. The optimization is carried out using the Lagrange multiplier formalism, and can be considered a constrained gradient descent search. The gradients are stochastically approximated, reducing the complexity from $O(N^2)$ to $O(MN)$, $M \ll N$. We have shown that the algorithm performs well on several data sets, and that it is capable of clustering data sets where the cluster boundaries are highly non-linear. We attribute this property to the information theoretic metric we use, combined with non-parametric Parzen density estimation.

Jenssen et al. [15] in fact discovered a relationship between the Cauchy-Schwarz pdf distance and the graph theoretic *cut*. This means that our proposed method can also be considered to belong to the family of graph-based clustering cost functions, and it is hence related to the Normalized Cut method and spectral clustering. However, in our method, there is no need to compute eigenvectors, which is known to be a computationally demanding procedure. In future work, we will further pursue this link between our information theoretic approach and graph theory. See also [16] for comments on this link.

References

1. A. K. Jain, M. N. Murty, and P. J. Flynn, "Data Clustering: A Review," *ACM Computing Surveys*, vol. 31, no. 3, pp. 264–323, 1999.
2. J. C. Bezdek, "A Convergence Theorem for the Fuzzy Isodata Clustering Algorithms," *IEEE Transactions on Pattern Analysis and Machine Learning*, vol. 2, no. 1, pp. 1–8, 1980.
3. G. J. McLachlan and D. Peel, *Finite Mixture Models*, John Wiley & Sons, New York, 2000.
4. K. Rose, E. Gurewitz, and G. C. Fox, "Vector Quantization by Deterministic Annealing," *IEEE Transactions on Information Theory*, vol. 38, no. 4, pp. 1249–1257, 1992.
5. T. Hofmann and J. M. Buhmann, "Pairwise Data Clustering by Deterministic Annealing," *IEEE Transactions on Pattern Analysis and Machine Intelligence*, vol. 19, no. 1, pp. 1–14, 1997.
6. S. J. Roberts, R. Everson, and I. Rezek, "Maximum Certainty Data Partitioning," *Pattern Recognition*, vol. 33, pp. 833–839, 2000.
7. N. Tishby and N. Slonim, "Data Clustering by Markovian Relaxation and the Information Bottleneck Method," in *Advances in Neural Information Processing Systems, 13*, MIT Press, Cambridge, 2001, pp. 640–646.
8. J. Principe, D. Xu, and J. Fisher, "Information Theoretic Learning," in *Unsupervised Adaptive Filtering*, S. Haykin (Ed.), John Wiley & Sons, New York, 2000, vol. I, Chapter 7.
9. E. Parzen, "On the Estimation of a Probability Density Function and the Mode," *The Annals of Mathematical Statistics*, vol. 32, pp. 1065–1076, 1962.
10. E. Gokcay and J. Principe, "Information Theoretic Clustering," *IEEE Transactions on Pattern Analysis and Machine Intelligence*, vol. 24, no. 2, pp. 158–170, 2002.

11. G. W. Milligan and M. C. Cooper, "An Examination of Procedures for Determining the Number of Clusters in a Data Set," *Phychometrica*, pp. 159–179, 1985.
12. B. W. Silverman, *Density Estimation for Statistics and Data Analysis*, Chapman and Hall, London, 1986.
13. J. Shi and J. Malik, "Normalized Cuts and Image Segmentation," *IEEE Transactions on Pattern Analysis and Machine Intelligence*, vol. 22, no. 8, pp. 888–905, 2000.
14. O.L Mangasarian and W. H. Wolberg, "Cancer Diagnosis via Linear Programming," *SIAM News*, vol. 5, pp. 1–18, 1990.
15. R. Jenssen, J. C. Principe, and T. Eltoft, "Information Cut and Information Forces for Clustering," in *Proceedings of IEEE International Workshop on Neural Networks for Signal Processing*, Toulouse, France, September 17-19, 2003, pp. 459–468.
16. R. Jenssen, D. Erdogmus, J. C. Principe, and T. Eltoft, "The Laplacian PDF Distance: A Cost Function for Clustering in a Kernel Feature Space," in *Advances in Neural Information Processing Systems 17*, MIT Press, Cambridge, 2005, pp. 625–632.

Concurrent Stereo Matching: An Image Noise-Driven Model

John Morris, Georgy Gimel'farb, Jiang Liu, and Patrice Delmas

Department of Computer Science, Tamaki Campus,
The University of Auckland, Auckland, Private Bag 92019, New Zealand
Tel: +64 9 3737599 ext 88744, Fax: +64 9 3082377
{j.morris, g.gimelfarb, p.delmas}@auckland.ac.nz,
jliu001@ec.auckland.ac.nz

Abstract. Most published techniques for reconstructing scenes from stereo pairs follow a conventional strategy of searching for a single surface yielding the best correspondence between the images. The search involves specific constraints on surface continuity, smoothness, and visibility (occlusions) embedded in a matching score - typically an *ad hoc* linear combination of distinctly different criteria of signal similarity. The coefficients or weighing factors are selected empirically because they dramatically effect accuracy of stereo matching. The single surface assumption is also too restrictive - few real scenes have only one surface.

We introduce a paradigm of concurrent stereo that circumvents in part these problems by separating image matching from a choice of the 3D surfaces. Concurrent stereo matching first detects all likely matching 3D volumes instead of single best matches. Then, starting in the foreground, the volumes are explored, selecting mutually consistent optical surfaces that exhibit high point-wise signal similarity. Local, rather than global, surface continuity and visibility constraints are applied.

1 Introduction

Many strategies for 3D reconstruction from stereo pairs have been proposed [1, 2]. Universally, matching corresponding points in the left and right images is a critical step. Stereo reconstruction remains an ill-posed inverse optical problem because many different optical surfaces may produce the same stereo pair due to homogeneous (i.e. uniform or repetitive) texture, partial occlusions and optical signal distortions. Occlusions result in image areas with no correspondence and texture homogeneity produces multiple equivalent matches.

Over many years, automated stereo matching has evolved from simple feature or gradient descent based algorithms (e.g. [4, 5]) to complex optimisation based on dynamic programming [6–9], graph minimum-cut [10–13], or belief propagation techniques [13–16] . Almost all these approaches follow the same paradigm of searching for a single optical surface yielding the best correspondence between images under specific constraints on surface continuity, smoothness, and visibility (or partial occlusions). Even the best performing minimum-cut algorithms

A. Rangarajan et al. (Eds.): EMMCVPR 2005, LNCS 3757, pp. 46–59, 2005.

use an *ad hoc* linear combination of signal similarity, surface smoothness, and surface visibility criteria with empirically chosen weights of each criterion. It has been shown that the choice of the weights strongly influences the reconstruction accuracy [18]. Moreover, few real scenes consist of a single surface, so this assumption is also too restrictive.

Recently a paradigm of searching for a minimal photo-consistent hull containing no spatial elements (voxels) resulting in dissimilar corresponding points was used to reconstruct a 3D surface from multiple images [19]. Also, humans tend to analyse a scene in 'strokes' - the eye's focus browsing from low to high frequency regions, from sharp points to smooth areas and vice versa rather than scanning line-by-line [20]. Starting with these ideas, we introduce a novel paradigm of concurrent binocular stereo reconstruction fusing advantages and reducing disadvantages of previous methods. In this paper, we show that a typical stereo pair contains many admissible matches, so that 'best' matching or minimization algorithms will make many incorrect decisions. To counter this, our paradigm separates image matching from a subsequent search for surfaces by considering all likely matching volumes instead of singleton local best matches and exploiting local surface constraints rather than global continuity ones. Concurrent matching has two main features. First, corresponding volumes are found by image-to-image matching at each fixed depth, or disparity value. This allows mutual photometric distortions of images to be taken into account. Secondly, reconstruction proceeds from foreground to background surfaces to account for occlusions - enlarging corresponding background volumes at the expense of occluded portions. An additional colour continuity criterion is used then to select most appropriate surfaces.

Section 2 discusses the ill-posed nature of binocular stereo using artificial scene profiles and slices of one real image pair (the "Tsukuba" set). Note that our aim in this paper is only to illustrate the main properties of the paradigm we are proposing. Basic steps of the concurrent paradigm are considered in Section 3, in particular, matching images to find corresponding spatial volumes and fitting surfaces to those volumes.

2   Ill-Posed Binocular Stereo

Figure 1 exemplifies the main problems that can be encountered with single surface binocular stereo reconstruction as well as with regularisation of a multiple surface scene. A section through a set of surfaces along with the corresponding piecewise-constant intensity profiles in the left and right images is shown in Figure 1(a). Grey areas in Figures 1(b)-(d) show matching regions. Figure 1(b) shows that an erroneous single surface profile may easily be constructed by applying smoothness and ordering constraints. Other reconstructions (from the many possible) are shown in Figures 1(c) and (d). Moreover, the corresponding (precisely matching) areas do not reflect the actual scene unless occlusions are taken into account. Without additional constraints, it is impossible to discriminate between possible solutions.

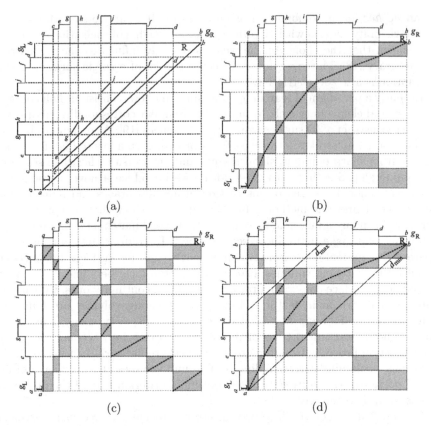

Fig. 1. Reconstructions from a stereo pair demonstrating the ill-posed nature of the problem - *even in the absence of noise*: (a) actual surface profiles with intensity profiles for the left and right images shown along vertical and horizontal axes - labels indicate correspondences between surfaces and regions in the intensity profiles; (b)-(d) possible surface reconstructions are shown by dotted lines through grey-shaded possible matching regions: (b) a single continuous profile, (c) one (extreme) disjoint variant, and (d) one restricted to a fixed disparity range - surface profiles above the line marked $'d_{max}'$ are excluded.

Furthermore, even low level signal noise that does not mask major signal changes in Fig. 1 hinders the conventional matching paradigm because it is based on the maximum similarity between the signals for a reasonably constrained surface. In our simple example, the closest similarity between the initially equal signals distorted with independent noise can lead to selection of a completely random surface from a set of admissible variants specified by both signal correspondences and surface constraints.

Given a noise model, a more realistic stereo matching goal is to estimate signal noise and specify a plausible range of differences between corresponding signals. The noise estimates allow us to outline 3D volumes that contain all the surfaces ensuring such a 'good matching'. Then the desired surface or surfaces may be chosen using surface constraints only.

Generally, stereo matching presumes the availability of a signal similarity model that accounts for changes in surface reflection for any potential noise sources. However, most stereo matching algorithms in computer vision, including the best-performing graph minimum-cut ones, use very simple similarity criteria such as the sum of absolute signal differences (SAD) or square differences (SSD) for all the binocularly visible surface points. The underlying signal model assumes equal corresponding signals distorted by an additive independent noise with the same zero-centred symmetric probability distribution. Such a simplification is justified for a few stereo pairs typically used for testing algorithms, e.g., for the Middlebury data set [2]. However, it is invalid in most practical applications, e.g. for aerial or ground stereo images of terrain collected at different times under changing illumination and image acquisition conditions. More realistic similarity models must take account of global or local offset and contrast signal distortions [7, 9].

For the "Tsukuba" pair, Table 1 shows empirical probability distributions of absolute pixel-wise signal differences, $\delta I(x, y, d) = |I_L(x, y) - I_R(x-d, y)|$, for the corresponding points in the supplied 'ground truth' and for three single-surface models reconstructed by symmetric dynamic programming stereo (SDPS), graph minimum cut (GMC), and belief propagation (BP) algorithms in a given x-disparity range $\Delta = [d_{\min} = 0, d_{\max} = 14]$. Effectively, this distribution shows the discrepancy in a real image pair from the assumed simple signal model: sources for this 'noise' are:

1. signal-based (circuit noise, quantization, . . .),
2. geometric (discrete pixel sensors, occlusions, perspective, . . .) and
3. optical (non-uniform scattering, specular reflections, . . .).

Fig. 2 plots these distributions (top left) and shows grey-coded signal correspondences for one epipolar line ($y = 173$) in terms of the pixel-wise absolute differences - black regions correspond to $\delta I = 0$. The multiplicity of possible

Table 1. Distribution of intensity differences for corresponding points in the "Tsukuba" scene: % of the corresponding points with the absolute intensity difference δI in the indicated range where x-disparities are derived from the ground truth (True) and the model reconstructed by SDPS, GMC and BP algorithms. The final column contains D, the sum of square distances between the distributions for the ground truth and the reconstructed models.

δI	0	1	2	3- 10	6- 20	11- 30	21- 60	31- 125	61- 255	126-	D $\times 10^{-4}$
True	18.5	29.6	19.5	19.1	6.6	3.7	1.4	1.2	0.4	0.0	
SDPS	20.9	30.9	18.1	17.9	6.7	3.7	1.2	0.6	0.0	0.0	8.5
GMC	17.2	25.3	15.5	17.3	8.9	6.9	3.3	2.2	1.4	0.0	60.9
BP	17.2	30.4	19.7	21.5	6.4	3.6	1.0	0.8	2.3	1.2	13.6

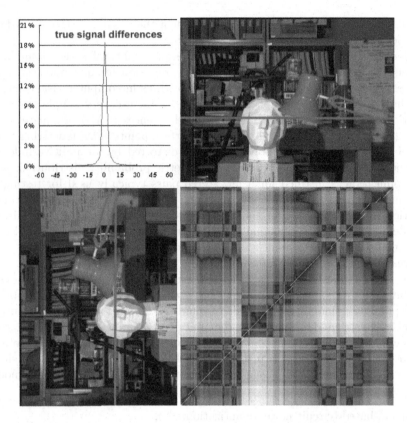

Fig. 2. "Tsukuba" stereo pair: (top left) distribution of signal differences, δI, for the pair of epipolar lines marked in the actual images ($y = 173$); (bottom right) grey-coded absolute signal differences, $|\delta I|$, for the whole image, with the actual profile marked. Dark regions indicate good matches: the multiplicity of *admissable* matches is clearly shown.

matches is clearly seen[1]. The distribution obtained with the symmetric dynamic programming stereo (SDPS) algorithm [9] is closest to the true one. Hence, in these experiments, we used the pixel-wise absolute signal differences from SDPS as estimates of the spatially variant image noise. The overlaid true surface profiles show that in this example the single-surface approximation is close to the actual disjoint scene only due to a small x-disparity range $\Delta = [0, 14]$.

3   Concurrent Stereo Matching - Basic Features

Concurrent stereo reconstruction first matches image pixels using a signal model to estimate random signal noise which generally is independent in both images

---

[1] Scene assumptions enable the matching regions to be delimited. Assuming no 'out-of-image' matching eliminates the lower right triangle. Assuming a closest approach (or maximum disparity) eliminates much of the upper left. However, plenty of candidate matches remain!

and can be spatially variant. The model takes into account possible global or local contrast or offset deviations between corresponding image areas. In contrast to conventional paradigms, rather than immediately trying to find the single optical surface or its minimal visual hull, it first delimits all 3D volumes which are reconstruction candidates, i.e. which contain all the candidate 3D points that ensure an admissible (or good) match according to the noise model[2]. The second step attempts to find surfaces fitting the candidate volumes using only smoothness and visibility constraints that rank the surfaces according to their appropriateness *for human visual perception*. The fundamentally ill-posed nature of the problem makes discovering the true surface an unrealistic goal. Thus, we set a more practical goal - to select from possible candidates a surface that closely resembles the choice that a human observer would make. In the final stage, one or more surfaces are selected and possible partial occlusions of the chosen surfaces are analyzed. In particular, this could be done by stratifying surfaces into foreground versus background and refining the occluded background after eliminating the foregrounds. By retaining all likely solutions for a given set of images, the imposition of constraints which are not always physically realistic is delayed until the final stage where they guide choices of possible solutions.

3.1   Admissible Point-Wise Correspondences

The artificial example in Fig. 1 presumes that corresponding volumes have zero matching error. If low-level noise is added to these signals, the pixel-wise correspondences for each disparity, d, have a zero-centred cluster of small signal differences that includes true matches and one or more distant clusters representing only mismatches. The noise distribution estimated from the central cluster allows us to recover the corresponding areas seen in Fig. 1.

Using the same simple model of signal distortions, natural cases such as the "Tsukuba" set (Fig. 2) produce continuous distributions of signal differences (see the top left quadrant of Fig. 2). Generally, the distribution of noise will be spatially variant and has to be locally estimated. For simplicity, the noise estimation process could focus on best matching scores under the same model. Table 1 shows that SDPS reconstruction along corresponding epipolar lines provides reasonably close estimates of the residual pixel-wise noise for the "Tsukuba" scene. Obviously, images with finer texture need more robust noise estimation models taking account of sub-pixel quantisation errors [21]. These noise estimates can be used to determine what is considered to be an admissible match.

Examples of the first step in our new paradigm are presented in Figs. 3–8 for four stereo pairs from the Middlebury database [2] ("Tsukuba", "Venus", "Map", and "Sawtooth", respectively). The middle panels in Figs. 3 and 6 and the upper panels in Figs. 5 and 8 show d-slices of the candidate (x, y, d) volumes. Black points indicate candidates with signal differences within the estimated noise ranges for each (x, y)-position, i.e., acceptable matches.

---

[2] All good matches are equivalent with respect to the estimated noise range and within other admissible contrast or offset image deviations.

Fig. 3. Stereo pair "Tsukuba" – First two rows: Ideal disparity map for selected disparities d. Middle two rows: First nine panels: Candidate (x, y, p) volumes sliced at selected values of d. Large black regions clearly indicate good candidates for the final surfaces. Tenth panel: SDPS-estimated spatial noise variation – black-to-white coding of a noise range from [0,0] to [0,27] (white indicates the largest range). Last two rows: Selection of reconstructed surfaces.

3.2   Surfaces for the Corresponding Volumes

Surfaces were successively fitted to each separate candidate volume working from foreground to background within a known disparity range, Δ. In the "Tsukuba" scene, this implies that the large black region of the lamp in the $d = 14$ slice was first accepted and then propagated 'back' into the scene as occluded points. To rank surface variants in the corresponding volumes in accord with typical

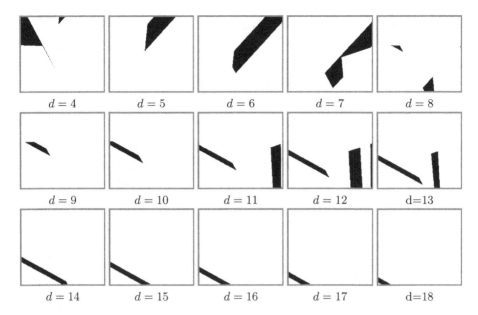

Fig. 4. Stereo pair "Venus" – Ideal disparity map for selected disparities d

visual perception, we used a preference criterion based on the surface planarity, area, and its local expansion or shrinkage at the adjacent d-slices. In our first set of experiments, the mean shift algorithm was used to segment the original left colour image into a dense set of connected regions. Then each connected region was examined for proportion of good matching points at the current d value. If this proportion was above a threshhold (0.65 for the results shown), then the region is labelled a 'survivor' for this d value and the holes filled in. Alternative approaches based on assumptions that any detectable 'feature' must have a minimum projection (in pixels) in the image plane could be used to remove noisy outliers. This latter approach would be a practical requirement that, in effect, requires us to ensure that the problem we are posing is realistic: accepting isolated pixels as representing candidate volumes implies that we are attempting to extract more information from the image pair than is physically realistic – given a noise model. In the "Tsukuba" pair, only a small textureless region in the background remained accepted after this criterion is applied. Note carefully, that this is not an empirical parameter used to evaluate a cost function - as in typical 'best matching' techniques: it is a criterion established at the experiment design stage which governs the parameters of the stereo camera configuration, including in particular, resolution in the imaging planes.

A selection of final volumes (represented by regions remaining at various d levels) is shown in the lower rows of Figs 3, 5, 6, and 8. From Fig 2, it can be noted that our model produces very sharp, correct edges for most objects – evidenced by the very strong edges running through the signal differences plot in the lower right quadrant (in comparison to the 'fuzzy' edges of window-

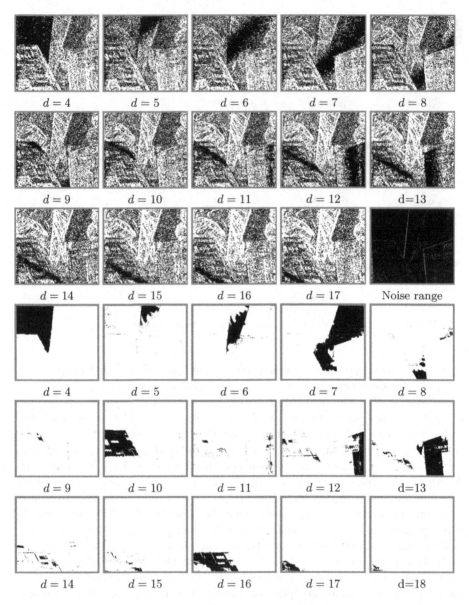

Fig. 5. Stereo pair "Venus" – First three rows: Candidate (x, y, p) volumes sliced at selected values of d (first 14 panels: large black regions clearly indicate good candidates for the final surfaces)and SDPS-estimated spatial noise variation (15th panel). Last three rows: Selection of reconstructed surfaces.

based correlation or 'slurred' edges of dynamic programming techniques). We also investigated region estimation using the mean shift algorithm and further suppression of likely matches by:

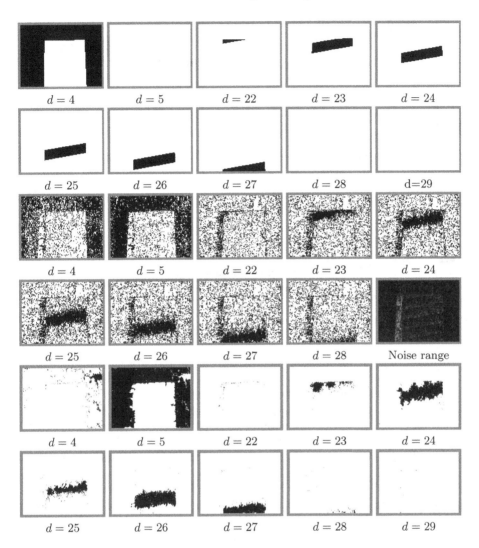

Fig. 6. "Map" image set: First two rows: Ideal disparity map for selected disparities. Middle two rows: Candidate (x, y, p) volumes sliced at selected values of d (first nine panels; large black regions clearly indicate good candidates for the final surfaces) and SDPS-estimated spatial noise variation (tenth panel). Last two rows: Selection of reconstructed surfaces.

1. generation of connected components based on region estimation,
2. estimating the ratio of likely matches in a connected cell versus the cell area for any given disparity slice, and
3. further processing of the connected components borders by intra- and inter-region statistical analysis.

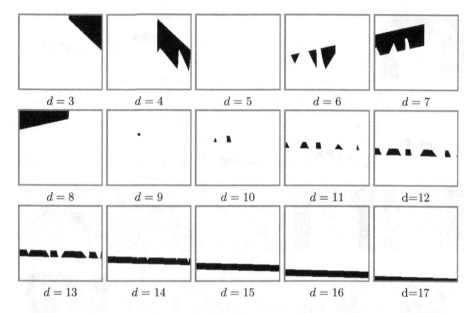

Fig. 7. Stereo pair "Sawtooth" – Ideal disparity map for selected disparities d

In Table 2, the performance of two variants of our concurrent stereo matching (CSM) algorithm are compared with the other algorithms ranked on the Middlebury web site. It can be seen that, with the exception of the stereo pair, "Map", the CSM algorithm is producing quite good results even before flexible surface models and optimization techniques are involved to ensure the best adjustment to the candidate volumes. The errors in the reconstructed "Map" surface are attributed to the original noise estimation step: the SDPS algorithm allows for significant signal mismatches in the regions where sharp jumps in disparity and thus large partial occlusions occur. Our oversimplified noise estimation takes no account of the occlusions, so that these mismatches translate into too large noise estimates for these regions. We expect that an improved noise estimation procedure, e.g. based on a Markov–Gibbs random field of noise ranges, will remove many of the poor matches accepted in this case.

4   Conclusion

Analysis of stereo images with ground truth shows that each stereo pair produces a large number of equivalent (with respect to the closest signal matching) solutions. Traditional stereo matching paradigms mix the matching and the selection of visually most appropriate surfaces. We propose that reconstruction should be separated into two steps:

1. independent noise or signal error range estimation to outline spatial volumes which are equivalent from the standpoint of image matching, and
2. selection of one or more surfaces to fit these volumes.

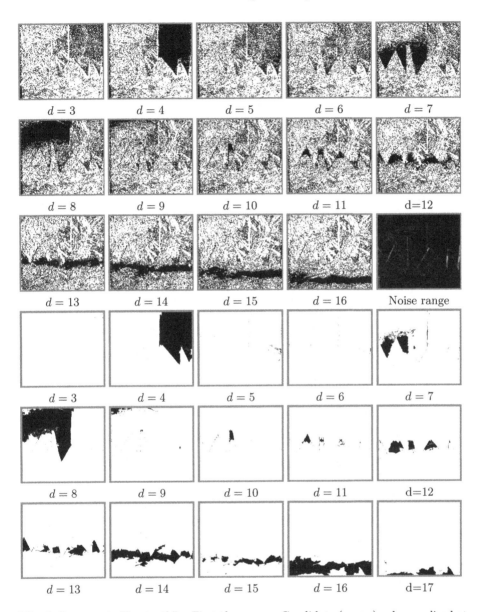

Fig. 8. Stereo pair "Sawtooth" – First three rows: Candidate (x, y, p) volumes sliced at selected values of d (first 14 panels; large black regions clearly indicate good candidates for the final surfaces) and SDPS-estimated spatial noise variation (15th panel). Last three rows: Selection of reconstructed surfaces.

The separation leads to more efficient stereo reconstruction techniques.

This key idea is that this new paradigm abandons the 'best match' or signal difference minimization criterion almost universally applied to date in favour of a likely match criterion based on a local signal noise model. The final reconstructed

Table 2. Comparison of concurrent stereo matching (CSM) with algorithms from the Middlebury web site `http://cat.middlebury.edu/stereo/` (MA): MA-SBPO – the best-performing symmetric belief propagation algorithm with occlusions[16]†; CSM-MSS and CSM-NS – CSM implementations with a conventional asymmetric stereo visibility model and with mean shift and noise based segmentation, respectively.

Algorithm	Tsukuba			Sawtooth			Venus			Map	
	all	untex.	disc.	all	untex.	disc.	all	untex.	disc.	all	disc.
MA-SBPO	0.97	0.28	5.45	0.19	0.00	2.09	0.16	0.02	2.77	0.16	2.20
Rank	1	3	3	1	1	3	3	2-3	7	1	1
Our:CSM-MSS	1.15	0.80	1.86	0.98	0.62	1.69	1.18	1.04	1.48	3.08	7.34
Rank	3	11	1	12	24	1	11	9	2	33	17
Our:CSM-NS	1.50	1.60	2.26	1.35	1.20	2.01	2.01	3.54	2.25	3.74	8.59
Rank	7	19	2	23	27	2	24	29	4	36	19
MA+CSM: rank 1	0.97	0.23	1.86	0.19	0.00	1.69	0.08	0.01	1.39	0.16	2.20
MA+CSM: rank 40	11.1	10.7	50.0	5.51	5.56	30.1	10.1	11.4	31.3	8.42	33.0

† The symmetric visibility model of Sun et al. [16] is close, although with no reference, to previously published models for symmetric dynamic programming stereo [6, 9, 17, 18].

surfaces exhibit excellent matching when compared to other reported algorithms even with an oversimplified implementation of the CSM paradigm. There is one exception – the stereo pair, "Map", with large disparity changes and thus large partially occluded regions that hinder our simple estimation of the image noise. We expect that with an improved noise model - for example, one that could easily be derived from calibrated camera systems - the errors resulting from using the SDPS generated disparity maps as noise estimators would be substantially reduced.

As a final note, we observe that this new paradigm is well suited to efficient parallel hardware implementations permitting high resolution, accurate, real-time, 3D scene reconstruction.

References

1. D. Burschka, M. Z. Brown, and G. D. Hager, Advances in computational stereo, *IEEE Trans. PAMI*, Vol. 25, pp. 993–1008, 2003.
2. D. Scharstein and R. Szeliski, A taxonomy and evaluation of dense two-frame stereo correspondence algorithms, *Int. J. Computer Vision*, Vol. 47, pp. 7–42, 2002.
3. T. Poggio, V. Torre, and C. Koch, Computational vision and regularization theory, *Nature*, no. 317, pp. 314–319, 1985.
4. Y. C. Hsieh, D. M. Mckeown Jr, and F.P. Perlant, Performance evaluation of scene registration and stereo matching for cartographic feature extraction, *IEEE Trans. PAMI*, Vol. 14, pp. 214–238, 1992.
5. C. L. Zitnick and T. Kanade, A cooperative algorithm for stereo matching and occlusion detection, *IEEE Trans. PAMI*, Vol. 22, pp. 675–684, 2000.
6. G. L. Gimel'farb, Symmetric approach to solution of the problem of automating stereo measurements in photogrammetry, *Cybernetics*, Vol. 15, pp. 235–247, 1979.

7. H. H. Baker, Surfaces from mono and stereo images, *Photogrammetria*, Vol. 39, pp. 217–237, 1984.

8. Y. Ohta and T. Kanade, Stereo by intra- and inter-scanline search using dynamic programming, *IEEE Trans. PAMI*, Vol. 7, pp. 139–154, 1985.

9. G. L. Gimel'farb, Intensity-based computer binocular stereo vision: signal models and algorithms, *Int. J. Imaging Systems and Technology*, Vol. 3, pp. 189–200, 1991.

10. S. Roy, Stereo without epiploar lines: A maximum-flow formulation, *Int. J. Computer Vision*, Vol. 34, pp. 147–161, 1999.

11. Yu. Boykov, O. Veksler, and R. Zabih, Fast approximate energy minimization via graph cut, *IEEE Trans. PAMI*, Vol. 23, pp. 1222–1239, 2001.

12. J. Kim, V. Kolmogorov, and R. Zabih, Visual correspondence using energy minimization and mutual information, in: *Proc. 9th IEEE Int. Conf. Computer Vision (ICCV 2003), Nice, France, 13–16 Oct. 2003*, IEEE Computer Society Press: Los Alamitos, Vol. 2, pp. 1003–1010, 2003.

13. M. F. Tappen and W. T. Freeman, Comparison of graph cuts with belief propagation for stereo, using identical MRF parameters, in: *Proc. 9th IEEE Int. Conf. Computer Vision (ICCV 2003), Nice, France, 13–16 Oct. 2003*, IEEE Computer Society Press: Los Alamitos, Vol. 2, pp. 900–906, 2003.

14. J. Sun, N. N. Zheng, and H. Y. Shum, Stereo matching using belief propagation, *IEEE Trans. PAMI*, Vol. 25, no. 7, pp. 787–800, 2003.

15. P. F. Felzenszwalb and D. P. Huttenlocher, Efficient belief propagation for early vision, *Proc. 2004 IEEE Computer Soc. Conf. Computer Vision and Pattern Recognition, 2004*, IEEE Computer Society Press, Vol. 1, pp. 261–268, 2004.

16. J. Sun, Y. Li, S. B. Kang, and H. Y. Shum, Symmetric stereo matching for occlusion handling, in: *Proc. 2005 IEEE Computer Soc. Conf. Computer Vision and Pattern Recognition, San Diego, CA, 20–26 June, 2005*, IEEE Computer Society Press, Vol. 2, pp. 399–406, 2005.

17. G. Gimel'farb, Probabilistic regularisation and symmetry in binocular dynamic programming stereo, *Pattern Recognition Letters*, Vol. 23, no. 4, pp. 431–442, 2002.

18. J. Liu and G. Gimel'farb, Accuracy of stereo reconstruction by minimum cut, symmetric dynamic programming, and correlation, in: *Proc. Image & Vision Computing New Zealand (IVCNZ'04) Conf., Akaroa, New Zealand, 21–23 Nov. 2004*, Landcare Research: Lincoln, pp. 65–70, 2004.

19. K. N. Kutulakos and S. M. Seitz, A theory of shape by space carving, *Int. J. Computer Vision*, Vol. 38, pp. 199–218, 2000.

20. A. Torralba. Modeling global scene factors in attention, *J. Optical Society of America*, Vol. 20A, pp. 1407–1418, 2003.

21. S. Birchfield and C. Tomasi, A pixel dissimilarity measure that is insensitive to image sampling, *IEEE Trans. PAMI*, Vol. 20, pp. 401–406, 1998.

Color Correction of Underwater Images
for Aquatic Robot Inspection

Luz A. Torres-Méndez and Gregory Dudek

Centre for Intelligent Machines, McGill University,
Montreal, Quebec, H3A 2A7, CA
{latorres, dudek}@cim.mcgill.ca,
http://www.cim.mcgill.ca/~latorres/research.html

Abstract. In this paper, we consider the problem of color restoration
using statistical priors. This is applied to color recovery for underwater
images, using an energy minimization formulation. Underwater images
present a challenge when trying to correct the blue-green monochrome
look to bring out the color we know marine life has. For aquatic robot
tasks, the quality of the images is crucial and needed in real-time. Our
method enhances the color of the images by using a Markov Random
Field (MRF) to represent the relationship between color depleted and
color images. The parameters of the MRF model are learned from the
training data and then the most probable color assignment for each pixel
in the given color depleted image is inferred by using belief propagation
(BP). This allows the system to adapt the color restoration algorithm to
the current environmental conditions and also to the task requirements.
Experimental results on a variety of underwater scenes demonstrate the
feasibility of our method.

1 Introduction

High quality image data is desirable for many underwater inspection and observation tasks. Particularly, vision systems for aquatic robots [3, 6, 9] must cope
with a host of geometrical distortions: colour distortions, dynamic lighting conditions and suspended particles (known as 'marine snow') that are due to inherent
physical properties of the marine environment. All these distortions cause poor
visibility and hinder computer vision tasks, e.g., those based on stereo triangulation or on structure from motion.

Image restoration in general, involves the correction of several types of degradation in an image. Traditionally, the most common sources of degradation are
due to imperfections of the sensors, or in transmission. Underwater vision is
plagued by poor visibility [11, 10] (even in the cleanest water). Additional factors
are the ambient light, and frequency-dependent scattering and absorption, both
between the camera and the environment, and also between the light source (the
sun) and the local environment (i.e. this varies with both depth and local water
conditions). The light undergoes scattering along the line of sight. The result
is an image that is color depleted (typically appearing bluish), blurry and out

A. Rangarajan et al. (Eds.): EMMCVPR 2005, LNCS 3757, pp. 60–73, 2005.

of focus. In this paper, we focus on the specific problem of restoring/enhancing the color of underwater images. The term *color* refers to the red, green and blue values (often called the color channels) for each pixel in an image. Prominent blue color of clear ocean water, apart from sky reflection, is due to selective absorption by water molecules. The quality of the water determines its filtering properties. The greater the dissolved and suspended matter, the greener (or browner) the water becomes. The time of day and cloudiness of the sky also have a great effect on the nature of the light available. Another factor is depth, once at sufficient depth, no amount of filtration can effectively restore color loss. Due to the nature of underwater optics, red light diminishes when the depth increases, thus producing blue to grey like images. By 3m in depth there is almost no red light left from the sun. By 5m, orange light is gone, by 10m most yellow is also gone. By the time one reaches 25m only blue light remains [4]. Since many (if not all) of the above factors are constantly changing, we cannot really know all the effects of water.

Color recovery is not a simple linear transform since it depends on distance and it is also affected by quantization and even light source variations. We propose a learning based Markov Random Field model for color correction based on training from examples. This allows the system to adapt the algorithm to the current environmental conditions and also to the task requirements. As proposed in[7], our approach is based on learning the statistics from training image pairs. Specifically, our MRF model learns the relationships between each of the color training images with its corresponding color depleted image. This model uses multi-scale representations of the color corrected (enhanced) and original images to construct a probabilistic enhancement algorithm that improves the observed video. This improvement is based on a combination of color matching correspondences from the training data, and local context via belief propagation (BP), all embodied in the Markov Random Field. Training images are small patches of regions of interest that capture the maximum of the intensity variations from the image to be restored.

This paper is structured as follows. Section 2 briefly consider some of the related prior work. Section 3 describes our method for color correction. Defining the MRF model and the inference approach using BP. Section 4 tests the proposed algorithm on two different scenarios with several types of experimental data each. Finally, in Section 5 we give some conclusions and future directions.

2   Related Work

There are numerous image retouching programs on the market that have easy-to-use, semi-automated image enhancement features. But since they are directed at land-based photography, these features do not always work with underwater images. Learning to manipulate the colors in underwater images with computer editing programs requires patience. Automated methods are essential, specially for real-time applications (such as aquatic inspection). Most prior work on image enhancement tend to approximate the lighting and color processes by idealized mathematical models. Such approaches are often elegant, but may not be well suited to the particular phenomena in any specific real environment. Color restoration is an ill-posed problem since there is not enough information in the poor colored image alone to determine the original image without ambiguity. In their work, Ahlen *et al.* [1] estimate a diffuse attenuation coefficient for three wavelengths using known reflectance values of a reference gray target that is present on all tested images. To calculate new intensity values they use Beer's Law, where the depth parameter is derived from images that are taken at different depths. Additional parameters needed are the image enhancements functions built into the camera. In general, their results are good, but the method's efficiency depends highly on the previously noted parameters. In [14] a method that eliminates the backscatter effect and improves the acquisition of underwater images with very good results is presented. Their method combines a mathematical formula with a physical filter normally used for land photography. Although the method does not perform color correction, the clarity achieved on the underwater images may allow for color correction.

3   Our MRF-BP Approach for Color Correction

The solution of the color correction problem can be defined as the minimum of an energy function. The first idea on which our approach is based, is that an image can be modeled as a sample function of a stochastic process based on the Gibbs distribution, that is, as a Markov Random Field (MRF) [8]. We consider the color correction a task of assigning a color value to each pixel of the input image that best describes its surrounding structure using the training image patches. The MRF model has the ability to capture the characteristics between the training sets and then used them to learn a marginal probability distribution that is to be used on the input images. This model uses multi-scale representations of the color corrected and color depleted (bluish) images to construct a probabilistic algorithm that improves the color of underwater images. The power of our technique is evident in that only a small set of training patches is required to color correct representative examples of color depleted underwater images, even when the image contains literally no color information. Each pair of the training set is composed by a color-corrected image patch with its corresponding color-depleted image patch. Statistical relationships are learned directly from the training data, without having to consider any lighting conditions of specific nature, location or environment type that would be inappropiate to a particular underwater scene. We use a pairwise MRF model, which is of particular interest in many low-level vision problems.

3.1   The Pairwise MRF Model

Denote the input color depleted image by $B = \{b_i\}, i = 1, ..., N$, where $N \in \mathbf{Z}$ is the total number of pixels in the image and b_i is a triplet containing the RGB channels of pixel location i. We wish to estimate the color-corrected image $C = \{c_i\}, i = 1, ..., N$, where c_i replaces the value of pixel b_i with a color value.

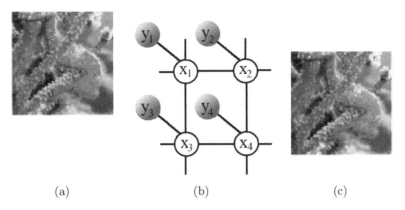

(a)   (b)   (c)

Fig. 1. (b) Pairwise Markov Random Field used to model the joint probability distribution of the system. Observation nodes, y, represent an image patch in the bluish image (a), and hidden nodes x, an image patch in the color image (b) to be inferred.

A pairwise MRF model (also known as *Markov network*) is defined as a set of hidden nodes x_i (white circles in the graph) representing local patches in the output image C, and the observable nodes y_i (shaded circles in the graph) representing local patches in the input bluish image B. Each local patch is centered to pixel location i of the respective images. Figure 1 shows the MRF model for color correction.

Denoting the pairwise potentials between variables x_i and x_j by ψ_{ij} and the local evidence potentials associated with variables x_i and y_i by ϕ_i (see Figure 2), the joint probability of the MRF model under variable instantiation $\mathbf{x} = (x_1, ..., x_N)$ and $\mathbf{y} = (y_1, ..., y_N)$, can be written [2, 8] as:

$$P(\mathbf{x}, \mathbf{y}) = \frac{1}{Z} \prod_{ij} \psi_{ij}(x_i, x_j) \prod_i \phi_i(x_i, y_i), \tag{1}$$

where Z is the normalization constant. We wish to maximize $P(\mathbf{x}, \mathbf{y})$, that is, we want to find the most likely state for all hidden nodes x_i, given all the evidence nodes y_i.

The compatibility functions allows to set high (or low) compatibilities to neighboring pixels according to the particular application. In our case, we wish

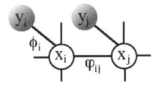

Fig. 2. The potential functions ϕ and ψ define the compatibilities between nodes in the Markov network

to preserve discontinuities (edges) in the input (color depleted) image to avoid over smoothing the color corrected image. Thus, we set high compatibility between neighboring pixels that have similar colors, and low compatibility between neighboring pixels with abrupt change in color values. These potentials are used in messages that are propagated between the pixels to indicate what color or combination of intensities each image pixel should have.

A color pixel value in C is synthesized by estimating the maximum a posteriori (MAP) solution of the MRF model using the training set. The MAP solution of the MRF model is:

$$\mathbf{x}_{MAP} = \arg \max_{\mathbf{x}} P(\mathbf{x} \mid \mathbf{y}), \tag{2}$$

where

$$P(\mathbf{x} \mid \mathbf{y}) \propto P(\mathbf{y} \mid \mathbf{x})P(\mathbf{x}) \propto \prod_i \phi_i(x_i, y_i) \prod_{(i,j)} \psi_{ij}(x_i, x_j) \tag{3}$$

Calculating the conditional probabilities in an explicit form to infer the exact MAP in MRF models is intractable. We cannot efficiently represent or determine all the possible combinations between pixels with its associated neighborhoods. Various techniques exist for approximating the MAP estimate, such as Markov Chain Monte Carlo (MCMC), iterated conditional modes (ICM), maximizer of posterior marginals (MPM), etc. See [5] for a comparison. In this work, we compute a MAP estimate, by using a learning-based framework on pairwise MRFs, as proposed by [7], using belief propagation (BP).

The compatibility functions $\phi(x_i, y_i)$ and $\psi(x_i, x_j)$ are learned from the training set using the patch-based method in [7]. They are usually assumed to obey a Gaussian distribution to model Gaussian noise. The $\phi_i(x_i, y_i)$ compatibility function is defined as follows

$$\phi_i(x_i, y_i) = e^{-|y_i - y_{x_i}|^2 / 2\sigma_i^2} \tag{4}$$

where x_i is a color-corrected patch candidate, y_{x_i} is the corresponding bluish patch of x_i, and y_i is the bluish patch in the input image.

The image is divided so that the corresponding color-corrected patches overlap. If the overlapping pixels of two node states match, the compatibility between those states is high. We define $\psi(x_i, x_j)$ as:

$$\psi_{ij}(x_i, x_j) = e^{-d_{ij}(x_i, x_j) / 2\sigma_i^2} \tag{5}$$

where d_{ij} is the difference between neighborhoods i and j (Section 3.3 defines the precise similarity measure we use).

Images in the training set are pairs of small image regions of the bluish image with its corresponding color-corrected image, thus the compatibility functions depend on each particular input image.

3.2 MRF-MAP Inference Using BP

Belief propagation (BP) was originally introduced as an exact algorithm for tree-structured models [12], but it can also be applied for graphs with loops, in which case it becomes an approximate algorithm, leading often to good approximate and tractable solutions [15]. For MRFs, BP is an inference method to efficiently estimate Bayesian beliefs in the network by the way of iteratively passing messages between neighboring nodes.

The message send from node i to any of its adjacent nodes $j \in N(i)$ is

$$m_{ij}(x_j) = Z \sum_{x_i} \psi(x_i, x_j) \phi(x_i, y_i) \prod_{k \in N(i) \setminus \{j\}} m_{ki}(x_i) \qquad (6)$$

where Z is the normalization constant. The maximum a posteriori scene patch for node i is:

$$x_{iMAP} = \arg \max_{\mathbf{x}_i} \phi(x_i, y_i) \prod_{j \in N(i)} m_{ji}(x_i). \qquad (7)$$

The BP algorithm is not guaranteed to converge, but if it does so, then it converges to a local stationary point of the Bethe approximation to the free energy [17]. In our experiments, the BP algorithm usually converges in less than 10 iterations. And it is also notable that BP is faster than many traditional inference methods.

Candidate states for each patch are taken from the training set. Fore each bluish patch in the image, we search the training set for patches that best resemble the input. The color-corrected patches corresponding the best k patches are used as possible states for the hidden nodes.

The algorithm for color correction can be summarized as follows:

---

1. Divide the training images (both the bluish and color images) into small patches, which form the sets of x_i's and y_i's.
2. For each input patch y_i, find the k closest y_{x_i}'s. The corresponding x_i's are the candidates for that patch. Calculate the compatibility function $\phi(x_i, y_i)$ according to Eq. 4.
3. For each pair of neighboring input patches, calculate the $k \times k$ compatibility function $\psi(x_i, x_j)$ according to Eq. 5.
4. Estimate the MRF-MAP solution using BP.
5. Assign the color value of the center pixel of each estimated maximum probability patch x_{iMAP} to the corresponding pixel in output image C.

3.3 Implementation Issues

Measuring the dissimilarity between image patches is of crucial for obtaining quality results, especially when there is a prominent color (blue or green) as in underwater images. Color information can be specified, created and visualized by different color spaces (see [16] for more information about color spaces). For example, the RGB color space, can be visualized as a cube with red, green and blue axes. Color distance is a metric of proximity between colors (e.g. Euclidean distance) measured in a color space. However, color distance does not necessarily correlate with *perceived* color similarity. Different applications have different needs which can be handled better using different color spaces. For our needs it is important to be able to measure differences between colors in a way that matches perceptual similarity as good as possible. This task is simplified by the use of *perceptually uniform* color spaces. A color space is perceptually uniform if a small change of a color will produce the same change in perception anywhere in the color space. Neither RGB, HLS or CIE XYZ is perceptually uniform.

The (nonlinear) conversions from RGB to CIE Lab are given by:[1]

$$
\begin{bmatrix} X \\ Y \\ Z \end{bmatrix} = \begin{bmatrix} 0.412453 & 0.357580 & 0.180423 \\ 0.212671 & 0.715160 & 0.072169 \\ 0.019334 & 0.119193 & 0.950227 \end{bmatrix} \begin{bmatrix} R \\ G \\ B \end{bmatrix}
$$

$$
L^* = \begin{cases} 116(Y/Y_n)^{1/3} - 16 & \text{if } Y/Y_n > 0.008856 \\ 903.3(Y/Y_n) & \text{otherwise} \end{cases}
$$

$$
a^* = 500[f(X/X_n)^{1/3} - f(Y/Y_n)^{1/3}]
$$

$$
b^* = 200[f(Y/Y_n)^{1/3} - f(Z/Z_n)^{1/3}]
$$

where

$$
f(t) = \begin{cases} t^{1/3} & \text{if } Y/Y_n > 0.008856 \\ 7.787t + 16/116 & \text{otherwise} \end{cases}
$$

We use the CIE *Lab* space which was designed such that the equal distances in the color space represent equal perceived differences in appearance. Color difference is defined as the Euclidean distance between two colors in this color space:

$$
\Delta E_{ab}^* = \sqrt{(\Delta L^*)^2 + (\Delta a^*)^2 + (\Delta b^*)^2} \tag{8}
$$

where ΔL^*, Δa^*, and Δb^* are the differences between two color pixel values.

This is the similarity measure used to select possible candidates to define the compatibility functions and also to evaluate the performance of our method. Our algorithm uses a pixel-based synthesis, i.e. one pixel (color) value c_i is estimated at a time.

4   Experimental Results

We test the proposed approach in two different scenarios. In the first scenario, we use color underwater images available on the web[2] as our ground truth data. These images were taken with a professional camera and in most of the cases they were also enhanced by using a commercial software. The second scenario, involves the acquisition of underwater video by our aquatic robot. Sections 4.1 and 4.2 describe these scenarios with the experimental results.

---

[1] Following ITU-R Recommendation BT.709, we use D_{65} as the reference white point so that $[X_n, Y_n, Z_n] = [0.9504511.088754]$ (see [13]).

[2] http://www.pbase.com/imagine

4.1   Scenario 1

In order to simulate the effects of water, an attenuation filter were applied to each of the color underwater image. Figure 3a shows the ground truth (color) image and Figure 3b, the simulated (color depleted) image after applying the attenuation filter. Since we have ground truth information, we can compute the performance of our algorithm. The images in the training set correspond to small image regions extracted from the ground truth image and the color depleted image (see Figure 4).

These images correspond to regions of interest in terms of the variations in pixel color values , thus the intention is that they capture the intrinsic statistical dependencies between the color depleted and ground truth pixel values. The size of the neighborhoods in all experiments were 5×5 pixels, the overlapping area between image patches 2×5 pixels, and the number of possible candidates k, was fixed to be 10. Figure 5a shows the training image patches from where our algorithm learns the compatibility functions and Figure 5b shows the resulted image after running our learning-based method. The color-corrected image *looks* good, the discontinuities and edges are preserved since our method assign colors pixel by pixel, thus avoiding over-smoothing. Also, there are no sudden changes in color which are typically both unrealistic and perceptually unappealing. To

(a)   (b)

Fig. 3. (a) The ground truth (color) image. (b) The simulated bluish image (this is the test image to be color corrected by our algorithm).

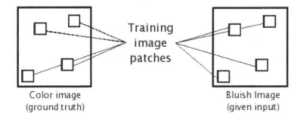

Fig. 4. Diagram showing how the training image pairs are acquired for the Scenario 1

Fig. 5. (a) The training image patches used to learn the compatibility functions. (b) The color corrected image.

evaluate the performance of our algorithm, we compute the mean absolute residual (MAR) error between the ground truth and the color corrected images. As mentioned in Section 3.3, the CIELab metric was used to calculate the similarities between pixels in the images. For this case, the MAR error is 6.5. For comparison purposes, we calculate the MAR error between the input (color depleted) image and the ground truth image, this is 22.03.

Fig. 6. Color correction results using different training sets. The input image is shown in Figure 3b. The training pairs (labeled) are shown in Figure 5a. Results using training pair (a) (1) and (3); (b) (2) and (3); (c) (1) and (2), and (d) (1).

Using the same input image (Figure 5b), we now show how the final result varies depending on the training data. In Figure 6, 4 examples when using different training pairs are shown. For example, Figure 6a shows a color-corrected image when using training pairs (1) and (3) (see Figure 5a). The MAR errors are 9.43, 9.65, 9.82, and 12.20, respectively. It can be seen that the resulting images are limited to the statistical dependencies captured by the training pairs.

Three more examples of underwater scenes are shown in Figure 7. Each row shows from left to right, the ground truth color image, the input bluish image and the color corrected image after running our algorithm. The training image regions are shown by squares in the corresponding color and bluish images. In general the results looks very good. For the last two examples, the size of the image patches in the training set is very small and enough to capture all the statistical dependencies between bluish and color information, as a result, the number of total comparisons in our algorithm is reduced and speed is achieved.

It was previously mentioned, that underwater images also contain some blurriness. In Figure 8, we show an example of applying our algorithm to a blurry and color depleted image at the same time. From left to right are, the ground

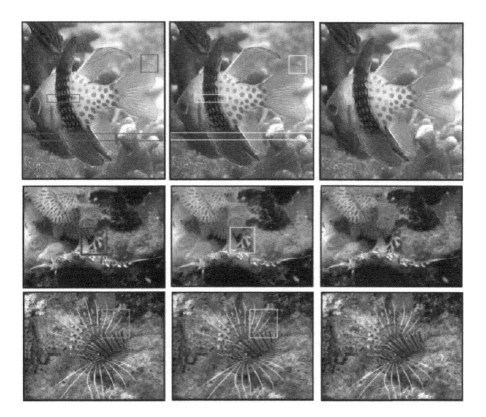

Fig. 7. More examples. The training pairs are indicated by the squares in the original and input images respectively.

(c)

Fig. 8. An example of color correcting and deblurring at the same time. The training pairs are indicated by the boxes in the original (a) and input images (b) respectively. (c) is the color-corrected and deblurred image.

truth image, the input image given to our algorithm and the color-corrected and deblurred image after running our algorithm.

4.2 Scenario 2: The Aquatic Robot in Action

As our aquatic robot [9] swims through the ocean, it takes video images. Figure 9 shows a picture of our aquatic robot in action.

In order to be able to correct the color of the images, training data from the environment that the robot is currently seeing needs to be gathered. How can better images be acquired? As light is absorbed selectively by water, not only does it get darker as you go deeper, but there is a marked shift in the light source

Fig. 9. The aquatic robot

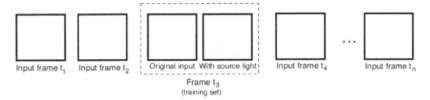

Input frame t_1 Input frame t_2 Original input With source light   Input frame t_4 Input frame t_n

Frame t_3
(training set)

Fig. 10. The scenario 2

color. In addition, there are non-uniformities in the source amplitude. Therefore, the aquatic robot needs to bring its own source of white light on it. However, due to power consumption, the light cannot be left turned on. Therefore, only at certain time intervals, the robot stops, turns its light on and take an image. These images are certainly much better, in terms of color and clarity, than the previous ones, and they can be used to train our algorithm to color correct neighboring frames (under the assumption that neighboring frames are similar). Figure 10 shows this scenario, here frame t_3 represents the image pair to be used to train our model for color correction.

Now we show an example. Figures 11a,b show the training image pair captured at time t. The robot moves around and then at time $t + \delta$ takes an image (Figure 11c), which is input to our algorithm. The resulting color-corrected image is shown in Figure 11d. Since we do not have ground truth data for this scenario, we cannot measure the performance of our algorithm, however it can be seen that the resulting image looks visually good.

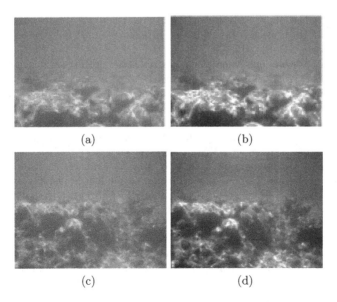

(a)   (b)

(c)   (d)

Fig. 11. (a)-(b) The training image pair captured at frame t. (c) Image taken at frame $t + \delta$ and input to our algorithm. (d) The color corrected image.

5   Summary and Conclusions

Color restoration and image enhancement are ubiquitous problems. In particular, underwater images contain distortions that arise from multiple factors making them difficult to correct using simple methods. In this paper, we show how to formulate color recovery and more general enhancement as an energy minimization problem using learned constraints. This approach's novelty lies in using a pair of images to constrain the reconstruction. There are some factors that influence the quality of the results, such as the adequate amount of reliable information as an input and the statistical consistency of the images in the training set.

Acknowledgments

We would like to thank photographer Ellen Muller for allowing the use of her underwater images for research purposes.

References

1. J. Åhlén and D. Sundgren. Bottom reflectance influence on a color correction algorithm for underwater images. In *Proc. SCIA*, pages 922–926, 2003.
2. J. Besag. Spatial interaction and the statistical analysis of lattice systems (with discussion). *J. Royal Statistics Society B*, 36:192–326, 1974.
3. T. Boult. DOVE: Dolphin omni-directional video equipment. In *Proc.Int. Conf. Robotics and Automation*, pages 214–220, 2000.
4. J. Dera. *Marine Physics*. Elsevier, 1992.
5. R.C. Dubes, A.K. Jain, S.G. Nadabar, and C.C. Chen. Mrf model-based algorithms for image segmentation. In *Proc. of IEEE Intl. Conf. on Pattern Recognition (ICPR)*, pages 808–814, 1990.
6. G.L. Foresti. Visual inspection of sea bottom structures by an autonomous underwater vehicle. *IEEE Trans. Syst. Man and Cyber., Part B*, 31:691–795, 2001.
7. W.T. Freeman, E.C. Pasztor, and O.T. Carmichael. Learning low-level vision. *International Journal of Computer Vision*, 20(1):25–47, 2000.
8. S. Geman and D. Geman. Stochastic relaxation, gibbs distributions, and the bayesian restoration of images. *IEEE Transactions on Pattern Analysis and Machine Intelligence*, 6:721–741, 1984.
9. C. Georgiades, A. German, A. Hogue, H. Liu, C. Prahacs, A. Ripsman, R. Sim, L. A. Torres-Méndez, P. Zhang, M. Buehler, G. Dudek, M. Jenkin, and E. Milios. AQUA: an aquatic walking robot. In *Proc. of IEEE/RSJ International Conference on Intelligent Robots and Systems*, volume 3, pages 3525–3531, Sendai, Japan, September 2004. IEEE/RSJ, IEEE Press.
10. S. Harsdorf, R. Reuter, and S. Tonebon. Contrast-enhanced optical imaging of submersible targets. In *Proc. SPIE*, volume 3821, pages 378–383, 1999.
11. J.S. Jaffe. Computer modeling and the design of optimal underwater imaging systems. *IEEE J. Oceanic Engineering*, 15:101–111, 1990.
12. J. Pearl. *Probabilistic Reasoning in Intelligent Systems: Networks of Plausible Inference*. Morgan Kaufmann Publishers, Inc., 1988.
13. C. Poynton. *A Technical Introduction to Digital Video*. Wiley, NewYork, 1996.

14. Y.Y. Schechner and N. Karpel. Clear underwater vision. In *Proc. of Intt. Conference of Vision and Pattern Recognition*, volume 1, pages 536–543, 2004.
15. Y. Weiss. Belief propagation and revision in networks with loops. Technical report, Berkeley Computer Science Dept., 1998.
16. G. Wyszecki and W.S. Stiles. *Color Science: Concepts and Methods, Quantitative Data and Formulae.* Wiley, NewYork, 1982.
17. J. Yedidia, W. Freeman, and Y. Weiss. Constructing free energy approximations and generalized belief propagation algorithms. Technical report, Mitsubishi Electrical Research Laboratories, Inc., 2004.

Bayesian Image Segmentation Using Gaussian Field Priors

Mário A.T. Figueiredo

Instituto de Telecomunicações,
and Department of Electrical and Computer Engineering,
Instituto Superior Técnico, 1049-001 Lisboa, Portugal
Phone: +351 218418464, Fax: +351 218418472
mario.figueiredo@lx.it.pt

Abstract. The goal of segmentation is to partition an image into a finite set of regions, homogeneous in some (e.g., statistical) sense, thus being an intrinsically discrete problem. Bayesian approaches to segmentation use priors to impose spatial coherence; the discrete nature of segmentation demands priors defined on discrete-valued fields, thus leading to difficult combinatorial problems.

This paper presents a formulation which allows using continuous priors, namely Gaussian fields, for image segmentation. Our approach completely avoids the combinatorial nature of standard Bayesian approaches to segmentation. Moreover, it's completely general, *i.e.*, it can be used in supervised, unsupervised, or semi-supervised modes, with any probabilistic observation model (intensity, multispectral, or texture features).

To use continuous priors for image segmentation, we adopt a formulation which is common in Bayesian machine learning: introduction of hidden fields to which the region labels are probabilistically related. Since these hidden fields are real-valued, we can adopt any type of spatial prior for continuous-valued fields, such as Gaussian priors. We show how, under this model, Bayesian MAP segmentation is carried out by a (generalized) EM algorithm. Experiments on synthetic and real data shows that the proposed approach performs very well at a low computational cost.

1 Introduction

Image segmentation has been one of the most studied problems in computer vision. Although remarkably successful approaches have been proposed for specific domains in which the goals are well defined (*e.g.*, segmentation of magnetic resonance images, segmentation of remote sensing images), a general purpose segmentation criterion remains an elusive concept. In the past couple of decades, many different approaches, formulations, and tools have been proposed.

Most segmentation methods work by combining cues from the observed image (via image features) with some form of regularization (or prior, in Bayesian terms), embodying the concept of "acceptable" (or "*a priori* probable") segmentation. Arguably, all the work on image segmentation can be classified as belonging to on one (or even both) of the following two research fronts:

A. Rangarajan et al. (Eds.): EMMCVPR 2005, LNCS 3757, pp. 74–89, 2005.
© Springer-Verlag Berlin Heidelberg 2005

(a) Development of image features, and feature models, which are as informative as possible for the segmentation goal. Some of the most recent proposals combine intensity, texture, and contour-based features, with the specific goal of mimicking human image segmentation [26]. Another recent approach combining several types of features is reported in [27]. Classical examples for texture-based segmentation include Gabor features [16], wavelet-based features [29], co-occurrence matrices [11], features derived from Markov random field local texture models [7], [8]. It's possible to perform segmentation using nonparametric statistical measures of texture similarity by resorting to pairwise clustering techniques [14]. The literature on texture features and models is vast; [25] provides a reasonably recent survey. There are many other examples of features developed for specific domains, such as color segmentation, segmentation of medical images, or segmentation of remote sensing images.

(b) Development of methods that impose some form of spatial regularity to the segmentation, *i.e.*, that integrate local cues (from features) into a globally coherent segmentation. The recent graph-based methods [28], [30], [32], achieve this by formulating image segmentation as the partitioning of a graph. Spatial coherence may also be achieved by constraining the class of image partitions which are considered by the segmentation algorithm (*e.g.*, [13] and [24] consider hierarchies of polygonal and quad-tree-like partitions, respectively) or by imposing some prior on the length or the smoothness of the region boundaries [34]; see recent work and many references in [17], which also advances research front (a). In a probabilistic Bayesian approach, as adopted in this paper, the preference for some form of spatial regularity is usually formulated via a Markov random field (MRF) prior (see [20], for a comprehensive set of references).

This paper belongs to research front (b): it describes a new way of introducing spatial priors for Bayesian image segmentation. The proposed approach uses priors on real-valued fields/images, rather than MRF priors for discrete labels, thus removing any combinatorial nature from the problem. Our formulation, is very general in that it can be used in supervised, unsupervised, or semi-supervised manners, as well as with generative or discriminative features.

To open the door to the use of priors on real-valued fields/images for image segmentation, we adopt an approach which is used in Bayesian machine learning: introduction of a (collection of) real-valued hidden field(s), to which the region labels are probabilistically related; these hidden field(s), being real-valued, can then be given any type of spatial prior, *e.g.*, it can be modelled as a (collection of) Gaussian field(s). This approach is used in the very successful approach to Bayesian learning of classifiers known as "Gaussian processes" [31]. In this paper, Gaussian field priors are adopted as a means of encoding a preference for spatially coherent segmentations. We show how the proposed approach can be used in supervised, unsupervised, and semi-supervised modes, by deriving (generalized) expectation-maximization (EM) algorithms for the three cases. In the supervised case, the resulting segmentation criterion consists in minimizing a convex cost function, thus initialization problems do not arise. If the underlying

Gaussian process prior is stationary, the M-step can be implemented in a very fast way using FFT-based processing in the Fourier domain. This is, arguably, one of the key advantages of the proposed approach.

Finally, we should mention that our formulation is close, in spirit, to the "hidden Markov measure fields" proposed in [22]; however, our hidden fields are real valued, and totally unconstrained, thus much easier to model and manipulate than measure fields. Recently, we have used a similar formulation to allow the use of wavelet-based spatial priors for image segmentation [9].

In the next section, we introduce notation and the proposed formulation. In Section 3, we present our segmentation criterion and derive the EM algorithm for implementing it. Section 4 describes the extensions to unsupervised, semi-supervised and discriminative segmentation. Finally, experiments are presented in Section 5, and Section 6 concludes the paper.

2 Formulation

2.1 Images and Segmentations

Let $\mathcal{L} = \{(n,m), \ n = 1, ..., N, \ m = 1, ..., M\}$ be a $2D$ lattice of $|\mathcal{L}| = MN$ sites/pixels on which observed images, and their segmentations, are defined. An observed image $\mathbf{x}$ is a set of (maybe vector valued) observations, indexed by the lattice $\mathcal{L}$, that is, $\mathbf{x} = \{x_i \in \mathbb{R}^d, \ i \in \mathcal{L}\}$. A segmentation $\mathcal{R} = \{R_k \subseteq \mathcal{L}, \ k = 0, ..., K - 1\}$ is a partition of $\mathcal{L}$ into K regions, in an exhaustive and mutually exclusive way:

$$\bigcup_{k=0}^{K-1} R_k = \mathcal{L} \quad \text{and} \quad \left(R_j \bigcap R_k = \emptyset\right) \Leftarrow (j \neq k).$$

In the sequel, it will be convenient to represent partitions by a set of binary indicator images $\mathbf{y}^{(k)} = \{y_i^{(k)}, \ i \in \mathcal{L}\}$, for $k = 0, ..., K - 1$, where $y_i^{(k)} \in \{0,1\}$, such that $(y_i^{(k)} = 1) \Leftrightarrow (i \in R_k)$. We denote as $\mathbf{y}$ the set of all these binary images, $\mathbf{y} = \{\mathbf{y}^{(0)}, ..., \mathbf{y}^{(K-1)}\}$, and as $\mathbf{y}_i$ the set of all $y_i^{(k)}$ for a given site i, that is, $\mathbf{y}_i = \{y_i^{(0)}, ..., y_i^{(K-1)}\}$. Of course, $\mathbf{y}$ and $\mathcal{R}$ carry exactly the same information.

2.2 Observation Model

Given a segmentation $\mathbf{y}$, we follow the standard assumption that the observed "pixels" are (conditionally) independently distributed,

$$p(\mathbf{x}|\mathbf{y}) = \prod_{k=0}^{K-1} \prod_{i \in R_k} p(x_i|\boldsymbol{\phi}^{(k)}) = \prod_{i \in \mathcal{L}} \prod_{k=0}^{K-1} \left[p(x_i|\boldsymbol{\phi}^{(k)})\right]^{y_i^{(k)}}, \quad (1)$$

where the $p(\cdot|\boldsymbol{\phi}^{(k)})$ are region-specific distributions. This type of model may be used for intensity-based segmentation, for texture-based segmentation (each x_i

is then a d-dimensional vector containing the values of d local texture features), or for segmentation of multi-spectral images (such as color images, or remote sensing images, with each x_i being in this case a d-dimensional vector, where d is the number of spectral bands). The region-specific densities $p(\cdot|\phi^{(k)})$ can be simple Gaussians, or any other arbitrarily complex models, such as finite mixtures, kernel-based density representations, or even histograms. When the $p(\cdot|\phi^{(k)})$ are fully known *a priori*, we are in the context of supervised segmentation with generative models. This is the case we will focus on first; later, it will be shown how the approach can be extended to unsupervised and semi-supervised scenarios, and to "discriminative features".

The goal of segmentation is, of course, to estimate $\mathbf{y}$, having observed $\mathbf{x}$. The maximum likelihood (ML) estimate, $\widehat{\mathbf{y}}_{\mathrm{ML}} = \arg\max_{\mathbf{y}} p(\mathbf{x}|\mathbf{y})$, can clearly be obtained pixel-by-pixel, due to the independence assumption. However, it's well known that pixel-wise segmentations may lack spatial coherence [20], [33]. To overcome this, one of the standard approaches consists in adopting an MRF prior $p(\mathbf{y})$, expressing the *a priori* preference for segmentations in which neighboring sites belong to the same region (see [20] for details and references). Given this prior, it is then most common to adopt the *maximum a posteriori* (MAP) criterion, $\widehat{\mathbf{y}}_{\mathrm{MAP}} = \arg\max_{\mathbf{y}}[\log p(\mathbf{y}) + \log p(\mathbf{x}|\mathbf{y})]$ (although there are other criteria). Due to the discrete nature of $\mathbf{y}$, finding $\widehat{\mathbf{y}}_{\mathrm{MAP}}$ involves a combinatorial optimization problem, to which much research has been devoted [20]. A recent breakthrough in MRF-type approaches (to segmentation [33] and other vision problems [5]) is the adoption of fast algorithms based on graph cuts[1].

2.3   Logistic Model

To keep the notation initially simple, consider the binary case ($K = 2$, thus each $\mathbf{y}_i = [y_i^{(0)}, y_i^{(1)}]$). Instead of designing a prior for $\mathbf{y}$ (the field of discrete labels), we consider a "hidden" (or latent) image $\mathbf{z} = \{z_i \in \mathbb{R}, \ i \in \mathcal{L}\}$, such that

$$p(\mathbf{y}|\mathbf{z}) = \prod_i p(\mathbf{y}_i|z_i) \quad \text{with} \quad p(y_i^{(1)} = 1|z_i) = \frac{e^{z_i}}{1 + e^{z_i}} \equiv \sigma(z_i), \qquad (2)$$

where $\sigma(\cdot)$ is called the *logistic* function and, obviously, $p(y_i^{(0)} = 1|z_i) = 1 - \sigma(z_i)$.

In general, for K regions, we need K hidden images $\mathbf{z} = \{\mathbf{z}^{(0)}, ..., \mathbf{z}^{(K-1)}\}$, where $\mathbf{z}^{(k)} = \{z_i^{(k)} \in \mathbb{R}, \ i \in \mathcal{L}\}$. The region label probabilities are obtained via a multinomial logistic model (also known as a "soft-max"),

$$p(y_i^{(k)} = 1|\mathbf{z}_i) = e^{z_i^{(k)}} \left(\sum_{j=0}^{K-1} e^{z_i^{(j)}} \right)^{-1}, \quad k = 0, ..., K-1, \qquad (3)$$

where $\mathbf{z}_i = \{z_i^{(0)}, ..., z_i^{(K-1)}\}$. Since these probabilities verify the normalization condition $\sum_{k=0}^{K-1} p(y_i^{(k)} = 1|\mathbf{z}_i) = 1$, one of the hidden images can be set to

---

[1] See http://www.cs.cornell.edu/~rdz/graphcuts.html for details and references.

zero; without loss of generality, we set $\mathbf{z}^{(0)} = \mathbf{0}$ (see, *e.g.*, [3]). Notice that $\mathbf{z} = \{\mathbf{z}^{(1)}, ..., \mathbf{z}^{(K-1)}\}$ is not under any type of constraint; any assignment of real values to its elements leads to valid probabilities for each site of $\mathbf{y}$.

2.4   Gaussian Random Field Prior

It is now formally simple to write priors for $\mathbf{z}$, due to its unconstrained real-valued nature. Among the several possibilities, we will focus here on what is arguably the simplest choice: a Gauss-Markov random field (GMRF) prior defined on the lattice $\mathcal{L}$.

The goal of the prior on $\mathbf{z}$ is to express preference for segmentations such that neighboring sites have high probability of belonging to the same region. This is achieved by encouraging neighboring values of each $\mathbf{z}^{(k)}$ to be close to each other. A GMRF prior that embodies this preference is

$$p(\mathbf{z}) \propto \exp\left\{ -\frac{1}{4} \sum_{i \sim j} \sum_{k=1}^{K-1} w_{i,j} \left(z_i^{(k)} - z_j^{(k)} \right)^2 \right\}, \tag{4}$$

where $i \sim j$ denotes that sites i and j are neighbors (in some neighborhood system defined in $\mathcal{L}$), and the $w_{i,j}$ are (non-negative) weights. It is clear that (4) models the set of hidden fields $\mathbf{z} = \{\mathbf{z}^{(1)}, ..., \mathbf{z}^{(K-1)}\}$ as *a priori* independent, *i.e.*,

$$p(\mathbf{z}) = \prod_{k=1}^{K-1} p(\mathbf{z}^{(k)}) \tag{5}$$

with

$$p(\mathbf{z}^{(k)}) \propto \exp\left\{ -\frac{1}{4} \sum_{i,j} w_{i,j} \left(z_i^{(k)} - z_j^{(k)} \right)^2 \right\}, \tag{6}$$

where the sum is now over all i, j because we encode the neighborhood structure in the $w_{i,j}$ by letting $w_{i,j} = 0$ when i and j are not neighbors. Let now $\mathbf{z}^{(k)} = [z_1^{(k)}, ..., z_{|\mathcal{L}|}^{(k)}]^T \in I\!\!R^{|\mathcal{L}|}$ denote an $|\mathcal{L}|$-vector obtained by stacking all the $z_i^{(k)}$ variables (for a given k) in standard lexicographical order. Also, let $\mathbf{W}$ be the $|\mathcal{L}| \times |\mathcal{L}|$ matrix with the $w_{i,j}$ weights. With this notation, we can write

$$p(\mathbf{z}^{(k)}) \propto \exp\left\{ -\frac{1}{2} (\mathbf{z}^{(k)})^T \boldsymbol{\Delta} (\mathbf{z}^{(k)}) \right\}. \tag{7}$$

where

$$\boldsymbol{\Delta} = \text{diag}\left\{ \sum_{j=1}^{|\mathcal{L}|} w_{1,j}, ..., \sum_{j=1}^{|\mathcal{L}|} w_{|\mathcal{L}|,j} \right\} - \mathbf{W} \tag{8}$$

is called the *graph-Laplacian matrix* [6]; in our case, the graph nodes are the sites of the lattice $\mathcal{L}$ and the edge weights are given by $w_{i,j}$ (with $w_{i,j} = 0$ denoting absence of edge between nodes i and j). Notice that $\boldsymbol{\Delta}$ has (at least) one zero eigenvalue since $\boldsymbol{\Delta}[1, 1, ..., 1]^T = \mathbf{0}$; thus, $p(\mathbf{z}^{(k)})$ is an improper prior (it can't be normalized [2]), but this is will not be a problem for MAP estimation. In the GMRF literature, $\boldsymbol{\Delta}$ is also called the *potential matrix* [1].

3 Estimation Criterion and Algorithm

3.1 Marginal MAP Criterion

Let us summarize our model: we have the observed field $\mathbf{x}$, and unobserved fields $\mathbf{y}$ and $\mathbf{z}$. These fields are probabilistically related by $p(\mathbf{x}|\mathbf{y})$, given by (1), $p(\mathbf{y}|\mathbf{z})$, given by (2) - (3), and a prior $p(\mathbf{z}) = p(\mathbf{z}^{(1)}) \cdots p(\mathbf{z}^{(K-1)})$ with each $p(\mathbf{z}^{(k)})$ given by (7). Given $\mathbf{x}$, the posterior probability of $\mathbf{y}$ and $\mathbf{z}$ is thus

$$p(\mathbf{z}, \mathbf{y}|\mathbf{x}) \propto p(\mathbf{x}|\mathbf{y})\, p(\mathbf{y}|\mathbf{z})\, p(\mathbf{z}). \tag{9}$$

Among the several possible Bayesian decision theoretic criteria, we consider the *marginal maximum a posteriori* (MMAP), given by

$$\widehat{\mathbf{z}} = \arg \max_{\mathbf{z}} \{p(\mathbf{z})p(\mathbf{x}|\mathbf{z})\} = \arg \max_{\mathbf{z}} \left\{ p(\mathbf{z}) \sum_{\mathbf{y}} p(\mathbf{x}|\mathbf{y})\, p(\mathbf{y}|\mathbf{z}) \right\} \tag{10}$$

where $p(\mathbf{x}|\mathbf{z}) = \sum_{\mathbf{y}} p(\mathbf{x}|\mathbf{y})\, p(\mathbf{y}|\mathbf{z})$ is the marginal likelihood obtained by summing over (the huge set of) all possible segmentations.

The estimate $\widehat{\mathbf{z}}$ is a probabilistic segmentation in the sense that it provides the probability that each pixel belongs to each region, via the logistic model (3). To obtain a hard segmentation, one can simply choose the *a posteriori* most probable class $\widehat{k}_i$ at each site i which is

$$\widehat{k}_i = \arg \max_k \{p(y_i^{(k)} = 1|\mathbf{z}_i)\}. \tag{11}$$

Clearly, the maximization in (10) can not be done directly, due to the combinatorial nature of $p(\mathbf{x}|\mathbf{z})$. In the next subsections, we will derive an EM algorithm for this purpose.

3.2 Why the EM Algorithm?

The following observations clearly suggest using the EM algorithm [23], treating $\mathbf{y}$ as missing data, to solve (10):

- If $\mathbf{y}$ was observed, estimating $\mathbf{z}$ would reduce to standard logistic regression under prior $p(\mathbf{z})$, that is, one could solve $\widehat{\mathbf{z}} = \arg \max_{\mathbf{z}} [\log p(\mathbf{y}|\mathbf{z}) + \log p(\mathbf{z})]$.
- The so-called complete log-likelihood $\log p(\mathbf{y}|\mathbf{z})$ (based on which we could estimate $\mathbf{z}$ if $\mathbf{y}$ was observed) is linear with respect to the hidden $y_i^{(k)}$ variables. In fact, $\log p(\mathbf{y}|\mathbf{z})$ is the standard logistic regression log-likelihood with an identity design matrix (see, e.g., [3], [12], [18]):

$$\log p(\mathbf{y}|\mathbf{z}) = \sum_i \sum_{k=0}^{K} y_i^{(k)} \log \frac{e^{z_i^{(k)}}}{\sum_{j=0}^{K-1} e^{z_i^{(k)}}} = \sum_i \left(\sum_{k=0}^{K} y_i^{(k)} z_i^{(k)} - \log \sum_{k=0}^{K} e^{z_i^{(k)}} \right). \tag{12}$$

The EM algorithm proceeds by iteratively applying the following two steps [23]:

E-step: Compute the expected value of the complete log-likelihood, given the current estimate $\widehat{\mathbf{z}}$ and the observations $\mathbf{x}$: $Q(\mathbf{z}|\widehat{\mathbf{z}}) = E_{\mathbf{y}}[\log p(\mathbf{y}|\mathbf{z})|\widehat{\mathbf{z}}, \mathbf{x}]$.

M-step: Update the estimate: $\widehat{\mathbf{z}} \leftarrow \widehat{\mathbf{z}}_{\text{new}} = \arg \max_{\mathbf{z}} \{Q(\mathbf{z}|\widehat{\mathbf{z}}) + \log p(\mathbf{z})\}$.

3.3   The E-Step

The fact that the complete log-likelihood is linear w.r.t. the missing variables is very important for EM: the E-step reduces to computing the expectation of the missing variables, with these expectations then plugged into the complete log-likelihood [23]. Moreover, as in finite mixtures [10], the missing $y_i^{(k)}$ are binary, thus their expected values are equal to their probabilities of being equal to one, which can be obtained via Bayes law:

$$\widehat{y}_i^{(k)} \equiv E[y_i^{(k)}|\widehat{\mathbf{z}}_i, \mathbf{x}] = p(y_i^{(k)} = 1|\widehat{\mathbf{z}}_i, \mathbf{x}_i) = \frac{p(x_i|\phi^{(k)})\, p(y_i^{(k)} = 1|\widehat{\mathbf{z}}_i)}{\displaystyle\sum_{j=0}^{K-1} p(x_i|\phi^{(j)})\, p(y_i^{(j)} = 1|\widehat{\mathbf{z}}_i)}. \tag{13}$$

Notice that this is essentially the same as the E-step for finite mixtures [10], with site-specific mixing probabilities given by $p(y_i^{(k)} = 1|\widehat{\mathbf{z}}_i)$ and with fixed component densities $p(x|\phi^{(k)})$ (recall that we're temporarily assuming that all the $\phi^{(k)}$ are known). Finally, $Q(\mathbf{z}|\widehat{\mathbf{z}})$ is obtained by plugging the $\widehat{y}_i^{(k)}$ (which depend on $\widehat{\mathbf{z}}$ via (13)) into the logistic log-likelihood (12):

$$Q(\mathbf{z}|\widehat{\mathbf{z}}) = \sum_i \left(\sum_{k=0}^{K} \widehat{y}_i^{(k)} z_i^{(k)} - \log \sum_{k=0}^{K} e^{z_i^{(k)}} \right). \tag{14}$$

Notice that $Q(\mathbf{z}|\widehat{\mathbf{z}})$ is formally a standard logistic regression log-likelihood, but with the usual hard (binary) training labels $y_i^{(k)} \in \{0,1\}$ replaced by "soft" labels $\widehat{y}_i^{(k)} \in [0,1]$.

3.4   Solving the M-Step

Our M-step, $\widehat{\mathbf{z}}_{\text{new}} = \arg\max_{\mathbf{z}} \{Q(\mathbf{z}|\widehat{\mathbf{z}}) + \log p(\mathbf{z})\}$, consists in solving a logistic regression problem with identity design matrix, given soft labels $\widehat{y}_i^{(k)}$, and under a prior $p(\mathbf{z})$. It is well known that this problem does not have a closed form solution and has to be solved by an iterative algorithm [3]. The standard choice for maximum likelihood logistic regression (i.e., for maximizing only $Q(\mathbf{z}|\widehat{\mathbf{z}})$ w.r.t. $\mathbf{z}$) is Newton's algorithm [12]. However, as shown below, we will obtain a much simpler method by adopting the bound optimization approach [19], introduced for logistic regression in [3] and [4] (see also [18]).

Let us temporarily ignore the log-prior $\log p(\mathbf{z})$ and consider only $Q(\mathbf{z}|\widehat{\mathbf{z}})$, simply denoted as $q(\mathbf{z})$ for notational economy. In the bound optimization approach, the maximization of $q(\mathbf{z})$ is achieved by iterating the two following steps

$$\widehat{\mathbf{z}}_{\text{new}} = \arg\max_{\mathbf{z}} l(\mathbf{z}|\widehat{\mathbf{z}}), \quad \widehat{\mathbf{z}} \leftarrow \widehat{\mathbf{z}}_{\text{new}}, \tag{15}$$

where $l(\mathbf{z}|\widehat{\mathbf{z}})$ is a so-called "surrogate" function verifying the following condition: $q(\mathbf{z}) - l(\mathbf{z}|\widehat{\mathbf{z}})$ attains its minimum for $\mathbf{z} = \widehat{\mathbf{z}}$ (see [19]). This condition is sufficient to guarantee that this iteration monotonically increases $q(\mathbf{z})$, i.e., $q(\widehat{\mathbf{z}}_{\text{new}}) \geq q(\widehat{\mathbf{z}})$.

Thus, by running iteration (15) one or more times, after each application of the E-step (equations (13)-(14)), the resulting procedure is a generalized EM (GEM) algorithm [23].

It is important to notice that, in the supervised mode, the objective function being maximized in concave (since the logistic log-likelihood and the logarithm of the GMRF prior are both concave) and so there are no initialization problems.

From this point on, we assume that $\mathbf{z}$ is organized into a $((K-1)|\mathcal{L}|)$-vector by stacking the several $\mathbf{z}^{(k)}$ vectors, i.e., $\mathbf{z} = [(\mathbf{z}^{(1)})^T, ..., (\mathbf{z}^{(K-1)})^T]^T$. In [3], the following surrogate for logistic regression was introduced:

$$l(\mathbf{z}|\hat{\mathbf{z}}) = q(\hat{\mathbf{z}}) + (\mathbf{z} - \hat{\mathbf{z}})^T \mathbf{g}(\hat{\mathbf{z}}) - \frac{(\mathbf{z} - \hat{\mathbf{z}})^T \mathbf{B}(\mathbf{z} - \hat{\mathbf{z}})}{2}, \tag{16}$$

where $\mathbf{g}(\hat{\mathbf{z}})$ is the gradient of $q(\mathbf{z})$ computed at $\hat{\mathbf{z}}$ and $\mathbf{B}$ is a positive definite matrix which provides a lower bounds for the (negative definite) Hessian $\mathcal{H}(\mathbf{z})$ of $q(\mathbf{z})$, i.e., $\mathcal{H}(\mathbf{z}) \succeq -\mathbf{B}$ (in the matrix sense, i.e., $\mathcal{H}(\mathbf{z}) + \mathbf{B}$ is positive semi-definite). Since $q(\mathbf{z}) - l(\mathbf{z}|\hat{\mathbf{z}}) \geq 0$, with equality if and only if $\mathbf{z} = \hat{\mathbf{z}}$, $l(\mathbf{z}|\hat{\mathbf{z}})$ is a valid surrogate function; any other function differing from it by an additive constant (irrelevant for (15)) is also a valid surrogate. Matrix $\mathbf{B}$ is given by

$$\mathbf{B} = \frac{1}{2} \left(\mathbf{I}_{K-1} - \frac{\mathbf{1}_{K-1} \mathbf{1}_{K-1}^T}{K} \right) \otimes \mathbf{I}_{|\mathcal{L}|}, \tag{17}$$

where $\mathbf{I}_a$ denotes an $a \times a$ identity matrix, $\mathbf{1}_a = [1, ..., 1]^T$ is an a-dimensional vector of ones, and $\otimes$ is the Kroenecker product.

The following simple Lemma (proved in the Appendix) will allow further simplification of the algorithm, by using a less tight, but simpler bound matrix.

Lemma 1. *Let us define* ξ_K *as*

$$\xi_K = \begin{cases} 1/2 & \text{if } K > 2 \\ 1/4 & \text{if } K = 2. \end{cases} \tag{18}$$

Then, $\mathbf{B} \preceq \xi_K \mathbf{I}_{(K-1)|\mathcal{L}|}$, *with equality if* $K = 2$.

This lemma allows us to replace $\mathbf{B}$ by $\xi_K \mathbf{I}_{(K-1)|\mathcal{L}|}$ in (16) and still have a valid surrogate; the advantage is that in this new surrogate the several $\mathbf{z}^{(k)}$ become decoupled. Performing some simple manipulation, using the fact that one is free to add to the surrogate any terms independent of $\mathbf{z}$ (thus irrelevant for the maximization), leads to

$$l(\mathbf{z}|\hat{\mathbf{z}}) = -\frac{\xi_K}{2} \sum_{k=1}^{K-1} \|\mathbf{z}^{(k)} - \mathbf{v}^{(k)}\|_2^2, \quad \text{with} \quad \mathbf{v}^{(k)} = \hat{\mathbf{z}}^{(k)} + \frac{\mathbf{d}^{(k)}}{\xi_K}, \tag{19}$$

where $\| \cdot \|_2^2$ denotes squared Euclidean norm,

$$\mathbf{d}^{(k)} = \begin{bmatrix} \hat{y}_1^{(k)} - p(y_1^{(1)} = 1|\hat{\mathbf{z}}_1) \\ \vdots \\ \hat{y}_{|\mathcal{L}|}^{(k)} - p(y_{|\mathcal{L}|}^{(k)} = 1|\hat{\mathbf{z}}_{|\mathcal{L}|}) \end{bmatrix}, \tag{20}$$

and the $p(y_1^{(k)} = 1|\widehat{\mathbf{z}}_1)$ are given by the logistic model (3).

Since a surrogate for $Q(\mathbf{z}|\widehat{\mathbf{z}})$ is also valid for $Q(\mathbf{z}|\widehat{\mathbf{z}}) + \log p(\mathbf{z})$, and (see (5)-(7))

$$\log p(\mathbf{z}) = \sum_{k=1}^{K-1} \log p(\mathbf{z}^{(k)}) = A - \frac{1}{2} \sum_{k=1}^{K-1} (\mathbf{z}^{(k)})^T \boldsymbol{\Delta} \, (\mathbf{z}^{(k)}), \qquad (21)$$

(A is an irrelevant constant) the following decoupled update equation results:

$$\widehat{\mathbf{z}}_{\text{new}}^{(k)} = \arg\min_{\mathbf{z}} \left\{ \|\mathbf{z} - \mathbf{v}^{(k)}\|_2^2 + \frac{\mathbf{z}^T \boldsymbol{\Delta} \, \mathbf{z}}{\xi_K} \right\} = \xi_K \left(\xi_K \mathbf{I}_{|\mathcal{L}|} + \boldsymbol{\Delta} \right)^{-1} \mathbf{v}^{(k)}, \qquad (22)$$

for $k = 1, ..., K - 1$.

3.5 FFT-Based Implementation of the M-Step

For a general matrix $\boldsymbol{\Delta}$ (i.e., an arbitrary choice of $\mathbf{W}$), (22) is computationally very expensive, requiring $O(|\mathcal{L}|^3)$ operations. However, for certain choices of $\mathbf{W}$ (correspondingly of $\boldsymbol{\Delta}$), we can resort to fast frequency-domain methods. Suppose that $w_{i,j}$ only depends on the relative position of i and j (the Gaussian field prior is stationary) and that the neighborhood system has periodic boundary condition; in this case, both $\mathbf{W}$ and $\boldsymbol{\Delta}$ are block-circulant matrices, with circulant[2] blocks [1]. It is well known that block-circulant matrices with circulant blocks can be diagonalized by a two-dimensional discrete Fourier transform (2D-DFT): $\boldsymbol{\Delta} = \mathbf{U}^H \mathbf{D} \mathbf{U}$, where $\mathbf{D}$ is a diagonal matrix, $\mathbf{U}$ is the matrix representation of the 2D-DFT, and the superscript $(\cdot)^H$ denotes conjugate transpose. Since $\mathbf{U}$ is an orthogonal matrix ($\mathbf{U}^H \mathbf{U} = \mathbf{U} \mathbf{U}^H = \mathbf{I}$), the inversion in (22) can be written as

$$\widehat{\mathbf{z}}_{\text{new}}^{(k)} = \xi_K \mathbf{U}^H \left(\xi_K \mathbf{I}_{|\mathcal{L}|} + \mathbf{D} \right)^{-1} \mathbf{U} \mathbf{v}^{(k)}, \qquad (23)$$

where $(\xi_K \mathbf{I}_{|\mathcal{L}|} + \mathbf{D})^{-1}$ is a trivial diagonal inversion, and the matrix-vector products by $\mathbf{U}$ and $\mathbf{U}^H$ (the 2D-DFT and its inverse) are not carried out explicitly but via the efficient ($O(|\mathcal{L}| \log |\mathcal{L}|)$) fast Fourier transform (FFT). Notice that this can be seen as a smoothing operation, applied to each $\mathbf{v}^{(k)}$ in the discrete Fourier domain. Since the computational cost of the E-step is essentially $O(|\mathcal{L}|)$, as is obvious from (13), the leading cost of the proposed algorithm is $O(|\mathcal{L}| \log |\mathcal{L}|)$.

Finally, we should mention that the condition of periodic boundary conditions can be relaxed; in that case, the resulting matrix $\boldsymbol{\Delta}$ is block-Toeplitz with Toeplitz blocks, but not block-circulant. Nevertheless, it is still possible to embed a block-Toeplitz matrix into a larger block-circulant one, and still work in the DFT domain [15].

---

[2] Recall that a circulant matrix is characterized by the fact that each row is a circularly shifted version of the first (or any other) row.

3.6   Summary of the Algorithm

We now summarize the algorithm, showing that it is in fact very simple.

Inputs: Observed image $\mathbf{x}$, number of regions K, observation models $p(\cdot|\boldsymbol{\phi}^{(k)})$,
matrix $\mathbf{W}$ or $\boldsymbol{\Delta}$, stopping threshold ε, number of inner iterations r.
Output: Estimates $\widehat{\mathbf{z}}^{(k)}$, for $k = 1, ..., K - 1$.
Initialization: For $k = 1, ..., K - 1$, set $\widehat{\mathbf{z}}^{(k)} = 0$.
Step 1: Run the E-step (13), producing K images $\{\widehat{\mathbf{y}}^{(0)}, ..., \widehat{\mathbf{y}}^{(K-1)}\}$.
Step 2: Store the current estimate: $\widehat{\mathbf{z}}_{\text{old}} \leftarrow \widehat{\mathbf{z}}$.
Step 3: Repeat r times (for $k = 1, ..., K - 1$):
    Step 3.a: Compute the images $\mathbf{d}^{(k)}$ (according to (20)).
    Step 3.b: Compute the images $\mathbf{v}^{(k)} = \widehat{\mathbf{z}}^{(k)} + \mathbf{d}^{(k)}/\xi_K$ (see (19)).
    Step 3.c: Compute $\widehat{\mathbf{z}}_{\text{new}}^{(k)}$ according to (23). Update $\widehat{\mathbf{z}}^{(k)} \leftarrow \widehat{\mathbf{z}}_{\text{new}}^{(k)}$.
    Step 3.d: Go back to **Step 3.a**.
Step 4: If $\max_k \|\widehat{\mathbf{z}}_{\text{old}}^{(k)} - \widehat{\mathbf{z}}^{(k)}\|_\infty < \varepsilon$, then stop; otherwise, return to **Step 1**.

4   Extensions

4.1   Unsupervised and Semi-supervised Segmentation

The model and algorithm above described can be extended to the unsupervised
case, where the parameters $\boldsymbol{\phi}^{(k)}$ of the observation models $p(\cdot|\boldsymbol{\phi}^{(k)})$ are consid-
ered unknown. In this case, the full posterior in (9) has to be modified to

$$p(\mathbf{z}, \boldsymbol{\phi}, \mathbf{y}|\mathbf{x}) \propto p(\mathbf{x}|\mathbf{y}, \boldsymbol{\phi})\, p(\mathbf{y}|\mathbf{z})\, p(\mathbf{z}). \tag{24}$$

where $\boldsymbol{\phi} = \{\boldsymbol{\phi}^{(0)}, ..., \boldsymbol{\phi}^{(K-1)}\}$, assuming the absence of any prior on $\boldsymbol{\phi}$ (although
one could easily be considered with little additional cost). Let us adopt again
the MMAP criterion, now jointly w.r.t. $\mathbf{z}$ and $\boldsymbol{\phi}$. The following observations can
now be added to those made in Section 3.2:

- If $\mathbf{y}$ was observed, estimating $\boldsymbol{\phi}$ would be a simple ML parameter estimation
  problem, based on the complete log-likelihood $\log p(\mathbf{x}|\mathbf{y}, \boldsymbol{\phi})$.
- The complete log-likelihood (see (1)) is linear w.r.t. the missing variables $\mathbf{y}$:

$$\log p(\mathbf{x}|\mathbf{y}, \boldsymbol{\phi}) = \sum_{i \in \mathcal{L}} \sum_{k=0}^{K-1} y_i^{(k)} \log p(x_i|\boldsymbol{\phi}^{(k)}).$$

The algorithm presented in Section 3.6 can thus be modified by inserting an
extra step, say between steps 2 and 3:

Step 2.5: Update the observation model parameters according to the following
weighted ML criterion:

$$\widehat{\boldsymbol{\phi}}^{(k)} = \arg\max_{\boldsymbol{\phi}} \sum_{i \in \mathcal{L}} \widehat{y}_i^{(k)} \log p(x_i|\boldsymbol{\phi}).$$

If, for example, the feature densities are Gaussians, $p(\cdot|\boldsymbol{\phi}^{(k)}) = \mathcal{N}(\cdot|\boldsymbol{\mu}^{(k)}, \mathbf{C}^{(k)})$, these update equations coincide with those of the EM algorithm for Gaussian mixture estimation:

$$\widehat{\boldsymbol{\mu}}^{(k)} = \frac{\sum_{i\in\mathcal{L}} \widehat{y}_i^{(k)} x_i}{\sum_{i\in\mathcal{L}} \widehat{y}_i^{(k)}}, \quad \widehat{\mathbf{C}}^{(k)} = \frac{\sum_{i\in\mathcal{L}} \widehat{y}_i^{(k)} (x_i - \widehat{\boldsymbol{\mu}}^{(k)})(x_i - \widehat{\boldsymbol{\mu}}^{(k)})^T}{\sum_{i\in\mathcal{L}} \widehat{y}_i^{(k)}}. \quad (25)$$

In the semi-supervised case, instead of previous knowledge of $\{\boldsymbol{\phi}^{(0)}, ..., \boldsymbol{\phi}^{(K-1)}\}$, one is given a subset of pixels for which the exact true label/region is known. In this case, the EM algorithm derived for the unsupervised case is applied, but holding the labels of the pre-classified pixels at their known values.

Of course, in the unsupervised or semi-supervised cases, the log-posterior is no longer concave, and the results will depend critically on the initialization.

4.2   Discriminative Features

The formulation presented above (and most of the work on probabilistic segmentation) uses what can be classified as "generative feature models": each $p(\cdot|\boldsymbol{\phi})$ is a probabilistic model that is assumed to describe how features/pixel values are generated in each region. However, discriminative models, such as logistic regression, Gaussian processes [31], support vector machines, or boosting (see references in [12]) are currently considered the state-of-the-art in classification.

Observe that all the EM segmentation algorithm requires, in the E-step defined in (13), is the posterior class probabilities, given the pixel values and the current estimates $\widehat{\mathbf{z}}^{(k)}$. These estimates provide some prior class probabilities in (13). Consider a probabilistic discriminative classifier, that is, a classifier that, for each pixel x_i, provides estimates of the posterior class probabilities $p(y_i^{(k)} = 1|x_i)$, for $k = 0, ..., K - 1$ (this can be obtained, $e.g.$, by logistic regression, or a tree classifier). Let us assume that this classifier was trained on balanced data, $i.e.$, using the same amount of data from each class. It can thus be assumed that these posterior class probabilities verify $p(y_i^{(k)} = 1|x_i) \propto p(x_i|y_i^{(k)} = 1)$, as can be easily verified by plugging uniform class priors $p(y_i^{(k)} = 1) = 1/K$ in Bayes rule. It is then possible to "bias" these classes, with given prior probabilities $p(y_i^{(k)} = 1)$, for $k = 0, ..., K - 1$, by computing

$$p_{\text{biased}}(y_i^{(k)} = 1|x_i) = \frac{p(y_i^{(k)} = 1|x_i)\, p(y_i^{(k)} = 1)}{\sum_{k=0}^{K-1} p(y_i^{(j)} = 1|x_i)\, p(y_i^{(j)} = 1)}.$$

This procedure allows using a pre-trained probabilistic discriminative classifier, which yields $p(y_i^{(k)} = 1|x_i)$, in our EM algorithm, by using the "biased" probabilities in the E-step. We have not yet performed experiments with this discriminative approach.

5   Experiments

In the first experiment, we consider a simple synthetic segmentation problem, with known class models. Each of the four regions follows a Gaussian distribution

Fig. 1. Top row: true regions and observed image. Bottom row: maximum likelihood segmentation and the one obtained by our algorithm.

with standard deviation 0.6 and means 1, 2, 3, and 4. We have used (in this and all the following examples) $r = 4$, and $\varepsilon = 0.001$. We choose the simplest possible GMRF prior: $w_{i,j} = \gamma$, if j is one of the four nearest neighbors of i, and is zero otherwise. The true regions, observed image, the maximum likelihood segmentation (obtained by maximizing (1) with respect to $\mathbf{y}$), and the (hard, obtained via (11)) segmentation produced by our algorithm are shown in Fig. 1. This is comparable to what would be obtained by an MRF-based method; however, it must be stressed that the algorithm herein proposed is optimal (in the sense that we are minimizing a convex objective function), fully deterministic, and fast (due to the use of the FFT-based M-step). This result illustrates the ability of the proposed method to use Gaussian priors to regularize image segmentation via the logistic modelling approach, producing well defined boundaries.

In Fig. 2 we show the final estimates $\widehat{\mathbf{z}}^{(1)}$, $\widehat{\mathbf{z}}^{(2)}$, and $\widehat{\mathbf{z}}^{(3)}$ as well as the corresponding $\widehat{\mathbf{y}}^{(1)}$, $\widehat{\mathbf{y}}^{(2)}$, $\widehat{\mathbf{y}}^{(3)}$, and $\widehat{\mathbf{y}}^{(4)}$, obtained from the $\widehat{\mathbf{z}}^{(k)}$ via the logistic model (3). Notice the higher uncertainty near the region boundaries. The hard segmentation shown in Fig. 1 was obtained by choosing, for each site, the maximum of the four $\widehat{\mathbf{y}}^{(k)}$ images.

The previous experiment was repeated using the unsupervised version of the algorithm; a threshold-based segmentation was used for initialization. The segmentation obtained is visually very similar to the one in Fig. 1, and it's not shown here, for the sake of space. The parameter estimates are within 1% of the true values.

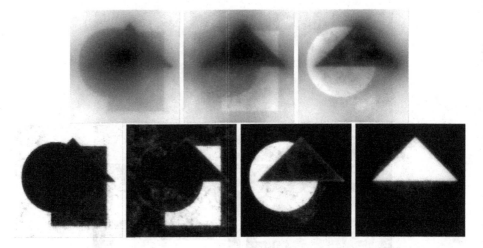

Fig. 2. Top row: final estimates $\widehat{\mathbf{z}}^{(1)}$, $\widehat{\mathbf{z}}^{(2)}$, and $\widehat{\mathbf{z}}^{(3)}$. Bottom row: corresponding $\widehat{\mathbf{y}}^{(1)}$, $\widehat{\mathbf{y}}^{(2)}$, $\widehat{\mathbf{y}}^{(3)}$, and $\widehat{\mathbf{y}}^{(4)}$, obtained by the logistic model (3).

Fig. 3. Observed image, maximum likelihood segmentation, and segmentation obtained by our algorithm

Fig. 4. Observed image, maximum likelihood segmentation, and segmentation obtained by our algorithm

For segmentation of real images, the results depend critically on the features and feature models used, and that is not the focus of this paper. We will only show two examples of color image segmentation ($d = 3$), using Gaussian densities for each region. In Fig. 3, the goal is to segment the image into three regions: clothe, skin, and background. Fig. 4 shows a figure-ground segmentation problem. The results shown were produced by the unsupervised version of our algorithm, initialized with the ML segmentations which result from fitting mixtures of Gaussians to the observed (RGB) pixels.

6   Summary and Conclusions

A new formulation for Bayesian image segmentation was introduced. This approach allows using priors for continuous-valued fields as regularizers for image segmentation; in particular, it was used with Gaussian field priors, which (if stationary) can be easily and efficiently manipulated in the frequency domain using the FFT algorithm. An EM algorithm was derived for supervised segmentation; it was shown how this algorithm is extended to handle unsupervised and semi-supervised problems, as well as discriminative features. Preliminary experiments show that the proposed approach has promising performance.

Future research will include a thorough experimental evaluation of the method, namely in comparison with graph-based and MRF-based methods. We are currently developing criteria for selecting the number of classes/regions, following the approach in [10].

Appendix: Proof of Lemma 1

Recall (see (17)) that

$$\mathbf{B} = \frac{1}{2} \left(\mathbf{I}_{K-1} - \frac{\mathbf{1}_{K-1} \mathbf{1}_{K-1}^T}{K} \right) \otimes \mathbf{I}. \tag{26}$$

For $K = 2$, it is obvious that $\mathbf{B} = \mathbf{I}/4$.

For $K > 2$, the matrix inequality $\mathbf{I}/2 \succeq \mathbf{B}$ is equivalent to $\lambda_{\min}(\mathbf{I}/2 - \mathbf{B}) \geq 0$. Now, since $\lambda_i(\mathbf{I}/2 - \mathbf{B}) = (1/2) - \lambda_i(\mathbf{B})$, we need to show that $\lambda_{\max}(\mathbf{B}) \leq (1/2)$.

To study the eigenvalues of $\mathbf{B}$, the following fact (see, e.g., [21]) is used: let $\mathbf{M}$ and $\mathbf{P}$ be $m \times m$ and $p \times p$ matrices, with eigenvalues $\{\lambda_1, ..., \lambda_m\}$ and $\{\gamma_1, ..., \gamma_p\}$, respectively; then, $\mathbf{M} \otimes \mathbf{P}$ has eigenvalues $\{\lambda_i \gamma_j, \ i = 1, ..., m, \ j = 1, ..., p\}$. Since $\mathbf{1}$ is a vector with $K - 1$ ones, $\mathbf{1}\mathbf{1}^T$ is a rank-1 matrix with eigenvalues $\{0, ..., 0, K - 1\}$; thus, the eigenvalues of $(\mathbf{I} - (1/K)\mathbf{1}\mathbf{1}^T)$ are $\{1, ..., 1, 1/K\}$. Because the eigenvalues of $\mathbf{I}$ are of course all ones, the maximum eigenvalue of $\mathbf{B}$ is $\lambda_{\max}(\mathbf{B}) = 1/2$. ∎

References

1. N. Balram and J. Moura, "Noncausal Gauss-Markov random fields: parameter structure and estimation", *IEEE Trans. Information Theory*, vol. 39, pp. 1333–1355, 1993.
2. J. Bernardo and A. Smith, *Bayesian Theory*, J. Wiley & Sons, 1994.
3. D. Böhning. "Multinomial logistic regression algorithm." *Annals Inst. Stat. Math.*, vol. 44, pp. 197–200, 1992.
4. D. Böhning and B. Lindsay. "Monotonicity of quadratic-approximation algorithms." *Annals Inst. Stat. Math.*, vol. 40, pp. 641–663, 1988.
5. Y. Boykov, O. Veksler, and R. Zabih, "Fast approximate energy minimization via graph cuts." *IEEE Trans. Patt. Anal. Mach. Intell.*, vol. 23, pp. 1222–1239, 2001.
6. F. Chung, *Spectral Graph Theory*, American Mathematical Society, 1997.
7. G. Cross and A. Jain. "Markov random field texture models." *IEEE Trans. Patt. Anal. and Mach. Intell.*, vol. 5, pp. 25-39, 1983.
8. H. Derin and H. Elliot. "Modelling and segmentation of noisy and textured images in Gibbsian random fields." *IEEE Trans. Patt. Anal. and Mach. Intell.*, vol. 9 , pp. 39-55, 1987.
9. M. Figueiredo, "Bayesian image segmentation using wavelet-based priors", *Proc. of IEEE CVPR'2005*, San Diego, CA, 2005.
10. M. Figueiredo and A.K.Jain. "Unsupervised learning of finite mixture models." *IEEE Trans. Patt. Anal. and Mach. Intell.*, vol. 24, pp. 381-396, 2002.
11. R. Haralick, K. Shanmugan, and I. Dinstein, "Textural features for image classification." em IEEE Trans. Syst., Man, and Cybernetics, vol. 8, pp. 610-621, 1973.
12. T. Hastie, R. Tibshirani, and J. Friedman, *The Elements of Statistical Learning*, Springer Verlag, New York, 2001.
13. L. Hermes and J. Buhmann, "A minimum entropy approach to adaptive image polygonization," *IEEE Trans. Image Proc.*, vol. 12, pp. 1243–1258, 2003.
14. T. Hofmann, J. Puzicha, and J. Buhmann. "Unsupervised texture segmentation in a deterministic annealing framework," *IEEE Trans. Patt. Anal. and Mach. Intell.*, vol. 20, pp. 803–818, 1998.
15. A. Jain. *Fundamentals of Digital Image Processing*, Prentice Hall, Englewood Cliffs, NJ, 1989.
16. A. Jain and F. Farrokhnia, "Unsupervised texture segmentation using Gabor filters." *Pattern Recognition*, vol. 24, pp. 1167-1186, 1991.
17. J. Kim, J. Fisher, A. Yezzi, M. Çetin, and A. Willsky, "A nonparametric statistical method for image segmentation using information theory and curve evolution," *IEEE Trans. Image Proc.*, to appear, 2005.
18. B. Krishnapuram, L. Carin, M. Figueiredo, and A. Hartemink. "Learning sparse Bayesian classifiers: multi-class formulation, fast algorithms, and generalization bounds", *IEEE-TPAMI*, vol. 27, no. 6, 2005.
19. K. Lange, D. Hunter, and I. Yang. "Optimization transfer using surrogate objective functions." *Jour. Comp. Graph. Stat.*, vol. 9, pp. 1–59, 2000.
20. S. Z. Li, *Markov Random Field Modelling in Computer Vision*. Springer Verlag, 2001.
21. J. Magnus and H. Neudecker. *Matrix Differential Calculus*. John Wiley & Sons, 1988.
22. J. Marroquin, E. Santana, and S. Botello. "Hidden Markov measure field models for image segmentation." *IEEE Trans. Patt. Anal. and Mach. Intell.*, vol. 25, pp. 1380–1387, 2003.

23. G. McLachlan and T. Krishnan. *The EM Algorithm and Extensions*, John Wiley & Sons, New York, 1997.

24. R. Nowak and M. Figueiredo, "Unsupervised progressive parsing of Poisson fields using minimum description length criteria," *Proc. IEEE ICIP'99*, Kobe, Japan, vol. II, pp. 26-29, 1999.

25. T. Randen and J. Husoy. "Filtering for texture classification: a comparative study." *IEEE Trans. Patt. Anal. Mach. Intell.*, vol. 21, pp. 291-310, 1999.

26. D. Martin, C. Fowlkes, and J. Malik. "Learning to detect natural image boundaries using local brightness, color and texture cues." *IEEE Trans. Patt. Anal. Mach. Intell.*, vol. 26, pp. 530-549, 2004.

27. E. Sharon, A. Brandt, R. Basri. "Segmentation and boundary detection using multiscale intensity measurements." *Proc. IEEE CVPR*, vol. I, pp. 469-476, Kauai, Hawaii, 2001.

28. J. Shi and J. Malik, "Normalized cuts and image segmentation." *IEEE Trans. Patt. Anal. Mach. Intell.*, vol.22, pp. 888-905, 2000.

29. M. Unser, "Texture classification and segmentation using wavelet frames." *IEEE Trans. Image Proc.*, vol. 4, pp. 1549 1560, 1995.

30. Y. Weiss, "Segmentation using eigenvectors: a unifying view." *Proc. Intern. Conf. on Computer Vision – ICCV'99*, pp. 975-982, 1999.

31. C. Williams and D. Barber. "Bayesian classification with Gaussian priors." *IEEE Trans. Patt. Anal. and Mach. Intell.*, vol. 20, pp. 1342–1351, 1998.

32. Z. Wu and R. Leahy, "Optimal graph theoretic approach to data clustering: theory and its application to image segmentation." *IEEE Trans. Patt. Anal. Mach. Intell.*, vol. 15, pp. 1101-1113, 1993.

33. R. Zabih and V. Kolmogorov, "Spatially coherent clustering with graph cuts." *Proc. IEEE-CVPR*, vol. II, pp. 437–444, 2004.

34. S. C. Zhu and A. Yuille, "Region competition: unifying snakes, region growing, and Bayes/MDL for multiband image segmentation," *IEEE Trans. Patt. Anal. Mach. Intell.*, vol. 18, pp. 884–900, 1996.

Handling Missing Data in the Computation of 3D Affine Transformations

Hanna Martinsson[1], Adrien Bartoli[2],
François Gaspard[1], and Jean-Marc Lavest[2]

[1] CEA LIST – LIST/DTSI/SARC/LCEI Bât 528, 91 191 Gif sur Yvette, France
Tel: +33(0)1 69 08 82 98, Fax: +33(0)1 69 08 83 95
hanna.martinsson@cea.fr
[2] LASMEA (CNRS / UBP) – 24 avenue des Landais, 63 177 Aubière, France
Tel: +33(0)4 73 40 76 61, Fax: +33(0)4 73 40 72 62
adrien.bartoli@univ-bpclermont.fr

Abstract. The reconstruction of rigid scenes from multiple images is a central topic in computer vision. Approaches merging partial 3D models in a hierarchical manner have proven the most effective to deal with large image sequences. One of the key building blocks of these hierarchical approaches is the alignment of two partial 3D models, which requires to express them in the same 3D coordinate frame by computing a 3D transformation. This problem has been well-studied for the cases of 3D models obtained with calibrated or uncalibrated pinhole cameras.

We tackle the problem of aligning 3D models – sets of 3D points – obtained using uncalibrated affine cameras. This requires to estimate 3D affine transformations between the models. We propose a factorization-based algorithm estimating simultaneously the aligning transformations and corrected points, exactly matching the estimated transformations, such that the reprojection error over all cameras is minimized. In the case of incomplete image data our algorithm uses an Expectation Maximization (EM) based scheme that alternates prediction of the missing data and estimation of the affine transformation.

We experimentally compare our algorithm to other methods using simulated and real data.

1 Introduction

Threedimensional reconstruction from multiple images of a rigid scene, often dubbed Structure-From-Motion (SFM), is one of the most studied problems in computer vision. The difficulties come from the fact that, using only feature correspondences, both the 3D structure of the scene and the cameras have to be computed. Most approaches rely on an initialisation phase optionally followed by self-calibration and bundle adjustment. Existing initialisation algorithms can be divided into three families, namely *batch*, *sequential* and *hierarchical* processes. Hierarchical processes [1] have proven the most successful for large image sequences. Indeed, batch processes such as the factorization algorithms [2] which reconstruct all features and cameras in a single computation step, do not easily

A. Rangarajan et al. (Eds.): EMMCVPR 2005, LNCS 3757, pp. 90–106, 2005.

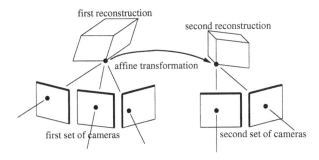

Fig. 1. The problem tackled in this paper is the Maximum Likelihood Estimation of 3D affine transformations between two affine reconstructions obtained from uncalibrated affine cameras

handle occlusions, while sequential processes such as [3] which reconstruct each view on turn, may typically suffer from accumulation of the errors. Hierarchical processes merge partial 3D models obtained from sub-sequences, which allows to distribute the error over the sequence, and efficiently handle open and closed sequences. A key step of hierarchical processes is the fusion or the *alignment* of partial 3D models, which is done by *computing 3D motion from 3D feature correspondences*. This problem has been extensively studied in the projective [4, 1] and the metric and Euclidean [5] cases.

We focus on the affine camera model [6], which is a reasonable approximation to the perspective camera model when the depth of the observed scene is small compared to the viewing distance. In this case, the partial 3D models obtained from sub-sequences, *i.e.* multiple subsets of cameras, are related by 3D affine transformations. We deal with the computation of such transformations from point correspondences, as illustrated on Fig. 1. We propose a Maximum Likelihood Estimator based on factorizing modified image point coordinates. We compute a 3D affine transformation and a set of 3D point correspondences which perfectly match, such that *the reprojection error in all sets of cameras is minimized.* It is intended to fit in hierarchical affine SFM processes of which the basic reconstruction block is, *e.g.* the affine factorization [2]. Our method does not make any assumption about the cameras, besides the fact that a reconstruction of each camera set using an affine camera model has been performed. The method relies on the important new concept of *orthonormal bases*. In the occlusion-free case, our algorithm needs one Singular Value Decomposition (SVD). However, in the case of incomplete measurement data, *i.e.* when some of the 3D points used for the alignment are not visible in all views, the factorization algorithm must be extended. We propose an Expectation-Maximization (EM) based scheme. The Expectation step predicts the missing data while the Maximization step maximizes the log likelihood.

We proposed the Maximum Likelihood Estimator in the case of complete data in [7]. The contribution of this paper with respect to the former one resides in the handling of missing data. We have also completed the experiments.

This paper is organized as follows. We give our notation and preliminaries in Sect. 2. In Sect. 3, we review the factorization approach to uncalibrated affine Structure-From-Motion. Our alignment method is described in Sect. 4, while other methods are summarized in Sect. 5. Experimental results are reported in Sect. 6. Our conclusions are given in Sect. 7.

2   Notation and Preliminaries

Vectors are typeset using bold fonts, *e.g.* $\mathbf{x}$, and matrices using sans-serif, calligraphic and greek fonts, *e.g.* A, $\mathcal{Q}$ and Λ. We do not use homogeneous co-ordinates, *i.e.* image point coordinates are 2-vectors: $\mathbf{x}^\mathsf{T} = (x \; y)$, where T is transposition. The different sets of cameras are indicated with primes, *e.g.* P_1 and P_1' are the first cameras of the camera sets. Index $i = 1 \ldots n$ is used for the cameras of a camera set and index $j = 1 \ldots m$ is used for the 3D points. The mean vector of a set of vectors, say $\{\mathbf{Q}_j\}$, is denoted $\bar{\mathbf{Q}}$. The Moore-Penrose pseudoinverse of matrix A is denoted $\mathsf{A}^\dagger$.

Let $\mathbf{Q}_j$ be a 3-vector and $\mathbf{x}_{ij}$ a 2-vector representing respectively a 3D and an image point. The uncalibrated affine camera is modeled by a (2×3) matrix P_i and a (2×1) translation vector $\mathbf{t}_i$, giving the projection equation

$$\mathbf{x}_{ij} = \mathsf{P}_i \mathbf{Q}_j + \mathbf{t}_i \; . \tag{1}$$

Calligraphic fonts are used for the measurement matrices, *e.g.*

$$\mathcal{X}_{(2n \times m)} = \begin{pmatrix} \mathcal{Y}_1 \cdots \mathcal{Y}_m \end{pmatrix} \quad \text{and} \quad \mathcal{Y}_j = \begin{pmatrix} \mathbf{x}_{1j}{}^\mathsf{T} \cdots \mathbf{x}_{nj}{}^\mathsf{T} \end{pmatrix}^\mathsf{T} ,$$

where $\mathcal{Y}_j$ contains all the measured image coordinates for the j-th point. The $(2n \times 3)$ 'joint projection' and $(3 \times m)$ 'joint structure' matrices are defined by

$$\mathcal{P} = \begin{pmatrix} \mathsf{P}_1{}^\mathsf{T} \cdots \mathsf{P}_n{}^\mathsf{T} \end{pmatrix}^\mathsf{T} \quad \text{and} \quad \mathcal{Q} = \begin{pmatrix} \mathbf{Q}_1 \cdots \mathbf{Q}_m \end{pmatrix} \; .$$

We assume that the noise on the image point positions has a Gaussian centered distribution and is i.i.d. Under these hypotheses, minimizing the reprojection error yields Maximum Likelihood Estimates.

3   Structure-from-Motion Using Factorization

Given a set of point matches $\{\mathbf{x}_{ij}\}$, the factorization algorithm is employed to recover all cameras $\{\hat{\mathsf{P}}_i, \hat{\mathbf{t}}_i\}$ and 3D points $\{\hat{\mathbf{Q}}_j\}$ at once [2]. Under the aforementioned hypotheses on the noise distribution, this algorithm computes Maximum Likelihood Estimates [8] by minimizing the reprojection error

$$\min_{\hat{\mathcal{P}}, \hat{\mathcal{Q}}, \{\hat{\mathbf{t}}_i\}} \mathcal{R}^2(\hat{\mathcal{P}}, \hat{\mathcal{Q}}, \{\hat{\mathbf{t}}_i\}) \quad \text{with} \quad \mathcal{R}^2(\mathcal{P}, \mathcal{Q}, \{\mathbf{t}_i\}) = \frac{1}{nm} \sum_{i=1}^{n} \sum_{j=1}^{m} d^2(\mathbf{x}_{ij}, \mathsf{P}_i \mathbf{Q}_j + \mathbf{t}_i) \; ,$$

$$\tag{2}$$

where $d(\mathbf{x}, \mathbf{y}) = \|\mathbf{x} - \mathbf{y}\|$ is the Euclidean distance between $\mathbf{x}$ and $\mathbf{y}$.

Step 1: Computing the translation. Given the uncalibrated affine projection (1), the first step of the algorithm is to compute the translation $\hat{\mathbf{t}}_i$ of each camera in order to cancel it out from the projection equation. This is achieved by nullifying the partial derivatives of the reprojection error (2) with respect to $\hat{\mathbf{t}}_i$: $\frac{\partial \mathcal{R}^2}{\partial \mathbf{t}_i} = 0$. A short calculation shows that if we fix the arbitrary centroid of the 3D points to the origin, then $\hat{\mathbf{t}}_i = \bar{\mathbf{x}}_i$. Each set of image points is therefore centered on its centroid, *i.e.* $\mathbf{x}_{ij} \leftarrow \mathbf{x}_{ij} - \bar{\mathbf{x}}_i$, to obtain *centered coordinates*: $\mathbf{x}_{ij} = \mathsf{P}_i \mathbf{Q}_j$.

Step 2: Factorizing. The problem is reformulated as

$$\min_{\hat{\mathcal{P}}, \hat{\mathcal{Q}}} \mathcal{R}^2(\hat{\mathcal{P}}, \hat{\mathcal{Q}}) \quad \text{with} \quad \mathcal{R}^2(\mathcal{P}, \mathcal{Q}) = \frac{1}{nm} \sum_{i=1}^{n} \sum_{j=1}^{m} d^2(\mathbf{x}_{ij}, \mathsf{P}_i \mathbf{Q}_j) \ .$$

The reprojection error can be rewritten by gathering the terms using the measurement, the 'joint projection' and the 'joint structure' matrices as

$$\mathcal{R}^2(\mathcal{P}, \mathcal{Q}) \propto \|\mathcal{X} - \mathcal{P}\mathcal{Q}\|^2 \ ,$$

and the problem is solved by computing the Singular Value Decomposition [9] of matrix $\mathcal{X}$, $\mathcal{X}_{2n \times m} = \mathsf{U}_{2n \times m} \Sigma_{m \times m} \mathsf{V}_{m \times m}^\mathsf{T}$. Let $\Sigma = \Sigma_u \Sigma_v$ be any decomposition of matrix Σ. The motion and structure are obtained by 'truncating' the decomposition or nullifying all but the 3 first singular values, which leads to

$$\mathcal{P} = \psi(\mathsf{U}\Sigma_u) \quad \text{and} \quad \mathcal{Q} = \psi^\mathsf{T}(\mathsf{V}\Sigma_v^\mathsf{T}) \ ,$$

where $\psi(\mathsf{W})$ returns the matrix formed with the 3 leading columns of matrix W. Note that the solution $\mathcal{P} = \psi(\mathsf{U})$ and $\mathcal{Q} = \psi^\mathsf{T}(\mathsf{V}\Sigma)$ has the property $\mathcal{P}^\mathsf{T}\mathcal{P} = \mathsf{I}$, which is useful for our alignment method, see Sect. 4.

The 3D model is obtained up to a global affine transformation. Indeed, for any (3×3) invertible matrix B,

$$\tilde{\mathcal{P}} = \hat{\mathcal{P}}\mathsf{B} \quad \text{and} \quad \tilde{\mathcal{Q}} = \mathsf{B}^{-1}\hat{\mathcal{Q}} \tag{3}$$

give the same reprojection error that $\mathcal{P}$ and $\mathcal{Q}$ since $\mathcal{R}^2(\tilde{\mathcal{P}}, \tilde{\mathcal{Q}}) = \|\mathcal{X} - \tilde{\mathcal{P}}\tilde{\mathcal{Q}}\| = \|\mathcal{X} - \hat{\mathcal{P}}\mathsf{B}\mathsf{B}^{-1}\hat{\mathcal{Q}}\|^2 = \|\mathcal{X} - \mathcal{P}\mathcal{Q}\|^2 = \mathcal{R}^2(\mathcal{P}, \mathcal{Q})$.

As presented above, the factorization algorithm do not handle occlusions. Though some algorithms have been proposed, see *e.g.* [10], they are not appropriate for Structure-From-Motion from large image sequences.

4   Alignment of 3D Affine Reconstructions

We formally state the alignment problem in the two camera set case and present our algorithm, dubbed 'FACTMLE-EM'.

4.1   Problem Statement

Consider two sets of cameras $\{(\mathsf{P}_i, \mathbf{t}_i)\}_{i=1}^{n}$ and $\{(\mathsf{P}_i', \mathbf{t}_i')\}_{i=1}^{n'}$ and associated structures $\{\mathbf{Q}_j \leftrightarrow \mathbf{Q}_j'\}_{j=1}^{m}$ obtained by reconstructing a rigid scene using *e.g.* the above-described factorization algorithm. Without loss of generality, we take $n = n'$ and the reprojection error over two sets is given by

$$\mathcal{C}^2(\mathcal{Q}, \mathcal{Q}') = \frac{1}{2nm} \left(\mathcal{R}^2(\mathcal{P}, \mathcal{Q}, \{\mathbf{t}_i\}) + \mathcal{R}'^2(\mathcal{P}', \mathcal{Q}', \{\mathbf{t}'_i\}) \right) . \qquad (4)$$

Letting $(\hat{\mathsf{A}}, \hat{\mathbf{t}})$ represent the aligning (3×3) affine transformation, the Maximum Likelihood Estimator is formulated by

$$\min_{\hat{\mathcal{Q}}, \hat{\mathcal{Q}}'} \mathcal{C}^2(\hat{\mathcal{Q}}, \hat{\mathcal{Q}}') \quad \text{s.t.} \quad \hat{\mathbf{Q}}'_j = \hat{\mathsf{A}}\hat{\mathbf{Q}}_j + \hat{\mathbf{t}} . \qquad (5)$$

4.2 A Factorization-Based Algorithm

Our method to solve problem (5) uses a three-step factorization strategy. We first describe it in the occlusion-free case and then propose an iterative extension for the missing data case.

Step 1: Orthonormalizing. We propose the important concept of *orthonormal bases*. We define a reconstruction to be in an orthonormal basis if the joint projection matrix is column-orthonormal. Given a joint projection matrix $\mathcal{P}$, one can find a 3D affine transformation represented by the (3×3) matrix N, which applies as B in (3), such that $\mathcal{P}\mathsf{N}$ is column-orthonormal, *i.e.* such that $\mathsf{N}^\mathsf{T}\mathcal{P}^\mathsf{T}\mathcal{P}\mathsf{N} = \mathsf{I}_{(3\times 3)}$. We call the transformation N an *orthonormalizing transformation*. The set of orthonormalizing transformations is 3-dimensional since for any 3D rotation matrix U, $\mathsf{N}\mathsf{U}$ still is an orthonormalizing transformation for $\mathcal{P}$. We use the QR decomposition $\mathcal{P} = \mathsf{QR}$, see *e.g.* [9], giving an upper triangular orthonormalizing transformation $\mathsf{N} = \mathsf{R}^{-1}$. Other choices are possible for computing an N, *e.g.* if $\mathcal{P} = \mathsf{U\Sigma V}^\mathsf{T}$ is an SVD of $\mathcal{P}$, then $\mathsf{N} = \mathsf{V\Sigma}^{-1}$ has the required property. Henceforth, we assume that all 3D models are expressed in orthonormal bases

$$\begin{cases} \mathcal{P} \leftarrow \mathcal{P}\mathsf{N} \\ \mathcal{P}' \leftarrow \mathcal{P}'\mathsf{N}' \end{cases} \quad \text{and} \quad \begin{cases} \mathcal{Q} \leftarrow \mathsf{N}^{-1}\mathcal{Q} \\ \mathcal{Q}' \leftarrow \mathsf{N}'^{-1}\mathcal{Q}' \end{cases} .$$

An interesting property of orthonormal bases is that $\mathcal{P}^\dagger = \mathcal{P}^\mathsf{T}$. Hence, triangulating points in these bases is simply done by $\mathcal{Q} = \mathcal{P}^\mathsf{T}\mathcal{X}$.

Note that the matrix $\mathcal{P}$ computed by factorization, see Sect. 3, may already satisfy $\mathcal{P}^\mathsf{T}\mathcal{P} = \mathsf{I}$. However, if at least one of the cameras is not used for the alignment, *e.g.* if none of the 3D point correspondences project in this camera, or if the cameras come as the result of the alignment of partial 3D models, then $\mathcal{P}$ will *not* satisfy $\mathcal{P}^\mathsf{T}\mathcal{P} = \mathsf{I}$, thus requiring the orthonormalization step.

Step 2: Eliminating the translation. The translation part of the sought-after transformation can not be computed directly, but can be eliminated from the equations. First, center the image points to eliminate the translation part of the cameras: $\mathbf{x}_{ij} \leftarrow \mathbf{x}_{ij} - \mathbf{t}_i$ and $\mathbf{x}'_{ij} \leftarrow \mathbf{x}'_{ij} - \mathbf{t}'_i$. Second, consider that the partial derivatives of the reprojection error (4) with respect to $\hat{\mathbf{t}}$ must vanish: $\frac{\partial \mathcal{C}^2}{\partial \mathbf{t}} = 0$. By using the constraint $\hat{\mathbf{Q}}'_j = \hat{\mathbf{A}}\hat{\mathbf{Q}}_j + \hat{\mathbf{t}}$ from (4) and expanding using (4), we get

$$\sum_{i=1}^{n'}\sum_{j=1}^{m}\left(\mathsf{P}'^{\mathsf{T}}_i\mathsf{P}'_i\hat{\mathbf{t}} - \mathsf{P}'^{\mathsf{T}}_i\mathbf{x}'_{ij} + \mathsf{P}'^{\mathsf{T}}_i\mathsf{P}'_i\hat{\mathbf{A}}\hat{\mathbf{Q}}_j\right) = 0$$

$$\sum_{j=1}^{m}\left(\mathcal{P}'^{\mathsf{T}}\mathcal{P}'\hat{\mathbf{t}} - \mathcal{P}'^{\mathsf{T}}\mathbf{y}'_j + \mathcal{P}'^{\mathsf{T}}\mathcal{P}'\hat{\mathbf{A}}\hat{\mathbf{Q}}_j\right) = 0$$

$$m\mathcal{P}'^{\mathsf{T}}\mathcal{P}'\hat{\mathbf{t}} - m\mathcal{P}'^{\mathsf{T}}\bar{\mathbf{y}}' + m\mathcal{P}'^{\mathsf{T}}\mathcal{P}'\hat{\mathbf{A}}\bar{\hat{\mathcal{Q}}} = 0 \ ,$$

which leaves us with $\hat{\mathbf{t}} = (\mathcal{P}'^{\mathsf{T}}\mathcal{P}')^{-1}(\mathcal{P}'^{\mathsf{T}}\bar{\mathbf{y}}' - \mathcal{P}'^{\mathsf{T}}\mathcal{P}'\hat{\mathbf{A}}\bar{\hat{\mathcal{Q}}})$ that, thanks to the orthonormal basis property $\mathcal{P}'^{\dagger} = \mathcal{P}'^{\mathsf{T}}$, further simplifies to

$$\hat{\mathbf{t}} = \mathcal{P}'^{\mathsf{T}}\bar{\mathbf{y}}' - \hat{\mathbf{A}}\bar{\hat{\mathcal{Q}}} \ . \tag{6}$$

Note that if the same entire sets of reconstructed points are used for the alignment, then we directly obtain $\hat{\mathbf{t}} = \mathbf{0}$ since $\bar{\mathbf{y}}' = \mathbf{0}$ and $\bar{\hat{\mathcal{Q}}} = \mathbf{0}$. This is rarely the case in practice, especially if the alignment is used to merge partial 3D models.

Third, consider that the m partial derivatives of the reprojection error (4) with respect to each $\hat{\mathbf{Q}}_j$ must vanish as well: $\frac{\partial \mathcal{C}^2}{\partial \hat{\mathbf{Q}}_j} = 0$, and expand as above

$$\sum_{i=1}^{n}\left(\mathsf{P}^{\mathsf{T}}_i\mathsf{P}_i\hat{\mathbf{Q}}_j - \mathsf{P}^{\mathsf{T}}_i\mathbf{x}_{ij}\right) + \sum_{i=1}^{n'}\left(\hat{\mathbf{A}}^{\mathsf{T}}\mathsf{P}'^{\mathsf{T}}_i\mathsf{P}'_i\hat{\mathbf{A}}\hat{\mathbf{Q}}_j - \hat{\mathbf{A}}^{\mathsf{T}}\mathsf{P}'^{\mathsf{T}}_i\mathbf{x}'_{ij} + \hat{\mathbf{A}}^{\mathsf{T}}\mathsf{P}'^{\mathsf{T}}_i\mathsf{P}'_i\hat{\mathbf{t}}\right) = 0$$

$$\mathcal{P}^{\mathsf{T}}\mathcal{P}\hat{\mathbf{Q}}_j - \mathcal{P}^{\mathsf{T}}\mathbf{y}_j + \hat{\mathbf{A}}^{\mathsf{T}}\mathcal{P}'^{\mathsf{T}}\mathcal{P}'\hat{\mathbf{A}}\hat{\mathbf{Q}}_j - \hat{\mathbf{A}}^{\mathsf{T}}\mathcal{P}'^{\mathsf{T}}\mathbf{y}'_j + \hat{\mathbf{A}}^{\mathsf{T}}\mathcal{P}'^{\mathsf{T}}\mathcal{P}'\hat{\mathbf{t}} = 0 \ .$$

The sum over j of all these derivatives also vanishes, giving

$$\mathcal{P}^{\mathsf{T}}\mathcal{P}\bar{\hat{\mathcal{Q}}} - \mathcal{P}^{\mathsf{T}}\bar{\mathbf{y}} + \hat{\mathbf{A}}^{\mathsf{T}}\mathcal{P}'^{\mathsf{T}}\mathcal{P}'\hat{\mathbf{A}}\bar{\hat{\mathcal{Q}}} - \hat{\mathbf{A}}^{\mathsf{T}}\mathcal{P}'^{\mathsf{T}}\bar{\mathbf{y}}' + \hat{\mathbf{A}}^{\mathsf{T}}\mathcal{P}'^{\mathsf{T}}\mathcal{P}'\hat{\mathbf{t}} = 0 \ .$$

By replacing $\hat{\mathbf{t}}$ by its expression (6), and after some minor algebraic manipulations, we obtain

$$\mathcal{P}^{\mathsf{T}}\mathcal{P}\bar{\hat{\mathcal{Q}}} - \mathcal{P}^{\mathsf{T}}\bar{\mathbf{y}} = 0 \quad\Longrightarrow\quad \bar{\hat{\mathcal{Q}}} = \mathcal{P}^{\dagger}\bar{\mathbf{y}} \tag{7}$$

and by substituting in (6) and using the orthonormal basis property, we get

$$\hat{\mathbf{t}} = \mathcal{P}'^{\mathsf{T}}\bar{\mathbf{y}}' - \hat{\mathbf{A}}\mathcal{P}^{\mathsf{T}}\bar{\mathbf{y}} \ . \tag{8}$$

It is common in factorization methods to center the data with respect to their centroid to cancel the translation part of the transformation. Equation (8) means that the data must be centered with respect to the *reconstructed centroid* of the image points, not with respect to the actual 3D centroid.

Obviously, if the 3D models have been obtained by the factorization method of Sect. 3, then the centroid of the 3D points corresponds to the reconstructed centroid, *i.e.* $\bar{\mathbf{Q}} = \mathcal{P}^{\mathsf{T}}\bar{\mathbf{y}}$ and $\bar{\mathbf{Q}}' = \mathcal{P}'^{\mathsf{T}}\bar{\mathbf{y}}'$, provided that the same sets of views are used for reconstruction and alignment.

To summarize, we cancel the translation part out of the sought-after transformation by translating the reconstructions and the image points as shown below

$$\begin{cases} \mathbf{Q}_j \leftarrow \mathbf{Q}_j - \mathcal{P}^\mathsf{T}\bar{\mathbf{y}} \\ \mathbf{Q}'_j \leftarrow \mathbf{Q}'_j - \mathcal{P}'^\mathsf{T}\bar{\mathbf{y}}' \end{cases} \quad \text{and} \quad \begin{cases} \mathbf{x}_{ij} \leftarrow \mathbf{x}_{ij} - \mathsf{P}_i\mathcal{P}^\mathsf{T}\bar{\mathbf{y}} \\ \mathbf{x}'_{ij} \leftarrow \mathbf{x}'_{ij} - \mathsf{P}'_i\mathcal{P}'^\mathsf{T}\bar{\mathbf{y}}' \end{cases} .$$

The reprojection error (4) is rewritten

$$\mathcal{C}^2(\mathcal{Q}, \mathcal{Q}') = \frac{1}{2nm} \left(\|\mathcal{X} - \mathcal{P}\mathcal{Q}\|^2 + \|\mathcal{X}' - \mathcal{P}'\mathcal{Q}'\|^2 \right) \tag{9}$$

and problem (5) is reformulated as

$$\min_{\hat{\mathcal{Q}},\hat{\mathcal{Q}}'} \mathcal{C}^2(\hat{\mathcal{Q}}, \hat{\mathcal{Q}}') \quad \text{s.t.} \quad \hat{\mathbf{Q}}'_j = \hat{\mathsf{A}}\hat{\mathbf{Q}}_j . \tag{10}$$

Step 3: Factorizing. Thanks to the orthonormal basis property $\mathcal{P}^\mathsf{T}\mathcal{P} = \mathsf{I}$, and since for any column-orthonormal matrix $\mathcal{A}$, $\|\mathcal{A}\mathbf{x}\| = \|\mathbf{x}\|$, we can rewrite the reprojection error for a single set of cameras as

$$\mathcal{R}^2(\mathcal{P}, \mathcal{Q}) \ \propto \ \|\mathcal{X} - \mathcal{P}\mathcal{Q}\|^2 \ = \ \|\mathcal{P}^\mathsf{T}\mathcal{X} - \mathcal{Q}\|^2 .$$

This allows to rewrite the reprojection error (9) as

$$\mathcal{C}^2(\hat{\mathcal{Q}}, \hat{\mathcal{Q}}') \ \propto \ \|\mathcal{P}^\mathsf{T}\mathcal{X} - \hat{\mathcal{Q}}\|^2 + \|\mathcal{P}'^\mathsf{T}\mathcal{X}' - \hat{\mathcal{Q}}'\|^2 \ = \ \| \underbrace{\begin{pmatrix} \mathcal{P}^\mathsf{T}\mathcal{X} \\ \mathcal{P}'^\mathsf{T}\mathcal{X}' \end{pmatrix}}_{\Lambda} - \underbrace{\begin{pmatrix} \hat{\mathcal{Q}} \\ \hat{\mathcal{Q}}' \end{pmatrix}}_{\Delta} \|^2 .$$

By introducing the constraint $\hat{\mathcal{Q}}' = \hat{\mathsf{A}}\hat{\mathcal{Q}}$ from (10) and, as in Sect. 3, an unknown global affine transformation B we can write

$$\Delta \ = \ \begin{pmatrix} \mathsf{I} \\ \hat{\mathsf{A}} \end{pmatrix} \mathsf{B}\mathsf{B}^{-1}\hat{\mathcal{Q}} \ = \ \underbrace{\begin{pmatrix} \mathsf{B} \\ \hat{\mathsf{A}}\mathsf{B} \end{pmatrix}}_{\tilde{\mathcal{M}}} \underbrace{\mathsf{B}^{-1}\mathcal{Q}}_{\tilde{\mathcal{Q}}} .$$

The problem is reformulated as

$$\min_{\tilde{\mathcal{M}},\tilde{\mathcal{Q}}} \|\Lambda - \tilde{\mathcal{M}}\tilde{\mathcal{Q}}\|^2 .$$

A solution is given by the SVD of matrix Λ

$$\Lambda_{(6\times m)} = \mathsf{U}_{(6\times 6)}\Sigma_{(6\times 6)}\mathsf{V}^\mathsf{T}_{(6\times m)} .$$

As in Sect. 3, let $\Sigma = \Sigma_u\Sigma_v$ be any decomposition of matrix Σ. We obtain $\tilde{\mathcal{M}} = \psi(\mathsf{U}\Sigma_u)$ and $\tilde{\mathcal{Q}} = \psi^\mathsf{T}(\mathsf{V}\Sigma_v^\mathsf{T})$. Using the partitioning $\tilde{\mathcal{M}} = \begin{pmatrix} \tilde{\mathsf{M}} \\ \tilde{\mathsf{M}}' \end{pmatrix}$, we get

$$\begin{cases} \mathsf{B} = \tilde{\mathsf{M}} \\ \hat{\mathsf{A}} = \tilde{\mathsf{M}}'\mathsf{B}^{-1} \\ \hat{\mathcal{Q}} = \mathsf{B}\tilde{\mathcal{Q}} \end{cases} .$$

Obviously, one needs to undo the effect of the orthonormalizing transformations, as follows

$$\begin{cases} \hat{A} \leftarrow N'\hat{A}N^{-1} \\ \hat{Q} \leftarrow N\hat{Q} \end{cases}.$$

This algorithm runs with $m \geq 4$ point correspondences.

Note that it is possible to solve the problem without using the orthonormalizing transformations. This solution requires however to compute the SVD of a $(2(n + n') \times m)$ matrix, made by stacking the measurement matrices $\mathcal{X}$ and $\mathcal{X}'$, and is therefore much more computationally expensive than the algorithm above, and may be intractable for large sets of cameras and points.

4.3   Dealing with Missing Data

The missing data case arises when some of the 3D points used for the alignment are not visible in all views. We propose an Expectation Maximization based extension of the algorithm to handle this case.

The EM algorithm is an iterative method which estimates the model parameters, given an incomplete set of measurement data. The main idea is to alternate between predicting the missing data and estimating the model. Since the log likelihood cannot be maximized using factorization, due to the missing data, it is replaced by its conditional expectation given the observed data, using the current estimate of the parameters. In the case where the log likelihood is a linear function of the missing data, this simply consists in replacing the missing data by their conditional expectations given the observed data at current parameter values. This approximated log likelihood is then maximized so as to yield a new estimate of the parameters. Monotone convergence to a local minimum of the Maximum Likelihood residual error (4) is shown *e.g.* in [11].

Since the reconstruction of both camera sets using factorization needs a complete data set, we are limited to the points visible in all views for the initial reconstruction. This allows to reconstruct all cameras, but only part of the 3D points. We then triangulate the missing points in order to complete the 3D point cloud. This preliminary expectation step yields a completed set of 3D data, that can be used in the alignement algorithm.

However, the reprojection error, *i.e.* the negative log likelihood, still cannot be minimized because of the incomplete measurement matrix $\mathcal{X}$. The expectation step predicts the missing image points by reprojecting them from the completed 3D points, namely for the missing point $\mathbf{x}_{ij}$, we set $\mathbf{x}_{ij} \leftarrow P_i\hat{Q}_j + \mathbf{t}_i$.

The maximization step consists in applying the algorithm described in the complete data case. This yields an estimate of the sought-after transformation $(\hat{A}, \hat{t})$ as well as corrected point positions $\{\hat{Q}_j \leftrightarrow \hat{Q}'_j\}$.

These two steps are alternated, thus forming an iterative procedure where the corrected points are used in the expectation at the next iteration. In order to decide whether convergence is reached, the change in reprojection error between two iterations is measured. When the reprojection error stabilizes, the final result is returned.

Table 1 gives a summary of the algorithm with its EM extension.

Table 1. The proposed Maximum Likelihood alignment algorithm

OBJECTIVE

Given $m \geq 4$ 3D point correspondences $\{\mathbf{Q}_j \leftrightarrow \mathbf{Q}'_j\}$ obtained by affine reconstruction and triangulation of the missing data from two sets of images, with respectively n cameras $\{(\mathsf{P}_i, \mathbf{t}_i)\}$ and n' cameras $\{(\mathsf{P}'_i, \mathbf{t}'_i)\}$, as well as measured image points $\{\mathbf{x}_{ij}\}$ and $\{\mathbf{x}'_{ij}\}$ forming an incomplete data set, compute the affine transformation $(\hat{\mathsf{A}}, \hat{\mathbf{t}})$ and corrected point positions $\{\hat{\mathbf{Q}}_j \leftrightarrow \hat{\mathbf{Q}}'_j\}$ such that the reprojection error e is minimized.

ALGORITHM

1. **Compute the orthonormalizing transformations:**

$$\left(\cdots \mathsf{P}_i^\mathsf{T} \cdots \right)^\mathsf{T} \overset{\text{QR}}{=} \mathcal{P}\mathsf{N}^{-1} \quad \text{and} \quad \left(\cdots \mathsf{P}_i'^\mathsf{T} \cdots \right)^\mathsf{T} \overset{\text{QR}}{=} \mathcal{P}'\mathsf{N}'^{-1} \ .$$

2. **Form the 'joint projection' and the measurement matrices:**

$$\mathcal{X} = \begin{pmatrix} \vdots \\ \cdots (\mathbf{x}_{ij} - \mathbf{t}_i) \cdots \\ \vdots \end{pmatrix} \quad \text{and} \quad \mathcal{X}' = \begin{pmatrix} \vdots \\ \cdots (\mathbf{x}'_{ij} - \mathbf{t}'_i) \cdots \\ \vdots \end{pmatrix} \ .$$

3. **Expectation-Maximization:**
   (a) **Expectation.** Predict the missing point $\mathbf{x}_{ij}$ by setting $\mathbf{x}_{ij} \leftarrow \mathsf{P}_i\hat{\mathbf{Q}}_j$. Compute the reconstructed centroids:

$$\mathbf{C} = \frac{\mathcal{P}^\mathsf{T}}{m} \sum_{j=1}^m \begin{pmatrix} \vdots \\ \mathbf{x}_{ij} \\ \vdots \end{pmatrix} \quad \text{and} \quad \mathbf{C}' = \frac{\mathcal{P}'^\mathsf{T}}{m} \sum_{j=1}^m \begin{pmatrix} \vdots \\ \mathbf{x}'_{ij} \\ \vdots \end{pmatrix} \ .$$

   Cancel the translations:

$$\mathcal{X} = \begin{pmatrix} \vdots \\ \cdots (\mathbf{x}_{ij} - \mathsf{P}_i\mathbf{C}) \cdots \\ \vdots \end{pmatrix} \quad \text{and} \quad \mathcal{X}' = \begin{pmatrix} \vdots \\ \cdots (\mathbf{x}'_{ij} - \mathsf{P}'_i\mathbf{C}') \cdots \\ \vdots \end{pmatrix} \ .$$

   (b) **Maximization.** Factorize:

$$\begin{pmatrix} \mathcal{P}^\mathsf{T}\mathcal{X} \\ \mathcal{P}'^\mathsf{T}\mathcal{X}' \end{pmatrix} \overset{\text{SVD}}{=} \mathsf{U}\Sigma\mathsf{V}^\mathsf{T} \quad \text{and set} \quad \begin{pmatrix} \tilde{\mathsf{M}} \\ \tilde{\mathsf{M}}' \end{pmatrix} = \psi(\mathsf{U}\sqrt{\Sigma}) \quad \text{and} \quad \tilde{\mathcal{Q}} = \psi^\mathsf{T}(\mathsf{V}\sqrt{\Sigma}) \ .$$

   (c) **Recover the corrected points.** Set $\hat{\mathcal{Q}} = \mathsf{N}\tilde{\mathsf{M}}\tilde{\mathcal{Q}}$ and $\hat{\mathcal{Q}}' = \mathsf{N}'\tilde{\mathsf{M}}'\tilde{\mathcal{Q}}$.
   (d) **Transfer the points to the original coordinate frames.** Extract the corrected points $\hat{\mathbf{Q}}_j$ from $\hat{\mathcal{Q}}$. Translate them as $\hat{\mathbf{Q}}_j \leftarrow \hat{\mathbf{Q}}_j + \mathbf{C}$.
   (e) **Compute the reprojection error:**
      Set $e^2 = \frac{1}{2nm}\left(\sum_{j=1}^m \left(\sum_{i=1}^n d^2(\mathbf{x}_{ij} - \mathsf{P}_i\hat{\mathbf{Q}}_j) + \sum_{i=1}^{n'} d^2(\mathbf{x}'_{ij} - \mathsf{P}'_i\hat{\mathbf{Q}}'_j) \right) \right)$.
   (f) **Loop.** If convergence is not reached (see Sect. 4.3), loop on step (a).
4. **Recover the transformation:** Set $\hat{\mathsf{A}} = \mathsf{N}'\tilde{\mathsf{M}}'\tilde{\mathsf{M}}^{-1}\mathsf{N}^{-1}$ and $\mathbf{t} = \mathbf{C}' - \hat{\mathsf{A}}\mathbf{C}$.

---

5 Other Algorithms

We briefly describe two other alignment algorithms. They do not yield Maximum Likelihood Estimates under the previously-mentioned hypotheses on the noise distribution. They rely on 3D measurements and therefore naturally handle missing image data.

5.1 Minimizing the Non-symmetric Transfer Error

This algorithm, dubbed 'TRERROR', is specific to the two camera set case. It is based on minimizing a non-symmetric 3D transfer error $\mathcal{E}(\hat{A})$ as follows

$$\min_{\hat{A},\hat{t}} \mathcal{E}^2(\hat{A}, \hat{t}) \quad \text{with} \quad \mathcal{E}^2(\hat{A}) = \frac{1}{m} \sum_{j=1}^{m} \|\mathbf{Q}'_j - \hat{A}\mathbf{Q}_j - \hat{t}\|^2 \; .$$

Differentiating $\mathcal{E}^2$ with respect to $\hat{t}$ and nullifying the result allows to eliminate the translation by centering each 3D point set on its centroid. By rewriting the error function and applying standard linear least-squares, one obtains

$$\hat{A} = \mathcal{Q}'\mathcal{Q}^\dagger \quad \text{and} \quad \hat{t} = \bar{\mathbf{Q}}' - \hat{A}\bar{\mathbf{Q}} \; .$$

5.2 Direct 3D Factorization

This algorithm, dubbed 'FACT3D', is based on directly factorizing the 3D reconstructed points. It is not restricted to the two camera set case, but for simplicity, we only describe this case. Generalization to multiple camera sets is trivial. The algorithm computes the aligning transformation $(\hat{A}, \hat{t})$ and perfectly corresponding points $\{\hat{\mathbf{Q}}_j \leftrightarrow \hat{\mathbf{Q}}'_j\}$. The reconstructed cameras are not taken into account by this algorithm, which entirely relies on 3D measures on the reconstructed points. Under certain conditions, this algorithm is equivalent to the proposed FACTMLE-EM.

The problem is stated as

$$\min_{\hat{\mathcal{Q}},\hat{\mathcal{Q}}'} \mathcal{D}^2(\hat{\mathcal{Q}}, \hat{\mathcal{Q}}') \quad \text{s.t.} \quad \hat{\mathbf{Q}}'_j = \hat{A}\hat{\mathbf{Q}}_j + \hat{t} \; ,$$

where the 3D error function employed is defined by

$$\mathcal{D}^2(\hat{\mathcal{Q}}, \hat{\mathcal{Q}}') = \frac{1}{2m} \left(\|\mathcal{Q} - \hat{\mathcal{Q}}\|^2 + \|\mathcal{Q}' - \hat{\mathcal{Q}}'\|^2 \right) \; .$$

Minimizing this error function means that if the noise *on the 3D point coordinates* were Gaussian, centered and i.i.d., which is *not* the case with our actual hypotheses, then this algorithm would yield the Maximum Likelihood Estimate.

Step 1: Eliminating the translation. By using the technique from Sect. 4.2, we obtain $\hat{t} = \bar{\mathbf{Q}}' - \hat{A}\bar{\mathbf{Q}}$. As in most factorization methods, cancelling the translation part out according to the error function $\mathcal{D}$ is done by centering each set of 3D points on its actual centroid: $\hat{\mathbf{Q}}_j \leftarrow \hat{\mathbf{Q}}_j - \bar{\mathbf{Q}}$ and $\hat{\mathbf{Q}}'_j \leftarrow \hat{\mathbf{Q}}'_j - \bar{\mathbf{Q}}'$. Henceforth, we assume to work in centered coordinates. The problem is rewritten as

$$\min_{\hat{\mathcal{Q}},\hat{\mathcal{Q}}'} \mathcal{D}^2(\hat{\mathcal{Q}}, \hat{\mathcal{Q}}') \quad \text{s.t.} \quad \hat{\mathbf{Q}}'_j = \hat{A}\hat{\mathbf{Q}}_j \; .$$

Step 2: Factorizing. Following the approach in Sect. 4.2, we rewrite $\mathcal{D}$ as

$$\mathcal{D}^2(\hat{\mathcal{Q}}, \hat{\mathcal{Q}}') \propto \| \begin{pmatrix} \mathcal{Q} \\ \mathcal{Q}' \end{pmatrix} - \begin{pmatrix} \hat{\mathcal{Q}} \\ \hat{\mathcal{Q}}' \end{pmatrix} \|^2 = \| \underbrace{\begin{pmatrix} \mathcal{Q} \\ \mathcal{Q}' \end{pmatrix}}_{\Lambda} - \underbrace{\begin{pmatrix} B \\ AB \end{pmatrix}}_{\tilde{\mathcal{M}}} \underbrace{B^{-1}\hat{\mathcal{Q}}}_{\tilde{\mathcal{Q}}} \|^2 \ .$$

Using SVD of matrix $\Lambda = U\Sigma V^\mathsf{T}$, we obtain $\tilde{\mathcal{M}} = \psi(U\Sigma_u)$ and $\tilde{\mathcal{Q}} = \psi^\mathsf{T}(V\Sigma_v^\mathsf{T})$. By using the partitioning $\tilde{\mathcal{M}} = (\tilde{M}\tilde{M}')^\mathsf{T}$, we get

$$\hat{A} = \tilde{M}'\tilde{M}^{-1} \quad \text{and} \quad \hat{\mathcal{Q}} = \tilde{M}\tilde{\mathcal{Q}} \ .$$

6   Experimental Evaluation

We evaluate our algorithm using simulated and real data. The implementation of all three compared algorithms, *i.e.* FACTMLE-EM, TRERROR and FACT3D, as well as the generation of simulated data, have been done in C++.

6.1   Simulated Data

We generate m 3D points and two sets of n weak perspective cameras each. The pose of a camera is defined by its three dimensional location, viewing direction and roll angle (rotation angle around the optical axis). The corresponding affine projection matrix is given by a (2×3), truncated, rotation matrix $\bar{R}_i$ together with a two-dimensional translation vector $\mathbf{t}_i$, both of which premultiplied by an internal calibration matrix. More precisly, we use weak perspective cameras $P_i = A_i\bar{R}_i$ and $\mathbf{t}_i = A_i\bar{T}_i$, where A_i is the internal calibration matrix

$$A_i = k_i \begin{pmatrix} \tau_i & 0 \\ 0 & 1 \end{pmatrix} \ .$$

The scale factor k_i models the average depth of the object and the focal length of the camera, and τ models the aspect ratio that we choose very close to 1. The 3D points are chosen from a uniform distribution inside a thin rectangular parallelepiped with dimensions $1 \times 1 \times (1-d)$, and the scale factors k_i are chosen so that the points are uniformly spread in 400×400 pixel images.

We generate three point sets containing the point visibles (i) in the first camera set, (ii) in the second one and (iii) in both camera sets. The third subset contains m_c points, whereas the two first subsets both contains $m - m_c$ points. Hence, m points are used to perform SFM on each camera set, while m_c points are used for the alignment. The points are projected onto the images where they are visible and gaussian noise with zero mean and standard deviation σ is added.

In order to assess the behaviour of the algorithms in the presence of non-perfectly affine cameras, we introduce the factor $0 \leq a \leq 1$. Let Z_{ij} be the depth of the j-th 3D point with respect to camera i, we scale the projected points $\mathbf{x}_{ij}$ by $\mathbf{x}_{ij} \leftarrow \frac{1}{\nu}\mathbf{x}_{ij}$ with $\nu = a + (1-a)Z_{ij}$, meaning that for $a = 1$, the points does not change and the projection is perfectly affine, and when a tends towards

0, the points undergo stronger and stronger perspective effects. The points are further scaled so that their standard deviation remains invariant, in order to keep them wellspread in the images.

So as to simulate the problem of incomplete data, $e.g.$ due to occlusions, we generate a list of missing image points. We introduce the probability p_{point} that any given 3D point is occluded in some images and the probability p_{image} that it is occluded in one particular image. For simplicity, we take $p_{point} = p_{image} = p$, which gives a rate of missing data of p^2.

A 3D model is reconstructed from each of the two camera sets using the factorization algorithm described in Sect. 3. Once the camera matrices and 3D points are estimated, only the m_c points common to the two camera sets are considered for the alignment. We define the overlap ratio of the two camera sets to be $\theta = m_c/m$, $i.e.$ for $\theta = 1$ all points are seen in all views, while for $\theta = 0$, the two sets of cameras do not share corresponding points.

Each of the three alignment algorithms yields estimates for the 3D affine transformation and corrected point clouds, except TRERROR which only gives the transformation. The comparison of the algorithms being based on the reprojection error, the point clouds used to compute it need to be re-estimated so that this error is minimized, given an estimated transformation. This must be done for TRERROR and FACT3D, but is useless for FACTMLE-EM.

We use the following default setting for the simulations: $n = 5$ views, $m = 250$ points, $\theta = 0.2$ ($i.e.$ a 20% overlap and $m_c = 50$ points common to the two 3D models), $\sigma = 3.0$ pixels, $d = 0.95$ (flat 3D scene), $a = 1$ (perfectly affine projections) and $p = 0.3$ (rate of missing data $p^2 = 0.09$). We vary each parameter at a time. Figures 2, 3 and 4 show the reprojection error averaged over 500 simulations for the three algorithms for different parameter values.

In Fig. 2, we vary the number of common points m_c (coupled with the total number of points m, so as to keep the overlap constant) and the number of cameras n, the former from 4 to 60, corresponding respectively to $m = 20$ and $m = 300$, and the latter from 2 to 15. We see that for $m_c > 20$, the number of points has a much smaller influence on the errors. Whereas FACT3D and TRERROR show similar behaviour, FACTMLE-EM is distinguished by its lower reprojection error. The difference between our method and the other two seems to be more important in the cases where we have few points or few cameras.

In Fig. 3, the rate of missing data and the overlap ratio (coupled with the number of common points m_c, so as to keep the total number of points m constant) are varied, the former from 0 to 0.5 and the latter from 0.1 to 1.0. In order to emphasize the contribution of the EM scheme, in Fig. 3(a) we also display the reprojection error of FACTMLE-EM after the first iteration. When the rate of missing data grows, the three methods show different tendencies. Whereas FACTMLE-EM handles missing data well, the other methods prove to be unstable. However, considering only one iteration of FACTMLE-EM, the reprojection error increases just as for the other methods. The difference in performance is thus provided by the EM iterations.

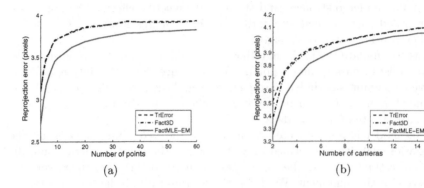

Fig. 2. Reprojection error against (a) the number of points m_c and (b) the number of cameras n

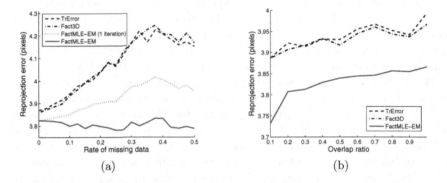

Fig. 3. Reprojection error against (a) the rate of missing data and (b) the extent of overlap θ between the two sets of cameras. For $\theta = 1$, all points are seen in all views.

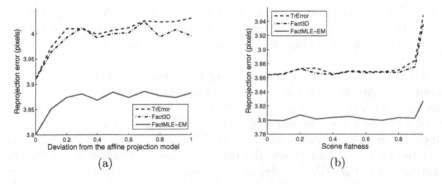

Fig. 4. Reprojection error against (a) the deviation a from the affine projection model and (b) the scene flatness d. For $a = 1$, the projection is perfectly affine. For $d = 1$, all 3D points lie on a plane.

In Fig. 4 the deviation from the affine model a varies from 0 to 1, from a perfectly affine projection, and the flatness of the simulated data d varies from 0 to 1, *i.e.* from a cube to a plane. Despite the fact that the alignement is affine, even completely projective cameras seem to be well modeled by the three methods. In fact, the error induced by the affine approximation is small compared to the added noise. The flatness of the scene does not change the result, except for very flat scenes making the algorithms unstable, FACT3D and TRERROR somewhat more than FACTMLE-EM. This result was expected since planar scenes are singular for the computation of a 3D affine transformation.

Simulations with varying σ reveal a quasi linear relationship between the the noise level and the reprojection error. The slope is somewhat less steep in the case of FACTMLE-EM than for the other two methods, indicating that our method is less sensitive to noise.

Although the three algorihtms have similar behaviour throughout the sequence of tests, except when varying the rate of missing data, FACTMLE-EM consistently outperforms the other ones.

6.2   Real Data

We applied the algorithms to real image sequences as follows. A number of images of a scene were taken from different angles and grouped into two sets. A certain number of point correspondences were defined within each one of the image sets, as well as for all the images, thus forming the measurement matrices $\mathcal{X}$ and $\mathcal{X}'$.

The camera used is an uncalibrated digital Nikon D100 with a lens of focal length $80 - 200$ mm, giving an image size of 2240×1488 pixels.

The 'books' sequence. We used a series of images of a rather flat scene, together with a large set of point correspondences, given by a tracking algorithm, shown

(a) One image from the 'books' sequence overlaid with the $m_c = 196$ point correspondences in white and reprojected points in black.

(b) A detail from the image in (a) showing the original points in black and reprojected points in white, from FACTMLE-EM (points), FACT3D (stars) and TRERROR (crosses).

Fig. 5. Results from the 'books' sequence

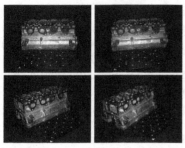

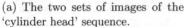

(a) The two sets of images of the 'cylinder head' sequence.

(b) The original points in black together with their FACTMLE-EM reprojections in white.

Fig. 6. Results from the 'cylinder head' sequence

in Fig. 5(a). So as to keep the experimental conditions close to the hypothesis of affine cameras, the photos are taken far away from the object using a large zoom. This group of images consists of two sets of respectively $n = 2$ and $n' = 3$ images, together with the $m_c = 196$ common point correspondences, and respectively $m = 628$ and $m' = 634$ correspondences for the two sets, giving an approximate overlap of 80%. The reprojection errors we obtained are:

FACTMLE-EM	1.90 pixels
FACT3D	1.97 pixels
TRERROR	2.17 pixels

A detail of an image with the reprojected points due to all three methods is shown in Fig. 5(b). As predicted by the tests on simulated data, FACTMLE-EM performs better than FACT3D and TRERROR.

The 'cylinder head' sequence. This sequence was acquired under different conditions than the previous one. The photos were taken with the same camera, using a lens with a focal length of 12 mm, at a distance of 60 cm of the object, which is 40 cm long. The points, shown in Fig. 6(b), were manually entered. Using these settings, the affine camera model does not apply and the reconstruction performed prior to the alignment is therefore less reliable. Nevertheless, the result of the alignment is rather good. This group of images consists of two sets of respectively $n = n' = 2$ images, together with the $m_c = 18$ common point correspondences, and respectively $m = 22$ and $m' = 23$ correspondences for the two sets, giving an approximate overlap of 31%. The reprojection errors are:

FACTMLE-EM	3.03 pixels
FACT3D	3.04 pixels
TRERROR	3.05 pixels

The two sets of images are displayed in Fig. 6(a) and the given point matches together with the FACTMLE-EM reprojections are displayed in Fig. 6(b).

 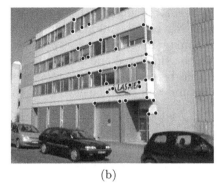

(a)   (b)

Fig. 7. The original common points in white together with their FACTMLE-EM re-projections in black. The two images are the first ones in the respective camera sets.

The 'building' sequence. The point correspondences are once again given by a tracking algorithm, but this time the data set is incomplete. We need at least two views of a 3D point in order to use it for the reconstruction, so we keep only those points that are present in two or more images. We then define a point correspondence to be common to the two sets and thus used for the alignment of the two reconstructions, as soon as it is present in (at least two images in each one of) the two sets. This group of images consists of two sets of respectively $n = n' = 5$ images, together with the $m_c = 40$ common point correspondences, and respectively $m = 94$ and $m' = 133$ correspondences for the two sets, giving an overlap of 43% and 30% respectively. The rates of missing data are for the first camera set 31% (13% for the common points) and for the second camera set 22% (11% for the common points). We note that the missing points are essentially not due to occlusions but to failure in the tracking algorithm or to the points being out of range in the images. The reprojection errors we obtained are:

FACTMLE-EM	0.78 pixels
FACT3D	0.84 pixels
TRERROR	0.85 pixels

As predicted by the simulations with varying rate of missing data, the difference between the methods is more important when processing incomplete data. Whereas FACT3D and TRERROR yield similar errors, FACTMLE-EM distinguishes itself with a significantly lower error. The results are displayed in Fig. 7.

7   Conclusions

We presented a method to compute the Maximum Likelihood Estimate of 3D affine transformations, under standard hypotheses on the noise distribution, aligning sets of 3D points obtained from uncalibrated affine cameras. The method computes all aligning transformations in a single computation step in the occlusion-free case, by minimizing the reprojection error over all points and all images. An iterative extension is presented for the missing data case. Experimental results on simulated and real data show that the proposed method consistently performs better than other methods based on 3D measurements.

Future work could be devoted to the incorporation of other types of features.

References

1. Fitzgibbon, A., Zisserman, A.: Automatic camera recovery for closed or open image sequences. In: ECCV. (1998) 311–326
2. Tomasi, C., Kanade, T.: Shape and motion from image streams under orthography: A factorization method. IJCV **9** (1992) 137–154
3. Beardsley, P., Zisserman, A., Murray, D.: Sequential updating of projective and affine structure from motion. IJCV **23** (1997) 235–259
4. Csurka, G., Demirdjian, D., Horaud, R.: Finding the collineation between two projective reconstructions. Comp. Vision and Image Underst. **75** (1999) 260–268
5. Walker, M., Shao, L., Volz, R.: Estimating 3D location parameters using dual number quaternions. Computer Vision, Graphics and Image Processing: Image Understanding **54** (1991) 358–367
6. Mundy, J., Zisserman, A., eds.: Geometric Invariance in Computer Vision. The MIT Press, Cambridge, MA, USA (1992)
7. Bartoli, A., Martinsson, H., Gaspard, F., Lavest, J.M.: On aligning sets of points reconstructed from uncalibrated affine cameras. In: SCIA. (2005) 531–540
8. Reid, I., Murray, D.: Active tracking of foveated feature clusters using affine structure. IJCV **18** (1996) 41–60
9. Golub, G., van Loan, C.: Matrix Computation. The Johns Hopkins University Press, Baltimore (1989)
10. Jacobs, D.: Linear fitting with missing data: Applications to structure-from-motion and to characterizing intensity images. In: CVPR. (1997) 206–212
11. McLachlan, G., Krishnan, T.: The EM algorithm and extensions. John Wiley & Sons, Inc. (1997)

Maximum-Likelihood Estimation of Biological Growth Variables

Anuj Srivastava[1], Sanjay Saini[1], Zhaohua Ding[2], and Ulf Grenander[3]

[1] Department of Statistics, Florida State University, Tallahassee, FL 32306
Phone: 850-222-4157, Fax: 850-644-5271
{anuj, sanjay}@stat.fsu.edu
[2] Institute of Imaging Sciences, Vanderbilt University, Nashville, TN 37232
zhaohua.ding@vanderbilt.edu
[3] Division of Applied Mathematics, Brown University, Providence, RI 02912
ulf-grenander@cox.net

Abstract. Shapes of biological objects, such as anatomical parts, have been studied intensely in recent years. An emerging need is to model and analyze *changes in shapes* of biological objects during, for example, growths of organisms. A recent paper by Grenander et al. [5] introduced a mathematical model, called GRID, for decomposing growth induced diffeomorphism into smaller, local deformations. The basic idea is to place focal points of local growth, called seeds, according to a spatial process on a time-varying coordinate system, and to deform a small neighborhood around them using radial deformation functions (RDFs). In order to estimate these variables – seed placements and RDFS - we first estimate optimal deformation from magnetic resonance image data, and then utilize an iterative solution to reach maximum-likelihood estimates. We demonstrate this approach using MRI images of human brain growth.

1 Introduction

There has been tremendous research in analysis of biological shapes in recent years. As a result, there exists a large variety of representations and metrics for comparing shapes of different objects. A related area that is gaining attention is analysis of *changes in shapes* of a biological object, an organism or an anatomical part, resulting from natural growth, a disease, or some other factor. Mathematical modeling and analysis of biological shape changes are of great interest in many areas dealing with physiology, evolution, medicine, and surgery. Applications include analysis and prediction of solid-tumor growth in animal tissues, testing normality of an organ's growth, analysis of shapes of anatomical structures in brain, and tracking of biological growth and decay in body parts. Shapes variations of anatomical parts are often important factors in deciding normality/abnormality of imaged patients. In many cases, the current clinical practice is to manually measure certain shape characteristics such as lengths, sizes or areas associated with the regions of interest, and use those indicators in diagnoses. Another common approach is to model objects via simple geometries,

A. Rangarajan et al. (Eds.): EMMCVPR 2005, LNCS 3757, pp. 107–118, 2005.

such as ellipsoids, spheres, rectangles, etc, and use resulting shape parameters for analysis. As an example, for measuring the growth of a tumor some techniques use "multicellular spheroid" models, where the growth of the inner core of a tumor is modeled by elliptical spheroids [10]. In general, however, one would like to measure and analyze complete shapes of objects, and not just certain indicators or their approximations by simple geometries, a goal that requires a comprehensive theory for statistical analysis of biological shapes. Growth and shape dissimilarities have also been modeled in the past using smooth deformations, or diffeomorphisms, of the underlying coordinate systems [4, 8, 12, 11, 9]. The set of all diffeomorphisms from $\mathbb{R}^n$ to $\mathbb{R}^n$, with $n = 2$ or 3, denoted by $\mathcal{D}$, forms an infinite-dimensional Lie group [8], and its differential geometry is often used to analyze deformations. An element $\phi \in \mathcal{D}$ denotes a diffeomorphism such that a pixel located at $x \in \mathbb{R}^n$ is mapped to the location $\phi(x) \in \mathbb{R}^n$ in a smooth fashion. For the identity map $id \in \mathcal{D}$, defined by $id(x) = x$, consider the space of all tangents to $\mathcal{D}$ at the point id, denoted by $T_{id}(\mathcal{D})$. An element $v \in T_{id}(\mathcal{D})$ is a vector field that assigns a vector $v(x) \in \mathbb{R}^n$ to each point in the coordinate system. The vector field v is said to *generate* a time-varying deformation ϕ_t according to the relation:

$$\phi_t(x) = x + \int_0^t v_\tau(\phi_\tau(x))d\tau \ .$$

In the context of deformations resulting from biological growth, a general goal is to derive biological motivated representations of ϕ_t and v_t.

In a recent paper, Grenander et al [5] introduced a mathematical representation of growth-induced deformation, called the GRID (Growth by Random Iterated Diffeomorphisms) model. This models provides a biologically-motivated representations of changes in shapes induced by growth. Our goal in this paper is to is to demonstrate the use of GRID model in representing ϕ. Taking a two-step approach, we: (i) estimate the optimal ϕ^* from the image data, and then (ii) develop a maximum-likelihood estimates (MLEs) of GRID variables from ϕ^* using an iterative approach. In this paper we restrict to $n = 2$ although the principles used here are easily extendible to $n = 3$.

In Section 2, we summarize the GRID model and refer the interested reader to [5] for details. In Section 3, we formulate estimation of ϕ^* as a problem in energy minimization, and use the estimated ϕ^* to form MLE of GRID variables in section 4. A summary is presented in Section 5.

2   General GRID Model

We start by summarizing the GRID model proposed by Grenander et al. [5]. The main motivation behind the GRID model is to model growth locally and biologically. It uses an evolving coordinate system, called Darcyan, that keeps track of genetic behavior of locations inside the object. GRID assumes that deformations are concentrated around genetically active points, called *seeds*, that turn on and off according to their genetic composition and bio-chemical environment. The placement of seeds is modeled as a Poisson process in the Darcyan coordinate system. Note that, in practice, this Poisson process will be heterogeneous in space and time.

2.1   A Model for Deformation ϕ

Around each seed, the deformation is modeled radially, using a *radial deformation function*, that captures the radial displacement as a function of angle around the seed. Studies of actual observed deformations, with examples shown in Figure 1, support the idea of radial deformation fields. In the GRID model, this deformation is formulated as depicted in the left panel of Figure 2: ξ denotes Darcyan coordinates of a genetic material, $x(\xi)$ denotes Cartesian coordinates of ξ, and $x(\xi_{seed})$ denotes the location of the seed ξ_{seed}. The displacement of any point, say $x(\xi)$, in a neighborhood of the seed, is defined as follows. Let (r, τ) be the polar coordinates of the vector $x(\xi) - x(\xi_{seed})$, i.e. (r, τ) are polar coordinates of $x(\xi)$ in a coordinate system centered at $x(\xi_{seed})$. The deformation takes (r, τ) radially to a new point with (local) polar coordinates $\rho(r, \tau), \tau)$. The radial displacement around the seed is given by $\rho(r, \tau) - r$.

How can we model this local, radial displacement ρ? The paper [5] suggest the following form:

$$\rho(r, \tau) - r = rR^{\alpha}(\tau)\exp(-(r^2/\delta^2)) . \tag{1}$$

where $R^{\alpha} : \mathbb{S}^1 \mapsto \mathbb{R}$ is called the **radial deformation function** (RDF) associated with that seed. The index α decides the nature of RDF. In future, we anticipate developing a pre-determined catalog of RDFs, and α will index elements of that set. For a given R^{α}, the active area is expanded (or contracted) at the rate given by $R^{\alpha}(\tau)$; $R(\tau) > 0$ means expansion or growth while $R^{\alpha}(\tau) < 0$ means contraction or decay. Plotted in the top right panel of Figure 2 are two examples of $(\rho(r, \tau) - r)$ versus r, for constant functions $R(\tau) = -0.5$ and 0.5. As the two curves show, major deformation lies in a region around the seed, denoted by $r = 0$ here, and goes to zero as r gets larger. The panel in right bottom plots the determinant of the Jacobian of the resulting deformation, as a function of r. For $R(\tau) = 0.5$, this plot shows an expansion for small r values, a

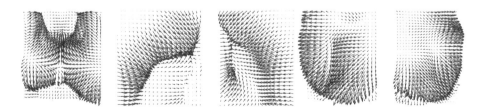

Fig. 1. Examples of growth-related deformation fields that motivate use of radial deformation fields around imaginary focal points called seeds

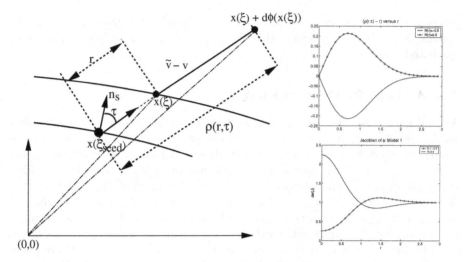

Fig. 2. Left: Illustration of displacement of (r, τ) to $(\rho(r, \tau), \tau)$. Right top: Examples of radial displacements given by $(\rho(r, \tau) - r)$ for $\delta = 1$. The displacement at distant points is zero. Right bottom: Plots of determinant of Jacobian of ϕ_t.

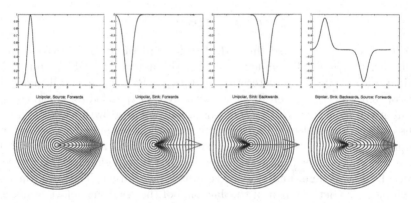

Fig. 3. Examples of elementary deformations obtained using different RDFs. Top row shows plots of RDFs and the bottom shows corresponding ϕ applied to a uniform polar grid.

compression in the medium r range, and no effect (determinant=1) for large r values. In other words, the growing interior pushes out and compresses the area around the boundary of this neighborhood. There is no effect on the points far away from the seed.

Figure 3 shows some examples of these elementary deformations ϕ generated by some simplistic RDFs. For each case, we display the function $R^{\alpha}(\tau)$ versus τ (top panel), with τ plotted in radians, and the resulting ϕ applied to a uniform polar grid (bottom panel).

2.2   Model for Displacement Field

In this paper, we will analyze deformations in form of displacement vector fields, and therefore we model them explicitly in this section. For a deformation ϕ, the displacement vector at any point x is given by $d\phi(x(\xi)) \equiv \phi(x(\xi)) - x(\xi)$. First, we derived a model for displacement field induced by the GRID model.

A unit displacement field, attributed to a single seed, is obtained using the Cartesian form of Eqn. 1, as

$$H(\xi) = x(\xi) \exp(-\|x(\xi)\|^2/\delta^2) R^\alpha(\tau(x(\xi))) .$$

(Here we simplify by assuming momentarily that the seed is located at the origin, i.e. $x(\xi_{seed}) = 0$.) As mentioned earlier, R^α is the radial deformation function (RDF) that captures the deformation around the seed. It is a function of the angle τ made by the vector $x(\xi)$ with the x_1 axis; we will use $\tau(\cdot)$ to denote the angle made by the argument vector with the x_1 axis. To simplify analysis, we introduce another condition that $|R^\alpha|$ integrates to one as a function of this angle. In the context of anatomical growth, we aim to define a finite catalog of RDFs, indexed by α, that are relevant for modeling deformations. To reduce notation, we assume that $x(\xi) = \xi$ at this time, i.e. the Darcyan coordinates match the Cartesian coordinates. This is valid at the start of the experiment where we initialize the Darcyan to be the Cartesian system. The deformation model simplifies to:

$$H(\xi; R^\alpha, \delta) = \xi \exp(-\|\xi\|^2/\delta^2) R^\alpha(\tau(\xi)) . \tag{2}$$

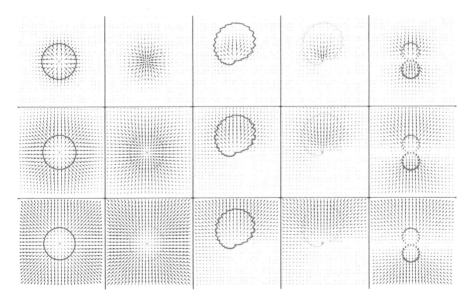

Fig. 4. Examples of deformation templates $H(\xi; R^\alpha, \delta)$ for different R^α and δ. Overlaid on deformation fields are polar plots of $|R(\tau)|$ versus τ; thick line denotes positive values and thin line denotes negative values. In each column δ increases from top to bottom.

H can be viewed as a "template displacement" of a uniform grid, induced by the RDF R^α. Shown in Figure 4 are some examples of such templates, drawn for different RDFs and δs. We have illustrated the corresponding RDF by drawing $|R(\tau)|$ as a function of τ over the vector field; thick line denotes positive value of $R(\tau)$ and thin line denotes the negative value. For later convenience, we define a vector field $G(\xi) = \xi \exp(-\|\xi\|^2/\delta^2)$, so that we can rewrite $H(\xi) = G(\xi)R^\alpha(\tau(\xi))$. Also, define $\mathcal{H}$ to be the Hilbert space:

$$\mathcal{H} = \overline{\mathrm{span}}\{H(\xi - \eta; R^\alpha, \delta)|\forall \eta \in \Xi,\ \forall \delta > 0,\ \forall \alpha\} .$$

Here, the span denotes all linear combinations of the elements of the set, and the bar denotes the closure of span using the $\mathbb{L}^2$ inner product $\int_\Xi \langle \eta_1(\xi), \eta_2(\xi) \rangle \, d\xi$. $\mathcal{H}$ is the space all possible displacement fields under the GRID model.

3   Estimation of Growth Deformation

The main goal of this paper is to demonstrate the estimation of GRID variables from image data of biological growth. We present some results on estimation of GRID variables from MRI growth data of a human brain. This estimation is performed in two steps: (i) Estimate full deformation ϕ^* from the image data, and (ii) estimate GRID variables from the estimated ϕ^*. In this section, we describe the first step of estimating ϕ^* from given image data at times t and $t + 1$. Let I be the image at time t and J be the image at time $t + 1$.

There is a large body of literature on estimation of deformations that model variations between given images. An important distinguishing factor between various techniques is the choice of cost function used in estimation of deformation. Ideas such as elastic matching [9], viscous modeling [2], spline-fitting [7], point-based matching [1], curve-based matching [6], and surface matching, have been used in the past. We perform this estimation using an energy that seeks to match both the images pixels and their boundaries. This energy has three components: (i) E_1 reflects the squared error between the deformed image and the target images, (ii) E_2 measures the mismatch between the (image) gradient vectors in the two images, and (iii) E_3 measures the smoothness of ϕ. The total energy function is:

$$E(\phi; c_1, c_2, c_3) = E_1 + E_2 + E_3$$
$$= c_1 \int_\Xi [I(\phi(x(\xi))) - J(x(\xi))]^2 d\xi + c_2 \int_{\mathbb{R}2} f(\langle \nabla I(\phi(x(\xi))), \nabla J(x(\xi))\rangle) d\xi \quad (3)$$
$$+ c_3 \int_\Xi \|\nabla(\phi(x(\xi)) - x(\xi))\|^2 d\xi$$

with $f(x) = -tanh(x/a); a > 0$, and c_1, c_2, c_3 are positive constants that denote relative weights of the three energy components. We want to solve for $\phi^* = \mathrm{argmin}_\phi E(\phi)$. Some important aspects of our approach are:

1. **Image Interpolation:** We will use a gradient approach to solve for $\phi^* = \mathrm{argmin}_\phi E(\phi)$. We need several gradients, for example $\frac{\partial E}{\partial \phi_k(x_1, x_2)}$ for $k = 1, 2$

and a vertex (x_1, x_2) on the discrete grid $G = \{1, ...l_1\} \times \{1...l_2\}$. In this setup $\phi : G \mapsto \mathbb{R}2$. Since ϕ takes values in $\mathbb{R}2$, the value of $I(\phi(x(\xi)))$ may not be readily available as I is defined only for grid vertices. We will use the bilinear interpolation to estimate image values between grid vertices to obtain $I(\phi(x(\xi)))$.

2. **Multi-Resolution Estimation:** Let $h_\sigma(x)$ be a 2D Gaussian filter, and let $I_\sigma = I * h_\sigma$ and $J_\sigma = J * h_\sigma$ be the smoothed versions of these two images. Let $\phi^*(\sigma) = \mathrm{argmin}_\phi E(\phi, \sigma)$, where $E(\phi, \sigma)$ is as defined in Eqn. 3, except I and J are replaced by I_σ and J_σ, respectively. Our strategy is to start with a large σ, implying a coarse resolution to estimate the mapping ϕ^*_σ. In the next iteration, decrease σ, thus increasing the resolution, and use the previous estimate to initialize the gradient search for ϕ at the next resolution.

3. **Rotation, Scaling and Translation (RST):** To remove rigid translation, rotation, and scale variability from observed images, we use a standard PCA-based approach in this paper. This uses singular decomposition of the matrix,

$$\sum_x \tilde{I}(x)(x - \bar{x})(x - \bar{x})^T, \quad \bar{x} = \sum_x x\tilde{I}(x), \quad \tilde{I}(x) = I(x)/\sum_y I(y).$$

to rotate and scale the image I (translation comes from $\bar{x}$) so that it is optimally aligned with J in the Euclidean norm. Shown Figure 5 is an example of this initialization.

Shown in Figures 5-7 are some estimation results using MRI images. Shown in Figure 5 is the first experimental setup. The left panel shows image I, the second panel shows image J, and the third image shows their initial difference $(I - J)$. Using a PCA-based transformation, we obtain an initial alignment RST of I that is shown in the last panel of this figure. Then, a multi-resolution approach is used to estimate the optimal ϕ^*. The results for estimating ϕ^* are shown in Figure 6, where the top left panel shows J, the second panel shows $I(\phi^*)$, and the last panel shows their difference $I(\phi^*) - J$. Deformations associated with the resulting ϕ^* are shown in the lower row using several ways – vector field (left), deformed grid (middle), and average magnitude (right) defined by:

$$P(x) = \frac{1}{|A_x|} \int_{A_x} \|d\phi^*(x)\| dx , \tag{4}$$

where A_x is a small neighborhood of x $(d\phi^*(x)$ is the optimal displacement given by $\phi^*(x) - x)$. Figure 7 shows another example of this estimation using a different pair of I and J.

Fig. 5. Left panel: I, second: J, third: initial different $I - J$, and right: I after RST

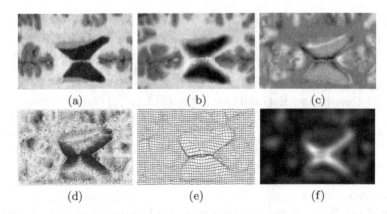

(a)   (b)   (c)

(d)   (e)   (f)

Fig. 6. (a) J, (b) $I(\phi^*)$, (c) $I(\phi^*) - J$, (d) deformation vector field generating ϕ^*, (e) optimal ϕ^* applied to a uniform grid, (f) an image of $P(x)$, that shows displacements averaged over small neighborhoods, in order to highlight active regions

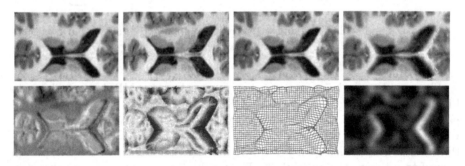

Fig. 7. Estimated deformation that optimally matched I with J. Top left: I, second: J, third: I after RST, and last: $I(\phi^*)$. Bottom left: $I(\phi^*) - J$, second: deformation vector field generating ϕ^*, third: optimal ϕ^* applied to a uniform grid, bottom right: $|\phi^*|$ averaged over small neighborhoods, to show active regions.

A quick look at estimated ϕ^*s supports the earlier claim that growth is local and the deformation field can be locally modeled using radial displacements around random seeds.

4   Estimation of GRID Variables

In this section, we present a statistical approach for estimating GRID variables - seed location, RDFs - from the displacement field $d\phi^*$ estimated in the previous section.

4.1   Observation Model

We are given a displacement vector field $d\phi^*$ such that for any $\xi \in \Xi$, $d\phi^*(\xi)$ is a two-dimensional vector. Our goal is to estimate GRID variables using the given deformation field. We first impose a data model on the observed deformation field that will allow us a framework for the estimation of unknowns. We assume that the observed deformation is a noisy version of the one dictated by the GRID model, i.e.

$$d\phi^*(\xi) = \sum_{i=1}^{n} \beta_i H(\xi - \xi_{i,seed}; R^{\alpha_i}, \delta_i) + N(\xi) , \qquad (5)$$

where $N(\xi) \in \mathbb{R}^2$ is a vector of independent, Gaussian random variables, with mean zero and a fixed variance σ^2. The number of seeds n is a random variable, and also needs to be estimated from the observed data. According to this model, the observed deformation is a weighted superposition of several template deformations, each having an associated R^α and a seed placement.

Remark: Note that Eqn. 5 is a simplification of the original GRID model that assumes that the seed placements are far enough to have non-overlapping displacements in the image. That is $\sum_\xi H(\xi - \xi_{i,seed}; R^{\alpha_i}, \delta_i) H(\xi - \xi_{j,seed}; R^{\alpha_j}, \delta_j) = 0$, for $i \neq j$. In case these displacements interact, the overall displacements will not be a simple linear combination. Instead, it will be a functional composition of the deformations introduced by each seed.

With this model, the negative of log-likelihood function, also referred to as likelihood energy, is therefore given by:

$$E = \int_\Xi \|d\phi^*(\xi) - \sum_{i=1}^{n} \beta_i H(\xi - \xi_{i,seed}, R^{\alpha_i}, \delta_i)\|^2 d\xi \qquad (6)$$

where $\|\cdot\|^2$ implies the 2-norm of a vector. Let Θ be the set of all unknowns: $\Theta = \{n, (\beta_i, \xi_{i,seed}, R^{\alpha_i}, \delta_i), i = 1, 2, \dots, n\}$.

4.2   Maximum Likelihood Estimation

Choosing MLE as the framework for variable estimation, we formulate the estimation problem: $\hat{\Theta} = \mathrm{argmin}_\Theta E(\Theta)$. This solution is equivalent to maximizing the magnitude of the projection of D onto $\mathcal{H}$.

We will estimate $\hat{\Theta}$ using an iterative approach, where the elements of Θ are updated iteratively. Since this approach is gradient based, it is important to have a good initialization of unknown variables. In this section, we derive and outline steps for updating components of Θ, while the remaining components are held fixed.

For each i, define the residual deformation, $d\phi_i^*(\xi) = d\phi^*(\xi) - \sum_{j \neq i} \beta_j H(\xi - \xi_{j,seed}; R^{\alpha_j}, \delta_j)$. $d\phi_i^*$ is the residual deformation field in D after removing the contribution of all other seeds except the ith seed. These residual are computed using the current values of GRID variables. To minimize computational cost, we first construct the templates $H_i \equiv H(\xi - \xi_{j,seed}; R^{\alpha_j}, \delta_j)$, $i = 1, 2, \dots, n$. Note that H_i's are non-zero only on a small subset of Ξ and zero on the remaining locations.

The GRID variables associated with the ith seed are updated as follows:

1. **Update** β: An update of the value of β_i is given by: for $i = 1, 2, \ldots, n$,

$$\beta_i = \frac{\int_{\Xi} \langle d\phi_i^*(\xi), H(\xi - \xi_{i,seed}; R^{\alpha_i}, \delta_i) \rangle \, d\xi}{\int_{\Xi} \langle H(\xi - \xi_{i,seed}; R^{\alpha_i}, \delta_i), H(\xi - \xi_{i,seed}; R^{\alpha_i}, \delta_i) \rangle \, d\xi} \, . \tag{7}$$

Here $H(\xi - \xi_{i,seed}; R^{\alpha_i}, \delta_i)$ denotes the deformation template $H(\xi; R^{\alpha_i}, \delta_i)$ centered at ξ_{seed}.

2. **Update** R^{α_i} according to:

$$R^{\alpha_i}(\tau) = \frac{1}{\beta_i} \frac{\int_{\xi \in \Xi_\tau} \langle d\phi_i^*(\xi), G(\xi - \xi_{seed}) \rangle \, d\xi}{\int_{\xi \in \Xi_\tau} \|G(\xi - \xi_{seed})\|^2 d\xi} \, , \tag{8}$$

where Ξ_τ denotes the set of all ξ such that the vector $\xi - \xi_{seed}$ makes the angle τ with the positive x_1 axis. We can drop β_i from this expression, as we are going to normalize by setting $\int_\tau |R^{\alpha_i}(\tau)| d\tau = 1$.

3. **Update** $\xi_{i,seed}$: Since the gradient-based update of ξ_{seed} seems complicated, we resort to a direct estimation of ξ_{seed} as follows:

$$\xi_{i,seed} = \operatorname*{argmin}_\eta \int_\xi \|d\phi_i^*(\xi) - \beta_i H(\xi - \eta; R^{\alpha_i}, \delta_i)\|^2 d\xi \tag{9}$$

The computation of this minimizer is cheap since the template $H(\xi; R^{\alpha_i}, \delta_i)$ need to be constructed only once. Decomposing the cost function:

$$\xi_{i,seed} = \operatorname*{argmin}_\eta \int_\xi \|d\phi_i^*(\xi) - \beta_i H(\xi - \eta; R^{\alpha_i}, \delta_i)\|^2 d\xi$$

$$= \operatorname*{argmin}_\eta \int_\xi \left(\|d\phi_i^*(\xi)\|^2 + \beta_i^2 \|H(\xi - \eta; R^{\alpha_i}, \delta_i)\|^2 - 2\beta_i \langle d\phi_i^*(\xi), H(\xi - \eta; R^{\alpha_i}, \delta_i) \rangle \right) d\xi$$

$$\approx \operatorname*{argmax}_\eta \int_\xi \langle d\phi_i^*(\xi), H(\xi - \eta; R^{\alpha_i}, \delta_i) \rangle \, d\xi \tag{10}$$

The last step results from assuming that δ_i is small enough and η lies in the interior of Ξ so that $\int_{\Xi} \|H(\xi - \eta; R^{\alpha_i}, \delta_i)\|^2 d\xi$ does not change with η. Defining $\bar{H}(\xi)$ to be $H(-\xi)$, the inner product in Eqn. 10 becomes the 2D convolution between $d\phi^*$ and $\bar{H}$. Define the 2D Fourier transforms,

$$F_d(\omega) = \int_\xi d\phi^*(\xi) e^{-i\xi\omega} d\xi, \quad F_H(\omega) = \int_\xi \bar{H}(\xi; R^{\alpha_i}, \delta_i) e^{-i\xi\omega} d\xi \, .$$

Then, we can obtain the maximizer as,

$$\xi_{i,seed} = \operatorname*{argmax}_\eta \int_\omega F_d(\omega) F_H(\omega) e^{i\omega\eta} d\omega \, .$$

Since the function to be maximized is the inverse Fourier transform of the product $F_d(\omega)F_H(\omega)$, it is fast to compute.

4. **Update** δ_i: Again, we perform this step using an exhaustive search since a gradient-based update will be computationally expensive. The update is:

$$\delta_i = \operatorname*{argmin}_{\delta} \int_{\xi} \|d\phi_i^*(\xi) - \beta_i H(\xi - \xi_{seed}, R^{\alpha_i}, \delta)\|^2 d\xi \qquad (11)$$

Shown in Figure 8 is a preliminary result. It shows a few examples of estimating the first seed location, for $d\phi^*$ estimated earlier in Section 3, with four different initial conditions.

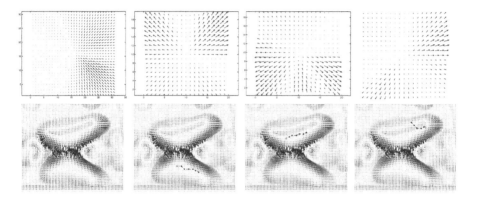

Fig. 8. Estimation of a seed location for displacement field estimated earlier. Four examples shown here represent four different initialization of the iterative search. In each case, we display the estimated location ξ_{seed} (green dot, bottom panels) and the displacement template H (top panel) resulting from the estimated R^α, δ for that seed. Red lines show the evolution of seed locations in iterative search.

The remaining issue is to estimate n, the number of seeds. Although we have not explored that issue in this paper, we suggest the use of birth/death processes [3], in a Bayesian framework, for estimating n.

5   Summary

In this paper, we have presented a maximum-likelihood framework for estimation of GRID variables using MRI growth data. The first step is to estimate the full deformation using an energy minimization technique. Once this deformation is estimated, we decompose it into its GRID components: focal points of local deformations called seeds, and radial deformation functions in small neighborhoods around those seeds. We demonstrate the estimation of seed locations and the radial deformation functions using an iterative procedure.

References

1. F. L. Bookstein. Size and shape spaces for landmark data in two dimensions. *Statistical Science*, 1:181–242, 1986.
2. G. E. Christensen, R. D. Rabbitt, and M.I. Miller. A deformable neuroanatomy textbook based on viscous fluid mechanics. In Jerry Prince and Thordur Runolfsson, editors, *Proceedings of the Twenty-Seventh Annual Conference on Information Sciences and Systems*, pages 211–216, Baltimore, Maryland, March 24-26 1993. Department of Electrical Engineering, The Johns Hopkins University.
3. U. Grenander and M. I. Miller. Representations of knowledge in complex systems. *Journal of the Royal Statistical Society*, 56(3), 1994.
4. U. Grenander and M. I. Miller. Computational anatomy: An emerging discipline. *Quarterly of Applied Mathematics*, LVI(4):617–694, 1998.
5. U. Grenander, A. Srivastava, and S. Saini. A pattern-theoretic characterization of biological growth. *IEEE Transactions on Medical Imaging*, in review, 2005.
6. N. Khaneja, M.I. Miller, and U. Grenander. Dynamic programming generation of curves on brain surfaces. *IEEE Transactions on Pattern Analysis and Machine Intelligence*, 20(11):1260–1264, Nov 1998.
7. B. Kim, J. L. Boes, K. A. Frey, and C. R. Meyer. Mutual information for automated unwarping of rat brain autoradiographs. *Neuroimage*, 5(1):31–40, 1997.
8. M. I. Miller and L. Younes. Group actions, homeomorphisms, and matching: A general framework. *International Journal of Computer Vision*, 41(1/2):61–84, 2002.
9. M.I. Miller, G.E. Christensen, Y. Amit, and U. Grenander. Mathematical textbook of deformable neuroanatomies. *Proceedings of the National Academy of Science*, 90(24), December 1993.
10. J. A. Sherratt and M. A. Chaplain. A new mathematical models for avascular tumour growth. *Journal of Mathematical Biology*, 43(4):291–312, 2001.
11. P. M. Thompson and A. W. Toga. A framework for computational anatomy. *Computing and Visualization in Science*, 5:13–34, 2002.
12. A. Trouve. Diffemorphisms groups and pattern matching in image analysis. *International Journal of Computer Vision*, 28(3):213–221, 1998.

Deformable-Model Based Textured Object Segmentation

Xiaolei Huang[1], Zhen Qian[2], Rui Huang[1], and Dimitris Metaxas[1,2]

[1] Division of Computer and Information Sciences, Rutgers University, NJ, USA
{xiaolei, ruihuang, dnm}@cs.rutgers.edu
[2] Department of Biomedical Engineering, Rutgers University, NJ, USA
zqian@eden.rutgers.edu

Abstract. In this paper, we present a deformable-model based solution for segmenting objects with complex texture patterns of all scales. The external image forces in traditional deformable models come primarily from edges or gradient information and it becomes problematic when the object surfaces have complex large-scale texture patterns that generate many local edges within a same region. We introduce a new textured object segmentation algorithm that has both the robustness of model-based approaches and the ability to deal with non-uniform textures of both small and large scales. The main contributions include an information-theoretical approach for computing the natural scale of a "texon" based on model-interior texture, a nonparametric texture statistics comparison technique and the determination of object belongingness through belief propagation. Another important property of the proposed algorithm is in that the texture statistics of an object of interest are learned online from evolving model interiors, requiring no other *a priori* information. We demonstrate the potential of this model-based framework for texture learning and segmentation using both natural and medical images with various textures of all scales and patterns.

1 Introduction

Deformable models, which are curves or surfaces that move under the influence of internal smoothness forces and external image forces, have been extensively studied and widely used for robust object segmentation. In the literature, there are two major classes of deformable models. One is the parametric deformable models [12, 25, 5] that explicitly represent curves and surfaces in their parametric form; the other class is the geometric deformable models [3, 14], which implicitly represent model shape as the zero level set of a higher-dimensional scalar function, and evolve the model based on front propagation using the theory of curve evolution. In the formulations for both types of models, the external image forces traditionally come from edge or image gradient information. However this makes the models unfit for finding boundaries of objects with complex large-scale texture patterns due to the presence of large variations in image gradient and many local edges inside the object.

There have been efforts to address this problem. Geodesic Active Regions [17] deal with supervised texture segmentation in a frame partition framework using level-set deformable model implementation. There are several assumptions in this supervised

A. Rangarajan et al. (Eds.): EMMCVPR 2005, LNCS 3757, pp. 119–135, 2005.
© Springer-Verlag Berlin Heidelberg 2005

method however, which include knowing beforehand the number of regions in an image and the statistics for each region are learned off-line using a mixture-of-gaussian approximation. These assumptions limit the applicability of the method to a large variety of natural images. Region Competition [27] performs texture segmentation by combining region growing and active contours using multi-band input after applying a set of texture filters. The method assumes multivariate Gaussian distributions on the filter-response vector inputs. Another texture segmentation approach in a deformable model framework [20] is based on deforming an improved active contour model [26] on a likelihood map instead of heuristically constructed edge map. However, because of the artificial neighborhood operations, the results from this approach suffer from blurring on the likelihood map, which causes the object boundary detected to be "dilated" versions of the true boundary. The dilate zone could be small or large depending on their neighborhood size parameter. Metamorphs [9] is recently proposed as a new class of deformable models that integrate boundary information and nonparametric region statistics for segmentation. It mostly dealt with intensity images with noise and complex intensity distributions however.

In this paper, we propose a new deformable-model based solution to accurate and robust texture segmentation. The key novelty and contribution is in the analysis and representation of model-interior texture statistics. The first step in analysis is to determine a best natural scale for the texons, which are the basic structural elements for the texture of interest. If this scale is small, then a nonparametric kernel-based approximation of the model-interior intensity distribution is sufficient to capture the statistics; if the scale is large which often means the texture consists of large-scale periodic patterns, a small bank of gabor filters is applied and the nonparametric statistics are evaluated on the filter responses. We then compute the likelihood map of texture consistency over the entire image domain by comparing local patch statistics with the model-interior statistics. This type of analysis enables our method to automatically and adaptively deal with both regions that are mostly homogeneous (intensity) and regions that consist of large-scale patterns, while keeping a sharp edge on the likelihood map right on the texture region boundary. The deformable model dynamics is derived from energy terms defined on the computed likelihood map, and when the model evolves, the model-interior statistics are re-analyzed and the likelihood map is updated. This adaptive online-learning process on one hand constraints the model to deformations that keep consistent model-interior statistics, and on the other hand enables the model to converge to true object boundary in the presence of not-perfectly uniform texture patterns.

1.1 Previous Work

Texture analysis and segmentation is an important problem in many areas of computer vision, because images of natural scenes, medical images and images of many other modalities are mainly composed of textured objects. Different texture segmentation approaches have been presented in the literature and they typically follow two steps: a modelling step to generate texture descriptors to describe texture appearance, and an optimization step to group pixels into regions of homogeneous texture appearance. In the modelling phase, Markov Random Fields [15], banks of filters [21], wavelets [2], etc. are some common techniques. In the classification/grouping phase, supervised methods

[17, 2] partition an image by maximizing likelihood given features or statistics learned from a set of texture patterns given *a priori*, while un-supervised methods [15, 13] apply clustering techniques to group pixels into homogeneous segments in the descriptor vector space.

Recently Graph Cuts [24] has been coupled with contour and texture analysis [13] to achieve un-supervised segmentation on varieties of images, and one of its extension, GrabCut [22], has shown promising results in interactive textured foreground extraction. Another work is Active Shape and Appearance Models [7, 6], which learns statistical models of object shape and appearance and use the prior models to segment textured objects.

Compared to previous work, the deformable model based texture segmentation method we propose integrates high-level model constraints with low-level processing and classification. It has the advantage of not requiring off-line supervised learning, yet it enjoys the benefits of having a likelihood map measuring texture consistency by means of online adaptive learning of model-interior statistics. Another advantage is in its elaborate information-theoretic texon scale analysis, which eliminates the classic blurring effect around texture boundaries on computed likelihood maps.

The remainder of the paper is organized as follows. We present an overview of our method in section 2. Then detailed algorithm in each step is described in section 3. Experimental results are presented in section 4, and we conclude with discussions in section 5.

2 Overview

The basic idea of our deformable-model based texture segmentation algorithm is depicted in Fig. 1, and the algorithm consists of the following steps:

1. Initialize a simple-shape deformable model centered around a seed point. In Fig. 1(a), the initial model is the circular model drawn in blue color, and the seed point is marked by the red asterisk.
2. Determine a "best" natural scale for the texture elements that are basic building blocks of the model interior texture. We call such texture elements "texons", following the naming convention in [10, 13, 28]. In Fig. 1(a), the determined texon scale is indicated by the red circle.
3. Compute nonparametric statistics of the model-interior texons, either on intensity or on gabor filter responses depending on the texon scale, and compare it with local-neighborhood statistics surrounding each pixel in the image. Thereafter a likelihood map is generated which measures the consistency of each local patch texture with the model-interior texture. Fig. 1(b) shows an example of such computed likelihood map given the model in Fig. 1(a).
4. Use the Belief-Propagation implementation of Markov Random Fields to update the likelihood map, taking into account contextual information from neighboring texture patches. For the cheetah image, the updated likelihood map is shown in Fig. 1(c).
5. Evolve the deformable model, for a fixed number of iterations, toward object boundary based on model dynamics derived from both texture energy terms defined on

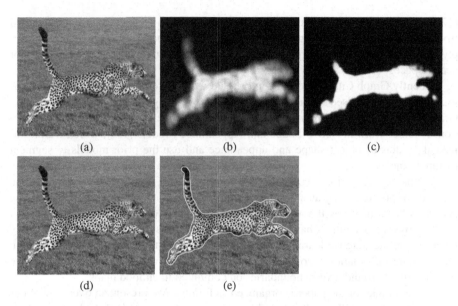

Fig. 1. (a) the original cheetah image. Initial Model: blue circle; Texon scale: red circle, (b) likelihood map computed based on texon statistics, (c) updated likelihood map after applying BP based MRF, (d) an intermediate model, (e) converged model.

the likelihood map and balloon-force energy terms defined on the model geometry. In Fig. 1(d), an intermediate model is drawn in green color.

6. Repeat steps 3-5 until convergence (e.g. when model deformation between iterations is sufficiently small). The converged model on the cheetah image is shown in Fig. 1(e).

3   Methodology

Next, we present the detailed algorithm in each step.

3.1   Implicit Model Representation

In our framework, we use the Euclidean distance transform to embed an evolving deformable model as the zero level set of a higher dimensional distance function [16, 18, 9]. In the 2D case, let $\Phi : \Omega \rightarrow R^+$ be a Lipschitz function that refers to the distance transform for the model shape $\mathcal{M}$. The shape defines a partition of the domain: the region that is enclosed by $\mathcal{M}$, $[\mathcal{R}_\mathcal{M}]$, the background $[\Omega - \mathcal{R}_\mathcal{M}]$, and on the model, $[\partial\mathcal{R}_\mathcal{M}]$. Given these definitions the following implicit shape representation is considered:

$$\Phi_\mathcal{M}(\mathbf{x}) = \begin{cases} 0, & \mathbf{x} \in \partial\mathcal{R}_\mathcal{M} \\ +ED(\mathbf{x}, \mathcal{M}) > 0, & \mathbf{x} \in \mathcal{R}_\mathcal{M} \\ -ED(\mathbf{x}, \mathcal{M}) < 0, & \mathbf{x} \in [\Omega - \mathcal{R}_\mathcal{M}] \end{cases} \quad (1)$$

where $ED(\mathbf{x}, \mathcal{M})$ refers to the min Euclidean distance between the image pixel location $\mathbf{x} = (x, y)$ and the model $\mathcal{M}$.

This implicit representation makes the model shape representation a distance map "image", which greatly facilitates the integration of boundary and region information. It also offers topology freedom and parameterization independence during model evolutions.

3.2   Texture Consistency Likelihood Map Given Model Interior

Given the current model shape, our first goal is to find a mathematical solution to determine a "best" local scale for the texture elements that are basic building blocks of the model interior texture.

Best Local Scale for Model Interior Texons. We approach this scale problem using a detector based on comparing a texon interior intensity probability density function (p.d.f.) with the whole model interior p.d.f., and we determine the scale of the texon as the smallest scale that provides a texon p.d.f that is sufficiently close to the overall model interior p.d.f.

Suppose the model is placed on image I, and the image region bounded by current model $\Phi_{\mathcal{M}}$ is $\mathcal{R}_{\mathcal{M}}$, we use a nonparametric kernel-based method to approximate the p.d.f. of the model interior intensity. Let us denote the random variable for intensity values by $i, i = 0, ..., 255$, then the intensity p.d.f. of the model-interior region is defined by:

$$\mathbf{P}(i|\Phi_{\mathcal{M}}) = \frac{1}{V(\mathcal{R}_{\mathcal{M}})} \iint_{\mathcal{R}_{\mathcal{M}}} \frac{1}{\sqrt{2\pi}\sigma} e^{\frac{-(i-I(\mathbf{y}))^2}{2\sigma^2}} d\mathbf{y} \qquad (2)$$

where $V(\mathcal{R}_{\mathcal{M}})$ denotes the volume of $\mathcal{R}_{\mathcal{M}}$, $\mathbf{y}$ are pixels in the domain $\mathcal{R}_{\mathcal{M}}$, and σ is a constant specifying the width of a gaussian kernel.

Similarly, the intensity p.d.f. for a local texon can be defined as in Eq. 2, the only difference being that the integration is over pixels inside the texon.

To measure the dissimilarity between two probability density functions, we adopt an information-theoretic distance measure, the Kullback-Leibler (K-L) Divergence [1]. Since the K-L divergence is asymmetric, we instead use one of its symmetrized relative – the Chernoff Information. The Chernoff Information between p_1 and p_2 is defined by:

$$C(p_2\|p_1) = \max_{0 \le t \le 1} -\log \mu(t)$$

where $\mu(t) = \int [p_1(i)]^{1-t} [p_2(i)]^t di$. A special case of Chernoff "distance" is the Bhattachayya "distance", in which t is chosen to be $\frac{1}{2}$, i.e., the Bhattachayya "distance" between p_1 and p_2 is:

$$B(p_2\|p_1) = -\log \mu(\frac{1}{2})$$

In order to facilitate notation, we write:

$$\rho(p_2\|p_1) = \mu(\frac{1}{2}) = \int [p_1(i)]^{\frac{1}{2}} [p_2(i)]^{\frac{1}{2}} di \qquad (3)$$

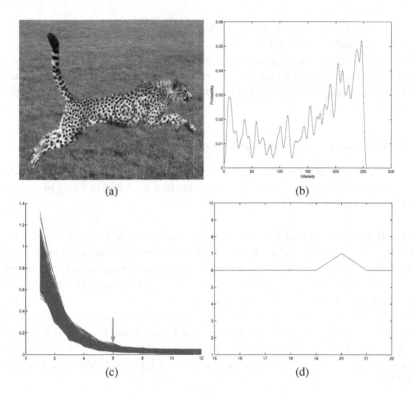

Fig. 2. (a) Cheeta image. Blue circle shows an initial model, red circle shows the determined best scale for model-interior texons. (b) Overall model interior p.d.f. (c) Y axis: K-L distance between texon p.d.f. and overall model-interior p.d.f.; X axis: changing scale (i.e. radius) of the texon under evaluation. Each curve represents a texon centered at a different pixel inside the model. (d) The best scale determined remains stable as we change the size of the initial model.

Clearly, when the value for ρ ranges from one to zero, the value for B goes from zero to infinity.

The Chernoff Information is an important information-theoretic distance measure, and it has been shown this measure is the exponential rates of optimal classifier performance probabilities [4]. The use of this measure is also justified in our experiments in which we observe a stable convergence in the distances between texon p.d.f and overall model interior p.d.f as the test scale increases.

The steps in determining the scale of texons inside the current model are as follows.

1. Approximate the intensity p.d.f. of the overall model interior (Eq. 2). Denote this p.d.f. as p_m.
   The p.d.f. for the cheetah example based on the blue curve model in Fig. 2(a) is displayed in Fig. 2(b).
2. Choose a best scale $\hat{s}$ for the model interior texons among all possible scales between $1...S$ [1].

---

[1] Here we assume that the current model interior contains at least one texon, and the largest test scale S is smaller than the size of the model.

Let us denote a texon of scale s centered at a pixel $\mathbf{x}$ by $T(\mathbf{x}, s)$, and its interior intensity p.d.f. by $p_{T(\mathbf{x},s)}$. To determine the best scale $\hat{s}$, we compute the Bhattachayya distance between p_m and $p_{T(\mathbf{x},s)}$, for all pixels $\mathbf{x}$ inside the model and for all scales $s = 1...S$. Fig. 2(c) visualizes the functional relationship between such distances and the scale in a graph. In the graph, each curve represents the "distance-scale" function for texons centered at a different pixel. From the graph, we can see that, as the scale increases, the Bhattachayya distance decreases asymptotically at all pixels, and all curves finally converge at a small value. This behavior proves the validity of the usage of this symmetrized K-L distance measure, and it also exposes to us a way to determine the natural scale of the model interior texons – the scale corresponding to the point of inflection on the Distance-Scale function curves. Since we get a scale value for every pixel inside the model this way, we use a robust estimator, the median estimator, to choose the best scale $\hat{s}$ as the median of the inflection-point scales chosen for all these pixels. On Fig. 2(a), the best scale such computed for the cheetah texture based on the initial blue-circle model is indicated by the red circle.

Based on our experiments, this "best" natural scale for model-interior texons determined using the method above is invariant to the size of the initial model. Fig. 2(d) shows the functional relation between the best scale chosen vs. initial size of the model for the cheetah example. We can see from the curve that the best scale remains stable as the size of the initial model changes. This behavior is also observed in many other examples that we tested.

Compute Texture Likelihood Map. Once we have determined the scale for model-interior texons, we can, for every pixel on the image, evaluate the likelihood of its neighborhood texon being consistent with the object texture learned from the model interior texture. We define this likelihood using the ρ value in Eq. 3, since it increases as the Bhattachayya distance between two distributions decreases. That is, the likelihood of any pixel $\mathbf{x}$ on the image I belonging to the object of interest is defined by:

$$\mathcal{L}(T(\mathbf{x}, \hat{s}) | \Phi_{\mathcal{M}}) \propto \rho(p_{T(x,\hat{s})} \| p_m) \qquad (4)$$

where $T(\mathbf{x}, \hat{s})$ represents the neighborhood texon centered at $\mathbf{x}$ and with scale $\hat{s}$, $p_{T(x,\hat{s})}$ is the intensity p.d.f. of the texon intensity, and p_m is the p.d.f. learned from interior intensity of the model initialized inside the object.

One limitation of using the nonparametric intensity p.d.f. to approximate texon(or model) interior texture statistics is that, the information on pixel order and spatial correlation between pixels within a texon is lost. For instance, if we take a texon inside the object, randomly re-permute all pixels within it to generate a new texon, then copy this new texon to locations surrounding the object, then the computation in Eq. 4 would have trouble differentiating these two kinds of texons, even though they appear different.

The importance of the texture pattern (i.e. pixel order) information depends on the scale $\hat{s}$ though, since this scale reveals to some extent the characteristics of the model-interior texture. In our framework, we separate two cases according to $\hat{s}$ and treat them differently when computing the likelihood map.

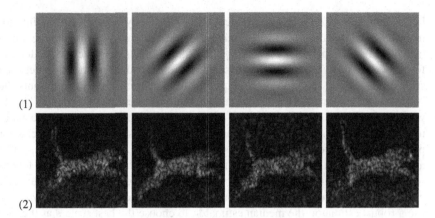

Fig. 3. (1) Gabor filters in a small bank with constant frequency and shape, and varying orientation. (2) Responses of the cheetah image to gabor filters in (1).

C1: In the first case, if $\hat{s}$ is very small (e.g. the radius of texons is less than 3 pixels wide), the model-interior texture is mostly homogeneous with some level of noise, hence it is not necessary to further consider the spatial correlation between pixels, and Eq. 4 should be sufficient in this case.

C2: In the second case, if $\hat{s}$ is rather large, we predict that the model-interior texture consists of periodic mosaics of large-scale patterns, and additional measures are necessary to capture the statistics in these patterns as well. We approach this by applying a small number of gabor filters [8] to the model interior, and learn statistics with respect to the gabor responses.

In our experiments, we choose $N (N = 4)$ gabor filter bases (Fig. 3(1)). The filters have constant frequency and shape, but with varying orientations. The frequency and Gaussian-envelop shape of the filters are computed based on the predetermined scale of model-interior texons. For each of the N gabor filters in the small filter bank, we get a response image $R_n, n = 1, ..., N$, as shown in Fig. 3(2). Suppose the random variable for the response value from filter n is X_n, we learn the probability density function of X_n, using the same nonparametric kernel-based approximation as in Eq. 2, for pixels inside the model. This way, we have N p.d.f.s, $p_n^{\mathcal{M}}, n = 1, ..., N$, to describe the statistics of the model-interior response to the different gabor filters.

When computing the likelihood map for pixels of the entire image, we use a mechanism similar to that in Eq. 4, but we combine the probabilities derived from all gabor filter responses. That is, for every pixel $\mathbf{x}$ on the image, we take its local neighborhood texon $T(\mathbf{x}, \hat{s})$, and compute its interior response-value p.d.f.s $p_n^T, n = 1, ..., N$. Then the likelihood of this texon being consistent with the model-interior texture pattern is measured by:

$$
\begin{aligned}
\mathcal{L}(T(\mathbf{x}, \hat{s})|\Phi_{\mathcal{M}}) &\propto P(T|p_1^{\mathcal{M}}, ..., p_N^{\mathcal{M}}) \\
&= \textstyle\prod_{n=1}^{N} P(T|p_n^{\mathcal{M}}) \\
&\propto \textstyle\prod_{n=1}^{N} \rho(p_n^T \| p_n^{\mathcal{M}})
\end{aligned} \tag{5}
$$

In the equation, we approximate the likelihood in terms of each gabor filter response using the ρ value, and the relations can be easily derived given that the responses from different gabor-filter bases are conditionally independent of each other

After computing the likelihood over the entire image domain, for each pixel, we denote the resulting likelihood map $\mathcal{L}(T(\mathbf{x}, \hat{s})|\Phi_\mathcal{M})$ as L_I.

Contextual Confirmation Through Belief Propagation. The likelihood map L_I quantifies the probability of every local texon belonging to part of the texture region of interest. However, all measurements are still local, and no context information between neighboring texons is accounted for. Markov Random Field (MRF) models are often used to capture dependencies between neighboring cliques (e.g. pixels, texons, etc.), and can be applied on the likelihood map to reduce noise and improve neighborhood consistency. Since the exact MAP inference in MRF models is computationally infeasible, we use an approximation technique based on the Belief Propagation (BP) algorithm, which is an inference method proposed by [19] to efficiently estimate Bayesian beliefs in the network by iteratively passing messages between neighbors.

Given a typical graphical-model illustration for MRF, as shown in Fig. 4, the graph has two kinds of nodes: hidden nodes (circles in Fig. 4, representing region labels) and observable nodes (squares in Fig. 4, representing image pixels). Edges in the graph depict relationships between the nodes.

Let n be the number of the hidden/observable states (i.e., the number of pixels in the image). A configuration of the hidden layer is:

$$\mathbf{h} = (h_1, ..., h_n), h_i \in V, i = 1, ..., n \tag{6}$$

where V is a set of region labels, such as $V = 0, 1$ where the value 0 indicates different texture from the model interior, and the value 1 indicates same texture as the model interior.

Similarly, a configuration of the observable layer is:

$$\mathbf{o} = (o_1, ..., o_n), o_i \in D, i = 1, ..., n \tag{7}$$

where D is a set of pixel values, e.g., the original likelihood values in the map L_I. The relationship between the hidden states and the observable states (also known as local evidence) can be represented as the compatibility function:

$$\phi(h_i, o_i) = P(o_i|h_i) \tag{8}$$

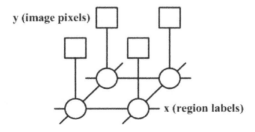

Fig. 4. The MRF Graphical Model

Similarly, the relationship between the neighboring hidden states can be represented as the second compatibility function:

$$\psi(h_i, h_j) = P(h_i, h_j) \tag{9}$$

Now the inference problem can be viewed as a problem of estimating the MAP solution of the MRF model:

$$\mathbf{h}_{MAP} = argmax_{\mathbf{h}} P(\mathbf{h}|\mathbf{o}) \tag{10}$$

where

$$P(\mathbf{h}|\mathbf{o}) \propto P(\mathbf{o}|\mathbf{h})P(\mathbf{h}) \propto \prod_i \phi(h_i, o_i) \prod_{(i,j)} \psi(x_i, x_j) \tag{11}$$

The exact MAP inference in MRF models is computationally infeasible, and we use an approximation technique based on the Belief Propagation (BP) algorithm, which is an inference method proposed by [19] to efficiently estimate Bayesian beliefs in the network by iteratively passing messages between neighbors. We assume the likelihood values in each region follow a Gaussian distribution:

$$\phi(h_i, o_i) = \frac{1}{\sqrt{2\pi\sigma_{x_i}^2}} exp\left(-\frac{(o_i - \mu_{x_i})^2}{2\sigma_{x_i}^2}\right) \tag{12}$$

and the compatibility function between neighboring hidden states is represented by:

$$\psi(o_i, o_j) = \frac{1}{Z} exp\left(\frac{\delta(o_i - o_j)}{\sigma^2}\right) \tag{13}$$

where $\delta(x) = 1$ if $x = 0$; $\delta(x) = 0$ if $x \neq 0$, σ controls the degree of similarity between neighboring hidden states, and Z is a normalization constant.

After this step of MRF contextual confirmation, the resulting new likelihood map is denoted by L_f^c. One example demonstrating the effect of this step can be seen in Fig. 1(c). In our experiments, we use the $\{0, 1\}$ region labels as the hidden states, hence by thresholding at 0.5, we can differentiate regions that have similar texture with the model-interior from other background regions.

3.3   Deformable Model Dynamics

In order to evolve the deformable model toward the boundary of the texture region of interest, we derive the model dynamics in a variational framework by defining energy terms leading to both external texture/image forces and internal balloon forces.

Free Form Deformations. The deformations a model in our framework can undergo are defined using a space warping technique, the Free Form Deformations (FFD) [23, 9]. The essence of FFD is to deform an object by manipulating a regular control lattice F overlaid on its volumetric embedding space, hence it integrates naturally with the implicit model shape representation (see section 1). In the Incremental FFD formulation used in [9], the deformation parameters, $\mathbf{q}$, are the deformations of the control points in both x and y directions:

$$\mathbf{q} = \{(\delta F_{m,n}^x, \delta F_{m,n}^y)\}; \ (m, n) \in [1, M] \times [1, N]$$

where the control lattice is of size $M \times N$. The deformed position of a pixel $\mathbf{x} = (x, y)$, given the deformation of the control lattice from an initial regular configuration F^0 to a new configuration F, is defined in terms of a tensor product of Cubic B-spline polynomials:

$$D(\mathbf{q}; \mathbf{x}) = \mathbf{x} + \delta D(\mathbf{q}; \mathbf{x}) = \sum_{k=0}^{3} \sum_{l=0}^{3} B_k(u) B_l(v) (F^0_{i+k,j+l} + \delta F_{i+k,j+l}) \tag{14}$$

where $i = \lfloor \frac{x}{X} \cdot (M - 1) \rfloor + 1$, $j = \lfloor \frac{y}{Y} \cdot (N - 1) \rfloor + 1$.

Since FFD imposes implicit smoothness constraints during model deformation, which guarantees C^1 continuity at control points and C^2 continuity everywhere else, we omit model smoothness energy terms that are common in traditional parametric or level-set based deformable models.

Data Terms for Texture/Image Forces. Given the likelihood map L^c_I computed based on the current model-interior texture statistics, we are able to segment out foreground regions that have similar texture with the model-interior (see section 3.2). Since there may be many disconnected foreground regions detected this way, we choose only the one overlapping the current model as the current region of interest (ROI). Suppose the binary mask of this ROI is I_r, we encode its boundary information by computing the Euclidean distance transform of the region boundary, which is denoted by Φ_r. Then we define a data energy term to evolve the model toward the ROI boundary as follows:

$$E_{data} = \frac{1}{V(\mathcal{R}_\mathcal{M})} \iint_{\mathcal{R}_\mathcal{M}} \left(\Phi_\mathcal{M}(\mathbf{x}) - \Phi_r(D(\mathbf{q}; \mathbf{x})) \right)^2 d\mathbf{x}$$

where $\Phi_\mathcal{M}$ is the implicit representation of the current model (Eq. 1), $\mathcal{R}_\mathcal{M}$ is the model interior region, $V(\mathcal{R}_\mathcal{M})$ refers to the volume of region $\mathcal{R}_\mathcal{M}$), and $D(\mathbf{q}; \mathbf{x})$ is the FFD definition for the position of a sample pixel $\mathbf{x}$ after deformation (Eq. 14).

Energy Term for Balloon Force. One additional energy term is defined on the model geometry to explicitly grow the model along its normal direction, which can expedite the model convergence process. It is also very important for accurate model convergence when the shape of the texture region has salient protrusions or concavities. The definition for the balloon-force energy term is as follows:

$$E_{balloon} = \frac{1}{V(\partial \mathcal{R}_\mathcal{M})} \iint_{\partial \mathcal{R}_\mathcal{M}} \left(\Phi_\mathcal{M}(D(\mathbf{q}; \mathbf{x})) \right) d\mathbf{x}$$

where $\partial \mathcal{R}_\mathcal{M}$ refers to the model affinity, which in practice we take as a narrow band around the model $\mathcal{M}$ (i.e. zero level set of the model representation $\Phi_\mathcal{M}$). The reason behind the form of this term is because of the definition for $\Phi_\mathcal{M}$, which has negative values outside the model, zero value on the model, and positive values inside the model.

Model Evolution. In our formulations above, both the data term and the balloon term are differentiable with respect to the model deformation parameters $\mathbf{q}$, hence a unified gradient-descent based parameter updating scheme can be derived. Let the overall energy functional be:

$$E = E_{data} + k E_{balloon} \tag{15}$$

(a)	(b)	(c)	(d)

Fig. 5. (a) Initial model in blue circle. (b) Likelihood map (after MRF) based on initial model. (c) An intermediate model. (d) Likelihood map re-computed based on the intermediate model.

where k is a constant balancing the contributions of the two terms. Then the following evolution equation for each element $\mathbf{q}_i$ in the model deformation parameters $\mathbf{q}$ can be derived:

$$\frac{\partial E}{\partial \mathbf{q}_i} = \frac{\partial E_{data}}{\partial \mathbf{q}_i} + k \frac{\partial E_{balloon}}{\partial \mathbf{q}_i} \qquad (16)$$

where

$$\frac{\partial E_{data}}{\partial \mathbf{q}_i} = \frac{1}{V(\mathcal{R}_\mathcal{M})} \iint_{\mathcal{R}_\mathcal{M}} 2(\Phi_\mathcal{M}(\mathbf{x}) - \Phi_r(D(\mathbf{q}; \mathbf{x}))) \cdot$$
$$\left(-\nabla \Phi_r(D(\mathbf{q}; \mathbf{x})) \cdot \frac{\partial}{\partial \mathbf{q}_i} D(\mathbf{q}; \mathbf{x}) \right) d\mathbf{x}$$

$$\frac{\partial E_{balloon}}{\partial \mathbf{q}_i} = \frac{1}{V(\partial \mathcal{R}_\mathcal{M})} \iint_{\partial \mathcal{R}_\mathcal{M}} \left(\nabla \Phi_\mathcal{M}(D(\mathbf{q}; \mathbf{x})) \cdot \frac{\partial}{\partial \mathbf{q}_i} D(\mathbf{q}; \mathbf{x}) \right) d\mathbf{x}$$

In the above formulas, the partial derivatives with respect to the deformation (FFD) parameters, $\frac{\partial}{\partial \mathbf{q}_i} D(\mathbf{q}; \mathbf{x})$, can be easily derived from the model deformation formula Eq. 14.

One important advantage of our framework is that, as the model evolves, the model interior changes, hence the model-interior texture statistics get updated and the new statistics are used for further model evolution. This online learning property enable our deformable model framework to segment objects with non-uniform texture patterns to some extent. In Fig. 5, we show the evolution in the likelihood map as the model evolves from an initial circular model to an intermediate model.

Change of Topology: Merging of Multiple Models. When multiple models are initialized in an image, each model evolves based on its own dynamics. At the end of each iteration, a collision detection step is applied by checking whether the interiors of more than one models overlap. If a collision is detected, the models involved are tested based on their interior texture statistics, and they are merged only if their statistics are sufficiently close.

Suppose a collision is detected between model K and model L. We first compare their model-interior texon scales. If the scales are very different, we do not merge the two models. If the scales are close, we further test their texture statistics. Let us denote their intensity p.d.f.s on the original image I by p_k and p_l respectively. Then we measure the Bhattachayya distance $B(p_k \| p_l)$ between the two distributions. Here we need

(a)   (b)   (c)   (d)

Fig. 6. (a) Two initial models in blue circles. (b) Two models evolving on their own before merging. (c) The two models are merged into one new model upon collision and the new model continues evolving. (d) The final converged model.

a definite threshold to determine whether the two distributions are sufficiently close enough. As discussed in [11], the error probability [2], P_e, of two distributions or processes, is related to the $\rho(p_k \| p_l)$ value by the following formula: $\frac{1}{8}\rho^2 \leq P_e \leq \frac{1}{2}$. In our algorithm, by allowing a 10% error probability (i.e., $P_e = 0.1$), we can derive the following threshold on the ρ value: $T_\rho \geq \sqrt{(8 * 0.1)} \approx 0.9$. That is, if the ρ value is less than T_ρ, then the two distributions are the result of two different signals (textures) with a 10% error probability; conversely, if the ρ value is greater than T_ρ, then we consider the two distributions are sufficiently close. More strict tests can be done by comparing gabor filter response statistics.

If we decide the statistics of two models in collision are sufficiently close, we merge the two models. Based on the model implicit representation in Eq. 1 (model interior has positive values), given the implicit representation of the two old models $\Phi_{\mathcal{M}_1}(\mathbf{x})$ and $\Phi_{\mathcal{M}_2}(\mathbf{x})$, then the implicit representation of the merged new model can be computed directly by:

$$\Phi_{\mathcal{M}}(\mathbf{x}) = \max\left(\Phi_{\mathcal{M}_1}(\mathbf{x}), \Phi_{\mathcal{M}_2}(\mathbf{x})\right)$$

Thereafter this new model evolves in place of the two old models.

Fig. 6 shows an example where we initialize two models, they first evolve on their own then they merge into one new model upon collision.

4   Experimental Results

We have run our algorithm on a variety of images with textures of different patterns and scales. Figures 7-9 show typical segmentation results. In all the cases, we initialize several seed points inside the textured regions of interest, then a texture-consistency likelihood map is computed based on each model interior, the models evolve on their own dynamics, and those models with similar texture statistics are allowed to merge upon collision. The likelihood map for each model is re-computed after every 5 iterations of model evolution since the model interior statistics change as the model deforms. The balance factor k between the two energy terms in Eq. 15 is kept constant at $k = 200$, which is a value that is tested once and works well in all our experiments. The implementation of our algorithm is mostly in Matlab, but the most computationally expensive

---

[2] This is the probability of mistakenly classifying two processes/distributions as the same when they are in fact different.

Fig. 7. (a) Original image with initial model. (b) Likelihood map based on gabor response statistics. (c) Likelihood map after BP. (d) The converged model. (e) Both cheetah boundaries detected after initializing another model in the other high-likelihood area.

parts – the texon scale determination, likelihood map computation and BP based MRF – are implemented in C and linked to Matlab by CMex. The running time on a 2 GHz Pentium PC station for images of size 210×280 pixels is under 3 minutes, with two initial circular models of radius 10.

Fig. 7 is another experiment run on an image containing two cheetahs. The likelihood maps computed based on the initial model are shown, and the converged model finds the boundary for one of the cheetahs. By initializing another model in another high-likelihood area, we are able to get the boundary for the other cheeta (Fig. 7(e)).

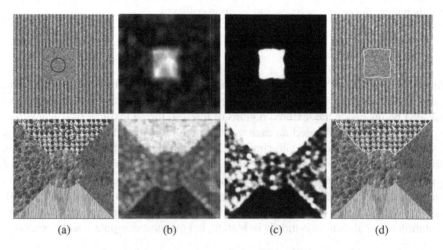

Fig. 8. (a) Original images. (b) Likelihood maps based on model-interior texture statistics. (c) Likelihood maps after BP. (d) The converged models at texture boundary.

In Fig. 8, we demonstrate our algorithm using two synthetic images. The image on the top row has a small-scale homogeneous region in the center, and large-scale periodic line patterns in the background. The line pattern is generated using a sinusoidal signal. To test the robustness of the method to noise, we randomly added high level of gaussian noise to the entire image. The segmentation result shows that our method can deal with both small-scale and large-scale texture patterns, and has good differentiation power even in the presence of high noise levels. On the bottom row, we show the performance on a synthetic texture mosaic image. The image consists of five texture regions of similar intensity distribution, and we demonstrate the likelihood map and segmentation of one of the regions. We are able to segment other four regions in the mosaic as well using the same method.

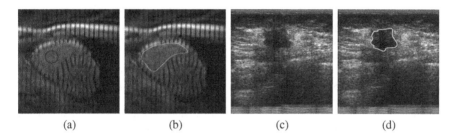

| (a) | (b) | (c) | (d) |

Fig. 9. (a) Original image and initial model for the tagged MR image. (b) segmentation result for tagged MR image. (c) original image and initial model for the ultrasound breast image. (d) segmented lesion in the breast image.

In Fig. 9, we show two examples of applying our model-based method to segment textured objects in medical images. On the left, we show segmentation of the right ventricle in a tagged MRI image of the heart. The result is shown in Fig. 9(b). And on the right is a ultrasound image of the breast. The goal is to segment the lesion on the breast. The final result is in Fig. 9(d). These results demonstrate the potential of our model-based method to deal with both large-scale tagging line patterns, and small-scale ultrasound speckle patterns.

5   Discussion and Conclusions

We have proposed a robust model-based segmentation method for finding boundaries of objects with complex textures of all scales and patterns. The novel ideas include an information-theoretic texon scale analysis algorithm and the online updating and learning of model-interior texture statistics to guide the model to achieve efficient, robust and accurate object segmentation.

Although we assume user-defined seed points to start the simple-shape initial deformable models, our method can be directly applied to full-field image segmentation by starting multiple initial models on a regular lattice covering the image. The topology freedom of the models enables evolving models with similar statistics to merge, and finally the image is partitioned into regions of homogeneous textures.

References

1. S. M. Ali and S. D. Silvey. A general class of coefficients of divergence of one distribution from another. *J. Roy. Stat. Soc.*, 28:131–142, 1966.
2. J. F. Aujol, G. Aubert, and L. Blanc-Feraud. Wavelet-based level set evolution for classification of textured images. *IEEE Trans. on Image Processing*, 12(12):1634–1641, 2003.
3. V. Caselles, R. Kimmel, and G. Sapiro. Geodesic active contours. In *IEEE Int'l Conf. on Computer Vision*, pages 694–699, 1995.
4. H. Chernoff. Large-sample theory: Parametric case. *Ann. Math. Stat.*, 27:1–22, 1956.
5. D. Cohen. On active contour models and balloons. *CVGIP: Image Understanding*, 53:211–218, 1991.
6. T. F. Cootes, G. J. Edwards, and C. J. Taylor. Active appearance models. In *Proc. of European Conf. on Computer Vision*, volume 2, pages 484–498, 1998.
7. T. F. Cootes, C. J. Taylor, D. H. Cooper, and J. Graham. Active shape models - their training and application. *Computer Vision and Image Understanding*, 61(1):38–59, 1995.
8. J. Daugman. Uncertainty relation for resolution in space, spatial frequency, and orientation optimized by two-dimensional visual cortical filters. *Journal of the Optical Society of America A*, 2(7):1160–1169, 1985.
9. X. Huang, D. Metaxas, and T. Chen. Metamorphs: Deformable shape and texture models. In *IEEE Conf. on Computer Vision and Pattern Recognition*, volume 1, pages 496–503, 2004.
10. B. Julesz. Texons, the elements of texture perception, and their interactions. *Nature*, 290(5802):91–97, 1981.
11. T. Kailath. The divergence and bhattacharyya distance measures in signal selection. *IEEE Trans. on Comm. Tech.*, 15(1):52–60, 1967.
12. M. Kass, A. Witkin, and D. Terzopoulos. Snakes: Active contour models. *Int'l Journal of Computer Vision*, 1:321–331, 1987.
13. J. Malik, S. Belongie, Leung T., and J. Shi. Contour and texture analysis for image segmentation. *Int'l Journal of Computer Vision*, 43(1):7–27, 2001.
14. R. Malladi, J. A. Sethian, and B. C. Vemuri. Shape modeling with front propagation: A level set approach. *IEEE Trans. on Pattern Analysis and Machine Intelligence*, 17(2):158–175, 1995.
15. B. Manjunath and Chellapa R. Unsupervised texture segmentation using markov random field models. *IEEE Trans. on Pattern Analysis and Machine Intelligence*, 13:478–482, 1991.
16. S. Osher and J. Sethian. Fronts propagating with curvature-dependent speed : Algorithms based on the Hamilton-Jacobi formulation. *Journal of Computational Physics*, 79:12–49, 1988.
17. N. Paragios and R. Deriche. Geodesic active regions for supervised texture segmentation. In *IEEE Int'l Conf. on Computer Vision*, pages 926–932, 1999.
18. N. Paragios, M. Rousson, and V. Ramesh. Matching Distance Functions: A Shape-to-Area Variational Approach for Global-to-Local Registration. In *European Conf. on Computer Vision*, pages II:775–790, 2002.
19. J. Pearl. *Reasoning in Intelligent Systems: Networks of Plausible Inference*. Morgan Kaufman Publishers, 1988.
20. O. Pujol and P. Radeva. Texture segmentation by statistical deformable models. *Int'l Journal of Image and Graphics*, 4(3):433–452, 2004.
21. T. Randen and J. H. Husoy. Texture segmentation using filters with optimized energy separation. *IEEE Trans. on Image Processing*, 8(4):571–582, 1999.
22. C. Rother, V. Kolmogorov, and A. Blake. Grabcut: Interactive foreground extraction using iterated graph cuts. *ACM Transactions on Graphics (SIGGRAPH)*, 23(3):309–314, 2004.

23. T. W. Sederberg and S. R. Parry. Free-form deformation of solid geometric models. In *Proceedings of the 13th Annual Conference on Computer Graphics*, pages 151–160, 1986.

24. J. Shi and J. Malik. Normalized cuts and image segmentation. *IEEE Trans. on Pattern Analysis and Machine Intelligence*, 22(8):888–905, 2000.

25. L. H. Staib and J. S. Duncan. Boundary finding with parametrically deformable models. *IEEE Transactions on Pattern Analysis and Machine Intelligence*, 14(11):1061–1075, 1992.

26. C. Xu and J. L. Prince. Generalized gradient vector flow external forces for active contours. *Signal Processing*, 71:131–139, 1998.

27. S. Zhu and A. Yuille. Region Competition: Unifying snakes, region growing, and Bayes/MDL for multi-band image segmentation. *IEEE Trans. on Pattern Analysis and Machine Intelligence*, 18(9):884–900, 1996.

28. S. C. Zhu, C. E. Guo, Y. Z. Wang, and Z. J. Xu. What are textons? *Int'l Journal of Computer Vision*, 62(1):121–143, 2005.

Total Variation Minimization and a Class of Binary MRF Models

Antonin Chambolle

CMAP (CNRS UMR 7641), Ecole Polytechnique,
91128 Palaiseau Cedex, France
antonin.chambolle@polytechnique.fr

Abstract. We observe that there is a strong connection between a whole class of simple *binary* MRF energies and the Rudin-Osher-Fatemi (ROF) Total Variation minimization approach to image denoising. We show, more precisely, that solutions to binary MRFs can be found by minimizing an appropriate ROF problem, and vice-versa. This leads to new algorithms. We then compare the efficiency of various algorithms.

1   Introduction

The goal of this note is to study the relationship between the Rudin-Osher-Fatemi Total Variation (TV) minimization model for image denoising, and a class of simple binary MRF models. In particular, we will show that some algorithms designed to solve one type of problem can be adapted to the other. Precisely, we will discuss the links between problems such as

$$\min_{\theta_{i,j}\in\{0,1\}} \lambda \sum_{i,j} |\theta_{i+1,j}-\theta_{i,j}|+|\theta_{i,j+1}-\theta_{i,j}| + \frac{1}{2}\sum_{i,j}\theta_{i,j}|g_{i,j}-a|^2 + (1-\theta_{i,j})|g_{i,j}-b|^2,$$

(1)

and

$$\min_{w_{i,j}\in\mathbb{R}} \lambda \sum_{i,j} |w_{i+1,j} - w_{i,j}| + |w_{i,j+1} - w_{i,j}| + \frac{1}{2}\sum_{i,j}|g_{i,j} - w_{i,j}|^2.$$

(2)

Here, i, j index the rows and columns of a digital image and run, for instance, from 1 to N and 1 to M, $N, M \geq 1$.

Problems such as (1) arise in simplified MRF image denoising models where one assumes, for instance, that an observation $g = (g_{i,j})_{i,j}$ results from an original binary signal $(b + \theta_{i,j}(a - b))_{i,j}$ taking only values a and b, to which a Gaussian noise is added. (Here, g, a, b could be vector valued.) But, in fact, similar problems involving binary fields appear in many branches of image processing and can be used in a much more elaborate way: for instance, in [24] the authors build a tree of binary MRFs to classify images in much more than two labels (see also [20, 21]).

It is known that (1) can be solved exactly using linear programming, and more exactly by finding a minimal cut in a graph, using a max-flow algorithm.

A. Rangarajan et al. (Eds.): EMMCVPR 2005, LNCS 3757, pp. 136–152, 2005.

This has been first observed by Greig, Porteous and Seheult [14], and these techniques have been then extended to much more general problems in the recent years [15, 6, 17, 18, 19, 22].

On the other hand, problem (2) has been first proposed in image processing by Rudin, Osher and Fatemi [23], as an efficient approach to edge-preserving image denoising or reconstruction. Here, g is the sum of a "clean" image w and a Gaussian noise, and the minimizer w of the energy is supposed to be a good approximation of the original signal.

Our main point, in this paper, is that problems (1) and (2) are easily derived one from the other, so that algorithms designed to solve one can be used to solve the other. We would like to discuss the consequences of these links and compare the algorithms. While a first version of this note was already submitted to the EMMCVPR conference, J. F. Aujol mentioned to us the recent work of Jérôme Darbon and Marc Sigelle [12, 13], which may be seen as the probabilistic counterpart of the present work. They show essentially the same results (including, in particular, Prop. 2), with very different proofs. Although we may claim our proofs are probably simpler, they reach the same conclusions and the algorithm they derive is essentially equivalent to the dyadic algorithm we present in section 3.3.

This note is organized as follows. In the next section we describe an abstract framework in which both (1) and (2) enter as a particular case. A first important result is a comparison principle for the solutions of (1) (Prop. 2). From this, we can deduce that these solutions are embedded in the level sets of the solutions of appropriate problems (2) (Prop. 3). This has interesting theoretical consequences: for instance, we can deduce that solutions of (1) are generically unique. But from a practical point of view, it also shows that one can use algorithms for one problem to solve the other one. This is discussed in Section 3. We describe some implementations of graph cuts algorithms that can be designed to solve (2). We then recall, in Section 4, the algorithm proposed in [9]. Numerical experiments are eventually performed to compare these algorithms.

2 The Abstract Framework

2.1 A Class of Regularizing Energies

We consider a vector space $X \sim \mathbb{R}^N$ with the Euclidean scalar product $(u, v) = \sum_{i=1}^N u_i v_i$. In practice, an element in X will represent a 2D scalar or multichannel image, but other situations could be encountered. The first part of the energies that appear in problems (1) and (2) is a particular case (as we will check in Section 3) of a function $J : X \to [0, +\infty]$ which is convex (i.e., $J(tu + (1-t)v) \leq tJ(u) + (1-t)J(v)$ for any $t \in [0, 1]$, $u, v \in X$), lower semicontinuous, positively one-homogeneous (i.e., $J(tu) = tJ(u)$ for any $t \geq 0$ and $u \in X$), and that satisfies the generalized co-area formula:

$$J(u) = \int_{-\infty}^{+\infty} J(u^t)\, dt \tag{3}$$

where for any $i = 1, \ldots, N$, $u_i^t = \begin{cases} 1 & \text{if } u_i > t, \\ 0 & \text{otherwise}, \end{cases}$

that is, $u^t = \chi_{\{u > t\}}$, the characteristic function (in $\{0,1,\ldots,N\}$) of the superlevel s of $u = (u_i)_{i=1}^N$. Observe that the one-homogeneity of J follows in fact easily from (3). Moreover, $J(u) = 0$ if $u_i = u_j$ for all i, j (otherwise the integral in (3) is always infinite).

2.2   Abstract Binary MRFs

We will check later on that problem (1) can be restated in the following abstract form

$$\min_{\theta \in X, \theta_i \in \{0,1\}} \lambda J(\theta) + \sum_{i:\theta_i=1} s - G_i \qquad (P_s)$$

where $G \in X$ would be a vector depending on g, a, b and $s \in \mathbb{R}$ a level depending on a, b. We now study problems of the form (P_s). A first observation, which is quite obvious, is the following:

Proposition 1. *Any solution θ of (P_s) is also a solution of the convex problem*

$$\min_{v \in X, v_i \in [0,1]} \lambda J(v) + \sum_{i=1}^N (s - G_i)v_i. \qquad (P_s')$$

Conversely, if v is a solution of (P_s'), then for any $t \in (0,1)$ v^t solves (P_s).

The proof is simple and based on the following identity: if $v_i \in [0,1]$ for any i, then $v_i = \int_0^{v_i} dt = \int_0^1 v_i^t \, dt$, so that

$$\lambda J(v) - \sum_{i=1}^N G_i v_i = \int_0^1 \left(\lambda J(v^t) - \sum_{i:v_i^t=1} G_i \right) dt.$$

This property shows that the minimization of the binary problem (P_s) is in fact a convex minimization problem. In the sequel, problems (P_0) and (P_0') are simply denoted by (P) and (P').

2.3   Comparison for Binary MRFs

Let us now mention the following comparison property, which does not seem to be well-known. It is also proved in J. Darbon and M. Sigelle's recent papers [12, 13], by a probabilistic approach. Our proof is quite simpler, and may be seen as the finite-dimensional counterpart of the proofs we proposed in [1, 2, 7].

Proposition 2. *Assume $G^1 > G^2$, i.e., for any $i = 1, \ldots, N$, $G_i^1 > G_i^2$. For $\alpha = 1, 2$, let v^α be solutions of (P') with G replaced with G^α. Then $v^1 \geq v^2$.*

Proof. The proof of this result relies on the following Lemma:

Lemma 1. *Let $v, w \in X$. Then $J(v \wedge w) + J(v \vee w) \leq J(v) + J(w)$.*

Here $(v \wedge w)_i = \min\{v_i, w_i\}$ and $(v \vee w)_i = \max\{v_i, w_i\}$, for any $i = 1, \ldots, N$. We do not prove Lemma 1 (first mentioned to us by Bouchitté [4]). It follows from (i) the convexity and 1-homogeneity of J, and (ii) the coarea formula (3), applied to the vector $\theta + \theta' = \theta \vee \theta' + \theta \wedge \theta'$, where $\theta_i, \theta'_i \in \{0, 1\}$ for all i. We compare the energies of v^1, v^2 with the energies of $v^1 \vee v^2$ and $v^1 \wedge v^2$:

$$\lambda J(v^1) - \sum_{i=1}^{N} G_i^1 v_i^1 \leq \lambda J(v^1 \vee v^2) - \sum_{i=1}^{N} G_i^1 (v_i^1 \vee v_i^2),$$
$$\lambda J(v^2) - \sum_{i=1}^{N} G_i^2 v_i^2 \leq \lambda J(v^1 \wedge v^2) - \sum_{i=1}^{N} G_i^2 (v_i^1 \wedge v_i^2).$$

Summing both inequalities and using the Lemma, we find

$$\sum_{i=1}^{N} G_i^1 ((v_i^1 \vee v_i^2) - v_i^1) \leq \sum_{i=1}^{N} G_i^2 (v_i^2 - (v_i^1 \wedge v_i^2)),$$

and since $(v_i^1 \vee v_i^2) - v_i^1 = v_i^2 - (v_i^1 \wedge v_i^2) = \max\{v_i^2 - v_i^1, 0\}$, we easily deduce that if $G_i^1 > G_i^2$ for every i, then $v_i^2 - v_i^1 \leq 0$. $\qquad\square$

In fact, the property in Lemma 1 is equivalent to the generalized coarea formula (3) (assuming J is a convex, l.s.c., one-homogeneous function such that $J(c + \cdot) = J(\cdot)$ for any $c \in \mathbb{R}$). Functions that satisfy the thesis of Lemma 1 appear in optimization theory as "sub-modular" functions, and it is observed in [18] that they are the only two-point interactions functions of binary variables that can be minimized using graph-cut algorithms.

2.4   The Abstract ROF Model

Let us now introduce the following minimization problem, which is the abstract version of (2):

$$\min_{w \in X} J(w) + \frac{1}{2\lambda} \|G - w\|^2. \tag{4}$$

Our main result is the following.

Proposition 3. *Let w solve (4). Then, for any $s \in \mathbb{R}$, both*

$$w_i^s = \begin{cases} 1 & \text{if } w_i > s, \\ 0 & \text{otherwise} \end{cases} \quad \text{and} \quad \overline{\overline{w}}_i^s = \begin{cases} 1 & \text{if } w_i \geq s, \\ 0 & \text{otherwise} \end{cases}$$

solve (P_s). Conversely, if θ solves (P_s) (resp, v solves (P'_s)), then $w^s \leq \theta \leq \overline{\overline{w}}_i^s$ (resp, $w^s \leq v \leq \overline{\overline{w}}^s$): that is, $w_i \geq s$ when $\theta_i = 1$, and $w_i \leq s$ when $\theta_i = 0$. In particular, if $w^s = \overline{\overline{w}}^s$ (which is true for all but a finite number of levels s), then the solution of (P_s) and (P'_s) is unique.

This means that solutions to the whole family of problems (P_s), $s \in \mathbb{R}$, could be computed by solving just one convex problem (4), and conversely, that (4) can be minimized by solving an appropriate family of binary problems (P_s).

We will explain later on how this is done. In the continuous setting, the same relationship has been observed in [8, 7]. In image processing, the observation that (1) can be solved by finding the appropriate superlevel of the solution of (4) was also mentioned recently in [10, 11].

Proof. We briefly sketch the proof of this result. The fact that the solutions of (P_s), for $s \in \mathbb{R}$, can be seen as the level sets of a $w \in X$, follows from Proposition 2. Indeed, if $s > s'$, one readily sees that any pair of solutions θ, θ' of (P_s) and $(P_{s'})$ will satisfy $\theta' \geq \theta$. Hence, letting for each $i = 1, \ldots, N$

$$w_i = \sup\{s \in \mathbb{R} : \exists \theta \text{ solving } (P_s) \text{ with } \theta_i = 1\},$$

it is not difficult to show that for any $s \in \mathbb{R}$, w^s is a solution of (P_s). Moreover, if $s \notin \{w_i : i = 1, \ldots, N\}$, then it is the unique solution, still because of the comparison principle. On the other hand, if $s \in \{w_i : i = 1, \ldots, N\}$, then also $\overline{\overline{w}}^s$ is a solution (and there might be other solutions in between).

We now explain why w is the solution of (4). For $v \in X$, and $s_* \leq \min_i v_i$,

$$\int_{s_*}^{+\infty} (s - G_i) v_i^s \, ds = \int_{s_*}^{v_i} s - G_i \, ds = \frac{1}{2} \left((v_i - G_i)^2 - (s_* - G_i)^2 \right).$$

By use of this formula and the coarea formula (3), one deduces (if $s_* \leq \min_i w_i$ as well) that the energy (4) of v must be larger than the energy of w. Hence w is the (unique) solution of the (strictly convex) problem (4). $\qquad\qquad\square$

2.5   Quantized ROF Model

We now consider the following quantized variant of (4):

$$\min \left\{ J(z) + \frac{1}{2\lambda} \|G - z\|^2 : z \in X, \ z_i \in \{l_0 \ldots, l_n\} \forall i = 1, \ldots, N \right\} \qquad (5)$$

where the real levels $(l_k)_{k=1}^n$ are given. That is, we minimize (4) only among functions that take values in a prescribed, finite set. Without loss of generality, we assume that $l_0 < l_1 < \cdots < l_n$, and for simplicity that for all $k = 1, \ldots, n$, $l_k - l_{k-1} = \delta l$ (adaption to other cases is straightforward). Then the following result is true.

Proposition 4. *Let z be a solution of (5), and w be the solution of (4). Then $\max_{i=1}^N |z_i - w_i| \leq \delta l / 2$, provided $l_0 \leq \min_i w_i$ and $l_n \geq \max_i w_i$.*

The last condition is certain if l_0 is chosen no larger than $\min_i G_i$, and l_n no less $\max_i G_i$. This results means that the quantized problem (5) produces exactly a quantization of the solution of (4).

Proof. For a z admissible, we can write

$$z = l_0 + \sum_{k=1}^n (l_k - l_{k-1}) \theta^k = l_0 + \delta l \sum_{k=1}^n \theta^k$$

where for each $k \geq 1$, θ^k is the binary vector defined by $\theta_i^k = 1$ iff $z_i \geq l_k$. Then, the fact $\theta^k \leq \theta^{k-1}$ for any $k \geq 2$, and the co-area formula (3), yield $J(z) = \sum_{k=1}^n \delta l\, J(\theta^k)$. On the other hand,

$$\|G - z\|^2 = \sum_{i=1}^N (G_i - l_0)^2 + 2\delta l \sum_{k=1}^n \sum_{i=1}^N \left(\frac{l_k + l_{k-1}}{2} - G_i \right) \theta_i^k,$$

hence, up to a constant, problem (5) is the same as

$$\min_{\theta^k} \sum_{k=1}^n \left(\lambda\, J(\theta^k) + \sum_{i=1}^N \left(\frac{l_k + l_{k-1}}{2} - G_i \right) \theta_i^k \right),$$

where the min is on the binary fields $(\theta^k)_{k=1}^n$, with the constraint that $\theta^k \leq \theta^{k-1}$ for any $k = 2, \ldots, n$. Each term in the sum is the energy that appears in problem (P_{s_k}), for $s_k = (l_k + l_{k-1})/2$. Now, by Lemma 2, if for each $k = 1, \ldots, n$, θ^k minimizes (P_{s_k}), then since $s_k > s_{k-1}$, $\theta^k \leq \theta^{k-1}$: hence the minimum problem above is in fact *unconstrained*. By Proposition 3, a solution of (P_{s_k}) is given by w^s, where w solves (4) – and any solution is between $\underline{w}^s$ and $\overline{\overline{w}}^s$. We find that a solution z of (5) is given by $z_i = l_0$ if $w_i \leq (l_1 + l_0)/2$, $z_i = l_k$, $k = 2, \ldots, n-1$, if $(l_k + l_{k-1})/2 < w_i \leq (l_{k+1} + l_k)/2$, and $z_i = l_n$ if $w_i > (l_n + l_{n-1})/2$. We also deduce that any solution z of (5) satisfies $|z_i - w_i| = \min_{k=0}^n |l_k - w_i|$ for any i: in particular, we deduce the thesis of Proposition 4.   □

2.6   Observation

One may check that all that has been said up to now can be adapted to problems of the form

$$\min_w J(w) + \sum_{i=1}^N H(i, w_i) \tag{6}$$

where for all i, $H(i, \cdot)$ is strictly convex, by replacing $s - G_i$ with $\partial_{w_i} H(i, \cdot)_{|s}$ in (P_s). The strict convexity of H (that is, the fact $\partial_{w_i} H(i, \cdot)$ is increasing) is important here, as it allows to use Proposition 2; however, many of our results remain valid with some adaption when the convexity is not strict.

3   Algorithms

The interaction energy appearing in (1), (2) is of the form

$$J(w) = \sum_{1 \leq i < j \leq N} \alpha_{i,j} |w_i - w_j|.$$

The weights $\alpha_{i,j}$ are always assumed to be nonnegative. We also introduce $\alpha_{j,i} = \alpha_{i,j}$, notice however that all the discussion that follows is still valid for the more general form of the energy $\sum_{i \neq j} \alpha_{i,j} (w_i - w_j)^+$, with directional and possibly different interaction weights $\alpha_{i,j}$ and $\alpha_{j,i}$ (we define $x^+ = \max\{x, 0\}$, $x^- = (-x)^+$ for any real number x). We will assume in the rest of the discussion that $\lambda = 1$, without loss of generality. Since for any two real numbers a, b, $|a - b| = \int_{-\infty}^{+\infty} |\chi_{\{a>s\}} - \chi_{\{b>s\}}| \, ds$, J clearly satisfies (3). (The same observation appears in a recent paper by B. A. Zalesky [25].)

The consequences of the previous discussion are, on one hand, that it is possible to solve a TV minimisation problem such as (4) by solving either binary MRF problems of type (P_s) for each level s (or rather for s in a finite, reasonably large set of levels $\{l_0, \ldots, l_n\}$), or by solving directly a quantized problem of type (5). All these can be solved by graph-flow techniques. Conversely, it is possible to find a solution of a binary problem such as (1) (or (P_s)) by solving an appropriate TV minimization problem, and thresholding the result. We will not discuss this alternative in the present paper (see [10, 11]), although it might be interesting for finding solutions to the whole family of problems (P_s) in one single pass. Let us first describe the "graph-cut" techniques for solving binary MRFs.

3.1   Algorithms for Binary MRFs

It has been observed first by Greig, Porteous and Seheult that a problem such as (1) or (P_s) is equivalent to finding a partition of an appropriate graph into two sets. We consider the problem written in the form (P) (remember (P) denotes problem (P_0)). Consider the graph $\mathcal{G} = (\mathcal{V}, \mathcal{E})$ made of vertices

$$\mathcal{V} = \{i : i = 1, \ldots, N\} \cup \{t\} \cup \{s\}$$

where the "terminals" s and t are called respectively the source and the sink, and of (oriented) edges

$$\begin{aligned} \mathcal{E} = \ &\{(i, j) : 1 \le i, j \le N \, i \ne j, \alpha_{i,j} > 0\} \\ &\cup \{(s, i) : 1 \le i \le N\} \cup \{(i, t) : 1 \le i \le N\} \,. \end{aligned}$$

The first two sets of edges represent the interactions between values, necessary to represent the potential J. The last set, that links each value to both terminals, is used to represent the potential $-\sum_i G_i \theta_i$ that appears in Problem (P). Now, assume each edge $e \in \mathcal{E}$ has a "capacity" $C(e)$. (For technical reasons, these capacities need be nonnegative.) Then, given a "cut" $(\mathcal{V}_s, \mathcal{V}_t)$ of the graph, that is, a partition of $\mathcal{V}$ into two sets, with $s \in \mathcal{V}_s$ and $t \in \mathcal{V}_t$, one can define the energy of the cut by

$$E(\mathcal{V}_s, \mathcal{V}_t) = \sum_{\substack{e = (\alpha, \beta) \in \mathcal{E} \\ \alpha \in \mathcal{V}_s, \beta \in \mathcal{V}_t}} C(e)$$

As shown in [14, 6, 18, 5, 15], there is a way to associate capacities to the graph $\mathcal{G}$ so that if we let $\theta_i = 1$ if $i \in \mathcal{V}_s$ and $\theta_i = 0$ otherwise, then

$$E(\mathcal{V}_s, \mathcal{V}_t) = J(\theta) - \sum_{i=1}^{N} G_i \theta_i + \text{constant} \qquad (7)$$

for any cut $(\mathcal{V}_s, \mathcal{V}_t)$. Indeed, to an edge $e = (i, j) \in \mathcal{E}$, we simply let $C(e) = \alpha_{i,j}$. Then, choosing $\overline{G} \geq \max_i G_i$, we let $C(s, i) = \overline{G}$ and $C(i, t) = \overline{G} - G_i$. It is then straightforward to check (7).

Now, it is possible to find, in polynomial time, an optimal cut (that is, a cut minimizing its total energy E) in such a graph, giving a solution to our binary MRF model. The idea is to find a "maximal flow" along the edges of the graph, from s to t. The equivalence between both problems is a duality result, due to Ford and Fulkerson. We refer to [5] for a very clear description of the method, and of an algorithm.

3.2   Minimization of (4) Using Graph Cuts

3.3   First Method

According to the discussion in section 2, one deduces the following method for minimizing (4) using the max flow algorithm for computing graph cuts. It consists simply in fixing $n + 1$ levels $l_0, \ldots, l_n$, with $l_0 = \min_i G_i$ and $l_k = \max_i G_i$, and $l_k - l_{k-1} = (l_n - l_0)/n = \delta l$, and to find a solution z of the quantized problem (5). Practically, one solves problem (P_{s_k}) for $s_k = (l_k + l_{k-1})/2$, for each $k = 1, \ldots, n$: the result is a field θ^k with $\theta^k = 1$ when $z > s_k$ and 0 else. One easily rebuilds z from the θ^k's. Now, there is a lot of redundancy in this method. Indeed, since $\theta^k \leq \theta^{k-1}$, once problem $(P_{s_{k-1}})$ is solved one should not need to reprocess the areas where $\theta^{k-1} = 0$ (since there, $\theta^k = 0$ is already known).

This observation yields a more efficient method for solving (4), up to an arbitrary, fixed precision. The algorithm that we propose here has already been presented, in a slightly different way, in two papers by J. Darbon and M. Sigelle [12, 13]. We denote by w the (unique) solution of (4). Given a "depth" $D \geq 1$, we fix a dyadic number of (increasing) thresholding levels s_k, for $k = 1, \ldots, n = 2^D - 1$. We introduce an array (K_i), $i = 1, \ldots, N$, of integers, whose meaning will be, at the end of the process, the following: if $K_i = k$, then $s_k \leq w_i \leq s_{k+1}$ (letting by convention $s_0 = -\infty$ and $s_{2^D} = +\infty$). We initialize this array with the value 0. Then, for d running from 0 to $D - 1$, we segment at each level s_k for $k = (2p - 1)2^{D-1-d}$, $p = 1, \ldots, 2^d$. First, for $d = 0$, we segment at level s_k for $k = 2^{D-1}$, by solving problem (P_{s_k}), and we get a map θ such that if $\theta_i = 1$, $w_i \geq s_k$, whereas if $\theta_i = 0$, $w_i \leq s_k$ (by Proposition 3). We let $K_i = k = 2^{D-1}$ when $\theta_i = 1$ and we leave the value 0 when $\theta_i = 0$.

Next, for $d = 1$, let us consider the levels s_k, $k = 2^{D-2}$, and $s_{k'}$, $k' = 3 \times 2^{D-2}$. If θ solve (P_{s_k}), we know that each time $K_i = 2^{D-1}$, then $\theta_i = 1$, in the same way, if θ' solve $(P_{s_{k'}})$, each time $K_i = 0$, then $\theta'_i = 0$. Thus, $(\theta_i)_{i:K_i=0}$ solves the problem

$$\min_{\theta_i \in \{0,1\}} \sum_{i<j, K_i = K_j = 0} \alpha_{i,j}|\theta_i - \theta_j| + \sum_{K_i = 0 \neq K_j} \alpha_{i,j}(1 - \theta_i) + \sum_{K_i = 0} (s_k - G_i)\theta_i \,,$$

while $(\theta'_i)_{i:K_i \neq 0}$ solves

$$\min_{\theta'_i \in \{0,1\}} \sum_{i<j, K_i = K_j \neq 0} \alpha_{i,j}|\theta'_i - \theta'_j| + \sum_{K_i \neq 0 = K_j} \alpha_{i,j}\theta'_i + \sum_{K_i \neq 0} (s_{k'} - G_i)\theta'_i \,.$$

These two problems can be solved independently, but they can also be merged in the following way: we let $\hat{\theta}_i = \theta_i$ when $K_i = 0$, and $\hat{\theta}_i = \theta'_i$ when $K_i = 2^{D-1}$, then $\hat{\theta}$ solves the problem

$$\min_{\hat{\theta}_i \in \{0,1\}} \sum_{i<j, K_i=K_j} \alpha_{i,j}|\hat{\theta}_i - \hat{\theta}_j| + \sum_{K_i<K_j}(\alpha_{i,j}(1-\hat{\theta}_i) + \alpha_{j,i}\hat{\theta}_j)$$

$$+ \sum_{i=1}^{N}(s_{K_i+2^{D-2}} - G_i)\hat{\theta}_i.$$

This problem is easily written on a graph $\mathcal{G} = (\mathcal{V}, \mathcal{E}')$ where $\mathcal{E}' \subset \mathcal{E}$ contains only the edges (i,j) with $K_i = K_j$: of course, this is fictitious in the sense that $\mathcal{V}\backslash\{s,t\}$ is now completely disconnected, and (at least) two different independent problems are solved. After $\hat{\theta}$ is computed, $(K_i)_{i=1}^{N}$ is updated as follows: if $K_i = 0$, then we let $K_i = 0$ if $\hat{\theta}_i = 0$ and $K_i = k = 2^{D-2}$ else, and if $K_i = 2^{D-1}$, we let $K_i = 2^{D-1}$ if $\hat{\theta}_i = 0$ and $K_i = k' = 3 \times 2^{D-2}$ else. Hence, K_i is updated according to the following rule:

$$K_i \leftarrow K_i + 2^{D-2}\hat{\theta}_i.$$

Now, the subsequent steps $(d \geq 2)$ are processed exactly in the same way. One solves the binary problem

$$\min_{\hat{\theta}_i \in \{0,1\}} \sum_{i<j, K_i=K_j} \alpha_{i,j}|\hat{\theta}_i - \hat{\theta}_j| + \sum_{K_i<K_j}(\alpha_{i,j}(1-\hat{\theta}_i) + \alpha_{j,i}\hat{\theta}_j)$$

$$+ \sum_{i=1}^{N}(s_{K_i+2^{D-1-d}} - G_i)\hat{\theta}_i.$$

Again, this is a disjoint union of at least 2^d problems, that can be solved on a graph with the same vertices as before (and less edges). One then updates K_i according to the rule

$$K_i \leftarrow K_i + 2^{D-1-d}\hat{\theta}_i.$$

At the end of the process, one finds an array (K_i) of values between 0 and $2^D - 1$, such that if $K_i = k$, then: if $k = 0$, $w \leq s_1$, if $k = n = 2^D - 1$, $w \geq s_n$, and in all other cases, $s_k \leq w \leq s_{k+1}$. This provides, of course, an approximation of w, with a precision controlled by 2^{-D}. In particular, we get an exact solution z of (5) for the levels $l_0 < l_1 < \cdots < l_n$, $n = 2^D - 1$, if for each $k \geq 1$, $s_k = (l_k + l_{k-1})/2$ and we let at the end of the process $z_i = l_{K_i}$.

3.4   Second Method (Ishikawa's Representation)

We briefly mention alternative approach to solve (5) using a max flow algorithm. It is based on a representation due to Ishikawa (see [15, 16]). The idea is to introduce an additional dimension and represent the field $z \in X$, $z_i \in \{l_0, \ldots, l_n\}$ for all i, in the following way: we let $Y = X^n$ and consider all *binary* fields $\Theta \in Y$,

$\Theta = (\Theta_i^k)_{i=1,\ldots,N}^{k=1,\ldots,n}$ such that $\Theta_i^k \leq \Theta_i^{k-1}$ for $2 \leq k \leq n$, and any i. Then, there is a one-to-one correspondence between admissible z for problem (5) and these binary fields, if to any such z we associate Θ given by $\Theta_i^k = 1$ if $z_i \geq l_k$, and 0 otherwise. If we define the energies (assuming, to simplify, that $l_k - l_{k-1} = \delta l$ is independent on k)

$$F(\Theta) = \delta l \sum_{k=1}^{n} \sum_{1 \leq i < j \leq N} \alpha_{i,j} |\Theta_i^k - \Theta_j^k| + \sum_{i=1}^{N} \sum_{k=2}^{n} \infty \cdot (\Theta_i^k - \Theta_i^{k-1})^+$$

$$+ \sum_{i=1}^{N} \sum_{k=1}^{n} \frac{(l_k - G_i)^2 - (l_{k-1} - G_i)^2}{2} \Theta_i^k$$

then one easily checks that for any $\Theta \in Y$, if $F(\Theta) < +\infty$ then Θ_i^k is nonincreasing with respect to k, so that Θ is in correspondence with an admissible $z \in X$, $z_i \in \{l_0, \ldots, l_n\}$. In this case, one has

$$F(\Theta) = J(z) + \frac{1}{2} \sum_{i=1}^{N} (z_i - G_i)^2 - N \frac{(l_0 - G_i)^2}{2}.$$

Hence, up to a constant, the energy of Θ is the same as the energy of z. The consequence is that problem (5) can be solved by finding the (unique) optimal cut in the graph associated to the energy F.

Let us observe that this construction is quite general: in [15], it is shown that as soon as J is convex an energy such as F can be found, whose minimization gives a solution to the initial problem. We will see that in our case this method is (by far) less efficient than the algorithm proposed in Section 3.3. However, it can be used for energies much more general than (4)-(5). In particular, it is important to notice that it will solve any (quantized) problem such as (6) where the function H *needs not be convex* in w_i. This is of particular interest in some situations, like for instance stereo correspondence problems.

4   TV Minimization

We now consider the case where our vector space X represents the grey-level values of a bidimensional image, that is, $X = \mathbb{R}^{N \times M}$, and a vector $w \in X$ is a matrix $(w_{i,j})_{i=1,\ldots,N, j=1,\ldots,M}$. We consider the simplest, anisotropic discretization of the TV, given by

$$J(w) = \sum_{i,j} |w_{i+1,j} - w_{i,j}| + |w_{i,j+1} - w_{i,j}|$$

where in the sum all terms that are well-defined appear. Extension of what will be said to more complex interactions (not nearest-neighbours, or nonuniform) is obvious.

We see that problem (2) is of the form (4). On the other hand, if a, b and $g_{i,j}$ are scalar quantities in (1), then clearly this problem is a particular 2-levels case of (5), with G simply given by g and λ by $\lambda/(b-a)$ (assuming $b > a$). If those quantities are vectorial, on the other hand, one can also rewrite (1) as

$$\min_{\theta_{i,j}\in\{0,1\}} \lambda \sum_{i,j} J(\theta) + \sum_{i,j} \left(\frac{b^2 - a^2}{2} - (b-a)\cdot g_{i,j}\right)\theta_{i,j} + \text{constant},$$

which is of the form (P_s).

We will compare the two algorithms described in sections 3.3 and 3.4 to the algorithm introduced in [9], for minimizing (2). Let us briefly recall this algorithm. First of all, we mention that also this algorithm could be described in the more general abstract setting of the previous section. However, it does not seem to be much more efficient than the first algorithm in section 3.3. Its strength, on the other hand, is that it also works with interaction energies of the form

$$J_{iso}(w) = \sum_{i,j} \sqrt{(w_{i+1,j} - w_{i,j})^2 + (w_{i,j+1} - w_{i,j})^2}, \tag{8}$$

that to our knowledge are not handled by the methods described previously. (In particular, J_{iso} does not satisfy (3), but it may be seen as a discretization of the "true" total variation, which satisfies, in the continuous setting, the co-area formula.) Also, it is easily generalized to the case where $w_{i,j}$ is vectorial (case of color/multispectral images). For these reasons, we prefer to stick to the description in [9], in the particular setting of a 2D, nearest-neighbours interaction energy. Let us briefly recall how the algorithm is implemented.

The energy J can be written

$$J(w) = \sum_{i,j} |(\nabla^x w)_{i,j}| + |(\nabla^y w)_{i,j}|$$

where $(\nabla w)_{i,j} = ((\nabla^x w)_{i,j}, (\nabla^y w)_{i,j}) \in X \times X$ is defined by $(\nabla^x w)_{i,j} = w_{i+1,j} - w_{i,j}$ when $i < N$ and 0 if $i = N$, and $(\nabla^y w)_{i,j} = w_{i,j+1} - w_{i,j}$ when $j < M$ and 0 if $j = M$. If both X and $X \times X$ are endowed with the standard Euclidean scalar product, then a discrete divergence is given by $\text{div} = -\nabla^*$, that is

$$(\text{div}\,\xi, w)_X = -(\xi, \nabla w)_{X\times X} \; \forall w \in X, \xi \in X \times X.$$

(It is easily computed, see [9].)

By standard duality arguments, it is shown in [9] that the solution of (2) is given by $\overline{w} = g + \lambda\text{div}\,\overline{\xi}$ where $\overline{\xi}$ is a solution to

$$\min\{\|g + \lambda\text{div}\,\xi\|^2 : \xi \in X \times X, |\xi^x_{i,j}| \leq 1 \text{ and } |\xi^y_{i,j}| \leq 1 \forall i, j\}. \tag{9}$$

and $\overline{\xi}_{i,j} \cdot (\nabla\overline{w})_{i,j} = |(\nabla^x\overline{w})_{i,j}| + |(\nabla^y\overline{w})_{i,j}|$ for all i, j. We observe that the field $\overline{\xi}$ which is found here is related to the flow computed by the max-flow algorithm of the previous sections.

The adaption of the iterative algorithm of [9] to problem (9) is as follows: we let $\xi^0 = 0$, and for all $n \geq 0$ we let

$$
\begin{cases}
w^n = g + \lambda \mathrm{div}\, \xi^n \\[2mm]
(\xi_{i,j}^{n+1})^x = \dfrac{(\xi_{i,j}^n)^x + (\tau/\lambda)(\nabla^x w^n)_{i,j}}{1 + (\tau/\lambda)|(\nabla^x w^n)_{i,j}|}, \\[4mm]
(\xi_{i,j}^{n+1})^y = \dfrac{(\xi_{i,j}^n)^y + (\tau/\lambda)(\nabla^y w^n)_{i,j}}{1 + (\tau/\lambda)|(\nabla^y w^n)_{i,j}|},
\end{cases}
\tag{10}
$$

where $\tau > 0$ is a fixed "time-step". One shows as in [9] that as $n \to \infty$, $w^n \to \overline{w}$, provided $\tau \leq 1/8$ (in fact, experimental convergence is observed as long as $\tau \leq 1/4$). The following variant, which is a simple gradient descent/reprojection method, seems to perform better:

$$
\begin{cases}
w^n = g + \lambda \mathrm{div}\, \xi^n \\[2mm]
(\xi_{i,j}^{n+1})^x = \dfrac{(\xi_{i,j}^n)^x + (\tau/\lambda)(\nabla^x w^n)_{i,j}}{\max\{1, |(\xi_{i,j}^n)^x + (\tau/\lambda)(\nabla^x w^n)_{i,j}|\}}, \\[4mm]
(\xi_{i,j}^{n+1})^y = \dfrac{(\xi_{i,j}^n)^y + (\tau/\lambda)(\nabla^y w^n)_{i,j}}{\max\{1, |(\xi_{i,j}^n)^y + (\tau/\lambda)(\nabla^y w^n)_{i,j}|\}}.
\end{cases}
\tag{11}
$$

It is easy to show the stability of this scheme up to $\tau \leq 1/4$ (indeed, $\xi^n \mapsto \xi^{n+1}$ is 1-Lipschitz); convergence is also probably true but not straigthforward (being $\nabla\mathrm{div}$ singular). Experiments show convergence up to $\tau \leq 1/4$, however, $\tau = 1/4$ seems not optimal, and a better convergence is obtained for $.24 \lesssim \tau \lesssim .249$.

We eventually observe that the error between w^n and the solution $\overline{w}$ of (2) can be estimated: indeed, since $w^n = g + \lambda\mathrm{div}\,\xi^n$ and $\overline{w} = g + \lambda\mathrm{div}\,\overline{\xi}$, one shows

$$
\|w^n - \overline{w}\|^2 \leq \lambda J(w^n) - (\xi^n, \nabla w^n)_{X \times X}.
\tag{12}
$$

5   Comparisons

We have compared four programs based on the two algorithms in Sections 3.3 and 3.4, and the two variants (fixed-point and gradient descent/projection) of the algorithm in Section 4, for the anisotropic problem (2).

We first performed the denoising of an image of $800 \times 600 = 480\,000$ pixels (corrupted with a noise of standard deviation 20, for original values in $[0, 255]$, with deviation ~ 90 – SNR $\simeq 13$), and of a smaller subimage of size $256 \times 256 = 65\,536$ pixels, see Figure 1. We chose a value of $\lambda = 20$ for the large image and 16 for the smaller. The results are shown in Figure 2.

All algorithms were programmed in C/C++ and were run on a 3.20 GHz-Pentium 4 Linux 2.6 system with 1 Mb of cache. The max flow algorithm program was the `maxflow-v2.2` implementation of [5], implemented by Vladimir Kolmogorov and that we downloaded from his web page. The type of the capacities was set to `double`, and it is likely that the results can be slightly improved

Fig. 1. The original and noisy image used in the experiments

Fig. 2. The results

by letting it to `short` or `int` and appropriately quantifying the values. This max-flow program was then linked with an appropriate C++ program organizing the dyadic decomposition of the levels. The execution times of the programs was measured using the `times()` C command.

Table 1 compares the algorithms for the small image. The RMSE and Absolute Difference are with respect to the "true" solution, computed using the dyadic graph-cut algorithm at depth 16 (precision $(1/2) \times 255/(2^{16}-1)$). The RMSE is renormalized (divided by 255) whereas the absolute difference is in pixel values (in $[0-255]$). For the fixed point algorithm and the projected gradient-descent

Table 1. Comparisons for the small 256 × 256 image

method	time (s)	iter.	RMSE	Abs. Diff. [0-255]
graph-cut, depth = 8	.43		.0011	.5 (theor.)
graph-cut, depth = 12	.84		.000067	.031 (theor.)
graph-cut, depth = 16	1.25		0	.002 (theor.)
fixed point, err = .01	.13	32	.0047	5.7
fixed point, err = .005	.35	88	.0022	3.0
proj. grad., err = .01	.17	37	.000717	4.0
proj. grad., err = .005	.38	81	.000371	2.2

("proj. grad.") algorithm (11), the estimate (12) (renormalized in order to be an RMSE estimate) was used as a stopping criterion. In the tables, "err=xxx" gives the corresponding value. We observe that for the projected gradient algorithm, the RMSE that is actually reached is about 7% of the stopping criterion, while it is almost 50% for the fixed point algorithm, the total number of iterations remaining of the same order: it shows that the projected gradient is more efficient. As a matter of fact, for a stopping criterion of .01, oscillations remain visible in the output of the fixed-point method, while they are much attenuated in the output of the projected gradient method. This algorithm seems to be the most efficient, however, the control of the error is more precise with the graph-cut algorithm. Another important observation is that the projected gradient algorithm is quite straightforward to implement. The comparisons for the larger image, in Table 2, yield the same conclusions. In both cases, both iterative algorithms had a "time-step" $\tau = .249$. Experiments with $\tau = .24$ show that the projected gradient iterations stop much earlier: after 37 iterations and 1.17 seconds for a stopping value of .01 and 110 iterations and 3.73 seconds for the stopping value of .005. However, in both cases, the RMSE that is attained is also proportionally higher than with $\tau = .249$: .001162 in the first case and .000535 in the second case. Still, this seems to show that it works better than the fixed-point iteration.

In the two previous experiments the SNR is quite high and the value of the regularizing parameter λ is tuned so that the output remains very close to the initial data. In this range, the superiority of the graph-cut approach is not so clear. We have run another experiment on a much noiser image (see Figure 3)

Table 2. Comparisons for the large 800 × 600 image

method	time (s)	iter.	RMSE	Abs. Diff. [0-255]
graph-cut, depth = 8	3.9		.0011	.5 (theor.)
graph-cut, depth = 12	8.6		.000067	.031 (theor.)
graph-cut, depth = 16	13.6		0	.002 (theor.)
fixed point, err = .01	1.60	50	.0047	6.6
fixed point, err = .005	4.90	154	.0022	3.0
proj. grad., err = .01	2.62	79	.000683	3.3
proj. grad., err = .005	5.50	163	.000387	2.4

Fig. 3. The noisy checkerboard and the reconstruction

Table 3. Comparisons for the (very) noisy 230 × 230 checkerboard

method	time (s)	iter.	RMSE	Abs. Diff. [0-255]
graph-cut, depth = 8	0.73		.0011	.5 (theor.)
graph-cut, depth = 12	1.42		.000067	.031 (theor.)
graph-cut, depth = 16	2.15		0	.002 (theor.)
fixed point, err = .01	1.97	625	.0045	4.3
fixed point, err = .005	5.48	1752	.0019	2.0
proj. grad., err = .01	1.33	453	.0021	3.8
proj. grad., err = .005	3.68	1235	.00087	1.6

of size $230 \times 230 = 52900$ pixels, of amplitude ~ 50 (without noise) and ~ 85 with a noise of standard deviation ~ 65 (SNR $\simeq 2$). For this image, $\lambda = 80$. In this range, the graph-cut approach clearly outperforms the more classical methods, as shown in Table 3. Again, the projected gradient method is sligthly more efficient than the fixed point.

Eventually, we also have run Ishikawa's algorithm of Section 3.4. Obviously, it is much slower than our dyadic graph-cut method (and gives exactly the same answer). Is also requires a huge amount of memory, so that we did not run it with 256 levels. With 16, 32, and 64 levels, it ran in respectively 1.61, 3.65 and 8.15 seconds, on the small image while the dyadic graph-cut method at depths 4, 5 and 6 ran respectively in .16, .21 and .31 seconds. However, we recall again that Ishikawa's method can be used in much more difficult (nonconvex) problems.

6   Conclusion

We compared three different techniques for solving the (anisotropic) Rudin-Osher-Fatemi minimization problem. One, based on the exact resolution of binary MRFs by integer optimization methods (and which is already found in [12, 13], has the advantage that it yields an exact solution of the problem, up to a known precision. However, it seems that the method proposed in [9] (or, even better, the simple gradient-descent/projection method given by (11)) yields comparable results, in the range of coefficients useful for the processing of not too noisy images. It is clearly outperformed when the SNR becomes very poor. On the other hand, it is easily adapted to process color or multidimensional images, and can be made more isotropic (using the penalization J_{iso} given by (8)) at no expense.

Acknowledgements

The author wishes to thank Guy Bouchitté (Univ. of Toulon, France) and Vicent Caselles (Univ. Pompeu Fabra, Barcelona, Spain): this research owes a lot to their collaboration on *apparently* quite different topics. Also, though the description of the max-flow algorithm in [5] is extremely clear, we were much helped thanks to a few C++ implementations of this algorithm that are available on the internet. We would like to thank the authors of these, Walter Bell [3] and Vladimir Kolmogorov. The latter's, that we found somewhat more efficient, is available at `http://www.cs.cornell.edu/People/vnk/software.html`. Eventually, we would like also to thank J. F. Aujol for mentioning to us the work of J. Darbon and M. Sigelle, and the two latter for interesting and helpful discussion.

The author is supported by the CNRS, and partially supported by the "Fonds national de la science", ACI "Nouvelles interfaces des mathématiques" MULTIM.

References

1. F. Alter, V. Caselles, and A. Chambolle. A characterization of convex calibrable sets in $\mathbb{R}^N$. *Math. Ann.*, 332(2):329–366, June 2005.
2. F. Alter, V. Caselles, and A. Chambolle. Evolution of characteristic functions of convex sets in the plane by the minimizing total variation flow. *Interfaces Free Bound.*, 7(1):29–53, 2005.
3. W. Bell. A C++ implementation of a Max Flow-Graph Cut algorithm. available at `http://www.cs.cornell.edu/vision/wbell/`, November 2001. Computer Science Dept, Cornell University.
4. G. Bouchitté. Recent convexity arguments in the calculus of variations. (lecture notes from the 3rd Int. Summer School on the Calculus of Variations, Pisa), 1998.
5. Y. Boykov and V. Kolmogorov. An experimental comparison of min-cut/max-flow algorithms for energy minimization in vision. *IEEE Trans. Pattern Analysis and Machine Intelligence*, 26(9):1124–1137, September 2004.
6. Y. Boykov, O. Veksler, and R. Zabih. Fast approximate energy minimization via graph cuts. In *International Conference on Computer Vision*, pages 377–384, September 1999.
7. V. Caselles and A. Chambolle. Anisotropic curvature-driven flow of convex sets. Technical Report 528, CMAP, Ecole Polytechnique, 2004.
8. A. Chambolle. An algorithm for mean curvature motion. *Interfaces Free Bound.*, 6(2):195–218, 2004.

9. A. Chambolle. An algorithm for total variation minimization and applications. *J. Math. Imaging Vision*, 20(1-2):89–97, 2004. Special issue on mathematics and image analysis.

10. T. F. Chan and S. Esedoglu. Aspects of total variation regularized L^1 function approximation. Technical Report 04-07, UCLA CAM, February 2004.

11. T. F. Chan, S. Esedoglu, and M. Nikolova. Algorithms for finding global minimizers of image segmentation and denoising models. Technical Report 04-54, UCLA CAM, September 2004.

12. J. Darbon and M. Sigelle. Exact optimization of discrete constrained total variation minimization problems. In R. Klette and J. Zunic, editors, *Tenth International Workshop on Combinatorial Image Analysis*, volume 3322 of *LNCS*, pages 548–557, December 2004.

13. J. Darbon and M. Sigelle. A fast and exact algorithm for total variation minimization. In J. S. Marques, N. Pérez de la Blanca, and P. Pina, editors, *2nd Iberian Conference on Pattern Recognition and Image Analysis*, volume 3522 of *LNCS*, pages 351–359, June 2005.

14. D.M. Greig, B.T. Porteous, and A.H. Seheult. Exact maximum a posteriori estimation for binary images. *J. R. Statist. Soc. B*, 51:271–279, 1989.

15. H. Ishikawa. Exact optimization for Markov random fields with convex priors. *IEEE Trans. Pattern Analysis and Machine Intelligence*, 25(10):1333–1336, 2003.

16. H. Ishikawa and D. Geiger. Segmentation by grouping junctions. In *IEEE Conf. Computer Vision and Pattern Recognition*, pages 125–131, 1998.

17. V. Kolmogorov and R. Zabih. Multi-camera scene reconstruction via graph cuts. In *European Conference on Computer Vision*, volume 3, pages 82–96, may 2002.

18. V. Kolmogorov and R. Zabih. What energy functions can be minimized via graph cuts? *IEEE Trans. Pattern Analysis and Machine Intelligence*, 2(26):147–159, 2004.

19. S. Paris, F. Sillion, and L. Quan. A surface reconstruction method using global graph cut optimization. *International Journal of Computer Vision*, 2005. to appear.

20. G. Poggi and A. R. P. Ragozini. Image segmentation by tree-structured Markov random fields. *IEEE Signal Processing Letters*, 6:155–157, 1999.

21. M. Rivera and J.C. Gee. Two-level MRF models for image restoration and segmentation. In *Proc. British Machine Vision Conference, London*, volume 2, pages 809–818, Sept. 2004.

22. S. Roy and I. J. Cox. A maximum-flow formulation of the n-camera stereo correspondence problem. In *ICCV*, pages 492–502, 1998.

23. L.I. Rudin, S. Osher, and E. Fatemi. Nonlinear total variation based noise removal algorithms. *Physica D*, 60:259–268, 1992.

24. G. Scarpa, G. Poggi, and J. Zerubia. A binary tree-structured MRF model for multispectral satellite image segmentation. Rapport de recherche RR-5062, INRIA Sophia Antipolis, December 2003.

25. B. A. Zalesky. Network flow optimization for restoration of images. *J. Appl. Math.*, 2(4):199–218, 2002.

Exploiting Inference for Approximate Parameter Learning in Discriminative Fields: An Empirical Study

Sanjiv Kumar, Jonas August, and Martial Hebert

The Robotics Institute, Carnegie Mellon University,
Pittsburgh, PA 15213 USA
{skumar, jonas, hebert}@cs.cmu.edu
http://www.cs.cmu.edu/~{skumar,jonas,hebert}

Abstract. Estimation of parameters of random field models from labeled training data is crucial for their good performance in many image analysis applications. In this paper, we present an approach for approximate maximum likelihood parameter learning in discriminative field models, which is based on approximating true expectations with simple piecewise constant functions constructed using inference techniques. Gradient ascent with these updates exhibits compelling limit cycle behavior which is tied closely to the number of errors made during inference. The performance of various approximations was evaluated with different inference techniques showing that the learned parameters lead to good classification performance so long as the method used for approximating the gradient is consistent with the inference mechanism. The proposed approach is general enough to be used for the training of, e.g., smoothing parameters of conventional Markov Random Fields (MRFs).

1 Introduction

In language processing, natural image analysis and many other applications, the input data show significant dependencies, which should be modeled appropriately to achieve good classification. In earlier work [1], we presented the Discriminative Random Field (DRF) model for image analysis, which discriminatively models the conditional distribution of the labels given the observed data directly as a Gibbs Field. DRFs allow one to relax the assumption of conditional independence of the observed data, which is invoked commonly in conventional generative MRF frameworks, and were shown to give better classification results than MRFs [1]. DRFs were inspired by Conditional Random Field (CRF), which was proposed by Lafferty et al. [2] and developed to analyze 1D sequence data for which exact maximum likelihood parameters can be computed efficiently, e.g., using iterative scaling [2], quasi-Newton methods [3], etc. Unfortunately, for graphs with loops, which are typical in image analysis, it is generally infeasible to exactly maximize the likelihood with respect to the parameters. Therefore, a critical issue in applying discriminative fields is the design of effective parameter learning techniques that can operate on arbitrary graphs. The objective of this paper is to address this central issue.

A. Rangarajan et al. (Eds.): EMMCVPR 2005, LNCS 3757, pp. 153–168, 2005.

In this work, we approximate the gradients of the log likelihood function directly using the inference techniques. Our experimental results may be summarized by the following two observations: First, *parameter learning* can be achieved by approximating the likelihood gradient using the label estimates obtained through methods such as Maximum A Posteriori (MAP) or Maximum Posterior Marginal (MPM) for the given conditional probability model. Second, good classification performance can be achieved by any of these approximations, so long as the method used for inference matches the method used for approximating the gradient in the parameter learning. We note that this *learning/inference coupling* is reasonable because the usual goal in classification problems is to minimize the number of errors, which is what our gradient approximation does, even though this may not necessarily maximize the likelihood. We also present a new experimental comparison of several learning and inference algorithm combinations for guiding what type of learning approximation should be adopted for a given choice of inference method.

2   Discriminative Random Field (DRF)

In this section, we review the formulation of discriminative fields. Although the formulation is general to arbitrary graphs with multiple class labels [4], we will discuss the problem of learning in the context of binary classification on 2D image lattices. Let $\boldsymbol{y}$ be the observed data from an input image, where $\boldsymbol{y} = \{\boldsymbol{y}_i\}_{i \in S}$, $\boldsymbol{y}_i$ is the data from i^{th} site, and S is the set of sites. Let the corresponding labels be given by $\boldsymbol{x} = \{x_i\}_{i \in S}$ where $x_i \in \{-1, 1\}$. The DRF formulation combines local discriminative models to capture the class associations at individual sites with the interactions in the neighboring sites as:

$$P(\boldsymbol{x}|\boldsymbol{y}) = \frac{1}{Z} \exp \left(\sum_{i \in S} \log P'(x_i|\boldsymbol{y}) + \sum_{i \in S} \sum_{j \in \mathcal{N}_i} \log P''(x_i, x_j|\boldsymbol{y}) \right), \quad (1)$$

where Z is the partition function (normalizing constant). Note that both the unary potential, $\log P'(x_i|\boldsymbol{y})$, and the pairwise potential, $\log P''(x_i, x_j|\boldsymbol{y})$, depend explicitly on all the observations $\boldsymbol{y}$. Unlike conventional generative MRFs, where the pairwise potential is a *data-independent* prior over the labels, the pairwise potential in DRFs depend on data $\boldsymbol{y}$ and thus allow *data-dependent* interactions among the labels. Hence, DRFs capture much richer contexts in images. For instance, while the pairwise potential in MRF priors can model smoothness of the labels, DRFs can modulate this smoothness by using local image context, e.g., the smoothness can be deactivated at edges in the image.

In (1), $P'(x_i|\boldsymbol{y})$ and $P''(x_i, x_j|\boldsymbol{y})$ are arbitrary unary and pairwise discriminative classifiers. This view gives us the flexibility to choose domain-specific discriminative classifiers suitable for specific tasks. In this paper, as in our previous work [1], we use a logistic link to give the local class posterior, i.e., $P'(x_i|\boldsymbol{y}) = \sigma(x_i \boldsymbol{w}^T \boldsymbol{h}_i(\boldsymbol{y}))$, where $\sigma(t) = 1/(1 + e^{-t})$. Here $\boldsymbol{w}$ is a parameter vector, and $\boldsymbol{h}_i(\boldsymbol{y})$ is a sitewise feature vector. Similarly, to model $P''(x_i, x_j|\boldsymbol{y})$

we use a pairwise logistic classifier, which can be written in a simplified form as, $P''(x_i, x_j | \boldsymbol{y}) = x_i x_j \boldsymbol{v}^T \boldsymbol{\mu}_{ij}(\boldsymbol{y})$. Here $\boldsymbol{v}$ is a parameter vector, and $\boldsymbol{\mu}_{ij}(\boldsymbol{y})$ is a pairwise feature vector. Note that these choices of discriminative classifiers lead to forms of unary and pairwise potentials that are linear in parameters, similar to the CRFs given in [2]. Therefore, this particular DRF form can be seen as a 2D extension of 1D CRFs. Again, the loops in these 2D graphs require more elaborate parameter learning methods, which is the main concern of this paper. It is interesting to note that by ignoring the dependence of the pairwise potential on the observed data $\boldsymbol{y}$, we obtain the conventional MRF smoothing potential, $\beta x_i x_j$, also known as the Ising model.

3   Parameter Learning Approaches

We take a supervised training approach to learning the parameters of the DRF model. The data required are the observed training images and their corresponding ground-truth labeling (e.g., known segmentation). In this work we focus on the standard maximum likelihood approach to learning the parameters. In the case of DRFs, this implies maximization of the *conditional* likelihood, $\log P(\boldsymbol{x} | \boldsymbol{y}, \theta)$[1].

3.1   Maximum Likelihood Parameter Learning

Let θ be the set of unknown DRF parameters, where $\theta = \{\boldsymbol{w}, \boldsymbol{v}\}$. Given M i.i.d. labeled training images, the maximum likelihood estimates of the parameters are given by maximizing the log-likelihood $l(\theta) = \sum_{m=1}^{M} \log P(\boldsymbol{x}^m | \boldsymbol{y}^m, \theta)$, i.e.,

$$\widehat{\theta} = \underset{\theta}{\mathrm{argmax}} \sum_{m=1}^{M} \left\{ \sum_{i \in S^m} \log \sigma(x_i^m \boldsymbol{w}^T \boldsymbol{h}_i(\boldsymbol{y}^m)) + \sum_{i \in S^m} \sum_{j \in \mathcal{N}_i} x_i^m x_j^m \boldsymbol{v}^T \boldsymbol{\mu}_{ij}(\boldsymbol{y}^m) - \log Z^m \right\},$$

$$(2)$$

where the partition function for the mth image is,

$$Z^m = \sum_{\boldsymbol{x}} \exp \left\{ \sum_{i \in S^m} \log \sigma(x_i \boldsymbol{w}^T \boldsymbol{h}_i(\boldsymbol{y}^m)) + \sum_{i \in S^m} \sum_{j \in \mathcal{N}_i} x_i x_j \boldsymbol{v}^T \boldsymbol{\mu}_{ij}(\boldsymbol{y}^m) \right\}.$$

Note that Z^m is a function of the parameters θ and the observed data $\boldsymbol{y}^m$. For learning the parameters using gradient ascent, the derivatives of the log-likelihood are

$$\frac{\partial l(\theta)}{\partial \boldsymbol{w}} = \frac{1}{2} \sum_m \sum_{i \in S^m} (x_i^m - \langle x_i \rangle_{\theta; \boldsymbol{y}^m}) \boldsymbol{h}_i(\boldsymbol{y}^m),$$

$$(3)$$

---

[1] Under the Bayesian view, maximum likelihood learning generally refers to the maximization of the joint distribution, $P(\boldsymbol{x}, \boldsymbol{y}; \theta) = P(\boldsymbol{x} | \boldsymbol{y}; \theta) P(\boldsymbol{x}; \theta)$, where $P(\boldsymbol{x}; \theta)$ is an explicit prior in a generative model.

$$\frac{\partial l(\theta)}{\partial \boldsymbol{v}} = \sum_{m} \sum_{i \in S^m} \sum_{j \in \mathcal{N}_i} (x_i^m x_j^m - \langle x_i x_j \rangle_{\theta;\boldsymbol{y}^m}) \boldsymbol{\mu}_{ij}(\boldsymbol{y}^m). \tag{4}$$

Here $\langle \cdot \rangle_{\theta;\boldsymbol{y}^m}$ denotes expectation with $P(\boldsymbol{x}|\boldsymbol{y}^m, \theta)$. Ignoring $\boldsymbol{\mu}_{ij}(\boldsymbol{y}^m)$, gradient ascent with (4) is exactly the learning problem for the smoothing parameter of the Ising model.

Generally the expectations in (3) and (4) cannot be computed analytically due to the combinatorial size of the label space. Sampling procedures such as Markov Chain Monte Carlo (MCMC) can be used to approximate the true expectations. Unfortunately, MCMC techniques have two main problems: a long 'burn-in' period (which makes them slow) and high variance in estimates [5]. Recently data-driven MCMC procedures have been proposed to address the problem of slow computation [6]. An alternative approach to avoid the above MCMC drawbacks, Contrastive Divergence (CD) was proposed by Hinton [5]. In CD, only a single MCMC move is made from the current empirical distribution of the data (P^0) leading to new distribution (P^1), thus eliminating the need for running the chain beyond burn-in. According to CD, $\langle x_i \rangle_{\theta;\boldsymbol{y}} \approx \langle x_i \rangle_{\theta;\boldsymbol{y}}^{P^1}$ and $\langle x_i x_j \rangle_{\theta;\boldsymbol{y}} \approx \langle x_i x_j \rangle_{\theta;\boldsymbol{y}}^{P^1}$. Even though CD is computationally simple and yields estimates with low variance, the bias in estimates can be a problem [7], which was also verified in our experiments in Section 6. However, this approximation of expectation using a single sample inspired the different approximations we propose in this work, as shown in the next section.

3.2   Coupling Parameter Learning and Inference

The approximations defined in the previous section replace the exact gradient of (3) and (4) by $\boldsymbol{J}(\boldsymbol{\theta}) = (\boldsymbol{J_1}(\theta), \boldsymbol{J_2}(\theta))$, where

$$\boldsymbol{J_1}(\theta) = \frac{1}{2} \sum_{m} \sum_{i \in S^m} (x_i^m - f_i(\theta; \boldsymbol{y}^m)) \boldsymbol{h}_i(\boldsymbol{y}^m), \tag{5}$$

$$\boldsymbol{J_2}(\theta) = \sum_{m} \sum_{i \in S^m} \sum_{j \in \mathcal{N}_i} (x_i^m x_j^m - g_{ij}(\theta; \boldsymbol{y}^m)) \boldsymbol{\mu}_{ij}(\boldsymbol{y}^m), \tag{6}$$

and f_i and g_{ij} are functions that approximate the true expectations in the gradient. Several approaches have been proposed that compute f_i and g_{ij} using pseudo-marginals [8][9]. In this work, we propose to directly construct f_i and g_{ij} using label estimates obtained through MAP and MPM inference at the current parameter estimates (Section 4.2 and 4.3).

Will the gradient ascent of the likelihood with such approximate gradients still converge? The answer is that, while the approximate gradient ascent is not strictly convergent in general, it is weakly convergent in that it oscillates within a set of good parameters, or converges to a good parameter with isolated large deviations, as shown experimentally in Section 5. But why should the parameters learned using a particular choice of approximating functions should yield good classification performance? Informally, if we use for parameter learning the same approximating function f_i that was obtained from inference (e.g., a MAP label estimate), then, given input training labels $\{x_i^m\}$,

$$N_E^\theta = \frac{1}{2} \sum_m \sum_{i \in S^m} |x_i^m - f_i(\theta; \boldsymbol{y}^m))| \tag{7}$$

can be interpreted as the number of errors in classification. Comparing (7) with (5) shows that the approximated gradient is directly related to the number of errors, so long as the *same approximation is used in both parameter learning and inference*. We provide more details in Section 7.1.

4   Candidate Approximations

We first review the form of f_i and g_{ij} based on pseudo-marginals, and then introduce two approximations directly based on two different inference algorithms for estimating the labels: Maximum A Posteriori (MAP), and Maximum Posterior Marginal (MPM). Given our focus on binary DRFs, approximate MAP estimates were obtained using the min-cut/max-flow algorithms as explained in [1], and the MPM estimates were obtained using the sum-product version of loopy Belief Propagation (BP) [10]. The approximations described below are designed to match these two classes of inference techniques.

4.1   Pseudo-Marginal Approximation (PMA)

It is easy to see that if we had true marginal distributions $P_i(x_i|\boldsymbol{y}, \theta)$ at each site i and $P_{ij}(x_i, x_j|\boldsymbol{y}, \theta)$ at each pair of sites i and $j \in \mathcal{N}_i$, we could compute exact expectations using

$$\langle x_i \rangle_{\theta; \boldsymbol{y}} = \sum_{x_i} x_i P_i(x_i|\boldsymbol{y}, \theta) \quad \text{and} \quad \langle x_i x_j \rangle_{\theta; \boldsymbol{y}} = \sum_{x_i, x_j} x_i x_j P_{ij}(x_i, x_j|\boldsymbol{y}, \theta).$$

Since computing exact marginal distributions is in general infeasible, a standard approach is to replace the actual marginals by pseudo-marginals [9]. Here, we again used loopy BP to get these marginals. Since loopy BP assumes a tree approximation of the graph [10], it is expected to produce better approximations of these marginals than mean-field, which assumes the nodes in the graph to be disconnected. McCallum et al. [9] use a similar approximation, where pseudo-marginals estimated using Tree-based Reparametrization (TRP) were used for parameter learning in Factorial CRFs.

4.2   Learning with MAP Inference: Saddle Point Approximation (SPA)

Here, we propose a very simple approximation inspired by CD [5], but uses MAP label estimates. It is based on approximating the partition function Z with the

Saddle Point Approximation (SPA) [11]. According to SPA, Z is approximated such that the summation over all the label configurations $\boldsymbol{x}$ in Z is replaced by the largest term in the sum, which occurs at the most probable label configuration[2]. In other words, if $\hat{\boldsymbol{x}} = \arg\max_{\boldsymbol{x}} P(\boldsymbol{x}|\boldsymbol{y},\theta)$, then the SPA implies,

$$
Z \approx \exp\left\{ \sum_{i \in S} \log \sigma(\hat{x}_i \boldsymbol{w}^T \boldsymbol{h}_i(\boldsymbol{y})) + \sum_{i \in S} \sum_{j \in \mathcal{N}_i} \hat{x}_i \hat{x}_j \boldsymbol{v}^T \boldsymbol{\mu}_{ij}(\boldsymbol{y}) \right\}.
$$

This leads to a very simple approximation to the expectation, i.e., $\langle x_i \rangle_{\theta;\boldsymbol{y}} \approx \hat{x}_i$. Observe that this approximation would be exact if $\boldsymbol{x}$ were Gaussian. If we further assume mean-field decoupling, i.e., $\langle x_i x_j \rangle_{\theta;\boldsymbol{y}} = \langle x_i \rangle_{\theta;\boldsymbol{y}} \langle x_j \rangle_{\theta;\boldsymbol{y}}$, it also follows that $\langle x_i x_j \rangle_{\theta;\boldsymbol{y}} \approx \hat{x}_i \hat{x}_j$. It is interesting to note that with the saddle point approximation of Z, the gradient ascent updates are similar to the perceptron-learning type updates used in [12] and [13] in nonprobabilistic settings.

4.3   Learning with MPM Inference: Maximum Marginal Approximation (MMA)

This is the second approximation based on BP inference in which Maximum Posterior Marginal (MPM) label estimates are used for approximating the expectations. Following the arguments of SPA-based parameter learning in the previous section, one can make a similar approximation of Z such that all the mass of Z is assumed to be concentrated on the maximum marginal configuration, $\tilde{x}_i = \arg\max_{x_i} P_i(x_i|\boldsymbol{y},\theta)$. The expectations in this case can be written as $\langle x_i \rangle_{\theta;\boldsymbol{y}} \approx \tilde{x}_i$ and $\langle x_i x_j \rangle_{\theta;\boldsymbol{y}} \approx \tilde{x}_i \tilde{x}_j$. Clearly, in the binary case, maximum marginals are just the thresholded sitewise marginals. Thus, MMA can be interpreted as a discrete approximation of PMA. We experimented with both MMA and SPA in order to gain a better understanding of the consequences of discretization (see Section 5 and 7.1).

5   Experimental Observations: Parameter Learning

To analyze the convergence behavior of various parameter learning procedures described in the previous section, we learned a DRF model for a binary image denoising application. The aim was to obtain true labels from corrupted binary images. A binary image (leftmost image in the top row of Figure 2) of size 64×64 pixels was corrupted by two types of noise: Gaussian noise and Bimodal (mixture of two Gaussians) noise. For each noise model, 10 noisy images were used as the training set for learning the parameters. The unary and pairwise features were defined as: $\boldsymbol{h}_i(\boldsymbol{y}) = [1, I_i]^T$ and $\boldsymbol{\mu}_{ij}(\boldsymbol{y}) = [1, |I_i - I_j|]^T$ respectively, where I_i and I_j are the pixel intensities at site i and site j. The details of the noise parameters for this dataset are given in [1]. Here, the parameter vectors $\boldsymbol{w}$ and $\boldsymbol{v}$ were both two-element vectors, i.e., $\boldsymbol{w} = [w_0 \quad w_1]^T$, and $\boldsymbol{v} = [v_0 \quad v_1]^T$.

---

[2] Seen from the Boltzmann distribution point of view, for the distribution $P(\boldsymbol{x}|\boldsymbol{y},\theta)$, this will happen at the zero-temperature limit.

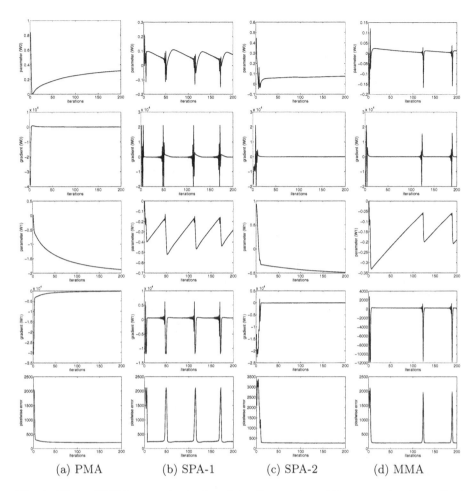

(a) PMA   (b) SPA-1   (c) SPA-2   (d) MMA

Fig. 1. Plots of DRF parameter (w_0) updates (top row), and the approximate gradient (second row) for different approximations. PMA shows a converging behavior while SPA shows oscillations which may be large-scale (SPA-1) or small-scale (SPA-2). MMA shows similar behavior as SPA. Rows 3 and 4 show the analogous plots for parameter w_1. The last row shows number of errors at each parameter update. The errors are low when the gradient magnitudes are small.

In all the experiments, parameters were initialized from random values and updates were based on gradient ascent. The step size η was fixed to a small value (10^{-5}). Fig. 1 shows, for each approximation, plots of the approximated gradients and the parameters at each iteration for a typical run with bimodal noise. For brevity we show plots only for parameters w_0 and w_1. The other parameters behaved similarly. The last row in Figure 1 shows the number of training errors (N_E^θ) made at the current estimate of the parameters using the same inference technique on which a particular gradient approximation is based.

Since the log likelihood in (2) is a convex function of parameters, the final parameter values at convergence will be independent of their initialization in the true gradient ascent. For the PMA based learning, this desirable behavior was seen (Fig. 1 (a)).

For SPA and MMA based learning, an interesting behavior emerges since both of them make discrete approximations of the true expectations. It was found that both SPA and MMA show two different stereotypical patterns of limit cycle convergence depending on the parameter initialization (see Section 7.1). For SPA, in the first case (Figure 1 (b)), the approximated gradients for all the parameters show oscillatory behavior. Initially there are large oscillations in gradients which later settle down to a low gradient zone. The gradients remain in this zone for a relatively long duration before showing large oscillations with changing sign again. Note that this will not occur for the gradient ascent with true gradients if suitably small η is chosen. One possibility of damping the oscillations is by annealing η according to a decrementing schedule for η. However such ad-hoc procedures of forcing convergence lead to bias in the final parameters. In the oscillatory case, one can choose any of the parameter selection heuristics commonly used in perceptron learning where convergence is also not guaranteed, e.g., the voted perceptron [14] [13]. In this work we simply used majority vote parameter setting, i.e., the parameters for which the training error was minimum.

The second kind of SPA behavior is seen in Figure 1 (c), where after initial oscillations, the gradients do not show 'periodic' large oscillations again but maintain microscopic oscillations within low gradient zones (not visible in the figure due to the scale of the plots). MMA-based learning behaved similar to the SPA-based learning indicating that these behaviors are related to the discrete, piecewise constant approximation of the actual expectations. An oscillating gradients case for MMA is shown in Figure 1 (d). In Section 7.1 we will discuss these limit cycle behaviors of SPA- and MMA-based learning procedures.

Finally, note that the number of errors for all approximations is small whenever gradient magnitudes are small, which indicates that all the three techniques tend to achieve parameter values that minimize the errors for that particular inference. This is especially interesting in the case of SPA and MMA because of the nature of the approximations. We will compare the performance of the parameter learning procedures with different inference techniques on a separate test set in Section 6.

6   Experimental Observations: Inference

The aim of these experiments was to compare the performance of different parameter learning procedures for a *fixed inference procedure*. For each noise model introduced in Section 5, a test set of 200 noisy images was generated using 50 noisy images each from four ground truth images shown in top row of Figure 2. For comparison, we also obtain the local MAP solution using Iterated Conditional Modes (ICM) [15] which has been shown to be robust to incorrect parameter settings. In addition, we also compare results with parameters learned through pseudo-Likelihood (PL), which uses a factored approximation

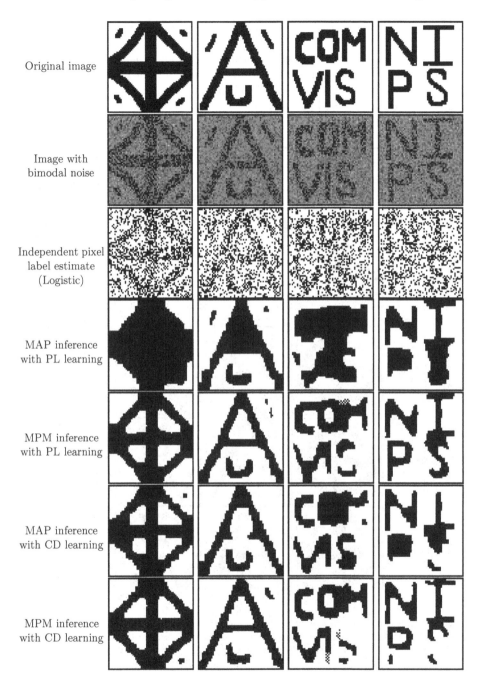

Fig. 2. Image denoising results on synthetic images with existing parameter learning methods (MAP: Maximum A Posteriori, MPM: Maximum Posterior Marginal, PL: Pseudo-Likelihood, CD: Contrastive Divergence). Both PL and CD yield poor estimates of the parameters.

of the partition function, Z, for tractability [1]. All results were computed on a 2.8 GHz CPU with code written in Matlab and C.

Figure 2 shows the denoising performance on four typical test images corrupted by the 'bimodal' noise. The parameters were first learned using existing techniques, i.e., pseudo-likelihood and contrastive divergence. It is clear from the figure that both the techniques give poor results with MAP or MPM inference.

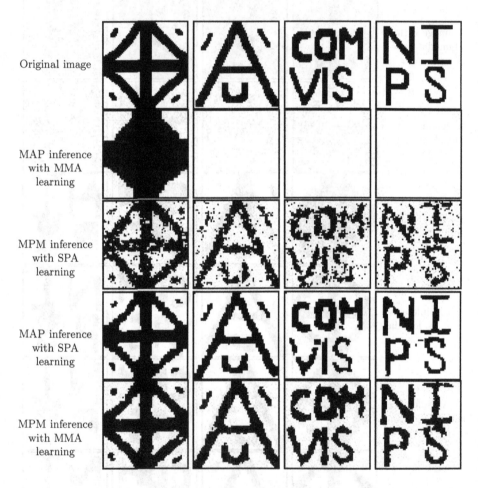

Fig. 3. Image denoising results on the noisy images shown in Figure 2 (MAP: Maximum A Posteriori, MPM: Maximum Posterior Marginal, SPA: Saddle Point Approximation, MMA: Maximum Marginal Approximation.) When inference algorithm is mismatched to the parameter learning method, the results are poor (rows 2 and 3). For example, oversmoothing is observed for MAP inference with MMA learning. MPM inference yields undersmoothed results with SPA learning. The results are good whenever the parameter learning is matched with the inference procedure (rows 4 and 5), i.e., MAP inference with SPA learning (both use min-cut) or MPM inference with MMA learning (both use BP).

The MAP inference with the matched learning technique, i.e., SPA, yields good results as shown in Figure 3. The same is true for MPM inference with MMA learning.

The overall pixelwise errors on the test set are given in Table 1. There are three key observations. Firstly, MAP inference works best with SPA parameters (both use min-cut [16]), and MPM works best with PMA and MMA parameters (all use BP), empirically verifying the claim of *learning/inference coupling*. Secondly, for MAP inference, SPA based learning is also the most efficient approach. The SPA learning is more than 14 times faster than the next most accurate method, PMA. Lastly, MMA is able to learn reasonable parameters for MPM inference (both use BP), at almost half the training time for PMA at the cost of slight decrease in performance from PMA. Note that both PMA and MMA use BP at the learning stage and slightly better results of PMA may be because PMA returns a single converged estimate of the parameters while in MMA one has to heuristically pick the best set of parameters. Better performance may be expected if a better heuristic is used instead of picking the majority voted parameters.

Three main observations help understand the differences between PMA and MMA. Firstly, since MMA is simply a discretized version of PMA, MMA will remain exact even if the pseudo-marginals converge to erroneous values, provided that the ranking of the labels implied by the pseudo-marginals is the same as that implied by the true marginals. This makes MMA more robust to errors in the estimate of marginals when pseudo-marginals tend to give poor estimates of the true marginals, e.g., in the presence of strong attractions or repulsion between nodes [17].

Secondly, this discretization accelerates parameter learning since we only need to run BP for enough iterations to stabilize the ranking of the labels, not the exact evaluations of the pseudo-marginals. The former is a coarse (low-resolution) computation, but the latter is a fine (high-resolution) computation. Empirically we noticed that most of the changes in the relative ranking of marginals generally occur in first few iterations. This partly explains faster learning through MMA in comparison to PMA as shown in Table 1.

Table 1. Pixelwise classification errors (%) on 200 test images (64×64 pixels each). The rows show different parameter learning procedures and the columns show different inference techniques used for two different noise models. See text for more.

Inference methods		Gaussian noise			Bimodal noise			Learning time
		MAP	MPM	ICM	MAP	MPM	ICM	(Sec)
	PMA	2.73	**2.51**	3.91	6.45	**5.48**	17.39	1183.13
Parameter	SPA	**2.49**	7.64	3.98	**5.82**	19.19	14.88	81.52
Learning	MMA	34.34	2.96	4.11	26.53	5.70	16.00	635.78
Methods	PL	3.82	3.10	**3.89**	17.69	7.31	22.22	299.75
	CD	3.78	2.82	4.09	8.88	6.29	**8.92**	206.93
Inference time (Sec)		5.52	90.04	5.20	5.96	113.84	5.20	

Thirdly, while learning the parameters using gradient ascent, MMA gives rise to oscillatory non-convergent behavior. Similar to SPA, this usually requires far fewer iterations of gradient ascent, as typically the *limit-cyclic* behavior in MMA implies that we can stop the gradient ascent iterations after one or two such 'cycles' to obtain sufficiently accurate estimate of the parameters.

An interesting observation is that the MAP inference is very poor with MMA parameters and the same is true for MPM inference with SPA parameters. This further enforces the idea that learning/inference coupling is rooted in minimizing the classification error for a learning/inference pair, rather than maximizing the true likelihood.

As a by-product of this comparison, we find that MPM inference is more robust to the parameters returned by other techniques than MAP which gives significantly worse results with parameters other than SPA and PMA. In addition, the PL and CD parameters generally give bad estimates while ICM does poor inference due to the problem of label initialization.

7   Discussion

7.1   Dynamics of SPA- and MMA-Based Learning

What is the origin of the complex dynamics of our proposed parameter learning methods (Figure 1)? In SPA and MMA we replace the expectations $\langle x_i \rangle_{\theta;y}$ and $\langle x_i x_j \rangle_{\theta;y}$ in the true likelihood gradient with approximations $f_i(\theta; y)$ and $g_{ij}(\theta; y) = f_i(\theta; y)f_j(\theta; y)$ obtained from MAP and MPM label estimates. These estimates are necessarily discrete values in the set $\{-1, +1\}$, and therefore $f_i(\theta; y)$ and $g_{ij}(\theta; y)$ are piecewise constant functions of the parameter $\theta \in \Theta$. In other words, the discrete label estimates induce a partition $\{\Theta_k\}$ of parameter space Θ into a disjoint union $\cup_k \Theta_k$ where $f_i(\theta; y)$ and $g_{ij}(\theta; y)$ are constant within each cell Θ_k. By substitution, the approximate gradient $J(\theta)$ is also piecewise constant for the same partition $\{\Theta_k\}$ of Θ.

As a consequence, integral curves through vector field $J(\theta)$ will be piecewise linear, with "kinks" at the boundaries between cells, say between Θ_k and $\Theta_{k'}$. Our approximate gradient ascent with its finite step size will therefore result in a sequence of parameters along piecewise linear trajectories.

One cannot generally expect these trajectories to terminate, as that would require $J(\theta)$ to be identically zero for all θ in some cell Θ_k. To understand why, consider the double sum in (5) as a product $\frac{1}{2}H(x - f)$ of the matrix $H = [h_i(y^m)]$ with vector $x - f$, where $x = [x_i^m]$ and $f = [f_i(\theta; y^m)]$. Now, $J(\theta) = 0$ requires that $x - f$ be in the nullspace of H. Because both training labels and the label estimates are discrete, the components $x_i^m - f_i(\theta; y^m)$ of $x - f$ will be one of the integers -2, 0, or +2. But the subset of real matrices H that have an integer vector in their nullspace has measure zero, and therefore the possibility that $(x - f) \in$ nullspace H is both unlikely and unstable. Generally, therefore, the approximate gradient ascent using SPA or MMA will not stop.

In the simpler case of true gradient ascent, for a sufficiently small step size η, the parameter updates converge (without stopping) in a neighborhood of a stationary point of the gradient vector field where the gradient is zero. Why does this ascent converge? Because this gradient vector field is smooth and thus the gradients along the ascent become arbitrarily small near the stationary point, automatically slowing the ascent.

Although our approximate gradients $J(\theta)$ may become small in the vicinity of the true maximum likelihood solution, they cannot become *arbitrarily* small because they are quantized, and therefore the trajectories never slow down beyond some nonzero lower bound. Indeed, our empirical results show a quasi-cyclical behavior of the parameter trajectories. Similar behavior, called *limit cycles*, is common in digital control systems and signal processing, and arises from quantizing states and coefficients in continuous dynamical systems. Such limit cycles have been observed with small oscillations after a single initial transient or with quasi-periodic transients followed by small oscillations. The small oscillation case corresponds to a parameter trajectory passing in a tight loop through nearby portions of abutting cells, say $\Theta_k, \Theta_{k'}$, and $\Theta_{k''}$, which all have small approximate gradients. But there is no guarantee that cells with small and large approximate gradients will not be adjacent. Thus the observed "wild" transient behavior in Figure 1 can arise from several adjacent cells with small approximate gradient linked by cells with large approximate gradient: most of the time is spent in the cells with small approximate gradient, but rapid change occurs in cells with large gradient. To summarize, discretization can account for these limit cycle dynamics.

7.2   The Role of Classification Errors in Parameter Learning

Given these limit cycle dynamics, how may one choose the best parameter along the trajectory? Approximate gradients alone may be misleading, as there may be large approximate gradients nearer to the optimal solution than some small approximate gradients. In true gradient ascent, one may use the likelihood itself as "yard stick" for choosing the best parameter, e.g., at the maximal likelihood observed on the trajectory. The likelihood is also useful in diagnosing pathological dynamics from too large a step size, e.g., if the likelihood decreased significantly. From a dynamical systems perspective, the likelihood exists because the gradient is, by construction, *integrable.*

Instead we have only approximate gradients, which may not be integrable: they may not be the actual gradient of any function. In other words, there may be no approximate likelihood for our approximate gradient!

To overcome this lack of an approximate likelihood, we guide our choice of parameter using the number of classification errors, a widely-employed performance criterion in parameter learning.[3] But what inference algorithm should one use to measure these classification errors? In keeping with the coupling of parameter learning and inference first discussed in Section 3.2, we compute the number

---

[3] Ideally, one would like to minimize the generalization error, i.e., expected error on the test set. This is a combination of the training error and the complexity of the learned classifier.

of errors N_E^θ at parameter estimate θ using the inference method used in the gradient approximation (7), i.e., $N_E^\theta = (1/2)\sum_m \sum_{i \in S} |x_i - f_i(\theta)| = (1/2)\|\boldsymbol{x} - \boldsymbol{f}\|$, where $\|\cdot\|$ is the L_1 norm. Formally, this choice is motivated by the following simple bound.

Lemma 1. $\|\boldsymbol{J}(\theta)\| \leq cN_E^\theta$, for some $c > 0$.

In other words, the number of errors provides an upper bound on the approximate gradient. Note that matching the inference method used in both the number of errors and the approximate gradient is required in the following proof of the lemma.

Proof. Recall that $\boldsymbol{J}(\theta) = (\boldsymbol{J_1}(\theta), \boldsymbol{J_2}(\theta))$. Using the form of $\boldsymbol{J_1}(\theta)$ in (5), $\|\boldsymbol{J_1}(\theta)\| \leq R N_E^\theta$, where $R = \max_{i,m} \|\boldsymbol{h}_i(\boldsymbol{y}^m)\|$. Now, define the pairwise error $N_P^\theta := (1/2)\sum_m \sum_{i \in S} \sum_{j \in \mathcal{N}_i} |x_i x_j - f_i(\theta; \boldsymbol{y}^m)f_j(\theta; \boldsymbol{y}^m)|$. Using the form of $\boldsymbol{J_2}(\theta)$ in (6) with $g_{ij}(\theta; \boldsymbol{y}^m) = f_i(\theta; \boldsymbol{y}^m)f_j(\theta; \boldsymbol{y}^m)$, it is easy to see that $\|\boldsymbol{J_2}(\theta)\| \leq 2Q \, N_P^\theta$, where $Q = \max_{ijm} \|\boldsymbol{\mu}_{ij}(\boldsymbol{y}^m)\|$. This implies that $\|\boldsymbol{J_2}(\theta)\| \leq 2QdN_E^\theta$, since $N_P^\theta \leq dN_E^\theta$, where d is the maximum degree of the graph, i.e., $d = \max_i |\mathcal{N}_i|$. Combining these results, we have $\|\boldsymbol{J}(\theta)\| = \|\boldsymbol{J_1}(\theta)\| + \|\boldsymbol{J_2}(\theta)\| \leq (R + 2Qd)N_E^\theta$, as required. QED.

This bound is useful in two ways. First, if $\|\boldsymbol{J}(\theta)\|$ is large, then N_E^θ is also large as verified in the plots in Figure 1. Second, if at some θ, N_E^θ is small, $\|\boldsymbol{J}(\theta)\|$ will also be small. Thus, for a suitably small step size η, the parameter change will also be small. This would mean that one will stay in a low error zone for a long period as seen in Figure 1.

Indeed, given the importance we put in the number of classification errors, one might ask whether minimizing N_E^θ itself should be used as a starting point for *deriving* parameter learning algorithms. Unfortunately, since the number of errors is piecewise constant in the parameters, its gradient is zero except on a set of measure zero. The number of errors is therefore useless to derive a gradient-based learning algorithm as known from the perceptron learning literature [18].

7.3   Related Work

The problem of learning the parameters of loopy discriminative graphs has been addressed before under different paradigms. In a non-probabilistic setting, Taskar et al. [19] learn the model parameters by maximizing the margin. Lecun and Huang [20] have described the sufficient conditions for the training of energy-based (unnormalized) graphical models. In our previous work [1], we proposed the use of penalized pseudo-likelihood that gives reasonable estimates of the parameters. However, this needs hand-tuning of the regularizing constant. Finally, taking the Bayesian view, Qi et al.[21] have argued for integrating the parameters while predicting the labels on a test input instead of using a point estimate of the parameters using maximum likelihood. Integrating the parameters, however, is generally a difficult task.

8   Conclusion and Future Work

We have presented an approach for learning the parameters of discriminative field models that uses inference to approximate the gradients used in maximum likelihood learning. We showed that the proposed approximations lead to a limit cycle convergence behavior of the learning procedures. Further, the learned parameters lead to good classification performance so long as the method used for approximating the gradient is consistent with the inference mechanism. We also provided an experimental comparison of commonly used learning and inference techniques for discriminative fields. For MAP inference, SPA based learning was found to be most accurate as well as efficient. Similarly, for MPM inference, PMA and MMA performed best. Although we restricted ourselves to binary fields in this paper, we have already used maximum marginal approximation to successfully learn more than 3000 parameters for multiclass DRFs applied to object detection [4]. We are currently evaluating the performance of the proposed approximate parameter learning procedures with conventional MRFs.

Acknowledgments. Our thanks to T. Minka for very helpful discussions on SPA based learning. Thanks to V. Kolmogorov, J. Lafferty and R. Mugizi for providing the min-cut code.

References

1. S. Kumar and M. Hebert. Discriminative fields for modeling spatial dependencies in natural images. *in adv. in Neural Information Processing Systems (NIPS)*, 2004.
2. J. Lafferty, A. McCallum, and F. Pereira. Conditional random fields: Probabilistic models for segmenting and labeling sequence data. *In Proc. Int. Conf. on Machine Learning*, 2001.
3. F. Sha and F. Pereira. Shallow parsing with conditional random fields. *In Proc. Human Language Technology-NAACL*, 2003.
4. S. Kumar and M. Hebert. Multiclass discriminative fields for parts-based object detection. *Snowbird Learning Workshop, Utah*, 2004.
5. G. E. Hinton. Training product of experts by minimizing contrastive divergence. *Neural Computation*, 14:1771–1800, 2002.
6. Z.W. Tu and S.C. Zhu. Image segmentation by data-driven markov chain monte carlo. *IEEE Trans on Pattern Analysis and Machine Intelligence*, 24(5):657–673, 2002.
7. C. K. I. Williams and F. V. Agakov. *An Analysis of Contrastive Divergence Learning in Gaussian Boltzmann Machines*. EDI-INF-RR-0120, Informatics Research Report, May 2002.
8. M. J. Wainwright, T. Jaakkola, and A. S. Willsky. Tree-reweighted belief propagation and approximate ml estimation by pseudo-moment matching. *9th Workshop on AI Stat*, 2003.
9. A. McCallum, K. Rohanimanesh, and C. Sutton. Dynamic conditional random fields for jointly labeling multiple sequences. *NIPS'03 workshop on Syntax, Semantics and Statistic*, 2003.
10. J. S. Yedidia, W. T. Freeman, and Yair Weiss. Generalized belief propagation. *In Advances Neural Information Processing Systems*, 13:689–695, 2001.

11. D. Geiger and F. Girosi. Parallel and deterministic algorithms from mrf's: Surface reconstruction. *IEEE Trans PAMI*, 5(5):401–412, May 1991.
12. Y. LeCun, L. Bottou, Y. Bengio, and P Haffner. Gradient-based learning applied to document recognition. *Proc. of the IEEE*, 86(11):2278–2324, 1998.
13. M. Collins. Discriminative training methods for hidden markov models: Theory and experiments with perceptron algorithms. *In Proc. EMNLP*, 2002.
14. Y. Freund and R. Schapire. Large margin classification using the perceptron algorithm. *Machine Learning*, 37(3):277–296, 1999.
15. J. Besag. On the statistical analysis of dirty pictures. *Journal of Royal Statistical Soc.*, B-48:259–302, 1986.
16. D. M. Greig, B. T. Porteous, and A. H. Seheult. Exact maximum a posteriori estimation for binary images. *Journal of Royal Statis. Soc.*, 51(2):271–279, 1989.
17. Kevin Murphy, Antonio Torralba, and William T. Freeman. Using the forest to see the trees:a graphical model relating features, objects and scenes. *in Advances in Neural Information Processing Systems (NIPS 03)*, 2003.
18. R. O. Duda, P. E. Hart, and D. G. Stork. *Pattern Classification*. John Wiley, New York, 2001.
19. B. Taskar, C. Guestrin, and D. Koller. Max-margin markov network. *Neural Information Processing Systems Conference (NIPS03)*, 2003.
20. Y. LeCun and F. J. Huang. Loss functions for discriminative training of energy-based models. *AI-Stats*, 2005.
21. Yuan Qi, Martin Szummer, and Thomas P. Minka. Bayesian conditional random fields. *AI & Statistics*, 2005.

Part II

Combinatorial Approaches

Probabilistic Subgraph Matching Based on Convex Relaxation

Christian Schellewald and Christoph Schnörr

Computer Vision, Graphics, and Pattern Recognition Group,
Department of Mathematics and Computer Science,
University of Mannheim, D-68131 Mannheim, Germany
{cschelle, schnoerr}@ti.uni-mannheim.de
http://www.cvgpr.uni-mannheim.de

Abstract. We present a novel approach to the matching of subgraphs for object recognition in computer vision. Feature similarities between object model and scene graph are complemented with a regularization term that measures differences of the relational structure. For the resulting quadratic integer program, a mathematically tight relaxation is derived by exploiting the degrees of freedom of the embedding space of positive semidefinite matrices. We show that the global minimum of the relaxed convex problem can be interpreted as probability distribution over the original space of matching matrices, providing a basis for efficiently sampling all close-to-optimal combinatorial matchings within the original solution space. As a result, the approach can even handle completely ambiguous situations, despite uniqueness of the relaxed convex problem. Exhaustive numerical experiments demonstrate the promising performance of the approach which – up to a single inevitable regularization parameter that weights feature similarity against structural similarity – is free of any further tuning parameters.

1 Introduction

Recognition of objects by matching relational structures of local features is a key problem of computer vision. Since such structures were suggested for image analysis in 1971 by Barrow and Popplestone [1], a very broad range of approaches have been suggested to cope with the inherent combinatorial complexity of the corresponding matching problem. A non-exhaustive list of relevant work includes tree search algorithms [2], evolutionary strategies [3], spectral approaches [4, 5], the expectation maximization framework [6], matching of structures in terms of generalized maximum clique search [7], interpolation-based matching [8], metric embedding [9], matching by graph seriation and sequence alignment [10], and exact probabilistic inference using sparse graphical models with computationally feasible junction trees [11]. Since a general discussion of related work is beyond the scope of this contribution, we refer to [12] for a recent survey.

The specific motivation for our work comes from two different directions. The first line of research originates from independent work of Gold and Rangarajan [13] and Ishii and Sato [14] on deterministic annealing strategies for the matching

A. Rangarajan et al. (Eds.): EMMCVPR 2005, LNCS 3757, pp. 171–186, 2005.
© Springer-Verlag Berlin Heidelberg 2005

of relational structures with *equal* number of nodes over the convex hull of all permutation matrices (cf. also [15, 16]). The second line of research concerns specific instances of the general pattern of convex relaxations of combinatorial integer programming problems [17, 18] to the specific problem addressed in [13, 14], the quadratic assignment problem [19, 20]. Using established benchmark tests [21], a thorough experimental comparison of both approaches [22] revealed similar performance, provided the used parameters for deterministic annealing [13, 14] are optimized for each problem instance, whereas no parameter tuning is necessary for a convex relaxation approach [19, 20].

The applicability of approaches related to the quadratic assignment problem is limited to the matching of relational structures with feature sets of (almost) equal cardinality. From the viewpoint of computer vision, such approaches are not applicable to the more frequent scenario of matching *smaller model graphs* representing typical object views, to *larger scene graphs* representing current observations – see Figure 1 for an illustration.

The present paper is an attempt to overcome this limitation by a novel optimization approach to subgraph matching. From the computational viewpoint, we consistently use semidefinite relaxation, as motivated by the discussion above, and by its performance in connection various combinatorial problems in computer vision [23, 24]. Besides obtaining parameter-free algorithms, we point out an additional benefit of this relaxation strategy – the interpretation of the globally optimal solution to the relaxed problem as probability distribution over the original combinatorial solution space. While this possibility is obvious from the mathematical viewpoint, it is by no means clear that this conveys useful information about the complex original solution space. This interpretation shows, however, that uniqueness in a larger embedding space is associated with the explicit representation of multiple hypotheses in the original space. In particular, our approach can cope with ambiguous situations. This accounts for a another novel aspect of our contribution.

Organization. We design a variational problem to subgraph matching in section 2. The domain of the resulting quadratic functional is the space of binary matching matrices. The optimality of the matchings is defined in terms of feature similarities and structural similarities, weighted by a single regularization parameter. In section 3, a semidefinite relaxation of this combinatorial optimization problem is derived. The additional degrees of freedom of the larger embedding space are exploited to incorporate constraints of the original problem formulation, thus tightening the relaxation mathematically. A probabilistic interpretation of the corresponding globally optimal solution and its ability to cope with ambiguous situations, is discussed in section 4. We summarize exhaustive numerical experiments in section 5 that characterize the performance of our approach.

Notation. We will use the following notation throughout this paper:

$x^\top$: transpose of x; I_n: $n \times n$ unit matrix; e_n: vector of all ones: $(e_n)_i = 1$, $i = 1, \ldots, n$; E_{nn}: matrix of all ones: $E_{nn} = ee^\top$; $\mathrm{Tr}[X]$ trace of the matrix X; $A \otimes B$:

Kronecker product of matrices A and B; δ_{ij}: Kronecker delta: $\delta_{ij} = 1$ if $i = j$, and 0 otherwise; $\mathcal{M}^{n \times m}$: set of $n \times m$ matching matrices; diag(X): vector of the diagonal elements of the matrix X.

2 Variational Approach

In this paper, we consider undirected graphs $G = (V, E)$ with nodes $V = \{1, \dots, n\}$ and edges $E \subset V \times V$. We denote the model graph with G_K and the scene graph with G_L. The corresponding sets V_K and V_L contain $K = |V_K|$ and $L = |V_L|$ nodes respectively. We assume $L \geq K$. Furthermore, we assume a distance function $w(i, j)$ to be given which measures the similarity of each pair of vertices $i \in V_K$ and $j \in V_L$.

Graphs representing object views are called *model graphs* or *object graphs* in this paper. In the same way as model graphs, *scene graphs* are computed by extracting local image features and spatial relationships in a preprocessing step. Our aim is to find a reasonable matching between the nodes of the model graph and the scene graph. In figure 1 a example for a subgraph matching problem is shown. The left object graph G_K has to be matched against the scene graph G_L. We do not discuss image preprocessing in this paper (cf. section 5.1, first paragraph) but assume the model and scene graphs to be given, along with a similarity between the nodes of the different graphs.

Fig. 1. The object graph G_K (left) with $K = 12$ nodes has to be matched against the scene graph (left) with $L = 41$ nodes. Local feature information is ambiguous.

2.1 Bipartite Matching

If we ignore the structure in both the model and the scene graph, then an optimal assignment of the K vertices of the model graph can be easily found as a matching in the bipartite graph $(V_K \cup V_L, E)$, with edges $(i, j) \in E$, defined for all pairs $i \in V_K, j \in V_L$ with corresponding weights $w(j, i)$.

Let $x \in \{0, 1\}^{KL}$ denote the 0/1-indicator vector for the bipartite matching between the nodes of the object and scene graph. A element $X_{ji} = 1$ indicates that the node i of the first set V_K is matched to the node j in the second set V_L. The elements of the indicator vector are ordered as follows:

$$x = (X_{11}, \cdots, X_{L1}, X_{12}, \cdots, X_{L2}, \cdots, X_{1K}, \cdots, X_{LK})^\top. \tag{1}$$

Thus the indicator vector x can be interpreted as a sequence of appended columns of a matching matrix $X \in \mathcal{M}^{L \times K}$. With the same order we denote the weight vector $(w(1,1), \cdots w(L,K))^\top$ with w.

Then using $A_K = I_K \otimes e_L^\top$ and $A_L = e_K^\top \otimes I_L$, the optimal bipartite matching between the two node sets can be found by solving the following linear integer program:

$$\min_x \; w^\top x \quad \text{s.t.} \; A_K x = e_K, \; A_L x \leq e_L, \; x \in \{0,1\}^{KL} \tag{2}$$

The constraints ensure that the feasible vectors x all represent a bipartite mapping. The totally unimodular matrix $A = (A_K^\top, A_L^\top)^\top$ along with the integer valued data of the equality and inequality constraints guarantees that (2) can easily be solved by the following linear program which has a integral solution (cf., e.g., [25, 26]):

$$\min_x \; w^\top x \quad \text{s.t.} \; A_K x = e_K, \; A_L x \leq e_L, \; x \geq 0 \tag{3}$$

2.2   Quadratic Integer Program

To incorporate the relational structure of both the model graph and the scene graph, we extend the linear integer program (2) with a quadratic term $x^\top Q x$. The non-negative parameter $\alpha \in \mathbb{R}^+$ is added to control the influence of these additional costs. Formally the quadratic integer program then reads:

$$\min_x \; w^\top x + \alpha x^\top Q x \quad \text{s.t.} \; A_K x = e_K, \; A_L x \leq e_L, \; x \in \{0,1\}^{KL} \tag{4}$$

As before, the matching constraints are defined by the linear constraints. The matrix $Q \in \mathbb{R}^{KL \times KL}$ in the quadratic term of (4) to be specified below involves the symmetric 0/1-adjacency matrices N_K, N_L of the model graph and the scene graph, respectively, which encode the neighborhood structure in these two graphs. To simplify the notation we define also the *Complementary Adjacency Matrices*.

Definition 1. *Complementary Adjacency Matrices*

$$\bar{N}_L = E_{LL} - N_L - I_L \qquad \bar{N}_K = E_{KK} - N_K - I_K$$

These matrices can be interpreted as indicator matrices for *non-adjacent* nodes. They have the element $(\bar{N})_{ij} = 1$ if the corresponding nodes i and j are not directly connected in the graph.

For example, the adjacency matrix N_K and the appropriate complementary adjacency matrix for a house-like model graph are shown in figure 2. With this

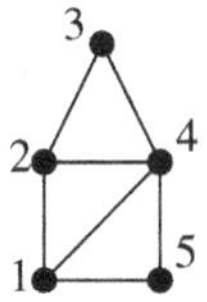

$$N_K = \begin{pmatrix} 0 & 1 & 0 & 1 & 1 \\ 1 & 0 & 1 & 1 & 0 \\ 0 & 1 & 0 & 1 & 0 \\ 1 & 1 & 1 & 0 & 1 \\ 1 & 0 & 0 & 1 & 0 \end{pmatrix}$$

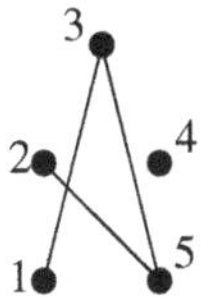

$$\bar{N}_K = \begin{pmatrix} 0 & 0 & 1 & 0 & 0 \\ 0 & 0 & 0 & 0 & 1 \\ 1 & 0 & 0 & 0 & 1 \\ 0 & 0 & 0 & 0 & 0 \\ 0 & 1 & 1 & 0 & 0 \end{pmatrix}$$

Fig. 2. Example object graph and its adjacency matrix N_K along with its complementary adjacency matrix $\bar{N}_K$

notation and referring to the order of the set of edges defined in (1), the symmetric *Relational Structure Matrix* Q in (4) incorporating the relational structure is defined in the following.

Definition 2. *Relational Structure Matrix*

$$Q = N_K \otimes \bar{N}_L + \bar{N}_K \otimes N_L \tag{5}$$

We explain in detail the two terms on the right hand side of (5) which are used to construct the matrix Q:

- The first term in the quadratic expression $x^\top Q x$ can be written as:

$$x^\top (N_K \otimes \bar{N}_L)x = \sum_{ar}^{KL} \sum_{bs}^{KL} (N_K)_{ab}(\bar{N}_L)_{rs} x_{ar} x_{bs} \tag{6}$$

The interpretation of this term is that if two nodes a and b in the model graph are neighbors, $(N_K)_{ab} = 1$, then a good assignment (no costs) involves corresponding nodes r and s in the scene graph which are neighbors, too: $(\bar{N}_L)_{rs} = 0$. For such a configuration no cost is added in (6). Otherwise if the corresponding nodes r and s are no neighbors in the scene graph, $(\bar{N}_L)_{rs} = 1$, then a cost of 1 is added. This two configurations are visualized in figure 3.

- Analogously, the second term in $x^T Q x$ gives:

$$x^\top (\bar{N}_K \otimes N_L)x = \sum_{ar}^{KL} \sum_{bs}^{KL} (\bar{N}_K)_{ab}(N_L)_{rs} x_{ar} x_{bs} \tag{7}$$

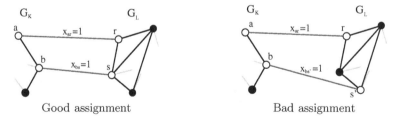

Good assignment   Bad assignment

Fig. 3. Left: Adjacent nodes a and b in the model graph G_K are assigned to adjacent nodes r and s in the scene graph G_L. **Right.** Adjacent model nodes a and b are no longer adjacent in the scene graph G_L after the assignment. The left assignment leads to no additional costs while the right undesired assignment adds 1 to the cost term (6).

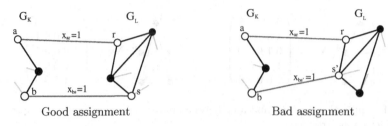

Good assignment   Bad assignment

Fig. 4. Left: Nodes a and b which are not adjacent in the object graph G_K are assigned to nodes which are also not adjacent in the scene graph G_L. **Right:** A pair of nodes a and b become neighbors r and s' after assignment. The left assignment is associated with no additional costs in (7). The undesired assignment on the right side adds 1 to these costs.

This term penalizes assignments where pairs of nodes in the object graph become neighbors in the scene graph which were not adjacent before. Figure 4 illustrates this situation in detail.

Note that due to the symmetry of the quadratic cost term $x^\top Q x$, every difference in the compared structure of the two graphs is penalized with a cost of 2.

In contrast to the linear bipartite matching problem (2), the computation of the global optimum of the quadratic optimization problem (4), which incorporates the object and scene structure, is intrinsically difficult (NP-hard). Therefore, we derive in the next section a tractable convex relaxation of this NP-hard problem in order to compute a "good" local minimum.

3   Convex Problem Relaxation

The combinatorial subgraph matching approach (4) will be relaxed to a (convex) semidefinite program (SDP) which has the following standard form:

$$\min \ \operatorname{Tr}\left[\tilde{Q}X\right]$$
$$\text{s.t. } \operatorname{Tr}[A_i X] = c_i \quad \text{for} \quad i = 1, \ldots, m \tag{8}$$
$$X \succeq 0$$

The last constraint in (8) says that X has to be positive semidefinite. We wish to emphasize once more that this convex optimization problem can be solved with standard methods like interior point algorithms. Note that the solution of the relaxation (8) provides a lower bound to (4).

Below, we describe step by step how we derive such a semidefinite program from (4). While in section 3.1, we derive an appropriate SDP objective function, we show in section 3.2 how the bipartite matching constraints can be incorporated into the SDP (8). For more information on semidefinite programming we refer to [27].

3.1   SDP Objective Function

In order to obtain an appropriate SDP relaxation for the combinatorial subgraph matching problem, we start with reformulating the objective function of (4) into a homogeneous quadratic form. And this can be stated directly in the appropriate trace formulation of objective function for the semidefinite relaxation (8) using the cyclic commutativity of the trace:

$$f(x) = w^\top x + \alpha x^\top Q x = \begin{pmatrix} 1 & x^\top \end{pmatrix} \begin{pmatrix} 0 & \frac{1}{2} w^\top \\ \frac{1}{2} w & \alpha Q \end{pmatrix} \begin{pmatrix} 1 \\ x \end{pmatrix} = \mathrm{Tr} \left[\tilde{Q} X \right] \qquad (9)$$

Here we denote with $\tilde{Q} \in \mathbb{R}^{(KL+1) \times (KL+1)}$ and $X \in \mathbb{R}^{(KL+1) \times (KL+1)}$ the following symmetric matrices:

$$\tilde{Q} = \begin{pmatrix} 0 & \frac{1}{2} w^\top \\ \frac{1}{2} w & \alpha Q \end{pmatrix} , \quad X = \begin{pmatrix} 1 \\ x \end{pmatrix} \begin{pmatrix} 1 & x^\top \end{pmatrix} = \begin{pmatrix} 1 & x^\top \\ x & x x^\top \end{pmatrix} \qquad (10)$$

Besides being symmetric, the matrix X is positive semidefinite and has rank 1. We relax the objective function by dropping the rank 1 condition of X which makes the set of feasible matrices convex [27]. This lifts the original problem (4) defined in a vector space with dimension KL into the space of symmetric, positive semidefinite matrices with the dimension $(KL + 1) \times (KL + 1)$.

3.2   SDP Constraints

We wish to incorporate several constraints into the SDP relaxation by specifying appropriate constraint matrices $A_i \in \mathbb{R}^{(KL+1) \times (KL+1)}$. These SDP constraints will have the form:

$$\mathrm{Tr}[A_i X] = c_i \quad \text{for} \quad i = 1, \ldots, m$$

In particular, we introduce four types of constraints which correspond to the homogeneous formulation of the problem, the 0/1-integer constraints, and the bipartite matching constraints, respectively.

We next discuss in detail how the appropriate constraint matrices A_i can be defined in terms of the Kronecker delta which make the implementation of our approach easier:

- The first constraint we take into account results from the homogenization (9). To restrict the element $X_{11} = 1$ in the matrix X, we introduce a constraint matrix $^{\mathrm{one}}A$ whose elements can be expressed as

$$^{\mathrm{one}}A_{kl} = \delta_{k1} \delta_{l1} \quad \text{for} \quad k, l = 1, \ldots, KL + 1 ,$$

where we make use of the Kronecker delta. Note that $^{\mathrm{one}}A$ has only $^{\mathrm{one}}A_{11} = 1$ as non-zero element.
- The second type of constraint we consider is derived from the integer constraints $x_i \in \{0, 1\}, i = 1, \ldots, KL$, which can be rewritten as $x_i^2 = x_i, i = 1, \ldots, KL$. If we consider the matrix X before it is relaxed (see (10)) we

observe that due to $x_i^2 = x_i$ the 0/1-integer elements on the diagonal of X must be equal to the 0/1-integer elements in the first column and row of X. Therefore the 0/1-integer constraints can be *weakly* enforced in the relaxed problem by requiring the first column and row of X to be equal to its diagonal. To implement these constraints, we introduce KL constraint matrices $^{\text{int}}A^j \in \mathbb{R}^{(KL+1)\times(KL+1)}, j = 2, \ldots, KL + 1$. We define these constraint matrices to have a 2 at the appropriate diagonal element and -1 at the corresponding elements in the first column and the first row. All other elements are zero. Using the Kronecker delta the elements of the j-th constraint matrix $^{\text{int}}A^j$ can be written as:

$$^{\text{int}}A_{kl}^j = 2\delta_{kj}\delta_{lj} - \delta_{kj}\delta_{l1} - \delta_{lj}\delta_{k1} \quad \text{for} \quad k, l = 1, \ldots, KL + 1$$

- The third type of constraint we take into account are the equality constraints $\sum_{j=1}^{L} x_{ij} = 1, i = 1, \ldots, K$, which are part of the bipartite matching constraints in (4). They represent the constraint that each node of the smaller graph is mapped to exactly one node of the scene graph. We define K constraint matrices $^{\text{sum}}A^j \in \mathbb{R}^{(KL+1)\times(KL+1)}, j = 1, \ldots, K$ which ensure (taking the order of the diagonal elements into account) that the sum of the appropriate portion of the diagonal elements of X is 1. We exploited again the fact that $x_i = x_i^2$ holds true for 0/1-variables. The matrix elements for the j-th constraint matrix $^{\text{sum}}A^j$ can be expressed as follows:

$$^{\text{sum}}A_{kl}^j = \sum_{i=(j-1)L+1}^{jL+1} \delta_{ik}\delta_{il} \quad \text{for} \quad k, l = 1, \ldots, KL + 1$$

- The fourth type of constraint is related to the observation that the bipartite matching constraints in (2) have a direct impact to certain matrix elements of the sub-matrix $\tilde{X} = xx^\top$ of X. If $x \in \{0,1\}^{KL}$ represents a bipartite matching then certain elements in $\tilde{X}$ must be zero. Affected elements can be determined by inspecting the following two cost terms which penalize matchings that do not meet the bipartite matching constraints.

$$x^\top(I_K \otimes (E_{LL} - I_L))x = \sum_{ar}^{KL}\sum_{bs}^{KL}(I_K)_{ab}(E_{LL} - I_L)_{rs}x_{ar}x_{bs} \qquad (11)$$

$$x^\top((E_{KK} - I_K) \otimes I_L)x = \sum_{ar}^{KL}\sum_{bs}^{KL}(E_{KK} - I_K)_{ab}(I_L)_{rs}x_{ar}x_{bs} \qquad (12)$$

The first of these two terms penalizes non-unique assignments of model nodes to scene nodes. Analogously, the second term penalizes assignments where different nodes of the model graph are mapped to the same node in the scene graph. Thus, in summary, the two terms penalize all assignments which do no lead to a bipartite matching. Figure 5 illustrates such configurations in detail. All integer solutions $\tilde{X} = xx^\top \in \mathbb{R}^{KL\times KL}$, where x represents a bipartite matching, have zero-values at those matrix positions where $I_K \otimes (E_{LL} - I_L)$

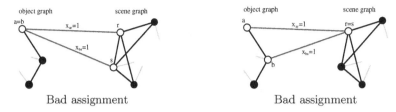

Fig. 5. Assignments which do not lead to bipartite matchings are penalized by the quadratic terms (11) and (12)

and $(E_{KK} - I_K) \otimes I_L$ have non-zero elements. Accordingly, we want to force the corresponding elements in $X \in \mathbb{R}^{(KL+1) \times (KL+1)}$ to be zero. Fortunately, this can be achieved with the constraint matrices $^{\text{zeros1}}A^{ars}$, $^{\text{zeros2}}A^{\hat{s}\hat{a}\hat{b}} \in \mathbb{R}^{(KL+1) \times (KL+1)}$ which are determined by the indices a, r, s and $\hat{s}, \hat{a}, \hat{b}$. They have the following matrix elements

$$^{\text{zeros1}}A^{ars}_{kl} = \delta_{k,(aL+r+1)}\delta_{l,(aL+s+1)} + \delta_{k,(aL+s+1)}\delta_{l,(aL+r+1)} \;, \tag{13}$$

$$^{\text{zeros2}}A^{\hat{s}\hat{a}\hat{b}}_{kl} = \delta_{k,(\hat{s}K+\hat{b}+1)}\delta_{l,(\hat{s}K+\hat{a}+1)} + \delta_{k,(\hat{s}K+\hat{a}+1))}\delta_{l,(\hat{s}K+\hat{b}+1)} \;, \tag{14}$$

where $k, l = 1, \ldots, KL + 1$. Note that each of these matrices has only two non-zero matrix elements at symmetric positions. The indices a, r, s and $\hat{s}, \hat{a}, \hat{b}$ attain all valid combinations of the following triples where $s > r$ and $\hat{b} > \hat{a}$:

$$(a, r, s): \; a = 1, \ldots, K; \; r = 1, \ldots, L; \; s = (r+1), \ldots, L$$

$$(\hat{s}, \hat{a}, \hat{b}): \; \hat{s} = 1, \ldots, L; \; \hat{a} = 1, \ldots, K; \; \hat{b} = (\hat{a}+1), \ldots, K$$

With this we define $(LL - L)K/2 + (KK - K)L/2$ additional constraints that ensure zero-values at the corresponding matrix positions of X.

Altogether we have the following $1 + KL + K + (LL - L)K/2 + (KK - K)L/2$ SDP constraints:

$$\text{Tr}[^{\text{one}}AX] = 1$$
$$\text{Tr}[^{\text{int}}A^j X] = 0 \quad \text{for} \quad j = 2 \ldots, KL + 1$$
$$\text{Tr}[^{\text{sum}}A^j X] = 1 \quad \text{for} \quad j = 1, \ldots, K$$
$$\text{Tr}[^{\text{zeros1}}A^{ars}X] = 0 \quad \forall(a, r, s) \quad , \text{Tr}[^{\text{zeros2}}A^{\hat{s}\hat{a}\hat{b}}X] = 0 \quad \forall(\hat{s}, \hat{a}, \hat{b})$$

The name *gangster operator* was introduced in [28] for the last two constraint operators because they "shoot holes",i.e. zeros, into the matrix X.

We note here that we dropped the additional linear *inequality* constraints of the bipartite matching, $\sum_{i=1}^{K} x_{ij} \leq 1, \forall j$, which, in principle, can be incorporated by lifting schemes (see e.g. [27]). This, however, would considerably increase the number of constraints and slow down the computation. Our experiments (section 5) show that this does not compromise the performance of our approach.

4   Combinatorial Solutions by Post-processing

The diagonal elements of the global optimum $X_{bound} \in \mathbb{R}^{(KL+1)\times(KL+1)}$ to the semidefinite relaxation (8) can be interpreted as a non-integer approximation $\hat{x}_{sol} = \mathrm{diag}(X_{bound})$ to the solution of (4). Omitting the first element in $\hat{x}_{sol} \in \mathbb{R}^{KL+1}$, which was added due to the homogenization (9), we obtain the approximation $x_{sol} \in \mathbb{R}^{KL}$ for the indicator vector $x \in \{0,1\}^{KL}$.

4.1   Probabilistic Interpretation of the Non-integer Solution

According to the constraints $A_K x_{sol} = e_K$, we have for each node i of the model graph $\sum_j^L (x_{sol})_{ji} = 1$, $i = 1, \dots, K$. Hence, $(x_{sol})_{ji}$ may be considered as the probability that model node i matches to scene node j. To illustrate this interpretation, figure 6 shows a completely ambiguous situation, whereas figure 7 depicts for each of the five model nodes $i = 1, \dots, 5$ the values $(x_{sol})_{ji}$. The presence of equally likely matchings clearly shows that multiple plausible hypotheses for matchings can be represented through the convex problem relaxation. As explained next, and as validated in section 5, this property can be exploited to compute the final matching from x_{sol}.

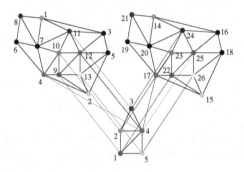

Fig. 6. Ambiguous situation with *two* global optima. The node colors indicate the similarity between the nodes of the object and the scene graph. Despite convexity and uniqueness, the semidefinite relaxation is able to represent multiple hypotheses for matching – see figure 7.

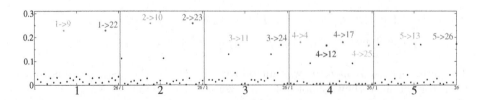

Fig. 7. The non-integer solution x_{sol} for the ambiguous matching situation shown in figure 6. The plot is subdivided into $K = 5$ segments, with the i-th segment ($i \in \{1, \dots, K\}$) representing all possible matchings from the model node i to all $L = 26$ nodes in the scene graph. In each segment the probabilities sum up to one.

4.2   Post-processing

Winner-Take-All Strategy. An obvious strategy for determining the final matching is to compute among all binary vectors x representing valid matchings the vector that is maximally aligned with x_{sol}:

$$\max_x x_{sol}^\top x \quad \text{s.t. } A_K x = e_K , \ A_L x \le e_L , \ x \in \{0,1\}^{KL} \tag{15}$$

The exact solution to (15), denoted with x_{lin}^*, can be computed by solving a linear program because the constraint matrices A_K and A_L are total unimodular (cf. section 2.1). According to the probabilistic interpretation, x_{lin}^* represents the most probable matching.

Sampling. To exploit alternative hypotheses for valid matchings as well, we may randomly select a node $i \in \{1, \ldots, K\}$ of the model graph and assign to it a scene node $j \in \{1, \ldots, L\}$ by sampling from the distribution $(x_{sol})_{ji}, j = 1, \ldots, L$. This assignment is only accepted if it results in a valid matching representing an *improved* combinatorial solution. In our experiments, we conducted $10 \cdot KL$ such sampling steps, starting with the solution x_{lin}^* to (15). The resulting matching is denoted with $x_{sampling}^*$.

5   Experiments

5.1   Real World Example

For the problem shown in figure 1, we computed feature similarities (weights w) by determining the earth mover distance [29] between local gray value histograms for each node. We point out that more elaborate feature selection or even learning is beyond the scope of this paper, whose main focus is the optimization.

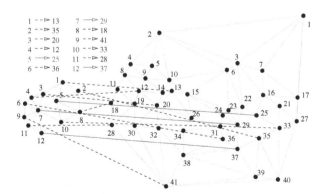

Fig. 8. Matching computed by the linear program (3) without regularization, i.e. sensitivity to relational structure. Only 3 out of the 12 assignments are correct (marked with red).

To demonstrate that the regularization in (4) is indeed necessary, we first computed the bipartite matching (3). The corresponding solution, shown in figure 8, just picks the locally best fitting scene graph nodes. Only the assignments drawn in red are correct.

The non-integer solution x_{sol} obtained by the SDP relaxation (8) of the approach (4), is shown in figure 9, where $(x_{sol})_{ji}$ is plotted for each model node $i = 1, \ldots, K$.

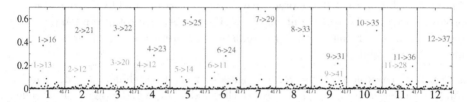

Fig. 9. The non-integer solution $(x_{sol})_{ji}$ for each model node $i = 1, \ldots, K = 12$, as obtained by the SDP relaxation. Only a few assignments have significantly large probabilities. The most likely ones are marked with red and green, respectively.

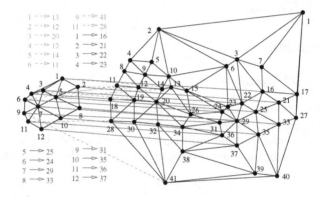

Fig. 10. SDP relaxation with winner take all post-processing results in the correct matching. An alternative hypothesis is shown by the green line segments.

Only a few mappings $i \mapsto j$ have significantly large probabilities $(x_{sol})_{ji}$. The most likely assignments are marked with red, and some alternative candidates with $(x_{sol})_{ji} \geq 0.1$ are marked with green. The corresponding matchings are shown in figure 10. The red assignments correspond to the optimal combinatorial solution which, in turn, corresponds to the solution x^*_{lin} to (15). Sampling, therefore, cannot lead to further improvements, in this case.

5.2   Generating Random Problem Instances

In order to get a more complete picture of the performance of our approach, we conducted a large series of experiments with randomly generated problem instances. Two kinds of experiments were considered:

Random Subgraph Problems. An object graph with K nodes is randomly created with an edge probability[1] equal to 0.5. Then the scene graph is created by copying the object graph and enlarging it to L nodes by adding $(L-K)$ random nodes and edges with edge probability 0.2. Hence, the model graph always forms a subgraph of the scene graph in this series of experiments. Costs $\{w_{ji}\}$ are selected randomly within the small range $0.4 \dots 0.6$ if the mapping of the object node i to the scene node j represents a desired mapping. Otherwise the costs are set randomly to a value within the wider range $0.4 \dots 1.0$. Note that the wider range includes the small range, which increases the probability that some undesired mappings have cheaper assignment costs w_{ji} than the desired mapping. Therefore, the linear matching approach (2), which ignores the graph structure, is likely to fail in all experiments.

We fixed the size of the object graph to $K = 9$ and varied the scene graph size from $L = 14$ to $L = 30$.

By construction, we know which subgraph of the scene corresponds to the object in each experiment. Accordingly, the corresponding matching is defined to be ground truth, irrespective of the existence of other accidental matchings with a better objective value (4) in some rare cases.

Random Model and Scene Graphs. In this series of experiments both object and scene graphs with K and L nodes, respectively, are created randomly, and independently from each other. The similarities w_{ji} are set randomly within the range $0.4 \dots 1.0$. The edge probability was set to 0.4 for the smaller model graph, and to 0.3 for the larger scene graph.

To compute ground truth, we have to rely on exhaustive search, forcing us to limit[2] the maximum size of the scene graph to $L = 19$.

For each size L, we created 1000 problem instances. The value of the regularization parameter α was 0.15 and 0.3 for the subgraph and purely random problems, respectively.

5.3   Evaluation

Fraction of Optimally Solved Problem Instances. Figure 11 shows the percentage of optimally[3] solved problem instances for various problem sizes K and L. We observe that for almost all smaller subgraph problems the global optimum is obtained by the convex relaxation followed by the winner take all post-processing step. The main observation, however, is that the sampling was always able to significantly increase the fraction of global optimal solutions. This confirms the usefulness of a probabilistic interpretation of the non-integer solution vector x_{sol} to the SDP relaxation. Furthermore, figure 11 shows that

---

[1] The edge probability is the probability that an edge of the underlying complete graph is present.

[2] The number of possible assignments growth as $L!/(L-K)!$.

[3] We count a solution as optimal if it has an equal or better objective value than the objective value of the correct matching.

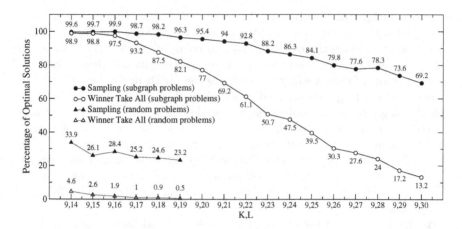

Fig. 11. Fraction of optimally solved problem instances for increasing problem sizes K and L. The sampling post-processing step significantly increases this fraction by exploiting the information in the non-integer solution vector x_{sol}.

the more structured subgraph matching problems are easier to solve than the purely random problem instances.

Quality of Optima. To get a more accurate picture of the performance of our approach, we investigated the quality of the combinatorial solutions. To this end, we computed the mean values along with the standard deviation of the ratios f^*_{lin}/f^*_{opt} and $f^*_{sampling}/f^*_{opt}$ for the solutions f^*_{lin} and $f^*_{sampling}$ obtained by the winner take all and the sampling post-processing step, respectively. A ratio close to 1 indicates that the obtained solution is close to the objective value f^*_{opt} of the true matching. The results are shown in table 1. We observe that the sampling post-processing step always improves the results obtained by the winner take all post-processing, and that the corresponding mean $f^*_{sampling}$ is very close to f^*_{opt}. For example, for the larger subgraph problems with $K = 9$, $L = 30$, the sampling improves the deviation from 35% to only 5%. Again, the random problems turn out to be more difficult to solve, but sampling still leads to good solutions close to the global optimum.

Table 1. Mean and standard deviation of the optima relative to the correct solution. A ratio close to 1 indicates that the computed solution is close to f^*_{opt}. Winner take all post-processing is always inferior to sampling. Note that the ratio for the subgraph problems can become smaller than 1 due to accidental matchings with smaller objective function value than that of the correct matching.

	K,L	9,15	9,17	9,19	9,25	9,30
subgraph problems	f^*_{lin}/f^*_{opt}	1.00 ± 0.01	1.01 ± 0.04	1.02 ± 0.08	1.17 ± 0.21	1.35 ± 0.24
	$f^*_{sampling}/f^*_{opt}$	0.99 ± 0.01	0.99 ± 0.01	1.00 ± 0.02	1.02 ± 0.06	1.05 ± 0.09
random problems	f^*_{lin}/f^*_{opt}	1.58 ± 0.36	1.74 ± 0.42	1.99 ± 0.49	n.a.	n.a.
	$f^*_{sampling}/f^*_{opt}$	1.10 ± 0.12	1.11 ± 0.12	1.14 ± 0.14	n.a.	n.a.

6   Conclusion

We proposed and investigated a novel approach to subgraph matching in computer vision using regularized bipartite matching, semidefinite relaxation, and a corresponding probabilistic post-processing step. A salient property of our approach is its mathematical simplicity: high-quality approximate solutions can be computed by just solving a *convex* optimization problem. As a consequence, no additional tuning parameters related to search heuristics, etc. are needed, apart from a single regularizing parameter penalizing structural differences of matchings. Extensive numerical experiments revealed a surprisingly good quality of the suboptimal solutions. Our approach provides a basis for learning optimal feature configurations for object recognition in future work.

References

1. H. G. Barrow and R.J. Popplestone. Relational descriptions in picture processing. *Machine Intelligence*, 6:377–396, 1971.
2. J.R. Ullmann. An algorithm for subgraph isomorphism. *Journal of the ACM*, 23(1):31–42, 1976.
3. A.D.J. Cross, R.C. Wilson, and E.R. Hancock. Inexact graph matching using genetic search. *Pattern Recog.*, 30(6):953–970, 1997.
4. S. Umeyama. An eigendecomposition approach to weighted graph matching problems. *IEEE Trans. Patt. Anal. Mach. Intell.*, 10(5):695–703, 1988.
5. B. Luo and E.R. Hancock. Structural graph matching using the em algorithm and singular value decomposition. *IEEE Trans. Patt. Anal. Mach. Intell.*, 23(10):1120–1136, 2001.
6. A.D.J. Cross and E.R. Hancock. Graph matching with a dual-step em algorithm. *IEEE Trans. Patt. Anal. Mach. Intell.*, 20(11):1236–1253, 1998.
7. M. Pavan and M. Pelillo. Dominant sets and hierarchical clustering. In *Proc. ICCV 2003 - 9th IEEE International Conference on Computer Vision*, volume 1, pages 362–369, 2003.
8. B.J. Van Wyk and M.A. Van Wyk. Kronecker product graph matching. *Patt. Recognition*, 36(9):2019–2030, 2003.
9. M.F. Demirci, A. Shoukoufandeh, Y. Keselman, S. Dickinson, and L. Bretzner. Many-to-many matching of scale-space feature hierarchies using metric embedding. In L.D. Griffin and M. Lillholm, editors, *Scale-Space 2003*, volume 2695 of *Lecture Notes in Computer Science*, pages 17–32. Springer, 2003.
10. A. Robles-Kelley and E.R. Hancock. Graph edit distance from spectral seriation. *IEEE Trans. Patt. Anal. Mach. Intell.*, 27(3):365–378, 2005.
11. T. Caelli and T.S. Caetano. Graphical models for graph matching: Approximate models and optimal algorithms. *Patt. Recog. Letters*, 26(3):339–346, 2005.
12. D. Conte, P. Foggia, C. Sansone, and M. Vento. Thirty years of graph matching in pattern recognition. *IJPRAI*, 18(3):265–298, 2004.
13. S. Gold and A. Rangarajan. A graduated assignment algorithm for graph matching. *IEEE Trans. Patt. Anal. Mach. Intell.*, 18(4):377–388, 1996.
14. S. Ishii and M. Sato. Doubly constrained network for combinatorial optimization. *Neurocomputing*, 43:239–257, 2002.
15. J.J. Kosowsky and A.L. Yuille. The invisible hand algorithm: Solving the assignment problem with statistical pyhysics. *Neural Networks*, 7(3):477–490, 1994.

16. A. Rangarajan, A. Yuille, and E. Mjolsness. Convergence properties of the softassign quadratic assignment algorithm. *Neural Computation*, 11(6):1455–1474, 1999.

17. F. Alizadeh. Interior point methods in semidefinite programming with applications to combinatorial optimization. *SIAM Journal on Optimization*, 5(1):13–51, 1995.

18. S. Poljak, F. Rendl, and H. Wolkowicz. A recipe for semidefinite relaxation for 0-1 quadratic programming. *Journal of Global Optimization*, (7):51–73, 1995.

19. Q. Zhao, S.E. Karisch, F. Rendl, and H. Wolkowicz. Semidefinite programming relaxations for the quadratic assignment problem. *J. Combinat. Optimization*, 2(1):71–109, 1998.

20. K. M. Anstreicher and N. W. Brixius. A new bound for the quadratic assignment problem based on convex quadratic programming. *Mathematical Programming*, 89(3):341–357, 2001.

21. R. E. Burkard, S. Karisch, and F. Rendl. QAPLIB-A Quadratic Assignment Problem Library. *European Journal of Operational Research*, 55:115–119, 1991.

22. C. Schellewald, S. Roth, and C. Schnörr. Evaluation of convex optimization techniques for the weighted graph-matching problem in computer vision. In B. Radig and S. Florczyk, editors, *Mustererkennung 2001*, volume 2191 of *Lect. Notes Comp. Science*, pages 361–368, Munich, Germany, Sept. 12–14 2001. Springer.

23. J. Keuchel, C. Schnörr, C. Schellewald, and D. Cremers. Binary partitioning, perceptual grouping, and restoration with semidefinite programming. *IEEE Trans. Patt. Anal. Mach. Intell.*, 25(11):1364–1379, 2003.

24. J. Keuchel, M. Heiler, and C. Schnörr. Hierarchical image segmentation based on semidefinite programming. In *Pattern Recognition, Proc. 26th DAGM Symposium*, volume 3175 of *Lecture Notes in Computer Science*, pages 120–128. Springer, 2004.

25. Alexander Schrijver. *Theory of linear and integer programming*. John Wiley & Sons, Inc. New York, NY, USA, 1986.

26. B. Korte and J. Vygen. *Combinatorial Optimization: Theory and Algorithms*. Algorithms and Combinatorics 21. Springer, Berlin Heidelberg New York, 2000.

27. H. Wolkowicz, R. Saigal, and L. Vandenberghe, editors. *Handbook of Semidefinite Programming*, Boston, 2000. Kluwer Acad. Publ.

28. Ph. L. Toint. On sparse and symmetric matrix updating subject to a linear equation. *Mathematics of Computation*, 31:954–961, 1977.

29. Y. Rubner, C. Tomasi, and L. J. Guibas. The earth mover's distance as a metric for image retrieval. *International Journal of Computer Vision*, 40(2):99–121, 2000.

Relaxation of Hard Classification Targets for LSE Minimization

Kar-Ann Toh[1], Xudong Jiang[2], and Wei-Yun Yau[3]

[1] Biometrics Engineering Research Center (BERC),
School of Electrical & Electronic Engineering,
Yonsei University, Seoul, Korea
katoh@ieee.org
[2] School of Electrical & Electronic Engineering,
Nanyang Technological University, Singapore
exdjiang@ntu.edu.sg
[3] Institute for Infocomm Research,
Heng Mui Keng Terrace, Singapore
wyyau@i2r.a-star.edu.sg

Abstract. In the spirit of stabilizing a solution to handle possible overfitting of data which is especially common for high order models, we propose a relaxed target training method for regression models which are linear in parameters. This relaxation of training target from the conventional binary values to disjoint classification spaces provides good classification fidelity according to a threshold treatment during the decision process. A particular design to relax the training target is provided under practical consideration. Extension to multiple class problems is formulated before the method is applied to a plug-in full multivariate polynomial model and a reduced model on synthetic data sets to illustrate the idea. Additional experiments were performed using real-world data from the UCI[1] data repository to derive certain empirical evidence.

Keywords: Pattern Classification, Parameter Estimation, Pattern Recognition, Multivariate Polynomials and Machine Learning.

1 Introduction

Apart from statistical means, learning from example constitutes a major paradigm in pattern classification (see e.g.[2, 3]). Under this paradigm, a classifier minimizes a certain energy function and forms a map between the input feature space and the output hypothesis space of possible functional solutions such as pattern classes. Although one usually does not have full access to the *expected* input-output spaces, a subset of the input-output spaces, which we called training set, is often available. A key question to perform empirical learning from this training set is the predictivity of learned algorithm for new data which is not found in the training set. This predictivity is also termed generalization in the context of pattern classification [4].

A. Rangarajan et al. (Eds.): EMMCVPR 2005, LNCS 3757, pp. 187–202, 2005.

Main reasons for poor predictivity come from two viewpoints, namely from the data perspective and from the classifier perspective. From the data perspective, the main concern is representativeness of training data, i.e. whether or not the training data covers the entire operating range of expected input-output spaces. From the classifier perspective, the major question is whether or not the classifier under-fits or over-fits the usually limited data available. As we may not always have the luxury to generate a sufficiently large data set for possible good coverage, we shall take the classifier perspective and address a narrower question upon an appropriate classification objective for stable prediction and hence reduce the chances of obtaining a largely biased solution or over-fitting the available finite training data set.

In this work, we propose to use a *relaxed target* for classification energy minimization, particularly for least-squares type of error objective (LSE) since it is widely used due to its simplicity and well developed theory (see e.g.[2, 3] for discriminant related functions). The main difference between our 'relaxed target' and the'soft classification' or 'partial classification' as seen in [5, 6] is that we are modifying the target vector to stabilize the solution and not concerned with whether or not the classification can be performed 'fully' or 'partially'. Moreover, all elements in the relaxed target vector can be varied according to its role in classification whereas soft classification in [5] refers only to data within the indecision zone. While not entrapping ourselves into arguing about good definition of terms, our relaxed target formulation inherits the merit of fast single step computation from the classical linear least squares error methods and at the same time maintaining, in some sense, the essence of classification objective. The classical linear least squares error methods adopting a binary target function attempt to map the input features onto distinct and usually discrete class values (e.g. labelled as '0' and '1' by intention) whereas in actual application, we only need to map the input features onto distinct classes described by disjoint spaces (e.g. '$(-\infty, 0]$' and '$[1, \infty)$'). This problem is addressed, and thus termed *relaxed target* labelling.

Main contributions of this work are summarized as follows: (i) Formulation of a new target relaxation method which modifies the commonly used least-squares error function from binary points mapping to disjoint spaces mapping in order to provide good classification fidelity according to a threshold treatment during the decision process. While providing good classification stability, the proposed formulation retains the simplicity of single step solution like that in least-squares formulation; (ii) Massive standardized experiments conducted to evaluate the proposed solution comparing with a benchmark classifier.

Organization of the presentation is as follows: Section 2 provides some classification preliminaries related to function mapping prior to motivating the idea of target relaxation. In Section 3, the main concept of target relaxation is first illustrated with an example. This is followed by a suggested target relaxation formulation in the same section. Section 4 reports statistical experiments on a synthetic data and Section 5 extends the experimentation to real-world problems. Finally, some concluding remarks are provided in Section 6.

2   Preliminaries and Problem Treatment

2.1   Pattern Classification

Let $\mathbb{R}$ denotes the set of real numbers and $\mathbb{N}$ denotes the set of natural numbers. We define $\mathbb{R}^- = (-\infty, t_0]$ and $\mathbb{R}^+ = [t_1, +\infty)$ where t_0 and t_1 denotes some real numbers with $t_1 \geqslant t_0$. Given an *inference* measure g, for two-class problems, we usually use the following classification function $cls : \mathbb{R} \to \{0, 1\}$ to segregate the two classes:

$$cls(g) = \begin{cases} 0, \, g < t_0 \\ 1, \, g \geqslant t_1. \end{cases} \tag{1}$$

For multi-class problems, given N_C pattern classes with decision inference $\boldsymbol{g} = \{g_1, g_2, \cdots, g_{N_C}\}$, we use the following classification function $cls : \mathbb{R}^l \to \{1, 2, ..., N_C\}$ for definition of each class label:

$$cls(\boldsymbol{g}) = argmax_i \, g_i, \; i = 1, 2, ..., N_C. \tag{2}$$

This is known as *winner-takes-all* technique.

2.2   Function Mapping

The above formulations for pattern classification can be treated from function mapping point of view. For two-class problems with l number of input features, we are interested in the following mapping:

$$g : \mathbb{R}^l \to [\mathbb{R}^-, \mathbb{R}^+], \; l \in \mathbb{N}. \tag{3}$$

For multi-class problems with l number of inputs and N_C pattern classes, we have

$$g : \mathbb{R}^l \mapsto [\mathbb{R}^-, \mathbb{R}^+]^{N_C}, \; l, N_C \in \mathbb{N}, \tag{4}$$

when we consider the *winner-takes-all* classification technique mentioned above. We shall utilize these mappings to establish the need for target relaxation and apply the idea on a recently proposed reduced model [7].

2.3   Motivation

The call for having a non-uniform treatment of training targets can be seen from the actual classification requirement point of view, i.e. mapping of pattern feature space onto disjoint target spaces (see (3) and (4)) that sufficiently provide each pattern class a label. Consider the two-class problems. What is needed here is merely $g : \mathbb{R}^l \to [\mathbb{R}^-, \mathbb{R}^+]$ because the final decision stage only uses a threshold function (1) to decide upon the class label and not performing a strict binary mapping in the training objective. The conventional training for binary target values does more than what is sufficient for this classification process. By relaxing the 'hard' requirement from mapping onto binary values, the least squares classification error objective becomes one that reflects more truly about the actual threshold treatment at the final stage of decision process.

Mathematically, a pattern classifier cannot be improved by replacing the hard target labels by soft/relaxed target labels when the size of training set is not limited [3]. Particularly, it has been shown that the class-specific discriminant functions are at the same time least mean-square estimates for Boolean class membership indicators as well as least mean-square estimates for the posteriori probabilities or soft/relaxed labels (see pages 113-116 of [3]). However in practice, the available training set size is always limited. The ambiguity or relevance of the supporting target labels can thus be adequately expressed by having a soft/relaxed target label. Moreover, to date, there is no known means to effectively assign the soft/relaxed target labels and solve the learning problem in a single step just like those of least mean-square estimates. Our relaxed target labelling method suggests some means to provide soft assignment of the target labels.

3   Learning of Relaxed Classification Targets

3.1   An Illustrative Example

We begin with an example for illustration purpose. Consider a 2-dimensional problem with two Gaussian classes, both with covariance matrices equal to identity and with means $\mu_1 = [1/\sqrt{2}, 1/\sqrt{2}]$ and $\mu_2 = [-1/\sqrt{2}, -1/\sqrt{2}]$. An instance of training data consisting of 100 samples (50 for each class) is shown in Fig. 1(a). For illustration purpose, we use a full bivariate polynomial model to learn the decision hyper-surface.

Based on a regularized least squares minimization algorithm, the learning target is conventionally chosen as a binary (zero and one) function as shown in Fig. 1(b) (see dashed curve). This results in decision boundary as shown in Fig. 1(a) (see dotted curve) for a 5th-order bivariate polynomial model. (FM5) If, however, we assign the target according to the distance between each data point and the known 'ideal' decision boundary[1] (linear dashed line in Fig. 1(a)), we get the decision boundary represented by the solid line as shown in Fig. 1(a). We label this 5th-order FM as FM5-RLX since the target was relaxed by values assigned according to distances from the ideal line. These newly assigned targets and the trained outputs are represented respectively as crossed points and solid line in Fig. 1(b). Here we see that by relaxing the target output from the two-values binary function, a near perfect fit is found for the trained output. Comparing the two decision boundaries resulted from two types of target vectors (binary and relaxed ones), we see that modification of learning target by relaxation according to classification requirement provides some means to shape the decision boundary.

To investigate into possible generalization properties on unseen test data, in the following experiments, we use the above data model to generate statistical

---

[1] This is distance from point (x_1^o, x_2^o) to line $ax_1 + bx_2 + c = 0$ given by $\frac{ax_1^o + bx_2^o + c}{\pm\sqrt{a^2+b^2}}$.

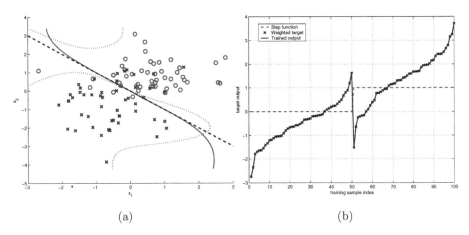

(a)   (b)

Fig. 1. (a): A two Gaussian classes example (dotted: FM5, solid: FM5-RLX, dashed: ideal); (b): Two learning target functions

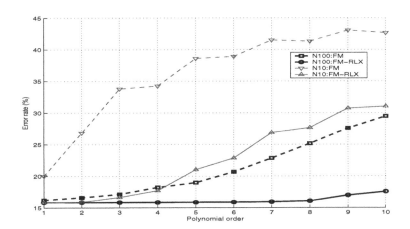

Fig. 2. Average error rates from 1000 runs versus polynomial order

runs. We perform two sets of training using, namely, (i) 100 training data points (denoted as N100), and (ii) 10 training data points (denoted as N10) on the full bivariate polynomial model. The test set contains 1000 samples with 500 samples in each pattern class. In all the following experiments on this Gaussian data, the error rates were obtained from the average of test errors taken from 1000 runs of randomly generated Gaussian data. The same set of randomly generated data for all 1000 runs was used in all compared algorithms.

Fig. 2 shows the average error rates for different polynomial orders using the regularized least squares formulation. The dashed curves correspond to use of the conventional binary target function (denoted as FM) and the solid curves correspond to use of relaxed target function (denoted as FM-RLX). Here, we see that for both cases (i)-(ii), the average error rate increases with the polynomial order. The error rates for FM-RLX for both cases are well below that of FM for all polynomial orders. These results show that target relaxation exhibits a much smaller performance degradation as the polynomial order increases when compared with the conventional binary target.

Since the desired 'distance-to-ideal-decision-boundary' of individual sample is not available in practice, we shall walk through a viable formulation to adjust the target output and discuss some design issues before an illustration of such application using Ripley's benchmark synthetic data.

3.2   A Suggested Method for Training Target Relaxation

Consider the regularized solutions corresponding to respectively two-class and multi-class problems [8] given by

$$\boldsymbol{\alpha} = (P^T P + bI)^{-1} P^T \mathbf{y}, \tag{5}$$

and

$$\Theta = (P^T P + bI)^{-1} P^T Y, \tag{6}$$

where $P \in \mathbb{R}^{m \times K}$, $\mathbf{y} \in \mathbb{R}^{m \times 1}$, $Y \in \mathbb{R}^{m \times N_C}$, I is a $(K \times K)$ identity matrix, and b is a regularization constant.

Without loss of generality, consider the prediction test output of a two-class problem given by

$$\begin{aligned} \hat{\mathbf{y}}_{test} = \mathbf{g}(\boldsymbol{\alpha}, \boldsymbol{x}, \mathbf{y}) &= P_{test}\, \boldsymbol{\alpha} \\ &= P_{test}\, (P^T P + bI)^{-1} P^T \mathbf{y}. \end{aligned} \tag{7}$$

The test output can be seen as a projection of test data (P_{test}) onto the learned parameter plane given by $\boldsymbol{\alpha}$. Since $\boldsymbol{\alpha}$ is dependent on the training data given by feature matrix P and target vector $\mathbf{y}$, the prediction test output is also dependent on P and $\mathbf{y}$. The traditional least squares approach had been used to fix the target vector in binary form and it attempted to minimize the squared errors with respect to this binary target output. The consequence is that training is rather 'hard' with respect to each and every target output since all training outputs from the same class are driven to equal values when constructing the decision surface.

Take the two-class problem and suppose we perform a validation[2] on the training set itself, i.e the training set is partitioned into two sets, one for training and one for validation. Denote symbols with a subscript v for validation set and those without for training set. Then the validation output is

$$\hat{\mathbf{y}}_v = P_v \boldsymbol{\alpha} = P_v (P^T P + bI)^{-1} P^T \mathbf{y}, \tag{8}$$

---

[2] Cross validation remains to be a viable means to assess generalization wherein a recent support can be seen from the connection between stability (of a certain cross validation) and predictivity (generalization) [4].

and the validation error can be written as

$$
\begin{aligned}
\hat{R}_v(\boldsymbol{\alpha}) &= (\mathbf{y}_v - \hat{\mathbf{y}}_v)^T (\mathbf{y}_v - \hat{\mathbf{y}}_v) \\
&= [\mathbf{y}_v - P_v (P^T P + bI)^{-1} P^T \mathbf{y}]^T [\mathbf{y}_v - P_v (P^T P + bI)^{-1} P^T \mathbf{y}] \\
&= [\mathbf{y}_v - P_v \boldsymbol{\Phi} \mathbf{y}]^T [\mathbf{y}_v - P_v \boldsymbol{\Phi} \mathbf{y}],
\end{aligned}
\tag{9}
$$

where $\boldsymbol{\Phi} = (P^T P + bI)^{-1} P^T$. A common treatment for possible good generalization is to optimize the validation through $\arg\min_{\boldsymbol{\alpha}} \hat{R}_v(b, \boldsymbol{\alpha})$ (Note: in the forthcoming derivations, only those variables which are treated as adjustable are included in the arguments of $\hat{R}_v$). Here, we propose to look at $\hat{R}_v(b, \boldsymbol{\alpha}, \mathbf{y})$ adjusting also the target vector used in training. First, consider $\min_{\mathbf{y}} \hat{R}_v(b, \boldsymbol{\alpha}, \mathbf{y}) + b' \|\mathbf{y}\|_2^2$ (b' is a real value regularization coefficient) and based on the similar solution form (5) from a regularized LSE, we obtain a relaxed target as

$$
\mathbf{y} = [(P_v \boldsymbol{\Phi})^T (P_v \boldsymbol{\Phi}) + b' I]^{-1} (P_v \boldsymbol{\Phi})^T \mathbf{y}_v,
\tag{10}
$$

in regularized form. Substitute (10) into (5), we have

$$
\boldsymbol{\alpha} = \boldsymbol{\Phi} (\boldsymbol{\Phi}^T P_v^T P_v \boldsymbol{\Phi} + b' I)^{-1} \boldsymbol{\Phi}^T P_v^T \mathbf{y}_v.
\tag{11}
$$

Here, we note that $\boldsymbol{\alpha}$ in (11) optimizes the newly formulated $\hat{R}_v(b, b', \boldsymbol{\alpha}, \mathbf{y})$ adjusting also the training target $\mathbf{y}$.

It is noted that the relaxed $\mathbf{y}$ obtained above can result in overlapping $\mathbb{R}^-$ and $\mathbb{R}^+$ containing the two pattern classes. The above formulation can thus include constraints to bound the values of $\mathbf{y}$ so as to segregate the two pattern classes. The minimization problem hence becomes $\min_{\mathbf{y}} \hat{R}_v(\mathbf{y})$ subject to a certain constraint function $h(\mathbf{y})$ which maps $\mathbf{y}$ onto disjoint $\mathbb{R}^-$ and $\mathbb{R}^+$.

Limiting the upper bound of target $\mathbf{y}^-$: Consider the first pattern class of a two-class problem and let the training target output for this pattern class falls below a certain threshold value, i.e. $y_i \leqslant t_0$ for all $i = 1, ..., k$ samples (we denote this class as $\mathbf{y}^- = [y_1^-, ..., y_k^-]^T \subset \mathbf{y}$). Define the constraint vector as $\mathbf{h}(\mathbf{y}^-) = [h(y_1^-), ..., h(y_k^-)]^T$ where

$$
h(y_i^-) = \begin{cases} y_i^- - t_0 & if\ y_i^- > t_0 \\ 0 & if\ y_i^- \leqslant t_0 \end{cases}, \quad i \in \{1, ..., k\}.
\tag{12}
$$

This means that the constraint is activated when the modified sample target y_i^- falls outside $\mathbb{R}^- = (-\infty, t_0]$. The minimization problem can then be written as

$$
\min_{\mathbf{y}^-} \hat{R}_v(\mathbf{y}^-) \ subject\ to\ \mathbf{h}(\mathbf{y}^-) \leqslant \mathbf{0}.
\tag{13}
$$

By the penalty function method, the constrained problem can be formulated as an unconstrained one as

$$
\min_{\mathbf{y}^-} \hat{R}_v(\mathbf{y}^-) + c\, \mathbf{h}(\mathbf{y}^-)^T \mathbf{h}(\mathbf{y}^-),
\tag{14}
$$

where c is a real value penalty coefficient.

Since h in (12) is non-smooth, and it results in nonlinear formulation if approximated by a log-like function, we consider only the differentiable part of **h** where the first derivative is

$$\frac{\partial \mathbf{h}(\mathbf{y}^-)}{\partial \mathbf{y}^-} = I \in \mathbb{R}^{k \times k}. \tag{15}$$

The solution $\hat{\mathbf{y}}^-$ solving (14) for this differentiable formulation is given by

$$\hat{\mathbf{y}}^- = [(P_v\Phi^-)^T(P_v\Phi^-) + cI]^{-1}[(P_v\Phi^-)^T\mathbf{y}_v + c\,\mathbf{t}_0], \tag{16}$$
$$= [\hat{y}_1^-, \hat{y}_2^-, ..., \hat{y}_k^-]^T,$$

with $\mathbf{t}_0 = [t_0, ..., t_0]^T \in \mathbb{R}^k$ and Φ^- being obtained based on data which constitute the first pattern class. To preserve the fast single-step computation of linear objective with linear constraints, we adopt the following approximation for the solution $\mathbf{y}^-$ accounting also the non-differentiable part of $\mathbf{h}(\mathbf{y}^-)$:

$$y_i^- = \begin{cases} \hat{y}_i^- & if \ \hat{y}_i^- \leqslant t_0 \\ t_0 & if \ \hat{y}_i^- > t_0 \end{cases}, \ i \in \{1, ..., k\}. \tag{17}$$

Limiting the lower bound of target $\mathbf{y}^+$: Similarly, for the second pattern class with target $y_i \geqslant t_1$ (i.e. $y_i \in [t_1, +\infty)$), we denote this class as $\mathbf{y}^+ = [y_{k+1}^+, ..., y_m^+]^T \subset \mathbf{y}$) for the rest of $i = k+1, ..., m$ samples, and the constrained function can be written as

$$h(y_i^+) = \begin{cases} -y_i^+ + t_1 \ if \ y_i^+ < t_1 \\ 0 \qquad\quad if \ y_i^+ \geqslant t_1 \end{cases}, \ i \in \{k+1, ..., m\}, \tag{18}$$

and the approximated constrained solution minimizing the penalized objective function (14) using the constraint $h(y_i^+) \leqslant 0$ in (18) is

$$y_i^+ = \begin{cases} \hat{y}_i^+ & if \ \hat{y}_i^+ \geqslant t_1 \\ t_1 & if \ \hat{y}_i^+ < t_1 \end{cases}, \ i \in \{k+1, ..., m\}, \tag{19}$$

where

$$\hat{\mathbf{y}}^+ = [(P_v\Phi^+)^T(P_v\Phi^+) - cI]^{-1}[(P_v\Phi^+)^T\mathbf{y}_v - c\,\mathbf{t}_1], \tag{20}$$
$$= [\hat{y}_{k+1}^+, \hat{y}_{k+2}^+, ..., \hat{y}_m^+]^T,$$

with $\mathbf{t}_1 = [t_1, ..., t_1]^T \in \mathbb{R}^{m-k}$, $I \in \mathbb{R}^{(m-k) \times (m-k)}$ and Φ^+ is obtained based on data which constitutes the second pattern class.

Relaxed solution: The above modified training target vectors (17) and (19) can be concatenated to form a single relaxed target vector $\mathbf{y}_{rlx}^T = [\mathbf{y}^{-T}, \mathbf{y}^{+T}]$ and substitute back into (5) for the validated training parameter estimation:

$$\boldsymbol{\alpha} = (P^TP + bI)^{-1}P^T\,\mathbf{y}_{rlx} = \Phi\begin{bmatrix} \mathbf{y}^- \\ \mathbf{y}^+ \end{bmatrix}. \tag{21}$$

3.3   Multi-class Problems

The above formulations can be generalized to multi-class problems where the validation error is written as

$$\hat{R}_v(\alpha) = (Y_v - \hat{Y}_v)^T(Y_v - \hat{Y}_v)$$
$$= [Y_v - P_v\Phi Y]^T[Y_v - P_v\Phi Y], \tag{22}$$

with $\Phi = (P^TP + bI)^{-1}P^T$. The solutions for the differentiable part of the constraint functions can be packed accordingly as

$$\hat{Y}^- = [(P_v\Phi^-)^T(P_v\Phi^-) + cI]^{-1}[(P_v\Phi^-)^TY_v + cT_0], \tag{23}$$

$$\hat{Y}^+ = [(P_v\Phi^+)^T(P_v\Phi^+) - cI]^{-1}[(P_v\Phi^+)^TY_v - cT_1], \tag{24}$$

where $T_0 = [t_0, ..., t_0] \in \mathbb{R}^{k \times N_C}$ and $T_1 = [t_1, ..., t_1] \in \mathbb{R}^{(m-k) \times N_C}$. The approximated solution form for (23)[3] and (24)[4] are concatenated to form a single relaxed target matrix $Y_{rlx}^T = [Y^{-T}, Y^{+T}]$ and substitute back into (6) for the validated training parameter estimation:

$$\Theta = (P^TP + bI)^{-1}P^T Y_{rlx} = \Phi \begin{bmatrix} Y^- \\ Y^+ \end{bmatrix}. \tag{25}$$

Remark 1: Here we note that SVM can also be considered to relax the target via the use of support vectors and find the solution through quadratic programming methods. The difference between SVM and the relaxed method is the optimization objective. SVM optimizes the separation margin between pattern classes while the relaxed method minimizes the *validated training error* (i.e. the solutions (21) and (25) minimize the least-squares error of training with relaxed training target based on validation).

The main advantage of our approach over the SVM approach is that computation of learning parameters (α using (21) and Θ using (25)) involved only a single step and no initialization is needed. The only intermediate step is to partition the data into respective pattern classes to compute the regression matrices Φ^- and Φ^+. The estimation of α and Θ, with estimation of relaxed target embedded, are least squares optimal.   □

3.4   Validation Data Selection

The above formulations immediately prompt us another question: how to select the validation data? Obviously, representative data gives rise to good prediction models. We do not simply select arbitrarily a subset of the training data for validation since we do not have much information about how this subset is biased with respect to the expected distribution. While not limiting ourselves from

---

[3] Y^- approximated from $\hat{Y}^-$ similar to that in (17) for each output.
[4] Y^+ approximated from $\hat{Y}^+$ similar to that in (19) for each output.

other possible choices, we propose in this paper to use the centroids obtained from the mean feature vector of each pattern class. There are two reasons for this choice: (i) it is likely to be unambiguously supported by the data[5], and thus representative; (ii) it does not hold back any data from training, i.e. all available training data can be used for training.

4   Ripley's Synthetic Data

In this section, we use Ripley's synthetic data to demonstrate the effectiveness of the relaxed target method for a reduced multivariate polynomial model (RM) as seen in [8] and a full multivariate polynomial model (FM). The data consists of a binary output indicating two pattern classes with each sample containing two feature elements. According to [9], a 100-example training set (randomly selected from Ripley's original 250) and a 1000-example test set was used to demonstrate the decision boundary and generalization capability of RVM. It was shown in [9, 10] that utilizing considerably small number of Gaussian kernel functions, the RVM produces comparable test error (slightly better) with that of SVM using similar kernel function.

In all the following experiments, we perform 1000 runs of training using each 100-example subset randomly selected from the original 250-example training set. The same set of randomly selected data for all 1000 runs was used in all compared algorithms. This is to provide a good statistical picture regarding the performances especially the generalization property.[6]

Fig. 3(a)-(b) shows the relative computing efforts for RVM, SVM, FM, FM-RLX, RM and RM-RLX in terms of CPU time running under similar computing platform (1.4GHz Pentium-Centrino, Matlab environment [12]). It is seen from this plot that the increment of CPU overheads to the original RM is relatively small as compared to those iterative methods (SVM and RVM).

Next, we compare relaxation with regularization alone. Besides RM, we demonstrate that the relaxed target method can also be applied to a conventional full multivariate polynomial model. Fig. 3(c) shows the corresponding average error rates (from 1000 runs) plotted against each polynomial order for several cases of multivariate polynomial regression: (i) FM: full multivariate polynomial with regularization $b = 0.1$, (ii) FM-RLX: full multivariate polynomial with regularization $b = 0.1$ plus relaxed target with constraint parameter $c = 1$, and (iii) RM: reduced polynomial RM [8] with regularization $b = 0.1$, (iv) RM-RLX: reduced polynomial RM [8] with regularization $b = 0.1$ plus relaxed target with constraint parameter $c = 1$. These results show that the relaxed target method provides possible room beyond regularization for good predictivity for both FM and RM.

---

[5] We say that a point is unambiguously supported by the data when it is surrounded by many labelled points of the same class. This will not be the case if the class distributions are non-convex and for such case the number of centroids can be increased to cover different regions. While not diverting to various possibilities, in this work we shall focus on applicability of the fundamental approach on single centroid per pattern class.

[6] For the Ripley's data, Tipping used a single run in [9] and Mário used 20 runs in [11].

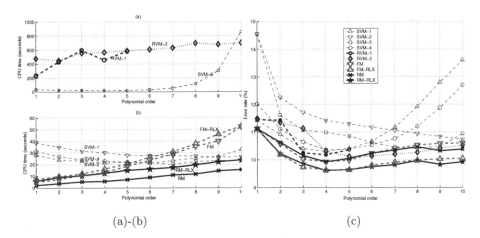

(a)-(b)   (c)

Fig. 3. (a)-(b): Total CPU times for 1000 runs versus polynomial order. FM, RM used $b = 0.1$, FM-RLX, RM-RLX used $(b,c) = (0.1,1)$, SVM-1 used $(C, Gamma, Coeff)$=(3,1,1), SVM-2 used (3,0.1,1), SVM-3 used (3,0.1,3), SVM-4 used (1,1,1), RVM-1 used default width=0.5, RVM-2 used width=1; (c): Average (1000 runs) test error rates versus polynomial order.

The average test errors of SVM [13] and RVM [14] are also plotted in Fig. 3(c) for comparison. For SVM, in order to demonstrate the effect of different parameter tunings for the 10 model orders, four settings of $(C, Gamma, Coeff)^7$ are experimented: (i) SVM-1 using (3,1,1); (ii) SVM-2 using (3,0.1,1); (iii) SVM-3 using (3,0.1,3) and (iv) SVM-4 using (1,1,1). The RVM-1 (using default settings: width=0.5, maximum number of iterations=500) in this figure has only error rates for 1st-5th orders because matrix singularities are frequently encountered for the experimented data set for higher order models. RVM-2 used a width of 1 with maximum number of iterations equal 500 for all model orders. The experiment shows that SVM tends to have high test error rates at low and high order models due to under-fitting and over-fitting. Both the RVMs and RM-RLX maintained relatively consistent test error rates throughout all experimented model orders. Overall, the average error rates for FM-RLX and RM-RLX are seen to be lower (approx. 0.5%-1%) than that of RVM. This is considered significant improvement as the range of operation is approaching the Bayes error of about 8%[9].

5   Experiments on UCI Data

To gain more insights into the effect of the proposed target relaxation method on real-world problems, we perform further experiments on 38 benchmark UCI data

---

[7] In [13], C is the cost of constraint violation, $Gamma$ and $Coeff$ are the parameters of the polynomial kernel which has the form of $[Gamma* < X(:,i), X(:,j) > + Coeff]^{Degree}$ where $< X(:,i), X(:,j) >$ is the inner-product of input vectors $X(:,i)$ and $X(:,j)$. $Degree$ is the order of the polynomial.

sets. These data sets were taken from [8] where 4 out of the total 42 data sets were left out due to computing memory limitation in current running platform. Both the RM and its respective relaxed target counterpart (RM-RLX) will be experimented. The full multivariate polynomials are not experimented because more than half of the total 42 data sets ran into problems of either matrix size too large to be computed or matrix singularity [8].

5.1   Experimental Setup

In all the following experiments, the regularization parameter was fixed at $b = 0.0001$ as our experience in [7] revealed that variation of b within $[10^{-6}, 10^{-2}]$ did not show large variation in performance, b is fixed here to save computational cost. Since our purpose here is to observed the impact of adjustment of target output on the test accuracy, the polynomial order r was fixed following the RM-Tuned algorithm for each data set as seen in [8]. Similar to [8], ten runs of 10-fold stratified cross-validation were performed for all accuracy results except for 6 cases which used the original training and test sets provided as they are considered as large data sets.

The target relaxed RM was labelled as RM-RLX where similar settings to above were based on, except that in this target relax mode an additional constraint parameter c was included. This constraint parameter c was chosen from $\{0.1, 1, 10, 100\}$ based on 10-fold validation using only the training set. The validation data was selected according to the mean of each pattern class as mentioned in section 3.4.

5.2   Results

(i) Relative Test Accuracy of RM-RLX to That of RM

The average test accuracies of RM-RLX are shown in Table 3 (average accuracies from 10 runs of 10-fold experiments). The relative performance of RM-RLX with respect to RM is shown in the last two columns of the table. As seen from the table, except for few cases with degradation of performance, the accuracy can improve from near zero to about 2.25% for RM-RLX over RM. The average accuracy of RM-RLX is found to be degraded for about 0.17% as compared to that of RM because of exceptionally poor performance of StatLog-vehicle data set due to numerical ill-conditioning. Overall, the observations for most data sets are in-lined with those from previous experiments on RM-RLX.

(ii) Comparing Test Accuracies of RM-RLX, SVM-Poly, and RVM-Poly

In the next set of experiments, we compare RM-RLX with SVM and RVM. A SVM Matlab toolbox [13] which has already implemented SVM with polynomial kernel for multi-class case is used. We choose the polynomial kernel in our experiments because: (i) in [15] the polynomial kernel showed good performance as compared to other kernels, and (ii) RM also applied multivariate polynomials in the implementation and this matches our goal to compare the different training objectives given by SVM and the relaxed method.

To observe the best performance of SVM for benchmarking, the parameters ([13] polynomial order *Degree*, cost of constraint violation C and scaling factor *Gamma*) of SVM-Poly are chosen based on an exhaustive search from cross-validation using only the training set[8]. The offset parameter *Coeff* is fixed at 1 for two reasons: (i) *Coeff* is relative to *Gamma* in $[Gamma* < X(:,i)$, $X(:,j) > +Coeff]^{Degree}$ and hence changing γ itself results in change of relative importance of *Coeff* with respect to $Gamma* < X(:,i), X(:,j) >$, and (ii) much computational cost can be saved from exhaustive search of fewer parameters.

The RVM (taken from a toolbox as seen in [14]) adopts the polynomial kernel for similar reasons stated above for SVM-Poly, and the only parameter polynomial order r was chosen similar to that of RM for comparative reason and to save computational time. Since the RVM toolbox does not extend to multi-class problems, only 2-class problems (data sets 1-16) are experimented.

The average accuracies for the standardized ten runs of 10-fold experiments using similar data partitioning are shown in Table 2 and Table 3 respectively for RVM-Poly and SVM-Poly. The results for SVM-Poly are tabulated along with the finally selected parameters from cross-validation using only the training set. For the given 16 sets of 2-class data, the RVM shows convergence for only 6 sets of data which are tabulated in Table 2. For both tables, the results with higher average accuracy are marked bold. It can be seen that the average accuracies for RM-RLX and SVM-Poly are comparable for the 38 data sets studied.

5.3   Summary of Results and Comments

The number of data sets which has better, equal and poorer performances for the relaxed target formulation over the original step target formulation are summarized in Table 1. Here, we see that x (better accuracy count) is significantly

Table 1. Summary of results

Method \ Number of data sets	x y z	$\frac{x}{x+y+z}$(%)	$\frac{y}{x+y+z}$(%)	$\frac{z}{x+y+z}$(%)
RM-RLX vs RM (total 38)	18 8 12	47.37	21.05	31.58
RM-RLX vs SVM-Poly (total 38)	16 2 20	42.11	5.26	52.63
RM-RLX vs RVM-Poly (total 6)	6 0 0	100.00	0	0

x: better performance, y: equal performance, z: poorer performance

---

[8] In tuning the SVM classifier, *Degree* is found from integers between 1 and 10, *Gamma* is found from the set $\{0.01, 0.1, 1\}$ and C is found from $\{1, 10, 100\}$. C is chosen from relatively low values because physical data sets are likely to be non-separable and much validation time can be saved from exhaustive search within a small parameter set. Finding of *Gamma* and C in geometric sequences is due to the observation that when theses parameters are small, a small change in the value of these parameters had a large effect on the performance than when they are big [16].

Table 2. Parameter settings and classification accuracy statistics for RVM-Poly

No	Name	RVM-Poly				
		r	min	ave	max	std
1	Shuttle-l-contr	2	0.9259	**0.9670**	0.9889	0.0226
2	BUPA-liver	2	0.6088	0.6429	0.6735	0.0202
5	Monk-3	2	0.8417	0.8800	0.9083	0.0221
6	Pima-diabetes	1	0.7671	0.7697	0.7750	0.0024
11	Votes	2	0.8143	0.9136	0.9381	0.0389
16	Sonar	1	0.7050	0.7320	0.7600	0.0166

Table 3. Parameter settings and classification accuracy statistics for SVM-Poly and RM-RLX

No	Name	SVM-Poly (Coeff=1.0)					RM-RLX					RM-RLX − RM	
		r	C	γ	ave	std	r	c	s	ave	std	diff	sign
1	Shuttle-l-contr	2	100	1.00	**0.9807**	0.0029	2	1	1	0.9630	0.0029	0.0052	+
2	BUPA-liver	4	1	1.00	0.7259	0.0090	2	100	1	**0.7274**	0.0098	0.0000	o
3	Monk-1	3	10	1.00	0.9450	0.0181	4	0.1	0.5	**0.9900**	0.0082	-0.0008	−
4	Monk-2	4	100	1.00	0.7575	0.0268	7	1	1	**0.7750**	0.0168	0.0081	+
5	Monk-3	2	10	1.00	0.9042	0.0168	2	10	1	**0.9158**	0.0087	0.0008	+
6	Pima-diabetes	10	100	0.01	0.7749	0.0037	1	1	1	**0.7759**	0.0048	0.0004	+
7	Tic-tac-toe	2	100	1.00	**0.9835**	0.0005	2	0.1	1	**0.9835**	0.0005	0.0000	o
8	Breast-cancer-W	1	1	0.01	**0.9716**	0.0020	3	1	1	0.9709	0.0021	0.0009	+
9	StatLog-heart	7	1	0.01	0.8404	0.0044	2	1	1	**0.8448**	0.0110	0.0007	+
10	Credit-app	3	10	0.10	0.8637	0.0014	1	1	1	**0.8644**	0.0023	0.0002	+
11	Votes	2	100	0.10	0.9443	0.0049	2	1	1	**0.9545**	0.0027	0.0002	+
12	Mushroom	6	100	1.00	**1.0000**	0.0000	2	0.1	0.1	0.9960	0.0002	0.0005	+
13	Wdbc	6	1	0.10	**0.9791**	0.0017	3	0.1	1	0.9511	0.0044	0.0013	+
14	Wpbc	4	100	1.00	0.8056	0.0045	1	100	0.1	**0.8117**	0.0115	0.0000	o
15	Ionosphere	6	100	1.00	**0.9071**	0.0068	3	0.1	0.05	0.8976	0.0061	0.0008	+
16	Sonar	7	100	0.01	**0.8355**	0.0164	1	1	1	0.7585	0.0179	0.0025	+
17	Iris	5	10	1.00	**0.9733**	0.0104	4	0.1	1	0.9693	0.0033	-0.0067	−
18	Balance-scale	2	100	1.00	**1.0000**	0.0000	2	10	1	0.9290	0.0013	0.0000	o
19	Teaching-assist	9	100	1.00	0.5521	0.0151	9	100	0.5	**0.5957**	0.0164	0.0007	+
20	New-thyroid	3	100	1.00	**0.9681**	0.0060	4	0.1	1	0.9381	0.0100	0.0014	+
21	Abalone	3	100	1.00	**0.6629**	0.0010	7	100	1	0.6475	0.0118	-0.0185	−
22	Contraceptive-mthd	3	1	1.00	**0.5440**	0.0068	5	10	1	0.5434	0.0048	-0.0002	−
23	Boston-housing	1	100	1.00	0.7645	0.0086	4	1	1	**0.7841**	0.0041	0.0006	+
24	Wine	5	100	0.01	0.9600	0.0084	1	0.1	1	**0.9875**	0.0028	0.0000	o
25	Attitude-smoking*	1	1	1.00	**0.6950**	0.0000	1	0.1	0.2	**0.6950**	0.0000	0.0000	o
26	Waveform*	8	1	1.00	0.8230	0.0000	1	1	1	**0.8310**	0.0000	-0.0020	−
27	Thyroid*	1	1	0.01	0.9271	0.0000	3	1	1	**0.9408**	0.0000	0.0009	+
28	StatLog-DNA*	1	10	1.00	0.8373	0.0000	3	100	1	**0.9452**	0.0000	0.0000	o
29	Car	4	100	1.00	**0.9958**	0.0010	3	100	1	0.8716	0.0019	-0.0001	−
30	StatLog-vehicle	3	10	1.00	**0.8122**	0.0097	6	100	1	0.7593	0.0327	-0.0636	−
31	Soyabean-small	1	1	0.10	**1.0000**	0.0000	1	0.1	0.1	0.9725	0.0135	0.0225	+
32	StatLog-satimage*	7	100	1.00	**0.8890**	0.0000	6	1	0.1	0.8640	0.0000	-0.0005	−
33	Glass	10	1	0.10	**0.6781**	0.0131	2	100	1	0.6405	0.0163	-0.0076	−
34	Zoo	4	10	1.00	0.9190	0.0099	1	100	0.1	**0.9790**	0.0083	0.0000	o
35	StatLog-image-seg	2	100	0.10	**0.9725**	0.0019	6	10	1	0.9338	0.0092	-0.0072	−
36	Ecoli	4	10	0.10	**0.8709**	0.0029	2	100	1	0.8620	0.0476	-0.0017	−
37	Led-display*	1	1	1.00	**0.7450**	0.0000	1	0.1	1	0.7290	0.0000	0.0015	+
38	Yeast	3	10	1.00	**0.6016**	0.0025	6	100	1	0.5931	0.0098	-0.0034	−
	Mean	3.95	47.66	0.68	**0.8529**	0.0057	3.05	30.34	0.79	**0.8471**	0.0080	-0.0017	−

* : Accuracy measured from the given training and test set instead of 10-fold validation.
r : Polynomial order of SVM-Poly and RM-RLX.
C : Cost of constraint in SVM-Poly.
γ : Polynomial scaling factor.
c : Cost of constraint in RM-RLX.
s : Input scaling factor for RM and RM-RLX.
Note: Data from the Attitudes Towards Smoking Legislation Survey - Metropolitan Toronto 1988, which was funded by NHRDP (Health and Welfare Canada), were collected by the Institute for Social Research at York University for Dr. Linda Pederson and Dr. Shelley Bull.

larger than z (poorer accuracy count) especially for relaxed target method versus original binary target, i.e. 47.37% versus 31.58% for RM. If we consider $(x + y)$, then we can say that about 70% data sets have comparable or better test performances for the relaxed target formulation than the original step target formulation. The accuracy improvement ranges from about 0.1% to more than 2% for RM.

It is noted that for all numerical well-conditioned cases, the performance of the relaxed formulation can be made equal to the original least square estimation adopting the binary target values by using a high value of c (e.g. $c \geqslant 1000$). This means that we have at worst the original estimate using step function for well-conditioned applications. However, for numerical ill-conditioned case, the test performance can degrade as much as 6.5% for the relaxed target formulation.

A comparison of superiority performance counts for RM-RLX are also summarized with respect to SVM-Poly and RVM-Poly in Table 1. While RVM-Poly may have insufficient successful runs for conclusive observations, it can be seen that RM-RLX has comparable performance with that of SVM-Poly which is well recognized to be among one of the top classifiers. The significance of this work can thus be seen from two aspects: (i) comparable accuracy to a top classifier, and (ii) fast deterministic single-step estimation process for target relaxation.

6   Conclusion

In this paper, a target relaxation method is proposed to provide good classification fidelity according to a threshold treatment during the decision process. The proposed method modifies the commonly used least-squares error function from binary points mapping to disjoint spaces mapping. With a particular centroid based validation design, we demonstrated that the relaxed target method provided means to stabilize the solution within a single computational step. While this particular design uses the polynomial models, the method is directly applicable to estimators which are linear in their parameters. Experiments on real-world data show the effectiveness of the method for many data sets. The relaxed classifier is also shown to have comparable average classification accuracy with SVM adopting the polynomial kernel. With this particular design on target relaxation, we hope that more effective relaxation means can be inspired for good classifier predictivity.

References

1. C. L. Blake and C. J. Merz, "UCI Repository of machine learning databases," in *http://www.ics.uci.edu/~mlearn/MLRepository.html*, 1998, university of California, Irvine, Dept. of Information and Computer Sciences.
2. R. O. Duda, P. E. Hart, and D. G. Stork, *Pattern Classification.* New York: John Wiley & Sons, Inc, 2001, (2nd Edition).
3. Jürgen Schürmann, *Pattern Classification: A Unified View of Statistical and Neural Approaches.* New York: John Wiley & Sons, Inc., 1996.

4. T. Poggio, R. Rifkin, S. Mukherjee, and P. Niyogi, "General Conditions for Predictivity in Learning Theory," *Nature*, vol. 428, pp. 419–422, March 2004.
5. Y. Baram, "Soft Nearest Neighbor Classification," in *International Conference on Neural Networks (ICNN)*, vol. 3, Houston, TX, June 1997, pp. 1469–1473.
6. ——, "Partial Classification: The Benefit of Deferred Decision," *IEEE Trans. Pattern Analysis and Machine Intelligence*, vol. 20, no. 8, pp. 769–776, 1998.
7. K.-A. Toh, W.-Y. Yau, and X. Jiang, "A Reduced Multivariate Polynomial Model For Multimodal Biometrics And Classifiers Fusion," *IEEE Trans. Circuits and Systems for Video Technology (Special Issue on Image- and Video-Based Biometrics)*, vol. 14, no. 2, pp. 224–233, 2004.
8. K.-A. Toh, Q.-L. Tran, and D. Srinivasan, "Benchmarking A Reduced Multivariate Polynomial Pattern Classifier," *IEEE Trans. Pattern Analysis and Machine Intelligence*, vol. 26, no. 6, pp. 740–755, 2004.
9. M. E. Tipping, "Sparse Bayesian Learning and the Relevance Vector machine," *Journal of Machine Learning Research*, vol. 1, pp. 211–244, 2001.
10. ——, "The Relevance Vector machine," in *Advances in Neural Information Processing Systems 12*, S. A. Solla, T. K. Leen, and K.-R. Müller, Eds., 2000, pp. 652–658.
11. M. A. T. Figueiredo, "Adaptive Sparseness for Supervised Learning," *IEEE Trans. Pattern Analysis and Machine Intelligence*, vol. 25, no. 9, pp. 1150–1159, 2003.
12. The MathWorks, "Matlab And Simulink," in *http://www.mathworks.com/*, 2003.
13. J. Ma, Y. Zhao, and S. Ahalt, "OSU SVM Classifier Matlab Toolbox (ver 3.00)," in *http://eewww.eng.ohio-state.edu/∼maj/osu_svm/*, 2002, the Ohio State University.
14. M. Tipping, "Sparse Bayesian Learning and the Relevance Vector Machine," in *http://research.microsoft.com/mlp/RVM*, 2004, (Microsoft Research).
15. V. N. Vapnik, *Statistical Learning Theory*. Wiley-Interscience Pub, 1998.
16. C. Soares, P. B. Brazdil, and P. Kuba, "A meta-learning method to select the kernel width in support vector regression," *Machine Learning*, vol. 54, no. 3, pp. 195–209, 2004.

Linear Programming Matching and Appearance-Adaptive Object Tracking

Hao Jiang, Mark S. Drew, and Ze-Nian Li

School of Computing Science, Simon Fraser University,
Burnaby BC, Canada V5A 1S6

Abstract. In this paper, we present a novel successive relaxation linear programming scheme for solving the important class of consistent labeling problems for which an L_1 metric is involved. The unique feature of the proposed scheme is that we use a much smaller set of basis labels to represent the label space. In a coarse to fine manner, the approximation improves during iteration. The proposed scheme behaves very differently from other methods in which the label space is kept constant in the solution process, and is well suited for very large label set matching problems. Based on the proposed matching scheme, we develop a robust multi-template tracking method. We also increase the efficiency of the template searching by a Markov model. The proposed tracking method uses a small number of graph templates and is able to deal with cases in which objects change appearance drastically due to change of aspect or object deformation.

1 Introduction

Matching is one of the most important tasks in computer vision, and is key for stereo, motion estimation, 3D object reconstruction, tracking, and object recognition. Matching can be mathematically formulated as a consistent labeling problem, in which we need to assign labels to sites such that a predefined energy function is minimized. For consistent matching problems, labels are usually defined in a metric space and therefore the distances of labels can be measured. Although simple in concept, consistent labeling is NP-hard in general. For some special cases, for instance, when sites have linear or tree order, dynamic programming can be applied to solve labeling problem in polynomial time. Another special case is when labels for each site have linear order, and the metric defined in the label space is convex. In this case, polynomial-time max-flow schemes [1] can be applied. Other searching schemes, e.g. branch and bound schemes [2], whose worst and average complexities are exponential, have also been applied to medium sized matching problems. For the general case in image matching, approximation algorithms are preferred. Relaxation labeling (RL) [3] was one of the earliest methods for solving labeling problems, and has had a great deal of influence on later matching schemes. RL uses local search, and therefore relies on a good initialization. ICM — Iterative Conditional Modes [4] — another widely applied method for solving labeling problems, is greedy and has been found to be easily trapped in a local minimum. In recent years, graph cut (GC) [5] and belief propagation (BP) [6][7][8] have become standard methods for solving consistent labeling problems. Graph cut based methods have been successfully applied in matching problems such as stereo [9] and

A. Rangarajan et al. (Eds.): EMMCVPR 2005, LNCS 3757, pp. 203–219, 2005.

motion [10]. Loopy belief propagation has also been widely applied in stereo [11] and object matching [12]. GC and BP are more robust than traditional labeling schemes and are also found to be faster than stochastic annealing based methods. But GC and BP are still very complex for large scale problems that involve a large number of labels. Besides GC and BP, many other schemes have been presented, such as spectrum graph theory based methods [13]. Although intensively studied, the large scale matching problem is still an unsolved problem. In this paper, we present methods based on linear programming to solve the class of consistent labeling problems with L_1 regularity terms. For this class of problems, an efficient LP method can be formulated, which is found to be faster and more robust in solving large label set problems than the standard methods such as BP and GC.

The work most related to the proposed scheme is the mathematical programming schemes, which have received much interest in formulating and solving labeling problems. The early RL schemes belong to this class. One of the major challenges of a labeling algorithm is to overcome the problem of local minima in the optimization process. Different schemes have been proposed. Deterministic annealing schemes [14][15] have been successfully applied for matching point sets and graphs. Quadratic programming schemes [16] and most recently semidefinite programming schemes [17] have been proposed for matching problems. Up to now, these schemes could only be applied to small scale problems. On the contrary, because of its efficiency, Linear Programming has been applied in many vision problems, such as estimating motion of rigid scenes [18]. A linear programming formulation [19] has been presented for uniform labeling problems and for approximating general problems by tree metrics. Another general LP scheme, studied in [20], is quite similar to the linear relaxation labeling formulation [3]. This LP formulation is found to be only applicable to small problems because of the large number of constraints and variables involved.

We present a linear programming relaxation scheme for L_1-regularity consistent labeling problems, and we study an efficient successive relaxation scheme to solve the optimization problem. Different from other methods, the proposed scheme uses a much smaller number of basis labels to represent the matching space. This is one key component of the method to speed up the algorithm. In our scheme, basis labels correspond to the coordinates of the 3D lower convex hull of the matching cost function for each site. We propose a successive relaxation scheme to increase the accuracy of the approximation iteratively. During the iteration, we shrink the trust region for each site and locate the new trust region based on the solution of the previous relaxation solution, but reconvexify the matching cost based on the *original* cost function. This process continues until the trust region becomes small. Since the convexification process eliminates many false local minima in the earlier stages of the solution process, the proposed scheme is able to find a good approximated solution quickly. Iteratively, the successive relaxation process refines the labeling result.

Based on the proposed matching scheme, we propose a robust template tracking scheme. In object tracking, handling drastic shape and appearance changes of objects, due to severe viewpoint and aspect changes and object shape deformation, is a difficult problem. Two classes of methods have been used to try to solve the problem. The first class uses features resistant to object aspect and deformation, such as the color histogram. The mean-shift based method [21] belongs to this class. Methods relying on invariant features cannot handle large appearance changes and usually do not produce an accurate correspondence in tracking. The second class of method is most correlated with the method studied in this paper, which is appearance-based and requires a set of key templates representing an object's appearance. Black and Jepson [22] propose a PCA based approach to select and represent templates. Researchers also study methods to learn the templates on-line [23]. In this paper, we present a scheme which does not rely on a complex training process. The system requires a very small number of exemplars. Graph templates are then generated and used in tracking. Apart from tracking objects of fixed appearance, the proposed scheme is also able to track an object that changes appearance dramatically by selecting the best template in matching. To further increase efficiency, the templates are organized into a digraph, so that one template can only be replaced by its scaled or rotated version or its neighbors with the same scale and rotation settings. The tracking process is then equivalent to finding a node transition sequence in the given digraph. Experiments show very promising results for tracking objects in cluttered backgrounds.

2   Matching by Linear Programming

The matching problem can be stated generally as the following consistent labeling problem,

$$\min_f \sum_{s \in S} c(s, f_s) + \sum_{\{p,q\} \in \mathcal{N}} \lambda_{p,q} d(f_p, f_q)$$

where $c(s, f_s)$ is the cost of assigning label f_s to site s; $d(f_p, f_q)$ is the distance between the labels assigned to neighboring sites p and q; S is a finite set of sites; $\mathcal{N}$ is the set of non-ordered neighboring site pairs; $\lambda_{p,q}$ are smoothing coefficients. For computer vision problems, labels can be discrete or continuous. When the labels are discrete, we denote a problem as a discrete labeling problem, and otherwise as a continuous labeling problem. For a discrete labeling problem, we can interpolate the cost $c(s, f_s)$ for each site piecewise-linearly such that $c(s, f_s)$ becomes a surface, and allow f_s to take values in the convex hull supported by the discrete labels: we thus obtain the *continuous extension* of a discrete problem. Continuous labeling problems such as motion estimation can be well approximated by such a continuous extension of a discrete system. In the following discussions, without loss of generality we assume both the set S and the label set $\mathcal{L}_s$ to be discrete. In this paper, we focus on that subset of consistent labeling problems such that $d(f_p, f_q) = ||f_p - f_q||$; $|| \cdot ||$ is the L_1 norm and f are vectors defined in the L_1 metric space. When f degenerate into scalars, a maximum-flow scheme can be used to solve the problem. For problems with label dimensionality greater than 1, the problem becomes much more complex. We rewrite the formulation as follows, with boldface symbols for site $\mathbf{s}$ and label $\mathbf{f}$ to emphasize that they are vectors:

$$\min_{\mathbf{f}} \sum_{\mathbf{s} \in S} c(\mathbf{s}, \mathbf{f_s}) + \sum_{\{\mathbf{p},\mathbf{q}\} \in N} \lambda_{\mathbf{p},\mathbf{q}} ||\mathbf{f_p} - \mathbf{f_q}||$$

In the following, we assume the **f** vectors are 2D. The methods proposed below can be easily extended to cases where the labels have higher dimensionality. To simplify notation, $c(\mathbf{s}, \mathbf{f_s})$ is also used to represent the continuous extension matching cost surfaces.

2.1   Approximation by Linear Programming

The above energy optimization problem is nonlinear and usually non-convex, which makes it difficult to solve in this original form without a good initialization process. We now show how to approximate the problem by a linear programming formulation via linear approximation and variable relaxation, as outlined in [24, 25] by Jiang et al. To linearize the first term, the following scheme is applied. A basis $\mathcal{B_s}$ is selected for the labels for each site s. Then the label $\mathbf{f_s}$ can be represented as a linear combination of the label basis as $\mathbf{f_s} = \sum_{\mathbf{j} \in \mathcal{B_s}} \xi_{\mathbf{s},\mathbf{j}} \cdot \mathbf{j}$, where $\xi_{\mathbf{s},\mathbf{j}}$ are real-valued weighting coefficients. The labeling cost of $\mathbf{f_s}$ can then be approximated by the linear combination of the cost of the basis labeling costs $c(\mathbf{s}, \sum_{\mathbf{j} \in \mathcal{B_s}} \xi_{\mathbf{s},\mathbf{j}} \cdot \mathbf{j}) \simeq \sum_{\mathbf{j} \in \mathcal{B_s}} \xi_{\mathbf{s},\mathbf{j}} \cdot c(\mathbf{s}, \mathbf{j})$. We also further set constraints $\xi_{\mathbf{s},\mathbf{j}} \geq 0$ and $\sum_{\mathbf{j} \in \mathcal{B_s}} \xi_{\mathbf{s},\mathbf{j}} = 1$ for each site s, so as to constrain the space spanned by the basis to the convex hull of the basis labels. Clearly, if $\xi_{\mathbf{s},\mathbf{j}}$ are constrained to be 1 or 0, and the basis contains all the labels, i.e. $\mathcal{B_s} = \mathcal{L_s}$, the above representation becomes exact. Note that $\mathbf{f_s}$ are *not* constrained to the basis labels, but can be any convex combination. To linearize the regularity terms in the nonlinear formulation we can represent a free variable by the difference of two nonnegative auxiliary variables and introduce the summation of the auxiliary variables into the objective function. If the problem is properly formulated, when the linear programming problem is optimized the summation will approach the absolute value of the free variable.

Based on this linearization process, a linear programming approximation of the problem can be stated as

$$\min \sum_{\mathbf{s} \in S} \sum_{\mathbf{j} \in \mathcal{B_s}} c(\mathbf{s}, \mathbf{j}) \cdot \xi_{\mathbf{s},\mathbf{j}} + \sum_{\{\mathbf{p},\mathbf{q}\} \in \mathcal{N}} \lambda_{\mathbf{p},\mathbf{q}} \sum_{m=1}^{2} (f_{\mathbf{p},\mathbf{q},m}^{+} + f_{\mathbf{p},\mathbf{q},m}^{-})$$

$$s.t. \quad \sum_{\mathbf{j} \in \mathcal{B_s}} \xi_{\mathbf{s},\mathbf{j}} = 1, \forall \mathbf{s} \in S$$

$$\sum_{\mathbf{j} \in \mathcal{B_s}} \xi_{\mathbf{s},\mathbf{j}} \cdot \phi_m(\mathbf{j}) = f_{\mathbf{s},m}, \ \forall \mathbf{s} \in S, \ m = 1, 2$$

$$f_{\mathbf{p},m} - f_{\mathbf{q},m} = f_{\mathbf{p},\mathbf{q},m}^{+} - f_{\mathbf{p},\mathbf{q},m}^{-}, \forall \{\mathbf{p}, \mathbf{q}\} \in \mathcal{N}, \ m = 1, 2$$

$$\xi_{\mathbf{s},\mathbf{j}}, \ f_{\mathbf{p},\mathbf{q},m}^{+}, f_{\mathbf{p},\mathbf{q},m}^{-} \geq 0$$

where $\mathbf{f_s} = (f_{\mathbf{s},1}, f_{\mathbf{s},2})$ and function ϕ_m returns the mth component of its argument. It is not difficult to show that the linear programming formulation is equivalent to the general nonlinear formulation if the linearization assumptions hold. In general situations, the linear programming formulation is an approximation of the original nonlinear optimization problem.

Property 1: *If* $\mathcal{B_s} = \mathcal{L_s}$, and *the cost function of its continuous extension* $c(\mathbf{s}, \mathbf{j})$ is *convex,* $\forall \mathbf{s} \in S$, *the LP exactly solves the continuous extension of the discrete labeling problem.* $\mathcal{L_s}$ *is the label set of s.*

Proof: We just need to show that when LP is optimized, the configuration $\{\mathbf{f}_s^* = \sum_{\mathbf{j}\in\mathcal{B}_s} \xi_{s,\mathbf{j}}^* \cdot \mathbf{j}\}$ also solves the continuous extension of the nonlinear problem. Since $c(\mathbf{s},\mathbf{j})$ is convex, $\sum_{\mathbf{j}\in\mathcal{L}_s} c(\mathbf{s},\mathbf{j})\xi_{s,\mathbf{j}}^* \geq c(\mathbf{s},\mathbf{f}_s^*)$. And, when the LP is minimized we have $\sum_{\{\mathbf{p},\mathbf{q}\}\in\mathcal{N}} \lambda_{\mathbf{p},\mathbf{q}} \sum_{m=1}^{2}(f_{\mathbf{p},\mathbf{q},m}^{+} + f_{\mathbf{p},\mathbf{q},m}^{-}) = \sum_{\{\mathbf{p},\mathbf{q}\}\in\mathcal{N}} \lambda_{\mathbf{p},\mathbf{q}}\|\mathbf{f}_{\mathbf{p}}^* - \mathbf{f}_{\mathbf{q}}^*\|$. Therefore

$$\min \sum_{\mathbf{s}\in S, \mathbf{j}\in\mathcal{L}_s} c(\mathbf{s},\mathbf{j})\xi_{s,\mathbf{j}} + \sum_{\{\mathbf{p},\mathbf{q}\}\in\mathcal{N}} \lambda_{\mathbf{p},\mathbf{q}} \sum_{m=1}^{2}(f_{\mathbf{p},\mathbf{q},m}^{+} + f_{\mathbf{p},\mathbf{q},m}^{-})$$

$$\geq \sum_{\mathbf{s}\in S} c(\mathbf{s},f_s^*) + \sum_{\{\mathbf{p},\mathbf{q}\}\in\mathcal{N}} \lambda_{\mathbf{p},\mathbf{q}}\|\mathbf{f}_{\mathbf{p}}^* - \mathbf{f}_{\mathbf{q}}^*\|$$

According to the definition of continuous extension, $\mathbf{f}_s^*$ are feasible solutions of the continuous extension of the non-linear problem. Therefore the optimum of the linear programming problem is not less than the optimum of the continuous extension of the nonlinear problem. On the other hand, it is easy to construct a feasible solution of LP that achieves the minimum of the continuous extension of the nonlinear problem. The property follows.

In practice, the cost function $c(\mathbf{s},\mathbf{j})$ is usually highly non-convex for each site $\mathbf{s}$. In this situation, the proposed linear programming model approximates the original non-convex problem by a convex programming problem.

Property 2: *For general cost function $c(\mathbf{s},\mathbf{j})$, and if $\mathcal{B}_s = \mathcal{L}_s$, $\forall s \in S$, the linear programming formulation solves the continuous extension of the reformulated discrete labeling problem, with $c(\mathbf{s},\mathbf{j})$ replaced by its lower convex hull for each site $\mathbf{s}$.*

The proof is similar to that of Property 1, by replacing $c(\mathbf{s},\mathbf{j})$ in the non-linear function with its lower convex hull. An example for lower convex hull and the coordinates of the lower convex hull vertices are illustrated in Fig. 1. Fig. 2(a) shows the convexification effect introduced by LP relaxation.

Property 3: *For general cost function $c(\mathbf{s},\mathbf{j})$, the most compact basis set $\mathcal{B}_s$ contains the vertex coordinates of the lower convex hull of $c(\mathbf{s},\mathbf{j})$, $\forall s \in S$.*

By Property 3, there is no need to include all the labeling assignment costs in the optimization: we only need to include those corresponding to the basis labels. This is one of the key steps to speed up the algorithm.

Property 4: *If the convex hull of the cost function $c(\mathbf{s},\mathbf{j})$ is strictly convex, nonzero weighting basis labels must be "adjacent".*

Proof: Here "adjacent" means the convex hull of the nonzero weighting basis labels cannot contain other basis labels. Assume this does not hold for a site $\mathbf{s}$, and the nonzero weighting basis labels are $\mathbf{j}_k$, $k = 1..K$. Then, there is a basis label $\mathbf{j}_r$ located inside the convex hull of $\mathbf{j}_k$, $k = 1..K$. Thus, $\exists \alpha_k$ such that $\mathbf{j}_r = \sum_{k=1}^{K} \alpha_k \mathbf{j}_k$ and $\sum_{k=1}^{K} \alpha_k = 1$, $\alpha_k \geq 0$. According to *Karush-Kuhn-Tucker Condition (KKTC)*, there exists $\lambda_1, \lambda_2, \lambda_3$ and $\mu_{\mathbf{j}}$ such that

$c(\mathbf{s},\mathbf{j}) + \lambda_1 + \lambda_2\phi_1(\mathbf{j}) + \lambda_3\phi_2(\mathbf{j}) - \mu_{\mathbf{j}} = 0$ and $\xi_{s,\mathbf{j}}\mu_{\mathbf{j}} = 0, \mu_{\mathbf{j}} \geq 0, \forall \mathbf{j} \in \mathcal{B}_s$

Therefore we have,

$c(\mathbf{s},\mathbf{j}_k) + \lambda_1 + \lambda_2\phi_1(\mathbf{j}_k) + \lambda_3\phi_2(\mathbf{j}_k) = 0, k = 1..K$

$c(\mathbf{s},\mathbf{j}_r) + \lambda_1 + \lambda_2\phi_1(\mathbf{j}_r) + \lambda_3\phi_2(\mathbf{j}_r) \geq 0$

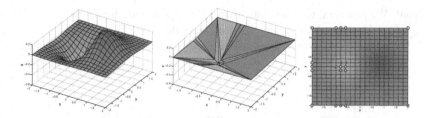

Fig. 1. Lower convex hull. Left: The surface; Middle: Lower convex hull facets; Right: Coordinates of the lower convex hull vertices.

On the other hand,

$$c(\mathbf{s}, \mathbf{j}_r) + \lambda_1 + \lambda_2 \phi_1(\mathbf{j}_r) + \lambda_3 \phi_2(\mathbf{j}_r)$$
$$= c(\mathbf{s}, \sum_{k=1}^{K} \alpha_k \mathbf{j}_k) + \lambda_1 + \lambda_2 \phi_1(\sum_{k=1}^{K} \alpha_k \mathbf{j}_k) + \lambda_3 \phi_2(\sum_{k=1}^{K} \alpha_k \mathbf{j}_k)$$
$$< \sum_{k=1}^{K} \alpha_k c(\mathbf{s}, \mathbf{j}_k) + \lambda_1 + \lambda_2 \sum_{k=1}^{K} \alpha_k \phi_1(\mathbf{j}_k) + \lambda_3 \sum_{k=1}^{K} \alpha_k \phi_2(\mathbf{j}_k) = 0$$

which contradicts the *KKTC*. The property follows.

It is not difficult to show that any basic feasible solution of the linear program has at most 3 basic variables from ξ of each site. Therefore, when using the simplex method, there will be at most 3 nonzero-weight basis labels for each site. After convexification, the original non-convex optimization problem turns into a convex problem and an efficient linear programming method can be used to yield a global optimal solution for the approximation problem. Note that, although this is a convex problem, standard local optimization schemes are found to work poorly because of quantization noise and large flat areas in the convexified objective function.

Approximating the matching cost by its lower convex hull is intuitively attractive since in the ideal case, the true matching will have the lowest matching cost and thus the optimization becomes exact in this case. In real applications, several target points may have equal matching cost and, even worse, some incorrect matching may have lower cost. In this case, because of the convexification process, in a one-step relaxation, the resulting fractional (continuous) labeling could be far from the true solution, as shown

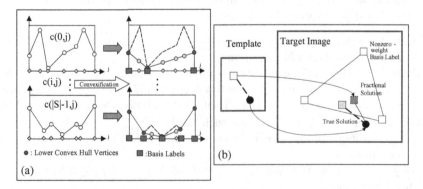

Fig. 2. (a): The convexification process introduced by LP relaxation. (b): An example when a single LP relaxation produces a fractional labeling.

in the Fig 2(b). In this simple example, there are 2 sites in the source image and we construct a simple 2-node graph template. There are 5 target points in the target image. The labels are displacement vectors. We assume that a white square will match a white square with zero cost. And the circles will match with zero cost. Matching between different shape points have large matching cost. The light gray square is in fact the true target for the white one in the source image, but the match cost is a very small positive number because of noisy measurement. By solving the LP relaxation problem, we get a fractional solution, as illustrated in Fig 2(b), that has zero cost for the LP's objective function but is not the true solution. Adjusting the smoothing parameter will not help because we already achieve the minimal (zero) cost. A traditional rounding scheme will try to round ξ into 0 and 1. Unfortunately, the rounding will drive the solution even farther from the true solution, in which the square template node will match one of the white squares in the target image. Intuitively, we can shrink the searching region for each site based on the current LP solution, and do a further search by solving a new LP problem in the smaller trust region. Clearly, if the trust region shrinks slowly, we will find the true optimal solution. In the following section, we expand this idea and propose a successive convexification scheme to improve the approximation iteratively.

3   Successive Relaxation Method

Here we propose a successive convexification linear programming method to solve the non-linear optimization problem, in which we construct linear programming problems recursively based on the previous searching result and gradually shrink the matching trust region systematically.

Assume $\mathcal{B}_\mathbf{s}^n$ is the basis label set for site $\mathbf{s}$ at stage n linear programming. The trust region $\mathcal{U}_\mathbf{s}^n$ of site $\mathbf{s}$ is determined by the previous relaxation solution $\mathbf{f}_\mathbf{s}^{n-1} = (f_{\mathbf{s},1}^{n-1}, f_{\mathbf{s},2}^{n-1})$ and a trust region diameter d_n. We define $\mathcal{Q}_\mathbf{s}^n = \mathcal{L}_\mathbf{s} \cap \mathcal{U}_\mathbf{s}^n$. $\mathcal{B}_\mathbf{s}^n$ is specified by $\mathcal{B}_\mathbf{s}^n = \{$the vertex coordinates of the lower convex hull of $\{c(\mathbf{s},\mathbf{j}), \forall \mathbf{j} \in \mathcal{Q}_\mathbf{s}^n\}\}$, where $c(\mathbf{s},\mathbf{j})$ is the cost of assigning label $\mathbf{j}$ to site $\mathbf{s}$.

Algorithm 1. *Successive Convexification Linear Programming*
1. Set $n = 0$; Set initial diameter $= d_0$;
2. FOREACH($\mathbf{s} \in S$)
3. {   Calculate the cost function $\{c(\mathbf{s},\mathbf{j}), \forall \mathbf{j} \in \mathcal{Q}_\mathbf{s}^0\}$;
4.   Convexify $\{c(\mathbf{s},\mathbf{j})\}$ and find basis $\mathcal{B}_\mathbf{s}^0$; }
5. Construct and solve $\mathcal{LP}_0$;
6. WHILE ($d_n \geq 1$)
7. { $n \leftarrow n+1$;
8. $d_n = d_{n-1} - \delta_n$;
9.   FOREACH($\mathbf{s} \in S$)
10.   {   IF ($\mathcal{Q}_\mathbf{s}^n$ is empty) $\mathcal{Q}_\mathbf{s}^n = \mathcal{Q}_\mathbf{s}^{n-1}; \mathcal{U}_\mathbf{s}^n = \mathcal{U}_\mathbf{s}^{n-1}$;
11.   ELSE update $\mathcal{U}_\mathbf{s}^n, \mathcal{Q}_\mathbf{s}^n$;
12.   Reconvexify $\{c(\mathbf{s},\mathbf{j})\}$ and relocate basis $\mathcal{B}_\mathbf{s}^n$; }
13.   Construct and solve $\mathcal{LP}_n$; }
14. Output $\mathbf{f}_\mathbf{s}^*, \forall \mathbf{s} \in S$;

It is not difficult to verify that the necessary condition for successive LP converging to the global minimum is that $\mathcal{LP}_n \leq \mathcal{E}^*$, where $\mathcal{E}^*$ is the global minimum of the non-linear problem. Since the global minimum of the function is unknown, we estimate an upper bound $\mathcal{E}^+$ of $\mathcal{E}^*$ in the iterative process. The configuration of targets that achieves the upper bound $\mathcal{E}^+$ is composed of *anchors* — an anchor is defined as the control point of the trust region for one site in the next iteration. A simple scheme is to select anchors as the solution of the previous LP, $\mathbf{r_s} = \mathbf{f_s}^{(n-1)}$. Unfortunately, in the worse case, this simple scheme has solutions whose objective function is arbitrarily far from the optimum. In fact, the fractional solution could be far away from the discrete label site. To solve this problem, we use a deterministic rounding process: we check the discrete labels and select the anchor that minimizes the non-linear objective function, given the configuration of fractional matching labels defined by the solution of the current stage. This step is similar to a single iteration of an ICM algorithm. In this step, we project a fractional solution into the discrete space. We call this new rounding selection scheme a *consistent rounding* process. Let $\mathbf{r_s}$ be the anchor; $\mathbf{m_s}$ be the global optimal solution; and $\mathbf{f_s}$ be the fractional labeling solution of LP.

Proposition 1: The energy with consistent rounding is bounded above by $3\varepsilon_{opt} + \sum_{\{\mathbf{p,q}\}\in\mathcal{N}} \lambda_{\mathbf{p,q}}(\|\mathbf{m_p}-\mathbf{f_p}\| + \|\mathbf{m_q}-\mathbf{f_q}\|)$, where ε_{opt} is the optimal energy.

Except for $\mathcal{LP}_1$, we further require that new anchors have energy not greater than the previous estimation: the anchors are updated only if new ones have smaller energy. The anchors are kept inside the new trust region for each site. The objective function for $\mathcal{LP}_n$ must be less than or equal to $\mathcal{E}^+$. This iterative procedure guarantees that the objective function of the proposed multi-step scheme is at least as good as a single relaxation scheme. In the following example, we use a simple scalar labeling problem to illustrate the solution procedure.

Example 1 (A scalar labeling problem): Assume there are two sites $\{1, 2\}$ and for each site the label set is $\{1..7\}$. The objective function is $\min_{\{f_1,f_2\}} c_{1,f_1} + c_{2,f_2} + \lambda|f_1 - f_2|$. In this example we assume that $\{c_{1,j}\} = \{2, 6, 1.7, 4, 5, 2, 2\}$; $\{c_{2,j}\} = \{5, 1, 3, 4, 1, 2, 5\}$, and $\lambda = 0.5$.

Based on the proposed scheme, the problem is solved by the sequential LPs: $\mathcal{LP}_0$, $\mathcal{LP}_1$ and $\mathcal{LP}_2$. In $\mathcal{LP}_0$ the trust regions for sites 1 and 2 both start as the whole label space $[1, 7]$. Constructing $\mathcal{LP}_0$ based on the proposed scheme corresponds to solving an approximated problem in which c for site 1 and 2 are replaced by their lower convex hulls respectively (see Fig. 3). Step $\mathcal{LP}_0$ uses convex hull basis labels $\{1, 3, 7\}$ for site 1 and $\{1, 2, 5, 6, 7\}$ for site 2. $\mathcal{LP}_0$ finds a solution with nonzero weights $\xi_{1,3} = 1$, $f_1 = 3$; and $\xi_{2,2} = 2/3$, $\xi_{2,5} = 1/3$, and resulting continuous label LP solution $f_2 = (2/3 * 2 + 1/3 * 5) = 3$. Based on the proposed rules for anchor selection, we fix site 1 at label 3 and search for the best anchor label for site 2 in $[1, 7]$ using the nonlinear objective function. This label is 2, which is selected as the anchor for site 2. Similarly, the anchor for site 1 is 3. At this stage $\mathcal{E}^+ = c(1, 3) + c(2, 2) + 0.5 * |3 - 2| = 3.2$. Further, the trust region for $\mathcal{LP}_1$ is shrunk to $[2, 6] \times [2, 6]$ by reducing the previous trust region diameter by a factor of 2. The solution of $\mathcal{LP}_1$ is $f_1 = 3$ and $f_2 = 3$. The anchor site is 3 for site 1 and 2 for site 2, with $\mathcal{E}^+ = 3.2$. Based on $\mathcal{LP}_1$, $\mathcal{LP}_2$ has new trust region $[3, 5] \times [2, 4]$ and its solution is $f_1 = 3$ and $f_2 = 2$. Since 3 and 2 are the anchors

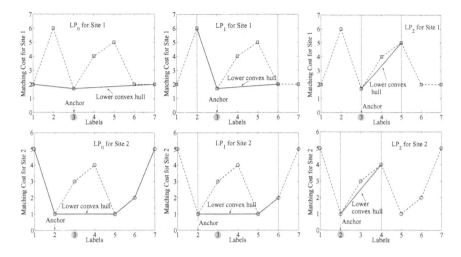

Fig. 3. Successive convexification LP in 1D. Labels in circles are LP fractional solutions.

for site 1 and 2 respectively and in the next iteration the diameter shrinks to unity, the iteration terminates. It is not difficult to verify that the configuration $f_1 = 3$, $f_2 = 2$ achieves the global minimum. Fig. 3 illustrates the proposed successive convexification process for this example.

Interestingly, for the above example, ICM or even the graph cut scheme only finds a local minimum, if initial values are not correctly set. For ICM, if f_2 is set to 5 and the updating is from f_1, the iteration will fall into a local minimum corresponding to $f_1 = 6$ and $f_2 = 5$. The GC scheme based on α-expansion will have the same problem if the initial values of f_1 and f_2 are set to 6 and 5 respectively.

A revised simplex method is used to solve the LP problem. Therefore, an estimate of the average complexity of successive convexification linear programming is $O(|S| \cdot |Q|^{1/2} \cdot (\log |Q| + \log |S|))$, where Q is the label set. Experiments also confirm that the average complexity of the proposed optimization scheme increases more slowly with the size of label set than previous methods such as the graph cut scheme, whose average complexity is linear with respect to $|Q|$.

4   Object Tracking with Multiple Templates

Based on the above matching framework, we present a robust multiple template tracking method that can be used to track objects with changing appearance. One assumption we use in the tracking process is that the template's scale and rotation remain continuous even if the template changes. This assumption is valid for appearance changes for most real-world objects, from simple rigid objects to complex articulated ones. We use a set of templates to represent possible object appearance in the tracking process. These templates can be further formulated as a digraph to represent the possible transitions from one appearance model to another. Models that can be reached in one step from the current model include the model itself and its neighbors. Other parameters in the tracking include the scale and rotation changes of the template. Based on this formulation, tracking becomes the process of locating the object with the best templates constrained by the model transition graph.

The deformable template defined includes feature nodes and neighbor relations. In this paper, the features are image blocks in the template images and target images centered on the edges. We use a very low edge detection threshold so as not to lose weak features. Usually we can downsample the feature points in the template and target images to reduce the complexity. To make the scheme resistant to changing illumination, we use chromaticity color space, in which the three color channels are normalized by their arithmetic mean. The L_1 norm is also used in calculating the cost of matching an image block with a target block. We also use non-square blocks at the boundary of the template, since values outside of the boundary are not defined. Therefore, each feature node also contains a feature mask in calculating the matching cost. We use baseline Delaunay triangulation to obtain the neighbor relations of the feature nodes. To simplify the matching problem, we decompose the geometrical transformation of the template into two cascaded transformations: a global transformation $\mathcal{G}$ and a local deformation $\mathcal{D}$. The global transformation is shared by all the sites in the template while the local deformation can be different for all sites. And, we assume that matching cost c is only influenced by global transformation but not local deformation. Intuitively, c is a function of the source pixel (site), the target pixel (label), and the global transformation (such as scaling and rotation). The energy minimization problem becomes:

$$\min_{\mathcal{G},\mathcal{D}} \mathcal{E} : \sum_{\mathbf{s} \in S} c_{\mathcal{G}}(\mathbf{s}, \mathcal{D} \circ \mathcal{G}(\mathbf{s})) + \sum_{\{\mathbf{p},\mathbf{q}\} \in \mathcal{N}} \lambda_{\mathbf{p},\mathbf{q}} \|\mathcal{D} \circ \mathcal{G}(\mathbf{p}) - \mathcal{D} \circ \mathcal{G}(\mathbf{q}) - \mathcal{G}(\mathbf{p}) + \mathcal{G}(\mathbf{q})\|$$

In the tracking process, the global transformation $\mathcal{G}$ is specified as the previous rotation and scale estimation and is updated after each matching process. With $\mathcal{G}$ fixed, the problem is reduced to the consistent labeling problem discussed in the last section and we can apply the proposed LP scheme to solve for $\mathcal{D}$ by the successive convexification LP scheme.

After finding the matches of the feature points in the template with corresponding points in the target image based on the proposed method, we need to further decide how similar these two constellations of matched points are and whether the matching result corresponds to the same event as in the exemplar. We use the following quantities to measure the difference between the template and the matching object. The first measure is P, defined as the average of pairwise length changes from the template to the target. To compensate for the global deformation, a global affine transform $\mathcal{A}$ is first estimated based on the matching and then applied to the template points before calculating P. P is further normalized with respect to the average edge length of the template. The second measure is the average warped template matching cost M, which is defined as the average absolute difference of the target image and the warped reference image in the region of interest. The warping is based on a cubic spline. The total matching cost is simply defined as $M + \alpha P$, where α has a typical value from 0.1 to 0.5. Experiments show that *only about 100 randomly selected feature points* are needed in calculating P and M.

Because of the constraints of the physical dynamics, we can safely consider only the neighboring templates equaling the current rotation and scale. The current template and its neighbors are used in the template selection process. The template with the lowest matching cost is chosen, its matching result is recorded, and the rotation θ and scale γ are updated based on the following smoothing model, in which α is typically 0.9:

$$(\theta, \gamma) = \alpha(\theta_{estimate}, \gamma_{estimate}) + (1 - \alpha)(\theta_{last}, \gamma_{last})$$

The proposed scheme is resistant to drifting because we do not track the object sequentially based on the features in the previous frame, and thus avoid template errors accumulated during the tracking process. But we do use parameters such as the rotation angle and scale estimated from previous frames to reduce the searching complexity. A model selection error may still possibly spread to future frames and make the tracker fail. In our scheme, tracking failure can be detected by comparing the minimum matching error with a threshold. When the matching error is too large, we infer a tracking failure and apply a restart process. In this process, all the templates in a rotation and scale range are used to match the target image and the best template is chosen.

5   Experimental Results

We start by comparing the proposed successive convexification LP scheme with the GC, BP, and ICM methods for local deformation estimation. We use the same energy formulation for all methods. GC uses the α-expansion scheme for symbol updating and a fixed order symbol sequence in the iteration. BP is the baseline belief propagation algorithm. BP was not conducted for all the images because of its high complexity. Fig. 4 shows comparison results for matching synthetic grayscale images with ground truth

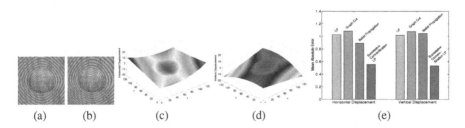

Fig. 4. (a, b): Reference and target image; (c, d): Ground truth horizontal and vertical displacement; (e): Lowest MAE is achieved for the different methods by adjusting the smoothing factors so that they each perform optimally

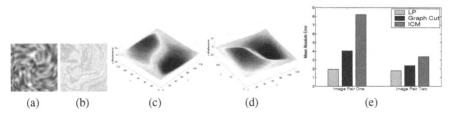

Fig. 5. (a, b): Two synthetic images. (c, d) Ground-truth x-motion and y-motion for images (a) and (b); (e): Mean absolute errors of LP, ICM and Graph Cut.

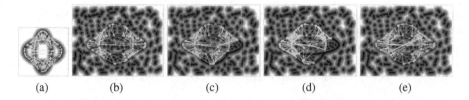

(a)   (b)   (c)   (d)   (e)

Fig. 6. (a): Template model showing distance transform; (b): Matching result of proposed scheme; (c): Matching result by GC; (d): Matching result by ICM. (e): Matching result by BP.

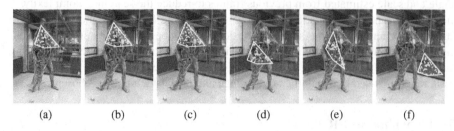

(a)   (b)   (c)   (d)   (e)   (f)

Fig. 7. Color template matching. (a): Template; (b): Matching result of successive relaxation LP with range the whole target image; (c): Matching result for GC with range $[-50, 50] \times [50, 50]$; (d): Matching result for GC with range the whole target image; (e, f): Matching results for ICM and direct sweeping search.

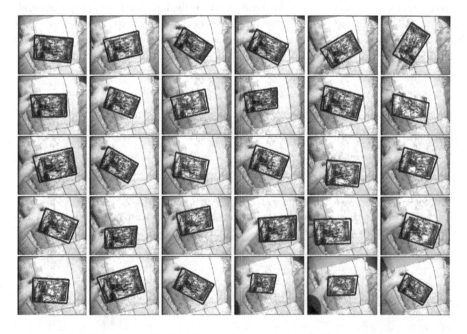

Fig. 8. Tracking result for video tape sequence. Selected from 600 frames.

displacement. The search window is $[-20,20] \times [-20,20]$. The proposed method achieves substantially better results. Fig. 5 shows another experiment result based on synthetic images. Two images and their warped versions based on a known displacement field are used in the experiment. Then, the proposed LP scheme, ICM, and GC are used to solve the L_1 norm consistent labeling problem. The target labels are all the pixels in the target image. The mean absolute error of the estimated matching for each method is then calculated based on the ground truth matching. The smoothing factor for each method is then adjusted such that a minimum matching error is obtained. These match errors for different methods are listed in Fig. 5. The proposed scheme achieves the minimum matching error. Fig. 6 shows another matching result for synthetic images. In this experiment, the pixel block size is 5 by 5 and the smoothing factor equals 1.5. The search range is the whole target image. The sites are selected on the zero-value pixels and the matching candidates for each site are all the zero-value pixels in the target image. The proposed scheme again performs the best among different schemes compared. Fig. 7 shows a template matching experiment for a color image of a wire-metal sculpture. The direct search scheme uses a fixed template shape and sweeps a search window over the target image. As shown in the figure, only our proposed scheme finds the correct target when the search range increases to the whole image. The matching energy for LP is 6.12e3, lowest compared to GC 7.45e3, ICM 11.5e3, and direct search 12.73e3.

Fig. 8 shows an experiment result for tracking a planar object under indoor lighting conditions. The glossy surface makes robust tracking a challenging task. In this experiment we use the first frame as the template image and the region of interest is indicated and a graph template is generated automatically based on random selected edge pixels and Delaunay triangulation. The scale and the rotation status of the template are adaptively updated based on the matching result. In the experiment, the smoothing factor α

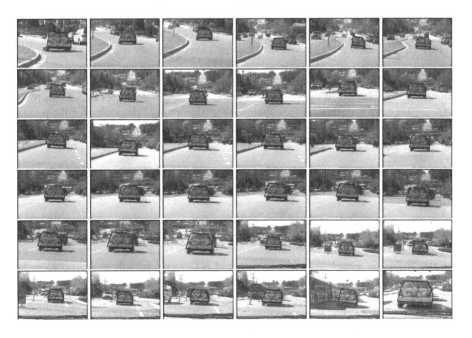

Fig. 9. Tracking result for car sequence. Selected from 1000 frames.

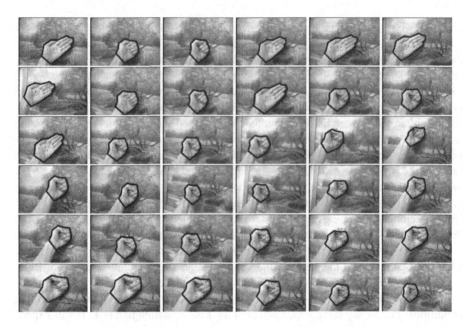

Fig. 10. Tracking result for hand sequence. Selected from 500 frames.

for scale and rotation update is set to 0.9. The proposed scheme successfully tracks the object over a long video sequence. Fig. 9 is another tracking result based on a single template, this time for a cluttered outdoor scene. The proposed scheme robustly and accurately follows the moving car in a video sequence with 1000 frames.

Fig. 10 shows a tracking result in which two exemplars are used. The hand undergoes dramatic shapes changes between the two gestures. There are also large scale and rotation changes of the hand involved in this sequence. The proposed scheme successfully tracks the movement of the hand in a poor, low-contrast video. Fig. 11 shows a result for tracking a walking person, using three exemplars. The posture of the person walking in the scene is accurately recovered. The template follows the object successfully in this very complex-background setting.

6   Conclusions

In this paper, we present a robust multiple-template object tracking scheme based on a robust linear programming based matching scheme — successive convexification linear programming. The proposed optimization method can be used for solving consistent labeling problems with L_1 regulary term, and is found to be able to converge to the global optimal solution with high probability. The successive convexification idea can also be generalized to other convex smoothing term problems. The proposed scheme is shown to be more efficient than the graph cut and belief propagation schemes for object matching problems. Based on the proposed optimization scheme, we study an object tracking framework in which multiple templates can be defined. Templates are updated

Fig. 11. Tracking result for walking sequence. Selected from 150 frames.

based on the estimation of the global transform resulting from mean square estimation of the matching patterns of the previous stage, and template matching is solved by the proposed LP based scheme. We further present measures to quantify the similarities of the template with target objects. By choosing the best template to its corresponding matching patterns, the proposed scheme can be used to robustly track objects changing appearance dramatically, using only a few templates. Since no training, but only several exemplars are needed, the proposed scheme is easier to deploy than appearance-model based schemes. Experiments show robust tracking results in cluttered environments. The proposed matching scheme can also be applied to other applications such as large scale motion estimation, wide baseline matching and 3D object reconstruction.

7 Appendix

Proposition 1: The energy with consistent rounding is bounded above by $3\varepsilon_{opt} + \sum_{\{p,q\}\in\mathcal{N}} \lambda_{p,q}(\|m_p - f_p\| + \|m_q - f_q\|)$, where ε_{opt} is the optimal energy.

Proof: The proof is simple but lengthy:

$$\sum_s c(s, r_s) + \sum_{\{p,q\}\in\mathcal{N}} \lambda_{p,q}\|r_p - r_q\|$$
$$\leq \sum_s c(s, r_s) + \sum_{\{p,q\}\in\mathcal{N}} \lambda_{p,q}(\|r_p - f_q\| + \|r_q - f_p\| + \|f_p - f_q\|)$$
$$= \sum_s c(s, r_s) + \sum_s \sum_{p\in\mathcal{N}(s)} \lambda_{s,p}\|r_s - f_p\| + \sum_{\{p,q\}\in\mathcal{N}} \lambda_{p,q}\|f_p - f_q\|$$

Recalling the anchor selection rule,

$$c(s, r_s) + \sum_{p\in\mathcal{N}(s)} \lambda_{s,p}\|r_s - f_p\| \leq c(s, m_s) + \sum_{p\in\mathcal{N}(s)} \lambda_{s,p}\|m_s - f_p\|$$

Therefore

$$\sum_s c(s, r_s) + \sum_{\{p,q\}\in\mathcal{N}} \lambda_{p,q}\|r_p - r_q\|$$
$$\leq \sum_s c(s, m_s) + \sum_s \sum_{p\in\mathcal{N}(s)} \lambda_{s,p}\|m_s - f_p\| + \sum_{\{p,q\}\in\mathcal{N}} \lambda_{p,q}\|f_p - f_q\|$$
$$= \sum_s c(s, m_s) + \sum_{\{p,q\}\in\mathcal{N}} \lambda_{p,q}(\|m_p - f_q\| + \|m_q - f_p\|) + \sum_{\{p,q\}\in\mathcal{N}} \lambda_{p,q}\|f_p - f_q\|$$
$$\leq \sum_s c(s, m_s) + \sum_{\{p,q\}\in\mathcal{N}} \lambda_{p,q}(\|m_p - m_q\| + \|f_q - m_q\|$$
$$+\|m_q - m_p\| + \|m_p - f_p\|) + \sum_{\{p,q\}\in\mathcal{N}} \lambda_{p,q}\|f_p - f_q\|$$
$$\leq \sum_s c(s, m_s) + 2\sum_{\{p,q\}\in\mathcal{N}} \lambda_{p,q}\|m_p - m_q\| + \sum_{\{p,q\}\in\mathcal{N}} \lambda_{p,q}\|f_p - f_q\|$$
$$+\sum_{\{p,q\}\in\mathcal{N}} \lambda_{p,q}(\|f_q - m_q\| + \|m_p - f_p\|)$$

Noticing that $\sum_{\{p,q\}\in\mathcal{N}} \lambda_{p,q}\|f_p - f_q\| \leq \varepsilon_{opt}$, the proof is complete.

References

1. H. Ishikawa. Global Optimization using Embedded Graphs, Ph.D. Dissertation. May 2000, NYU.
2. T.M. Breuel. A comparison of search strategies for geometric branch and bound algorithms. ECCV, III:837-850, 2002.
3. A. Rosenfeld, R.A. Hummel, and S.W. Zucker. Scene labeling by relaxation operations. IEEE Trans. Systems, Man, and Cybernetics, 6(6):420-433, 1976.
4. J. Besag. On the statistical analysis of dirty pictures. J. R. Statis. Soc. Lond. B, 48:259-302, 1986.
5. Y. Boykov, O. Veksler, and R. Zabih. Fast approximate energy minimization via graph cuts. PAMI, 23:1222-1239, 2001.
6. J. Pearl. Probabilistic reasoning in intelligent systems – Networks of plausible inference. Morgan-Kaufmann, 1988.
7. Y. Weiss and W.T. Freeman. On the optimality of solutions of the max-product belief propagation algorithm in arbitrary graphs. IEEE Trans. on Information Theory, 47(2):736-744, 2001.

8. P.F. Felzenszwalb and D.P. Huttenlocher. Efficient belief propagation for early vision. CVPR, I:261-268, 2004.

9. V. Kolmogorov and R. Zabih. Multi-camera scene reconstruction via graph cuts. ECCV, III:82-96, 2002.

10. V. Kolmogorov and R. Zabih. Computing visual correspondence with occlusions using graph cuts. ICCV, II:508-515, 2001.

11. J. Sun, H.Y. Shum and N.N. Zheng. Stereo matching using belief propagation. PAMI, 25(7):787-800, 2003.

12. J.M. Coughlan and S.J. Ferreira. Finding deformable shapes using loopy belief propagation. ECCV, III:453-468, 2002.

13. B. Luo and E.R. Hancock. Structural matching using the EM algorithm and singular value decomposition. PAMI, 23:1120-1136, 2001.

14. H. Chui and A. Rangarajan. A new algorithm for non-rigid point matching. CVPR, II:44-51, 2000.

15. A. Rangarajan, H.L. Chui and F.L. Bookstein. The softassign procrustes matching algorithm. Information Processing in Medical Imaging, pages 29-42, Springer, 1997.

16. P. D. Tao, T. Q. Phong, R. Horaud, and L. Quan. Stability of Lagrangian duality for nonconvex quadratic programming solution methods and applications to computer vision. Mathematical Modelling and Numerical Analysis, 31(1):57-90, 1997.

17. X. Bai, H. Yu, E. Hancock. Graph matching using embedding and semidefinite programming. BMVC, 2004.

18. M. Ben-Ezra, S. Peleg, and M. Werman. Real-time motion analysis with linear programming. ICCV, pages 703-709, 1999.

19. J. Kleinberg and E. Tardos. Approximation algorithms for classification problems with pairwise relationships: metric labeling and Markov random fields. IEEE Symposium on Foundations of Computer Science, pages 14-23, 1999.

20. C. Chekuri, S. Khanna, J. Naor, and L. Zosin. Approximation algorithms for the metric labeling problem via a new linear programming formulation. Symp. on Discrete Algs, pages 109-118, 2001.

21. D. Comaniciu, V. Ramesh, and P. Meer. Real-time tracking of non-rigid objects using mean shift. CVPR, II:142-149, 2000.

22. M. J. Black and A. D. Jepson. Eigentracking: robust matching and tracking of articulated objects using a view-based representation. ECCV, pages 329-342, 1996.

23. L.P. Morency, A. Rahimi, and T. Darrell. Adaptive view-based appearance models. CVPR, I:803-810, 2003.

24. H. Jiang, Z.N. Li, and M.S. Drew. Optimizing motion estimation with linear programming and detail-preserving variational method. CVPR, I:738-745, 2004.

25. H. Jiang, Z.N. Li, and M.S. Drew. Posture recognition with convex programming. ICME, 2005.

Extraction of Layers of Similar Motion
Through Combinatorial Techniques

Romain Dupont[1,2], Nikos Paragios[1], Renaud Keriven[1], and Phillipe Fuchs[2]

[1] Atlantis Research Group, CERTIS
ENPC, Marne-La-Vallee, France
Fax: (+33) 1 64 15 21 99, Tel: (+33) 1 64 15 21 72
{dupont, paragios, keriven}@certis.enpc.fr
[2] Centre de Robotique, CAOR
ENSMP, Paris, France
fuchs@ensmp.fr

Abstract. In this paper we present a new technique to extract layers in a video sequence. To this end, we assume that the observed scene is composed of several transparent layers, that their motion in the 2D plane can be approximated with an affine model. The objective of our approach is the estimation of these motion models as well as the estimation of their support in the image domain. Our technique is based on an iterative process that integrates robust motion estimation, MRF-based formulation, combinatorial optimization and the use of visual as well as motion features to recover the parameters of the motion models as well as their support layers. Special handling of occlusions as well as adaptive techniques to detect new objects in the scene are also considered. Promising results demonstrate the potentials of our approach.

1 Introduction

Motion perception is an important characteristic of biological vision used as input in various tasks like to determine the focus of attention, etc. Therefore, motion analysis has been a long time objective of computational vision, a low to mid-level task.

The segmentation of an image sequence into regions with homogeneous motion is a challenging task in video processing [1, 2, 3, 4, 5, 6] that can be used for various purposes such as video-based surveillance and action recognition. In addition, it can be considered for video compression [1] since the motion model and the corresponding supporting layers provide a compact representation of the scene.

Motion/displacement is a well-defined measurement in the real world. On the other hand, one can claim that recovering the corresponding quantity in the image plane is a tedious task. Optical flow calculation [7, 8, 9, 10, 5] is equivalent with the estimation of a motion displacement vector for each pixel of the image plane that satisfies the visual constancy constraint. Such a task refers to an ill-posed problem where the number of unknown variables exceeds the number

A. Rangarajan et al. (Eds.): EMMCVPR 2005, LNCS 3757, pp. 220–234, 2005.

of constraints. The use of smoothness constraints [11] and other sophisticated techniques were consider to address such an issue.

Parametric motion models are an alternative to dense optical flow estimation [12, 10, 13, 5]. The basic assumption of such a technique is that for an image block, the 2D motion in the image plane can be modeled using a parametric transformation. Such assumption is valid when the block refers to a projection of 3D planar patch.

The objective of this work is to recover different planar surfaces, or motion layers, and the motion parameters describing their apparent displacements. In the literature, a K-mean clustering algorithm [1] on the motion estimates, or a minimum description length (MDL) [3] were considered to determine the number of motion planes. In the latter case, the extraction is done according to a maximum likelihood criterion, followed by optimization by the Expectation-Maximization algorithm [14, 3]. More recent approaches [15] refer to region growing techniques within combinatorial optimization [16].

In this paper, we present an iterative technique to estimate the motion parameters, the support of each layer as well as its visual properties. The latter is used to overcome cases where motion information is not enough to estimate the support. Our approach addresses in a very efficient fashion motion estimation through a robust incremental technique, accounts for occlusions through a forward/backward transformation and recover the layer support through a MRF-based formulation that is optimized with the graph cut approach and the α-expansion algorithm. To this end, motion residuals, visual appearance as well as spatial and temporal smoothness constraints are considered.

The reminder of this paper is organized according to the following fashion. In section 2, we briefly introduce the problem under consideration while in section 3, an iterative approach to recover the motion parameters is presented. The extraction of the support regions of the different layers is part of section 4, while in section 5 we discuss the implementation details of our approach and provide experimental results and future directions.

2   Decomposition of Scenes in Motion Layers

Let us consider a static scene that consists of several planes, a moving observer on the scene, and a sequence of 2D images acquired by the observer. Due to the camera's ego motion from one image to the next, one will be able to observe motion on the static parts of the scene. Such motion (2D projection) depends on the camera projection model and the depth level of the different planes in the 3D scene. Here, we consider the projective camera model. The concept of motion decomposition in layers [1] consists of separating the image domain into n support regions $\mathcal{S}_i, i \in [1, n]$ with their corresponding motion models $(\mathcal{A}_i, \sigma_i)$. The i-th layer $\mathcal{L}_i, i \in [1, n]$ is defined as the couple $(\mathcal{S}_i, \mathcal{A}_i)$.

The image domain Ω is partioned into n disjoint sets $\mathcal{S}_i$ such that $\cup_{i=1}^{n} \mathcal{S}_i = \Omega$, $\mathcal{S}_i \cap \mathcal{S}_j = \emptyset, i \neq j$ and neither the number of layers, not their support regions, nor their motion parameters are known. In the reminder of this paper, we will propose efficient methods to address the estimation of these unknown variables.

In terms of motion, one can find in the literature parametric models of various degrees of freedom like rigid, similarity, homographic, quadratic, etc. Affine model is a reasonable compromise between low complexity and fairly good approximation of the non-complex motions of objects at about the same depth. It consists of 6 degrees of freedom,

$$\mathcal{A}(x, y) = \begin{pmatrix} a_0 \cdot x + a_1 \cdot y + a_2 \\ a_3 \cdot x + a_4 \cdot y + a_5 \end{pmatrix}$$

Such a model describes accurately (as detailed in [2]) the motion induced by a planar object viewed from a moving camera. Furthermore, this model describes well the 2D motion of the projection of an arbitrary 3D scene undergoing camera rotations, zoom and small camera translations [17]. Likewise, when the overall depth of the object is greater than the depth within the object, the model describes the image motion with a sub-pixel accuracy.

Motion estimation consists of recovering the parameters of this model such that a correspondence between the projections of the same 3D patch within two consecutive images is established. In principle, motion estimation refer to an ill-posed problem since neither the projection model, neither the internal parameters of the cameras are known and therefore constraints are to be deduced from the images toward its estimation.

3   Recovering the Parameters of the Motion Models

The intensity preservation constraint (equivalent to the brightness constancy assumption) [7] is often used to address motion estimation. The essence of this constraint is that under the assumption of planar, Lambertian surfaces and without global illumination changes, the appearance of the 2D projection of the same 3D patch will not change over time. Therefore if a motion vector $\mathbf{dx} = (dx, dy)$ is assumed for the pixel $\mathbf{x} = (x, y)$, then the following condition is to be satisfied:

$$I(\mathbf{x}; t) \approx I(\mathbf{x} + \mathbf{dx}; t + 1), \quad (i)$$
$$I(\mathbf{x}; t) \approx I(\mathbf{x} + \mathcal{A}(\mathbf{x}); t + 1), \quad (ii)$$

for the case of dense motion (i) and for the case of affine motion (ii). Given such a condition, one can define the total motion residual according to:

$$E(\mathcal{A}) = \int_\Omega |I(\mathbf{x}; t) - I(\mathbf{x} + \mathcal{A}(\mathbf{x}); t + 1)|^2 \, d\mathbf{x} \tag{1}$$

Solving the inference problem, that is recovering the parameters of the affine model through the lowest potential of the above function is a common practice in computational vision. One can consider an iterative process using a well adopted first order linear form of optical flow constraint:

$$\mathcal{A}(\mathbf{x}) \cdot \nabla I(\mathbf{x}; t) + \nabla_t I(\mathbf{x}) = 0 \tag{2}$$

where ∇I to the spatial gradient and $\nabla_t I$ to the temporal gradient. One can consider minimizing the corresponding cost function

$$E(\mathcal{A}) = \int_\Omega |\mathcal{A}(\mathbf{x}) \cdot \nabla I(\mathbf{x}; t) + I(\mathbf{x}; t + 1) - I(\mathbf{x}; t)|^2 \, d\mathbf{x} \qquad (3)$$

with standard linear methods that will fail though to capture large displacements between two successive frames. To overcome this limitation, we consider an iterative process as prescribed in [12]. To this end, one can consider an incremental update of the motion parameters where at each step, given the current estimates $\mathcal{A}$, we seek to recover an improvement of the estimation $\Delta\mathcal{A}$ such that the accumulation of existing parameters and the improvement minimizes the following residual error:

$$E(\Delta\mathcal{A}) = \int_\Omega [I(\mathbf{x}; t) - I(\mathbf{x} + \mathcal{A}(\mathbf{x}); t + 1) - \Delta\mathcal{A}\nabla I(\mathbf{x} + \mathcal{A}(\mathbf{x}); t + 1)]^2 \, d\mathbf{x} \quad (4)$$

that has a closed form solution. While one can claim that such an incremental method will improve the estimation process, it will still suffer from the presence of outliers resulting an estimation bias. Robust estimation process like an M-estimator can be used to overcome this limitation. Such a method assigns weights $we(\mathbf{x})$ to the constraints at the pixel level that are disproportional to their residual error, thus rejecting the motion outliers. To this end, one should define the influence function, $\psi(x)$ like for example the Tukey's estimator [FIG. 1]:

$$\psi(x) = \begin{cases} x(K_\sigma{}^2 - x^2)^2 & \text{if } |x| < K_\sigma \\ 0 & \text{otherwise} \end{cases} \qquad (5)$$

where K_σ characterizes the shape of the robust function. The weights $we(\mathbf{x})$ are then computed as following: $we(\mathbf{x}) = \frac{\psi(r(\mathbf{x}))}{r(\mathbf{x})}$ ([12]).

One can now consider such a process for each layer in an independent fashion, that consists of minimizing the following cost function

$$E(\Delta\mathcal{A}_1, ..., \Delta\mathcal{A}_n) = \qquad (6)$$

$$\sum_{k=1}^n \int_\Omega \chi_{\mathcal{S}_i}(\mathbf{x}) \rho \left[I(\mathbf{x}; t) - I(\mathbf{x} + \mathcal{A}_i(\mathbf{x}); t + 1) - \Delta\mathcal{A}_i \nabla \, I(\mathbf{x} + \mathcal{A}_i(\mathbf{x}); t + 1) \right] d\mathbf{x}$$

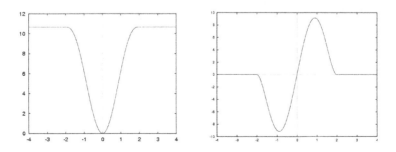

Fig. 1. Tukey function ρ (on the left) and its derivative ψ (on the right)

where $\chi_{\mathcal{S}_i}$ is the characteristic function of the region $\mathcal{S}_i$. Once the support layers are known, one can proceed to a straightforward estimation of the motion models. Occlusions due to motion of the observer and the scene often arise in motion and stereo reconstruction and must be taken into account. Such a case can be accounted for through the joint estimation of the backward/forward motion;

Let (i) $\mathcal{A}_1, ..., \mathcal{A}_n$ be the motion models that create visual correspondences between the images t and $t+1$ (such that $I(\mathbf{x};t) = I((\mathbf{x}+\mathcal{A}(\mathbf{x});t+1))$ and (ii) $\mathcal{A}'_1, ..., \mathcal{A}'_n$ the ones that create visual correspondences between the images $t+1$ and t (such that $I(\mathbf{x};t+1) = I((\mathcal{A}'(\mathbf{x});t))$). Then, we seek for a simultaneous estimate of the improvements of both models forward/backward according to:

$$E(\Delta\mathcal{A}_1, ..., \Delta\mathcal{A}_n, \Delta\mathcal{A}'_1, ..., \Delta\mathcal{A}'_n) = \tag{7}$$

$$\sum_{k=1}^{n} \int_{\Omega} \chi_{\mathcal{S}_i}(\mathbf{x})\rho\left[I(\mathbf{x};t+1) - I(\mathbf{x}+\mathcal{A}'_i(\mathbf{x});t) - \Delta\mathcal{A}'_i(\mathbf{x})\nabla\, I(\mathbf{x}+\mathcal{A}'_i(\mathbf{x});t)\right]$$

$$+\sum_{k=1}^{n} \int_{\Omega} \chi_{\mathcal{S}_i}(\mathbf{x})\rho\left[I(\mathbf{x};t) - I(\mathbf{x}+\mathcal{A}_i(\mathbf{x});t+1) - \Delta\mathcal{A}_i(\mathbf{x})\nabla\, I(\mathbf{x}+\mathcal{A}_i(\mathbf{x});t+1)\right]$$

Under the assumption on the absence of occlusion, one can consider that for a given pixel, both transformations capture its real motion and therefore, posing $\mathbf{x}' = \mathbf{x} + \mathcal{A}(\mathbf{x})$, the following condition will be satisfied:

$$\mathbf{x}' + \mathcal{A}'(\mathbf{x}') = \mathbf{x} \tag{8}$$

Such a concept is presented in [FIG. (2)]. The distance between the origins of the pixel $\mathbf{x}$ and its position upon the application of forward/backward motion models;

$$\mathcal{D}(\mathbf{x}) = \|\mathbf{x}' + \mathcal{A}'(\mathbf{x}') - \mathbf{x}\|^2 \tag{9}$$

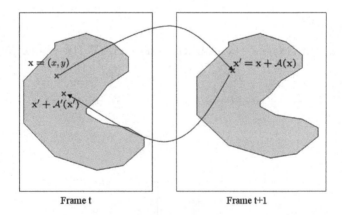

Frame t   Frame t+1

Fig. 2. Occlusion Detection: the Euclidean distance between the pixel origin and the corresponding one after being transformed through the forward/backward motion is used to detect occlusions

can be considered as an indicator on the presence of occlusions and used to ponderate the influence function ψ defined in equation 5:

$$\psi(x) = \psi(x) \cdot \frac{1}{1 + \mathcal{D}(\mathbf{x})} \tag{10}$$

Hence, occlusions will have low influence on the estimation process. However, given the robust estimation process that was considered for any given partition of the image, we will be able to recover affine motion models that, to some extent, describe the observed motion. Therefore, we refer to the egg and the chicken problem where it is crucial to have a consistent estimation of the support layers.

4   Extraction of Support Layers

Let us consider a partition of the image into n segments

$$\{\mathcal{S}_1, ..., \mathcal{S}_n\} : \cup_{i=1}^n \mathcal{S}_i = \Omega, \quad \mathcal{S}_i \cap \mathcal{S}_j = \emptyset, i \neq j$$

The problem of extracting support within the layer decomposition process consists of selecting for each pixel of Ω, the label among these n that dictates the most appropriate motion model for this image patch. One can see such a task in the form of a labeling problem, where one should assign to the pixel $\mathbf{x}$ a label $\omega(\mathbf{x}) \in [1, n]$ according to a certain criterion. Within our approach we adopt motion and appearance terms to address such a labeling process while imposing certain spatial and temporal smoothness constraints on the label space.

4.1   Motion Criterion

Let us consider the distribution of the residual errors within a layer. Under the assumption of proper motion estimation as well as correct classification, one can consider that residual errors are due to the presence of noise that in the most general case white.

Therefore, the motion residual $r_i(\mathbf{x}) = |I(\mathbf{x}, t) - I(\mathbf{x} + \mathcal{A}_i(\mathbf{x}), t + 1)|$ for the layer $\mathcal{L}_i$ obeys a normal law $G(\mu_i, \sigma_i)$. Consequently, the probability for given a pixel within the region $\mathcal{L}_i$ to actually being part of this region according to the observed residual is:

$$p\left(r_i(\mathbf{x}) | \mathcal{A}_i, \sigma_i\right) = \frac{1}{\sqrt{2\pi}\sigma_i} \exp\left(\frac{-r_i^2(\mathbf{x})}{2\sigma_i^2}\right) \tag{11}$$

where σ_i is the standard deviation computed during the motion estimation for each layer support. We consider the following robust estimator which tolerates 50% of outliers efficiently:

$$\sigma_i = 1.4826 \left\{ \underset{\mathbf{x} \in \mathcal{S}_i}{\text{median}} |r_i(\mathbf{x})| \right\} \tag{12}$$

One can assume independence on the distribution of the residual errors within the pixels of a support layer $\mathcal{S}_i$ and given the expected distribution, would like to maximize the conditional density,

$$p_i(r_i(\mathbf{x})|\mathcal{A}_i, \sigma_i) = p\left(\bigcap_{\mathbf{x} \in \mathcal{S}_i} \{r_i(\mathbf{x})|\mathcal{A}_i, \sigma_i\}\right)$$

$$= \prod_{\mathbf{x} \in \mathcal{S}_i} p(r_i(\mathbf{x})|\mathcal{A}_i, \sigma_i) \tag{13}$$

Furthermore, independence on the residual errors is assumed between the different support layers. Then, using the Bayes rule, one can consider the posterior for the labeling process ω according to the motion characteristics in the following fashion:

$$p(r_i(\mathbf{x})|\mathcal{A}_i, \sigma_i, \omega) = \prod_{\mathbf{x} \in \Omega} p_{\omega(\mathbf{x})}(r_{\omega(\mathbf{x})}(\mathbf{x})|\mathcal{A}_{\omega(\mathbf{x})}, \sigma_{\omega(\mathbf{x})}) \tag{14}$$

where the assumption that all labelings are equal probable was made. Maximizing the posterior is equivalent with minimizing the negative log-likelihood of such a density:

$$E_{motion}(\omega) = -\int_\Omega \log\left[p_{\omega(\mathbf{x})}\left(r_{\omega(\mathbf{x})}(\mathbf{x})|\mathcal{A}_{\omega(\mathbf{x})}, \sigma_{\omega(\mathbf{x})}\right)\right] d\mathbf{x}$$

$$= \int_\Omega \left(\log\left[\sigma_{\omega(\mathbf{x})}\right] + \frac{r_{\omega(\mathbf{x})}^2(\mathbf{x})}{2\sigma_{\omega(\mathbf{x})}^2}\right) d\mathbf{x} \tag{15}$$

The lowest potential of this objective function will classify image pixels according to their residual errors. Such classification will reflect the maximum posterior according to the expected distribution of the residual error for each layer. However, motion estimates are reliable when image structure is present and consequently motion-based classification may be ambiguous in some cases, like in the lack of texture.

4.2 Visual Appearance Criterion

We overcome this limitation through the introduction of a visual grouping constraint, where a classification according to the observed intensities is to be considered. To this end, we consider a flexible parametric density function - Gaussian mixture - to describe the visual properties of each layer;

$$p_i(I) = \sum_{k=1}^{m_i} \pi_{\{i,k\}}\ p_{\{i,k\}}\left(I|\mu_{\{i,k\}}, \Sigma_{\{i,k\}}\right) \tag{16}$$

where $p_i()$ is the colour distribution of the i-th layer that consists of m_i Gaussian components with $\pi_{\{i,k\}} \in [0,1]$ being the prior of the component k (or its proportion in the mixture) and $(\mu_{\{i,k\}}, \Sigma_{\{i,k\}})$ the mean and the covariance matrix of this component. These parameters are estimated from an observed distribution through an EM algorithm [18]. To efficiently determine the number of Gaussian components per mixture, a Minimum Description Length (MDL) criterion is considered. Such a colour distribution has been chosen because it provides a simple and efficient way to learn the visual characteristics of each layer while not being constraint to be a unimodal. Therefore even regions with very different colour characteristics that belong to the same plane will be accounted for. Then, the posterior segmentation probability can be considered as the most efficient metric to recover the separation of the image domain into regions of support for the different layers according to their expected appearance properties. Similar to the case of motion, we consider that layers as well as pixels within regions are independent and all possible labelings are equally probable, leading to the following objective function

$$E_{visual}(\omega) = -\int_\Omega \log\left[p_{\omega(\mathbf{x})}\left(I(\mathbf{x})\right)\right] d\mathbf{x} \tag{17}$$

$$= \int_\Omega \log\left(\sum_{k=1}^{m_{\omega()}} \pi_{\{\omega(),k\}} \; p_{\{\omega(),k\}}\left(I()|\mu_{\{\omega(),k\}}, \Sigma_{\{\omega(),k\}}\right)\right) d\mathbf{x}$$

where $\mathbf{x}$ were omitted from the notation due to the lack of space. One can seek the lowest potential of these two terms weighted according to some constant to recover the most appropriate image partition in terms of support layers. Such a method will be able to determine support through an independent decision process according to the similarity between the observed image and the expected properties in terms of appearance and residual error. Such an independent process will form several discontinuities that will be quite disrupting to the human eye and will violate the condition that images are assumed to be consistent at a local scale.

4.3   Spatial Smoothness

Such a limitation is often addressed using local smoothness constraints on the label domain, that consists of saying that neighborhood pixels should belong to the same layer;

$$E_{smooth}(\omega) = \int_\Omega \left[\int_{\mathcal{N}(\mathbf{x})} \mathcal{V}(\omega(\mathbf{x}), \omega(\mathbf{u})) d\mathbf{u}\right] d\mathbf{x} \tag{18}$$

where $\mathcal{N}(\mathbf{x})$ is the local neighborhood of $\mathbf{x}$. Here, the function $\mathcal{V}$ has the following form (named Pott's model):

$$\mathcal{V}(\omega(\mathbf{x}), \omega(\mathbf{u})) = \begin{cases} +\alpha_{diff} & , \omega(\mathbf{x}) \neq \omega(\mathbf{u}) \\ 0 & , \omega(\mathbf{x}) = \omega(\mathbf{u}) \end{cases} \tag{19}$$

with $\alpha_{diff} > 0$ and the local neighborhood consists of pixels that are 4- or 8-connected. Such a term will penalize discontinuities in the support space that are also discontinuities in the motion space. While such an assumption seems natural, it is not valid when considering pixels that refer to real discontinuities of the observed scene. In that case, we should tolerate label discontinuities, which is satisfied through a multiplicative factor applied to the smoothness potential that is inversely proportional to the image gradient [19], or:

$$\mathcal{V}^g(\omega(\mathbf{x}), \omega(\mathbf{u})) = \mathcal{V}(\omega(\mathbf{x}), \omega(\mathbf{u})) \exp\left(-\frac{\|I(\mathbf{x}) - I(\mathbf{u})\|^2}{2\sigma^2}\right) \qquad (20)$$

Such a term will produce smoothness on the label space in rather uniform regions while it will relax the constraint in areas where physical discontinuities are present.

One can further explore smoothness in the temporal domain. Given that we are treating sequences of images observing the same scene, the assumption of smoothness within the labeling in the temporal space is valid.

4.4   Temporal Smoothness

Let us consider a sequence of images $I(;1), I(;2), ..., I(;\tau)$, as well as a sequence of labelings $\omega(;1), \omega(;2), ..., \omega(;\tau)$. We assume that we are currently treating the image $t \in [1, \tau]$ and the motion models $\mathcal{A}_1, ..., \mathcal{A}_{t-1}$ have correctly been estimated. Then, we define a smoothness function on the temporal space that takes into account the motion models and the support layers of the previous frame:

$$\mathcal{V}^t(\omega(\mathbf{x};t)) = \begin{cases} +\alpha_{diff} & , \omega(\mathbf{x};t) \neq \omega(\mathcal{A}_{t-1}^{-1}(\mathbf{u});t-1) \\ 0 & , \omega(\mathbf{x};t) = \omega(\mathcal{A}_{t-1}^{-1}(\mathbf{u});t-1) \end{cases} \qquad (21)$$

where $\mathcal{A}_{t-1}^{-1}$ is the inverse motion model that establishes correspondences between the frames $I(;t)$ and $I(;t-1)$. One can now introduce an additional temporal smoothness term:

$$E_{tsmooth}(\omega) = \int_{\Omega} \mathcal{V}^t(\omega(\mathbf{x}))d\mathbf{x} \qquad (22)$$

where particular attention is to be paid to address the presence of new objects in the scene. Motion residual errors, visual consistency and spatial and temporal smoothness can now be considered to recover the optimal partition of the image given the expected characteristics of each layer, or:

$$E(\omega) = E_{motion}(\omega) + \alpha E_{visual}(\omega) + \beta E_{smooth}(\omega) + \gamma E_{tsmooth}(\omega) \qquad (23)$$

The lowest -sub-optimal- potential of the discrete form of the above function can be determined using several techniques of various complexity like the iterated conditional modes [20], the highest confidence first [21], the mean field and simulated annealing [22] and the min-cut max flow approach [23]. Because of its efficiency, the graph-cut framework is retained to recover the optimal solution on the label assignement problem [23].

5   Graph-Cuts and Implementation

The graph $\mathcal{G} = \langle \mathcal{V}, \mathcal{E} \rangle$ is a set of nodes $\mathcal{V}$ and directed edges $\mathcal{E}$ connecting them. Two special *terminal* nodes are present: the *source* s and the *sink* t. Each edge connecting nodes p and q is assigned a weight $w(p, q)$. We break all edges in two groups: n-links and t-links. A n-link is an edge connecting two non-terminal nodes. A t-link connects a non-terminal node with a terminal node, s or t. The cut C is a partitioning of the nodes of the graph into two disjoint subsets S et T such that the source $s \in S$ and the sink $t \in T$. Its cost $c(S, T)$ is the sum of the weights of all edges (p, q) such that $p \in S$ and $q \in T$. The minimum cut is the cut with minimal cost and can be determined in polynomial time with a max-flow extraction algorithm.

For the energy (23), finding directly the optimal solution is not feasible in practical. Indeed, the problem of multi-labeling is NP-hard and no polynomial method is available to obtain the optimal solution. However, the α-expansion algorithm [23] gives fastly a good approximation of this energy which is guaranteed to be within a factor of 2 from the optimal one. To minimize the energy (23), we proceed as follows: we start with an initial layer assignments, obtained at the previous iteration. Then, for each $\alpha \in [1, n]$, we improve this energy by modifying some labelings to the label α via an α-*expansion move* which we describe here: considering a binary graph $\mathcal{G}$, each pixel $\mathbf{x} \in \Omega$ is representd by a non-terminal node p connected to the source with a weight $t_{s,p}$ and to the sink with a weight $t_{p,t}$. Each pair of neighbouring nodes (p, q) - if their layer assignments are different - are linked through an intermediate node a with weights $t_{s,a}$, $t_{p,a}$ and $t_{a,q}$ respectively. For t-link weights, we define the data cost function $D_p(\omega)$ as $D_p(\omega) = E_{motion}(\omega) + \alpha E_{visual}(\omega) + \gamma E_{tsmooth}(\omega)$. The table 1 summarizes all the weights associated to the n- and t-links. The minimal cut gives the new layer assignments which is optimal considering label α against all the others.

Table 1. Weights associated to each nodes of the α-expansion graph

link	weight	for
$t_{s,p}$	$D_p(\omega(\mathbf{x}))$	$\omega(\mathbf{x}) \neq \alpha$
$t_{s,p}$	∞	$\omega(\mathbf{x}) = \alpha$
$t_{p,t}$	$D_p(\alpha)$	$\forall\, \omega(\mathbf{x})$
$t_{s,a}$	$\mathcal{V}(\omega(\mathbf{x}), \omega(\mathbf{u}))$	$\omega(\mathbf{x}) \neq \omega(\mathbf{u})$
$t_{p,a}$	$\mathcal{V}(\omega(\mathbf{x}), \alpha)$	$\omega(\mathbf{x}) \neq \omega(\mathbf{u})$
$t_{a,q}$	$\mathcal{V}(\alpha, \omega(\mathbf{u}))$	$\omega(\mathbf{x}) \neq \omega(\mathbf{u})$
$t_{p,q}$	$\mathcal{V}(\omega(\mathbf{x}), \alpha)$	$\omega(\mathbf{x}) = \omega(\mathbf{u})$

5.1   Implementation Details

Once appropriate modules have been presented to address each sub-task, now we can proceed to the definition of the overall concept. In the first image, a random sampling into $\mathcal{N}$ segments is considered. These segments are used as support layers, and the motion as well as visual properties are obtained. Such measures are then introduced to the α-expansion algorithm that will provide a new image partition with different visual and motion properties. The process is repeated until convergence. Initialization of the layer support from one image to the next is done through the motion models and the same process as the one of the first frame is considered. One critical step is the estimation of the number of layers. Toward this end, we use two techniques sequentially. The first one reduces the number of layers and the second one detects new layers (or new objects) which appear in the video.

5.2   On the Number of Layers

We merge two layers if their motions are similar. As motion parameters does not define uniquely the motion over all the layer support, rather than considering them directly, we consider the optical flow generated by the two motion models. Hence, using the notation introduced in section 3, the motion similarity criterion r_{ij} between two layers i and j is computed as follows:

$$r_{ij} = \frac{1}{|\mathcal{S}_i|} \int_{\Omega} (\mathcal{A}_i(\mathbf{x}) - \mathcal{A}_j(\mathbf{x}))^2 \chi_{\mathcal{S}_i}(\mathbf{x}) d\mathbf{x}$$
$$+ \frac{1}{|\mathcal{S}_j|} \int_{\Omega} (\mathcal{A}_i(\mathbf{x}) - \mathcal{A}_j(\mathbf{x}))^2 \chi_{\mathcal{S}_j}(\mathbf{x}) d\mathbf{x}$$

where $|\mathcal{S}_i| = \int_{\Omega} \chi_{\mathcal{S}_i}(\mathbf{x}) d\mathbf{x}$ (similarly for $|\mathcal{S}_j|$). If r_{ij} drops down under a certain threshold, the two layers i and j are merged together. Furthermore, layers with too small support (and so giving bad motion estimation) or with too important variance (due to too many outliers in the support) are deleted.

New objects which appear must be detected and classified in new layers. Toward this end, we proceed as follows: first, warp residual is computed for the whole frame, giving a residual map. We apply a binary threshold $\mathcal{T}$ to this map. All pixels whose residual is higher than $\mathcal{T}$ are extracted and pixels which do not belong to a large connected region (the minimal size $\mathcal{T}_{min}$ of the region is defined empirically) are ignored. These connected regions which contain the remaining pixels are considered as new layer support.

6   Discussion and Conclusion

6.1   Experimental Results

The validation was also done on two classical sequences (calendar sequence FIG. 3 and flowers sequence FIG. 4) to permit comparisons with previous methods. One can see that the algorithm extracts well the different layers for both sequences. In FIG. 3, if the calendar and the train are well segmented, the ball is over-segmented (due to lack of texture and similar colors with the background) and is classified in the same layer than the train.

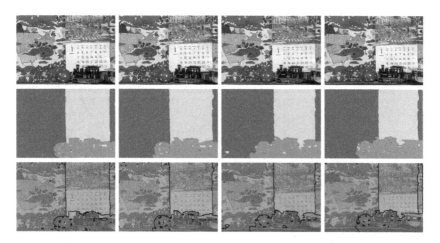

Fig. 3. Results on calendar sequence (one frame on four is considered). Each column represent a frame: frames 0,12,24,36 are represented here. First row, original sequence; second row, the layers extracted ; third row, superposition of layers boundaries with original sequence.

For the flowers sequence, the first frame is over-segmented but the number of layers is then well determined. The background is well distinguished from the middle-plane (the house and the flowers). Colors criterion permits to overcome ambiguities in the sky due to lack of texture. However, branches are not well classified with the good layer. Indeed, due to the small distance between the tree and the camera, as branches do not belong to the same 3D plane, their motion can not be represented with the same affine model than the one of the tree.

6.2 Conclusion

In this paper, a method to robust motion estimation and layered reconstruction of scene according to parametric motion models is presented. Our method performs robust motion estimation while being able to account for occlusions through a forward/backward iterative estimation process. Furthermore, within an forward/backward schema, our approach groups the image domain into layers according to motion, appearance and spatial and temporal smoothness constraints. Promising experimental results demonstrate the potential of the proposed method as shown in [FIG. 3 and 4].

Computational complexity is the most important limitation of the proposed approach. In particular the motion estimation step is time consuming and can lead to sub-optimal results. Hardware implementation of the method in Graphics Processing Units is under consideration. The sequential nature of the proposed approach is also a limitation. To this end, one can consider a combinatorial approach where the parameters of the affine models are also recovered through an α-expansion algorithm.

Fig. 4. Results on flowers sequence. Each column represent a frame: frames 0,3,6,...,18 are represented here. First row, original sequence; second row, the layers extracted ; third row, superposition of layers boundaries with original sequence. One can note that layers become more accurate and stay constant throughout the sequence. Main parameters: $\alpha = 0.25$, $\beta = 10$, $\gamma = 1$, $\mathcal{T}_{min} = 0.2$.

Acknowledgments

The authors would like to thank Olivier Juan, for providing the EM algorithm used for the estimation of the Gaussian mixture model parameters and Yuri Boykov from the University of Western Ontarion for fruitful discussions.

References

1. Wang, J., Adelson, E.: Representing Moving Images with Layers. IEEE Transactions on Image Processing **3** (1994) 625–638
2. Bergen, J.R., Anandan, P., Hanna, K.J., Hingorani, R.: Hierarchical model-based motion estimation. In: ECCV '92: Proceedings of the Second European Conference on Computer Vision, Springer-Verlag (1992) 237–252
3. Ayer, S., Sawhney, H.: Layered Representation of Motion Video Using Robust Maximum-Likelihood Estimation of Mixture Models and MDL Encoding. In: IEEE International Conference in Computer Vision, Caibridge, USA (1995) 777–784
4. Weiss, Y.: Smoothness in layers: Motion segmentation using nonparametric mixture estimation. In: CVPR '97: Proceedings of the 1997 Conference on Computer Vision and Pattern Recognition (CVPR '97), Washington, DC, USA, IEEE Computer Society (1997) 520
5. Shanon X. Ju, Michael J. Black, A.D.J.: Skin and bones: Multi-layer, locally affine, optical flow and regularization with transparency. In: CVPR '96: Proceedings of the 1996 Conference on Computer Vision and Pattern Recognition (CVPR '96), Washington, DC, USA, IEEE Computer Society (1996) 307
6. Cremers, D., Soatto, S.: Variational space-time motion segmentation. In: International Conference on Computer Vision (ICCV). (2003) 886–893
7. Horn, B., Schunck, B.: Determinating Optical Flow. Artificial Intelligence **17** (1981) 185–203
8. Barron, J., Fleet, D., Beauchemin, S., Burkitt, T.: Performance of optical flow techniques. Computer Vision and Pattern Recognition (CVPR) (1992) 236–242
9. Brox, T., Bruhn, A., Papenberg, N., Weickert, J.: High accuracy optical flow estimation based on a theory for warping. In: 8th European Conference on Computer Vision (ECCV). (2004) 25–36
10. Black, M.J., Anandan, P.: The robust estimation of multiple motions: parametric and piecewise-smooth flow fields. Comput. Vis. Image Underst. **63** (1996) 75–104
11. Tikhonov, A.: Ill-Posed Problems in Natural Sciences. Coronet (1992)
12. Odobez, J.M., Bouthemy, P.: Robust multiresolution estimation of parametric motion models. Journal of Visual Communication and Image Representation **6** (1995) 348–365
13. Black, M.J., Jepson, A.D.: Estimating optical flow in segmented images using variable-order parametric models with local deformations. IEEE Trans. Pattern Anal. Mach. Intell. **18** (1996) 972–986
14. Darrell, T., Pentland, A.P.: Cooperative robust estimation using layers of support. IEEE Trans. Pattern Anal. Mach. Intell. **17** (1995) 474–487
15. Xiao, J., Shah, M.: Motion layer extraction in the presence of occlusion using graph cut. In: CVPR (2). (2004) 972–979
16. Zabih, R., Kolmogorov, V.: Spatially coherent clustering using graph cuts. In: IEEE Computer Society Conference on Computer Vision and Pattern Recognition (CVPR). (2004) 437–444

17. Irani, M., Anandan, P.: A unified approach to moving object detection in 2d and 3d scenes. IEEE Trans. Pattern Anal. Mach. Intell. **20** (1998) 577–589
18. Duda, R., Hart, P.: Pattern Classification and Scene Analysis. John Wiley & Sons (1973)
19. Boykov, Y., Jolly, M.P.: Interactive graph cuts for optimal boundary and region segmentation of objects in n-d images. In: ICCV. (2001) 105–112
20. Besag, J.: On the statistical analysis of dirty images. Journal of Royal Statistics Society **48** (1986) 259–302
21. Chou, P., Brown, C.: The theory and practice of bayesian image labeling. International Journal of Computer Vision **4** (1990) 185–210
22. Geman, S., Geman, D.: Stochastic Relaxation, Gibbs Distributions, and the Bayesian Restoration of Images. IEEE Transactions on Pattern Analysis and Machine Intelligence **6** (1984) 721–741
23. Boykov, Y., Veksler, O., Zabih, R.: Fast Approximate Energy Minimization via Graph Cuts. IEEE Transactions on Pattern Analysis and Machine Intelligence **23** (2001) 1222–1239

Object Categorization by
Compositional Graphical Models

Björn Ommer and Joachim M. Buhmann

ETH Zurich, Institute of Computational Science,
CH-8092 Zurich, Switzerland
{bjoern.ommer, jbuhmann}@inf.ethz.ch

Abstract. This contribution proposes a compositionality architecture for visual object categorization, i.e., learning and recognizing multiple visual object classes in unsegmented, cluttered real-world scenes. We propose a sparse image representation based on localized feature histograms of salient regions. Category specific information is then aggregated by using relations from perceptual organization to form compositions of these descriptors. The underlying concept of image region aggregation to condense semantic information advocates for a statistical representation founded on graphical models. On the basis of this structure, objects and their constituent parts are localized.

To complement the learned dependencies between compositions and categories, a global shape model of all compositions that form an object is trained. During inference, belief propagation reconciles bottom-up feature-driven categorization with top-down category models. The system achieves a competitive recognition performance on the standard CalTech database[1].

1   Introduction

The automatic detection and recognition of objects in images has been among the prime objectives of computer vision for several decades. There are several levels of semantic granularity on which classification of objects can be conducted, e.g. recognizing different appearances of the same object as opposed to different representations of the same category of objects. Object categorization aims at recognizing visual objects of some general class in scenes and labeling the images accordingly. Therefore, a given set of training samples is used to learn category-specific properties which are then represented in a common model. Based on this model, previously unknown instances of the learned categories are then to be recognized in new visual scenes.

The large variations among appearances and instantiations of the same visual object category turn learning and representing models for various categories into a key challenge. Therefore, common characteristics of objects in a category have to be captured while at the same time a great flexibility with respect to variability or absence of such features has to be offered. Consequently, we propose a system that infers scene labels based on learned category-dependent agglomerations

---

[1] http://www.vision.caltech.edu/html-files/archive.html

A. Rangarajan et al. (Eds.): EMMCVPR 2005, LNCS 3757, pp. 235–250, 2005.

of features which are robust with respect to intra-class variations and are thus reliably detectable. This approach to categorization has its origin in the principle of *compositionality* [9]. It is not only observed in human vision (see [2]) but also in cognition in general that complex entities are perceived as compositions of simpler, more unspecific, and widely usable parts. Objects are then defined by their components and the relations between those components. Therefore, the relationships between parts compensate for the limited information provided by each individual part. Moreover, a comparably small number of these lower-level constituents suffices to enable perception of various objects in diverse scenes. We like to emphasize that we see key contribution of our approach in the probabilistic coupling of different components which have been discussed in the literature. The homogeneity of this compositionality architecture and the common probabilistic framework for information processing yields the demonstrated robustness which we consider indispensible for object recognition.

Our architecture detects features of salient image regions and represents them using a small codebook that has been learned on the training set. Consecutively relations between the regions are acquired and used to establish compositions of these image parts. Therefore the part representations, the compositions, as well as the overall image categorization are all combined in a single graphical model, a Bayesian network [19]. Thus the probabilities of compositions and overall image categorization can be inferred from the observed evidence using model parameters that are learned from the training data. This learning is based on category labels of complete training images as the only information, e.g., images labeled as belonging to the car category contain a car somewhere in the image without marking the car region specifically. Therefore, the intermediate representation, that is the set of relevant compositions, is learned with no user supervision. Furthermore, the spatial configuration of all object components of a given category are learned and captured in a global, probabilistic shape model. Categorization hypotheses are then refined based on this information and objects can be localized in an image. The architecture has been trained and evaluated on the standard CalTech database (cars, faces, motorbikes, and airplanes). An additional background category of natural sceneries from the COREL image database has been incorporated for learning the hidden compositions. In summary, the architecture combines bottom-up, feature-driven recognition with top-down, category model driven hypotheses in a single Bayesian network and performs them simultaneously during belief propagation to infer image categorization.

This contribution outlines our approach in Section 3. An evaluation of the categorization model follows in Section 4 before we conclude this presentation with a final discussion. Related work is summarized in the next section.

2   Related Work

Object categorization has previously been mainly based on local appearance patches (e.g. [1, 12, 13, 6, 7]). That is, image regions are extracted, converted to grayscale and subsampled to obtain limited invariance with respect to minor variations in such patches. The resulting features are clustered to acquire a codebook of typically some thousand local patch representatives that are category specific.

To incorporate additional information beyond extracted local patches and features, a sequence of recognition models have been proposed in the class of *constellation models*. Originally, Fischler and Elschlager [8] described a spring model with local features to characterize objects. In the same spirit, Lades et al [11] proposed a face recognizer which has been inspired by the *Dynamic Link Architecture* for cognitive processes with a neurobiologically plausible dynamics. Similar to this model, Weber et al. [21] have introduced a joint model for all features present in an object. Fergus et al. [7] extend this approach and estimate the joint spatial, scale, appearance, and edge curve distributions of all detected patches which they normalize with respect to scale. However, due to the complexity of the joint models used by these approaches, only a small number of parts can be used. In contrast to this, Agarwal et al. [1] build a comparably large codebook of distinctive parts and learn spatial configurations of part tuples which belong to objects of a single category. However, since the individual appearance patches are highly specific the joint model is restricted in terms of its generalization ability and requires large training sets. To overcome these difficulties, Leibe et. al [12, 13] estimate the mean of all shifts between positions of codebook patches in training and test images. Using a probabilistic Hough voting strategy one object category is distinguished from a background category. Moreover, the spatial information is used to segment images and to take account of multiple objects in a scene. We further refine this approach and reconcile conflicting categorization hypotheses proposed by compositions of parts and those proposed by spatial models. Therefore, compositions and spatial models are coupled in a Bayesian network and beliefs are propagated between them in an alternating manner.

The approach in [12] to incorporate top-down information into segmentation has been proposed previously by Borenstein and Ullman in [5] where learned object fragments are aligned based on bottom-up coherence criteria. This improves especially segmentation boundaries, but they do not use this process for recognition. In [4] an extension is presented that uses the sum-product algorithm [19, 10] to solve local contradictions and to obtain a globally optimal segmentation.

The approach of forming an object representation based on compositions of unspecific, and reliably detectable features has strong support by visual cognition [2]. Geman et al. [9, 3] present this concept in the context of stochastic grammars and use it for recognizing handwritings. However, compositionality in the scenario of object categorization is a novel technique. In [18] we have proposed an architecture for forming compositional grouping hierarchies based on the psychological principles of perceptual organization [14]. Therefore different types of perceptual relations between parts are established to build salient compositions of reduced description length and increased robustness.

3   Categorization Based on Interacting Compositions

Our architecture which represents compositionality in a graphical model for performing object categorization has several stages. The following sketches the

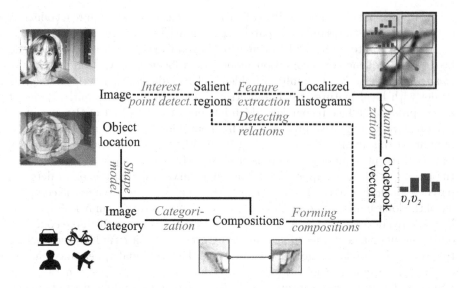

Fig. 1. Outline of the processing pipeline and information flow. Belief is being propagated along the solid lines, whereas the dotted ones indicate the capturing of evidence.

recognition process and states how learning is involved (see Figure 1): At first a scale invariant Harris interest point detector is used [16] to detect salient image regions. Every region is then captured by several feature histograms, each being localized with respect to the interest point. The features are represented using a probability distribution over a codebook that has been obtained by a histogram quantization in the learning stage. This codebook captures locally typical feature configurations of the categories under consideration. In a next step relations are detected between the regions and are being used to infer compositions. This inference is based on previously learned category specific grouping probabilities. Thereafter, all these compositions are taken into account to yield the overall categorization probability for the image. In addition to a maximum a-posteriori estimate for the category, this also yields a confidence in this classification. Finally, a learned model of object shapes is used to infer the object position in the image based on all compositions and the categorization hypothesis. This spatial probability distribution is in turn used to refine compositions and overall categorization. Thereby, both bottom-up image classification which depends on features and top-down recognition which depends on category models are corroborating another by running in an interleaved manner during belief propagation.

The following section gives a detailed account of the different stages and describes the learning of models which are underlying the inference procedure used for recognition with the network illustrated in Figure 2. Due to the independence properties represented by this Bayesian network, the categorization probabilities factorize and their computation is split into separate parts [19]. This factorization is significant to dividing up the procedure into the different stages and making inference feasible. In [19] a message-passing algorithm is introduced that propa-

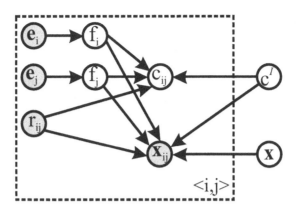

Fig. 2. Illustration of the Bayesian network. The evidence nodes (shaded variables) are $E = \{\mathbf{e}_i\}_i \cup \{r_{ij}, \mathbf{x}_{ij}\}_{<i,j>}$. Where $< i, j >$ denotes pairs of parts that are agglomerated into compositions—the dotted structure is therefore replicated for all these tuples, see text for details.

gates evidence through polytrees to estimate the *belief* of unobserved variables, that is their posterior given the evidence. For some random variable Y it is

$$BEL(y) := P(Y = y|E) \ , \tag{1}$$

where E denotes the observed evidence. Moreover, it has been widely advocated that this so called *sum-product algorithm* [10] yields good approximations even for Bayesian networks with loops (cf. [17]).

3.1 Localized Feature Histograms for Compositionality

As outlined above, representations of object categories have to deal with large intra-class variations. However, the local appearance patches that have been widely used in the field of object categorization are basically subsampled image patches. The clustering that is then performed to obtain patch representatives is usually based on normalized grayscale correlation whereby invariance to illumination changes of patches as a whole is obtained. However, since the resulting invariances are just established by a global subsampling and intensity normalization, translations or local alterations still have an overproportional influence on the complete feature. Moreover, due to the low-pass filtering, only information on the strongest edges is preserved while the remaining patch content is blurred.

To overcome these problems we follow the concept of compositionality [9] where models for complex objects are decomposed into more unspecific, robustly detectable and thus widely usable components. This strategy results in fairly short representations for components and facilitates robust estimation of the statistics that model the grouping of parts. This section starts by outlining the part representation, while later sections continue to present relations and compositions.

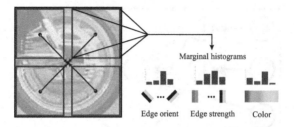

Fig. 3. Sketch of localized feature histograms

A crucial problem of forming a scene representation is the trade-off between its invariance properties, e.g. to varying influences of the imaging process, and its specificity for a certain task, e.g. distinguishing object categories. As delineated above, current approaches to categorization base their class recognition mainly on highly distinctive local appearance patches (e.g. [1, 12, 6]) and incorporate only limited invariance with respect to alteration of patch contents. An alternative approach at the other end of the modeling spectrum is that of using histograms over complete images (cf. [20]). Thereby, utmost invariances with respect to changes of individual pixels can be obtained. In conclusion, the former approach facilitates almost perfect localization while the latter one offers maximal invariance with respect to local distortions. We therefore aim at a representation whose invariance properties are transparently adjusted between these two classical extremes and add the specificity lost by invariance through the relations that are used for forming the compositions.

To process an image, we start by applying the interest point detector to obtain some 10^2 to 10^3 interest points together with rough local scale estimates. Although our implementation incorporates multiple scales, our current approach is based on a single estimated scale selected by the interest point detector. Therefore we extract quadratic image patches (with a side length of 10 to 20 pixel depending on scale) and subdivide them into a number of subpatches with fixed location relative to the patch center (see Figure 3). In each of these subwindows three types of marginal histograms are computed (four bins allocated for each), measuring edge strengths, edge orientations, and color. The statistics of each feature channel are estimated independently from another to make the estimates robust by having enough data support. In the following, the vector of measurements $\mathbf{e}_i$ denotes the combination of the features extracted in all the subpatches at interest point i. These vectors serve as evidence in our Bayesian network. The trade-off between invariance and localization is represented by the number of subpatches—in the current implementation a patch is divided up into four of these subwindows.

The proposed representation differs from the SIFT features [15] not only in that color is used. Whereas SIFT features aim at distinguishing different instances of the same object from another, we seek a representation that is invariant to the specificities of individual object instances and environment configurations. To obtain a small codebook of atomic representatives for compositionality, we reduce the complexity of the very features whereas the other approach would have to perform this indirectly by clustering in a high-dimensional space with few prototypes.

3.2 Codebook Representation of Atomic Compositional Parts

To facilitate a robust estimation of statistics in subsequent stages of the architecture, a small codebook for features is generated during learning. This set forms a representation of atomic compositional parts. The codebook is generated by clustering the features detected in training images of all the different categories with k-means—resulting in a set of 300 centroids in our current implementation. It should be emphasized that this representation is shared by all the different categories. During recognition the squared euclidean distance $d_\nu(\mathbf{e}_i)$ of a measured feature $\mathbf{e}_i$ to all the centroids $\mathbf{a}_\nu$ from the codebook is computed. The objective is to represent measurements not merely by their nearest prototype but by a distribution over the codebook, thereby leading to increased robustness. Now, for each measurement $\mathbf{e}_i$, a new random variable F_i is introduced that takes on cluster indices ν as its values. Each of these variables is coupled with the corresponding measurement using the same Gibbs distribution [22]

$$P(F_i = \nu|\mathbf{e}_i) := Z(\mathbf{e}_i)^{-1} \exp\left(-d_\nu(\mathbf{e}_i)\right) \ , \tag{2}$$

$$Z(\mathbf{e}_i) := \sum_\nu \exp\left(-d_\nu(\mathbf{e}_i)\right) \ . \tag{3}$$

Subsequently, $P(F_i = \nu)$ is abbreviated using its realization $f_i = \nu$ and simply writing $P(f_i)$ which models the first stage of the Bayesian network in Figure 2.

3.3 Forming Compositions

The part representations have to be augmented by additional evidence. Therefore, relations between image regions are taken into account. From the various principles of perceptual organization, investigated in [18] for grouping processes, we apply *good continuation*. This concept basically groups those entities together that form a common smooth contour. Hence we consider pairs of patches which lie on a common edge curve and measure their distance. To facilitate a later robust statistical estimation, this distance is discretized into three ranges (i.e. close/medium/far) which depend on a histogram over all these distances measured in the training data. The edge curves are obtained by performing Canny edge detection twice, once with a scale parameter that is the mean of the lower half of all scales detected at the interest points, and once with scale being equal to the mean of the upper half. The edge images are then added up. Now consider two patches at interest points i and j. If they are observed to lie on the same contour and have a discretized gap of r_{ij} they establish the relation $R_{ij} = r_{ij}$. The two parts are then forming a composition which we denote by $< i, j >$, i.e.,

$$< i, j > \Leftrightarrow \text{part } i \ \& \ \text{part } j \text{ form a composition} \ . \tag{4}$$

Since the relations between image regions are observed, all the random variables R_{ij} enter as evidence into the Bayesian network in Figure 2. It should be emphasized that this is a sparse set of nodes—iff both patches lie on a common contour, such a random variable is introduced. In conclusion, a grouping based on such relations incorporates additional edge information that takes compositions beyond a mere proximity or co-occurrence grouping.

Based on the detected relations the following modelling heuristic describes how compositions of parts are formed. Let the random variable C_{ij} represent a composition of the two image regions i, j. Each such composition is of a certain category. That is, it has a certain state $c_{ij} \in \mathcal{C}_C$, where this state space of compositions is a superset of the set $\mathcal{C}_I = \{\text{face}, \text{airplane}, \dots\}$ of all categories for images, i.e. $\mathcal{C}_I \subset \mathcal{C}_C$. Consider the illustrating example of an image that is recognized to contain a motorbike. Then compositions representing subparts such as tires might be added to the set of allowed image categories. In our current implementation both sets differ by an additional category for *background* that we have incorporated for compositions, i.e. $\mathcal{C}_C = \mathcal{C}_I \cup \{\text{background}\}$.

The distribution of a composition of the two parts i, j depends only on the representations of the involved parts, their relation, as well as on the categorization of the image, denoted by C^I, where $c^I \in \mathcal{C}_I$. Thereby, the invariances represented in the Bayesian network from Figure 2 are reflected,

$$P(C_{ij} = c_{ij} | F_i = f_i, F_j = f_j, R_{ij} = r_{ij}, C^I = c^I) . \tag{5}$$

All C_{ij} are assumed to be identically distributed and this distribution is split into

$$P(c_{ij} | f_i, f_j, r_{ij}, c^I) \propto P(c^I | c_{ij}) P(c_{ij} | f_i, f_j, r_{ij}) \tag{6}$$

using Bayes formula and dropping a normalization constant. The first factor models category confusion probabilities which are assumed to be independent from features and relations ($P(c^I | c_{ij}) = P(c^I | c_{ij}, f_i, f_j, r_{ij})$) when compositions c_{ij} are given. With no further assumptions on categories, we have made the following choice,

$$P(c^I | c_{ij}) = \begin{cases} |\mathcal{C}_I|^{-1}, & \text{if } c_{ij} = \text{background} \\ \eta, & \text{if } c^I = c_{ij} \\ 1 - \eta, & \text{otherwise} . \end{cases} \tag{7}$$

In our current implementation we simply set $\eta = 1$. The second distribution in Eq. (6) is the categorization probability of compositions: The underlying nonparametric model is obtained in the learning stage by processing all the training images as follows: for each detected grouping, the category label of the whole image is taken as c_{ij} and the distribution is estimated from the empirical histogram of all observed compositions. Figure 4 and 9 visualize the category beliefs of compositions for the different classes.

3.4   Modeling Object Shape

In the following, a model of the spatial configuration of object components is presented. This model is used to refine the image categorization by propagating

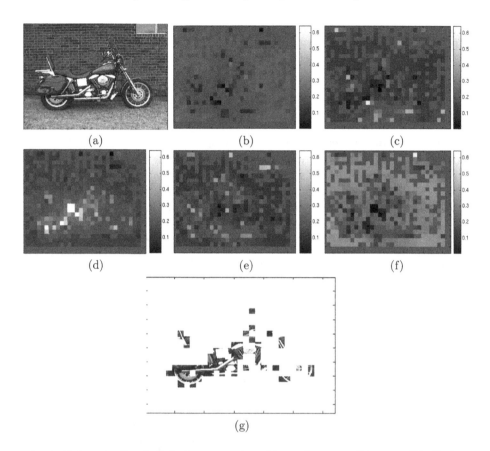

Fig. 4. Categorization belief of compositions. For each composition c_{ij}, (b) displays $P(C_{ij} = \text{car}|E)$ at the position of patches i and j. Image regions that are not used to form compositions are displayed with the uniform distribution over all categories. Regions that are involved in multiple compositions show the average belief of these compositions. (c) Displays the posterior for class *face*, (d) for *motorbike*, (e) for *airplane*, and (f) for *background*. Where the last category facilitates a figure-ground segregation of compositions. (g) Shows the regions selected by the algorithm to categorize the image as *motorbike*.

information on the estimated object location. The shape of an object of a given category is modeled by the displacement $\mathbf{s}_{ij}$ of all of its components from its center $\mathbf{x}$. Letting $\mathbf{x}_{ij}$ denote the location of a composition (the midpoint between its components) detected in the training data, its shift is computed as

$$\mathbf{s}_{ij} = \mathbf{x} - \mathbf{x}_{ij}. \tag{8}$$

During learning, the object centers are computed by

$$\mathbf{x} = \sum_{I \in \text{train data}} \sum_{<i,j> \in I} \mathbf{x}_{ij} \cdot P(C_{ij} = c^I | f_i, f_j, r_{ij}) \ . \tag{9}$$

To predict the location of the object center, a Parzen window density estimation is performed. The probability of a shift, given the features of a composition and the object category, is represented by the following non-parametric model

$$p(S = \mathbf{s}|f_i, f_j, r_{ij}, c^I) = \frac{1}{N} \sum_{l=1}^{N} \frac{K_{\sigma_N}\left(\mathbf{s} - \mathbf{s}_{ij}^{(l)}\right)}{\sigma_N}. \tag{10}$$

Here K_σ is a Gaussian kernel function with diagonal covariance matrix $\Sigma = \sigma \cdot \mathbf{I}$. Moreover, $\mathbf{s}_{ij}^{(l)}$ is the l-th shift vector found in the training data for a composition of parts represented by (f_i, f_j, r_{ij}). The number of shift vectors observed for such a composition in the training set is denoted $N = N(f_i, f_j, r_{ij})$. Therefore, the spatial density of the object center given one composition is

$$p(X = \mathbf{x}|f_i, f_j, r_{ij}, \mathbf{x}_{ij}, c^I) = p(S = \mathbf{x} - \mathbf{x}_{ij}|f_i, f_j, r_{ij}, c^I) . \tag{11}$$

Using this equation the conditional probability to observe a composition at location $\mathbf{x}_{ij}$ can be written as

$$p(\mathbf{x}_{ij}|f_i, f_j, r_{ij}, c^I, \mathbf{x}) \propto p(S = \mathbf{x} - \mathbf{x}_{ij}|f_i, f_j, r_{ij}, c^I) \, p(\mathbf{x}_{ij}|f_i, f_j, r_{ij}, c^I) . \tag{12}$$

To simplify the representation in the graphical model the locations $\mathbf{x}_{ij}$ are discretized on a regular 10×10 grid. The latter term is then approximated during learning by histogramming over the observed positions of compositions in the training data. Figure 5 gives an example for the estimation of object locations.

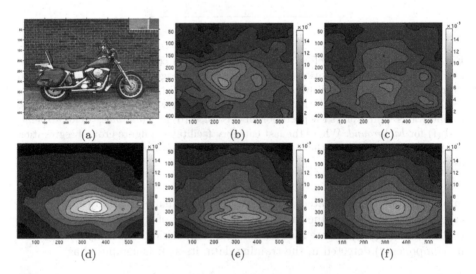

(a)   (b)   (c)

(d)   (e)   (f)

Fig. 5. Spatial density of the object location, given some categorization C^I. (b) displays $p(\mathbf{x}|\{f_i, f_j, r_{ij}, \mathbf{x}_{ij}\}_{<i,j>}, C^I = car)$. In (c) the category C^I is *face*, in (d) *motorbike*, in (e) *airplane*. (f) shows the inferred final belief for the object center position, $p(\mathbf{x}|E)$. Note that the density for the true category in (d) and the final belief are both nicely peaked at the true center.

3.5   Inference of Image Categorization

During recognition, loopy belief propagation is performed using the evidence $E = \{e_i\}_i \cup \{r_{ij}, x_{ij}\}_{<i,j>}$ to categorize the scene as a whole, i.e. we are interested in the belief of the random variable C^I. Belief propagation simplifies the complex problem of optimizing a marginalization of the joint distribution over all model variables. This is rendered possible by using the independence properties represented in the graphical model and taking only the resulting local interactions into account. To simplify the computation scheme we transform the Bayesian network from Figure 2 into the factor graph (cf. [10]) displayed in Figure 6(a). Function nodes represent the conditional probability distributions, whereas the remaining variable nodes correspond to the random variables of the Bayes net. To propagate beliefs each vertex in this graph has to compute and send messages to its neighbors as follows: Consider some variable node v that has function node neighbors $\mathcal{F}_v$ and $\mathcal{F}_{w_1}, \ldots, \mathcal{F}_{w_n}$ as depicted in Figure 6(b). Adjacent to each $\mathcal{F}_{w_i}$ is again some variable node w_i and $\mathcal{F}_v$ has variable node neighbors v and $u_1, \ldots, u_m$. Now an unobserved variable sends messages to its function node neighbors by taking all the incoming messages into account [10],

$$\mu_{v \to \mathcal{F}_v}(v) := \prod_i \mu_{\mathcal{F}_{w_i} \to v}(v) \ . \tag{13}$$

If v is an evidence variable and observed to be in state v' then this message is just $\mu_{v \to \mathcal{F}_v}(v) = \mathbf{1}\{v = v'\}$, where $\mathbf{1}\{.\}$ denotes the characteristic function. Moreover a function node sends the following messages to its neighbors

$$\mu_{\mathcal{F}_v \to v}(v) := \sum_{u_1, \ldots, u_m} \mathcal{F}_v(v, u_1, \ldots, u_m) \prod_j \mu_{u_j \to \mathcal{F}_v}(u_j) \ . \tag{14}$$

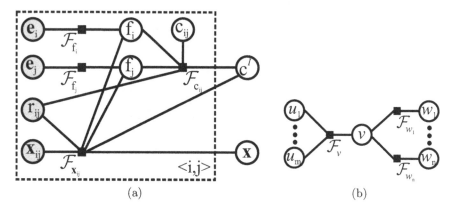

(a)   (b)

Fig. 6. (a) Conversion of the Bayesian network from Figure 2 into a factor graph representation. The function nodes $\mathcal{F}_\bullet$ represent the posterior of the corresponding random variable, e.g. $\mathcal{F}_{f_i} = P(f_i|e_i)$, see text for details. (b) A simple factor graph used for illustrating belief propagation.

The belief of v given all the present evidence E is then the product of all of its incoming messages

$$P(v|E) \propto \mu_{\mathcal{F}_v \to v}(v) \prod_i \mu_{\mathcal{F}_{w_i} \to v}(v) \ . \tag{15}$$

In conclusion, our architecture propagates beliefs not only in a bottom-up manner from the observed image features to infer categorization and object location. The system also propagates information backwards in a top-down fashion from object localization and categorization to composition and part hypotheses, c_{ij} and f_i respectively. While the bottom-up feature-driven and the top-down category model driven updates are performed concurrently, hypotheses get improved by finding those which have optimal mutual agreement.

4   Evaluation

In the following, the proposed architecture is evaluated on the CalTech image database. During learning, some 700 images are presented to the system together

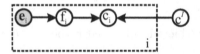

Fig. 7. A simple Bayesian network for categorization used to evaluate the gain of compositionality

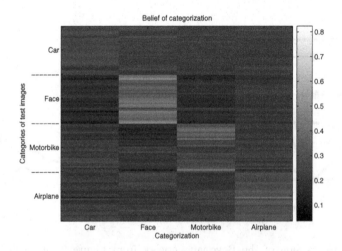

Fig. 8. Category confusion matrix for categorization without using compositionality. The predicted class is shown on the x-axis, whereas the true class is on the y-axis. This model achieves an overall classification rate of 82.5%.

with the image category labels as the only additional information. The test scenario is then to classify previously unknown images as belonging to one of the categories. Moreover, a confidence in this categorization is returned.

In order to evaluate the gain of compositionality in categorization, we first investigate a simpler model. It is based on the same image representation but with neither compositions nor a shape model (see Figure 7). Therefore the categorizations c_{ij} of compositions are replaced by the classification c_i of single parts, where $P(c_i|f_i, c^I)$ is empirically estimated from the training data in the same way as the c_{ij} in Section 3.3. Figure 8 displays the resulting category confusion matrix. The confidence in a categorization of class c^I (shown on the x-axis) of images with a given ground truth category (shown on the y-axis) is visualized in this figure. Therefore a row represents the beliefs of the different categories

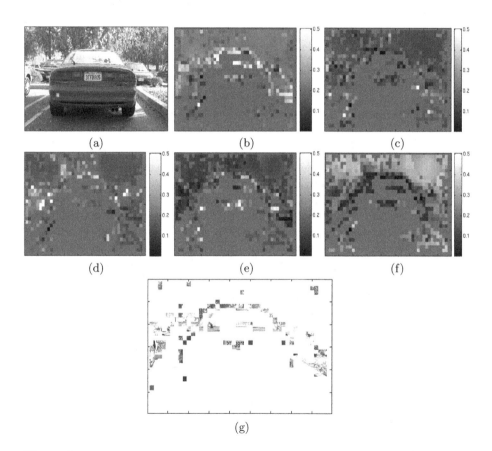

Fig. 9. Categorization belief of compositions. For each composition c_{ij}, (b) displays $P(C_{ij} = \mathrm{car}|E)$ at the position of patches i and j. See Figure 4 for details. (c) Shows the posterior for class *face*, (d) for *motorbike*, (e) for *airplane*, and (f) for *background*. Where the last category facilitates a figure-ground segregation of compositions. (g) Shows the regions that support categorizing the image as *car*.

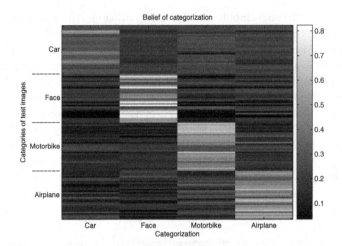

Fig. 10. Category confusion matrix for categorization based on the full model with compositionality and shape. This approach achieves an overall classification rate of 91.7% and has a significantly higher confidence than the previous one. Considering only the last three categories a recognition rate of 94.4% is achieved (see text for details). Compare this with the 93.0% reported in [6] for the same three categories.

for one test image. This model achieves an overall correct classification rate of 82.5%. However, the categorization confidence is quite low.

Subsequently, this simple model is to be compared with the full approach outlined in Section 3. Figure 10 displays the category confusion matrix of the model that is based on compositions and their spatial arrangement. When comparing the two plots it becomes evident that the system with compositionality and shape achieves a significantly increased confidence in the correct categorizations. Moreover, the recognition rate has increased to 91.7%. This illustrates that the relations used for compositions add crucial information to that already present in the individual parts. As one can see, most of the error results from falsely classified car images. This is due to the fact that the interest point detector returns only very few votes for the large homogeneous parts of the body of a car. Most detections are in the background or at the outline of the vehicle. This is also apparent in the illustration of compositions in Figure 9. Although for this specific dataset the background features would provide good indications for the presence of cars, we do not want to introduce such dependencies as they are to a great deal database specific and would very likely lead to an overfitting to this image collection. In a future extension of the approach we therefore plan to revise the interest point detection stage to also incorporate homogeneous regions. When leaving out the car category and considering only the remaining three ones, the present approach achieves an overall recognition rate of 94.4%. Compare this with the average recognition rate of 93.0% reported by Fergus et al. in [6] for the same three categories.

5   Conclusion and Future Work

Inspired by Geman's compositionality approach [9], we have devised a novel model for object categorization on the basis of a Bayesian network. The underlying image representation emphasizes keypoint relations and it accounts for large intra-class variations as they are usually encountered in general object categorization. Models for compositions and global object shape have been introduced and tightly combined in a single graphical model to infer image categorizations based on the underlying statistical framework. As a result, the system not only propagates information on an image category in a feature-driven, bottom-up manner. It also uses category models to corroborate such hypotheses by a model-driven, top-down inference, thereby reconciling different locally proposed categorization hypotheses by belief propagation. The system achieves competitive recognition performance on a standard image database used for categorization.

The approach shows significant potential for future extensions at several stages. First, feature representation should incorporate multiple scales and segmentation or other prior information to deal with homogeneous regions. Moreover, compositions could be formed in a recursive manner to yield a representation that is semantically closer to the final image categorization. Also, additional types of relations should add significant information on the objects present in a scene. All these refinements are expected to be necessary for large-scale experiments with hundreds of classes and a diverse nature of rigid, articulate and flexible objects.

References

1. S. Agarwal, A. Awan, and D. Roth. Learning to detect objects in images via a sparse, part-based representation. *IEEE Trans. Pattern Anal. Machine Intell.*, 26(11), 2004.
2. I. Biederman. Recognition-by-components: A theory of human image understanding. *Psychological Review*, 94(2):115–147, 1987.
3. E. Bienenstock, S. Geman, and D. Potter. Compositionality, mdl priors, and object recognition. In *NIPS*, volume 9, 1997.
4. E. Borenstein, E. Sharon, and S. Ullman. Combining top-down and bottom-up segmentation. In *CVPR Workshop on Perceptual Organization in Computer Vision*, 2004.
5. E. Borenstein and S. Ullman. Class-specific, top-down segmentation. In *ECCV*, 2002.
6. R. Fergus, P. Perona, and A. Zisserman. Object class recognition by unsupervised scale-invariant learning. In *CVPR*, 2003.
7. R. Fergus, P. Perona, and A. Zisserman. A visual category filter for google images. In *ECCV*, 2004.
8. M. A. Fischler and R. A. Elschlager. The representation and matching of pictorial structures. *IEEE Trans. Comput.*, 22(1), 1973.
9. S. Geman, D. F. Potter, and Z. Chi. *Composition Systems*. Technical report, Division of Applied Mathematics, Brown University, Providence, RI, 1998.
10. F. R. Kschischang, B. J. Frey, and H.-A. Loeliger. Factor graphs and the sum-product algorithm. *IEEE Trans. Inform. Theory*, 47(2), 2001.

11. M. Lades, J. C. Vorbrüggen, J. M. Buhmann, J. Lange, C. von der Malsburg, R. P. Würtz, and W. Konen. Distortion invariant object recognition in the dynamic link architecture. *IEEE Trans. Comput.*, 42, 1993.

12. B. Leibe, A. Leonardis, and B. Schiele. Combined object categorization and segmentation with an implicit shape model. In *ECCV Workshop on Stat. Learning in Computer Vision*, 2004.

13. B. Leibe and B. Schiele. Scale-invariant object categorization using a scale-adaptive mean-shift search. In *Pattern Recognition, DAGM*, 2004.

14. D. G. Lowe. *Perceptual Organization and Visual Recognition*. Kluwer Academic Publishers, Norwell, MA, 1985.

15. D. G. Lowe. Distinctive image features from scale-invariant keypoints. *Int. J. Computer Vision*, 60(2), 2004.

16. K. Mikolajczyk and C. Schmid. Scale & affine invariant interest point detectors. *Int. J. Computer Vision*, 60(1), 2004.

17. K. Murphy, Y. Weiss, and M. Jordan. Loopy-belief propagation for approximate inference: An empirical study. In *UAI*, 1999.

18. B. Ommer and J. M. Buhmann. A compositionality architecture for perceptual feature grouping. In *EMMCVPR*, 2003.

19. J. Pearl. *Probabilistic Reasoning in Intelligent Systems: Networks of Plausible Inference*. Morgan Kaufmann, 1988.

20. R. C. Veltkamp and M Tanase. Content-based image and video retrieval. In O. Marques and B. Furht, editors, *A Survey of Content-Based Image Retrieval Systems*. Kluwer, 2002.

21. M. Weber, M. Welling, and P. Perona. Unsupervised learning of models for recognition. In *ECCV*, 2000.

22. G. Winkler. *Image Analysis, Random Fields and Markov Chain Monte Carlo Methods—A Mathematical Introduction*. Springer, 2nd edition, 2003.

Learning Hierarchical Shape Models from Examples

Alex Levinshtein[1], Cristian Sminchisescu[1,2], and Sven Dickinson[1]

[1] University of Toronto, Canada
{babalex, sven}@cs.toronto.edu
Phone number: (416) 978-3853
[2] TTI-C, Chicago, USA
crismin@cs.toronto.edu

Abstract. We present an algorithm for automatically constructing a decompositional shape model from examples. Unlike current approaches to structural model acquisition, in which one-to-one correspondences among appearance-based features are used to construct an exemplar-based model, we search for many-to-many correspondences among qualitative shape features (multi-scale ridges and blobs) to construct a generic shape model. Since such features are highly ambiguous, their structural context must be exploited in computing correspondences, which are often many-to-many. The result is a Marr-like abstraction hierarchy, in which a shape feature at a coarser scale can be decomposed into a collection of attached shape features at a finer scale. We systematically evaluate all components of our algorithm, and demonstrate it on the task of recovering a decompositional model of a human torso from example images containing different subjects with dissimilar local appearance.

1 Introduction

The early generic object models proposed by researchers such as Marr and Nishihara [11] and Brooks [10] not only decomposed a 3-D object into a set of volumetric parts and their attachments, but supported the representation of objects at multiple scales, using an abstraction hierarchy. Marr's classical example of a human consists of a single cylindrical part at the highest level, a torso, head, and arms appearing at the next level, an upper arm and lower arm appearing at the next level, etc. Modeling an object at different levels of abstraction is a powerful paradigm, offering a mechanism for coarse-to-fine object recognition. Unfortunately, such models were constructed manually, and the feature extraction and abstraction machinery required to effectively recover volumetric parts, much less their abstractions, was not available at the time.

The recognition community has recently returned to the problem of modeling objects as configurations of parts and relations, with the goal of automatically recovering (or learning) such descriptions from examples. For example, collections of interest points [1, 7] or affine-invariant image patches [2], forming a "constellation" of features, capture the "parts" and their geometric relations that define a view-based object category. Armed with powerful new machine learning techniques, complex configuration models can be automatically recovered from image collections or image sequences. For example, one can extract models based on motion and persistent appearance [4, 6, 12, 3, 5]. Global detectors that combine both motion and appearance have also been successfully applied to pedestrian tracking tasks [13].

A. Rangarajan et al. (Eds.): EMMCVPR 2005, LNCS 3757, pp. 251–267, 2005.

As powerful as these part-based techniques are, they all rely on computing a one-to-one correspondence between low-level, appearance-based features. However, two exemplars belonging to the same class may not share a single appearance-based feature. Yet at some higher level of abstraction, the two exemplars may share the same coarse part structure. Local, appearance-based features simply do not lend themselves to the types of abstract object representations proposed by Marr and his peers – abstractions in which a single part may cover an entire subcollection of local, appearance-based features. One approach might be to try and group the appearance-based features into local collections each of which defines an abstract part. However, appearance-based features are texture encodings of neighborhoods centered at interest points, and do not reflect the underlying shape structure required for perceptual grouping. Granted, the analysis of moving interest point-based features can support their partitioning into groups. But again, this requires the tracking of an exemplar, for which one-to-one feature correspondence is assured. Moreover, it is not clear how to abstract a coarse part model from a sparse set of local features.

In this paper, we address the problem of recovering a Marr-like abstraction hierarchy from a set of examples. We begin by applying a multi-scale blob and ridge detector [18] to a set of images containing exemplars drawn from the same class. The extracted features become the nodes in a *blob graph* whose edges reflect nonaccidental proximity relations between pairs of features. Blobs and ridges capture the coarse part structure of an object, and represent low-order projections of restricted classes of volumetric part models, including generalized cylinders, superquadric ellipsoids, and geons. Unfortunately, as feature complexity increases, so does its reliability decrease, as seen in Figure 1, showing the extracted blob graphs from a set of images of different humans with varying appearance and arm articulations. Some parts are over-segmented, some are under-segmented, some are missing, and some are spurious (possibly representing background clutter). These segmentation errors all pose a significant challenge to a matching algorithm whose goal is to find common structure in a set of images. Whereas one-to-one matching of local appearance-based features can exploit the high dimensionality of the features to ensure robust matching, one-to-one matching of noisy blobs and ridges is ripe with ambiguity, and structural relations and context must be exploited for successful matching.

Still, there is an even more challenging problem to be solved here. In Figure 1, sometimes an arm may appear as a single, elongated ridge (when the arm is extended), while at other times, an arm is broken into two smaller ridges (due to articulation at the elbow). Any matching algorithm that assumes a one-to-one correspondence between features cannot match these two descriptions, therefore failing to capture the notion that a coarser feature can be decomposed (at a finer level of abstraction) into two smaller features. Detecting these decompositional or abstraction relations between features requires a matching strategy that can match features many-to-many. Only then can we recover the multi-scale abstraction models that support true generic object recognition or categorization.

In this paper, we propose a framework for learning a shape abstraction hierarchy from a set of examples with dissimilar local appearance. From a set of noisy, poorly-segmented blob graphs, capturing the articulated part structure of objects at different

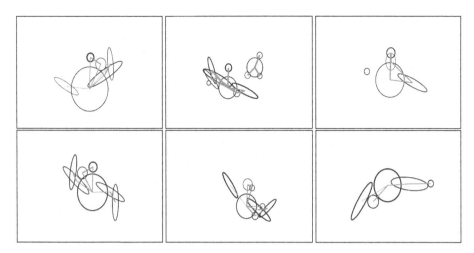

Fig. 1. Blob graphs extracted from a set of images, each containing the upper body of a different person (with different clothing). The high level of feature abstraction comes at the cost of increased segmentation errors in the form of under- and over-segmentation, missing features, and spurious features (including background clutter). Notice also that features may be extracted at different levels of abstraction, such as a straight arm (single ridge) or bent arm (two smaller ridges). Edges between blobs reflect a commitment to nonaccidental proximity-based grouping (see text) with edge width reflecting strength of grouping.

levels of abstraction, we construct an abstraction hierarchy, in the form of a graph, that contains both coarse-to-fine decompositional (abstraction) relations as well as attachment relations. Relaxing the one-to-one feature correspondence assumption common to most structure learning frameworks, we draw on recent results in many-to-many graph matching to match blob graphs many-to-many, allowing the matching of two exemplars whose parts may appear *at different levels of abstraction*. An analysis of the many-to-many matching results over all pairs of input exemplars ultimately yields the nodes and edges (both abstraction and attachment) in the final model.

We begin with a summary of related work (Section 2) and proceed to present our graph construction computed over a multi-scale blob and ridge decomposition (Section 3). We then describe our many-to-many graph matching technique (Section 4), our technique for identifying persistent parts (Section 5.1), and our technique for defining both attachment and abstraction relations (and their probabilities) (Section 5.2). We evaluate each stage of the pipeline using ground truth data, and explore the sensitivity of each step to changes in parameters (Section 6). Finally, we offer some conclusions (Section 8) as well as directions for future research.

2   Related Work

Many authors have attempted to learn categorical models from examples, and we highlight only a few due to space limitations. Constellation models have emerged as a popular representation for modeling general categories, such as motorbikes, faces, and cars

[1, 7]. Constellation models represent objects as configurations of local, appearance-based descriptors together with their spatial distributions. Learning these models can be accomplished robustly since appearance-based patches can be matched effectively and independently across training examples, therefore providing an efficient model boot-strapping step. The domain of human structural modeling from examples has also received considerable recent attention [8, 6, 5, 3]. Specific human structural tree models have been used in conjunction with efficient dynamic programming search methods by [8], while others [6, 4] assume an unknown (but tree-shaped) model structure and rely on ribbon detectors or temporal tracking [3] and clustering of body parts to recover a kinematic human representation using maximum weight spanning tree algorithms [9].

There are three critical differences between our approach and the above frameworks. The first is our use of generic shape features, as opposed to specific appearance-based features. Using appearance-based features not only constrains the training set to the same object exemplars, but yields a simple correspondence problem. Our generic features, in the form of ridges and blobs, are highly ambiguous, and cannot be tracked across training examples on the basis of their properties alone. This gives rise to the second major difference, whereby the context of a feature, i.e., the nature of its structural connections to nearby blobs, is critical to computing blob/ridge correspondence across training examples. The use of perceptual grouping to commit to this necessary structure *prior* to matching is in contrast to approaches in which the use of robust, local feature correspondences allows structural relations to be computed *following* matching. The final, and perhaps most critical difference, is our recovery of decompositional relations between features, allowing us to capture a coarse-to-fine representation of an object. Recovering such relations hinges on being able to match features many-to-many, as opposed to assuming a one-to-one feature correspondence. Without motion (of a single exemplar), appearance-based features cannot be matched many-to-many, due to their lack of generic structure.

3   Representing Qualitative Image Structure

We seek a decomposition of an image into a set of qualitative parts and attachment relations, and adopt the multi-scale blob and ridge decomposition proposed in [18]. Since blobs are generic features, they encode no appearance-specific information. Consequently, matching a blob in one image to a blob in another cannot be done on the basis of a blob's parameters, which include only a blob vs. ridge feature type, position (not translation or articulation invariant), orientation (not rotation invariant), ridge extent (not viewpoint invariant), and saliency. To overcome this tremendous ambiguity during matching, we need to draw on a blob's context, i.e., the structure of nearby blobs thought to be part of the same object. Specifically, we seek a set of edges that span features that are unlikely to be in close proximity by chance. Given our desire to describe objects at multiple levels of abstraction, spatial coherence and continuity dictate that, for example, when a coarse, elongated shape is decomposed into a set of smaller, elongated shapes, the latter will likely be attached end-to-end.

To set the edge weights, we must look ahead slightly to how they will be used at matching time. The many-to-many graph matching algorithm (to be described in more

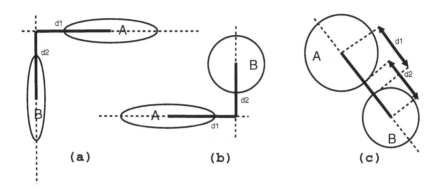

Fig. 2. Edge construction: (a) ridge-ridge; (b) ridge-blob; and (c) blob-blob. The total length of the bold lines represents the assigned edge weight between the two features in the graph.

detail later) first embeds the nodes of two graphs to be matched into two weighted point sets in Euclidean space. In this geometric space, a powerful many-to-many weighted point matching algorithm, the *Earth Mover's Distance (EMD)* [14], yields a solution which, in turn, specifies a many-to-many node correspondence between the original graphs. EMD will map (or "spread") a point from one graph to a collection of points from another graph if the members of the collection are in close geometric proximity. Therefore, if we want multiple parts at a finer scale in one graph to match a single part at a coarser scale in another graph, the edge weights (distances) linking the finer scale parts to be grouped must be relatively small.

A connectivity measure is computed for each pair of features, according to:

$$max\{d_1/major(A), d_2/major(B)\}, \tag{1}$$

where $major(X)$ is the length of the major axis of blob X. If this measure is greater than a threshold (whose sensitivity we evaluate in Section 6.1), the blobs are considered disconnected; if the measure is less than the threshold, an edge is inserted between the blobs whose weight is a function of d_1 and d_2, as shown in Figure 2. Due to scene clutter, the graph may have a number of connected components, representing multiple objects. We greedily choose the largest (in terms of number of nodes) connected component as a simple method for figure-ground separation, and discard the other components. Ultimately, a distance matrix over these remaining features is necessary to construct an embedding of the graph into a geometric space. To ensure that the distance matrix is invariant to part articulation, the distance between any two nodes is defined as the shortest path distance (along graph edges) between the nodes.

4   Computing Many-to-Many Blob Correspondences

Given an input training set of blob graphs, we compute a many-to-many matching between each pair of graphs. In the graph domain, this is an intractable problem that would require matching (perhaps connected) subsets of nodes in one graph to subsets of nodes in another. Our technique is based on a recent approach to this problem, proposed by Demirci et al. [16], which transforms the many-to-many graph matching problem to a many-to-many weighted point matching problem, for which an efficient algorithm exists. Given a shortest-path distance matrix encoding node-to-node distances, the algorithm employs a spherical coding technique to yield a low-distortion embedding of the nodes in a low-dimensional Euclidean space (we adopt a simpler, spectral embedding technique). The approach essentially throws out the original graph edges, and locates the points in space such that the Euclidean distances between points in the embedded space is close (with low distortion) to shortest path distances between nodes in the original graph.

The embedded points can now be matched many-to-many using the Earth Mover's Distance (EMD) under transformation [15]. If the points corresponding to one graph are viewed as piles of earth, while the points corresponding to the other graph are viewed as holes, the EMD algorithm computes the assignment of earth to holes that minimizes the amount of work required to move the earth to the holes. If we assume that mass is approximately conserved through levels of abstraction, then points should be assigned a weight that's proportional to the areas of their corresponding blobs. Returning to our "arm" example, the mass of the straight arm blob should roughly equal the sum of the masses of the broken arm blobs. The EMD under transformation is an iterative assignment/alignment process that quickly converges on a solution which can be mapped to a many-to-many node correspondence between the original graphs. In the following subsections, we provide the details on these steps.

4.1 Graph Embedding

A number of techniques are available for embedding the distance matrix into Euclidean space; examples include metric tree embedding [17], spherical codes [16], and ISOMAP [19]. We adopt a spectral embedding of a distance matrix computed in terms of shortest paths between nodes in a blob graph, similar to [19]. Each blob in the graph maps to a point which encodes the blob's embedded position and mass (blob area). The matching of two blob graphs can now be formulated as the matching of their embedded weighted point sets, in which a source point's mass can flow to multiple target points and a target point can receive flow from multiple source points. For our experiments, we embed the graph into a 2-D space. Though higher dimensional embeddings will result in a lower distortion and a more accurate many-to-many matching, the alignment computation may become underconstrained since more point correspondences will be needed. A 2-D space was chosen since it requires only 3 point correspondences for an affine alignment computation. Most of our exemplar images do share at least 3 feature correspondences. It is possible to adapt the dimensionality of the embedding space for each particular matching, the subject of future work.

4.2 Weighted Point Matching

The Earth Mover's Distance (EMD) algorithm under transformation [15] allows us to compute a many-to-many matching of the embedded points which, in turn, specifies

Fig. 3. Many-to-many matching of blob graphs using Earth Mover's Distance under transformation in embedded (Euclidean) space. Left two images show the detected blobs with green lines indicating blob connections and line width indicating edge strength (nonaccidental, proximity-based grouping strength). The right figure shows the embedded features (red for left image, blue for right image) after alignment, using the modified EMD under transformation. The flows are shown in green, with line width indicating amount of flow; note that since the blobs are well aligned, the flow distances are very small. The sizes of the circles correspond to the point masses (blob areas).

a many-to-many node correspondence between the nodes in the original graphs. The EMD is a global assignment problem, and assumes that the total masses of the two graphs are the same. However, with noise, occlusion, and clutter, this assumption is violated, and we must modify the algorithm to take a more local approach. Specifically, the mass of each feature in the first image is distributed among its nearby features in the second image in a greedy fashion, with both small flows and flows over large distances eliminated. If we compute the flows in the opposite direction, i.e., from the second image to the first image, the flows may be different, due to our greedy approximation. Augmenting the EMD cost function (the amount of work required to redistribute the mass) with terms that penalize for unmatched masses in the two images by adding the sum of untransferred masses in source nodes and the sum of unfilled masses in target nodes to the cost, we select the direction with minimum cost.

The flows associated with a given direction are used to compute an affine transformation between the corresponding point sets using a least-squares minimization of the sum of squared differences between the location of a point in the one set and a weighted (by the flows) average location of its matched points in the other set:

$$\sum_i \|(Pos(i) - T(\sum_j Flows(i,j) \times Pos(j)))\|^2, \tag{2}$$

where T is an N−dimensional affine transformation. In this approximation to the iterative **FT** (an optimal **F**low and an optimal **T**ransformation) algorithm [15], which alternates between computing the EMD flows and computing the affine transformation, the algorithm typically converges in 3-4 iterations. Figure 3 shows two blob graphs and the final matching, as computed by EMD under transformation. The final flow matrix computed by Algorithm 1 defines a direction of minimum cost. This matrix can be "inverted" to yield a consistent flow matrix for the opposite direction. These two matrices will play a key role in our procedure for extracting the parts in the final decompositional model.

Algorithm 1. EMD Under Transformation for Many-to-Many Matching of Two Weighted Point Sets

1: Compute the distance matrix $d(i, j) = \|P_{1_i} - P_{2_j}\|$.
2: Compute the $Flows$ matrix using the above distance matrix d.
3: **repeat**
4:     Compute   the   transformation T that   minimizes $\sum_i \|(P_{1_i} - T(\sum_j Flows(i, j) \times P_{2_j}))\|^2$.
5:     Transform each point P_{2_j} from the second set with the computed transformation T.
6:     Compute a new distance matrix $d(i, j) = \|P_{1_i} - P_{2_j}\|$.
7:     Compute a new $Flows$ matrix using the new distance matrix d.
8: **until** the change in the $Flows$ matrix is small
9: Assign a cost to the computed $Flows$ matrix.
10: Return computed flow matrix $Flows$ and its cost.

5   Model Construction

Using the above feature matching framework, each pair of the P input exemplars is matched, resulting in $O(P^2)$ pairs of mass flow matrices (one per direction). Furthermore, each pair of flow matrices can be row normalized to 1, with each row entry indicating the fraction of mass flowing from the feature specified by the row to the feature specified by the column. These matrices are combined to form a single $N \times N$ matching matrix, M, where N is the total number of blobs in all of the exemplar images. M is a block matrix, where the (i, j)-th block stores the flows from features in image i to features in image j; diagonal blocks are identity matrices, reflecting the perfect one-to-one matching that would result from matching an image to itself.

The final decompositional model is derived from the matching matrix M and the original blob graphs. First, the one-to-one flows are analyzed to yield consistently appearing parts, i.e., parts that match one-to-one across many pairs of input images. Next, the many-to-many flows (M) between these extracted parts are analyzed to yield the decompositional relations among parts detected in the first step. Finally, the input blob graphs are analyzed to yield the attachment edges between the extracted parts. The extracted parts and their relations are used to construct the final decompositional model. The following subsections outline these steps in more detail.

5.1   Extracting Parts

Our goal in populating the final model is to select parts that occur frequently across many input exemplars, i.e., parts that match one-to-one. Recall that entry (p, q) in the matching matrix M contains the computed flow from blob p (in the image in which it was detected) to q (in the image it was detected) when the two images were matched; (q, p) contains the flow in the other direction. If both flows are close to 1.0, then the blobs are said to be in one-to-one correspondence. However, if part p or q is involved in a many-to-one decompositional relation, the flow in one direction will be less than 1.0.

By redefining both entries to be the minimum of the two flows, the entries representing one-to-one correspondences will retain their high values (close to 1.0) and the matrix becomes symmetric. Subtracting the entry from 1 turns the symmetric flow matrix into a symmetric distance matrix, setting up a clustering problem where clusters represent collections of nodes in one-to-one correspondences. Again, we draw on spectral techniques to embed the distance matrix in a low-dimensional space, and use the k-means[1] algorithm for clustering. The quality $[0, 1]$ of the cluster is proportional to the "cliqueness" of the one-to-one matches among the members of the cluster. If a cluster is of sufficient size and quality, it becomes a node in the final decompositional model.

5.2   Extracting Relations

Two types of edges are used to link together the extracted parts (nodes). Decompositional edges are directed from one part to multiple parts, and capture the notion that a feature can appear alternatively as a set of component features, due to finer scale or articulation (or, in the reverse direction, a set of features can be abstracted to form a single feature). Attachment relations are the same nonaccidental proximity relations found in the blob graphs computed from the training images. An attachment edge is undirected, and implies that the blobs spanning the edge are connected. The many-to-many matching results (flows) between the extracted parts will be analyzed to extract the decompositional edges, while the attachment relations (in the original blob graphs) between the extracted parts will be analyzed to extract the attachment relations.

The K extracted parts represent clusters of matching blobs in the matrix M. For attachment relations, we compute the likelihood with which any two such parts not only co-appear in the images in which they were found, but are attached as well. If this likelihood of attachment exceeds a threshold, we define an attachment relation between the two extracted parts. The likelihood $[0, 1]$ of attachment between parts i and j is defined by the $K \times K$ matrix PA (part attachment) as:

$$PA(i, j) = \frac{\sum_{p=1}^{P} \sum_{k=1}^{B(p)} \sum_{l=1}^{B(p)} [C_p(k) = i][C_p(l) = j] conn_p(k, l)}{\sum_{p=1}^{P} \sum_{k=1}^{B(p)} \sum_{l=1}^{B(p)} [C_p(k) = i][C_p(l) = j]} \tag{3}$$

where P is the number of training images, $B(p)$ is the number of blobs in training image p, $C_p(k)$ is the cluster that blob k in image p is assigned to, $[C_p(k) = i]$ is an indicator function whose value is 1 when $C_p(k) = i$ and 0 otherwise, and $conn_p(k, l)$ has value 1 if there is an attachment between blobs k and l in image p (and 0 otherwise). The expression captures the number of times blobs drawn from the two clusters were attached, normalized by the number of times blobs from the two clusters co-appeared in an image. Part attachment relations above a threshold T_{attach} are inserted into the final model. We found that $T_{attach} = 0.6$ worked well for our complete set of experiments, representing the condition that co-occurring blobs belonging to two different parts are connected in at least 60% of the input images.

---

[1] We first run k-means with a large value of k, resulting in over-segmented clusters. In a post-processing step, we reassign some blobs to more compatible clusters, remove noisy blobs from clusters, remove weak clusters, and merge similar clusters. The resulting procedure yields stable clusters that are less sensitive to the initial choice of k.

For decompositional relations, we restrict ourselves to one-to-many decompositional relations. A directed, one-to-many decompositional relation between one extracted part (parent) and a set of two or more extracted parts (children) must satisfy three conditions:

1. Most of the mass of the parent flows to the children.
2. In the reverse (many-to-one) direction, most of the mass of each child flows to the parent.
3. The children form a connected component, implying a spatial coherence constraint.

Testing the first two (flow) conditions requires a $K \times K$ part flow matrix, $PF(i, j)$, constructed by averaging the flows from all blobs in extracted part i's cluster to all blobs in extracted part j's cluster:

$$PF(i, j) = \frac{\sum_{k=1}^{N} \sum_{l=1}^{N} [C(k) = i][C(l) = j] M(k, l)}{(\sum_{k'=1}^{N} [C(k') = i]) \times (\sum_{l'=1}^{N} [C(l') = j])} \qquad (4)$$

where N is the total number of blobs extracted from all images, $C(l)$ is the cluster that blob l is assigned to, and M is the $N \times N$ matching matrix. The expression represents the sum of all flows from blobs in cluster i to blobs in cluster j, normalized by the number of flows, yielding a mean flow. The entries in the matrix PF are in the range $[0, 1]$.

Given the part flow (PF) and part attachment (PA) matrices, Algorithm 2 extracts the part decomposition relations among the extracted parts in the final model. T_{child} (0.6) is determined empirically and reflects the degree to which a conservation of

---

Algorithm 2. Extracting Decompositional Relations

1: **for** $i = 1$ to K **do**
2:     Find all parts $j \neq i$, s.t. $PF(j, i) \geq T_{child}$. Let D be the set of all such parts, representing the potential children of i.
3:     **for all** subsets D' of D **do**
4:         Let $PA_{D'}$ be the upper triangular matrix of $PA(k, l)$, where $k, l \in D'$.
5:         The quality of the decomposition of part i into the set D' is $e^{-|1 - \sum_{j \in D'} PF(i,j)|} \times min\{1, \frac{\sum_{k,l \in D'} PA_{D'}(k,l)}{|D'|-1}\}$ {The first term in the quality measure cost is high when most of the parent's mass flows to the children (and low otherwise). The second term encourages the children to form a connected component, where a connected component of D' children implies at least $D' - 1$ attachment edges among them.}
6:     **end for**
7: **end for**
8: Choose decompositions whose quality exceeds T_{decomp}

---

mass constraint can be imposed between the children and their parent in a many-to-one mapping. A higher threshold, reflecting a stronger constraint, implies less blob over- or under-segmentation in the image domain in which the models are being learned. T_{decomp} is also set to 0.6, reflecting the fact that a parent distributes most of its mass to its children and that the children are attached (the product of the two terms needs to be larger than 0.6).

5.3   Assembling the Final Model Graph

The final model is a graph whose nodes represent the extracted parts and whose edges represent the extracted attachment and decompositional relations. Associated with each node is a saliency value, defined as the average of all the compatibility values of the blobs in a given cluster (defined in Section 5.1). The attachment relation between parts i and j has an associated likelihood, defined by $PA(i, j)$. The decompositional relation between a parent part and its constituent children has both an associated quality, defined by the algorithm above, and a probability reflecting how likely the decomposition is, i.e., the probability that the set of children will be observed in an image in lieu of the parent.

6   Experimental Results

We evaluate our model on a database of 86 torso images containing different individuals with different arm articulations; the blob graphs extracted from some of these images can be seen in Figure 1. Ground truth is provided for each input image in the form of a labeling of the extracted blobs in terms of the parts in an ideal torso decompositional model, shown in Figure 4; blobs that are not deemed (by a human observer) to correspond to a part on the ideal model are labelled as noise. This allows us to systematically evaluate each component of the system, including the detection of the blobs and attachment relations forming the input graphs, the many-to-many matching results, the detection of parts (clustering) that become the nodes in the final graph[2], and the attachment and decompositional relations that link the nodes together. Moreover, we can evaluate the sensitivity of each step as a function of any underlying parameters.

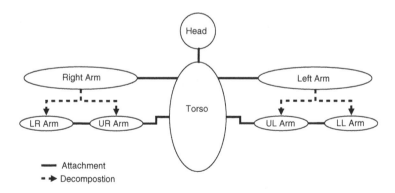

Fig. 4. The ideal torso decompositional model, representing ground truth for the experiments

---

[2] Since the clustering step is not deterministic (due to the random initialization of clusters), the clustering experiments, as well as all experiments that rely on the clustering results, were conducted 20 times for each value of the parameter being evaluated.

6.1 Evaluation of Input Blob Graphs

As mentioned in Section 1, the detection of blobs is a noisy process, resulting in over- and under-segmentation, spurious blobs, missing blobs, and poorly localized blobs. Given the ground truth labeling, we can evaluate the blob detection process. According to the part labels shown in Figure 4, the percentage of images in which the designated part was detected was: head (47%), torso (83%), left arm (50%), right arm (51%), left upper arm (37%), left lower arm (36%), right upper arm (40%), and right lower arm (37%). These relatively low percentages reflect the significant degree of noise in the detection of blobs (note that a straight arm and its two components cannot simultaneously appear). The attachment relations are governed by a single proximity threshold. Large threshold values cause all blobs to be attached and thus produce false positive attachment relations among parts, whereas small threshold values create sparse graphs with false negative attachment relations among parts. Figure 5(a) shows the error in individual attachment, representing the sum of the SSD error in the attachment matrices of all exemplar blob graphs.

6.2 Evaluation of Many-to-Many Matching

The error in the many-to-many matching component is computed by finding the sum of the SSD errors in the flow matrices of each pair of exemplars. Given the optimal proximity threshold, our matching algorithm yields a 9% error based on an element-by-element comparison of the computed matching matrix M to the ground truth data.

6.3 Evaluation of Part Extraction

The error in the clustering step comprising part extraction is a function of two parameters. The cluster error is computed by first finding the best cluster for every part in the ideal model. Given a labeling of each image in terms of the ideal model, we can then compute both precision and recall for each model part. The minimum (worst-case) of the precision and recall values is averaged across all clusters and then inverted to yield a final error measure. Figure 5(b) plots smoothed error as a function of embedding dimension. From the figure, we conclude that the choice of the embedding dimension is not critical. The second parameter is k, representing an upper bound on the true number of clusters. Figure 5(c) plots smoothed error as a function of k (maximum number of clusters). Since the minimum is rather shallow, our algorithm is not very sensitive to the choice of k.

6.4 Evaluation of Edge Extraction

Errors in the extraction of part attachment and part decomposition edges are computed by first finding the correspondence between the ideal model (ground truth) parts and the computed clusters, from which the SSD errors in the attachment and decomposition edges can be computed. Since the correspondence between ground truth and computed clusters is not necessarily one-to-one, and since a computed cluster does not necessarily correspond to any ground truth cluster, an additional error term is added to account for

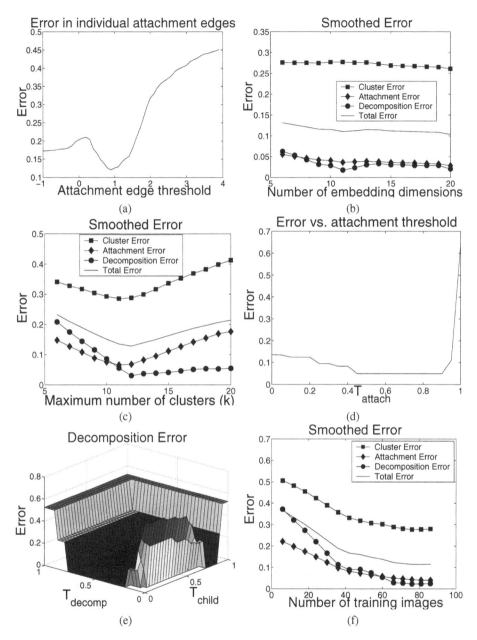

Fig. 5. Evaluating the Model: (a) Input attachment relation error as function of proximity-based grouping threshold; (b,c,f) The four curves represent clustering error, recovered attachment edge error, recovered decomposition edge error, and final decompositional model error as a function of dimensionality of embedding, the upper bound k on the number of putative clusters, and training set size, respectively; (d) Recovered attachment edge error as a function of T_{attach}; (e) Recovered decomposition edge error as a function of T_{child} and T_{decomp}

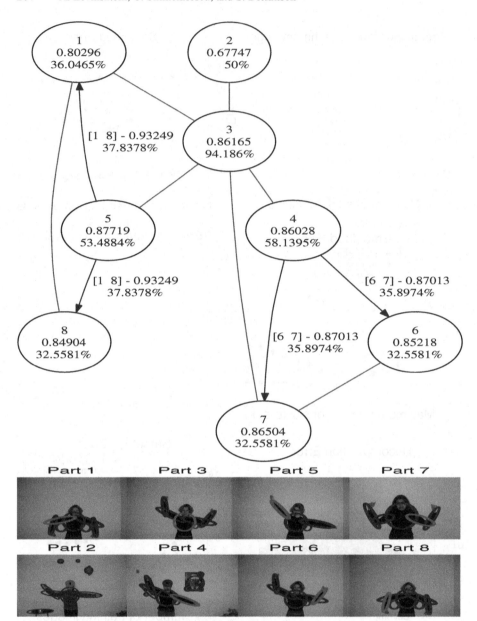

Fig. 6. Final decompositional model obtained by our system on 86 input images. Red edges indicate part attachment, while blue edges indicate part decomposition (or, inversely, abstraction). The values on the decomposition edges specify the children (square brackets), the quality of the decomposition, and the probability of the decomposition. The top number inside a node is its part number, the middle number is its cluster quality, and the bottom number is the probability of occurrence of the part. At the bottom is one example image for each part (shown in red), sampled from its cluster. The model not only captures the correct attachments between parts, but also captures the decompositional relations between each arm and its constituent subparts.

the dissimilarity in the number of edges between the ground truth model and the final recovered model. The error term is the difference in the number of edges relative to the maximum number of edges in the ground truth and retrieved models. Figures 5(d) and 5(e) show the error in attachment edges, as a function of the threshold T_{attach}, and decomposition edges, as a function of the thresholds, T_{child} and T_{decomp}. The same clustering results are used throughout these two experiments. As can be seen from the figures, there is a range of thresholds that results in good attachments and decomposition edges.

6.5 Evaluation of the Final Model

From the above experiments, we determined optimal values for the different parameters and manually entered them into the system. In our final experiment, we evaluate the error of the final decompositional model as a function of the size of the input training set. The error is defined by averaging the clustering error, the recovered part attachment error, and the recovered part decomposition error. Figure 5(f) shows the smoothed final model error and its three components as a function of training set size. It can be clearly seen that the errors decrease as the number of training images increases. The automatically generated model (for the full training set) is shown in Figure 6. The recovered model is isomorphic to the ideal model, reflecting our algoithm's ability to correctly recover a decompositional model from noisy examples.

7 Limitations

The many-to-many matching component of our framework can handle spurious noise in the form of missing features and small extraneous features. However, the presence of a large noise feature or large occluder may result in incorrect assignments during the EMD stage, for it may draw too much mass from correct features (if it's a "hole") or flood too many correct features (if it's a "pile"). The impact of such features can be minimized by assigning additional properties to the features, such as shape or appearance, and then using these properties as constraints in computing the mass flows during EMD. Another important limitation arises from the fact that positional information of the blobs is lost during the embedding. Although the use of distance between features yields articulation invariance, it also means that feature ordering may be lost, as exemplified by a head on one torso matching a similarly sized noise blob on the bottom or side of another torso. Again, the role of additional blob properties as constraints may help to alleviate this problem.

8 Conclusions and Future Work

We have presented an algorithm for automatically recovering a decompositional, generic shape model from examples; parts of the model can be represented at different levels of abstraction – an important representational goal originally proposed by Marr. Two important challenges face this task: 1) the inherent ambiguity in generic shape features, such as ridges and blobs; and 2) the need, due to articulation, scale, and segmentation error, to match such features many-to-many. By imposing a graph-based perceptual grouping on the parts, we provide the structural context necessary to match ambiguous parts many-to-many. Our algorithm requires a number of parameters, and we have established the relative insensitivity of the results to changes in the parameters. We have demonstrated the approach on recovering a decompositional torso model from example images of different subjects. Although our features and grouping rules are tuned for articulated objects, such as humans, the framework could be applied to other features and grouping rules that are more suitable for other categories. The correctness of the recovered model as a function of the size of the training set has been evaluated with respect to ground truth. Preliminary results are very encouraging, and current efforts are aimed at recovering more complex models having a higher incidence of decompositional structure. Moreover, we seek to augment the recovered model with both node and relation constraints, derived from the input data. Finally, we plan to apply machine learning techniques to recover optimal perceptual grouping parameters, and develop object recognition techniques adapted to part-based decompositional models.

Acknowledgements

The authors would like to thank Lars Bretzner for his blob extraction software. Fatih Demirci and Ali Shokoufandeh provided both feedback and support in the development of the many-to-many graph matching module, and also provided the EMD software. We are very grateful for their assistance. The authors would also like to thank Allan Jepson for his thoughtful feedback on the work. The support of NSERC, the NSF, CITO, and PREA is gratefully acknowledged.

References

1. Fei-Fei, L., Fergus, R., and Perona, P., A Bayesian Approach to Unsupervised One-Shot Learning of Object Categories, ICCV, Nice, 2003.
2. Lazebnik, S., Schmid, C., and Ponce, J., Semi-Local Affine Parts for Object Recognition, BMVC, 2004.
3. Song, Y., Goncalves, L., and Perona, P., Unsupervised Learning of Human Motion, *IEEE PAMI*, Vol. 25, No. 7, 2003.
4. Ramanan, D. and Forsyth, D.A., Using Temporal Coherence to Build Models of Animals, ICCV, 2003.
5. Ramanan, D. and Forsyth, D.A., Finding and Tracking People From the Bottom Up, IEEE CVPR, 2003.
6. Ioffe, S. and Forsyth, D.A., Human tracking with mixtures of trees, ICCV, 2001.
7. Fergus, R., Perona, P., and Zisserman, A., Object Class Recognition by Unsupervised Scale-Invariant Learning, IEEE CVPR, 2003.
8. P. Felzenszwalb and D. Huttenlocher, Efficient Matching of Pictorial Structures, IEEE CVPR, 2000.
9. Chow, C.K., Liu, C.N., Approximating discrete probability distributions with dependence trees, *IEEE Trans. Info. Theory*, IT-14, No.3, 1968, pp. 462-467.
10. Brooks, R.A., Model-Based Three Dimensional Interpretations of Two Dimensional Images, *IEEE PAMI*, March 1983.

11. Marr. D. and Nishihara, H.K., Representation and recognition of the spatial organization of three dimensional shapes, Proc. of Royal Soc. of London, 1978.
12. Jepson, A.D., Fleet, D.J., and Black, M.J., A layered motion representation with occlusion and compact spatial support, ECCV, 2002.
13. Viola, P., Jones, M.J., and Snow, D., Detecting Pedestrians Using Patterns of Motion and Appearance, ICCV, 2003.
14. Rubner, Y, Tomasi, C., and Guibas, L.J., A metric for distributions with applications to image databases, ICCV, 1998.
15. Cohen, S. and Guibas, L.J., The Earth Mover's Distance under Transformation Sets, ICCV, 1999.
16. Demirci, M.F., Shokoufandeh, A. Dickinson, S., Keselman, Y., Bretzner, L., Many-to-Many Feature Matching Using Spherical Coding of Directed Graphs, ECCV, 2004.
17. Matoušek, J., On Embedding Trees into Uniformly Convex Banach Spaces, *Israel J. of Mathematics*, Volume 237, 1999.
18. Lindeberg, T. and Bretzner, L., Real-time scale selection in hybrid multi-scale representations, Proc. Scale-Space'03, 2003.
19. Tenenbaum, J.B., de Silva, V., and Langford, J.C., A Global Geometric Framework for Nonlinear Dimensionality Reduction, *Science*, 290 (5500), 2000.

Discontinuity Preserving Phase Unwrapping Using Graph Cuts*

José M. Bioucas-Dias and Gonçalo Valadão

Instituto de Telecomunicações,
Instituto Superior Técnico, Torre Norte, Piso 10,
Av. Rovisco Pais, 1049-001 Lisboa, Portugal
{bioucas, gvaladao}@lx.it.pt

Abstract. We present a new algorithm for recovering the absolute phase from modulo-2π phase, the so-called phase unwrapping (PU) problem. PU arises as a key step in several imaging technologies, from which we emphasize interferometric synthetic aperture radar/sonar (InSAR/SAS), magnetic resonance imaging (MRI), and optical interferometry. We adopt a discrete energy minimization viewpoint, where the objective function is a *first-order Markov random field*. The minimization problem is dealt with via a binary iterative scheme, with each iteration step cast onto a graph cut based optimization problem. For convex clique potentials we provide an exact energy minimization algorithm; namely we solve exactly the PU classical L^p norm, with $p \geq 1$. For nonconvex clique potentials, it is well known that PU performance is particularly enhanced, namely, the discontinuity preserving ability; however the problem is NP-hard. Accordingly, we provide an approximate algorithm, which is a modified version of the first proposed one. For simplicity we call both algorithms PUMF, for Phase Unwrapping Max-Flow. The state-of-the-art competitiveness of PUMF is illustrated in a series of experiments.

1 Introduction

Phase is an important property of many classes of signals [1]. For instance, interferometric SAR (InSAR) uses two or more antennas to measure the phase between the antennas and the terrain; the topography is then inferred from the difference between those phases [2]. In magnetic resonance imaging (MRI), phase is used, namely, to determine magnetic field deviation maps, which are used to correct echo-planar image geometric distortions [3]. In optical interferometry, phase measurements are used to detect objects shape, deformation, and vibration [4].

In all the examples above, in spite of phase being a crucial information, the acquisition system can only measure phase modulo-2π, the so-called principal phase value, or wrapped phase. Formally, we have

$$\phi = \psi + 2k\pi, \tag{1}$$

* This work was supported by the Fundação para a Ciência e Tecnologia, under the project PDCTE/CPS/49967/2003.

A. Rangarajan et al. (Eds.): EMMCVPR 2005, LNCS 3757, pp. 268–284, 2005.

where ϕ is the true phase value (the so-called absolute value), $\psi \in [-\pi, \pi[$ is the measured (wrapped) modulo-2π phase value, and $k \in \mathbb{Z}$ an integer number of wavelengths [5, Chap. 1].

Phase unwrapping (PU) is the process of recovering the absolute phase ϕ from the wrapped phase ψ. This is, however, an ill-posed problem, if no further information is added. In fact, an assumption taken by most phase unwrapping algorithms is that the absolute value of phase differences between neighbouring pixels is less than π, the so-called Itoh condition [6]. If this assumption is not violated, the absolute phase can be easily determined, up to a constant. Itoh condition might be violated if the true phase surface is discontinuous, or if only a noisy version of the wrapped phase is available. In either cases, PU becomes a very difficult problem, to which much attention has been devoted [5], [7], [8], [9], [10], [11], [12], [13],[14].

Phase unwrapping approaches belong to one of the following classes: path following [7], minimum L^p norm [10], Bayesian [8], [15], [16], and parametric modelling [17].

Path following algorithms apply line integration schemes over the wrapped phase image, and basically rely on the assumption that Itoh condition holds along the integration path. Wherever that condition is not met, different integration paths may lead to different unwrapped phase values. Techniques employed to handle these inconsistencies include the so-called *residues branch cuts* [7] and *quality maps* [5, Chap. 4].

Minimum norm methods exploit this fact: if Itoh condition is met, the differences between absolute phases of neighbour pixels are equal to the wrapped differences between correspondent wrapped phases. Thus, these methods try to find a phase solution ϕ for which the L^p norm of the difference between absolute phase differences and wrapped phase differences (so a second order difference) is minimized. This is, therefore, a global minimization in the sense that all the observed phases are used to compute a solution. With $p = 2$ we have a least squares method [18]. The exact solution with $p = 2$ is developed in [14] using network programming techniques. An approximation to the least squares solution can be obtained by relaxing the discrete domain $\mathbb{Z}^{MN}$ to $\mathbb{R}^{MN}$ and applying FFT or DCT based techniques[1][19]. A drawback of the L^2 norm is that this criterion tends to smooth discontinuities, unless they are provided as binary weights. L^1 norm performs better than L^2 norm in what discontinuity preserving is concerned. Such a criterion has been solved exactly by Flynn [11] and Costantini [12] using network programming. With $0 \leq p < 1$ the ability of preserving discontinuities is further increased at stake, however, of more complex optimization algorithms [5, Chap. 5], [20].

The Bayesian approach relies on a data-observation mechanism model and on a prior density expressing the *a priori* knowledge of the phase. For instance in [21] a non-linear optimal filtering is applied, while in [22] an InSAR observation model is considered taking into account not only the image phase, but also

---

[1] M and N are the number of lines and columns, respectively.

the *backscattering coefficient* and *correlation factor* images, which are jointly recovered from InSAR image pairs.

Finally, parametric algorithms constrain the unwrapped phase to a parametric surface. Low order polynomial surfaces are used in [17]. Very often in real applications just one polynomial is not enough to describe accurately the complete surface. In such cases the image is partitioned and different parametric models are applied to each partition [17].

1.1 Proposed Approach

This paper proposes a new phase unwrapping methodology based on discrete energy minimization. The objective function considered is a first-order Markov random field, where the associated energy has only pairwise interactions. The energy minimization is worked out through a binary iterative scheme, similar to the one presented in [14], [23]. Each iteration step is casted onto a graph min-cut/max-flow problem, relying mainly on [24] but also on [25] and [26].

If the chosen clique potentials are convex, we devise a low-order polynomial exact algorithm. In particular we solve exactly the phase unwrapping classical L^p norm [10], with $p \geq 1$. Otherwise, for nonconvex clique potentials, even though our problem turns out to be NP-hard [24], [25], it is well known that in image reconstruction and namely in phase unwrapping, discontinuity preserving abilities are greatly enhanced [5, Chap. 5], [20], [27], [28], [29], [30], [31]; it also happens that in a nonconvex setting, nor the iterative scheme, nor the graph cut casting employed in the algorithm are possible. Accordingly, we further present a discontinuity preserving phase unwrapping algorithm. This is an approximate algorithm that is a modified version of the first one, building on two main ideas: 1) widening of the configuration space of each binary problem; 2) applying majorize minimize (MM) [32] concepts to our energy function, which allows the graph cut casting. For simplicity we call both algorithms PUMF, for Phase Unwrapping Max-Flow.

2   Problem Formulation

Figure 1 shows a pixel and its first-order neighbours along with the variables h and v signalling horizontal and vertical discontinuities respectively.

The L^p norm of the difference between neighbouring pixel phases, 2π-congruent with wrapped phases, is given by $\sum_{ij \in \mathbb{Z}_1} |\Delta\phi_{ij}^h|^p \overline{v}_{ij} + |\Delta\phi_{ij}^v|^p \overline{h}_{ij}$, where $(\cdot)^h$ and $(\cdot)^v$ denotes pixel horizontal and vertical differences given by

$$\Delta\phi_{ij}^h = \left[2\pi(k_{ij} - k_{ij-1}) - \Delta\psi_{ij}^h \right], \; k \in \mathbb{Z} \tag{2}$$

$$\Delta\phi_{ij}^v = \left[2\pi(k_{ij} - k_{i-1j}) - \Delta\psi_{ij}^v \right], \; k \in \mathbb{Z} \tag{3}$$

$$\Delta\psi_{ij}^h = \psi_{ij-1} - \psi_{ij} \tag{4}$$

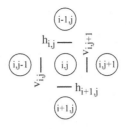

Fig. 1. Representation of the pixel (i,j) and its first order neighbours along with the variables h and v signalling horizontal and vertical discontinuities respectively

$$\Delta\psi_{ij}^v = \psi_{i-1j} - \psi_{ij}, \tag{5}$$

with ψ being the wrapped (observed) phase, $\overline{h}_{ij} = 1 - h_{ij}$ and $\overline{v}_{ij} = 1 - v_{ij}$ ($h_{ij}, v_{ij} \in \{0,1\}$) being binary horizontal and vertical discontinuities respectively, and $(i,j) \in \mathbb{Z}_1$ where $\mathbb{Z}_1 = \{(i,j) : i = 1,\ldots,M, \; j = 1,\ldots,N\}$, with M and N denoting the number of lines and columns respectively (i.e., the usual image pixel indexing 2D grid). Similarly our energy function is given by

$$E(\mathbf{k}|\boldsymbol{\psi}) = \sum_{ij\in\mathbb{Z}_1} V\left(\Delta\phi_{ij}^h\right)\overline{v}_{ij} + V\left(\Delta\phi_{ij}^v\right)\overline{h}_{ij}, \tag{6}$$

where the clique potential V is a real-valued function.

Our goal is to find the integer image $\mathbf{k}$ that minimizes energy (6), $\mathbf{k}$ being such that $\boldsymbol{\phi} = 2\pi\mathbf{k} + \boldsymbol{\psi}$, where $\boldsymbol{\phi}$ is the estimated unwrapped image and $\boldsymbol{\psi}$ is the observed wrapped image; $\mathbf{k}$ is the so-called *wrap-count* image. To achieve this goal, we cast this integer problem into a series of graph flow calculations for which efficient max-flow/min-cut algorithms exist. This relies on an energy minimization lemma given in section 3.1, and results on binary energy minimization through graph cuts [24].

We should point out that the variables conveying discontinuity information h_{ij} and v_{ij} are to be introduced when available. In SAR jargon these images are the so-called quality maps. They can also be used as continuous variables expressing prior knowledge on phase variability. Quality maps can be derived from correlation maps for InSAR, or from phase derivative variance in a more general setting [5, Chap. 3]. Nevertheless, we must stress that in practice quality maps are very often unavailable, at least partially, which requires clique potentials to have discontinuity preserving abilities, and therefore, calls for nonconvexity.

Although energy (6) was succinctly introduced in a deterministic and natural way, it can also be derived under a Bayesian perspective as in [14]. Consider a first-order Markov random field prior on the absolute phase image, given by $p(\phi) = \frac{1}{Z}e^{-U(\phi)}$ where $U(\phi) = \sum_{ij\in\mathbb{Z}_1} V\left(\Delta\phi_{ij}^h\right)\overline{v}_{ij} + V\left(\Delta\phi_{ij}^v\right)\overline{h}_{ij}$, and Z is a normalizing constant. Assuming that the wrapped phase is noiseless, then $\phi = \psi + 2k\pi$. Therefore, the maximum a posteriori (MAP) estimate exactly amounts to minimize $E(\mathbf{k}|\boldsymbol{\psi})$ with respect to $\mathbf{k}$.

2.1   The Clique Potential V

Setting $V(\cdot) = |\cdot|^p$ in energy (6), the L^p norm energy expression above mentioned is recovered. The 2π-quantized version of this clique potential [23] has been extensively used in phase unwrapping and it is the so-called classical L^p norm. With $p = 2$, we have the least-squares type approach, which, as referred above, tends to oversmooth the inferred phase. To cope with oversmoothing and to preserve discontinuities, low values of p should be used. However, $p < 1$ leads to NP-hard algorithms [20], [24], [25]. L^1 has then been a compromise between discontinuity preserving and algorithm complexity. Flynn in [11] and Costantini in [12] presented exact L^1 norm PU algorithms.

In this paper we consider the family of clique potentials $V(\cdot)$ schematized in Fig. 2. Please note that the plots therein presented show $V(x)$ as a function of x. However, our potentials are not centred; in fact, as can be seen from expressions (6), (2), and (3) V depends on $\Delta\psi$: this means that the clique potential as function of the labels k_{ij} is off-centred. Curves plotted in Fig. 2 are quadratic in an origin neighbourhood, and given by $|\cdot|^p$ outside of it. This shape, which has been used in edge preserving image restoration, accounts for Gaussian noise and simultaneously preserves discontinuities [27]. In spite of considering a particular shape for the clique potential V, the concepts and algorithms next developed do not depend on the particular shape of V.

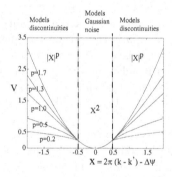

Fig. 2. Five instances of clique potentials V. These functions contain distinct branches in order to attempt both discontinuity preserving and noise smoothing. Note that cliques are off-centred as function of labels k.

3   Minimizing E by a Sequence of Binary Optimizations

In Subsections 3.1 and 3.2 we derive an exact algorithm assuming that the clique potential V is convex. With a nonconvex V, as referred, the computational problem turns out to be extremely difficult, namely, NP-hard; since we are especially interested in this nonconvex case, we propose an approximate algorithm in Subsection 3.3. As will be illustrated, this gives very good results in practice.

3.1   An Existence Lemma for Energy Minimization

The following lemma, an extension of Lemma 1 in [14], assures that if the minimum of $E(\mathbf{k}|\boldsymbol{\psi})$ [$E(\mathbf{k}|\boldsymbol{\psi})$ given by (6)] is not yet reached and if V is convex, then there exists a binary image $\delta\mathbf{k}$ (i.e., the elements of $\delta\mathbf{k}$ are all 0 or 1) such that $E(\mathbf{k} + \delta\mathbf{k}|\boldsymbol{\psi}) < E(\mathbf{k}|\boldsymbol{\psi})$.

Lemma 1. *Let* $\mathbf{k}_1$ *and* $\mathbf{k}_2$ *be two wrap-count images such that*

$$E(\mathbf{k_2}|\boldsymbol{\psi}) < E(\mathbf{k_1}|\boldsymbol{\psi}). \tag{7}$$

Then, if V *is convex, there exists a binary image* $\delta\mathbf{k}$ *such that*

$$E(\mathbf{k_1} + \delta\mathbf{k}|\boldsymbol{\psi}) < E(\mathbf{k_1}|\boldsymbol{\psi}). \tag{8}$$

Proof. The proof follows the same lines as the proof of Lemma 1 in [14], replacing quadratic potentials by convex ones.   □

According to Lemma 1, we can iteratively compute $\mathbf{k}^{t+1} = \mathbf{k}^t + \delta\mathbf{k}$, where $\delta\mathbf{k} \in \{0,1\}^{MN}$ minimizes $E(\mathbf{k}^t + \delta\mathbf{k}|\boldsymbol{\psi})$, until the the minimum energy is reached.

3.2   Mapping Binary Optimizations Onto Graph Min-Cuts

Let $k_{ij}^{t+1} = k_{ij}^t + \delta k_{ij}^t$ be the wrap-count at time $t+1$ and pixel (i,j). Introducing k_{ij}^{t+1} into (2) and (3), we obtain, respectively,

$$\Delta\phi_{ij}^h = \left[2\pi(k_{ij}^{t+1} - k_{ij-1}^{t+1}) - \Delta\psi_{ij}^h\right] \tag{9}$$

$$\Delta\phi_{ij}^v = \left[2\pi(k_{ij}^{t+1} - k_{i-1j}^{t+1}) - \Delta\psi_{ij}^v\right]. \tag{10}$$

After some simple manipulation, we get

$$\Delta\phi_{ij}^h = \left[2\pi(\delta k_{ij}^t - \delta k_{ij-1}^t) + a^h\right] \tag{11}$$

$$\Delta\phi_{ij}^v = \left[2\pi(\delta k_{ij}^t - \delta k_{i-1j}^t) + a^v\right], \tag{12}$$

where

$$a^h = 2\pi(k_{ij}^t - k_{ij-1}^t) - \Delta\psi_{ij}^t \tag{13}$$

$$a^v = 2\pi(k_{ij}^t - k_{i-1j}^t) - \Delta\psi_{ij}^t. \tag{14}$$

Now introducing (11) and (12) into (6), we can rewrite energy $E(\mathbf{k}|\boldsymbol{\psi})$ as a function of binary variables $\delta k_{ij}^t \in \{0,1\}$, i.e.,

$$E(\mathbf{k}|\psi) = \sum_{ij\in\mathbb{Z}_1} \underbrace{V\left(2\pi(\delta k_{ij}^t - \delta k_{ij-1}^t) + a^h\right)\overline{v}_{ij}}_{E_h^{ij}(x_{ij-1},x_{ij})} + \underbrace{V\left(2\pi(\delta k_{ij}^t - \delta k_{i-1j}^t) + a^v\right)\overline{h}_{ij}}_{E_v^{ij}(x_{i-1j},x_{ij})}, \tag{15}$$

where $x_{ij} = \delta k_{ij}^t$.

The minimization of energy (15) will be now mapped into a max-flow/min-cut calculation. Since the seminal work [33] of Greig et al., a considerable amount of research effort has been devoted to energy minimization via graph methods (see, e.g., [24], [25], [26], [34], [35], [36]). Namely, the mapping of a minimization problem into a sequence of binary minimizations, computed by graph cut techniques, has been addressed in works [25] and [26]. Nevertheless, these two works assume the potentials to be either a metric or a semi-metric, which is not the case for the clique potentials that we are considering: from (15) it can be seen that $V(x, y) \neq V(y, x)$ as a consequence of the presence of a^h and a^v terms[2]. For this reason, we adopt the method proposed in [24], which generalizes the class of binary minimizations that can be solved by graph cuts. Furthermore, the graph structures therein proposed are simpler.

We now establish a one-to-one mapping between energy function (15) and cuts on a certain graph $\mathcal{G} = (\mathcal{V}, \mathcal{E})$, having n vertices and two terminals, source and sink. This mapping relies, basically, on the observation that any graph-cut leaves every vertex either on the source side or the sink side, and so this corresponds to an assignment of a binary variable to each vertex.

For simplicity, let us denote for a moment terms E_h^{ij} and E_v^{ij} by $E^{ij}(x_k, x_l)$. We have, thus,

$$
\begin{aligned}
E^{ij}(0,0) &= V(a)\,\overline{d}_{ij}, \\
E^{ij}(1,1) &= V(a)\,\overline{d}_{ij}, \\
E^{ij}(0,1) &= V(2\pi + a)\,\overline{d}_{ij}, \\
E^{ij}(1,0) &= V(-2\pi + a)\,\overline{d}_{ij},
\end{aligned}
$$

where a represents a_h or a_v and $\overline{d}_{ij}$ represents $\overline{h}_{ij}$ or $\overline{v}_{ij}$. So we have

$$E^{ij}(0,0) + E^{ij}(1,1) = 2V(a)\overline{d}_{ij} \tag{16}$$

and

$$E^{ij}(0,1) + E^{ij}(1,0) = [V(2\pi + a) + V(-2\pi + a)]\,\overline{d}_{ij}. \tag{17}$$

It follows then that

$$2V(a)\overline{d}_{ij} \leq [V(2\pi + a) + V(-2\pi + a)]\,\overline{d}_{ij}.$$

In fact, since V is convex:

$$V(a)\overline{d}_{ij} \leq [(1 - t)V(-2\pi + a) + tV(2\pi + a)]\,\overline{d}_{ij}, t \in [0, 1]$$

and setting $t = 1/2$ we have,

$$
\begin{aligned}
V(a)\overline{d}_{ij} &\leq [1/2V(-2\pi + a) + 1/2V(2\pi + a)]\,\overline{d}_{ij} \Longleftrightarrow \\
2V(a)\overline{d}_{ij} &\leq [V(-2\pi + a) + V(2\pi + a)]\,\overline{d}_{ij},
\end{aligned} \tag{18}
$$

which, from expressions (16) and (17), can be stated as

$$E^{ij}(0,0) + E^{ij}(1,1) \leq E^{ij}(0,1) + E^{ij}(1,0). \tag{19}$$

---

[2] By definition either a metric or a semi-metric must satisfy the symmetry property.

Using results presented in [24][3], expression (19) assures, by definition, that our binary energy (15) is so-called *regular* and accordingly *graph representable*. This means that there exists a one-to-one mapping between configurations $(x_1, \ldots, x_n)$ [the arguments of energy (15)] and cuts on a certain graph. This mapping is such that the cost of the cuts equals the energy value at the corresponding configuration[4]. Therefore, minimizing the energy corresponds to computing a max-flow/min-cut on the appropriate graph.

Work [24] also details how to construct the graph. First, build vertices and edges corresponding to each pair of neighbouring pixels, and then join these graphs together based on the additivity theorem also given in [24]. So, for each energy term E_h^{ij} and E_v^{ij} (see expression 15), we construct an "elementary" graph with four vertices $\{s, t, v, v'\}$, where $\{s, t\}$ represents source and sink, common to all terms, and $\{v, v'\}$ represents the two pixels involved (v being the left (up) pixel and v' the right (down) pixel). Following very closely [24], we define a directed edge (v, v') with the weight $E(0, 1) + E(1, 0) - E(0, 0) - E(1, 1)$. Moreover, if $E(1, 0) - E(0, 0) > 0$ we define an edge (s, v) with the weight $E(1, 0) - E(0, 0)$ or, otherwise, we define an edge (v, t) with the weight $E(0, 0) - E(1, 0)$. In a similar way for vertex v', if $E(1, 1) - E(1, 0) > 0$ we define an edge (s, v') with weight $E(1, 1) - E(1, 0) > 0$ or, otherwise, we define an edge (v', t) with the weight $E(1, 0) - E(1, 1)$. Figure 3(a) shows an example where $E(1, 0) - E(0, 0) > 0$ and $E(1, 0) - E(1, 1) > 0$. Figure 3(b) illustrates the complete graph obtained at the end.

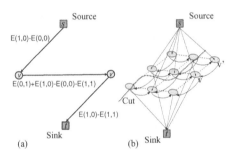

Fig. 3. (a) Elementary graph for a single energy term, where s and t represent source and sink respectively, and v and v' represent the two pixels involved in the energy term. In this case $E(1, 0) - E(0, 0) > 0$ and $E(1, 0) - E(1, 1) > 0$. (b) The graph obtained at the end results from adding elementary graphs.

As we have shown above, building on results from [14] and from [24], we can iteratively find the energy minimum through binary optimizations, based on max-flow/min-cut calculation on a certain graph[5].

---

[3] There are also interesting developments in [37].

[4] Up to an additive constant.

[5] For a proof that the number of iteration steps is finite see [23].

Algorithm 1. (PUMF) Graph cuts based phase unwrapping algorithm

Initialization: $\mathbf{k} \equiv \mathbf{k}' \equiv \mathbf{0}$, possible_improvement $\equiv 1$
1: **while** possible_improvement **do**
2:     Compute $E(0,0), E(1,1), E(0,1)$, and $E(1,0)$ {for every horizontal and vertical pixel pairs}.
3:     Construct elementary graphs and merge them to obtain the main graph.
4:     Compute the min-cut (S,T) {S- source set; T-sink set}.
5:     **for all** pixel (i,j) **do**
6:         **if** pixel $(i,j) \in S$ **then**
7:             $k'_{i,j} = k_{i,j} + 1$
8:         **else**
9:             $k'_{i,j} = k_{i,j}$ {remains unchanged}
10:        **end if**
11:    **end for**
12:    **if** $E(\mathbf{k}'|\psi) < E(\mathbf{k}|\psi)$ **then**
13:        $\mathbf{k} = \mathbf{k}'$
14:    **else**
15:        possible_ improvement $= 0$
16:    **end if**
17: **end while**

Algorithm 1 shows the pseudo-code for the Phase Unwrapping Max-Flow (PUMF) algorithm.

In the convex scenario we have proposed an exact minimizer for our class of energies. At this point we should mention work [36]. There, the author proposes a minimizer for convex energies, by computing a single cut on a certain graph. Nevertheless, for a general convex potential that graph can be huge, imposing in practice heavy computational demands.

3.3   Approximate Algorithm for a Non-convex V

When V is non-convex the previous exact algorithm is not valid and the reason is twofold. First, Lemma 1 only works for a convex V. Let us use the terminology of [25] and call a $1-$jump move the operation of adding a binary image $\delta\mathbf{k}$; so, if V is non-convex it is not possible, in general, to reach the minimum through 1-jump moves only. Second, with a non-convex V energy (6) is not regular, i.e., (19) does not hold with generality for every horizontal or vertical pairwise interactions (see [23]). This means that we *cannot* make the energy graph-representation used in the binary optimization that was employed on each algorithm iteration.

Our approximate algorithm arises as a minor modification of PUMF to handle those two issues. Regarding the latter, as the problem relies on the non-regularity of some energy terms $E^{ij}(x_i, x_j)$, i.e., they do not verify (19), our procedure consists of approximating them by regular ones. We do that by leaning on majorize minimize MM [32]. The basic idea is the following: consider the regular energy

$$E'^{ij}(x_i, x_j) \equiv \begin{cases} E'^{ij}(x_i, x_j) \geq E^{ij}(x_i, x_j), \text{ if } (x_i, x_j) \neq (0,0) \\ E'^{ij}(0,0) = E^{ij}(0,0) \end{cases} \qquad (20)$$

Algorithm 2. Approximate PUMF

Initialization: $\mathbf{k} \equiv \mathbf{k}' \equiv 0$
1: **for all** i in $[1, 2..., m, 1, 2, ..., m]$ (m is the maximum jump size) **do**
2:     possible_improvement $\equiv 1$
3:     **while** possible_improvement **do**
4:         Compute $E(0,0), E(1,1), E(0,1),$ and $E(1,0)$ {for every horizontal and vertical pixel pairs}.
5:         Find any non-regular pixel pairs $[E(0,1) + E(1,0) - E(0,0) - E(1,1) < 0]$. If there is any set it to zero.
6:         Construct elementary graphs and merge them to obtain the main graph.
7:         Compute the min-cut (S, T) {S- source set; T-sink set}.
8:         **for all** pixel (i, j) **do**
9:             **if** pixel $(i, j) \in S$ **then**
10:                 $\mathbf{k}'_{i,j} = \mathbf{k}_{i,j} + i$
11:             **else**
12:                 $\mathbf{k}'_{i,j} = \mathbf{k}_{i,j}$ {remains unchanged}
13:             **end if**
14:         **end for**
15:         **if** $E(\mathbf{k}'|\psi) < E(\mathbf{k}|\psi)$ **then**
16:             $\mathbf{k} = \mathbf{k}'$
17:         **else**
18:             possible_ improvement $= 0$
19:         **end if**
20:     **end while**
21: **end for**

---

then, necessarily,

$$E^{ij}(x_i^\star, x_j^\star) \leq E^{ij}(0,0), \tag{21}$$

where $(x_i^\star, x_j^\star)$ minimizes $E'^{ij}(x_i, x_j)$.

So, by replacing the nonregular energy terms $E^{ij}(x_i, x_j)$ with regular ones $E'^{ij}(x_i, x_j)$, we have the guarantee of energy decreasing and so approximate the minimum, on each binary optimization[6]. A possible solution to obtain the replacement terms can be, for instance, to increase term $E^{ij}(0,1)$ until $[E^{ij}(0,1) + E^{ij}(1,0) - E^{ij}(0,0) - E^{ij}(1,1)]$ equals zero; we choose this solution in the results presented in the next section, yet others are possible [23].

With respect to the first referred reason for non validity of PUMF, our strategy is extending the range of allowed moves. Instead of only 1-jumps we now use sequences of i-jumps, which correspond to add an $(i\delta)\mathbf{k}$ image (pixels can have the 0 or i values).

The above presented approximate algorithm has proved outperforming results in all the experiments we have put it through; in the next section we illustrate some of those experiments. Algorithm 3.3 shows the pseudo-code of the modified PUMF algorithm.

A final word about i-jumps is worthy. This kind of moves is used in work [25] (from which we take the terminology) to solve minimization problems through

---

[6] Work [38] that uses graph cuts based optimization, also approximates non regular cliques employing a theorem that is equivalent to the proposed majorize minimize (MM) procedure. We thank Vladimir Kolmogorov for pointing out that work.

a sequence of binary problems, namely via α-expansions for which the author derives a bound on the energy under the nonconvex scenario. We should stress again that, nevertheless, we cannot use that kind of algorithms, as our clique potentials are not symmetric (thus, not a metric nor a semi-metric).

4   Experimental Results

The results presented in this section were obtained with MATLAB coding (max-flow algorithm is implemented in C++[7]). We first present images illustrating the

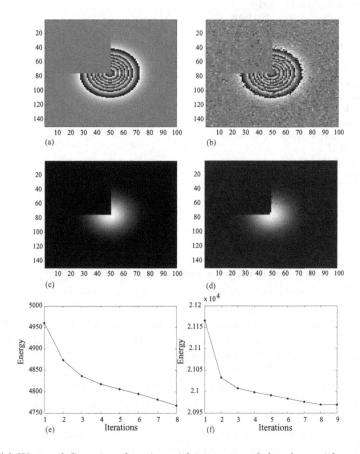

Fig. 4. (a) Wrapped Gaussian elevation with a quarter of the plane with zero height. The associated noise standard deviation is $0°$. (b) Wrapped Gaussian elevation with a quarter of the plane with zero height. The associated noise standard deviation is $41.2°$. (c) Image in (a) unwrapped by PUMF. (d) Image in (b) unwrapped by PUMF. (e) Energy decreasing for the unwrapping of image in (a). (f) Energy decreasing for the unwrapping of image in (b). Notice that no discontinuities are supplied to the algorithm.

---

[7] Code made available in http://www.cs.cornell.edu/People/vnk/software.html by V. Kolmogorov. See [39] for more details.

performance of PUMF on three representative phase unwrapping problems; then we compare the performances of PUMF and state-of-the-art PU algorithms. We have employed nonconvex potentials in all the presented experiments (please see Section 2.1).

Figures 4(a) and 4(b) display two phase images (100×150 pixels) to be unwrapped; they are synthesized from an original absolute phase surface formed by a Gaussian elevation with a height of 14π rad, and standard deviations $\sigma_i = 15$ and $\sigma_i = 10$ pixels; additionally in a quarter of the plane the Gaussian has zero height, introducing surface discontinuities, and therefore rendering a quite difficult unwrapping problem. We stress that we did not supply discontinuities as an input to the algorithm. The wrapped images are generated according to an InSAR observation statistics (see, e.g., [14]), producing an interferometric pair, with correlation coefficient 1.0 and 0.95, respectively. This corresponds to an interferometric noise standard deviation of $0°$ and $41.2°$, respectively. The wrapped phase images are obtained (for each pair), by computing the product of one image by the complex conjugate of the other, and finally taking the argument. The noise standard deviation of $41.2°$ is high enough to induce a large number of phase jumps (*residues*), making the unwrapping an even harder task. Figures 4(c) and 4(d) show the corresponding unwrapped surfaces by PUMF (V as in Fig. 2, with $p = 0.2$), taking 8 and 9 iterations respectively and around 4 seconds in a 2GHz PC. We can see that, even with low-correlation induced discontinuities, PUMF successfully accomplishes a meaningful unwrapping. Figures 4(e) and 4(f) show the energy evolution with the algorithm iterations. It is noticeable a great energy decreasing in the first few iterations.

Figure 5(a) shows a phase image analogous to Fig. 4(a) but now the original phase corresponds to a (simulated) InSAR acquisition for a real steep-relief mountainous area[8] inducing, therefore, many discontinuities and posing a very tough PU problem. Figure 5(d) shows a quality map computed from the InSAR coherence estimate (see [5, Chap.3] for further details). However, to illustrate the discontinuity preserving ability of the PUMF method with nonconvex potentials, we have reduced the number of supplied discontinuities in the algorithm to a minimum set[9]. This map is shown in Fig. 5(c). The resulting phase unwrapped (it was used V as in Fig. 2, with $p = 0.2$) is "3-D" rendered in Fig. 5(b), corresponding to an error norm (variance) of 1.9 square radians. Figure 5(e) illustrates the energy evolution with the algorithm iterations.

Figure 6(a) shows another phase image to be unwrapped, which was synthesized from an original surface consisting of two "intertwined" spirals built on two sheared planes. It should be noticed that the original phase surface has many discontinuities, which make this an extremely difficult unwrapping problem if no information is supplied about discontinuities locations. PUMF is able to blindly unwrap (perfectly) this image as is shown in Fig. 6(b) (V as in Fig. 2, with $p = 0.01$). Figure 6(c) shows a "3-D" rendering of the unwrapped surface

---

[8] Long's Peak, Colorado,USA. Data distributed with book [5].
[9] Experimentally evidence shows that below that minimum results are catastrophic.

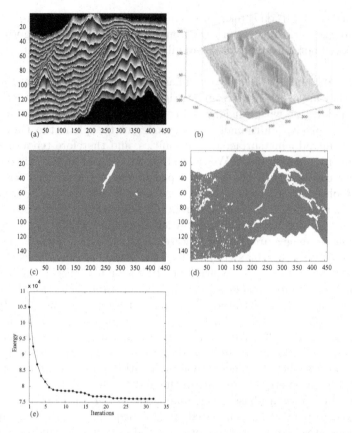

Fig. 5. (a) Wrapped phase image obtained from a simulated InSAR acquisition from Long's Peak, Colorado, USA (Data distributed with [5]). (b) Image in (a) unwrapped by PUMF (32 iterations). (c) Discontinuity information given as input to the unwrapping process. White pixels signal discontinuity locations. (d) The total discontinuity information at disposal. White pixels signal discontinuity zones. (e) Energy decreasing for the unwrapping of image in (a).

and Fig. 6(d) shows the decreasing of the energy, along 39 iterations, in the unwrapping process.

Next, in table 1, we summarize the performance of PUMF and some reference and state-of-the-art PU algorithms, applied to the above illustrated problems, with the exception of last one; in fact all the algorithms, but PUMF, have a very poor performance in unwrapping the spiral. The performance is measured by the variance of the absolute error between original and unwrapped phase images. The comparing algorithms are:

- **Path following type:** Goldstein's branch cut (GBC) [7]; quality guided (QG) [40]; and mask cut (MC) [41].
- **Minimum norm type:** Flynn's minimum discontinuity (FMD) [11]; weighted least-squares (WLS) [19]; and L^0 norm (L0N) (see [5, ch. 5.5]).

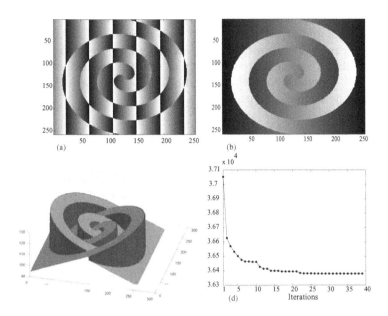

Fig. 6. (a) Wrapped phase image corresponding to an original phase surface of two intertwined spirals in two sheared planes (Data distributed with [5]). (b) Image in (a) blindly unwrapped by PUMF (39 iterations). (c) A "3-D" rendering of the unwrapped image. (d) Energy decreasing for the unwrapping of image in (a). Notice that no discontinuities are supplied to the algorithm.

Table 1. Comparative performance of PUMF and reference PU algorithms

| Algorithm | Error (squared radians) | | |
	Gauss. (corr=1)	Gauss. (corr=0.95)	Peaks
PUMF	0	0.8	1.9
WLS	35.9	17.3	1270.7
L0N	29.7	3.5	1275.5
MC	4.7	17.7	851.8
FMD	1.5	4.7	991.1
QG	0.1	8.5	85.3
GBC	1.2	3.6	73.9

5   Concluding Remarks

We developed a new graph cuts based phase unwrapping algorithm, in the vein of the minimum L^p norm class of PU algorithms. An iterative binary optimization scheme was adopted from $\mathbb{Z}\pi M$ algorithm [14], and the results on energy minimization from [24] were applied to perform the optimization, casting it on a series of graph max-flow/min-cut computations. In particular, we solved exactly the PU L^p minimum norm problem for $p \geq 1$. Instead of the strict L^p norm, PUMF concepts and algorithm are valid for a general real valued potential V; PUMF is an exact minimizer if V is convex and an approximate one otherwise. More particularly, we considered a family of non-convex discontinuity preserving potentials, for which, in a set of experiments, the proposed PUMF algorithm outperforms the state-of-the-art methods.

Acknowledgments

The authors acknowledge Vladimir Kolmogorov both for the max-flow/min-cut C++ code made available on the web, and for pointing out his work on approximating non-regular functions.

References

1. A. V. Oppenheim and J. S. Lim. The importance of phase in signals. *Proceedings of the IEEE*, 69(5):529–541, May 1981.
2. P. Rosen, S. Hensley, I. Joughin, F. LI, S. Madsen, E. Rodriguez, and R. Goldstein. Synthetic aperture radar interferometry. *Proceedings of the IEEE*, 88(3):333–382, March 2000.
3. P. Jezzard and R. Balaban. Correction for geometric distortion in echo-planar images from B_0 field variations. *Magnetic Resonance in Medicine*, 34:65–73, 1995.
4. S. Pandit, N. Jordache, and G. Joshi. Data-dependent systems methodology for noise-insensitive phase unwrapping in laser interferometric surface characterization. *Journal of the Optical Society of America*, 11(10):2584–2592, 1994.
5. D. Ghiglia and M. Pritt. *Two-Dimensional Phase Unwrapping. Theory, Algorithms, and Software*. John Wiley & Sons, New York, 1998.
6. K. Itoh. Analysis of the phase unwrapping problem. *Applied Optics*, 21(14), 1982.
7. R. Goldstein, H. Zebker, and C. Werner. Satellite radar interferometry: Two-dimensional phase unwrapping. In *Symposium on the Ionospheric Effects on Communication and Related Systems*, volume 23, pages 713–720. Radio Science, 1988.
8. J. Marroquin and M. Rivera. Quadratic regularization functionals for phase unwrapping. *Journal of the Optical Society of America*, 12(11):2393–2400, 1995.
9. J. Buckland, J. Huntley, and S. Turner. Unwrapping noisy phase maps by use of a minimum cost matching algorithm. *Applied Optics*, 34(23):5100–5108, 1995.
10. D. Ghiglia and L. Romero. Minimum L^p norm two-dimensional phase unwrapping. *Journal of the Optical Society of America*, 13(10):1999–2013, 1996.
11. T. Flynn. Two-dimensional phase unwrapping with minimum weighted discontinuity. *Journal of the Optical Society of America A*, 14(10):2692–2701, 1997.
12. M. Costantini. A novel phase unwrapping method based on network programing. *IEEE Transactions on Geoscience and Remote Sensing*, 36(3):813–821, May 1998.
13. J. Strand. *Two-dimensional Phase Unwrapping with Applications*. PhD thesis, Department of Mathematics, Faculty of Mathematics and Natural Sciences, University of Bergen, 1999.
14. J. Dias and J. Leitão. The $\mathbb{Z}\pi$M algorithm for interferometric image reconstruction in SAR/SAS. *IEEE Transactions on Image Processing*, 11:408–422, April 2002.

15. J. Marroquin, M. Tapia, R. Rodriguez-Vera, and M. Servin. Parallel algorithms for phase unwrapping based on markov random field models. *Journal of the Optical Society of America A*, 12(12):2578–2585, 1995.
16. G. Nico, G. Palubinskas, and M. Datcu. Bayesian approach to phase unwrapping: theoretical study. *IEEE Transactions on Signal Processing*, 48(9):2545–2556, Sept. 2000.
17. B. Friedlander and J. Francos. Model based phase unwrapping of 2-d signals. *IEEE Transactions on Signal Processing*, 44(12):2999–3007, 1996.
18. D. Fried. Least-squares fitting a wave-front distortion estimate to an array of phase-difference measurements. *Journal of the Optical Society of America*, 67(3):370–375, 1977.
19. D. Ghiglia and L. Romero. Robust two-dimensional weighted and unweighted phase unwrapping that uses fast transforms and iterative methods. *Journal of the Optical Society of America A*, 11:107–117, 1994.
20. C. Chen. *Statistical-Cost Network-Flow Approaches to Two-Dimensional Phase Unwrapping for Radar Interferometry*. PhD thesis, Stanford University, 2001.
21. J. Leitão and M. Figueiredo. Absolute phase image reconstruction: A stochastic non-linear filtering approach. *IEEE Transactions on Image Processing*, 7(6):868–882, June 1997.
22. J. Dias and J. Leitão. Simultaneous phase unwrapping and speckle smoothing in SAR images: A stochastic nonlinear filtering approach. In *EUSAR'98 European Conference on Synthetic Aperture Radar*, pages 373–377, Friedrichshafen, May 1998.
23. J. Bioucas-Dias and G. Valadão. Phase unwrapping via graph cuts. Submitted to IEEE Transactions on Image Processing, 2005.
24. V. Kolmogorov and R. Zabih. What energy functions can be minimized via graph cuts? *IEEE Transactions on Pattern Analysis and Machine Intelligence*, 26(2):147–159, February 2004.
25. O. Veksler. *Efficient Graph-Based Energy Minimization Methods In Computer Vision*. PhD thesis, Cornell University, 1999.
26. Y. Boykov, O. Veksler, and R. Zabih. Fast approximate energy minimization via graph cuts. *IEEE Transactions on Pattern Analysis and Machine Intelligence*, 23(11):1222–1239, 2001.
27. A. Blake and A. Zisserman. *Visual Reconstruction*. MIT Press, Cambridge, M.A., 1987.
28. A. Blake. Comparison of the efficiency of deterministic and stochastic algorithms for visual reconstruction. *IEEE Transactions on Pattern Analysis and Machine Intelligence*, 11(1):2–12, January 1989.
29. T. Hebert and R. Leahy. A generalized EM algorithm for 3-D Bayesian reconstruction from Poisson data using Gibbs priors. *IEEE Trans. on Medical Imaging*, 8(2):194–202, June 1989.
30. S. Geman and G. Reynolds. Constrained restoration and the recovery of discontinuities. *IEEE Trans. Pattern Analysis and Machine Intelligence*, 14(3):367–383, March 1992.
31. C. Bouman and K. Sauer. A generalized Gaussian image model for edge-preserving MAP estimation. *IEEE Transactions on Image Processing*, 2(3):296–310, July 1993.
32. K. Lange. *Optimization*. Springer Verlag, New York, 2004.
33. D. Greig, B. Porteous, and A. Seheult. Exact maximum a posteriory estimation for binary images. *Jounal of Royal Statistics Society B*, 51(2):271–279, 1989.

34. P. Ferrari, M. Gubitoso, and E. Neves. Reconstruction of gray-scale images. *Methodology and Computing in Applied Probability*, 3:255–270, 2001.
35. Z. Wu and R. Leahy. An optimal graph theoretic approach to data clustering: Theory and its application to image segmentation. *IEEE Transactions on Pattern Analysis and Machine Intelligence*, 15(11):1101–1113, November 1993.
36. H. Ishikawa. Exact optimization for markov random fields with convex priors. *IEEE Transactions on Pattern Analysis and Machine Intelligence*, 25(10):1333–1336, October 2003.
37. D. Freedman and P. Drineas. Energy minimization via graph cuts: settling what is possible. In *Proceedings of the IEEE Computer Society Conference on Computer Vision and Pattern Recognition - CVPR'05*, San Diego, CA, June 2005.
38. C. Rother, S. Kumar, V. Kolmogorov, and A. Blake. Digital tapestry. In *Proceedings of the IEEE Computer Society Conference on Computer Vision and Pattern Recognition - CVPR'05*, San Diego, CA, June 2005.
39. Y. Boykov and V. Kolmogorov. An experimental comparison of min-cut/max-flow algorithms for energy minimization in vision. *IEEE Transactions on Pattern Analysis and Machine Intelligence*, 26(9):1124–1137, 2004.
40. H. Lim, W. Xu, and X. Huang. Two new practical methods for phase unwrapping. In *Proccedings of the 1995 International Geoscience and Remote Sensing Symposium-IGARSS'95*, pages 196–198, Firenze, Italy, 1995.
41. T. Flynn. Consistent 2-D phase unwrapping guided by a quality map. In *Proceedings of the 1996 International Geoscience and Remote Sensing Symposium-IGARSS'96*, volume 4, pages 2057–2059, Lincoln, NE, 1996.

Retrieving Articulated 3-D Models Using Medial Surfaces and Their Graph Spectra

Juan Zhang[1], Kaleem Siddiqi[1], Diego Macrini[2],
Ali Shokoufandeh[3], and Sven Dickinson[2]

[1] McGill University, School of Computer Science & Centre for Intelligent Machines
[2] University of Toronto, Department of Computer Science
[3] Drexel University, Department of Computer Science

Abstract. We consider the use of medial surfaces to represent symmetries of 3-D objects. This allows for a qualitative abstraction based on a directed acyclic graph of components and also a degree of invariance to a variety of transformations including the articulation and deformation of parts. We demonstrate the use of this representation for both indexing and matching 3-D object models. Our formulation uses the geometric information associated with each node along with an eigenvalue labeling of the adjacency matrix of the subgraph rooted at that node. We present comparative results against the techniques of shape distributions [17] and harmonic spheres [12] on a database of 320 models representing 13 object classes. The results demonstrate that medial surface based graph matching significantly outperforms these techniques for objects with articulating parts.

Keywords: 3-D model matching, indexing, medial surfaces, graph spectra.

1 Introduction

With an explosive growth in the number of 3-D object models stored in web repositories and other databases, the graphics community has begun to address the important and challenging problem of 3-D object retrieval and matching, a problem which traditionally falls in the domain of computer vision research. Recent advances include query-based search engines which employ promising measures including spherical harmonic descriptors [12] and shape distributions [17]. Such systems can yield impressive results on databases including hundreds of 3-D models, in a matter of a few seconds.

Thus far the emphasis in the computer graphics community has broadly been on the use of qualitative measures of shape that are typically global. Such measures are robust in the sense that they can deal with noisy and imperfect models, and at the same time are simple enough so that efficient algorithmic implementations can be sought. However, an inevitable cost is that such measures are inherently coarse, and are sensitive to deformations of objects or their parts. As a motivating example, consider the 3-D models in Fig. 1. These four exemplars of an object class were created by articulations of parts and changes of pose. For such examples, the very notion of a center of mass or a rigid reference point[1], which is crucial for the computation of descriptions such as shape histograms (sectors or shells) [3] or spherical extent functions [30], can be nonintuitive and arbitrary. In fact, the centroid of such models may actually lie in the background.

A. Rangarajan et al. (Eds.): EMMCVPR 2005, LNCS 3757, pp. 285–300, 2005.

Fig. 1. Exemplars of the object class "human" created by changes in pose and articulations of parts (top row). The medial surface (or 3-D skeleton) of each is computed using the algorithm of [27] (bottom row). The medial surface is automatically partitioned into distinct parts, each shown in a different color.

To complicate matters, it is unclear how to obtain a global alignment of such models. As well, measures based on reflective symmetries [11], and signatures based on 3-D moments [7] or chord histograms [17] are not invariant under such transformations.

The computer vision community has grappled with the problem of *generic* level object recognition by suggesting representations based on volumetric parts, including generalized cylinders, superquadrics and geons [5, 16, 19, 4]. Such approaches build a degree of robustness to deformations and movement of parts, but their representational power is limited by the vocabulary of geometric primitives that are selected. Motivated in part by such considerations there have been attempts to encode 3D shape information using probabilistic descriptors. These allow intrinsic geometric information to be captured by low dimensional signatures. An elegant example of this is the geodesic shape distribution of [9] where information theoretic measures are used to compare probability distributions representing 3D object surfaces. In the domain of graph theory there have also been attempts to address the problem of 3D shape matching using representations based on Reeb graphs [24, 10]. These allow for topological properties to be captured, at least in a coarse sense.

An alternative approach is to use 3-D medial loci (3-D skeletons), obtained by considering the locus of centers of maximal inscribed spheres along with their radii [6]. As pointed out by Blum, this offers the advantage that a graph of parts can be inferred from the underlying local mirror symmetries of the object. To motivate this idea, consider once again the human forms of Fig. 1. A medial surface-based representation (bottom row) provides a natural decomposition, which is largely invariant to the articulation and bending of parts.

In this article, we build on a recent technique to compute medial surfaces [27] by proposing an interpretation of its output as a directed acyclic graph (DAG) of parts. We then use refinements of algorithms based on graph spectra [26] to tackle the problems of indexing and matching 3-D object models. These and related algorithms have already shown promise in the computer vision community for generic level view-based object indexing and matching using 2-D skeletal graphs [28, 25, 18, 22]. They have also been demonstrated in the context of matching 3-D object models with tubular parts, using a centerline approximation of the 3-D skeleton [29]. We demonstrate their significant potential for medial surface-based 3-D object retrieval with experimental results on a database of 320 models representing 13 object classes, including exemplars of both rigid objects and ones with significant articulation of parts. Comparative results using the information retrieval notion of *precision versus recall* demonstrate that this method significantly outperforms the popular techniques of shape distributions [17] and harmonic spheres [12] for objects with articulating parts. To our knowledge these are the first comprehensive empirical results on the use of medial surfaces and their graph spectra in the context of 3-D object model retrieval and indexing.

2 Medial Surfaces and DAGs

Recent approaches for computing 3-D skeletons include the *power crust* algorithm [2], the *shock scaffold* [13] and *average outward flux-based* skeletons [27]. The first two methods have the advantage that they can be employed on input data in the form of points sampled from an object's surface, and theoretical guarantees on the quality of the results can be provided. Unfortunately, automatic segmentation of the resulting skeletons remains a challenge. The last method assumes that objects have first been voxelized, and this adds a computational burden. However, once this is done the limiting behavior of the average outward flux of the Euclidean distance function gradient vector field can be used to characterize 3-D skeletal points. We choose to employ this latter method since it has the advantage that the digital classification of [15] allows for the taxonomy of generic 3-D skeletal points [8] to be interpreted on a rectangular lattice, leading to a graph of parts.

Under the assumption that the initial model is given in triangulated form, we begin by scaling all the vertices so that they fall within a rectangular lattice of fixed dimension and resolution. We then sub-divide each triangle to generate a dense intersection with this lattice, resulting in a binary (voxelized) 3-D model. The average outward flux of the Euclidean distance function's gradient vector field is computed through unit spheres centered at each rectangular lattice point, using Algorithm 1. This quantity has the property that it approaches a negative number at skeletal points and goes to zero elsewhere [27], and thus can be used to drive a digital thinning process, for which an efficient implementation is described in Algorithm 2. This thinning process has to be implemented with some care, so that the topology of the object is not changed. This is done by identifying each *simple* or removable point $\mathbf{x}$, for which a characterization based on the 26-neighborhood of each lattice point $\mathbf{x}$ is provided in [15]. With O being the set of points in the interior of the voxelized object and N_{26}^* being the 26-neighborhood of $\mathbf{x}$, not including $\mathbf{x}$ itself, this characterization is based on two numbers:

1. C^*: the number of 26-connected components 26-adjacent to $\mathbf{x}$ in $O \cap N_{26}^*$, and
2. $\bar{C}$: the number of 6-connected components 6-adjacent to $\mathbf{x}$ in $\bar{O} \cap N_{18}$.

It can be shown that a digital point $\mathbf{x}$ is *simple* if $C^*(\mathbf{x}) = 1$ and $\bar{C}(\mathbf{x}) = 1$.

The taxonomy of generic 3-D skeletal points in the continuum, i.e., those which are stable under small perturbations of the object, is provided in [8]. Using the notation

---

Algorithm 1: Average Outward Flux

Data   : Voxelized 3-D Object Model.

Result   : Average Outward Flux Map.

Compute the Euclidean distance transform D of the model ;

Compute the gradient vector field ∇D;

Compute the average outward flux of ∇D:

For (each point **x**) $AOF(\mathbf{x}) = \dfrac{1}{26} \sum_{i=1}^{26} < \hat{\mathbf{N}}_{\mathbf{i}}, \nabla D(\mathbf{x}_i) >$;

(where $\mathbf{x}_i$ is a 26-neighbor of **x** in 3-D and $\hat{\mathbf{N}}_{\mathbf{i}}$ is the outward normal at $\mathbf{x}_i$ of the unit sphere centered at **x**)

Algorithm 2: Topology Preserving Thinning

Data   : 3-D Object Model, Average Outward Flux Map.

Result   : 3-D Skeleton (Medial Surface).

for *(each point* **x** *on the boundary of the object)* **do**

    if *(***x** *is simple)* **then**

       insert(**x**, maxHeap) with $AOF(\mathbf{x})$ as the sorting key for insertion;

while *(maxHeap.size > 0)* **do**

    x = HeapExtractMax(maxHeap);

    if *(***x** *is simple)* **then**

       if *(***x** *is an end point) and (*$AOF(\mathbf{x}) < Thresh$*)* **then**

          mark **x** as a medial surface (end) point;

       else

          Remove **x**;

          for *(all neighbors* **y** *of* **x***)* **do**

             if *(***y** *is simple)* **then**

                insert(**y**, maxHeap) with $AOF(\mathbf{y})$ as the sorting key for insertion;

A_n^k, where n denotes the number of points of contact of the maximal inscribed sphere with the surface and k the order of these contacts, the taxonomy includes: 1) A_1^2 points which form a smooth medial manifold, 2) A_3 points which correspond to the rim of a medial manifold, 3) A_1^3 points which represent the intersection curve of three medial manifolds, 4) an A_1^4 point at the intersection of four A_1^3 curves, and 5) an $A_1 A_3$ point at the intersection between an A_3 curve and an A_1^3 curve.

It is clear from this classification that 3-D skeletons are essentially comprised of medial manifolds, their rims and intersection curves, and this is why we refer to this as a *medial surface* representation. As shown in [15], the numbers C^* and $\bar{C}$ can also be used to classify surface points, rim points, junction points and curve points on a rectangular lattice. These results are summarized in Table 1. This suggests the following 3-step approach for segmenting the (voxelized) medial surface into a set of connected parts:

Table 1. The topological classification of [15]

$\bar{C}$	C^*	TYPE
0	any	interior point
any	0	isolated point
1	1	border (simple) point
1	2	curve point
1	> 2	curves junction
2	1	surface point
2	> 2	surface-curve(s) junction
> 2	1	surfaces junction
> 2	≥ 2	surfaces-curves junction

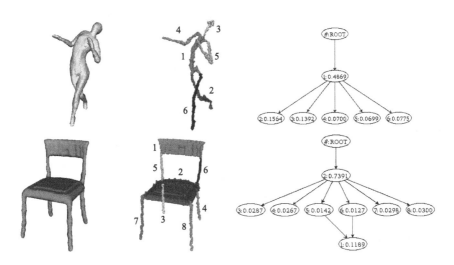

Fig. 2. A voxelized human form and chair (left) and their segmented medial surfaces (middle). A hierarchical interpretation of the medial surface, using a notion of part saliency, leads to a directed acyclic graph DAG (right). The nodes in the DAGs have labels corresponding to those on the medial surface, and the saliency of each node is also shown.

1. Identify all manifolds comprised of 26-connected surface points and border points.
2. Use junction points to separate these manifolds, but allow junction points to belong to all manifolds that they connect.
3. Form connected components with the remaining curve points, and consider these as parts as well.

This process of automatic skeletonization and segmentation is illustrated for two object classes, a chair and a human form, in Fig. 2.

We now propose an interpretation of the segmented medial surface as a directed acyclic graph (DAG), where we shall treat each component as a node. This will in turn allow the subsequent matcher and indexer to cope with both changes in part structure, as reflected by connectivity in the graph, as well as changes in part shape, as reflected by the geometric information associated with each node. We begin by introducing a notion of *saliency* which captures the relative importance of each component. Consider that the envelope of maximal inscribed spheres of appropriate radii placed at all skeletal points reconstructs the original object's volume [6]. The contribution of each component to the overall volume can thus be used as a measure of its significance. Since the spheres associated with adjacent components can overlap, an objective measure of component j's saliency is given by:

$$Saliency_j = \frac{\text{Voxels}_j}{\sum_{i=1}^{N} \text{Voxels}_i},$$

where N is the number of components and Voxels_i is the number of voxels *uniquely* reconstructed by component i. We propose the following construction of a DAG, using each component's saliency. Consider the most salient component as the root node (level 0), and place components to which it is connected as nodes at level 1. Components to which these nodes are connected are placed at level 2, and this process is repeated in a recursive fashion until all nodes are accounted for. The graph is completed by drawing edges between all pairs of connected nodes, in the direction of increasing levels, hence avoiding the occurrence of any cycles. However, to allow for 3-D models comprised of disconnected parts we introduce a single dummy node as the parent of all DAGs for a 3-D model.

This process is illustrated in Fig. 2 (right column) for the human and chair models, with the saliency values shown within the nodes. Note how this representation captures the intuitive sense that the human is a torso with attached limbs and a head, a chair is a seat with attached legs and a back, etc. Our DAG representation of the medial surface is quite different than the graph structure that follows from a direct use of the taxonomy of 3-D skeletal points in the continuum [8]. Our motivation is to be able to exploit the hierarchical structure indexing and matching algorithms reported in [28, 26].

3 Indexing

A linear search of the 3-D model database, i.e., comparing the query 3-D object model to each 3-D model and selecting the closest one, is inefficient for large databases. An indexing mechanism is therefore essential to select a small set of candidate models to which the matching procedure is applied. When working with hierarchical structures, in the form of DAGs, indexing is a challenging task, and can be formulated as the fast selection of a small set of candidate model graphs that share a subgraph with the query. But how do we test a given candidate without resorting to subgraph isomorphism and its intractability? The problem is further compounded by the fact that due to perturbation and noise, no significant isomorphisms may exist between the query and the (correct) model. Yet, at some level of abstraction, the two structures (or two of their substructures) may be quite similar. Thus, our indexing problem can be reformulated as finding model (sub)graphs whose structure is *similar* to the query (sub)graph.

Choosing the appropriate level of abstraction with which to characterize a DAG is a challenging problem. We seek a description that, on the one hand, provides the low dimensionality essential for efficient indexing, while on the other hand, is rich enough to prune the database down to a tractable number of candidates. In recent work [26], we draw on the eigen-space of a graph to characterize the topology of a DAG with a low-dimensional vector that will facilitate an efficient nearest-neighbor search in a database.

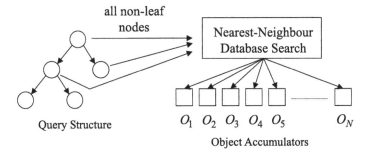

Fig. 3. Indexing Mechanism. Each non-trivial node (whose TSV encodes a topological abstraction of the subgraph rooted at the node) votes for models sharing a structurally similar subgraph. Models receiving strong support are candidates for a more comprehensive matching process.

The eigenvalues of a graph's adjacency matrix encode important structural properties of the graph, characterizing the degree distribution of its nodes. Moreover, we have shown that the magnitudes of the eigenvalues are stable with respect to minor perturbations of graph structure due to, for example, noise, segmentation error, or minor within-class structural variation. For every rooted directed acyclic subgraph (i.e., part) of the original DAG, we compute a function of the eigenvalues of the subgraph's antisymmetric $\{0, 1, -1\}$ node-adjacency matrix which yields a low-dimensional *topological signature vector* (TSV) encoding of the "shape" of the subgraph. Details of the TSV, along with an analysis of its stability, can be found in [26].

Indexing now amounts to a nearest-neighbor search in a model database, as shown in Fig. 3. The TSV of each non-leaf node (the root of a graph "part") in each model DAG defines a vector location in a low-dimensional Euclidean space (the model database) at which a pointer to the model containing the subgraph rooted at the node is stored. At indexing time, a TSV is computed for each non-leaf node, and a nearest-neighbor search is performed using each "query" TSV. Each TSV "votes" for nearby "model" TSVs, thereby accumulating evidence for models that share the substructure defined by the query TSV. Indexing could, in fact, be accomplished by indexing solely with the root of the entire query graph. However, in an effort to accommodate large-scale perturbation (which corrupts all ancestor TSVs of a perturbed subgraph), indexing is performed locally (using all non-trivial subgraphs, or "parts") and evidence combined. The result is a small set of ranked model candidates which are verified more extensively using the matching procedure described next.

4 Matching

Each of the top-ranking candidates emerging from the indexing process must be verified to determine which is most similar to the query. If there were no noise our problem could be formulated as a graph isomorphism problem for vertex-labeled graphs. With limited noise, we would search for the largest isomorphic subgraph between query and model. Unfortunately, with the presence of significant noise, in the form of the addition and/or deletion of graph structure, large isomorphic subgraphs may simply not exist.

This problem can be overcome by using the same eigen characterization of graph structure we use as the basis of our indexing mechanism [28].

As we know, each node in a graph (query or model) is assigned a TSV, which reflects the underlying structure in the subgraph rooted at that node. If we simply discarded all the edges in our two graphs, we would be faced with the problem of finding the best correspondence between the nodes in the query and the nodes in the model; two nodes could be said to be in close correspondence if the distance between their TSVs (and the distance between their domain-dependent node labels) was small. In fact, such a formulation amounts to finding the maximum cardinality, minimum weight matching in a bipartite graph spanning the two sets of nodes. In a modification of Reyner's algorithm [20], we combine the above bipartite matching formulation with a greedy, best-first search in a recursive procedure to compute the corresponding nodes in two rooted DAGs which, in turn, yields an overall similarity measure that can be used to rank the candidate. Details of the algorithm can be found in [28, 14].

4.1 Node Similarity

The above matching algorithm requires a node similarity function that compares the shapes of the 3-D parts associated with two nodes. A variety of the measures used in the literature as signatures for indexing entire 3-D models could be used to compute similarities between two parts (nodes) [17, 3, 30, 7, 11]. Some care would of course have to be taken in the implementation of methods which require a form of global alignment. We have opted for a much simpler measure, which is based on the use of a mean curvature histogram.

First, consider the volumetric part that a node i represents, along with its Euclidean distance function D. At any point within this volume, the mean curvature of the iso-distance level set is given by $\text{div}(\frac{\nabla D}{\|\nabla D\|})$. On a voxel grid with unit spacing the observable mean curvatures are in the range $[-1, 1]$. We compute a histogram of the mean curvature over all voxels in the volumetric part, over this range, using a fixed number of bins N. A mean curvature histogram vector $\hat{M}_i$ is then constructed with entries representing the fraction of total voxels in each bin. The similarity between two nodes i and j is then given by the following measure, which uses the sum of squared distances between the corresponding entries k of each node's mean curvature histogram vector:

$$Similarity(i,j) = [1 - \underbrace{\sqrt{\sum_{k=1}^{N} [\hat{M}_i(k) - \hat{M}_j(k)]^2}}_{Distance(i,j)}].$$

By construction, this similarity function is in the interval $[0, 1]$. This measure could be further modified to take into account overall part sizes. In our experiments we choose not to do this since our object models have undergone a global size normalization.

5   Experimental Results

In order to test the power of our indexing and matching algorithms using medial surface-based DAGs, we have considered using the Princeton Shape Benchmark [23]. This

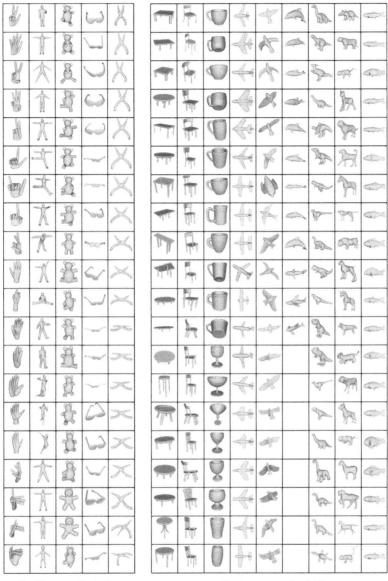

significant articulation   moderate or no articulation

Fig. 4. Database Exemplars. 20 members are shown from each of the object classes (with the exception of the class dolphins which has fewer exemplars). Exemplars from classes on the left have significant part articulation of a complexity not seen in the Princeton Shape Benchmark. Note that we treat the dinosaurs and the four-legged animals as members of a single object class "four-limbs".

standardized database, which contains 1,814 3-D object models organized by class, is an effective one for comparing the performance of a variety of methods including those in [11, 17, 3, 30, 7]. A majority of the models in the database correspond to rigid, man-made objects for which a notion of a centroid applies. The natural objects include a variety of animals (including humans), trees, plants and body parts. However, only a limited number of these have articulated or deformed parts. When such models are present, the precise nature of part articulation typically defines a unique base level category. For example, *animal-biped-human* contains human models which are upright, *animal-biped-human-arms-out* contains similar models with outstretched hands and *animal-biped-human-walking* contains those in a walking pose. Results reported in [23] indicate that a number of global shape descriptors perform suitably at such base levels of classification, but degrade rapidly at coarser levels, e.g., the classification *human*. In the context of *generic* 3-D model retrieval, such coarser levels in fact correspond to the notion of a *basic level* or *entry level* categorization [21, 4], whose exemplars might reflect a variety of complex poses and articulations, such as those seen in Fig. 1. Our matching and indexing algorithms have the potential to work at this more challenging level, because they use intuitive part-based representations.

To demonstrate this, we have constructed our own database adopting some of the models in the Princeton repository, but adding several of our own. Our database includes a total of 320 exemplars taken from several *basic level* object classes (hands, humans, teddy bears, glasses, pliers, tables, chairs, cups, airplanes, birds, dolphins, dinosaurs, four-legged animals, fish). A large number of these models are shown in Fig. 4. We divide these classes into two categories, those with significant part articulation, and those with moderate or no part articulation. In our experiments we merge the categories "four-legged" and "dinosaurs", treating them as a single category "four-limbs"

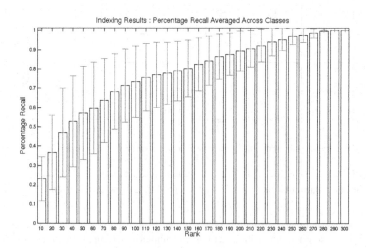

Fig. 5. Indexing Results: Percentage Recall. For several rank thresholds, $N = 10, 20, ...$, we plot the percentage of models in the database in the same category as the query (not including the query itself) with indexing rank $\leq N$. The results averaged across all classes are shown along with error bars depicting +/- 1 standard deviation.

Indexing Results: In order to test our indexing algorithm, which utilizes only the topological structure of medial surface-based DAGs, we carried out two types of experiments. In the first we evaluated percentage recall. For a number of rank thresholds the percentage of models in the database in the same category as a query (not including the

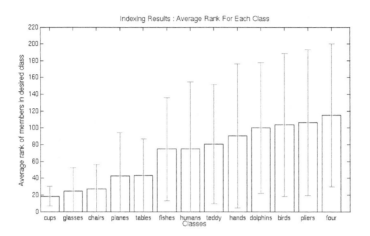

Fig. 6. Indexing Results: Average Ranks. For all queries in a class the rank of all other objects in that class are computed. The ranks averaged across that class are shown, along with error bars depicting +/- 1 standard deviation.

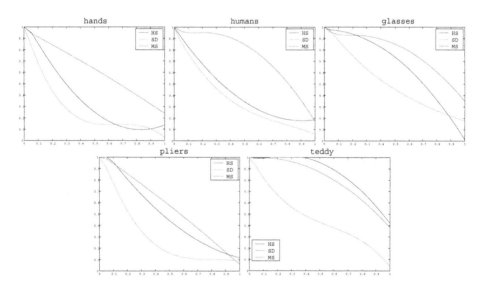

Fig. 7. Precision (y axis) versus Recall (x axis): Objects with articulating parts. The results using medial surfaces (MS) are shown in red, those using harmonic spheres (HS) are shown in blue and those using shape distribution (SD) are shown in green. The results obtained using MS are superior for all categories with the exception of the category "teddy" for which both HS and MS give excellent results.

query itself) with higher indexing rank, are shown in Fig. 5. The results indicate that on average 70% of the desired models are in the top 80 (25% of 320) ranks. In the second experiment we examine the average ranks according to object classes. For all queries in a class the rank of all other objects in that class is computed. The ranks averaged across that class are shown in Fig. 6. The results indicate that for 9 of the 13 object classes the average rank is in the top 80 (25% of 320). The higher average ranks for the remaining classes are due to the fact that certain categories have similar part decompositions. In such cases topological structure on its own is not discriminating enough, and part shapes also have to be taken into account.

It should be emphasized that the indexer is a fast screener which can quickly prune the database down to a much smaller set of candidates to which the matcher can be applied. Furthermore, the eigen characterization used to compute the index is also used at matching time, so the same eigen structure calculation is exploited for both steps.

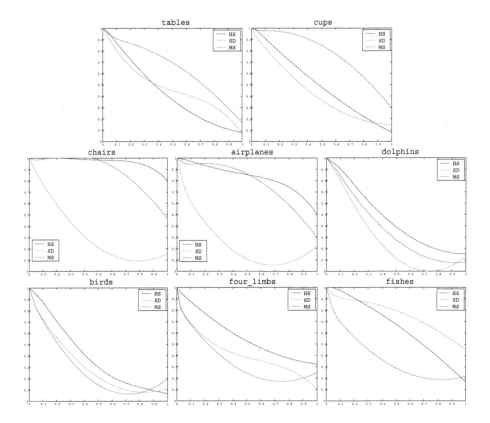

Fig. 8. Precision (y axis) versus Recall (x axis): Objects with moderate or no articulation. The results using medial surfaces (MS) are shown in red, those using harmonic spheres (HS) are shown in blue and those using shape distribution (SD) are shown in green. For categories in the top row MS gives superior results. For categories in the middle row HS gives slightly better results than MS, but both are superior to SD. For categories in the third row the results are comparable for birds, but for four-limbs and fishes, both HS and SD out perform MS.

The systems against which we evaluate the matcher in the following section run a linear search on the entire database for each query. This approach does not scale well, since the indexing problem is essentially ignored.

Matching Results: On a large database we envision running the indexing strategy first to obtain a smaller subset of candidate 3-D models and to match the query only against these. However, given the moderate size of our database we were able to generate the $320 \times 320 = 102,400$ pairs of matches in a matter of 15-20 minutes on a 3.0 GHz desktop PC. We compare the results using medial surfaces (MS) with those obtained using harmonic spheres (HS) [12] and shape distributions (SD) [17]. The pair-wise distances between models using harmonic spheres were obtained using Michael Kazhdan's executable code (http://www.cs.jhu.edu/~misha) and those using shape distributions were based on our own implementation of the algorithm described in [17]. For both HS and SD we used as input a mesh representation of the bounding voxels of the voxelized model used for MS. The comparisons are performed using the standard information re-

Table 2. Average Matching Results Using MS. Each object in the database is matched against all the other objects in the database. Each cell shows the average similarity between objects selected from two fixed object classes. In each row red and blue boxes are drawn, respectively, around the two highest average similarity scores. In all cases the highest score coincides with the correct object class. In most cases there is also a very significant difference between the top two average similarity scores.

Instance	✈	✈	🪑	☕	🐟	🐘	✋	🧍	🪑	🧸	🐟	👓	✂
✈	.61	.37	.00	.45	.23	.20	.02	.02	.10	.00	.09	.16	.26
✈	.37	.38	.00	.21	.25	.18	.12	.10	.18	.02	.18	.23	.25
🪑	.00	.00	.51	.29	.17	.15	.07	.03	.00	.15	.02	.00	.07
☕	.45	.21	.29	.64	.34	.23	.04	.04	.00	.01	.05	.04	.28
🐟	.23	.25	.17	.34	.43	.24	.16	.15	.12	.04	.22	.06	.19
🐴	.20	.18	.15	.23	.24	.28	.20	.22	.14	.07	.26	.05	.14
✋	.02	.12	.07	.04	.16	.20	.51	.46	.37	.08	.45	.00	.09
🧍	.02	.10	.03	.04	.15	.22	.46	.53	.29	.03	.47	.02	.06
🪑	.10	.18	.00	.00	.12	.14	.37	.29	.58	.04	.31	.02	.23
🧸	.00	.02	.15	.01	.04	.07	.08	.03	.04	.48	.08	.15	.07
🐟	.09	.18	.02	.05	.22	.26	.45	.47	.31	.08	.56	.02	.12
👓	.16	.23	.00	.04	.06	.05	.00	.02	.02	.15	.02	.71	.21
✂	.26	.25	.07	.28	.19	.14	.09	.06	.23	.07	.12	.21	.40

trieval notion of *recall versus precision*, where curves shifted upwards and to the right indicate superior performance.

The results for objects with articulating parts are presented in Fig. 7. For the category "teddy" both MS and HS give excellent results and for all other categories MS outperforms the other two techniques. Fig. 8 shows the results for objects with moderate or no part articulation. For categories in the top row MS gives superior results. For categories in the middle row HS gives slightly better results than MS, but both are significantly superior to SD. For categories in the third row the results are comparable for birds, but for four-limbs and fishes, both HS and SD out perform MS. In Table 2 we show the average similarity scores using MS, organized by object class. Red and blue boxes are drawn, respectively, around the two highest similarity scores. In all cases the highest score coincides with the correct object class. Overall these results demonstrate the significant potential of medial surface based representations and their graph spectra for *generic* level 3-D model retrieval, despite substantial articulation of parts.

6   Conclusion

We advance the state-of-the-art in 3-D object model retrieval by: 1) introducing a modification of a Euclidean distance function-based method for computing and segmenting medial surfaces, 2) proposing a DAG representation of the medial surface which captures a notion of part saliency, 3) building on algorithms in the computer vision literature to address the problem of 3-D model indexing and matching in a uniform framework and 4) presenting indexing and matching results on a database of object models organized according to an *entry* level of categorization, with categories having significant part articulation. Whereas all the pieces of this system have been developed in past work, putting them together and demonstrating them in the context of 3-D model retrieval with comparative results against competing methods has been the focus of this article.

The major current limitations of our work include: 1) the assumption that the original object models can be voxelized, 2) the coarse nature of the part similarity measure based on mean curvature histograms, and 3) the assumption that objects with complex part topologies can yield stable graph structures using medial surface decompositions on a digital lattice. First, it is feasible to "patch" models with a few missing triangles, so that voxelization becomes possible. It might also be fruitful to explore Voronoi methods for computing medial surface-based DAGs that could in principle be applied directly to point clouds, provided that the sampling density is high enough [2] or to use the shock scaffold technique [13]. However, for models with incomplete surfaces and large holes, and hence no well defined notion of an interior and an exterior, medial surface-based DAGs would not be appropriate. With regard to the second limitation, indeed we expect that the performance of graph theoretic algorithms for comparing medial surface based representations will improve with more discriminating part similarity measures, and any one of a number suggested in the literature can be investigated. Finally, the third concern (as exemplified by the poorer results on the four-limbed animals) points to some limitations of the current representation. It is well known that certain regions of the medial locus are less stable than others, such as Blum's ligatures [6]. Thus, there is more work to be done both in the direction of developing robust techniques for segmenting 3D skeletons as well as in selecting its stable manifolds for building representations.

References

1. H. Alt, O. Aichholzer, and G. Rote. Matching Shapes With a Reference Point. In *Proceedings of the Tenth Annual Symposiusm On Computational Geometry*, pages 85–92, 1994.
2. N. Amenta, S. Choi, and R. Kolluri. The Power Crust, Unions of Balls, and the Medial Axis Transform. *Computational Geometry: Theory and Applications*, 19(2):127–153, 2001.
3. M. Ankerst, G. Kastenmüller, H. Kriegel, and T. Seidl. 3-D Shape Histograms for Similarity Search and Classification in Spatial Databases. In *Advances in Spatial Databases, 6th International Symposium*, volume 18, pages 700–711, 1999.
4. I. Biederman. Recognition–By–Components: A Theory of Human Image Understanding. *Psychological Review*, 94(2):115–147, 1987.
5. T. O. Binford. Visual Perception by Computer. In *IEEE Conference on Systems and Control*, December 1971.
6. H. Blum. Biological Shape and Visual Science. *Journal of Theoretical Biology*, 38:205–287, 1973.
7. M. Elad, A. Tal, and S. Ar. Content Based Retrieval of VRML Objects- An Iterative and Interactive Approach. In *6th Europgraphics Workshop on Multimedia*, pages 107–118, Manchester, UK, 2001.
8. P. J. Giblin and B. B. Kimia. A formal Classification of 3D Medial Axis Points and Their Local Geometry. *IEEE Transactions on Pattern Analysis and Machine Intelligence*, 26(2):238–251, February 2004.
9. A. B. Hamza and H. Krim. Geodesic Object Representation and Recognition. In *Proceedings of DGCI*, volume LNCS 2886, pages 378–387, 2003.
10. M. Hilaga, Y. Shinagawa, T. Kohmura, and T. L. Kunii. Topology Matching for Fully Automatic Similarity Estimation of 3D Shapes. In *Proceedings of ACM SIGGRAPH*, pages 203–212, 2001.
11. M. Kazhdan, B. Chazelle, D. Dobkin, T. Funkhouser, and S. Rusinkiewicz. A Reflective Symmetry Descriptor for 3-D Models. *Algorithmica*, 38(1):201–225, October 2003.
12. M. Kazhdan, T. Funkhouser, and S. Rusinkiewicz. Rotation Invariant Spherical Harmonic Representation of 3D Shape Descriptors. In *Symposium on Geometry Processing*, jun 2003.
13. F. F. Leymarie and B. B. Kimia. Computation of the Shock Scaffold for Unorganized Point Clouds in 3D. In *Proceedings of the IEEE Conference on Computer Vision and Pattern Recognition*, pages 821–827, Madison, Wisconsin, 2003.
14. D. Macrini. *Indexing and Matching for View-Based 3-D Object Recognition Using Shock Graphs*. PhD thesis, University of Toronto, 2003.
15. G. Malandain, G. Bertrand, and N. Ayache. Topological Segmentation of Discrete Surfaces. *International Journal of Computer Vision*, 10(2):183–197, 1993.
16. D. Marr and K. H. Nishihara. Representation and Recognition of the Spatial Organization of Three Dimensional Structure. *Proceedings of the Royal Society of London*, B 200:269–294, 1978.
17. R. Osada, T. Funkhouser, B. Chazelle, and D. Dobkin. Shape Distributions. *ACM Transactions on Graphics*, 21(4):807–832, oct 2002.
18. M. Pellilo, K. Siddiqi, and S. W. Zucker. Matching Hierarchical Structures Using Association Graphs. *IEEE Transactions on Pattern Analysis and Machine Intelligence*, 21(11):1105–1120, 1999.
19. A. Pentland. Perceptual organization and the representation of natural form. *Artificial Intelligence*, 28:293–331, 1986.
20. S. W. Reyner. An Analysis of a Good Algorithm for the Subtree Problem. *SIAM J. Comput.*, 6:730–732, 1977.

21. E. Rosch. Principles of Categorization. In *Cognition and Categorization*. L. Erlbaum Associates, 1978.
22. T. Sebastian, P. Klein, and B. Kimia. Recognition of shapes by editing their shock graphs. *IEEE Transactions on Pattern Analysis and Machine Intelligence*, 26:551–571, 5 2004.
23. P. Shilane, P. Min, M. Kazhdan, and T. Funkhouser. The Princeton Shape Benchmark. In *Shape Modeling International*, Genova, Italy, June 2004.
24. Y. Shinagawa, T. L. Kunii, and Y. L. Kergosien. Surface Coding Based on Morse Theory. *IEEE Transactions On Computer Graphics and Applications*, 11(5):66–78, 1991.
25. A. Shokoufandeh, S. J. Dickinson, K. Siddiqi, and S. W. Zucker. Indexing Using a Spectral Encoding of Topological Structure. In *IEEE Conference on Computer Vision and Pattern Recognition*, pages 491–497, Fort Collins, CO, June 1999.
26. A. Shokoufandeh, D. Macrini, S. Dickinson, K. Siddiqi, and S. Zucker. Indexing Hierarchical Structures Using Graph Spectra. *IEEE Transactions On Pattern Analysis and Machine Intelligence*, 27(7), 2005.
27. K. Siddiqi, S. Bouix, A. Tannenbaum, and S. W. Zucker. Hamilton-Jacobi Skeletons. *International Journal of Computer Vision*, 48(3):215–231, 2002.
28. K. Siddiqi, A. Shokoufandeh, S. J. Dickinson, and S. W. Zucker. Shock Graphs and Shape Matching. *International Journal of Computer Vision*, 35(1):13–32, 1999.
29. H. Sundar, D. Silver, N. Gagvani, and S. Dickinson. Skeleton Based Shape Matching and Retrieval. In *International Conference On Shape Modeling International and Applications*, pages 130–142, Seoul, Korea, May 2003.
30. D. Vranic and D. Saupe. 3-D Model Retrieval With Spherical Harmonics and Moments. In *Proceedings of the DAGM*, pages 392–397, 2001.

Spatio-temporal Segmentation Using Dominant Sets

Andrea Torsello, Massimiliano Pavan, and Marcello Pelillo

Dipartimento di Informatica, Università Ca' Foscari di Venezia,
Via Torino 155, 30172 Venezia Mestre, Italy
{torsello, pavan, pelillo}@dsi.unive.it

Abstract. Pairwise data clustering techniques are gaining increasing popularity over traditional, feature-based central grouping techniques. These approaches have proven very powerful when applied to image-segmentation problems. However, they are computationally too demanding to be applied to video-segmentaton problems due to their scaling behavior with the quantity of data. On a dataset containing N examples, the number of potential comparisons scales with $O(N^2)$, thereby rendering the approaches unfeasible for problems involving very large data sets. It is therefore of primary importance to develop strategies to reduce the number of comparisons required by subsampling the data and extending the grouping to out-of-sample points after the clustering process has taken place. In this paper we present an approach to out-of-sample clustering based on the dominant set framework [10] and apply it to video segmentation. The method is compared against two recent pairwise clustering algorithms which provide out-of-sample extensions: the Nyström method [3], and the minimal-shift embedding approach [14]. Our results show that our approach performs comparably against the competition in terms of quality of the segmentation, being, however, much faster.

1   Introduction

Proximity-based, or pairwise, data clustering techniques are gaining increasing popularity over traditional central grouping techniques, which are centered around the notion of "feature" (see, e.g., [5, 15, 16, 14]). In many application domains, in fact, the objects to be clustered are not naturally representable in terms of a vector of features. On the other hand, quite often it is possible to obtain a measure of the similarity/dissimilarity between objects. Although such a representation lacks geometric notions such as scatter and centroid, it is attractive as no feature selection is required and it keeps the algorithm generic and independent from the actual data representation and metric involved. Further, it allows one to use non-metric similarities and it is applicable to problems that do not have a natural embedding to a uniform feature space, such as the grouping of structural or graph-based representations.

These appraoches have proven very powerful when applied to image segmentation problems [16, 7, 5, 2]. However the application of these method to video

A. Rangarajan et al. (Eds.): EMMCVPR 2005, LNCS 3757, pp. 301–315, 2005.

segmentation is, in general, unfeasible, due to the scaling behavior with the number of data items. On a dataset containing N examples, the number of potential comparisons scales with $O(N^2)$, thereby rendering the approach too demanding, both in terms of computation time and of space, to be used to segment video feeds. A way of overcoming this drawback is to drastically reduce the number of objects to be clustered and then extend the partition to the full data-set. Unfortunately, there is no straightforward way of extending the clustering results to new data within the pairwise grouping paradigm short of recomputing the complete cluster structure.

In an attempt to address this shortcoming of the pairwise approach, Fowlkes et al. [3] have recently proposed to use the Nyström approximation to extend normalized cut to out-of-sample data, while Bengio et al. [1] use the Nyström extension to extend other spectral clustering appraoches. Roth et al. [14] propose to perform pairwise clustering by embedding the distance data in an Euclidean space, and show how this embedding can be extended to new points.

Recently, a new framework for pairwise data clustering based on the graph-theoretic concept of a *dominant set* has emerged [10]. An intriguing connection between dominant sets and the solutions of a (continuous) quadratic optimization problem makes them related in a non-trivial way to spectral-based cluster notions, and allows one to use straightforward dynamics from evolutionary game theory to determine them [17]. A nice feature of this framework is that it naturally provides a principled measure of a cluster's cohesiveness as well as a measure of a vertex participation to its assigned group. The approach has proven to be a powerful one when applied to problems such as intensity, color, and texture segmentation, and is competitive with spectral approaches such as normalized cut [10, 11].

Motivated by the previous arguments, in this paper we address the problem of applying the dominant set approach to spatio-temporal segmentation of video sequences. In order to do this we propose an efficient approach to assigning out-of-sample data to one of a set of previously determined dominant sets. This allows us to substantially reduce the computational burden associated to the processing of the huge amount of data involved in video segmentation. We compare the segmentation obtained with our results to those obtained using the Nyström extension [3] and the minimal-shift embedding method [14], both on video sequences and synthetic data.

2   The Dominant Set Framework

In the pairwise clustering framework the data to be clustered are represented (possibly implicitly) as an undirected edge-weighted graph with no self-loops $G = (V, E, w)$, where $V = \{1, \ldots, n\}$ is the vertex set, $E \subseteq V \times V$ is the edge set, and $w : E \to \mathbb{R}_+^*$ is the (positive) weight function. Vertices in G correspond to data points, edges represent neighborhood relationships, and edge-weights reflect similarity/dissimilarity between pairs of linked vertices. As customary, we represent the graph G with the corresponding weighted adjacency (or similarity/dissimilarity) matrix, which is the $n \times n$ nonnegative, symmetric matrix $A = (a_{ij})$ defined as:

$$a_{ij} = \begin{cases} w(i,j) \,, & \text{if } (i,j) \in E \\ 0 \,, & \text{otherwise} \,. \end{cases}$$

The dominant set framework has been presented in [10]. Let $S \subseteq V$ be a non-empty subset of vertices and $i \in V$. The *(average) weighted degree* of i w.r.t. S is defined as:

$$\text{awdeg}_S(i) = \frac{1}{|S|} \sum_{j \in S} a_{ij} \tag{1}$$

where $|S|$ denotes the cardinality of S. Moreover, if $j \notin S$ we define $\phi_S(i,j) = a_{ij} - \text{awdeg}_S(i)$ which is a measure of the similarity between nodes j and i, with respect to the average similarity between node i and its neighbors in S.

Let $S \subseteq V$ be a non-empty subset of vertices and $i \in S$. The *weight* of i w.r.t. S is

$$\text{w}_S(i) = \begin{cases} 1, & \text{if } |S| = 1 \\ \displaystyle\sum_{j \in S \setminus \{i\}} \phi_{S \setminus \{i\}}(j,i)\,\text{w}_{S \setminus \{i\}}(j), & \text{otherwise} \end{cases} \tag{2}$$

while the *total weight* of S is defined as:

$$W(S) = \sum_{i \in S} \text{w}_S(i) \,. \tag{3}$$

Intuitively, $\text{w}_S(i)$ gives us a measure of the overall similarity between vertex i and the vertices of $S \setminus \{i\}$ with respect to the overall similarity among the vertices in $S \setminus \{i\}$, with positive values indicating high internal coherency.

A non-empty subset of vertices $S \subseteq V$ such that $W(T) > 0$ for any non-empty $T \subseteq S$, is said to be *dominant* if:

1. $\text{w}_S(i) > 0$, for all $i \in S$
2. $\text{w}_{S \cup \{i\}}(i) < 0$, for all $i \notin S$.

The two previous conditions correspond to the two main properties of a cluster: the first regards internal homogeneity, whereas the second regards external inhomogeneity. The above definition represents our formalization of the concept of a cluster in an edge-weighted graph.

Now, consider the following quadratic program, which is a generalization of the so-called Motzkin-Straus program [8]:

$$\begin{array}{ll} \text{maximize} & f(\mathbf{x}) = \mathbf{x}' A \mathbf{x} \\ \text{subject to} & \mathbf{x} \in \Delta_n \end{array} \tag{4}$$

where

$$\Delta_n = \{\mathbf{x} \in \mathbb{R}^n \ : \ x_i \geq 0 \text{ for all } i \in V \text{ and } \mathbf{1}'\mathbf{x} = 1\}$$

is the standard simplex of $\mathbb{R}^n$, and $\mathbf{1}$ is a vector of appropriate length consisting of unit entries. The *support* of a vector $\mathbf{x} \in \Delta_n$ is defined as the set of indices corresponding to its positive components, that is $\sigma(\mathbf{x}) = \{i \in V : x_i > 0\}$. In [10], an intriguing connection between dominant sets and local solutions of program (4) is established. Specifically, it is proven that if S is a dominant subset of vertices, then its (weighted) characteristic vector $\mathbf{x}^S$, which is the vector of Δ_n defined as

$$x_i^S = \begin{cases} \frac{w_S(i)}{W(S)}, & \text{if } i \in S \\ 0, & \text{otherwise} \end{cases} \tag{5}$$

is a strict local solution of program (4). Conversely, if $\mathbf{x}$ is a strict local solution of program (4) then its support $S = \sigma(\mathbf{x})$ is a dominant set, provided that $w_{S \cup \{i\}}(i) \neq 0$ for all $i \notin S$.

By virtue of this result, a dominant set can be found by localizing a local solution of program (4) with an appropriate continuous optimization technique, such as replicator dynamics from evolutionary game theory [17], and then picking up its support. In order to get a partition of the input data into coherent groups, a simple approach is to iteratively find a dominant set and then remove it from the graph, until all vertices have been grouped.

Note that the components of the weighted characteristic vectors give us a natural measure of the participation or "centrality" of the corresponding vertices in the cluster, whereas the value of the objective function measures the homogeneity or cohesiveness of the class.

3   Out-of-Sample Extension of a Dominant Set Classification

Suppose we are given a set V of n unlabeled items and let $G = (V, E, w)$ denote the corresponding similarity graph. After determining the dominant sets (i.e., the clusters) for these original data, we are next supplied with a set of m new data items and are asked to assign each of them to one of the previously extracted clusters. A recent approach to the out-of-sample extension of the dominant set framework was presented in [12]. The approach tested each new point against each set to see whether it increased its "cohesiveness". In particular, if $w_{S \cup \{i\}}(i) > 0$, then the new item i was assigned to cluster S. There are, however, a number of problems with this approach. First, it does not provide a partition of the data, since each point can be assigned to more than one cluster or to none at all. More importantly, the approach needs the distances between all the samples and the new item to be avaiable to perform the extension, and has, hence, $O(nm)$ time-complexity, where n is the number of samples and m is the number of out-of-sample items. A similar approach can be found in [4]

In a central-clustering framework a straightforward way to do it is to assign each new vector x to the cluster with the closest centroid, i.e.,

$$C(x) = \underset{\nu}{\operatorname{argmin}}(\|y_\nu - x\|),$$

where y_ν is the centroid of cluster ν. In a pairwise clustering framework, however, the cluster-centroid is not explicit. However, with sufficient samples, we can assume that at least one element of the cluster is "close" to the centroid. Previous experience show that the weight x_i^S of the characteristic vector is a measure of the centrality of item i with respect to the dominat set S. Hence, we take the sample with maximum weight to be the prototype $P(S)$ of S, that is:

$$P(S) = \operatorname*{argmax}_i(x_i^S) \,.$$

A similar definition of prototype was recently proposed in [4]. There, however, the prototype was not used for clustering purposes and had no implicit relation to the centroid.

With the prototype at hand, we perform the cluster extension by assigning each new item j to the cluster S_ν with the closest prototype, i.e.,

$$C(j) = \operatorname*{argmax}_\nu(\operatorname{Sim}\left(P(S_\nu), j\right)) \,,$$

where $\operatorname{Sim}(i, j)$ is the similarity between items i and j.

The proposed extension is very efficient, since, for each new point to be clustered, it only requires the computation of one distance per cluster. Hence, having a $O(km)$ time complexity, where k is the number of clusters and m the number of out-of-sample items. Furthermore, the extension can be done *on-line* since each new point is assigned to a cluster in isolation, without any information about the similarity structure of the other out-of-sample points.

4   Experimental Results

To assess the ability of the proposed approach to perform meaningful segmentation on large data-sets, we apply the algorithm to spatio-temporal segmetnation of video sequences. We compare the performance, both in terms of quality and computation time, to two recent out-of-sample pairwise clustering approaches described in [3] and [14].

4.1   The Nyström Method

In a recent paper, Fowlkes et al. propose to use the Nyström Method to extend the Normalized Cut framework to out-of-sample data [3]. The Nyström method is a technique for finding numerical approximations to eigenfunctions problems of the form

$$\int_a^b W(x, y)\phi(y) \, dy = \lambda\hat\phi(x) \,.$$

It is based on the idea that this equation can be approximated using a simple quadrature rule on a set of sample points $\zeta_1, \ldots, \zeta_n$ in the interval $[a, b]$:

$$\frac{b-a}{n} \sum_{j=1}^n W(x, \zeta_j)\hat\phi(\zeta_j) = \lambda\hat\phi(x) \,, \tag{6}$$

where $\hat{\phi}(x)$ is the approximation of $\phi(x)$. Let $A_{i,j} = W(\zeta_i, \zeta_j)$ be the matrix obtained by sampling the weight function W at points $\zeta_1, \ldots, \zeta_n$, the set $\Phi = \{\phi_1, \ldots, \phi_n\}$ of the eigenvector of A are solutions of the system:

$$\frac{b-a}{n} \sum_{j=1}^{n} W(\zeta_i, \zeta_j)\hat{\phi}(\zeta_j) = \lambda\hat{\phi}(\zeta_i) \quad \forall i \in \{1, \ldots, n\}.$$

Substituting back into (6) yields the *Nyström extension*

$$\hat{\phi}_i(x) = \frac{1}{n\lambda_i} \sum_{j=1}^{n} W(x, \zeta_j)\phi_i(\zeta_j).$$

Let the complete weight matrix W be

$$W = \begin{bmatrix} A & B \\ B' & C \end{bmatrix},$$

where matrix A holds the similarities between the samples points, B the similarities between sample and out-of-sample points, and C the similarities between out-of-sample points. The Nystöm approach implicitly approximates C with $B'A^{-1}B$, leading to the extended weight matrix

$$\hat{W} = \begin{bmatrix} A & B \\ B' & B'A^{-1}B \end{bmatrix}.$$

To apply the Nyström approximation to Normalized Cut, it is necessary to compute the row sums $\hat{d}$ of the extended weight matrix $\hat{W}$

$$\hat{d} = \hat{W}1_{n+m} = \begin{bmatrix} A1_n + B1_m \\ B'1_n + B'A^{-1}B1_m \end{bmatrix},$$

where n is the number of samples, m is the number of out-of-sample points. This requires the (implicit) computation of $B1_m$. Hence the approach cannot easily be expressed as an *on-line* extension and, at least in the implementation provided in [3] and used in our experiments, requires the full matrix B to be in memory. This severely limits the dimension of the video sequences that can be segmented with this approach.

4.2   Minimal-Shift Embedding

In a recent paper, Roth et al. present an embedding of possibly non-Euclidean distance data that preserve the clustering properties of the k-means functional [14]. The approach derives from the observation that the k-means functional

$$H^{km} = \sum_{\nu=1}^{k} \sum i = 1^n M_{i\nu} \|x_i - y_\nu\|^2, \tag{7}$$

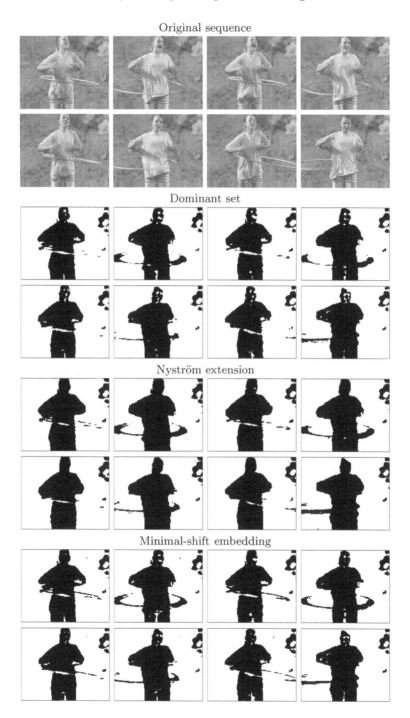

Fig. 1. The hula sequence. Top to Bottom: dominant set, Nyström extension, and minimal-shift embedding.

where y_ν is the centroid of cluster ν and $M_{i\nu} = 1$ if item i is assigned to cluster ν, $M_{i\nu} = 0$ otherwise, can be expressed in terms of pairwise distances between the points to be clustered as: In fact, by setting the prototype vectors we can write (7) as

$$H^{km} = \frac{1}{2} \sum_{\nu=1}^{k} \frac{\sum_{i=1}^{n} \sum_{j=1}^{n} M_{i\nu} M_{j\nu} \|x_i - x_j\|^2}{\sum_{l=1}^{n} M_{l\nu}}. \tag{8}$$

Furthermore, the authors show that this functional is invariant under a constant shift of the distance matrix D, i.e., $H^{km}(D) = H^{km}(D + d_0(\mathbf{11'} - I))$ where d_0 is an arbitrary constant, $\mathbf{1}$ is the vector of all ones and I is the identity matrix. Let us define the matrix

$$S_{ij}^c = \frac{1}{2} \left[D_{ij} - \frac{1}{n} \sum_{k=1}^{n} D_{ik} - \frac{1}{n} \sum_{k=1}^{n} D_{kj} + \frac{1}{n^2} \sum_{k,l=1}^{n} D_{kl} \right].$$

Clearly, $D_{ij} = S_{ii}^c + S_{jj}^c - 2S_{ij}^c$. It is a well known result that D derives from a Euclidean distance, or, equivalently, can be embedded in an Euclidean space, if and only if S^c is positive semidefinite. However, the shifted matrix $\tilde{S} = S - \lambda_n T$, where λ_n is the least eigenvector of S, is clearly positive semidefinite, and the distance matrix $\tilde{D}_{ij} = \tilde{S}_{ii} + \tilde{S}_{jj} - 2\tilde{S}_{ij}$ can be obtained from D with a constant shift $\tilde{D} = D - 2\lambda_n(\mathbf{11'} - I)$. Hence, $\tilde{D}$ is embeddable in an Euclidean space and has the same k-means functional as the original matrix D. To perform the clustering, Roth et al. propose to compute the shifted matrix $\tilde{D}$, embed it into an Euclidean space and run the k-means clustering algorithm on the embedding space. To reduce the noise dimensional reduction approaches such as principal component analysis can be applied to the embedding space. This is equivalent to performing multi-dimensional scaling on $\tilde{D}$.

One interesting property of this approach, mentioned in [14], is that it is possible to extend the embedding to new data. First, note that we can write the embedding in the form $X_p = \tilde{S} V_p \Lambda_p^{-1/2} v$, where V_p is the matrix containing the first p eigenvector of $\tilde{S}$ and Λ_p the corresponding eigenvalues matrix. Given the matrix D^n of distances between the new and the old data, we define

$$S_{ij}^n = \frac{1}{2} \left[D_{ij}^n - \frac{1}{n} \sum_{k=1}^{n} D_{ik}^n - \frac{1}{n} \sum_{k=1}^{n} \tilde{D}_{kj} + \frac{1}{n^2} \sum_{k,l=1}^{n} \tilde{D}_{kl} \right]$$

and project the new points as $X_p^n = S^n V_p \Lambda_p$. The new point is then assigned to the cluster with the closest centroid. While this approach allows each new point to be clustered on-line, that is without any information about the other out-of-sample points, it requires the computation of the full set of distances between the new point and the original samples to perform the embedding, and hence, the extension is computationally more demanding than using our approach, being of order $O(nm)$, where n is the number of samples and m the number of out-of-sample items.

Original sequence

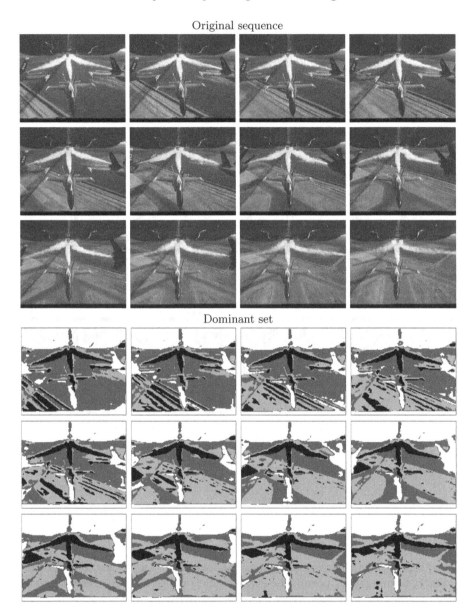

Dominant set

Fig. 2. The flight sequence. Original sequence and the segmentation obtained with the dominant set framework.

4.3   Similarity Measures

To measure the similarity/distance between two points in a video sequence we make use of both color and texture information. To measure the difference in texture we convolve each frame with a bank of linear spatial filters. The filters

Nyström extension*

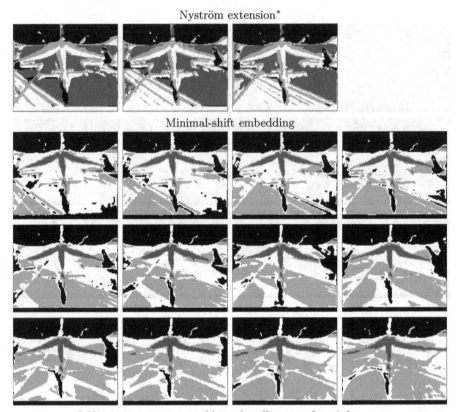

Minimal-shift embedding

* Nyström extension could not handle more than 3 frames.

Fig. 3. The flight sequence. Segmentaion obtained with the Nyström extension, and the minimal-shift embedding.

consist of pairs odd- and even-symmetric oriented filters in various scales and orientations, plus a set of center-symmetric filters. The odd-symmetric filters are re-orientation and re-scaling of the base $f_o(x, y) = c_o G'_{\sigma 1}(y) G_{\sigma 2}(x)$, where $G_\sigma(x)$ represents a Gaussian with standard deviation σ and c_o is a constant that forces f_o to unitary L_1 norm. The even-symmetric filters are re-orientation and re-scaling of the base $f_e(x, y) = c_e G'_{\sigma 1}(y) G_{\sigma 2}(x)$, while the center symmetric filters have basis $f_c(x, y) = c_c(G_{\sigma 1}(y) G_{\sigma 1}(x) - G_{\sigma 2}(y) G_{\sigma 2}(x))$. Here the constants c_e and c_c guarantee that all the basis have unitary L_1 norm. Similarly to what was presented in [7], in our experiments we have 6 different orientations uniformly separated by 30°, and 4 different scales, for a total of 40 filters, hence the filter-responses are vectors in a 40-dimensional space. The difference in texture is measured as the Euclidean distance between the filter-responses, while the difference between two colors is defined as the Euclidean distance of the RGB representations of the two colors. For each two points p and q in the video sequence, we extract their 5x5 spatial neighborhoods and, for each point of in-

Original sequence

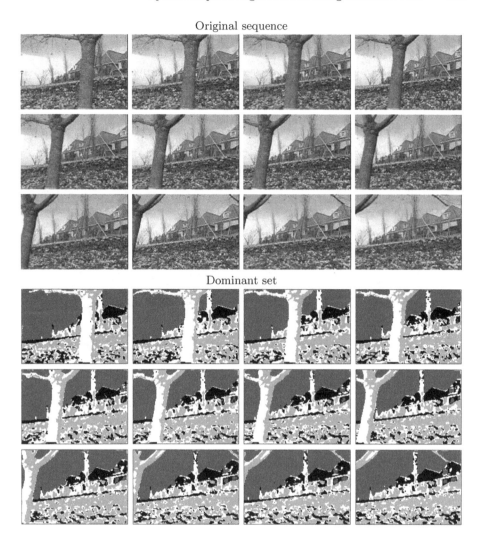

Dominant set

Fig. 4. The flower garden sequence. Original sequence and the segmentation obtained with the dominant set framework.

dex (i, j) in the neighborhoods, we compute the color vectors c_{ij}^p and c_{ij}^q around points p and q respectively. Similarly, we compute the filter-response vectors f_{ij}^p and f_{ij}^q. We define the color-distance function d_c and the filter-distance function d_f as the weighted combination of distances

$$d_c(p, q) = \sum_{i,j=1}^{5} w_{ij} \| c_{ij}^p - c_{ij}^q \| \quad d_f(p, q) \sum_{i,j=1}^{5} w_{ij} \| f_{ij}^p - f_{ij}^q \| ,$$

where, in our experiments, the weight w_i is a Gaussian centered at the center of the neighborhood and with unitary standard deviation.

Nyström extension[*]

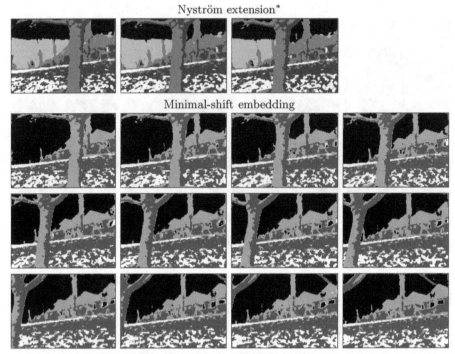

Minimal-shift embedding

[*] Nyström extension could not handle more than 3 frames.

Fig. 5. The flower garden sequence. Segmentaion obtained with the Nyström extension, and the minimal-shift embedding.

To obtain a similarity measure to be used with the dominant set approach and the Nyström extension, we combine the two distances with the formula

$$s(p,q) = e^{-\frac{1}{2}\left(\frac{d_c(p,q)}{k_1} + \frac{d_f(p,q)}{k_2}\right)}$$

where k_1 and k_2 are scaling constants determined experimentally. On the other hand, the distance used for the minimal shift embedding algorithm is a simple convex combination of the two distances:

$$d(p,q) = \alpha d_c(p,q) + (1-\alpha)d_f(p,q).$$

4.4   Video Segmentation

In order to test the performance of the segmentation algorithms, we applied the methods to three video sequences. All the experiments where run on a Pentium 4 PC with with a 1.2GHz CPU and 512Mb of RAM. To ensure a fair comparison, the clustering and extension algorithms where all coded in Matlab, while the

Table 1. Computation time required to cluster the video sequences

	Hula (sec.)	Flight (sec.)	Flower garden (sec.)
Dominant set	73	277	279
Nyström extension	871	618*	572*
Minimal-shift embedding	546	1236	1218

* Nyström extension could not handle more than 3 frames.

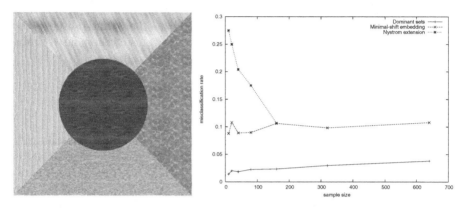

Fig. 6. Sensitivity of the clustering algorithms to the number of samples

feature extraction and distance/similarity calculation where performed using non-optimized C++ code. The parameters defining the similarities/distances were experimentally selected to provide the best results, and the number of cluster to be extracted was set to be the same for all three algorithms.

Figures 1–5 show the segmentations obtained from the three sequences, while Table 1 displays the time required to segment the videos.

In Figure 1 we can see the results on the "Hula" sequence. This sequence consists of 8 frames of 160x128 pixels each and 100 samples were used to extract the clusters. Lines 2 to 4 of Figure 1 show the segmentation obtained using the dominant set approach, the Nyström extension and the minimal-shift embedding approach respectively. In the segmentation images every grey-level represent a different cluster. In the video there is a clear separation between figure and ground and all three algorithms provide similar segmentations. Note however, that there is a dramatic difference in computation time, with the dominant set approach clearly outperforming the other two. Figures 2 and 3 display the segmentation obtained from the "flight" sequence. This sequence consists of 12 frames of 160x128 pixels each and 300 samples were used to extract the clusters. It is important to note that, already with this small example, the size of matrix B of the similarities between out-of-sample points and sample points was too big to fit in memory, rendering the Nyström method infeasible. In fact The approach could not be applied to more than 3 frames. The other two approaches, on the other hand, did not suffer from this limitation due to their ability to perform the extension *on-line*. The sequence was much harder to segment, and all three approaches provide rather poor, yet comparable, segmentations. However, in this case as well the dominant set approach clearly outperforms both methods in terms of execution time. Finally, Figures 4 and 5 present the segmentation obtained from the "flower garden" sequence. This sequence consists of 12 frames of 176x120 pixels each. 300 samples were used to extract the clusters, and in this case as well the Nyström method could not go beyond the first 3 frames. In this case the dominant set, not only proved much faster than the other approaches, but also provided a better segmentation than those obtained with the other algorithms. In fact it was the only method that proved to be able to separate the tree in the foreground from the roofs of the houses in the background.

4.5 Sensitivity Analysis

To complement these real world experiments we have performed some sensitivity analysis aimed at assessing the performance of the clustering algorithms as the number of samples is reduced. To this end we have applied the segmentation approaches to an artificial image with 5 patches of different texture. The segmentation were repeated using 10, 20, 40, 80, 160, 320, and 640 color and texture samples. Figure 6 displays the image to be segmented and the rate of misclassified points as the number of samples increases. Note that the Nyström approach did not scale beyond 160 samples. The results show that both the dominant set approach and the minimal-shift embedding method are insensitive to the number of samples, with the dominant set approach having the edge in terms of average misclassification rate. The Nyström method, however, shows a clear dependency on the number of samples.

5 Conclusions

In this paper we have addressed the problem of applying the dominant set approach to spatio-temporal segmentation of video feeds. In order to do this we proposed an efficient approach to assigning out-of-sample data to one of a set of previously determined clusters. This allowed us to substantially reduce the computational burden associated to the processing of the huge amount of data involved in video segmentation. We compared the performance of the approach to two state-of-the-art out-of-sample cluster-extension algorithms: the Nyström extension applied to normalized cut and the minimal-shift embedding method. The experiments show that, in terms of quality, the algorithm performs comparably to the minimal shift embedding and the Nyström extension. In terms of computation time, the dominant set approach proved to be consistently the fastest of the three algorithms.

References

1. Y. Bengio, J.-F. Paiement, P. Vincent, O. Delalleau, N. Le Roux, and M. Ouimet. Out-of-sample extensions for LLE, isomap, MDS, eigenmaps, and spectral clustering. In *Advances in Neural Information Processing Systems 16*, MIT Press, Cambridge, MA, 2004.

2. B. Fischer, J. M. Buhmann. Path-based clustering for grouping of smooth curves and texture segmentation. *IEEE Trans. Pattern Anal. Machine Intell.* 25(4):513–518, 2003.

3. C. Fowlkes, S. Belongie, F. Chun, and J. Malik. Spectral grouping using the Nyström method. *IEEE Trans. Pattern Anal. Machine Intell.* 26:214–225, 2004.

4. R. Hamid et al. Detection and explanation of anomalous activities: representing activities as bags of event n-grams. To appear *CVPR* 2005.

5. T. Hofmann and J. M. Buhmann. Pairwise data clustering by deterministic annealing. *IEEE Trans. Pattern Anal. Machine Intell.* 19:1–14, 1997.

6. D. Luenberger. *Linear and nonlinear programming*. Addison-Wesley, Reading, MA, 1984.

7. J. Mailk, S. Belongie, T. Leung, and J. Shi. Contour and texture analysis for image segmentation. *Int. J. of Computer Vision* 43(1):7–27, 2001.

8. T. S. Motzkin and E. G. Straus. Maxima for graphs and a new proof of a theorem of Turán. *Canad. J. Math.* 17:533–540, 1965.

9. A. Y. Ng, M. I. Jordan, and Y. Weiss. On spectral clustering: Analysis and an algorithm. In *Advances in Neural Information Processing Systems 14*, MIT Press, Cambridge, MA, pp. 849–856, 2002.

10. M. Pavan and M. Pelillo. A new graph-theoretic approach to clustering and segmentation. In *Proc. IEEE Conf. Computer Vision and Pattern Recognition*, pp. 145–152, 2003.

11. M. Pavan, M. Pelillo. Unsupervised texture segmentation by dominant sets and game dynamics. In *Proc. 12th Int. Conf. on Image Analysis and Processing*, pp. 302–307, 2003.

12. M. Pavan and M. Pelillo. Efficient out-of-sample extension of dominant-set clusters. In *Advances in Neural Information Processing Systems 17*, MIT Press, Cambridge, MA, pp. 1057–1064, 2005

13. P. Perona and W. Freeman. A factorization approach to grouping. In: H. Burkhardt and B. Neumann (Eds.), *Computer Vision—ECCV'98*, pp. 655–670. Springer, Berlin, 1998.

14. V. Roth, J. Laub, M. Kawanabe, and J. M. Buhmann. Optimal cluster preserving embedding of nonmetric proximity data. *IEEE Trans. Pattern Anal. Machine Intell.* 25:1540–1551, 2003.

15. S. Sarkar and K. Boyer. Quantitative measures of change based on feature organization: Eigenvalues and eigenvectors. *Computer Vision and Image Understanding* 71:110–136, 1998.

16. J. Shi and J. Malik. Normalized cuts and image segmentation. *IEEE Trans. Pattern Anal. Machine Intell.* 22:888–905, 2000.

17. J. W. Weibull. *Evolutionary game theory*. MIT Press, Cambridge, MA, 1995.

18. Y. Weiss. Segmentation using eigenvectors: A unifying view. In *Proc. 7th Int. Conf. on Computer Vision*, pp. 975–982, 1999.

Stable Bounded Canonical Sets and Image Matching

John Novatnack[1], Trip Denton[1], Ali Shokoufandeh[1], and Lars Bretzner[2]

[1] Department of Computer Science, Drexel University
{jmn27, tdenton, ashokouf}@cs.drexel.edu
[2] Computational Vision and Active Perception Laboratory,
Department Of Numerical Analysis and Computer Science, KTH, Stockholm, Sweden
bretzner@nada.kth.se

Abstract. A common approach to the image matching problem is representing images as sets of features in some feature space followed by establishing correspondences among the features. Previous work by Huttenlocher and Ullman [1] shows how a similarity transformation - rotation, translation, and scaling - between two images may be determined assuming that three corresponding image points are known. While robust, such methods suffer from computational inefficiencies for general feature sets. We describe a method whereby the feature sets may be summarized using the *stable bounded canonical set* (SBCS), thus allowing the efficient computation of point correspondences between large feature sets. We use a notion of stability to influence the set summarization such that stable image features are preferred.

1 Introduction

Image matching remains an important open problem in computer vision with numerous applications. One common approach to the problem is to represent images as features in some feature space. Given two images, the matching problem is then to establish a correspondence between the features. Increasing the difficulty is that two images may not be exact copies as one may have undergone some transformation. The transformations between the images must be determined solely from the features representing the image. Previous work by Huttenlocher and Ullman on point matching [1] shows how a similarity transformation - rotation, translation, and scaling - between two images in 2D may be determined assuming that three corresponding points are known. Of course one cannot assume that such a correspondence is known, and therefore a transformation must be found for each set of possible features correspondences. The combinatorial number of possible transformations is unrealistic to compute as the number of features increases.

In this paper we present a technique to reduce the number of candidate features for Huttenlocher and Ullman's algorithm using a smaller canonical set. The canonical set consists of maximally stable features that are representations for a single image. The notion of stability in the feature space is a measure of the invariance of the features under changes in lighting conditions, as well as invariance under image transformations. The definition of stability is purposely left loosely defined here, as our approach is general in that it may be applied to any feature extraction method which augments points with a notion of stability. The features used in this paper are the centers of scale-space blobs and ridges [2, 3], where the stability of a feature is a function of the multi-scale detector used to detect either the blob or ridge. Figure 2 shows an image marked

A. Rangarajan et al. (Eds.): EMMCVPR 2005, LNCS 3757, pp. 316–331, 2005.

with blobs and ridges detected in scale-space. In order to simplify the presentation of the features in this paper, while visualizing as many as possible, we show only the centers of the blobs and ridges.

Figure 1 shows an overview of the technique. Two images, one a transformed copy of the other, are represented as a large number of features. Using our algorithm we extract stable canonical elements from each set of features (Figure 3), and compute a transformation between each possible feature correspondence in the canonical sets. The transformation which results in the minimum distance between the features in the feature space is selected as the best. In the case shown in Figure 1 the transformation aligns the images with negligible error. Notice that because of the high number of features we detect in our experiments (approximately two hundred) a number of features are detected in the black area surrounding the images. Although the features are detected by the scale-space filter, the low feature detector responses in this area result in low feature stability.

In order to determine the maximally stable defining subset of the points in feature space we propose the notion of *stable bounded canonical set* (SBCS) and show a tech-

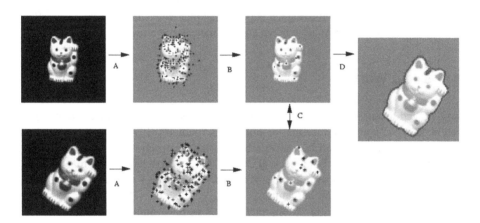

Fig. 1. A) Blob and ridge feature extraction with centroids of blobs and ridges denoted, B) Stable Bounded Canonical Set (SBCS) construction, C) Determine transformation, D) Outline shows transformation determined from SBCS

Fig. 2. Blobs and ridges detected in scale-space

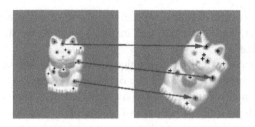

Fig. 3. Corresponding SBCS Features

nique for finding approximate solutions using semidefinite programming [4]. The stable bounded canonical set problem extends our previous work [5, 6] where we studied the usefulness of canonical sets in representing defining views of an object rotated in three-dimensions. In this paper we formulate the stable bounded canonical set problem first as an integer programming problem, then show a reformulation as a quadratic programming problem which may be relaxed and solved approximately using semidefinite programming. Experimental evidence is presented that shows the usefulness of SBCS in determining the transformation between two images in feature space.

2   Related Work

Most related to our work is unsupervised feature selection via quantization, rate distortion theory [7], and the information bottleneck method [8]. Work has been done on image segmentation viewed as a clustering problem that may be solved by applying the method of information bottleneck [9, 10, 11]. Our approach differs in that we try to pick representative features from the given data set instead of arbitrary elements that are centroids of some cluster in feature space.

The notion of SBCS stems from our previous work in finding canonical views of a three-dimensional object [5, 6]. In developing an approximation framework for computing canonical sets, we take the novel view expressed by Cyr and Kimia [12] that "the shape similarity metric between object outlines endows the viewing sphere with a metric which can be used to cluster views into aspects, and to represent each aspect with a prototypical view." In this paper we reduce the SBCS problem to a graph optimization problem and approximate it using semidefinite programming. The work of Goemans and Williamson [13] on the MAX-CUT problem in graphs, showed SDP relaxations to be useful in obtaining improved approximation algorithms for several optimization problems. See Goemans [14] and Mahajan and Ramesh [15] for a survey of recent results and applications of SDP.

A method of solving similarity transformations using aligning correspondence points was originally discovered by Huttenlocher and Ullman [16, 17]. By assuming that three corresponding points are known between a model and a target, they present a number of formulas to solve for the translation, scaling, and rotation. The algorithm has since been applied to a number of applications including randomized point matching [18], object recognition [19], and shape tracking [20].

Early methods of image matching using local features stemmed from Harris's corner and edge detector [21]. The corners and edges detected using Harris's method depended on the current scale of the image. Matching techniques using the features were unable to differentiate two images of the same object residing at different scales. Further work has been done on representing images in scale-space, where images are represented by a set of features residing at a number of different scales. Lindeberg has worked on the problem of extracting features in scale-space with automatic scale selection [2]. More recently, Lowe has introduced a method named scale invariant feature transform (SIFT), which extracts local scale-space features which include a number of scale-space characteristics [22]. Vectors containing the feature's location in scale-space as well as scale-space characteristics are used for image matching.

The problem of feature or attribute selection has also been studied in the context of the dimensionality curse and dimensionality reduction [23, 24, 25]. This is mainly motivated by that fact that in large semi-structured databases there are many attributes which are correlated with the others, and the need for feature reduction and attribute selection is motivated by the fact that many datasets can largely be well-approximated in fewer dimensions.

The notion of SBCS is not meant to create a feature based matching technique superior to current existing work, but rather to enhance the computational efficiency at the expense of a slight reduction in the robustness in the matching procedure.

3   SBCS Construction

In this section, we describe our method for constructing stable bounded canonical sets in polynomial time. Starting with a set of features $\mathcal{P} = \{p_1, ..., p_n\}$ of an object, a similarity function $\mathcal{S} : \mathcal{P} \times \mathcal{P} \to \mathbb{R}^{\geq 0}$, and a set of stabilities associated with each feature $\{t_1, ..., t_n\}$, we construct an edge weighted graph $G = G(\mathcal{P})$, where the features $\{p_1, ..., p_n\}$ are represented by vertices with weights given by their stability values, and the edges between the vertices have weights corresponding to the measure of similarity between the vertices. We use V^* to denote the vertices in V, the vertex set of G, corresponding to the SBCS.

The problem of maximizing the weight of cut-edges in a graph is known to be NP hard [26]. Goemans and Williamson [13] explored the problem MAX-CUT in graphs, and used semidefinite programming (SDP) relaxations to provide good approximate solutions. Inspired by their results, we formulate SBCS as an integer programming problem, and then use SDP to produce an approximate solution.

The formulation of the SBCS problem requires a number of definitions. First let $\mathbf{t}$ be a vector $[t_1, ..., t_n]^T$ that contains the stabilities of each feature in $\mathcal{P} = \{p_1, ..., p_n\}$. For each feature p_i, $1 \leq i \leq n$, we also introduce an indicator variable y_i. The variable y_i has a binary range $\{-1, +1\}$, indicating whether the corresponding feature belongs to V^* or V/V^*, respectively. Let $y \in \{-1, +1\}^n$ be the column vector $[y_1, ..., y_n]^T$ and let $\mathcal{W} \in \mathbb{R}^{n \times n}$ denote the edge weight matrix of graph G where

$$\mathcal{W}_{i,j} = \begin{cases} \mathcal{S}(p_i, p_j) & \text{if } (p_i, p_j) \in E, \\ 0 & \text{otherwise.} \end{cases}$$

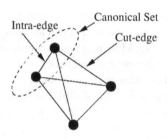

Fig. 4. SBCS Edges

It is important to note that the weight between two vertices is the *similarity* between the two features, which is the inverse of the distance between them in feature space. Figure 4 shows the edges of the SBCS construction. We refer to an edge (u, v) as a cut-edge if one vertex is a member of the canonical set and the other is not, that is $u \in V^*$ and $v \notin V^*$ or $u \notin V^*$ and $v \in V^*$. We refer to an edge (u, v) as an intra-edge if both elements are members of the canonical set that is, $u \in V^*$ and $v \in V^*$. In order to enforce the desired structure of the canonical sets, we introduce three objective functions. First we seek to minimize the similarity between the intra-edges, which forces the elements in the canonical set to be as dissimilar as possible. Secondly we maximize the similarity of the cut-edges, which enforces the local structure of the vertices adjacent to a canonical element. Lastly we maximize the stability of the elements in the canonical set.

3.1   Integer Programming Formulation

In this section we formalize the SBCS problem as an integer optimization. Specifically, we wish to formalize the maximization of the weights (similarities) of the cut-edges, minimization of the weights (similarities) of the intra-edges, and maximization of the stability of the elements in the canonical set. The problem of maximizing the sum of the weights of the cut-edges can be formulated as

$$\text{Maximize } \frac{1}{2} \sum_{i,j} \mathcal{W}_{ij} (1 - y_i y_j),$$

or equivalently

$$\text{Minimize } \frac{1}{2} \sum_{i,j} \mathcal{W}_{ij} (1 + y_i y_j). \tag{1}$$

Similarly, minimizing the sum of the weights of the intra-edges becomes

$$\text{Minimize } \frac{1}{4} \sum_{i,j} \mathcal{W}_{ij} (1 + y_i)(1 + y_j). \tag{2}$$

The problem of maximizing the stability of the elements in the canonical set may be formulated as

$$\text{Maximize } \frac{1}{2} \sum_{i=1}^{n} (1 + y_i) t_i,$$

or equivalently

$$\text{Minimize } \frac{1}{2}\sum_{i=1}^{n}(1 - y_i)t_i. \tag{3}$$

Our constraints for the problem are

$$\frac{1}{2}\sum_{i=1}^{n}(1 + y_i) - k_{min} \geq 0, \tag{4}$$

which ensures that the cardinality of the SBCS is at least k_{min},

$$k_{max} - \frac{1}{2}\sum_{i=1}^{n}(1 + y_i) \geq 0, \tag{5}$$

which ensures that the cardinality of the SBCS is at most k_{max}, and $y_i \in \{-1, +1\}$ for all $i \in \{1, ..., n\}$, which ensures that every vertex is either in the SBCS or it is not. Our final integer programming formulation is

$$\textbf{(IP):} \text{ Minimize } \frac{1}{2}\sum_{i,j}\mathcal{W}_{ij}(1 + y_i y_j)$$

$$\text{Minimize } \frac{1}{4}\sum_{i,j}\mathcal{W}_{ij}(1 + y_i)(1 + y_j)$$

$$\text{Minimize } \frac{1}{2}\sum_{i=1}^{n}(1 - y_i)t_i$$

$$\text{Subject to } \frac{1}{2}\sum_{i=1}^{n}(1 + y_i) - k_{min} \geq 0,$$

$$k_{max} - \frac{1}{2}\sum_{i=1}^{n}(1 + y_i) \geq 0,$$

$$y_i \in \{-1, +1\} \; \forall \; 1 \leq i \leq n.$$

3.2 Quadratic Programming Formulation

The integer programming formulation described by (1) is unfortunately known to be NP-hard [27]. In order to develop an approximate solution, our approach is to give a reformulation as a quadratic integer programming problem, and then to use vector labeling and a semidefinite programming (SDP) relaxation to obtain an approximate solution in polynomial time. Since (1) is quadratic we reformulate (2) and (3) so that our problem is homogeneous. First we introduce a *set indicator* variable $y_{n+1} \in \{-1, +1\}$, that is, $p_i \in V^*$, $1 \leq i \leq n$, if and only if $y_i = y_{n+1}$. Observe that $y_i y_{n+1} = 1$ if y_i is in the SBCS and $y_i y_{n+1} = -1$ otherwise. This gives us

$$p_i \in V^* \Leftrightarrow \frac{1 + y_i y_{n+1}}{2} = 1, \; p_i \notin V^* \Leftrightarrow \frac{1 - y_i y_{n+1}}{2} = 1.$$

We can reformulate the objective of minimizing the sum of the weights of the intra-edges (2) as

$$\text{Minimize } \frac{1}{4}\sum_{i,j} W_{ij}(1 + y_i y_{n+1})(1 + y_j y_{n+1}). \tag{6}$$

We can then combine equation (1) and (6) along with the fact that $y_i^2 = 1$ for all $i \in \{1, ..., n+1\}$ to produce

$$\text{Minimize } \frac{3}{4}\sum_{i,j} W_{ij} y_i y_j + \frac{1}{2}\sum_{i=1}^{n} y_{n+1} y_i \sum_{j=1}^{n} W_{ij} - \frac{1}{4}\sum_{ij} W_{ij}. \tag{7}$$

Additionally formulate the stability objective (3) as

$$\text{Minimize } \frac{1}{2}\sum_{i=1}^{n}(1 - y_i y_{n+1})t_i.$$

We can also rewrite our constraints on the size of the SBCS (4,5) as

$$\frac{1}{2}\sum_{i=1}^{n}(1 + y_{n+1}y_i) - k_{min} \geq 0$$

and

$$k_{max} - \frac{1}{2}\sum_{i=1}^{n}(1 + y_{n+1}y_i) \geq 0.$$

We then arrive at our quadratic formulation for the SBCS problem

$$\textbf{(QIP): Minimize } \frac{3}{4}\sum_{i,j} W_{ij} y_i y_j + \frac{1}{2}\sum_{i=1}^{n} y_{n+1} y_i \sum_{j=1}^{n} W_{ij} - \frac{1}{4}\sum_{ij} W_{ij}$$

$$\text{Minimize } \frac{1}{2}\sum_{i=1}^{n}(1 - y_i y_{n+1})t_i$$

$$\text{Subject to } \frac{1}{2}\sum_{i=1}^{n}(1 + y_{n+1}y_i) - k_{min} \geq 0,$$

$$k_{max} - \frac{1}{2}\sum_{i=1}^{n}(1 + y_{n+1}y_i) \geq 0,$$

$$y_i \in \{-1, +1\} \ \forall \ 1 \leq i \leq n+1.$$

3.3   Semidefinite Programming Formulation

Since **(QIP)** is still intractable, we use vector labeling to reformulate the problem as a semidefinite program. As is conventional in SDP relaxations of quadratic integer programming problems, we introduce a vector for each indicator variable. We replace each

y_i with a vector $x_i \in S_{n+1}$, where $1 \le i \le n+1$ and S_{n+1} is the unit sphere in $\mathbb{R}^{n+1}$. We can reformulate the combined objective (7) as

$$\text{Minimize } \frac{3}{4} \sum_{i,j} \mathcal{W}_{ij} x_i^T x_j + \frac{1}{2} \sum_{i=1}^{n} x_{n+1}^T x_i \sum_{j=1}^{n} \mathcal{W}_{ij} - \frac{1}{4} \sum_{ij} \mathcal{W}_{ij}. \qquad (8)$$

The stability of the canonical set (7) may be reformulated using vectors as

$$\text{Minimize } \frac{1}{2} \sum_{i=1}^{n} (1 - x_i^T x_{n+1}) t_i. \qquad (9)$$

In order to formulate the problem as a semidefinite program, equations (8) and (9) must be expressed in terms of matrices. First let the matrix $\mathcal{V}$ be defined as

$$\mathcal{V} = \begin{bmatrix} x_i & \cdots & x_n & x_{n+1} & \tilde{\mathbf{0}} & \tilde{\mathbf{0}} \\ & \tilde{\mathbf{0}}^T & & 0 & 1 & 0 \\ & \tilde{\mathbf{0}}^T & & 0 & 0 & 1 \end{bmatrix}.$$

Where $\tilde{\mathbf{0}}$ is an all-zeros vector in $\mathbb{R}^n$. Define $\mathcal{X} = \mathcal{V}^T \mathcal{V}$. Clearly, $\mathcal{X}$ is a semidefinite matrix, since

$$x^T \mathcal{X} x = x^T \mathcal{V}^T \mathcal{V} x = ||\mathcal{V}x||_2^2, \ \forall x \in \mathbb{R}^{n+1}.$$

Next let $w_\Sigma = \sum_{ij}^{n} \mathcal{W}_{ij}$, and $t_\Sigma = \sum_{i=1}^{n} t_i$. We can then express (8) as

$$\text{Minimize } \mathcal{C} \bullet \mathcal{X},$$

where $\mathcal{A} \bullet \mathcal{B}$ denotes the Frobenius inner product of matrices $\mathcal{A}$ and $\mathcal{B}$, i.e. $\mathcal{A} \bullet \mathcal{B} = \text{Trace}(\mathcal{A}^T \mathcal{B})$, and $\mathcal{C}$ encodes the combined objective function and is defined as

$$\mathcal{C} = \begin{bmatrix} \frac{3}{4}\mathcal{W} & d & \tilde{\mathbf{0}} & \tilde{\mathbf{0}} \\ d^T & -\frac{1}{4}w_\Sigma & 0 & 0 \\ \tilde{\mathbf{0}}^T & 0 & 1 & 0 \\ \tilde{\mathbf{0}}^T & 0 & 0 & 1 \end{bmatrix},$$

where the vector d is a vector in $\mathbb{R}^n$ whose i^{th} entry has value $d_i = \frac{1}{2} \sum_{j=1}^{n} \mathcal{W}_{i,j}$. Observe that

$$\sum_{i=1}^{n} x_i^T x_{n+1} = \frac{1}{2} \mathcal{E} \bullet \mathcal{X},$$

where

$$\mathcal{E} = \begin{bmatrix} \hat{\mathbf{0}} & e & \tilde{\mathbf{0}} & \tilde{\mathbf{0}} \\ e^T & 0 & 0 & 0 \\ \tilde{\mathbf{0}}^T & 0 & 0 & 0 \\ \tilde{\mathbf{0}}^T & 0 & 0 & 0 \end{bmatrix},$$

and $\hat{\mathbf{0}}$ is a $(n \times n)$ matrix of all zeroes and e is a column vector of n ones. In order to encode the stability objective (equation 9), define the matrix $\mathcal{T}$ as

$$\mathcal{T} = \begin{bmatrix} \hat{\mathbf{0}} & -\frac{1}{4}\mathbf{t} & \tilde{\mathbf{0}} & \tilde{\mathbf{0}} \\ -\frac{1}{4}\mathbf{t}^T & \frac{1}{2}t_\Sigma & 0 & 0 \\ \tilde{\mathbf{0}}^T & 0 & 0 & 0 \\ \tilde{\mathbf{0}}^T & 0 & 0 & 0 \end{bmatrix}.$$

We require that both objectives in our SDP formulation to be convex functions for reasons that will be evident in the following section. Recall that the objective functions are convex if the Jacobians of both $\mathcal{C} \bullet \mathcal{X}$ and $\mathcal{T} \bullet \mathcal{X}$ are non-negative semidefinite. In order to make this true we reformulate the objective matrix $\mathcal{C}$ as

$$
\tilde{\mathcal{C}} = \begin{bmatrix} \frac{3}{4}\mathcal{W} & d & \tilde{\mathbf{0}} & \tilde{\mathbf{0}} \\ d^T & 1 & 0 & 0 \\ \tilde{\mathbf{0}}^T & 0 & 1 & 0 \\ \tilde{\mathbf{0}}^T & 0 & 0 & 1 \end{bmatrix}.
$$

This is possible as the term $\frac{1}{4}w_\Sigma$ in (8) is constant. In order to redefine the matrix $\mathcal{T}$ we require additional notation. Let $\tilde{\mathbf{t}}^T$ be a column vector where $\tilde{t}_i = \frac{1}{1+t_i}$. We may now redefine $\mathcal{T}$ as $\tilde{\mathcal{T}}$, where the Jacobian of $\tilde{\mathcal{T}} \bullet X$ is non-negative semidefinite, as

$$
\tilde{\mathcal{T}} = \begin{bmatrix} \hat{\mathbf{0}} & \frac{1}{2}\tilde{\mathbf{t}} & \tilde{\mathbf{0}} & \tilde{\mathbf{0}} \\ \frac{1}{2}\tilde{\mathbf{t}}^T & \frac{1}{2}t_\Sigma & 0 & 0 \\ \tilde{\mathbf{0}}^T & 0 & 0 & 0 \\ \tilde{\mathbf{0}}^T & 0 & 0 & 0 \end{bmatrix}.
$$

The canonical set stability objective can then be rewritten as

$$
\text{Minimize } \tilde{\mathcal{T}} \bullet \mathcal{X},
$$

and the SDP formulation of SBCS can be stated as follows

(SDP): Minimize $\tilde{\mathcal{C}} \bullet \mathcal{X}$
          Minimize $\tilde{\mathcal{T}} \bullet \mathcal{X}$
          Subject to $\mathcal{D}_i \bullet \mathcal{X} \geq 0, \ \forall \, i = 1\ldots,m,$
          $x_{ii} = 1 \, \forall \, 1 \leq i \leq n+1,$
          $\mathcal{X} \succeq 0,$

where $m = n + 3$ and denotes the number of constraint matrices. $\mathcal{A} \bullet \mathcal{B}$ denotes the Frobenius inner product of matrices $\mathcal{A}$ and $\mathcal{B}$ as before, and $\mathcal{X} \succeq 0$ means that $\mathcal{X}$ is positive semidefinite. Our first $n + 1$ constraint matrices,matrices $\mathcal{D}_1$ to $\mathcal{D}_{n+1}$ are all zeros with a single "one" that moves along the main diagonal. This enforces the $x_{ii} = 1$ constraints. The constraint matrix corresponding to the lower bound in (4) has the following matrix form

$$
\mathcal{D}_{n+2} = \begin{bmatrix} \hat{\mathbf{0}} & e & \tilde{\mathbf{0}} & \tilde{\mathbf{0}} \\ e^T & 0 & 0 & 0 \\ \tilde{\mathbf{0}}^T & 0 & 2n - 4k_{min} & 0 \\ \tilde{\mathbf{0}}^T & 0 & 0 & 0 \end{bmatrix},
$$

where as before $\hat{\mathbf{0}}$ is an $n \times n$ matrix of zeroes, e is an all-ones vector in $\mathbb{R}^n$, and $\tilde{\mathbf{0}}$ is an all-zeros vector in $\mathbb{R}^n$. Also, the upper bound constraint in (5) has the following matrix form

$$
\mathcal{D}_{n+3} = \begin{bmatrix}
\hat{\mathbf{0}} & -\mathbf{e} & \tilde{\mathbf{0}} & \tilde{\mathbf{0}} \\
-\mathbf{e}^T & 0 & 0 & 0 \\
\tilde{\mathbf{0}}^T & 0 & 0 & 0 \\
\tilde{\mathbf{0}}^T & 0 & 0 & 4k_{max} - 2n
\end{bmatrix}.
$$

Through this construction the approximately optimal stable bounded canonical set may be found in polynomial time.

3.4 Combining Optimization Functions

In order to solve the semidefinite program expressed in Section 3.3 we must combine the two objective functions. Optimization problems that involve multiple objectives can be formulated as follows [28, 29]

$$\text{Minimize } \mathcal{F}(\mathcal{X}) = \{f_1(\mathcal{X}), f_2(\mathcal{X}), \ldots, f_m(\mathcal{X})\}$$
$$\text{Subject to } \mathcal{X} \in \Gamma,$$

where $\mathcal{F}(\mathcal{X}) = \{f_1(\mathcal{X}), \ldots, f_m(\mathcal{X})\}$ is the set of objective functions and Γ is the feasible set.

Observe that the objective functions for the SBCS are somewhat competitive. A solution that minimizes the canonical set objective may not minimize the stability objective and vice versa. A trade-off optimality condition known as *Pareto* optimality is used [28]. Specifically, a solution $\mathcal{X}^*$ is called Pareto optimal if there is no $\mathcal{X} \in \Gamma$ such that $\mathcal{F}(\mathcal{X}) \leq \mathcal{F}(\mathcal{X}^*)$; that is, $\mathcal{X}^*$ is lexicographically optimal compared to any suboptimal solution $\mathcal{X}$. Observe that such a solution is not necessarily unique. The set of all Pareto optimal solutions $\mathcal{X}^* \in \Gamma$ is denoted by Γ_{Par}, the *Pareto set*. The Pareto set can be thought of as the boundary of the image of the feasible set, and a Pareto optimal solution is a point on the boundary.

If the objective functions in a multi-objective optimization problem $f_i(\mathcal{X})$, $1 \leq i \leq m$ are all convex functions, then the optimal solution $\mathcal{X}^*$ of the following single-objective problem belongs to the Pareto set of problem $\mathcal{F}(\mathcal{X})$ [29]

$$\text{Minimize } \sum_{i=1}^{m} \alpha_i f_i(\mathcal{X})$$
$$\text{Subject to } \mathcal{X} \in \Gamma,$$
$$\text{where } \sum_{i=1}^{m} \alpha_i = 1, \text{ and } \alpha_i \geq 0 \quad \forall 1 \leq i \leq m,$$

Our approach for combining the cardinality and similarity objectives of the SBCS formulation is based on using a convex combination of the two objective functions. Specifically, we let $\mathcal{C}_1 = \alpha \tilde{\mathcal{C}}$ and $\mathcal{C}_2 = (1 - \alpha)\tilde{\mathcal{T}}$ for a convexity parameter $\alpha \in [0, 1]$. The combined objective function then satisfies

$$\mathcal{C}_1 \bullet \mathcal{X} + \mathcal{C}_2 \bullet \mathcal{X} = \mathbf{Trace}(\mathcal{C}_1^T \mathcal{X}) + \mathbf{Trace}(\mathcal{C}_2^T \mathcal{X}) = \mathbf{Trace}((\mathcal{C}_1 + \mathcal{C}_2)^T \mathcal{X}).$$

Letting $\mathcal{C}(\alpha) = \mathcal{C}_1 + \mathcal{C}_2$, our combined multi-objective SDP formulation is

$$\textbf{(CoSDP):} \quad \text{Minimize } \mathcal{C} \bullet \mathcal{X}$$
$$\text{Subject to } \mathcal{D}_i \bullet \mathcal{X} \geq 0, \ \forall \, i = 1, \ldots, m$$
$$x_{ii} = 1 \ \forall \, 1 \leq i \leq n+1,$$
$$\mathcal{X} \succeq 0.$$

Finally, for every $\alpha \in [0,1]$ the optimal solution $\mathcal{X}^* = \mathcal{X}^*(\alpha)$ can be computed in polynomial time using the algorithm [30] (for details on a SDP solver the reader is referred to [31]).

3.5   Rounding

Once the solution to the semi-definite program described in section 3.4 is computed, a rounding step must be performed to obtain an integer solution. This step identifies the set of values for indicator variables $y_1, ..., y_n$ and the set indicator variable y_{n+1}. In our experiments, we have used a rounding scheme based on Cholesky decomposition and a multivariate normal hyperplane method that can be effectively derandomized. (See [15] for details.)

Let $\mathcal{X}^* = \mathcal{X}^*(\alpha)$ denote the optimal solution of the **(CoSDP)** for a given $\alpha \in [0,1]$. Since $\mathcal{X}^*$ is a symmetric positive semidefinite matrix, using Cholesky decomposition it can be represented as $\mathcal{X}^* = \mathcal{V}^t \mathcal{V}$ [32]. This provides us with $n + 1$ vectors for the relaxed SBCS problem. Specifically, column x_i, $1 \leq i \leq n$, of $\mathcal{V}$ forms the vector associated with vertex $v_i \in G$ in the optimal SDP relaxation of the SBCS set problem, and column x_{n+1} corresponds to the set indicator variable. Finally, we pick a random vector $\rho \in \mathbb{R}^{n+1}$ with multivariate normal distribution, with 0 mean, and with covariance $\mathcal{X}^*$, to generate the indicator variables y_i, $i \leq 1 \leq n+1$ and the canonical set V^* as $y_i = \textbf{sign}\,(\rho^t x_i)$ and $V^* = \{v_i \,|\, y_i = y_{n+1}, 1 \leq i \leq n\}$. We perform this rounding step multiple times, each time checking that the constraints are not violated, and keeping track of the solution with the best objective value.

4   Experiments

In order to verify the effectiveness of recovering transformations from elements in the canonical set we performed three experiments. In the first experiment we randomly chose three objects from the COIL-20 [33] database, and applied a random transformation which included rotation in the image plane, scaling, and translation. We then confirmed that we could recover the known transformation using the SBCS computed between the images. In the second experiment we took the same four objects from the COIL-20 database, and the same four objects rotated in depth five, ten, and fifteen degrees. Again we computed the canonical sets of both images and showed their invariance under small rotations in depth. The out-of-plane rotation experiments show that the method does not rely on seeing exactly the same view as the model view and can establish correspondence among stable features obtained by SBCS. In the last experiment we tested the effectiveness of our method under the presence of occlusion. We created an image containing each of the four objects with occlusion, and then found the best transformation between each object and the composite image.

For each one of the images used in the experiments we extracted approximately two-hundred blobs and ridges in scale-space using previously existing techniques [2, 3]. The features used for matching were the centers of the respective blobs and ridges. Blobs and ridges are found at local maxima in scale-space. The response of the multi-scale detector at a feature is used as the stability of that feature. From these features we computed a SBCS with a minimum cardinality of twelve and a maximum cardinality of sixteen. In order to determine the transformation between two images we found a transformation for each possible feature correspondence set amongst the elements in the canonical sets. After determining the transformation for a given feature set correspondence, we use a many-to-many matching algorithm [34] based on the earth mover's distance to compute the distance between the transformed image and the target image. The distance computed using the many-to-many matching algorithm allows the transformations to be ranked. After a transformation is found for each feature set correspondence, the one which returns the minimum distance is returned as optimal.

Figure 5 shows the results of the first experiment. Column one of the figure shows three images from the COIL-20 database and the canonical sets computed using our semidefinite programming formulation. The second column shows the same image rotated in the image plane and scaled, and the respective canonical set. In order to apply Ullman and Huttenlocher's algorithm, three feature correspondences are needed, however it may be visually confirmed that the intersection of the canonical sets of the two images contain many more correspondences. The third column of the figure shows the

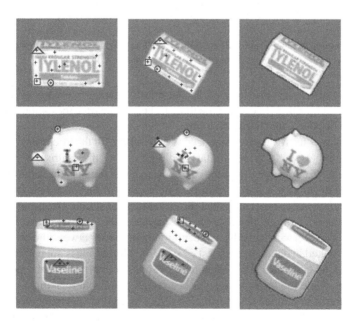

Fig. 5. Left: reference images with SBCS features, Middle: images rotated and scaled with SBCS features, Right: outline of reference images transformed onto rotated images

Fig. 6. Left: reference images with SBCS features, Middle: images rotated in depth with SBCS features, Right: outline of reference images transformed onto rotated images

outline of the first image transformed by the transformation found using Ullman and Huttenlocher's algorithm. In each of the three test cases the transformation computed is highly similar to the actual transformation.

Figure 6 shows the results from the second experiment for the fifteen degree rotations in depth (the other results were similar). Column one of the figure is repeated from experiment one. Column two shows the canonical features found in the same four objects rotated in depth fifteen degrees. Again the intersection of these canonical sets can be visually be confirmed to be greater than three features, the number required to compute the transformation. Column three shows the outline of the original image transformed by the transformation which results in the minimum distance between the original image and its copy rotated in depth. In each test case the transformation is not perfectly correct, as our technique computes a two-dimensional rotation matrix from the points in the feature space, while the target image has been rotated in depth by a three-dimensional rotation. Still, the computed transformation serves as a good approximation.

We have also conducted limited preliminary experiments to study the matching in the presence of occlusion. Clearly, a systematic study of occlusion and cluttered scenes is in order. As a proof of concept we have included one of our occlusion experiments.

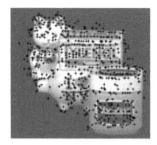

Fig. 7. Left: reference image with scale-space features Middle: image with SBCS features Right: outline of query images on reference image

The composite image is a synthetic scene consisting of four objects from the COIL-20 database with varying amounts of occlusion. Using this as a reference image we selected each of the four objects from the COIL-20 database and found the best transformation between the object and the composite image. Figure 7 shows the results of this experiment. Column one shows the composite image with several hundred scale-space features. Column two shows the fifty-five points of the SBCS computed from the features. Using the SBCS of the individual objects, shown in the previous experiments, we identified the transformation which minimizes the distance between the query and the reference image. Column three shows the outlines of the best transformations found for the four objects.

5   Summary and Future Work

Our work was motivated by the desire to reduce the complexity of applying Huttenlocher and Ullman's algorithm. If n is the number of features in the first image and m is the number of features in the second, then their algorithm requires $O\left(\binom{n}{3}\binom{m}{3}\right)$ correspondence evaluations. We have shown through a limited series of experiments that the Stable Bounded Canonical Set of image features can be used to provide acceptable results with a substantial savings in computation time.

This paper serves as evidence of the application of SBCS to image matching. We plan a more extensive set of experiments to further confirm our preliminary findings. We also plan to test the ability of our approach to match images under varying lighting conditions and degrees of occlusion. In addition we would like to test the approach with feature graphs that are more highly attributed, in an effort to incorporate deeper structure.

Acknowledgments

The authors would like to thank M. Fatih Demirci (Drexel University) for his help. Funded in part by a grant from the Office of Naval Research (ONR-N000140410363).

References

1. Huttenlocher, D.P., Ullman, S.: Recognizing solid objects by alignment with an image. International Journal of Computer Vision **5:2** (1990) 195–212
2. Lindeberg, T.: Detecting Salient Blob–Like Image Structures and Their Scales With a Scale–Space Primal Sketch—A Method for Focus–of–Attention. IJCV **11** (1993) 283–318
3. Bretzner, L., Lindeberg, T.: Qualitative multi-scale feature hierarchies for object tracking. In: Journal of Visual Communication and Image Representation. Volume 11. (2000) 115–129
4. Goemans, M.X., Williamson, D.P.: Improved Approximation Algorithms for Maximum Cut and Satisfiability Problems Using Semidefinite Programming. J. Assoc. Comput. Mach. **42** (1995) 1115–1145
5. Denton, T., Abrahamson, J., Shokoufandeh, A.: Approximation of canonical sets and their application to 2d view simplification. In: CVPR. (2004) Volume 2, p550–557
6. Denton, T., Demirci, M.F., Abrahamson, J., Shokoufandeh, A.: Selecting canonical views for view-based 3-d object recognition. In: ICPR. (2004) pp. 273–276
7. Cover, T., Thomas, J.: Elements of Information Theory: Rate Distortion Theory. John Wiley & Sons (1991)
8. Tishby, N., Pereira, F., Bialek, W.: The information bottleneck method. In: Proceedings of the 37-th Annual Allerton Conference on Communication, Control and Computing. (1999) 368–377
9. Hermes, L., Zoller, T., Buhmann, J.M.: Parametric distributional clustering for image segmentation. In: Proceedings, European Conference on Computer Vision. (2002) 577–591
10. Gordon, S., Greenspan, H., Goldberger, J.: Applying the information bottleneck principle to unsupervised clustering of discrete and continuous image representations. In: Proceedings, International Conference on Computer Vision, Nice, France (2003)
11. Liu, H., Motoda, H.: Feature transformation and subset selection. IEEE Intelligent Systems **13** (1998) 26–28
12. Cyr, C.M., Kimia, B.: 3d object recognition using shape similarity-based aspect graph. In: 8th Inter. Conf. Comp. Vision. (2001) 254–261
13. Goemans, M.X., Williamson, D.P.: .878-approximation algorithms for max cut and max 2sat. In: Twenty-sixth Annual ACM Symposium on Theory of Computing, New York (1994) 422–431
14. Goemans, M.X.: Semidefinite programming in combinatorial optimization. Mathematical Programming **79** (1997) 143–161
15. Mahajan, S., Ramesh, H.: Derandomizing approximation algorithms based on semidefinite programming. SIAM Journal on Computing **28** (1999) 1641–1663
16. Huttenlocher, D., Ullman, S.: Object recognition using alignment. In: Proceedings, First International Conference on Computer Vision, London, UK (1987) 102–111
17. Huttenlocher, D., Ullman, S.: Recognizing solid objects by alignment with an image. International Journal of Computer Vision **5** (1990) 195–212
18. Irani, S., Raghavan, P.: Combinatorial and experimental results for randomized point matching algorithms. In: SCG '96: Proceedings of the twelfth annual symposium on Computational geometry, New York, NY, USA, ACM Press (1996) 68–77
19. Ratan, A.L., Grimson, W.E.L., W. M. Wells, I.: Object detection and localization by dynamic template warping. International Journal on Computer Vision **36** (2000) 131–147
20. Meer, P., Lenz, R., Ramakrishna, S.: Efficient invariant representations. Int. J. Comput. Vision **26** (1998) 137–152
21. Harris, C., Stephens, M.: A combined corner and edge detector. In: In 4th ALVEY vision conference. (1988) 147 – 151

22. Lowe, D.G.: Object recognition from local scale-invariant features. In: Proc. of the International Conference on Computer Vision ICCV, Corfu. (1999) 1150–1157

23. Blum, A.L., Langley, P.: Selection of relevant features and examples in machine learning. Artificial Intelligence **97** (1997) 245–271

24. Berchtold, S., Böhm, C., Kriegel, H.P.: The pyramid-tree: Breaking the curse of dimensionality. In Haas, L.M., Tiwary, A., eds.: SIGMOD 1998, Proceedings ACM SIGMOD International Conference on Management of Data, June 2-4, 1998, Seattle, Washington, USA, ACM Press (1998) 142–153

25. Pagel, B.U., Korn, F., Faloutsos, C.: Deflating the dimensionality curse using multiple fractal dimensions. In: ICDE '00: Proceedings of the 16th International Conference on Data Engineering, Washington, DC, USA, IEEE Computer Society (2000) 589

26. Gary, M.R., Johnson, D.S.: Computers and Intractability: A Guide to the Theory of NP-completeness. Freeman, San Francisco (1979) (ND2,SR1).

27. Garey, M.R., Johnson, D.S.: Computers and intractability: A guide to the theory of NP-completeness. W.H. Freeman and Co., Baltimore (1979)

28. Ehrgott, M.: Multicriteria Optimization. Volume 491 of Lecture Notes in Economics and Mathematical Systems. Springer-Verlag, New York (2000)

29. Miettinen, K.M.: Nonlinear Multiobjective Optimization. Kluwer Academic Publishers, Dordrecht, Netherlands (1999)

30. Alizadeh, F.: Interior point methods in semidefinite programming with applications to combinatorial optimization. SIAM J. Optim. **5** (1995) 13–51

31. Toh, K.C., Todd, M.J., Tutuncu, R.: SDPT3 — a Matlab software package for semidefinite programming. Optimization Methods and Software **11** (1999) 545–581

32. Golub, G., Loan, C.: Matrix Computations. The Johns Hopkins University Press, Baltimore (1996)

33. Nene, S.A., Nayar, S.K., Murase, H.: Columbia object image library: Coil (1996)

34. Demirci, M.F., Shokoufandeh, A., Dickinson, S., Keselman, Y., Bretzner, L.: Many-to-many graph feature matching using spherical coding of directed graphs. In: ECCV. (2004)

Coined Quantum Walks Lift the Cospectrality of Graphs and Trees

David Emms[1], Simone Severini[1], Richard C. Wilson[2], and Edwin R. Hancock[2]

[1] Departments of Computer Science and Mathematics,
[2] Department of Computer Science,
University of York, York YO10 5DD, UK
demms@york.ac.uk

Abstract. In this paper we consider the problem of distinguishing graphs that are cospectral with respect to the standard adjacency and Laplacian matrix representations. Borrowing ideas from the field of quantum computing, we define a new matrix based on paths of the coined quantum walk. Quantum walks exhibit interference effects and their behaviour is markedly different to that of classical random walks. We show that the spectrum of this new matrix is able to distinguish many graphs which cannot be distinguished by standard spectral methods. We pay particular attention to strongly regular graphs; if a pair of strongly regular graphs share the same parameter set then there is no efficient algorithm that is proven to be able distinguish them. We have tested the method on large families of co-parametric strongly regular graphs and found it to be successful in every case. We have also tested the spectra's performance when used to give a distance measure for inexact graph matching tasks.

1 Introduction

Quantum algorithms have recently attracted considerable attention in the theoretical computer science community. This is primarily because they offer considerable speed-up over classical algorithms. For instance, Grover's [12] search method is polynomially faster than its classical counterpart, and Shor's factorisation method is exponentially faster than classical methods. However, quantum algorithms also have a richer structure than their classical counterparts since they use qubits rather than bits as the basic representational unit [19]. For instance, this structure is exploited in Shor's algorithm where the Fourier transform is use to locate prime factors. The interference and entanglement of qubits may also be exploited to develop interesting protocols, and one fascinating example is Braunstein's quantum teleportation idea [6].

It is this issue of richer representations that is the subject of this paper. We are interested in the problem of random walks on graphs and how they can be used to distinguish graphs which cannot be distinguished efficiently by other methods. Random walks are useful tools in the analysis of the structure of graphs. The steady state random walk on a graph is given by the leading

A. Rangarajan et al. (Eds.): EMMCVPR 2005, LNCS 3757, pp. 332–345, 2005.

eigenvector of the transition probability matrix, and this in turn is related to the eigenstructure of the graph Laplacian. Hence, the study of random walks has been the focus of sustained research activity in spectral graph theory. For instance, Lovász has written a useful review of the subject [16], and spectral bounds have been placed on the properties of random walks including the mixing times and hitting times [25].

From a practical perspective, there have been a number of useful applications of random walks. One of the most important of these is the analysis of routing problems in network and circuit theory. Of more recent interest is the use of ideas from random walks to define the page-rank index for internet search engines such as Googlebot [7]. In the pattern recognition community there have been several attempts to use random walks for graph matching. These include the work of Robles-Kelly and Hancock [21, 20] which has used both a standard spectral method [21] and a more sophisticated one based on ideas from graph seriation [20] to convert graphs to strings, so that string matching methods may be used. Gori, Maggini and Sarti [11] on the other hand, have used ideas borrowed from page-rank to associate a spectral index with graph nodes and have then used standard subgraph isomorphism methods for matching the resulting attributed graphs.

One of the problems that limits the use of random walks, and indeed any spectral method, is that of cospectrality. This is the situation in which structurally distinct graphs present the same pattern of eigenvalues. Classic examples are strongly regular graphs [8] and certain trees [22, 17]. In these cases standard methods will fail to distinguish between such non-isomorphic graphs, however, we provide a method that has been able to distinguish all such graphs that we have tested. We also extend the method to the problem of inexact graph matching by using this method to define a distance measure for pairs of graphs.

Recently, quantum walks have been introduced as quantum counterparts of random walks [13, 3]. Their behaviour is governed by unitary rather than stochastic matrices. Quantum walks posses a number of interesting properties not exhibited by classical random walks. For instance, because the evolution of the quantum walk is unitary and therefore reversible, the walks are non-ergodic and what is more they do not have a limiting distribution. The present applications of quantum walks are fast quantum algorithms for database searching [24], graph traversal [9, 14], and the problem of element distinctness [4].

Although the analysis of quantum walks may seem detached from the practical problems listed above, they may offer a way of lifting the problems of cospectrality. In this paper, we borrow ideas from quantum walks and combine the state space of the walk with a 'coin space' which dictates the quantum amplitudes of the various paths. The unitary matrix governing this walk is used to construct a new representation for graphs. Our main conclusion is that by making use of this representation of the adjacency structure, problems of cospectrality can be lifted and random walks can be used to distinguish otherwise indistinguishable graph structures.

The remainder of the paper is organised as follows: Section 2 gives a brief introduction to some basics of quantum computing. Section 3 describes the classical and quantum random walks and as an example describes the quantum walk on the line. Section 4 describes representations of graphs based on the coined quantum walk. Section 5 examines these representations for the case of strongly regular graphs. Section 6 details the experiments. Finally Section 7 presents our conclusions.

2   Quantum Computing

Quantum computing is interested in taking advantage of the vastly different behaviour of quantum systems to carry out computations in a fundamentally different way. Whereas a classical computer manipulates classical states to carry out computation, a quantum computer would manipulate quantum states such as the polarisation of photons [15] or the excitation states of trapped ions [10].

The state space of a quantum computer that manipulates a quantum system with n simultaneously distinguishable modes is represented by a vector in a Hilbert space $\mathcal{H}^n \cong \mathbb{C}^n$. Let $\{|i\rangle : 1 \leq i \leq n\}$ be the standard basis of $\mathcal{H}^n$. A general state is a complex linear combination of the n basis states; let $|\Psi_1\rangle$ and $|\Psi_2\rangle$ be two such states:

$$|\Psi_1\rangle = \sum_{a=1}^{n} \alpha_a |a\rangle, \quad |\Psi_2\rangle = \sum_{a=1.}^{n} \beta_a |a\rangle.$$

We write as $\langle\Psi_1|$ the linear functional that maps every vector $|\Psi_2\rangle \in \mathcal{H}^n$ to the inner product

$$\langle\Psi_1|\Psi_2\rangle = (|\Psi_1\rangle, |\Psi_2\rangle) = \sum_{a=1}^{n} \overline{\alpha_a}\beta_a,$$

where $\overline{\alpha}$ is the complex conjugate of α. It is the inner product that is used to determine the probabilities of various observations when a measurement is made as explained later. The time evolution is linear and norm preserving, hence the state at time t, $|\psi_t\rangle$, is related to the initial state, $|\psi_0\rangle$, by

$$|\psi_t\rangle = U_t|\psi_0\rangle,$$

where U_t is unitary.

The power quantum computation comes from quantum parallelism. Consider a qubit, which is the quantum analogue of a bit. A state of a qubit can be represented by a vector, $|\psi\rangle \in \mathbb{C}^2$, whereas that for a bit would be $x \in \mathbb{Z}_2 = \{0,1\}$. However, due to the laws of quantum mechanics, the state space of a system of n qubits is the tensor product $\mathbb{C}^{\otimes 2n}$ whereas the state space for n bits is the Cartesian product $\mathbb{Z}_2^{\oplus n}$. Thus a system with n bits has $2n$ possible states whereas a system of n qubits is a complex vector space of dimension 2^n. Crucially this means that a linear combination of basis states, known as a 'superposition' of states can be manipulated simultaneously. However, not all the information contained in a quantum state is accessible. For the state $|\Psi_1\rangle$, if a projective measurement is made (in the standard basis) then only one of the basis states is observed. A particular state, $|a\rangle$, is observed with probability $P(|a\rangle) = |\langle a|\Psi\rangle|^2$.

3   Classical and Quantum Random Walks

Random walks are a model of diffusion important in statistical physics, applied probability, randomized algorithms, *etc.* (see, *e.g.*, [2, 16, 25]).

Let $G = (V, E)$ be a graph on n vertices, we write $i \sim j$ if $\{i, j\} \in E$. Let $P : V \times V \to [0, 1]$ be the function determining the transition probabilities, then

- $P(i, j) > 0$ if $\{i, j\} \in E$,
- $P(i, j) = 0$ if $\{i, j\} \notin E$
- and for every $i \in V$, $\sum_i P(i, j) = 1$.

The function P induces a stochastic matrix, M, called the *transition matrix*, such that $M_{ij} := P(i, j)$.

A (probability) distribution for the walk at time, t, is encoded by a vector $\mathbf{x}^{(t)} \in \mathbb{R}^n$, where $\sum_{i=1}^n x_i^{(t)} = 1$. A *random walk* on G induced by M is a discrete Markov chain $\{X_t\}_{t=0}^\infty$ with state-set V, which starts at $X_0 = i$ and moves with transition probabilities $\Pr[X_{t+1} = i | X_t = j] = P(i, j)$, for every $i, j \in V$. The state after t steps is given by

$$\mathbf{x}^{(t)} = M^t \mathbf{x}^{(0)}$$

and the random variables $\{X_t\}_{t=0}^\infty$ are such that

$$\Pr[X_t = j | X_0] = M^t \mathbf{x}^{(0)} \cdot F_j,$$

where F_j is the projector onto the one dimensional subspace spanned by $\mathbf{j}$.

A random walk is said to be *simple* when the ij-th entry of the transition matrix is $\frac{1}{d(j)}$ if $(i, j) \in E$, where $d(j)$ is the degree of the vertex i. A random walks is *ergodic* if there is a unique limiting distribution π which satisfies $\lim_{t \to \infty} M^t \mathbf{x}^{(0)} = \pi$, independent of $\mathbf{x}^{(0)}$; this is equivalent to saying that M is irreducible and aperiodic. Moreover, if M is symmetric, the rate of convergence of $\mathbf{x}^{(t)}$ to π, depends on the real number $1 - |\lambda_2|$, where λ_2 is the second largest eigenvalue of M. The greater this quantity the faster the rate of convergence.

3.1   The Coined Quantum Walk on the Line

By way of introduction to the coined quantum walk on general graphs, we first describe the coined quantum walk on the line [18]. A state of the walk is the product of a 'position space' describing the position of the walk and a 'coin space' describing along which edge the walk arrived at/will leave that position. A step of the walk involves applying a 'coin operator' to the 'coin space' which assigns quantum amplitudes to the various edges leaving a given position state and a transition operator acting on the whole state space.

We define an orthonormal basis $\{|i\rangle \otimes |e\rangle : i \in \mathbb{Z}, e = l, r\}$ for the state space of the walk where i represents the position, l and r represent the edge to its left and right respectively and $\otimes$ is the symbol for the Kronecker tensor product.

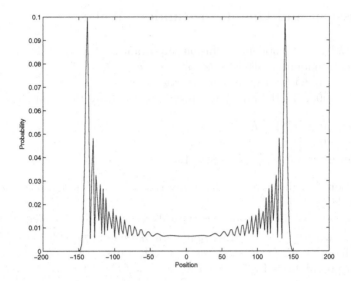

Fig. 1. The probability distribution after 200 steps for the quantum walk on the line using the Hadamard coin and a symmetric starting state. Only even positions are plotted since odd positions have probability zero.

To best compare the quantum walk with its classical counterpart we use the symmetric starting state $|\psi_0\rangle = \frac{1}{\sqrt{2}}|0\rangle \otimes (|l\rangle + |r\rangle)$ and the Hadamard coin,

$$H = \frac{1}{\sqrt{2}} \begin{bmatrix} 1 & 1 \\ 1 & -1 \end{bmatrix}.$$

If the walk is allowed to evolve without measurement then, after 200 steps, we have the probability distribution in Fig. 1. The distribution is in stark contrast to that observed for the classical walk, which tends towards a Gaussian distribution with $\mu = 0$ and $\sigma^2 = n$, where n is the number of steps. The probability distribution for the quantum walk has $\mu = 0$ and $\sigma^2 \sim n^2$. It is almost uniform in the interval $[-\frac{n}{\sqrt{2}}, \frac{n}{\sqrt{2}}]$ and heavily peaked, with the modal positions at the limits of the distribution.

An observation that can be made of the walk on the line is that the quantum walk spreads quadratically faster than the classical walk and it turns out that this is generally the case for walks on graphs [1]. However, there are cases where there is an exponential speed-up in the hitting time of a certain node in some graphs. This was observed on the hypercube by Kempe [14] and for graphs constructed by joining two n-level binary trees at their leaves by Childs, Farhi and Gutmann [9].

The quantum walk on the hypercube was the basis of a quantum search algorithm for a marked item in an unordered database by Shenvi, Kempe and Whaley [24], giving a different formulation of Grover's algorithm for the same problem [12].

3.2 Coined Quantum Walks on Graphs

Quantum walks are quantum counterparts of random walks, and were recently introduced with the aim of applying them to the design of new quantum algorithms [1, 5, 13, 3]. The constraints imposed by unitarity do not allow one to define a unitary transition matrix for all digraphs [23]. In order to carry out a discrete quantum walk on a general graph it is necessary for the state of the walk to encode both the current state of the walk and the previous state by which it got there. This was done by the the authors of [1, 5] by defining the notion of coined quantum walks as follows. Let G be a graph on n vertices and $E[i] = \{e \in E : i \in e\}$ be the set of edges incident upon the vertex i, we define an orthonormal basis for the state space of the walk to be $\{|i\rangle \otimes |e\rangle : i \in V, e \in E$ with $e \in E[i]\}$. Equivalently, one can view the state space of the walk as the set of ordered pairs of vertices, (i, j), $i, j \in V$ such that $\{i, j\} \in E$, we will use this notation later for labelling the entries of the transition matrix. A *step* of a coined quantum walk on G consists of the following:

1. A unitary matrix C_i is applied to $|i\rangle \otimes |e\rangle$, for every $i \in V(G)$. The matrix C_i produces the vector $|i\rangle \otimes \sum_{e \in E[i]} \alpha_e |e\rangle$ such that $\sum_{e \in E[i]} |\alpha_e|^2 = 1$. The matrix C_i is called the *coin* and determines the quantum amplitudes for the various transitions.
2. A permutation matrix S is applied so that, if $e = \{i, j\}$ then $S|i\rangle \otimes |e\rangle = |j\rangle \otimes |e\rangle$ and $S|j\rangle \otimes |e\rangle = |i\rangle \otimes |e\rangle$. That is, it brings about the transitions along the edges of the graph determined by the coin state. The matrix S is called the *shift*.

Note that for a coined quantum walk the set of coins can be chosen freely, however, the choice is not arbitrary. It is natural to chose a set that are invariant under permutations of the node and edge labels. The *Grover matrices*, $G^{(n)} = I_n - \frac{2}{n} J_n$ (where J_n is the $n \times n$ all-ones matrix) are such a set. In addition, Grover matrices are the real-orthogonal matrices that maximize the distance from the identity in terms of the matrix norm, and hence should produce the smallest mixing parameters.

If the graph is regular then the same coin can be used for each vertex and a single step of the walk can be written as $|\psi_t\rangle = S(I \otimes C)|\psi_{t-1}\rangle = U|\psi_{t-1}\rangle$. If the graph is not regular then the transition matrix for the walk cannot be separated in this way. However, for all graphs we the transition operator is given by:

$$U_{ij,kl} = \begin{cases} \frac{2}{d_j} - \delta_{il} & \text{if } j = k \\ 0 & \text{if } j \neq k \end{cases}$$

where we have labelled a state $|i\rangle \otimes |e\rangle$, such that $e = \{i, j\}$, by the ordered pair (i, j). The coins used here are the Grover matrices; since these matrices have real entries, note that this matrix is real-orthogonal.

Let $|\psi_t\rangle = U^t|\psi_0\rangle$ be the state induced by the coined quantum walk after t steps. A *coined quantum walk* on G is a sequence $\{X_t\}_{t=0}^{\infty}$ of random variables starting at $X_0 = \{j, f\}$ ($j \in V$ and $f \in E[j]$) and $\Pr[X_t = i, e, |X_0] =$

$\sum_{e \in E[i]} \langle \psi_t | P^{(i,e)} | \psi_t \rangle$, where $P^{(i,e)}$ is the projector onto the one dimensional subspace spanned by $|i\rangle \otimes |e\rangle$.

Observe that non-trivial quantum walks are non-ergodic, since unitary operators are norm-preserving and linear. They do not approach a limiting distribution, however for other notions of convergence(*e.g.*, the Cesaro mean), the same quantum walk induces a variety of limiting distributions that are dependent on the initial state.

The Hamiltonian for the Coined Quantum Walk. The classical random walk can be viewed as an energy minimization problem. Consider a walk on some graph G, and let L be its Laplacian matrix. Then the classical random walk is the walk that minimizes the energy function

$$\varepsilon_c = \sum_{xy} A_{xy}(v_x - v_y)^2, \quad \text{such that } \mathbf{v} \perp \mathbf{1},$$

where $\mathbf{1}$ is the all-one's vector. This function is minimized by the Fiedler vector, that is the eigenvector of the Laplacian with the second smallest eigenvalue. The coined quantum walk can be viewed in the same way, although the energy function cannot be written down as easily. Let U be the matrix for the coined quantum walk, then the Hamiltonian for the walk, H, is such that $U = e^{-iH}$. The matrix U has a spectral decomposition, $U = W\Lambda W^{-1}$, with $W = [w_{(1)} | w_{(2)} | \dots | w_{(n)}]$ and $\Lambda = \text{diag}(\lambda_{(1)}, \lambda_{(2)}, \dots, \lambda_{(n)})$ where the $\lambda_{(k)}$ are the eigenvalues of U with corresponding eigenvectors $w_{(k)}$. The entries of H can therefore be expressed as:

$$H_{xy} = i \sum_k \ln(\lambda_{(k)}) W_{xk}(W^{-1})_{ky}$$

and the walk is such that it minimizes the energy function

$$\varepsilon_q = \sum_{xy} H_{xy}(v_x - v_y)^2, \quad \text{such that } \mathbf{v} \perp \mathbf{1}.$$

4   Matrix Representations Based on U

We wish to concentrate on the how the idea of quantum walks can be used classically. The spectrum of the unitary matrix governing the evolution of a quantum walk turns out to be related to the spectrum of the transition matrix for the classical random walk. The unitary matrix can be written as

$$U_{ij,kl} = A_{ik} A_{jl} \delta_{jk} \left(\frac{2}{d_k} - \delta_{il} \right).$$

Let $\mathbf{e}$ be an eigenvector of T with eigenvalue μ, then U has eigenvalues $\lambda = \mu \pm \sqrt{1 - \mu^2}$ with corresponding eigenvectors

$$v_{ij} = \frac{A_{ij}}{d_j} - \bar{\lambda} \frac{A_{ij} e_i}{d_i}.$$

The remaining eigenvalues are ± 1 each with multiplicity $|E| - |V|$ each. So the spectrum of U is completely determined by the spectrum of the transition matrix T. However, the random walk induced by U still has advantages over its classical analogue. In the next section we consider how we can make use of the differences between the walks.

4.1 Interference on the Coined Quantum Walk and the Positive Support of U^t

The quantum walk traverses all possible paths simultaneously with amplitudes corresponding to the probability of each path. These walks are not independent but are able to constructively or destructively interfere, giving rise to probability distributions dependent upon this effect. This appears to allow the walk to probe and distinguish graphs more effectively than happens classically. The state of the walk after t steps is given by U^t, the (i, j) entry giving the amplitude in the state $|i\rangle$ at time t for a walk starting in the state $|j\rangle$. Define the positive support, $S^+(V)$ of the unitary matrix V to be the matrix with entries

$$S^+(V) = \begin{cases} 1 & \text{if } V_{ij} > 0; \\ 0 & \text{otherwise.} \end{cases}$$

The matrix can be viewed as an adjacency matrix of a digraph with vertex set $\{(i, j), (j, i) : \{i, j\} \in E(G)\}$. The matrix for the positive support of the real-orthogonal U^t has a non-zero (x, y) entry if and only if there is a positive quantum amplitude for the walk starting in the state y being observed in the state x after t steps, where each state corresponds to an ordered pair of vertices. For small values of t this pattern of non-zero entries is more complex than is the case for the classical walk. We make use of the matrices $S^+(U^t)$ in order to distinguish strongly regular graphs, as described below.

5 Strongly Regular Graphs

A strongly regular graph (SRG) with parameters (n, k, λ, μ) is a k-regular graph on n vertices such that every pair of adjacent vertices share λ common neighbours and every pair of non-adjacent vertices share μ common neighbours [8]. The spectra of the generalised adjacency and Laplacian matrices of a SRG are completely determined by its parameters, however, large sets of coparametric non-isomorphic SRG exist. Such graphs cannot be distinguished using standard spectral methods and are in fact very hard to distinguish; the best known algorithm for distinguishing SRG runs in time $n^{O(n^{1/3})}$. Thus, SRG provide a hard case for distinguishing non-isomorphic graphs. Below we consider the spectra of $S^+(U_G^t)$ for small values of t.

5.1 Spectra of $S^+(U^t)$ for SRG

Let G be a SRG with parameters (n, r, s, t), adjacency matrix A and transition matrix for the discrete quantum walk U. Let γ be an eigenvalue of A with corresponding eigenvector v. Then $S^+(U_G)$ has eigenvalues

$$\delta = \frac{\gamma}{2} \pm i\sqrt{r - 1 - \gamma^2/4},$$

the remaining $n(r - 2)$ eigenvalues of $S^+(U)$ are ± 1. Furthermore, $S^+(U^2)$ has eigenvalues

$$\delta = \frac{\gamma^2}{2} + 2 - r \pm i\gamma\sqrt{r - 1 - \gamma^2/4}$$

the remaining $n(r - 2)$ eigenvalues of $S^+(U^2)$ take the value 2. However, the spectrum of $S^+(U^3)$ is not determined by the parameters of the SRG G. As an example, consider the pair of SRG with parameters $(16, 6, 2, 2)$ shown in Figure 3. We have:

$$\mathrm{sp}(A_G) = \mathrm{sp}(A_H) = \{[-2]^9, [2]^6, [6]\}.$$

and

$$\mathrm{sp}(L_G) = \mathrm{sp}(L_H) = \{[0]^1, [4]^6, [8]^9\}.$$

However,

$$\mathrm{sp}(S^+(U_G^3)) = \{[-7 - 2i]^{15}, [-7 + 2i]^{15}, [-5]^9, [-1]^{18}, [1]^{27}, [3]^5, [5]^6, [45]^1\}$$

and

$$\mathrm{sp}(S^+(U_H^3))) = \{[-7 - 2i]^{15}, [-7 + 2i]^{15}, [-5]^6, [-1]^{24}, [1]^{21}, [3]^2, [5]^9, [45]^1\}.$$

That is, we are able to distinguish the pair of SRG using the spectra of the matrices $S^+(U^3)$. Consequently, we propose the use of the spectrum of the matrix representation $S^+(U^3)$ for a graph G for distinguishing it from other graphs that are cospectral with respect to standard matrix representations.

5.2   Constructing $S^+(U^3)$

For a SRG G with parameters (n, r, s, t) and adjacency matrix A, the matrix representation can be constructed directly. $S^+(U_G^3)_{(i,j),(k,l)} = 1$ if and only if one of the following conditions holds:

1. $i = m$, $j \neq l$ and

$$t + (s - t) A_{j,l} - r + \frac{r^2}{4} > 0$$

(which always holds if $i = m$, $j \neq l$ and $r > 4$);
2. $i = l$, $m \neq j$ and $A_{j,m} < \frac{2s}{r}$;
3. $i = l$ and $m = j$;
4. $i \neq l$, $m = j$ and $A_{i,l} < \frac{2s}{r}$;
5. $i \neq l$, $i \neq m$, $j \neq l$, $j \neq m$ and

$$\frac{2}{r}[t + (s - t)A_{j,l}] > A_{i,l} + A_{j,m}.$$

Thus the matrix $S + (U_G^3)$ for a SRG G can be constructed directly, without the need to first construct U and carry out matrix multiplication. The spectrum of $S + (U_G^3)$ can then be used to represent the graph G, this can be calculated in time $O(n^3 r^3)$.

6   Experiments

In this section we experiment with the method outlined earlier in the paper. We commence by considering the case of strongly regular graphs, and then illustrate the utility of the method on graphs extracted from image data.

6.1   Strongly Regular Graphs

As noted earlier, traditional spectral methods for various graph matching tasks rely on the use of the spectrum of either the adjacency or Laplacian matrices. However, these methods fail when confronted with of non-isomorphic graphs which share the same adjacency and Laplacian spectra. Strongly regular graphs furnish examples of such graphs. We have tested the effectiveness of the spectrum of $S^+(U^3)$ for distinguishing co-parametric non-isomorphic SRG and have found that it works for all graphs tested so far. A summary of the graphs studied can be found in Table 1. In addition, this method was also able to distinguish between pairs of co-immanantal trees as constructed in [17].

To characterise the results we computed a vector, $\vec{e}$, of the ordered eigenvalues of $S^+(U_G^3)$, for every graph G in a number of the co-parametric families. The matrix with entries $D_{GH} = |\vec{e}_G - \vec{e}_H|$, for all G and H in the family was then constructed. We found that $D_{GH} = 0$ only when $G = H$, thus distinguishing all non-isomorphic graphs. As an example, the matrix for the SRG with parameters $(26, 10, 3, 4)$ is

$$
D = \begin{pmatrix}
0 & 4.13 & 42.88 & 26.64 & 22.90 & 26.21 & 45.13 & 26.11 & 23.54 & 23.36 \\
4.13 & 0 & 45.49 & 25.43 & 22.30 & 24.60 & 51.95 & 29.34 & 24.85 & 23.79 \\
42.88 & 45.49 & 0 & 53.42 & 55.58 & 58.84 & 15.50 & 96.27 & 53.68 & 57.49 \\
26.64 & 25.43 & 53.42 & 0 & 3.08 & 3.86 & 53.24 & 75.14 & 3.63 & 3.06 \\
22.90 & 22.30 & 55.58 & 3.08 & 0 & 2.46 & 53.46 & 68.05 & 2.49 & 1.17 \\
26.21 & 24.60 & 58.84 & 3.860 & 2.46 & 0 & 57.21 & 71.88 & 3.38 & 2.53 \\
45.13 & 51.95 & 15.50 & 53.24 & 53.46 & 57.21 & 0 & 94.33 & 51.90 & 55.51 \\
26.11 & 29.34 & 96.27 & 75.14 & 68.05 & 71.88 & 94.33 & 0 & 71.37 & 68.36 \\
23.54 & 24.85 & 53.68 & 3.63 & 2.49 & 3.38 & 51.90 & 71.37 & 0 & 1.89 \\
23.36 & 23.79 & 57.49 & 3.06 & 1.17 & 2.53 & 55.51 & 68.36 & 1.89 & 0
\end{pmatrix}.
$$

We visualise the results of performing spectral decomposition by applying multidimensional scaling to the distance matrix. This allows us to embed the graphs on a plane using the leading two eigenvectors of the distance matrix. Cospectral pairs of graphs will appear as co-incident points under the embedding, and sets of graphs which are not cospectral will be distributed across the plane. Fig. 2 shows two embeddings of the four sets of co-parametric SRG; the first using distances calculated from the spectrum of their adjacency matrix and the second using distances from the spectra of $S^+(U^3)$. Although the embedding using the spectrum of the adjacency matrix separates the individual sets, all graphs with the same set of parameters are mapped to the same point. The embedding using the spectra of $S + (U^3)$, on the other hand, also distinguishes all the graphs within each set.

Table 1. The SRG used to test the algorithm. These SRG were obtained from [26].

(n, k, λ, μ)	Number of co-parametric SRG
$(16, 6, 2, 2)$	2
$(16, 9, 4, 6)$	2
$(25, 12, 5, 6)$	15
$(26, 10, 3, 4)$	10
$(28, 12, 6, 4)$	4
$(29, 14, 6, 7)$	41
$(35, 18, 9, 9)$	227
$(36, 14, 4, 6)$	180
$(36, 15, 6, 6)$	32, 548
$(40, 12, 2, 4)$	28
$(45, 12, 3, 3)$	78
$(64, 18, 2, 6)$	167

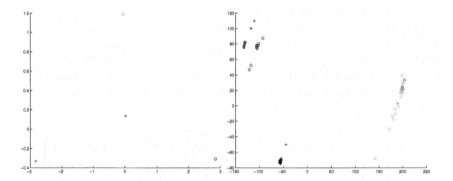

Fig. 2. MDS embeddings of SRG with distances calculated using the spectra of A on the left and the spectra of $S^+(U^3)$ on the right. The sets are those with parameters $(25, 12, 5, 6)$, red $*$; $(26, 10, 3, 4)$, blue $\circ$; $(29, 14, 6, 7)$, black $+$; and $(40, 12, 2, 4)$, green $\square$.

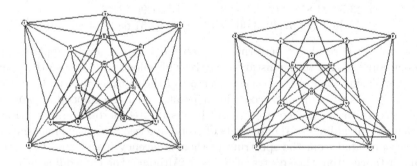

Fig. 3. Two non-isomorphic SGR (G left, H right) with the parameter set $(16, 6, 2, 2)$ (The graphs were drawn using Bill Kocay's "Graphs and Groups" program available at http://bkocay.cs.umanitoba.ca/G&G/G&G.html)

6.2   Inexact Graph Matching

We have seen that the spectra of $S^+(U^3)$ are able to distinguish graphs that are cospectral with respect to standard matrix representations. In this subsection we present the results of tests performed using the spectra of $S^+(U^3)$ for inexact graph matching tasks. The tests were carried out on Delaunay graphs derived from images in the COIL database. Some sample images from the database are shown in Fig. 4. The embeddings obtained by applying MDS to the distance-matrices of the spectra are shown in Fig. 5. The results are are similar to those obtained using the spectrum of the Laplacian matrix. However, carrying out embeddings using the spectra of $S^+(U^3)$ has the advantage that the method is robust when used with graphs that were previously cospectral.

Fig. 4. The objects from the COIL database (http://www1.cs.columbia.edu/CAVE/ research/softlib/coil-100.html) embedded using PCA on the spectrum of $S^+(U^3)$ of the Delauny graphs

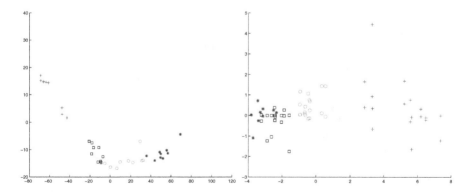

Fig. 5. The objects from the COIL database embedded using PCA on the spectrum of $S^+(U^3)$ of the Delauny graphs on the left and using PCA on the spectrum of the Laplacian on the right. White cup +, Earthenware cup ○, cat toy *, wooden shape □ and car ◇.

7   Conclusions

In this paper we have shown how a matrix representation based on the idea of
a coined quantum walk can be used to lift the cospectrality of strongly regular
graphs. We have reviewed how unitary matrices inducing coined quantum walks
are constructed and have shown how their spectra are related to the spectra of the
transition matrix of the classical random walk. We have looked at the positive
support of powers of such unitary matrices and shown that the spectrum of
$S^+(U_G^3)$ for a SRG, G, is not determined by the parameters of G. Consequently
we proposed the use of the spectra of $S^+(U_G^3)$ to distinguish otherwise cospectral
graphs. We have tested this method extensively on SRG and found it to be
successful in every case.

In addition, we have examined the efficacy of using its spectra for inexact
graph matching tasks. Having found it to perform well, we propose its use in
order to make standard spectral methods robust when dealing with graphs that
were previously cospectral.

References

1. D. Aharonov, A. Ambainis, J. Kempe, and U. Vazirani. Quantum walks on graphs.
   In *Proc. 33th STOC*, pages 50–59, New York, NY, 2001. ACM.
2. D. Aldous and J. Fill. Reversible markov chains and random walks on graphs.,
   2005.
3. A. Ambainis. Quantum walks and their algorithmic applications. *International
   Journal of Quantum Information*, 1:507–518, 2003.
4. A. Ambainis. Quantum walk algorithm for element distinctness. In *Proc. of 45th
   Annual IEEE Symposium on Foundations of Computer Science (FOCS'04)*, 2004.
5. A. Ambainis, E. Bach, A. Nayak, A. Vishwanath, and J. Watrous. One-dimensional
   quantum walks. In *Proc. 33th STOC*, pages 60–69, New York, NY, 2001. ACM.
6. S.L. Braunstein. Quantum teleportation without irreversible detection. *Physical
   Review A*, pages 1900–1903, 1996.
7. Sergey Brin and Lawrence Page. The anatomy of a large-scale hypertextual Web
   search engine. *Computer Networks and ISDN Systems*, 30(1–7):107–117, 1998.
8. P. J. Cameron. *Topics in Algebraic Graph Theory*, chapter Strongly regular graphs,
   pages 203–221. Cambridge University Press, 2004.
9. A. Childs, E. Farhi, and S. Gutmann. An example of the difference between quantum and classical random walks. *Quantum Information Processing*, 1:35, 2002.
10. J. Cirac, P. Zoller, H. J. Kimble, and H. Mabuchi. Quantum state transfer and
    entanglement distribution among distant nodes in a quantum network. *Phys. Rev.
    Lett.*, 78:3221–3224, 1997.
11. Marco Gori, Marco Maggini, and Lorenzo Sarti. Graph matching using random
    walks. In *IEEE 17th International Conference on Pattern Recognition*, August
    2004.
12. L. Grover. A fast quantum mechanical algorithm for database search. In *Proc.
    28th Annual ACM Symposium on the Theory of Computation*, pages 212–219, New
    York, NY, 1996. ACM Press, New York.
13. J. Kempe. Quantum random walks – an introductory overview. *Contemporary
    Physics*, 44(4):307–327, 2003.

14. J. Kempe. Quantum random walks hit exponentially faster. In *Proc. of 7th Intern. Workshop on Randomization and Approximation Techniques in Comp. Sc. (RANDOM'03)*, pages 354–69, 2003.

15. P. Kwiat, J. R. Mitchell, P. D. D. Schwindt, and A. G. White.

16. László Lovász. *Combinatorics, Paul Erdös is Eighty*, volume 2, chapter Random Walks on Graphs: A Survey, pages 353–398. János Bolyai Mathematical Society, Budapest, 1996.

17. Russell Merris. Almost all trees are coimmanantal. *Linear Algebra and its Applications*, 150:61–66, 1991.

18. A. Nayak and A. Vishwanath. Quantum walk on a line, 2000. DIMACS Technical Report 2000-43.

19. Michael A. Nielson and Issac L. Chuang. *Quantum Computing and Quantum Information*. Cambridge University Press, Cambridge, 2000.

20. Antonio Robles-Kelly and Edwin R. Hancock. Edit distance from graph spectra. In *Proc. of the IEEE International Conference on Computer Vision*, pages 234–241, 2003.

21. Antonio Robles-Kelly and Edwin R. Hancock. String edit distance, random walks and graph matching. *International Journal of Pattern Recognition and Artificial Intelligence*, 18(3):315–327, 2004.

22. Allen J. Schwenk. Almost all trees are cospectral. In Frank Harary, editor, *New Directions in the Theory of Graphs*, pages 275–307. Academic Press, 1973.

23. Simone Severini. On the digraph of a unitary matrix. *SIAM Journal on Matrix Analysis and Applications*, 25(1):295–300, 2003.

24. N. Shenvi, J. Kempe, and K. B. Whaley. A quantum random walk search algorithm. *Phys. Rev. A*, 67(5), 2003.

25. Alistair Sinclair. *Algorithms for random generation and counting: a Markov chain approach*. Birkhauser Verlag, Boston, 1993.

26. E. Spence. *Strongly Regular Graphs*. www.maths.gla.ac.uk/ es/srgraphs.htm, 2004.

Part III

Variational Approaches

Geodesic Image Matching: A Wavelet Based Energy Minimization Scheme

Laurent Garcin[1] and Laurent Younes[2]

[1] Laboratoire MATIS, Institut Géographique National
[2] Center for Imaging Science,
Department of Appplied Mathematics and Statistics, Johns Hopkins University

Abstract. In this paper, we first detail the geodesic matching of images which consists in minimizing an energy resulting from a Riemannian metric on a manifold of images, which itself comes from the projection of a Riemannian metric on a deformation group onto the image manifold. We will then present an energy minimization technique based on a wavelet analysis of the deformation and finally some applications with face images and 3D medical data.

1 Introduction

This paper develops a new multiscale image matching technique, to implement image metamorphoses [15]. The method demonstrates significant improvements over previously designed algorithms, offering more numerical stability, and the ability of estimating very large deformations in a completely unsupervised framework.

Metamorphoses provide a generic approach to design a metric distance on Riemannian manifolds which are acted upon by a Lie group. The interested reader may refer to [15] for a theoretical presentation, and we here restrict to the particular context of 2D or 3D images and the action of diffeomorphisms. The point of view is to define image evolutions which combine diffeomorphic deformations and gray level variation, and minimize a time integrated cost function to obtain an optimal evolution, which, in the case of images, provides outputs similar to image morphings made popular in computer graphics. However, unlike standard image morphing methods, this approach works free of any user interaction (like the definition of landmarks or curve correspondences).

The graphical aspect is, however, not our primal interest. The advantage of metamorphic image matching is that it allows to estimate optimal point to point correspondences from grey-level information, and provides a quantitative measure of deformation which is a metric distance between the compared shapes. Moreover, because it estimates geodesics, it provides, as decribed below, a template-based coordinate system which is a one-to-one signature of the deformed image relative to the template.

We introduce some notation: d-dimensional images are defined on an open set $\Omega \subset \mathbb{R}^d$, and we denote $\mathcal{I}$ the set of square integrable images on Ω. A diffeomorphism of Ω is a continuously differentiable one-to-one correspondence g from Ω onto Ω, which also has a C^1 inverse. The set of all diffeomorphisms of Ω forms a group which is denoted $Diff(\Omega)$.

A. Rangarajan et al. (Eds.): EMMCVPR 2005, LNCS 3757, pp. 349–364, 2005.

An interesting class of diffeomorphisms are those which can be expressed as flows of ordinary differential equations (ODEs), as follows. Let $(t, x) \mapsto \mathbf{v}_t(x)$ be a time-dependent vector field on Ω: it is defined for t in $[0, 1]$ and $x \in \Omega$ and takes values in $\mathbb{R}^d$. The associated ODE is $\dot{y} = \mathbf{v}_t(y)$ where the dot refers to time derivative, and the flow associated to this equation is $\mathbf{g}_t : x \mapsto y_t$ where y_t is the value at time t of the solution of the ODE with initial condition $y_0 = x$. Existence and uniqueness of the flow for any initial condition in Ω and over all times come from regularity assumptions of the *velocity field* $\mathbf{v}_t$, namely that $\mathbf{v}_t$ is Lipschitz in its x variable, uniformly with respect to the t variable. Also, $\mathbf{g}_t$ is at all times a diffeomorphim of Ω, under adequate boundary conditions on $\mathbf{v}_t$ (e.g. that it vanishes, or remains tangent, on $\partial\Omega$).

The diffeomorphisms that we consider belong to this class, under the additional restriction that $\mathbf{v}_t$ belongs, at all times, to a specified Hilbert space, denoted $\mathfrak{G}$, with $\sup_t \|\mathbf{v}_t\|_{\mathfrak{G}} < \infty$. If $\mathfrak{G}$ is assumed to be continuously embedded in the space of C^1-functions on Ω (with its ususal norm), the resulting set of diffeomorphisms forms a subgroup G of $\mathit{Diff}(\Omega)$, which is entirely specified by the Hilbert space $\mathfrak{G}$. This is the "large deformation" setting used in [4, 11, 10, 12, 15], for example.

If I_0 is an image on Ω, its deformation under the action of a diffeomorphism g is $g.I_0 = I_0 \circ g^{-1}$. If $\mathbf{g}_t$ is the flow associated to $\dot{y} = \mathbf{v}_t(y)$, and $\mathbf{I}_t = \mathbf{g}_t.I_0$, the following advection equation holds

$$\frac{d\mathbf{I}_t}{dt} + \nabla\mathbf{I}_t.\mathbf{v}_t = 0.$$

The theory of metamorphoses in this context introduces a right-hand term to the conservation equation, and considers the evolution

$$\frac{d\mathbf{I}_t}{dt} + \nabla\mathbf{I}_t.\mathbf{v}_t = \sigma^2\mathbf{Z}_t.$$

where $\mathbf{Z}_t$ is the residual image variation and σ^2 an error parameter. This is an evolution equation for the image, which is controlled by the velocity fields $\mathbf{v}_t$ and scalar fields $\mathbf{Z}_t$. Our goal is to adjust these controls in order to evolve an image $I_0 = I_{temp}$ (template) into $I_1 = I_{targ}$ (target) with a minimal cost. In this paper, the cost is defined by

$$U = \int_0^1 \|\mathbf{v}_t\|_{\mathfrak{G}}^2 dt + \sigma^2 \int_0^1 \|\mathbf{Z}_t\|_{L^2}^2 dt$$

$$= \int_0^1 \|\mathbf{v}_t\|_{\mathfrak{G}}^2 dt + \frac{1}{\sigma^2} \int_0^1 \|\frac{d\mathbf{I}_t}{dt} + \nabla\mathbf{I}_t.\mathbf{v}_t\|_{L^2}^2 dt \qquad (1)$$

This corresponds to the computation of a geodesic for some Riemannian metric in the image space (specifically, the metric is $\|j\|_I^2 = \inf\{|v|_{\mathfrak{G}}^2 + \sigma^2|Z|^2 : Z = j + \nabla I.v\}$). Because of this, the Euler-Lagrange equations for the optimal $(\mathbf{v}, \mathbf{Z})$ also are evolution equations which can be solved from the knowledge of initial conditions I_{temp} and Z_0. Assuming that the template is fixed, the initial Z_0 characterizes the target I_{targ} (it characterizes in fact the optimal evolution from I_{temp} to I_{targ}). As a consequence, this is a template-centered signature of the target.

Our main contributions to this setting are: (i) the design of a suitable Hilbert space $\mathfrak{G}$ based on a wavelet representation of the vector fields; (ii) the description of a stable and efficient numerical procedure to minimize U and compute the initial signature Z_0.

Wavelet methods have already been applied for the estimation of optical flows or deformations, for example in [2, 1], but is never has been combined with the present approach based on the estimation of a velocity *path*. Doing so, as will be shown in section 4, provides strong improvements to both methods when used separately.

The paper is organized as follows: first we introduce the wavelet model of the deformation path $\mathbf{v}$ and relations between the regularization norm $|.|_\mathfrak{G}$ and the Lipschitz regularity of $\mathbf{v}$ with respect the space variable. Then we will detail our energy minimization algorithm which takes advantage of the multiresolution decomposition of the velocity field $\mathbf{v}$. Eventually, we will show some results on both $2D$ (face images) and 3D (medical images) data.

2   Wavelet Based Deformation

The Hilbert space $\mathfrak{G}$ and the associated norm must be selected to ensure enough smoothness for the velocity field $\mathbf{v}_t$ with respect to the space variable. In this paper, we use a norm based on wavelet decomposition of each component of the velocity field.

The first motivation is the fact that this will allow us to easily implement a multiscale minimization procedure. Such an approach has often been shown to improve the efficiency of the method, as well as its accuracy (in avoiding local minima).

Let us review the notation related to the wavelet decomposition in d dimensions. Let ψ and ϕ are respectively the mother wavelet function and the mother scaling function in a 1D wavelet analysis (we refer to [6, 7, 3] for a general description of wavelet theory). The associated d dimensional wavelet basis is

$$\psi_{sk}^n(x) = 2^{ds} \prod_{i=1}^d \left(n_i \psi(2^s x_i - k_i) + (1 - n_i)\phi(2^s x_i - k_i) \right).$$

Here, $s \in \mathbb{Z}$ is the resolution, and $k = (k_1, \ldots, k_d) \in \mathbb{Z}^d$ is the position in space.. Finally, $n \in \{0, 1\}^d - \{\mathbf{0}_d\}$ is the wavelet type (there are $2^d - 1$ types in d dimensions).

The family (ψ_{sk}^n) form an orthonormal basis of $L^2(\mathbb{R}^d)$. If one needs an initial coarse resolution, this family can be truncated to $s \geq s_0 \in \mathbb{Z}$ and combined with the family $\phi_{s_0 k}, k \in \mathbb{Z}^d$, with

$$\phi_{sk}(x) = 2^{ds} \prod_{i=1}^d \phi(2^s x_i - k_i).$$

We will use this last basis, with the convention $s_0 = 0$ to simplify notation. The wavelet analysis of the velocity field $\mathbf{v}_t$ is:

$$\mathbf{v}_t = \sum_k \mathbf{v}_{s_0 k}(t)\phi_{s_0 k} + \sum_{s,k,n} \mathbf{v}_{sk}^n(t)\psi_{sk}^n$$

where $\mathbf{v}_{sk}^n(t) \in \mathbb{R}^d$, defined by $\mathbf{v}_{sk}^n(t) = (\langle \mathbf{v}_1(t), \psi_{sk}^n \rangle, \ldots, \langle \mathbf{v}_d(t), \psi_{sk}^n \rangle)$.

We define a (uniform in scale) operator R on L^2 by

$$Rv = \kappa_{s_0} \sum_k v_{s_0 k}(t)\phi_{s_0 k} + \sum_{s,k,n} \kappa_s^n v_{sk}^n \psi_{sk}^n.$$

This defines in turn our Hilbert space by $\mathfrak{G} = \{v \in L^2(\Omega) | Rv \in L^2(\Omega)\}$, and $\|v\|_{\mathfrak{G}} = \|Rv\|_{L^2}$. Therefore, $v \in \mathfrak{G}$ if and only if

$$\sum_{s,k,n} \kappa_s^{n\,2} |v_{sk}^n|^2 < \infty.$$

(since, for $v \in L^2$, $\sum_k |v_{s_0k}(t)|^2 < \|v\|_{L^2}^2$, the first part of the decomposition is not needed here). We need enough smoothness for the elements of $\mathfrak{G}$, which are ensured by suitably selecting the eigenvalues of R (i.e. the κ_s^n's). The guidelines are provided in the next section.

2.1 Link Between Smoothness and Eigenvalues

Since we use a wavelet decomposition of the velocity field $\mathbf{v}$, it seems natural to relate the smoothness of the field $\mathbf{v}$ to its Lipschitz regularity with respect to the space variable: indeed, there exists a relationship between the Lipschitz regularity of a mapping and the decay of its wavelet coefficients (cf. Thm. 1). We will enforce the decay of the wavelet coefficients of $\mathbf{v}$ by choosing appropriate eigenvalues for the operator R (cf. Prop. 1,2).

Definition 1. *A mapping is α-Lipschitz with $\alpha = n + r$ ($n \in \mathbb{N}, 0 \leq r < 1$) iff there exists a constant C and a polynomial P of degree n such that*

$$\forall x, y, |f(x) - P(y)| < C|x - y|^\alpha$$

Then we can give the following theorem [5, 9, 8].

Theorem 1. *Let ψ_{sk}^n a d-dimensional wavelet basis with N vanishing moments. A mapping $f = \sum f_{sk}^n \psi_{sk}^n$, where $f_{sk}^n = \langle f, \psi_{sk}^n \rangle$, is α-Lipschitz with $\alpha \leq N$ iff there exists a constant C such that:*

$$|f_{sk}^n| < C2^{-ds(\alpha + \frac{1}{2})} \tag{2}$$

The two following propositions give a connection between the eigenvalues of the operator R and the smoothness of the elements of $\mathcal{G}$.

Proposition 1. *If the eigenvalues κ_s of the operator R are $\mathcal{O}(2^{ds\beta})$, then every compactly supported and α-Lipschitz mapping v for $\alpha > \beta$, belongs to the Hilbert space $\mathcal{G}$ defined by the norm $\|R.\|_{L^2}$.*

Proposition 2. *If the eigenvalues κ_s of the operator R are $\mathcal{O}(2^{ds\beta})$, then each element v of $\mathcal{G}$ is α-Lipschitz for $\alpha < \beta - \frac{1}{2}$.*

These propositions are proved in appendix.

From now on, we assume that the wavelet basis has a sufficient number of vanishing moments and that the mother wavelet is compactly supported (for instance, Daubechies's wavelets fulfil these conditions [3]) so that we are able to control the smoothness of the deformation through the operator R's eigenvalues.

3   Energy Minimization

3.1   Algorithm

The wavelet based energy allows us to compute the optimal deformation at different scales. Indeed, it suffices to project the velocity field onto a part of the wavelet basis: we only take into account the coefficients $\mathbf{v}_{sk}^n$ for $s \leq S$ where S stands for the desired scale. The energy minimization scheme is a coarse to fine strategy which consists in minimizing the energy at a given scale and then using the minimization result as the starting point of the energy minimization at a finer scale (cf. Alg. 1). At the difference of most multigrid methods, this has the advantage of always minimizing the same function, but simply adding more degrees of freedom at each stage. This avoids intricate subdiscretization issues which occur when changing scales in multigrid methods.

Algorithm 1. Multi resolution matching of two images I_0 and I_1

Initialize velocity path: $\forall t, \mathbf{v}(t) = 0$
Initialize image path: $\mathbf{I}(t) = (1 - t)I_0 + tI_1$
Initialize resolution: $S = 0$
repeat
   repeat
      Gradient descent w.r.t. deformation $\Rightarrow$ computing $\mathbf{v}_{sk}^n$ for $s \leq S$
      Gradient descent w.r.t. image
   until $\Delta U < \epsilon$
   $S \leftarrow S + 1$
until $S > S_{max}$

3.2   Discretization

We first describe both the time and space discretization schemes for (1). The gradient descent will then be based on the true gradient of the energy, so that the discretization step is essential for the accuracy of the method.

We start with time discretization, over T time steps. We therefore introduce a sequence $\mathbf{v}_0, \ldots, \mathbf{v}_{T-1}$ of vector fields on Ω, and $\mathbf{I}_0, \ldots, \mathbf{I}_T$ of images, with $\mathbf{I}_0 = I_{temp}$ and $\mathbf{I}_T = I_{targ}$. The difficulty comes from the discretization of the advection term $d\mathbf{I}/dt + \nabla \mathbf{I}_t.\mathbf{v}_t$. A simple discretization with finite differences leads to numerical unstabilities. A common way of addressing this problem is to let the partial derivatives of I (in space) depend on the sign of v ("upwind" scheme described in [13, 14]), which would be appropriate if we were to solve the initial value problem associated to this equation. Besides the fact that this creates a very complicated nonlinear term in the energy, this does not completely remove unstabilities. Our choice here is to use an implicit form of this total derivative, and approximate it by $\mathbf{I}(t + 1, x + \mathbf{v}(t, x)) - \mathbf{I}(t, x)$. This choice is legitimate since we have:

$$\lim_{\epsilon \to 0} \frac{\mathbf{I}(t + \epsilon, x + \epsilon \mathbf{v}(t, x)) - \mathbf{J}(t, x)}{\epsilon} = \frac{\partial \mathbf{I}}{\partial t}(t, x) + \frac{\partial \mathbf{I}}{\partial x}(t, x).\mathbf{v}(t, x)$$

This term is unfortunately nonlinear in $\mathbf{v}$, which will complicate the implementation, but this guarantees stable numerical results.

Given this, the time-discretized energy is

$$U(\mathbf{I}, \mathbf{v}) = \sum_{t=0}^{T-1} \|\mathbf{v}_t\|_{\mathcal{G}}^2 + \lambda \sum_{t=0}^{T-1} \int_{\Omega} |\mathbf{I}_{t+1}(x + \mathbf{v}_t(x)) - \mathbf{I}_t(x)|^2 \, dx$$

Now consider the space discretization, for which we consider a rectangular grid, and take $\Omega = \mathbb{R}^d$ to simplify (we will see later how to formally extend the images to this infinite domain). The discretized $\mathbf{I}$ and $\mathbf{v}$ are assumed to be defined on $\mathbb{Z}^d$, taking values respectively in $\mathbb{R}$ and $\mathbb{R}^d$. Since $x + \mathbf{v}_t(x)$ does not take integer values, we introduce a linear interpolation operator $\mathfrak{I}$. Also, $\|\mathbf{v}_t\|_{\mathfrak{G}}^2$ is defined using the same formula as before, using the discrete wavelet transform (DWT) of $\mathbf{v}_t$.

$$U(\mathbf{I}, \mathbf{w}) = \sum_{t=0}^{T-1} \left[\|\mathbf{v}_t\|_{\mathfrak{G}}^2 + \lambda |\mathfrak{I}(\mathbf{I}_{t+1})(x + \mathbf{v}_t(x)) - \mathbf{I}_t(x)|^2 \right] \qquad (3)$$

Denoting $\|z\|_2^2 = \sum_x z(x)^2$ for a discrete function z, this is also

$$U(\mathbf{I}, \mathbf{w}) = \sum_{t=0}^{T-1} \|\mathbf{v}_t\|_{\mathfrak{G}}^2 + \lambda \|\mathfrak{I}(\mathbf{I}_{t+1})(. + \mathbf{v}_t(.)) - \mathbf{I}_t\|_2^2 \qquad (4)$$

In practice, we use a bilinear interpolation for $\mathfrak{I}$:

$$\mathfrak{I}(I)(x) = \sum_{\epsilon \in \{0,1\}^d} c_\epsilon(x) I(\lfloor x_1 \rfloor + \epsilon_1, \ldots, \lfloor x_d \rfloor + \epsilon_d)$$

$\lfloor z \rfloor$ being the integer part of the real z and $\{z\} = z - \lfloor z \rfloor$ its fractional part. The coefficient $c_\epsilon(x)$ is defined as:

$$c_\epsilon(x) = \prod_{i=1}^d (\epsilon_i + (1 - 2\epsilon_i)\{x_i\}).$$

Computing the Image Gradient. Since (3) is now completely specified in the discrete variables, we are in position to compute its exact gradient.

For a mapping $v : \mathbb{Z}^d \to \mathbb{R}^d$, we note $\aleph_v$ the linear operator which associates to a discrete image $I : \mathbb{Z}^d \to \mathbb{R}$ its interpolation on the grid $G_v = \{x + v(x) | x \in \mathbb{Z}^d\}$ that is to say:

$$(\aleph_v I)(x) = (\mathfrak{I}I)(x + v(x)).$$

With this notation, the discretized energy is:

$$U(\mathbf{I}, \mathbf{v}) = \sum_{t=0}^{T-1} \left[\|\mathbf{v}(t)\|_{\mathfrak{G}}^2 + \lambda \|\aleph_{\mathbf{v}(t)} \mathbf{I}(t+1) - \mathbf{I}(t)\|^2 \right]$$

and the energy gradient w.r.t. $\mathbf{I}(t)$ is:

$$\frac{1}{2\lambda}\nabla_{\mathbf{I}(t)}U = \mathbf{I}(t) - \aleph_{\mathbf{v}(t)}\mathbf{I}(t+1) + \aleph_{\mathbf{v}(t-1)}^{T}(\aleph_{\mathbf{v}(t-1)}\mathbf{I}(t) - \mathbf{I}(t-1)) \qquad (5)$$

We now derive an explicit expression for the operator $\aleph_v^T$ in the case of bilinear interpolation. Let $x_0 \in \mathbb{Z}^d$ and I_0 be an image such that for all $x \in \mathbb{Z}^d$, $I(x) = \delta(x, x_0)$ where δ is the Kronecker symbol. For $k \in \mathbb{Z}^d$, denote $P_k = \{x \in \mathbb{R}^d | \forall\, 1 \le i \le d, k_i \le x_i < k_i + 1\}$. For all discrete image I:

$$(\aleph_v I_0, I) = \sum_{\epsilon \in \{0,1\}^d} \sum_{x \in \mathbb{Z}^d | x' \in P_{x_0^\epsilon}} \prod_{i=1}^{d}(\epsilon_i + (1 - 2\epsilon_i)r(x_i'))I(x, y)$$

with $x' = x + v(x)$ and $x_0^\epsilon = x_0 + \epsilon - \mathbf{1}_d$.

By definition of the transposition, we have $(\aleph_v I, J) = (I, \aleph_v^T J)$ for all I, J so, in the case $I = I_0$:

$$(\aleph_v I_0, I) = (I_0, \aleph_v^T I) = (\aleph_v^T I)(x_0, y_0).$$

which completely specifies the gradient with respect to the image part.

Computing the Deformation Gradient. Denote by ψ_{sk}^n the discrete wavelet filters and $\mathbf{v}_{sk}^n(t)$ the coefficients of the discrete wavelet transform of $\mathbf{v}(t)$. We can express the energy (3) according to these coefficients:

$$U(\mathbf{I}, \mathbf{v}) = \sum_{t=0}^{T-1}\sum_{s,k,n}\kappa_s^2\mathbf{v}_{sk}^n(t)^2 + \sum_{t=0}^{T-1}\int_{\Omega}|\mathbf{I}_{t+1}(x + \sum_i \mathbf{v}_{sk}^n(t)\psi_{sk}^n(x)) - \mathbf{I}_t(x)|^2 dx$$

and if we let $\mathbf{f}$ be the trajectory on $\mathbb{Z}^d$ defined by

$$\mathbf{f}_t(x) = (\mathbf{I}_{t+1}(x + \mathbf{v}_t(x)) - \mathbf{I}_t(x))\nabla\mathbf{I}_{t+1}(x + \mathbf{v}_t(x))$$

the gradient of the energy w.r.t. the coefficients $\mathbf{v}_{sk}^n(t)$ is

$$\frac{1}{2}\nabla_{\mathbf{v}_{sk}^n(t)}U = \kappa_s^2\mathbf{v}_{sk}^n(t) + \lambda\langle\mathbf{f}_t, \psi_{sk}^n\rangle \qquad (6)$$

The important fact is that $\langle\mathbf{f}(t), \psi_{sk}^n\rangle$ is a wavelet coefficient of $\mathbf{f}_t$, and therefore can be directly computed via a discrete wavelet transform. Note that, in order to compute $\mathbf{f}_t$, the expansion of $\mathbf{v}_t$ on the grid must be known, which requires running an inverse wavelet transform on the v_{sk}^n. Also, the gradient $\nabla\mathbf{I}_{t+1}$ is computed using the space derivatives of the interpolation scheme $\mathfrak{I}$.

Remark. In practice, images are not defined on all $\mathbb{Z}^d$ but on subsets of the form $\prod_{i=1}^{d}\{0, \ldots, N_i - 1\}$. We extend this image I into an image $\tilde{I}$ in the following way:

$$\tilde{I}(x) = I(\min(\max(x_1, 0), N_0 - 1), \ldots, \min(\max(x_d, 0), N_d - 1))$$

for all $x \in \mathbb{Z}^d$. In practice, it is sufficient to extend the image only on a subset of $\mathbb{Z}^d$ where the deformation is non zero. If W is the size of the discrete mother wavelet, we only need to extend I on $\prod_{i=1}^{d}\{-W, \ldots, N_i - 1 + W\}$.

4   Results

4.1   An Example of Geodesic Image Matching

First, we give an example of a minimizing path between two images in Fig. 1, where we can see both the image path $\mathbf{J}$ and the associated diffeomorphism path $\mathbf{g}$ (the discrete diffeomorphism path $\mathbf{g}$ is computed from the velocity path $\mathbf{v}$ and the relationship $\mathbf{g}_{t+1} = (Id + \mathbf{v}_t) \circ \mathbf{g}_t$ which is the time discretized analog of the ODE $d\mathbf{g}/dt = \mathbf{v}_t \circ \mathbf{g}_t$). We can see the bright patch on the shoulder expand in both the image and the deformation paths.

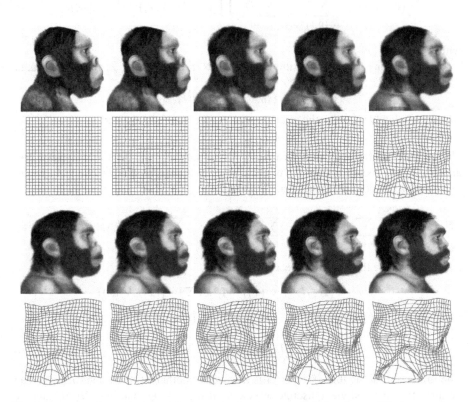

Fig. 1. Example of a geodesic path between the first image and the last image. The intermediate images were computed by the energy minimzation algorithm. The grids below the images depict the corresponding diffeomorphism at that time.

4.2   Comparison to Other Algorithms

Then we compare our algorithm Alg. 1 (we will refer to it as case LDWAVEMR in our experiments) to several other algorithms:

– large deformation without mutiresolution (case LDWAVENOMR), that is to say that the minimization is computed immediately over all deformation scales as opposed to the coarse to fine scheme of Alg. 1,

– small deformation with multiresolution (case SDWAVEMR), which consists in modeling the deformation as a displacement field as opposed to a diffeomorphism (in practice, it suffices to take only one time step in the minimization algorithm Alg. 1),
– Gaussian smoothing (case LDGAUSS), which corresponds to the case when $\mathfrak{G}$ is a reproducible kernel Hilbert space with a Gaussian kernel

We present some results for both synthetic and real data. In both cases the image used were of size 128×128. In the cases with wavelet-based smoothing (LDWAVEN-OMR, LDWAVEMR, SDWAVEMR), all scales available for the input images were used (that is s scales for images of size $2^s \times 2^s$). The wavelet was a Daubechies wavelet with 10 coefficients for the synthetic data and 20 coefficients for the real data. The eigenvalues κ_s of the operator R (see section 2) decreased as $\kappa_s = \kappa_{s_0} 2^{(s0-s)}$ for the synthetic data and $\kappa_s = \kappa_{s_0} 4^{(s0-s)}$ for the real data. In the large deformation cases (LDWAVEN-OMR, LDWAVEMR,LDGAUSS), we chose a discretization of 10 time steps. Finally, the Gaussian kernel used for Gaussian smoothing had a standard deviation of 5 pixels.

The synthetic input data were the two portions of annulus appearing at the beginning and the end of the sequences of Fig. 2, 3 and 4. We do not present the results for case SDWAVEMR, because the algorithm did not succeed into reaching a "reasonable" solution (the deformation was highly irregular due to the lack of the diffeomorphism constraint present in the other cases). We can see that in case LDWAVEMR, the initial

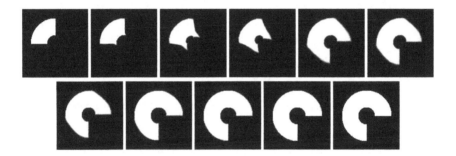

Fig. 2. Synthetic data: case LDWAVEMR

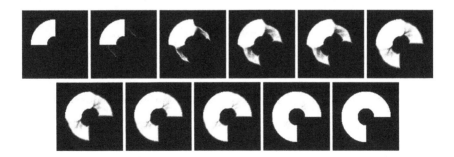

Fig. 3. Synthetic data: case LDWAVENOMR

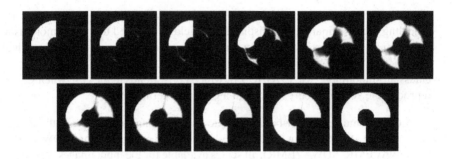

Fig. 4. Synthetic data: case LDGAUSS

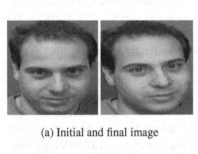

(a) Initial and final image

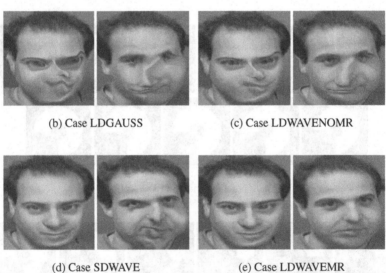

(b) Case LDGAUSS   (c) Case LDWAVENOMR

(d) Case SDWAVE   (e) Case LDWAVEMR

Fig. 5. In each pair: final image warped by the inverse deformation (to be compared with the initial image) and initial image warped by the direct deformation (to be compared with the final image)

shape evolves smoothly towards the final shape, whereas in the two other cases, we notice that two white patches appear outside of initial shape and then inflate and connect to the initial shape to form the final shape.

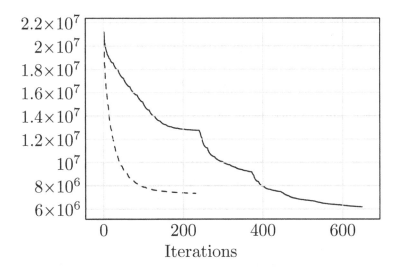

Fig. 6. Evolution of the energy for case LDWAVENOMR (dashed) and case LDWAVEMR (plain) with the input images of Fig. 5(a)

Then we tested our algorithm on face images (see Fig. 5). The deformation between the initial and final image was smaller than with the synthetic data so we managed to get results for the small deformation case SDWAVEMR. However, we can see that the deformation provided by our multiresolution algorithm is "visually" more satisfying than with the other algorithms. The registrations of the initial image onto the final image and of the final image onto the initial image are really improved by the large deformation and the multiresolution schemes.

The superiority of the multiresolution scheme depicted in Alg. 1 as compared to the straightforward energy minimization over all scales can also be seen in Fig. 6, which shows the energy evolutions in both cases for the input images of Fig. 5(a). Indeed, we notice that the final energy for the multiresolution algorithm is less than the final energy of the straightforward algorithm, which probably got stuck in a local minimum of the energy.

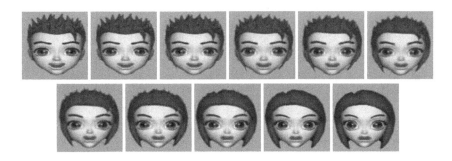

Fig. 7. Minimizing image path for vector data

4.3 Application to Vector Data

We also point the fact that our algorithm is also able to process vector data such as color images with only slight modifications. Namely, it suffices:

- to replace the single image gradient (5) by the gradients of each image channel and to perform a gradient descent on each channel,
- to replace f_t in (6) by the sum of the f_t's corresponding to each image channel.

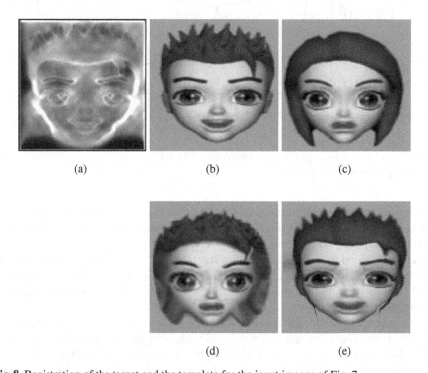

(a)   (b)   (c)

(d)   (e)

Fig. 8. Registration of the target and the template for the input images of Fig. 7.
(a) Jacobian of the estimated deformation (black: low values, white: high values). (b) Template.
(c) Target. (d) Template registered onto the target. (e) Target registered onto the template.

Fig. 9. Minimizing image path for vector data (bis)

We show an example of this kind of matching in Fig. 7 and 8. Thanks to Fig. 8(a), we can check that the main deformations occur on the outline of the face which is thinned during the process. We can also notice that our algorithm, though based on photometric information, responded well to the difference of eye color since it did not generate any unnecessary deformations in this region. Eventually, we present another result of minimizing path for more complex images in Fig. 9.

4.4   Application to Image Averaging

We present another application of our algorithm to image averaging. Indeed, the energy U defined in (1) defines a geodesic distance on the image manifold:

$$d(I_0, I_1) = \min\{\sqrt{U(I, v)} : I(0) = I_0, I(1) = I_1\}$$

so that it is possible to define an explicit average $\bar{I}$ of several images $I_1, \ldots, I_N$:

$$\bar{I} = argmin \sum_n U(I, I_n).$$

We can still use a slightly modified version of our algorithm to solve the minimization of the sum of the energies if we notice that the common extremity I of the N image paths $I \rightarrow I_n$ is free as opposed to the classical matching algorithm where the two

(a) Input images

(b) Mean image for the Eu-   (c) Mean image for the
clidean metric   Riemannian metric

Fig. 10. Computing the mean image

extremities are fixed. In Fig. 10, we show the result of the averaging of 4 face images. The mean image for the Riemannian metric corresponds to the result of our algorithm whereas the mean image for the Euclidean metric corresponds to the image $\bar{I}$ such that $\bar{I}(x) = \frac{1}{N} \sum_{n=1}^{N} I_n(x)$.

4.5 Application to 3D Medical Images

Finally, we present a 3D application of our algorithm. We compare two binary images representing hippocampi (brain structures); these images are provided by the Center for Imaging Science (Johns Hopkins University) as a part of the BIRN project. The non zero value represents the inside of the shape. We apply our matching algorithm to these two 3D images. In Fig. 11, we can see both the template and the target shapes defined as the boundaries of the respective sets of points with non zero values. We can also see in blue the deformed template set superimposed onto the target in red. The last image

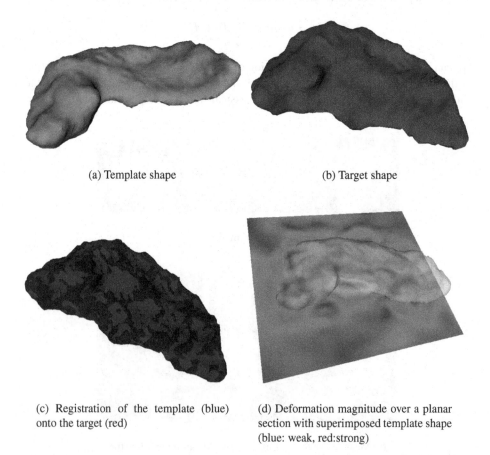

(a) Template shape

(b) Target shape

(c) Registration of the template (blue) onto the target (red)

(d) Deformation magnitude over a planar section with superimposed template shape (blue: weak, red:strong)

Fig. 11. Registration and computing of the deformation between two 3D binary images representing hippocampi

shows the intensity of the deformation over a planar section of the 3D template image. We can verify that the template hippocampus is heavily deformed in its concave part which no longer exists in the target hippocampus.

A   Proof of Proposition 1

Notation 2 *For points $a, b \in \mathbb{R}^d$, we denote by $[a, b]$ the d-dimensional interval* $\prod_{n=1}^{d} [a_n, b_n]$.

Proof. Let v be a compactly supported and α-Lipschitz mapping v with $\alpha > \beta$. Then, according to Thm. 1, there exists a constant C such that

$$|v_{sk}^n| < C2^{-ds(\alpha + \frac{1}{2})}$$

Besides, v being compactly supported, one can assume that there exist $p_0, p_1 \in \mathbb{R}^d$ such that:

$$Supp(v) \subset [p_0; p_1]$$

If we also assume that

$$Supp(\psi) \subset [q_0; q_1]$$

then

$$Supp(\psi_{sk}^n) \subset [2^{-s}(k + q_0); 2^{-s}(k + q_1)]$$

So the multi-indices $k \in \mathbb{Z}^d$ such that v_{sk}^n is non zero belong to the d-dimensional interval $[2^s p_0 + q_0, 2^s p_1 + q_1]$.

Hence, the number N_s of such indices k at resolution s is less than $\prod_{n=1}^{d}(2^s(p_1^n - p_0^n) + (q_1^n - q_0^n) + 1))$. So if we take $A = \prod_{n=1}^{d}((p_1^n - p_0^n) + (q_1^n - q_0^n) + 1))$, we have $s \geq 0$, $N_s \leq A2^{ds}$. Besides there exists a constant B such that $\kappa_s \leq B2^{ds\beta}$. So at a given resolution s:

$$a_s = \kappa_s^2 \sum_k |v_{sk}^n|^2 \leq AB^2 C2^{ds} 2^{2ds\beta} 2^{-2ds(\alpha + \frac{1}{2})}$$
$$= \mathcal{O}(2^{2ds(\beta - \alpha)})$$

The series $\sum_{s \geq 0} a_s$ converges and consequently, v belongs to $\mathcal{G}$.

B   Proof of Proposition 2

Proof. There exists a constant B such that $\kappa_s \leq B2^{ds\beta}$. Let $b_s = \sum_k |v_{sk}^n|^2$ for a given resolution s. The fact that v belongs to $\mathcal{G}$ is equivalent to:

$$\sum_{s,k,n} \kappa_s^2 |v_{sk}^n|^2 \leq B^2 \sum_s b_s 2^{2ds\beta} < \infty$$

This means that the convergence radius of the power series $\sum b_s z^s$ is at least $2^{2d\beta}$. Hence, we can write:

$$\limsup(b_s)^{\frac{1}{s}} \leq 2^{-2d\beta}$$

Consequently, for all $\alpha < \beta - \frac{1}{2}$, there exists a constant C such that:

$$\forall s, b_s \leq C2^{-2ds(\alpha+\frac{1}{2})}$$

Since $|v_{sk}^n| \leq b_s$ for all k, we get the relation (2) which ensures that v is α-Lipschitz.

References

1. C. Bernard. Fast optic flow computation with discrete wavelets. Technical Report RI365, Centre de Mathématiques Appliquées, École Polytechnique, May 1997.
2. C. P. Bernard. Discrete wavelet analysis for fast optic flow computation. *Applied and Computational Harmonic Analysis*, 11(1):32–63, July 2001.
3. I. Daubechies. *Ten lectures on wavelets*. SIAM, Philadelphia, PA, 1992.
4. P. Dupuis and U. Grenander. Variational problems on flows of diffeomorphisms for image matching, 1998.
5. S. Jaffard and P. Laurençot. *Orthonormal wavelets, analysis of operators, and applications to numerical analysis*, pages 543–601. Academic Press Professional, Inc., 1992.
6. S. Mallat. A theory for multiresolution signal decomposition: The wavelet representation. *IEEE Trans. Pat. Anal. Mach. Intell.*, 11:674–693, 1989.
7. S. Mallat. *A wavelet tour of signal processing*. Academic Press, 1998.
8. S. G. Mallat and W. L. Hwang. Singularity detection and processing with wavelets. *IEEE Transactions on Information Theory*, 38(2):617–643, 1992.
9. Y. Meyer. Wavelets and operators. In *Analysis at Urbana, Vol. I (Urbana, IL, 1986–1987)*, volume 137 of *London Mathematical Society Lecture Note Series*, pages 256–365. Cambridge University Press, Cambridge, 1989.
10. I. Miller, M and L. Younes. Group action, diffeomorphisms and matching: a general framework. *International Journal of Computer Vision*, 41:61–84, 2001.
11. M. I. Miller, S. C. Joshi, and G. E. Christensen. Large deformation fluid diffeomorphisms for landmark and image matching. In A. W. Toga, editor, *Brain Warping*, chapter 7. Academic Press, 1999.
12. M. I. Miller, A. Trouvé, and L. Younes. Geodesic shooting in computational anatomy. Technical report, Center for Imaging Science, Johns Hopkins University, 2003.
13. S. Osher and J. A. Sethian. Fronts propagating with curvature-dependent speed: Algorithms based on Hamilton-Jacobi formulations. *Journal of Computational Physics*, 79:12–49, 1988.
14. J. A. Sethian. *Fast Marching Methods and Level Set Methods: Evolving Interfaces in Computational Geometry, Fluid Mechanics, Computer Vision and Materials Sciences*. Cambridge University Press, Cambridge, 1999.
15. A. Trouvé and L. Younes. Metamorphoses through Lie group action. *Foundations of Computational Mathematics*, 2004.

Geodesic Shooting and Diffeomorphic Matching Via Textured Meshes

Stéphanie Allassonnière[1], Alain Trouvé[2], and Laurent Younes[3]

[1] LAGA, Institut Galilée, University Paris 13, France
Stephanie.Allassonniere@cmla.ens-cachan.fr
[2] CMLA, Ecole Normale Supérieure, Cachan, France
Alain.Trouve@cmla.ens-cachan.fr
[3] CIS, Johns Hopkins University, Baltimore MD
laurent.younes@jhu.edu

Abstract. We propose a new approach in the context of diffeomorphic image matching with free boundaries. A region of interest is triangulated over a template, which is considered as a grey level textured mesh. A diffeomorphic transformation is then approximated by the piecewise affine deformation driven by the displacements of the vertices of the triangles. This provides a finite dimensional, landmark-type, reduction for this dense image comparison problem. Based on an optimal control model, we analyze and compare two optimization methods formulated in terms of the initial momentum: direct optimization by gradient descent, or root-finding for the transversality equation, enhanced by a preconditioning of the Jacobian. We finally provide a series of numerical experiments on digit and face matching.

1 Introduction

The theory of deformable templates [10, 4, 3] provides a large range of applications to pattern and shape analysis and matching, with specific important achievements in object recognition and medical imaging. The large deformation diffeomorphic approach, initiated in [18, 6], has proved particularly accurate and robust in this framework. Several algorithms have been developed, ranging from landmark matching [13, 5, 1, 9, 7, 14] to images [16, 2], shape matching via measures [8] or currents [20]. These algorithms come with a strong theoretical support, regarding their well-posedness [6, 18, 19], and their properties, in terms of metric distances [23, 16], and in relation to infinite dimensional mechanics, yielding the notion of conservation of momentum and its normality [15, 21, 11]. As noticed in [21], this can also be embedded in a Hamiltonian, or optimal control, framework. We shall adopt this last point of view in the present paper.

Assume that a template and a target images are given. Assume also that a region of interest is extracted from the template, on which a triangulation is overlayed, resulting in a textured mesh. We shall develop a dense matching algorithm which computes a piecewise affine deformation between the images. This deformation is controlled by a dynamical evolution of the vertices of the

A. Rangarajan et al. (Eds.): EMMCVPR 2005, LNCS 3757, pp. 365–381, 2005.

triangulation (through an ordinary differential equation), which will end-up in a formulation closely related to diffeomorphic landmark matching [13, 5, 21]. Because of this, we will henceforth refer to the vertices of the triangulation as landmarks, although they do not need to correspond to any point of interest within the images.

From the evolution of the landmark, we will deduce an evolution of the triangulation, and build from it a piecewise affine deformation. The quality of the matching is measured by a data term based on the mean squared error between the deformed template and the target within the region of interest covered by the triangulation. The whole procedure is therefore governed by the ordinary differential equation (ODE) satisfied by the landmarks, which will be specified in term of a non-autonomous (time-dependent) vector field on the image plane. This vector field can be seen as a control for the final matching, and its cost will be defined as an integrated measure of smoothness of the vector field along time.

The problem can be handled by an optimal control (or Hamiltonian) approach, which, thanks to the maximum principle, can be parametrized by what is called the initial momentum, which evolves through a conservation equation and allows to recover the ODE and the deformation. In our context, this point of view has been introduced in [15] and used in [21] for landmark matching, using gradient descent algorithms. We will here adapt the gradient descent algorithms to our image matching framework, and analyze an alternative optimization method, also applicable to standard landmark matching, called shooting in the optimal control literature. This is a root-finding method (using Newton's algorithm), designed to solve the transversality equation associated to the problem.

The paper is organized as follows. We start with describing a generic landmark based matching problem in terms of optimal control, first as an infinite dimensional problem, and then reduce it to finite dimensions, using usual arguments of the theory of smoothing splines. We then describe our approaches for solving this problem: direct minimization by gradient descent and root-finding by Newton's method. This last method will be briefly illustrated by landmark matching examples. We will then focus on our image matching problem, introducing notation and computing the elements needed for the two algorithms. The paper will end with a presentation of some experiments with 2D images.

We first fix notation. Images are assumed to be defined on Ω, an open bounded set of $\mathbb{R}^n$ with regular boundary (piecewise C^1). We assume that a template image (denoted I_0) has been selected, and that a triangulation has been overlayed on the template, and denote $(x_1, ..., x_N)$ the vertices of the triangulation. Typically, $(x_1, ..., x_N)$ are chosen first, as landmarks, and the triangulation is deduced, using in our case Delaunay's triangulation. We denote by x_i^d the dth coordinate of the vector x_i. The landmarks will serve as control points to estimate a diffeomorphism ϕ which will provide a dense matching between I_0 and a target image I_1.

For vectors x, y, the notation $\langle x, y \rangle$ will be used for the standard dot product $x^T y$. For dot products on a Hilbert space V, the notation $\langle x, y \rangle_V$ will be used.

2   Optimal Control Problem

2.1   Context

We provide a Hamiltonian formulation of the landmark matching large deformation setting, originally introduced in [13]. The interpretation already appeared in [15], [21], and can be summarized as follows. The evolution of the landmarks is driven by a single non-autonomous ODE $dy/dt = v_t(y)$. This defines N landmark trajectories, denoted $t \mapsto q_i(t), i = 1, \ldots, N$, each satisfying the system

$$\begin{cases} \dfrac{dq_i(t)}{dt} = v_t(q_i(t)) \\ \\ q_i(0) = x_i \,. \end{cases} \tag{1}$$

Here, $(t, y) \mapsto v_t(y)$ is a time dependent velocity vector field, which serves as a control variable for our system of N landmarks.

As done in the optimal control theory for image matching, developped among others by Dupuis et al. ([6]), we introduce an energy which has to be minimized under constraints. This energy stems from a tradeoff between a deformation constraint and a data attachment term. The deformation term is equal to the integration over time (between 0 and 1) of the kinetic energy of the transformation.

The instantaneous kinetic energy is defined as the norm $\|v_t\|_V^2/2$ of the velocity field introduced in (1). The total energy is $E_k(v) = \frac{1}{2} \int_0^1 \|v_t\|_V^2 dt$. This norm is a Hilbert norm (defined on a Hilbert space V); it is designed to ensure that v_t is sufficiently smooth. For this purpose, V is assumed to be continuously embedded in $C_0^1(\Omega)$, the set of continuously differentiable functions which vanish on the boundary of Ω. Because of this, V is a so-called self-reproducing kernel Hilbert space, which implies that there exists a kernel k_V, defined on $\Omega \times \Omega$, taking values in the set of symmetric (n, n) matrices, such that: (i) for all $x \in \Omega$, and for all $\alpha \in \mathbb{R}^n$, the vector field $k_V(x)\alpha : y \mapsto k_V(x, y)\alpha$ belongs to V and (ii) $\langle k_V(x)\alpha, w \rangle_V = \langle w(x), \alpha \rangle_{\mathbb{R}^n}$, for all $w \in V$.

If a set of landmarks: $q = (q_1, \ldots, q_N)$ is given, we denote by $K(q)$ the $nN \times nN$ matrix consisting on the $n \times n$ blocks $k_V(q_i, q_j)$: $K(q) = (k_V(q_i, q_j)_{1 \leq i,j \leq N})$.

We assume that the data attachment term only depends on the final configuration of the landmarks: $q(1)$, and of other constants of the problem (in our case: the template and target images I_0 and I_1). We will denote it by $g_{I_0, I_1}(q(1))$, or simply $g(q(1))$ if there is no ambiguity on the compared images. This will be detailed in section 3 for our image comparison algorithm. However, since most of the developments can be done by only assuming that $q \mapsto g(q)$ is twice differentiable, we carry on this discussion assuming a generic data attachment term satisfying this property.

With this notation, introducing a positive weight λ, the complete energy is

$$E(v, q(1)) = \frac{1}{2} \int_0^1 \|v_t\|_V^2 dt + \lambda g(q(1)) \,. \tag{2}$$

Remark 1. *The dynamical aspect of the formulation can be compared to linear smoothing spline approaches, which will essentially remove the time variable, using a single $v \in V$, and replace (1) by $q_i(1) = q_i(0) + v(q_i(0))$, with the integral in the energy term replaced by $\|v\|_V^2$. As already demonstrated in [13, 5], our formulation ensures non-ambiguous and smoother deformation when interpolated to Ω, and is consistent with the constraint of building diffeomorphisms, which is not the case with linear splines.*

The smoothness assumptions on $(v_t, t \in [0,1])$ ensures existence and uniqueness of the solutions of the ODE, so that the landmarks $q(.)$ are defined at all times.

2.2   Reduction of Dimension

Standard arguments, similar to those used in the theory of smoothing splines, and relying on the kernel k_V of the Hilbert space V, allow to characterize the velocity field v_t by a finite dimensional time dependent system [22], [13]. In our case, this has an interesting Hamiltonian interpretation [21], which can also be derived from Pontryagin's maximum principle in optimal control [12]. The result is the existence at all times t of N vectors $p_i(t) \in \mathbb{R}^n$, such that:

$$v_t = \sum_{i=1}^{N} k_V(q_i(t))p_i(t) . \qquad (Interpolation\ Formula) \qquad (3)$$

The vector $p_i(t)$ is called the *momentum of the ith landmark at time t*. The joint evolution of the landmarks and the momentum can be written in a standard Hamiltonian form for $H(q,p) = \frac{1}{2}\langle p, K(q)p \rangle$ (see Appendix)

$$
\begin{cases}
\dfrac{dq}{dt} = \dfrac{\partial H}{\partial p}(q,p) = K(q(t))p(t) \\[2mm]
\dfrac{dp}{dt} = -\dfrac{\partial H}{\partial q}(q,p) = -\dfrac{1}{2}\nabla_{q(t)}K(p(t),p(t))
\end{cases}
\qquad (4)
$$

where $\nabla_q K(p,p)$ is defined as follows. Let $d_q K$ be the differential of $q \mapsto K(q)$: since K is a matrix, the linear map $h \mapsto d_q K.h$ is matrix valued. We define $\nabla_q K(p,p)$ to be the vector w such that, for all $h \in \mathbb{R}^n$, $\langle (d_q K.h)p, p \rangle = \langle w, h \rangle$. From the definition of K, we have $H(q(t), p(t)) = \|v_t\|_V^2/2$ and the Hamiltonian remains constant along the trajectories of (4), yielding

$$E_k(v) = \frac{1}{2}\int_0^1 \|v_t\|_V^2 dt = \frac{1}{2}\langle K(q(0))p(0), p(0) \rangle . \qquad (5)$$

Using system (4), the time evolution of the momentum and landmarks can be computed from the initial momentum and landmarks. In particular, since the initial position of the landmarks is fixed, their final position, $q(1)$, can be seen as a function of the initial momentum, $p(0)$, alone. According to this, our energy function can be seen as only depending on this initial momentum, a finite dimensional variable.

$$\mathcal{E}(p(0)) = \frac{1}{2}\langle K(q(0))p(0), p(0)\rangle + \lambda g(q(1)) \ . \tag{6}$$

Remark 2. *Because of the formula (3) we can reconstruct a global deformation by integrating the equation $dy/dt = v_t(y)$ with various initial conditions: this is the flow associated to the ODE, and provides a diffeomorphism on Ω which only depends on the initial momentum and initial landmarks, since this was the case for v_t. We will refer to it as the reconstructed diffeomorphism.*

Returning to our optimal control problem, the optimal trajectory must satisfy an **additional transversality condition** (see Appendix for a brief derivation and [8] for a more general case). This is given by

$$p(1) + \lambda\nabla_{q(1)}g = 0 \ . \tag{7}$$

Since $p(1)$ and $q(1)$ can be considered as functions of $p(0)$, this is a non-linear equation in the initial momentum.

We now analyze and describe two methods for the solution of our variational problem. The first one is to directly minimize the energy by gradient descent, with respect to the initial momentum $p(0)$. The second is to solve (7), again with respect to $p(0)$.

2.3   Algorithms

Gradient Descent. Several gradient descent algorithms which minimize the landmark-based energies with respect to the landmark trajectories have been developed in [13, 1, 5]. An algorithm working with the initial momentum has been proposed in [21], yielding the following gradient descent algorithm:

Algorithm 1. Gradient Descent on $p(0)$

`Choose an initial` $p(0)$`, and` $\delta \in \mathbb{R}_+^*$`, then iterate until convergence:`

$$p(0)^{new} = p(0)^{old} - \delta\nabla_{p(0)^{old}}\mathcal{E}$$

where $\nabla_{p(0)}\mathcal{E} = K(q(0))p(0) + \lambda\left(\frac{\partial q(1)}{\partial p(0)}\right)^T\nabla_{q(1)}g$.

Solving the transversality Equation. To solve (7), we use a variant of Newton's algorithm. The advantage of this algorithm is its convergence speed. Choosing an initial point in a neighborhood of the solution provides a quadratic convergence rate. This yields the following iterations : let $G(p(0)) = p(1) + \lambda\nabla_{q(1)}g$.

Here we have, denoting $d_q^2 g$ the Hessian matrix (second derivative) of g,

$$d_{p(0)}G = \frac{\partial p(1)}{\partial p(0)} + \lambda d_{q(1)}^2 g\frac{\partial p(1)}{\partial p(0)} \ . \tag{8}$$

Algorithm 2. Newton's Algorithm on transversality Condition
***

`Choose an initial p(0), then iterate until convergence :`

$$p(0)^{new} = p(0)^{old} - (d_{p(0)^{old}}G)^{-1}G(p(0)^{old})$$

However, Newton's method must be used with care, since its convergence is not guaranteed. It is sometimes a good idea to combine gradient descent and Newton's algorithm: use gradient descent as long as it is efficient (large variations of the energy), and switch to the second algorithm when it slows down (hopefully in a close neighborhood of a local minimum). Note however that such an approach was unnecessary in our handwritten digit and face experiments for which we could start directly with the root-finding algorithm and always achieve convergence.

There is an other issue in Newton's algorithm : to compute each iteration, we have to invert a matrix. Depending on its conditioning, the inversion could make the algorithm diverge. To avoid this issue, before the inversion, we pre-condition the matrix. The choice we made is to project the matrix on its main singular directions.The resulting vector p_r is an approximation of the real solution of (7) which converge when r increases. So that the resulting algorithm is :

Algorithm 3. Newton's Algorithm on Transversality Condition, Preconditioning
***

`Choose an initial value of p(0), then iterate until convergence`

$$p_0^{k+1} = p_0^k - V^T D_r U^T G(p_0^k) \text{ where } [U\ S\ V] = svd\left(\frac{\partial p(1)}{\partial p(0)} + d^2_{q(1)}g\frac{\partial q(1)}{\partial p(0)}\right)$$

and $D_r = \text{diag}(1/\lambda_1, \cdots, 1/\lambda_r, 0, \cdots, 0)$ where the λ_i's are the singular values of S sorted in decreasing order.

Variation of the Hamiltonian System. Both algorithms require the computation of the differential of the end-points of system (4) with respect to the initial momentum $p(0)$. This is obtained by differentiating the system, yielding a new evolution providing the required differentials.

$$\begin{cases} \frac{d}{dt}\left(\frac{\partial q(t)}{\partial p(0)}\right) = \frac{\partial K(q(t))}{\partial q(t)}\frac{\partial q(t)}{\partial p(0)} + K(q(t))\frac{\partial p(t)}{\partial p(0)} \\ \\ \frac{d}{dt}\left(\frac{\partial p(t)}{\partial p(0)}\right) = -\frac{\partial p(t)}{\partial p(0)}\frac{\partial K(q(t))}{\partial q(t)}p(t) - p(t)\frac{\partial}{\partial p(0)}\left(\frac{\partial K(q(t))}{\partial q(t)}\right)p(t) - p(t)\frac{\partial K(q(t))}{\partial q(t)}\frac{\partial p(t)}{\partial p(0)}. \end{cases} \quad (9)$$

Remark 3. *This additionnal transversality equation enables the use of Newton's algorithm which wouldn't have been so easy working only on the energy: running this algorithm to solve $\nabla_{p(0)}E = 0$ requires to compute $\frac{d^2q(1)}{dp(0)^2}$ and so to differentiate twice then solve the Hamiltonian system (4).*

2.4   A First Application : Landmark Matching

As a first application of this framework, we discuss landmark matching: in this special case, the data attachment term is equal to the sum of squared distances between the final landmarks and the target landmarks $y = (y_i)_{1 \leq i \leq N}$: $g(q(1)) = \sum_{i=1}^{N} ||q_i(1) - y_i||_{\mathbb{R}^n}^2$. In this case, the first and second derivatives of the data attachment term are easy to compute : $\nabla_{q(1)} g = 2 \sum_{i=1}^{N} q_i(1) - y_i$ and $d_{q(1),q(1)}^2 g = 2 Id_{nN}$, Id_{nN} being the identity matrix in $\mathcal{M}_{nN}(\mathbb{R})$. This yields the two following algorithms :

Gradient descent: Choose an initial $p(0)$, and a constant δ, then iterate until convergence: $p(0)^{new} = p(0)^{old} - \delta(K(q(0))p(0) + 2\lambda \left(\frac{\partial q(1)}{\partial p(0)} \right)^T (q(1) - \mathbf{y}))$

Newton's method: Choose an initial value of $p(0)$, then iterate until convergence : $p(0)^{new} = p(0)^{old} - (\frac{dp(1)}{dp(0)} + 2\lambda Id_{nN})^{-1}(p(1) + \lambda(q(1) - \mathbf{y}))$

Figure 1 shows the results of Newton's Method for 2 sets of landmarks.

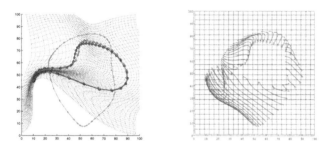

Fig. 1. Landmark matching : left : template (+), targets (∘), final landmarks (◇) and deformation of the inherent space ; right : landmarks trajectories

3   Image Matching on Piecewise Affine Triangulations

We now focus on our primary application: image matching, which goes as follows. We start with a template image which has previously been annotated with landmarks. This will define a region of interest in the template which will then be warped to the target image so that it delimitates a region with similar content.

The region of interest is provided by a triangulation associated to the landmarks, for example, Delaunay's triangulation whose advantage is among others that no triangle is included in an other. For this particular case, this yields a convex region which is partitioned into triangles (or simplices in higher dimension), as illustrated in figures 2. We now define the data attachment term $g_{I_0,I_1}(q(1))$. Denote by $T_1, \ldots, T_r$ the family of triangles forming the partition of the region

Fig. 2. Triangulation (2D), tessellation (3D), and examples of template triangulations

of interest in the template. Each triangle T_k have vertices from the initial landmarks, say $T_k = (x_{i_{k1}}, x_{i_{k2}}, x_{i_{k3}})$. The landmark evolution (4) displaces T_k into the triangle $T'_k = (q_{i_{k1}}(1), q_{i_{k2}}(1), q_{i_{k3}}(1))$ in the target. There exists a unique affine transformation ϕ_k which transforms T_k onto T'_k, and, assuming that the orientation of T'_k is consistent with the one of T_k, we define the piecewise affine homeomorphism

$$\phi : R := \bigcup_{k=1}^{r} T_k \mapsto R' := \bigcup_{k=1}^{r} T'_k \tag{10}$$

by $\phi_{|T_k} = \phi_k$. (Although this does not appear in the notation, ϕ depends on the landmark trajectories.) To keep the consistency of the triangle orientations, a sufficient condition is to choose the kernel variance according to the constant λ. (cf : Annexes) The data attachment term g is then defined by

$$g(q(1)) = \int_{R'} (I_0 \circ \phi^{-1} - I_1)^2 dy \ . \tag{11}$$

3.1   Reformulation of the Data Attachment Term

We now express g into a form which will simplify the computation of its derivatives (recall that we need the first derivative for gradient descent, and the second for Newton's method). First, introducing the triangulation, we have, with the notation above,

$$g(q(1)) = \sum_{k=1}^{r} \int_{T'_k} |I_1(y) - I_0 \circ \phi_k^{-1}(y)|^2 dy \ . \tag{12}$$

In order to lighten the notation, we only focus, from now, on the 2D case. Higher dimension is adressed with an identical argument (simply replacing triangles by simplices).

We can remove the dependence of the integration domain on ϕ by a change of variables yielding

$$g(q(1)) = \sum_{k=1}^{r} \int_{T_k} |I_1(\phi_k(x)) - I_0(x)|^2 |d_x\phi_k| dx \ . \tag{13}$$

Note that, because ϕ_k is affine, the jacobian is equal to the ratio between the surfaces of the target and template triangles, and will be easily handled in the computation of derivatives. We now make the computation explicit by introducing a local parametrization of the interior of each triangle.

Using our notation, each point in the interior of T_k is uniquely described by 2 coordinates (α, β), with $0 \leq \alpha \leq 1$, $0 \leq \beta \leq 1 - \alpha$, by $x = \psi_{0k}(\alpha, \beta)$ with $\psi_{0k}(\alpha, \beta) = \alpha(x_{i_{k2}} - x_{i_{k1}}) + \beta(x_{i_{k3}} - x_{i_{k1}}) + x_{i_{k1}}$.

Since the deformation is affine on the triangle, we have $\phi_k(x) = \psi_{1k}(\alpha, \beta)$ with $\psi_{1k}(\alpha, \beta) = \alpha(q_{i_{k2}}(1) - q_{i_{k1}}(1)) + \beta(q_{i_{k3}}(1) - q_{i_{k1}}(1)) + q_{i_{k1}}(1)$.

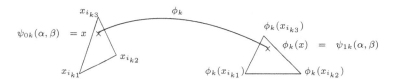

Fig. 3. Image of a point x in the template triangle T_k through the affine function ϕ_k

Using the coordinates (α, β) is in fact equivalent to making a new change of variable from the triangle T_k to the standard simplex $T_0 = \{\alpha + \beta < 1, \alpha, \beta > 0\}$ so that, denoting $A(T)$ for the area of a triangle T, and $s = (\alpha, \beta)$:

$$\int_{T_k} |I_1(\phi_k(x)) - I_0(x)|^2 |d_x\phi_k| dx = \int_{T_0} |I_1(\psi_{1k}(s)) - I_0(\psi_{0k}(s))|^2 A(T_k')ds . \quad (14)$$

This yields the final expression of the energy : $\mathcal{E}(p(0)) =$

$$\frac{1}{2}\langle K(q(0))p(0), p(0)\rangle + \lambda \sum_{k=1}^{r} \int_{T_0} |I_1(\psi_{1,k}(s)) - I_0(\psi_{0,k}(s))|^2 A(T_k')ds . \quad (15)$$

4   Computation of the Derivatives

4.1   Gradient

We compute the first derivative of g, which is needed for the gradient descent algorithm and the computation of the transversality equation. To compute this gradient we use formula (15) which can be differentiated without requiring Green's formula which would involve an integration over the edges of the triangles. We expect in particular more numerical accuracy from surface intergrals than from interpolated line integrals.

Proposition 1. *Denote $z_k = (q_{k1}^1(1), q_{k2}^1(1), q_{k3}^1(1), q_{k1}^2(1), q_{k2}^2(1), q_{k3}^2(1)) \in \mathbb{R}^6$, considered as a column vector and with a slight abuse of notation, denote $A(z_k) = A(T_k')$. Let $z = (z_1, ..., z_N)^T$ be the vector containing all the vertices of the triangles. We can notice that in z, some of the landmarks are repeated, but this* *does not affect the computation, since we treat each triangle separately. Let $\tilde{I}_{i,k} = I_i \circ \psi_{i,k}$ for $i = 0, 1$. The gradient of the data attachment term is equal to:*

$$\nabla g(z) = \sum_{k=1}^{r} \int_{T_0} \left(2(\tilde{I}_{1,k}(s) - \tilde{I}_{0,k}(s)) A(z_k) (\partial_{z_k} \psi_{1,k}(s))^T \nabla I_1(\psi_{1,k}(s)) \right.$$

$$\left. + |\tilde{I}_{1,k}(s) - \tilde{I}_{0,k}(s)|^2 \nabla A(z_k)) ds \right) \quad (16)$$

where : $\nabla A(z_k) = \begin{pmatrix} 0 & 0 & 0 & 0 & -1 & 1 \\ 0 & 0 & 0 & 1 & 0 & -1 \\ 0 & 0 & 0 & -1 & 1 & 0 \\ 0 & 1 & -1 & 0 & 0 & 0 \\ -1 & 0 & 1 & 0 & 0 & 0 \\ 1 & -1 & 0 & 0 & 0 & 0 \end{pmatrix} z_k$ *and* $\partial_{z_k} \psi_{1,k} = \begin{pmatrix} 1-\alpha-\beta & \alpha & \beta & 0 & 0 & 0 \\ 0 & 0 & 0 & 1-\alpha-\beta & \alpha & \beta \end{pmatrix}$.

4.2   Second Differential of g

We now compute the Hessian matrix of g which is needed for the implementation of Newtons's method.

Proposition 2. *Using the same notation as before, the second derivative of the data attachment term with respect to the final landmarks equals :*

$$d_z^2 g(\delta z, \delta z) = \sum_{k=1}^{r} \int_{T_0} (\delta z_k)^T \left(2A(z_k) (\partial_{z_k} \psi_{1,k})^T \nabla I_1(\psi_{1,k}) \nabla I_1(\psi_{1,k})^T \partial_{z_k} \psi_{1,k} \right.$$

$$+ A(z_k)(\tilde{I}_{1,k} - \tilde{I}_{0,k}) (\partial_{z_k} \psi_k)^T \, Hess_{I_1}(\psi_{1,k}) \, \partial_{z_k} \psi_{1,k}$$

$$+ 2(\tilde{I}_{1,k} - \tilde{I}_{0,k})(\partial_{z_k} \psi_{1,k})^T \nabla I_1(\psi_{1,k})(\nabla A(z_k))^T$$

$$\left. + (\tilde{I}_{1,k} - \tilde{I}_{0,k})^2 Hess_A(z_k) \, ds \right) \delta z_k \quad (17)$$

where $Hess_A(z_k) \equiv \begin{pmatrix} 0 & 0 & 0 & 0 & -1 & 1 \\ 0 & 0 & 0 & 1 & 0 & -1 \\ 0 & 0 & 0 & -1 & 1 & 0 \\ 0 & 1 & -1 & 0 & 0 & 0 \\ -1 & 0 & 1 & 0 & 0 & 0 \\ 1 & -1 & 0 & 0 & 0 & 0 \end{pmatrix}$ *and $Hess_f$ denotes for the hessian matrix of f.*

Proof: We use the same notation as in the computation of the first derivative. We can notice that $\partial_{z_k} \psi_{1,k}$ is independent of z_k and $\nabla A(z_k)$ is linear on z_k, so that the second derivative of $\psi_{1,k}$ with respect to z_k is null and we easily get the expression of $Hess_A(z_k)$ as the matrix involved in its gradient. This yields :

$$d_z^2 g(\delta z, \delta z) =$$

$$\sum_{k=1}^{r} \int_{T_0} \left(2\langle \nabla I_1(\psi_{1,k}), \partial_{z_k} \psi_{1,k}(\delta z_k) \rangle \langle \nabla I_1(\psi_{1,k}), \partial_{z_k} \psi_{1,k}(\delta z_k) \rangle A(z_k) \right.$$

$$+ 2d_{\psi_{1,k}}^2 I_1(\partial_{z_k} \psi_{1,k}(\delta z_k), \partial_{z_k} \psi_{1,k}(\delta z_k))(I_1(\psi_{1,k}) - I_0(\psi_{0,k})) A(z_k)$$

$$+ 2(I_1(\psi_{1,k}) - I_0(\psi_{0,k})) \langle \nabla I_1(\psi_{1,k}), \partial_{z_k} \psi_{1,k}(\delta z_k) \rangle \langle \nabla A(z_k), \delta z_k \rangle$$

$$\left. + 2(I_1(\psi_{1,k}) - I_0(\psi_{0,k}))^2 d_{z_k}^2 A(\delta z_k, \delta z_k) \right) ds . \quad (18)$$

Equation (17) is the matrix form of (18).

5   Experiments and Discussion

In the experiments showed in figure 4, the first line corresponds to the final results of the gradient descent in the initial momentum space. The second line corresponds to the results of Newton's method. The deformation ϕ (fourth column) and the transformation of the template (third column) are computed using the interpolation formula ; it is the reconstructed diffeomorphism and no more its approximation by a piecewise affine function.

The mesh can be either adapted to the template or be shared by every images. The choice depends on the goal we pursue. Using a common mesh enables a comparison of the resulting energies on the same area of the images (see table 1 and 2). In case of image detection or classification, we try to explain an image made of two different parts: a specific zone where the information is located and the background. If we want to give a probalistic model to each part, localizing the information, that is to say using an adaptative mesh, will probably enable to reach better results. The risk with object adapted triangulation is the data attachment term can be small when the deformed template is included in the target, but not perfectly aligned to it. This can happen in particular when the grey-level information is weak within the shape, espescially with binary images.

In each case, more iterations are needed by the gradient descent, often with less accurate results than with Newton's method.

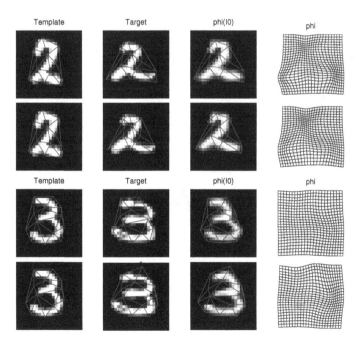

Fig. 4. Comparison between gradient descent (line 1 and 3) and root-finding (line 2 and 4) methods on an adaptative mesh for 2 different digits

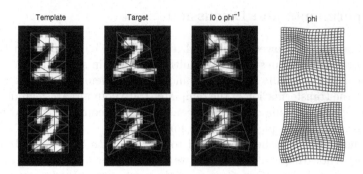

Fig. 5. Combination of gradient descent and root-finding methods for 2 regular mesh (15 and 24 landmarks)

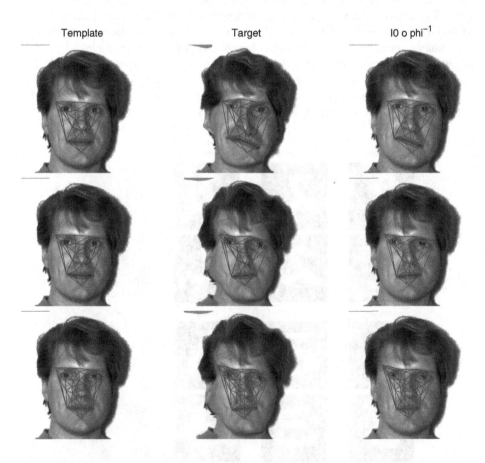

Fig. 6. Newton's method results on 2 synthetic face matchings (line 1 and 2), using 2 different meshes (line 2 and 3)

The number of singular directions used for Newton's method is computed automatically: we start with 10% of singular directions and keep adding new ones unless the norm of $G(p_0) = p_1(p_0) + \lambda \nabla g$ increases. The resulting energy is smaller using Newton's method as well as the averaged numerical value of $|G(p_0)|$. Typical initial values are larger than 300 for the energy and than 4 for the average of $|G(p_0)|$. Note that this value is not always 0 at the end of the iteration, essentially due to interpolation errors.

In figure 5, we can see the final results of the combination of both gradient and Newton's methods for a common regular mesh with 15 or 24 landmarks. If we increase the number of points, a good initialization of Newton's method is required. One solution is to combine the two methods as previously described. Handwritten digit images are almost binary, small images; this creates a risk of numerical unstability for the computation of their gradient and second derivative. For face images (100 times bigger), Newton's algorithm is more stable and uses almost every singular values in the last steps. The final result depends on the two parameters λ and σ_V. Increasing λ allows larger deformations to better fit the data, but the minimum is harder to achieve. The kernel parameter, σ_V, needs to be large enough to ensure triangle consistency, but small enough to avoid too rigid deformations (like in figure 6, 3rd line). The tradeoff we made is choose σ_V almost equal to the size of the triangles. The design of the triangulation is important too. Indeed, since the deformation is affine on each triangle, all elements in one triangle will have a homogeneous displacement. Thus, it is reasonable to ensure that every triangle holds only one structure of the image, for example the mouth or the cheeks but not both.

6   Conclusion

We have presented here a new method for image matching using a triangulation of a restricted part of the image domain, and a piecewise affine transformation on this triangulation. We also introduced a new way for finding the transformation by directy solving the transversality equation. The motivation was to take advantage of the dimensionality reduction that is provided by the landmark dependence of the deformation and the linearity of the affine function that enables an explicit computation of the derivatives of the data attachement term. Solving the transversality equation by Newton's algorithm also provided significant acceleration of the convergence of our matching algorithm. A 3D generalization of the computations is also almost straightforward.

References

1. M. F. BEG, M. I. MILLER, J. T. RATNANATHER, A. TROUVÉ, L. YOUNES *Computing Metrics on Diffeomorphisms for Computational Anatomy*, International Journal of Computer Vision, (2004)
2. M. F. BEG, M. I. MILLER, A. TROUVÉ, L. YOUNES, *Computing large deformation metric mappings via geodesic flow of diffeomorphisms*, Int. J. Comp. Vis., 61 (2005), pp 139-157

3. F.L. BOOKSTEIN *Morphometric tools for landmark data; geometry and biology*, Cambridge University Press, (1991)
4. R. BROIT, C. BAJCSY, *Matching of deformed images*, Proc. 6th Int. Conf. of Pattern Recogition, München, (1982) pp 351-353
5. V. CAMION, L. YOUNES *Geodesic Interpolating Splines*, In M. Figueiredo, J. Zerubia, and A.K. Jain, editors, Proceedings of EMMCVPR 2001, volume 2134 of Lecture Notes in Computer Science, Springuer (2001), pp 513-527
6. P. DUPUIS, U. GRENANDER, M. I. MILLER *Variational problems on flows of diffeomorphisms for image matching*, Quart. Appl. Math., vol. LVI, pp 587-600, (1998)
7. L. GARCIN, A RANGARAJAN, L.YOUNES *Non rigid registration of shapes via diffeomorphic point matching and clustering*
8. J. GLAUNES, A. TROUVÉ, L. YOUNES *Modeling planar shape variation via hamiltonian flow of curves* (Submitted)
9. J. GLAUNES, M. VAILLANT, M. I. MILLER *Landmark matching via large deformation diffeomorphisms on the sphere*, J. Math. Imaging Vision 20 no. 1-2, (2004) pp 179-200.
10. U. GRENANDER, M.I. MILLER *Computational anatomy: An emerging discipline*, Quaterly of Applied Mathematics, LVI (1998) pp 617-694
11. D.D. HOLM, J.T. RATNANATHER, A. TROUVÉ, L. YOUNES *Solition Dynamics in Computational Anatomy*, Neuroimage (2004)
12. D.G. HULL *Optimal Control Theory for Applications*, XIX, Sringer, (2003)
13. S. JOSHI, M. I. MILLER *Landmark matching via Large Deformation diffeomorphisms*, IEEE transaction in image processing 9 (2000) pp 1357-1370
14. S. MARSLAND, C TWINING *Clamped-plate splines and the optimak flow bounded diffeomorphisms*, Complex Stochastic Systemp and Engineering, Oxford: Clarendon press (2002), pp 85-103.
15. M. I. MILLER, A. TROUVÉ, L. YOUNES *On the metrics and Euler Lagrange Equations of Computational Anatomy*, Annual Review of Biomedical Engeneering 4 (2002) pp 375-405
16. M. I. MILLER, L. YOUNES *Group action, diffeomorphism and matching: a general framework*, Int. J. Comp. Vis., 41, (2001) pp 61-84
17. F. RICHARD, L. COHEN *A new image registration technique with free boundary constraints : application to mammography*, Computer Vision and Image Understanding, vol. 89/2-3 pp 166-196, Special Issue on Nonrigid Registration, 2003
18. A. TROUVÉ *Diffeomorphisms Groups and Pattern Matching in Image Analysis*, International Journal of Computer Vision 28(3) (1998) pp 213-221
19. A. TROUVÉ, L. YOUNES *Local geometry of deformable template*, SIAM Journal of Numerical Analysis (2004-5)
20. M. VAILLANT, J. GLAUNES *Surface Matching via Currents*, Proceedings of Information Processing in Medical Imaging (IPMI 2005), pp. 381-392, 2005.
21. M. VAILLANT, M. I. MILLER, A. TROUVÉ, L. YOUNES *Statistics on diffeomorphisms via tangent space representaion*, NeuroImage 23 (2004) S161-169
22. G. WAHBA *Spine Models for Observational Data*, Philadelphia, PA, SIAM, (1990)
23. L. YOUNES *Optimal matching between shapes via elastic deformations*, Image and Vision Computing, (1999)
24. L. YOUNES *Computable elastic distances between shapes*, SIAM J Appl Math, 58 (1998) pp 565-586

Appendix

* We provide here for completness, a sketch of the derivation of the Hamiltonian formulation given in (4) and of the transversality condition (7).

  Let $(v_t, q(t))_{t \in [0,1]}$ be a minimizer of (2) with $v \in L^2([0,1], V)$. For any perturbation $v_t \to v_t + \epsilon h_t$ with $h \in L^2([0,1], V)$, we get at $\epsilon = 0$

$$\partial_\epsilon \dot{q}(t) = d_{q(t)} v_t \partial_\epsilon q(t) + h_t(q(t)) \tag{19}$$

where $h_t(q(t)) \doteq (h_t(q_i(t)))_{1 \le i \le N}$. Let $(P_{s,t})$ be the matrix semi-group satisfying

$$P_{s,s} = \mathrm{Id}_{nN} \text{ and } \partial_t P_{s,t} = d_{q(t)} v_t P_{s,t}, \ \forall t \ge s. \tag{20}$$

From (19) and (20), we get at $\epsilon = 0$, $\partial_\epsilon q(1) = \int_0^1 P_{s,1} h_s(q(s)) ds$ and

$$\partial_\epsilon E(v, q(1)) = \int_0^1 \langle v_s, h_s \rangle_V ds + \int_0^1 \langle \nabla_{q(1)} g, P_{s,1} h_s(q(s)) \rangle_{\mathbb{R}^{nN}} ds = 0.$$

Since h is arbitrary, we get $v_s(q(s)) = \dot{q}(s) = K(q(s))p(s) = \frac{\partial H}{\partial p}(q(s), p(s))$ where $p(s) + P_{s,1}^* \nabla_{q(1)} g = 0$ which gives the first equation of (4) and also (7) for $s = 1$. From (20), we get $\partial_s P_{s,t} = -P_{s,t} d_{q(s)} v_s$ so that eventually

$$\dot{p}(s) = \partial_s P_{s,1}^* p_1 = -(d_{q(s)} v_s)^* p(s) = -\frac{\partial H}{\partial q}(q(s), p(s)). \tag{21}$$

* We provide here a proposition concerning the triangle consistency.

Table 1. Comparison of the 2 metods for solving the Image matching problem for handwritten digits (images normalized in $[-1, 1]$)

Fig	Energy value		Mean value $|G(p(0))|$	
	Gradient desc.	Newton's method	Gradient desc.	Newton's method
Fig 4 1st line	62.87	60.43	0.95	0.48
Fig 4 2nd line	166	156	1.30	0.62
Fig 5 15 pts	107	76.9	0.76	0.33
Fig 5 24 pts	71.1	65.5	0.58	0.40

Table 2. Newton's method results on face images (images normalized in $\{0, \dots, 255\}$)

Fig	Energy value	Mean value of the $|G(p(0))|$ vector
Fig 6 1st line	$3.39 \cdot 10^3$	1.08
Fig 6 2nd line	$1.98 \cdot 10^3$	0.40
Fig 6 3rd line	$1.32 \cdot 10^3$	0.09

Proposition 3. Let $\gamma(t) = \sin(\theta(t))$ where $\theta(t)$ is one of the triangle angles. Let V be a self reproducing kernel Hilbert space, with a σ^2 variance gaussian kernel and ϕ_t be the diffeomorphism solution of $d\phi/dt = v_t \circ \phi_t$ for a velocity vector field $v_t \in L^1([0,1], V)$. Denoting $\psi(x) = 2xe^{2x}$, a sufficient condition to keep the triangle consistency is given by

$$\psi\left(\frac{\sqrt{2\lambda g_{I_1, I_0}(q(0))}}{\sigma}\right) \leq \frac{|\gamma(0)|}{(1 + |\gamma(0)|)} .$$

Proof: Let A, B, C be the 3 vertices of a triangle, $a(t) = \phi_t(B) - \phi_t(A)$ and $b(t) = \phi_t(C) - \phi_t(A)$. We want to control the sign of the sine of the $\widehat{BAC}$ angle, θ_t. To avoid reversal of the triangle this quantity must not change its sign. Let $\alpha(t) = |a(t) \, b(t)| = |a(t) \wedge b(t)|$; we can notice that : $\alpha(t) = |a(t)||b(t)|\sin(\theta_t)$. Then, using Cauchy-Schwarz inequality:

$$\partial_t \alpha(t) = \langle \partial_t a(t) \wedge b(t) + a(t) \wedge \partial_t b(t), \frac{a(t) \wedge b(t)}{|a(t) \wedge b(t)|} \rangle$$

$$\leq (|\partial_t a(t)||b(t)| + |\partial_t b(t)||a(t)|) .$$

But, $\partial_t a(t) = \partial_t(\phi_t(B) - \phi_t(A)) = v_t(\phi_t(B)) - v_t(\phi_t(A))$. So that:

$$\partial_t \alpha(t) \leq 2\|dv_t\|_\infty |a(t)||b(t)| . \tag{22}$$

Let $\gamma(t) = \sin\theta_t = \frac{\alpha(t)}{|a(t)||b(t)|}$; we try to quantify the difference between $\sin(\theta_t)$ and $\sin(\theta_0)$ to find a suffitient condition.

$$\partial_t \gamma(t)$$
$$= \frac{\partial_t \alpha(t)}{|a(t)||b(t)|} - \frac{\alpha(t)}{|a(t)|^2|b(t)|^2}(|b(t)|\langle \partial_t a(t), \frac{a(t)}{|a(t)|}\rangle + |a(t)|\langle \partial_t b(t), \frac{b(t)}{|b(t)|}\rangle)$$
$$\leq \frac{1}{|a(t)||b(t)|}\left(|\partial_t \alpha(t)| + |\alpha(t)|\left(\left|\langle \frac{\partial_t a(t)}{|a(t)|}, \frac{a(t)}{|a(t)|}\rangle\right| + \left|\langle \frac{\partial_t b(t)}{|b(t)|}, \frac{b(t)}{|b(t)|}\rangle\right|\right)\right) .$$

Using (22), $\partial_t \gamma(t) \leq 2\|dv_t\|_\infty + |\gamma(t)|\left(\left|\frac{\partial_t a(t)}{a(t)}\right| + \left|\frac{\partial_t b(t)}{b(t)}\right|\right) \leq 2\|dv_t\|_\infty(1 + |\gamma(t)|)$. And $|\gamma(0) - \gamma(t)| \leq \int_0^t |\partial_t \gamma(t)|dt \leq \int_0^t 2\|dv_t\|_\infty(1 + |\gamma(0)|)dt + \int_0^t 2\|dv_t\|_\infty|\gamma(0) - \gamma(t)|dt$. Applying Gronwall's lemma to this last inequality, we finally get:

$$|\gamma(0) - \gamma(t)| \leq 2(1 + |\gamma(0)|)\left(\int_0^1 \|dv_t\|_\infty dt\right)\exp\left(2\int_0^1 \|dv_t\|_\infty dt\right) .$$

As we are using a self reproducing gaussian kernel Hilbert space: $\forall x \in \mathbb{R}^d$ $|v(x)| = \sup_{|a|\leq 1} \langle v(x), a\rangle_{\mathbb{R}^d} = \sup_{|a|\leq 1} \langle K_x a, v\rangle_V$, so: $\|v\|_\infty \leq \||K_{x,x}\|| \|v\|_V = \|v\|_V$, where $\||K_{x,x}\||$ is the matrix norm subordinate to the Euclidian norm in $\mathbb{R}^d$, and, using a Taylor development of the kernel, $\|dv_t\|_\infty \leq \frac{1}{\sigma}\|v_t\|_V$. So we get: $\int_0^1 \|dv_t\|_\infty dt \leq \frac{1}{\sigma}\sqrt{2E_k(v)} \leq \frac{\sqrt{\lambda}}{\sigma}\tilde{G}$ where $\tilde{G} \doteq \sqrt{2g_{I_1,I_0}(q(0))}$. And finally: $\forall v \in L^1([0,1], V)$,

$$|\gamma(0) - \gamma(t)| \leq (1 + |\gamma(0)|)\psi(\frac{\sqrt{\lambda}}{\sigma}\tilde{G}) \text{ where } \psi(x) = 2xe^{2x}, \ \forall x \geq 0. \quad (23)$$

To avoid the reversal of a triangle, it suffices that $|\gamma(0) - \gamma(t)| \leq |\gamma(0)|$ for any $t \in [0,1]$. A sufficient condition is $\psi(\frac{\sqrt{\lambda}}{\sigma}\tilde{G}) \leq \left(\frac{|\gamma(0)|}{(1+|\gamma(0)|)}\right)$, which gives the result.

An Adaptive Variational Model for Image Decomposition

Stacey E. Levine*

Department of Mathematics and Computer Science,
440 College Hall, Duquesne University, Pittsburgh, PA, 15282
Phone: (412) 396-5489, Fax (412) 396-5197
sel@mathcs.duq.edu

Abstract. We propose a new model for image decomposition which separates an image into a cartoon, consisting only of geometric objects, and
an oscillatory component, consisting of textures and noise. The model
is given in a variational formulation with adaptive regularization norms
for both the cartoon and texture part. The energy for the cartoon interpolates between total variation regularization and isotropic smoothing,
while the energy for the textures interpolates between Meyer's G norm
and the H^{-1} norm. These energies are dual in the sense of the Legendre-
Fenchel transform and their adaptive behavior preserves key features
such as object boundaries and textures while avoiding staircasing in what
should be smooth regions. Existence and uniqueness of a solution is established and experimental results demonstrate the effectiveness of the
model for both grayscale and color image decomposition.

1 Introduction

One of the fundamental objectives in image processing is to extract useful information from an image. This often requires decomposing an image into meaningful
parts. A classic example is the image denoising problem in which the goal is to
decompose a given degraded image I into a component u which is the 'true' image and a component v containing 'noise'. These quantities are usually related by
$I = u + v$. Most denoising methods aim to only recover u, the 'true' image since
in this setting the residual v is thought to contain no meaningful information.

Traditionally, variational approaches for image denoising search for a solution
u in BV, the set of functions of bounded variation. This is the natural space
for modeling 'cartoon' type images, since elements of BV consist of smoothly
varying regions with sharp object boundaries. However, Gousseau and Morel [15]
showed that real images which contain natural oscillations or textures cannot
be modeled in BV. To overcome this problem, Meyer [18] formulated the image
decomposition problem as follows. Given a degraded image, I, decompose I
into a 'cartoon' part u containing only geometric objects, and an oscillatory
part v containing noise and textures. I, u, and v should be still be related by

---

* This work was supported in part by NSF Grant DMS 0505729.

A. Rangarajan et al. (Eds.): EMMCVPR 2005, LNCS 3757, pp. 382–397, 2005.
© Springer-Verlag Berlin Heidelberg 2005

the equation $I = u + v$. However, when solving this problem, the goal is to simultaneously recover both u and v, assuming they both contain meaningful information.

Several different approaches have been used to determine such a *'cartoon + texture'* decomposition. One class of models is based on statistical methods or wavelet techniques, e.g. [7,12,17,18]. Meyer's work [18] has inspired several variational formulations for solving this problem, e.g. [3,4,16,20,22]; this is the approach we take here.

In this work we propose a new variational model for image decomposition which separates an image into a cartoon and texture component. The main feature of the proposed model is that the regularization norms for both the cartoon and texture part are adaptive to the local image information and remain in duality. At locations with high gradient (likely edges or textures in I), total variation based regularization is used for the cartoon u and a minimization energy which favors highly oscillatory functions is used for v. At locations with low gradient (likely homogeneous regions in I), isotropic smoothing is used to prevent staircasing for u and a more regularizing energy is used for v.

More precisely, for $\Omega \subset R^2$ and $1 \leq q < \infty$ denote the Sobolev spaces

$$W^{1,q}(\Omega) = \{u \in L^q(\Omega) \mid \nabla u \in L^q(\Omega)\} \text{ and } H^1(\Omega) = W^{1,2}(\Omega).$$

Then $W^{-1,p}(\Omega)$ is the dual space of $W_0^{1,q}(\Omega)$ (functions in $W^{1,q}(\Omega)$ that vanish on the boundary of Ω) where $\frac{1}{q} + \frac{1}{p} = 1$. Using this notation, the proposed model behaves as follows. Depending on the strength of the gradient, the minimization energy for the cartoon interpolates between the total variation semi-norm ($\approx$ $W^{1,1}$ norm) and the $W^{1,2} = H^1$ norm while that for the oscillating component simultaneously interpolates between their dual norms in the spaces $W^{-1,\infty}$ and $W^{-1,2} = H^{-1}$. The duality between the energies for u and v enables the model to correctly self-adjust when handling key features in the image, specifically, object boundaries, textures and noise. This also prevents false edge generation (or 'staircasing') in the cartoon part yielding a truly piecewise smooth image.

The paper is organized as follows. Section 2 provides a brief survey of related variational decomposition models. In section 3, the proposed model is described. Section 4 contains the numerical implementation for both grayscale and color images, and section 5 contains the experimental results. Section 6 will have the concluding remarks. The appendix contains the proof of existence and uniqueness of a solution.

2 Total Variation (TV) Based Image Decomposition Models

The 'cartoon + texture' decomposition problem considered here for two dimensional grayscale images is formulated as follows: Given an image $I : \Omega \subset R^2 \to R$, find a decomposition $I = u + v$ where $u : \Omega \to R$ is piecewise smooth consisting only of geometric objects and their boundaries and $v : \Omega \to R$ contains only oscillating features such as textures and noise. The space most widely accepted for modeling piecewise smooth 'cartoon' type images u is the set of functions of bounded variation, $BV(\Omega) = \{u \in L^1(\Omega) \mid \int_\Omega |Du| < \infty\}$ [14], where the total variation semi-norm of u is

$$\int_\Omega |Du| := sup\{\int_\Omega u(x)\mathrm{div}(\xi(x)) \mid \xi \in C_c^1(\Omega; R^2),\ ||\xi||_{L^\infty(\Omega)} \le 1\}.$$

Rudin-Osher-Fatemi [21] proposed the now classic total variation (TV) denoising model which can be formulated as follows:

$$\min_{\substack{I=u+v, u \in BV \times L^2(\Omega)}} \int_\Omega |Du| + \lambda||v||^2_{L^2(\Omega)} \tag{1}$$

The fundamental strength of TV based denoising is its ability to keep sharp boundaries in the cartoon u while removing noise. However, if the desired goal is to create a 'cartoon + texture" decomposition, the L^2 norm may not be most appropriate minimization energy for the oscillatory component v. While u, the part of the image containing geometric structures, can still be modeled in BV, the oscillating patterns in v should be modeled in a space which lies somewhere between BV and L^2 [15].

In addition, Meyer showed there are simple cases in which (1) will not create a true $u+v$ decomposition. For example, if $I \in BV$ is the characteristic function of a region with smooth boundary, it would be reasonable to assume the (1) should yield the decomposition $u = I$ and $v = 0$. However, this is not always the case for $\lambda > 0$ [18]. The problem does not necessarily stem from assuming $v \in L^2(\Omega)$, but from using the L^2 norm as the minimization energy for v. Meyer proposed several alternate norms for v which allow for more oscillations. The one this work will focus on is that of the Banach space

$$G(R^2) = \{f = \mathrm{div}\xi \mid \xi \in L^\infty(R^2, R^2)\},\ \text{with norm}$$

$$||v||_{G(R^2)} = \inf\{|| |\xi| ||_{L^\infty(R^2, R^2)} \mid \xi \in L^\infty(R^2, R^2),\ |\xi| = \sqrt{\xi_1^2 + \xi_2^2}\}$$

where $\xi = (\xi_1, \xi_2)$. Very oscillatory signals have small G norm (see [18] for examples), so this energy will preserve both textures and noise. Meyer modified (1) using the $G(R^2)$-norm for v and proposed the following model:

$$\inf_{\substack{(u,v) \in BV \times G(R^2), \\ I=u+v}} \int_{R^2} |Du| + \frac{1}{2\lambda}||v||^2_{G(R^2)} \tag{2}$$

The notion of duality in the decomposition $u + v$ exists, as $G(R^2)$ is precisely the space $W^{-1,\infty}(R^2)$, the dual of $W_0^{1,1}(R^2)$ which is very close to the space $BV(R^2)$. The duality also gives some insight into the presence of the divergence operator in the definition of $G(R^2)$, since the gradient and the divergence are dual operators.

Aubert and Aujol [2] studied a natural analogue of Meyer's model (2) on a bounded domain $\Omega \subset R^2$. In order to do this, they replaced $G(R^2)$ with the space

$$G(\Omega) := \{v \in L^2(\Omega) \mid v = \mathrm{div}\xi,\ \xi \in L^\infty(\Omega, R^2),\ \xi \cdot N = 0\ \text{on}\ \partial\Omega\} \tag{3}$$

which is contained in $W^{-1,\infty}(\Omega)$. Here, N is the unit outward normal to the boundary of Ω, $\partial\Omega$.

Remark 1. If an image $I \in L^2(\Omega)$ is decomposed using a $u + v$ model where $u \in BV(\Omega) \subset L^2(\Omega)$, then regardless of the minimization energy imposed on v, it must be that $v \in L^2(\Omega)$. So (2) still yields a $u + v$ decomposition with $v \in L^2(\Omega)$. However, the $u + v$ decomposition obtained by (2) is different than that obtained by (1) (see [2, 16, 18, 22] for examples).

Vese and Osher [22, 23] proposed the first numerical implementation of (2). Their method decomposes an image into a cartoon part, u, and further separates the textures into two components, ξ_1 and ξ_2, which model the oscillating patterns in the horizontal and vertical directions respectively. They proposed the model

$$\inf\{\int_\Omega |Du| + \lambda||I - (u + \operatorname{div}\xi)||^2_{L^2(\Omega)} + \mu|| |\xi| ||_{L^p(\Omega)} | \qquad (4)$$

$$(u, \xi) \in BV(\Omega) \times L^p(\Omega, R^2))\}$$

where $\xi = (\xi_1, \xi_2)$, $|\xi| = \sqrt{\xi_1^2 + \xi_2^2}$, $\lambda, \mu > 0$ and $p \geq 1$ are fixed, and $\Omega \subset R^2$ is a bounded open set. Their model differs from (2) in the second and third terms. The second term is a data term enforcing fidelity with the initial data, I, that is, it forces $I \approx u + v = u + \operatorname{div}\xi$. The third term is an approximation of the energy for v in Meyer's model in the sense that $\inf_\xi || |\xi| ||_{L^p} \to ||v||_G$ as $p \to \infty$.

Following the the success of the Vese-Osher model, these two authors along with Solé [20] proposed a higher order denoising method based on (4) for the case $p = 2$. Recently, Le and Vese [16] proposed another decomposition in which the textures are modeled in $\operatorname{div}(BMO)$, a slightly larger space than G, thus

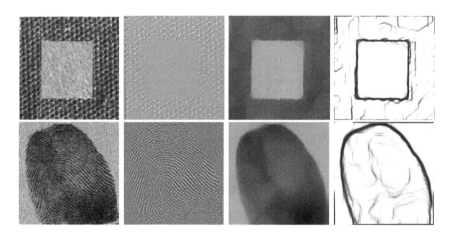

Fig. 1. Image decomposition using the TV-based model (4) with $\mu = .001$ and $\lambda = .025$. FIRST COLUMN: Initial Images I; SECOND COLUMN: texture part v; THIRD COLUMN: cartoon part u; FOURTH COLUMN: edge maps (18) of above cartoon images u. Both images were run for 250 iterations.

allowing more oscillatory components. An alternate discrete approximation of the G-norm was proposed by Aujol et.al. [3, 4] based on Chambolle's duality based projection method for implementing the discrete TV model [6].

All of the above mentioned models have demonstrated that variational decomposition methods are computationally stable, efficient and effective. Furthermore, they are based on mathematically sound foundations. In [2, 3, 4, 16] the authors prove the existence of a solution, as well as analyze the nature of the solutions.

Current variational decomposition models have focused on developing more appropriate norms for modeling oscillating features v which are in some sense dual to the TV semi-norm. In all of the above mentioned models, the TV semi-norm is used to model the cartoon u. However, the cartoon part still exhibits staircasing when using the TV energy for u (see figure 1). In this paper, we investigate different energies for both the cartoon $u \in BV$ and oscillating component $v \in L^2$ which show less evidence of staircasing in u while still preserving sharp object boundaries in u and textures in v.

3   Image Decomposition Via Adaptive Regularization

3.1   Adaptive Cartoon Reconstruction

Variational methods with cost functionals that interpolate between total variation based $W^{1,1}$ smoothing and isotropic $W^{1,2} = H^1$ smoothing overcome the problems of staircasing in cartoon image reconstruction while still preserving sharp object boundaries. Several denoising models using this kind of interpolation have been studied (e.g. [5, 8, 11] and references there-in). In [11] the following adaptive model was proposed

$$\min_{I=u+v, u \in BV \cap L^2(\Omega)} \int_\Omega \phi(x, \nabla u) + \lambda ||v||^2_{L^2(\Omega)}. \tag{5}$$

where

$$\int_\Omega \phi(x, \nabla u) = \begin{cases} \frac{1}{q(x)} |\nabla u|^{q(x)}, & |\nabla u| < \epsilon \\ |\nabla u| - \frac{q(x)\epsilon - \epsilon^{q(x)}}{q(x)}, & |\nabla u| \geq \epsilon \end{cases}, \tag{6}$$

and $q(x) = q(|\nabla \widetilde{I}(x)|)$ satisfies

$$\lim_{|\nabla \widetilde{I}| \to 0} q(|\nabla \widetilde{I}|) = 2 \quad \lim_{|\nabla \widetilde{I}| \to \infty} q(|\nabla \widetilde{I}|) = \alpha > 1 \tag{7}$$

and $q(|\nabla \widetilde{I}|)$ is monotonically decreasing

(here $\widetilde{I}$ is a smoothed version of I). For example, one could choose

$$q(x) = 1 + \frac{1}{1 + k|\nabla G_\sigma * I|^2} \tag{8}$$

where $G_\sigma = \frac{1}{\sigma} exp\left(-|x|^2/4\sigma^2\right)$ is the Gaussian filter and $\sigma, k > 0$ are fixed.

The main feature of this model is that the type of regularization depends on the local image information. At likely edges, or regions with sufficiently high gradient, TV based regularization is used. In likely homogeneous regions where the gradient is very low, $q(x) \approx 2$ and isotropic smoothing is used. At all other locations, ϕ self adjusts to use the appropriate combination of TV and isotropic smoothing.

Furthermore, the functional (6) is both convex and lower semi-continuous. In particular, when the threshold, ϵ, is set to 1 we have that

$$\int_\Omega \phi(x, \nabla u) = \begin{cases} \frac{1}{q(x)} |\nabla u|^{q(x)}, & |\nabla u| < 1 \\ |\nabla u| - \frac{q(x)-1}{q(x)}, & |\nabla u| \geq 1 \end{cases},$$

$$= \sup_{|\xi| \leq 1, \xi \in C^1(\Omega, R^2)} \int_\Omega \left(-u \mathrm{div}\xi - \frac{1}{p(x)} |\xi|^{p(x)} \right) dx \qquad (9)$$

where $\frac{1}{q(x)} + \frac{1}{p(x)} = 1$ for all $x \in \Omega$. This leads to a mathematically sound model which is established in [11].

3.2   New Model: Adaptive Cartoon + Texture Decomposition

The relationship (9) gives insight into the decomposition model proposed in this paper. Since $\int_\Omega \phi(x, \nabla u)$ is proper, convex, and lower-semicontinuous, it demonstrates that the functionals

$$\Phi(u) := \int_\Omega \phi(x, \nabla u) \text{ and } \Psi(\xi) := \int_\Omega \frac{1}{p(x)} |\xi|^{p(x)} \qquad (10)$$

are essentially conjugate in the sense of the Legendre-Fenchel transform [13], where $\phi(x, \nabla u)$ is defined in (6), $1 < \alpha \leq q(x) = q(|\nabla \tilde{I}(x)|) \leq 2$ satisfies (7), and

$$\frac{1}{q(x)} + \frac{1}{p(x)} = 1 \text{ for all } x \in \Omega. \qquad (11)$$

Based on the notion of duality between the cartoon and oscillatory components, we define a functional $F : BV(\Omega) \times L^2(\Omega, R^2) \to R$ by

$$F(u, \xi) := \Phi(u) + \lambda ||I - u - \mathrm{div}\xi||^2_{L^2(\Omega)} + \mu \Psi(\xi) \qquad (12)$$

for $I \in L^2(\Omega)$ and propose the following image decomposition model:

$$\inf_{(u,\xi) \in BV(\Omega) \times L^2(\Omega, R^2)} \{ F(u, \xi) \mid \mathrm{div}\xi \in L^2(\Omega) \text{ and } \int_\Omega u dx = \int_\Omega I dx \} \qquad (13)$$

using definitions (10)-(12) with $\lambda, \mu > 0$.

Remark 2. We mention the key features of the model (12)-(13).

1. The adaptive nature of the model is exploited by the conjugacy of the variable exponents (11). At locations with large gradient such as edges, textures,

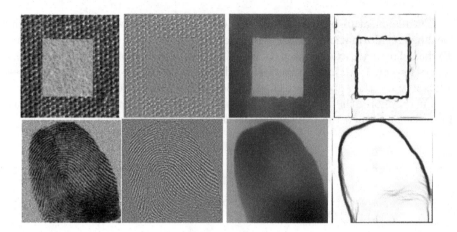

Fig. 2. Image decomposition using the proposed model (13) with $\mu = .1$ and $\lambda = .05$. FIRST COLUMN: Initial Images I; SECOND COLUMN: texture part v; THIRD COLUMN: cartoon part u; FOURTH COLUMN: edge maps (18) of above cartoon images u. Both images were run for 250 iterations.

and noise, Meyer's model (1) should be used since these are the main features used to distinguish between geometric objects and oscillating patterns. In this case, TV ($\approx W^{1,1}$) regularization for the cartoon u retains sharp object boundaries. Furthermore, $W^{-1,\infty}$ regularization for the oscillatory component keeps only smaller scale patterns in v. The proposed model (12)-(13) has this feature since as $|\nabla \widetilde{I}| \to \infty$,

$$q(|\nabla \widetilde{I}|) \to 1 \quad \text{and} \quad p(|\nabla \widetilde{I}|) \to \infty.$$

On the other hand, isotropic smoothing should be used in likely homogeneous regions in order to reduce the effects of staircasing (see figure 2). In this case, H^1 smoothing should be used for the cartoon and H^{-1} for the oscillatory component. The H^{-1} norm was proposed and analyzed in [20] for modeling the residual v in order to solve the image denoising problem. The authors demonstrate that it successfully contributes to a smoother cartoon image. Again, the conjugacy of the exponents yields this behavior since as $|\nabla \widetilde{I}| \to 0$,

$$q(|\nabla \widetilde{I}|) \to 2 \quad \text{and} \quad p(|\nabla \widetilde{I}|) \to 2.$$

2. The coefficient $\frac{1}{p(x)}$ in $\Psi(\xi)$ (see (10)) not only preserves the notion of duality between the energies for the cartoon, u, and oscillations $v = \text{div}\xi$, but it also provides a natural scaling for the oscillations. At highly oscillatory features, $\frac{1}{p(x)}$ will be very small, thus allowing more oscillations to be preserved in ξ. Since $1 < \alpha \leq q(x) \leq 2$ we have that $2 \leq p(x) \leq \frac{\alpha}{\alpha-1} < \infty$ so the coefficient is never zero.
3. The fidelity term $\lambda \|I - (u + \text{div}\xi)\|_{L^2}^2$ ensures that $I \approx u + \text{div}\xi = u + v$ as in (4).

4. The constraints $\mathrm{div}\xi \in L^2(\Omega)$ and $\int_\Omega u\,dx = \int_\Omega I\,dx$ in (13) arise naturally in this decomposition problem. Since $I \in L^2(\Omega)$, it is necessary that $v = \mathrm{div}\xi \in L^2(\Omega)$. Then the texture component $v = \mathrm{div}\xi$ lies in the space

$$\{v \in L^2(\Omega) \mid v = \mathrm{div}\xi \text{ with } \xi \in L^2(\Omega, R^2)\}$$

which is slightly bigger than $G(\Omega)$ (see (3)). This may allow for more oscillatory features to be captured in $v = \mathrm{div}\xi$. The requirement that $\int_\Omega u\,dx = \int_\Omega I\,dx$ forces $\int_\Omega v\,dx \approx 0$, a natural assumption for oscillating patterns. Furthermore, it ensures that the model is well-posed.

5. The model (12)-(13) is well-posed. The proof of existence and uniqueness can be found in the appendix.

We refer the reader to new related work in staircase-reducing decomposition models using higher order energies for the cartoon in [10, 9].

4   Numerical Implementation

We implemented (12)-(13) by solving it's corresponding Euler-Lagrange equations

$$u = I - \mathrm{div}(\xi_1, \xi_2) + \frac{1}{2\lambda}\mathrm{div}\left(|\nabla u|^{\hat{q}(x)-2}\nabla u\right) \tag{14}$$

$$\mu\xi_1\sqrt{\xi_1^2 + \xi_2^2}^{\,p(x)-2} = 2\lambda\frac{\partial}{\partial x}(u - I + \mathrm{div}(\xi_1, \xi_2)) \tag{15}$$

$$\mu\xi_2\sqrt{\xi_1^2 + \xi_2^2}^{\,p(x)-2} = 2\lambda\frac{\partial}{\partial y}(u - I + \mathrm{div}(\xi_1, \xi_2)) \tag{16}$$

where $\xi = (\xi_1, \xi_2)$ and

$$\hat{q}(x) = \begin{cases} q(x), & |\nabla u| < \epsilon, \\ 1, & |\nabla u| \geq \epsilon \end{cases} \quad \text{and} \quad \frac{1}{q(x)} + \frac{1}{p(x)} = 1 \text{ for all } x \in \Omega \tag{17}$$

with $q(x)$ chosen as in (8). Our initial data is $u(x,0) = I(x)$, $\xi_1(x,0) = -\frac{1}{2\lambda}\frac{I_x}{|\nabla I|}$ and $\xi_2(x,0) = -\frac{1}{2\lambda}\frac{I_y}{|\nabla I|}$, and the natural Neumann boundary conditions are used. To avoid dependency on the threshold ϵ, this value was automatically updated to ensure that at least 75% of the pixels were using adaptive smoothing, $\hat{q}(x) = q(x)$. Division by zero is avoided in the diffusion term by approximating $\mathrm{div}\left(|\nabla u|^{\hat{q}(x)-2}\nabla u\right)$ with $\mathrm{div}\left(\sqrt{|\nabla u|^2 + \delta^2}^{\,\hat{q}(x)-2}\nabla u\right)$ for small $\delta > 0$. In the case $\hat{q}(x) \equiv 1$, this approximation yields the correct solution as $\delta \to 0$ [1]. Our experimental results found this approximation is also stable for general $1 \leq \hat{q}(x) \leq 2$. We approximated (14)-(16) using a semi-implicit scheme with central differences. We obtained similar results using a minmod approximation [21] for the diffusion term and believe other difference schemes should work as well.

4.1 Parameters

We tested the proposed model for different values of λ and μ. In (12)-(13), the parameter λ controls the level of fidelity between the initial image I and it's decomposition $u + v$. The parameter μ controls the level of oscillatory features retained in v. These parameters play the same role as in the models (2) and (4). Meyer [18] showed that as μ decreases, more oscillatory features are kept in v. We found that the adaptive coefficient $\frac{1}{p(x)}$ reduced the effect of μ on the v component in the proposed model. For both parameters, values less than one yielded optimal results. The parameter k in the exponent $q(x)$ determines the interpolation between the $W^{1,1}$ and H^1, and the $W^{-1,\infty}$ and H^{-1} norms respectively. All of our images ranged in intensity from 0 to 255, and we found that a value of $k = .05$ worked well in each case. The threshold, ϵ, in (17) is set so that 75% of the pixels use adaptive smoothing, $\hat{q}(x) = q(x)$, and the others use TV-based regularization, $\hat{q}(x) \equiv 1$.

4.2 Comparison with TV-Based Decomposition Model (4)

We chose to compare our model with (4) as the representative TV-based decomposition model since it was straightforward to implement, yields very good results, and both inspired and is most closely related to (12)-(13). When comparing with (4), we used the implementation proposed by the authors [22] and follow their example of setting the exponent on the oscillatory component to $p = 1$. They reported finding similar results for $1 \leq p \leq 10$ and when p is too large, only smaller scale textures were preserved. The parameters λ and μ were chosen so that both models yielded optimal results and v had roughly the same standard deviation for both (4) and (12)-(13).

4.3 Color Image Decomposition

A simple modification of the proposed model (12)-(13) yields similar decomposition results for color images, $I : \Omega \subset R^2 \to R^3$. Our main goal in this work was to verify that the adaptive nature of the model would be preserved when applied to color images. Therefore, for our experiments, we used a straightforward channel by channel processing. Specifically, we decomposed the color image into it's RGB components, processed each channel separately using (14)-(16), and then recombined to get the final results. There are other, potentially more optimal, color image representations that will further enhance the decomposition, however we found this one to be easy to implement and yielded results comparable to that for grayscale images $I : \Omega \subset R^2 \to R$. We used a similar modification for the TV based model (4).

5   Experimental Results

5.1   Grayscale Image Decomposition

Figures 1-2 provide a series of comparisons of the proposed model and (4). We first tested the TV image decomposition model (4) on two textured images (figure

1) in an effort to examine the nature of the cartoon image. The TV-based model successfully decomposes the image, however, false edges still appear in u in what should represent smoothly varying regions. This indicates that the cartoon u has undergone staircasing, visible in the cartoons' edge maps. All edge maps in our examples were obtained by applying a standard gradient based edge detector

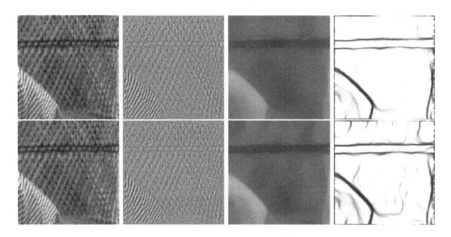

Fig. 3. TOP ROW: Decomposition using the proposed model (12)-(13) with $\mu = .001$ and $\lambda = .001$. BOTTOM ROW: Decomposition using the TV-based model (4) with $\mu = .001$ and $\lambda = .001$; FIRST COLUMN: Initial Images I; SECOND COLUMN: texture part v; THIRD COLUMN: cartoon part u; FOURTH COLUMN: edge maps (18) of above cartoon images u. Both images were run for 200 iterations.

Fig. 4. TOP ROW: Decomposition using the proposed model (12)-(13) with $\mu = .1$ and $\lambda = .005$ for 300 iterations. BOTTOM ROW: Decomposition using the TV-based model (4) with $\mu = .001$ and $\lambda = .005$ for 400 iterations; FIRST COLUMN: Initial Images I; SECOND COLUMN: texture part v; THIRD COLUMN: cartoon part u; FOURTH COLUMN: edge maps (18) of above cartoon images u.

$$\frac{1}{1 + .05|\nabla G_\sigma * u|^2} \tag{18}$$

In figure 2, the same series of images were obtained using the proposed model (12)-(13). The proposed model also successfully decomposes the image and on closer examination of the cartoon image u, it is evident that the geometric regions remain piecewise smooth. This is further demonstrated by examining the corresponding edge maps. It is also interesting to note that while the textures are accurately separated into v, small details such as corners are well preserved in the cartoon. Figures 3 and 4 contains several more examples demonstrating the effectiveness of the proposed model (12)-(13) in reducing the effect of staircasing in grayscale image decomposition.

5.2   Color Image Decomposition

When decomposing color images, we separated the image into it's RGB components, processed each channel separately using (4) or (12)-(13) respectively, and then recombined to get the final results.

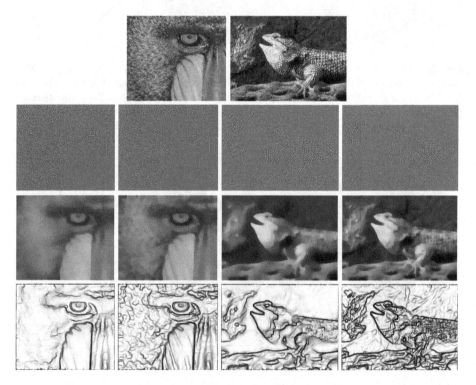

Fig. 5. TOP ROW: original images, SECOND ROW: texture part v, THIRD ROW: cartoon part u, FOURTH ROW: edge maps (18) of cartoon u. The bottom three rows were decomposed using: 1st AND 3rd COLUMNS: proposed model (12)-(13) with $\mu = .001$, $\lambda = .005$ for 100 and 75 iterations respectively, 2nd AND 4th COLUMNS: TV-based decomposition model (4) with $\mu = .001$, $\lambda = .005$ for 200 and 75 iterations respectively.

The decompositions in figure 5 demonstrate that both (4) and (12)-(13) can be easily and successfully modified for decomposing color images. The presence or absence of staircasing for both models was similar to that for grayscale image decomposition. The staircasing effect for the cartoon u is still reduced using the adaptive method (12)-(13). Furthermore, the oscillating features are well preserved in v while the boundaries of objects such as the baboon's eye or the rock under the lizard's foot remain sharp in u.

In figures 6 and 7 we give an example where the proposed model can identify regions which are obstructed, but not necessarily segmented by textures. Figure

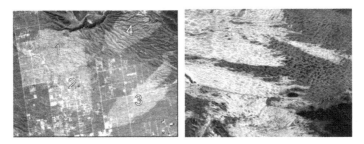

Fig. 6. TOP ROW: *left*: ASTER image of 4 fire scars in the Phoenix, Arizona valley (numbered areas indicate burned regions); *right*: ASTER image of a remote region near Ayers Rock in Australia (yellow indicates burned regions)

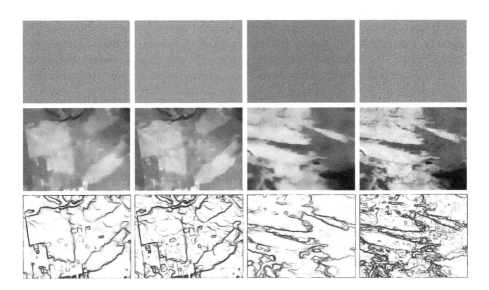

Fig. 7. FIRST ROW: texture part v, SECOND ROW: cartoon part u, THIRD ROW: edge maps (18) of cartoon u. The images were decomposed using: FIRST AND THIRD COLUMNS: proposed model (12)-(13) with $\mu = .001$ and $\lambda = .005$ for 100 and 75 iterations respectively, SECOND AND FOURTH COLUMNS: TV-based decomposition model (4) with $\mu = .001$ and $\lambda = .005$ for 200 iterations each.

6 contains two multi-spectral ASTER (Advanced Spaceborne Thermal Space-borne Emission and Reflectance Radiometer) images which have both been the site of several wildfires. Identification of the fire scar boundaries is difficult to obtain with spectral information information alone given continuously changing properties such as those of the vegetation, atmosphere, etc. [19]. Gradient based edge detection would be insufficient in detecting the boundaries of the target regions given the presence of textures such as road patterns and topography. Furthermore, the textures retain the same oscillatory features both inside and outside the scars, so a proper segmentation could not be based solely on texture analysis. However, we found that performing an appropriate decomposition will leave the target regions intact in the cartoon while removing the textures obstructing their boundaries.

We compare the results of the adaptive and TV based decomposition models applied to both ASTER images. Both models preserve the textures in v as well as the fidelity of the scar edges in u. As in the previous examples, the adaptive model (12)-(13) retains piecewise smooth regions with clear boundaries in u with less evidence of staircasing both inside and outside the target regions.

6   Concluding Remarks

We presented a new model for image decomposition which separates an image into a cartoon and texture component. The model automatically adapts to the local image information while preserving duality between the cartoon and oscillatory component. Sharp object boundaries are preserved while staircasing is avoided in the cartoon, while oscillating features are simultaneously preserved in the texture component. This model is mathematically sound (see appendix) and is successful in decomposing both grayscale and color images.

ACKNOWLEDGEMENTS. We thank Michael Ramsey and Tamara Misner at the University of Pittsburgh for providing the LANDSAT images in Figure 6.

Appendix: Existence and uniqueness of a solution to (12)-(13)

Lemma 1. *The functional* $\Phi(u) = \int_\Omega \phi(x, \nabla u)$, *where* ϕ *is defined in (6), is convex and lower-semicontinuous on* $L^1(\Omega)$; *that is, if* $u_j, u \in BV(\Omega)$ *satisfy* $u_j \to u$ *in* $L^1(\Omega)$ *as* $j \to \infty$ *then*

$$\Phi(u) \leq \liminf_{j \to \infty} \Phi(u_j). \tag{19}$$

Proof. See [11]

Lemma 2. *The functional* $\Psi : L^2(\Omega, R^2) \to R$ *defined by* $\Psi(\xi) := \int_\Omega \frac{1}{p(x)} |\xi|^{p(x)} dx$
$(2 \leq p(x) \leq \beta < \infty$ *for* $x \in \Omega)$ *is convex and lower-semicontinuous on*
$L^1(\Omega, R^2)$; *that is, if* $\xi_j, \xi \in L^2(\Omega, R^2)$ *satisfy* $\xi_j \to \xi$ *in* $L^1(\Omega, R^2)$ *as* $n \to \infty$,
then

$$\Psi(\xi) \leq \liminf_{j \to \infty} \Psi(\xi_j).$$

Proof. Straightforward computations give us that

$$\Psi(\xi) = \sup_{r \in C(\Omega, R^2)} \int_\Omega r \cdot \xi - \frac{1}{q(x)} |r|^{q(x)} dx$$

where $\frac{1}{q(x)} + \frac{1}{p(x)} = 1$ for all $x \in \Omega$. Therefore, Ψ is the pointwise supremum
of a family of continuous affine functions on $L^1(\Omega, R^2)$ and is thus convex and
lower-semicontinuous.

To prove existence and uniqueness of a solution to (12)-(13), we follow a
similar argument to that used in [2, 3, 16].

Theorem 1. *Let* $I \in L^2(\Omega)$. *Then there exists a solution* $(\hat{u}, \hat{\xi}) \in BV(\Omega) \times$
$L^2(\Omega, R^2)$ *of (12)-(13). If* $\int_\Omega I dx \neq 0$, *then the solution is unique.*

Proof. Let (u_n, ξ_n) be a minimizing sequence for $F(u, \xi)$. Then there exists a
constant $C > 0$ such that

$$|u_n|_{BV(\Omega)} \leq C \tag{20}$$

$$||I - u_n - \text{div}\xi_n||^2_{L^2(\Omega)} \leq C \tag{21}$$

$$||\xi_n||_{L^2(\Omega)} \leq C \tag{22}$$

The Poincare-Wirtinger inequality $(||u_n - \int_\Omega u_n||_{L^2(\Omega)} \leq |u_n|_{BV(\Omega)})$ and the
fact that $\int_\Omega u_n dx = \int_\Omega I dx$, give us that

$$||u_n||_{L^2(\Omega)} \leq C. \tag{23}$$

By (20) and (23), there exists a function $\hat{u} \in BV(\Omega)$ such that

$$u_n \to \hat{u} \text{ strongly in } L^1(\Omega) \tag{24}$$

$$u_n \rightharpoonup \hat{u} \text{ weakly in } L^2(\Omega) \tag{25}$$

$$\text{and} \int_\Omega \hat{u} dx = \int_\Omega I dx. \tag{26}$$

For each n, let $v_n = \text{div}\xi_n$. Then $v_n \in L^2(\Omega)$ and by (21) and (23) we also have
that $||v_n||_{L^2(\Omega)} \leq C$. Therefore, there exists $\hat{v} \in L^2(\Omega)$ such that

$$v_n \rightharpoonup \hat{v} \text{ in } L^2(\Omega) \text{ weak} \tag{27}$$

and by (22), there exists $\hat{\xi} \in L^2(\Omega)$ such that

$$\xi_n \rightharpoonup \hat{\xi} \text{ in } L^2(\Omega) \text{ weak.} \tag{28}$$

Therefore, for $\phi \in C_c^\infty(\Omega)$ we have that

$$\int_\Omega v_n\phi dx = \int_\Omega \mathrm{div}\xi_n\phi dx = -\int_\Omega \xi_n \cdot \nabla\phi dx \xrightarrow{n\to\infty} -\int_\Omega \hat\xi \cdot \nabla\phi dx = \int_\Omega \mathrm{div}\hat\xi \phi dx$$

$$\text{and} \quad \int_\Omega v_n\phi dx \xrightarrow{n\to\infty} \int_\Omega \hat v\phi dx.$$

So $\hat v = \mathrm{div}\hat\xi$ in the sense of distribution, but since $\hat v \in L^2(\Omega)$,

$$\hat v = \mathrm{div}\hat\xi \; a.e. \tag{29}$$

From (24), (27), (28), lemmas 1 and 2, and the weak lower-semicontinuity of the L^2 norm, we have that $F(\hat u, \hat\xi) \leq \liminf_{n\to\infty} F(u_n, \xi_n) = \inf F(u, \xi)$. Since the minimizer $(\hat u, \hat\xi)$ satisfies (26) and (29), existence of a solution to (12)-(13) is established.

Finally, we claim that if $\int_\Omega I dx \neq 0$ then the minimizer is unique. We observe that $||I - u - \mathrm{div}\xi||^2_{L^2(\Omega)}$ is strictly convex on $BV(\Omega) \times L^2(\Omega, R^2)$ except along the direction $(u + tu, \mathrm{div}\xi - tu)$, $t \in R$. However, if $(\hat u, \hat\xi)$ is a solution of (12)-(13), then for $t \neq 0$, $(\hat u + t\hat u, \xi)$ cannot be for any $\xi \in L^2(\Omega)$. If it were, then $\int_\Omega \hat u dx = \int_\Omega I dx = (t+1) \int_\Omega \hat u dx$ which is impossible.

References

1. R. Acar and C. R. Vogel. Analysis of bounded variation penalty methods for ill-posed problems. *Inverse Problems*, 10(6):1217–1229, 1994.
2. G. Aubert and J.-F. Aujol. Modeling very oscillating signals. Application to image processing. *Appl. Math. Optim.*, 51(2):163–182, 2005.
3. J.-F. Aujol, G. Aubert, L. Blanc-Feraud, and A. Chambolle. Image decomposition application to sar images. In *Scale space methods in computer vision : 4th international conference, Scale Space 2003, Isle of Skye, UK, June 10-12, 2003 : proceedings/ Lewis D. Griffin, Martin Lillholm (eds.).*, Lecture Notes in Computer Science, pages 297–312. Spring: New York, Berlin, 2003.
4. J.-F. Aujol and A. Chambolle. Dual norms and image decomposition models. *Int. J. Computer Vision*, 63(1):85–104, 2005.
5. P. Blomgren, T. F. Chan, P. Mulet, L. Vese, and W. L. Wan. Variational PDE models and methods for image processing. In *Numerical analysis 1999 (Dundee)*, volume 420 of *Chapman & Hall/CRC Res. Notes Math.*, pages 43–67. Chapman & Hall/CRC, Boca Raton, FL, 2000.
6. A. Chambolle. An algorithm for total variation minimization and applications. *J. Math. Imaging Vision*, 20(1-2):89–97, 2004.
7. A. Chambolle, R. A. DeVore, N.-y. Lee, and B. J. Lucier. Nonlinear wavelet image processing: variational problems, compression, and noise removal through wavelet shrinkage. *IEEE Trans. Image Process.*, 7(3):319–335, 1998.
8. A. Chambolle and P.-L. Lions. Image recovery via total variation minimization and related problems. *Numer. Math.*, 76(2):167–188, 1997.
9. T. F. Chan, S. Esedoglu, and F. Park. A fourth order dual method for staircase reduction in texture extraction and image restoration problems. *Technical Report, University of California, Los Angeles, CA*, CAM05-28, 2005.

10. T. F. Chan, S. Esedoglu, and F. Park. Image decomposition combining staircase reduction and texture extraction. *Technical Report, University of California, Los Angeles, CA*, CAM05-18, 2005.

11. Y. Chen, S. Levine, and M. Rao. Variable exponent, linear growth functionals in image processing. *submitted to SIAM J. Appl. Math.*, 2004.

12. D. L. Donoho and I. M. Johnstone. Adapting to unknown smoothness via wavelet shrinkage. *J. Amer. Statist. Assoc.*, 90(432):1200–1224, 1995.

13. I. Ekeland and R. Temam. *Convex analysis and variational problems.* Translated from the French, Studies in Mathematics and it's Applications, Vol. 1. North-Holland Publishing Co., Amsterdam, 1976.

14. L. C. Evans and R. F. Gariepy. *Measure theory and fine properties of functions.* Studies in Advanced Mathematics. CRC Press, Boca Raton, FL, 1992.

15. Y. Gousseau and J.-M. Morel. Are natural images of bounded variation? *SIAM J. Math. Anal.*, 33(3):634–648 (electronic), 2001.

16. T. M. Le and L. Vese. Image decomposition using total variation and div(bmo). *CAM04-76, UCLA*, 2004.

17. F. Malgouyres. Minimizing the total variation under a general convex constraint for image restoration. *IEEE Trans. Image Process.*, 11(12):1450–1456, 2002.

18. Y. Meyer. *Oscillating patterns in image processing and nonlinear evolution equations*, volume 22 of *University Lecture Series*. American Mathematical Society, Providence, RI, 2001. The fifteenth Dean Jacqueline B. Lewis memorial lectures.

19. T. Misner, M. Ramsey, and J. Arrowsmith. Multi-frequency, multitemporal brush fire scar analysis in a semi-arid urban environment: Implications for future fire and flood hazards. *2002 meeting of the American Geological Society*, 2002.

20. S. Osher, A. Solé, and L. Vese. Image decomposition and restoration using total variation minimization and the H^{-1} norm. *Multiscale Model. Simul.*, 1(3):349–370 (electronic), 2003.

21. L. Rudin, S. Osher, and E. Fatemi. Nonlinear total variation based noise removal algorithms. *Physica D*, 60:259–268, 1992.

22. L. A. Vese and S. J. Osher. Modeling textures with total variation minimization and oscillating patterns in image processing. *J. Sci. Comput.*, 19(1-3):553–572, 2003. Special issue in honor of the sixtieth birthday of Stanley Osher.

23. L. A. Vese and S. J. Osher. Image denoising and decomposition with total variation minimization and oscillatory functions. *J. Math. Imaging Vision*, 20(1-2):7–18, 2004. Special issue on mathematics and image analysis.

Segmentation Informed by Manifold Learning

Qilong Zhang, Richard Souvenir, and Robert Pless

Department of Computer Science and Engineering,
Washington University, St. Louis, MO, 63130, USA
{zql, rms2, pless}@cse.wustl.edu

Abstract. In many biomedical imaging applications, video sequences are captured with low resolution and low contrast challenging conditions in which to detect, segment, or track features. When image deformations have just a few underlying causes, such as continuously captured cardiac MRI without breath-holds or gating, the captured images lie on a low-dimensional, non-linear manifold. The manifold structure of such image sets can be extracted by automated methods for manifold learning. Furthermore, the manifold structure of these images offers new constraints for tracking and segmentation of relevant image regions. We illustrate how to incorporate these new constraints within a snake-based energy minimization approach, and demonstrate improvements in using snakes to segment a set of cardiac MRI images in challenging conditions.

1 Introduction

Many diagnostic and medical applications require segmenting particular tissue structures in every frame of a long 2D or 3D data set. This is challenging because medical video images often have low resolution and low contrast. Combining cues between frames is difficult because often tissues move significantly between frames, and this motion may include complicated deformations that do not lend themselves to simple parameterized models. Creating automated tools to understand and parameterize image data that is affected by a small set of deformations has the potential to impact a large set of relevant medical imaging problems.

For the purpose of segmentation or boundary detection, a collection of tools support imposing various priors on the expected solution. Snakes [1], for instance, are a tool for integrating cues from image data with priors on the expected smoothness of a contour. Within video sequences, these smoothness constraints can be extended to enforce temporal consistency, minimizing variation between consecutive frames, providing cues for segmentation in image regions that have particularly low contrast or high noise.

However, there is often additional structure in a set of images beyond consistency between consecutive frames. In particular, medical image sequences often vary due to a small number of factors. For example, in cardio-pulmonary imaging, the patient breathing cycle causes a deformation of the chest cavity, and the heartbeat leads to large deformations of the shape of the heart. It is complicated

A. Rangarajan et al. (Eds.): EMMCVPR 2005, LNCS 3757, pp. 398–413, 2005.

to define parametric models of these deformations that fit multiple patients. For any one patient, however, a collection of cardio-pulmonary images forms a 2 dimensional manifold, where each image is indexed by the current phase of the breathing and heartbeat cycles.

The observation within this paper is that the manifold structure of these data sets provides *stronger* constraints between images than temporal consistency. In [2], a method is proposed to incorporate a statistical prior on the shape of the segmenting contour, while our work can be viewed as a method to use manifold learning to help enforce priors on the changes of shape. We offer an example mechanism to exploit automated manifold learning tools as a pre-processing step to provide a new multi-image constraint to be used in energy-minimization based segmentation procedures. We implement these tools for the specific case of extracting left ventricle wall contours in cardio-pulmonary MRI. In this example domain, a variation in the breathing cycle leads to a uniform translation of the heart. Variation in the heartbeat cycle leads to variations in the shape of the heart, but, largely, not its position. These deformations suggest that strong constraints can be placed on the expected variation of the heart contour between images — constraints more specific than general smoothness constraints.

The following section gives a brief overview of related work in manifold learning and image segmentation. This is followed by an explanation of how to use Isomap in order to extract the cardiopulmonary manifold structure. Then, the primary contribution of this paper is presented – the classical snake-based energy function is extended in order to exploit using this manifold structure to fit snakes simultaneously in many images. We conclude by demonstrating the efficacy of these constraints on both simulated and real data.

1.1   Background and Previous Work

This work integrates ideas from snake-based energy minimization and manifold learning. To our knowledge, these ideas have not been explicitly considered together before. In order to ground our later presentation, we first introduce, very briefly, some recent research in the use of snakes in biomedical image analysis and an overview of manifold learning.

Snakes for Medical Image Segmentation. The enormous amount of prior work on snakes is a testimony to the effectiveness of active contours on a wide variety of problems in medical imagery (for general reviews, see example [3, 4]). With respect to tracking in cardiovascular imagery, an important use of deformable models is to measure the dynamic behavior of the human heart, especially the left ventricle. Accurately characterizing heart wall motion is necessary to diagnose and estimate the severity and extent of diseases such as ischemia [5].

For this task, one approach uses a 2D deformable contour model to segment the LV boundary in each slice of an initial image volume. These contours are then used as the initial approximation of the LV boundaries in corresponding slices of the image volume at the next time instant and are then deformed to extract the new set of LV boundaries [6, 7].

A traditional snake is a parametric contour embedded in the image plane, represented as a closed curve $C(s) = (x(s), y(s))^\top$, where x and y are the coordinate functions and $s \in [0, 1]$ is the parametric domain. The shape of the contour minimizes the following functional:

$$E = \int_0^1 E_{int}(C(s)) + E_{img}(C(s)) + E_{con}(C(s))ds, \qquad (1)$$

where E_{int} represents the internal energy of the snake due to bending, E_{img} is the image energy derived from the image, and its local minima coincide with intensity extrema, edges, and other image features of interest, and E_{con} is a place holder for additional constraints appropriate for a given context, including prior shape models and limitations on changes between consecutive images. Our contribution within this work is to offer a method for having these additional constraints depend upon the automatically extracted manifold structure of an image set.

Once the energy function is specified, one can obtain the snake minimizing the functional in Equation 1 by solving the following Euler-Lagrange equation:

$$C_t = -\alpha \frac{\partial^2 C}{\partial s^2} + \beta \frac{\partial^4 C}{\partial s^4} + \nabla E_{img} \qquad (2)$$

where C_t is the partial derivative of $C(s, t)$ with respect to the introduced time variable t, which tracks the evolution of the snake. Equilibrium is achieved when the internal force and image force balance and the left-hand side term C_t vanishes.

The *internal energy* can be written as:

$$E_{int} = \frac{1}{2}\left(\alpha \left| \frac{\partial C}{\partial s} \right|^2 + \beta \left| \frac{\partial^2 C}{\partial s^2} \right|^2 \right) \qquad (3)$$

where α and β are blending parameters that control the snake tension and rigidity, respectively.

A commonly used *external* image force is gradient vector flow (GVF) [8, 9]. This is a bidirectional image force ∇E_{img} that can capture the object boundaries from either side and can deal with concave regions. A GVF field $\mathbf{v}(x, y)$ is defined as the equilibrium solution of the following system of partial equations:

$$\mathbf{v}_t = g(|\nabla f|)\nabla^2 \mathbf{v} - h(|\nabla f|)(\mathbf{v} - \nabla f)$$
$$\mathbf{v}(x, y, 0) = \nabla f \qquad (4)$$

where $\mathbf{v}_t$ is the partial derivative of $\mathbf{v}(x, y, t)$ with respect to t, and ∇f is the gradient of the image edge map. The steady state of this update equation depends on the scalar parameter κ which affects the relative weight of the smoothness term $g(|\nabla f|) = \exp\{-(\frac{|\nabla f|}{\kappa})^2\}$ and the term that fits the GVF to the image gradient $h(|\nabla f|) = 1 - g(|\nabla f|)$.

In section 3 we offer a definition of a new E_{con} term that is used to enforce constraints that are available from an understanding the intrinsic manifold structure of an image set. The next section gives a brief background on these automated manifold learning methods, and their recent specialization for medical imagery.

Manifold Learning. Image data can be naturally represented as points in a high dimensional data space (one dimension for each pixel). Often, however, a set of images has a lower *intrinsic* dimensionality, and the image data set can be mapped onto a lower dimensional space. Classical dimensionality reduction techniques for image sets rely on Principle Component Analysis (PCA) [10] and Independent Component Analysis (ICA) [11]. These seek to represent data as linear combinations of a small number of basis vectors. However, many natural image data sets have an intrinsic dimensionality that is much less than the number of basis images required to linearly reconstruct them.

This has led to a number of methods seeking to parameterize low-dimensional, non-linear manifolds. These methods measure local distances or approximate geodesic distances between points in the original data set, and seek low-dimensional embeddings that preserve these properties. Isomap [12] extends classic multidimensional scaling (MDS) by substituting an estimate of the geodesic distance along the image manifold for the inter-image Euclidean distance as input. LLE [13] attempts to represent the image manifold locally by reconstructing each image as weighted combination of its neighbors. SDE [14] applies semi-definite programming to learn kernel matrices which can be used to create isometric embeddings.

Isomap performs well for image sets sampled from convex manifolds. LLE and SDE do not fail in the case of non-convexity, but do not provide minimal parameterizations for cyclic manifolds (i.e., they give points on a sphere three coordinates instead of two). One algorithm which explicitly addresses cyclic manifolds is [15]. These algorithms, and others [16, 17, 18] have been used in various applications, including classification, recognition, tracking, and to a limited extent, biomedical image analysis [19]. Using image distance measures that explicitly reflect the variations within the image set (for instance, using estimates of the local deformation instead of pixel intensity differences) has been shown to be advantageous for medical imagery, and leads to low-dimensional embeddings that more accurately reflect the underlying intrinsic degrees of freedom [20, 21].

2   Cardio-Pulmonary Image Manifolds

Cardio-pulmonary MRI imagery is an outstanding candidate for manifold analysis. The appearance and deformations of MRI imagery of the chest varies greatly from patient to patient. However, images of a particular patient vary with the global deformation of the chest cavity due to breathing, deformation of the heart and nearby tissues due to heartbeats, and image noise.

The analysis of these images, even the *capture* of MR imagery, is affected by these parameters. Diagnostic imaging often requires "held-breath" and cardiac-gated imaging. These protocols offer two distinct methods to minimize variation in the captured imagery. The "held-breath" protocols require the patient to minimize variation due to breathing (by capturing all the imagery while the patient holds their breath and minimizes lung motion). Cardiac-gated imaging triggers the image capture to always occur at the same part of the cardiac cycle.

When the diagnostic value of imaging comes from analysis of motion, the imaging process takes unconstrained samples of the cardiopulmonary image manifold — a set of images that vary due to the heart and lung deformation. In this section we consider the post hoc analysis of samples of the cardiopulmonary image manifold. Although heartbeat monitors are relatively unobtrusive and common in diagnostic environments, we explore methods that operate only on the images without any additional knowledge, and focus on tools that will be effective in the presence of significant noise. To make this presentation concrete, we focus on a particular, noisy MRI image set, which is illustrated in Figures 1,4,5.

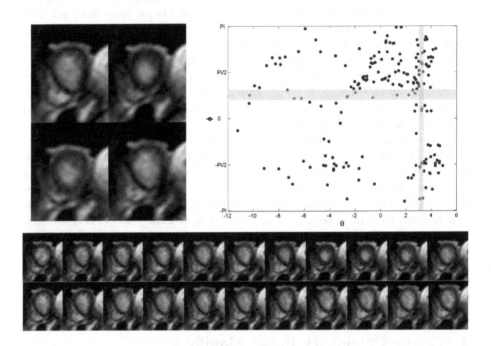

Fig. 1. The top left shows four images from a 200 image cardio-pulmonary MRI cine sequence of the heart. Note the variation both in the shape of the left ventricle (the white blob roughly centered in the image) and the position of the heart (shifting vertically). The top right shows the cylindrical Isomap embedding of this data set (using the algorithm of [15]). The scale of the axes is the same, and is proportional to the distance between images (measured, as discussed in the text, as the sum of the phase difference of a grid of complex Gabor filters). Cylindrical Isomap imposes a scale factor so that the y-axis (the cyclic axis) is embedded in the range $[-\pi, \pi)$. The bottom of the figure shows two sequences, example images from two paths through the Isomap embedding. The top sequence shows ordered image from a vertical path (drawn in yellow) at $\theta \approx 3.1$. Notice that in these images the heart deforms due to its beating, but there is no translation of the heart. The bottom sequences shows image for which $\phi \approx \pi/4$. Notice here that the heart is not deforming, but rather there is a translation (due to breathing).

2.1   Isomap Embedding of Cardiopulmonary Manifolds

The Isomap procedure for dimensionality reduction starts by computing the distance between all pairs of images (using some distance function such as SSD pixel intensities). Then, a graph is defined with each image as a node and undirected edges connecting each image to its k-closest neighbors (usually choosing k between 5 and 10). A complete pair-wise distance matrix is calculated by solving for the all-pairs shortest paths in this sparse graph. Finally, this complete distance matrix is embedded into low dimensions, by solving an Eigenvalue problem using a technique called Multidimensional Scaling (MDS) [22]. The low-dimensional embedding can be chosen as desired, but ideally is the number of degrees of freedom in the image set, in our case 2 (the two intrinsic dimensions of variability are the heartbeat and breathing).

One previous work that applied manifold learning to biomedical image analysis suggests modifying Isomap to use image distance functions other than pixel intensity differences [21]. For data sets with deformable motion, the suggested distance function is computed as the phase difference of local Gabor filters, where the filters have a reasonable magnitude:

$$||I_1 - I_2||_{motion} = \sum_{x,y} \Psi(G_{(\omega,V,\sigma)} \otimes I_1, G_{(\omega,V,\sigma)} \otimes I_2) + \Psi(G_{(\omega,H,\sigma)} \otimes I_1, G_{(\omega,H,\sigma)} \otimes I_2)$$

where $G_{(\omega,\{V|H\},\sigma)}$ is defined to be the 2D complex Gabor filter with frequency ω, oriented either vertically or horizontally, with σ as the variance of the modulating Gaussian, and Ψ returns the phase difference of the pair of complex Gabor responses above some threshold τ; we choose τ to be the 50-th percentile filter magnitude. A technical modification to the Isomap procedure also allows the images to be embedded on a cylindrical manifold instead of a flat plane [15]. Figure 1 illustrates the cylindrical embedding of 185 frame cardiac MRI image set, captured each 72 ms. The figure also illustrates that the manifold embedding separates the non-rigid deformation of the heart from the translation of the heart due to breathing. In the next section, we consider how to exploit this manifold structure to provide new constraints for defining contours over every image of a data set undergoing such deformations.

3   Segmentation Constraints

The manifold embedding provides an automated tool to parameterize the cardiac image data, in terms of the motion caused by the heartbeat and the breathing. In this section we propose a method to solve for contours of the left ventricle in all images in the data set simultaneously. This solution uses two new constraints, first, a generic smoothness constraint that penalizes variation in contours that fit images nearby in the manifold, and second, a term that uses the specific nature of the image changes along different manifold directions to provide stronger constraints on manifold shape.

For a cardiopulmonary image sequence, heart deformation through time is defined by cardiac phase ϕ and pulmonary phase θ. Therefore, we seek to define the shape of the heart contour as a function of ϕ and θ, described by $C(s, \phi, \theta) = (x(s, \phi, \theta), y(s, \phi, \theta))^\top$. For a fixed ϕ, θ varying the arc-length parameter s traces out the contour boundary. Varying ϕ, θ defines all possible contours of the heart observed. A given cardiopulmonary image sequence specifies this contour by minimizing the following functional:

$$E = \oint E_{int}(C(s, \phi, \theta)) + E_{img}(C(s, \phi, \theta)) + E_{con}(C(s, \phi, \theta)) \ ds \ d\phi \ d\theta \quad (5)$$

The generic smoothness constraints (between nearby images on the manifold), can be written naturally as a parallel to the internal energy of the snake model, as follows:

$$E_{int} = \frac{1}{2} \left[\alpha \left| \frac{\partial C}{\partial s} \right|^2 + \beta \left| \frac{\partial^2 C}{\partial s^2} \right|^2 + \mu \left(\left| \frac{\partial C}{\partial \phi} \right|^2 + \left| \frac{\partial C}{\partial \theta} \right|^2 \right) + \gamma \left(\left| \frac{\partial^2 C}{\partial \phi^2} \right|^2 + \left| \frac{\partial^2 C}{\partial \theta^2} \right|^2 \right) \right]$$
$$(6)$$

where parameter μ and γ control the snake's tension and rigidity along ϕ and θ, respectively.

More specific constraints are available when the manifold dimensions correspond to specific kinds of motion. The breathing of the patient, while causing a complicated deformation of the chest cavity as a whole, results, largely, in a translation of the heart. The cardiac cycle, absent motion caused by breathing, causes deformation with minimal overall translation. Both of these types of motion allow stronger constraints on the relationship of a contour between frames than simple temporal continuity. Therefore, there are additional constraints between images that are embedded at either the same ϕ coordinate or the same θ coordinate. These constraints can be written as:

$$E_{con} = \frac{\eta}{2} \left| \frac{\partial C}{\partial \theta} - \int_0^1 \frac{\partial C}{\partial \theta} ds \right|^2 + \frac{\rho}{2} \left| \int_0^1 \frac{\partial C}{\partial \phi} ds \right|^2, \quad (7)$$

where the first term penalizes non-rigid changes in the snake (by integrating the squared difference between the motion of points on the contour and the mean motion of the contour), and the second term penalizes the overall mean translational motion of the snake, which is minimal when motion is caused only by the heartbeat. The rest of this section details our implementation of these constraints.

3.1   Implementation

Splines are a widely used function approximation tool [23]. A snake can be modeled by a closed cubic b-spline with N control points $\{p_i = (x_i, y_i)^\top, i = 1 \cdots N\}$, and a closed curve $C(s)$ as a collection of n curve segments $g_i(s), s \in [0, 1]$. Each curve segment is controlled by four nearby control points, as follows:

$$g_i(s) = \sum_{j=0}^{3} b_j(s) p_{i+j-1}, i = 1, \cdots, N \quad (8)$$

where $p_0 = p_N, p_{N+1} = p_1$ and $p_{N+2} = p_2$. Uniform cubic B-spline basis functions, $b_0 \sim b_3$, are defined by:

$$b_0(s) = \frac{1}{6}(1-s)^3$$
$$b_1(s) = \frac{1}{6}(3s^3 - 6s^2 + 4)$$
$$b_2(s) = \frac{1}{6}(-3s^3 + 3s^2 + 3s + 1)$$
$$b_3(s) = \frac{1}{6}s^3 \tag{9}$$

Then, the snake contour $C(s)$ is represented by multiplying a vector $\mathbf{P}$ of snake control points with its associated b-spline basis functions:

$$\underbrace{\begin{bmatrix} g_1 \\ g_2 \\ \vdots \\ g_N \end{bmatrix}}_{\mathbf{C}(s)} = \underbrace{\begin{bmatrix} b_1 & b_2 & b_3 & & \cdots & & b_0 \\ b_0 & b_1 & b_2 & b_3 & \cdots & & \\ & b_0 & b_1 & b_2 & b_3 & \cdots & \\ \vdots & & \ddots & \ddots & \ddots & \ddots & \\ & & \cdots & b_0 & b_1 & b_2 & b_3 \\ b_3 & & \cdots & & b_0 & b_1 & b_2 \\ b_2 & b_3 & & \cdots & & b_0 & b_1 \end{bmatrix}}_{\mathbf{H}(s)} \underbrace{\begin{bmatrix} p_1 \\ p_2 \\ \vdots \\ p_N \end{bmatrix}}_{\mathbf{P}} \tag{10}$$

Using b-spline representation, one can analytically compute the snake's k-th order of derivatives with respect to s as:

$$\frac{\partial^k \mathbf{C}(s)}{\partial s^k} = \frac{\partial^k \mathbf{H}(s)}{\partial s^k} \mathbf{P}. \tag{11}$$

To create a set of samples along each curve segment p_i, we can choose a set of parametric variables $\{s_j, \; j = 1, \cdots, k\}$, such that $0 \leq s_1 < s_2 < \ldots < s_k < 1$. Then the snake can be written in a discrete form:

$$\mathbf{C} = \begin{bmatrix} \mathbf{C}(s_1) \\ \mathbf{C}(s_2) \\ \vdots \\ \mathbf{C}(s_k) \end{bmatrix} = \underbrace{\begin{bmatrix} \mathbf{H}(s_1) \\ \mathbf{H}(s_2) \\ \vdots \\ \mathbf{H}(s_k) \end{bmatrix}}_{\mathbf{H}} \mathbf{P} \tag{12}$$

Because it is our intention to solve simultaneously for snakes in every image, we parameterize the snake control points in each image as a function of position of each image on the manifold. Given an image sequence of M frames, we use the manifold learning procedure to estimate the breathing phase θ and cardiac phase ϕ for each image. For the i-th frame, let these values be (ϕ_i, θ_i). Let

$\mathbf{C}(\phi_i, \theta_i)$ denote the snake defined by a discrete set of control points $\mathbf{P}(\phi_i, \theta_i) = [p_1(\phi_i, \theta_i), p_2(\phi_i, \theta_i), \cdots, p_n(\phi_i, \theta_i)]^\top$. Then we can express the set of all snakes in all images as:

$$
\underbrace{\begin{bmatrix} \mathbf{C}(\phi_1, \theta_1) \\ \mathbf{C}(\phi_2, \theta_2) \\ \vdots \\ \mathbf{C}(\phi_M, \theta_M) \end{bmatrix}}_{\mathbb{C}} = \underbrace{\begin{bmatrix} \mathbf{H} & & & \\ & \mathbf{H} & & \\ & & \ddots & \\ & & & \mathbf{H} \end{bmatrix}}_{\mathbb{H}} \underbrace{\begin{bmatrix} \mathbf{P}(\phi_1, \theta_1) \\ \mathbf{P}(\phi_2, \theta_2) \\ \vdots \\ \mathbf{P}(\phi_M, \theta_M) \end{bmatrix}}_{\mathbb{P}}
\tag{13}
$$

For any control point $p_i(\phi, \theta)$, its position changes in different frames as a function of ϕ and θ. To model the relationship of the positions of control point p_i between different frames, we use a cubic B-spline surface to represent the position of each point p_i. Any point on that surface presents the position of control point p_i in the frame specified by (ϕ, θ). Therefore, the change of the control point position should be locally small and continuous.

The cubic b-spline surface for the i-th snake control point is defined by a two-dimensional set of control points $\{q_{u,v}^{(i)}, u = 1, \cdots, n; v = 1, \cdots, m\}$. The following is the equation of a cubic b-spline surface defined by n rows and m columns of surface control points:

$$
p_i(\phi, \theta) = \sum_{u=1}^{n} \sum_{v=1}^{m} B_u(\phi) B_v(\theta) q_{u,v}^i
$$

$$
= \underbrace{\begin{bmatrix} B_1(\phi)B_1(\theta) \\ B_2(\phi)B_1(\theta) \\ \vdots \\ B_n(\phi)B_1(\theta) \\ B_1(\phi)B_2(\theta) \\ \vdots \\ B_n(\phi)B_m(\theta) \end{bmatrix}}_{\mathbf{B}(\phi,\theta)}^{\top} \underbrace{\begin{bmatrix} q_{1,1}^{(i)} \\ q_{2,1}^{(i)} \\ \vdots \\ q_{m,1}^{(i)} \\ q_{1,2}^{(i)} \\ \vdots \\ q_{m,n}^{(i)} \end{bmatrix}}_{\mathbf{Q}_i}
\tag{14}
$$

where $B_i(\phi)$ and $B_j(\theta)$ are cubic b-spline basis functions. Then we can analytically compute the k-th order of derivatives of control point p_i with respect to ϕ (or θ) as

$$
\frac{\partial^k p_i(\phi, \theta)}{\partial \phi^k} = \frac{\partial^k \mathbf{B}(\phi, \theta)}{\partial \phi^k} \mathbf{Q}_i, \quad \frac{\partial^k p_i(\phi, \theta)}{\partial \theta^k} = \frac{\partial^k \mathbf{B}(\phi, \theta)}{\partial \theta^k} \mathbf{Q}_i
\tag{15}
$$

Considering all control points over all frames, we have

$$\mathbb{P} = \begin{bmatrix} \mathbf{P}(\phi_1,\theta_1) \\ \mathbf{P}(\phi_2,\theta_2) \\ \vdots \\ \mathbf{P}(\phi_n,\theta_n) \end{bmatrix} = \underbrace{\begin{bmatrix} \mathbf{B}(\phi_1,\theta_1) & & & & & \\ & \mathbf{B}(\phi_1,\theta_1) & & & & \\ & & \ddots & \mathbf{B}(\phi_1,\theta_1) & & \\ \vdots & & & \vdots & & \\ \mathbf{B}(\phi_m,\theta_m) & & & & & \\ & \mathbf{B}(\phi_m,\theta_m) & & & & \\ & & & & \ddots & \mathbf{B}(\phi_m,\theta_m) \end{bmatrix}}_{\mathbb{B}} \underbrace{\begin{bmatrix} \mathbf{Q}_1 \\ \mathbf{Q}_2 \\ \vdots \\ \mathbf{Q}_m \end{bmatrix}}_{Q} \tag{16}$$

Finally, we have a single form which expresses the contours in all images:

$$\mathbb{C} = \mathbb{H}\mathbb{P} = \mathbb{H}\mathbb{B}Q. \tag{17}$$

Using the calculus of variations, the snake minimizing the functional in (5) can be found by solving for the following Euler-Lagrange equation:

$$\frac{\partial E}{\partial C} = \frac{\partial E_{int}}{\partial C} + \nabla E_{img} + \frac{\partial E_{con}}{\partial C} = 0$$

$$\Rightarrow -\alpha \frac{\partial^2 C}{\partial s^2} + \beta \frac{\partial^4 C}{\partial s^4} - \mu \left(\frac{\partial^2 C}{\partial \phi^2} + \frac{\partial^2 C}{\partial \theta^2} \right) + \gamma \left(\frac{\partial^4 C}{\partial \phi^4} + \frac{\partial^4 C}{\partial \theta^4} \right)$$

$$+ \nabla E_{img} - \rho \left(\frac{\partial^2 C}{\partial \theta^2} - \int_0^1 \frac{\partial^2 C}{\partial \theta^2} \, ds \right) - \eta \int_0^1 \frac{\partial^2 C}{\partial \phi^2} \, ds = 0$$

$$\Rightarrow \mathbf{A}_{int}\mathbb{C} + \mathbf{A}_{con}\mathbb{C} - \mathbf{V} = 0 \tag{18}$$

where $\mathbf{A}_{int}$ and $\mathbf{A}_{con}$ are matrices corresponding to internal energy and external constraint energy term, respectively, and they can be directly computed using equations in (17), (15),and (11). $\mathbf{V}$ is the matrix presenting the collection of GVF $\mathbf{v}$ sampled along $C(s,\phi,\theta)$ over all images. Since the snake is implemented using cubic b-spline, all 4-th order of partial derivatives of C with respect to s, ϕ and θ are zero. Hence, in the later sections, we will ignore the blending parameters β and γ in the equations in (18).

In order to obtained desired solution of the Euler equation (18), the snake $C(s,\phi,\theta)$ is treated as a function evolves with respect to time variable t, and the resulting equation is

$$\mathbf{A}_{int}\mathbb{C}^{t+1} - \mathbf{V} + \mathbf{A}_{con}\mathbb{C}^{t+1} = -\delta(\mathbb{C}^{t+1} - \mathbb{C}^t) \tag{19}$$

where δ denotes a step size. At equilibrium, the time derivative vanishes and we end up from equation (19) and (17) the following update rules as:

$$\mathbb{C}^{t+1} = (\mathbf{A}_{int} + \mathbf{A}_{con} + \delta \mathbf{I})^{-1}(\delta \mathbb{C}^t + \mathbf{V})$$

$$\Rightarrow Q^{t+1} = [(\mathbf{A}_{int} + \mathbf{A}_{con} + \delta \mathbf{I})\mathbb{H}\mathbb{B}]^+ (\delta \mathbb{H}\mathbb{B}Q^t + \mathbf{V}) \tag{20}$$

where $\mathbf{I}$ denotes identity matrix.

4   Experimental Results

This section describes preliminary results of a system that implements the constraints defined in the last section. We first consider a collection of artificially generated data, for which we can control the deformation and noise parameters, and test our approach versus standard snake approaches. We follow this with an application to finding the left ventricle wall shape in a noise cardiac MRI sequence. In both cases, we used $\alpha = 0.1$ for all snakes, and $\mu = 0.1$, $\rho = 0.1$ and $\eta = 0.01$ for manifold constraints. Deriving optimal choices for these parameters, or other methods to automate the process of finding good parameters is in further investigation.

4.1   Simulation Data

We construct an artificial data set by defining a shape and deforming it with a composition of a non-rigid deformation and a rigid translation. Thus, this data set has a 2D manifold structure, indexed by the magnitude of each deformation. One hundred images were created, each was then corrupted by additive white Gaussian noise, and the contrast was decreased in a randomly selected patch of the image. The two deformation types are depicted in the top of Figure 2, and 8 selected frames among the 100 generated images are shown at the top right.

The noise in the image and the low contrast patches make this a challenging data set for snakes to converge to the correct boundary. The second column of Figure 2 gives results for classical snakes (using only a single image) with the starting condition shown in the first column. While some optimization is possible to improve these results for this data set, for this work it is our goal to illustrate the advantages of using the manifold structure of these images.

The third column of Figure 2 gives the contours which are the results of applying the algorithm of the previous section, which exploits the manifold structure of these images. These can be compared to the ground truth contours shown in the rightmost column.

4.2   Example Application

In cardiovascular imagery, an important application is to measure the dynamic behavior of the human heart, especially the left ventricle. Figure 3 illustrates one example of coupled snakes [24, 25] that outline the interior and exterior wall of the left ventricle. Often, For continuously captured cine-MRI images, the available resolution and contrast is more limited than this example shows, and extracting ventricle wall contours on each image individually is difficult. By imposing manifold constraints, we solved the problem with a modified version of [25].

Figure 4 shows examples of cine-MRI images (from the same data set as shown in Figure 1). The rectangular region of the heart is blown up and the results of fitting pairs of snakes to the inner and outer ventricle wall on individual images is shown in the middle column. On the right of this figure are

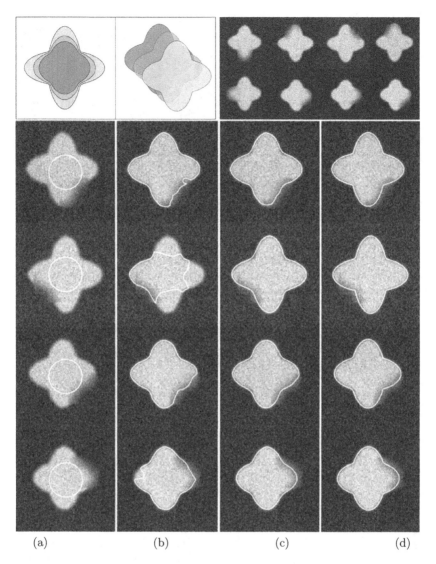

(a)   (b)   (c)   (d)

Fig. 2. An artificial data set constructed by composing 2 deformations (shown in the top row), a non-rigid variation to a shape and a rigid translation. The bottom four rows show results fitting snakes to these images which are corrupted by zero mean Gaussian noise and by a patch of reduced contrast. Column (a) shows the image and the initial condition, column (b) shows the classical snake result on this image, column (c) shows the result (for that image) of using the manifold based constraints to solve for all snakes simultaneously, and (d) is the ground truth contour used to generate each image.

the results when enforcing the additional constraints from understanding the manifold image structure, following the algorithm outlined in Section 3. While these results are not perfect, they are an improvement and encourage further

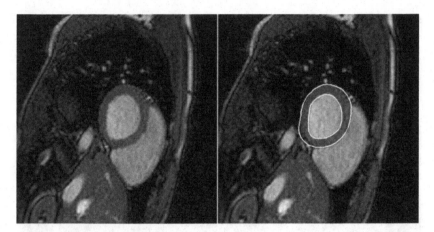

Fig. 3. Important applications in cardiac imagery include measuring the thickness of ventricle walls. For relatively high contrast, and high resolution images, a pair of snakes can find both the inner and outer wall. Applying this algorithm to lower resolution images (in Figure 4) fails because of insufficient image resolution and contrast.

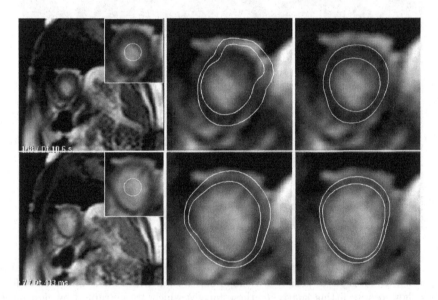

Fig. 4. For continuously captured cine-MRI images, there are currently limits on the available resolution and contrast. Extracting ventricle wall contours on each image individually is difficult. The original image is shown on the left, and a subwindow shows an expansion of the heart region, and the initial snake contour (for the interior wall). The contours extracted from a single image are shown in the middle. On the right are the results when enforcing the additional shape constraints from the manifold structure extracted in Figure 1.

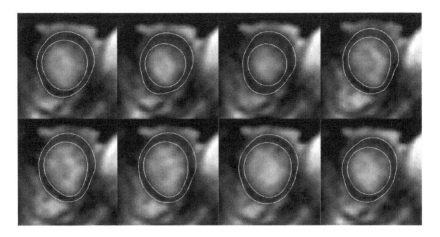

Fig. 5. Additional segmentation results obtained by imposing our manifold constraints over the whole image sequence. Here we show 8 consecutive frames of the 200 frame sequence. Notice that in these cardio-plumonary images, the heart deformation is sometimes large between consecutive images due to the relatively low sampling rate. In these cases, naive temporal smoothness constraints on heart deformation may fail.

work in integrating manifold constraints with energy minimization tools for contour fitting. Additional results are shown in Figure 5, for 8 consecutive images of the cine sequence. The frame to frame deformation is in some cases quite large, so naive smoothness constraints between consecutive images may not be successful.

5   Conclusion

This work presents preliminary efforts towards incorporating manifold learning as a tool to provide additional constraints for finding contours using energy minimization tools. The advantages of combining these two techniques were illustrated for a collection of simulation data and demonstrated on a low-resolution, high-noise cardiac MRI video sequence.

It is also possible to extend the manifold constraints to a level set based segmentation framework for handling topological changes and numerical stability of evolving curves [26]. We believe that many algorithms may be improved through better understanding and exploitation of non-linear image manifold learning algorithms, and tight integration of these with classical analysis tools.

Acknowledgements

This research was supported by NSF grant IIS-0413291.

References

1. Kass, M., Witkin, A., Terzopoulos, D.: Snakes: Active contour models. International Journal of Computer Vision 1 (1988) 321–331
2. Cremers, D., Tischhäuser, F., Weickert, J., Schnörr, C.: Diffusion snakes: Introducing statistical shape knowledge into the mumford-shah functional. International Journal of Computer Vision 50 (2002) 295–313
3. Duncan, J.C., Ayache, N.: Medical image analysis: Progress over two decades and the challenges ahead. IEEE Trans. Pattern Anal. Mach. Intell. 22 (2000) 85–106
4. Frangi, A.F., Rueckert, D., Duncan, J.S.: Three-dimensional cardiovascular image analysis. IEEE Trans. Med. Imaging 21 (2002) 1005–1010
5. McInerney, T., Terzopoulos, D.: Deformable models in medical images analysis: a survey. Medical Image Analysis 1 (1996) 91–108
6. Ueda, N., Mase, K.: Tracking moving contours using energy-minimizing elastic contour models. International Journal of Pattern Recognition and Artificial Intelligence 9 (1995) 465–484
7. Geiger, D., Gupta, A., Costa, L.A., Vlontzos, J.: Dynamic programming for detecting, tracking, and matching deformable contours. IEEE Trans. Pattern Anal. Mach. Intell. 17 (1995) 294–302
8. Xu, C., Prince, J.L.: Gradient vector flow: A new external force for snakes. In: Proceedings of the Conference on Computer Vision and Pattern Recognition, Washington, DC, USA (1997) 66
9. Xu, C., Prince, J.L.: Generalized gradient vector flow external forces for active contours. Signal Process. 71 (1998) 131–139
10. Jolliffe, I.T.: Principal Component Analysis. Springer-Verlag (1986)
11. Hyvärinen, A., Karhunen, J., Oja, E.: Independent Component Analysis. John Wiley and Sons (2001)
12. Tenenbaum, J.B., de Silva, V., Langford, J.C.: A global geometric framework for nonlinear dimensionality reduction. Science 290 (2000) 2319–2323
13. Roweis, S.T., Saul, L.K.: Nonlinear dimensionality reduction by locally linear embedding. Science 290 (2000) 2323–2326
14. Weinberger, K.Q., Saul, L.K.: Unsupervised learning of image manifolds by semidefinite programming. In: Computer Vision and Pattern Recognition. (2004)
15. Pless, R., Simon, I.: Embedding images in non-flat spaces. In: Proc. of the International Conference on Imaging Science, Systems, and Technology. (2002)
16. Donoho, D.L., Grimes, C.: Hessian eigenmaps: Locally linear embedding techniques for high-dimensional data. PNAS 100 (2003) 5591–5596
17. Brand, M.: Charting a manifold. In S. Becker, S.T., Obermayer, K., eds.: Advances in Neural Information Processing Systems 15. MIT Press, Cambridge, MA (2003) 961–968
18. Belkin, M., Niyogi, P.: Laplacian eigenmaps and spectral techniques for embedding and clustering. In: Advances in Neural Information Processing Systems. (2002)
19. Lim, I.S., Ciechomski, P.d.H., Sarni, S., Thalmann, D.: Planar arrangement of high-dimensional biomedical data sets by isomap coordinates. In: Proceedings of the 16th IEEE Symposium on Computer-Based Medical Systems. (2003) 50–55
20. Pless, R.: Differential structure in non-linear image embedding functions. In: Articulated and Nonrigid Motion. (2004)
21. Souvenir, R., Pless, R.: Isomap and non-parametric models of image deformation. In: In Proc. IEEE Workshop on Motion and Video Computing, Breckenridge, CO (2005)

22. Borg, I., Groenen, P.: Modern Multidimensional Scaling: Theory and Applications. Springer-Verlag (1997)
23. Dierckx, P.: Curve and surface fitting with splines. Oxford University Press, Inc., New York, NY, USA (1993)
24. Paragios, N.: A variational approach for the segmentation of the left ventricle in cardiac image analysis. International Journal of Computer Vision **50** (2002) 345–362
25. Malpicaa, N., Ledesma-Carbayoa, M., Santosa, A., Prezb, E., Garca-Fernandezb, M., Descob, M.: A coupled active contour model for myocardial tracking in contrast echocardiography. In: Image Understanding and Analysis, Imperial College London, UK (2004)
26. Zhang, Q., Pless, R.: Segmenting cardiopulmonary images using manifold learning with level sets. In: ICCV workshop on Computer Vision for Biomedical Image Applications: Current Techniques and Future Trends, Beijing, China (2005)

One-Shot Integral Invariant Shape Priors for Variational Segmentation*

Siddharth Manay[1,**], Daniel Cremers[2], Anthony Yezzi[3], and Stefano Soatto[4]

[1] Lawrence Livermore National Laboratory
smanay.ece98@gtlaumni.org
[2] Siemens Corporate Research
daniel.cremers@siemens.com
[3] Georgia Institute of Technology
anthony.yezzi@gatech.edu
[4] University of California at Los Angeles
soatto@cs.ucla.edu

Abstract. We match shapes, even under severe deformations, via a smooth re-parametrization of their integral invariant signatures. These robust signatures and correspondences are the foundation of a shape energy functional for variational image segmentation. Integral invariant shape templates do not require registration and allow for significant deformations of the contour, such as the articulation of the object's parts. This enables generalization to multiple instances of a shape from a single template, instead of requiring several templates for searching or training. This paper motivates and presents the energy functional, derives the gradient descent direction to optimize the functional, and demonstrates the method, coupled with a data term, on real image data where the object's parts are articulated.

1   Introduction

As computational vision continues the transition from low-level representations of knowledge (edges, features) to high-level representations, shape has become a key component in the detection and recognition of objects. Unfortunately, shape is an elusive concept; shape is the object data left after removing all the "uninteresting" (in this context) dependencies: translation, rotation, scale [1], photometry, articulation, class variation, etc.

Fig. 1 briefly illustrates the difficulties that arise when segmenting an object from an image. The varying illumination, textured/noisy background, and similar intensity values in the fore/background make intensity-based segmentation methods alone useless.

---

* UCRL-CONF-212393. This work was performed under the auspices of the U. S. Department of Energy by Univesity of California Lawrence Livermore National Laboratory under contract No. W-7405-Eng-48. Supported by NSF IIS-0208197, AFOSR F49620-03-1-0095, ONR N00014-03-1-0850.

** Corresponding author can be reached at: Center for Applied Scientific Computing, Lawrence Livermore National Laboratory, P.O. Box 808, L-551, Livermore, CA 94551-9900. (925) 423-7431.

A. Rangarajan et al. (Eds.): EMMCVPR 2005, LNCS 3757, pp. 414–426, 2005.

Fig. 1. Similar objects with a variation of its articulated parts. We desire a shape template for segmenting these images that will handle these variations.

A shape template would help; but several templates or a learned probabilistic model of the templates (which in turn requires several templates in the form of a training set) would be needed to segment all the images. Yet humans understand the shape and its variations as well as the backs of their own hands.

This paper proposes to extend the recent work on integral invariant shape descriptors [2, 3, 4] for shapes represented as closed planar contours. These functions are by construction invariant to many of the nuisance factors that make shape analysis difficult (photometry and group actions) and robust to other such nuisances (local deformation of the shape due to articulations or parts, occlusions, or noise). These properties make integral invariants ideal for shape recognition despite nuisances. For the same reasons, integral invariants make ideal candidates for shape templates.

Our contribution is to propose a method for matching shapes undergoing severe deformations, and develop a segmentation scheme that enforces prior shape knowledge through integral invariant representations. This includes using a local representation in terms of an integral invariant signatures, as done by several authors before (reviewed in Sections 1.1 and 2.1), with a smooth re-parametrization of the shape domain to allow for large deformations (Section 2.2). We apply this model to derive an energy functional to enforce shape priors for segmentation (Section 4) and illustrate promising preliminary results for segmentation tasks (Section 5).

1.1 Prior Shapes in Variational Segmentation

Shape has a long history; we only make a few notes on the works that provide context for the interested reader. There are many representations of shape and frameworks for their study, decomposition, and comparison. Statistical methods based landmarks on parameterized contours were pursued in [5, 6, 7, 8]. Representations of shape independent of parameterization began in [9] and continues today [10, 3]. This work ties closely with representations of shape as points on an infinite dimensional manifold, where the deformations are the actions of Lie groups [11, 12, 13, 14, 10]. These approaches based on an explicit representation of shape enable the definition of correspondences between shapes [15, 16, 10].

For variational contour-evolution methods for segmentation [17, 18, 19, 20, 21], a statistical representation of shape is used to cope with class variability [22, 23, 24, 25, 26, 7] Unlike statistical methods which require a training set, we propose a determin-istic method that spans these variations with a *single template shape* by exploiting the locality property of an integral invariant. In contrast to some of the literature on shape where a method is termed group-invariant when the group parameters are an optimized input for the function (i. e. [7]), we call a function invariant if the value is *independent of an action belonging to the group*. (We make this precise in Sec. 2.1.)

2   Integral Invariants and Shape Distance

In this section, we briefly review integral invariants and describe a intuitively meaning-ful shape distance defined between these invariants.

2.1   Integral Invariants

For a shape represented as a closed planar curve $\gamma : \mathbb{S} \mapsto \mathbb{R}^2$ and a group G acting on $\mathbb{R}^2$, an *integral G-invariant* is an integral function of the curve that does not vary due to the action of any $g \in G$. Formally, for a kernel $h : \mathbb{R}^2 \times \mathbb{R}^2 \mapsto \mathbb{R}$,

$$I_\gamma(p) = \int_{\bar{\gamma}} h(p, x) d\mu(x) \tag{1}$$

is an integral invariant if

$$I_\gamma(p) = I_{g\gamma}(gp) \quad \forall g \in G. \tag{2}$$

These invariants share several desirable qualities of their more well-known cousins, dif-ferential invariants, including locality. However, unlike differential invariants, integral invariants are far more robust to noise. Specific examples include the "observed trans-port" shape measure [2] and the local area invariant [3]. Both of these invariants are parameterized by r, the radius of a circular kernel.

Due to its noise-robustness, we favor the so-called local area Euclidean-invariant. Specifically, the invariant is based on a kernel $h(p, x) = \chi(B_r(p) \cap \bar{\gamma})(x)$, which rep-resents the indicator function of the intersection of a small circle of radius r centered at the point p with the interior of the curve γ. For a radius r, the corresponding integral invariant

$$I_\gamma^r(p) \doteq \int_{B_r(p) \cap \bar{\gamma}} dx \tag{3}$$

can be thought of as a function from the interval $[0, 1]$ to the positive reals, bounded above by the area of the region bounded by the curve γ. Alternately, normalizing the

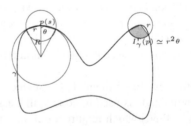

Fig. 2. Integral area invariant defined by eq. (3)

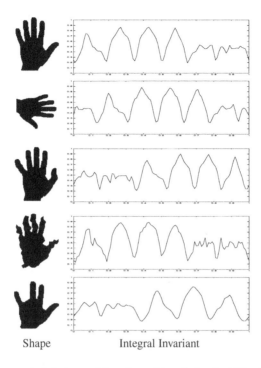

Shape   Integral Invariant

Fig. 3. *Sample shapes and their integral invariants.* Kernel size is 15% of the curve's bounding box. Note the missing "hump" on the last invariant due to the missing arclength (finger) in last row.

functional by the area of B_r maps the interval $[0, 1]$ to $[0, 1]$. This is illustrated in Fig. 2 and examples are shown in Fig. 3, which demonstrates (in the first four rows) the effectiveness of this representation for comparing shapes under Euclidean transformations, articulation of parts, and in global additive noise. However, Fig. 3 (last row) demonstrates that the local area invariant, like all other integral and differential invariants, is not robust to a highly localized perturbation such as an occlusion. In the next section we present a method to warp the parameterization of the curves so that such comparisons can be made robustly.

2.2   Shape Distance and Warping Integral Invariants

While invariants can be designed to be invariant to group actions, and integral invariants are robust to noise, an invariant for highly localized, high energy perturbations of a shape, such as the addition of spikes, slivers, or other parts, or the "disappearance" of parts due to occlusion or change in configuration (i.e. Fig. 3, first, third, and fifth row) is much more problematic. A naive distance defined on an invariant would yield a relatively large distance between the two hands in the last two rows of Fig. 3 (implying they are very different) while intuitively these shapes should have a small distance between them.

From the perspective of invariants, the large difference between shapes with local variation is due to the parameterization of the curves, as demonstrated in Fig. 3. If the "stub" could be mapped to the ring finger (which has much longer arclength), the distance between the two shapes would be limited to the error caused by that finger. This warping of the parameterization of one shape, or more symmetrically both shapes, would allow the computation of an intuitively more satisfying distance while effectively inducing point correspondences between the two curves.

Thus we wish to find an optimal correspondence between the contours and concurrently measure the shape distance based on the correspondence. Intuitively, two corresponding points on two contours should have similar invariant value, which leads us to define the optimal correspondence in terms of an energy functional $E(I_1, I_2, d; s)$ for the discrepancy between two integral invariants I_1, I_2, in terms of the disparity function $d(s)$, as follows:

$$E(I_1, I_2, d; s) = E_1(I_1, I_2, d; s) + E_2(d'; s)$$
$$= \int_0^1 \|I_1(s - d(s)) - I_2(s + d(s))\|^2 ds \tag{4}$$
$$+ \alpha \int_0^1 \|d'(s)\|^2 ds$$

where $\alpha > 0$ is a constant. The first term E_1 of the energy functional measures the similarity of two curves by integrating the local difference of the integral invariant at corresponding points. A cost functional based on a local comparisons minimizes the impact of articulations and local changes of a contour because the difference in invariants is proportionally localized in the domain of the integral; contrast this with a global descriptor where local changes influence the descriptor everywhere. The second term E_2 of the energy functional is associated with the elastic energy of the disparity function $d(s)$ with the control parameter α that penalizes stretching or shrinking of the disparity.

The shape matching of two curves is obtained by finding a correspondence between their integral invariants. The correspondence between two curves is determined by the disparity function $d(s)$ that minimizes the energy functional as follows:

$$d^*(s) = \arg\min_{d(s)} E(I_1, I_2, d; s) \tag{5}$$

Given the correspondence d^*, the shape matching between two curves (γ_1, γ_2) is given as:

$$\gamma_1(s - d^*(s)) \sim \gamma_2(s + d^*(s)), \quad \forall s \in [0, 1] \subset \mathbb{R} \tag{6}$$

where $\sim$ denotes the point-wise correspondence between curves [4].

Suggested methods for the implementation of this optimization include graph-based methods as in [27, 2, 28, 29], where d^* is the shortest path through a graph where the nodes represent pointwise correspondences.

3   Estimating Shape and Correspondence Via Bayesian Inference

In this work, we address the following problem: Given an image $I : \mathbb{R}^2 \to \mathbb{R}$ and given a *single* template shape $\gamma_0 : \mathbb{S} \to \mathbb{R}^2$, determine the optimal segmentation $\gamma : \mathbb{S} \to \mathbb{R}^2$

of the image plane and the optimal correspondence (or reparameterization) function $q : \mathbb{S} \to \mathbb{S}$ which associates the parts of the contour γ with corresponding parts on the template γ_0. (In Section 4 we discuss the connections between the reparameterization $q(s)$ and disparity $d(s)$ in Equation 4.)

Clearly, the estimation of the optimal contour γ and the optimal correspondence function q are highly coupled problems. Therefore we propose to solve this problem by maximizing the conditional probability

$$\mathcal{P}(\gamma, q | I, \gamma_0) \tag{7}$$

simultaneously with respect to both the contour γ and the correspondence function q.

According to the Bayesian formula, we can rewrite (7) as:

$$\mathcal{P}(\gamma, q | I, \gamma_0) = \frac{\mathcal{P}(I | \gamma) \mathcal{P}(\gamma, q | \gamma_0)}{\mathcal{P}(I)}. \tag{8}$$

Here we have made the two assumptions that the conditional probability $\mathcal{P}(I | \gamma, q, \gamma_0)$ in the numerator of (8) does not depend on the given template γ_0 or on the correspondence function q.

Maximizing this conditional probability for a given image I is equivalent to minimize the energy

$$E(I, \gamma, q) = \alpha E_{data}(I, \gamma) + (1 - \alpha) E_{shape}(\gamma, \gamma_0, q), \tag{9}$$

where the data energy and the shape energy correspond to the negative logarithms of the two probabilities given in the numerator of (8). Since the focus of this paper is on modeling a novel shape prior, for simplicity we choose the Chan-Vese energy as a data term, and alternate the minimization of each energy term. In the following, we will focus on modeling the shape energy.

Minimizing the above joint energy will accomplish two goals. The first is to favor segmentation contours γ that separate the domain of the image data I into object and background. The second is to favor contours that have a shape similar to a template contour γ_0. In contrast to existing methods to introduce shape priors into variational segmentation, the proposed shape prior is not learnt as a statistical model inferred from a set of training shapes. We only use a single template shape, and the flexibility of the shape prior arises through the use of a more sophisticated shape dissimilarity measure which can handle stretching or shrinking and the correspondence of subparts.

Based on the assumption that the intensities of object and background are Gaussian-distributed, one can derive a data term E_{data} given by the piecewise constant Mumford-Shah functional [30, 31]:

$$E_{cv}(I, \gamma) = \int_{\bar{\gamma}} (I - c_1)^2 dx + \int_{\Omega/\bar{\gamma}} (I - c_2)^2 dx + \nu \int_{\gamma} ds \tag{10}$$

here c_1, c_2 are the constant approximation of u (i. e. the mean) inside and outside γ. This functional can be minimized by evolving an initial contour and model in the gradient direction

$$\gamma_{t,cv} = ((c_1 - c_2)(I - c_1 + I - c_2) - \nu\kappa) \, \mathbf{N} \tag{11}$$

where κ denotes the local curvature. This functional will provide the connection between the segmenting contour γ and the image data. However, any other variational segmentation model proposed in the literature could be substituted.

4 Integral Invariant Templates for Curve Evolution

In this section, we will construct an appropriate shape prior E_{shape} in (9) for variational segmentation based on the notion of integral invariant shape descriptions and pointwise correspondence. Intuitively, we reason that the best way to update the portion of a contour that will become, say, a finger, is to compare it to the relevant part of the template, the corresponding finger. As discussed in Section 2.2, integral invariant based shape distances allow us to do exactly this; with the invariant and correspondence in hand, the evolution of the contour is governed by only the shape of the template, and is not influenced by nuisance factors.

Section 2.2 hints at our design of the energy term that will achieve the second goal. Following [32], which evolves a contour so that its invariant has a certain property, we evolve the contour to reduce its shape distance with a template invariant. This shape term has all the advantages of integral invariant methods: (1) the resulting flow will also be G-invariant, eliminating contour motions that do not instruct the shape of the contour, or alternately eliminating the need to align or register the contour to the template; (2) the resulting flow will be more noise robust; and (3) the resulting flow will be less sensitive to articulation of parts, allowing a template to better represent a class of shapes. For instance, with a method that is not insensitive to articulation, a hand template could only be used when the target hand's fingers *are configured exactly like the template*; with the integral invariant representation of the hand, hands with splayed or bent fingers have similar invariants to the template.

These advantages are realized with a shape energy term

$$E_{shape}(\gamma, \gamma_0, q) = \frac{1}{2} \int_\gamma (I(s) - I_0(q(s)))^2 ds \tag{12}$$

based on the integral invariant from Section 2.1 rewritten as

$$I(s) = \int_{\tilde{\gamma}} B(\gamma(s) - \tilde{s}, r) d\tilde{s}. \tag{13}$$

$q(s) = s - 2d(s)$ is an asymmetric expression of the warping function. For convenience, we define $f(s) = I(s) - I_0(q(s))$. In anticipation of the time-dependence of the arclength parametrization, we rewrite the energy with a change of variables

$$E(\gamma, q) = \frac{1}{2} \int_\gamma f(p)^2 ||\gamma_p|| dp. \tag{14}$$

Taking the time derivative yields

$$E_t(\gamma, q) = \int_\gamma f(p) f_t(p) ||\gamma_p|| dp + \frac{1}{2} \int_\gamma f(p)^2 ||\gamma_p||_t dp, \tag{15}$$

$f_t(p) = I_t(p) - (I_o(q(p)))_t$ The second term is the well known curve shortening flow, so we concentrate on the first term. Two notes at this point aid the simplification of the expression. First, we must compute the derivative of the integral invariant I_t. Via the divergence theorem, an area-based energy of the form $E(s) = \int_{\bar{\gamma}} F(s)ds$ (for a general function $F(s)$) has a derivative that can be expressed as a contour integral $E_t(s) = \int_\gamma \langle \gamma_t, F(s)N \rangle ds$, where $\langle \cdot, \cdot \rangle$ is the dot product and N is the normal direction. Applying this formula to I_t yields

$$I_t(p) = -\int_\gamma \langle \gamma_t, B(|\gamma(p) - \tilde{s}|, r)N \rangle d\tilde{s} \qquad (16)$$

Second, we note that $I_o(\cdot)$ is the constant shape template, so its derivative is 0. Rewriting and reversing the change of variables

$$E_t(\gamma, q) = -\int_\gamma f(s) \int_\gamma \langle \gamma_t, B(|\gamma(s) - \tilde{s}|, r)N \rangle d\tilde{s} ds + \dots \qquad (17)$$

Re-arranging the nested integral allows us to introduce another convenient quantity,

$$g(s) = \int_\gamma f(s)B(|\gamma(s) - s|, r)ds, \qquad (18)$$

and write

$$E_t(\gamma, q) = \int_\gamma \langle \gamma_t, -\int_\gamma g(s)ds N \rangle d\tilde{s} + \dots \qquad (19)$$

Including the omitted curvature shortening term,

$$E_t(\gamma, q) = \int_\gamma \langle \gamma_t, (-\int_\gamma g(s)ds + f(s)^2 \kappa)N \rangle d\tilde{s}. \qquad (20)$$

In order to maximally reduce this energy, we chose γ_t to be the negative of the second term of the inner product

$$\gamma_t = \int_\gamma (-g(s) + f(s)^2 \kappa(s))N. \qquad (21)$$

The $g(s)$ term has a straightforward interpretation; at a point on the contour, it is simply the integral of difference of the invariant values on the sections of γ inside the kernel.

In the next section, we integrate this shape term into a segmentation functional.

5   Energy Minimization with Integral Invariant Shape Templates

In this section we will detail how to minimize the joint energy (9) to simultaneously compute a segmentation and a correspondence of the parts of the segmentation to respective parts of the given shape template. We will apply this segmentation functional to real data to demonstrate the flexibility of integral invariant shape templates.

We will minimize the functional (9) with the partial differential equation

$$\gamma_t = \gamma_{t,data} + \alpha\gamma_{t,shape} \tag{22}$$

where $\gamma_{t,shape}$ is (21) and $\gamma_{t,data}$ is the flow in (11). α is a user-defined weighting term.

The curve γ is embedded in a higher-dimensional function $\Phi : \mathbb{R}^2 \mapsto \mathbb{R}$ to make use of the well-known level-set implementation of curve evolution methods [33, 19, 21]. The level-set function is constructed so that $\{x|\Phi(x) = 0\} = \gamma$; the evolution of γ in the $\gamma_t = \beta N$ direction is realized through the evolution of Φ in the

$$\Phi_t = -\beta|\nabla\Phi| \tag{23}$$

direction.

We employ a dual representation of the contour to speed the computations. A polygonal representation is used for the computation of $d(s)$, $f(s)$, and $g(s)$. These terms, computed on the vertices of a polygon, are then mapped to the level-set domain and nearest-neighbor extrapolated. N, κ, the data terms, and Φ_t are computed directly in the image/level-set domain, per usual. At each timestep, we recompute the integral invariant and correspondence, so that we are alternating the two optimizations (correspondence, segmentation).

In the remainder of this section we show an experiment that demonstrates the power of an integral invariant based template over more traditional shape-template methods. Specifically, we will address the case where an affine transformation is not adequate to map the shape template to the object in the image. In this case, a more general, local deformation is required; the goal is to demonstrate that the locality of the integral invariant translates into energy penalties that are proportional to the size of the deformation.

We compare our implementation to a implementation that seeks to optimize the distance from the contour to a shape prior

$$E_{shape}(\gamma) = \int_{\gamma} d(\gamma(s), g\gamma_0)ds \tag{24}$$

where $g \in G$, a group. For a traditional method that aligns the shape template to the object during the segmentation process, an affine transformation in two dimensions requires the optimization of six parameters. Many methods in the literature restrict themselves to lower-dimensional groups (Euclidean, similarity) but the generalization is straightforward. The optimization is usually implemented with two steps per iteration; first an update of the contour

$$\gamma_{t,shape} = \nabla d(\gamma, g\gamma_0) \tag{25}$$

and second an update of the transformation parameters g. In the remainder of this section, we demonstrate results on real images that show the potential of the integral invariant as a shape template.

Fig. 4 shows the segmentation of the image of a hand, taken with varying illumination against a busy background. While the contrast is strong, it should be noted that the gray values of the object and background are in a similar range, making segmentation by image data alone (via the Chan-Vese method with a strong curvature prior) difficult,

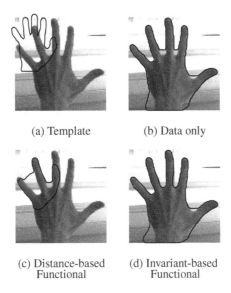

(a) Template   (b) Data only

(c) Distance-based   (d) Invariant-based
   Functional   Functional

Fig. 4. Segmentation with a shape template. $\alpha=0.85$.

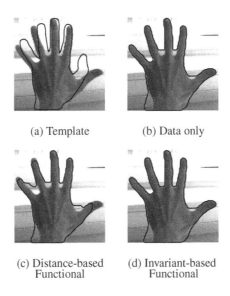

(a) Template   (b) Data only

(c) Distance-based   (d) Invariant-based
   Functional   Functional

Fig. 5. Segmentation with a shape template. $\alpha=0.85$.

as shown in Fig. 4(b). A shape template may assist in the segmentation, but the choice of template is important. An unregistered template (as in Fig. 4) has a strong influence on the contour. This is because the segmentation contour cannot both be near the template and edges in the image; the energy functional converges to a "compromise" between the two criteria. Unfortunately, this compromise serves neither criteria well. In contrast, the integral invariant shape template is not dependent on the location of the template. Regardless of the alignment, the template does not compete with the data term for the location of the contour (d).

Figure 5 shows the added flexibility of the integral invariant shape template. While optimization of transform parameters allows the alignment of the distance function template to the data (a), the template cannot capture the articulated thumb (c). Again, the integral invariant template generalizes to better capture this object (d). Here, due to the locality of the invariant, the deviations of the segmentation from the template are penalized *only at the differing bends in the contour* This allows for a much better "compromise" between the shape and data terms; now a single template shape can be used despite the many variations (finger poses) inherent in this class of object.

6 Open Issues

The method we have proposed relies on the uniqueness of the integral invariant representation. In [3] Manay et. al. outline the relationship between curvature, which is a unique representation of the contour, with the integral invariant in the limit as kernel size goes to 0. For finite kernel size the uniqueness of the invariant is the topic of continuing investigation.

If the invariant is not unique, the contour flow will not necessarily converge to the shape template, but may converge to other shapes that have the same invariant. Indeed, this may explain the instabilities we have observed in the contour flow in synthetic experiments where the image data term is discarded. However, in practice, the data terms of the flow help restrict the contour to the desired solution. A more rigorous solution would be to base the flow on an integral invariant that is unique; the development of which is also the topic of our continuing research.

7 Summary and Conclusions

In this paper we draw on the emerging work on local integral invariant shape descriptions to first present a shape distance between two contours based on optimal correspondences between the parts of the contours that have similar integral invariant. Based on this shape distance we construct a shape energy functional for variational segmentation. This new shape energy term fundamentally differs from previously proposed statistical shape priors which allow for shape deformations that are statistically learnt from an entire set of training shapes. Our shape prior only uses a single template shape, it is not dependent on the relative position and rotation of the template, eliminating the need for registration of the data to the template. Further, due to the locality properties of the integral invariant, the more sophisticated shape distance allows for certain deformations of the given template, such as local stretching or shrinking and the articulation of parts. Preliminary results show the effectiveness of integral invariant templates in a curve evolution segmentation framework implemented via level set methods and applied to real data.

References

1. Kendall, D.G.: The diffusion of shape. Advances in Appl. Probability **9** (1977) 428–430
2. Pitiot, A., Delingette, H., Toga, A., Thompson, P.: Learning Object Correspondences with the Observed Transport Shape Measure. In: Information Processing in Medical Imaging IPMI'03. (2003)
3. Manay, S., Hong, B., Yezzi, A., Soatto, S.: Integral invariant signatures. In: European Conf. Comp. Vis. (2004)
4. Manay, S., Hong, B., Cremers, D., Yezzi, A., Soatto, S.: Integral invariants and shape matching. Pat. Anal. and Mach. Intell. (2005) Submitted.
5. Bookstein, F.: The Measurement of Biological Shape and Shape Change. Springer, New York (1978) volume 24 of *Lect. Notes in Biomath.*
6. Cootes, T.F., Taylor, C.J., Cooper, D.M., Graham, J.: Active shape models – their training and applications. Comp. Vision Image Underst. **61** (1995) 38–59
7. Cremers, D., Osher, S., Soatto, S.: Kernel density estimation and instrinsic alignment for knowledge-driven segmentation: Teaching level sets to walk. In: DAGM. (2004)
8. Dryden, I.L., Mardia, K.V.: Statistical Shape Analysis. Wiley, Chichester (1998)
9. Fréchet, M.: Les courbes aléatoires. Bull. Inst. Int'l Stat. **38** (1961) 499–504
10. Klassen, E., Srivastava, A., Mio, W., Joshi, S.H.: Analysis of planar shapes using geodesic paths on shape spaces. Pat. Anal. and Mach. Intell. **26** (2004) 373–383
11. Grenander, U.: Lectures in Pattern Theory. Springer, Berlin (1976)
12. Grenander, U., Chow, Y., Keenan, D.M.: Hands: A Pattern theoretic Study of Biological Shapes. Springer, New York (1991)
13. Trouvé, A.: Diffeomorphisms, groups, and pattern matching in image analysis. Int. J. Computer Vision **28** (1998) 213–221
14. Younes, L.: Computable elastic distances between shapes. SIAM J. Appl. Math **58** (1998) 565–586
15. Basri, R., Costa, L., Geiger, D., Jacobs, D.: Determining the similarity of deformable shapes. Vision Research **38** (1998) 2365–2385
16. Gdalyahu, Y., Weinshall, D.: Flexible syntactic matching of curves and its application to automatic hierarchical classication of silhouettes. Pat. Anal. and Mach. Intell. **21** (1999) 1312–1328
17. Kass, M., Witkin, A., Terzopoulis, D.: Snakes: Active contour models. Int. J. Computer Vision **1** (1987) 321–323
18. Kichenassamy, S., Kumar, A., Olver, P.J., Tannenbaum, A., Yezzi, A.: Analysis of planar shape influence in geodesic active contours. In: Int. Conf. Comp. Vis. (1995) 810–815
19. Chan, T., Vese, L.: Active contours without edges. IEEE Trans. on Image Proc. **10** (2001) 266–277
20. Caselles, V., Kimmel, R., Sapiro, G.: Geodesic active contours. In: Int. Conf. Comp. Vis. (1995) 694–699
21. Tsai, A., Yezzi, A., Willsky, A.: Curve evolution implementation of the Mumford Shah functional for image segmentation, denoising, interpolation, and magnification. IEEE Trans. on Image Proc. **10** (2001) 1169–1186
22. Leventon, M.E., Grimson, W.E.L., Faugeras, O.: Statistical shape influence in geodesic active contours. In: Proc. Conf. Comput. Vision and Pat. Rec. Volume 1. (2000) 316–323
23. Tsai, A., Yezzi, A., Wells, W., Tempany, C., Tucker, D., Fan, A., Grimson, E., Willsky, A.: Model-based curve evolution technique for image segmentation. In: Proc. Conf. Comput. Vision and Pat. Rec. (2001) 463–468
24. Chen, Y., Tagare, H., Thiruvenkadam, S., Huang, F., Wilson, D., Gopinath, K.S., Briggs, R.W., Geiser, E.: Using shape priors in geometric active contours in a variational framework. Int. J. Computer Vision **50** (2002) 315–328

25. Rousson, M., Paragios, N.: Shape priors of level set represenations. In: European Conf. Comp. Vis. (2002) 78–92
26. Rousson, M., Paragios, N., Deriche, R.: Implicit active shape models for 3D segmentation in MRI imaging. In: Int. Conf. Medical Image Computing and Computer Assited Intervention. (2004) 209–216
27. Bakircioglu, M., Grenander, U., Khaneja, N., Miller, M.I.: Curve matching on brain surfaces using frenet distances. Human Brain Mapping **6** (1998) 329–333
28. Sebastian, T., Klein, P., Kimia, B.: Alignment-based recognition of shape outlines. Lecture Notes in Computer Science **2059** (2001) 606–??
29. Tomasi, C., Manduchi, R.: Stereo without search. In: European Conf. Comp. Vis. (1996) 452–465
30. Mumford, D., Shah, J.: Optimal approximations by piecewise smooth functions and associated variational problems. Comm. on Pure and Applied Math. **42** (1989)
31. Zhu, S.C., Yuille, A.: Region competition: Unifying snakes, region growing, and Bayes/MDL for multiband image segmentation. Pat. Anal. and Mach. Intell. **18** (1996) 884–900
32. Nain, D., Yezzi, A., Turk, G.: Vessel segmentation using a shape driven flow. In: Int. Conf. Medical Image Computing and Computer Assited Intervention. (2004)
33. Osher, S., Sethian, J.: Fronts propagating with curvature dependent speed: Algorithms based on Hamilton-Jacobi formulations. J. of Comp. Physics **79** (1988) 12–49

Dynamic Shape and Appearance Modeling Via Moving and Deforming Layers

Jeremy D. Jackson[1], Anthony Yezzi[1], and Stefano Soatto[2]

[1] School of Electrical and Computer Engineering,
Georgia Institute of Technology, Atlanta, GA 30332
gtg120d@mail.gatech.edu, ayezzi@ece.gatech.edu
[2] UCLA Computer Science Department, 4732 Boelter Hall,Los Angeles, CA 90095-1596
soatto@ucla.edu

Abstract. We propose a model of the shape, motion and appearance of a sequence of images that captures occlusions, scene deformations, arbitrary viewpoint variations and changes in irradiance. This model is based on a collection of overlapping layers that can move and deform, each supporting an intensity function that can change over time. We discuss the generality and limitations of this model in relations to existing ones such as traditional optical flow or motion segmentation, layers, deformable templates and deformotion. We then illustrate how this model can be used for inference of shape, motion, deformation and appearance of the scene from a collection of images. The layering structure allows for automatic inpainting of partially occluded regions. We illustrate the model on synthetic and real sequences where existing schemes fail; we implement our gradient-based infinite-dimensional optimization using level set methods.

1 Introduction

We are interested in modeling video sequences where changes occur over time due to viewer motion, motion or deformation of objects in the scene – including occlusions – and appearance variations due to the motion of objects relative to the illumination. A suitable model will trade off generality, by allowing variations of shape, motion and appearance, with tractability, by being amenable to inference and analysis. The goal of modeling is to support inference, and depending on the application one may be more interested in recovering shape (e.g. in shape analysis, classification, recognition, registration), or recovering motion (e.g. tracking, optical flow), or appearance variations (e.g. segmentation). Traditionally, therefore, the modeling task has been approached by making strict assumptions on some of the unknowns in order to recover the others, for instance the brightness-constancy assumption in optical flow, or the affine warping in shape analysis and registration. This is partly justified because in any image-formation model there is ambiguity between the three factors – shape, motion and appearance – and therefore the most general inference problem is ill-posed. In some applications, for instance video compression, the ambiguity is moot since all that matters is for the model to capture the sequence as faithfully and parsimoniously as possible. Nevertheless, since all three factors affect the generation of the image, a more germane approach

A. Rangarajan et al. (Eds.): EMMCVPR 2005, LNCS 3757, pp. 427–438, 2005.

would call for modeling all three jointly, then letting the analysis dictate the responsibility of each factor, and the application dictate the choice of suitable regularizers to make the inference algorithms well posed. We therefore concentrate our attention on modeling, not on any particular application. So, this is not yet another paper on tracking, nor on motion segmentation, nor on optical flow, nor on shape registration. It is a little bit of each.

We propose a model of image formation that is general enough to capture shape, motion and appearance variations (Sect. 2), and simple enough to allow inference (Sect. 3). We want to be able to capture *occlusion phenomena*, hence our model will entail a notion of *hierarchy* or *layering*; we want to capture image variability due to arbitrary *changes in viewpoint* for non-planar objects, hence our model will entail *infinite-dimensional deformations* of the image domain. Such deformations can be due to changes in viewpoint for a rigid scene, or changes of shape of the scene seen from a static viewpoint, or any combination thereof. Our model will not attempt to resolve this ambiguity, since that requires higher-level knowledge. Furthermore, we want to capture large-scale motion of objects in the scene, as opposed to deformations, hence we will allow for a choice of a finite-dimensional group, e.g. Euclidean or affine. Finally, we want to capture changes in appearance, hence scene radiance will be one of the unknowns in our model. Changes in radiance can come from changes in reflectance or changes in illumination, including changes in the mutual position between the light sources and the scene; again we do not attempt to resolve this ambiguity, since that requires higher-level knowledge. The image-formation model we propose is not the most general that one can conceive; far from it. Indeed, it is far less general than the simplest models considered acceptable in Computer Graphics, and we illustrate the lack of generality in Sect. 2.1. Nevertheless, it is more general than any other model used so far for motion analysis in Computer Vision, as we discuss also in Sect. 2.1, and is complex enough to be barely tractable with the analytical and computational tools at our disposal today. We pose the inference problem within a variational framework, involving partial differential equations, integrated numerically in the level set framework [15], although any other computational scheme of choice would do, including stochastic gradients or Markov-chain Monte Carlo. The point of this paper is to propose a model and show that it can be inferred with at least one particular computational scheme, not to advocate a particular optimization technique.

1.1 Relation to Existing Work

This work relates to a wide body of literature in scene modeling, motion estimation, shape analysis, segmentation, and regsitration which cannot be properly reviewed in detail in the limited space available. In Sect. 2.1 we illustrate the specific relationship between the model we propose and existing models. These include Layers [20, 12], which only model affine deformations of the domain and can therefore only capture planar scenes under small viewer motion or small aperture, and where there is no explicit spatial consistency within each layer and the appearance of each layer is fixed. As we will illustrate, our model allows deformations that can model arbitrary viewpoint variation, layer deformation and enforce spatial coherence within each layer. One could think of our work as a generalization of existing work on Layers to arbitrary viewpoint changes, or arbitrary scene shape, and to changes in radiance (texture), all cast within a principled variational framework. Our work relates to a plethora of variational algorithms for optical flow computation, for instance [18, 1, 8] and references therein, except that we partition the domain and allow arbitrary smooth deformations as well as changes in appearance (that would violate the brightness constancy constraints that most work on optical flow is based on, with a few exceptions, e.g. [10]). It also relates to various approaches to motion segmentation, where the domain is also partitioned and allowed to move with a simple motion, e.g. Euclidean or affine, see for instance [7] and references therein. Such approaches do not allow deformations of the region boundaries, or changes in the intensity within each region. Furthermore, they realize a partition, rather than a hierarchy, of domain deformations, so our model can be thought of as motion segmentation with moving and deforming layers with changes in intensity and inpainting [3]. In this, our work relates to [19], except that we allow layers to overlap. So, our work can be though of as a layered version of Deformotion with changes in region intensities. Also very related to our work is work done by [17] in registering one distance function to another using a rigid and non-rigid transformation. Our work relates to deformable templates [14, 9], in the sense that each of our layers will be a deformable template. However, we do not know the shape and intensity profile of the template, so we estimate that along with the layering structure. Our work is also related to active appearance models [6, 2], in that we seek the same goal, although rather than imposing regularization of shape and appearance by projection onto suitably inferred linear subspaces we employ generic regularizers. One can therefore think of our work as a generalization of active appearance models to smooth shape and intensity deformations, cast in a variational framework. Of course this work relates more generically to active contours, e.g. [4, 13, 5, 16] and references therein. In the next section we introduce our model, and in Sect. 3 we illustrate our approach to infer its (infinite-dimensional) constitutive elements.

2   Modeling

We represent a scene as a collection of L overlapping *layers*. Each layer, labeled by an index $l = 1, \ldots, L$, is a function that has associated with it a domain, or *shape* $\Omega^l \subset \mathbb{R}^2$, and a range, or *radiance* $\rho^l : \Omega^l \to \mathbb{R}^+$. Layer boundaries model the occlusion process, and each layer l undergoes a *motion*, described by a (finite-dimensional) group action g^l, for instance $g^l \in SE(2)$ or $\mathbb{A}(2)$, and a *deformation*, or *warping*, described by a diffeomorphism $w^l : \Omega^l \to \mathbb{R}^2$, in order to generate an image I at a given time t. Warping models changes of viewpoint for non-planar scenes, or actual changes in the shape of objects in the scene. Since each image is obtained from the given scene after a different motion and deformation, we index each of them by t: g_t^l, w_t^l, and I_t. Finally, since layers occlude each other, there is a natural ordering in l which, without loss of generality, we will assume to coincide with the integers: Layer $l = 1$ is occluded by layer $l = 2$ and so on. So, the only layer that will contribute to the intensity at a pixel in a given image is the frontmost that intersects the warped domain. For simplicity we assume that $\Omega^0 = \mathbb{R}^2$ (the backmost layer, or "the background"). With this notation, the model of how the value of the generic image $I_t : \Omega^0 \to \mathbb{R}^+$ at the location $x \in$

$\Omega^0 \subset \mathbb{R}^2$ is generated can be summarized as $I_t\big(g_t^l \circ w_t^l(x)\big) = \rho^l(x)$, with $x \in \Omega^l$, $l = \max\{k \mid x \in \Omega^k\}$. To simplify the notation, we call $x_t^l \doteq g_t^l \circ w_t^l(x)$, which sometimes we indicate, for simplicity, as x_t, so that

$$
\begin{cases}
I_t\big(x_t^l\big) = \rho^l(x), & x \in \Omega^l \\
x_t^l = g_t^l \circ w_t^l(x), & l = \max\{k \mid x \in \Omega^k\}.
\end{cases}
\tag{1}
$$

Our goal in this work is to infer the radiance family $\{\rho^l\}_{l=1,\ldots,L}$, the shape family $\{\Omega^l\}_{l=1,\ldots,L}$, the motions $\{g_t^l\}_{l=1,\ldots,L;t=1,\ldots,N}$ and the deformations $\{w_t^l\}_{l=1,\ldots,L;t=1,\ldots,N}$ that minimize the discrepancy of the measured images from the ideal model (1), subject to generic regularity constraints. Such a discrepancy is measured by a cost functional $\phi(\Omega^k, \rho^k, w_t^k, g_t^k)$ to be minimized as

$$
\phi \doteq \sum_{t=1}^{N} \int_{\Omega^0} \left(I_t(x_t) - \rho^l(w_t^{l-1} \circ g_t^{l-1}(x_t)) \right)^2 dx_t +
$$

$$
+ \lambda \sum_{k=1}^{L} \int_{\Omega^k} \|\nabla \rho^k(x)\|^2 dx + \mu \sum_{k,t=1}^{L,N} \int_{\Omega^l} r(w_t^k(x)) dx
\tag{2}
$$

$$
\text{subject to } l = \max\{k \mid x \in \Omega^k\}.
$$

Here r is a regularizing functional, for instance $r(w) \doteq |\dot{w}| + \frac{1}{|\dot{w}|}$, and λ, μ are positive constants. Note that l is a function, specifically $l : \Omega^0 \to \mathbb{Z}^+$.

2.1   Generality of the Model

It can be easily shown that eq. (1) models images of 3-D scenes with piecewise smooth geometry exhibiting Lambertian reflection with piecewise smooth albedo[1] viewed under diffuse illumination from an arbitrarily changing viewpoint. It does not capture global or indirect illumination effects, such as cast shadows or inter-reflections, complex reflectance, such as specularities, anisotropies or sub-surface scattering. These are treated as modeling errors and are responsible for the discrepancy between the model and the images, which is measured by ϕ in eq. (2). We lump these discrepancies together with sensor errors and improperly call them "noise." Although far from general, (1) is nevertheless a more ambitious model than has ever been used in the context of motion estimation and tracking. In fact, the reader can easily verify that many existing models are special cases of (1). In particular, $L = 0$, $g = Id$, $\lambda = 0$ yields traditional **optical flow**, where $\rho = I_{t+1}$. There are too many variants of this model to review here, depending on the choice of norm and regularizers, stemming from the ancestor [11]. Choosing $L = 1$, $w = Id$, $\lambda = 0$ yields **motion segmentation**, that has also been addressed by many, see for instance [7] and references therein for the case of affine motion $g \in \mathbb{A}(2)$. $L = 1, \rho = \text{const}, r(w) = \|w\|$ yields a model called **Deformotion**

---

[1] The model can be further generalized by allowing ρ^l to be vector-valued to capture a set of radiance statistics such as the coefficients of a filter bank or other texture descriptors, but this is beyond the scope of this paper.

in [19], and has also been extended to grayscale images $L = 1$, $r(w) = \|w\|$. Choosing $L > 1$, $w = Id$, Ω^k unconstrained and $g \in \mathbb{A}(2)$ would yield a variational version of the **Layers** model [20], that to the best of our knowledge has never been attempted. Note that this is different than simpler variational multi-phase motion segmentation, since in that case the motion of a phase affects the shape of neighboring phases, whereas in the model (1) layers can overlap without distorting underlying domains. One can think of the Layer model as a multi-phase motion segmentation with inpainting [3] of occluded layers and shape constraints. The model also relates to **deformable templates**, where $\rho = const$ in the traditional model [9] and $\rho = smooth$ in the more general version [14]. Another relevant approach is **Active Appearance Models** where the regions, warping and radiances are modeled as points in a linear space. The model (1) does not impose such restrictions, and render the problem well-posed by generic regularization instead.

3   Inference

Minimizing the cost functional in (2) is a tall order. It depends upon each domain boundary (a closed planar contour) Ω^k, its deformation (a flow of planar diffeomorphisms) w_t^k, the radiance (a piecewise smooth function) ρ^k, all of which are infinite-dimensional unknowns. In addition, it depends on a group action per layer per instant, g_t^k, and on the occlusion model, which is represented by the discrete-valued function $l(x) = \max\{k \mid x \in \Omega^k\}$, and all of this for each layer $k = 1, \ldots, K$. The first simplification is to notice that, as long as each layer is a compact region bounded by a simple smooth curve, there is no loss of generality in assuming that Ω^k are fixed. This is because each diffeomorphism w_t^k will act transitively on it. Therefore, we assume that each region Ω^k is a circle in most of the examples. While there is no loss of generality, there is a loss of energy, in that if we were allowed to also optimize with respect to the initial regions we would be able to reach each deforming layer with less energy. This, however, does not enhance the generality of the model, hence we will forgo it (see Fig. 1 for an illustration of this effect).

Apart from this simplification, we proceed by minimizing the functional (2) using simultaneous gradient flows with respect to the groups (motion), the radiances (appearance) and the diffeomorphisms (deformation). The detailed evolution equations are a bit complicated depending upon the number of layers and the occlusion structure between layers. To help avoid excessive subscripting and superscripting and multiple-case definitions according to occlusion relationships, we will outline some of the key properties of the various gradient flows for the case of a background layer Ω^0, a single image I, and a single foreground layer Ω^1. We will also, to help keep the illustration simple, assume that the group action g^0 and the warp w^0 for the background layer are simply the identity transforms. This is the simplest possible scenario that will allow us to still show the key properties of the gradient flows.

Let $\hat{x} = g^1(w^1(x))$ and $\hat{\Omega}^1 = g^1(w^1(\Omega^1))$. With this notation, we may write image-dependent terms in our energy functional as follows.

$$E = \int_{\hat{\Omega}^1} \left(I(\hat{x}) - \rho^1(x) \right)^2 d\hat{x} + \int_{\Omega^0 \setminus \hat{\Omega}^1} \left(I(x) - \rho^0(x) \right)^2 dx \tag{3}$$

If g denotes any single parameter (e.g. horizontal translation) of the group g^1, then differentiating yields

$$\frac{\partial E}{\partial g} = \int_{\partial \hat{\Omega}^1} \left\langle \frac{\partial \hat{x}}{\partial g}, \hat{N} \right\rangle \left(\left(I(\hat{x}) - \rho^1(x) \right)^2 - \left(I(\hat{x}) - \rho^0(\hat{x}) \right)^2 \right) d\hat{s} \qquad (4)$$
$$+ 2 \int_{\hat{\Omega}^1} \left(I(\hat{x}) - \rho^1(x) \right) \left\langle \nabla \rho(x), \mathrm{inv} \left[(w^1)' \right] \frac{\partial}{\partial g} \mathrm{inv}[g^1](\hat{x}) \right\rangle d\hat{x}$$

where $\hat{N}$ and $d\hat{s}$ denote the outward unit normal and the arclength element of $\partial \hat{\Omega}^1$ respectively. We are able to note two things. First, the update equations for the group involve measurements both along the boundary of its corresponding layer (first integral) as well as measurements within the layer's interior (second integral). Notice that this later integral vanishes if a constant radiance ρ is utilized for the layer. We also see that it is not necessary to differentiate the image data I. Derivatives land on the estimated smooth radiance ρ instead, which is a significant computational perk of our model that results in considerable robustness to image noise.

A similar gradient structure arises for the case of the infinite dimensional warp w (boundary based terms and region based terms for each layer similar to previous integrals). However, additional terms arise in the gradient flow equations for w depending upon the choice of regularization terms in the energy functional (smoothness penalties, magnitude pentalties etc.).

The curve evolution is also similar to the boundary based term for the evolution of the g's:

$$\frac{\partial C}{\partial t} = - \left(\left(I(\hat{x}) - \rho^1(x) \right)^2 - \left(I(\hat{x}) - \rho^0(\hat{x}) \right)^2 \right) \hat{N} \qquad (5)$$

Finally, the optimality conditions for the smooth radiance functions ρ^0 and ρ^1 are given by the following Poisson-type equations.

$$\Delta \rho^1(x) = \lambda \left(\rho^1(x) - I(\hat{x}) \right), \qquad x \in \Omega^1 \qquad (6)$$
$$\Delta \rho^0(x) = \begin{cases} 0, & x \in \hat{\Omega}^1 \\ \lambda \left(\rho^0(x) - I(x) \right), & x \in \Omega^0 \setminus \hat{\Omega}^1 \end{cases} \qquad (7)$$

Notice that the background radiance ρ^0 is "inpainted" in regions occluded by the foreground layer Ω^1 by harmonic interpolation (as it satisfies Laplace's equation $\Delta \rho^0 = 0$) of values along the boundary of $\hat{\Omega}^1$.

4   Experiments

The first simple experiment is meant to illustrate that there is no lack of generality in the model by assuming that the shape of the initial regions Ω is fixed. This is because the transformations g and w act transitively to obtain regions bounded by general simple, closed, smooth planar contours. In Fig. 1 we illustrate this point by allowing a circular region to capture the motion and deformation of a rectangle. This simulation involves one background layer, one foreground layer, and one set of transformations g and w. We

Fig. 1. Rectangle Captured By a Circle: The shape of the region is fixed to be a circle (left), and the appearance of the images (in this case a simple binary image of a rectangular domain) is captured by its motion g (middle) and deformation w (right) without loss of generality

can simultaneously find g and w, but in this experiment the similarity transformation g is allowed to reach steady state and then the warp w is found. The data fidelity term used is a Mumford-Shah term, so the radiances representing each layer are smooth functions. Figure 1 shows the initial circle placed over the image and then the image with the similarity transformation at steady state; Finally, the warp w is applied. Adding the regions Ω to the model, therefore, would only simplify the optimization procedure, and allow us to reach various shapes with less energy, but not add to the generality of the model.

In the next experiment we illustrate the capability of our model to track deforming layers. In Figure 2 we show three sequences of an image where a deflating balloon is undergoing a rather errating motion while deforming from an initial waterdrop shape to a circular one, finally to a spermatozoidal shape. On the top row of Fig. 2 we show the layer boundaries for a model that only allow for affine deformations of the initial contour (a circle). This is essentially a variational implementation of the model of [20]. As it can be seen, it captures the gross motion of the balloon, but it cannot capture the subtler

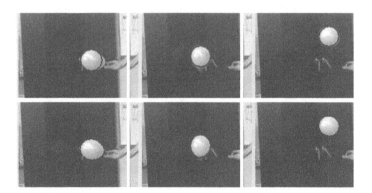

Fig. 2. Tracking a Balloon: Three sample views are shown from a sequence of a deflating baloon moving with an erratic motion while changing its shape from a drop-like shape to a circle. In the top row we show the boundary of the first layer as estimated by an affine layer model that does not allow for layer deformation, akin to a variational implementation of traditional layer models. As it can be seen, the model tracks the motion of the layer, but it fails to capture its deformation. On the bottom row we show the same three images with the first layer superimposed, where the layer is allowed to both move (affinely) and deform (diffeomorphically), yielding 12% lower RMS residual error, and capturing the subtler shape variations.

Fig. 3. Original Tree Background 300x300 image

shape variations. The second row shows the same three sample images with the boundary of the first layer superimposed, where the layer is allowed to deform according to the model we have introduced. Again the data fidelity term used is a Mumford-Shah term so the radiances representing each layer are smooth functions. As it can be seen, the layer changes shape to adapt to the deforming baloon, all while capturing its rather erratic motion. The average RMS error per image for the affine layer model is **30.87**, whereas the residual for the case of the deforming layers is **5.51**, corresponding to a 12% improvement. More importantly, the phenomenology of the scene, visible in the figure, has been correctly captured.

Figure 3 shows a 300x300 image of a tree that was used in an experiment that allows the foreground boundary (contour) to move and allows separate transformations for the foreground and background layers to be found. Figure 4 shows 100x100 images that have been cut out of Figure 3 that were used for this experiment. Figure 4 shows this example that has a rigid transformation for the foreground layer and has a separate rigid transformation for the background layer. The contour that bounds the

Fig. 4. Curve evolution with background and foreground transformations: The 100x100 images here are taken from Fig 3. The top row shows the initial curve, the bottom row shows the final segmentation and registration of the tree. A transform is computed for the background as well and gives rise to the next Figure 5.

Fig. 5. Reconstructed Tree Background: This image is the smooth approximation of the background ρ^0 given by the background regions from the three images in Figure 4

foreground layer is allowed to evolve to capture the tree. The reconstructed background function is shown in Figure 5.

In the next experiment we illustrate all the features of our model by showing how it allows recovering the background behind partially occluded layers while recovering their motion and deformation. In Figure 6 we show a few samples from this dataset where the silhouette of a moving hand forms a victory sign while moving the relative position between the fingers. The background, which is partially occluded, is a spiral. Here we use the average shape as the initial shape of the foreground layer to find its

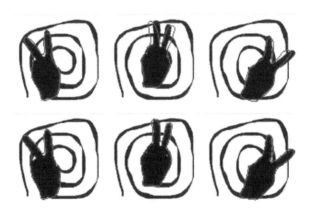

Fig. 6. Victory sign, with deforming hand, moving in front of a partially occluded background portraying a spiral. The goal here is to recover the radiance of each layer (the spiral in the background and the constant black intensity of the hand), as well as the motion and deformation of the foreground layer. Note that current layer models based only on affine motion would fail to capture the phenomenology of this scene by over-segmenting the region into three regions, each moving with independent affine motion. Our model captures the overall motion of the layer with an affine group, and then the relative motion between the fingers as a deformation, as we illustrate in the next figure 7.

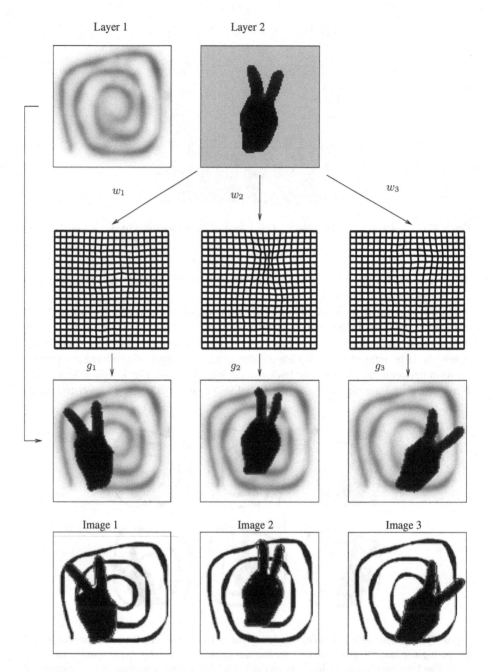

Fig. 7. Multiple Layers Mapping onto Multiple Images: The inference process returns an estimate of the albedo in each layer (top). Since we are assuming smooth albedo, the spiral is smoothed. The deformation of each layer is estimated (second row) together with its affine motion, to yield an approximation of the image (third row). This is used for comparison with the measured images (bottom row) that drives the optimization scheme.

affine motion, and then the diffeomorphic warp w_i. Again we assume smooth radiance within each layer, so when we recover the background layer we will only be able to show a slightly smoothed version of the spiral (of course we could further segment the black spiral from the background and thus obtain sharp boundaries, but this is standard and therefore we do not illustrate it here.)

In Fig. 7 we illustrate the results of this experiments, arranged to summarize the modeling process. On the top row we show the recovered layers. Since we are assuming a smooth radiance within each layer, we can only recover a smoothed version of the spiral. These layers are deformed according to a diffeomorphism, one per layer, defined on the domain of the layer (second row) and then moved according to an affine motion. The third row shows the image generated by the model, which can therefore be though of as a generative (although deterministic) model since it performs comparison at the image level, not via some intermediate feature. The corresponding images are displayed in the last row, with the layers superimposed for comparison.

5   Discussion

We have presented a generative model of the appearance (piecewise smooth albedo), motion (affine transformation) and deformation (diffeomorphism) of a sequence of images that include occlusions. We have used this model as a basis for a variational optimization algorithm that simultaneously tracks the motion of a number of overlapping layers, estimates their deformation, and estimates the albedo of each layer, including portions that were partially occluded. Where no information is available, the layers are implicitly impainted by their regularizers.

This model generalizes existing layer models to the case of deforming layers. Alternatively, one can think of our algorithm as a layered version of deformable tracking algorithms, or as a generalized version of optical flow or motion segmentation where multiple layers are allowed to occlude each other without disturbing the estimate of adjacent and occluded ones.

Our numerical implementation of the flow-based algorithm uses level set methods, and is realized without taking derivatives of the image, a feature that yields significant robustness when compared with boundary-based of optical flow algorithms. We have illustrated our approach on simple but representative sequences where existing methods fail to capture the phenomenology of the scene by either over-segmenting it, or by failing to capture its deformation while only matching its affine motion.

References

1. L. Alvarez, J. Weickert, and J. Sanchez. A scale-space approach to nonlocal optical flow calculations. In *In ScaleSpace '99*, pages 235–246, 1999.
2. S. Baker, I. Matthews, and J. Schneider. Image coding with active appearance models. Technical report, Carnegie Mellon University, The Robotics Institute, 2003.
3. M. Bertalmio, G. Sapiro, V. Caselles, and C. Ballester. Image inpainting. In Kurt Akeley, editor, *Siggraph 2000, Computer Graphics Proceedings*, pages 417–424. ACM Press / ACM SIGGRAPH / Addison Wesley Longman, 2000.

4. A. Blake and M. Isard. *Active contours*. Springer Verlag, 1998.
5. V. Caselles, R. Kimmel, and G. Sapiro. Geodesic active contours. *Int. J. of Computer Vision*, 22(1):61–79, 1997.
6. T. F. Cootes, G. J. Edwards, and C. J. Taylor. Active appearance models. In *Proc. of the Eur. Conf. on Comp. Vis.*, pages 484–496, 1998.
7. D. Cremers. Multiphase levelset framework for variational motion segmentation. In *Intl. Conf. on Scale-Space Theories in Computer Vision*, pages 599–614, June 2003.
8. R. Deriche, P. Kornprobst, and G. Aubert. Optical flow estimation while preserving its discontinuities: a variational approach. In *Proc. of ACCV*, volume 2, pages 290–295, 1995.
9. U. Grenander. *General Pattern Theory*. Oxford University Press, 1993.
10. H. W. Haussecker and D. J. Fleet. Computing optical flow with physical models of brightness variation. *IEEE Trans. Pattern Anal. Mach. Intell.*, 23(6):661–673, 2001.
11. B. K. P. Horn and B. G. Schunk. Determining optical flow. *Artificial Intell.*, 17:185–203, 1981.
12. S. Hsu, P. Anandan, and S. Peleg. Accurate computation of optical flow by using layered motion representations. In *Proc. IEEE Conf. on Comp. Vision and Pattern Recogn.*, pages 1621–1626, 1992.
13. M. Kass, A. Witkin, and D. Terzopoulos. Snakes: active contour models. *Int. J. of Computer Vision*, 1(4):321–331, 1987.
14. M. I. Miller and L. Younes. Group action, diffeomorphism and matching: a general framework. In *Proc. of SCTV*, 1999.
15. S. Osher and J. Sethian. Fronts propagating with curvature-dependent speed: algorithms based on hamilton-jacobi equations. *J. of Comp. Physics*, 79:12–49, 1988.
16. N. Paragios and R. Deriche. Geodesic active contours and level sets for the detection and tracking of moving objects. *IEEE Transactions on Pattern Analysis and Machine Intelligence*, 22(3):266–280, 2000.
17. Nikos Paragios, Mikael Rousson, and Visvanathan Ramesh. Non-rigid registration using distance functions. *Comput. Vis. Image Underst.*, 89(2-3):142–165, 2003.
18. C. Schnörr. Computation of discontinuous optical flow by domain decomposition and shape optimization. *Int. J. of Computer Vision*, 8(2):153–165, 1992.
19. S. Soatto and A. Yezzi. Deformotion: deforming motion, shape average and the joint segmentation and registration of images. In *Proc. of the Eur. Conf. on Computer Vision (ECCV)*, volume 3, pages 32–47, 2002.
20. J. Wang and E. Adelson. Representing moving images with layers. In *IEEE Trans. on Image Processing*, volume 3(5), pages 625–638, 1994.

Energy Minimization Based Segmentation and Denoising Using a Multilayer Level Set Approach*

Ginmo Chung and Luminita A. Vese

Department of Mathematics, University of California, Los Angeles,
405 Hilgard Avenue, Los Angeles, CA 90095-1555, USA
senninha@math.ucla.edu, lvese@math.ucla.edu

Abstract. This paper is devoted to piecewise-constant segmentation of images using a curve evolution approach in a variational formulation. The problem to be solved is also called the minimal partition problem, as formulated by Mumford and Shah [20]. The proposed new models are extensions of the techniques previously introduced in [9], [10], [27]. We represent here the set of boundaries of the segmentation implicitly, by a multilayer of level-lines of a continuous function. In the standard approach of front propagation, only one level line is used to represent the boundary. The multilayer idea is inspired from previous work on island dynamics for epitaxial growth [14], [4]. Using a multilayer level set approach, the computational cost is smaller and in some applications, a nested structure of the level lines can be useful.

1 Introduction

We model here images by functions $f : \Omega \to \mathbb{R}$, where Ω is an open and bounded domain in $\mathbb{R}^n$. In particular, $n = 1$ corresponds to signals, $n = 2$ corresponds to planar images, while $n = 3$ corresponds to volumetric images, such as MRI data.

An important problem in image analysis is the segmentation or the partition of an image f into regions and their boundaries, such that the regions correspond to objects in the scene. Here, we deal with the case where we look for an optimal piecewise-constant approximation of the function f, our starting point being the minimal partition problem, as formulated by D. Mumford and J. Shah [20]. The general problem is, given a function f in $L^\infty(\Omega)$ (induced by the L^2-topology), find a set of disjoint open regions Ω_i, such that $u = c_i$ in each Ω_i is a minimizer of [20]

$$F(u, \Gamma) = \sum_i \int_{\Omega_i} |f - c_i|^2 dx + \mu \mathcal{H}^{n-1}(\Gamma), \tag{1}$$

* This work has been supported in part by the National Science Foundation (Grants NSF ITR ACI-0113439 and NSF DMS 0312222), by an Alfred P. Sloan Fellowship, by the National Institute of Mental Health and the National Institute of Neurological Disorders and Stroke (Grant MH65166), and by the Institute of Pure and Applied Mathematics.

A. Rangarajan et al. (Eds.): EMMCVPR 2005, LNCS 3757, pp. 439–455, 2005.
© Springer-Verlag Berlin Heidelberg 2005

where $\Gamma = \cup_i(\partial\Omega_i)$, $\Omega = (\cup_i\Omega_i) \cup \Gamma$, $\mu > 0$ is a scale parameter, and $\mathcal{H}^{n-1}$ is the Hausdorff $(n-1)$-dimensional measure in $I\!\!R^n$. In one dimension $\mathcal{H}^0(\Gamma)$ is the counting measure, in two dimensions $\mathcal{H}^1(\Gamma)$ is the length of the curve Γ, while in three dimensions $\mathcal{H}^2(\Gamma)$ is the surface area.

The existence of minimizers has been proved by Mumford-Shah for continuous data f [20], and later by Morel-Solimini [19], for data $f \in L^\infty(\Omega)$. Elliptic convergent approximations of the minimal partition problem in the weak formulation (and also of the full Mumford and Shah model) have been proposed by Ambrosio-Tortorelli [1], [2], where the minimizer u is approximated by smoother functions, and the unknown set of discontinuities is also approximated by a smooth function v, essentially supported outside Γ. A constructive convergent algorithm for solving (1) has been proposed by Koepfler-Lopez-Morel [16], based on region growing and merging (a piecewise-constant minimizer u is obtained, and not only a smooth approximation, by contrast with [1], [2]). Also, it has been proved by Mumford-Shah [20] that a minimizer u of (1) has a finite number of regions Ω_i and of constant intensities c_i.

Curve evolution techniques and implicit representations for global segmentation have been proposed, that can be seen as particular cases of the minimal partition problem, where the number of regions Ω_i or an upper bound are assumed to be known. Thus, in [9], [10], [8], [27], [28], restrictions of the energy (1) to piecewise-constant functions taking a finite number of regions and intensities, in a variational level set approach [29], have been introduced. The energy has been minimized for restrictions to $\{u(x) = c_1H(\phi(x))+c_2H(-\phi(x))\}$, or $\{u(x) = c_{11}H(\phi_1(x))H(\phi_2(x)) + c_{10}H(\phi_1(x))H(-\phi_2(x)) + c_{01}H(-\phi_1(x))H(\phi_2(x)) + c_{00} H(-\phi_1(x))H(-\phi_2(x))\}$, and so on, where $\phi, \phi_i : \Omega \to I\!\!R$ are Lipschitz continuous functions, and H denotes the Heaviside function. The variational level set approach from Zhao, Chan, Merriman, and Osher [29] has been used, and the boundaries were represented by zero level lines of ϕ_i.

The multiphase formulation from [29] has been used in [24], [25] for computing the boundaries $\partial\Omega_i$ in the case of a finite and known number of regions, and where the corresponding intensity averages c_i where given.

The advantage of the multiphase method in [27] is that triple junctions can be represented, as in [29], [24], [25], but the regions Ω_i are disjoint and covering of Ω by definition. In addition, a smaller number of level set functions ϕ_i was needed to represent the partition, for the same number of distinct intensities c_i.

In the above mentioned work, together with other related work, the unknown boundaries $\partial\Omega_i$ are represented by the zero level line of a Lipschitz continuous function ϕ. In general, such function $\phi : \Omega \to I\!\!R$, as used for active contours [5], [18], [6], [15] partitions the domain Ω in at most two open regions $\{x \in \Omega : \phi(x) > 0\}$ and $\{x \in \Omega : \phi(x) < 0\}$, with a common boundary given by the zero level line of ϕ, $\{x \in \Omega : \phi(x) = 0\}$. For image partition, active contours, and image segmentation, such functions ϕ are thus used to represent boundaries of regions of different characteristics. In order to represent more than two regions, several functions ϕ_i can be combined and used, as we have mentioned in [29], [24], [25], [27]. For instance, in [11], [27], only two functions ϕ_i, $i = 1, 2$ were used to represent up to four disjoint regions making up Ω, and only three functions ϕ_i, $i = 1, 2, 3$ were used to represent up to eight disjoint regions.

Here, we continue the approaches from [9], [10], [27], and we show that we can use even fewer level set functions to represent disjoint regions making up Ω. The applications illustrated in this paper include active contours for object detection, image segmentation and partition, image denoising. The main idea is to use more than one level-line of the Lipschitz continuous function ϕ to represent the discontinuity set of u, and the computational cost is decreased. The idea is inspired from a different application of implicit curve evolution and free boundaries, introduced in [14], [4], where island dynamics for epitaxial growth is modeled. A first layer of islands is represented by $\{x : \phi(x) = 0\}$, then a second layer of islands, growing on the top of the previous one is represented as $\{x : \phi(x) = 1\}$, etc.

In summary, here we combine the techniques from [9], [10], [27] for image partition, with the multilayer technique for modeling epitaxial growth from [14], [4], to obtain new and improved curve evolution models for image segmentation. Another recent independent work for image segmentation is Lie, Lysaker and Tai [17], where the authors propose an interesting and efficient multi-phase image segmentation model using a polynomial approach, but different than the methods proposed in the present work.

The proposed minimization methods are non-convex, and with no uniqueness for global minimizers (these theoretical properties are inherited from the Mumford and Shah model). Moreover, we do not guarantee that our multilayer formulation computes a global minimizer of the energy. It is possible sometime to obtain only a local minimizer by the computational algorithm. Also, the final result may depend on the choice of the initialization. However, in practice, we have obtained very satisfactory results; the numerical algorithm is stable and the computed energy is decreasing function of iterations, to a local or global minimizer. The method is computationally more efficient than the one introduced in [27]. Related prior work for region based segmentation using curve evolution implementation is by L. Cohen [12], [13], Paragios-Deriche [21], [22], [23], Tsai, Yezzi and Willsky [26], among other work mentioned in [27]. We also mention the segmentation model by Zhu-Yuille, in a probabilistic energy minimization approach [30].

2   Description of the Proposed Models

2.1   The Case of One Function

We consider in this subsection the case when the contours in the image f can be represented by level lines of the same level set function ϕ.

Two Levels. Let us consider a Lipschitz continuous function $\phi : \Omega \to \mathbb{R}$. Using for instance two levels $l_1 = 0$ and $l_2 = l > 0$, the function ϕ partitions the domain into three disjoint open regions, making up Ω, together with their boundaries:

$$R_1 = \{x : \ \phi(x) < 0\}, \ R_2 = \{x : \ 0 < \phi(x) < l\}, \ R_3 = \{x : \ \phi(x) > l\}.$$

We can thus extend the binary piecewise-constant level set segmentation model from [9], [10], to the following model, again as an energy minimization algorithm, in a level set form:

$$\inf_{c_1,c_2,c_3,\phi} F(c_1, c_2, c_3, \phi) = \int_\Omega |f(x) - c_1|^2 H(-\phi(x))dx \tag{2}$$

$$+ \int_\Omega |f(x) - c_2|^2 H(\phi(x))H(l - \phi(x))dx + \int_\Omega |f(x) - c_3|^2 H(\phi(x) - l)dx$$

$$+ \mu\Big[\int_\Omega |\nabla H(\phi)| + \int_\Omega |\nabla H(\phi - l)|\Big],$$

where H is the one-dimensional Heaviside function, and $\mu > 0$ is a weight parameter. The terms $\int_\Omega |\nabla H(\phi)|$ and $\int_\Omega |\nabla H(\phi - l)|$ correspond to the length of the boundary between R_1, R_2 and R_2, R_3, respectively. The segmented image in this case will be given by

$$u(x) = c_1 H(-\phi(x)) + c_2 H(\phi(x))H(l - \phi(x)) + c_3 H(\phi(x) - l).$$

To minimize the above energy, we approximate the Heaviside function by a regularized version H_ε, as $\varepsilon \to 0$, such that $H_\varepsilon \to H$ pointwise and $H_\varepsilon \in C^1(I\!R)$. We denote by $\delta_\varepsilon := H_\varepsilon'$. Examples of such approximations, that we use in practice, are [9], [10]:

$$H_\varepsilon(z) = \frac{1}{2}\Big(1 + \frac{2}{\pi}arctan(\frac{z}{\varepsilon})\Big), \quad \delta_\varepsilon(z) = H_\varepsilon'(z) = \frac{1}{\pi} \cdot \frac{\varepsilon}{\varepsilon^2 + z^2}.$$

Minimizing the corresponding approximate energy F_ε alternately with respect to the unknowns, yields the associated Euler-Lagrange equations, parameterizing the descent direction by an artificial time $t \geq 0$:

$$\phi(0, x) = \phi_0(x), \tag{3}$$

$$c_1(t) = \frac{\int_\Omega f(x)H(-\phi(t, x))dx}{\int_\Omega H(-\phi(t, x))dx}, \tag{4}$$

$$c_2(t) = \frac{\int_\Omega f(x)H(\phi(t, x))H(l - \phi(t, x))dx}{\int_\Omega H(\phi(t, x))H(l - \phi(t, x))dx}, \tag{5}$$

$$c_3(t) = \frac{\int_\Omega f(x)H(\phi(t, x) - l)dx}{\int_\Omega H(\phi(t, x) - l)dx}, \tag{6}$$

$$\frac{\partial \phi}{\partial t} = \delta_\varepsilon(\phi)\Big[|f - c_1|^2 - |f - c_2|^2 H(l - \phi) + \mu div\Big(\frac{\nabla \phi}{|\nabla \phi|}\Big)\Big] \tag{7}$$

$$+ \delta_\varepsilon(\phi - l)\Big[H(\phi)|f - c_2|^2 - |f - c_3|^2 + \mu div\Big(\frac{\nabla \phi}{|\nabla \phi|}\Big)\Big],$$

$$\frac{(\delta_\varepsilon(\phi) + \delta_\varepsilon(\phi - l))\nabla \phi}{|\nabla \phi|} \cdot \boldsymbol{n} = 0 \text{ on } \partial\Omega, \ t > 0, \tag{8}$$

where n is the exterior unit normal to $\partial\Omega$. At steady state, a local or global minimizer of the energy (2) will be obtained. Note that the energy (2) is non-convex and it may have more than one global minimizer, these being properties inherited from the Mumford and Shah model [20]. In practice, we do not guarantee that our computational algorithm converges to a global minimizer. Therefore, sometime only a local minimizer may be obtained, but close to a global minimizer, and this may also depend on the choice of the initialization of the algorithm.

m **Levels.** More levels $\{l_1 < l_2 < ... < l_m\}$ can be considered, instead of only two $\{l_1 = 0 < l_2 = l\}$. The energy in this more general case will be:

$$\inf_{c_1,c_2,...,c_{m+1},\phi} F(c_1, c_2, ..., c_{m+1}, \phi) = \int_\Omega |f(x) - c_1|^2 H(l_1 - \phi(x))dx$$

$$+ \sum_{i=2}^m \int_\Omega |f(x) - c_i|^2 H(\phi(x) - l_{i-1})H(l_i - \phi(x))dx$$

$$+ \int_\Omega |f(x) - c_{m+1}|^2 H(\phi(x) - l_m)dx + \mu \sum_{i=1}^m \int_\Omega |\nabla H(\phi - l_i)|.$$

The associated Euler-Lagrange equations in this more general case, can be expressed in a similar way, as follows: in a dynamical scheme, starting with $\phi(0, x) = \phi_0(x)$, solve for $t > 0$

$$c_1(t) = \frac{\int_\Omega f(x)H(l_1 - \phi(t,x))dx}{\int_\Omega H(l_1 - \phi(t,x))dx},$$

$$c_i(t) = \frac{\int_\Omega f(x)H(\phi(t,x) - l_{i-1})H(l_i - \phi(t,x))dx}{\int_\Omega H(\phi(t,x) - l_{i-1})H(l_i - \phi(t,x))dx},$$

$$c_{m+1}(t) = \frac{\int_\Omega f(x)H(\phi(t,x) - l_m)dx}{\int_\Omega H(\phi(t,x) - l_m)dx},$$

for $i = 2, ..., m$, and

$$\frac{\partial\phi}{\partial t} = \delta_\varepsilon(l_1 - \phi)|f - c_1|^2 + \sum_{i=2}^m \left[-\delta_\varepsilon(\phi - l_{i-1})H(l_i - \phi)|f - c_i|^2 \right.$$

$$+ \delta_\varepsilon(l_i - \phi)H(\phi - l_{i-1})|f - c_i|^2 \Big] - \delta_\varepsilon(\phi - l_m)|f - c_{m+1}|^2$$

$$+ \mu \sum_{i=1}^m \left[\delta_\varepsilon(\phi - l_i)\text{div}\left(\frac{\nabla\phi}{|\nabla\phi|}\right) \right],$$

together with the corresponding boundary conditions on $\partial\Omega$, for $t > 0$.

We show in Fig. 1 examples of partitions of the domain Ω, using two and three level lines of a Lipschitz continuous function ϕ.

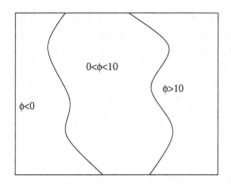 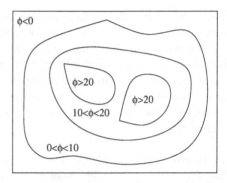

Fig. 1. Left: the level lines $\{x \in \Omega : \phi(x) = 0\}$, $\{x \in \Omega : \phi(x) = 10\}$ partition the domain Ω into 3 disjoint regions. Right: the level lines $\{x \in \Omega : \phi(x) = 0\}$, $\{x \in \Omega : \phi(x) = 10\}$, $\{x \in \Omega : \phi(x) = 20\}$ partition the domain Ω into 4 disjoint regions.

We present next experimental results applied to synthetic and real images obtained with the models with one level set function and multiple layers just introduced. In each figure, we show the evolution over time of the segmented image u of averages (left column), and the evolving set of curves superposed over the initial image f (right column). We also give the main parameters used in the calculations and the CPU times.

In Fig. 2 we illustrate how the model works on a noisy synthetic image, in the case $m = 3$, where m is the number of the nested level lines of the function ϕ used to partition the domain Ω. In Fig. 3-4, we illustrate how the models work on real noisy images of poor resolution, representing blood cells. Here, the model with two level lines of the function ϕ has been applied, producing very satisfactory results. In Fig. 5, application to brain data segmentation is illustrated.

We note that in all these cases, in the piecewise-constant segmentation models from [24], [25], and [27], we would have needed more than one function ϕ for the segmentation, therefore more computational storage is required. In practice, we do not impose that ϕ is Lipschitz continuous (this aspect will be discussed again at the end). The parameter levels l_1, l_2, ... are here kept constant and fixed for all our different experimental calculations. These can also be specified by the user. We have not implemented an automatic procedure of selection of these parameter levels. Sometimes, these could be estimated if a statistical prior exists about the contours or level lines of the data. We note that the algorithm is not sensitive with respect to the change of these parameter levels l_i. As in the model from [27], only an upper bound of the phases is needed. For instance we can segment an image into 2 regions, using the model with one level set function and 2 levels (therefore with 3 regions in theory, but only two regions will appear in practice). Note that in all cases, the energy reaches a minimum (local or global) very fast, only after a small number of iterations. The only varying parameter in this set of results is the coefficient of the length term, which has a scaling role.

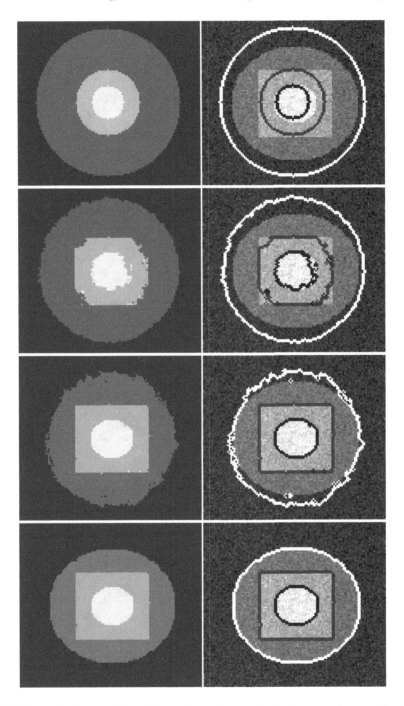

Fig. 2. Segmentation and denoising of a noisy synthetic image using one level set function ϕ and 3 levels. Parameters: $l_1 = 0$, $l_2 = 25$, $l_3 = 35$, $\triangle t = 0.1$, $\mu = 0.0217 \cdot 255^2$, 30 iterations, cpu time 0.41 sec.

Fig. 3. Segmentation and denoising of a real noisy blood cells image using one level set function and two levels. Parameters: $l_1 = 0$, $l_2 = 25$, $\triangle t = 0.1$, $\mu = 0.03 \cdot 255^2$, 200 iterations, cpu time 2.51 sec.

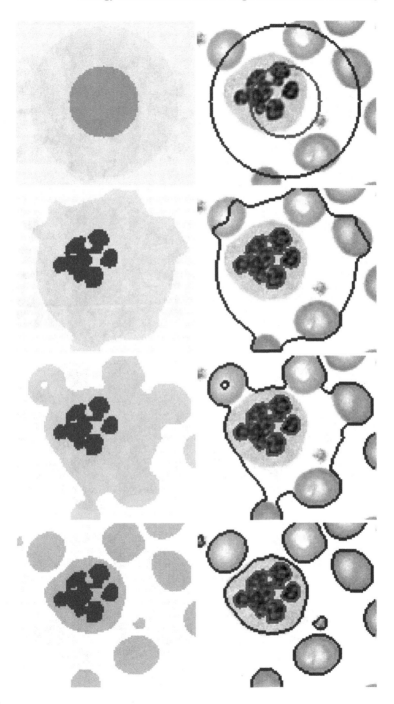

Fig. 4. Segmentation and denoising of a real noisy blood cells image using one level set function and two levels. Parameters: $l_1 = 0$, $l_2 = 25$, $\triangle t = 0.1$, $\mu = 0.043 \cdot 255^2$, 200 iterations, cpu time 2.493 sec.

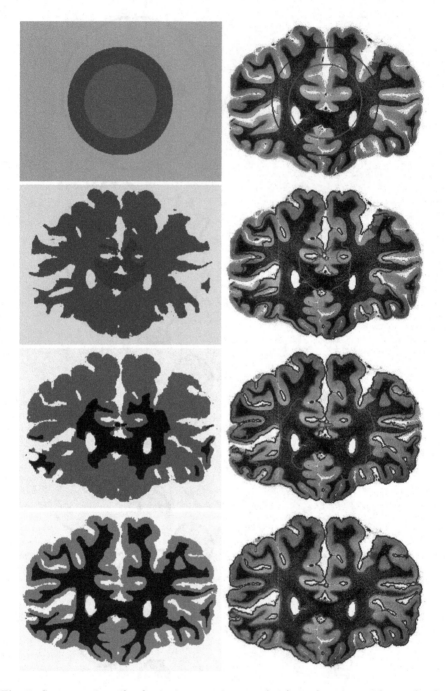

Fig. 5. Segmentation of a brain image using one level set function with two levels. Parameters: $l_1 = 0$, $l_2 = 25$, $\triangle t = 0.1$, $\mu = 0.1 \cdot 255^2$, 1500 iterations, cpu time 183.544 sec.

2.2   The Case of Two Functions

As in [11], [27], we can extend the multilayer model from the previous section to the case of more than one level set function. This may be needed for instance for images with triple junctions. Here, we will use only two level set functions, to represent up to nine distinct regions of different intensities, making up Ω. We will work with the functions ϕ_1 and ϕ_2, and with two levels $\{0, l\}$, with $l > 0$.

The nine regions defined by the two level set functions and two levels are:

$$R_{11} = \{x : \phi_1 < 0, \ \phi_2 < 0\}, R_{21} = \{x : 0 < \phi_1 < l, \ \phi_2 < 0\},$$
$$R_{31} = \{x : \phi_1 > l, \ \phi_2 < 0\},$$
$$R_{12} = \{x : \phi_1 < 0, 0 < \phi_2 < l\}, R_{22} = \{x : 0 < \phi_1 < l, 0 < \phi_2 < l\},$$
$$R_{32} = \{x : \phi_1 > l, 0 < \phi_2 < l\},$$
$$R_{13} = \{x : \phi_1 < 0, \ \phi_2 > l\}, R_{23} = \{x : 0 < \phi_1 < l, \ \phi_2 > l\},$$
$$R_{33} = \{x : \phi_1 > l, \ \phi_2 > l\}.$$

Following the previous section and [27], the associated energy for image segmentation is:

$$\inf_{c,\Phi} F(c,\Phi) = \int_\Omega \Big[|f(x) - c_{11}|^2 H(-\phi_1(x)) H(-\phi_2(x))$$
$$+ |f(x) - c_{21}|^2 H(\phi_1(x)) H(l - \phi_1(x)) H(-\phi_2(x))$$
$$+ |f(x) - c_{31}|^2 H(\phi_1(x) - l) H(-\phi_2(x))$$
$$+ |f(x) - c_{12}|^2 H(-\phi_1(x)) H(\phi_2(x)) H(l - \phi_2(x))$$
$$+ |f(x) - c_{22}|^2 H(\phi_1(x)) H(l - \phi_1(x)) H(\phi_2(x)) H(l - \phi_2(x))$$
$$+ |f(x) - c_{32}|^2 H(\phi_1(x) - l) H(\phi_2(x)) H(l - \phi_2(x))$$
$$+ |f(x) - c_{13}|^2 H(-\phi_1(x)) H(\phi_2(x) - l)$$
$$+ |f(x) - c_{23}|^2 H(\phi_1(x)) H(l - \phi_1(x)) H(\phi_2(x) - l)$$
$$+ |f(x) - c_{33}|^2 H(\phi_1(x) - l) H(\phi_2(x) - l) \Big] dx$$
$$+ \mu \Big[\int_\Omega |\nabla H(\phi_1)| + \int_\Omega |\nabla H(\phi_1 - l)| + \int_\Omega |\nabla H(\phi_2)| + \int_\Omega |\nabla H(\phi_2 - l)| \Big],$$

where $c = (c_{11}, c_{21}, c_{31}, c_{12}, c_{22}, c_{32}, c_{13}, c_{23}, c_{33})$ is the unknown vector of averages, and $\Phi = (\phi_1, \phi_2)$ is a vector-valued unknown function.

Embedding the minimization in a dynamical scheme, starting with $\phi_1(0, x) = \phi_{1,0}(x)$, $\phi_2(0, x) = \phi_{2,0}(x)$, we have that the unknown constants $c_{11}, c_{21}, ...$ are given by the averages of the data f on their corresponding regions $R_{11}, R_{21}, ...$, as follows:

$$c_{11}(t) = \frac{\int_\Omega f H(-\phi_1) H(-\phi_2) dx}{\int_\Omega H(-\phi_1) H(-\phi_2) dx}, \quad c_{21}(t) = \frac{\int_\Omega f H(\phi_1) H(l-\phi_1) H(-\phi_2) dx}{\int_\Omega H(\phi_1) H(l-\phi_1) H(-\phi_2) dx},$$
$$c_{31}(t) = \frac{\int_\Omega f H(\phi_1 - l) H(-\phi_2) dx}{\int_\Omega H(\phi_1 - l) H(-\phi_2) dx}, \quad c_{12}(t) = \frac{\int_\Omega f H(-\phi_1) H(\phi_2) H(l-\phi_2) dx}{\int_\Omega H(-\phi_1) H(\phi_2) H(l-\phi_2) dx},$$
$$c_{22}(t) = \frac{\int_\Omega f H(\phi_1) H(\phi_2) H(l-\phi_1) H(l-\phi_2) dx}{\int_\Omega H(\phi_1) H(\phi_2) H(l-\phi_1) H(l-\phi_2) dx},$$

$$c_{32}(t) = \frac{\int_\Omega f(x)H(\phi_1-l)H(\phi_2)H(l-\phi_2)dx}{\int_\Omega H(\phi_1-l)H(\phi_2)H(l-\phi_2)dx},$$

$$c_{13}(t) = \frac{\int_\Omega fH(-\phi_1)H(\phi_2-l)dx}{\int_\Omega H(-\phi_1)H(\phi_2-l)dx},$$

$$c_{23}(t) = \frac{\int_\Omega fH(\phi_1)H(l-\phi_1)H(\phi_2-l)dx}{\int_\Omega H(\phi_1)H(l-\phi_1)H(\phi_2-l)dx},$$

$$c_{33}(t) = \frac{\int_\Omega fH(\phi_1-l)H(\phi_2-l)dx}{\int_\Omega H(\phi_1-l)H(\phi_2-l)dx}.$$

The unknown functions ϕ_1 and ϕ_2 are solutions of the following equations:

$$\phi_1(0,x) = \phi_{1,0}(x), \quad \phi_2(0,x) = \phi_{2,0}(x),$$

$$\frac{\partial\phi_1}{\partial t} = \delta_\varepsilon(\phi_1)\Big[|f-c_{11}|^2H(-\phi_2) - |f-c_{21}|^2H(l-\phi_1)H(-\phi_2)$$

$$+|f-c_{12}|^2H(\phi_2)H(l-\phi_2) - |f-c_{22}|^2H(l-\phi_1)H(\phi_2)H(l-\phi_2)$$

$$+|f-c_{13}|^2H(\phi_2-l) - |f-c_{23}|^2H(l-\phi_1)H(\phi_2-l) + \mu\mathrm{div}\Big(\frac{\nabla\phi_1}{|\nabla\phi_1|}\Big)\Big]$$

$$+\delta_\varepsilon(\phi_1-l)\Big[|f-c_{21}|^2H(\phi_1)H(-\phi_2) - |f-c_{31}|^2H(-\phi_2)$$

$$+|f-c_{22}|^2H(\phi_1)H(\phi_2)H(l-\phi_2) - |f-c_{32}|^2H(\phi_2)H(l-\phi_2)$$

$$+|f-c_{23}|^2H(\phi_1)H(\phi_2-l) - |f-c_{33}|^2H(\phi_2-l) + \mu\mathrm{div}\Big(\frac{\nabla\phi_1}{|\nabla\phi_1|}\Big)\Big],$$

$$\frac{\partial\phi_2}{\partial t} = \delta_\varepsilon(\phi_2)\Big[|f-c_{11}|^2H(-\phi_1) - |f-c_{12}|^2H(-\phi_1)H(l-\phi_2)$$

$$+|f-c_{21}|^2H(\phi_1)H(l-\phi_1) - |f-c_{22}|^2H(\phi_1)H(l-\phi_1)H(l-\phi_2)$$

$$+|f-c_{31}|^2H(\phi_1-l) - |f-c_{32}|^2H(\phi_1-l)H(l-\phi_2) + \mu\mathrm{div}\Big(\frac{\nabla\phi_2}{|\nabla\phi_2|}\Big)\Big]$$

$$+\delta_\varepsilon(\phi_2-l)\Big[|f-c_{12}|^2H(-\phi_1)H(\phi_2) - |f-c_{13}|^2H(-\phi_1)$$

$$+|f-c_{22}|^2H(\phi_1)H(l-\phi_1)H(\phi_2) - |f-c_{23}|^2H(\phi_1)H(l-\phi_1)$$

$$+|f-c_{32}|^2H(\phi_1-l)H(\phi_2) - |f-c_{33}|^2H(\phi_1-l) + \mu\mathrm{div}\Big(\frac{\nabla\phi_2}{|\nabla\phi_2|}\Big)\Big].$$

We show in Fig. 6 an example of partition of the domain Ω, using two level lines corresponding to $l_1 = 0$, $l_2 = 10$, and two continuous functions ϕ_1, ϕ_2.

Note that, as in the multi-phase models from [27] and [28], when two distinct level set functions are used to represent the contours, as in this subsection, then it is possible that two level lines of the different functions ϕ_1 and ϕ_2 may partially overlap, and therefore by the above formulation the length of the common contour will be counted more than once and will have a different weight. This is different from the Mumford and Shah energy [20]. This is not a problem in practice, as seen in the numerical approximations. Moreover, this can also be simply avoided, as explained in [28].

We show next experimental results on images with triple junctions, where only two level set functions ϕ_1, ϕ_2 with two levels are used to represent up to nine disjoint regions, making up Ω.

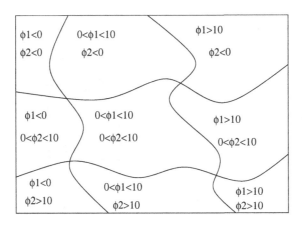

Fig. 6. The level lines $\{x \in \Omega : \phi_i(x) = 0\}$ and $\{x \in \Omega : \phi_i(x) = 10\}$, $i = 1, 2$, partition the domain Ω into 9 disjoint regions

We present in Fig. 7 a numerical result of segmentation and partition of a noisy synthetic image, composed of 5 regions of distinct intensities. All regions and corresponding intensities are correctly detected and represented. The model uses 9 phases in theory, but at steady state only 5 appear. The proposed model performs faster than the one in [27]; both multi-phase models give similar qualitative results. In Fig. 8 we have a numerical result for a noisy synthetic color image consisting of 9 regions of distinct intensities, in a vector-valued fashion, as in [8].

We note that in all the above numerical results, we do not use the reinitialization to the distance function of the level set functions ϕ, ϕ_i. Also, using the length regularization only of the level lines $\{\phi = l_i\}$, the function ϕ may become discontinuous away from these levels. This is true in practice, however, it does not appear to be an inconvenience. If, however, we would need to keep the function ϕ more regular, we can use different regularizations that act on all level lines of ϕ. We have tested and compared in practice several regularizations for ϕ, instead of the length of the levels l_i: these are $\int_\Omega |\nabla\phi|dx$ (total variation regularization, still decreases the perimeter of each level line independently, and produces a function ϕ that tends to be piecewise-constant, with jumps near the detected contours), $\int_\Omega |\nabla\phi|^2 dx$ (which will guarantee a smooth function ϕ, but may smooth corners also); $\||\nabla\phi|\|_{L^\infty(\Omega)}$, that leads to the infinity-Laplacian, or the second order derivative in the normal direction to the level lines of ϕ (this regularization formally keeps the function ϕ Lipschitz, in $W^{1,\infty}(\Omega)$, and the gradient magnitude is strictly positive near the contours, therefore preventing the surface to become too flat). All these regularizations give satisfactory and similar results. We conclude the paper by showing in Fig. 9 the iso-contours of the final function ϕ for the real image used in Fig. 4, obtained with length regularization, and with the sup-norm of the gradient regularization. We see that in the last case, the function ϕ is closer to a "distance" function, in the sense that distinct level lines stay at constant distance of each other, and do not become too close.

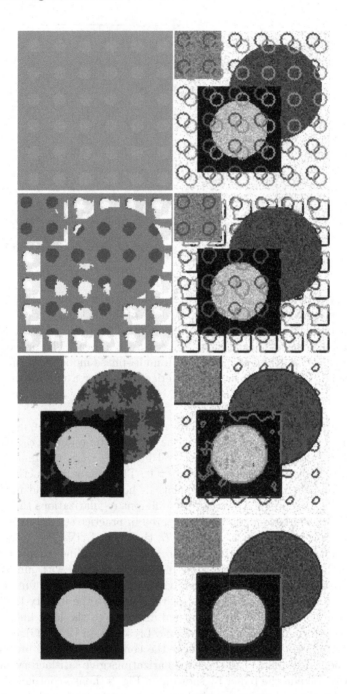

Fig. 7. Segmentation and denoising of a synthetic noisy image with triple junctions, using two functions ϕ_1, ϕ_2 and two levels. Parameters: $l_1 = 0$, $l_2 = 25$, $\triangle t = 0.4$, $\mu = 0.023 \cdot 255^2$, 200 iterations, cpu time 13.985 sec.

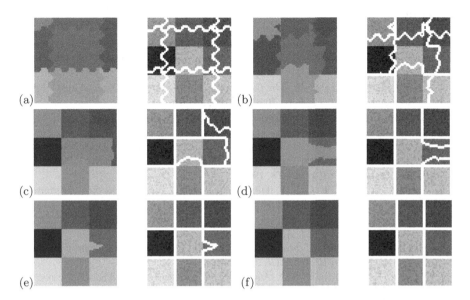

Fig. 8. Segmentation and denoising of a synthetic noisy color image with junctions, using two functions ϕ_1, ϕ_2 and two levels. Parameters: $l_1 = 0$, $l_2 = 25$, $\triangle t = 0.01$, $\mu = 0.335 \cdot 255^2$, 160 iterations, cpu time 10.975 sec. Note that the image contains nine different regions, all correctly detected and segmented in an efficient approach.

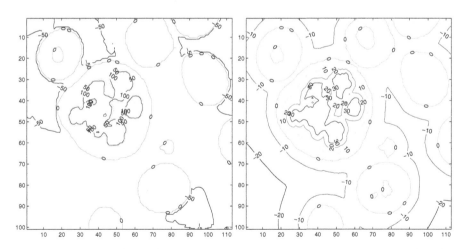

Fig. 9. Left: iso-contours of final ϕ using length regularization only, $\mu\delta_\varepsilon(\phi)\mathrm{div}\left(\frac{\nabla\phi}{|\nabla\phi|}\right) + \mu\delta_\varepsilon(\phi - l)\mathrm{div}\left(\frac{\nabla\phi}{|\nabla\phi|}\right)$. Right: iso-contours of final ϕ using the sup-norm of the gradient $\||\nabla\phi|\|_{L^\infty(\Omega)}$ as regularization, minimized using the infinity Laplacian $\mu\triangle_\infty\phi = \frac{\phi_{xx}(\phi_x)^2 + 2\phi_x\phi_y\phi_{xy} + \phi_{yy}(\phi_y)^2}{|\nabla\phi|^2}$, therefore ensuring that ϕ remains Lipschitz (see Aronsson [3], Caselles, Morel, Sbert [7], among others).

References

1. L. Ambrosio, V.M. Tortorelli, *Approximation of functionals depending on jumps by elliptic functionals via Γ-convergence*, Comm. Pure Appl. Math., 43, 999-1036, 1990.
2. L. Ambrosio, V.M. Tortorelli, *On the Approximation of Free Discontinuity Problems*, Bollettino U.M.I. (7) 6-B, 105-123, 1992.
3. G. Aronsson, *Minimization problems for functionals* $\sup_x F(x, f(x), f'(x))$, Arkiv for mathematik 6(1): 33-&, 1965.
4. R.E. Caflisch, M.F. Gyure, B. Merriman, S.J. Osher, C. Ratsch, D.D. Vvedensky, J.J. Zinck, *Island dynamics and the level set method for epitaxial growth*, Applied Mathematics Letters 12(4): 13-22, 1999.
5. V. Caselles, F. Catté, T. Coll, F. Dibos, *A geometric model for active contours in image-processing*, Numerische Mathematik, 66(1): 1-31, 1993.
6. V. Caselles, R. Kimmel, G. Sapiro, *Geodesic active contours*, IJCV 22(1): 61-79, 1997.
7. V. Caselles, J.M. Morel, C. Sbert, *An axiomatic approach to image interpolation*, IEEE Transactions on IP 7(3): 376-386, 1998.
8. T.F. Chan, B.Y. Sandberg, L.A. Vese, *Active contours without edges for vector-valued images*, JVCIR, 11(2): 130-141, 2000.
9. T. F. Chan, L. Vese, *An active contour model without edges*, LNCS 1682, 141-151, 1999.
10. T.F. Chan, L.A. Vese, *Active contours without edges*, IEEE Transactions on IP 10(2): 266 -277, 2001.
11. T.F. Chan, L.A. Vese, *Level Set Algorithm for Minimizing the Mumford-Shah Functional in Image Processing*, IEEE Workshop on VLSM, 161-168, 2001.
12. L.D. Cohen, *Avoiding local minima for deformable curves in image analysis*, in *Curves and Surfaces with Applications in CAGD*, A. Le Méhauté, C. Rabut, and L.L. Schumaker (eds.), 77-84, 1997.
13. L. Cohen, E. Bardinet, and N. Ayache, *Surface reconstruction using active contour models*, Proc. SPIE 93 Conference on Geometric Methods in Computer Vision, San Diego, CA, July 1993.
14. M.F. Gyure, C. Ratsch, B. Merriman, R.E. Caflisch, S. Osher, J.J. Zinck, D.D. Vvedensky, *Level-set methods for the simulation of epitaxial phenomena*, Physical Review E 58(6): R6927-R6930 Part A, 1998.
15. S. Kichenassamy, A. Kumar, P. Olver, A. Tannenbaum, A. Yezzi Jr., *Conformal curvature flows: from phase transitions to active vision*, Arch. Rational Mech. Anal. 134(3): 275-301, 1996.
16. G. Koepfler, C. Lopez, J.-M. Morel, *A multiscale algorithm for image segmentation by variational method*, SIAM J. Num. Analysis, 31(1): 282-299, 1994.
17. J. Lie, M. Lysaker, X.-C. Tai, *Piecewise Constant Level Set Methods and Image Segmentation*, LNCS 3459: 573-584, 2005.
18. R. Malladi, J.A. Sethian, B.C. Vemuri, *Shape modeling with front propagation - a level set approach*, IEEE Tr. PAMI, 17(2): 158-175, 1995.
19. J.M. Morel, S. Solimini, *Density estimates for the boundaries of optimal segmentations*, CRASS I-Mathématique 312(6): 429-432, 1991.
20. D. Mumford, J. Shah, *Optimal approximation by piecewise smooth functions and associated variational problems*, Comm. Pure Appl. Math. 42:577-685, 1989.
21. N. Paragios, R. Deriche, *Unifying boundary and region-based information for geodesic active tracking*, Proc. CVPR 1999, Vol. 2: 23-25, 1999.

22. N. Paragios, R. Deriche, *Geodesic active regions: A new framework to deal with frame partition problems in computer vision*, JVCIR 13(1-2): 249-268, 2002.

23. N. Paragios, R. Deriche, *Geodesic active regions and level set methods for supervised texture segmentation*, IJCV 46(3): 223-247, 2002.

24. C. Samson, L. Blanc-Féraud, G. Aubert, J. Zérubia, *A level set model for image classification*, LNCS 1682, 306-317, 1999.

25. C. Samson, L. Blanc-Féraud, G. Aubert, J. Zérubia, *A level set model for image classification*, IJCV 40(3): 187-197, 2000.

26. A. Tsai, A. Yezzi, A.S. Willsky, *Curve evolution implementation of the Mumford-Shah functional for image segmentation, denoising, interpolation, and magnification*, IEEE Transactions on IP, 10(8):1169 - 1186, 2001.

27. L.A. Vese and T.F. Chan, *A Multiphase Level Set Framework for Image Segmentation Using the Mumford and Shah Model*, IJCV 50(3): 271-293, 2002.

28. L. Vese, *Multiphase Object Detection and Image Segmentation* in "Geometric Level Set Methods in Imaging, Vision and Graphics", S. Osher and N. Paragios (eds), Springer Verlag, 175-194, 2003.

29. H.-K. Zhao, T. Chan, B. Merriman, and S. Osher, *Variational level set approach to multiphase motion*, JCP 127(1): 179-195, 1996.

30. S.C. Zhu and A. Yuille, *Region competition: Unifying snakes, region growing, and Bayes/MDL for multiband image segmentation*, IEEE Transactions on PAMI, 18(9): 884-900, 1996.

Constrained Total Variation Minimization and Application in Computerized Tomography

Xiao-Qun Zhang* and Jacques Froment

LMAM, Université de Bretagne Sud,
Campus de Tohannic - Y. Coppens, BP573, 56017 Vannes, France

Abstract. We present a simple framework for solving different ill-posed inverse problems in image processing by means of constrained total variation minimizations. We argue that drawbacks commonly attributed to total variation algorithms (slowness and incomplete fit to the image model) can be easily bypassed by performing only a few number of iterations in our optimization process. We illustrate this approach in the context of computerized tomography, that comes down to inverse a Radon transform obtained by illuminating an object by straight and parallel beams of x-rays. This problem is ill-posed because only a finite number of line integrals can be measured, resulting in an incomplete coverage of the frequency plane and requiring, for a direct Fourier reconstruction, frequencies interpolation from a polar to a Cartesian grid. We introduce a new method of interpolation based on a total variation minimization constrained by the knowledge of frequency coefficients in the polar grid, subject to a Lipschitz regularity assumption. The experiments show that our algorithm is able to avoid Gibbs and noise oscillations associated to the direct Fourier method, and that it outperforms classical reconstruction methods such as filtered backprojection and Rudin-Osher-Fatemi total variation restoration, in terms of both PSNR and visual quality.

1 Introduction

Many ill-posed problems in image processing may be solved by minimizing the total variation (TV) of an image, subject to a constraint : the TV functional provides an appropriate solution to the visual perception, while the constraint ensures that the solution satisfies all the conditions stated in the problem.

1.1 The Total Variation and the Rudin-Osher-Fatemi Approach

If the image f is defined on the bounded, open and convex region Ω of $\mathbb{R}^2$ such that $f \in L^1(\Omega)$, one sets

$$\mathrm{TV}(f) := \int_\Omega |\nabla f| dx \qquad (1)$$

* X. Zhang is partially supported by *La Région Bretagne* under grant B/1042/2003/300/MIRIM.

A. Rangarajan et al. (Eds.): EMMCVPR 2005, LNCS 3757, pp. 456–472, 2005.

where ∇f is the weak gradient of f that is, the vector of the partial derivatives of f taken in the distributional sense. The set of functions of Bounded Variation (BV) is defined as the Banach space of L^1 functions with finite TV, using the TV-seminorm.

The TV functional has been first introduced by Rudin, Osher and Fatemi (ROF) in [1] in the context of image denoising. It has proved to be particularly relevant in recovering piecewise smooth functions without smoothing sharp discontinuities (edges). The ROF problem is formulated in the constraint minimization form by

$$\inf_f TV(f) \quad (2i) \quad \text{subject to} \quad \int_\Omega (o - f)^2 = \sigma^2 \quad (2ii), \tag{2}$$

where o is the observed image, which is assumed to be corrupted by a Gaussian noise of variance σ^2. Introducing a Lagrange multiplier λ, (2) is equivalent to the following unconstrained minimization problem [2], that can be viewed as a particular Tikhonov regularization :

$$\inf_f TV(f) + \lambda \int_\Omega (o - f)^2. \tag{3}$$

The ROF algorithm consists in solving (3) by using a time marching scheme to reach the steady state of a nonlinear diffusion process. The parameter $\lambda \geq 0$ in the data-fidelity term is chosen so that the constraint (2ii) is satisfied. Unfortunately such choice is not always possible, leading to a solution not consistent with the problem. Notice that to avoid non-differentiability of the TV-functional in constant areas, a small perturbation is added. This may significantly alter the original energy functional.

1.2   Following Developments

The introduction of the ROF algorithm has been of great interest in image denoising and deblurring, and recent years have seen number of developments of TV-minimization methods. Lot of work has been done to obtain more efficient minimization algorithms or better mathematical properties, most often by slightly modifying the TV functional to ensure differentiability [3][4][5][6][7][8], by using level sets thanks to the Coarea formula [9][10], or more recently by using subgradients methods [11][12][13]. The ROF approach has also been enlarged to various restoration problems, sometimes in combination with cosine or wavelets bases [14][15][16][17][18]. A few authors have proposed to enhance the TV model by using a more appropriate norm in the fidelity constraint. The l_1 norm can be found in [19] in relation with recursive median filters. In [20][21], M. Nikolova uses a l_1 data-fidelity term that involves an implicit detection of outliers. An exact optimization scheme in the case of L^1 or L^2 norms is given in [10].

A major deception in the mathematical image processing community was to discover that the BV space is still not the appropriate space to model physical images : natural images are not, in general, of finite TV because of microtextures generating oscillations at every scales [22]. In order to measure textural parts removed by the TV functional, Y. Meyer has introduced in [23] a dual norm called the G-norm and he has proposed to use it for the data-fidelity term. This was the beginning of promising researchs for new dual norms [24][25] and new functionals allowing the decomposition of the image f into $f = u + v + w$ where u is the cartoon-part (detected by minimizing the TV), v the textural part, and where the residue w contains the undesirable noise [26][27].

1.3   Our Contribution

In this article, we present a constrained TV-minimization framework that we believe to be mathematically and numerically simple, flexible enough to be used to solve various ill-posed inverse problems in image processing, and that avoids the main drawbacks commonly attributed to TV-minimization : slowness of basic gradient algorithms and incomplete fit to the image model. Such a framework has already be applied by one of us, together with S. Durand and F. Alter, to denoise signals using wavelet shrinkage [12] and to restore JPEG-compressed images [28]. One of the main goal of this present article is to emphasize that a complete mathematical model of images may not always be necessary, nor even suitable, to obtain efficient image reconstruction or restoration algorithms. Indeed, a solution of a formal optimization problem is numerically found as the result of an iterative procedure when the number of iterations tends to infinity. Therefore, the practitioner is facing the following choice : should I try to obtain a good approximation, and then to keep the algorithm running a long time, or should I perform only a small number of iterations, to preserve a low computational complexity ? We claim that the BV space, as an incomplete image model unable to contain the thinest details, should sometimes be see as a chance to build algorithms with best results after a small number of iterations only (typically less than 10, see Fig.3).

After these remarks, we introduce our main original contribution : an application of our constrained TV-minimization framework to Computerized Tomography (CT). CT is the typical ill-posed inverse problem in image reconstruction. Besides, obtaining noiseless high quality tomographic images in limited time (low hardware cost) is of great importance for improving public health. A CT scanner contains a rotating x-ray device to create cross-sectional images of the body. The input is the set of x-ray projections called sinogram and which corresponds to the Radon transform of the image f that has to be reconstructed. If the Radon transform can be theoretically inverted using Fourier transforms, it requires however a complete set of projections. In practice only a finite number of projections can be measured, resulting in an incomplete coverage of the frequency plane. Solving the CT problem involves therefore to perform (implicitly or explicitly) a frequency interpolation, from a polar to a Cartesian grid. This is the critical point of CT. As far as we know, it does not exist any CT interpolation method based on a mathematical model that tells us what should be the reconstructed image in accordance with the visual perception. As a result of, the two main families of reconstruction methods, direct Fourier methods

(DFM) and filtered backprojection (FBP), generate visual artefacts : DFM are by far those suffering worse artefacts, with unpleasant oscillations due to noisy data in high frequencies. In presence of noise, the performance of FBP is fair since it consists of averaging backprojections for all sinogram lines. Moreover, a Hamming window is often applied to deemphasize high frequencies. This explains why windowed FBP is currently considered as the best reconstruction method. However, windowed FBP is unable to remove the noise while keeping edges sharp. We claim that the BV model is particularly adapted to model CT images. No doubt, as for other images, the TV is not able to model the finest details. However, CT scanners cannot deliver very thin details as they are mixed with the noise. The technology seems not ready to offer textured CT images, and the common test image is still the famous Shepp-Logan phantom [29], an image made by piecewise-constant functions (for which level lines are ellipses).

In the constrained TV-minimization framework applied to CT, the key point is to define the constraint space. The solution we are currently proposing is based on a local Lipschitz regularity assumption of the Fourier spectrum. From the input data in the polar grid, we compute the local Lipschitz constants and we assume that, locally, those constants are the same in the Cartesian grid. This allows to set intervals of frequency values in the Cartesian grid, resulting in defining the constraint as a frequency hypercube. Following our constrained TV-framework, the numerical scheme performs a subgradient "descent" combining a projection on this hypercube. The method does converge, but the practitioner is warned not to try to reach the convergence zone. Indeed, and this seems to be a characteristic shared by all instantiations of our constrained TV-framework, the first iterations of the subgradient algorithm make edges sharper while removing the noise but not meaningful structures. If too many iterations would be performed, the constraint space may be too large to avoid loss of thin details, and the visual quality of the solution would decrease. As a result of, the numerical scheme is pretty fast and remain of the same order than classical methods DFM and FBP. However, the reconstructed image is of better quality both visually and in term of PSNR.

2   A Simple Constrained-TV Framework

2.1   The Subgradient Projection Method

As noted before, the ROF method is implemented using the unconstrained minimization (3), and it does not guarantee the condition (2ii) to be satisfied. In addition, the practitioner has to deal with the parameter λ. By explicitly defining a set $U \subset$ BV of admissible solutions, we avoid such drawbacks and the formulation is more flexible that the one based on a data-fidelity term. The set U models the knowledge on the image, computed from the input data. In the following, we will assume U to be a convex set. The constrained optimization problem can be simply written as

$$\text{find } f^* \in U \quad \text{such that } \text{TV}(f^*) = \min_{f \in U} \text{TV}(f). \tag{4}$$

In the numerical analysis of the TV minimization, the difficulty comes from the non-differentiable argument $|\nabla|$. Most authors introduce a form of relaxation as

$$\text{TV}(f) = \int_\Omega \sqrt{|\nabla f|^2 + \beta} \, dx \qquad (5)$$

where β is a small positive parameter [5][6][7][8]. However, by smoothing the TV functional one loses more or less the main advantage of the BV model: allowing restoration of sharp discontinuities. This smooth approximation approach has other serious shortcomings, see [11] for details. Therefore, as some other authors [4][11][13][30], we propose to compute the TV without any regularization and to overcome the singularity, we adjust the standard gradient descent algorithm to subgradients.

Since TV is a convex function and U a convex set, any solution f^* of (4) is given by

$$t > 0, \quad f^* = \text{P}(f^* - t \cdot g(f^*)), \qquad (6)$$

where P is the projector onto U that minimizes the distance and $g(f)$ a subgradient of $\text{TV}(f)$ at f. This equation leads to the following iterative process, known as Polyak's subgradient projection method [31] [11] :

$$f^{k+1} = P(f^k - t_k g(f^k)), \quad t_k > 0, \quad f^0 \in U. \qquad (7)$$

A classical condition to ensure the convergence of this algorithm is for step-sizes $(t_k)_k$ to converge to zero not too rapidly [31][28] :

$$\text{If } \sum_{k=0}^{+\infty} t_k = +\infty \text{ and } \sum_{k=0}^{+\infty} t_k^2 < +\infty, \text{ then } \exists f^* \in U / \lim_{k \to +\infty} f^k = f^*. \qquad (8)$$

As a result of, the subgradient projection method is considered as a slow algorithm and several strategies may be developed to speed it [11]. However our opinion is that, in the context of constrained TV-minimization, this point is not crucial since the practitioner would have advantage to stop the algorithm after a few number of iterations.

2.2   A Simple Algorithmic Framework

A more annoying point is the computation of the projection $P(f)$. When it cannot be implemented in a straightforward fashion, it requires sophisticated algorithms that can be time-consuming (see works of P. Combettes [32][11]). Our simple constrained-TV framework is obtained by noticing that various ill-posed inverse problems in image processing involve an orthogonal linear transform T applied on pixel's values. If f is a discrete image of size $N \times N$, one introduces

$$T : \mathbb{R}^{N^2} \to \mathbb{R}^{N^2}, \ T \in \text{Orthogonal group of } \mathbb{R}^{N^2}. \qquad (9)$$

If the knowledge on the data is given in the domain $T(f)$, one may define the constraint set as

$$U = \left\{ f \in \mathbb{R}^{N^2} : \ (T(f))_n \in [T_n^-, T_n^+] \ \forall n \in I \right\}, \qquad (10)$$

where $I \subset \{1, \ldots, N\}^2$ is a set of indices and where T_n^-, T_n^+ are fixed, depending of the input data only. With such a constraint the computation of the projection is straightforward, and the method leads the following simple, although general, algorithm:

1. Get $f^0 \in U$, usually by running a basic existing algorithm;
2. Choose a maximal (small) number of iterations K;
3. Choose t_k, for example (but not necessarily) according to (8), e.g. $t_k = 1/(k+1)$;
4. Compute $v^k = f^k - t_k g(f^k)$;
5. Compute $w^k = T(v^k)$;
6. Set any $(w^k)_n < T_n^-$ to T_n^-, set any $(w^k)_n > T_n^+$ to T_n^+;
7. Set $f^{k+1} = T^{-1}(w^k)$;
8. Increment k; loop to step 3 while $k < K$.
9. End. The result is the image f^K.

2.3   Examples

The specific form of the constraint U in (10) may be seen very restrictive. However in low-level computer vision, number of approaches involves the use of an orthogonal transform to process the image. Here are some examples we have successfully implemented, and which significantly improve most of existing algorithms.

Image Denoising. This is the most basic example, in the spirit of the ROF algorithm. Assume that the observed image o is corrupted by a noise of variance σ^2. Set $f^0 = o$, $T = \text{Identity}$, $I = \{1, \ldots, N\}^2$, $T_n^- = o_n - 2\sigma$, $T_n^+ = o_n + 2\sigma$.

Image Deblurring. Assume that the observed image o is blurred by a known convolution kernel $h : o = h * f$. At frequencies for which the Fourier transform $\hat{h}$ vanishes, a direct restoration is not possible. To recover missing frequencies in $\hat{f}$ set $T = \text{2D-FFT}$, $I = \{n : |\hat{h}_n| > \varepsilon\}$, $T_n^- = T_n^+ = \hat{o}_n/\hat{h}_n$. In presence of frequency noise, one may take $\varepsilon > 2\sigma$ and add to T_n^-, T_n^+ the previous deviation (for a more sophisticated algorithm, see e.g. [33]). This approach may also be applied to perform digital zooming by means of TV spectral extrapolation [34]. In that case, simply choose h to be the ideal low-pass filter given by the Shannon sampling rate.

Signal Denoising Via Wavelet Shrinkage [35][12]. Signal (or image) denoising by means of a wavelet shrinkage consists of decomposing the noisy data o into a orthogonal wavelet basis, suppressing the wavelet coefficients smaller than a given amplitude, and transforming the data back into the original domain [36]. Let f^0 be the noiseless signal obtained in this way. To remove visual artefacts due to missing wavelet coefficients set $T = \text{orthogonal wavelet transform}$, $I = $ map of the retained wavelet coefficients, $T_n^- = T_n^+ = (T(o))_n$.

JPEG Restoration [14][28]. The observed image o has been compressed by the JPEG lossy coder [37]. To remove blocking artefacts and Gibbs oscillations due to a compression at low bit rates, set f^0 = decoded JPEG image, T = block cosine transform, and compute T_n^-, T_n^+ from the quantization table given in the bit-stream such that

$$(T(h))_n \in [T_n^-, T_n^+] \ \ \forall n \in \{1, \ldots, N\}^2, \tag{11}$$

for h the original (unknown) image.

3   Application in Computerized Tomography

Our main original contribution is in the following : we provide another example of our simple framework in the context of CT.

3.1   Computerized Tomography Issue

In CT the observed body slice is modeled as a two-dimensional distribution $(x, y) \mapsto f(x, y)$ of the x-ray attenuation constant, and a line integral called projection represents the total attenuation suffered by a beam of x-ray as it travels through the body. The line integrals are measured to approximate the distribution of the object. Let (r, θ) be such a line, r being the perpendicular distance from the line to the origin and θ the angle between the perpendicular vector and the x-axis. A projection obtained by illuminating the object along the line is given by

$$P_\theta(r) = \int_{(r,\theta)} f(x, y)dxdy = \int_{-\infty}^{\infty} \int_{-\infty}^{\infty} f(x, y)\delta(x\cos\theta + y\sin\theta - r)dxdy, \tag{12}$$

where δ denotes the Dirac delta-distribution. The function $(r, \theta) \mapsto P_\theta(r)$ is called the Radon transform of f. The main result that allows reconstruction of f from its Radon transform is the Fourier slice theorem, which relates the 2D Fourier transform of f to the 1D Fourier transform P_θ : for a given angle θ, let $\omega \mapsto \widehat{P_\theta}(\omega)$ be the 1D Fourier transform of $r \mapsto P_\theta(r)$ and $(u, v) \mapsto \widehat{f}(u, v)$ the 2D Fourier transform of f. One reads [38]

$$\widehat{P_\theta}(\omega) = \widehat{f}(u, v), \tag{13}$$

where (u, v) is the frequency that belongs to the radial line passing through the origin with angle θ and which is located at distance ω from the origin : $u = \omega\cos\theta$, $v = \omega\sin\theta$.

Since only a finite number of line integrals can be measured, the function $\widehat{f}$ is known for a limited number of points (u, v), which are radial points since they are distributed among a polar grid (see Fig. 1). Notice that the density of radial points becomes sparser as one gets farther away from the center that is, when one considers higher frequency components. A straightforward image reconstruction in the frequency domain can be sketched as follows : using a 1D Discrete Fourier Transform (DFT), the sequence $(\widehat{P_\theta}(\omega))_\theta$ is computed for all measured angles θ; the non-uniformly spaced data $(\widehat{f}(u, v))_{(u,v)}$ are then interpolated to a uniform Cartesian grid; afterwards, the inverse Fourier transform is computed using a 2D inverse DFT. Thanks to the efficiency of the Fast Fourier Transform (FFT), such approach, called Direct Fourier Method (DFM), requires only $O(N^2 \log N)$ arithmetic operations for an image of size $N \times N$.

The main drawback of frequency domain reconstruction remains the occurrence of visual artifacts, due especially to inaccuracies in the high frequency band. The approach comes up against two difficulties [39] : the interpolation to perform in the frequency space [40] and sharp contours in the image producing Gibbs oscillations when high frequencies are missing. Therefore, the standard reconstruction algorithm in clinical application, which is the filtered backprojection (FBP), does not work on the frequency domain but on the spatial one. The reconstruction is done by applying a ramp filter and by summing over the image plane the inverse Fourier transforms of the filtered projections [38]. The backprojection computes for each pixel in the reconstructed image the sum of all line integrals that pass through that pixel, and requires therefore $O(N^3)$ arithmetic operations.

The goal of our application is not to propose one of the fastest algorithms, but rather to introduce a method which offers better reconstructed images than standard ones, while its computational cost remains in the $O(N^2 \log N)$ (or $O(N^3)$) bound. The idea is to formulate the image reconstruction issue as a constrained optimization problem in the frequency space, the constraints being the knowledge of $(\widehat{f}(u, v))$ in the polar grid while the functional to minimize will be chosen in order to eliminate visual artifacts. Although such formulation appears to be new in tomographic imaging, optimization methods have already been proposed, especially in the spatial-domain approach. Let A denote the discrete Radon transform and s the sinogram. A common optimization formulation is

$$\min_f \|Af - s\| \tag{14}$$

where the norm is usually the quadratic one. The solution is found iteratively using, for example, the conjugate gradient algorithm. This requires to efficiently compute both A and its adjoint operator and it can be done in $O(N^2 \log N)$ using one of the fast Radon transform algorithms [41] or by sparse matrix multiplication. A frequency-domain version of (14) has been proposed by Bronstein et al. in [42] in the context of diffraction ultrasound tomography. In this case A is a projection operator in an oversampled Fourier basis, computed using a non-uniform Fourier transform [43], while s is the projection of the sinogram. The authors propose to incorporate into the solution some types of a priori information, using the Tikhonov-regularized form [5]

$$\min_f \|Af - s\| + \lambda\phi(f) \tag{15}$$

where ϕ is the regularization functional, and where the parameter λ controls the tradeoff between a good fit to the data and the smoothness of the solution.

3.2 TV in Computerized Tomography

Classical norms such as the quadratic one are not well-suited to be used as the regularization functional ϕ, since they tend to reconstruct images with blurred edges. For tomographic images, the most meaningful visual information is given by the shape of the objects (such as tumors), and therefore edges and enclosed areas have to be reconstructed sharply and without artifact. As the TV functional penalizes oscillations but not sharp discontinuities, the BV set appears to constitute a particularly relevant space of analysis.

We propose therefore the choice $\phi = $ TV, and we adapt our simple TV-minimization framework to the ill-posed problem of tomographic imaging. Solving this problem formulated in the Fourier domain leads implicitly to solve the polar to Cartesian interpolation, in an optimal way regarding the BV image model. To the best of our knowledge, other approaches using TV-minimization in the Fourier domain are up to now limited to extrapolation and interpolation of the spectrum [30][34] in order to enhance image resolution (zoom). One may consider our method as a very particular case of spectrum extrapolation and interpolation, where known and missing values follow a specific geometry. Up to now, only very few articles combine TV with tomography reconstruction [42] [44]. These two works do not consider a constrained problem as we do, but rather an unconstrained one like the formulation (15), and they do not apply to x-ray parallel beams tomography (although they probably could be adapted to). Another unconstrained TV-minimization framework is experimented in [45], in conjunction with denoising by means of curvelet thresholding. A very recent article [46] introduces the TV in the context of binary tomography : it is used to enforce a set of constraints while the energy to minimize is the quadratic error with the FBP reconstructed image.

3.3 Definition of the Constraint

Let $P_\theta(r)$ be the sinogram, given at the grid points

$$(r_k, \theta_l) := (k \cdot \Delta r, \, l \cdot \Delta \theta); \quad k = -\frac{K}{2}, \cdots, \frac{K}{2} - 1; \quad l = 0, \cdots, L-1; \quad \Delta \theta = \frac{\pi}{L}. \quad (16)$$

Adapting the Fourier slice theorem (13) to the discrete setting and using L univariate DFT of length K, we get

$$S_{k,l} := \widehat{P}_{\theta_l}(\omega_k) = \Delta r \sum_{s=-\frac{K}{2}}^{\frac{K}{2}-1} P_{\theta_l}(r_s) e^{-2\pi j \cdot \frac{sk}{K}}. \quad (17)$$

They are 2D-Fourier coefficients of the image f we have to reconstruct. However, these coefficients are given over the polar grid

$$Q_{k,l} := (\omega_k, \theta_l) \quad (18)$$

and in order to perform the bivariate inverse DFT, we must guess frequency coefficients over the Cartesian grid

$$C_{m,n} := (m\Delta x, n\Delta x) \tag{19}$$

of size $N \times N$. Let $(F_{m,n})$ be those Fourier coefficients.

The constraint space (10) may be rewritten as

$$U = \left\{ f \in \mathbb{R}^{N^2} : \quad \forall m, n = -\frac{N}{2}, \cdots, \frac{N}{2} - 1, \quad F_{m,n} \in [F_{m,n}^-, F_{m,n}^+] \right\}, \tag{20}$$

where the bounds $[F_{m,n}^-, F_{m,n}^+]$ are computed over a polar neighborhood using a local Lipschitz regularity assumption.

3.4   Polar Neighborhood

By allowing frequency $F_{m,n}$ to freely vary inside $[F_{m,n}^-, F_{m,n}^+]$, one permits to smooth the reconstructed image regarding to the TV functional. The geometry of polar neighborhoods has to be designed with care : on one side, neighborhoods should not be too wide in order to use all known information. On the other side, they should not be too narrow so that the algorithm could be able to smooth the image enough to remove the noise. We consider disks of constant radius r and centered at coordinates (m, n) of the Cartesian grid. Over the polar grid, points representing low frequencies are dense enough, whereas high frequency points are sparse (see Fig. 1). For coordinates (m, n) near the origin, the disk neighborhood might include too many polar points and so the constraint $[F_{m,n}^-, F_{m,n}^+]$ may be too large. We therefore limit the number of polar points to a fixed integer M, see Fig. 2. More precisely, the disk neighborhood of $C_{m,n}$ is defined by

$$V_{m,n} = \{(k, l) : d(Q_{k,l}, C_{m,n}) < r\}, \tag{21}$$

the list of points (k, l) being ordered in increasing distance from $C_{m,n}$ and limited to at most M points. At high frequency it may exist (m, n) such that $V_{m,n} = \emptyset$ and $F_{m,n}$ cannot be recovered by the knowledge of its neighborhood. In such a case we do not set any constraint on (m, n), and therefore highest frequencies are reconstructed by means of TV spectral extrapolation [34]. Experiments show that parameters r and M may be fixed to $r = 3$ and $M = 40$; they do not appear to depend of the image. As the FFT requires the number of samples to be a power of two, projection data are zero-padded before computing the 1D transform of every row. This operation generates a denser polar grid and this pre-interpolation eases to get non-empty $V_{m,n}$ at high frequencies. Accordingly, the Cartesian grid is oversampled by reducing the interval of frequency samples.

3.5   Local Lipschitz Regularity

We compute bounds $F_{m,n}^-$, $F_{m,n}^+$ on each neighborhood $V_{m,n}$ using a local Lipschitz assumption. As the Shepp-Logan phantom is made by piecewise-constant functions, its Fourier transform is a combination of cardinal sine functions and is therefore, in the continuous model, infinitely many times differentiable. However, real sinograms suffer from noise and the hypothesis $\widehat{f} \in C^\infty$ would be surely unrealistic. We believe however that assuming $\widehat{f}$ to be locally Lipschitz continuous is a reasonable condition, and such a weak assumption would be enough to compute intervals bounds. On each $V_{m,n}$, we estimate the Lipschitz constant by

$$L_{m,n} = \max_{(k,l),(k',l') \in V_{m,n}} \frac{|S_{k,l} - S_{k',l'}|}{d(Q_{k,l}, Q_{k',l'})}, \tag{22}$$

and we define the intervals bounds by averaging deviations from all known values in the neighborhood :

$$F_{m,n}^\pm = \begin{cases} \dfrac{1}{\#V_{m,n}} \displaystyle\sum_{(k,l)V_{m,n}} S_{k,l} \pm L_{m,n} d(Q_{k,l}, C_{m,n}) & \text{if } V_{m,n} \neq \emptyset, \\ \pm\infty & \text{if } V_{m,n} = \emptyset. \end{cases} \tag{23}$$

3.6   Experimental Results

With the above definitions and $T = $ 2D-FFT, the algorithm sketched in Section 2.2 is applied to reconstruct CT images. To start the algorithm, one may choose $f^0 = $ image reconstructed by DFM or by FBP. As r and M are fixed, the only remaining parameter is the number of iterations K (or, equivalently, the constant c used to define step-sizes $t_k = \frac{c}{k+1}$) and Fig.3 tells us that K should be chosen small, leading to a fast algorithm : pre-computation of the constraint space U needs $O(N^2)$ operations while other computations are of the same order of the FFT, that is $O(N^2 \log N)$. The overall complexity of our algorithm remains therefore in the same complexity class than the standard algorithm used to compute f^0 ($O(N^2 \log N)$ with DFM, $O(N^3)$ with FBP).

We have experimented the algorithms on the Shepp and Logan head phantom, for which projection data have been computed using a discrete Radon transform. Several image sizes have been checked, but in the following we only report experiments corresponding to $N = 256$. We set $\Delta r = \Delta x$ so there are $K = \sqrt{2} \times N \approx 367$ parallel beams for each angle. In order to reconstruct the image reliably [38], the number of angles L is chosen to be N. Each row of projection data are zero-padded to obtain the size $K = 1024$ and the Cartesian grid is oversampled to the size 512×512. Without any noise, all algorithms perform well with visually almost indistinguishable differences, but our constrained-TV method is the one that achieves the highest PSNR. However in real tomography, noise is always disturbing the reconstruction process. As noticed in [47], inverting a noisy Radon transform is a hard task since the Radon transform is a smoothing operator and projections have, roughly speaking, one-half derivative more smoothness than the original image. The most used method, windowed FBP, exhibits degradation in recovering f from noisy data, since high-frequency components are considered as noise and the reconstruction is done mainly with low-frequency ones. Our approach allows to keep the information in the high-frequency bands while the noise is removed by the action of the TV functional. As a result of, our algorithm clearly outperforms classical ones when noise is added to the Radon transform. Fig. 4 shows simulation results in the presence of Gaussian white noise in the sinogram. The following algorithms have been experimented : DFM with linear interpolation in the Fourier space; plain FBP; FBP with Hamming filter to reduce the noise; ROF-like approach (space-based Tikhonov regularization (15) with $\phi = $ TV); and at last our constrained-TV framework. The efficiency of DFM and plain FBP in presence of noise is very poor, with noisy reconstructed images. Applying a Hamming window with FBP increases noticeably the visual quality, by reducing the noise without altering edges (removing more high-frequencies would decrease the noise further, but edges would be smoothed). TV-regularization using Tikhonov model performs well in denoising data, but the image is slightly blurred by the relaxation (5) and by the absence of strong constraints. Best results are by far obtained with our constrained-TV minimization method, that denoises the image without significantly affecting edges. Also, the PSNR is much greater than the other ones and surprisingly than the ROF-like one (with a difference greater than 3 db). We believe that, by projecting on a *had hoc* constraint space, our algorithm is able to denoise data without affecting too much edges (compare plots of ROF versus constrained-TV in Fig.4 : the noise amplitude is greater with ROF while main peaks - corresponding to the white ellipse - are lower).

Besides, in order to obtain fair results with ROF one has to perform a much greater number of iterations (30 in our experiment). As already noted in the beginning our algorithm, although convergent, exhibits best results after a small number of iterations only (7 in our experiment, see Fig.3). Indeed, if in the first steps the algorithm tends to reduce the noise and oscillatory artifacts (ringing), after a while the TV functional is known to produce staircase effects and to erode peaks [48][49][33]. The constraint we are using protects somewhat from this phenomenon, but is too weak in highest frequencies to avoid it completely.

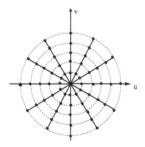

Fig. 1. Points (u, v) where $\widehat{f}(u, v)$ is known are distributed among a polar grid, they are therefore radial points. Due to this particular geometry, the density of radial points becomes sparser when frequencies are increasing : reconstruction of missing high frequency components is the major issue of tomographic imaging.

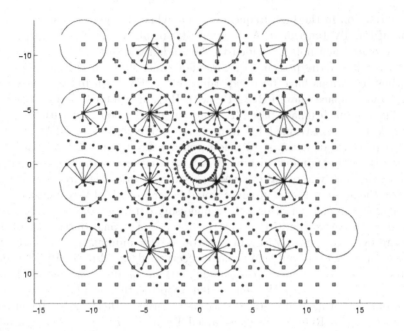

Fig. 2. The disk neighborhoods with $r = \sqrt{2}$ and $M = 16$ (these values are for illustration). Points $Q_{m,n}$ of the polar grid are marked as black dots while points $C_{m,n}$ of the Cartesian one are marked as grey squares.

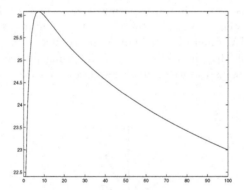

Fig. 3. PSNR versus number of iterations. The quality of the reconstructed image is firstly rapidly increasing, and decreases after a given threshold has been reached. This optimal number of iterations is 3 for noiseless sinograms and increases with the quantity of noise, but does not exceed 10. This graph corresponds to the experiment reported in Fig. 4 (last line), with noise level SNR=20.1. The same kind of graph has been obtained with any implementation of our constrained-TV framework, including examples of Section 2.3.

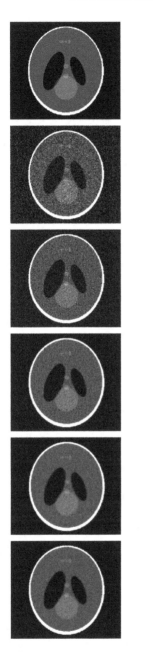 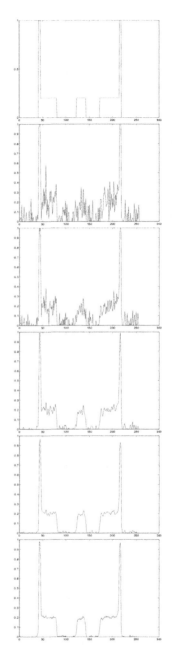

Fig. 4. Reconstruction with noisy data added on the sinogram (noise level: SNR=20.1). Left column : reconstructed images. Right column : plots of an horizontal section (located at the middle of the image). Lines, from up to down : original Shepp-Logan phantom; DFM with linear interpolation (PSNR=20.3); FBP (PSNR=22.4); FBP with Hamming window (PSNR=24.1); ROF (PSNR=22.9, 30 iterations); our constrained-TV algorithm (PSNR=26.1, 7 iterations).

References

1. Rudin, L., Osher, S., Fatemi, E.: Nonlinear total variation based noise removal algorithms. Physica D **60** (1992) 259–268
2. Chambolle, A., Lions, P.L.: Image recovery via total variation minimization and related problems. Numer. Math. **76** (1997) 167–188
3. Acar, R., Vogel, C.: Analysis of total variation penalty methods for ill-posed problems. Inverse Problems **10** (1994) 1217–1229
4. Li, Y., Santosa, F.: A computational algorithm for minimizing total variation in image restoration. IEEE Trans. on Image Proc. **5** (1996) 987–995
5. Vogel, C., Oman, M.: Iterative method for total variation denoising. SIAM J. Sci. Comput. **17** (1996) 227–238
6. Dobson, D.C., Vogel, C.R.: Convergence of an iterative method for total variation denoising. SIAM J. Numer. Anal. **34** (1997) 1779–1791
7. Vogel, C., Oman, M.: Fast, robust total variation-based reconstruction of noisy, blurred images. IEEE Trans. on Image Proc. **7** (1998) 813–824
8. Chan, T., Golub, G., Mulet, P.: A nonlinear primal-dual method for total variation-based image restoration. SIAM J. Sci. Comput. **20** (1999) 1964–1977
9. Dibos, F., Koepfler, G.: Global total variation minimization. SIAM J. Numer. Anal. **37** (2000) 646–664
10. Darbon, J., Sigelle, M.: Exact optimization of discrete constrained total variation minimization problems. In Klette, R., Zunic, J., eds.: Tenth International Workshop on Combinatorial Image Analysis. Lecture Notes in Computer Science 3322 (2004) 548–557
11. Combettes, P., Luo, J.: An adaptive level set method for nondifferentiable constrained image recovery. IEEE Trans. on Image Proc. **11** (2002) 1295–1304
12. Durand, S., Froment, J.: Reconstruction of wavelet coefficients using total variation minimization. SIAM J. Sci. Comput. **24** (2003) 1754–1767
13. Chambolle, A.: An algorithm for total variation minimization and applications. J. Math. Imaging Vis. **20** (2004) 89–97
14. Alter, F., Durand, S., Froment, J.: Deblocking DCT-based compressed images with weighted total variation. In: Proc. of ICASSP 2004, Montréal. Volume 3. (2004)
15. Coifman, R., Sowa, A.: Combining the calculus of variations and wavelets for image enhancement. Applied and Comput. Harmonic Ana. **9** (2000) 1–18
16. Chan, T.F., Zhou, H.: Total variation improved wavelet thresholding in image compression. In: Proc. of ICIP'2000. (2000)
17. Malgouyres, F.: Combining total variation and wavelet packet approaches for image deblurring. In: Proc. of IEEE work. on VLSM 2001, Vancouver, Canada. (2001) 57–64
18. Malgouyres, F.: Minimizing the total variation under a general convex constraint for image restoration. IEEE Trans. on Image Proc. **11** (2002) 1450–1456
19. Aliney, S.: A property of the minimum vectors of a regularizing functional defined by means of the absolute norm. IEEE Trans. on Signal Proc. **45** (1997) 913–917
20. Nikolova, M.: Minimization of cost-functions with non-smooth data-fidelity terms to clean impulsive noise. In Rangarajan, A., Figueiredo, M.A.T., Zerubia, J., eds.: EMMCVPR. Volume 2683 of Lecture Notes in Computer Science., Springer (2003) 391–406
21. Nikolova, M.: Minimization of cost-functions involving nonsmooth data-fidelity terms. application to the processing of outliers. SIAM J. Numer. Anal. **40** (2002) 965–994

22. Gousseau, Y., Morel, J.M.: Are natural images of bounded variation ? SIAM J. Math. Anal. **33** (2001) 634–648
23. Meyer, Y.: Oscillating patterns in image processing and in some nonlinear evolution equations. In: The Fifteenth Dean Jacquelines B. Lewis Memorial Lectures. Volume 22., American Mathematical Society (2001)
24. Osher, S., Solé, A., Vese, L.: Image decomposition and restoration using total variation minimization and the H^{-1} norm. SIAM Multiscale Model. Simul. **1** (2003) 349–370
25. Vese, L., Osher, S.: Image denoising and decomposition with total variation minimization and oscillatory functions. J. Math. Imaging Vis. **20** (2004) 7–18
26. Aujol, J., Aubert, G., Blanc-Féraud, L., Chambolle, A.: Image decomposition into a bounded variation component and an oscillating component. J. Math. Imaging Vis. **22** (2005)
27. Aujol, J., Chambolle, A.: Duals norms and image decomposition models. Int. Jour. of Computer Vision **63** (2005) 85–104
28. Alter, F., Durand, S., Froment, J.: Adapted total variation for artifact free decompression of JPEG images. J. Math. Imaging Vis. **23** (2005)
29. Shepp, L., Logan, B.: The Fourier reconstruction of a head section. IEEE Trans. Nucl. Sci. **21** (1974) 21–43
30. Guichard, F., Malgouyres, F.: Total variation based interpolation. In: Proc. of EUSIPCO'98. Volume 3. (1998) 1741–1744
31. Polyak, B.: Introduction to Optimization. Optimization Software (1987)
32. Combettes, P.L.: Convex set theoretic image recovery by extrapolated iterations of parallel subgradient projections. IEEE Trans. on Image Proc. **6** (1997) 493–506
33. Durand, S., Malgouyres, F., Rougé, B.: Image deblurring, spectrum interpolation and application to satellite imaging. ESAIM:COCV Control, Opt. and Cal. of Var. **5** (2000) 445–475
34. Moisan, L.: Extrapolation de spectre et variation totale pondérée. In: Proc. of Gretsi'01, Toulouse, France. (2001)
35. Durand, S., Froment, J.: Artifact free signal denoising with wavelets. In: Proc. of ICASSP'01, Salt Lake City. Volume 6. (2001)
36. Donoho, D., Johnstone, I.: Ideal spatial adaptation via wavelet shrinkage. Biometrika **81** (1994) 425–455
37. Wallace, G.: The JPEG still picture compression standard. Communications of the ACM **34** (1991) 31–44
38. Kak, A., Slaney, M.: Principles of Computerized Tomographic Imaging. SIAM (2001)
39. Gottlieb, D., Gustafsson, B., Forssén, P.: On the direct Fourier method for computer tomography. IEEE Trans. Medical Imaging **19** (2000) 223–232
40. Waldén, J.: Analysis of the direct Fourier method for computer tomography. IEEE Trans. Medical Imaging **19** (2000) 211–222
41. Averbuch, A., Coifman, R., Donoho, D., Israeli, M., Waldén, J.: Fast slant stack: A notion of radon transform for data in a cartesian grid which is rapidly computable, algebraically exact, geometrically faithful and invertible. SIAM J. Sci. Comput. (to appear)
42. Bronstein, M., Bronstein, A., Zibulevsky, M., Azhari, H.: Reconstruction in ultrasound diffraction tomography using non-uniform FFT. IEEE Trans. Medical Imaging **21** (2002) 1395–1401
43. Fessler, J., Sutton, B.: Nonuniform fast Fourier transforms using min-max interpolation. IEEE Trans. on Signal Proc. **51** (2003) 560–574

44. Jonsson, E., Huang, S., Chan, T.: Total variation regularization in positron emission tomography. UCLA CAM Report 98-48, University of California, Los Angeles, CA, http://www.math.ucla.edu/~chan/papers.html (1998)
45. Candès, E., Guo, F.: New multiscale transforms, minimum total variation synthesis: Applications to edge-preserving image reconstruction. Signal Processing **82** (2002) 1519–1543
46. Capricelli, T.D., Combettes, P.L.: Parallel block-iterative reconstruction algorithms for binary tomography. In: Special issue of Electronic Notes in Discrete Mathematics : Workshop on discrete tomography and its applications, June 13-15, 2005, New York City, Elsevier (to appear)
47. Lee, N.Y., Lucier, B.J.: Wavelet methods for inverting the radon transform with noisy data. IEEE Trans. on Image Proc. **10** (2001) 79–94
48. Chan, T., Marquina, A., Mulet, P.: High-order total variation-based image restoration. SIAM J. Sci. Comput. **22** (2000) 503–516
49. Dobson, D., Santosa, F.: Recovery of blocky images from noisy and blurred data. SIAM J. Appl. Math. **56** (1996) 1181–1199

Some New Results on Non-rigid Correspondence and Classification of Curves

Xiqiang Zheng, Yunmei Chen, David Groisser, and David Wilson

Department of Mathematics, University of Florida, Gainesville, FL 32611
Tel: (352)392-0281
{xzheng, yun, groisser, dcw}@math.ufl.edu

Abstract. We present two new algorithms for correspondence and classification of planar curves in a non-rigid sense. In the first algorithm we define deforming energy based on aligning curves using certain of their properties, namely Multi-Step-Size Local Similarity (MSSLS) and the difference between the angle changes of beginning and ending tangent lines of two corresponding curve segments, as well as local scale of stretching. MSSLS overcomes the noise of local shape information of curves to be aligned. In the second algorithm, we improve the computation of shape context so that it catches the local information of ordered sets representing planar curves better. The optimal correspondence is found by a modified dynamic-programming method. Based on deforming energy, we can do pattern recognition among curves, which is very important in many areas such as recognition of hand-written characters and cardiac curves where rigid transformations and scaling do not work well. Finally, the effect of correspondence and classification is shown in application to hand-written characters and cardiac curves.

Keywords: Curve alignment, recognition, correspondence, dynamic programming.

1 Introduction

For non-rigid curve alignment, as pointed out in [1], Cohen in [2] pioneered the *deformation-based* approach to curve matching. Their approach was to find a function mapping one curve into another such that high curvature points of one curve mapped to high curvature points of another curve while maintaining a smooth displacement field. Tagare, O'Shea, and Groisser in [3] and [6] proposed *bi-morphisms* and a new criterion for non-rigid shape comparison. Bi-morphisms treat two curves symmetrically and give a hint to measure deforming energy of the region near the connecting points in the discrete formulation. The new criterion in [3] and [6] overcomes some deficiencies of [2]. Belongie, Malik, and Puzicha in [7] and [8] introduced *shape context*, a rich shape descriptor that aids in judging shape similarity between similar shape points. It is applied on the more general problem of matching between two unordered sets. Sebastian, Klein, and Kimia in [1] defined a *dissimilarity metric* (or deforming energy) based on the alignment curve using two intrinsic properties of the curve, namely, length and curvature. The optimal correspondence is found by a dynamic-programming method.

A. Rangarajan et al. (Eds.): EMMCVPR 2005, LNCS 3757, pp. 473–489, 2005.

Frenkel and Basri in [9] used both curvature and shape context, and employed Sethian's *Fast Marching Method* in [10] to find the solution with sub-resolution accuracy and in consistence with the underlying continuous problem. Although a lot of progress has been made, when those methods above are used to classify hand-written characters, some characters are still difficult to classify well. For example, Figure 3 of [9] shows that the characters 3,7,1, and y are not well classified using a curvature-based method. *The problem of curvature-based methods* is that just *local shape information* such as curvature and local scale of stretching between two corresponding points is used to compute the deforming energy. But shape information of a local region is very noisy in many applications and hence the classification effect may not be good. *Shape context* takes into account all the points instead of being confined to a local region. From the computation of shape context, we can see that shape context does not catch the local shape information very precisely. Figure 5 of [9] shows that U and V, or y and g, are not well distinguished using shape context. Based on the previous work above, we formulate one more desirable property which is *Multi-Step-Size Local Similarity* (shortened as *MSSLS*). It not only catches the local information very well, but also catches the overall shape information better and hence overcomes the noise of local information. We improve the usual *substructure property* for the case of discrete formulation so that the total bending energy is well counted. The computation of dissimilarity is based on non-overlapping area which is very stable. The optimal solution is found by a modified dynamic-programming method. Because we are dealing with planar curves represented by ordered point sets, we can compute the tangent lines at each point easily and apply restricted template matching to catch the local shape information better than the usual shape context. The resulting algorithm is called the algorithm of *improved shape context* or *restricted template matching*, which is implemented in Section 4. What we implemented are the actual bi-morphisms, and hence the deforming energy of the region near the connecting points in the discrete formulation is also well measured as shown at the beginning of the 3rd section. Some results for the classification and correspondence of hand-written characters are shown in Figures 2 and 3, and the classification of some cardiac curves are shown in later figures.

2   Formulation of the Energy Functional

Suppose we are given two planar curves C_1 and C_2, and a parameterized bi-morphism $\mu : [0, 1] \to C_1 \times C_2$. Let $p_k : C_1 \times C_2 \to C_k$ denote the projection onto the kth factor for $k = 1, 2$. In the following, a curve segment means a part of a given curve such that the arc length of that curve segment is positive. If we divide the interval $[0, 1]$ into n equal subintervals $I_i = [\frac{i-1}{n}, \frac{i}{n}]$ for $i = 1, 2, ..., n$, and if we assume that $p_k \circ \mu$ does not compress any of these subintervals to a single point, then the curve C_k is divided into n segments C_{kt} for $k = 1, 2$ and $t = 1, 2, ..., n$.

Definition 1. *For any curve segment C_{kt}, the line segment connecting its beginning and ending points is called the* base *of that curve segment.*

Definition 2. *For any given curve segment C_{kt} and a point Q of C_{kt}, the distance of Q to the base of C_{kt} is called the* height *of Q.*

For two curve segments C_{1t} and C_{2t}, let us denote the length of their bases as d_k for $k = 1, 2$, and assume that $d_1 \leq d_2$ temporarily. If we enlarge C_{1t} and compress C_{2t} by a factor r so that their bases can match after rotation and translation, then $rd_1 = \frac{d_2}{r}$ and hence $r = \sqrt{\frac{d_2}{d_1}}$. After this alignment, the length of their common base is $d = \sqrt{d_1 d_2}$. r is called the stretching factor of mapping C_{1j} to C_{2j}. If $d_1 > d_2$, $r = \sqrt{\frac{d_2}{d_1}}$ is called a compressing factor of mapping C_{1t} to C_{2t}. In both cases, r is called a scaling factor in Definition 3. We also denote by $\tilde{A}_k$ the region enclosed by the curve segment C_{kt} and its base for $k = 1, 2$. Then let $\Delta \tilde{A}_{12} = (\tilde{A}_1 - \tilde{A}_2) \bigcup (\tilde{A}_2 - \tilde{A}_1)$, the symmetric difference between $\tilde{A}_1$ and $\tilde{A}_2$, and let ΔA_{12} be the area of $\Delta \tilde{A}_{12}$.

Definition 3. *The scaling factor r mapping curve segment C_{1t} to C_{2t} is defined as* $r = \sqrt{\frac{d_2}{d_1}}$.

Definition 4. *Define the dissimilarity between curve segments C_{1t} and C_{2t} as* $\rho(C_{1t}, C_{2t}) = \frac{\Delta A_{12}}{d^2}$, *where ΔA_{12} is the area of the symmetric difference between $\tilde{A}_1$ and $\tilde{A}_2$ and $d = \sqrt{d_1 d_2}$ is the length of their common base after scaling and rigid transformations as above.*

For example, the dissimilarity between an arc of degree 2α of a unit circle and its base is $f(\alpha) = \frac{2\alpha - sin2\alpha}{8sin^2\alpha}$. It is easy to show that $f(\alpha)$ approaches zero when α goes to zero. Since $f'(\alpha) = \frac{tan\alpha - \alpha}{2sin^2\alpha tan\alpha}$, $f(\alpha)$ is increasing when $\alpha \in (0, \pi)$. So the arc segment of degree α behaves like a straight line when α approaches zero. When α is bigger in the range $(0, 2\pi)$, the arc segment is more different from a straight line. Also $f(2\alpha) \neq 2f(\alpha)$, hence this function is not additive: $f(\alpha + \beta) \neq f(\alpha) + f(\beta)$. When $\alpha \in (0, \frac{\pi}{2}]$, $f(2\alpha) > 2f(\alpha)$. As we subdivide a smooth curve into smaller and smaller segments, the segments become better approximated by circular arcs. Hence the energy function we are going to define in Equation 1 usually will decrease when two curves are divided into more pairs. In the MSSLS-based algorithm we introduce later, we fix the number of pairs. Then Equation 1 of deforming energy becomes Equation 4 and hence is additive as explained in the 3rd section.

Definition 5. *Define the angle difference between curve segments C_{1t} and C_{2t} as* $\Delta\theta(C_{1t}, C_{2t}) = |\Delta\theta_1 - \Delta\theta_2|$, *where $\Delta\theta_k$ is the angle between beginning and ending tangent line of the curve segment C_{kt} for $k = 1, 2$.*

Now we can formulate our energy function. Let C_1 and C_2 be two given planar curves. For simplicity, we assume that they have a given starting point and ending point. Up to a scaling, we can also assume that curves C_1 and C_2 have unit arc length. For a given n and parameterized bi-morphism $\mu : [0, 1] \rightarrow C_1 \times C_2$, define the subintervals $I_i \subseteq [0, 1]$ and curve segments C_{kt} for $k = 1, 2$ and $i, t = 1, 2, ..., n$ as in the beginning of this section (once again we assume no C_{kt} is a single point). Then we define the deforming energy between C_1 and C_2 corresponding to this bi-morphism μ as following:

$$E_{C_1,C_2;n}(\mu) = \sum_{i=1}^{n} \lambda_1 \, \rho(P_i) + k_\theta \, \Delta\theta(P_i) + k_r |l(P_i, 1) - l(P_i, 2)|$$
$$+ \sum_{j=1}^{n_2} \lambda_2 \, \rho(Q_j) + k_\theta \, \Delta\theta(Q_j) + k_r |l(Q_j, 1) - l(Q_j, 2)| +$$
$$\sum_{g=1}^{n_3} \lambda_3 \, \rho(R_g) + k_\theta \, \Delta\theta(R_g) + k_r |l(R_g, 1) - l(R_g, 2)| \qquad (1)$$

where $P_i = (p_1(\mu(I_i)), p_2(\mu(I_i)))$ is the ith pair in the matching, $\rho(P_i)$ the dissimilarity of the pair P_i as in Definition 4, $\Delta\theta(P_i)$ the angle difference as in Definition 5, and $l(P_i, k)$ the length of the base of the curve segment of curve C_k corresponding to the pair P_i as in Definition 1; $Q_j = (p_1(\mu(I_j \cup I_{j+1})), p_2(\mu(I_j \cup I_{j+1})))$ is the jth pair in the matching whose step size is twice as much as that of P_i, and $n_2 = n - 1$, which is the number of such pairs (see Figure 1); and $R_g = (p_1(\mu(I_g \cup I_{g+1} \cup I_{g+2})), p_2(\mu(I_g \cup I_{g+1} \cup I_{g+2})))$ is the gth pair in the matching whose step size is 3 times that of P_i, and $n_3 = n - 2$. λ_i, k_θ, and k_r are parameters.

Remark: In Equation 1, the terms for Q_j measure the local similarity near the connecting point between the $(i-1)th$ pair and ith pair, and catch the global shape information better than the terms for P_i. Similarly the terms for R_g catch the global information better than the terms for Q_j. We can make the step size bigger and bigger until the whole curve is included in one step, but the classification effect might not become better. How much the step size should be depends on how curved are those curves. For example, for hand-written characters, some of them have loops and hence the classification is usually better if the step size is less than the arc lengths of loops. If there are not many concave and convex regions in one curve, the *angle difference of the longer segments* R_g and Q_j in Equation 1 helps to catch the overall shape difference of two curves. If there are many concave and convex regions in one curve, the longer segments R_g and Q_j probably contain more than one such region. In such cases the angle difference no longer reflects the amount of bending and hence the effect may be better if those angle terms are not included in Equation 1 (In principle, we could increase the number n of pairs to avoid this problem, but there are computational limitations on how large we can take n). In such cases, the dissimilarity measures the amount of bending very well as long as the longer segments do not contain loops.

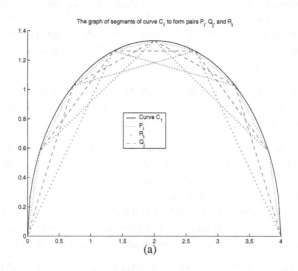

Fig. 1. Show different kinds of pairs P_i for $i = 1, 2, ..., n$, Q_j for $j = 1, 2, ..., n_2$, and R_t for $t = 1, 2, ..., n_3$ where $n = 8, n_2 = 7, n_3 = 6$

Now our goal is to find an optimal bi-morphism μ^* such that

$$E_{C_1,C_2;n}(\mu^*) = \min_{\mu} E_{C_1,C_2;n}(\mu). \tag{2}$$

Because the space of bi-morphisms is infinite, it is hard to find such a minimizer precisely. But we can restrict our search space to a reasonable subset of that space so that an approximate minimizer can be found. Based on the actual application, we don't need to consider those bi-morphisms which cannot be the minimizer, which reduces the size of search space. Other application-based criteria can be used to reduce the search space further (see Section 3).

To apply dynamic programming to find the minimizer in the restricted space, we need to deduce the following substructure.

Proposition 1. *For any bi-morphism μ, let P_i, Q_j and R_g have the same meaning as in Equation 1, $M_{k,t-1}$ and $M_{k,t}$ be the starting and ending point of the curve segment C_{kt} for $k = 1, 2$ and $t = 1, 2, ..., n$. Denote $C_k(u, v)$ be the part of the curve C_k composed of segments corresponding to pairs P_{u+1} through P_v for $1 \leq u < v \leq n$ and $k = 1, 2$. In other words, $C_k(u, v)$ be the part of the curve C_k whose starting point is $M_{k,u}$ and the ending point is $M_{k,v}$. Then we have*

$$\begin{aligned}
E_{C_1,C_2;n}(\mu) = & E_{C_1(0,n-1),C_2(0,n-1);n-1}(\mu) + E_{C_1(n-1,n),C_2(n-1,n);1}(\mu) \\
& + \lambda_2 \, \rho(Q_{n_2}) + k_\theta \, \Delta\theta(Q_{n_2}) + k_r |l(Q_{n_2}, 1) - l(Q_{n_2}, 2)| \\
& + \lambda_3 \, \rho(R_{n_3}) + k_\theta \, \Delta\theta(R_{n_3}) + k_r |l(R_{n_3}, 1) - l(R_{n_3}, 2)|.
\end{aligned} \tag{3}$$

Proof. By Equation 1, it is easy to check the validity of Equation 3.

Proposition 1 can easily be generalized to the following proposition.

Proposition 2. *For any bi-morphism μ, if we use the same notation as in Proposition 1, then for any $2 < i < n - 2$ we have*

$$\begin{aligned}
E_{C_1,C_2;n}(\mu) = & E_{C_1(0,i),C_2(0,i);i}(\mu) + E_{C_1(i,n),C_2(i,n);n-i}(\mu) \\
& + \lambda_2 \, \rho(Q_i) + k_\theta \, \Delta\theta(Q_i) + k_r \, |l(Q_i, 1) - l(Q_i, 2)| \\
& + \lambda_3 \, \rho(R_{i-1}) + k_\theta \, \Delta\theta(R_{i-1}) + k_r \, |l(R_{i-1}, 1) - l(R_{i-1}, 2)| \\
& + \lambda_3 \, \rho(R_i) + k_\theta \, \Delta\theta(R_i) + k_r \, |l(R_i, 1) - l(R_i, 2)|.
\end{aligned} \tag{4}$$

With a bit of care, Proposition 2 can be applied for any $0 \leq i \leq n$. For example, when $i = 1$ the terms for R_{i-1} disappear.

3   The MSSLS-Based Algorithm

For any given bi-morphism μ in Equation 4, $E_{C_1(0,i),C_2(0,i);i}(\mu)$ is a term which measures the *deforming energy* of the part of curve composed of the first i segments and $E_{C_1(i,n),C_2(i,n);n-i}(\mu)$ is a term which measures deforming energy of the part of curve composed of the last $n - i$ segments. The remaining terms of Equation 4 measure the deforming energy of the region connecting those two parts. Without those remaining terms, Equation 4 would become

$$E_{C_1,C_2;n}(\mu) = E_{C_1(0,i),C_2(0,i);i}(\mu) + E_{C_1(i,n),C_2(i,n);n-i}(\mu)$$

which is the *usual additive property* (see the definition in Equation 2 of [1]). In the discrete formulation, using the usual additive property the local similarity of the region near the point connecting the two parts $C_1(0, i)$ and $C_1(i, n)$ cannot be well measured. For example, if we don't assume curve C_1 is smooth at the connecting point between its two parts $C_1(0, i)$ and $C_1(i, n)$. Then $C_1(0, i)$ and $C_1(i, n)$ can be connected in many different ways but all of them result in the same deforming energy using the usual additive property which is not desired. Although in many applications we can assume all curves to be aligned are smooth, there are still such cases that the direction (angle) of tangent line changes a lot over some very small arc length. Then the computation of tangent line is very noisy over such segments. When the curves are smooth and n is big, the remaining terms of Equation 4 can be omitted, and those terms are 0 in the continuous formulation. But for finite n, our experiments with the dynamic programming approach show that those remaining terms make the classification effect better.

In many applications, one segment cannot be stretched or compressed too much. In terms of Definition 3, this entails constraining the scaling factor for each pair of segments to lie between $\frac{1}{3}$ and 3, as in [1]. We impose an analogous restriction as follows. Let us divide each curve C_k into n equal segments C_{kt} for $k = 1, 2$ and $t = 1, 2, ..., n$. We restrict our search space of bi-morphisms to those bi-morphisms such that one segment of a curve can only be matched to the part of another curve which is composed of one segment, or two segments, or three segments, or $\frac{1}{3}$ or $\frac{2}{3}$ segments. Then we can apply dynamic programming to find the minimizer using Equation 4.

We now detail the programming technique. To make notation simpler, we divide the first curve C_1 into n equal (arc length) segments, denoted C_{1t} for $t = 1, 2, ..., n$, and divide the second curve C_2 into $3n$ equal (arc length) segments, denoted $\tilde{C}_{2j}$ for $j = 1, 2, ..., 3n$. Then we first restrict the search space of bi-morphisms to the set $\bar{B}_1$ which consists of those bi-morphisms matching C_{1t} of curve C_1 to at most 9 segments of the form $\tilde{C}_{2j}$ of the curve C_2. Use $\tilde{M}_{2,j-1}$ to denote the starting point and $\tilde{M}_{2,j}$ to denote the ending point of the segment $\tilde{C}_{2j}$ for $j = 1, 2, ..., 3n$. As in Proposition 1, let $C_1(u, v)$ be the part of curve C_1 starting from point M_{1u} and ending at M_{1v} for each $0 \le u < v \le n$, and let $\tilde{C}_2(u, v)$ be the part of curve C_2 starting from point $\tilde{M}_{2u}$ and ending at $\tilde{M}_{2v}$ for each $0 \le u < v \le 3n$.

Let $\delta(i_1, i_1 + k; j_1, j_2; k) = min_{\mu \in \bar{B}_1} E_{C_1(i_1,i_1+k),\tilde{C}_2(j_1,j_2);k}(\mu)$. Also let $d(i, j; i) = \delta(0, i; 0, j; i)$ for $i = 1, 2, ..., n$ and $j = 1, 2, ..., 3n$. Then what we want is to compute

$$\min_{\mu \in \bar{B}_1} E_{C_1,C_2;n}(\mu) = \min_{\mu \in \bar{B}_1} E_{C_1(0,n),\tilde{C}_2(0,3n);n}(\mu) = d(n, 3n; n). \tag{5}$$

To find it, we need the following proposition, whose proof like that of Proposition 1, is just a careful application of Equation 1.

Proposition 3. *For any bi-morphism $\mu \in \bar{B}_1$, let the point $M_{1,i-c}$ of curve C_1 be matched to the point $\tilde{M}_{2,j_c}$ of curve C_2 under bi-morphism μ for $c = 1, 2, 3$. Then we* *have* $1 \leq j_1 - j_2 \leq 9$ *and* $1 \leq j_2 - j_3 \leq 9$ *since* $\mu \in \bar{B}_1$. *Moreover if we let* $\bar{Q}_{i,j;p,q}$ *be the pair matching* $C_1(i,j)$ *to* $\tilde{C}_2(p,q)$ *and similarly let* $\bar{R}_{i,j;p,q}$ *be the pair matching* $C_1(i,j)$ *to* $\tilde{C}_2(p,q)$, *then we have*

$$E_{C_1(0,i),\tilde{C}_2(0,j);i}(\mu) = E_{C_1(0,i-1),\tilde{C}_2(0,j_1);i-1}(\mu) + E_{C_1(i-1,i),\tilde{C}_2(j_1,j);1}(\mu)$$
$$+\lambda_2 \rho(\bar{Q}_{i-2,i;j_2,j}) + k_\theta \, \Delta\theta(\bar{Q}_{i-2,i;j_2,j}) + k_r |l(\bar{Q}_{i-2,i;j_2,j},1) - l(\bar{Q}_{i-2,i;j_2,j},2)|$$
$$+\lambda_3 \rho(\bar{R}_{i-3,i;j_3,j}) + k_\theta \, \Delta\theta(\bar{R}_{i-3,i;j_3,j}) + k_r |l(\bar{R}_{i-3,i;j_3,j},1) - l(\bar{R}_{i-3,i;j_3,j},2)| \quad (6)$$

Definition 6. *Let* i, j, j_1 *be integers such that* $0 \leq i \leq n$, $0 \leq j \leq 3n$ *and* $0 \leq j_1 < j$. *If* $0 < j - j_1 \leq 9$ *and* $i - 1 \leq j_1 \leq 9(i-1)$, *then we call* j_1 *a* feasible J-index preceding (i,j), *which means that only for those feasible* j_1 *can* $C_1(i-1,i)$ *be matched to* $\tilde{C}_2(j_1,j)$. *Let* $\Lambda(i,j)$ *be the set of* feasible J-indices preceding (i,j).

For any $0 \leq i \leq n$ and $0 \leq j \leq 3n$, we have

$$d(i,j;i) = \delta(0,i;0,j;i) = \min_{\mu \in \bar{B}_1} E_{C_1(0,i),\tilde{C}_2(0,j);i}(\mu). \quad (7)$$

Then there is $\mu^* \in \bar{B}_1$ such that $d(i,j;i) = E_{C_1(0,i),\tilde{C}_2(0,j);i}(\mu^*)$. Let $\tilde{M}_{2,j_1^*} \in C_2$ be the matching point of $M_{1,i-1} \in C_1$ under μ^*. j_1^* is needed for tracing the pairs of the form Q_j and R_g which is very important because, at each step of the dynamic programming of the following Algorithm 1, the corresponding terms for Q_j and R_g are added as well as the terms for P_i. Obviously j_1^* can be seen as a function of (i,j) and we give a name for such a function in the following.

Definition 7. *For any* $0 \leq i \leq n$ *and* $0 \leq j \leq 3n$, *define* $Pre(i,j) = j_1^*$.

To compute $d(n,3n;n)$, we first compute $d(1,j;1)$ for $j = 1, 2, ..., 3n$. Then compute $d(2,j;2)$ for $j = 1, 2, ..., 3n$ until $d(n,3n;n)$. Each time we check whether (i,j) is feasible or not, and record the *feasible J-index preceding (i,j)* defined in Definition 6. If (i,j) is not feasible, set $d(i,j;i) = \infty$. For example, we should set $d(1,10;1) = \infty$ since C_{11} is not allowed to be matched to 10 segments of curve C_2. For each (i,j), we not only record $d(i,j;i)$ but also record the index $Pre(i,j)$ which is defined above and will be used in the next step as shown in the following Proposition 4. The following Proposition 4 provides the mechanism of the dynamic programming of MSSLS-based algorithm. The idea is similar to the usual dynamic programming except that at each step we have more terms to add and that some terms depend on the results of previous 2 and 3 steps.

Proposition 4. *For any* $0 \leq i \leq n$, $0 \leq j \leq 3n$ *and* $j_1 \in \Lambda(i,j)$, *let* $j_2 = Pre(i-1,j_1)$, $j_3 = Pre(i-2,j_2)$, *and*

$$\beta(i,j,j_1) = d(i-1,j_1;i-1) + \delta(i-1,i;j_1,j;1) + \lambda_2 \, \rho(\bar{Q}_{i-2,i;j_2,j})$$
$$+k_\theta \, \Delta\theta(\bar{Q}_{i-2,i;j_2,j}) + k_r \, |l(\bar{Q}_{i-2,i;j_2,j},1) - l(\bar{Q}_{i-2,i;j_2,j},2)| + \lambda_3 \, \rho(\bar{R}_{i-3,i;j_3,j})$$
$$+k_\theta \, \Delta\theta(\bar{R}_{i-3,i;j_3,j}) + k_r \, |l(\bar{R}_{i-3,i;j_3,j},1) - l(\bar{R}_{i-3,i;j_3,j},2)|. \quad (8)$$

Also let $\eta = \min_{j_1 \in \Lambda(i,j)} \beta(i,j,j_1)$. *Then* $\eta \geq d(i,j;i)$.

Proof. By the Definition of η, there exists $j_1^* \in \Lambda(i,j)$ such that $\eta = \beta(i,j,j_1^*)$. Let $j_2^* = Pre(i-1, j_1^*)$ and $j_3^* = Pre(i-2, j_2^*)$. Then

$$\eta = d(i-1, j_1^*; i-1) + \delta(i-1, i; j_1^*, j; 1) + \lambda_2\, \rho(\bar{Q}_{i-2,i;j_2^*,j})$$
$$+ k_\theta\, \Delta\theta(\bar{Q}_{i-2,i;j_2^*,j}) + k_r\, |l(\bar{Q}_{i-2,i;j_2^*,j}, 1) - l(\bar{Q}_{i-2,i;j_2^*,j}, 2)| + \lambda_3\, \rho(\bar{R}_{i-3,i;j_3^*,j})$$
$$+ k_\theta\, \Delta\theta(\bar{R}_{i-3,i;j_3^*,j}) + k_r\, |l(\bar{R}_{i-3,i;j_3^*,j}, 1) - l(\bar{R}_{i-3,i;j_3^*,j}, 2)|. \qquad (9)$$

Then by the Definition of d and δ, there exist μ_1^* and μ_2^* such that $d(i-1, j_1^*; i-1) = E_{C_1(0,i-1),\tilde{C}_2(0,j_1^*);i-1}(\mu_1^*)$ and $\delta(i-1, i; j_1^*, j; 1) = E_{C_1(i-1,i),\tilde{C}_2(j_1^*,j);1}(\mu_2^*)$. Since $j_1^* \in \Lambda(i,j)$, we can construct a new bi-morphism μ^* whose action on all possible pairs are determined by μ_1^*, μ_2^*, $\bar{Q}_{i-2,i;j_2^*,j}$, and $\bar{R}_{i-3,i;j_3^*,j}$. Then $\mu^* \in \bar{B}_1$ and $\eta = E_{C_1(0,i),\tilde{C}_2(0,j);i}(\mu^*) \geq d(i,j;i)$.

Let us examine more closely how it can happen that η might not equal $d(i,j;i)$. By the Definition of d, there exists $\hat{\mu} \in \bar{B}_1$ such that $d(i,j;i) = E_{C_1(0,i),\tilde{C}_2(0,j);i}(\hat{\mu})$. Let $\hat{j}_1, \hat{j}_2$, and $\hat{j}_3$ be the points of C_2 which correspond to $M_{1,i-1}, M_{1,i-2}$ and $M_{1,i-3}$ of curve C_1 under the bi-morphism $\hat{\mu}$ respectively. By Equations 6 and 8, we have

$$E_{C_1(0,i),\tilde{C}_2(0,j);i}(\hat{\mu}) = E_{C_1(0,i-1),\tilde{C}_2(0,\hat{j}_1);i-1}(\hat{\mu}) + E_{C_1(i-1,i),\tilde{C}_2(\hat{j}_1,j);1}(\hat{\mu})$$
$$+ \lambda_2\rho(\bar{Q}_{i-2,i;\hat{j}_2,j}) + k_\theta\, \Delta\theta(\bar{Q}_{i-2,i;\hat{j}_2,j}) + k_r|l(\bar{Q}_{i-2,i;\hat{j}_2,j}, 1) - l(\bar{Q}_{i-2,i;\hat{j}_2,j}, 2)|$$
$$+ \lambda_3\rho(\bar{R}_{i-3,i;\hat{j}_3,j}) + k_\theta\, \Delta\theta(\bar{R}_{i-3,i;\hat{j}_3,j}) + k_r|l(\bar{R}_{i-3,i;\hat{j}_3,j}, 1) - l(\bar{R}_{i-3,i;\hat{j}_3,j}, 2)| \quad (10)$$

If we expand $\beta(i, j, \hat{j}_1)$ using Equation 8, we can see that the first two terms of this expansion are less than or equal to the first two terms of the right side of Equation 10 but this may not be true for the remaining terms. Hence η might not equal $d(i,j;i)$. In Equation 8, the first term contains the deforming energy of the previous $i-1$ segments, and the remaining terms just contain the deforming energy of the ith segment and the deforming energy measuring the connection with previous 2 segments. Hence the first term should dominate as i goes larger. When we cannot get the accurate value of $d(i,j;i)$, we need to make the first part as small as possible, in other words, use sequential minimization (see Algorithm 1 below). Instead of computing $d(i,j;i)$ exactly, we estimate it using the slightly larger quantity η in Proposition 4. Then we use dynamic programming to estimate $d(n, 3n; n)$. Whenever we apply Proposition 4 once, one new pair is generated. Finally we get n pairs. Using this approach we have the following Algorithm 1. In the following, the *cost* means exactly the *deforming energy* between two curves. For all algorithms in this paper, we assume that the lengths of all input curves are not drastically different, so that we are not comparing a part of one curve with another whole curve.

Algorithm 1: *Step 1* Smooth each set of data a little bit.

Step 2 Normalize each curve so that all curves have the same arc length.

Step 3 Apply cubic spline to fit each data-set to get a continuously differentiable curve. Also we need it to compute the non-overlapping area (see the detailed instruction after Step 9) to get the local dissimilarity.

Step 4 Refine the first curve into n segments (method of choosing n is discussed below) and the second curve into $3n$ segments based on the cubic splines.

Step 5 Compute the tangent line and the corresponding angle at each point.

Step 6 Estimate the parameters λ_i, k_θ, and k_r in Equation 1 by the method detailed below.

Step 7 Start from curve 1 and apply Proposition 4 recursively to get the total cost $d(n, 3n)'$.

Step 8 Start from curve 2 and similarly do step 7 to get the total cost $d(3n, n)''$.

Step 9 Compute the total cost $d(C_1, C_2; n) = d(n, 3n)' + d(3n, n)''$.

Choose a Suitable Sampling Size n: For a given application, we need to choose suitable n in Algorithm 1. If n is too small, some curves can not be well represented. As shown in Figure 4, the computational time increases quickly when n is increasing. If n is very big and just 3 different step sizes are used in Algorithm 1, global information is not caught well and hence the goals of correspondence and classification may not be achieved well. In some cases there are also limitations for choosing suitable step sizes as explained in the remark following Equation 1. By experimenting on given data, we are available to find suitable n.

Computation of Local Dissimilarity: For each i, j and t, 10,20 and 30 points from segment pairs P_i, Q_j and R_t are sampled respectively to compute the corresponding local dissimilarity. After the alignment of each pair, their bases are the same. Hence we can estimate the symmetric area differences of height at corresponding sample points.

Method of Choosing Parameters in Step 6: First we determine suitable λ_1, λ_2, and λ_3 of Equation 1 as follows. We sample 48 points from each curve. The terms $\rho(Q_j)$ and $\rho(R_g)$ are very important in catching the features of those curves. From experiments, the terms $\rho(R_g)$ are a few times bigger than the terms $\rho(Q_j)$. The terms $\rho(P_i)$ are more noisy and hence not so important as the terms of $\rho(Q_j)$ and $\rho(R_g)$. So we set $\lambda_1 = 2, \lambda_2 = 3$, and $\lambda_3 = 1$. To choose k_θ and k_r in Equation 1, let $E_1 = \sum_{i=1}^n \lambda_1 \rho(P_i) + \sum_{j=1}^{n_2} \lambda_2 \rho(Q_j) + \sum_{j=1}^{n_3} \lambda_3 \rho(R_g)$, $E_2 = k_\theta(\sum_{i=1}^n \Delta\theta(P_i) + \sum_{j=1}^{n_2} \Delta\theta(Q_j) + \sum_{j=1}^{n_3} \Delta\theta(R_g))$, and

$$E_3 = k_r\left(\sum_{i=1}^n |l(P_i, 1) - l(P_i, 2)| + \sum_{j=1}^{n_2} |l(Q_j, 1) - l(Q_j, 2)| + \sum_{g=1}^{n_3} |l(R_g, 1) - l(R_g, 2)|\right).$$

E_1 represents the deforming energy of MSSLS which is more important than E_2 and E_3. E_3 represents the among of stretching which is the least important. We need to choose k_θ and k_r such that E_1 is a bit bigger than E_2, and E_2 is a few times bigger than E_3 by testing some curves. So we set $k_\theta = 10$, and $k_r = 40$. We did many experiments using different parameters and found that the algorithm is very stable.

We applied our algorithms to some data of hand-written characters and cardiac curves where each curve is normalized to have unit length 1. The correspondence of some cardiac curves and numerals is shown in Figure 3. To compare the result using the curvature-based dissimilarity shown in Figure 3 of [9], for the same database we get the result shown in Figure 2(a) of this paper. In Figure 2(a), we used the curve which has the smallest cost to all curves in the same class as the average shape in that class (the first entry of each row). From Figure 2(a), we can see that all characters in the class of 3's are very well classified by the MSSLS-based algorithm and their cost to

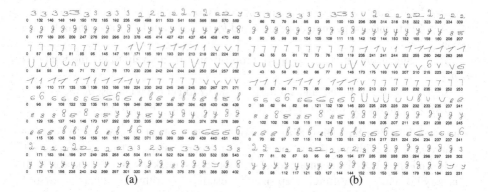

(a)   (b)

Fig. 2. (a) Matches using MSSLS-based method. (b) Matches using the Improved Shape Context. The left-most curve of each row is the average shape of some character. The number underneath each curve represents its cost from the left most curve of the same row. For example the left-most curve of the first row is the average shape of class 3 and the remaining curves of that row are closest (among all curves in the database) to this average shape.

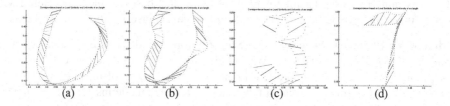

(a)   (b)   (c)   (d)

Fig. 3. Correspondence based on MSSLS. (a),(b) are for cardiac curves.

characters of other classes is much bigger than the cost to any letter of its own class. But as shown in the first row and then third row of Figure 3 of [9], only 7 out of 10 threes are classified and only 4 out of 10 sevens are classified using curvature-based algorithm. For other characters, we also got better results. By comparing Figure 2(a) of this paper with Figure 3 of [9], we can see that MSSLS-based algorithm is much better than curvature-based algorithm. It is also rotation invariant. For example,in Figure 2(a) the upside-down U is still recognized and ranked in the fifth place of that class. There are two characters of class 8 that are not recognized because for one of them, the starting point is very different from the starting point of most of the 8's, and for the others, the orientation of the curve is opposite to the customary one drawing an 8. So the local shape information is caught very well by MSSLS-based algorithm, but it is still not very efficient in catching the overall shape information. For example, in Figure 2(a), the numeral 7 with a very curly arm is just on the 20th place of that row.

4   Improve Shape Context for Ordered Point Sets

Shape context is introduced and used in [7] and [8] to solve a more general problem of matching sets of unordered points of R^2. If we have two such sets $\mathcal{P} = \{\mathbf{p}_1, \mathbf{p}_2, ..., \mathbf{p}_n\}$

$\subset R^2$ and $\mathcal{Q} = \{\mathbf{q}_1, \mathbf{q}_2, ..., \mathbf{q}_n\} \subset R^2$, we should match each point $\mathbf{p}_s$ of the first set to a point $\mathbf{q}_t$ of the second set for $1 \leq s, t \leq n$. If we use polar coordinates and start from two corresponding points p_s and q_t, the orientations of other points from the starting point are quantized into 12 bins and their distance from the starting point is quantized into 5 bins in log scale. Then the corresponding 60 regions partition two sets $\mathcal{P}$ and $\mathcal{Q}$ into subsets. In [7], the cost of matching $\mathbf{p}_s$ with $\mathbf{q}_t$ is defined as

$$C(\mathbf{p}_s, \mathbf{q}_t) = \frac{1}{2} \sum_{k=1}^{60} \frac{[h_s(k) - h_t(k)]^2}{h_s(k) + h_t(k)} \tag{11}$$

where $h_s(k)$ and $h_t(k)$ are the number of points of the set $\mathcal{P}$ and $\mathcal{Q}$ in the region k respectively.

In our situation, two sets to be matched are ordered. Hence we can consider local information better in this simpler case. After a suitable logarithmic transformation, the further a region is from the starting point the more it is compressed. If we use template matching after the log transform, then all points are considered but closer points get more weight and hence both local and global shape information can be captured. The usual template-matching is very computationally expensive and is not necessary in our case. For each curve, make one translation so that $\mathbf{p}_s$ and $\mathbf{q}_t$ become the origin, and make one rotation so that the positively-oriented tangent direction at the origin becomes the positive x-axis. Then apply a logarithm to make compression, and after those 3 transformations let $\mathcal{P}' = \{\mathbf{p}_1', \mathbf{p}_2', ..., \mathbf{p}_n'\}$ be the new coordinates of the set $\mathcal{P}$ and $\mathcal{Q}' = \{\mathbf{q}_1', \mathbf{q}_2', ..., \mathbf{q}_n'\}$ new coordinates of $\mathcal{Q}$. For any $X, Y \in R^2$, let $d(X, Y)$ be the distance between X and Y. For $j = 1, 2, ..., n$, let $d1_j = min\{d(\mathbf{p}_j', Y) \mid Y \in \mathcal{Q}'\}$ and $d2_j = min\{d(X, \mathbf{q}_j') \mid X \in \mathcal{P}'\}$. We define

$$C(\mathbf{p}_s, \mathbf{q}_t) = \sum_{j=1}^{n} (d1_j + d2_j) \tag{12}$$

to be the cost of this *restricted template matching* or *improved shape context*.

To deal with bi-morphisms, we need the notations for finding a suitable bi-morphism $\mu : [0, 1] \to C_1 \times C_2$ where C_1 and C_2 are two given planar curves. As in Section 3, divide the curve C_k into n equal segments denoted C_{kt} for $k = 1, 2$ and $t = 1, 2, ..., n$, and let $M_{k,t-1}$ and $M_{k,t}$ be the starting and ending point of the curve segment C_{kt}. As in Equation 1, let $P_i = (p_1(\mu(I_i)), p_2(\mu(I_i)))$ be the ith pair in the matching for $i = 1, 2, ..., n$. Let E_{ki} be the end point of the curve segment $p_k(\mu(I_i))$ for $k = 1, 2$. Now we translate the curve C_k so that E_{ki} becomes the origin, and rotate C_k so that the positively-oriented tangent direction of C_k at the origin is aligned with the positive x-axis. Denote the new coordinates of $M_{k,t}$ after those two transformations and a logarithm as $M_{k,t}'$ for $k = 1, 2$ and $t = 0, 1, 2, ..., n$. For $j = 0, 1, 2, ..., n$, let $d1_j = min\{d(M_{1,j}', M_{2,t}') \mid t \in \{0, 1, 2, ..., n\}\}$ and $d2_j = min\{d(M_{1,t}', M_{2,j}') \mid t \in \{0, 1, 2, ..., n\}\}$. Let $\nu(P_i) = \sum_{j=0}^{n} (d1_j + d2_j)$. Whenever we use dynamic programming to add a new pair, the left end points of two curve segments of a pair going to be added are already fixed and hence the positions of their right end points represent the (improved) shape context of that pair. So $\nu(P_i)$ measures the cost of Improved Shape

Context mapping $p_1(\mu(I_i))$ to $p_2(\mu(I_i))$. We define the deforming energy of the improved shape-context-based algorithm as following:

$$E_{C_1,C_2;n}(\mu) = \sum_{i=1}^{n} k_s \, \nu(P_i) + k_\theta \, \Delta\theta(P_i) + k_r |l(P_i, 1) - l(P_i, 2)|. \qquad (13)$$

Algorithm 2: Do *Step 1* through *Step 6* of Algorithm 1 but with the new cost function (13).

Step 7 Start from curve 1 and apply Proposition 4 recursively to get the total cost $d(n, 3n)'$. But in this algorithm, when we apply Proposition 4 the terms for Q_j and R_g are not needed and the energy terms are replaced by those in Equation 13.

Step 8 Start from curve 2 and do similarly as in Step 7 to get the total cost $d(3n, n)''$.

Step 9 Compute the total cost $d(C_1, C_2; n) = d(n, 3n)' + d(3n, n)''$.

Figure 2(b) shows us that the Improved Shape Context gives us better results than the *usual shape context* which is shown in Figure 5 of [9]. For example, in the fourth row of Figure 5 of [9], one V is classified 7th in the U class and 3 out of 10 U's are not shown in that row. Because we use tangent lines as x-axes, our algorithm is rotation invariant. There is one U missing from the fourth row of Figure 2(b) of this paper because the data of that U are reversed. If we allow searching for flipping, then that U should be classified but more computation would be needed. In the last row of Figure 2(b) of this paper, there are still two characters of y class misclassified. That is reasonable because they are quite different from the previous ones and hence should be in a separate class.

As is shown in Figure 4, when we use 48 points to represent a curve, the computational time using Improved Shape Context is less than that using the Usual Shape Context. But when we use 97 points to represent a curve, the computational time using Improved Shape Context is much bigger than that using the Usual Shape Context. However in the computation of $d1_k$ of Equation 12, we can set $Q' = \{q'_u, ..., q'_k, ..., q'_v\}$ where $v = min(k + d, n)$ and $u = max(k - d, 1)$, n is the number of point representing a curve, and $d = ceil(0.2k)$ is the smallest integer exceeding $0.2k$. Then the computational time shown in Figure 4 is not much, and the result (shown in a figure) is still very good. If we use more points to represent a curve, then we should change 0.2 to a smaller number. Let us call this algorithm (using a restricted search space) *Algorithm 2'*.

Algorithm	CB	MSSLS	USC	ISC
Hours(48 points)	2.37	3.23	7.01	6.68
Hours(97 points)	5.01	8.24	27.97	73.4(27.1)

Fig. 4. Running time of Matlab programs for different algorithms to classify 30 curves on a 2.8 GHz PC. The 2nd (3rd) row is the running time when 48 (97) points are used to represent a curve. CB means Curvature Based, MSSLS means Multi-Step-Size Local Similarity, USC means Usual Shape Context, and ISC means Improved Shape Context. The number 27.1 inside the parentheses is the computational time using Algorithm 2'.

5   Curve Classification Based on the Cost of Non-rigid Correspondence

Let us consider the set Γ of all smooth curves. For any two curves C_1 and C_2 in Γ, let $d(C_1, C_2; n)$ be the deforming energy between C_1 and C_2 computed using Algorithm 1 or Algorithm 2, where n is the number of pairs when we search for the best bimorphism. Then we have the following proposition.

Proposition 5. *For any given $C_1, C_2 \in \Gamma$, the deforming energy $d(C_1, C_2; n)$ satisfies the following:*

1). $d(C_1, C_1; n) = 0$;

1'). If C_1 is similar to C_2 as oriented curves, then $d(C_1, C_2; n) = 0$; if $d(C_1, C_2; n)$ denotes the deforming energy between C_1 and C_2 computed using Algorithm 1, and we assume that there are enough number of points (not just 10,20,and 30 points) sampled when we compute the similarity of each pair of curve segments, then $d(C_1, C_2; n) = 0$ implies that C_1 is similar to C_2 as oriented curves.

2). $d(C_1, C_2; n) = d(C_2, C_1; n)$.

Proof. 1) and 2) follow directly from the algorithms to compute $d(C_1, C_2; n)$. To prove 1'), if C_1 is similar to C_2, then after a scaling they are the same in rigid sense and hence $d(C_1, C_2; n) = 0$. Now assume that $d(C_1, C_2; n)$ be the deforming energy between C_1 and C_2 computed using Algorithm 1, and we assume that there are enough number of points sampled when we compute the similarity of each pair of curve segments. If $d(C_1, C_2; n) = 0$, then all scaling factors equal 1 and the dissimilarity between any two curve segments paired by Algorithm 1 equals 0. Hence any two curve segments paired are the same in rigid sense because the curve segments are smooth and sufficient

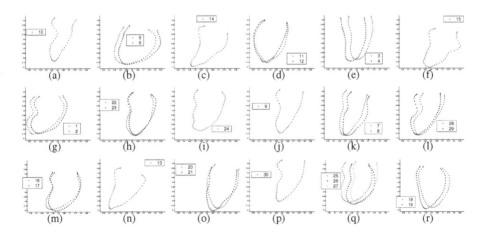

Fig. 5. Classification among 30 cardiac curves using MSSLS where 48 points are sampled on each curve. Numbers from 1 to 15 are abnormal and the meaning of those numbers is mentioned in the paragraph "Classification of some Cardiac Curves" of Section 5.

number of points are sampled. Then C_1 and C_2 are the same (after their bases are aligned) because of the smoothness, and hence C_1 is similar to C_2 as oriented curves.

Now suppose we have a set of m curves and we want to classify them into several groups based on their similarity which is in non-rigid sense. Based on the algorithms of previous sections we can compute the cost of matching between any two curves among the m curves, which turned out to be an $m \times m$ matrix. This matrix can be used to pattern recognition among those curves.

Classification of some Cardiac Curves: We tried 30 cardiac curves. Among them 15 curves are abnormal and numbered from 1 to 15, and others are normal. Here we just applied our algorithm to the data of ES_{Endo} (for each patient, 4 kinds of data available which are $ED_{Epi}, ED_{Endo}, ES_{Epi}$ and ES_{Endo}) to see how promising the algorithm is. If some curves are thought very similar by experts, their sequential numbers in the database are very close. The experts want to classify their cardiac curves into some groups. Preferably each of those groups should contain only abnormal or only normal cardiac curves. Figures 5 through 8 show the classification results of different algorithms.

Selection of Seeds: We first make some experiments to determine the number of groups, indicated as k, to get good separation of the 30 curves based on the suggestion of experts. Then use the 30×30 cost matrix to select k seeds (representatives). Because here the total number of curves tested is just 30, we don't need randomization to select seeds. First we choose two curves which have greatest cost to each other as seeds. The third seed should be chosen among the remaining curves so that it has greatest cost to previous two seeds. We iterate this process until we get k seeds. Our method of selecting seeds is more suitable than the method with randomization for the purpose of comparing different algorithms.

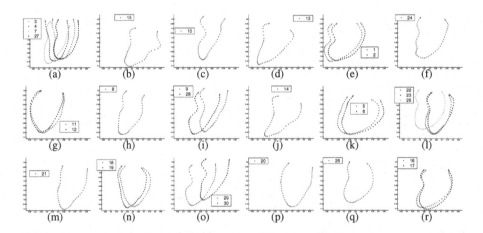

Fig. 6. Classification among 30 cardiac curves using curvature based algorithm. The numbers mean the same as in Fig. 5.

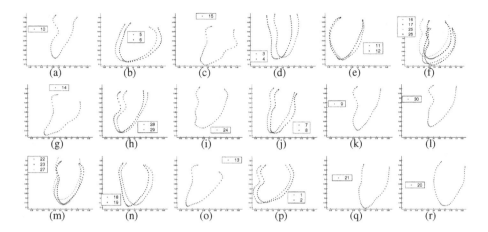

Fig. 7. Classification among 30 cardiac curves using Improved Shape Context (Algorithm $2'$). The numbers mean the same as in Fig. 5.

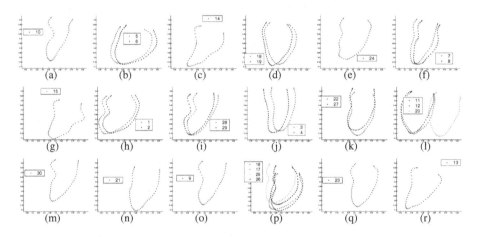

Fig. 8. Classification among 30 cardiac curves using the Usual Shape Context. The numbers mean the same as in Fig. 5.

6   Conclusion

We have shown two new good algorithms for non-rigid correspondence and curve classification. Both algorithms are used to classify planar curves. Since the MSSLS-based algorithm catches overall shape information better and ensures a bi-morphism in the discrete formulation, it has some advantages over curvature-based algorithm. It is also better in catching local shape information than the Improved Shape Context algorithm. The Improved Shape Context algorithm catches local information better than the Usual Shape Context for the ordered sets representing planar curves. For example, Figure 2 shows us that using MSSLS the characters $3,g,7,1,8,b,2,$and y are classified better. The computation of local dissimilarity is robust since it does not involve any derivatives. The Improved Shape Context catches overall shape better than does the MSSLS-based algorithm. For example, Figure 2(b) shows that, using Improved Shape Context the members of the class of numeral 7 are all well-classified even though some of them have very curly arms. For cardiac curves, Figure 5 shows the effect of classification using the MSSLS-based algorithm. We obtained good results for classification among 30 cardiac curves using this algorithm. As shown in Figure 8(c),(g),(l), the Usual Shape Context catches global information very well. The dynamic programming approach can only solve the corresponding minimization problem approximately, but its computation is efficient. To classify 30 cardiac curves, if we set the scaling between $\frac{1}{3}$ and 3, the running time for different algorithms is shown in Figure 4. The MSSLS-based algorithm uses dynamic programming and hence the running time is not too large. Experimental results show that restricting relative scale factors to lie between $\frac{1}{3}$ and 3 does not impair the classification of these data.

Acknowledgments

The authors would like to thank Dr. Tagare for his talk given in year 2003 at the university of Florida about nonrigid correspondence, and Dr. Frenkel for generously providing the data of hand-written characters. We also thank the reviewers for their detailed comments and recommendations on earlier versions of this paper.

References

1. T.B. Sebastian, P.N. Klein, and B.B. Kimia. On Aligning Curves. *IEEE Trans. on Pattern Analysis and Machine Intelligence*, Vol. 25, no. 1, 116-124, 2003.
2. I. Cohen, N. Ayache, and P. Sulger. Tracking Points on Deformable Objects Using Curvature Information. *Proc. European Conf. Computer Vision*, 458-466, 1992.
3. H.D. Tagare. Shape-Based Non-Rigid Correspondence with Application to Heart Motion Analysis. *IEEE Trans. Medical Imaging*, Vol. 18, no. 7, 570- 578, 1999.
4. R. Basri, L. Costa, D. Geiger, and D. Jacobs. Determining the Similarity of Deformable Shapes. *Vision Research*, Vol. 38, 2365-2385, 1998.
5. L. Younes. Computable Elastic Distance between Shapes. *SIAM J. Applied Math.*, Vol. 58, 565-586, 1998.
6. H.D. Tagare, D.O'Shea, and D. Groisser. Non-Rigid Shape Comparison of Plane Curves in Images. *J. Mathematical Imaging and Vision*, Vol. 16, no. 1, 57-68, 2002.
7. S. Belongie, J. Malik, and J. Puzicha. Shape Contexts: A New Descriptor for Shape Matching and Object Recognition. *NIPS*, Vol.13, 831-837, 2001.
8. S. Belongie, J. Malik,and J. Puzicha. Shape Matching and Object Recognition Using Shape Contexts. *IEEE Trans. on Pattern Analysis and Machine Intelligence*, Vol. 24, no. 24, 509-522, 2002.
9. M. Frenkel and R. Basri. Curve Matching Using the Fast Marching Method. *Lecture Notes in Computer Science* , Vol. 2683, 35-51, 2003.
10. J. Sethian. A Fast Marching Level Set Method for Monotonically Advancing Fronts. *Proc. Nat. Acad. Sci.*, Vol. 93, no. 4, 1591-1595, 1996.
11. A. Rangarajan, H. Chui, and E. Mjolsness. A relationship between spline-based deformable models and weighted graphs in non-rigid matching. *IEEE Computer Vision and Pattern Recognition (CVPR)*, Vol. 1, 897-904, 2001.

12. H. Chui and A. Rangarajan. A new point matching algorithm for non-rigid registration. *Computer Vision and Image Understanding (CVIU)*, Vol. 89, 114-141, 2003.

13. A. Marzal and E. Vidal. Computation of Normalized Edit Distances and Applications. *IEEE Trans. Pattern Analysis and Machine Intelligence, Vol. 15*, 926-932, 1993.

14. M. Sermesant, C. Forest, X. Pennec, H. Delingette, and N. Ayache. Deformable biomechanical models: Application to 4D cardiac image analysis. *Medical Image Analysis*, Vol. 7, no. 4, 475-488, 2003.

15. H.C. Liu and M.D. Srinath. Partial Shape Classification Using Contour Matching in Distance Transformation. *IEEE Trans. Pattern Analysis and Machine Intelligence*, Vol. 12, no. 11, 1072-1079, 1990.

Edge Strength Functions as Shape Priors in Image Segmentation

Erkut Erdem, Aykut Erdem, and Sibel Tari

Middle East Technical University,
Department of Computer Engineering, Ankara, TR-06531, Turkey
{erkut, aykut}@ceng.metu.edu.tr, stari@metu.edu.tr

Abstract. Many applications of computer vision requires segmenting out of an object of interest from a given image. Motivated by unlevel-sets formulation of Raviv, Kiryati and Sochen [8] and statistical formulation of Leventon, Grimson and Faugeras [6], we present a new image segmentation method which accounts for prior shape information. Our method depends on Ambrosio-Tortorelli approximation of Mumford-Shah functional. The prior shape is represented by a by-product of this functional, a smooth edge indicator function, known as the "edge strength function", which provides a distance-like surface for the shape boundary. Our method can handle arbitrary deformations due to shape variability as well as plane Euclidean transformations. The method is also robust with respect to noise and missing parts. Furthermore, this formulation does not require simple closed curves as in a typical level set formulation.

1 Introduction

In many vision applications, one searches an object of interest whose pose may vary and whose shape may exhibit variability. Deliniating the object boundary correctly and estimating the pose becomes particularly challenging when corrupting influences due to missing regions and noise appear. As a remedy, use of prior shape models are considered. During the last five years, quite interesting works addressing shape prior integration directly into segmentation process appeared [4, 5, 6, 8, 9, 11].

These methods differ in terms of

- How they represent shape prior;
- Boundary detection rule which forms the backbone;
- Extension of the boundary detection rule to allow the influence of the prior;
- Computation.

In Cremers et.al. [5], a variational framework is used for the integration of shape statistics and segmentation. Shape boundaries are represented explicitly as spline curves. Aligned shape variability is captured by a Gaussian distribution model whose mean and covariance matrix are computed from a group of splines. A shape energy that maximizes the shape probability is combined with Mumford-Shah [7] segmentation energy and minimized by applying gradient descent.

A. Rangarajan et al. (Eds.): EMMCVPR 2005, LNCS 3757, pp. 490–502, 2005.

In Leventon et.al. [6], a shape boundary is embedded as the zero level curve of a level set function (distance function). Shape prior is represented via coefficients of the principal components computed from a group of distance functions whose zero-levels correspond to the various appearances of a shape of interest. A two step procedure is employed. First, the level set function is evolved such that its zero level curve converges to the shape boundary. Second, pose and shape variables are computed via MAP estimation on the Gaussian probability space.

In Tsai et.al. [11], a shape based curve evolution technique is proposed. The implicit shape representation proposed by Leventon et.al. [6] is embedded into region-based active contour models as in [3]. Again a two step procedure is employed. However, pose and shape variables are computed by applying gradient descent.

In Chen et. al. [4], prior shape is represented by the average of aligned contours. A shape term which measures the similarity between evolving and prior contours is added into a variational active contours framework. Hence, evolution of the active contour is controlled by a force which depends on both image gradients and prior shape.

In Rousson et.al. [9], a probabilistic approach to generate shape priors using level set representations which can also handle local shape variability is proposed. From a set of training samples, represented as level sets, a probability density function is constructed by maximum likelihood estimation. A shape energy is defined and incorporated into a level set based segmentation method depending on the proposed model.

In Raviv et.al. [8], shape variability is ignored. Quite elegant formulation is obtained by utilizing a generalized cone whose cross sections are the various appearances of a given object under pose changes. This cone also functions as a level set function which evolves according to a constraint derived from the prior. The cost function is an extension of Chan-Vese approximation [3] of Mumford-Shah functional with a shape prior term.

Inspired by Raviv et.al. [8] and Leventon et.al. [6], we present a new method for shape prior incorporation into segmentation process. Backbone of our method is Ambrosio-Tortorelli [1] approximation (AT) of Mumford-Shah functional. We employ a by-product of this functional, a smooth edge indicator function which is known as the "edge strength function" as a distance-like surface which embeds the shape boundary. Shape similarity term which is a normalized difference between "deformed" shape prior and the evolving edge strength function is added to Ambrosio-Tortorelli functional.

The edge strength function has some nice properties which makes it a quite versatile tool for different vision tasks. Despite its shortcomings as a segmentation tool, it has been proven to be quite useful in capturing essential shape characteristics [10] and recently applied to object recognition very successfully [2]. An interesting property of the edge strength function is that it encodes the local symmetry information [10]. This makes possible the integration of boundary and local symmetry information and design shape energies which will force morphological equivalence. As an example, it is possible to change the shape energy by simply adding a weight that is proportional to local symmetry strength. Furthermore, the embedding provided by the edge strength function does not require simple closed curves as in a typical level set formulation.

The paper is organized as follows. Section 2 is on Ambrosio-Tortorelli functional. Representation of a set of prior shapes is explained in Section 3. In Section 4, the combined energy and its minimization is discussed. Experimental results are presented in Section 5. Finally, Section 6 is the summary.

2   Ambrosio-Tortorelli Segmentation Functional

A prototype for energy based minimization is Mumford and Shah [7] approach. In this approach, image segmentation problem is formulated as a functional minimization via which a piecewise smooth approximation of an image and a set of discontinuity locus corresponding to object boundaries are to be recovered. The energy to be minimized is:

$$E_{MS} = \alpha \int \int_{R \backslash \Gamma} \|\nabla u\|^2 dx dy + \beta \int \int_{R} (u - g)^2 dx dy + length(\Gamma) \quad (1)$$

where $R \subset \Re^2$ is connected, bounded, open subset representing the image domain, $g(x,y)$ is an image, Γ is a curve segmenting R, $u(x,y)$ is the smoothed image, α and β are the weights. Let $\sigma = \sqrt{\frac{\alpha}{\beta}}$. Then, σ may be interpreted as the smoothing radius in $R \backslash \Gamma$. With σ fixed, the higher the value of α, the lower the penalty for $length(\Gamma)$, hence the more detailed is the segmentation. Unknown edge set Γ makes the minimization mathematically difficult. A convenient approximation is suggested by Ambrosio and Tortorelli in [1] where they introduce a smooth edge indicator function $v(x,y)$ which is more convenient than the original edge indicator. On the edges, $v(x,y) \rightarrow 1$ and on the smooth regions $v(x,y) \rightarrow 0$. Ambrosio-Tortorelli functional

$$E_{AT} = \int \int_{R} \left(\alpha((1-v)^2 \|\nabla u\|^2) + \beta(u-g)^2 + (\frac{\rho}{2}\|\nabla v\|^2 + \frac{v^2}{2\rho}) \right) dx dy \quad (2)$$

is shown to converge to the original functional as $\rho \rightarrow 0$.

3   Representation of the Prior Shape

For the proper choice of ρ, edge strength function provides a smooth embedding surface whose one-level curve correspond to shape boundary which is not necessarily a simple closed curve(Fig. 1). Prior edge strength function $v_p(x,y)$ can be computed from a binary prior image as the minimizer of the following energy [10]

$$\frac{1}{2} \int \int \rho\|\nabla v\|^2 + \frac{v^2}{\rho} dx dy \quad (3)$$

subject to $v = 1$ on the shape boundary.

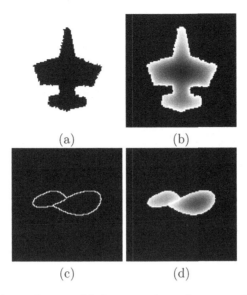

(a)   (b)

(c)   (d)

Fig. 1. (a) An airplane silhoutte. (b) Corresponding edge strength function computed with $\rho = 32$. (c) a line drawing with self intersections. (d) Corresponding edge strength function computed with $\rho = 16$.

Fig. 2. Differential properties of v capture local symmetry strength

A quite curious property of the edge strength function computed with large ρ is that the local symmetry information is encoded via differential properties. Consider Fig. 2 which displays the quantity $1 - \left| \frac{d}{ds} \|\nabla v\| \right|$ where

$$\left| \frac{d}{ds} \|\nabla v\| \right| = \frac{|(v_y^2 - v_x^2)v_{xy} - v_x v_y(v_{yy} - v_{xx})|}{\|\nabla v\|^2}$$

If a shape does not exhibit variations other than pose, $v_p(x, y)$ captures the prior information. Suppose we are given an ensemble of pose and scale aligned shapes[1] whose boundaries are given by the curves $\Gamma_{p_1}, \cdots, \Gamma_{p_n}$ respectively. Following an idea presented by Leventon et.al. [6] and later adopted in [11], we

---

[1] The alignment algorithm proposed in [11] is used in the experiments.

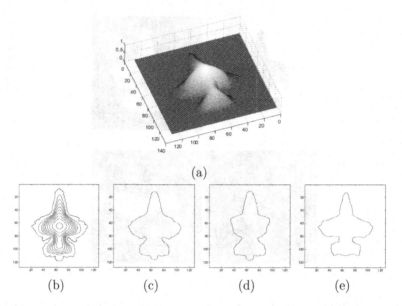

(a)

(b)   (c)   (d)   (e)

Fig. 3. (a) Mean edge strength function extracted from the set of airplane images shown in Fig. 4. (b) Corresponding level curves. (c)-(e) 1-level curves of $\Phi_{\mathbf{w}}$ for three different choices of $\mathbf{w}$.

Fig. 4. Set of airplane shapes taken from [11]

use coefficients of the principal components as shape variability parameters. Specifically, let $v_{p_1}(x,y), \cdots, v_{p_n}(x,y)$ be an ensemble of prior edge strength functions. The mean edge strength function $\overline{\Phi}(x,y)$ is the ordinary average of $v_{p_1}(x,y), \cdots, v_{p_n}(x,y)$. Let $\Phi_1, \cdots, \Phi_n$ be the principal components computed by Karhunen-Loeve Transformation, then a possible shape from this ensemble has

$$\Phi_{\mathbf{w}}(x,y) = \overline{\Phi}(x,y) + \sum w_i \Phi_i(x,y) \tag{4}$$

as its edge strength function. Fig. 3 illustrates the concept for the edge strength functions computed from the set of images shown in Fig. 4.

4   Shape Energy: Similarity of the Embedding Surface

In the previous section, a representation for the shape prior in terms of a mean edge strength function and principle components is developed. Now we will discuss how this representation captured by equation (4) can be used to integrate prior shape information into Ambrosio-Tortorelli functional. The simplest solution is adding two energies to arrive at a combined energy:

$$E = E_{AT} + \mu E_{shape} \tag{5}$$

where μ is the parameter which enforces the shape similarity of the embedding surface in the overall segmentation process.

A straight forward choice for shape energy is simply

$$E_{shape}(v, t_x, t_y, h, \theta, \mathbf{w}) = \int \int_R (v - T(\Phi_{\mathbf{w}}))^2 dx dy \tag{6}$$

where the pose transformation function T applied to the shape prior $\Phi_{\mathbf{w}}$ is defined as follows:

$$
\begin{bmatrix} x' \\ y' \\ T(\Phi_{\mathbf{w}}) \end{bmatrix} = \underbrace{\begin{bmatrix} h & 0 & 0 \\ 0 & h & 0 \\ 0 & 0 & 1 \end{bmatrix}}_{scale} \underbrace{\begin{bmatrix} \cos\theta & -\sin\theta & 0 \\ \sin\theta & \cos\theta & 0 \\ 0 & 0 & 1 \end{bmatrix}}_{rotation} \begin{bmatrix} x \\ y \\ \Phi_{\mathbf{w}} \end{bmatrix} + \underbrace{\begin{bmatrix} t_x \\ t_y \\ 0 \end{bmatrix}}_{translation} \tag{7}
$$

However, we observed that such a straight forward choice may cause segmentation process to trap into local minima. Hence we considered the normalized difference:

$$E_{shape}(v, t_x, t_y, h, \theta, \mathbf{w}) = \frac{\int \int_R (v - T(\Phi_{\mathbf{w}}))^2 dx dy}{\int \int_R (v + T(\Phi_{\mathbf{w}}))^2 dx dy} \tag{8}$$

Upon casting the problem into a discrete setting, we arrive to the following minimization problem:

$$
\min E(u, v, t_x, t_y, h, \theta, \mathbf{w}) = \sum_{i=1}^{width} \sum_{j=1}^{height} \beta(u_{i,j} - g_{i,j})^2 + \alpha(1 - v_{i,j})^2(u_x^2 + u_y^2)
$$

$$
+ \frac{\rho}{2}(v_x^2 + v_y^2) + \frac{v_{i,j}^2}{2\rho}
$$

$$
+ \mu \frac{\sum_{i=1}^{width} \sum_{j=1}^{height} (v_{i,j} - T(\Phi_{\mathbf{w}})_{i,j})^2}{\sum_{i=1}^{width} \sum_{j=1}^{height} (v_{i,j} + T(\Phi_{\mathbf{w}})_{i,j})^2} \tag{9}
$$

subject to constraints

$$0 \le u_{i,j} \le 255$$
$$0 \le v_{i,j} \le 1$$

where u_x, u_y, v_x, v_y are the central difference approximations for x and y derivatives of $u_{i,j}$ and $v_{i,j}$ respectively:

$$u_x = \frac{u_{i+1,j} - u_{i-1,j}}{2} \quad u_y = \frac{u_{i,j+1} - u_{i,j-1}}{2}$$
$$v_x = \frac{v_{i+1,j} - v_{i-1,j}}{2} \quad v_y = \frac{v_{i,j+1} - v_{i,j-1}}{2}$$

Our algorithm recovers both pose transformation parameters t_x, t_y, θ, h and shape variability parameters $\mathbf{w}$ simultaneously along with a piecewise smooth approximation of the image u and the corresponding edge strength function v. These parameters are evaluated via gradient descent equations obtained by minimizing the energy functional with respect to each parameter. These equations are given in the appendix.

We can summarize our overall algorithm as follows:

1. Take an input image g and a set of pose and scale aligned prior edge strength functions $v_{p_1}, \cdots, v_{p_n}$.
2. Using $v_{p_1}, \cdots, v_{p_n}$, determine mean edge strength function $\overline{\Phi}$ and the principal components $\Phi_1, \cdots, \Phi_n$.
3. Initialize evolving image u with g.
4. Initialize the edge strength function using the following equation:

$$v_0 = \frac{2\alpha\rho\|\nabla u\|^2}{1 + 2\alpha\rho\|\nabla u\|^2}$$

5. Set initial values for pose transformation parameters t_x, t_y, θ, h.
6. Set initial values of shape variability parameters $w_1, \cdots, w_n$.
7. Update u according to the gradient descent equation (10).
8. Update v according to the gradient descent equation equation (11).
9. Update t_x and t_y using the equations (12) and (13) respectively.
10. Update h using equation (14).
11. Update θ using equation (15).
12. Compute the new shape variability parameters $w_1, \cdots, w_n$ using equation (16).
13. Repeat steps 7-12 until convergence.

5   Segmentation Results

We demonstrate the segmentation results of our algorithm on various images. If the image to be segmented contains a shape that does not exhibits variations other than pose, we can use a single edge strength function of the shape as the shape prior. Otherwise, to capture the shape variability, we perform Karhunen-Loeve Transform on a set of edge strength functions generated from pose and scale aligned shapes of similar type. In our experiments, we use $\mu = 1$ unless otherwise stated. In order to prevent over-smoothing, we use a small smoothing radius, i.e. $\sqrt{\frac{\alpha}{\beta}} = 0.1$. Typical ρ values are $8, 16, 32$.

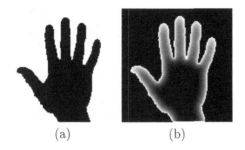

(a)   (b)

Fig. 5. (a) Prior hand shape. (b) Corresponding edge strength function computed with $\rho = 8$.

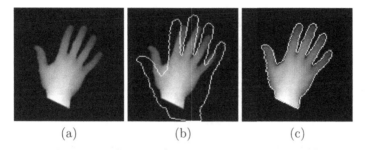

(a)   (b)   (c)

Fig. 6. Segmentation of a hand image. (a) Input image. (b) Initial 1-level curve of prior edge strength function. (c) Segmentation result.

Consider the 'hand' shape shown in Fig. 5(a), its edge strength function computed with $\rho = 8$ (given in Fig. 5(b)) is used as shape prior. Fig. 6(a) is generated from the grayscale 'hand' image by performing some translation, rotation and scaling. While the initial 1-level curve of the prior edge strength function is shown in Fig. 6(b), the final segmentation result is presented in Fig. 6(c). The recovered transformation parameters are $t_x = 4.4492$, $t_y = -7.3222$, $\theta = 24.6474°$, $h = 1.2513$.

We next consider a case with both occlusion and missing part. Fig. 7(a) is generated from the 'hand' image shown in Fig. 6(a). The thumb is occluded by a ring type shape and some part of the pointer finger is cut off. Fig. 7(b) shows the initial 1-level curve of the prior edge strength function, Fig. 7(c) shows the final segmentation result. The recovered transformation parameters are $t_x = 4.2945$, $t_y = -5.9638$, $\theta = 25.3761°$, $h = 1.2810$. Instead of taking μ constant and equal to 1, if we increase its value throughout the iterations, we can speed up the recovery process of the transformation parameters. The missing and occluded parts become apparent in the evolving edge strength function in less number of iterations(see Fig. 8).

Fig. 9(a) is generated from the 'hand' image shown in Fig. 6(a) by adding a noise. While Fig. 9(b) shows the initial 1-level curve of the prior edge strength function, Fig. 9(c) show the final segmentation result. The recovered transformation parameters are $t_x = 4.3475$, $t_y = -6.4416$, $\theta = 24.9079°$, $h = 1.2719$.

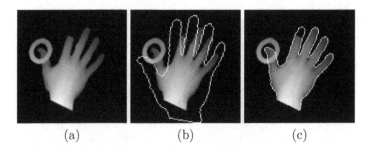

Fig. 7. Segmentation of a hand image with both occlusion and missing part. (a) Input image. (b) Initial 1-level curve of prior edge strength function. (c) Segmentation result.

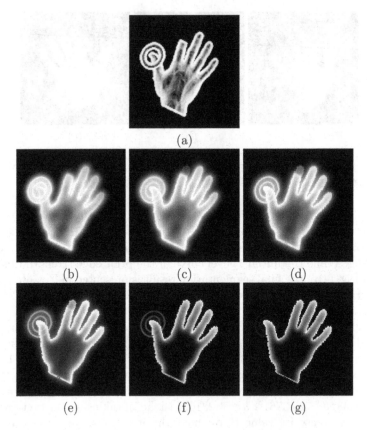

Fig. 8. Evolution of the edge strength function of the hand image given in Fig. 7(a) throughout iterations. (a) $t = 0$. (b) $t = 32$. (c) $t = 36$. (d) $t = 40$. (e) $t = 44$. (f) $t = 48$. (g) $t = 52$.

To demonstrate that our algorithm can handle shape variability in segmentation process, we have used the set of 'airplane' shapes shown in Fig. 4. After extracting the edge strength functions of each image in this data set, the mean

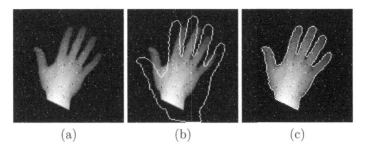

(a)   (b)   (c)

Fig. 9. Segmentation of a noisy hand image. (a) Input image. (b) Initial 1-level curve of prior edge strength function. (c) Segmentation result.

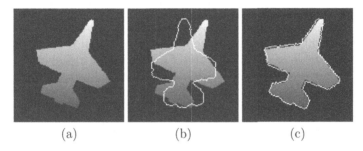

(a)   (b)   (c)

Fig. 10. Segmentation of an airplane image. (a) Input image. (b) Initial estimate of the boundary obtained from the mean edge strength function. (c) Segmentation result.

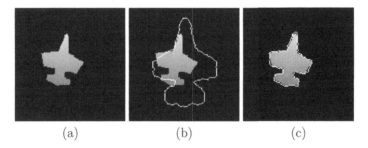

(a)   (b)   (c)

Fig. 11. Segmentation of another airplane image. (a) Input image. (b) Initial estimate of the boundary obtained from the mean edge strength function. (c) Segmentation result.

edge strength function(see Fig. 3(a)) and the principal components are computed which are used to define the shape prior. For the 'airplane' images shown in Fig. 10(a) and 11(a), initial estimates of the boundary obtained from the mean edge strength function and segmentation results are shown in 10(b)-(c) and 11(b)-(c) respectively. For the first 'airplane' image the recovered parameters are $t_x = -3.6578$, $t_y = -3.3881$, $\theta = 22.9083°$, $h = 0.9522$ and coefficients of the principle components, $\mathbf{w} = [-0.4094, -0.1463, -0.4080, -0.0919,$

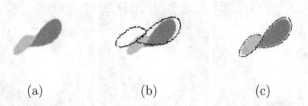

(a)   (b)   (c)

Fig. 12. (a) Input image. (b) Initial 1-level curve of prior edge strength function. (c) Segmentation result.

0.1621, 0.0832, 0.1295, 0.2282, 0.0556, 0.0264, 0.0390, 0.0053]. For the second one $t_x = 16.8324$, $t_y = -3.7704$, $\theta = 10.7317°$, $h = 1.5759$ and coefficients of the principle components, $\mathbf{w} = [-0.3846, -0.0776, -0.1361, 0.3473, -0.1117, -0.0737, -0.0053, -0.1174, 0.0958, -0.1269, 0.1143, -0.1388$.

Fig. 1(c)-(d) illustrates a case where the prior is given in the form of a line drawing with junctions. Since the curve Γ_p is no longer a simple closed curve, a level set formulation can not be devised. As Fig. 12 illustrates, the algorithm is able to extract both blobs simultaneously. The recovered transformation parameters are $t_x = -1.5529$, $t_y = 6.3731$, $\theta = -30.6071°$, $h = 1.1079$.

6   Summary

We have demonstrated the potential use of Ambrosio-Tortorelli edge strength function as an aid for incorporating shape priors into image segmentation. For large ρ values the edge strength function v provides a representation equivalent to level set representation without explicitly requiring 2 phases(inside and outside). Differential properties such as the cross derivative $\frac{d}{ds}\|\nabla v\|$ captures the local symmetry information and $1 - \left|\frac{d}{ds}\|\nabla v\|\right|$ may be interpreted as the symmetry strength and may be used as a weight to force the equivalence of the evolving v and transformed prior more on local symmetry points. These issues will be studied further.

Acknowledgments. This work is partially funded by TUBITAK-BAYG through PhD scholarships to Erkut Erdem and Aykut Erdem. The authors would like to thank Kemal Leblebicioglu and Cagri Aslan for their helpful discussions.

A   Gradient Descent Equations

The piecewise smooth image u, the edge strength function v, the translation parameters t_x, t_y, rotation angle θ, scale factor h, and shape variability parameters $\mathbf{w}$ are to be recovered as the minimizers of equation (9) by applying gradient descent:

$$\frac{\partial u_{i,j}}{\partial t} = \frac{\alpha}{2}\left[(1 - v_{i-1,j})^2(u_{i,j} - u_{i-2,j}) - (1 - v_{i+1,j})^2(u_{i+2,j} - u_{i,j})\right]$$

$$+ (1 - v_{i,j-1})^2 (u_{i,j} - u_{i,j-2}) - (1 - v_{i,j+1})^2 (u_{i,j+2} - u_{i,j})]$$
$$+ 2\beta(u_{i,j} - g_{i,j}) \tag{10}$$

$$\frac{\partial v_{i,j}}{\partial t} = -2\alpha(1 - v_{i,j})(u_x{}^2 + u_y{}^2) + \frac{v_{i,j}}{\rho}$$
$$+ \frac{\rho}{4}\left[(v_{i,j} - v_{i-2,j}) - (v_{i+2,j} - v_{i,j}) + (v_{i,j} - v_{i,j-2}) - (v_{i,j+2} - v_{i,j})\right]$$
$$+ 2\mu\left[\frac{(v_{i,j} - T(\Phi_{\mathbf{w}})_{i,j})}{S} - \frac{D(v_{i,j} + T(\Phi_{\mathbf{w}})_{i,j})}{S^2}\right] \tag{11}$$

$$\frac{\partial t_x}{\partial t} = 2\mu\left[\frac{\sum_{i=1}^{width}\sum_{j=1}^{height}(v_{i,j} - T(\Phi_{\mathbf{w}})_{i,j})\left(-\frac{\partial T(\Phi_{\mathbf{w}})}{\partial x'}\right)_{i,j}}{S}\right.$$
$$\left.- \frac{D\sum_{i=1}^{width}\sum_{j=1}^{height}(v_{i,j} + T(\Phi_{\mathbf{w}})_{i,j})\left(\frac{\partial T(\Phi_{\mathbf{w}})}{\partial x'}\right)_{i,j}}{S^2}\right] \tag{12}$$

$$\frac{\partial t_y}{\partial t} = 2\mu\left[\frac{\sum_{i=1}^{width}\sum_{j=1}^{height}(v_{i,j} - T(\Phi_{\mathbf{w}})_{i,j})\left(-\frac{\partial T(\Phi_{\mathbf{w}})}{\partial y'}\right)_{i,j}}{S}\right.$$
$$\left.- \frac{D\sum_{i=1}^{width}\sum_{j=1}^{height}(v_{i,j} + T(\Phi_{\mathbf{w}})_{i,j})\left(\frac{\partial T(\Phi_{\mathbf{w}})}{\partial y'}\right)_{i,j}}{S^2}\right] \tag{13}$$

$$\frac{\partial h}{\partial t} = 2\mu\left[\frac{\sum_{i=1}^{width}\sum_{j=1}^{height}(v_{i,j} - T(\Phi_{\mathbf{w}})_{i,j})\left(-\frac{\partial T(\Phi_{\mathbf{w}})}{\partial x'}\frac{\partial x'}{\partial h} - \frac{\partial T(\Phi_{\mathbf{w}})}{\partial y'}\frac{\partial y'}{\partial h}\right)_{i,j}}{S}\right.$$
$$\left.- \frac{D\sum_{i=1}^{width}\sum_{j=1}^{height}(v_{i,j} + T(\Phi_{\mathbf{w}})_{i,j})\left(\frac{\partial T(\Phi_{\mathbf{w}})}{\partial x'}\frac{\partial x'}{\partial h} + \frac{\partial T(\Phi_{\mathbf{w}})}{\partial y'}\frac{\partial y'}{\partial h}\right)_{i,j}}{S^2}\right] \tag{14}$$

$$\frac{\partial \theta}{\partial t} = 2\mu\left[\frac{\sum_{i=1}^{width}\sum_{j=1}^{height}(v_{i,j} - T(\Phi_{\mathbf{w}})_{i,j})\left(-\frac{\partial T(\Phi_{\mathbf{w}})}{\partial x'}\frac{\partial x'}{\partial \theta} - \frac{\partial T(\Phi_{\mathbf{w}})}{\partial y'}\frac{\partial y'}{\partial \theta}\right)_{i,j}}{S}\right.$$
$$\left.- \frac{D\sum_{i=1}^{width}\sum_{j=1}^{height}(v_{i,j} + T(\Phi_{\mathbf{w}})_{i,j})\left(\frac{\partial T(\Phi_{\mathbf{w}})}{\partial x'}\frac{\partial x'}{\partial \theta} + \frac{\partial T(\Phi_{\mathbf{w}})}{\partial y'}\frac{\partial y'}{\partial \theta}\right)_{i,j}}{S^2}\right] \tag{15}$$

$$\frac{\partial w_l}{\partial t} = 2\mu\left[\frac{\sum_{i=1}^{width}\sum_{j=1}^{height}(v_{i,j} - T(\Phi_{\mathbf{w}})_{i,j})(-T(\Phi_l)_{i,j})}{S}\right.$$
$$\left.- \frac{D\sum_{i=1}^{width}\sum_{j=1}^{height}(v_{i,j} + T(\Phi_{\mathbf{w}})_{i,j})(T(\Phi_l)_{i,j})}{S^2}\right] \tag{16}$$

where

$$D = \sum_{i=1}^{width}\sum_{j=1}^{height}(v_{i,j} - T(\Phi_{\mathbf{w}})_{i,j})^2$$

$$S = \sum_{i=1}^{width}\sum_{j=1}^{height}(v_{i,j} + T(\Phi_{\mathbf{w}})_{i,j})^2$$

References

1. L. Ambrosio and V. Tortorelli. On the approximation of functionals depending on jumps by elliptic functionals via Γ-convergence. *Commun. Pure Appl. Math.*, 43(8):999–1036, 1990.

2. C. Aslan. Disconnected skeletons for shape recognition. Master's thesis, Department of Computer Engineering, Middle East Technical University, May 2005.

3. T. Chan and L. Vese. Active contours without edges. *IEEE Trans. Image Processing*, 10(2):266–277, 2001.

4. Y. Chen, H. Tagare, S. Thiruvenkadam, F. Huang, D. Wilson, K. S. Gopinath, R. W. Briggs, and E. A. Geiser. Using prior shapes in geometric active contours in a variational framework. *Int. J. Comput. Vision*, 50(3):315–328, 2002.

5. D. Cremers, F. Tischhäuser, J. Weickert, and C. Schnörr. Diffusion snakes: Introducing statistical shape knowledge into the mumford-shah functional. *Int. J. Comput. Vision*, 50(3):295–313, 2002.

6. M. E. Leventon, W. Eric L. Grimson, and O. D. Faugeras. Statistical shape influence in geodesic active contours. In *CVPR*, pages 1316–1323, 2000.

7. D. Mumford and J. Shah. Optimal approximations by piecewise smooth functions and associated variational problems. *Commun. Pure Appl. Math.*, 42(5):577–685, 1989.

8. T. Riklin-Raviv, N. Kiryati, and N. A. Sochen. Unlevel-sets: Geometry and prior-based segmentation. In *ECCV (4)*, pages 50–61, 2004.

9. M. Rousson and N. Paragios. Shape priors for level set representations. In *ECCV (2)*, pages 78–92, 2002.

10. S. Tari, J. Shah, and H. Pien. Extraction of shape skeletons from grayscale images. *CVIU*, 66(2):133–146, May 1997.

11. A. Tsai, A. J. Yezzi, W. M. Wells III, C. Tempany, D. Tucker, A. Fan, W. E. L. Grimson, and A. S. Willsky. A shape-based approach to the segmentation of medical imagery using level sets. *IEEE Trans. Med. Imaging*, 22(2):137–154, 2003.

Spatio-temporal Prior Shape Constraint for Level Set Segmentation

Timothée Bailloeul[1,2,3,*], Véronique Prinet[1],
Bruno Serra[2], and Philippe Marthon[3]

[1] LIAMA, Institute of Automation, Chinese Academy of Sciences,
P.O Box 2728, Beijing 100080, China
Phone: (+86 10) 82 61 44 62 / Fax : (+86 10) 62 64 74 58
`tbailloeul@liama.ia.ac.cn, prinet@nlpr.ia.ac.cn`
[2] Alcatel Space, 100 bd du Midi, 06156 Cannes La Bocca, France
Phone: (+33) 4 92 92 67 26 / Fax: (+33) 4 92 92 76 60
`Bruno.Serra@space.alcatel.fr`
[3] LIMA (IRIT), 2 rue Camichel, 31071 Toulouse, France
Phone/Fax: (+33) 5 61 58 83 53
`Philippe.Marthon@enseeiht.fr`

Abstract. This paper exposes a novel formulation of prior shape constraint incorporation for the level set segmentation of objects from corrupted images. Applicable to variational frameworks, the proposed scheme consists in weighting the prior shape constraint by a function of time and space to overcome local minima issues of the energy functional. Pose parameters which make the prior shape constraint invariant from global transformations are estimated by the downhill simplex algorithm, which is more tractable and robust than the traditional gradient descent. The proposed scheme is simple, easy to implement and can be generalized to any variational approach incorporating a single prior shape. Results illustrated with different kinds of images demonstrate the efficiency of the method.

1 Introduction

Since the early nineties the incorporation of *a priori* and geometric high level information within active contours frameworks has become popular to segment objects from physically corrupted images. A constraint applied on the shape of a free form deformable model is a common approach to address the issue of object segmentation from altered data. Unlike generic geometric constraints such as contour regularization, a prior shape constraint is specific and derived from extrinsic information. It aims at restricting the space of possible shapes embodied by a segmenting curve and therefore enables to overcome image artifacts

---

* This project is supported by the Chinese MOST 863 programme and Alcatel Space. We thank Wanlin Zhu for providing the medical image used in our experiments and Ian Jermyn for the discussions we had about the proposed approach. We thank the anonymous reviewers for their remarks and suggestions.

A. Rangarajan et al. (Eds.): EMMCVPR 2005, LNCS 3757, pp. 503–519, 2005.

which influence is penalized by the shape prior constraint. The Medical Imaging community was the first to use shape constrained deformable models as it has to deal with images frequently distorted by noise, occlusions and poor contrast of organs to be segmented [1, 2, 3, 4]. The application of these model-based schemes was later extended to manufactured and natural scenes objects as well as object tracking from video sequences [5, 6, 7, 8, 9, 10, 11].

The prior shape constraint can be derived from a single or a collection of reference shapes. In the latter case statistical frameworks take advantage of the geometric variability across the different instances of the object, which conveys a larger although restricted space of possible shapes of the active contour. As a result, the segmenting curve has a globally constrained shape while being able to include local disparities contained in the training samples. Shape samples are first aligned to remove pose differences which could bias the retrieval of intrinsic shape variabilities from the database. Then a statistical prior shape model is built to determine the variability across the family of shapes. Finally the shape model is integrated in the segmentation model: the constraint could be naturally incorporated in the active contour evolution equation, exerted in the training shapes space or inserted extrinsically as a corrective term. The shape constraint integration is often invariant from a global transformation which parameters need to be estimated as the segmenting curve evolves. In [1] shapes are represented by their projection on an elliptic Fourier basis. Prior probability distributions are calculated on the representation parameters from the training samples and are used in a maximum *a posteriori* (MAP) framework to constrain the segmenting curve that captures image high gradients. In [2, 5, 3, 12] shape samples are projected in an orthogonal subspace by principal component analysis (PCA), which retains the main variations modes from the different instances. Differences arise among these schemes towards the representation of the shapes as well as the way the shape constraint is applied. In [2] the active contour is explicitly represented as a snake [13], and in [5] shapes are projected on a B-spline basis. The main limitation of the aforementioned works is their inability to make the evolving contour undergo topological changes which are naturally handled by the distance level set representation of curves [14, 15]. In [3, 12] shapes are implicitly represented by their level set functions. In [2, 12] the shape constraint is directly applied in the PCA subspace whereas it is achieved by a corrective term to the evolution equation in a MAP approach in [3]. In [5] the shape constraint incorporation is achieved through the input in an energy functional of a Mahalanobis distance measuring the discrepancy between the evolving curve and the statistical prior shape model. In [6] Paragios and Rousson propose a non-stationary pixel-wise Gaussian model which fully takes advantage of the level set representation of shapes and preserves the ability to capture local deformations.

In case the different instances of the object reduce to a sole shape prior, the training shapes space contracts to a singleton set and statistical schemes for prior shape modeling are no longer valid. As a consequence shape prior incorporation is achieved in a harder fashion as local variabilities of the contour from the reference shape are only governed by the balance between image and prior shape information. Incorporation of the shape prior can be achieved through the formulation of a distance measuring the dissimilarity between the segmenting curve and the reference shape, modulo a global transformation. In [4] shape constrained geodesic active contours are used to retrieve boundaries of corrupted objects from medical images. In this variational framework the shape distance is formalized as the sum of the squared distances between the evolving contour points and the shape prior. Unlike this edge-to-edge dissimilarity measure, surface terms comparing the active contour and the shape prior were proposed for level set segmentation [9, 10, 8]. The dissimilarity energy can be either the squared difference between the level set functions embedding the contour and the shape prior [9], or the difference of areas contained by the contour and the reference shape [8]. In the latter case, the shape energy does not depend on the image domain Ω. Further works towards shape energy independent from Ω and the extension to shape prior with multiple components can be found in [10] with the formulation of a symmetric pseudo-distance. In [7] Foulonneau *et al.* formulate a distance between high order geometric moments of the evolving curve and the shape prior to apply the constraint. The moments are projected on a Legendre polynomial basis to decrease the redundancy of the shape representation.

In this paper we argue about the sensitivity to local minima of shape constrained level segmentation in variational frameworks. We propose to address the issue of the balance between shape and image information responsible for local minima occurrence. We tackle this problem while considering a segmenting curve constrained by a single shape prior. The next section states and details further the problem we aim at resolving. The present paper formalizes and extends the work undertaken in [16] and applied to remote sensing imagery.

2   Problem Statement

Assuming the evolving active contour is implicitly represented by a signed Euclidean distance level set function ϕ [14, 15], the shape prior incorporation in variational frameworks can be generally formalized as follows:

$$J(\phi, \psi) = J_{image}(\phi) + \lambda J_{shape}(\phi, \psi) \qquad (1)$$

where J is the energy functional, J_{image} is the image-based energy which aims at driving the segmenting curve to the object boundaries and J_{shape} is the shape constraint energy that restricts possible shapes embodied by the contour. J_{shape} measures the dissimilarity between the evolving contour and a shape reference ψ. The higher the discrepancy, the higher J_{shape}:

$$J_{shape}(\phi, \psi) = \int_{\Omega} \mathcal{D}(\phi(\mathbf{x}), \psi(\mathbf{x})) \, d\mathbf{x} \qquad (2)$$

where $\mathcal{D}$ is a function measuring the distance over the image domain Ω between the active contour embedded in ϕ and the shape prior represented by the level set function ψ. The constant $\lambda \in \mathbb{R}^+$ balances the influence of the shape constraint with respect to the image information. A first issue referring to the value of the constant λ arises from equation (1). On the one hand, a too low value of λ will not enable to overcome image artifacts, i.e. the local minima of J corresponding to wrong segmentations will be numerous (in the rest of the paper these minima will be denoted as local minima of the first kind). On the other hand, a high value of λ will restrict too much the freedom of movement of the contour, thus drastically limiting the ways it can escape from local minima (second kind). To find an optimal value for λ, which could fairly balance shape and image information is not trivial since this optimum may depend on the image to be analyzed as well as the type and level of corruption of image data, which are not always known in advance. The tuning of the constant λ is a difficult task which is even more intractable when the target object to be retrieved in the image is surrounded by peripheral objects with similar statistical properties or when it is poorly discriminated from the background. Indeed in such case image information which drives the contour to the object boundaries is weakened regarding to the shape constraint which therefore becomes predominant. The shape information is then over-weighted, which leads to the second aforementioned local minima problem. This unwelcome effect is even more severe when the segmenting curve initialization is distant from the target as the convergence to the right solution become hazardous. The issue of local minima inherent to the unsuitable balance between the shape constraint and the image information is addressed in this paper. To alleviate this problem we propose to embed the shape prior in a soften fashion while spatially and temporally relaxing and reinforcing the shape constraint during the convergence process. Such flexible incorporation that we will describe in section three conveys a better control of the degrees of freedom of the segmenting curve to overcome local minima obstacles.

The distance $\mathcal{D}$ in (2) is made invariant from a global transformation which best maps the prior shape to the evolving active contour:

$$\psi = \psi_0 \circ T_\xi \tag{3}$$

where T is a global transformation which parameters are $\xi = \{\xi_1, \ldots, \xi_n\}$; ψ_0 is the static shape prior level set. Invariance from global transformation is achieved while finding the optimal parameters ξ_{opt} which minimize J_{shape}:

$$\xi_{opt} = \arg\min_{\xi} J_{shape}(\phi, \psi_0 \circ T_\xi) \tag{4}$$

The second problem we address in this paper relates to the estimation of the optimum parameters ξ_{opt} which minimize J_{shape}. According to the expression of J_{shape} it may not always be possible to analytically deduce ξ_{opt} from:

$$\left(\frac{\partial J_{shape}}{\partial \xi_i}\right)_{i=1,\ldots,n} = 0 \tag{5}$$

As a consequence numerical schemes have to be used to retrieve ξ_{opt}. A commonly adopted method is a gradient descent scheme which sequentially estimates ξ_i by

n iterative descents [2, 17, 12, 4, 6, 8]. Practical implementation of such scheme is challenging as a wrong estimation in the ith descent may bias the estimation of the $n - 1$ remaining parameters, preventing in the end to retrieve T. Cremers *et. al* touched on the problem of tuning such gradient-descent scheme for parameters optimization in [11]. They proposed an alternative way avoiding numerical optimization: invariance from translation and isotropic scaling is achieved in projecting the level set functions ϕ and ψ in their intrinsic reference systems. In his approach the scale and translation parameters are not derived from (5) but are equal to the first and second order moments of the shape. Invariance from rotation with such scheme is more challenging and not achieved yet. In this article we propose an alternative to the gradient descent scheme for pose parameters estimation during the segmentation process. The section four details our alternative based on the downhill simplex optimization method, which is parameter free and estimates the pose parameters simultaneously and more robustly. The combination of the soften shape constraint with the simplex pose parameters estimation yields some promising experimental results that are showed in section five with different kinds of images. We compare our proposed scheme with constant and simpler spatio-temporal prior shape incorporations. The performances difference between the simplex and gradient descent schemes is also investigated. Finally we discuss the proposed approach and the results illustrated in this paper and conclude in section six.

3   Spatio-temporal Shape Constraint Weight

To address the practical problem of local minima, we first turn the shape prior weight λ in equation (1) into a function of space. It is meant to relax the shape prior influence within a restricted area close to the 0-level set of the reference template ψ while preserving the original uniform shape constraint far from it. Such spatially restricted relaxation will convey a limited freedom to the evolving active contour which shape space is therefore enlarged. Consequently, the contour may globally keep the reference template shape while allowing local variations, which may be a desirable property to avoid local minima of the second kind. We propose to formalize this spatial relaxation by a symmetric function of the distance to the shape prior:

$$\lambda\left(\psi\left(\mathbf{x}\right)\right) = 1 - e^{-\left(\frac{\psi(\mathbf{x})}{d}\right)^2} \tag{6}$$

This one-parameter function has a minimum value at the 0-level set of the prior template while it increases and asymptotically tends to a constant farther. d is the parameter controlling the size of the area where the prior shape is spatially relaxed. Simpler or more intuitive formulations than (6) such as piecewise linear functions of $\psi(\mathbf{x})$ would fulfill the same relaxation requirements. However as we may empirically demonstrate and discuss further in section 5.3, the derivability and the presence of a stationary point at $\psi(\mathbf{x}) = 0$ is a property which improves the present method.

The existence of the freedom space is intended to prevent the segmenting curve from being trapped by local minima of the second kind, nevertheless it would not enable to deal with corrupted images as allowed local variations may correspond to artifacts we aim at overcoming (local minima of the first kind). We propose to temporally decrease the freedom space to $\{\emptyset\}$ in the iterative convergence process starting from time t_1. As the freedom space narrows the active contour shape space decreases, which augments the shape constraint efficiency uniformly all over the image domain. The underlying idea is to reach a rough segmentation while the prior shape constraint is spatially relaxed ($t < t_1$) and to enhance the shape penalty in a second time to overcome image alterations ($t \geq t_1$). As a result, the prior shape weight function depends on space and on time as well. The decrease of the freedom space is to be achieved in turning the parameter d into a decreasing linear function of time:

$$d(t) = \begin{cases} d_0 & \text{if } t < t_1 \\ (\varepsilon - d_0)\frac{t - t_1}{t_2 - t_1} + d_0 & \text{if } t_1 \leq t < t_2 \\ \varepsilon & \text{if } t_2 \leq t \end{cases} \tag{7}$$

where $(d_0, \varepsilon) \in \mathbb{R}^{*+}$ with $d_0 > \varepsilon$ and $\varepsilon \ll 1$.

Finally, we enhance prior shape relaxation and reinforcement in multiplying (6) by an increasing function $\lambda_a(t)$ of the convergence time t and which will globally rule the amplitude of the prior shape weight function. At the beginning of the iterative process, the amplitude of the prior shape weight is low to convey more flexibility to the evolving active contour. Starting from t_1, the amplitude increases to reach a maximum value which supports the shape constraint and enables the segmentation of corrupted objects in the image. In the end, the spatio-temporal prior shape weight function $\lambda : \mathbb{R} \times \mathbb{R} \to \mathbb{R}^+$ can be formalized as follows:

$$\lambda(t, \psi(\mathbf{x})) = \lambda_a(t)\lambda_{space}(\psi(\mathbf{x})) \tag{8}$$

where $\lambda_a(t)$ is ranging from λ_{min} and λ_{max} and is akin to the opposite function of (7) and $\lambda_{space}(\psi(\mathbf{x})) = 1 - e^{-\left(\frac{\psi(\mathbf{x})}{d(t)}\right)^2}$. The shape energy is then reformulated as:

$$J_{shape}(\phi, \psi, t) = \int_\Omega \lambda(t, \psi(\mathbf{x})) \mathcal{D}(\phi(\mathbf{x}), \psi(\mathbf{x})) d\mathbf{x} \tag{9}$$

A spatio-temporal variation of the shape prior constraint has already been carried out in [9] for a different purpose. The authors introduced a labelling function which defines where the shape constraint is applied and which evolves in space and time. As a result the segmentation scheme is able to segment familiar and corrupted objects as well as unfamiliar ones. This method was extended in [8] to similarity transformation invariance and with a different formulation of the dynamic labelling function. Satisfying results are showed for segmenting object lacking discrimination from the background, which is the point we also address here. However our approach does not make use of extrinsic labelling function, which makes our scheme simpler and more self-consistent. The figure 1

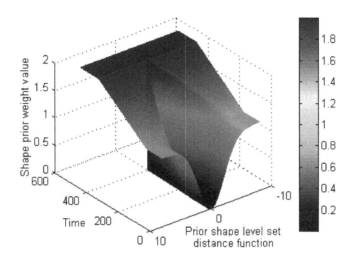

Fig. 1. Spatio-temporal shape prior weight function with $d_0 = 3$, $t_1 = 100$, $t_2 = 400$, $\lambda_{min} = 1.25$ and $\lambda_{max} = 2$

illustrates the spatio-temporal profile in three dimensions. Two questions arise from the definition of the proposed spatio-temporal shape constraint. The first deals with the choice of t_1 which should depend on the image features. As we already mentioned, a solution would be to reach a rough segmentation with a low and spatially constrained shape prior and subsequently increase the shape constraint efficiency. In that case t_1 is the time needed to reach the convergence of the coarse segmentation. The second issue applies to the influence on pose parameters estimation of discrepancies between the contour and the shape prior. Since variations from the reference template are allowed within the freedom space, it might be crucial to robustly retrieve pose parameters in spite of local discrepancies. We address the latter issue in the next section.

4   Shape Prior Invariance: A Simplex Optimization Scheme for Parameters Estimation

The sequential estimation of pose parameters by gradient descent as well as the tuning of the time step for each descent make the use of this scheme unsuitable. As the descents estimate parameters with different geometric meanings (e.g. rotation, scaling, translation, etc...), it is not clear how fast should one descent be with respect to the others. Since the n gradient descents are dependent, a slightly wrong parameter estimation in one descent might impact the $n-1$ remaining ones to finally make the pose parameters retrieval diverge. We propose to use the downhill simplex method [18] to solve the optimization problem stated in equation (4). The simplex method is an efficient zero-order iterative scheme designed to minimize non-linear cost functions. Unlike the gradient descent technique, the simplex does not use derivatives and it estimates robustly the optimal parameters. A simplex is a n-dimensional convex polyhedron defined in the parameters space by $n + 1$ vertices which evaluate the cost function with different sets of parameters ξ. Initially, the first vertex of the simplex is derived from some given initial parameters ξ_0 and the rest of the polyhedron is built in the same way while adding an individual variation δ_i to each component of ξ_0. The subsequent iterative algorithm is as follows:

1. The simplex vertices are sorted according to their corresponding cost function values. Let be **b** the best vertex among them (minimum cost function value), **w** the worst and **a** the best after **b**. As the method intends to find a minimum of the cost function, it attempts to build a new simplex far from the worst vertex **w**. To do so, one tries to replace **w** by a vertex **c** better than **b**:

2. A better candidate **c** is tested as the reflexion of **w** with respect to the hyperplane $\mathcal{H}$ opposite to **w** (reflexion of the simplex). If such **c** is better than **b** it is possible to look farther in this direction (expansion of the simplex). The best candidate among the reflexion and expansion results is chosen to replace **w**.

3. If none of the previous attempts is better than **b**, one tries two candidates $\mathbf{c_1}$ and $\mathbf{c_2}$ laying on each side of $\mathcal{H}$ and belonging to the hyper-line normal to $\mathcal{H}$ which goes through **w**. The best candidate will replace **w** if it is better than **a** (contraction of the simplex).

4. If neither $\mathbf{c_1}$ nor $\mathbf{c_2}$ is better than **a**, it means **b** is already close to the expected solution. In that case the best vertex **b** is kept and each remaining vertex is replaced by the middle point of the segment connecting it to **b**.

5. Once the new simplex is built, the algorithm loops from steps 1 to 5 until the score difference between two consecutive best vertices is below a given threshold $\varepsilon_{simplex}$. The estimated optimal parameters $\hat{\xi}_{opt}$ are the ones corresponding to the last best vertex **b**.

The main advantage of the simplex algorithm over the gradient descent scheme is the simultaneous estimation of the parameters. In that way the uneasy and intricate tuning of the n dependent gradient descents is avoided. Besides, the simplex is known to estimate more robustly parameters which values are far from ξ_0. Indeed the simplex does not need to follow gradient descent curves in the cost function space, which makes it less sensitive to local minima. However one limitation of the simplex method is its computational cost as it needs numerous evaluations of the cost function to be minimized. We will see in section 5.2 how to decrease the computational load for evaluating the cost function by using the narrow band technique. A too high number of parameters to be estimated might also increase the complexity of the simplex method. However in two dimensions, affine and projective transformations have less than ten parameters, which is manageable by the simplex. Finally, the performances of the simplex algorithm also depend on the size of the initial simplex as well as the value of $\varepsilon_{simplex}$: a large initial simplex might enable to retrieve optimal parameters far from ξ_0

at the cost of a higher computational load; a smaller $\varepsilon_{simplex}$ would yield finer estimates $\hat{\xi}_{opt}$ with longer convergence times. In the experiments detailed in the next section, we chose to estimate pose parameters after each evolution of the active contour and with $\varepsilon_{simplex} = 10^{-4}$.

5   Experiments

5.1   Image-Based and Shape Constraint Models

In our experiments we make use of the region-based formulation of the Bayesian MAP deformable model formerly proposed in [19] in order to drive the active contour to the target object in the image. This approach best befits segmentation of piecewise smooth components of an image I:

$$J_{image}(\phi) = \int_\Omega \left(\frac{(I(\mathbf{x}) - \bar{I}_{in}(\phi(\mathbf{x},t)))^2}{2\sigma_{in}^2(\phi(\mathbf{x},t))} + \ln \sqrt{2\pi\sigma_{in}^2(\phi(\mathbf{x},t))} \right) H_a(\phi(\mathbf{x},t)) \, d\mathbf{x}$$

$$+ \int_\Omega \left(\frac{(I(\mathbf{x}) - \bar{I}_{out}(\phi(\mathbf{x},t)))^2}{2\sigma_{out}^2(\phi(\mathbf{x},t))} + \ln \sqrt{2\pi\sigma_{out}^2(\phi(\mathbf{x},t))} \right) (1 - H_a(\phi(\mathbf{x},t))) \, d\mathbf{x}$$

$$(10)$$

where $\bar{I}$ and σ^2 respectively denote the image mean and variance grey level. Subscripts in and out refer to the computation of these statistical quantities inside and outside the evolving active contour:

$$\bar{I}_{in}(\phi(\mathbf{x},t)) = \frac{\int_\Omega I(\mathbf{x}) H_a(\phi(\mathbf{x},t)) \, d\mathbf{x}}{\int_\Omega H_a(\phi(\mathbf{x},t)) \, d\mathbf{x}} \tag{11}$$

$$\bar{I}_{out}(\phi(\mathbf{x},t)) = \frac{\int_\Omega I(\mathbf{x}) (1 - H_a(\phi(\mathbf{x},t))) \, d\mathbf{x}}{\int_\Omega (1 - H_a(\phi(\mathbf{x},t))) \, d\mathbf{x}} \tag{12}$$

$$\sigma_{in}^2(\phi(\mathbf{x},t)) = \frac{\int_\Omega (I(\mathbf{x}) - \bar{I}_{in}(\phi(\mathbf{x},t)))^2 H_a(\phi(\mathbf{x},t)) \, d\mathbf{x}}{\int_\Omega H_a(\phi(\mathbf{x},t)) \, d\mathbf{x}} \tag{13}$$

$$\sigma_{out}^2(\phi(\mathbf{x},t)) = \frac{\int_\Omega (I(\mathbf{x}) - \bar{I}_{out}(\phi(\mathbf{x},t)))^2 (1 - H_a(\phi(\mathbf{x},t))) \, d\mathbf{x}}{\int_\Omega (1 - H_a(\phi(\mathbf{x},t))) \, d\mathbf{x}} \tag{14}$$

The active contour is embedded as a level set function ϕ, which is assumed to be positive inside the contour. H_a represents a regularized approximation of the Heaviside function. Edge-based and contour regularization terms have been intentionally omitted in (10) since we only investigate region-based active contours. Besides, the shape constraint to be introduced will act as a contour regularizer. We chose the shape constraint energy independent from the domain Ω and proposed in [8]. It measures the discrepancy between areas included in the evolving active contour and the shape prior:

$$\mathcal{D}(\phi(\mathbf{x}), \psi(\mathbf{x})) = (H_a(\phi(\mathbf{x})) - H_a(\psi(\mathbf{x})))^2 \tag{15}$$

The gradient of the overall energy functional J with respect to the level set function ϕ yields the following active contour evolution equation:

$$\phi\left(\mathbf{x},t\right)_t = \delta_a\left(\phi\left(\mathbf{x},t\right)\right)\left\{-\frac{\left(I\left(\mathbf{x}\right) - \bar{I}_{in}\left(\phi\left(\mathbf{x},t\right)\right)\right)^2}{2\sigma_{in}^2\left(\phi\left(\mathbf{x},t\right)\right)} + \frac{\left(I\left(\mathbf{x}\right) - \bar{I}_{out}\left(\phi\left(\mathbf{x},t\right)\right)\right)^2}{2\sigma_{out}^2\left(\phi\left(\mathbf{x},t\right)\right)}\right.$$

$$\left. + \ln\left(\frac{\sigma_{out}^2\left(\phi\left(\mathbf{x},t\right)\right)}{\sigma_{in}^2\left(\phi\left(\mathbf{x},t\right)\right)}\right) + 2\lambda\left(t,\psi\left(\mathbf{x}\right)\right)\left[H_a\left(\phi\left(\mathbf{x},t\right)\right) - H_a\left(\psi\left(\mathbf{x},t\right)\right)\right]\right\} \quad (16)$$

5.2   Invariance from Similarity Transformation and Algorithm

In these experiments we propose to consider invariance from a similarity transformation which includes isotropic scaling, rotation and translation:

$$T\mathbf{x} = s\begin{bmatrix} \cos\theta & -\sin\theta \\ \sin\theta & \cos\theta \end{bmatrix}\mathbf{x} + \begin{bmatrix} \mu_x \\ \mu_y \end{bmatrix} \quad (17)$$

with the scaling factor noted as s ($s \in \mathbb{R}^{*+}$), θ refers to the rotation angle and μ to the translation. As demonstrated in [20], the relationship between a level set function and its transformed by similarity is solved analytically, which eases the computation of $\psi\left(\mathbf{x},t\right)$. We use the narrow banding technique to decrease the computational cost of our algorithm. The reason for using such technique is twofold. First it decreases the cost for evolving the active contour and re-distancing the level set function ϕ. Second, it can also decrease the computational cost of the simplex-based pose parameters estimation. Indeed the evaluation of the cost function J_{shape} using equation (9), which is needed to build the simplex vertices, can be reduced by computing shape discrepancies within a narrow band around the 0-level set of ϕ:

$$J_{shape}\left(\phi,\psi\right) = \int_\Omega N\left(\phi\left(\mathbf{x}\right),\varepsilon_b\right)\lambda\left(t,\psi\left(\mathbf{x}\right)\right)\mathcal{D}\left(\phi\left(\mathbf{x}\right),\psi\left(\mathbf{x}\right)\right)d\mathbf{x} \quad (18)$$

where the function $N\left(\phi\left(\mathbf{x}\right),\varepsilon_b\right)$ is equal to 1 if $\left|\phi\left(\mathbf{x}\right)\right| \leq \varepsilon_b$, otherwise it is equal to 0. The band half size ε_b is then a compromise between computational efficiency and the pose parameters accuracy: a too narrow band will not yield a discriminative measure of discrepancy, which may lead the simplex optimization to erroneous results. A systematic re-initialization of the level set function ϕ is also needed to provide a good measure of dissimilarity with the shape prior and therefore an accurate pose parameters estimation. The segmentation algorithm can be expressed as follows:

1. For a given prior shape, initialize pose parameters: $s\left(t = 0\right) = 1$, $\theta\left(t = 0\right) = 0$, $\mu\left(t = 0\right) = \mathbf{0}$ and build $\psi\left(\mathbf{x},t = 0\right)$. Initialize $\phi\left(\mathbf{x},t = 0\right)$ within a narrow band.
2. Evolve the active contour according to (16).
3. Re-initialize $\phi\left(\mathbf{x},t\right)$ within a narrow band.
4. Retrieve and update pose parameters ($s\left(t\right)$, $\theta\left(t\right)$, $\mu\left(t\right)$) using the simplex.

5. While the contour has not converged loop steps 2 to 5. Otherwise trigger the shape constraint weight function increase ($t = t_1$).
6. Repeat steps 2 to 4 until final convergence.

In our experiments a narrow band half size of three pixels yields satisfying results and re-initialization is achieved in using the fast scheme presented in [21]. We adapted the latter method to preserve sub-pixel accuracy of the segmenting curve.

5.3   Results and Discussion

We show experimental results with three different kinds of 2D grey-level images. The first image depicts a manufactured toy extracted from the Amsterdam Library of Object Images (ALOI). The second and third apply to remote sensing and medical imaging respectively. Prior shapes used in experiments represent the exact boundaries of the object we aim at segmenting. In the case of remote sensing imagery, prior shape knowledge might come from cartographic data as we showed in [16]. A perfect single prior shape is however not realistic in the case of medical imaging since shape variabilities of organs across patients, views and acquisition means compel to use statistical frameworks. Nevertheless, we performed experiments with the brain image in order to demonstrate the robustness our scheme on a wider range of images which exhibit a lack of discrimination of the target from the background. In the following experiments, the initial contour is similar to the shape prior and transformed by a similarity transformation which parameters are called $\xi_{ini} = (s_{ini}, \theta_{ini}, \mu_{ini})$ in the rest of the paper. We propose to quantify and compare the performances of the simplex and gradient descent schemes in computing the absolute error between ξ_{ini} and their estimates $\hat{\xi}_{opt}$ retrieved by each method (table 1). We refer the reader to [8] for implementation details about the gradient descent technique. As the shape priors perfectly match the objects to be segmented in the images, the quantitative results of table 1 also measure the accuracy of the segmentation achieved

Table 1. Absolute errors between the initial similarity transformation parameters ξ_{ini} and their estimates $\hat{\xi}_{opt}$ by the simplex and gradient descent schemes

Experiments	Absolute	error	
	$\Delta\theta$ in degrees	Δs	$\Delta\mu$ in pixels
1. Spatio-temporal λ + simplex, fig. 2.c	-0.6	0.05	$(-0.2, -0.05)$
2. Spatio-temporal λ + simplex, fig. 3.a	-0.1	-0.01	$(-0.04, -0.60)$
3. Spatio-temporal λ + simplex, fig. 3.b	1.0	0.00	$(0.65, -0.15)$
4. Spatio-temporal λ + simplex, fig. 3.c	-0.2	0.00	$(0.25, -0.02)$
5. $\lambda = cst$ + simplex, fig. 5.a	0.9	0.05	$(-0.12, -0.20)$
6. $\lambda = cst$ + grad. desc, fig. 5.b	0.9	0.05	$(-0.15, -0.20)$
7. Spatio-temporal λ + grad. desc, fig. 5.c	-4.0	-0.08	$(0.65, -3.30)$
8. Spatio-temporal λ + grad. desc, fig. 5.d	122.6	-0.20	$(0.50, -3.70)$

by the spatio-temporal weighting technique.The first experiment illustrates the efficiency of the proposed scheme with a simple case and $s_{ini} = 2$, $\theta_{ini} = \pi$, $\mu_{ini} = (10, -10)$ (fig. 2). We compare the results obtained with a constant prior shape weight ($\lambda = 100$, $\lambda = 10$) and our scheme. The case ($\lambda = 100$) illustrates the lack of flexibility of the active contour because of a predominant shape constraint (fig. 2.a where λ is intentionally high). The constraint prevents and penalizes the motion of the active contour which image-based force is not significant enough to segment accurately the border of the object. In that case the correct pose parameters can not be estimated and the contour finally reached a local minimum of the functional corresponding to an unsatisfying segmentation result. In the second case ($\lambda = 10$), the shape constraint is not strong enough to cope with the erasure which corrupts the object in the image (fig. 2.b), which also corresponds to a local minimum of the energy. Finally the spatio-temporal scheme shows how a low and spatially constrained shape prior weight enables to reach a rough segmentation which is at the end improved when the constraint is reinforced. The resulting segmentation is satisfying (fig. 2.c) and the pose parameters are estimated with a good accuracy (table 1, row 1). The second set of experiments is performed with images which exhibit lack of discrimination of the target object from the background and the proposed spatio-temporal scheme (fig. 3). In the first case the toy pattern was flipped, resized and duplicated to make a background with similar local radiometric properties to the target. In the first experiment (fig. 3.a), the initial contour is transformed according to $s_{ini} = 0.75$, $\theta_{ini} = \pi/4$, $\mu_{ini} = (10, -10)$. We can see that peripheral patterns

(a)

(b)

(c)

Fig. 2. Segmenting curve evolution from left to right: comparison between constant and spatio-temporal shape prior weight. (a) $\lambda = 100$, (b) $\lambda = 10$ (c) spatio-temporal function with $d_0 = 10$, $\lambda_{min} = 20$ and $\lambda_{max} = 100$.

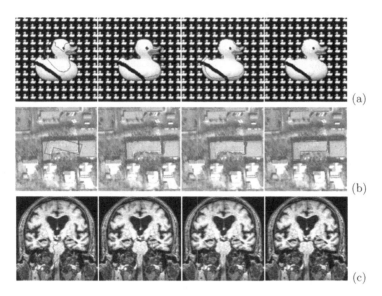

Fig. 3. Segmenting curve evolution (from left to right) with spatio-temporal shape prior weight function and lack of discrimination of the target from the background. (a) $d_0 = 15$, $\lambda_{min} = 15$ and $\lambda_{max} = 100$ (b) $d_0 = 7$, $\lambda_{min} = 27$ and $\lambda_{max} = 70$ (c) $d_0 = 10$, $\lambda_{min} = 50$ and $\lambda_{max} = 100$.

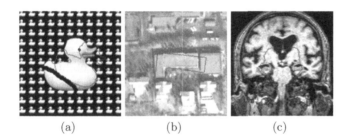

(a)   (b)   (c)

Fig. 4. Failed segmentations with constant shape prior weight and lack of discrimination from background. (a) $\lambda = 20$ (b) $\lambda = 50$ (c) $\lambda = 70$.

similar to the target do not affect the final segmentation result. Indeed, during the convergence process the prior shape is flexible enough to allow segmentation of the patterns and topology changes. At the end of the process, the target is correctly segmented as the erasure artifact is overcome by constraint enhancement. The effect of the freedom space is visible in figure 3.a as small toy patterns are segmented within a neighborhood of the main segmenting curve. The figure 4.a shows the unsuccessful segmentation result obtained with a constant shape constraint ($\lambda = 20$). The over-estimated shape weight restricts the motion of the active contour which is trapped by a local minimum. The second case applies to a remote sensing image depicting two buildings with similar radiometric properties (fig. 3.b, fig. 4.b). In this case we expect to segment the L-shaped building in the center of the image. The initial contour is transformed according to $s_{ini} = 1.0$, $\theta_{ini} = 0.3$, $\mu_{ini} = (7, -5)$. The segmentation process in figure 3.b shows how the spatio-temporal scheme conveys flexibility to the segmenting curve while avoiding to segment the squared building nearby the target. A hard and constant shape prior incorporation yields the unsuccessful segmentation of parts of both buildings (fig. 4.b). The main reason of such result is the inability of the segmenting curve to split at the border between the two buildings because of a two high shape constraint. As a result, a part of the second building is also segmented as it shares similar image statistical properties to the target. Finally the ability of the segmenting curve to undergo topological changes is yet illustrated with the medical image in figure 3.c ($s_{ini} = 1.1$, $\theta_{ini} = 0.7$, $\mu_{ini} = (3, 3)$). The spatially constrained active contour prevents from spreading all over the image while retaining local flexibility within the freedom space and yields the correct solution opposed to the constant shape constraint (fig. 4.c). The quantitative results of these three cases (table 1, rows 2 to 4) validate the performances of the simplex algorithm as well as our spatio-temporal scheme. Indeed, the absolute error between the initial transform and its estimate is less than one degree for the angle, less than one pixel for the translation and less than 0.05 for the scale factor. Results displayed in figure 5 compare the simplex and gradient descent schemes for the estimation of the similarity transformation parameters. The two first experiments carried out with a simple case ($s_{ini} = 1.5$, $\theta_{ini} = \pi/4$, $\mu_{ini} = (2, 0)$) show comparable good results with a constant prior shape weight, which is confirmed by the parameter estimate errors (table 1, rows 5-6). However the two last results are wrong segmentations with the spatio-temporal schemes and the gradient descent (fig. 5.c-d) whereas they were successful with the simplex algorithm (fig. 3.a, fig. 2.c). Sensitivity to local minima of the gradient descent scheme might explain these incorrect segmentations. The comparison of the parameters estimations (table 1, rows 2&7 and 1&8) also demonstrates that the simplex outperforms the gradient descent in these cases. In the end, we com-

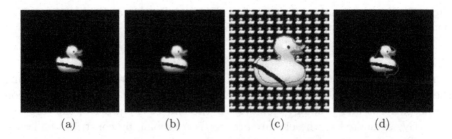

(a)   (b)   (c)   (d)

Fig. 5. Segmentation results comparison with the simplex and the gradient descent schemes. (a-b) successful results with $\lambda = 75$: (a) simplex method (b) gradient descent. (c-d) unsuccessful results of the grad. desc method with the spatio-temporal scheme: (c) $d_0 = 15$, $\lambda_{min} = 15$ and $\lambda_{max} = 100$ (d) $d_0 = 10$, $\lambda_{min} = 20$ and $\lambda_{max} = 100$.

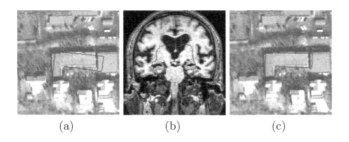

(a)   (b)   (c)

Fig. 6. Failed segmentations with: (a) sole temporal variation of the shape prior weight amplitude between $\lambda_{min} = 30$ and $\lambda_{max} = 70$ (no spatial relaxation). (b) spatio-temporal model with ramp-like spatial profile. (c) spatio-temporal model with no time transition (Heaviside step function for $\lambda_a(t)$ and $d(t)$).

pare our spatio-temporal shape constraint scheme exposed in (8) with simpler temporal and spatial profiles functions. In figure 6.a is displayed the segmentation result with a sole temporal weight variation (no spatial relaxation) using the same $(\lambda_{min}, \lambda_{max})$ values as the experiment carried out in figure 3.b. This result is unsuccessful unlike the spatio-temporal case. With the purely temporal method, the low shape constraint applied at the beginning of the convergence process does not allow to overcome image artifacts because of the lack of spatial flexibility. As a consequence, the segmenting curve diverges from the target and biases pose parameters estimation. When the shape constraint is reinforced at the end, the curve is far from the target with a significant shape weight, which makes the segmentation process very sensitive to local minima and explain the erroneous result. The second experiment similar to the one in figure (3.c) was carried out with the proposed spatio-temporal technique but with a different spatial profile. Instead of the exponential formulation, a simpler piecewise linear function was used: $\lambda_{space}(\psi(\mathbf{x})) = |\psi(\mathbf{x})| / (2d(t))$ if $|\psi(\mathbf{x})| < 2d(t)$, else $\lambda_{space}(\psi(\mathbf{x})) = 1$. With this more intuitive ramp-like spatial profile, the result is incorrect (fig. 6.b). Such profile reinforces too much the weight in a very close neighborhood of the prior shape. As a result, the segmenting curve is not flexible enough to roughly capture the object in the image and prevents from a good result when the shape constraint is enhanced. Attempts with a larger freedom space to cope with this drawback would not yield better results as the shape constraint would be too loose in space. The proposed spatial profile in (8) alleviates this problem since it enables a low weight close to the reference template while retaining a strong constraint farther. Finally, we repeat the experiment of figure 3.b while replacing the temporal profiles $\lambda_a(t)$ and $d(t)$ by two Heaviside step functions. The shape constraint is then suddenly enhanced instead of progressively. The unsuccessful result of figure 6.c shows that the spatio-temporal scheme proposed originally performs better. Before shape constraint reinforcement, the pose parameters estimation can be slightly biased as the contour roughly segments the object in the image. A progressive reduction of the freedom space and increase of the constraint amplitude is therefore needed for the parameters estimation scheme to catch up with the evolving curve which converges to the target because of its gradually enhanced regularization. Such adjusting procedure is not possible with a sudden constraint application as the active contour directly embodies the prior shape with inaccurate pose parameters. As a consequence, the evolving curve might be far from the target with a high and uniform shape constraint, which makes it sensitive to local minima and prevents from satisfying segmentation (fig. 6.c).

6 Conclusion

We have presented a soften single shape prior incorporation for model-based level set segmentation of objects from corrupted data in variational frameworks. The proposed scheme is intended to circumvent the difficult tuning of the weight balancing shape and image information. Most of the time this constant parameter is under or over-estimated, which yields unsuccessful segmentation results corresponding to local minima of the energy functional. The proposed shape constraint is spatially relaxed in a neighborhood of the prior shape to overcome the issue of local minima. The constraint is later enhanced to overcome image data corruptions. Experiments carried out with different kinds of images demonstrated the efficiency of our spatio-temporal approach compared to the shape prior integration achieved by a constant constraint. We also empirically demonstrated the good performances of our approach with respect to simpler temporal and spatial profile functions. Future works may be dedicated to the building up of a theoretical basis enabling to retrieve such profile functions from the image and shape prior information instead of the exposed ad hoc definitions. Besides, we have proposed an alternative to the gradient descent scheme for pose parameters estimation by using the downhill simplex method. The simplex algorithm is easier to tune and estimates more robustly pose parameters than the gradient descent scheme. Practically more tractable, the proposed method is simple, easy to implement and can be applied to any segmentation problem incorporating single prior shape constraints.

References

1. Staib, L.H., Duncan, J.S.: Boundary finding with parametrically deformable models. IEEE Transactions on Pattern Analysis and Machine Intelligence **14** (1992) 1061-1075
2. Cootes, T., Cooper, D., Taylor, C., Graham, J.: Active shape models - their training and application. Computer Vision and Image Understanding. **61** (1995) 38-59
3. Leventon, M., Grimson, E., Faugeras., O.: Statistical shape influence in geodesic active contours. Comp. Vision and Patt. Recon. (CVPR) (2000)
4. Chen, Y., Tagare, H., Thiruvenkadam, S., Huang, F., Wilson, D., Gopinath, K., Briggs, R., Geiser, E.: Using prior shapes in geometric active contours in a variational framework. International Journal of Computer Vision 50(3): 315-328 (2002)
5. Cremers, D., Tischhauser, F., Weickert, J., Schnorr, C.: Diffusion snakes : introducing statistical shape knowledge into the mumford-shah functional. ICCV (2002)

6. Paragios, N., Rousson, M.: Shape priors for level set representations. European Conference in Computer Vision **2** (2002) 78–92
7. Foulonneau, A., Charbonnier, P., Heitz, F.: Geometric shape priors for region-based active contours. IEEE Int. Conf. Image Processing, ICIP 2003 (2003)
8. Chan, T., Zhu, W.: Level set based shape prior segmentation. Technical report, UCLA (2003)
9. Cremers, D., Sochen, N., Schnörr, C.: Towards recognition-based variational segmentation using shape priors and dynamic labeling. Intl. Conf. on Scale-Space Theories in Computer Vision (2003)
10. Cremers, D., Soatto, S.: A pseudo-distance for shape priors in level set segmentation. Proc. ICCV'2003 (2003)
11. Cremers, D., Osher, S., Soatto, S.: Kernel density estimation and intrinsic alignment for knowledge-driven segmentation: teaching level sets to walk. DAGM'04: 26th Pattern Recognition Symposium (2004)
12. Tsai, A., Yezzi, A., Wells, W., Tempany, C., Tucker, D., Fan, A., Grimson, E., Willsky, A.: Model-based curve evolution technique for image segmentation. IEEE Conference on Computer Vision and Pattern Recognition **1** (2001) 463–468
13. Kass, M., Witkin, A., Terzopoulos, D.: Snakes : active contour models. 1st International Conference on Computer Vision, pp. 259-268 (1987)
14. Osher, S., Sethian, J.: Fronts propagating with curvature-dependent speed: algorithms based on Hamilton-Jacobi formulations. Journal of Computational Physics, 79, pp. 12-49 (1988)
15. Sethian, J.: Level set methods and fast marching methods: evolving interfaces in computational geometry, fluid mechanics, computer vision and materials science. Cambridge University Press (1999)
16. Bailloeul, T., Prinet, V., Serra, B., Marthon, P., Chen, P., Zhang, H.: Digital building map refinement from knowledge-driven active contours and very high resolution optical imagery. Proc. ISPRS Hannover Workshop (2005)
17. Chen, Y., Thiruvenkadam, S., Tagare, H., Huang, F., Wilson, D., Geiser, E.A.: On the incorporation of shape priors into geometric active contours. IEEE 1st Worshop on Vatiational Framework and Level Sets methods (2001)
18. Nelder, J., Mead, R.: A simplex method for function minimization. Computer Journal **7** (1965) 308–313
19. Paragios, N., Deriche, R.: Geodesic active regions: A new paradigm to deal with frame partition problems in computer vision. Journal of Visual Communication and Image Representation, **13** (2002) 249–268
20. Paragios, N., Rousson, M., Ramesh, V.: Matching distance functions: A shape-to-area variational approach for global-to-local registration. European Conference in Computer Vision (2002)
21. Yui, S., Hara, K., Zha, H., Hasegawa, T.: A fast narrow band method and its application in topology-adaptative 3-d modeling. 16th Intl Conf. on Pattern Recognition (ICPR'02) Vol. 4 (2002)

A New Implicit Method for Surface Segmentation by Minimal Paths: Applications in 3D Medical Images

Roberto Ardon[1,2], Laurent D. Cohen[2], and Anthony Yezzi[3]

[1] MEDISYS-Philips France, 51, rue Carnot, 92156 Suresnes, France
[2] CEREMADE-Université Paris Dauphine,
Place du Marchal de Lattre de Tassigny, 75775 Paris Cedex 16, France
[3] Georgia Institute of Technology, Atlanta, GA, USA
roberto.ardon@philips.com, cohen@ceremade.dauphine.fr,
ayezzi@ece.gatech.edu

Abstract. We introduce a novel implicit approach for single object segmentation in 3D images. The boundary surface of this object is assumed to contain two known curves (the constraining curves), given by an expert. The aim of our method is to find this surface by exploiting as much as possible the information given in the supplied curves. As for active surfaces, we use a cost potential which penalizes image regions of low interest (most likely areas of low gradient or away from the surface to be extracted). In order to avoid local minima, we introduce a new partial differential equation and use its solution for segmentation. We show that the zero level set of this solution contains the constraining curves as well as a set of paths joining them. These paths globally minimize an energy which is defined from the cost potential. Our approach is in fact an elegant, implicit extension to surfaces of the minimal path framework already known for 2D image segmentation. As for this previous approach, and unlike other variational methods, our method is not prone to local minima traps of the energy. We present a fast implementation which has been successfully applied to 3D medical and synthetic images.

Keywords: Image segmentation, Active contours, Minimal Paths, Level Set method, Object Extraction, Stationary Transport Equation.

1 Introduction

Since their introduction by Kass et al. [15], deformable models have been extensively used to find single and multiple objects in 2D and 3D images. The common use of these models consists in introducing an initial object in the image and deforming it until it reaches a desired target. In most applications, the evolution of the object is chosen in order to most rapidly reduce an energy involving the image data, until a steady state is reached. One of the main drawbacks of this approach is that it suffers from local minima 'traps'. This is the case when the steady state, reached by the active object, does not correspond to the target but to another local minimum of the energy. An immediate consequence of this behavior is that the active object's initialization is a crucial step, since the final result depends strongly upon it. Since the publication of [15], much work has been done in order to free active models from the problem of local minima.

A. Rangarajan et al. (Eds.): EMMCVPR 2005, LNCS 3757, pp. 520–535, 2005.

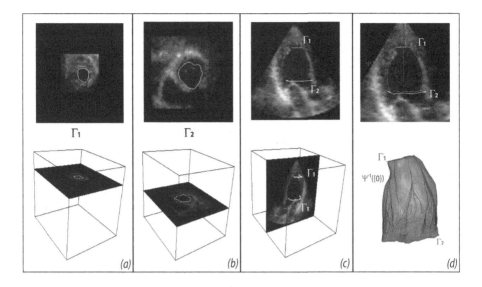

Fig. 1. 3D ultrasound volume of a left ventricle: (a) and (b) show the two parallel slices where the user given curves Γ_1 and Γ_2 are drawn. (c) shows a slice perpendicular to the curves in order to show their position with respect to the ventricle. Finally (d) shows the surface containing the constraint curves obtained with our approach. In the upper position we have shown the intersection of the zero level set of Ψ with a vertical plane. In the lower position we have traced some minimal paths between the two constraining curves and a 3D representation of the zero level set, the minimal paths are traced on this surface.

A balloon force was early proposed in [8] to make the model more active and to cope with the shrinking problem, but this force assumes a known direction in the evolution. The introduction of region dependent energies [9, 27, 19] and the use of shape priors approaches [26], contributed to create a more robust framework. In order to avoid local minima of the active contours, [10] proposed an approach to find a global minimum of the energy. However their approach cannot be extended to find the global minimum for an active surface in a 3D image.

In this work, we focus on a novel approach for 3D single object segmentation where the resulting surface globally minimizes a given energy. Our aim is to generate a surface that contains a couple of 'constraining' curves (Γ_1 and Γ_2) and which is also a segmentation of an object. Γ_1 and Γ_2 are supposed to be traced by an expert[1] on the surface to be segmented. Our approach is based on implicitly generating a surface that contains the set of paths globally minimizing an image energy and connecting Γ_1 and Γ_2. Moreover, the constraining curves are the only input for the initialization of our model. The paths linking Γ_1 and Γ_2 are globally minimal with respect to an energy of the form $\int_\Gamma \widetilde{\mathcal{P}}$. If the incremental cost $\widetilde{\mathcal{P}}$ is chosen to take lower values on the contours of the 3D image, in particular on the surface of the object to be extracted, global min-

---

[1] Notice that the expert may obtain these curves with a 2D active contour or interactive tool like with the minimal path approach in [13].

imal paths will help finding the boundary of the object (see section 2 and [10]). This fact has been exploited in previous work [2, 3], where a network of a *finite* number of minimal paths was computed between the two constraining curves and then extended, by means of interpolation, to a segmentation surface of the object.

Although this approach gave good results, particularly in ultrasound 3D images, the topology of the network was often problematic (paths tend to merge and only few points of Γ_1 are to be reached, see figure 1.d) considerably complicating the generation of the segmenting surface and, in the worst cases, leading to bad segmentations (figure 3.b).

Our work presented herein, although based on similar ideas, is much more than an implicit extension of the network approach. The surface generated by our algorithm is *completely* composed of *globally* minimal paths, and in particular, it contains all the minimal paths of the network introduced in [3]. Indeed, by solving a stationary transport equation of the form: $\nabla \Psi . \nabla U = 0$, where U is the action map (defined in section 3) and Ψ is the unknown, we show in section 4 that Ψ is such that: *any* minimal path between the constraining curves is contained in its zero level set $\Psi^{-1}(\{0\})$. We also prove that for almost any point of this level set, the minimal path between this point and Γ_1 is contained as well in $\Psi^{-1}(\{0\})$. This property is the key point explaining the good performance of our algorithm. In section 5 we give some results obtained by our method on synthetic and real data.

As an illustration of our problem, we give in figures 1.a, 1.b and 1.c an example of the user input to our algorithm. We perform the segmentation of a 3D ultrasound volume of the left ventricle. In figure 1.d we show the output of our method, which is the zero level set of function Ψ. We have also traced, for demonstration purposes, some minimal paths joining points of Γ_2 to Γ_1, which are clearly displayed on the segmented surface.

2   Minimal Paths in 2D Images

2.1   Active Contour Model

The first active contour model was introduced by Kass *et al.* in the seminal paper [15]. Their model, the well known 'snakes', consists in finding a curve $\mathcal{C}$ (parametrized on interval $[0, 1]$ and traced on the image) that minimizes the energy,

$$E_s(\mathcal{C}) = \int_0^1 \left\{ \alpha \left\| C'(x) \right\|^2 + \beta \left\| C''(x) \right\|^2 + \mathcal{P}(\mathcal{C}(x)) dx \right\}, \qquad (1)$$

where α and β are positive constants. The minimization of the first two terms of E_s induces the curve $\mathcal{C}$ to have a relatively high regularity, while the minimization of the latter is intended to drive the curve toward significant edges of the image. In fact, Finding a curve that minimizes energy E is not a simple task; this functional is defined on the infinitely dimensioned space of regular curves and, generally, it is non-convex. The potential function $\mathcal{P}$ usually represents an edge detector that has lower values along edges. A common choice for this function is $\mathcal{P} = (1 + |\nabla I|^2)^{-1}$, if I is the image. Finding a curve that minimizes the energy E_s is not a simple task; this functional is defined on an infinite dimensional space and, generally, it is non-convex. The usual approach is based on finding a local minimum of E_{snake} by evolving an initial curve C_0 under the time dependent equation: $\frac{\partial C(x,t)}{\partial t} - \alpha\frac{\partial^2 C(x,t)}{\partial x^2} + \beta\frac{\partial^4 C(x,t)}{\partial x^4} = -\nabla P(C)$, with $C(\cdot,0) = C_0$. By this approach, the final curve C is strongly dependent on the initialization C_0. Since the method was originally intended to interactively segment a single object in the image, this behavior is rather natural. Nonetheless, if C_0 is too far from the object to extract, the evolving curve can be trapped in another local minimum, thus giving an unsatisfactory result.

2.2   Active Contours and Minimal Paths

In order to obtain global minimization in the active contours framework, Cohen and Kimmel [10] simplified the energy by choosing $\beta = 0$ in the expression (1) of E_s. Additionally, they propose to use arclength parameterization (here noted s). Thus, they look for the curve minimizing energy

$$E(C) = \int_0^L \left\{\alpha + P\big(C(s)\big)\right\} ds \tag{2}$$

where L is the length of curve C and s its arclength parameterization (in the rest of this paper we shall note $\widetilde{P} = \alpha + P$). Even though this is the same energy proposed by Caselles *et al.*[6] and Yezzi *et al.* [24], used in the well-known geodesic active contour model, Cohen and Kimmel choose a completely different approach for the minimization of E. Instead of using an evolution equation as in [6, 15, 24], they exploit a method capable of building a curve between two points (p_1 and p_2) which is the global minimum of E among all the curves joining these points. This minimum is called a minimal path. Their approach is based on the fact that a minimal path between p_2 and p_1 can be obtained by 'back propagation', solving : $\frac{dC}{dx}(x) = -\nabla U_{p_1}\big(C(x)\big)$ with $C(0) = p_2$. Where the real function U_{p_1}, called the minimal action map, is defined at each point q of the image domain by: $U_{p_1}(q) = \inf\left\{\int_0^L \widetilde{P}(C(s))ds\right\}$. Where the inf is taken among all curves such that $C(0) = p_1$ and $C(L) = q$. In order to compute U_{p_1}, Cohen and Kimmel [10] use the fact (a proof of this fact can be found in [5]) that this map is solution to the well known Eikonal equation :

$$\|\nabla U_{p_1}\| = \widetilde{P} \text{ and } U_{p_1}(p_1) = 0. \tag{3}$$

This equation is numerically solved by Cohen and Kimmel using the 'Fast marching' algorithm in order to compute a minimal path ([10]).

3   From Global Minimal Paths to 3D Surface Extraction

The method introduced in [10] can easily be extended for the construction of minimal paths between two points in a 3D image [12]. In that case, the formalism given in the previous section is unchanged, except for the fact that the functions $\widetilde{P}, U_{p_1}$ are defined (and C takes its values) on a 3D domain. The authors of [12] used it to find centerlines in 3D tubular structures. As in the previous section, the cost function $\widetilde{P}$ is supposed to have lower values on a surface to be extracted from the 3D image. Before reviewing ideas in [2, 3], where the minimal path framework was extended to the extraction of surfaces between two given curves Γ_1 and Γ_2, we give for comparison purposes a brief description of the (now classical) geodesic active surface approach.

3.1 Background on Active Surfaces

The active surface model, introduced in [7], is a variational approach for the segmentation of objects in 3D images. In the same spirit as geodesic active contours, it is based on finding a surface which minimizes an energy of the form:

$$E_S(S) = \int_O \mathcal{P}(S) \left\| \frac{\partial S}{\partial u} \wedge \frac{\partial S}{\partial v} \right\| du dv, \tag{4}$$

where (u, v) are the parameters of S, defined on the open set $O \subset \mathbb{R}^2$. The most common procedure for finding a local minimum of this energy is to deform, until convergence, an initial surface S_0, according to the evolution equation:

$$\frac{\partial S}{\partial t} = \mathcal{P} H N_S - (\nabla \mathcal{P} . N_S) N_S \text{ with } S(\cdot, \cdot, 0) = S_0, \tag{5}$$

H being the mean curvature of S and N_S its normal. This implies that the final surface is the local minimum of E_S which is "closest" to S_0. As with geodesic active contours, this method lacks robustness with respect to S_0. In [2] a method was suggested, based on minimal paths, that provided this model with a convenient initialization. This was done by incorporating the information given by the user through the two constraining curves, Γ_1, Γ_2. We give a description of this approach in the next section since our algorithm, further proposed, elaborates on ideas that are related.

3.2 Minimal Path Set Between Two Curves

Active surfaces are usually initialized with simple geometric structures like ellipsoids or cylinders which do not always lead to a good segmentation after evolution to a steady state. Here, instead, the user is asked to introduce into the 3D image a couple of curves (not necessarily planar) drawn on the surface to be extracted. These curves, Γ_1 and Γ_2, are exploited as the initialization of the model and as incorporated user information. The approach is based on considering a network of paths that globally minimizes an energy associated to the image. This network is used to generate a surface that contains the constraining curves and which provides a segmentation of the object lying between them.

We say that a curve $\gamma_{\Gamma_1}^q$ is a path between a point q and curve Γ_1 if $\gamma_{\Gamma_1}^q(0) = q$ and $\gamma_{\Gamma_1}^q(L) \in \Gamma_1$. A path network $\mathcal{N}_{\Gamma_1}^{\Gamma_2}$, between the points of Γ_2 and curve Γ_1, is the set

$$\mathcal{N}_{\Gamma_1}^{\Gamma_2} = \left\{ \gamma_{\Gamma_1}^q \right\}_{q \in \Gamma_2},$$

where it is supposed that every point q of Γ_2 is visited only once. Using the geodesic energy of each path composing the network, we define the following energy on the set of all possibles networks:

$$E_{Net}\left(\mathcal{N}_{\Gamma_1}^{\Gamma_2}\right) = \int_{q\in\Gamma_2} \int_0^{L(q)} \widetilde{\mathcal{P}}\left(\gamma_q^{\Gamma_1}(s)\right) ds dq. \tag{6}$$

Since the potential function $\widetilde{\mathcal{P}}$ is positive, the minimization of E_{Net} can be obtained by finding every globally minimal path between the points of Γ_2 and curve Γ_1. Moreover, these minimal paths are easily found. Indeed, similar to section 2.2, the minimal path between Γ_1 and a point q (further noted $\mathcal{C}_{\Gamma_1}^q$), with respect to the energy E (defined by (2)), is solution of the ordinary differential equation:

$$\frac{d\mathcal{C}_{\Gamma_1}^q}{dx}(x) = -\nabla U_{\Gamma_1}\left(\mathcal{C}_{\Gamma_1}^q(x)\right) \text{ with } \mathcal{C}_{\Gamma_1}^q(0) = q. \tag{7}$$

U_{Γ_1} is the action map defined on each point $q \in \Omega$ by :

$$U_{\Gamma_1}(q) = \inf\left\{\int_0^L \widetilde{\mathcal{P}}(\mathcal{C}(s))ds\right\},$$

where the inf is taken among all curves such that $C(0) = q$ and $\mathcal{C}(L) \in \Gamma_1$. Furthermore, it follows that $U_{\Gamma_1}(q) = \inf_{p\in\Gamma_1}\{U_p(q)\}$. This implies, as a consequence of relation (3), that U_{Γ_1} is also a solution to the Eikonal equation but with a different initial condition :

$$\|\nabla U_{\Gamma_1}\| = \widetilde{\mathcal{P}}, \text{ and } \forall p \in \Gamma_1, U_{\Gamma_1}(p) = 0. \tag{8}$$

By solving equation (7), using each point of Γ_2 as part of the initial condition, we globally minimize the energy E_{Net}, producing the minimal energy network:

$$\mathcal{S}_{\Gamma_1}^{\Gamma_2} = \bigcup_{q\in\Gamma_2} \{\mathcal{C}_{\Gamma_1}^q\}.$$

The minimal network is thus the set of all solutions of the ordinary differential equation (7) when varying its initial condition along Γ_2. Up to a reparameterization, assume every minimal path (respectively curve Γ_2) is parameterized on an interval J (respectively I). $\mathcal{S}_{\Gamma_1}^{\Gamma_2}$ can then be considered as a mapping (since minimal paths cannot cross without merging) from $I \times J$ to Ω, such that for all pair $(u, v) \in I \times J$ $\mathcal{S}_{\Gamma_1}^{\Gamma_2}(u, v) = \mathcal{C}_{\Gamma_1}^{\Gamma_2(u)}(v)$. Using this map for segmentation follows the same intuition as in [2, 3], where the hypothesis is made that each path of $\mathcal{S}_{\Gamma_1}^{\Gamma_2}$ is within a small distance from the surface to extract. Unfortunately, as can be understood from [18], in the general case the map $\mathcal{S}_{\Gamma_1}^{\Gamma_2}(\cdot, \cdot)$ lacks the fundamental property of continuity. For that reason, it is insufficient for segmentation. In order to cope with this difficulty, *Ardon* and *Cohen* [2, 3], proposed two different solutions :

– An analytical interpolation method was used to generate a surface from a finite number of paths belonging to $\mathcal{S}_{\Gamma_1}^{\Gamma_2}$. This approach gave satisfactory segmentation results only in very particular cases (the topology of the surface being such that the gaps created by the discontinuities uncover relatively small areas of the surface), and was thus preferred as an initialization of other active object methods [2].

- A different network was generated by solving a projected version of the ordinary differential equation (7) [3]. The projection was made on planes whose definition depended on Γ_1 and Γ_2. Even though satisfactory results were obtained in medical images under some restrictions applied to the two constraining curves (they should neither intersect nor be open), with this approach the network is no longer minimal for energy E_{Net}. Furthermore, paths can cross without merging thus no mapping can be defined. Last but not least, this approach can only extract surfaces of objects whose topology is cylindrical.

In order to solve the problems mentioned above, we introduce in the next section a novel approach for the generation of a surface using the minimal path network. This surface shall be defined as the zero level set of a function Ψ which solves a certain transport equation.

4   Implicit Definition of a Surface Containing the Minimal Paths Set

In order to simplify our description, Γ_1 and Γ_2 are assumed to be two non-intersecting planar, closed curves. We look for a real function Ψ, defined on the image domain Ω, such that $S_{\Gamma_1}^{\Gamma_2}$ is contained in its zero level set (further noted $\Psi^{-1}(\{0\})$). Having no *a priori* knowledge on the properties Ψ should satisfy, we shall suppose that Ψ is continuously differentiable and we first look for a necessary condition based on our knowledge of the minimal path network. Further, this condition is exploited to formulate a sufficient condition and finally give a consistent description of function Ψ.

4.1   Searching for an Implicit Function

As in section 3.2, we denote by $\mathcal{C}_{\Gamma_1}^q$ a minimal path from a point $q \in \Omega$ to curve Γ_1, and we suppose that J is its parameterization interval. The minimal paths set $S_{\Gamma_1}^{\Gamma_2}$ can also be considered as a subset of Ω, $p \in S_{\Gamma_1}^{\Gamma_2}$ means that p is a point belonging to a minimal path. Let us first assume that a continuously differentiable function Ψ, defined in Ω is such that $S_{\Gamma_1}^{\Gamma_2} \subset \Psi^{-1}(\{0\})$. This means that for all minimal path $\mathcal{C}_{\Gamma_1}^q$ we have $\forall x \in J, \Psi\big(\mathcal{C}_{\Gamma_1}^q(x)\big) = 0$. From the derivative with respect to x of this relation we obtain

$$\forall x \in J, \nabla\Psi\big(\mathcal{C}_{\Gamma_1}^q(x)\big).\frac{d\mathcal{C}_{\Gamma_1}^q}{dx}(x) = 0.$$

Using relation (7) we deduce the following proposition:

Proposition 4.11 (Necessary condition). *For any real differential function Ψ defined on Ω such that $S_{\Gamma_1}^{\Gamma_2} \subset \Psi^{-1}(\{0\})$, we have for every point p of $S_{\Gamma_1}^{\Gamma_2}$:*

$$\nabla\Psi(p).\nabla U_{\Gamma_1}(p) = 0. \tag{9}$$

The perpendicularity of the two gradient vector fields is only necessary on the points of the minimal path network. Hardening this condition and demanding that Ψ satisfies relation (9) everywhere in Ω, should lead to a sufficient relation for the minimal paths to be contained in $\Psi^{-1}(\{0\})$.

Proposition 4.12 (Sufficient condition). *If Ψ is a C^1 function satisfying :*

$$
\begin{cases}
(C_1) \; \forall p \in \Omega, \nabla\Psi(p).\nabla U_{\Gamma_1}(p) = 0 \\[2mm]
(C_2) \qquad\qquad \forall q \in \Gamma_2, \Psi(q) = 0
\end{cases}
\quad then \; \mathcal{S}_{\Gamma_1}^{\Gamma_2} \subset \Psi^{-1}(\{0\}).
$$

Proof: for every point $q \in \Gamma_2$, the values taken by function Ψ along the minimal path $\mathcal{C}_{\Gamma_1}^q$ are given by function $f_q = \Psi \circ \mathcal{C}_{\Gamma_1}^q$. The derivative of f_q, for all $x \in J$, gives:

$$
\frac{df_q}{dx}(x) \;=\; \nabla\Psi\big(\mathcal{C}_{\Gamma_1}^q(x)\big).\frac{d\mathcal{C}_{\Gamma_1}^q}{dx}(x)
$$
$$
\underset{\text{from (7)}}{=} -\nabla\Psi\big(\mathcal{C}_{\Gamma_1}^q(x)\big).\nabla U_{\Gamma_1}\big(\mathcal{C}_{\Gamma_1}^q(x)\big) \underset{\text{from }(C_1)}{=} 0.
$$

Thus, function f_q is constant on J. Furthermore, recall that $\mathcal{C}_{\Gamma_1}^q(0) = q$ and $q \in \Gamma_2$. Condition (C_2) establishes then that $f_q(0) = 0$ and finally that f_q is zero on J, which means that Ψ is zero along any minimal path.

In the previous reasoning, the fact that point q belongs to Γ_2 is not relevant for establishing that f_q is a constant function. As a matter of fact, for every point $p \in \Psi^{-1}(\{0\})$ (not necessary on Γ_2), along the minimal path between this point and curve Γ_1, function Ψ also has zero values (since $f_p = 0$). This means that the set $\Psi^{-1}(\{0\})$ contains a set of minimal paths which is much larger than $\mathcal{S}_{\Gamma_1}^{\Gamma_2}$. More interestingly, we have:

Proposition 4.13 ($\Psi^{-1}(\{0\})$ structure). *If Ψ satisfies the same conditions as in property 4.12, then for all $p \in \Psi^{-1}(\{0\})$, the minimal path $\mathcal{C}_{\Gamma_1}^p$ joining p to Γ_1 satisfies $\mathcal{C}_{\Gamma_1}^p \subset \Psi^{-1}(\{0\})$.*

This establishes that the zero level set of the function Ψ is in fact a set of minimal paths joining Γ_1. Being minimal with respect to the geodesic energy E (see section 2.2), these paths tend to be traced on the object to extract (as Γ_1 and Γ_2). This explains the better results, compared to [3], obtained with our method, more information is injected into the model. A good example is given in figure 3, which demonstrates, on a synthetic image, how this approach gives good results where clearly $\mathcal{S}_{\Gamma_1}^{\Gamma_2}$ is insufficient for segmentation. In the next sections we outline two different manners to derive advantages from these propositions. The first one, is a direct implementation of the transport problem, the second is a combination with other active object approaches such as the active surface model.

4.2 Segmenting with the Transport Equation

We further denote by Π_1, Π_2 the intersection of the planes containing Γ_1 and Γ_2 with the image domain. The functions d_1, d_2 are the signed distance functions to these curves, positive in their interior and defined on Π_1 and Π_2 respectively. Notice that at each point $q \in \Gamma_2, d_2(q) = 0$.

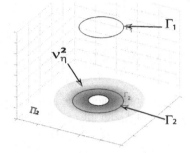

Fig. 2. Boundary conditions for the transport problem

Consider now the closed set

$$V_\eta^2 = \{p \in \Pi_2 \text{ such that } |d_2(p)| \leqslant \eta\},$$

where η is a real positive value (see figure 2). Inspired by proposition 4.12, we consider the open set $\mathcal{O} = \text{int}(\Omega) - V_\eta^2$, where $\text{int}(\Omega)$ is the interior of the image domain, and search for Ψ as the solution to the Cauchy problem defined on Ω:

$$\begin{cases} \nabla\Psi(p).\nabla U_{\Gamma_1}(p) = 0 & \text{if } p \in \mathcal{O}, \\ \Psi(p) = d_2(p) & \text{if } p \in V_\eta^2, \\ \Psi(p) = \min_{p \in \Pi_2}\big(d_2(p)\big) & \text{if } p \in \delta\Omega. \end{cases}$$
(10)

$\delta\Omega$ is the boundary of the image domain Ω. Problem (10) is known as a stationary transport problem: its solution Ψ, being constant along minimal path, "transports" the values taken along the boundary $V_\eta^2 \cup \delta\Omega$.

The transport problem (10) has been studied from a theoretical point of view (see for example [1] and references within), and results of existence and uniqueness have been given by Bouchut *et. al.* in [4] and L. Ambrosio in [1]. It is beyond the scope of this paper to present the theoretical details. As a matter of fact, numerical approaches (see section 4.4) that take in consideration the presence of possible discontinuities of the function Ψ were proposed before a theoretical framework was established. Section 4.4 describes a fast algorithm for solving this problem.

4.3 A New Force for Active Models

Another approach for solving the stationary transport problem is to look for the steady state of the time dependent equation: $\frac{\partial \Psi}{\partial t} = \nabla\Psi.\nabla U_{\Gamma_1}$. In the level set formulation of the active surface model (see section 3.1 and [7]), the time dependent equation to solve, in the Level Set formulation [21], is: $\frac{\partial \Phi}{\partial t} = \nabla\Phi.\nabla\widetilde{\mathcal{P}} + \widetilde{\mathcal{P}}\|\nabla\Phi\| \text{div}\left(\frac{\nabla\Phi}{\|\nabla\Phi\|}\right)$. The first term of the right hand side is a transport term that drives the level sets of Φ to the minima of $\widetilde{\mathcal{P}}$. The second induces a regularization of Φ, which is dominant in areas where $\widetilde{\mathcal{P}}$ is strong. It is thus natural to introduce the same regularization in our problem and solve

$$\frac{\partial \Psi}{\partial t} = \nabla\Psi.\nabla U_{\Gamma_1} + U_{\Gamma_1}\|\nabla\Psi\| \text{div}\left(\frac{\nabla\Psi}{\|\nabla\Psi\|}\right)$$

(because Ψ would minimize a geodesic energy where U_{Γ_1} plays the role of the potential). A small inconvenience arises near Γ_2 since U_{Γ_1} can be strong in that area, thereby enforcing too much smoothing. The final surface may not strictly contain the constraining curves.

A different option is to consider our transport term as a new external force that drives the model toward the minimal path network, thus introducing the information given by the user through the constraining curves as well as the global information contained in the function U. The dynamic equation to solve is then of the form:

$$\frac{\partial \Psi}{\partial t} = \nabla \Psi . \nabla \widetilde{\mathcal{P}} + \widetilde{\mathcal{P}} \left\| \nabla \Psi \right\| \operatorname{div} \left(\frac{\nabla \Psi}{\left\| \nabla \Psi \right\|} \right) + \underbrace{\nabla \Psi . \frac{\nabla U_{\Gamma_1}}{\left\| \nabla U_{\Gamma_1} \right\|}}_{\text{normalized force}} .$$

We have here considered the active surface model but our 'minimal path' force can be added to other active surface models as well. Of course, unlike the direct segmentation with the transport equation, while this new force contributes to avoiding unwanted local minima of the energy, it does not ensure the reaching of a global minimum. In what follows we will concentrate on the numerical solution to the transport problem and will leave further development of the method presented in this section to future papers.

4.4   Implementation of the Transport Problem

We now describe an efficient algorithm for the numerical implementation of the transport problem (10). Unlike [3], minimal paths are not to be computed directly in this implicit approach. We only numerically calculate solutions to the Eikonal and to the stationary transport equations.

To numerically solve the Eikonal equation (8) classic finite difference schemes tend to be unstable. Generally it is preferable to use consistent algorithms using *upwind* differences (derivative approximations are chosen looking in the direction from which the information is flowing) as fast marching [23, 20] or fast sweeping [14]. Numerical complexity of $O(N)$ (N being the number of grid points) can then be achieved and only one grid pass is needed to obtain a first order approximation of the solution U_{Γ_1}.

The stationary transport equation, as with most first order partial differential equations whose characteristics intersect, is difficult to solve numerically. In fact, in the general case ($\widetilde{\mathcal{P}}$ is supposed to be a bounded and continuous function), there is no classical solution defined in all Ω, and the weak solution Ψ can present discontinuities. Many implementations of the transport equation in its non-static expression have been proposed in the modeling of geophysical phenomena. In 1964, Lax and Wendorff proposed in [16] a scheme using centered finite differences for the approximation of derivatives. Then, in 1968, Crowley suggested in [11] a scheme that achieved second order precision in time and space, and which inspired other numerous publications. In particular, a generalization to multiple dimensions was proposed by Smolarkiewicz in [22]. These are only some early publications from a long list of papers treating this topic. Here we will concentrate on a first order, fast algorithm which is less constrained since only the zero level set of the solution matters in our approach.

In order to simplify notation, the symbol V shall be used to refer to the gradient ∇U_{Γ_1}. One of the first numerical approaches for solving the transport equation proposes a first order approximation of the gradient $\nabla \Psi$ that follows the direction in which information propagates. This discretization is the *upwind* approach and consists in choosing the approximation of $\frac{\partial \Psi}{\partial \alpha}$ following the sign of the components V_α (where $\alpha = x, y$ ou z) of V. Recently, A. Yezzi and J. L. Prince used this scheme in [25] for the numerical solution of equation $\nabla \Psi . T = 1$ (where T was a known vector field). Lastly, although this scheme is of relatively low precision and dissipative [17], it gives satisfactory results in our experiments with an acceptable convergence speed.

If $\Psi^{i,j,k}$ is the value of the numerical approximation of Ψ at point $[i; j; k]$ of the discrete square grid, we shall denote the left and right approximations of the partial derivatives by:

$$D^{-x}\Psi = \frac{\Psi^{i,j,k} - \Psi^{i-1,j,k}}{h}, \quad D^{+x}\Psi = \frac{\Psi^{i+1,j,k} - \Psi^{i,j,k}}{h}$$

(similarly in the y and z directions) where h is the discretization step, identical in all three spatial directions. Our scheme for solving the stationary transport problem $V.\nabla\Psi = 0$ is then

$$V_x^{i,j,k}.\left(D^{-x}\Psi^{i,j,k} \text{ or } D^{+x}\Psi^{i,j,k}\right) + V_y^{i,j,k}.\left(D^{-y}\Psi^{i,j,k} \text{ or } D^{+y}\Psi^{i,j,k}\right) + V_z^{i,j,k}.\left(D^{-z}\Psi^{i,j,k} \text{ or } D^{+z}\Psi^{i,j,k}\right) = 0.$$

In our problem, the direction in which information propagates is given by the vector $-V$. Therefore, denoting by H the heaviside function defined by $H(x) = \begin{cases} 1, & \text{if } x \geqslant 0 \\ 0, & \text{else.} \end{cases}$,

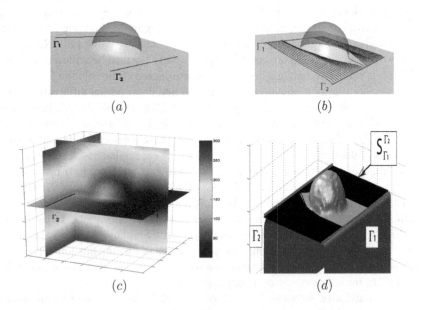

Fig. 3. (a) represents a half-sphere blended with a plane (transparent visualization) and Γ_1 and Γ_2 (black segments). (b) shows some minimal paths of $S_{\Gamma_1}^{\Gamma_2}$ taking a short cut around the sphere. (c) shows the values taken by Ψ on three perpendicular planes. (d) shows the superposition of $\Psi^{-1}(0)$ and the set $S_{\Gamma_1}^{\Gamma_2}$ (see please the electronic color version).

the *upwind* approximation is:

$$
\begin{aligned}
V_x^{i,j,k} \cdot \left(D^{-x}\Psi^{i,j,k} H(-V_x^{i,j,k}) + D^{+x}\Psi^{i,j,k} H(V_x^{i,j,k}) \right) + \\
V_y^{i,j,k} \cdot \left(D^{-y}\Psi^{i,j,k} H(-V_y^{i,j,k}) + D^{+y}\Psi^{i,j,k} H(V_y^{i,j,k}) \right) + \\
V_z^{i,j,k} \cdot \left(D^{-z}\Psi^{i,j,k} H(-V_z^{i,j,k}) + D^{+z}\Psi^{i,j,k} H(V_z^{i,j,k}) \right) = 0.
\end{aligned}
$$

Then, if $I = (i+1)$ if $V_x > 0$, $i-1$ otherwise, and similarly for J and K, we have

$$
\begin{aligned}
\left| V_x^{i,j,k} \right| \left[\Psi^{I,j,k} - \Psi^{i,j,k} \right] + \left| V_y^{i,j,k} \right| \left[\Psi^{i,J,k} - \Psi^{i,j,k} \right] \\
+ \left| V_z^{i,j,k} \right| \left[\Psi^{i,j,K} - \Psi^{i,j,k} \right] = 0,
\end{aligned}
$$

which, by grouping terms with $\Psi^{i,j,k}$, finally leads to the update expression of our algorithm:

$$
\Psi^{i,j,k} = \frac{|V_x^{i,j,k}|\Psi^{I,j,k} + |V_y^{i,j,k}|\Psi^{i,J,k} + |V_z^{i,j,k}|\Psi^{i,j,K}}{|V_x^{i,j,k}| + |V_y^{i,j,k}| + |V_z^{i,j,k}|}. \tag{11}
$$

This equality can be exploited, as presented in [25], in a fast marching type scheme that achieves a first order approximation of the solution to our problem in only one grid

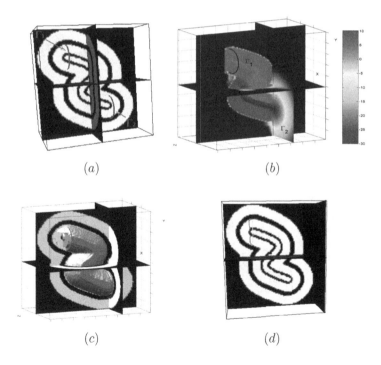

(a) (b)

(c) (d)

Fig. 4. (a) shows the intersection of a plain with a binary image where three 'S' shaped tubes are one inside the other, Γ_1 and Γ_2 are shown in red. (b) shows the values taken by Ψ on three perpendicular planes (see please the electronic color version). (c) shows the superposition of $\Psi^{-1}(0)$ and the original image and (d) the intersection of this surface with a plane of the image.

pass and with a $N \log(N)$ complexity. In the end, our algorithm consists in solving the Eikonal equation first, then the transport equation by means of the same implementation. We thus can achieve very rapid computing times. In the next section we give some results.

5   Applications

We apply our method to some synthetic and real 3D images. In all our examples we used a potential of the form: $\widetilde{\mathcal{P}} = \alpha.h(|\nabla I_\sigma|) + (1 - \alpha).h_{gap}(\Delta I_\sigma)$, where h and h_{gap} are two functions bounded between 0 and 1 and where I_σ is the convolution of the given image with a Gaussian kernel of variance σ. Typically, $h(x) = \frac{1}{1+x^2/\lambda^2}$, where λ is a user defined contrast factor that can be computed as an average gradient value, and h_{gap} is chosen to be a zero crossing detector.

Figure 3 represents a sphere blended with a plane. This surface is to be extracted between two curves which are parallel lines (see figure 3.a). This configuration does not exactly satisfy the hypothesis taken in section 3 (we are not dealing with closed curves) but the extension is straightforward (the boundary conditions have to be slightly modified). The set of minimal paths $\mathcal{S}_{\Gamma_1}^{\Gamma_2}$ is unable to provide enough information for

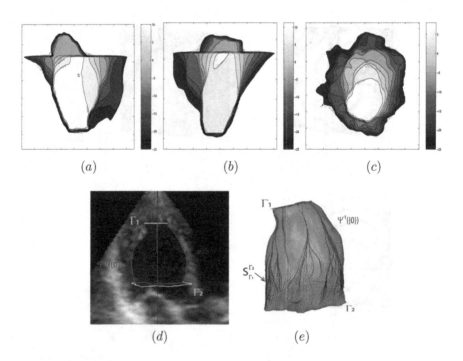

(a) (b) (c)

(d) (e)

Fig. 5. Left ventricle segmentation : (a),(b) and (c) display some level sets of our solution Ψ on three orthogonal planes. (d) shows the intersection of the zero level set of Ψ with a slice of the image and (e) shows a volume representation of $\Psi^{-1}(\{0\})$ (see please the electronic color version).

the extraction of the surface, since no minimal path 'climbs' on the sphere surface. Nonetheless, the zero level set of the corresponding Ψ function reconstructs perfectly the surface. Our implicit method recovers more information than the minimal paths and we obtain the complete surface.

Figure 4 illustrates with a synthetic binary volume the behavior of our algorithm when various local minima of energy E_S (4) are present. In this volume three 'S' shaped tubes are displayed one inside the other. The constraining curves are traced on the second tube, without the information they bring, segmenting this tube is a hard task.

In figure 5 we show the extraction of the surface of the left ventricle from the 3D ultrasound image shown in figure 1. For this ultrasound image of size $256 \times 256 \times$

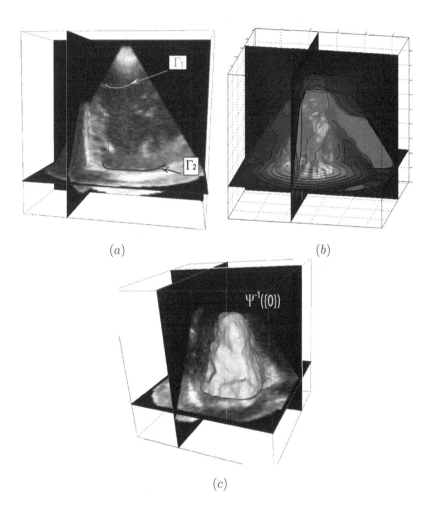

(a) $\qquad\qquad\qquad\qquad\qquad\qquad$ (b)

(c)

Fig. 6. (a) shows a plane of a 3D ultrasound volume obtained from a patient whose echogenicity is low. This image is difficult to segment. (b) shows some level sets of our solution Ψ and a volume representation of the zero level set. (c) displays the segmentation obtained with our method(see please the electronic color version).

256 we used a personal computer with a 1.4Ghz processor and 512 Mb of RAM. The segmentation is obtained in less than 15 seconds.

In our last example, shown in figure 6, we display the segmentation of a left ventricle. In this case the information given by the two constraining curves is crucially important, since the echogenicity of the patient generates a very low visibility.

6 Conclusion

In this paper we have presented a method that generalizes globally minimal paths for curve segmentation in 2D to surface segmentation in 3D. Our model is initialized by two user-supplied curves which we maximally exploit partly by the fact that the surface we generate is constrained to contain them. We have developed a novel implicit approach that, through a linear partial differential equation, exploits the solution to the Eikonal equation and generates a function whose zero level set contains all the globally minimal paths between the constraining curves. Hence, our approach is not prone to local minima traps as are other active surface approaches. It is especially well suited for medical image segmentation, in particular for ultrasound images segmentation. In cases where the image quality is very poor, our approach handles the introduction of additional information coming from the practitioner in a very natural manner: a few 2D segmentations can be enough to generate a coherent, complete surface.

References

1. L. Ambrosio. Transport equation and Cauchy problem for BV vector fields. *Preprints Scuola Normale Superiore, Department of Mathematics: http://cvgmt.sns.it/people/ambrosio/*, 2003.
2. R. Ardon and L.D. Cohen. Fast constrained surface extraction by minimal paths. *2nd IEEE Workshop on Variational, Geometric and Level Set Methods in Computer Vision*, pages 233–244, October 2003.
3. R. Ardon and L.D. Cohen. Fast Constrained Surface Extraction by Minimal Paths. *To appear in IJCV*, 2005.
4. F. Bouchut, F. James, and S. Mancini. Uniqueness and weak stability for multi-dimensional transport equations with one-sided lipschitz coefficient. *Prépublications du département Mathématiques et Applications, Physique Mathématique d'Orléans*, 2004.
5. A.M. Bruckstein. On shape from shading. *CVGIP*, 44(2):139–154, November 1988.
6. V. Caselles, R. Kimmel, and G. Sapiro. Geodesic active contours. *IJCV*, 22(1):61–79, 1997.
7. V. Caselles, R. Kimmel, G. Sapiro, and C. Sbert. Minimal-surfaces based object segmentation. *IEEE Transactions On Pattern Analysis and Machine Intelligence*, 19(4):394–398, April 1997.
8. L.D. Cohen. On active contour models and balloons. *CVGIP*, 53(2):211–218, 1991.
9. L.D. Cohen. Avoiding local minima for deformable curves in image analysis. In *Curves and Surfaces with Applications in CAGD*, Nashville, 1997. Vanderbilt Univ. Press.
10. L.D. Cohen and R. Kimmel. Global minimum for active contour models: A minimal path approach. *IJCV*, 24(1):57–78, August 1997.
11. W. P. Crowley. Numerical advection experiments. *Monthly Weather Review*, 96:1–11, 1968.
12. T. Deschamps and L.D. Cohen. Fast extraction of minimal paths in 3D images and applications to virtual endoscopy. *Medical Image Analysis*, 5(4), December 2001.

13. O. Gerard, T. Deschamps, M. Greff, and L. D. Cohen. Real-time interactive path extraction with on-the-fly adaptation of the external forces. *European Conference on Computer Vision*, june 2002.
14. C. Y. Kao, S. Osher, and J. Qian. Lax-Friedrichs sweeping scheme for static Hamilton-Jacobi equations. *Journal of Computational Physics*, 26:367–391, Mai 2004.
15. M. Kass, A. Witkin, and D. Terzopoulos. Snakes: Active contour models. *International Journal of Computer Vision*, 1(4):321–331, 1988.
16. P. D. Lax and B. Wendorff. Systems of conservation laws. *Communications on Pure and Applied mathematics*, 17:381–398, 1964.
17. R. J. LeVeque. High-resolution conservative algorithms for advection in incompressible flow. *SIAM Journal on Numerical Analysis*, 33(2):627–665, April 1996.
18. C. Mantegazza and A. C. G. Mennucci. Hamilton-Jacobi equations and distance functions on Riemannian manifolds. *Appl. Math. Opt.*, 47(1):1–25, 2003.
19. N. Paragios. *Geodesic Active Regions and Level Set Methods: Contributions and Applications in Artificial Vision*. PhD thesis, Université de Nice Sophia-Antipolis, France, 2000.
20. J.A. Sethian. A fast marching level set method for monotonically advancing fronts. *Proceedings of the National Academy of Sciences*, 93(4):1591–1595, February 1996.
21. J.A. Sethian. *Level set methods: Evolving Interfaces in Geometry, Fluid Mechanics, Computer Vision and Materials Sciences*. Cambridge University Press, University of California, Berkeley, 2nd edition, 1999.
22. P. K. Smolarkiewicz. The multi-dimensional crowley advection scheme. *Monthly Weather Review*, 110:1968–1983, 1982.
23. J. N. Tsitsiklis. Efficient algorithms for globally optimal trajectories. *IEEE Transactions on Automatic Control*, 40(9):1528–1538, September 1995.
24. A. Yezzi, S. Kichenassamy, A. Kumar, P. Olver, and A. Tannenbaum. A geometric snake model for segmentation of medical imagery. *IEEE Transactions On Medical Imaging*, 16(2):199–209, Avril 1997.
25. A. Yezzi and J. L. Prince. An Eulerian PDE Approach for Computing Tissue Thickness. *IEEE Transactions On Medical Imaging*, 22:1332–1339, October 2003.
26. A.L. Yuille, P.W. Hallinan, and D.S. Cohen. Feature extraction from faces using deformable templates. *International Journal of Computer Vision*, 8(2):99–111, August 1992.
27. S.C. Zhu and A. Yuille. Region competition: Unifying snakes, region growing, and bayes/mdl for multiband image segmentation. *IEEE Transactions On Pattern Analysis and Machine Intelligence*, 18(9):884–900, September 1996.

Part IV

Other Approaches and Applications

Increasing Efficiency of SVM by Adaptively Penalizing Outliers

Yiqiang Zhan[1,2,3] and Dinggang Shen[2,3]

[1] Dept. of Computer Science, The Johns Hopkins University, Baltimore, MD
[2] Center for Computer-Integrated Surgical Systems and Technology,
The Johns Hopkins University, Baltimore, MD
[3] Section of Biomedical Image Analysis, Dept. of Radiology,
University of Pennsylvania, Philadelphia, PA
yzhan@cs.jhu.edu, Dinggang.Shen@uphs.upenn.edu

Abstract. In this paper, a novel training method is proposed to increase the classification efficiency of support vector machine (SVM). The efficiency of the SVM is determined by the number of support vectors, which is usually large for representing a highly convoluted separation hypersurface. We noted that the separation hypersurface is made unnecessarily over-convoluted around extreme outliers, which dominate the objective function of SVM. To suppress the domination from extreme outliers and thus relatively simplify the shape of separation hypersurface, we propose a method of adaptively penalizing the outliers in the objective function. Since our reformulated objective function has the similar format of the standard SVM, the idea of the existing SVM training algorithms is borrowed for training the proposed SVM. Our proposed method has been tested on the UCI machine learning repository, as well as a real clinical problem, i.e., tissue classification in prostate ultrasound images. Experimental results show that our method is able to dramatically increase the classification efficiency of the SVM, without losing its generalization ability.

1 Introduction

Support vector machine (SVM), proposed by Vapnik in 1995 [1], is a new generation of learning systems, based on statistical learning theory. Considering a two-class classification problem with m labeled training samples,

$$\{(\bar{x}_i, y_i) \mid \bar{x}_i \in R^n, y_i \in \{-1, 1\}, i = 1 \cdots m\},$$

SVM is able to generate a hypersurface that has maximum margin to separate these two classes. During the applications, a testing sample $\bar{x}$ is classified by calculating its distance to the hypersurface:

$$d(\bar{x}) = \sum_{i=1}^{m} \alpha_i y_i K(\bar{x}_i, \bar{x}) + b \qquad (1)$$

where α_i and b are the parameters determined by SVM's learning algorithm, and $K(\bar{x}_i, \bar{x})$ is the kernel function. Samples $\bar{x}_i$ with nonzero parameters α_i are called "support vectors".

A. Rangarajan et al. (Eds.): EMMCVPR 2005, LNCS 3757, pp. 539–551, 2005.

SVM has several striking properties. *First*, SVM is developed based on the idea of structural risk minimization [1]. It can achieve high generalization ability by minimizing the Vapnik-Chervonenkis dimension. *Second*, by using the kernel trick [2], the samples are implicitly mapped to a higher dimensional space. Therefore, SVM can generate a convoluted hypersurface to non-linearly separate different classes. *Finally*, the training procedure of SVM can be eventually formulated as a constraint quadratic optimization problem, which has a unique global minimum.

Accordingly, SVM shows superior performances in pattern recognition problems and has drawn considerable attentions in various research areas [3-8]. However, while confronting large data classification problem, SVM usually needs a huge number of support vectors to parameterize the separation hypersurface. Since it is computationally expensive to calculate the decision function with many non-zero parameters α_i in Eq. (1), SVM exhibits substantially slower classification speed than that of neural network [9]. This disadvantage unavoidably limits the capability of SVM in the applications that require a massive number of classifications [5] or real-time classification [11].

In this paper, we will propose a novel training method to increase the classification efficiency of SVM. The basic idea of our method is to prevent the separation hypersurface from being locally over-convoluted, usually incurred by extreme outliers in the training set. To achieve this goal, we reformulate the objective function of the standard soft-margin SVM by designing an adaptive penalty term to outliers. Therefore, the objective function will be no longer dominated by extreme outliers and the separation surface can be simplified without losing its generalization ability. We will further show that the reformulated objective function can be eventually transformed to a quadratic optimization problem with adaptive constraints, which has similar format as the dual problem of the standard soft-margin SVM. In this way, our training method can be easily implemented in an iterative framework, which can be embedded by any existing SVM training methods.

The remaining of this paper is organized as following. In Section 2, we will first analyze the problem in details, and then reformulate SVM by an adaptive penalty term to outliers. The training method of reformulated SVM will also be provided. Section 3 will present the experimental results of our method on the UCI machine learning repository, as well as a real clinical problem, i.e., tissue classification in a set of prostate ultrasound images. This paper concludes in Section 4.

2   Methods

2.1   Problem Description

As indicated in Eq. (1), the computational cost of SVM is directly related to the number of the support vectors, i.e. training samples with non-zero parameters α_i. According to their relative positions to the separation hypersurface, support vectors can be categorized into two types. The first type of support vectors are the training samples that exactly locate on the margins of the separation hypersurface, i.e., $d(\vec{x}_i) = \pm 1$, such as red circles/crosses shown in Fig 1. The second type of support vectors are the training samples that locate beyond their corresponding margins, i.e., $y_i d(\vec{x}_i) < 1$, such as blue and green circles/crosses shown in Fig 1. For a SVM, the second type of

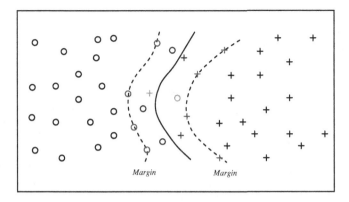

Fig. 1. Schematic explanation of the separation hypersurface (solid curves), margins (dashed curves), and support vectors of SVM (colored circles/crosses). The positive and the negative training samples are indicated by circles and crosses, respectively.

support vectors are regarded as misclassified samples, although some of them still locate at the correct side of the hypersurface (shown as blue circles/crosses).

SVM usually has a huge number of support vectors, when the distributions of the positive and the negative training samples from a large dataset highly overlap with each other. This unfavorable situation can be contributed to two reasons: (1) a large number of the first-type support vectors are needed to construct a highly convoluted hypersurface, in order to separate two classes; (2) even the highly convoluted separation hypersurface has been constructed, a lot of confounding samples will be misclassified, thus selected as the second type of support vectors.

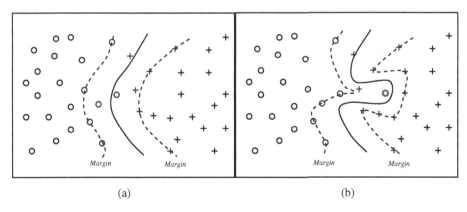

(a)   (b)

Fig. 2. Schematic explanation of the over-convoluted separation hypersurface incurred by an outlier. The solid and dashed curves denote the separation hypersurface and margins, respectively. Circles and crosses denote the positive and the negative training samples, respectively. The blue ones denote the support vectors. The red circle in (b) is an outlier that incurs the hypersurface over-convoluted. Notably, except the red circle in (b), other samples in (a) and (b) are identical.

Some support vectors might be redundant to parameterize the separation hypersurface. Based on this hypothesis, researchers have proposed efficient SVM training methods [11][13]. Compared to [13], the method proposed by Osuna *et al* in [11] is more feasible, and it offered a principle for controlling the accuracy of approximation. This method approximates the separation hypersurface with a subset of the support vectors by using a Support Vector Regression Machine (SVRM). If the separation hypersurface is relatively simple, Osuan's method is quite effective to reduce the number of support vectors without system degradation. However, in many large dataset classification problems, SVM usually generates a highly convoluted separation hypersurface, which is difficult to be parameterized by a small number of support vectors as Osuan's method did. Therefore, the only way for decreasing the number of support vectors is to simplify the over-convoluted separation hypersurface.

It is widely accepted that the convoluted hypersurface of SVM is critical for nonlinear separation of classes, which might overlap with each other in the original feature space. However, in certain cases, the hypersurface generated by SVM is unnecessarily over-convoluted in some local regions without increasing the generalization ability of the SVM. Fig 2 presents a toy problem to illustrate those cases. In Fig 2(a), the separation hypersurface of the SVM is relatively simple and it has 12 support vectors (denoted by blue crosses or circles). The distribution of the training samples in Fig 2(b) is almost the same as that of Fig 2(a) except an additional positive sample (denoted by the red circle). However, the separation hypersurface in Fig 2 (b) became much more convoluted, in order to satisfy this additional sample, and the trained SVM has 16 support vectors. Notably, since this additional training sample locates in an isolated region that is far from samples of the same class, it might be an outlier produced by noise or error. Therefore, the over-convoluted hypersurface, used to satisfy this sample, will decrease the generalization ability of SVM, but increase its computational cost. Obviously, this unfavorable situation should be avoided, in order to increase the classification efficiency and generalization of the SVM. In the next section, we will investigate this problem in detail, and finally prevent it by reformulating a new objective function for SVM.

2.2   Reformulation of Objective Function in SVM

It is necessary to briefly introduce the objective function of SVM, before investigating the reason for over-convoluted separation hypersurface in some classification cases. According to the statistical learning theory [1], SVM tries to generate a separation hyperplane, $\bar{w} \cdot \bar{x} + b = 0$, which has the maximum generalization ability. Here, $\bar{w}$ is the normal of the hyperplane, and b is the distance from the hyperplane to the origin. Given m labeled training samples, i.e. $\{(\bar{x}_i, y_i) \mid \bar{x}_i \in R^n, y_i \in \{-1,1\}, i = 1 \cdots m\}$, the training of SVM can be formulated as solving a quadratic optimal problem:

$$\min_{\bar{w},b,\xi_i} \frac{1}{2}\|\bar{w}\|^2 + C\sum_{i=1}^{m} \xi_i$$
$$s.t. \; y_i(\bar{w} \cdot \phi(\bar{x}_i) + b) \geq 1 - \xi_i \qquad (2)$$
$$\xi_i \geq 0$$

Here, $\|\cdot\|$ is the norm of a vector, and $\phi(\cdot)$ maps samples into a higher dimensional space and can be implicitly implemented by the kernel trick [2].

In the objective function of Eq. (2), the first term $\|\vec{w}\|$ measures the inverse of the margin distance that should be minimized to obtain the minimum structural risk [2]. The second term is a penalty term consisting of a number of non-negative slack variables ξ_i, used to construct a soft margin hyperplane [12]. By using the relaxed separation constraints $y_i(\vec{w} \cdot \phi(\bar{x}_i) + b) \geq 1 - \xi_i$, some training samples are allowed to locate beyond their corresponding margins, i.e. $y_i(\vec{w} \cdot \phi(\bar{x}_i) + b) < 1$. The linear summation of all slack variables ξ_i is constrained by the second term in the objective function, in order to avoid the trivial solution that all ξ_i take large values.

According to Eq. (2), it is not difficult to understand the reason why the case described in Fig 2 happens. The separation hypersurface in Fig 2(b) has to be convoluted in order to satisfy that additional red positive sample; otherwise, the corresponding ξ_i of that additional sample will be very large, thus dominating the objective function. However, as the additional sample locates in an isolated region far from samples of the same class, it is an outlier that might be generated by noise or error. Therefore, the hypersurface convoluted around the additional sample is unnecessary, and it will only decrease the generalization of the trained SVM. To solve this problem, we introduce a non-linear penalty term, instead of the linear penalty term in Eq. (2) that makes the effect of outliers overwhelming over the whole objective function. The objective function of SVM is reformulated as following:

$$\min_{\vec{w},b,\xi_i} \frac{1}{2}\|\vec{w}\|^2 + C\sum_{i=1}^{m} erf\left(\xi_i;\sigma\right)$$
$$s.t. \; y_i(\vec{w} \cdot \phi(\bar{x}_i) + b) \geq 1 - \xi_i \quad \xi_i \geq 0$$
(3)

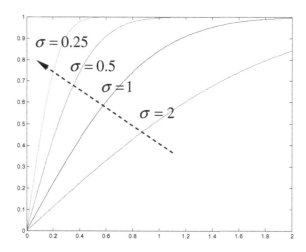

Fig. 3. A nonlinear error function for suppressing the slack variables with large value, thus adaptively penalizing outliers. The curves of different colors denote the error functions *with respect to* different parameter σ used. The dashed arrow indicates the decrease of σ with the progress of iterative training, i.e., transferring linear penalty to nonlinearly-mapped penalty.

where $erf(\xi;\sigma)$ is a nonlinear error function, defined by $erf(\xi;\sigma)=\dfrac{2}{\sqrt{\pi}\sigma}\int_0^\xi e^{-z^2/\sigma^2}dz$, to adaptively penalize outliers. As indicated by the function plot in Fig 3, the error function erf will suppress the slack variables when they are large. In this way, the objective function will be no longer dominated by the large slack variables, and thus the resulting separation hypersurface will not be over-convoluted around extreme outliers. On the other hand, if there are a considerable number of same-class samples clustering in an isolated region that is distant from other samples of this class, the generated hypersurface could still be convoluted to satisfy these samples, in order to decrease the total error for these samples. In this way, the generalization ability of the SVM is preserved.

2.3 Training of the Reformulated SVM

In this section, we will discuss the training algorithm for the reformulated SVM. Similarly, the Lagrangian theory is employed here to solve the reformulated constrained quadratic problem. After introducing Lagrangian multipliers α_i and η_i, we obtain the primary Lagrangian of Eq. (3) as:

$$L(\bar{w},b,\xi_i)=\frac{1}{2}\|\bar{w}\|^2+C\sum_{i=1}^{m}erf(\xi_i)-\sum_{i=1}^{m}\left[\alpha_i\left(y_i\left(\bar{w}\cdot\phi(\bar{x}_i)+b\right)-(1-\xi_i)\right)+\eta_i\xi_i\right] \quad (4)$$

According to Kuhn-Tucker condition, we can express Eq. (4) as a dual problem given next, by differentiating Eq. (4) with respect to the primary variables $\bar{w}$ and b, setting the derivatives as zero and resubmitting the relations obtained by these equations.

$$\min_{\alpha_i,\xi_i}\sum_{i,j=1}^{m}y_iy_j\alpha_i\alpha_j-\sum_{i=1}^{m}\alpha_i+C\sum_{i=1}^{m}\left[\xi_ierf'(\xi_i;\sigma)-erf(\xi_i;\sigma)\right]$$

$$s.t.\ \ 0\le\alpha_i\le C\cdot erf'(\xi_i;\sigma)\ \ \xi_i\ge 0 \quad (5)$$

where $erf'(\xi_i)$ is the derivative of the nonlinear error function, i.e., a Gaussian function with the standard deviation σ.

Notably, compared to the dual problem expressed for the standard SVM, the Lagrangian multiplier α_i in Eq. (5) is no longer constrained by a global constant C, but $C\cdot erf'(\xi_i;\sigma)$, which is adaptive to each sample according to its corresponding ξ_i. Since $erf'(\xi_i;\sigma)$ is actually a Gaussian function, the Lagrangian multiplier α_i of a training sample with large slack variable ξ_i is actually restricted by a very low upper bound. Therefore, this sample has very little contribution in constructing the separation hypersurface, even if it is selected as a support vector. Actually, the reformulated SVM offers a soft selection mechanism to adaptively determine the importance of different training samples, thus the effect of the outliers is suppressed. On the other hand, our method can be interpreted as an algorithm of adaptively and softly selecting samples for training, which is significantly different from the method proposed by Lee et al [14], which randomly selects a subset of training samples in order to speed up SVM.

Since the objective function in Eq. (5) has a very similar format with respect to the standard SVM, we can design an iterative framework to train the reformulated SVM, by borrowing any existing SVM training methods. *First*, α_i are optimized using a similar training method for the standard SVM, except using the adaptive constraints $0 \le \alpha_i \le C \cdot erf'(\xi_i; \sigma)$. *Then*, ξ_i can be calculated by the following equation,

$$\xi_i = \sum_{i=1}^{m} \alpha_i y_i K(\bar{x}_i, \bar{x}) + b - 1 \cdot \tag{6}$$

In the initial iterations, the parameter σ is set to be a large value, thus the error function performs as a linear slack term used in the standard SVM (c.f. Fig 3). With progress of the training, the parameter σ becomes smaller and smaller, thereby the nonlinear error function starts to suppress the large slack variables more. After the training procedure converges, we thus generate an optimal separation hypersurface for the reformulated SVM. *Finally*, Osuna's method [11], which employs the SVRM to approximate the hypersurface by a subset of support vectors, is employed to further decrease the number of support vectors and thus increase the classification efficiency of the SVM.

3 Experiments

To validate the effectiveness of our method, we applied it to the UCI Machine Learning Repository, as well as a real clinical problem, i.e., tissue classification in the prostate ultrasound images. The experimental results are presented next.

3.1 Experiments on UCI Machine Learning Repository

UCI Machine Learning Repository contains a set of data that is used by the machine learning community for the empirical analysis of machine learning algorithms. From the repository, we select the datasets "Adult" (45222 samples, 14 features), "Breast Caner" (687 samples, 10 features), "Ionosphere" (351 samples, 34 features), and "Monks" (432 samples, 6 features), to test our method.

For the datasets of "Breast Cancer", "Ionosphere" and "Monks", we randomly divided each dataset into several groups, with each group having 50 samples. In the training stage, one group is left out as testing samples, and other remaining groups are used as training samples. This leave-one-group-out cross validation is repeated. The averages on the correct classification rate and the number of support vectors from all tests are reported.

For the "Adult" dataset, we use the standard training and testing sets, which have 30162 samples and 15606 samples, respectively.

Table 1 summarizes the average number of support vectors and the average correct classification rate, obtained by the standard SVM, Osuna's method and our method, respectively. Compared to the standard SVM, our method is able to dramatically reduce the number of support vectors, without losing the generalization ability of the classifier. In some cases, the classification rate is even higher, indicating the increased generalization of our method. Compared to Osuna's method, our method is able to generate more efficient SVM with similar classification rate, except for the "Breast Cancer" dataset that has a relatively simple distribution of samples.

Table 1. Comparison on the classification performances obtained by standard SVM, Osuna's method, and our method. SV below denotes 'support vector'.

	Standard SVM		Osuna's Method		Our Method	
Problem	# SV	correct rate	# SV	correct rate	# SV	correct rate
Adult	9996	85.80%	1000	84.91%	338	85.38%
Breast	50.8	96.46%	6.8	96.92%	7.1	97.25%
Iono-sphere	161.3	93.43%	160.4	93.43%	37.5	94.28%
Monks	96.8	97.51%	53.9	97.50%	25.9	97.00%

3.2 Experiments on Tissue Classifications in Prostate Ultrasound Images

In our study of 3D prostate segmentation from ultrasound images [5], SVM is used for texture-based tissue classification. The input of SVM is a set of texture features extracted by the Gabor filter bank [16], and the output is a soft label denoting the likelihood of the voxel belonging to the prostate. In this way, prostate tissues are differentiated from the surrounding tissues. In this study, the computational cost of SVM for tissue classification is a particularly critical problem to be concerned, as the tissue classification is operated for lots of times (i.e., 10^6) in the segmentation stage and also the real-time segmentation is usually required for clinical applications. Therefore, the training method proposed in this paper is applied to speeding up the SVM for tissue classification.

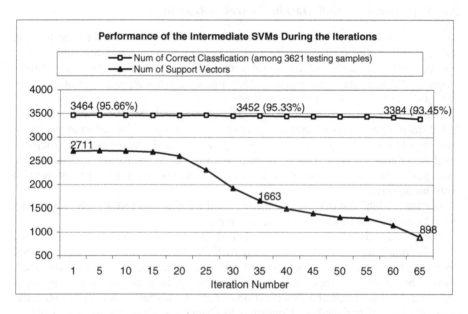

Fig. 4. Performance of intermediately trained SVMs, by different numbers of iteration

In preparing the experimental dataset, we first randomly select prostate and non-prostate samples from six manually labeled ultrasound images, in which 3621 samples from one ultrasound image are used as testing samples and 18105 samples from other five images are used as training samples. Each sample has 10 texture features, extracted by Gabor filters.

The SVM is used for tissue classification, and it is trained by the proposed iterative training method. After each iteration, we record the number of support vectors used and the correct classification of the intermediate SVM; the results from all possible numbers of iteration are provided in Fig 4. As shown in Fig 4, the number of support vectors is reduced quickly with the increase of iterations, while the classification rate keeps similar. The finally trained SVM has 898 support vectors, which is only 33.1% of those of the original SVM (2711); but its classification rate still reaches 93.45%. Compared to 95.66% classification rate achieved by the original SVM, the loss of classification rate is relatively trivial, thereby it will not affect the performance of our model-based segmentation algorithm [5]. Notably, the intermediate SVM can be selected as a classifier to satisfy different classification requirements, i.e., choosing the intermediate SVM generated in 35th iteration, with 1663 support vectors, to obtain a more accurate classification.

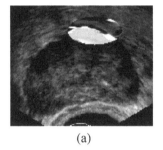 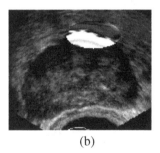

       (a)   (b)

Fig. 5. Comparison on tissue classification results obtained by (a) the original SVM with 2711 support vectors, and (b) our trained SVM with 898 support vectors. The tissue classification results are shown only in the regions surrounded by dashed ellipsoids.

To further validate the performance of our trained SVM in tissue classification, the SVM with 898 support vectors (denoted by the white triangle in Fig 4) is applied to a real ultrasound image for tissue classification. By comparing results in Fig 5(a) and Fig 5(b), the result of our trained SVM in Fig 5(b) is not inferior to that of the original SVM with 2711 support vectors in Fig 5(a), in terms of differentiating prostate tissues from the surrounding ones.

We further compare the performances of SVMs generated by different training methods. Four methods are implemented for comparison: (1) a method of slackening the training criterion by decreasing the linear penalty factor [2]; (2) a heuristic method, which assumes the training samples distributing in a multi-variant Gaussian way, then excludes the "outliers" distant from the respective distribution centers, and finally trains a SVM only by the remaining samples; (3) Osuna's method [11]; (4) our proposed method. The performances of these four methods are evaluated in Fig 6 (a),

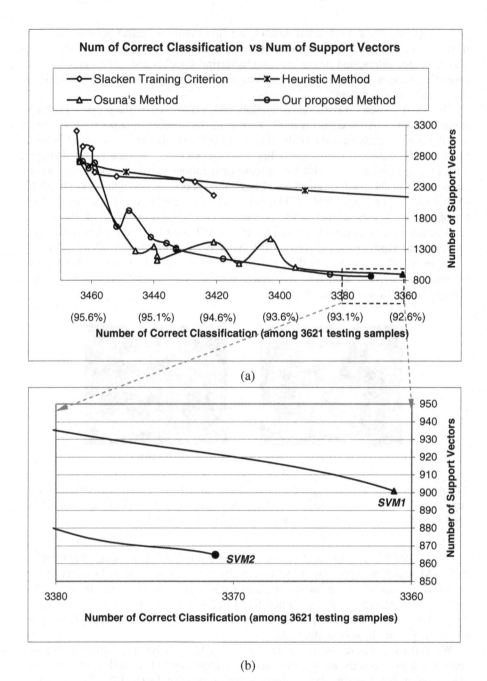

Fig. 6. (a) Comparison on the performances of four training methods in increasing the classification efficiency of SVM. (b) The zoomed version of the area surrounded by the dashed rectangle in (a), for clearly illustrating the classification rate and the number of support vectors obtained by the two SVMs under comparison.

by the number of support vectors used vs the number of correct classifications achieved. In these four methods, our proposed method is most effective in reducing the number of support vectors.

The classification abilities of two SVMs, respectively trained by Osuna's method and our proposed method, are further compared. The SVM trained by Osuna's method, as denoted by the black triangle in Fig 6 (b), needs 901 support vectors and its classification rate is 92.81%. The SVM trained by our proposed method, as denoted by the black circle in Fig 6 (b), needs only 865 support vectors, while its classification rate is 93.10%, higher than that produced by Osuna's method. Moreover, our trained SVM actually has much better generalization ability than the SVM trained by Osuna's method, once checking the histograms of their classification outputs. As shown in Fig 7, the classification outputs of Osuna's SVM concentrate around 0, which means the margins between the positive and the negative samples are narrow. In contrast, most classification outputs of our trained SVM are either larger than 1.0 or smaller than -1.0. This experiment further proves that our training method is better in achieving the generalization ability of the SVM after increasing its efficiency.

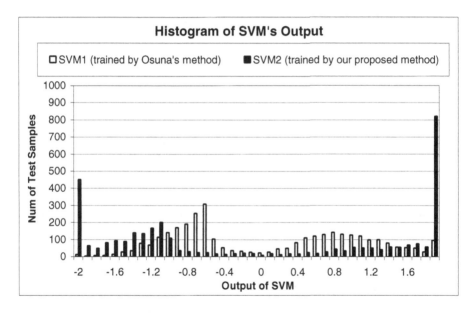

Fig. 7. Histograms of classification outputs on a testing dataset, respectively from our trained SVM (black bars) and Osuna's SVM (white bars)

4 Conclusion

In this paper, we proposed a method to increase the classification efficiency of the SVM, by reducing the number of support vectors used. We noted that the optimal separation hypersurface generated by the standard training method might be unnecessarily over-convoluted around extreme outliers, thus requesting more computational cost without increasing the generalization ability. This situation is actually resulted from the slack variables of outliers that dominate over the objective function, since all slack variables are linearly summed. To overcome this problem, we introduced a nonlinear mapping function to suppress the large slack variables of the outliers. Thus, the separation hypersurface can be simplified and the number of support vectors can be reduced, while the generalization ability of SVM is not sacrificed. To train our reformulated SVM, we modeled it as a dual problem, similar to that of the standard SVM. Therefore, we can borrow any existing SVM training algorithms to iteratively train the reformulated SVM.

Our method has been tested on the UCI machine learning repository, as well as a real clinical problem, i.e., tissue classification in prostate ultrasound images. Compared to the SVM trained by the standard training method and Osuna's method, our method is able to achieve a much more efficient SVM, without losing its generalization ability.

References

1. V.N. Vapnik, "The Natural of Statistical Learning Theory". Springer Verlag, New York, 1995.
2. C.J.C. Burges, "A Tutorial on Support Vector Machines for Pattern Recognition", *Data Mining and Knowledge Discovery,* Vol. 2, pp. 121-167, 1998.
3. E. Osuna, R. Freund and F. Giosi, "Training Support Vector Machines: An Application to Face Detection", Proc. IEEE. Conf. Computer Vision and Pattern Recognition, pp. 130-136, 1997.
4. T. Joachims, "A statistical learning learning model of text classification for support vector machines", Proceedings of the 24th annual international ACM SIGIR conference on Research and development in information retrieval, New Orleans, 2001.
5. Y. Zhan, D. Shen, "Automated Segmentation of 3D US Prostate Images Using Statistical Texture-Based Matching Method", *Medical Image Computing and Computer-Assisted Intervention (MICCAI), 2003,* Nov 16-18, Canada.
6. V.Wan and S. Renals, "Speaker Verification using Sequence Discriminant Support Vector Machines", IEEE Transactions on Speech and Audio Processing, Vol. 13, No. 2, pages 203-210, March 2005.
7. M. P. S. Brown, W. N. Grundy, D. Lin, N. Cristianini, C. W. Sugnet, T. S. Furey, M. Ares Jr. and D. Haussler, "Knowledge-based analysis of microarray gene expression data by using support vector machines", Genetics, Vol. 97, Issue 1, 262-267, January 4, 2000.
8. C. Davatzikos, D. Shen, Z. Lao, Z. Xue and B. Karacali "Morphological classification of medical images using nonlinear support vector machines", *IEEE International Symposium on Biomedical Imaging (ISBI),* Arlington, VA, April 15-18, 2004.
9. Y. Lecun, L. Jackel, L. Bottou, A. Brunot, C. Cortes, J. Denker, H. Drunker, I. Guyon, U. Muller, E. Sackinger, P. Simard and V. Vapnik, "Comparison of Learning Algorithms for Handwritten Digit Recognition", International Conference on Artificial Neural Networks, pp. 53-60, 1995.
10. Y-L. Tian, L. Brown, A. Hampapur, S. Pankanti, A. W. Senior, and R. M. Bolle, "Real World Real-time Automatic Recognition of Facial Expressions", IEEE workshop on performance evaluation of tracking and surveillance, Graz, Austria, March 31, 2003.
11. E. Osuna and F. Girosi, "Reducing the run-time complexity of Support Vector Machines", *ICPR,* Brisbane, Australia, 1998.

12. B. Scholkopf and A. J. Smola, "Learning with Kernels", The MIT Press, Cambridge, 2002.
13. C.J.C Burges, "Simplified support vector decision rules", Proceedings of the 13th International Conference on Machine Learning, pp. 71-77, 1996.
14. Y.-J. Lee and O.L. Mangasarian, "RSVM: Reduced support vector machines", Proceedings of the First SIA International Conference on Data Mining, 2001.
15. S. Hettich, C.L. Blake and C.J. Merz, "Repository of machine learning databases", http://www.ics.uci.edu/~mlearn/MLRepository.html, 1998.
16. B.S. Manjunath and W.Y. Ma, "Texture Features for Browsing and Retrieval of Image Data", *IEEE Trans. on Pattern Anal. Mach. Intell.*, Vol.18, pp. 837-842, 1996.

Locally Linear Isometric Parameterization

Xianfang Sun[1,2] and Edwin R. Hancock[2]

[1] School of Automation Science and Electrical Engineering,
Beihang University, Beijing 100083, P.R. China
[2] Department of Computer Science, The University of York, York YO10 5DD, UK
{xfsun, erh}@cs.york.ac.uk

Abstract. A general algorithm framework for 3D mesh parametrization is proposed in this paper. Under this framework, a parametrization
algorithm is divided into three steps. In the first step, the linearly reconstructing weights of each vertex with respect to its neighbours are computed. These weights are then used to computed a initial parametrization mesh, and in the third step, this initial mesh is rotated and scaled
to obtain a parametrization mesh with high isometric precision. Four
parametrization algorithms are proposed based on this framework. Examples show the effectiveness and applicability of the parametrization
algorithms proposed in the paper.

1   Introduction

Triangular mesh parametrization aims to determine a 2D triangular mesh with
its vertices, edges, and triangles corresponding to that of the original 3D triangular mesh, satisfying an optimality criterion. The technique has been applied in
a wide range of problems in computer graphics and image processing, including
texture mapping [13], morphing [9], and remeshing [5]. Extensive research has
been undertaken into the theoretical issues underpinning the method and its
practical application. For a tutorial and survey, the reader is referred to [4].

A well-known parametrization method is that proposed by Floater [2]. It is a
generalization of the basic procedure originally proposed by Tutte [11] which was
used to draw planar graphs. The basic idea underpinning this method is to use
the vertex coordinates of the original 3D triangular mesh to compute reconstructing weights of each interior vertex with respect to its neighbour vertices. These
weights are subsequently used together with the boundary vertex coordinates
on a plane to compute the interior vertex coordinates of a 2D triangular mesh.
A drawback of Floater's parametrization method is that the boundary vertex
coordinates must be determined manually beforehand.

Another parametrization method is that proposed by Zigelman et al. [13]. It
first uses the Dijkstra algorithm to compute the geodesic distances between each
pair of the vertices, and then uses multidimensional scaling (MDS) to determine
the vertex coordinates on a 2D plane. This method does not need the boundary
vertex coordinates to be determined manually beforehand. However, it is highly
time-consuming because it needs to compute the geodesic distances between
every pair of vertices.

A. Rangarajan et al. (Eds.): EMMCVPR 2005, LNCS 3757, pp. 552–567, 2005.
© Springer-Verlag Berlin Heidelberg 2005

In fact, the parametrization method proposed by Zigelman et al. [13] is a special case of a newly emerging nonlinear dimensionality reduction method, Isomap, proposed by Tenenbaum et al. [10]. Isomap maps high-dimensional data points into a low dimensional space. Naturally, it can be used to map the 3D vertices into a 2D plane as is required in the parametrization of 3D triangular meshes. The only difference between Zigelman's method and Isomap is that the former attempts to improve the precision of the geodesic distance computation by incorporating the geometry of the problem into the solution.

Another important nonlinear dimensionality reduction method is the Locally Linear Embedding (LLE) method proposed by Roweis and Saul [6]. This method uses an analytical method to compute the low dimensional embedding, and hence is more computationally efficient. Like Isomap, it could also potentially be used for mesh parametrization. Unfortunately, because it rotates and scales the vertex coordinates, it can not preserve inter-vertex distances, and thus its use for mesh parametrization is limited.

Motivated by the basic idea of the LLE method, we propose a general algorithm framework of 3D mesh parametrization in this paper. The aim of this framework is to develop parametrization algorithms which have the properties of both fast computation and minimization of the distance errors. In addition, the algorithms should remove the requirement that the boundary vertex coordinates of the parametrization mesh must by determined beforehand.

The paper is organised as follows. Section 2 describes the general algorithm framework which consists of three steps. Sections 3 to 5 give some detailed optimal criteria and algorithms for each step of this framework. Based on the framework and the algorithms described in Section 2 to 5, Section 6 gives four possible algorithms for mesh parametrization and use three examples to show the properties of these algorithms. Finally, in Section 7 we conclude the paper.

2   Algorithm Framework

Consider a triangular mesh $T = T(V, E, F, X)$ with vertex set $V = \{i : i = 1, 2, ..., N\}$ and corresponding coordinate set $X = \{x_i : x_i \in R^d, i \in V\}$ ($d = 2$ or 3), edge set $E = \{(i, j) : (i, j) \in V \times V\}$, and triangular face set $F = \{(i, j, k) : (i, j), (i, k), (j, k) \in E\}$. Here an edge (i, j) is represented by a straight line segment between vertices i and j, and a triangular face (i, j, k) is a triangular facet bounded by three edges (i, j), (i, k) and (j, k). When $d = 2$, T is drawn on a plane and represents a planar triangular mesh, while $d = 3$, T is drawn in a 3-dimensional space and represents a 3D triangular mesh. A triangular mesh is called valid if the only intersections between edges are at common end points (vertices) and the only intersections between triangular faces are on the common edges. Hereafter, when a triangular mesh is referred to without qualification, it implies that the triangular mesh is valid.

The parametrization here is made on a valid 3D triangular mesh. A parametrization of a valid 3D triangular mesh $T = T(V, E, F, X)$ is any valid planar triangular mesh $T_p = T_p(V, E, F, Y)$ with $Y = \{y_i : y_i \in R^2, i \in V\}$ being the corresponding coordinates of V.

For each vertex i, let $T_i = T_i(V_i, E_i, F_i, X_i)$ be the sub-mesh of T, whose vertex set V_i consists of vertex i and its neighbours in V, and whose edge set E_i consists of edges in E which connect pairs of vertices in T_i. The parametrization algorithm framework proposed in this paper consists of the following three steps.

- For each 3D sub-mesh T_i, construct a local planar sub-mesh $T_{Li} = T_{Li}(V_i, E_i, F_i, Y_{Li})$, and then compute weights $W_{i,j}$, such that using these weights, Y_{Li} can be best linearly reconstructed from its neighbours' coordinates Y_{Lj};
- Using all the weights $W_{i,j}$ obtained in the above step, construct an initial global planar mesh $T_I = T_I(V, E, F, Y_I)$ such that Y_I give the best linear reconstruction of their neighbours;
- Make coordinate transformation on Y_I to obtain the final coordinates Y such that the total distortion of the planar parametrization $T_p = T_p(V, E, F, Y)$ with respect to the original 3D triangular mesh $T = T(V, E, F, X)$ is minimized.

Note that the algorithm framework proposed here is very general. One can have different definitions on the distortion or the quality of the best reconstruction. In the following sections, we provide detailed explanations about each step and describe some algorithms based on different definitions on these concepts.

3   Best Linearly Reconstructing Weights

The first step of this algorithm consists of two stages. In the first stage, each 3D sub-mesh T_i is flattened to yield a local parametrization $T_{Li} = T_{Li}(V_i, E_i, F_i, Y_{Li})$, and in the second stage, weights $W_{i,j}$ are computed using Y_{Li}.

3.1   Sub-mesh Flattening

There are different ways of mapping T_i into the plane [2]. Some of them are unstable when there are large angles between the triangular facets in T_i. Others have poor performance according to some distortion criteria. A potentially good method is that proposed by Welch and Witkin [12], which was also adopted by Floater [2]. Although this method preserves the arc length in each radial direction from the vertex i, there are large errors in the boundary arc lengths. In this section, we provide a new mapping method that couples the errors in the radial directions and the boundary arcs. We will apply the classical MDS method to map the 3D mesh T_i into the 2D plane such that the total distortion associated with the geometric distances of the edges is minimized.

To use the MDS method, we need to compute the geodesic distances between each pair of vertices. Let us first consider an interior vertex i of the 3D triangular mesh (refer to Figure 1(a)). We cut the sub-mesh T_i along any one radial arc (e.g., the edge (i, j_{m_i}) in Figure 1(a)), and then develop it onto the plane (Figure 1(b)). The geodesic distances $d_{0,k}$ between vertex i and j_k ($k = 1, ..., m_i$),

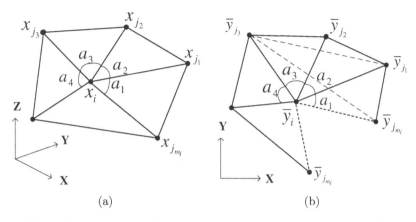

Fig. 1. A sub-mesh T_i (a) and its cut and development on a plane (b)

$d_{k,k+1}$ ($k = 1, ..., m_i - 1$) and d_{1,m_i} between adjacent vertices are the same as their corresponding Euclidean distances $l_{0,k}$, $l_{k,k+1}$ and l_{1,m_i}. The other required distances between the two boundary vertices j_a and j_b can be computed using the following formula

$$d_{a,b} = \sqrt{l_{0,a}^2 + l_{0,b}^2 - 2l_{0,a}l_{0,b}\cos\alpha_{a,b}} \ . \tag{1}$$

Here $\alpha_{a,b}$ is the short path angle between edges (i, j_a) and (i, j_b), which is computed by (without loss of generality, assuming $b > a$)

$$\alpha'_{a,b} = \sum_{k=a+1}^{b} \alpha_k, \quad \alpha_{\text{sum}} = \sum_{k=1}^{m_i} \alpha_k \ , \tag{2}$$

$$\alpha_{a,b} = \begin{cases} \alpha'_{a,b} \ , & \text{if } \alpha'_{a,b} \leq \alpha_{\text{sum}}/2 \\ \alpha_{\text{sum}} - \alpha'_{a,b} \ , & \text{if } \alpha'_{a,b} > \alpha_{\text{sum}}/2 \end{cases} \ , \tag{3}$$

where α_k ($k = 2, \cdots, m_i$) is the angle between edges (i, j_{k-1}) and (i, j_k), and α_1 is the angle between edges (i, j_{m_i}) and (i, j_1). The justification of the above computations is clear from Figure 1.

If the vertex i is a boundary vertex, then we can directly develop the sub-mesh T_i on the 2D plane. The computation formula is the same as that for an interior vertex other than that α_1 is equal to the angle between developed edges (i, j_{m_i}) and (i, j_1), and thus $\alpha_{\text{sum}} = 2\pi$.

After all the required geodesic distances have been obtained the classical MDS method proceeds according to the following steps [1].

– Form the matrix of squared geodesic distances D_I. For our case, D_I is defined as

$$D_I = \begin{bmatrix} d_{0,0}^2 & d_{0,1}^2 & \cdots & d_{0,m_i}^2 \\ d_{1,0}^2 & d_{1,1}^2 & \cdots & d_{1,m_i}^2 \\ \vdots & \vdots & \ddots & \vdots \\ d_{m_i,0}^2 & d_{m_i,1}^2 & \cdots & d_{m_i,m_i}^2 \end{bmatrix} \ . \tag{4}$$

Note that because the distance between two vertices is nondirectional, $d_{a,b} = d_{b,a}$, hence the matrix D_I is symmetric;
- Apply double centering to D_I, to obtain the centred distance matrix

$$B = -\frac{1}{2} J D_I J \ , \tag{5}$$

where $J = I - \frac{1}{m_i+1} \mathbf{1}\mathbf{1}^T$, I is identity matrix, and $\mathbf{1}$ is a vector of ones of length $m_i + 1$;
- Compute the eigendecomposition $B = Q \Lambda Q^T$;
- Denote the matrix of the first two largest positive eigenvalues as Λ_+, and the corresponding first two columns of Q as Q_+. The local parametrization coordinates are now given by $Y_{Li} = Q_+ \Lambda_+^{\frac{1}{2}}$, where the transpose of the first row of Y_{Li} is the coordinate y_{Li} of vertex i, and the transpose of the second to the (m_i+1)'th rows are the coordinates y_{Lj_1} to $y_{Lj_{m_i}}$ of vertices j_1 to j_{m_i}.

Because the classical MDS method minimizes the loss function $L(Y_{Li}) = \|\frac{1}{2} J[\hat{D}_I(Y_{Li}) - D_I]J\|$, where $\hat{D}_I(Y_{Li})$ is the squared Euclidean distances computed by Y_{Li}, this local parametrization has the property of minimizing the distance distortion.

3.2   Computation of the Linearly Reconstructing Weights

The locally linear reconstructing weights $W_{i,j}$ are those satisfying the condition

$$y_{Li} = \sum_{k=1}^{m_i} W_{i,j_k} y_{Lj_k} \ , \quad \sum_{k=1}^{m_i} W_{i,j_k} = 1 \ . \tag{6}$$

There are some alternative methods for computing the weights. Floater proposed a shape-preserving scheme [2]. The weights computed using this scheme can result in a good parametrization in the case that the original 3D triangular mesh is an embedding on an intrinsic 2D manifold, and that the boundary vertices can be determined properly beforhand. However, these weights do not have a physically meaningful optimal property when the original 3D triangular mesh is an embedding on an intrinsic 3D manifold. In addition, since this scheme requires that the boundary vertices be determined beforehand, it does not provide a method of computing the weights for the boundary vertices.

Roweis and Saul computed the weights using a least-squares method [6]. Because the solution to the least-squares problem is singular for most of the vertices, they introduced a modification on the solution. However, this modification makes the weights suboptimal.

In this section, we introduce a new method for computing the weights, which is optimal in the sense that the coordinate errors are minimized.

From (6), it can be seen that when y_{Lj_k} has error Δy_{Lj_k} $(k = 1, \cdots, m_i)$, the error of y_{Li} will be

$$\Delta y_{Li} = \sum_{k=1}^{m_i} W_{i,j_k} \Delta y_{Lj_k} = \Delta Y_{Lj}^T W_i \ , \tag{7}$$

where $W_i = [W_{i,j_1}, \cdots, W_{i,j_{m_i}}]^T$, and $\Delta Y_{Lj} = [\Delta y_{Lj_1}, \cdots, \Delta y_{Lj_{m_i}}]^T$. The squared magnitude of Δy_{Li} is

$$\|\Delta y_{Li}\|^2 = W_i^T \Delta Y_{Lj} \Delta Y_{Lj}^T W_i \leq \lambda_{\max}(\Delta Y_{Lj} \Delta Y_{Lj}^T)\|W_i\|^2 \ , \tag{8}$$

where $\lambda_{\max}(\cdot)$ is the maximum eigenvalue.

Since the distribution of ΔY_{Lj} is unknown, we can only deal with the worst case error of Δy_{Li} caused by ΔY_{Lj}. From (8) it can be seen that when the magnitude of ΔY_{Lj} is given, the worst case squared error is proportional to $\|W_i\|^2$. Hence, by minimizing $\|W_i\|^2$ we also minimize the worst case error. Thus, we need to solve the following minimization problem

$$\begin{aligned} &\min \|W_i\|^2 \\ &\text{s.t.} \quad y_{Li} = \sum_{k=1}^{m_i} W_{i,j_k} y_{Lj_k} , \quad \sum_{k=1}^{m_i} W_{i,j_k} = 1 \end{aligned} \ . \tag{9}$$

Let $z_i = \begin{bmatrix} y_{Li} \\ 1 \end{bmatrix}$, $Z_j = [Y_{Lj} \ 1]$, then (9) becomes

$$\begin{aligned} &\min W_i^T W_i \\ &\text{s.t.} \quad z_i = Z_j^T W_i \end{aligned} \ . \tag{10}$$

The solution of this minimisation problem can be easily obtained using the Lagrange operator method, which yields

$$W_i = Z_j (Z_j^T Z_j)^{-1} z_i \ . \tag{11}$$

Note that for any interior vertex i of the triangular mesh, the number of its neighbours $m_i \geq 3$, and none of the neighbours are on the same straight line. Hence, $Z_j^T Z_j$ is not singular, and (11) has a unique solution. For a boundary vertex i, however, the number of its neighbours m_i may be equal to 2. And even if $m_i \geq 3$, its neighbours may occasionally be distributed on the same straight line. In these cases, $Z_j^T Z_j$ is singular, and we can not obtain a unique solution of W_i from (11). The trick to overcome this problem is to introduce a new vertex, which is itself the neighbour of one of the neighbours of vertex i. This new vertex combined with the neighbours of vertex i forms the new set of neighbours, and the new $Z_j^T Z_j$ is nonsingular. A unique solution of W_i can now be computed.

3.3 Mean Value Coordinates

It is worth mentioning that the two stages of the first step can be merged in some cases. For example, when the LLE method [6] is used for computing the linear reconstructing weights, the first stage is actually omitted. We usually directly use the original 3D coordinates to compute the weights. However, just as suggested in [8], introducing the first stage may result in linear reconstructing weights with better optimal property.

Floater [3] also dispensed with the first stage when he used the mean-value coordinate scheme to compute linearly reconstructing weights, but this does not affect the optimal property when the original 3D mesh is an embedding on an intrinsic 2D manifold. However, Floater did not discuss the computation of the linear reconstructing weights of the boundary vertices. In this section, we explain this problem in more detail.

The linear reconstructing weights, or the mean value coordinates as called by Floater [3], of an interior vertex i can be computed using the formulae

$$W_{i,j} = \frac{\lambda_{i,j}}{\sum_{(i,k) \in E} \lambda_{i,k}}, \quad \lambda_{i,j} = \frac{\tan(\alpha_{i,j-1}/2) + \tan(\alpha_{i,j}/2)}{\|x_j - x_i\|}, \quad (12)$$

where $\alpha_{i,j-1}$ and $\alpha_{i,j}$ are the angles between the edge (i,j) and its two neighbouring edges $(i, j-1)$ and $(i, j+1)$ (see Fig. 2(a)).

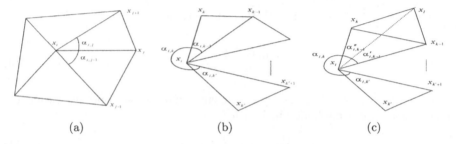

(a)   (b)   (c)

Fig. 2. Elements for the computation of mean value coordinates: (a) interior vertex, (b) general boundary vertex, (c) boundary vertex in case with additional neighbour vertex

We can use similar formulae to compute the mean value coordinates of a boundary vertex. However, some special problems must be paid attention to. For a boundary vertex i, the coefficients $\lambda_{i,k}$ and $\lambda_{i,k'}$ of its neigbouring boundary vertices k and k' are computed using the formulae (refer to Fig. 2(b))

$$\lambda_{i,k} = \frac{\tan(\alpha_{i,k-1}/2) + \tan(\alpha_{i,k}/2)}{\|x_k - x_i\|}, \quad \lambda_{i,k'} = \frac{\tan(\alpha_{i,k}/2) + \tan(\alpha_{i,k'}/2)}{\|x_{k'} - x_i\|}, \quad (13)$$

Because $\alpha_{i,k}$ is not strictly less than π, two problems arise when (12) and (13) are used to compute $W_{i,j}$. The first problem occurs when $\alpha_{i,k} = \pi$, i.e. $\tan(\alpha_{i,k}/2) = \infty$, which causes a computational overflow. The solution of this problem is to simply set $\lambda_{i,k} = 1/\|x_k - x_i\|$, $\lambda_{i,k'} = 1/\|x_{k'} - x_i\|$, and $\lambda_{i,j} = 0$ for all other $j \in V$. The second problem occurs when $\sum_{(i,j) \in E} \lambda_{i,j} = 0$, which causes a divide-by-zero error when $W_{i,j}$ is computed. In this case, an additional vertex l, which is originally not the neighbour vertex of i, but that of one of i's neighbouring vertices, is now taken as the neighbour vertex of i in computing the mean value coordinates (see Fig. 2(c)).

4   Initial Local Planar Mesh

After the W_i's have been obtained, we proceed to Step 2. In this step, we compute an initial parametrization mesh $T_I = T_I(V, E, F, Y_I)$. The problem can be solved by minimizing the cost function

$$\Phi(Y_I) = \sum_{i=1}^{N} \left\| y_{Ii} - \sum_{k=1}^{m_i} W_{i,j_k} y_{Ij_k} \right\|^2 , \tag{14}$$

where N is the number of vertices.

Two cases exist in solving this problem. The first case is that when the boundary vertices are given beforehand. Floater discussed this case and gave the solution [2]. In this case, the minimum cost of (14) is 0, and the solution of Y_I is determined by the linear system of equation

$$L_W Y_I = 0 , \tag{15}$$

where $L_W = I - W$ is the general normalized Laplacian operator, $W = [W_{i,j}]$ with $W_{i,j} = 0$ for j not being a neighbour of i. Let Y_{IB} be the known boundary vertex coordinates, and Y_{II} be the unknown interior vertex coordinates, then after its redundant rows were eliminated, equation (15) becomes

$$L_W^{II} Y_{II} = L_W^{IB} Y_{IB} , \tag{16}$$

where L_W^{II} is the sub-matrix of L_W corresponding to the rows and columns of the interior vertices, and L_W^{IB} is the sub-matrix corresponding to the rows of the interior vertices and the columns of the boundary vertices. Many numerical method can be used to solve the linear equation system (16) efficiently.

The second case is that when the boundary vertices are not given beforehand. The problem is now the same as that in [6], and we can borrow the method from that paper.

It is clear that all the coordinates, i.e. the Y_{Ii}'s, can be translated by a constant displacement and rotated by a constant angle without affecting the cost. We remove the translational and rotational degrees of freedom by forcing the following constraints.

$$\sum_{i=1}^{N} y_{Ii} = 0 , \tag{17}$$

$$\frac{1}{N} \sum_{i=1}^{N} y_{Ii} y_{Ii}^T = I , \tag{18}$$

Note that in the second constraint, we have fixed the scale of coordinates to avoid degenerate solutions.

Let $M = L_W^T L_W$. Spectral decomposition of M gives the lowest 3 eigenvectors (corresponding to smallest 3 eigenvlues). The lowest eigenvector of M has eigenvalue 0 and corresponds to the all-ones vector, is discarded here. The remaining two eigenvectors then form the initial 2D coordinates Y_I.

5   Global Parametrization

The initial coordinates Y_I obtained in the last section have the property that they are the optimal linear reconstructions of the original 3D triangular mesh subjecting to scaling the coordinates. When we use Y_I to construct a 2D triangular mesh, the shape of the mesh can best approach that of the original 3D triangular mesh. However, because of the scaling, the errors of edge lengths between the original mesh and the new one may be significant. To obtain a global optimal parametrization, these errors should be minimized. In this section, we rotate and re-scale Y_I to generate new coordinates, such that the errors of edge lengths are minimized.

Let the rotation matrix be R and the diagonal re-scaling matrix be S, then for each y_{Ii}, we can compute a new coordinate y_i by

$$y_i = SRy_{Ii} \ . \tag{19}$$

To minimize the errors of edge lengths, we use the following cost function

$$\Psi = \sum_{(i,j) \in E} (d_{i,j}^2 - l_{i,j}^2)^2 \ , \tag{20}$$

where $d_{i,j}$ and $l_{i,j}$ are the lengths of the edge (i, j) in the 2D and 3D triangular mesh, respectively. From (19), we have

$$\begin{aligned}
d_{i,j}^2 &= (y_i - y_j)^T (y_i - y_j) = (y_{Ii} - y_{Ij})^T R^T S^2 R (y_{Ii} - y_{Ij}) \\
&= (y_{Ii} - y_{Ij})^T A (y_{Ii} - y_{Ij}) = (y_{Ii1} - y_{Ij1})^2 A_{11} \\
&\quad + 2(y_{Ii1} - y_{Ij1})(y_{Ii2} - y_{Ij2}) A_{12} + (y_{Ii2} - y_{Ij2})^2 A_{22}
\end{aligned} \tag{21}$$

where we have defined

$$A = \begin{bmatrix} A_{11} & A_{12} \\ A_{12} & A_{22} \end{bmatrix} = R^T S^2 R \ . \tag{22}$$

Substituting (21) into (20), we see that minimizing (20) becomes a least-squares problem, and we can easily obtain (A_{11}, A_{12}, A_{22}) through solving the least-squares problem. Then according to (22), S and R can be obtained through spectral decompotion of the matrix A. After S and R are obtained, y_i can be computed through (19). Finally, a parametrization $T_p = T_p(V, E, F, Y)$ is obtained, which has the property that the global edge lengths errors are minimized.

6   Examples

In this section, three examples are provided to illustrate some properties of the algorithms based on the algorithm framework proposed in this paper. Four algorithms are applied, which are different in the main first step, and the same in the remaining two steps. The first algorithm uses the two-stage optimal method described in Sections 3.1 and 3.2 as its first step and is called the iso-optimal algorithm for short. The second one chooses the enhanced mean value coordinate method described in Section 3.3 as its first step and is called the iso-MVC algorithm. The third one applies the original LLE method [6] for the computation of the linear reconstructing weights and is called the iso-LLE-O algorithm. Finally, the fourth algorithm also applies the LLE method for the computation of the linear reconstructing weights, but it uses the natural neighbours of the triangular mesh, not the K-nearest neighbours as in the third algorithm. The fourth algorithm is called the iso-LLE-N algorithm for short.

We will first compare the parametrization results of the proposed algorithms with the Isomap method [10] through two synthetic examples using two measures – the isometric precision and the CPU time cost. Then, we will compare these algorithms and Floater's original mean value coordinate method [3] through an example of texture mapping application. Note that in the first two examples, we do not compare our method with Floater's [2, 3] because an apparent advantage of our method over Floater's is that Floater's method requires that the boundary vertices of the parametrization mesh be determined manually beforehand, while ours does not. We also do not compare our algorithms with Zigleman's method [13] because in our experimental cases, the properties of Zigleman's method are not better than that of the Isomap method.

In the first example, we consider an S-shaped manifold [7]. It is an intrinsically two dimensional manifold. We have performed experiments on this manifold in two different sampling cases. In the first case, we have sampled points on the manifold regularly, and constructed the Delaunay triangulation of the sample points. Experiments with different numbers of points show that the iso-optimal algorithm results in a perfect parametrization. As a matter of fact, in all the experiments using our algorithm, the residual variances of the edge lengths are of an order of magnitude less than 10^{-21}, while the residual variances of other algorithms including the Isomap method are of the order of magnitude $10^{-3} \sim 10^{-5}$.

Figure 3(a) shows a regular sample of $N = 600$ data points and its triangulation in 3D. Figures 3(b)∼(f) show its parametrization using our algorithms method and the Isomap method, respectively. It can be seen that the result from the iso-optimal algorithm is almost the same as the development of the original 3D triangular mesh, but obvious errors appear in the result of the other algorithms. The resulting parametrization mesh obtained using the iso-LLE-N algorithm even overlaps. It is worth mentioning that the different number of neighbours K in the iso-LLE-O algorithm may result in greatly different results. Too large or too small a value of K may result in an overlapping mesh. Figure 3(d) is the best result that we have obtained through carefully choosing K. In the remainder of this section, whenever the result of the iso-LLE-O algorithm is given, it is always the best result we have obtained.

In the second case of the first example, we have placed sample points on the S-shaped manifold randomly, and again constructed the Delaunay triangulation of the sample points. Figure 4(a) shows a random sample of $N = 600$ data points on the S-shaped manifold. Figure 4(b)∼(f) show its parametrization using different

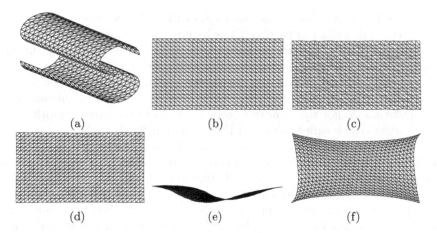

Fig. 3. Parametrization of a regular mesh (a) using iso-optimal (b), iso-MVC (c), iso-LLE-O (K=8) (d), iso-LLE-N (e), and the Isomap method (f)

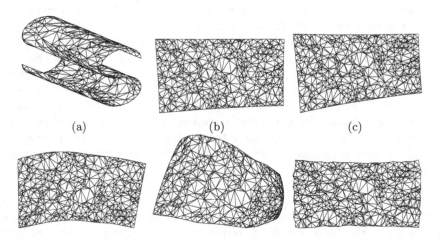

Fig. 4. Parametrization of an irregular mesh (a) using iso-optimal (b), iso-MVC (c), iso-LLE-O (K=12) (d), iso-LLE-N (e), and the Isomap method (f)

algorithms. It can be seen that the appearance of the parametrization using the iso-optimal algorithm is closer to the development of the original mesh than that using the other algorithms.

Figure 5 (a) and (b) give a comparison of the residual variances and CPU time cost of different algorithms for different numbers of points in the random sampling case. In order to show the difference clearly, we have divided each figure into two parts. Note that we have not provided the results of the iso-LLE-N algorithm because in many cases the iso-LLE-N algorithm yielded an overlapping mesh, and it almost always performed worse than the iso-LLE-O algorithm.

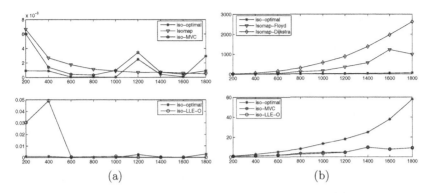

Fig. 5. Comparison of the residual variance (a) and the CPU time (seconds) (b)

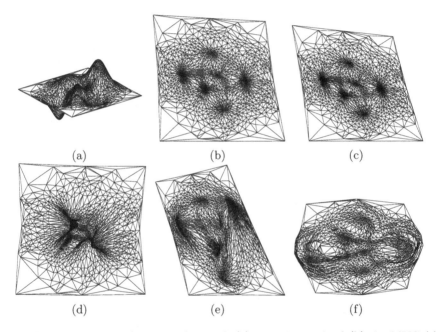

Fig. 6. Parametrization of an irregular mesh (a) using iso-optimal (b), iso-MVC (c), iso-LLE-O (K=12) (d), iso-LLE-N (e), and the Isomap method (f)

From Figure 5 (a) it can be seen that the precision of the iso-optimal algorithm is mostly better than that of the other algorithms, while the precision of the Isomap is mostly worse than the others.

To be fair in the comparison of CPU time cost, we have used Matlab 7.0 to code all algorithms with no special coding optimization for any one. For the Isomap method, we have used both Floyd's algorithm and Dijkstra's algorithm to compute the geodesic distances. The times shown in the figure were obtained when the programs were run on a PC with Pentium 4 CPU 2.40GHz and 2.41GHz, 512MB of RAM. From Figure 5 (b) it can be seen that the CPU time cost by the Isomap method is significantly more than that used by the other algorithms, and the CPU time cost by the iso-optimal algorithm is more than that used by the iso-MVC and the iso-LLE-O algorithm. With an increasing number of vertices, the difference in CPU times grows rapidly. It can also be seen that in the Isomap method, the Dijkstra algorithm is more time-consuming than Floyd's algorithm.

The second example uses the *peaks* function of Matlab. We have scaled down the z-coordinates by 1/3 for an efficient parametrization. Figure 6(a) shows an irregular triangulation of this function. It consists of 1688 vertices and 5049 edges. Figure 6(b)~(f) show its parametrization using different algorithms. It can be seen that the iso-LLE-O and iso-LLE-N algorithms and the Isomap method all yield a parametrization with some edges folded over, while the iso-optimal and iso-MVC algorithms do not. Interestingly, however, the residual variances of the Isomap and iso-LLE-N algorithms are less than that of the iso-optimal and iso-MVC. They are 6.2×10^{-3}, 7.2×10^{-3}, 8.6×10^{-3}, and 9.1×10^{-3}, correspondingly. The variance of the iso-LLE-O algorithm is 1.2×10^{-2}.

The CPU time cost by the iso-optimal algorithm is 23.49 seconds, iso-MVC 15.05 seconds, iso-LLE-O 11.05 seconds, iso-LLE-N 9.17 seconds, while that of

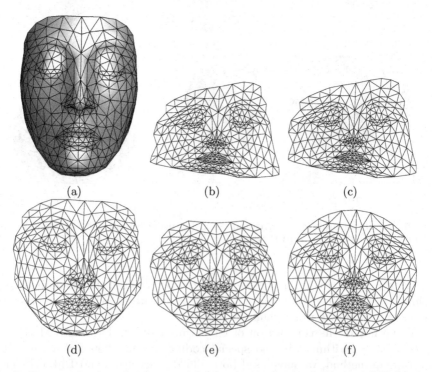

Fig. 7. Parametrization of a face model (a) using iso-optimal (b), iso-MVC (c), iso-LLE-O (K=11) (d), Isomap (e), and the original mean value coordinate algorithm (f)

the Isomap method using Floyd's and Dijkstra's algorithms for geodesic distance computation are 769.67 and 2747.90 seconds, respectively. Although the CPU time cost of the iso-optimal algorithm is greater than that of the iso-MVC, iso-LLE-O, and iso-LLE-N algorithms, it is significantly smaller than that of the Isomap algorithm. Even using the faster Floyd algorithm, the Isomap method takes more than 32 times the CPU time as the iso-optimal algorithm.

In the third example, we use a face model to demonstrate the application of the parametrization in texture mapping. Figure 7(a) shows a triangular mesh on this face. Figures 7(b)∼(f) show its parametrization using different algorithms. Here we have not given the result of the iso-LLE-N algorithm because it resulted in an overlapping mesh, and we have given the result of the original mean value coordinate method [3] with the boundary vertices distributed on a circle because the parametrization results from the other algorithm are actually very close to a circle. The algorithms listed in the order of increasing residual variances are the original mean value coordinate, the iso-LLE-O, the iso-MVC, the iso-optimal, and the Isomap. Note that although the residual variance of the original mean value coordinate is the smallest here, it does not mean that the mean-value

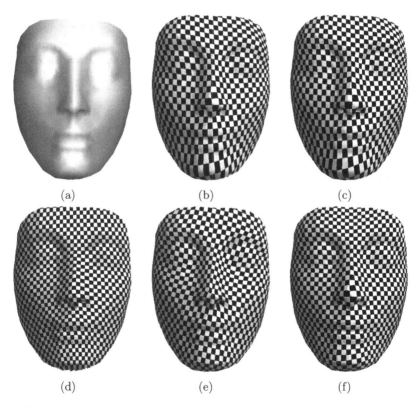

Fig. 8. Texture mapping of a face (a) using iso-optimal (b), iso-MVC (c), iso-LLE-O (K=11) (d), Isomap (e), and the original mean value coordinate parametrization (f)

coordinate algorithm is the best. The reason for this is that if the boundary vertices are wrongly determined, the residual variance may become very large.

Figure 8(a) shows the rendering of the face model. Figures 8(b)~(f) show the texture mapping results using using different parametrization algorithms. Visually, the iso-LLE-O algorithm results in the best texture mapping (see Figure 8(d)), while the iso-optimal and the iso-MVC algorithms result in a poorer texture mapping. However, all these algorithms have demonstrated their applicability in the field of texture mapping.

7   Conclusion

The parametrization method proposed by Floater [2, 3] has the drawback that the boundary vertex coordinates must be determined manually beforehand. Moreover, the parametrization method proposed by Zigelman et al. [13], which is similar to the Isomap method [10], has the drawback that it is highly time-consuming. In this paper, we have proposed a general parametrization algorithm framework to overcome these two drawbacks. Under this framework, a parametrization algorithm consists of three steps, and in each step, different optimal criteria can be chosen to yield different parametrization algorithms. We have provided isometric precision criteria in each step and developed four algorithms based on the different criteria. Examples show that the proposed iso-optimal algorithm can overcome the two above-mentioned drawbacks and has both high isometric precision and low CPU time cost.

References

1. Borg, I., Groenen, P.: Modern Multidimensional Scaling Theory and Application. Springer-Verlag, Berlin Heidelberg New York (1997)
2. Floater, M. S.: Parametrization and smooth approximation of surface triangulations. Comp. Aided Geom. Design. **14** (1997) 231–250
3. Floater, M. S.: Mean value coordinates. Comp. Aided Geom. Design. **20** (2003) 19–27
4. Floater, M. S., Hormann, K.: Surface parameterization: a tutorial and survey. In: Dodgson, N. A., Floater, M. S., Sabin, M.A.(eds.): Advances in Multiresolution for Geometric Modelling. Springer-Verlag, Berlin Heidelberg New York (2004) 157–186
5. Praun, E., Hoppe, H.: Spherical parametrization and remeshing. ACM Trans. Graphics. **22** (2003) 340–349
6. Roweis, S. T., Saul, L. K.: Nonlinear dimensionality reduction by locally linear embedding. Science. **290** (2000) 2323–2326
7. Saul, L. K., Roweis, S. T.: An introduction to locally linear embedding. Technical report, AT & T Labs-Research. (2000)
8. Saul, L. K., Roweis, S. T.: Think globally, fit locally: unsupervised learning of low dimensional manifolds. Journal of Machine Learning Research, **4** (2003) 119–155
9. Surazhsky, V., Gotsman, C.: Intrinsic morphing of compatible triangulations. Int. J. Shape Modelling. **9** (2003) 191–201

10. Tenenbaum, J. B., de Silva, V., Langford, J. C.: A global geometric framework for nonlinear dimensionality reduction. Science. **290** (2000) 2319–2323
11. Tutte, W. T.: How to draw a graph. Proc. London Math. Soc. **13** (1963) 743–768
12. Welch, W., Witkin, A.: Free-form shape design using triangulated surfaces. In: Computer Graphics, SIGGRAPH 94. (1994) 247–256
13. Zigelman, G., Kimmel, R., Kiryati N.: Texture mapping using surface flattening via multi-dimensional scaling. IEEE Trans. Visualization Comp. Graphics **8** (2002) 198–207

A Constrained Hybrid Optimization Algorithm for Morphable Appearance Models

Cuiping Zhang and Fernand S. Cohen

Electrical and Computer Engineering department,
Drexel University, Philadelphia PA 19104, USA
{zcp, fscohen}@cbis.ece.drexel.edu

Abstract. In this paper, we propose a constrained hybrid optimization algorithm that incorporates several shape constraints into a gradient descent procedure using a novel unbiased cost function. Shape constraints are heuristically derived from face images where the face shape can be directly estimated based on "motion" analysis. To better locate face contour points regardless of the background, local projection models are used. Experiments show that our algorithm benefits significantly from these shape constraints and achieves a much higher convergent rate compared to the inverse compositional optimization algorithm. We test our algorithm on different face databases, and demonstrate its robustness in presence of various illuminations, background patterns, as well as variations in face expressions.

1 Introduction

A widely adopted strategy in face analysis and recognition is analysis by synthesis, i.e., describing and analyzing a human face through modelling. In recent years, many flexible model-based algorithms have been proposed based on the analysis by synthesis approach and have been shown to be fruitful in wide applications ranging from face coding, to face reconstruction, to facial expression recognition etc. Two such models that have received a great deal of attention are: the Active Appearance Model (AAM) [1] and the Multidimensional Morphable Model (MMM) [2]. These are by and large generative parametric models that are customized to model a lot of phenomena.

The AAM, the MMM and most of their variants, follow several basic rules. Raw face shape and texture are extracted from the face image and are stored (in a vector form) as two distinct measurements. Face parameters are formed by treating face shape (or texture) as a linear combination of a set of exemplar basis shapes (or textures). Fitting a face model to a face image is an optimization process that minimizes a cost function. Modelling quality is evaluated using the cost function, which usually measures the minimum mean square error (MSE) between a synthesized model face and input face. Successful face modelling mainly depends on the design of the cost function, and the optimization scheme.

Face modelling amounts to finding the global minimum of the cost function, and is usually attained with standard gradient descent algorithms. It is well

A. Rangarajan et al. (Eds.): EMMCVPR 2005, LNCS 3757, pp. 568–583, 2005.
© Springer-Verlag Berlin Heidelberg 2005

known that for the solution to be a desired global minimum, the cost function has to be convex, which is hard to meet in reality. Besides, heavy computation is inevitable as gradient and Hessian information of the cost function need to be updated iteratively. The MMM originally adopts a stochastic gradient descent algorithm, which is comparatively fast and can to some extent avoid the trapping in local minima. The AAM takes a totally different approach. It assumes a fixed linear relationship between the texture error and the necessary update in the parameter space. This relationship is learned from a training set. The AAM is very fast, but it also has obvious drawbacks. First, the assumption of a fixed linear relationship is incorrect [3]. Secondly, the face image background is encoded, which may result in degraded performance when modelling a novel face with an unseen background. Matthews etc. [3] proposed an inverse compositional AAM that is as efficient as the AAM, yet is more theoretically founded. Its main advantage over standard gradient descent algorithms is its computational efficiency due to constant gradient and Hessian information. The inverse compositional AAM is reported to have similar convergence rate as the original AAM [4], and is therefore used as a test bed to compare with our algorithm.

Global algorithms attempt to find the bottom of the deepest valley for the cost function over a region of parameter space. Simulated annealing algorithms and genetic algorithms are two typical global optimization methods. M. Stegmann [5] studied various AAM extensions in his thesis, and compared several global and local optimization schemes. Global algorithms have broader view of the cost function's terrain and seek for a possibly better solution.

Treating the fitting problem as a general function minimization problem and seeking an analytical solution can hardly achieve both a decent convergent rate and algorithm efficiency. Fortunately there are alternative methods from a different perspective. The Active Shape Model (ASM) [6] is such a good example. It fully utilizes the heuristic information from face image and moves facial landmark points in a way so that extracted local terrain features conform to typical local distributions. The Active Morphable Model (AMM) [7] directly estimates face shape using a standard optical flow algorithm. Its model fitting algorithm is robust with a large region of convergence. However its iterative hierarchical optical flow estimation inside each iterative step makes it a less efficient model.

In this paper, we propose a constrained hybrid optimization algorithm to efficiently fit a morphable model to frontal face images. This algorithm takes advantage of abundant heuristic information in face image while preserving the gradient descent power of an analytical cost function. Based on our observation of one weakness of the widely adopted cost function, a novel unbiased error evaluation function is proposed. Two different algorithms are adopted to estimate face shape directly from face image. One is the block "motion" estimation algorithm that adjusts crucial landmark points for better local fitting. Another one consists of local projection models along face contour. For most appearance model-based algorithms, face contour points are especially hard to locate due to 2 facts: face cheek is almost textureless; face background is unpredictable and unreliable. Local projection models prove to be effective and computationally efficient by making use of intermediate piecewise affine transforms between face meshes. The directly estimated shape is incorporated as shape constraint within the framework of the standard inverse compositional fitting algorithm. At the initial phase of our model fitting process, the directly estimated shape dominates so that the search has better chance to move toward a global solution. As the model fitting error becomes smaller, gradient descent direction of the evaluation function takes control. Experiment indicates that a much higher convergent rate is achieved. The hierarchical motion estimation algorithm helps lock to the neighborhood of true minimum. In this sense, it is a global optimization scheme. Yet, it is much more efficient than general global optimization algorithms like simulated annealing algorithms and genetic algorithms. Average shape from training set is good enough to serve as the initial model estimate. Another merit of our algorithm is that it is truly background independent compared to various AAM or MMM algorithms.

The paper is organized as follows: Section 2 briefly introduces the AAM face model and the normalized inverse compositional optimization method; Section 3 starts with a novel definition of error evaluation function, followed by two direct shape estimating methods: block motion estimation and local projection models. Then we show how the estimated shape is incorporated to the inverse compositional optimization scheme; Section 4 gives our experimental results and analysis; Last section is conclusion part.

2   Preliminaries: Face Model and Normalized Inverse Compositional Optimization Algorithm

2.1   Face Model Definition

We follow the face model definition used by the AAM as it has a more concise shape definition than the MMM (where shape is in the form of dense flow field). Constructing training sets is straightforward with manually labelled landmark points. For any face image, its face shape $\mathbf{S}_{img} = \{x_0, y_0, x_1, y_1, \ldots, x_n, y_n\}$ is defined as a sequence of coordinates of facial landmark points, as shown in Fig. 1(a). Face texture is obtained by warping all pixels enclosed by a triangulated face mesh $\mathbf{S}_{img}$ to a common mesh $\mathbf{S}_0$, which is usually the average shape of all training images. The warped texture is shapeless in the sense it is generated on the base image coordinate and contains no shape information about the specific face. We use the same notation $\mathbf{S}_{img}$ to refer to the face shape, the triangular mesh and the set of all enclosed pixels.

After normalization using a similarity transformation with parameters $\mathbf{q}$, the face shape can be expressed as a linear combination of prototype shapes $\{S_k\}$ as $\mathbf{S} = \mathbf{S}_0 + \sum_{k=1}^{m_0} p_k \cdot \mathbf{S}_k$. The coefficients $\mathbf{p} = \{p_k\}$ are also referred as shape parameters. The orthogonal prototype shapes are usually generated using a SVD analysis on the training shapes. Similarly, texture is expressed as linear combination of prototype textures $\{\mathbf{T}_k\}$ with the base texture $\mathbf{T}_0$ and coefficients $\alpha = \{\lambda_k\}$, i.e., $\mathbf{T} = \mathbf{T}_0 + \sum_{k=1}^{n_0} \lambda_k \cdot \mathbf{T}_k$.

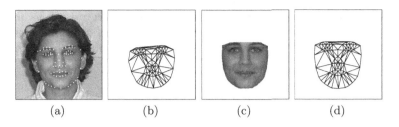

| (a) | (b) | (c) | (d) |

Fig. 1. (a)Definition of 73 landmark points. (b)Face mesh. (c)Warped shapeless texture. (d)Base face mesh.

$\{\mathbf{q}, \mathbf{p}, \alpha\}$ forms the complete face model parameter set. Model face can be rendered by warping a synthesized texture $\mathbf{T}$ from base mesh $\mathbf{S}_0$ to the reconstructed face mesh $\mathbf{S}_{img}$.

Modelling a face in a given image is equivalent to finding the optimal parameters so that the difference between the model face and the given face image is minimized. Any pixel u inside the base face $\mathbf{S}_0$ is mapped to a new position $w(u; \mathbf{p}, \mathbf{q})$ in the image according to the shape parameters $\mathbf{p}$ and the similarity parameters $\mathbf{q}$. The cost function usually takes the form of the sum of the squares of the texture difference (also referred as difference image) in accordance with:

$$G(\mathbf{p}, \mathbf{q}, \alpha) = \sum_{u \in S_0} \left[\mathbf{T}_0(u) + \sum_{k=1}^{n_0} \lambda_k \cdot \mathbf{T}_k(u) - \mathbf{I}(w(u; \mathbf{p}, \mathbf{q})) \right]^2. \tag{1}$$

In the original AAM, the difference image is directly used to update the current model parameters using a linear regression model. This updating rule is efficient and empirically driven, but it doesn't fall into any traditional optimization category.

2.2   Normalized Inverse Compositional Optimization Algorithm

Given the function $G(\mathbf{p}, \mathbf{q}, \alpha)$, a variety of gradient descent optimization algorithms could be applied. Generally, given a current estimate of model parameters, the function $G(\mathbf{p} + \mathbf{\Delta p}, \mathbf{q} + \mathbf{\Delta q}, \alpha + \mathbf{\Delta}\alpha)$ can be approximated to be a quadratic function of the incremental updates $\mathbf{\Delta p}, \mathbf{\Delta q}$ and $\mathbf{\Delta}\alpha$, using a Taylor series expansion. Closed form solutions to the updates of the current estimate in the parameter space are found. This operation is repeated till a minimum is reached. Unfortunately, gradient descent algorithms are slow due to heavy computation. The inverse compositional algorithm is a principled gradient descent algorithm that performs model fitting very efficiently. It is derived from the canonical Lucus-Kanade image alignment algorithm. For the time being, assume texture is fixed from the base texture image $\mathbf{T}_0$ to an input image $\mathbf{I}$, and the cost function is:

$$E(\mathbf{p}, \mathbf{q}) = \sum_{u \in S_0} \left[\mathbf{T}_0(u) - \mathbf{I}(w(u; \mathbf{p}, \mathbf{q})) \right]^2. \tag{2}$$

Basically in the iteration, the base texture image $\mathbf{T}_0$ is warped according to the underlying parameters $\Delta\mathbf{p}$ and $\Delta\mathbf{q}$ so that the warped base image resembles the input image at the current warp $w(u; \mathbf{p}, \mathbf{q})$. Mathematically, it equals to minimize:

$$E(\Delta\mathbf{p}, \Delta\mathbf{q}) = \sum_{u \in S_0} \left[\mathbf{T}_0(w(u; \Delta\mathbf{p}, \Delta\mathbf{q})) - \mathbf{I}(w(u; \mathbf{p}, \mathbf{q})) \right]^2. \tag{3}$$

The real warp between the base texture image and the input image is then updated as a composition of current warp and the inverse of the incremental warp parameters resulting from minimizing (3). The updating rule in (4) also explains how the inverse compositional AAM got its name.

$$w(u; \mathbf{p}, \mathbf{q}) \leftarrow w(u; \mathbf{p}, \mathbf{q}) \circ w(u; \Delta\mathbf{p}, \Delta\mathbf{q})^{-1}. \tag{4}$$

The cost function $E(\mathbf{p}, \mathbf{q})$ doesn't consider the texture variation between the base image and the input image. In the normalized inverse compositional algorithm, the texture parameters α are iteratively updated given the pose parameters $\mathbf{q}$ and the shape parameters $\mathbf{p}$. The closed form solution is:

$$\lambda_i = \sum_{u \in S_0} \mathbf{T}_k(u) \cdot \left[\mathbf{I}(w(u; \mathbf{p}, \mathbf{q})) - \mathbf{T}_0(u) \right]. \tag{5}$$

The difference image is accordingly adjusted for the inverse compositional algorithm.

The merit of the inverse compositional AAM is its efficiency. In the Gaussian-Newton gradient descent algorithm, approximating $\mathbf{T}_0(w(u; \Delta\mathbf{p}, \Delta\mathbf{q}))$ in (3) with its first order Taylor expansion requires the evaluation of $\frac{\partial w}{\partial p}$ at warp $\mathbf{w}(u, \mathbf{0}, \mathbf{0}) = u$, the identity transform. This leads to constant gradient descent images and Hessian matrix. Therefore, the computation time is cut greatly. It's not been demonstrated or proved in [3] that inverse compositional AAM might be superior to other gradient descent algorithms in terms of its convergent rate. It is just a special form of general gradient descent algorithm and fast enough for real-time applications.

When a global minimum is desired, gradient descent methods are suitable only when the objective function is convex. However, the sum of squared texture error is far from a convex function. Most likely gradient descent methods will end up in an undesired local minimum. It is of great interest to design an efficient and global optimization method for fitting this kind of morphable models.

3   Inverse Compositional Algorithm Constrained with Direct Shape Estimate

3.1   Unbiased Error Evaluation Function

Intuitively, we seek for the model parameters so that a synthesized model face best resembles the face in the unknown image. Naturally the fitting quality should be evaluated as summed squares of the texture error on the image frame. For most appearance-based models, however, the fitting error is computed on the base shape frame as sum of squared difference of synthesized texture and shape-less texture warped from input unknown image. Though measuring the fitting error on a standard base frame is straightforward and efficient, it can't reflect the real model fitting quality. This is caused by the piecewise affine transform during the image warping. As a result, the underlying optimization process is affected. Therefore, we propose a revised error function so that the error computed on the standard base frame could impartially reflect the fitting quality on the image frame.

On the test image frame, assume the nth triangle $\mathbf{L}_n$ has area $\tau_n(\mathbf{p}, \mathbf{q})$. All pixels inside this triangle contribute to the sum of squared error as:

$$\varepsilon_n(\mathbf{p}, \mathbf{q}, \alpha) = \sum_{u \in \mathbf{L}_n} \left[\mathbf{T}_0(u) + \sum_{k=1}^{n_0} \lambda_k \cdot \mathbf{T}_k(u) - \mathbf{I}(w(u; \mathbf{p}, \mathbf{q})) \right]^2. \tag{6}$$

The total error on the image frame is then the sum over all n_t triangles:

$$G_1(\mathbf{p}, \mathbf{q}, \alpha) = \sum_{n=1}^{n_t} \varepsilon_n(\mathbf{p}, \mathbf{q}, \alpha). \tag{7}$$

Accordingly, denote the corresponding n^{th} triangle $\mathbf{L}'_n$ on the standard base frame has area as τ'_n. It is easy to see that under affine transform mapping, the pixels inside this triangle have the same mean squared error as its counterpart triangle on the image frame. Apparently, the canonical error function on standard frame shown in (1) can be expressed as:

$$G(\mathbf{p}, \mathbf{q}, \alpha) = \sum_{n=1}^{n_t} \frac{\tau'_n}{\tau_n(\mathbf{p}, \mathbf{q})} \varepsilon_n(\mathbf{p}, \mathbf{q}, \alpha). \tag{8}$$

As an effort to minimize (8), general optimization algorithms might tend to maximize $\tau_n(\mathbf{p}, \mathbf{q})$ for large $\varepsilon_n(\mathbf{p}, \mathbf{q}, \alpha)$, therefore are more likely to converge to a local minimum. Such an effect is not desirable since the fitting error on the image frame is still large, indicating a bad model fitting. This problem is inherent in all model fitting algorithms based on the shapeless texture error measurement. On the other hand, computing a cost function on the standard frame is computationally efficient and better controlled. It is not difficult to rewrite $G_1(\mathbf{p}, \mathbf{q}, \alpha)$ on the standard frame as:

$$G_1(\mathbf{p}, \mathbf{q}, \alpha) = \sum_{n=1}^{n_t} \frac{\tau_n(\mathbf{p}, \mathbf{q})}{\tau'_n} \sum_{u \in \mathbf{L}'_n} \left[\mathbf{T}_0(u) + \sum_{k=1}^{n_0} \lambda_k \cdot \mathbf{T}_k(u) - \mathbf{I}(w(u; \mathbf{p}, \mathbf{q})) \right]^2. \tag{9}$$

Because the total area of the face mesh on the image frame depends on the parameters $\mathbf{p}$ and $\mathbf{q}$, it is more reasonable to use mean squared error (MSE) to evaluate the model fitting quality. The MSE on the image frame can then be computed on the standard model frame as:

$$G_{mse}(\mathbf{p}, \mathbf{q}, \alpha) = \sum_{u \in S_0} \rho_n(\mathbf{p}, \mathbf{q}) \cdot \left[\mathbf{T}_0(u) + \sum_{k=1}^{n_0} \lambda_k \cdot \mathbf{T}_k(u) - \mathbf{I}(w(u; \mathbf{p}, \mathbf{q})) \right]^2 . \quad (10)$$

G_{mse} is our new cost function. It is nothing but a weighted error function. The weight function varies for different triangles. In [8], it is explained how to minimize a weighted error function under the framework of inverse compositional algorithm. In short, Gradient and Hessian matrix of the new cost function are now respectively weighted sum of gradient and Hessian matrices for all triangles, which can be pre-computed before the iterative optimization.

3.2   Direct Shape Estimate from Motion Estimation

Motion estimation is one of the many applications of morphable models. Our focus in this paper is however the opposite. We would like to examine how a general motion estimation algorithm could help the model fitting process of our parameterized face model.

Motion estimation, literally, means estimating the motion of an object or camera from consecutive video images. In a standard morphable model fitting process, a parameterized model is fitted to an unknown image in an analysis-by-synthesis fashion. A cost function is minimized so that the synthesized model image is aligned with the input image. In other words, the fitting process tries to estimate the arbitrary "motion" between the synthesized image and the unknown image. Since facial landmark points are carefully defined in salient facial areas with a rich texture. It is of particular interest to estimate the motions of blocks centered at all landmark points.

Block motion model is one of the fundamental motion estimation methods. For a block β centered at current landmark point u_0 in the synthesized image $\mathbf{I}_s$, assume that its counterpart best-matching block in the unknown image $\mathbf{I}_0$ is displaced by a flow vector $\mathbf{v}$. Vector $\mathbf{v}$ can then be obtained by minimizing the sum of squared error as follows:

$$E_\beta(u) = \sum_{u \in \beta} (\mathbf{I}_s(u) - \mathbf{I}_0(u + \mathbf{v}))^2 = \sum_{u \in \beta} (\Delta\mathbf{I} - \nabla\mathbf{I}_0 \cdot v)^2, \quad (11)$$

where $\Delta\mathbf{I} = \mathbf{I}_s(u) - \mathbf{I}_0(u)$ is the difference block image. $\nabla\mathbf{I}_0$ is the gradient of the unknown image. The solution to (11) is:

$$\left[\sum (\nabla\mathbf{I}_0^T \cdot \nabla\mathbf{I}_0) \right] \cdot \mathbf{v} = \sum (\nabla\mathbf{I}_0^T \cdot \Delta\mathbf{I}). \quad (12)$$

The incremental flow vector will be accepted if it leads to a smaller block fitting error. Figure 2 shows a synthesized model image and how it looks like when overlapped to the unknown image.

(a)   (b)   (c)

Fig. 2. From left to right: a) Synthesized image. b) Input image. c) Synthesized face overlapped on the original face with current landmark points.

This simple block motion estimation algorithm is very efficient and fast. In (11), the block motion error is computed on the image frame and only difference image and gradient of unknown image are required to estimate the flow vector. Applying the motion estimation with various block sizes hierarchically on a down-sampled image generates more robust estimation. In a standard gradient descent optimization procedure, the motion estimation procedure only adds little extra computation.

Another merit of conducting motion estimation on the image frame is the background independence. Synthesized face is confined by the convex hull of landmark points as shown in Fig. 2. This convex hull serves as a face mask. During the block motion estimation, blocks are examined against this face mask so that only inner facial pixels participate in the motion estimation procedure. In this way, background independence is achieved. On the other hand, by subjecting the whole unknown image to motion estimation, heuristic information is fully explored.

3.3 Face Boundary Detection with Local Projection Models

Appearance-based morphable models seek for the optimal shape based on image intensity variation. Take another look at the masked face in Fig. 2(a), its background pattern in its original image could be arbitrary and unpredictable. It is not surprising that most morphable models often fail to locate face boundary correctly. To solve this problem, we come up with a method similar to the ASM based on the fact that landmark points on the face contour are usually the strongest local edge points. In the ASM algorithm, a landmark point moves along local normal direction so that its profile conforms to a typical distribution.

Instead of using the edge strength along the profile directly, we believe that edge information would be more prominent and stable after taking local average. This could be implemented by opening a narrow window and accumulating the edge map along the boundary direction to create a projection model for each landmark point. This is illustrated in Fig. 3.

Building local projection models in the original face image, as the ASM does, would be a time consuming task. All contour points and boundary directions

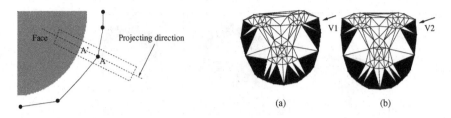

Fig. 3. Building local projection model

Fig. 4. Mesh definition. (a)Shape of the person in Fig. 1(a). (b)Base shape mesh.

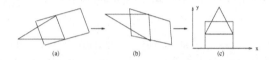

Fig. 5. Triangle-parallelogram pairs. (a)Image frame. (b)Base frame. (c)Standard pair.

need to be updated iteratively. Secondly, the scale of local projection model should be made proportional to the size of the whole face. These two problems are easily solved in our approach by associating the local projection models with the base shape mesh. Fig. 4(a) is the mesh of landmark points for the person in Fig. 1(a). Fig.4(b) shows the base shape mesh.

Triangles sitting on the face boundary are filled with black color. Their bottom sides form the face contour. Assume each black triangle is associated with a parallelogram with the bottom side of the triangle being the parallelogram's middle line. Our local projection models are built based on the analysis of the edge map inside these parallelograms. Instead of working on the edge map in the original face image, we equivalently work on the warped image edge map on the base frame. Suppose a triangle in the original mesh is V_1. It corresponding transformed triangle in the base mesh is V_2. We also introduce an isosceles triangle as a standard triangle V_0. As long as the bottom side of the triangle is transformed to the horizontal or vertical position, the projection along the face contour direction in the face image is now simplified to summation along the x (or y axis) after two affine transforms. Fig. 5 illustrates how a triangle-parallelogram pair in the face image is warped to the base frame and subsequently to the standard triangle-parallelogram pair.

The piece-wise affine transform parameters between V_1 and V_2 are available in the basic model fitting process (to generate a shapeless texture vector from the current face patch). The transforms between V_0 and all the triangles in the base shape could also be computed in advance. Clearly, with the help of a base shape and a standard triangle-parallelogram pair, the local projection models can lock the face contour points to the locally strongest edge points. It is much faster and easier compared to the ASM. The regions of interest for our local projection models are defined according to current face landmark points. Therefore there is no scaling problem at all.

3.4   Constrained Gradient Descent Optimization

Assume 3.2 and 3.3 yields estimated face shape as $\mathbf{S}^*$, it is desirable to minimize the distance between parameterized face shape $w(\mathbf{S}_0; \mathbf{p}, \mathbf{q})$ and $\mathbf{S}^*$. Mathematically, we construct a new cost function $F(\mathbf{p}, \mathbf{q})$ as sum of squared distance:

$$F(\mathbf{p}, \mathbf{q}) = \|w(\mathbf{S}_0; \mathbf{p}, \mathbf{q}) - \mathbf{S}^*\|^2. \tag{13}$$

In section 3.1, our cost function is defined as weighted mean squared texture error. Since $F(\mathbf{p}, \mathbf{q})$ is squared shape error, it provides complementary knowledge. To effectively benefit from both functions, we construct a hybrid function as combination of $F(\mathbf{p}, \mathbf{q})$ and $G_{mse}(\mathbf{p}, \mathbf{q}, \alpha)$:

$$R(\mathbf{p}, \mathbf{q}) = G_{mse}(\mathbf{p}, \mathbf{q}, \alpha) + K \cdot F(\mathbf{p}, \mathbf{q}). \tag{14}$$

The function $R(\Delta \mathbf{p}, \Delta \mathbf{q})$ is minimized to generate the incremental update $\Delta \mathbf{p}, \Delta \mathbf{q}$. Optimization based purely on texture error function $G_{mse}(\mathbf{p}, \mathbf{q}, \alpha)$ has a small region of convergence by nature. In the iterative realization, weight K starts with a large initial value, so that shape error function $F(\mathbf{p}, \mathbf{q})$ plays a major role at the initial stage. As search continues, K decreases till texture error function $G_{mse}(\mathbf{p}, \mathbf{q}, \alpha)$ totally dominates the optimization. We discriminate gradient-descent generative function $R(\mathbf{p}, \mathbf{q})$ from fitting error evaluation function $G_{mse}(\mathbf{p}, \mathbf{q}, \alpha)$ and accept new parameters when they imply a smaller fitting error.

The inverse compositional optimization algorithm is chosen to minimize function $R(\mathbf{p}, \mathbf{q})$ due to its efficiency and effectiveness. The general framework about how to minimize a constrained function like (14) is introduced in [8]. In this section, we briefly show how to minimize (14) when the shape transform is a piece-wise affine transform for morphable face models.

An unique feature of inverse compositional algorithm is that model parameters are updated indirectly according to (4). The real incremental updates $\Delta \mathbf{p}', \Delta \mathbf{q}'$ to current model parameters $(\mathbf{p}, \mathbf{q})$ are $(\Delta \mathbf{p}'; \Delta \mathbf{q}') = \mathbf{J} \cdot (\Delta \mathbf{p}; \Delta \mathbf{q})$, where $\mathbf{J}$ is the Jacobian matrix. The hybrid function is then updated according to:

$$R(\boldsymbol{\Delta} \mathbf{p}, \boldsymbol{\Delta} \mathbf{q}) = G_{mse}(\boldsymbol{\Delta} \mathbf{p}, \boldsymbol{\Delta} \mathbf{q}) + K \cdot F((\mathbf{p}, \mathbf{q}) + \mathbf{J} \cdot (\boldsymbol{\Delta} \mathbf{p}, \boldsymbol{\Delta} \mathbf{q})). \tag{15}$$

Let $\mathbf{U}_s$ be a matrix whose columns are orthogonal prototype shapes, $\mathbf{U}_s = [\mathbf{S}_1, \mathbf{S}_2, \ldots, \mathbf{S}_{m0}]$. Let $\mathbf{U}_g$ be a matrix of orthogonal global shape basis so that $\mathbf{S} = \mathbf{U}_g \cdot \mathbf{q}$ implies the equivalent global affine transform (refer to [3] for details). Assume j^{th} triangle $\mathbf{V}_0$ in the base face mesh $\mathbf{S}_0$ is mapped to its counterpart triangle $\mathbf{V}_1$ on the image frame by a general affine transform as $\mathbf{V}_1 = \mathbf{R}_j \cdot \mathbf{V}_0 + \mathbf{b}_j$, it is easy to find the Jacobian matrix J to be

$$J = \begin{bmatrix} \frac{\partial \mathbf{p}}{\partial \boldsymbol{\Delta} \mathbf{p}} & \mathbf{0} \\ \mathbf{0} & \frac{\partial \mathbf{q}}{\partial \boldsymbol{\Delta} \mathbf{q}} \end{bmatrix}, \tag{16}$$

where $\frac{\partial \mathbf{p}}{\partial \Delta \mathbf{p}}$ is the derivative of shape parameters $\mathbf{p}$ w.r.t. $\Delta \mathbf{p}$ and $\frac{\partial \mathbf{q}}{\partial \Delta \mathbf{q}}$ is the derivative of $\mathbf{q}$ w.r.t. $\Delta \mathbf{q}$. In detail,

$$\begin{cases} \frac{\partial \mathbf{p}}{\partial \Delta \mathbf{p}} = -\mathbf{U}_s \cdot \mathbf{A}_p \cdot \mathbf{U}_s \\ \frac{\partial \mathbf{p}}{\partial \Delta \mathbf{p}} = -\mathbf{U}_g \cdot \mathbf{A}_q \cdot \mathbf{U}_g \end{cases} \tag{17}$$

$\mathbf{A}_p$ is a matrix of all zeros except its two by two sub-matrices along the main diagonal direction:

$$\overline{\mathbf{R}^i} = \begin{bmatrix} \mathbf{A}_p(2 \cdot i - 1, 2 \cdot i - 1) & \mathbf{A}_p(2 \cdot i - 1, 2 \cdot i) \\ \mathbf{A}_p(2 \cdot i, 2 \cdot i - 1) & \mathbf{A}_p(2 \cdot i, 2 \cdot i) \end{bmatrix} \text{ for } i = 1, 2, ..., n_v, \tag{18}$$

where n_v is the number of mesh vertices. $\overline{\mathbf{R}^i}$ is the affine transform matrix associated with the ith vertex of the face mesh (superscript is used to discriminate it from $\mathbf{R}_j$, which denotes transform matrix for j^{th} triangle). $\overline{\mathbf{R}^i}$ is generated by averaging affine transforms of all triangles associated with this specific vertex. $\overline{\mathbf{R}^i} = mean(\mathbf{R}_j)$. $\mathbf{A}_q$ is defined in the same way, but much simpler as it corresponds to a single global affine transform, so $\overline{\mathbf{R}^i} = \mathbf{R}_j = \mathbf{R}$ for $\mathbf{A}_q$. In a typical morphable model fitting procedure, all the piecewise affine transforms are already computed. Computing the Jacobian matrix $\mathbf{J}$ is easy and fast based on (17) and (18).

Because $R(\Delta \mathbf{p}, \Delta \mathbf{q})$ is a sum of two summed squared measurements, it is easy to see that its Gaussian-Newton Hessian is the sum of Gaussian-Newton Hessian for the weighted texture error function and K times Gaussian-Newton Hessian of the shape error function. The same conclusion is true for steepest gradient descent images. With the computed Jacobian matrix, the optimization procedure is nothing special other than a normal inverse compositional algorithm.

4   Experiment Results and Discussion

4.1   Face Database

Our face database includes 138 nearly frontal images from various different face databases [9][10][11]. All images were roughly resized and cropped to 256 by 256. Various lighting conditions and image background patterns impose challenge to our model fitting algorithm. Nevertheless, we believe a versatile face database is the best way to test the robustness of our model fitting algorithm. We sequentially picked 80 images to train face shape subspace. 40 shape parameters are used to capture 98% of the shape variation, and texture subspace has a dimension of 66 to account for 98% of the texture variation. With four extra global pose parameters, we have totally 44 model parameters. Some samples from our database are shown in Fig.6.

4.2   Constrained Hybrid Model Fitting Optimization

In our constrained hybrid optimization scheme, shape is directly estimated from block motion estimation and local projection models. Integration of such heuristic information is the key for a high convergent rate with only around 10% extra

Fig. 6. Sample images in our face database

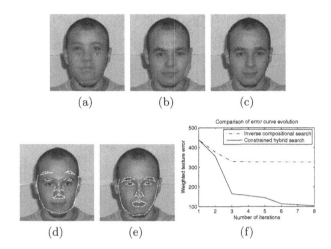

(a)   (b)   (c)

(d)   (e)   (f)

Fig. 7. Comparison of hybrid search and original inverse compositional AAM search.
(a)-(c)Hybrid search process at iteration 1,2 and 6. (d)Inverse compositional AAM
search. (e) Constrained hybrid search. (f)Evolution of error curve.

computation. Our algorithm is compared to standard inverse compositional algorithm. Fig. 7(d) shows the fitting with standard inverse compositional algorithm.
Almost all landmark points are displaced. It is commonly seen that model eye
points converge to eyebrow area in the image. Fitting with our algorithm is shown
in Fig. 7(e). Figures 7(a) to (c) show a typical scenario of our hybrid search. Fig.
7(f) compares texture error evolution curve of our constrained hybrid model fitting algorithm with standard normalized inverse compositional AAM algorithm.

Though the weighted texture error is used as evaluation function, it couldn't
reflect the model fitting quality strictly, especially when the novel face texture
pattern is beyond the representation power of the trained texture subspace. In
that case, the texture reconstruction error might remain large even when all
landmark points are perfectly located. A reasonable evaluation is to measure how
good the model points converge to their desired positions in the image. For all
138 images, we manually labelled the landmark points and created distance map
for each image. The model fitting quality is then measured by the average point
to edge distance. Fig. 8 compares the performance of the inverse compositional
algorithm and our proposed algorithm by plotting the average point to edge
error for all images in the training set and the test set. The superiority of our
constrained hybrid algorithm is clearly manifested.

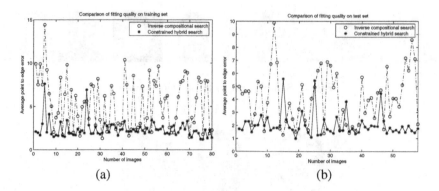

(a)   (b)

Fig. 8. Fitting errors on (a)Training set. (b)Test set.

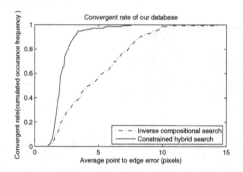

Fig. 9. Cumulative functions

All the tests are conducted with exactly the same initial model parameters and stop criterions. Inverse compositional search has a quite bad performance due to the fact that our face database consists of images originating from various sources. With our constrained hybrid optimization method, the average point to edge error reduces from 4.3900 to 2.0359 on the training set, and 5.3869 to 2.4713 on the test set. Both show considerable improvement.

Based on the results in Fig.8, we could further generate error density functions. All 138 images are used to estimate their probability density functions of the fitting error. Their cumulative functions are plotted in Fig. 9. Given a threshold from x-axis, we can read a number from y-axis, which is the percentage of images that have equal or less fitting errors than the threshold. If we assume the model fitting is successful when the point to edge error is below a threshold, then Fig. 9 is actually a plot of the convergent rate versus threshold. Apparently our hybrid optimization has a significantly higher convergent rate compared to standard inverse compositional algorithm.

There are 3 key components in our constrained hybrid optimization scheme: the unbiased evaluation function, the integration of direct shape estimation from block motion estimation, and the local projection models. To see how each of

Table 1. Average point to edge error for different algorithms

Database	NIC	NIC_MO	NIC_MO_LPM	NIC_MO_LPM_cr
Training set	4.3900	2.3924	2.3440	2.0359
Test set	5.3869	2.7506	3.0055	2.4713

these components plays a role in the hybrid optimization, we tested 4 different algorithms: Original normalized inverse compositional algorithm (NIC), NIC with motion integration (NIC_MO), NIC with both motion integration and local projection models (NIC_MO_LPM), hybrid model with unbiased evaluation function (NIC_MO_LPM_cr). Table 1 summarized their performance with average point to edge errors.

Table 1 demonstrates that our constrained hybrid optimization scheme has the best performance. Unbiased error function proves to be a better evaluation function than traditional error function as it truly reflects the fitting quality on the image frame. An exception is NIC_MO_LPM error is larger than NIC_MO error on the test set. This might just because we only have 55 test images. In fact, if we look at this problem from a different perspective, 27 images of the 55 perform better with local projection models, comparing to 20 of the 55 perform better without projection models. It is still justified that local projection models improve the overall performance.

4.3 Experiments on the JAFFE Face Database

We also tested on Japanese Female Facial Expression database (JAFFE)[12], which contains 213 images of 7 facial expressions of 10 female models. In our training database, all 80 images are without any facial expression. Nevertheless, our constrained hybrid model fitting algorithm performs very well on JAFFE database. The only pre-processing we conducted is to scale original 200 by 200 images to standard size 256 by 256.

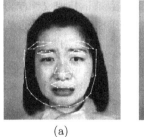 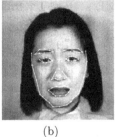

(a)   (b)

Fig. 10. Model fitting results: (a)Inverse compositional algorithm. (b)Constrained hybrid algorithm.

Table 2. Average point to edge error for different algorithms

Database	NIC	NIC_MO	NIC_MO_LPM	NIC_MO_LPM_cr
JAFFE	6.3646	4.1144	3.3958	2.9133

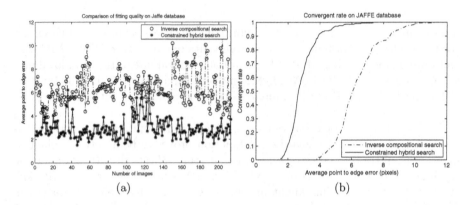

(a)   (b)

Fig. 11. (a)Model fitting errors on JAFFE. (b)Cumulative density functions.

Fig. 10 shows an example of converged face model overlapped to images. Fig. 11 plots average point to edge error for all images in JAFFE. Table 2 shows average point to edge error for different algorithms. From our face database to JAFFE, the performance only degenerates very slightly with an average point to edge error of 2.9. It proves the efficiency and robustness of our algorithm even in the presence of rich facial expressions, unseen in our training set.

5   Conclusions

In this paper, we presented a constrained hybrid optimization algorithm to solve the general morphable model fitting problem. Designing a robust and efficient modelling algorithm is very important as feature detection is an inevitable step for a lot of face applications. Our constrained hybrid algorithm features a novel error evaluation function which is an unbiased error estimate of model fitting quality on the image frame. Shape estimate from block motion estimation and local projection models is incorporated into the gradient-descent optimization procedure. They play a role in the parameter updating by acting as a shape constraint in the optimization process. As a result, our model fitting algorithm performs much better than general optimization algorithms that purely rely on analytic solutions. One apparent conclusion is that heuristic information in an image itself is abundant and could see better of image local terrains. Blindly minimizing a texture error is inefficient and error-prone. Experiments on our face database and JAFFE database shows that our constrained hybrid model fitting algorithm could achieve a high convergent rate even when presented with images of a large variety of illuminations, image backgrounds and facial expressions. Large image scaling, rotation and partial occlusion are not tested. These topics should be covered in the future and it is possible to extend our algorithm to multiple views and 3D face modelling.

References

1. Cootes, T., Edwards, G., Taylor, C.: Active appearance models. IEEE Trans. PAMI **23** (2001) 681–685
2. M.J.Jones, Poggio, T.: ultidimensional morphable models. In: Proc. Of the International Conference on Computer Vision. (1998) 683–688
3. Matthews, I., Baker, S.: Active appearance models revisited. International Journal of Computer Vision **60** (2004)
4. Cootes, T.F., P.Kittipanya-ngam: Comparing variations on the active appearance model algorithm. In: Proceedings of the British Machine Vision Conference, Cardiff, UK (2002)
5. Stegmann, M.: Active appearance models: Theory, extensions and cases. Master's thesis, Department of Mathematical Modelling, Technical University of Denmark, Department of Mathematical Modelling, Lyngby, Denmark (2000)
6. Cootes, T., Taylor, C., Cooper, D., Graham, J.: Active shape models: Their training and application. CVGIP: Imaging Understanding **61** (1995) 38–59
7. Xu, X., Zhang, C., Huang, T.S.: Active morphable model: An efficient method for face analysis. In: Sixth IEEE International Conference on Automatic Face and Gesture Recognition, Seoul, Korea (2004)
8. Baker, S., R.Gross, Matthews, I.: Lucas-kanade 20 years on: A unifying framework: Part 2. Technical Report Technical Report CMU-RI-TR-03-01, Robotics Institute, Carnegie Mellon University (2004)
9. Zhang, C., Cohen, F.: Face shape extraction and recognition using 3d morphing and distance mapping. In: 4th IEEE International Conference on Automatic Face and Gesture Recognition, Grenoble, France (2000)
10. Phillips, P., Moon, H., Rauss, P., Rizvi, S.: The feret evaluation methodology for face recognition algorithms. In: Proceedings of IEEE Computer Vision and Pattern Recognition. (1997) 137–143
11. : The phychological image collection at stirling. (http://pics.psych.stir.ac.uk/)
12. Lyons, M.J., Akamatsu, S., Kamachi, M., Gyoba, J.: Coding facial expressions with gabor wavelets. In: Third IEEE International Conference on Automatic Face and Gesture Recognition, Nara, Japan (1998) 200–205

Kernel Methods for Nonlinear Discriminative Data Analysis

Xiuwen Liu[1,*] and Washington Mio[2]

[1] Department of Computer Science, Florida State University, Tallahassee, 32306
Phone: (850) 644-0050, Fax: (850) 644-0058
liux@cs.fsu.edu
[2] Department of Mathematics, Florida State University, Tallahassee, FL 32306

Abstract. Optimal Component Analysis (OCA) is a linear subspace technique for dimensionality reduction designed to optimize object classification and recognition performance. The linear nature of OCA often limits recognition performance, if the underlying data structure is nonlinear or cluster structures are complex. To address these problems, we investigate a kernel analogue of OCA, which consists of applying OCA techniques to the data after it has been mapped nonlinearly into a new feature space, typically a high (possibly infinite) dimensional Hilbert space. In this paper, we study both the theoretical and algorithmic aspects of the problem and report results obtained in several object recognition experiments.

1 Introduction

Modeling nonlinearity in observed data for tasks such as dimensionality reduction in data representation for efficient classification and recognition of objects and patterns is a problem that arises in numerous contexts. For example, in image-based object recognition, nonlinearity often arises as a result of varying poses, illumination and other factors. Kernel methods have been widely used as a general strategy for simplifying data structure so that it becomes amenable to linear methods. One typically maps a given dataset in Euclidean space $\mathbb{R}^n$ nonlinearly into a very high (possibly infinite) dimensional Hilbert space $\mathbb{H}$ and analyzes the transformed data with more standard techniques. Such methods have been investigated in the context of support vector machines [12], principal component analysis [10], independent component analysis [1], and Fisher discriminant analysis [2]. For practical feasibility, the usual assumption is that the nonlinear map $\Phi \colon \mathbb{R}^n \to \mathbb{H}$ is not known explicitly, only the relative positions of the points $\Phi(x)$, $x \in \mathbb{R}^n$, given by the inner products $k(x, y) = \Phi(x) \cdot \Phi(y)$, $x, y \in \mathbb{R}^n$. The function $k(x, y)$ is referred to as a *kernel function*. Thus, dimension reduction techniques and classifiers should only require knowledge of the kernel k, not the function Φ.

In this paper, we present a kernel analogue of a linear subspace technique developed by Liu et al. in [7, 11] that has been termed Optimal Component Analysis (OCA). Given training data for a specific classification problem, OCA is a technique for finding an

---

* Corresponding author.

A. Rangarajan et al. (Eds.): EMMCVPR 2005, LNCS 3757, pp. 584–599, 2005.

optimal subspace of feature space for dimensionality reduction for classification and recognition. Although originally developed in the context of images for the nearest-neighbor classifier, the method applies to more general data classification based on other criteria, as well. We address both the theoretical and computational aspects of kernel OCA. For the methodology to be useful in practice, it is crucial that we develop an algorithmic approach that leads to effective computational tools. This will be achieved by exploiting the differential geometric properties of Grassmann manifolds [5, 13], as discussed in more detail below. Several object recognition experiments will illustrate the fact that high recognition rates can be achieved with kernel OCA in a computationally efficient manner. A special case of kernel OCA was studied in [14], where the kernel function is required to satisfy the additional constraint that Φ preserves orthonormality. Under this assumption, the problem can be more easily reduced to OCA in Euclidean space.

The paper is organized as follows. In Sect. 2, we give a brief overview of optimal component analysis in Euclidean space, which is followed by a formulation of the corresponding problem in kernel space in Sect. 3. Sect. 4 shows how an efficient stochastic gradient search algorithm can be devised by exploiting a special representation of elements of Grassmann manifolds. Sect. 5 contains a systematic set of experiments and Sect. 6 concludes the paper with a discussion of future research.

2   Optimal Component Analysis

We begin with a brief review of Optimal Component Analysis (OCA) in Euclidean space $\mathbb{R}^m$. Suppose that a given dataset is divided in *training* and *validation* sets, each consisting of representatives of P different classes of objects. For $1 \leq c \leq P$, we denote by $x_{c,1}, \ldots, x_{c,t_c}$ and $y_{c,1}, \ldots, y_{c,v_c}$ the elements in the training and validation sets, resp., that belong to class c. Given an r-dimensional subspace U of $\mathbb{R}^m$ and $x, y \in \mathbb{R}^m$, we let $d(x, y; U)$ denote the distance between the orthogonal projections of x and y onto U. The quantity

$$\rho(y_{c,i}; U) = \frac{\min_{c \neq b, j} d^2(y_{c,i}, x_{b,j}; U)}{\min_j d^2(y_{c,i}, x_{c,j}; U) + \epsilon} \tag{1}$$

measures how well the *nearest-neighbor classifier* applied to the data projected onto U identifies the element $y_{c,i}$ as belonging to class c; a large value $\rho(y_{c,i}; U)$ indicates that, after projection, $y_{c,i}$ is much closer to the class it belongs than to other classes. Here, $\epsilon > 0$ is a small number used to prevent vanishing denominators. The function ρ is a mild variant of that used in [7], with the distance d squared to ensure smoothness. Note that (1) can be modified to reflect the performance of a more general K-nearest-neighbor classifier. Define a performance function by

$$F(U) = \frac{1}{P} \sum_{c=1}^{P} \left(\frac{1}{v_c} \sum_{i=1}^{v_c} h\left(\rho(y_{c,i} : U) - 1 \right) \right), \tag{2}$$

where h is a monotonically increasing bounded function. A common choice is

$$h(x) = \frac{1}{1 + e^{-2\beta x}},$$

for which the limit value of $F(U)$, as $\beta \to \infty$, is precisely the recognition performance of the nearest-neighbor classifier after projection to the subspace U. Unlike the actual recognition performance, $F(U)$ is smooth so that we can approach the search for its maxima using gradient-type algorithms. The function h is used to control bias with respect to particular classes in measurements of performance.

Let $\mathcal{G}(m, r)$ be the Grassmann manifold [5, 13] of r-planes in $\mathbb{R}^m$. An optimal r-dimensional subspace for the given classification problem from the viewpoint of the available data is given by

$$\hat{U} = \underset{U \in \mathcal{G}_{m,r}}{\operatorname{argmax}} F(U).$$

An algorithmic procedure for estimating $\hat{U}$ on $\mathcal{G}(m, r)$ using a stochastic gradient search is described in [7]. Notice that, in practice, for this approach to classification and recognition to be feasible, the estimation of the gradient of F must be carried out efficiently.

3   Subspace Representation

In data analysis using kernel methods, one typically maps a given set of data $x_1, \ldots, x_M$ in $\mathbb{R}^n$ to a Hilbert space $(\mathbb{H}, \langle , \rangle)$ using a nonlinear map $\Phi \colon \mathbb{R}^n \to \mathbb{H}$, and then applies linear subspace techniques to the collection $\Phi(x_1), \ldots, \Phi(x_M)$. The typical assumption is that Φ is not known explicitly, only the kernel function $k(x, y) = \Phi(x) \cdot \Phi(y)$. The problem of determining what functions $k(x, y)$ are kernels associated with a mapping Φ has been studied in [4, 12, 10]. Some of the most commonly used kernel functions are

$$k(x, y) = (x \cdot y)^d,$$

which corresponds to mapping $\mathbb{R}^n$ into a higher dimensional space using all monomials of order d in the input variables [9], and the *Gaussian kernel*

$$k(x, y) = \exp\left(-\frac{\|x - y\|^2}{2\sigma^2}\right).$$

We shall adapt OCA to this setting, by projecting vectors of the form $\Phi(x)$, $x \in \mathbb{R}^n$, onto subspaces of

$$V = \operatorname{span}\{\Phi(x_1), \ldots, \Phi(x_M)\} \subseteq \mathbb{H},$$

where we use the nearest-neighbor (or more generally K-nearest-neighbor) criterion for classification and recognition. For this purpose, we must be able to measure distances between projected vectors solely in terms of the kernel function.

Remarks.

(a) Note that OCA, in its original formulation, does not restrict subspaces to the span of the data points. This is an important difference and philosophically reflects the fact that, in the kernel approach, cluster structures are expected to be simplified by applying a non-linear map Φ to the original data, so that high recognition rates can be achieved only using projections to low-dimensional subspaces of the span of the kernelized data. This will lead to significant gains in computational efficiency.

(b) If the need arises, one can allow other subspaces of the Hilbert space $\mathbb{H}$, for example, by taking a set of vectors $\{\bar{x}_1, \ldots, \bar{x}_N\} \subset \mathbb{R}^n$ and replacing V above with

$$V = \text{span}\left\{\Phi(\bar{x}_1), \ldots, \Phi(\bar{x}_N)\right\}.$$

Thus, the formulation given here is not limited to the span of the training images. This raises the problems of learning and selecting $\{\bar{x}_1, \ldots, \bar{x}_N\}$ either from data or based on associated physical processes; these issues require further investigation.

Each element $a = (a_1, \ldots, a_M)^T \in \mathbb{R}^{M \times 1}$ defines a vector $v \in V$ given by $v = \sum_{i=1}^{M} a_i \Phi(x_i)$. Form the symmetric Gram matrix $K \in \mathbb{R}^{M \times M}$, whose entries are

$$K_{ij} = \Phi(x_i) \cdot \Phi(x_j).$$

If $a, b \in \mathbb{R}^{M \times 1}$ represent $v, w \in V$, then

$$\langle v, w \rangle = a^T K b. \tag{3}$$

Our first goal is to find an orthonormal basis of V in the a-representation. For this, we diagonalize the Gram matrix, and let $d_j^* = (d_{1j}^*, \ldots, d_{Mj}^*)^T$, $1 \leq j \leq m$, be an orthonormal set (with respect to the standard inner product on $\mathbb{R}^M$) associated with the nonzero eigenvalues $\lambda_1, \ldots, \lambda_m$ of K, where $m = \dim V = \text{rank } K$. It follows from (3) that

$$d_1 = d_1^*/\sqrt{\lambda_1}, \ldots, d_m = d_m^*/\sqrt{\lambda_m} \tag{4}$$

represent an orthonormal basis of V. This fact can be expressed as $D^T K D = I_m$, where D is the $M \times m$ matrix whose columns are $d_1, \ldots, d_m$. Note that D can be constructed as indicated since the Gram matrix K is positive semi-definite. In addition, one can choose a subset of the eigenvectors (with nonzero eigenvalues) to further reduce computational costs if needed.

3.1 Subspaces of V

Subspaces of V of dimension r will be represented by spanning orthonormal r-frames. For each $1 \leq j \leq r$, let $\alpha_j = (\alpha_{1j}, \ldots, \alpha_{Mj})^T$ represent a vector $v_j \in V$, and let α be the $(M \times r)$-matrix whose entries are α_{ij}; that is, the columns of α are α_j. From Eqn. 3, it follows that $\{v_j, 1 \leq j \leq r\}$ is orthonormal if and only if

$$\alpha^T K \alpha = I_r, \tag{5}$$

where I_r is the $r \times r$ identity matrix. The collection of all $M \times r$ matrices satisfying Eqn. 5 will be denoted $\mathcal{A}$. Given $\alpha \in \mathcal{A}$, let $[\alpha]$ be the r-dimensional subspace of V associated with α; i.e.,

$$[\alpha] = \text{span}\left\{v_j, 1 \leq j \leq r\right\},$$

with $v_j = \sum_{i=1}^{M} \alpha_{ij} \Phi(x_i)$. We denote by $\pi_\alpha \colon \mathbb{R}^m \to [\alpha]$ be the orthogonal projection of $\mathbb{H}$ onto $[\alpha]$. For $x \in \mathbb{R}^n$, we derive an expression for $\Phi^\alpha(x) = \pi_\alpha(\Phi(x))$. The product $\langle \Phi^\alpha(x), v_j \rangle = \langle \pi_\alpha(\Phi(x)), v_j \rangle = \langle \Phi(x), v_j \rangle$, for $1 \le j \le r$, can be calculated as

$$\langle \Phi(x), v_j \rangle = \sum_{i=1}^{M} \alpha_{ij} \langle \Phi(x), \Phi(x_i) \rangle = \sum_{i=1}^{M} \alpha_{ij} k(x, x_i),$$

which implies that

$$\Phi^\alpha(x) = \sum_{j=1}^{r} \left(\sum_{i=1}^{M} \alpha_{ij} k(x, x_i) \right) v_j. \tag{6}$$

3.2 Distance in $[\alpha]$

In applications using nearest-neighbor classifiers, we will be primarily interested in the distance between $\Phi^\alpha(x)$ and $\Phi^\alpha(y)$, for $x, y \in \mathbb{R}^n$. Since

$$\begin{aligned}
\|\Phi^\alpha(x) - \Phi^\alpha(y)\|^2 &= \langle \Phi^\alpha(x), \Phi^\alpha(x) \rangle - 2\langle \Phi^\alpha(x), \Phi^\alpha(y) \rangle \\
&\quad + \langle \Phi^\alpha(y), \Phi^\alpha(y) \rangle,
\end{aligned} \tag{7}$$

it suffices to derive expressions for inner products of the form $\langle \Phi^\alpha(w), \Phi^\alpha(z) \rangle$, $w, z \in \mathbb{R}^n$. From Eqn. 6, we obtain

$$\begin{aligned}
\Phi^\alpha(w) \cdot \Phi^\alpha(z) &= \sum_{\ell=1}^{r} \left(\sum_{i=1}^{M} \alpha_{i\ell} k(w, x_i) \right) \left(\sum_{j=1}^{M} \alpha_{j\ell} k(z, x_j) \right) \\
&= \alpha^T h(w) \cdot \alpha^T h(z),
\end{aligned}$$

where $h(w)$ denotes the vector $(k(w, x_1), \ldots, k(w, x_M))^T \in \mathbb{R}^{M \times 1}$, $h(z)$ is defined similarly, and $\cdot$ is the standard inner product in $\mathbb{R}^r$. In (7), we obtain

$$\begin{aligned}
\|\Phi^\alpha(x) - \Phi^\alpha(y)\|^2 &= \|\alpha^T h(x)\|^2 - 2\alpha^T h(x) \cdot \alpha^T h(y) \\
&\quad + \|\alpha^T h(y)\|^2.
\end{aligned} \tag{8}$$

This expresses the distance solely in terms of α and the kernel function k, as desired.

4 Kernel OCA

The results of Sec. 3.1 allow us to define a performance function G for KOCA similar to the function F given by (2). If $\alpha \in \mathcal{A}$, the definition of $G([\alpha])$ is identical to that of the function $F(U)$ in (2), with distances $d(y_{c,i}, x_{d,j}; U)$ between training and cross-validation points replaced by

$$d(y_{c,i}, x_{d,j}; [\alpha]) = \left(\|\alpha^T h(x)\|^2 - 2\alpha^T h(x) \cdot \alpha^T h(y) + \|\alpha^T h(y)\|^2 \right)^{1/2}. \tag{9}$$

To complete the description of kernel OCA, we address the problem of maximizing G over the Grassmann manifold $\mathcal{G}(V, r)$ formed by all r-dimensional subspaces of V. If $v_1, \ldots, v_m$ is an orthonormal basis of V and $e_1, \ldots, e_m$ is the standard basis of $\mathbb{R}^m$, the correspondence $e_j \mapsto v_j$ induces an identification of $\mathcal{G}(m, r)$ with $\mathcal{G}(V, r)$. This will allow us to reduce the question to an optimization problem over $\mathcal{G}(m, r)$.

4.1 Grassmann and Stiefel Manifolds

Let $\mathcal{V}(m, r)$ denote the *Stiefel* manifold of orthonormal r-frames $(u_1, \ldots, u_r)$ in $\mathbb{R}^m$, which we represent by the $m \times r$ matrix U whose jth column is u_j, $1 \le j \le r$. A matrix $U \in \mathbb{R}^{m \times r}$ represents an element of $\mathcal{V}(m, r)$ if and only if $U^T U = I_r$. The Grassmann manifold $\mathcal{G}(m, r)$ may be viewed as the quotient space of $\mathcal{V}(m, r)$ under the following equivalence relation: $U_1 \sim U_2$ if there exists an orthogonal matrix $H \in O(r)$ such that $U_1 = U_2 H$. This just formalizes the simple fact that if we represent r-planes in $\mathbb{R}^m$ using their orthonormal basis, we have to account for all possible choices. We abuse notation and use $U \in \mathbb{R}^{m \times r}$ to denote both an element in the Stiefel manifold and its equivalence class in the Grassmannian.

Let J be the $m \times r$ matrix formed by the first r columns of the identity matrix I_m. The matrix J represents the orthonormal r-frame formed by the first r elements of the standard basis of $\mathbb{R}^m$. It can be shown that tangent vectors to $\mathcal{G}(m, r)$ at J can be identified uniquely with matrices of the form

$$\begin{bmatrix} 0 & B \\ -B^T & 0 \end{bmatrix} J \in \mathbb{R}^{m \times r},$$

where $B \in \mathbb{R}^{r \times (m-r)}$. Let E_{ij}, $1 \le i \le r$ and $r < j \le m$, be the $m \times m$ matrix whose (k, l) entry is

$$E_{ij}(k, l) = \begin{cases} 1/\sqrt{2}, & \text{if } k = i \text{ and } l = j; \\ -1/\sqrt{2}, & \text{if } k = j \text{ and } l = i; \\ 0, & \text{otherwise}, \end{cases}$$

Then, $\{E_{ij} J, 1 \le i \le r, r < j \le m\}$ represents an orthonormal basis of the tangent space $T_J \mathcal{G}(m, r)$.

Any two orthonormal r-frames in $\mathbb{R}^m$ differ by the action of an orthogonal matrix. Thus, for any $U \in \mathcal{G}(m, r)$, there is an orthogonal matrix $Q \in O(n)$ such that $J = QU$. Any such matrix Q has the property that $Q^T = [U, W]$, where W is some $m \times (m - r)$ matrix satisfying $W^T W = I_{m-r}$ and $U^T W = 0$; the role of V is to complete U to an $m \times m$ orthogonal matrix. Since left multiplication by Q^T induces an isometry on $\mathcal{G}(m, d)$, it follows that $\{Q^T E_{ij} J, 1 \le i \le r, r < j \le m\}$, represents an orthonormal basis of the tangent space $T_U \mathcal{G}(m, r)$. Another important consequence of the fact that left multiplication by Q^T is an isometry is that the geodesic $\gamma_{ij}(t; U)$ in $\mathcal{G}(m, r)$ starting at U with initial velocity $Q^T E_{ij} J \in T_U \mathcal{G}(m, r)$ is given by the action of Q^T on the geodesic $\gamma_{ij}(t; J) = e^{t E_{ij}} J$. In other words,

$$\gamma_{ij}(t; U) = Q^T e^{t E_{ij}} J. \tag{10}$$

4.2 Maximizing G

Let $U \in \mathcal{G}(m, r)$. The mapping $U \mapsto [DU]$, where D is the $M \times m$ matrix whose column vectors are given by (4) and $[DU]$ denotes the subspace of V associated with $\alpha = DU$, induces an identification $\mathcal{G}(m, r) \approx \mathcal{G}(V, r)$. Thus, maximizing the performance function $G \colon \mathcal{G}(V, r) \to \mathbb{R}$ is equivalent to maximizing $H \colon \mathcal{G}(m, r) \to \mathbb{R}$, where

$$H(U) = G([DU]). \tag{11}$$

The Gradient of H. The partial derivatives of H at $U \in \mathcal{G}(m, r)$ in the direction $Q^T E_{ij} J$, $1 \le i \le r$, $r < j \le m$, can be evaluated as

$$\partial_{ij} H(U) = \lim_{\epsilon \to 0} \frac{G\left([DQ^T e^{\epsilon E_{ij}} J] - G([DU])\right)}{\epsilon}. \tag{12}$$

Note that D is fixed and Q depends only on U. To estimate the partial derivatives at U using finite differences, we first compute DQ^T. If we write the $m \times m$ identity matrix as $I_m = [e_1 \ldots e_m]$, the exponential $e^{\epsilon E_{ij}}$ can be obtained from I_m by the following column replacements:

$$e_i \mapsto \cos(\epsilon/\sqrt{2})e_i - \sin(\epsilon/\sqrt{2})e_j \quad \text{and} \quad e_j \mapsto \sin(\epsilon/\sqrt{2})e_i + \cos(\epsilon/\sqrt{2})e_j.$$

Then, the $M \times r$ matrix $DQ^T e^{\epsilon E_{ij}} J$ can be calculated by first performing the same column replacements on DQ^T and then deleting the last $m - r$ columns.

Also, to evaluate the performance function G at $[DQ^T e^{\epsilon E_{ij}} J]$, we need to compute the distances $d(y_{c,i}, x_{d,j}; [DQ^T e^{\epsilon E_{ij}} J])$ between training and cross-validation points. Since $DQ^T e^{\epsilon E_{ij}} J$ and DQ^T differ in a single column, Eqns. 9 and 7 show that significant gains in computational efficiency can be realized by first calculating $d(y_{c,i}, x_{d,j}; [DU])$ and storing the intermediate results.

To summarize, given U_t at time t, we first compute Q such that $Q^T = [U_t, W_t]$, where the columns of W_t form an orthonormal basis for the null space of U_t. Using Eqn. 12, we estimate the partial derivatives $\partial_{ij} H(U_t)$ and then add a stochastic component to $\partial_{ij} H(U_t)$ to carry out a stochastic gradient optimization of H; details of the implementation of the stochastic search can be found in [7].

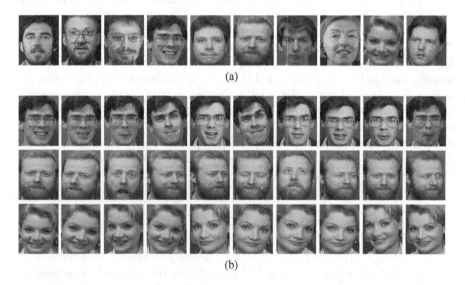

(a)

(b)

Fig. 1. Part of the ORL dataset: (a) 10 subjects used in the experiments; (b) images of three selected subjects taken at different facial expression and illumination conditions

5 Experimental Results

We present the results of several image-based object recognition experiments. By pre-computing $\Phi(w, x_i), i = 1, \ldots, M$, for each validation image w, the implementation of the proposed algorithm is at least as efficient as the OCA algorithm in Euclidean space. Recall that if n is much larger than the size of the training set M, a substantial additional computational gain is realized by considering only subspaces in the span of $\Phi(x_i), 1 \leq i \leq M$, as remarked in Sect. 3. Compared to a direct implementation in kernel space [8], on a face recognition data set, the computational time is reduced from several hours to just a few seconds. Furthermore, the techniques developed provide an adaptive way of balancing efficiency and accuracy as illustrated in Fig. 5.

As in other gradient-based methods and the original OCA algorithms, the choice of free parameters may affect results significantly. Additionally, for KOCA, the choice of kernel functions is also important. Instead of pursuing asymptotic convergence results, we have conducted numerical simulations to demonstrate the effectiveness of the proposed algorithm. We varied the subspace dimension, as well as the kernel functions.

Using part of the ORL face database, we have applied the proposed algorithm to the search for optimal linear basis in the context of face recognition in the kernel space. The dataset consists of faces of 40 different subjects with 10 images each. The subjects are shown in Fig. 1(a) and the images of three particular subjects are shown in Fig. 1(b) to illustrate the variation of facial expression and lighting condition. Here we used 10 subjects for the plots in the Figures 2-8 and 20 subjects for the results shown in Tab. 1. Figure 2 shows the evolution of the optimization performance using a Gaussian kernel with a fixed width σ. Fig. 2(a) and (b) show two cases with random initial subspace while Fig. 2(c) shows the case using the kernel PCA as the initial subspace. In each case, the plot on the left shows the evolution of the performance function $F(U_t)$ with $\beta = 0.5$; the middle plot shows the corresponding recognition rate. Note that the recognition rate is piecewise constant and does not have a meaningful gradient for stochastic optimization while $F(U_t)$ is smooth. The right plot shows the distance of U_t from the initial one (Frobenius norm), indicating that the optimization process is effective. In all these cases, the optimization is successful in maximizing the recognition performance.

We have also used polynomial kernel of different degrees. Fig. 3 shows three such examples. As in the previous example, the performance improves significantly with the number of iterations in all the cases. Compared to the results in Fig. 2, here the performance function itself is worse than that using the Gaussian kernel, indicating the importance of the kernel function for performance.

For dimension reduction, the choice of the subspace dimension is an important parameter. Using the proposed method, we can significantly reduce the required dimension for a given level of performance. To show this, Fig. 4 shows three examples of Gaussian kernel for different values of the subspace dimension r. As expected, when r is larger, it takes fewer iterations to achieve a given performance. With $r = 3$, the proposed algorithm achieves maximum recognition performance. For applications where the computational complexity is critical, the proposed method may reduce the required dimension effectively.

As pointed out earlier, significant computational efficiency can be realized by restricting subspaces to those contained in the span of the kernelized data. To illustrate

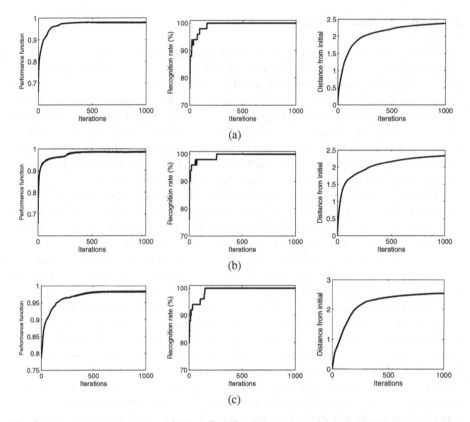

Fig. 2. Plots of the performance function F (left), the corresponding recognition rate (middle), and the distance from the initial subspace (right) versus the number t of iterations using projections onto a 4-dimensional subspace. Here Gaussian kernel with proper σ is used. (a) and (b) Two random initial subspaces. (c) Initial subspace given by KPCA, whose recognition performance is 80%.

that the gain in efficiency usually does not lead to significant loss in discriminative power, we show in Fig. 5(a) a plot of the distribution of eigenvalues of K matrix given by a Gaussian kernel; Fig. 5(b) shows the percentage of energy captured by the first given number of eigenvectors. Clearly we can reduce the dimension to a much smaller number and still have most of the information for classification. Fig. 6 shows three examples with a different number of eigenvectors. As the examples in Fig. 6(b) and (c) show, one can reduce the dimension of the search space without much loss of performance as compared to that given in Fig. 2, where the span of all the training images is used. It is expected that when the search space is reduced too much, the performance loss can become significant, as shown in Fig. 6(a). In the extreme case, when $m = r$, KOCA is reduced to KPCA or other method, depending how the initial subspace is generated.

To summarize the experiments and compare the performance using the proposed algorithm and that of KPCA [10], Tab. 1 shows the performance of both methods using

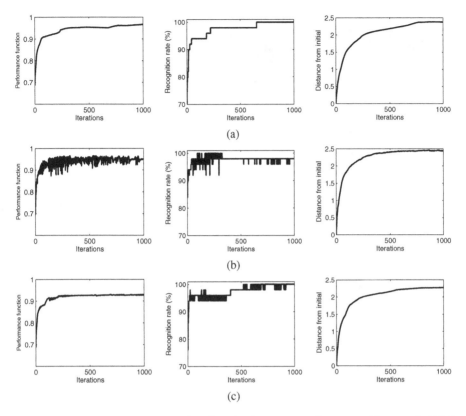

Fig. 3. Plots of the performance function F (left), the corresponding recognition rate (middle), and the distance from the initial subspace (right) versus the number t of iterations using projections onto a 4-dimensional subspace. Here polynomial kernels $k(x, y) = (x \cdot y)^d$ with different d's are used. The initial subspace is given randomly. (a) Polynomial kernel of $d = 2$. (b) Polynomial kernel of $d = 3$. (c) Polynomial kernel of $d = 4$.

different kernel functions with different dimension of subspaces (r) using 20 subjects of the ORL face dataset. It is clear that the proposed algorithm is significantly more effective than KPCA in all the cases. Additionally, this shows again the importance of kernel functions and how to learn the kernel functions is an important problem.

While the above experiments demonstrate clearly the effectiveness of the proposed KOCA technique, for real world applications, one is interested in the generalization performance, i.e., the performance on images that are not part of the training. To simulate this situation, we divide the face dataset into a training set, a cross validation set, and a separate test set, i.e., images in the test set are not used in the optimization performance. To visualize the effectiveness of KOCA, we use five classes here and set $r = 2$. Fig. 7 shows the 2-dimensional representation of the training, cross validation, and test images given by KPCA and KOCA. Here each image is shown at the center given by its 2-dimensional representation. It is clear that some of images from the same class do not form good clusters in the space given by KPCA. In comparison, images

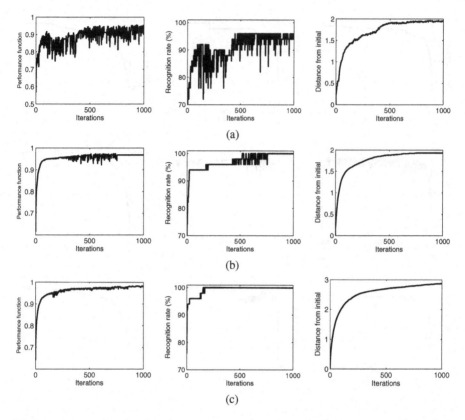

Fig. 4. Plots of the performance function F (left), the corresponding recognition rate (middle), and the distance from the initial subspace (right) versus the number t of iterations using projections onto r-dimensional subspaces with different r's. Here Gaussian kernel with proper σ is used and the initial subspace is given randomly. (a) $r = 2$. (b) $r = 3$. (c) $r = 6$.

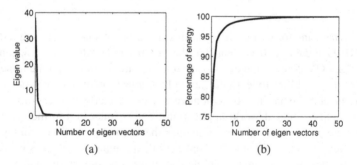

Fig. 5. Distribution of eigen values (a) and the energy captured by the first given eigen vectors (b)

from each of the five classes form a compact cluster that is away from clusters of other classes. Here we used a modified version of (2), which is related to a 4-nearest neighbor performance.

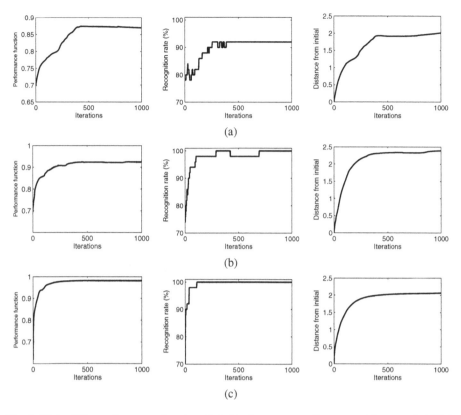

Fig. 6. Plots of the performance function F (left), the corresponding recognition rate (middle), and the distance from the initial subspace (right) versus the number t of iterations using projections onto an 4-dimensional subspace. Here Gaussian kernel with proper σ is used and the initial subspace is given randomly. (a) $m = 8$ that captures 98% of the energy. (b) $m = 16$ that captures 99.25% of the energy. (c) $m = 35$ that captures 99.99% of the energy.

Table 1. Comparison of recognition performance of KPCA and the proposed algorithm

Kernel function	Dimension r	KPCA	Proposed	Kernel function	Dimension r	KPCA	Proposed
Gaussian	2	48%	91%	$(x,y)^2$	4	82%	96%
Gaussian	4	82%	99%	$(x,y)^3$	4	80%	97%
Gaussian	6	83%	100%	$(x,y)^4$	4	82%	95%

To show the significance of KOCA, we computed the nearest neighbor classifier, the 4-nearest neighbor classifier, and $F(U)$ (given by (2)) in the original image space (each image is $92 \times 112 = 10,304$), the 2-dimensional KPCA space, and a 2-dimensional KOCA space using a Gaussian kernel. Tab. 2 shows the results. Note that while the nearest neighbor performance is high in all the cases for this small set, the 4-nearest neighbor performance is significantly different. KOCA achieves a much better 4-nearest neighbor performance due to the much better clustering structure as shown in Fig. 7(b).

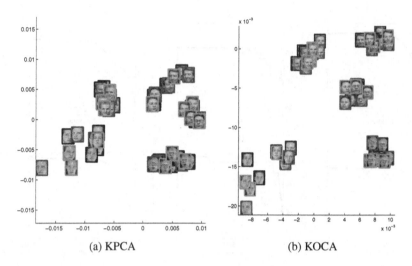

(a) KPCA   (b) KOCA

Fig. 7. 2-dimensional representation of training (blue), cross validation (green), and test (red) images using (a) KPCA and (b) KOCA. It is clear that clusters are much better organized using the representation given by KOCA. Here the axes are the projections given the corresponding 2-dimensional projection matrix.

Table 2. Recognition performance of different representations on a five-class subset

Set	F	Nearest neighbor (%)	4-nearest neighbor(%)
10,304-dimensional original feature			
Cross validation	0.542	100.0	86.7
Test	0.545	100.0	86.7
2-dimension KPCA feature			
Cross validation	0.719	100.0	80.0
Test	0.715	100.0	80.0
2-dimension KOCA feature			
Cross validation	0.994	100.0	100.0
Test	0.955	**100.0**	**100.0**

To demonstrate the significance of the proposed technique, we repeated the above experiments on the full ORL dataset using $r = 10$. Tab. 3 shows the performance. Clearly KOCA not only reduces the dimension of the images significantly, but also increases the performance on both the cross validation set and more importantly on the test set.

Note that the proposed technique is not limited to images and applies to any recognition problem, where the input can be represented as a vector of a fixed length. As an example, we have applied our technique on an optical character recognition (OCR) dataset from the UCI machine learning repository [1]. Since there is no cross validation set in the given setting, (2) was modified to relate to the leave-one-out performance

---

[1] Obtained from http://www.ics.uci.edu/~mlearn/MLRepository.html.

Table 3. Recognition performance of different representations on the full 40-class ORL dataset

Set	F	Nearest neighbor (%)	4-nearest neighbor(%)
10,304-dimensional original feature			
Cross validation	0.521	96.7	71.7
Test	0.524	94.2	73.3
10-dimension KPCA feature			
Cross validation	0.529	83.3	52.9
Test	0.526	92.5	63.3
10-dimension KOCA feature			
Cross validation	0.995	100.0	100.0
Test	0.937	**100.0**	**99.17**

Table 4. Recognition performance of different representations on an OCR dataset

Set	F	Nearest neighbor (%)	11-nearest neighbor(%)
Original 64-dimensional feature			
Training (leave-one-out)	0.637	95.2	94.4
Test	0.638	94.7	93.9
10-dimensional KICA feature			
Training (leave-one-out)	0.280	22.9	28.0
Test	0.288	24.4	17.8
10-dimensional KOCA feature			
Training (leave-one-out)	0.919	98.4	98.0
Test	0.862	**96.1**	**96.1**

on the training set. Tab. 4 shows the performance in the original space, the initial 10-dimensional space given by the FastICA algorithm [6] in the kernel space, and a 10-dimensional space given by KOCA that uses KICA as the initial condition. As in the previous example, KOCA not only reduces the dimensionality significantly but also improves the performance on the test compared to that in the original space.

6   Conclusion and Discussion

In this paper, we presented a kernel analogue of Optimal Component Analysis (OCA), addressing both theoretical and computational aspects of the problem. The kernel approach allows one to model nonlinearity in data structure, overcoming a fundamental limitation of OCA, as proposed in [7]. To achieve computational efficiency, the algorithms developed exploit the geometric structure of Grassmann manifolds. Several experiments were carried out and results compared to those obtained via kernel PCA.

As with other kernel methods, performance is often tied to the choice of the kernel function. Thus, in applications, the choice of the kernel function for a specific classification problem is of critical importance. To illustrate this point, Fig. 8 shows plots of the performance functions associated with three Gaussian kernels of different widths. In each column, the top panel shows a contour plot of the matrix K and the bottom panel shows the performance function with respect to the number t of iterations. Clearly the

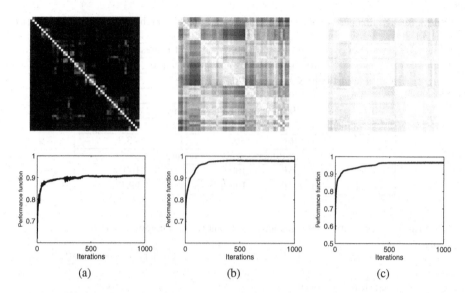

Fig. 8. The K matrix using Gaussian kernel of different σ's. subspace is given randomly. In each panel, the top image shows the K matrix and the bottom plot shows the corresponding performance function with respect to t. (a) A Gaussian kernel with σ that is too small. (b) A Gaussian kernel with a proper σ. (c) A Gaussian kernel with σ that is too large.

performance is affected by the choice of kernel function parameters. Note that in the proposed formulation one can treat the kernel function parameters in the search space and one can perform optimization in the joint space to obtain optimal subspace and kernel function parameters. This needs to be investigated further.

The geometric optimization techniques developed in this paper were applied to a performance function derived from the nearest-neighbor classifier, but they are adaptable to performance functions based on other criteria. For example, if the choice of bases is relevant in addition to the choice of subspaces, the solution space becomes a Stiefel manifold; one such criterion is to impose both sparseness and recognition performance [11]. The formulation given here can be used directly to extend the corresponding algorithms and techniques to the kernel space. Thus, the methodology developed yields a general framework and efficient algorithms for learning optimal low-dimensional representations in the presence of nonlinearity.

Acknowledgment. This work was supported in part by NSF grants IIS-0307998 and CCF-0514743, and an ARO grant W911NF-04-01-0268.

References

1. F. Bach and M. I. Jordan. Kernel independent component analysis. *Journal of Machine Learning Research*, vol. 3, pp. 1–48, 2003.
2. G. Baudat and F. Anouar. Generalized discriminant analysis using a kernel approach. *Neural Computation*, 12:2385–2404, 2000.

3. P. N. Belhumeur, J. P. Hepanha, and D. J. Kriegman. Eigenfaces vs. fisherfaces: Recognition using class specific linear projection. *IEEE Transactions on Pattern Analysis and Machine Intelligence*, 19(7):711–720, 1997.

4. B. Boser, I. Guyon, and V. Vapnik. A training algorithm for optimal margin classifiers. In *Proc. of the 5th Annual Workshop on Computational Learning Theory*, pages 144–152, 1992.

5. W. M. Boothby. *An Introduction to Differential Manifolds and Riemannian Geometry*. Academic Press, 1986.

6. A. Hyvarinen. Fast and robust fixed-point algorithm for independent component analysis. *IEEE Transactions on Neural Networks*, 10:626–634, 1999.

7. X. Liu, A. Srivastava, and Kyle Gallivan, "Optimal linear representations of images for object recognition," *IEEE Transactions on Pattern Recognition and Machine Intelligence*, vol. 26, no. 5, pp. 662–666, 2004.

8. W. Mio, Q. Zhang and X. Liu, "Nonlinearity and optimal component analysis," In *the Proceedings of the International Conference on Neural Networks*, 2005.

9. T. Poggio. On optimal nonlinear associative recall. *Biological Cybernetics*, 19:201–209, 1975.

10. B. Schölkopf, A. Smola, and K. R. Müller. Nonlinear component analysis as a kernel eigenvalue problem. *Neural Computation*, 10:1299–1319, 1998.

11. A. Srivastava and X. Liu, "Tools for Application-Driven Dimension Reduction," *Neurocomputing*, in press, 2005.

12. V. Vapnik. *The Nature of Statistical Learning Theory*. Springer-Verlag, New York, 1995.

13. F. W. Warner, *Foundations of Differentiable Manifolds and Lie Groups*, Springer, New York, 1983.

14. Q. Zhang and X. Liu, "Kernel optimal component analysis," In *the Proceedings of the IEEE Workshop on Learning in Computer Vision and Pattern Recognition*, 2004.

Reverse-Convex Programming
for Sparse Image Codes

Matthias Heiler and Christoph Schnörr

Computer Vision, Graphics, and Pattern Recognition Group,
Department of Mathematics and Computer Science,
University of Mannheim, 68131 Mannheim, Germany
{heiler, schnoerr}@uni-mannheim.de

Abstract. Reverse-convex programming (RCP) concerns global optimization of a specific class of non-convex optimization problems. We show that a recently proposed model for sparse non-negative matrix factorization (NMF) belongs to this class. Based on this result, we design two algorithms for sparse NMF that solve sequences of convex second-order cone programs (SOCP).

We work out some well-defined modifications of NMF that leave the original model invariant from the optimization viewpoint. They considerably generalize the sparse NMF setting to account for uncertainty in sparseness, for supervised learning, and, by dropping the non-negativity constraint, for sparsity-controlled PCA.

1 Introduction and Related Work

Reverse-convex programming (RCP) is a powerful framework from global optimization which, among others, subsumes d.c. programming [1]. Motivated by a recently proposed model for *sparse non-negative matrix factorization* [2], we employ RCP for solving sparsity-controlled NMF.

NMF was originally proposed to model processes in the physical sciences [3, 4]. In recent years, it has become increasingly popular in machine learning, signal processing, and computer vision as well [5, 6, 7]. One reason for this popularity is that NMF codes naturally favor sparse, parts-based representations [8, 9] which in the context of recognition can be more robust than non-sparse, global features. Especially for computer vision applications, where robustness against occlusion is a constant concern, researchers suggested various extensions of NMF in order to enforce very localized representations [10, 11]. Locality is closely related to *sparseness* which is a desirable property from a machine-learning perspective [12, 13] as well as from biological considerations [14]. We found (Sec. 3) that a particularly accurate sparsity measure introduced in [2] is accurately modeled using *second order conic constraints*.

From a computational viewpoint, second order conic constraints are attractive: Being convex, efficient and robust solvers are available [15, 16] that cover a surprisingly large variety of problems [17]. However, with *sparsity-controlled NMF* difficulties arise since the conic constraints are *reversed*: Admissible are

A. Rangarajan et al. (Eds.): EMMCVPR 2005, LNCS 3757, pp. 600–616, 2005.

points lying *outside* a second order cone. For such *reverse-convex programs* solvers were proposed that find a globally optimal solution [18, 19, 1]. However, to the best of our knowledge, there currently exists no globally optimal algorithm that is practical for solving the large-scale problems common in computer vision and pattern recognition.

In this paper we exploit the geometry of the sparsity-controlled NMF optimization problem to derive two algorithms that efficiently yield *locally* optimal solutions of the respective reverse-convex problems. The algorithms complement existing solvers based on projected gradient descent [2]. However, with our approach, there is *no need to select optimization parameters* (e.g., stepsize) and *performance* is superior in some relevant situations (Sec. 6). In addition, the reverse-convex framework allows to *easily extend the sparsity-controlled NMF model* by additional constraints. As proof-of-concept we show how additional convex constraints can *account for prior knowledge* available in supervised classification. Along a similar line, we present an algorithm for *sparsity-controlled PCA* [20, 21, 22] that uses reverse-convex solvers as subroutine.

In summary, the contributions of this paper[1] are

- two algorithms based on reverse-convex optimization for solving variations of the NMF problem,
- extensions of the sparsity-controlled NMF model to account for prior knowledge and uncertainty in sparseness, and
- a reverse-convex algorithm for sparsity-controlled PCA.

Outline. In Section 2 we present the models considered in this paper. This includes the original model by Hoyer [2] as well as some useful extensions. In Section 3 we explain how, precisely, the sparsity measure used relates to second order cones. Section 4 presents the tangent-plane approach, a fast and practical algorithm based on first-order approximation of the sparsity constraints. Section 5 gives an algorithm based on a dual optimization idea. We present experimental results in Section 6 before we conclude in Section 7.

Notation. For any $m \times n$-matrix M, we denote its i-th column by M_{*i}, and its row by M_{i*}. Unless stated otherwise, $V \in \mathbb{R}_+^{m \times n}$ is a non-negative matrix containing n data points, and $W \in \mathbb{R}_+^{m \times r}$ is a corresponding basis with r-dimensional coefficients $H \in \mathbb{R}_+^{r \times n}$. $\|x\|_p$ denotes the ℓ_p-norm for vectors x, and $\|M\|_F$ the Frobenius norm for matrices: $\|M\|_F = \sqrt{\text{tr}(M^\top M)}$. Further, $\otimes$ denotes Kronecker's matrix product and $\odot$ the element-wise matrix multiplication. $\text{vec}(M)$ is the concatenation of the columns of M. Special matrices we will encounter are $I_{r \times r}$, the $r \times r$ identity matrix, and $E_{a \times b}$, the $a \times b$ matrix with all entries equal to unity. Finally, e is the vector with entries equal to unity.

---

[1] Note that a shorter paper with focus on Computer Vision appears in ICCV. In this shorter paper translation-invariant image bases were treated, but the tangent-plane approach (Sec. 4) and the sparse PCA algorithm (Sec. 5.1) as well as some theoretical and experimental results had to be omitted due to lack of space.

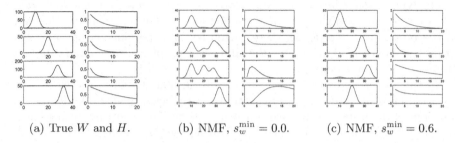

(a) True W and H.   (b) NMF, $s_w^{\min} = 0.0$.   (c) NMF, $s_w^{\min} = 0.6$.

Fig. 1. Paatero experiments. The data set is displayed in Fig. 1(a): Gaussian and exponential distributions are multiplied to yield matrix V. In the experiments, a small amount of Gaussian noise $\eta \sim \mathcal{N}(0, 0.1)$ is added to the product. The results for different values of the min-sparsity constraint are shown in Fig. 1(b) and 1(c): Only a non-trivial sparsity constraint makes recovery of W and H successful.

2   Sparsity Control for NMF and PCA

2.1   Sparse NMF

We consider the NMF optimization problem:

$$
\min_{W,H} \quad \|V - WH\|_F^2
$$
$$
\text{s.t.} \quad 0 \leq W, H.
$$

(1)

Although NMF codes are often sparse, it has been suggested to control sparsity by more direct means. This can lead to considerably improved basis functions (Fig. 1). We will employ the following sparseness measure recently introduced in the NMF context by Hoyer [2]:

$$
\mathrm{sp}(x) := \frac{1}{\sqrt{n}-1}\left(\sqrt{n} - \frac{\|x\|_1}{\|x\|_2}\right), \quad x \in \mathbb{R}^n \setminus \{0\}.
$$

(2)

Since $\frac{1}{\sqrt{n}}\|x\|_1 \leq \|x\|_2 \leq \|x\|_1$, (2) is bounded: $0 \leq \mathrm{sp}(x) \leq 1$. In particular, $\mathrm{sp}(x) = 0$ for minimal sparse vectors with equal non-zero components, and $\mathrm{sp}(x) = 1$ for maximally sparse vectors with all but one vanishing components. By a slight abuse of notation, we will sometimes write $\mathrm{sp}(M) \in \mathbb{R}^n$, meaning $\mathrm{sp}(\cdot)$ is applied to each column of matrix $M \in \mathbb{R}^{m \times n}$.

Originally, it was proposed to use $\mathrm{sp}(x) = const.$ to constrain the set of admissible solutions of (1) [2]. Slightly generalizing, we formulate:

$$
\min_{W,H} \quad \|V - WH\|_F^2
$$
$$
\text{s.t.} \quad 0 \leq W, H
$$
$$
s_w^{\min} \leq \mathrm{sp}(W) \leq s_w^{\max}
$$
$$
s_h^{\min} \leq \mathrm{sp}(H^\top) \leq s_h^{\max},
$$

(3)

where $s_w^{\min}, s_h^{\min}, s_w^{\max}, s_h^{\max}$ are user parameters to control sparsity. To obtain a feasible set with non-void interior, we usually choose $s_{h/w}^{\min}$ strictly smaller than $s_{h/w}^{\max}$.

Alternatively, it can be convenient to trade sparsity for reconstruction accuracy by relaxing the hard constraints:

$$\min_{W,H} \quad \|V - WH\|_F^2 - \lambda_h e^\top \mathrm{sp}(H^\top) - \lambda_w e^\top \mathrm{sp}(W)$$
$$\text{s.t.} \quad 0 \le W, H. \tag{4}$$

Furthermore, for object recognition it is generally useful to integrate available information about object labels into the process of learning basis functions [11]. With our approach it is particularly efficient to restrict, for each class i and for each of its vectors j, the coefficients H_{j*} to a cone around the class center μ_i

$$\min_{W,H} \quad \|V - WH\|_F^2$$
$$\text{s.t.} \quad 0 \le W, H \tag{5a}$$
$$\|\mu_i - H_{j*}\|_2 \le \lambda \|\mu_i\|_1 \quad \forall i, \forall j \in \text{class}(i). \tag{5b}$$

Given class label information, the μ_i are completely determined by the coefficient matrix H. Thus, they are computed implicitly during optimization.

2.2 Sparse PCA

For data that is non-negative by nature, e.g., image data, certain physical properties, probabilities, or equities, NMF is particularly well-suited. However, in situations where negative values occur we want to allow for negative bases and coefficient vectors as well. This leads to a sparsity-controlled setting similar to PCA [20, 21, 22]. In particular, the problem considered reads

$$\min_{W,H} \quad \|V - WH\|_F^2$$
$$\text{s.t.} \quad s_w^{\min} \le \mathrm{sp}(W) \le s_w^{\max} \tag{6}$$
$$s_h^{\min} \le \mathrm{sp}(H^\top) \le s_h^{\max},$$

which equals (3) except for the non-negativity constraints that are omitted.

3 Sparsity and Second Order Cones

In this section we show how our sparsity measure relates to second order cones. Through their close link algorithms based on convex programming become useful for sparsity-controlled NMF.

The *second order cone* $\mathcal{L}^{n+1} \subset \mathbb{R}^{n+1}$ is the convex set [17]:

$$\mathcal{L}^{n+1} := \left\{ \begin{pmatrix} x \\ t \end{pmatrix} = (x_1, \ldots, x_n, t)^\top \;\middle|\; \|x\|_2 \le t \right\}, \tag{7}$$

The problem of minimizing a linear objective function, subject to the constraints that several affine functions of the variables are situated in $\mathcal{L}^{n+1}$, is called a *second order cone program (SOCP)*:

$$\inf_{x \in \mathbb{R}^n} f^\top x$$

$$\text{s.t.} \begin{pmatrix} A_i x + b_i \\ c_i^\top x + d_i \end{pmatrix} \in \mathcal{L}^{n+1}, \qquad i = 1, \ldots, m \tag{8}$$

Note, that linear constraints and, in particular, the condition $x \in \mathbb{R}_+^n$ are important special cases. Our approach to sparsity-constrained NMF, to be developed subsequently, is based on this class of convex optimization problems for which efficient and robust solvers exist in software [15, 16].

On the non-negative cone we can model the sparseness-measure (2) using the family of *convex* sets parametrized by sparsity-parameter $s \in [0,1]$:

$$C(s) := \left\{ x \in \mathbb{R}^n \ \middle| \ \begin{pmatrix} x \\ e^\top x/c_{n,s} \end{pmatrix} \in \mathcal{L}^{n+1} \right\}, \qquad c_{n,s} := \sqrt{n} - (\sqrt{n} - 1)s. \tag{9}$$

Inserting the bounds $0 \leq \mathrm{sp}(x) \leq 1$ for s, we obtain

$$C(0) = \{\lambda e, \ 0 < \lambda \in \mathbb{R}\} \qquad \text{and} \qquad \mathbb{R}_+^n \subset C(1). \tag{10}$$

This raises the question as to when we must impose non-negativity constraints explicitly.

Proposition 1. *The set $C(s)$ contains non-positive vectors $x \neq 0$ if:*

$$\frac{\sqrt{n} - \sqrt{n-1}}{\sqrt{n} - 1} < s \leq 1, \quad n \geq 3 \tag{11}$$

Proof. We observe that if $x \in C(s)$, then $\lambda x \in C(s)$ for arbitrary $0 < \lambda \in \mathbb{R}$, because $\|\lambda x\|_2 - e^\top(\lambda x)/c_{n,s} = \lambda(\|x\|_2 - e^\top x/c_{n,s}) \leq 0$. Hence it suffices to consider vectors x with $\|x\|_2 = 1$. According to definition (9), such vectors tend to be in $C(s)$ the more they are aligned with e. Therefore, w.l.o.g., put $x_n = 0$ and $x_i = (n-1)^{-1/2}$, $i = 1, \ldots, n-1$. Then $x \in C(s)$ if $c_{n,s} < \sqrt{n-1}$, and the result follows from the definition of $c_{n,s}$ in (9). Finally, for $n = 2$ the lower bound for s equals 1, i.e., no non-positive vectors exist for all admissible values of s. □

This argument shows that $C(s') \subseteq C(s)$ for $s' \leq s$. To represent the feasible set of problem (3), we combine the convex non-negativity condition with the convex upper bound constraint:

$$\{x \in \mathbb{R}_+^n \mid \mathrm{sp}(x) \leq s\} = \mathbb{R}_+^n \cap C(s), \tag{12}$$

and impose the *non-convex* lower bound constraint by subsequently removing $C(s')$:

$$\{x \in \mathbb{R}_+^n \mid s' \leq \mathrm{sp}(x) \leq s, \ s' < s\} = (\mathbb{R}_+^n \cap C(s)) \setminus C(s') \tag{13}$$

To reformulate (3), we define accordingly, based on (9):

$$\mathcal{C}_w(s) := \left\{ W \in \mathbb{R}^{m \times r} \mid W_{*i} \in C(s), \ i = 1, \dots, r \right\} \tag{14}$$

$$\mathcal{C}_h(s) := \left\{ H \in \mathbb{R}^{r \times n} \mid H_{i*} \in C(s), \ i = 1, \dots, r \right\} \tag{15}$$

As a result, the sparsity-constrained NMF problem (3) now reads:

$$\min_{W,H} \quad \|V - WH\|_F^2$$
$$\text{s.t.} \quad W \in \left(\mathbb{R}_+^{m \times r} \cap \mathcal{C}_w(s_w^{\max}) \right) \setminus \mathcal{C}_w(s_w^{\min}) \tag{16}$$
$$H \in \left(\mathbb{R}_+^{r \times n} \cap \mathcal{C}_h(s_h^{\max}) \right) \setminus \mathcal{C}_h(s_h^{\min})$$

This formulation makes explicit that enforcing sparse NMF solutions introduces a single additional *reverse-convex* constraint for W and H, respectively. Consequently, not only the joint optimization of (W, H) is non-convex, but individual optimization of W and H are also.

4   Tangent-Plane Approach

In this section, we present an optimization scheme for sparsity-controlled NMF which relies on linear approximations of the reverse-convex constraint in (16). We process W and H alternately, leaving one fixed while optimizing the other. For presentation, we consider the H-step:

$$\min_{H} \quad f(H) = \|V - WH\|_F^2$$
$$\text{s.t.} \quad H \in \left(\mathbb{R}_+^{r \times n} \cap \mathcal{C}_h(s_h^{\max}) \right) \setminus \mathcal{C}_h(s_h^{\min}). \tag{17}$$

The W-step is analogous. Throughout this paper, we assume $s_h^{\min} < s_h^{\max}$, i.e., the interior of the feasible set is non-empty. Furthermore, we assume that every basis vector W_{*i} contains at least one non-zero entry.

Step one. The algorithm starts by setting $s_h^{\min} = 0$ in (17), and by computing the global optimum of the convex problem: $\min f(H), H \in \mathbb{R}_+^{r \times n} \cap \mathcal{C}_h(s_h^{\max})$, denoted by $\tilde{H}^0$. Rewriting the objective function:

$$f(H) = \|V^\top - H^\top W^\top\|_F^2$$
$$= \|\text{vec}(V^\top) - (W \otimes I)\text{vec}(H^\top)\|_2^2, \tag{18}$$

we observe that $\tilde{H}^0$ solves the SOCP:

$$\min_{\mathbb{R}} t, \quad H \in \mathbb{R}_+^{r \times n} \cap \mathcal{C}_h(s_h^{\max}), \quad \begin{pmatrix} \text{vec}(V^\top) - (W \otimes I)\text{vec}(H^\top) \\ t \end{pmatrix} \in \mathcal{L}^{r \cdot n + 1}. \tag{19}$$

Note that $\tilde{H}^0$ will in general be infeasible w.r.t. the original problem because the reverse-convex constraint of (17) is not imposed in (19). In case $\tilde{H}^0$ already is feasible the reverse-convex min-sparsity constraint is superfluous and the algorithm terminates returning $\tilde{H}^0$ as solution.

Table 1. Tangent-plane approximation algorithm in pseudocode

1.)	$H^0 \leftarrow$ solution of (19), $J^0 \leftarrow \emptyset$, $k \leftarrow 0$
2.)	repeat
3.)	$\tilde{H}^k \leftarrow H^k$
4.)	repeat
5.)	$J^k \leftarrow J^k \cup \{j \in 1, \ldots, r : \tilde{H}^k_{j*} \in \mathcal{C}_h(s^{\min}_h)\}$
6.)	$t^k_j \leftarrow \nabla \mathcal{C}(s^{\min}_h)(\pi(\tilde{H}^k_{j*}))$ $\forall j \in J^k$
7.)	$\tilde{H}^k \leftarrow$ solution of (20) replacing H^k by $\tilde{H}^k$
8.)	until $\tilde{H}^k_{j*}$ feasible
9.)	$H^{k+1} \leftarrow \tilde{H}^k$, $J^{k+1} \leftarrow J^k$, $k \leftarrow k+1$
10.)	until $|f(H^k) - f(H^{k-1})| \leq \epsilon$

Step two. Using an iteration counter k initialized to 0 we determine in step two the index set $J^k \subseteq \{1, \ldots, r\}$ of those vectors $\tilde{H}^k_{j*}$ violating the reverse-convex constraint, that is $\tilde{H}^k_{j*} \in C(s^{\min}_h)$. Let $\pi(\tilde{H}^k_{j*})$ denote the projections of $\tilde{H}^k_{j*}$ onto $\partial C(s^{\min}_h)$, $\forall j \in J^k$, and t^k_j the normals to $\mathcal{C}_h(s^{\min}_h)$ at these points, and H^k the matrix $\tilde{H}^k$ rectified accordingly. Given J^k, we re-solve (19) with additional linear constraints enforcing feasibility of each H^k_{j*}, $j \in J^k$:

$$\min_{\mathbb{R}} t \, , \quad H \in \mathbb{R}^{r \times n}_+ \cap \mathcal{C}_h(s^{\max}_h) \, , \quad \begin{pmatrix} \text{vec}(V^\top) - (W \otimes I)\text{vec}(H^\top) \\ t \end{pmatrix} \in \mathcal{L}^{r \cdot n + 1}$$

$$\langle t^k_j, H_{j*} - \pi(H^k_{j*}) \rangle \geq 0 \, , \quad \forall j \in J^k \qquad (20)$$

Geometrically, the linear constraints force $H^k_{j*}, j \in J^k$ onto the non-negative side of the plane tangential to the min-sparsity cone running through $\pi(H^k_{j*})$. Thus, in the solution $\tilde{H}^{k+1}$ of (20) all $\tilde{H}^{k+1}_{j*}$, $j \in J^k$, will be feasible. However, it is possible that new vectors $\tilde{H}^{k+1}_{j*}$ corresponding to unconstrained indices $j \notin J^k$ have become infeasible. When this happens we augment J^k accordingly, adjust the tangent planes to reflect the new position of $\tilde{H}^{k+1}_{j*}$, and re-solve (20) until the solution is feasible. The result is denoted by H^{k+1}, the corresponding index set by J^{k+1}. Finally, we increment the iteration counter: $k \leftarrow k+1$ and check whether H^{k+1} satisfies the termination criterion $|f(H^{k+1}) - f(H^k)| \leq \epsilon$. If it does not we continue with step two. The algorithm is summarized in Tab. 1.

4.1   Convergence Properties

In the following discussion we will use matrices $T^k = (t^k_j)_{j \in J}$ that have tangent plane vector t^k_j as j-th column when $j \in J^k$ and zeros elsewhere.

Proposition 2. *If the cone constraints are regular[2] the tangent-plane algorithm yields a sequence $H^1, H^2, \ldots$ of feasible points, every cluster point of which is a local optimum.*

Proof. (Sketch). Our proof follows [18–Prop. 3.2]. First, note that for every $k > 0$ the solution H^k of iteration k is a feasible point for the SOCP solved in iteration $k + 1$. Therefore, $\{f(H^k)\}_{k=1,\ldots}$ is a decreasing sequence, bounded from below and thus convergent. By assumption, no column of $W \geq 0$ equals the zero vector. Then, $\{H : f(H) \leq f(H^k)\}$ is bounded for each k. Consequently, the sequence $\{H^k\}_{k=1,\ldots}$ of solutions of (20) and the corresponding sequences $\{T^k\}_{k=1,\ldots}$ of tangent planes are bounded and contain converging subsequences. Let $\{H^{k_\nu}\}_{\nu=1,\ldots}$ and $\{T^{k_\nu}\}_{\nu=1,\ldots}$ be subsequences converging to cluster points $\bar{H}$ and $\bar{T}$.

Because H^{k_ν} is the global solution of a convex program we have

$$f(H^{k_\nu}) \leq f(H), \qquad \forall H \in \mathcal{C}(s_h^{\max}) \text{ with } T^{k_\nu \top} H \geq 0, \tag{21}$$

and in the limit $\nu \to \infty$

$$f(\bar{H}) \leq f(H), \qquad \forall H \in \mathcal{C}(s_h^{\max}) \text{ with } \bar{T}^\top H \geq 0. \tag{22}$$

We assumed the tangent plane constraints are regular. Then the constraints active in $\bar{T}$ correspond to entries $\bar{H}_{j*} \in \partial \mathcal{C}_h(s_h^{\min}), j \in J$. According to (22) there is no feasible descent direction at $\bar{H}$ and, thus, it must be a stationary point. Since the target function is quadratic positive-semidefinite it is an optimum. $\square$

While the individual optimization of H for given W converges (and vice versa), the same cannot be claimed for the *alternating* sequence of optimizations in W and H necessary to solve (3): The intervening optimization of W prevents us from deriving a bound on $f(H)$ from a previously found locally optimal H. In rare cases, this can lead to undesirable oscillations.

4.2   Practical Remarks

Two things are remarkable regarding the tangent-plane algorithm: First, multiple tangent-planes with reversed signs can also be used to approximate the convex max-sparsity constraints. Then (20) reduces to a *quadratic programming* (QP) problem. Except for linear programming, QP solvers are often among the most efficient mathematical programming codes available. Thus, a speedup might be gained by using QP instead of SOCP solvers, in particular, for the important case when no max-sparsity constraints are specified (i.e., $s_h^{\max} = s_w^{\max} = 1$).

A second remark concerns the termination criterion (step 10 in Tab. 1). While it can be chosen almost arbitrarily rigid, an overly small ϵ does not help in the overall optimization w.r.t. W *and* H. As long as, e.g., W is known only approximately, there is no need to compute the corresponding H to the last digit. In Sec. 6 we chose relatively large ϵ so that the outer loop (steps 2 to 10 in Tab. 1) executed only once or twice before the variable was switched.

---

[2] According to Proposition 1 this is the case iff $s \neq \frac{\sqrt{n} - \sqrt{n-1}}{\sqrt{n-1}}$ and the interior of the feasible set is non-empty.

5   Sparsity-Maximization Approach

In this section we present an algorithm that alternately maximizes sparsity and minimizes the objective function, in effect replacing the reverse-convex constraint by a sequence of convex proximity constraints. Unlike the tangent-plane approach presented above, this algorithm can easily be employed to yield monotonically decreasing sequences of objective values in H *and* in W, i.e., $f(H^k, W^k) \geq f(H^{k+1}, W^k) \geq f(H^{k+1}, W^{k+1}) \geq \cdots$, with $f(H, W) = \|V - WH\|_F^2$. This rules out oscillations that are rare, but cumbersome to avoid with the tangent-plane approach.

5.1   Sparse NMF

In order to solve (16) we again alternately optimize for W and for H, keeping the other constant. Since both optimizations are symmetric, we focus our presentation on the H step.

Our algorithm is motivated by results from global optimization [18] and consists of two complementary steps: One maximizes sparsity subject to the constraint that the objective value must not increase. Dually, the other optimizes the objective function $f(H) = \|V - WH\|_F^2$ under the condition that the min-sparsity constraint may not be violated.

Initialization. Let $H^0 \in \partial \mathcal{C}_h(s_h^{\min})$ be an initialization on the boundary of the min-sparsity cone. It may be computed by solving (19) for H, i.e., ignoring min-sparsity constraints and projecting the solution onto $\partial \mathcal{C}_h(s_h^{\min})$. Set $k \leftarrow 0$.

Step one. In the first step, consider the program

$$\max_{H} \quad g(H) = \min_{j} \{\mathrm{sp}(H_{j*})\}$$
$$\mathrm{s.t.} \quad H \in \mathbb{R}_+^{r \times n} \cap \mathcal{C}_h(s_h^{\max}) \tag{23}$$
$$f(H) \leq f(H^k)$$

that maximizes sparsity of the least sparse H_{j*} subject to the constraint that the solution may not measure worse than H^k in terms of the target function f. This is a convex maximization problem on a bounded domain. As such, it can in principle be solved to global optimality [18]. However, practical algorithms exist for small-scale problems only.

Thus, we will content ourselves with a local improvement that is obtained by replacing $\mathrm{sp}(x)$ by its first order Taylor expansion at H^k, resulting in the SOCP

$$\max_{H,t} \quad t$$
$$\mathrm{s.t.} \quad H \in \mathbb{R}_+^{r \times n} \cap \mathcal{C}_h(s_h^{\max}) \tag{24}$$
$$\begin{pmatrix} \mathrm{vec}(V^\top) - (W \otimes I)\mathrm{vec}(H^\top) \\ f(H^k) \end{pmatrix} \in \mathcal{L}^{rn+1}$$
$$t \leq \mathrm{sp}(H_{j*}) + \langle \nabla_{H_{j*}} \mathrm{sp}(H_{j*}^k)^\top, H_{j*} - H_{j*}^k \rangle \quad \forall j.$$

Table 2. Sparsity-maximization algorithm in pseudocode

1.) $H^0 \leftarrow$ solution of (19) projected on $\partial \mathcal{C}_h(s_h^{\min})$, $k \leftarrow 0$
2.) repeat
3.) $H^{\mathrm{sp}} \leftarrow$ solution of (24)
4.) $H^{k+1} \leftarrow$ solution of (25)
5.) $k \leftarrow k+1$
6.) until $|f(H^k) - f(H^{k-1})| \leq \epsilon$

Let H^{sp} denote the corresponding solution. Note that H^k is a feasible point of (24) and the sparsity cone is convex. Thus, optimization will in fact yield $g(H^{\mathrm{sp}}) \geq g(H^k)$.

Step two. In the second step we solve the SOCP

$$\min_{H,t} \quad t$$

$$\text{s.t.} \quad \begin{pmatrix} \mathrm{vec}(V^\top) - (W \otimes I)\mathrm{vec}(H^\top) \\ t \end{pmatrix} \in \mathcal{L}^{rn+1} \tag{25}$$

$$\begin{pmatrix} H_{j*} - H_{j*}^{\mathrm{sp}} \\ \min_{q \in \mathcal{C}(s_h^{\min})} \|q - H_{j*}^{\mathrm{sp}}\|_2 \end{pmatrix} \in \mathcal{L}^{n+1} \quad \forall j$$

$$H \in \mathbb{R}_+^{r \times n} \cap \mathcal{C}_h(s_h^{\max}).$$

This problem is identical to (16) restricted to H, except for the reverse-convex min-sparsity constraint that is replaced by a convex proximity constraint: Each H_{j*} is restricted to lie within a "save" distance from H_{j*}^{sp}.

Akin to [18], convergence to a local optimum can be proven under mild restrictions (notably, that W is not degenerate and contains at least one non-zero entry in each column). A proof will be presented in an extended paper.

Assuming convergence for a moment, it is easy to see that for any given feasible H^0 the algorithm terminates with an H^k that performs at least as well as H^0 in terms of f, i.e., $f(H^k) \leq f(H^0)$. This is, because in each iteration i the current estimate H^i is a feasible point of the convex program (25) minimizing f so that $f(H^{i+1}) \leq f(H^i)$, $i = 0, \ldots, k-1$. When the sparsity-maximization algorithm runs multiple times, alternately optimizing H for fixed W and vice versa, one will, after the first iteration, not initialize the algorithm by solving (19) and projecting subsequently, but use the current estimates for H and W as initializations. This way, one obtains a monotonically decreasing sequence of objective values $\|V - W^k H^k\|_F^2$.

Relaxed Formulation. The relaxed form of sparsity-controlled NMF described in (4) is optimized similarly by linearizing $\mathrm{sp}(x)$ around H^k, yielding the SOCP

$$\min_{H,t,s} \quad t - \lambda_h e^\top s$$

$$\text{s.t.} \quad \begin{pmatrix} \text{vec}(V^\top) - (W \otimes I)\text{vec}(H^\top) \\ t \end{pmatrix} \in \mathcal{L}^{rn+1} \tag{26}$$

$$s_j \leq \text{sp}(H_{j*}^k) + \langle \nabla_{H_{j*}} \text{sp}(H_{j*}^k)^\top, H_{j*} - H_{j*}^k \rangle \quad \forall j$$

$$H \in \mathbb{R}_+^{r \times n}.$$

Thus, in order to solve (4) for H we iteratively solve instances of (26) until convergence.

Exploiting Information from Class Labels. The supervised variant (5) of the NMF problem is readily solved by above algorithms since (5b) translates, for each class i and for each coefficient vector H_{j*} belonging to class i, into a second order constraint

$$\begin{pmatrix} 1/n_i H_{(i)} e - H_{j*} \\ \lambda/n_i e^\top H_{(i)} e \end{pmatrix} \in \mathcal{L}^{n+1}, \quad \forall i, \forall j \in \text{class}(i). \tag{27}$$

Here, the $r \times n_i$-matrix of coefficients belonging to class i is abbreviated $H_{(i)}$ and we recognize $\mu_i = 1/n_i H_{(i)} e$. Adding these constraints to, e.g., (24) and (25) yields an algorithm for solving supervised NMF.

5.2   Sparse PCA

Next, we show how to optimize for H when both, W and H may contain negative entries. The idea is that we can factorize any non-zero matrix $M \in \mathbb{R}^{m \times n}$ into $M_\pm \equiv \text{sign}(M) \in \mathbb{R}^{m \times n}$ and $M_+ \in \mathbb{R}_+^{m \times n}$ s.t. $M = M_\pm \odot M_+$. Since sparsity is not affected by sign changes or multiplicative constants we observe

$$\text{sp}(M) = \text{sp}(M_+), \tag{28}$$

i.e., it is *sufficient to exercise sparsity control on the non-negative part* of x. Thus, the sparsity-controlled NMF algorithms presented above can be used on W_+ and H_+. Finally, for those entries in W and H that are close to 0 we subsequently optimize signs using convex programming.

Step one. E.g., in the H-step we first optimize for H_+, by solving

$$\min_{H_+,t} \quad t$$

$$\text{s.t.} \quad \begin{pmatrix} \text{vec}(V) - ((I \otimes W) \odot H_S)\text{vec}(H_+) \\ t \end{pmatrix} \in \mathcal{L}^{rn+1} \tag{29}$$

$$H_+ \in (\mathbb{R}_+^{r \times n} \cap \mathcal{C}_h(s_h^{\max})) \setminus \mathcal{C}_h(s_h^{\min})$$

using any of the techniques presented above. Note that (29) is identical to the NMF case, i.e., it minimizes the original problem for $H = H_\pm \odot H_+$ but the signs of H are not allowed to change. The matrix H_S is given by

$$H_S = (I_{r \times r} \otimes E_{n \times n}) \odot (\text{vec}(H_\pm)e^\top)^\top. \tag{30}$$

Step two. In a second step, we solve for $H_\pm$ using the convex program

$$\min_{t, H_\pm \in H_\epsilon} \quad t$$

$$\text{s.t.} \quad \begin{pmatrix} \text{vec}(V) - ((I \otimes W) \odot H_A)\text{vec}(H_\pm) \\ t \end{pmatrix} \in \mathcal{L}^{rn+1} \qquad (31)$$

$$-1 \le H_\pm \le 1,$$

where H_A is constructed from H_+ analogously to (30):

$$H_A = (I_{r \times r} \otimes E_{n \times n}) \odot (\text{vec}(H_+)e^\top)^\top. \qquad (32)$$

H_ϵ denotes those entries in H_+ that are within ϵ from 0. Entries in $H_\pm$ corresponding to larger entries in H_+ are *not* optimized in order to prevent an entry in $H_\pm$ with small norm cancel out an entry with large norm in H_+, thus possibly modifying sparseness of the product $H = H_\pm \odot H_+$.

6 Experiments

6.1 Comparison with Established Algorithms

To see how our algorithms compare against an established method we computed sparsity-controlled decompositions into $r = 4$ basis functions for a subset of the USPS handwritten digits data set using our methods and projected gradient descent (pgd) as proposed in [2]. For different choices of sparseness we report mean and standard deviation of the runtime and mean residual error[3] averaged over 10 runs in Tab. 3. Note that the stopping criterion used was different for our algorithms and for pgd: We stopped when after a full iteration the objective value did not improve at least by a constant, the pgd implementation used[4] stopped as soon as the norm of the gradient was smaller than some ϵ. As the error measurements shown in Tab. 3 demonstrate, both stopping criteria yield comparable results. Regarding running time we see that the tangent-plane approach was usually fastest, followed by sparse-maximization. Also, our algorithms usually showed relatively small variation between individual runs while the runtime of pgd varied strongly, dependent on the randomly chosen starting points.

6.2 Global Approaches

A potential source of difficulties with the sparsity-maximization algorithm is that the lower bound on sparsity is optimized only locally in (24). Through the proximity constraint in (25) the amount of sparsity obtained in effect limits the

---

[3] Standard deviation of the residual error was equally negligible for all algorithms.

[4] We used the pgd code kindly provided by the author of [2], and removed all logging and monitoring parts to speed up calculation. Our SOCP solver was Mosek 3.2 from MOSEK ApS, Denmark, running under Linux.

Table 3. Performance comparison. Comparison of the tangent-plane (tgp) approach and the sparsity-maximization algorithm (spm) with projected gradient descent (pgd). Sparse decompositions of the digit data set were computed. Statistics collected over 10 repeated runs are reported for runtime (sec.) and residual error $\|V - WH\|_F^2$. tgp and spm are usually faster than pgd while keeping errors small.

sparsity	0.1	0.2	0.3	0.4	0.5	0.6	0.7	0.8	0.9
mean time tgp	34.35	35.46	41.30	64.97	66.80	60.86	56.33	51.82	42.50
mean time spm	94.81	106.20	133.52	159.30	173.14	167.06	114.36	78.42	74.96
mean time pgd	517.02	1038.99	218.17	70.24	177.35	189.48	167.94	430.36	322.88
stdv time tgp	3.17	2.64	3.84	5.50	8.51	7.05	4.25	0.76	0.38
stdv time spm	3.48	12.67	23.67	16.45	11.51	11.64	7.69	1.22	1.29
stdv time pgd	278.24	21.21	128.00	8.90	78.12	52.54	95.53	439.34	174.81
mean error tgp	0.82	0.76	0.73	0.72	0.78	0.89	0.99	1.08	1.12
mean error spm	0.81	0.77	0.74	0.73	0.78	0.89	1.00	1.08	1.13
mean error pgd	0.85	0.79	0.74	0.72	0.77	0.88	0.99	1.07	1.12

step size of the algorithm. Insufficient sparsity optimization may, in the worst case, lead to convergence to a bad local optimum.

To see if this worst-case scenario is relevant in practice, we discretized the problem by sampling the sparsity cones using rotated and scaled version of the current estimate H^k and then evaluated g in (23) using samples from each individual sparsity cone. Then we picked one sample from each cone and computed (24) replacing the starting point H^k by the sampled coordinates. For an exhaustive search on r cones each sampled with s points we have s^r starting points to consider.

For demonstration we used the artificial Paatero data set [23] consisting of products of Gaussian and exponential functions (Fig. 1). This data set is suitable since it is not overly large and sparsity control is crucial for its successful factorization (cf. [23] and Fig. 1).

In the sparsity-maximization algorithm we first sampled the four sparsity cones corresponding to each basis function of the data for $s_w \geq 0.6$ sparsely, using only 10 rotations on each cone. We then combined the samples on each cone in each possible way and evaluated g for all corresponding starting points. In a second experiment we placed 1000 points on each sparsity cone, and randomly selected 10^4 combinations as starting points. The best results obtained over four runs and 80 iterations with our local linearization method and the sparse enumeration (first) and the sampling (second) strategy, are reported below:

Algorithm	min-sparsity	objective value
local linearization	0.60	0.24
sparse enumeration	0.60	0.26
sampling	0.60	0.26

We see that the local sparsity maximization yields results comparable to the sampling strategies. In fact, it is better: Over four repeated runs with each of the sampling strategies we observed outliers with very bad objective values (not

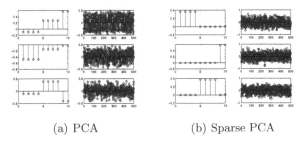

(a) PCA   (b) Sparse PCA

Fig. 2. Sparse PCA experiment. Basis and coefficients for an artificial data set are shown. Only sparsity-controlled PCA successfully recovers the structure of the data.

shown). This is most likely caused by severe under-sampling of the sparsity cones. This problem is not straightforward to circumvent: With above sampling schemes a run over 80 iterations takes about 24h of computing[5], so more sampling is not an option. In comparison, the proposed algorithm finishes in few seconds.

6.3   Sparse PCA

As proof-of-concept we factorized the artificial data set examined in [20] using PCA and sparsity-controlled PCA. The data set consists of three factors sampled from $V_1 \sim \mathcal{N}(0, 290), V_2 \sim \mathcal{N}(0, 300), V_3 \sim -0.3V_1 + 0.925V_2 + \eta$ and additional Gaussian noise. The sparse PCA algorithm iteratively solved (29) and (31) using the relaxed optimization framework (26) with $\lambda_w = 0.6$ and a constraint limiting the admissible reconstruction error.

In Fig. 2 we depict the factors and factor-loadings for PCA and sparsity-controlled PCA (best result out of three repeated runs). It is apparent that sparsity-controlled PCA correctly factorizes the data, while classical PCA fails.

6.4   Modeling a Low-Entropy Image Class

A sample application using real-world data is face modeling: Human faces, aligned, cropped and evenly lit, lead to highly structured images. With such images, sparse NMF appears robust against quantization: We learned a sparse image code ($r = 6, s_h^{\min} = 0.3$) for face images [24] and a PCA code for comparison. Then we enumerated possible reconstructions by setting each entry of the coefficient vector to 0 or to 1. The resulting $2^6 = 64$ images are shown in Fig. 3: While most NMF "reconstructions" look remarkably natural the corresponding PCA images mostly suffer severe degradation.

To measure qualitatively how quantization affects reconstruction performance we used PCA and NMF to find a large image base ($r = 100$) on a subset of the face data. Then, we quantized the reconstruction coefficients H using k-means on each individual row of coefficients H_{j*}. The results are shown

---

[5] On machines with 3GHz P4, 2GB RAM, running Matlab under Linux.

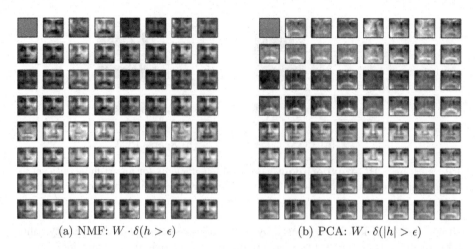

(a) NMF: $W \cdot \delta(h > \epsilon)$ (b) PCA: $W \cdot \delta(|h| > \epsilon)$

Fig. 3. Robustness against quantization. The 64 faces corresponding to previously learned 6bit NMF/PCA image codes after quantization of the coefficients. The top left image corresponds to the binary coefficient vector #b000000, the bottom right image to #b111111. The NMF faces suffer less from quantization than their PCA counterparts.

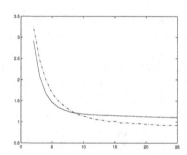

Fig. 4. Robustness against quantization. An basis for face images was trained using NMF (solid blue line) and PCA (dashed black line). The reconstruction coefficients H where quantized using k-means for $k = 2, \ldots, 25$ (x-axis) and the reconstruction error $f(W, H)$ was determined (y-axis) for the training data set. NMF is more robust against strong quantization.

in Fig. 4: As expected, PCA offers slightly better reconstruction performance for large values of k. With stronger quantization, however, it looses its advantage and NMF performs better.

This is surprising as quantization robustness was not an original design goal of NMF codes. From a Bayesian perspective we can explain this result by the fact that as quantization (or noise) increases the influence of prior information becomes more important. NMF models the prior information that images are non-negative. PCA has no such constraint and thus suffers more from strong quantization.

6.5 Supervised Training

To show that the supervised label constraints (5b) can be useful we trained NMF codes ($r = 4$) on only 100 samples from the USPS handwritten digit data set. We used different values for the parameter λ and a very simple conditional maximum entropy model $p(y|h)$ with mean coefficient values $\mathbb{E}[h_i]$ as only features for classification. The number of errors on a 300 sample test dataset is given below:

λ	1e4	1e2	1	1e-2	1e-4	1e-6
#errors	108	82	75	60	58	56

When λ is large, i.e., the supervised label constraint is inactive, the error is about 36% (108 out of 300 samples). This is slightly worse than a corresponding PCA basis (95 errors) would achieve. As the label constraint is strengthened the classification performance improves and finally is almost twice as good as in the unsupervised case.

7 Conclusion

We presented two algorithms for sparse coding based on ideas from reverse-convex programming and non-negative matrix factorization. The algorithms are conceptually clean, easy to use (no free parameters), and show attractive performance characteristics. Most importantly, they are flexible enough to be extended along various dimensions. For instance, prior information can be accounted for by adding a single conic constraint, and sparsity-controlled PCA is possible by separate optimization of absolute value and signs of the factors.

References

1. R. Horst and H. Tuy, *Global Optimization*. Springer, Berlin, 1996.
2. P. O. Hoyer, "Non-negative matrix factorization with sparseness constraints," *J. of Mach. Learning Res.*, vol. 5, pp. 1457–1469, 2004.
3. J. Shen and G. W. Israël, "A receptor model using a specific non-negative transformation technique for ambient aerosol," *Atmospheric Environment*, vol. 23, no. 10, pp. 2289–2298, 1989.
4. P. Paatero and U. Tapper, "Positive matrix factorization: A non-negative factor model with optimal utilization of error estimates of data values," *Environmetrics*, vol. 5, pp. 111–126, 1994.
5. W. Xu, X. Liu, and Y. Gong, "Document clustering based on non-negative matrix factorization," in *SIGIR '03: Proc. of the 26th Ann. Intl. ACM SIGIR Conf. on Res. and Developm. in Info. Retrieval*, pp. 267–273, ACM Press, 2003.
6. P. O. Hoyer and A. Hyvärinen, "A multi-layer sparse coding network learns contour coding from natural images," *Vision Research*, vol. 42, no. 12, pp. 1593–1605, 2002.
7. P. Smaragdis and J. C. Brown, "Non-negative matrix factorization for polyphonic music transcription," in *IEEE Workshop on Appl. of Sign. Proc. to Audio and Acoustics*, pp. 177–180, 2003.
8. D. D. Lee and H. S. Seung, "Learning the parts of objects by non-negative matrix factorization," *Nature*, vol. 401, pp. 788–791, Oct. 1999.

9. D. Donoho and V. Stodden, "When does non-negative matrix factorization give a correct decomposition into parts?," in *Adv. in NIPS*, vol. 17, 2004.
10. S. Z. Li, X. W. Hou, H. J. Zhang, and Q. S. Cheng, "Learning spatially localized, parts-based representation," in *Proc. of CVPR*, 2001.
11. Y. Wang, Y. Jia, C. Hu, and M. Turk, "Fisher non-negative matrix factorization for learning local features," in *Proc. Asian Conf. on Comp. Vision*, 2004.
12. N. Littlestone and M. Warmuth, "Relating data compression, learnability, and the Vapnik-Chervonenkis dimension," tech. rep., Univ. of Calif. Santa Cruz, 1986.
13. R. Herbrich and R. C. Williamson, "Algorithmic luckiness," *J. of Mach. Learning Res.*, vol. 3, pp. 175–212, 2002.
14. B. A. Olshausen and D. J. Field, "Sparse coding with an overcomplete basis set: A strategy employed by V1?," *Vision Research*, vol. 37, pp. 3311–3325, Dec. 1997.
15. J. F. Sturm, *Using SeDuMi 1.02, a Matlab toolbox for optimization over symmetric cones (updated version 1.05)*. Department of Econometrics, Tilburg University, Tilburg, The Netherlands, 2001.
16. M. ApS, ed., *The MOSEK optimization tools version 3.2 (Revision 8) User's manual and reference*. MOSEK ApS, Denmark, 2005.
17. M. S. Lobo, L. Vandenberghe, S. Boyd, and H. Lebret, "Applications of second-order cone programming," *Linear Algebra and its Applications*, 1998.
18. H. Tuy, "Convex programs with an additional reverse convex constraint," *J. of Optim. Theory and Applic.*, vol. 52, pp. 463–486, Mar. 1987.
19. R. Horst and P. M. Pardalos, eds., *Handbook of Global Optimization*. Kluwer Academic Publisher, 1995.
20. A. d'Aspremont, L. E. Ghaoui, M. I. Jordan, and G. R. Lanckriet, "A direct formulation for sparse PCA using semidefinite programming," in *Adv. in NIPS*, 2004.
21. H. Zou, T. Hastie, and R. Tibshirani, "Sparse principal component analysis," (J. of Comp. a. Graph. Statistics, to appear).
22. C. Chennubholta and A. Jepson, "Sparse PCA extracting multi-scale structure from data," in *Proc. of ICCV*, pp. 641–647, 2001.
23. P. Paatero, "Least squares formulation of robust non-negative factor analysis," *Chemometrics and Intelligent Laboratory Systems*, vol. 37, 1997.
24. CBCL, "CBCL face database #1." MIT Center For Biological and Computational Learning, http://cbcl.mit.edu/software-datasets, 2000.

Stereo for Slanted Surfaces:
First Order Disparities and Normal Consistency

Gang Li and Steven W. Zucker

Department of Computer Science, Yale University, New Haven, CT 06520, USA
{gang.li, steven.zucker}@yale.edu

Abstract. Traditional stereo algorithms either explicitly use the frontal parallel plane assumption by only considering position (zero-order) disparity when computing similarity measures of two image windows, or implicitly use it by imposing a smoothness prior bias towards frontal parallel plane solution. However this introduces two types of systematic error for slanted or curved surfaces. The first type is structural, and relates to discrete pixel coordinates and neighborhood structure. The second is geometric, and relates to differential properties of surfaces. To eliminate these systematic errors we extend stereo matching to include first-order disparities. Contextual information is then expressed geometrically by transporting surface normals over overlapping neighborhoods, which takes a particularly simple (and efficient) form in the tangent plane approximation. In particular, we develop a novel stereo algorithm that combines first-order disparity information with position (zero-order) disparity for slanted surfaces, and illustrate its use.

1 Introduction

Two view dense stereo correspondence algorithms have made significant progress in recent years [1, 7, 25, 5]. Working with a rectified image pair [9, 11], most of these algorithms exploit the *frontal parallel plane assumption* either explicitly or implicitly. In particular, it assumes position disparity (or depth) is constant (with respect to the rectified stereo pair) over a region under consideration. However, real world objects possess surfaces rich in shape, which generically violate the frontal parallel plane assumption (Fig. 1).

To find correspondence, traditional area based methods compare a window of the same size and shape in the left and right images and compute the similarity measure, where the frontal parallel plane assumption is explicitly used. Several algorithms address this problem. [12] uses a parameterized planar or quadratic patch fit to the images as a local model for the disparity surface. In [14] variable window size (but fixed shape) is used. In [6] disparity derivatives are used to deform the matching window in a refined correlation algorithm. In [3, 18] slanted and curved surfaces are explicitly modeled for each segmented region, where segmentation and correspondence are iteratively obtained from the multiway-cut algorithm [4]. [21] develops a slanted scanline algorithm.

A. Rangarajan et al. (Eds.): EMMCVPR 2005, LNCS 3757, pp. 617–632, 2005.

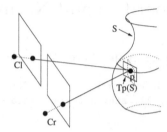

Fig. 1. For a regular surface $S \subset \mathbb{R}^3$, the tangent plane $T_p(S)$ (in solid lines) at a point $p \in S$ is well defined. However traditional stereo algorithms use the frontal parallel plane (in dotted lines) to represent the (local) surface geometry at p, which is incorrect.

Taken individually, point-wise geometric constraints (e.g. epipolar constraint) and similarity measure (e.g. SSD) cannot always resolve matching ambiguities. Thus requiring neighboring matching pairs to be "consistent" is natural. An early cooperative algorithm[19] uses a local excitatory neighborhood of the same disparity level to support the current matching pair. In the refined cooperative algorithm [29] local support is defined as the sum of all match values within a 3D local support volume, designed to include a small disparity range as an extra dimension. In [24] local support at different disparity hypotheses is diffused iteratively, and the amount of diffusion is controlled by the quality of the disparity estimate. In [4] a smoothness term over neighboring pixels is introduced in an energy function minimized by graph cuts. In [26, 27] messages (similarity measure weighted by gaussian smoothed disparity difference) are passed between nearby matching pairs in a Markov network by belief propagation. However these algorithms implicitly use the frontal parallel plane assumption since the neighboring matching pairs interact in a way such that frontal parallel plane solution is preferred.

Both the explicit and the implicit use of the frontal parallel plane assumption introduces systematic errors to stereo corrspondence (see experiment section for details). To move beyond this assumpltion, locally it implies that the tangent plane $T_p(S)$ deviates from the frontal parallel plane. Our geometric observation then arises in several forms: (i) the shape of matching patches in the left/right image must vary; (ii) integer coordinates must be interpolated; (iii) disparity derivatives are related to surface differential geometric property; and (iv) continuity over overlapping neighborhoods must include (at least) surface normal consistency. To take full advantage of (iii) and (iv), which follow directly from differential geometry, we futher observe that some form of (Cartan) transport is required to combine information from different surface normals in a neighborhood around a putative matching point.

In this paper our task is to develop a new constraint for planar surfaces not in the frontal parallel plane using basic surface differential geometry. Specifically, we develop a novel stereo algorithm that explicitly takes into account first-order disparities for non-frontal-parallel surfaces. This amounts to: (1) the local deformation of the SSD window, which gives us continuous (interpolated) disparity as well as first order disparities (surface orientation); and (2) describing geometric consistency between nearby matching pairs by using depth (position disparity) and surface normal (first-order disparities), which *does* help the matching process. The second part behaves like an *extra geometric constraint* for stereo correspondence. While the epipolar constraint is well studied and utilized in stereo correspondence, geometric contextual constraints among nearby matching pairs are largely unexplored. In this paper we explore the simplest such geometric constraint for slanted or curved surfaces by taking into account their orientation. One implementation illustrates how well these constraints perform in practice, extending performance beyond traditional algorithms on several scenes. We hope this novelty will inspire researchers since our constraint could be used in more elaborate stereo algorithms.

2 Background

Assume the image pair is rectified [11]. For a 3D point p with disparity d, 3D planes (centered at p) in $\mathbb{R}^3$ can be classified as frontal parallel, horizontally slanted, vertically slanted, and in general configuration, respectively (Fig. 2(a-d)). First order disparities ($\{\frac{\partial d}{\partial u}, \frac{\partial d}{\partial v}\}$) do not vanish simultaneously for non-frontal parallel planes. Thus they cannot be ignored, otherwise systematic error will arise. In this section we describe how to take this effect into account for any local (window-based) algorithms with an aggregation step. In the next section we show how these first order disparities can be used to impose geometric contextual information by transporting surface normals over overlapping neighborhoods.

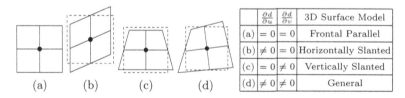

		$\frac{\partial d}{\partial u}$	$\frac{\partial d}{\partial v}$	3D Surface Model
	(a)	$= 0$	$= 0$	Frontal Parallel
	(b)	$\neq 0$	$= 0$	Horizontally Slanted
	(c)	$= 0$	$\neq 0$	Vertically Slanted
(a) (b) (c) (d)	(d)	$\neq 0$	$\neq 0$	General

Fig. 2. (LEFT: a-d) 3D plane types in $\mathbb{R}^3$: frontal parallel, horizontally slanted, vertically slanted, and in general configuration, respectively (frontal parallel plane also drawn in dashed lines for comparison); (RIGHT) First order disparities for different 3D plane types

2.1 Deforming Matching Window by First-Order Disparities

To find correspondence, traditional area based methods use a small window (e.g. 9x9) centered at (u, v) in the left image, and compare it with a window of the same size and shape at $(u - d, v)$ in the right image using similarity measure such as normalized cross correlation (NCC), sum of squared difference (SSD), or sum of absolute difference (SAD), etc. Disparity estimate d is obtained by selecting the one that gives the best similarity measure. When the scene within

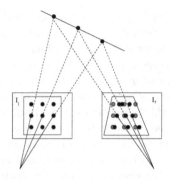

Fig. 3. Computing a similarity measure using an image window of size 3x3. To overcome the limitation of the frontal parallel plane assumption, the other image window must be deformed according to the shape of the (disparity) surface. This involves both window shape and corresponding pixels. Shown are true corresonding points (as black dots) in the right image of a slanted surface, which are different from measured gray dots.

each window satisfies the frontal parallel plane assumption the above method is valid. However when the 3D surfaces are slanted in depth or curved the problem formulation has to be modified, otherwise systematic errorr will arise. In Fig. 7, traditional SSD yields a stepwise scalloped pattern (frontal parallel planes at different depth) due to such systematic error.

To illustrate, we consider a small image window of a slanted planar surface (Fig. 3) for similarity measure (SSD). If the correspondence of (u, v) in the left image is $(u - d, v)$ in the right image, then to a first order approximation the correspondence of $(u + \Delta u, v + \Delta v)$ (black dots) in the neighborhood (in the left image) is $(u + \Delta u - d - \frac{\partial d}{\partial u} \Delta u - \frac{\partial d}{\partial v} \Delta v, v + \Delta v)$ (also black dots) in the right image, with $\frac{\partial d}{\partial u}$ and $\frac{\partial d}{\partial v}$ the partial derivatives of disparity d with respect to u and v, respectively; Δu and Δv the small step size in each direction. Typically $\Delta u, \Delta v \in \{0, \pm 1, \pm 2, \cdots\}$. When the 3D surface is not frontal parallel, these black dots are different from the measured gray dots. This effect can not be neglected. The effect of $\frac{\partial d}{\partial u}$ and $\frac{\partial d}{\partial v}$ on the location of the true correspondence is magnified by Δu and Δv. The bigger the window size, the stronger the effect, and to compute the similarity measure between the left and right image windows integer indexes in the right image no longer suffice. Matching window in the right image must be deformed accordingly.

The deformed window SSD is:

$$dw\_SSD(u, v, d, \frac{\partial d}{\partial u}, \frac{\partial d}{\partial v}) =$$

$$\sum_{(u+\Delta u, v+\Delta v) \in \mathcal{N}_{uv}} (I_l(u + \Delta u, v + \Delta v) - \tag{1}$$

$$\hat{I}_r(u + \Delta u - d - \frac{\partial d}{\partial u} \Delta u - \frac{\partial d}{\partial v} \Delta v, v + \Delta v))^2$$

where $\mathcal{N}_{uv}$ denotes the window centered at (u, v), and $\hat{I}_r$ is the linearly interpolated intensity of two nearest integer index positions in the right image.

With this new formulation of the similarity measure, the correspondence problem is then: for every (u, v) in the left image to select $\{d, \frac{\partial d}{\partial u}, \frac{\partial d}{\partial v}\}$ that gives the best similarity measure:

$$\arg \min_{\{d, \frac{\partial d}{\partial u}, \frac{\partial d}{\partial v}\}} dw\_SSD(u, v, d, \frac{\partial d}{\partial u}, \frac{\partial d}{\partial v}) \tag{2}$$

We use direction set method [22], a multidimensional minimization method, initialized with the integer disparity d_I (obtained from traditional SSD) and zeros for the first order disparities. The results are the (interpolated) floating point disparity d and first order disparities $\{\frac{\partial d}{\partial u}, \frac{\partial d}{\partial v}\}$ that achieve the best similarity measure at (u, v). In [6] such a deformed window was also used. Our contribution is to relate the deformation to surface orientation and impose geometric consistency over overlapping neighborhoods by using surface orientation, which provides extra geometric constraints for stereo correspondence. In the next section details will be given.

Note that several recent algorithms [4, 16, 26] use a pixel dissimilarity measure [2], which is insensitive to sampling by using linearly interpolated intensity functions. This measure is pixel-wise. To compute the similarity between two image windows using correlation or SSD, this measure has to be adjusted according to the deformation described above, otherwise systematic error may still arise.

3   Geometric Consistency from First-Order Disparities

This is the central part of our paper. Since ambiguities (along the epipolar line) cannot always be resolved using the local measurements described previously, we require neighboring matching pairs to be consistent. Unlike others [29], we derive this consistency geometrically, with surface orientation playing an important role.

Assume cameras are calibrated. The stereo pair has a baseline B and focal length α (pixels), and the depth of a point with disparity d is [9]:

$$Z(u, v) = \frac{B\alpha}{d(u, v)}$$

Differentiating Z we have:

$$Z_u = \frac{\partial Z}{\partial u} = -\frac{B\alpha}{d^2} \frac{\partial d}{\partial u} \tag{3}$$

$$Z_v = \frac{\partial Z}{\partial v} = -\frac{B\alpha}{d^2} \frac{\partial d}{\partial v} \tag{4}$$

The surface normal at this point is then $(1, 0, Z_u)^T \times (0, 1, Z_v)^T$, which after normalization is:

$$\mathbf{N} = \frac{(-Z_u, -Z_v, 1)^T}{\sqrt{Z_u^2 + Z_v^2 + 1}} \tag{5}$$

With the (putative) surface depth and normal at hand, we can then utilize contextual information geometrically. The basic idea is in the spirit of the Cartan moving frame model [15,8], which specifies how adapted frame fields change when they are transported along an object. And this model can be used to integrate local (geometric) information with (geometric) information in the neighborhood. We use i to denote a candidate match, i.e. $\{d, \frac{\partial d}{\partial u}, \frac{\partial d}{\partial v}\}$ at pixel (u, v), or equivalently $(u, v) < - > (u - d, v)$ with first order disparities $\{\frac{\partial d}{\partial u}, \frac{\partial d}{\partial v}\}$.

Geometric consistency means that, for a matching pair i, when it is transported along the object to a neighboring position, it is consistent with a neighboring matching pair j (Fig. 4). Note that the local surface approximation around i (computed from the information $at\ i$) serves as the object along which geometric information is transported, and is formally known as the *osculating object*. In this paper, the osculating object for a surface S takes its simplest form, which is the tangent plane $T_p(S)$ at $p \in S$. Since i and j refer to matching pairs, they each encode position disparity (depth) separately. Note that first order disparities at i and j further encode surface normals at these two points. Fig. 4 shows the geometric consistency between a matching pair i and its neighboring matching pair j (in solid lines). The tangent planes provide a natural description of the *geometric compatibility* r_{ij} between i and j:

$$r_{ij} = 1 - \frac{1}{m}(|\mathbf{v}_{ij} \cdot \mathbf{N}_i| + |\mathbf{v}_{ji} \cdot \mathbf{N}_j|) \tag{6}$$

where $\mathbf{v}_{ij}$ denotes the vector from i to j, $\mathbf{N}_i$ is the surface normal at i, and m is a normalization constant. Also shown are different neighbors j (dashed lines) of different depth and orientation, to illustrate the importance of both zero-order

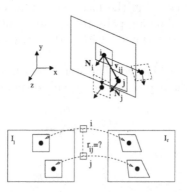

Fig. 4. Illustration of the geometry for the basic matching constraint. Surface patch i on a slanted surface in $\mathbb{R}^3$ projects to patches in the left and right images. For a nearby patch j in $\mathbb{R}^3$, the surface normal $\mathbf{N}_j$ must be parallel to $\mathbf{N}_i$, and the two patches must both lie on the same surface. Possible patches (dashed lines) which lie off the (tangent) plane at i, or at the wrong orientation, are not consistent. Both zero-order (position) disparity and first-order disparities are essential in determining such geometric consistency.

disparity (depth) and first-order disparities (surface orientation) in determining such consistency measure.

The geometric constraint (eqn. (6)) can be used as follows. For a matching pair i (hypothesis), we initialize its support s_i^0 according to its deformed window SSD (denoted by c_i) and iteratively update s_i by the geometric support it receives from its neighboring matching pair j:

$$s_i^0 = 1 - \frac{c_i}{c} \tag{7}$$

$$s_i^{t+1} = \frac{\sum_{j \in \mathcal{N}_i} r_{ij} s_j^t}{\sum_{j \in \mathcal{N}_i} s_j^t} \tag{8}$$

with c a normalization factor, $\mathcal{N}_i$ denotes the neighbors of i (in our experiments we use a 5x5x3 (u, v, d) region). The true correspondence will be supported by its neighbors since their local surface geometry estimates are geometrically consistent. False matches are unlikely to get support from neighbors.

Assuming the noise in the surface normals is roughly zero mean Gaussian i.i.d. (independent and identically distributed), the "best fit" (in a least-squares sense) unit normal at i is updated as [23]:

$$\mathbf{N}_i^{t+1} = \frac{\sum_{j \in \mathcal{N}_i} \mathbf{N}_j^t}{\sigma} \tag{9}$$

with $\sigma > 0$ and

$$\sigma^2 = \left(\sum_{j \in \mathcal{N}_i} N_{jx} \right)^2 + \left(\sum_{j \in \mathcal{N}_i} N_{jy} \right)^2 + \left(\sum_{j \in \mathcal{N}_i} N_{jz} \right)^2$$

Note that even without calibration information, such gometric consistency support can still perform in the disparity space. Surface normal in the disparity space is then $\mathbf{N} = \frac{(-\frac{\partial d}{\partial u}, -\frac{\partial d}{\partial v}, 1)^T}{\sqrt{(\frac{\partial d}{\partial u})^2 + (\frac{\partial d}{\partial v})^2 + 1}}$.

For a line segment in the 3D plane, the orientation difference between its projections in the left and right images is called the *orientation disparity* [13, 28], which is widely studied in psychophysics. Note that first order disparities $\{\frac{\partial d}{\partial u}, \frac{\partial d}{\partial v}\}$ encode such orientation disparity.

3.1   Relation to Energy Minimization Formulation

Our problem formulation consists of two parts: (1) It requires zero and first order disparities ($\{d, \frac{\partial d}{\partial u}, \frac{\partial d}{\partial v}\}$) to be consistent with image measurement, or "data" consistency; and (2) It requires neighboring matching pairs i and j to be geometrically consistent, or "smoothness" consistency. Accroding to the taxonomy [25], our algorithm is neither a *local method* (e.g. SSD) nor a *global method* (e.g. graph cuts). It is in the spirit of a cooperative algorithm [19, 20, 29], which iteratively performs local computations and uses nonlinear operations resulting in a final effect similar to global optimization. Nevertheless, to facilitate intuition here we show its relation to global optimization method (graph cuts) that uses an energy minimization formulation. Graph cut algorithms [4, 16] for stereo find the disparity labeling d for every pixel p in the reference image such that the following energy is minimized:

$$E(d) = E_{smooth}(d) + E_{data}(d) \tag{10}$$
$$= \sum_{\{p,q\} \in \mathcal{N}_{\mathcal{I}}} V_{p,q}(d_p, d_q) + \sum_{p \in \mathcal{I}} D_p(d_p)$$

where in the first term $\mathcal{N}_{\mathcal{I}}$ is the set of all neighboring pairs of image pixels $\{p, q\}$ (determined by 4-neighborhood, for instance), and E_{smooth} measures the extent to which d is not smooth; E_{data} measures the disagreement between d and the observed data, and the sum is over all image pixels p in the reference image $\mathcal{I}$. A popular smoothness prior is the Potts model [4] which is a piecewise constant model. To overcome the difficulty of such a model for handling non-frontal parallel planes, a piecewise smooth prior has been introduced [4] by using either a truncated quadratic or a truncated linear function ($V_{p,q}(d_p, d_q) = C \cdot \min(K, |d_p - d_q|)$) centered at zero disparity difference. But still this model prefers a frontal parallel plane solution. To illustrate, Fig. 5 shows a truncated linear piecewise smooth prior $V_{p,q}(d_p, d_q)$ centered at disparity d_p of pixel p. Since this smooth model is not oriented according to surface orientation at (p, d_p), a point that comes from the same surface at a neighboring pixel q with disparity d_q still has a large penalty in the smooth term. This model still prefers an erroneous space point with disparity d_p at q, which lies in the frontal parallel plane at (p, d_p). It is just the consideration of the surface orientation that allows us to encode the true (up to first order approximation) geometric contextual information in the algorithm.

Fig. 6 shows the problem when first order disparities (surface orientation) are not considered. It consists of a horizontally slanted plane with $\frac{\partial d}{\partial u} = 0.25$

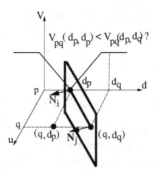

Fig. 5. Shown is the smoothness prior ($V_{p,q}$) as a function of disparity difference ($d_p - d_q$) for neighboring pixels p and q along the epipolar line. The classical prior $V_{p,q}$ has its valley oriented parallel to the frontal parallel plane. Our constraint amounts to a rotation of the valley according to surface orientation (surface shown in bold).

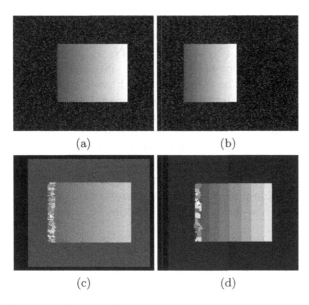

(a)   (b)

(c)   (d)

Fig. 6. Synthetic pair to illustrate the importance of surface orientation on smoothness term: (a)(b) Left and right images. (c) Our result. (d) Disparity map by graph cuts.

and $\frac{\partial d}{\partial v} = 0$. Fig. 6(d) shows the result by graph cuts [4]. Their result has staircases because their contextual structure is biased towards frontal parallel planes. Without modeling the orientation of the 3D surface, such results will generically arise. On the other hand, by considering the orientation, a correct disparity map can be obtained (Fig. 6(c), please see electronic version for better comparison), also note the smooth disparity change. This agrees with the observation by Tappen and Freeman [27]: "the greatest increase in performance will be found by improving the formulation of the MRF, rather than improving the solutions found for the MRF's currently being used."

In summary, without considering surface orientation, the piecewise smooth model still implies frontal parallel plane assumption. Zero-order disparity (position disparity) alone does not suffice, first-order disparities (surface orientation) have to be considered as well.

In the context of the energy minimization problem, our new formulation of stereo correspondence, without a bias towards frontal parallel plane solution, is to find the disparity labeling d and its differential d' to minimize the energy functional:

$$E(d, d') = E_{smooth}(d, d') + E_{data}(d, d') \tag{11}$$
$$= \sum_{\{p,q\} \in \mathcal{N}_{\mathcal{I}}} V_{p,q}(d_p, d_q, d'_p, d'_q) + \sum_{p \in \mathcal{I}} D_p(d_p, d'_p)$$

An example smooth prior is $V_{p,q}(d_p, d_q, d'_p, d'_q) = 1 - r_{ij}$, with r_{ij} the compatibility (eqn. (6)) between i (pixel p with disparity d_p and differential d'_p), and j

(pixel q with disparity d_q and differential d'_q). To make the data term meaningful here D_p could be the aggregated data cost. Note that when surface patch at i and j are frontal parallel ($\mathbf{N}_i = \{0,0,1\}^T$, $\mathbf{N}_j = \{0,0,1\}^T$), in the disparity space the new smooth prior becomes $\frac{1}{m}(|\mathbf{v}_{ij} \cdot \mathbf{N}_i| + |\mathbf{v}_{ji} \cdot \mathbf{N}_j|) = \frac{1}{2m}|d_p - d_q|$, which after truncation is the piecewise smooth prior used in [4].

This new geometric compatibility requirement between nearby candidate matching pairs, or contextual information expressed geometrically, can be used in graph cuts algorithms [4, 16] or belief propagation algorithms [26, 27]. It amounts to the formulation of different Markov Random Fields. However, it would be expensive to compute directly. In the next subsection we describe an approximation that efficiently accomplishes "data" consistency and "smoothness" consistency separately. Although our solution cannot guarantee the global optimization, experimental results show it works well in practice.

3.2   Stereo Algorithm

In this section we describe our stereo algorithm:

(1) Use traditional similarity measure (e.g. SSD) for integer disparity values at each (u,v), keep only the top $\delta\%$ (we use 3 non-immediate neighboring ones in our experiments) as the initial disparity hypotheses.

(2) For each disparity hypothesis at every (u,v), use optimization method (we use direction set method [22]) to obtain $\{d, \frac{\partial d}{\partial u}, \frac{\partial d}{\partial v}\}$ that minimizes dw_SSD in equation (1) based on the deformed window. The input to the optimization method are the initial integer disparity hypotheses, together with the first order derivatives initialized to zeros. Note that d obtained this way is interpolated in the continuous domain. At each pixel (u,v) we could have several local minima based on dw_SSD. Geometric contextual information will be explored in the next few steps. $\{d, \frac{\partial d}{\partial u}, \frac{\partial d}{\partial v}\}$ could also be obtained by enumerating different combinations of these parameters if they are properly quantized, and selecting the set that minimizes dw_SSD.

(3) Compute the initial support s_i^0 at each matching pair i by equation (7), which encodes the similarity measure based on the deformed window SSD.

(4) Iteratively update the geometric support s_i at every i by equation (8) until it converges (in practice we run a preset number (e.g. 8) of iterations), using the compatibilities between nearby matching pairs r_{ij} (eqn. (6)) which denotes how geometrically consistent they are. Also update surface normal $\mathbf{N}_i$ at i (eqn. (9)) based on the normals of neighbors, to reduce the effect of local noisy measurements.

(5) For each (u,v) select the the disparity with the highest support s, output disparity and surface normal.

Observe that steps (3)-(5) are the unique geometric content of our algorithm.

4   Experimental Results

In this section we report our experimental results on synthetic and real stereo images. The first example is the synthetic "Corridor" pair [10] from University of Bonn, The image size is 256x256 pixels with a disparity range 11. Fig. 7 shows the results. Next to the original image pair we show the disparity map and surface normal by our algorithm (first row). For comparison, in the second row we show disparity maps of traditional SSD (same window size, 9x9), graph cuts [4], belief propagation [27], respectively. They are obtained (and similarly for all other examples) from the stereo package provided by Scharstein and Szeliski [25]. In particular, the α-β-swap algorithm [4] for graph cuts, and max-product (contributed by [27]) for belief propagation. Also shown is the cooperative algorithm [29] (software kindly provided by the authors) result. Note that other algorithms obtain stepwise scalloped pattern because of the frontal parallel plane assumption being used, either explicitly or implicitly. Also note the gradual (continuous) disparity change in our result, we achieve such better result because we explicitly model 3D surface geometry.

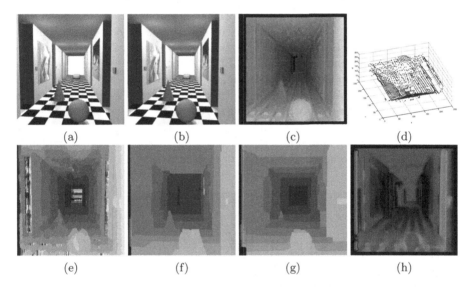

Fig. 7. (a) Left (reference) image. (b) Right image. (c) Disparity map by our algorithm. (d) Surface orientation by our algorithm. (e)(f)(g)(h) Disparity maps by traditional SSD, graph cuts, belief propagation, and cooperative algorithm, respectively. See text for details.

Disparity Error	SSD	GC	BPA	BPS	Our
RMS error (pixel)	1.31	0.65	0.75	0.62	0.35
% of errors > ±1	14.0	7.4	10.1	5.4	3.4
% of errors > ±0.5	32.5	26.4	30.3	24.3	11.6

Fig. 8. Disparity error statistics on Corridor pair. RMS error and Percentange of bad matching pixels (δ_d=1 and δ_d=0.5), for SSD, Graph cuts, Belief propagation (accelerated), Belief propagation (synchronous), and Our algorithm, respectively. Our algorithm outperforms other algorithms for such scenes with slanted surfaces because we explicitly model 3D surface geometry.

Our algorithm takes 538 seconds; the synchronous belief propagation algorithm [27] takes 552 seconds, while the accelerated version [27] takes 75 seconds; the graph cuts algorithm [4] takes 95 seconds. The results are obtained with Pentium III M 1.0GHz CPU. The disparity map scale factor is 21.25. We use the taxonomy package [25] to compute the disparity error statistics (Fig. 8). Two measures are used here: (i) RMS (root-mean-squared) error (measured in disparity units); and (ii) Percentage of bad mathing pixels with absolute disparity error larger than a threshold δ_d. Note that in [25] δ_d is set to 1.0, here we also report the results when δ_d is 0.5. Our algorithm outperforms other leading algorihtms and has only about half of their errors. (cooperative result is included for visual inspection, its error statistics is not reported, partially due to the unspecified built in disparity scale factor in their software [29].) Also note that our goal is not to provide a complete stereo algorithm but to emphasize the importance of considering surface differential geometry (e.g. surface normal consistency) in dealing with slanted surfaces. The performance comparison should be viewed with this in mind. As we stated earlier, our new geometric constraint could be used in more elaborate algorithms (e.g. belief propagation [26, 27], graph cuts [4, 16]), but it is beyond the discussion of the current paper.

The second example is the "Parking meter" pair from the well-known JISCT database. In Fig. 9 we show our results (first row), together with results from other algorithms (second row). Once again other algorithms obtain stepwise scalloped pattern because of the frontal parallel plane assumption being used, either explicitly or implicitly. But we acheive better result because we explicitly model 3D surface geometry. The disparity map scale factor is 25.

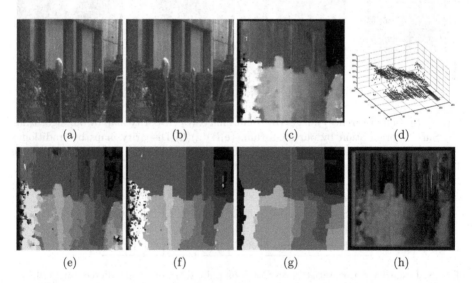

Fig. 9. (a) Left (reference) image. (b) Right image. (c) Disparity map by our algorithm. (d) Surface orientation by our algorithm. (e)(f)(g)(h) Disparity maps by traditional SSD, graph cuts, belief propagation, and cooperative algorithm, respectively. See text for details.

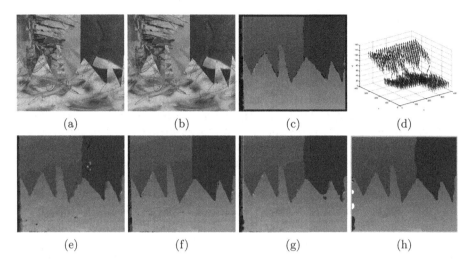

Fig. 10. (a) Left (reference) image. (b) Right image. (c) Disparity map by our algorithm. (d) Surface orientation by our algorithm. (e)(f)(g)(h) Disparity maps by traditional SSD, graph cuts, belief propagation, and cooperative algorithm, respectively. See text for details.

In recent years the Middlebury stereo database [25] has been very influential in providing a fair testbed and a taxonomy [25] for quantitatively evaluating algorithms' performance. However we observe that this dataset is very limited in terms of 3D geometry of objects such as slanted or curved surfaces, as objects are largely frontal parallel in this dataset. (This is why we include images from other databases as well.) Without the "slant" effect, our algorithm degrades roughly to the cooperative algorithm [29], and has similar error statistics using the taxonomy [25]. Due to space limit here we only report the results on one example from this dataset — the "sawtooth" pair. In Fig. 10 we show our results (first row), together with results from other algorithms (second row). Since the object is roughly frontal parallel, the difference between our result and other results is not obvious, as expected. Fig. 11 reports the error statistics (cooperative algorithm result provided by the authors [29]). For these three examples, the geometric consistenty support is performed in the disparity space.

Disparity Error	SSD	GC	BPA	BPS	CO	Our
RMS error (pixel)	1.65	1.42	1.67	1.45	1.46	1.30
% of errors > ±1	8.7	3.9	4.5	4.7	4.2	4.5

Fig. 11. Disparity error statistics on Sawtooth pair. RMS error and Percentage of bad matching pixels ($\delta_d = 1$), for SSD, Graph cuts, Belief propagation (accelerated), Belief propagation (syncrhonous), Cooperative algorithm, and Our algorithm, respectively. Our algorithm is comparable to other algorithms for such scenes with frontal parallel surfaces.

Note that the disparity sub-pixel refinement post-processing stage cannot be performed for belief propagation and graph cuts here. At pixel (u, v), sub-pixel refinment stage takes the "cost" at the winning disparity $C(d)$, and the "costs" at the immediate two disparities $C(d-1)$, $C(d+1)$ (also at pixel (u, v)), and then fits a parabola for these three costs. Finally it outputs the floating number disparity which gives the minimum of this parabola. Essentially this step uses the frontal parallel plane solution at the floating number disparity to replace the frontal parallel plane solution at integer disparity. Although this step *does* alleviate some problems caused by the frontal parallel plane assumption, it *does not* solve the problem. The remaining "soft staircasing" is still noticeable (see [25] for examples). Furthermore, this post-processing step *does not* help the matching process. We use the Scharstein and Szeliski [25] software package (for SSD and Graph Cuts) with extention (for Belief Propagation) by Tappen and Freeman [27]. In this package, both Belief Propagation and Graph Cuts find the Maximum A Posteriori (MAP) estimates, which means the "costs" at other disparities are not necessarily meaningful, thus sub-pixel refinement cannot be performed. As a result, we did not perform such a sub-pixel refinement step in our comparison (except for cooperative algorithm, which has this step built in).

5   Conclusion

In this paper we show a novel stereo algorithm that explicitly takes into account first-order disparities of non-frontal parallel surfaces; it then relates these to surface normal and further impose geometric consistency between neighboring matching pairs. Our algorithm outperforms state-of-the-art algorithms on general surfaces (e.g. slanted surfaces), which suggests the power of surface differential geometry in obtaining a smooth solution for stereo correspondence. Our constraints could be used in more elaborate graph cuts or belief propagation algorithms. Based on similar underlying ideas, a curve based stereo algorithm that performs well on complicated scenes rich in curve structure has been developed [17].

However, there are several limitations of the current algorithm: First, as most local area based methods, it needs texture or shading variations to get a reliable local estimation. Possible solution to this limitation is to combine surface occluding contours where reliable information can be propagated to unreliable estimates. Second, occlusion is not considered in the current model. And third, object boundaries are not used, which provide information on depth discontinuities. We consider all these as our future work.

Acknowledgments

We thank the authors of [4, 16, 25, 27, 29] for providing their software packages.

References

1. S. T. Barnard and M. A. Fischler. Computational stereo. *ACM Computing Surveys*, 14(4):553–572, 1982.
2. S. Birchfield and C. Tomasi. A pixel dissimilarity measure that is insensitive to image sampling. *IEEE Transactions on Pattern Analysis and Machine Intelligence*, 20(4):401–406, 1998.
3. S. Birchfield and C. Tomasi. Multiway cut for stereo and motion with slanted surfaces. In *Proc. of IEEE International Conference on Computer Vision*, 1999.
4. Y. Boykov, O. Veksler, and R. Zabih. Fast approximate energy minimization via graph cuts. *IEEE Transactions on Pattern Analysis and Machine Intelligence*, 23(11):1222–1239, 2001.
5. M. Z. Brown, D. Bruschka, and G. D. Hager. Advances in computational stereo. *IEEE Transactions on Pattern Analysis and Machine Intelligence*, 25(8):993–1008, 2003.
6. F. Devernay and O. D. Faugeras. Computing differential properties of 3-d shapes from stereoscopic images without 3-d models. In *Proc. of IEEE Conference on Computer Vision and Pattern Recognition*, 1994.
7. U. R. Dhond and J. K. Aggarwal. Structure from stereo – a review. *IEEE Trans. on Systems, Man, and Cybernetics*, 19(6):1489–1510, 1989.
8. M. P. do Carmo. *Differential Geometry of Curves and Surfaces*. Prentice-Hall, Inc., 1976.
9. O. Faugeras. *Three-Dimensional Computer Vision*. The MIT Press, 1993.
10. T. Frohlinghaus and J. M. Buhmann. Regularizing phase-based stereo. In *Proc. of ICPR*, 1996.
11. R. Hartley and A. Zisserman. *Multiple View Geometry in Computer Vision*. Cambridge Univ. Press, 2000.
12. W. Hoff and N. Ahuja. Surfaces from stereo: Integrating feature matching, disparity estimation, and contour detection. *IEEE Transactions on Pattern Analysis and Machine Intelligence*, 11(2):121–136, 1989.
13. D. G. Jones and J. Malik. Determining three-dimensional shape from orientation and spatial frequency disparities. In *Proc. of European Conference on Computer Vision*, 1992.
14. T. Kanade and M. Okutomi. A stereo maching algorithm with an adaptive window: Theory and experiment. *IEEE Transactions on Pattern Analysis and Machine Intelligence*, 16(9):920–932, 1994.
15. J. J. Koenderink. *Solid Shape*. The MIT Press, 1990.
16. V. Kolmogorov and R. Zabih. Computing visual correspondence with occlusions using graph cuts. In *Proc. of IEEE International Conference on Computer Vision*, 2001.
17. G. Li and S. W. Zucker. A differential geometrical model for contour-based stereo correspondence. In *Proc. IEEE Workshop on Variational, Geometric, and Level Set Methods in Computer Vision (at ICCV'03)*, 2003.
18. M. H. Lin and C. Tomasi. Surfaces with occlusions from layered stereo. *IEEE Transactions on Pattern Analysis and Machine Intelligence*, 26(8):1073–1078, 2004.
19. D. Marr and T. Poggio. Cooperative computation of stereo disparity. *Science*, 194:283–287, 1976.
20. D. Marr and T. Poggio. A computational theory of human stereo vision. *Proc. Royal Soc. London B,*, 204:301–328, 1979.

21. A. S. Ogale and Y. Aloimonos. Stereo correspondence with slanted surfaces: Critical implications of horizontal slant. In *Proc. of IEEE Conference on Computer Vision and Pattern Recognition*, 2004.
22. W. H. Press, S. A. Teukolsky, W. T. Vetterling, and B. P. Flannery. *Numerical Reciples in C*. Cambridge University Press, second edition, 1992.
23. P. T. Sander and S. W. Zucker. Inferring surface trace and differential structure from 3-d images. *IEEE Transactions on Pattern Analysis and Machine Intelligence*, 12(9):833–854, 1990.
24. D. Scharstein and R. Szeliski. Stereo matching with nonlinear diffusion. *International Journal of Computer Vision*, 28(2):155–174, 1998.
25. D. Scharstein and R. Szeliski. A taxonomy and evaluation of dense two-frame stereo correspondence algorithms. *International Journal of Computer Vision*, 47(1/2/3):7–42, 2002.
26. J. Sun, N.-N. Zheng, and H.-Y. Shum. Stereo matching using belief propagation. *IEEE Transactions on Pattern Analysis and Machine Intelligence*, 25(7):787–800, 2003.
27. M. F. Tappen and W. T. Freeman. Comparison of graph cuts with belief propagation for stereo, using identical mrf parameters. In *Proc. of IEEE International Conference on Computer Vision*, 2003.
28. R. P. Wildes. Direct recovery of three-diemensional scene geometry from binocular stereo disparity. *IEEE Transactions on Pattern Analysis and Machine Intelligence*, 13(8):761–774, 1991.
29. C. Zitnick and T. Kanade. A cooperative algorithm for stereo mathching and occlusion detection. *IEEE Transactions on Pattern Analysis and Machine Intelligence*, 22(7):675–684, 2000.

Brain Image Analysis Using Spherical Splines

Ying He, Xin Li, Xianfeng Gu, and Hong Qin

Center for Visual Computing (CVC) and Department of Computer Science,
Stony Brook University, Stony Brook, NY, 11794-4400, USA
{yhe, xinli, gu, qin}@cs.sunysb.edu

Abstract. We propose a novel technique based on spherical splines for brain surface representation and analysis. This research is strongly inspired by the fact that, for brain surfaces, it is both necessary and natural to employ spheres as their natural domains. We develop an automatic and efficient algorithm, which transforms a brain surface to a single spherical spline whose maximal error deviation from the original data is less than the user-specified tolerance. Compared to the discrete mesh-based representation, our spherical spline offers a concise (low storage requirement) digital form with high continuity (C^{n-1} continuity for a degree n spherical spline). Furthermore, this representation enables the accurate evaluation of differential properties, such as curvature, principal direction, and geodesic, without the need for any numerical approximations. Thus, certain shape analysis procedures, such as segmentation, gyri and sulci tracing, and 3D shape matching, can be carried out both robustly and accurately. We conduct several experiments in order to demonstrate the efficacy of our approach for the quantitative measurement and analysis of brain surfaces.

1 Introduction

The human cortical surface is a highly complex, folded structure with rich geometric, anatomical, and functional information. The outward folds (called gyri) and the cortical grooves (called sulci) encode important anatomical features which provide a parcellation of the cortex surface into anatomically distinct areas. Surface-based modeling is valuable in brain imaging to help analyze anatomical shape, to statistically combine or compare 3D anatomical models across subjects, and to map functional imaging parameters onto anatomical surfaces. Thus, various novel data analysis tools towards the quantitative study and better understanding of cortical surfaces have been developed in recent years. For example, Avants and Gee [1] develop a technique to estimate the shape operator and computes principal directions and curvatures. Cachia et al. present a mean curvature based primal sketch, which derived from a scale space computed for the mean curvature of the cortical surface [2]. Gu et al. study the conformal brain mapping [3] and present an algorithm for 3D shape matching using 2D conformal representations [4]. Tao et al. present a method for automatically finding curves of sulcal fundi on human cortical surfaces using statistical models [5, 6]. Thompson et al. present a technique for brain image warping in [7] and then apply it to detect disease-specific patterns in [8].

Recent developments in brain imaging have accelerated the collection of high-resolution data sets for cortical surfaces. Typically, the acquired digital models of corti-

A. Rangarajan et al. (Eds.): EMMCVPR 2005, LNCS 3757, pp. 633–644, 2005.
© Springer-Verlag Berlin Heidelberg 2005

cal surfaces are in the form of triangular meshes. It is desirable and necessary to reverse-engineer a spline-based surface from meshes for many medical applications, leading to many advantages. For example, a continuous spline representation for a cortical surface facilitates the quantitative and accurate study of the anatomy of cortical surfaces, and consequently, provides a means for mapping functional activation sites over complicated geometry. In particular, we can precisely compute all the differential quantities such as geodesics, curvatures, and areas anywhere on cortical surfaces. In general, these local and global differential attributes will enable many medical imaging applications such as image segmentation/classification, tracking brain change in an individual over time, and surface quality analysis and control.

At present, tensor-product B-spline and NURBS are widely used for surface representation because of their many attractive geometric properties. Nevertheless, due to their rectangular structures, they are less suitable for the effective modeling and shape analysis of cortical surfaces. In contrast, because of the topological equivalence between spheres and brain surfaces, spherical splines appear to be more ideal for modeling brain surfaces, both in theory and in practice, than tensor product B-splines and NURBS. In this paper, we present a general framework to model brain surfaces with spherical triangular B-splines proposed by Pfeifle and Seidel [9]. These spline surfaces are defined on an arbitrary spherical triangulation and exhibit no degeneracies that frequently arise when attempting to employ planar parametric splines for modeling sphere-like, closed surfaces. Our specific contributions are as follows:

1. The shape is represented by a single degree n spline without any patching and stitching work. The maximal error deviation from the original data is less than any user-specified tolerance. The reconstructed surface is C^{n-1} continuous everywhere. The surface approximation procedure is automatic.
2. Based on its analytical representation, we can compute the differential properties, including normals, curvatures, geodesics, etc, without the need for any numerical approximations via frequently-used bilinear interpolation and/or local algebraic surface fitting. Therefore, the shape analysis procedures, such as segmentation, can be done robustly and accurately.
3. By analyzing the extrema of the derivative of principal curvatures with respect to the curvature directions, we can automatically detect the gyri and sulci curves to achieve quantitatively accurate results.
4. With the analytical formulation of conformal factor and mean curvature, we compare the 3D shapes using conformal representation robustly and accurately.

2 Surface Approximation Using Spherical Triangular B-Splines

In this section, we briefly review the definition of spherical triangular B-splines and then introduce the algorithm for automatic conversion of the brain surface into a spherical triangular B-spline.

2.1 Spherical Triangular B-Spline

Denote by $\mathbb{S}^2 = \{\mathbf{x} | \mathbf{x} \in \mathbb{R}^3, \|\mathbf{x}\| = 1\}$ a unit sphere in $\mathbb{R}^3$. Let points $\mathbf{t}_i \in \mathbb{S}^2$, $i \in \mathbb{N}$, be given and define a spherical triangulation

$$T = \{\Delta(I) = [\mathbf{t}_{i_0}, \mathbf{t}_{i_1}, \mathbf{t}_{i_2}] : I = (i_0, i_1, i_2) \in I \subset \mathbb{N}^3\},$$

where every triangle is oriented counter-clockwise (or clockwise). Next, with every vertex $\mathbf{t}_i$ of T we associate a cloud of knots $\mathbf{t}_{i,0}, \ldots, \mathbf{t}_{i,n}$ such that $\mathbf{t}_{i,0} = \mathbf{t}_i$. For every spherical triangle $I = [\mathbf{t}_{i_0}, \mathbf{t}_{i_1}, \mathbf{t}_{i_2}] \in T$,

1. all the triangles $X_\beta^I = [\mathbf{t}_{i_0,\beta_0}, \mathbf{t}_{i_1,\beta_1} \mathbf{t}_{i_2,\beta_2}]$ with $\beta = (\beta_0, \beta_1, \beta_2)$ and $|\beta| = \beta_0 + \beta_1 + \beta_2 \le n$ are non-degenerate.
2. the set $\Omega_n^I = interior(\cap_{|\beta| \le n} X_\beta^I)$ must be non-empty.

Then the spherical triangular B-spline basis function N_β^I, $|\beta| = n$, is defined by means of spherical simplex splines $M(\mathbf{u}|V_\beta^I)$ as $N(\mathbf{u}|V_\beta^I) = |\det(X_\beta^I)|M(\mathbf{u}|V_\beta^I)$ where $V_\beta^I = \{\mathbf{t}_{i_0,0}, \ldots, \mathbf{t}_{i_0,\beta_0}, \mathbf{t}_{i_1,0}, \ldots, \mathbf{t}_{i_1,\beta_1}, \mathbf{t}_{i_2,0}, \ldots, \mathbf{t}_{i_2,\beta_2}\}$.

A degree n spherical triangular B-spline surface $\mathbf{F}$ over T is then defined as

$$\mathbf{F}(\mathbf{u}) = \sum_{I \in T} \sum_{|\beta|=n} \mathbf{c}_{I,\beta} N(\mathbf{u}|V_\beta^I), \tag{1}$$

where $\mathbf{c}_{I,\beta} \in \mathbb{R}^3$ are the control points.

The spherical triangular B-spline has many useful properties, including:

- *Piecewise polynomial:* $\mathbf{F}(\mathbf{u})$ is a degree n piecewise polynomial defined on the sphere.
- *Locality:* The movement of a single control point $\mathbf{c}_{I,\beta}$ only influences the surface on the triangle I and on the triangles directly surrounding I.
- *Smoothness:* If the knots of each set V_β^I are in "spherical" general position (i.e., no three knots in V_β^I lie on the same great circle), then $\mathbf{F}(\mathbf{u})$ is C^{n-1} continuous everywhere.

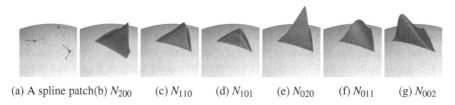

(a) A spline patch (b) N_{200} (c) N_{110} (d) N_{101} (e) N_{020} (f) N_{011} (g) N_{002}

Fig. 1. Six basis functions of a quadratic spherical spline patch

Figure 1(a) shows a quadratic spherical spline patch defined on $\{\mathbf{t}_0, \mathbf{t}_1, \mathbf{t}_2\}$. We associate two sub-knots $\mathbf{t}_{i,j}$, $j = 1, 2$ with each vertex $\mathbf{t}_i$. The six basis functions are shown in Figure 1(b)-(g). Since no three knots are co-circular, every basis function is C^1 everywhere.

2.2   Surface Reconstruction Algorithm

The goal of surface reconstruction is to obtain a continuous representation of a surface described by a cloud of points or a mesh. The problem can typically be stated as follows:

given a set $P = \{\mathbf{p}_i\}_{i=1}^m$ of points $\mathbf{p}_i \in \mathbb{R}^3$, find a smooth spherical spline $\mathbf{F} : \mathbb{S}^2 \to \mathbb{R}^3$ that approximates P.

A general framework for surface reconstruction is to minimize a linear combination of interpolation and fairness functionals, i.e.,

$$\min E = E_{dist} + \lambda E_{fair}. \tag{2}$$

The first part is

$$E_{dist} = \sum_{i=1}^m \|\mathbf{F}(\mathbf{u}_i) - \mathbf{p}_i\|^2$$

where $\mathbf{u}_i \in \mathbb{S}^2$ is parameter for $\mathbf{p}_i$, $i = 1, \ldots, m$. The second part E_{fair} in (2) is a smoothing term. A frequently used example is the thin plate energy, $E_{fair} = \iint_{\mathbb{S}^2} (\mathbf{F}_{uu}^2 + 2\mathbf{F}_{uv}^2 + \mathbf{F}_{vv}^2) du dv$. Both parts are quadratic functions of the unknown control points. For example, the approximation functional E_{dist} has the following form:

$$E_{dist} = \frac{1}{2} \mathbf{x}^T Q \mathbf{x} + \mathbf{c}^T \mathbf{x} + f,$$

where $\mathbf{x} = (\ldots, c_{I,\beta}, \ldots)^T$,

$$Q = \begin{pmatrix} & \vdots & \\ \cdots & 2\sum_{i=1}^m N_{I,\beta}(\mathbf{u}_i) N_{I',\beta'}(\mathbf{u}_i) & \cdots \\ & \vdots & \end{pmatrix},$$

$$\mathbf{c} = (\ldots, -2\sum_{i=1}^m \mathbf{p}_i N_\beta^I(\mathbf{u}_i), \ldots)^T,$$

and $f = \sum_{i=1}^m \|\mathbf{p}_i\|^2$.

The fairness functional E_{fair} is also a quadratic function in the unknown control points, and can be written in a similar fashion. However, the computation of the fairness functional is usually time-consuming since it requires the integration over a product of two splines. Similar to [10], we do not use the traditional fairness functional, which requires integration of products of spherical splines. Instead, we employ a set of linear constraints on the control points.

Let $[\mathbf{t}_{0,\beta_0}, \mathbf{t}_{1,\beta_1}]$ be an edge of the spherical triangulation. Denote $I = (\mathbf{t}_0, \mathbf{t}_1, \mathbf{t}_2)$ and $J = (\mathbf{t}_0, \mathbf{t}_1, \mathbf{t}_3)$ its two adjacent triangles. Let $\mathbf{F}^I = \sum_{|\beta|=n} c_{I,\beta} N(\mathbf{u}|V_\beta^I)$ be the polynomial on triangle I and similarly for $\mathbf{F}^J$. Let f^I and f^J be the polar forms of $\mathbf{F}^I$ and $\mathbf{F}^J$, respectively. Then, we require

$$c_{I,\beta} = f^J(X_\beta^I), \forall \beta, |\beta| = n, \beta_2 \leq r \tag{3}$$

where $0 \leq r \leq n - 1$ is an integer ($r = 2$ and $n \geq 5$ in our implementation) which controls the fairness of the spline surface. Equation (3) is a linear equation of the control points. We refer the readers to [11, 12, 10] for the detailed information about the polar form and fairing triangular B-spline surfaces.

Therefore, the above optimization problem can be stated as follows:

$$\min \quad \frac{1}{2}\mathbf{x}^T Q\mathbf{x} + \mathbf{c}^T\mathbf{x} + f \tag{4}$$
$$\text{subject to} \quad A\mathbf{x} = \mathbf{b},$$

which is a typical constrained convex quadratic programming problem, and can be solved by the interior-point based method efficiently.

Algorithm 1: automatic conversion brain surface to spherical spline

Input: brain surface M with m points, $\{\mathbf{p}_i\}_{i=1}^m$, degree n, maximal fitting tolerance ε, number of triangles N in the initial spherical domain.

Output: a degree n spherical triangular B-spline $\mathbf{F}$ which approximates M.

1. *Calculate the spherical conformal parameterization of M using Gu et al. method [3]. Denote by $h : M \to \mathbb{S}^2$ this conformal map, i.e., $h(\mathbf{p}_i) = \mathbf{u}_i \in \mathbb{S}^2$.*
2. *Decimate M to a simplified mesh $\tilde{M}$ with N triangles. Map $\tilde{M}$ to the sphere. Construct an initial spherical triangular B-spline of degree n based on the spherical triangulation of $\tilde{M}$.*
3. *Solve Equation (4) by considering control points as free variables.*
4. *Check the maximal fitting error for each spherical triangle Δ_I. If it violates the criterion, i.e., $\max_{\mathbf{u}_i \in \Delta_I} \|\mathbf{F}(\mathbf{u}_i) - \mathbf{p}_i\| > \varepsilon$, subdivide the triangle Δ_I using 1-to-4 scheme and then split the neighboring triangles to avoid T-junctions.*
5. *If the maximal fitting error on each triangle satisfies the user-specified fitting tolerance ε, exit; Otherwise, go to step 3.*

3   Brain Surface Analysis

By converting dense meshes/point clouds to spherical splines, we achieve a compact and highly continuous representation. More importantly, we have the analytical form of the underlying shape. Thus, we can compute the normals, curvatures, geodesics, areas, etc., anywhere on the surface. These differential properties are crucial in the brain image analysis. In this section we demonstrate the efficacy of analyzing the brain surface using spherical splines.

3.1   Segmentation by the Mean Curvature

The computation of curvature is essential in shape analysis, segmentation and registration. There are many techniques to estimate the curvature on polygonal meshes, e.g., [13, 14, 15, 16, 17, 18]. These methods use either discrete differential operators or local polynomial fitting to approximate the curvature tensor. Therefore, the estimation results closely rely on the connectivity and quality of the input meshes.

In our framework, we convert the brain surface into a single spherical spline of high continuity. Thus, the Gaussian curvature K and mean curvature H can be computed analytically and efficiently without resorting to any numerical approximations.

Curvature features such as zero contours and maxima are useful for surface matching and object recognition. After computing the curvature values, we can easily locate the curvature zero contours, which are helpful for segmenting the brain surface into regions (the gyri and the sulci).

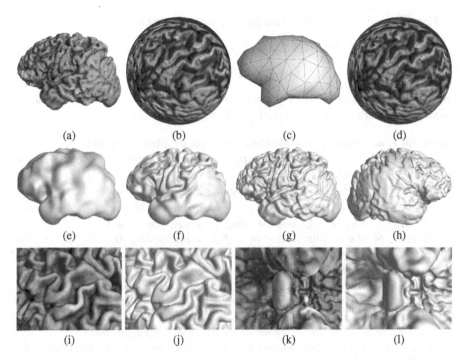

(a)   (b)   (c)   (d)

(e)   (f)   (g)   (h)

(i)   (j)   (k)   (l)

Fig. 2. Illustration of surface reconstruction using spherical splines. The input is a triangular mesh M with $131K$ triangles (a). We first compute its conformal spherical parameterization shown in (b). Then we simplify the mesh to 280 triangles (shown in (c)) and map it to the sphere as the initial spherical domain (shown in (d)). From (e) to (g), we fit the mesh M using a degree 5 spherical spline with 280, 1048 and 2086 spherical triangles. The root-mean-square error (r.m.s.) are 0.328%, 0.0951%, 0.0196% of the diagonal of the input mesh, respectively. (h) shows the back view of the reconstructed spline. (i) and (k) show the closeup of the original mesh. (j) and (l) show the closeup of the reconstructed spline. Note that the high continuity (C^4-continuous) of our spline surface.

3.2   Tracing the Sulci and Gyri Lines

The major sulci and gyri on the cortical surface have distinct geometric properties and are conserved between individuals, making them useful landmarks for morphometric comparisons. From computer vision's point of view, these sulci and gyri are closely related to the ridge-valley lines, which are curves on a surface along which the surface bends sharply. The ridge-valley lines are powerful shape descriptors that provides us with important information about the shapes of objects. Therefore, robust extraction of ridge-valley structures is important for brain image analysis.

In [19], Belyaev et al. present a mathematical description of such surface creases by the extrema of the principal curvatures along their curvature lines. For a spherical spline surface $\mathbf{F}(u,v)$, denote by $k_{max}(u,v)$ and $k_{min}(u,v)$ the maximal and minimal principal curvatures, $k_{max} \geq k_{min}$. Let $\mathbf{t}_{max}(u,v)$ and $\mathbf{t}_{min}(u,v)$ be the corresponding principal directions. Consider the derivatives of the principal curvatures along their corresponding directions $e_{max}(u,v) = \partial k_{max}/\partial \mathbf{t}_{max}$ and $e_{min}(u,v) = \partial k_{min}/\partial \mathbf{t}_{min}$. The extrema of the principal curvatures along their curvature directions are given by the zero-crossings of e_{max} and e_{min}, and the ridges and valleys are characterized by

$$e_{max} = 0, \partial e_{max}/\partial \mathbf{t}_{max} < 0, k_{max} > |k_{min}|, (ridges), \qquad (5)$$

$$e_{min} = 0, \partial e_{min}/\partial \mathbf{t}_{min} > 0, k_{min} < -|k_{max}|, (valleys). \qquad (6)$$

Note that if we change the surface orientation, then the ridges turn into the ravines and vice versa.

Similar to [20], we measure the strength of a ridge line by the integral of k_{max} along the line, i.e., $\int k_{max} ds$. The ridges whose strength are less than the user-specified threshold are ignored.

Algorithm 2: automatic tracing the sulci and gyri lines
Input: a spherical spline $\mathbf{F}$, N resolution of the output mesh, λ_{thres}
Output: a set of ridge (gyri) curves and a set of valley (sulci) curves.

1. *Evaluate the spline $\mathbf{F}$ and get the mesh M_s containing N triangles.*
2. *For each vertex $\mathbf{v} \in M_s$, compute e_{max} and e_{min}. Mark $\mathbf{v}$ as feature point if it satisfies Equation (5) and (6).*
3. *For each edge $(\mathbf{v}_i, \mathbf{v}_j) \in M_s$, let $h(\mathbf{v}_i) \in \mathbb{S}^2$ and $h(\mathbf{v}_j) \in \mathbb{S}^2$ be the spherical parameters of vertex $\mathbf{v}_i$ and $\mathbf{v}_j$ respectively. If $e(h(\mathbf{v}_i))e(h(\mathbf{v}_j)) < 0$, perform the 1-D search on the edge to get the vertex $\tilde{\mathbf{v}} \in (\mathbf{v}_i, \mathbf{v}_j)$ such that $e(h(\tilde{\mathbf{v}})) = 0$. Mark $\tilde{\mathbf{v}}$ as feature point.*
4. *Trace the feature points to get feature curves.*
5. *Compute the strength $T = \int k_{max} ds$ of each feature curve. Output the curve if $T \geq \lambda_{thres}$.*

The output of Algorithm 2 usually contains large number of sulci and gyri. Sometimes, the doctors are interested only in part of them. For example, seven major sulci are used in [6]. Our system allows the user to interactively select the desired sulci from the output of Algorithm 2. We also provide the functionality to automatically connect two user-specified sulci.

3.3 3D Shape Comparison Using Conformal Representation

In [4], Gu and Vemuri present a systematic method for 3D shape comparison using conformal representations. By stereographic projection, the unit sphere (except the north pole) can be mapped to the (u, v) plane, the mapping can be represented as

$$(x, y, z) \rightarrow (u, v) : (u, v) = \frac{1}{1-z}(x, y).$$

The metric (first fundamental form) of the sphere is represented as

$$ds_0^2 = \frac{4(du^2 + dv^2)}{(1 + u^2 + v^2)^2}.$$

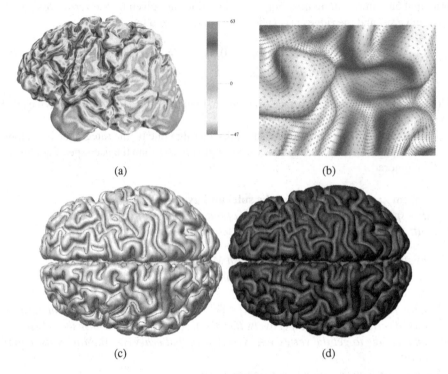

(a)

(b)

(c)

(d)

Fig. 3. Computing the curvature on the cortical surface: (a) Mean curvature; (b) Close-up of the principal directions; (c) The zero contour of the mean curvature; (d) Segmentation of gyri and sulci by the sign of mean curvature

Any closed genus zero surface Σ can be mapped to the unit sphere by a diffeomorphism $\phi : \Sigma \to S^2$. Therefore, (u,v) is also a local parameter coordinate system of Σ, such that the metric of Σ can be represented as

$$ds_\Sigma^2 = \lambda(u,v)ds_0^2, \lambda(u,v) \in \mathbb{R}^+.$$

It can be demonstrated that ϕ preserves the angles; namely, any two intersecting curves on Σ will be mapped to two curves on S^2 such that the intersecting angle is preserved. These kinds of mappings are called *conformal* maps, and $\lambda(u,v)$ is called the *conformal factor*. There are infinite conformal maps from Σ to S^2. Assume $\phi_i : \Sigma \to S^2, i = 0, 1$ are two conformal maps, then their difference $\phi_1 \circ \phi_0 : S^2 \to S^2$ is a *Möbius* transformation. In (u,v) coordinates, it has the form

$$\frac{az+b}{cz+d}, z = u + iv, a, b, c, d \in \mathbb{C}, ad - bc = 1.$$

Gu and Vemuri demonstrated that Σ can be determined by the conformal factor $\lambda(u,v)$ and its mean curvature $H(u,v)$ uniquely up to rigid motion in $\mathbb{R}^3$. Therefore,

(λ, H) under the conformal parameterization (u, v) is the *conformal representation* of the surface Σ.

In order to compare shape Σ_1 and Σ_2, it is sufficient to measure the distance between their conformal representations. Suppose (λ_1, H_1) and (λ_2, H_2) are the conformal representations of Σ_1 and Σ_2 respectively; the distance between them is formulated as

$$E(\Sigma_1, \Sigma_2) = \inf_{\tau} \int_{S^2} (\lambda_1 - \lambda_2 \circ \tau)^2 + (H_1 - H_2 \circ \tau)^2 ds, \tau \in Mobius\ Group \qquad (7)$$

In [4], the conformal factor is approximated using a piecewise linear function, and mean curvature is approximated by the discrete Laplace-Beltrai operator. The approximation is brute force and inaccurate.

In our current implementation, we represent the brain surfaces using C^4 smooth splines with the user specified tolerance. Since we use spherical conformal parametrization to construct the spherical spline, the computation of the conformal factor and mean curvature are direct and without any approximation.

4 Experimental Results

We have implemented a prototype system on a 3GHz Pentium IV PC with 1GB RAM. We perform experiments on two brain surfaces (shown in Figure 6(a) and (b)) which

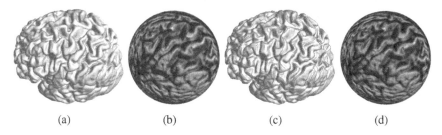

(a) (b) (c) (d)

Fig. 4. Automatic tracing the sulci and gyri: (a) Sulci (cyan curves) on the brain surface; (b) Sulci (green curves) on the spherical domain; (c) Gyri (cyan curves) on the brain surface; (d) Sulci (green curves) on the spherical domain. The number of detected sulci and gyri are 412 and 528, respectively.

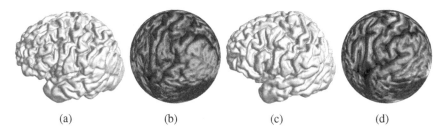

(a) (b) (c) (d)

Fig. 5. Illustration of seven major sulci of the left brain hemisphere of two different brain surfaces. Only few user interactions are needed to specify the desired sulci.

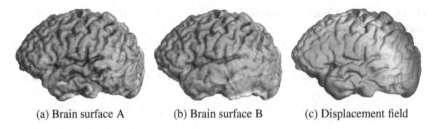

(a) Brain surface A   (b) Brain surface B   (c) Displacement field

Fig. 6. 3D shape comparison using conformal representation. (a) and (b) show two brain surfaces. The displacement field is color-encoded as shown in (c).

Table 1. Statistics of the surface approximation algorithm. Mesh size: M_v, # of vertices, M_f, # of faces; Spline configuration: n, degree of spherical splines, N_t, # of domain triangles, N_c, # of control points, *r.m.s.*, root mean square error, L_∞, maximal error.

Subject	M_v	M_f	n	N_t	N_c	r.m.s.	L_∞
A	65,538	131,072	5	2,086	26,077	0.0196%	0.155%
B	65,538	131,072	5	2,012	25,152	0.0201%	0.176%

are obtained from 3D $256 \times 256 \times 124$ T1 weighted SPGR (spoiled gradient) MRI images, by using an active surface algorithm that deforms a triangulated mesh onto the brain surface [21]. In order to compare the fitting qualities for different test cases, we uniformly scale the data into a unit cube.

We first convert these brain images into spherical triangular B-spline representation by Algorithm 1. In order to compute the ridge and valley curves accurately, we need to compute the fourth order derivative of the spline surface. Therefore, in our experiments, we use degree 5 spherical splines which are C^4-continuous everywhere. The fitting procedure takes about 30 to 40 minutes for each test case. Figure 2 illustrates the pipeline of our surface reconstruction algorithm on test case A. Table 1 shows the input mesh size, spline configuration and fitting quality. Compared to the discrete mesh representation, our spherical spline based representations have low storage requirements and can achieve high accuracy (e.g., root-mean-square error $\leq 0.02\%$) as well as high continuity (C^4).

Figure 3 shows the computation of mean curvature, principal directions, and the zero-crossing of the mean curvature of the reconstructed brain surface A.

Figure 4 shows the detected sulci and gyri on the reconstructed brain surface A and its spherical domain. The number of detected sulci and ridges for are 412 and 528 respectively. The time for tracing feature curves is less than 1 minute for both test cases. Figure 5 shows seven major sulci of the left brain hemisphere of two different brain surfaces. These sulci are selected by the users with only very few interactions.

Figure 6 shows the results of 3D shape comparison using conformal representation. The conformal factor $\lambda(u,v)$ and mean curvature $H(u,v)$ are computed analytically using spherical splines.

5 Conclusion

In this paper, we propose a spherical spline based framework for brain surface analysis. We present automatic algorithm to convert a brain mesh into a spherical triangular *B*-spline whose maximal error deviation from the original data is less than the user-specified tolerance. With the analytical representation of the brain model, we can easily compute various differential properties, such as conformal factor, mean curvature, principal directions, geodesics, etc, accurately and robustly. By studying the extrema of the principal curvatures with respect to the curvature directions, we present an automatic algorithm to trace the gyri and sulci. Furthermore, we can solve the 3D shape comparison using conformal representation directly without resorting to any numerical approximation. Experimental results show the efficacy of using spherical splines in brain image analysis.

References

1. Avants, B.B., Gee, J.C.: The shape operator for differential analysis of images. In: IPMI. (2003) 101–113
2. Cachia, A., Mangin, J.F., Rivière, D., Boddaert, N., Andrade, A., Kherif, F., Sonigo, P., Papadopoulos-Orfanos, D., Zilbovicius, M., Poline, J.B., Bloch, I., Brunelle, F., Régis, J.: A mean curvature based primal sketch to study the cortical folding process from antenatal to adult brain. In: MICCAI. (2001) 897–904
3. Gu, X., Wang, Y., Chan, T.F., Thompson, P.M., Yau, S.T.: Genus zero surface conformal mapping and its application to brain surface mapping. In: IPMI. (2003) 172–184
4. Gu, X., Vemuri, B.C.: Matching 3d shapes using 2d conformal representations. In: MICCAI (1). (2004) 771–780
5. Tao, X., Han, X., Rettmann, M.E., Prince, J.L., Davatzikos, C.: Statistical study on cortical sulci of human brains. In: IPMI. (2001) 475–487
6. Tao, X., Prince, J.L., Davatzikos, C.: An automated method for finding curves of sulcal fundi on human cortical surfaces. In: ISBI. (2004) 1271–1274
7. Thompson, P.M., Toga, A.W.: A surface-based technique for warping 3-dimensional images of the brain. IEEE Trans. Medical Images **15** (1996) 402–417
8. Thompson, P.M., Mega, M.S., Vidal, C., Rapoport, J.L., Toga, A.W.: Detecting disease-specific patterns of brain structure using cortical pattern matching and a population-based probabilistic brain atlas. In: IPMI. (2001) 488–501
9. Pfeifle, R., Seidel, H.P.: Spherical triangular b-splines with application to data fitting. Comput. Graph. Forum **14** (1995) 89–96
10. He, Y., Gu, X., Qin, H.: Fairing triangular *B*-splines of arbitrary topology. In: Proceedings of Pacific Graphics '05. (2005) to appear
11. Seidel, H.P.: Polar forms and triangular *B*-spline surfaces. In Du, D.Z., Hwang, F., eds.: Euclidean Geometry and Computers, 2nd Edition. World Scientific Publishing Co. (1994) 235–286
12. Gormaz, R.: *B*-spline knot-line elimination and Bézier continuity conditions. In: Curves and surfaces in geometric design. A K Peters, Wellesley, MA (1994) 209–216
13. Meyer, M., Desbrun, M., Schröder, P., Barr, A.H.: Discrete differential-geometry operators for triangulated 2-manifolds. In: VisMath '02. (2002)
14. Taubin, G.: Estimating the tensor of curvature of a surface from a polyhedral approximation. In: ICCV. (1995) 902–907

15. Goldfeather, J., Interrante, V.: A novel cubic-order algorithm for approximating principal direction vectors. ACM Trans. Graph. **23** (2004) 45–63
16. Rusinkiewicz, S.: Estimating curvatures and their derivatives on triangle meshes. In: 3DPVT. (2004) 486–493
17. Surazhsky, T., Magid, E., Soldea, O., Elber, G., Rivlin, E.: A comparison of gaussian and mean curvatures estimation methods on triangular meshes. In: ICRA. (2003) 1021–1026
18. Theisel, H., Rössl, C., Zayer, R., Seidel, H.P.: Normal based estimation of the curvature tensor for triangular meshes. In: Pacific Conference on Computer Graphics and Applications. (2004) 288–297
19. Belyaev, A.G., Pasko, A.A., Kunii, T.L.: Ridges and ravines on implicit surfaces. In: Computer Graphics International. (1998) 530–535
20. Ohtake, Y., Belyaev, A.G., Seidel, H.P.: Ridge-valley lines on meshes via implicit surface fitting. ACM Trans. Graph. **23** (2004) 609–612
21. Thompson, P.M., Toga, A.W.: A framework for computational anatomy. Computing and Visualization in Science **5** (2002) 1–12

High-Order Differential Geometry of Curves for Multiview Reconstruction and Matching*

Ricardo Fabbri[1,2] and Benjamin B. Kimia[1]

[1] Brown University, Division of Engineering, Providence RI 02912, USA
{rfabbri, kimia}@lems.brown.edu
www.lems.brown.edu
[2] Funded by CNPq – Brazil

Abstract. The relationship between the orientation and curvature of projected curves and the orientation and curvature of the underlying space curve has been previously established. This has allowed a disambiguation of correspondences in two views and a transfer of these properties to a third view for confirmation. We propose that a higher-order intrinsic differential geometry attribute, namely, curvature derivative, is necessary to account for the range of variation of space curves and their projections. We derive relationships between curvature derivative in a projected view, and curvature derivative and torsion of the underlying space curve. Regardless of the point, tangent, and curvature, any pair of curvature derivatives are possible correspondences, but most would lead to very high torsion and curvature derivatives. We propose that the minimization of third order derivatives of the reconstruction, which combines torsion and curvature derivative of the space curve, regularizes the process of finding the correct correspondences.

1 Introduction

The key bottleneck to successful reconstruction of structure from multiple images is the disambiguation of correspondences. A large body of literature has been developed based on correlating unorganized and often sparse feature points by matching some aspects of the local region surrounding the feature [1, 2, 3], and oriented edges to disambiguate correspondences [4, 5, 6, 7]. A number of criteria such as smoothness, uniqueness, ordering, limited disparity, and limited orientation disparity, have been used to deal with the inherent ambiguity. However, these can break down, especially with wide baseline, with multiple nearby structures, or when discontinuities and branching structures exist [8]. An alternative approach to using unorganized features is to use longer curve segments such as lines, conics, and planar and non-planar higher order algebraic curves to disambiguate correspondences [9, 10, 11, 12, 13, 14], but a large number of views of the same curve are required (seven views are required of an electric wire in [14].)

The idea that the differential geometry of curves can be used to correlate structure in multiple images was presented in the work of Ayache and Lust-

---

* This research is supported by NSF under grant 5.26422, and CNPq - Brazil Proc. 200875/2004-3 generously funded the first author's activities.

A. Rangarajan et al. (Eds.): EMMCVPR 2005, LNCS 3757, pp. 645–660, 2005.

man [15], who proposed a trinocular constraint for matching line segments arising from polygonal edge linking. The main idea is that a 3D point and its tangent reconstructed from a pair of potentially corresponding points and tangents in two views determine a point and tangent in a third view, which can be compared to observations; see also [16, 17, 18]. Robert and Faugeras [19] extended Ayache's method of transferring points and tangents from two views to a third to include curvature: 3D curvature and normal can be reconstructed from 2D curvatures at two views, which in turn determine the curvature in a third view. This leads to improved precision and density in the reconstruction since curvature provides an additional constraint and reinforces figural continuity in propagating strong hypotheses to neighboring curve samples. This allows then to discard the use of heuristics such as the ordering constraint [20]. Schmid and Zisserman [21] also derived a formula for transferring curvatures from two views to a third, using a projective geometry formalism in which the osculating circle is transfered as a conic.

Li and Zucker [8] derived formulas for the curvature of a projected curve from the curvature of a 3D space curve. They also derived a system of linear equations for reconstructing 3D curvature from 2D, as previously done by Faugeras [19], but with a different proof. Their stereo method assesses the compatibility of *two* neighboring point-tangent-curvature matches according to a cost, which is then minimized through relaxation labeling. While tangents and curvatures can be reconstructed, torsion cannot be constrained. Therefore their process minimizes the torsion of the resulting 3D curve, assuming real-world curves tend to have low variation.

The motivation underlying the use of differential geometry in matching curves across views can be described as follows. Consider a curve $\gamma_1(s)$ in image 1, where s is some length parameter, and which is a projected view of a space curve $\Gamma(s)$.[1] Assuming calibrated cameras are available, what is the space of curves γ_2 which is a projected view of Γ in another camera? In this space, what are the most likely curves to arise? Which curves occur so infrequently that they can be discarded without penalty? The use of such a prior, which is necessary to disambiguate correspondences, can be potentially applied to (*i*) the shape of the second curve γ_2, (*ii*) the variations in depth of the reconstructed space curve Γ from γ_1 [22], or (*iii*) the shape of the space curve. It is our position that limiting the shape of γ_2 or the depth variation of Γ would both rule out some practically occurring situations, thus leading to significant errors. The least restrictive regularization can be realized by imposing a smoothness constraint directly on the space curve Γ.

The idea of directly regularizing the space curve as a way of constraining the correspondences was proposed by Li and Zucker [8], who suggested minimizing total torsion and by Kahl and August [23], who suggested minimizing total curvature. The idea of minimizing total curvature is an extension of "elastica" priors on 2D curves [24, 25]. One can view this as limiting second-order derivatives of the curve. Consider the Taylor expansion of Γ to the third order:

---

[1] We assume Γ does not change with views, as arising from a sharp ridge or a reflectance edge.

$$\boldsymbol{\Gamma}(\tilde{S}) = \boldsymbol{\Gamma}_0 + \tilde{S}\boldsymbol{T}_0 + \frac{\tilde{S}^2}{2}K_0\boldsymbol{N}_0 + \frac{\tilde{S}^3}{6}\left[-K_0^2\boldsymbol{T}_0 + \dot{K}_0\boldsymbol{N}_0 + K_0\tau_0\boldsymbol{B}_0\right] + \boldsymbol{O}(\tilde{S}^4) \ ,$$

$$(1.1)$$

where $\tilde{S}$ is arc-length along $\boldsymbol{\Gamma}$, $(\boldsymbol{T}_0, \boldsymbol{B}_0, \boldsymbol{N}_0)$ is the Frenet frame at point $\boldsymbol{\Gamma}_0$, K_0, $\dot{K}_0$ τ_0 are curvature, curvature derivative, and torsion, respectively. Then, minimizing $\int \|\boldsymbol{\Gamma}''(\tilde{S})\|^2 d\tilde{S}$ gives the elastica in 3D. We will argue below that this is too restrictive as it penalizes rapidly turning space curves, and it is more appropriate to minimize $\int \|\boldsymbol{\Gamma}'''(\tilde{S})\|^2 d\tilde{S}$. The third derivative motivates considering the relationship between torsion and curvature derivative of the space curve with the curvature derivative of the projected curve.

The idea that the use of curvature alone is too restrictive can be illustrated by the problem of curve completion in 2D, where the completion of the gap between a near pair of point-tangents (edgels) requires more than a circle (constant curvature). It was shown in [26] that an Euler spiral segment (in which curvature derivative is constant but not necessarily zero) can interpolate any pair of point-tangent pairs, resulting in intuitive completion curves. In the case of multiview reconstruction, a hypothetically corresponding pair of point-tangent pairs in another image can be interpolated in each image using the Euler spiral, resulting in both curvature and curvature variation, which when reconstructed give curvature, curvature derivative, and torsion, i.e., the full elements of a third-order approximation are available, and $\|\boldsymbol{\Gamma}'''(s)\|$ can be used as the regularization term. The requirement that curvature derivatives across views be related to reconstructed curvature derivative and torsion of the space curve is a motivation of this paper.

Li and Zucker extended the idea of cocircularity of a pair of edge elements, used in a relaxation framework for edge linking, to compatibility of two point-tangent (edge) pairs in stereo, with one pair in one view (potentially) corresponding to a pair in another view. They use an osculating circle approximation for the 3D point underlying the first edge correspondence. The compatibility of a match pair is taken as the degree in which this planar local approximation is consistent with the other match. By doing this, they argue, torsion of the reconstructed space curve, which accounts for its non-planarity, is being minimized. The idea of minimizing torsion is obtained by taking the dominant element in the Taylor expansion along each of the directions of the Frenet frame separately. Specifically, reorganizing the terms of Equation 1.1 by direction:

$$\boldsymbol{\Gamma}(\tilde{S}) = \boldsymbol{\Gamma}_0 + \left(\tilde{S} - \frac{\tilde{S}^3}{6}K_0^2\right)\boldsymbol{T}_0 + \left(\frac{\tilde{S}^2}{2}K_0 + \frac{\tilde{S}^3}{6}\dot{K}_0\right)\boldsymbol{N}_0 + \frac{\tilde{S}^3}{6}K_0\tau_0\boldsymbol{B}_0 + \boldsymbol{O}(\tilde{S}^4) \ ,$$

$$(1.2)$$

and taking only the dominant terms in each one, they get:

$$\boldsymbol{\Gamma}(\tilde{S}) \approx \boldsymbol{\Gamma}_0 + \tilde{S}\boldsymbol{T}_0 + \frac{\tilde{S}^2}{2}K_0\boldsymbol{N}_0 + \frac{\tilde{S}^3}{6}K_0\tau_0\boldsymbol{B}_0 \ ,$$

$$(1.3)$$

which also appears in [27, 28]. We believe that the independent approximation along each direction ignores the interaction among them: third order changes are along a vector not typically aligned with B_0, see Equation (1.1). Curvature and its derivative play roles along with torsion in the reconstruction. In Sect. 3, we show how to obtain a full third-order Taylor expansion for the space curve given third-order expansions in its perspective projections.

The above ideas can also be intuitively expressed by taking a sequence of ordered points along a curve in one view and a corresponding sequence on a corresponding curve in another view. Assuming that the points are closely spaced, a pair of points approximates the curve tangent, a triplet approximates curvature, and a quadruplet of points approximates curvature derivative. We can illustrate the interaction of correspondence ambiguity among n-tuples of ordered points in two views as follows.

Consider a pair of images to be matched, taken from arbitrary viewpoints. Given a point in one image, Fig. 1(a) illustrates the ambiguity in selecting a match in the right image, which is along the epipolar line and its vicinity (a neighborhood around the epipolar line arises from discretization, calibration, and other errors, but is not drawn here for simplicity). Points $(A_1, A_2, \ldots, A_n)$ are all equally good matches for A. Consider now a neighboring point B to A on the curve, as in Fig. 1(b). Given a particular selection for A's corresponding point, say A_1, any selection for B's mate is possible. Certain choices, however, are more likely than others based on limiting orientation disparity [29, 2, 30]. Although limiting the choice of tangents does reduce ambiguity, it also rules out a portion of practically occurring cases, thus leading to errors.

Similarly, as in Fig. 1(c), given corresponding points for both A and B, any selection from the epipolar line corresponding to C is a suitable match for C, but again certain choices are more likely. Since three nearby points deter-

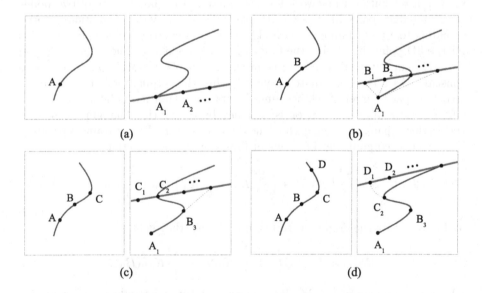

Fig. 1. Matching with differential constraints

mine curvature, limiting curvature disparity or limiting the total curvature [23] of the reconstructed curve places a measure of suitability for each potential match. However, in analogy to [26], where penalizing total curvature of completion curves (elastica) can lead to unintuitive completion curves, penalizing total curvature could also lead to reconstruction errors in the vicinity of highly curving space curves. Continuing this process by considering a fourth point D, and given corresponding points for A, B, and C, as shown in Fig. 1(d), it is again clear that all selections from the epipolar line corresponding to D are theoretically possible, but most selections are extremely unlikely. Four nearby points determine curvature derivatives in the image curve in each view, both intrinsic quantities. Limiting the third-order properties of the reconstructed curve allows for a significant variety of space curves while regularizing the choice of correspondences.

The above discrete picture illustrates the idea that placing shape priors on low-order derivatives is limiting because they are broadly-tuned, while the prior becomes narrowly-turned in higher-order derivatives. What limits the process is the fact that computing high-order derivatives can be numerically challenging. In our previous work, we have been able to compute third-order derivatives such as curvature derivatives and torsion stably using ENO schemes [31, 32], see Fig. 2.

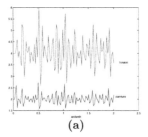
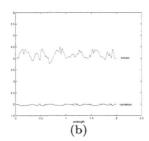

(a)   (b)

Fig. 2. (From [31]). Curvature and torsion versus arc-length using ordinary difference scheme (a), and using ENO scheme (b), using 100 points on a helix ($K = 2$ and $\tau = 4$).

We should emphasize that attributing points with differential geometric signatures such as tangents, curvatures, curvature derivative, etc., does not by itself disambiguate correspondences using only two views. That these attributes provide no direct constraints in two views was shown for tangent and curvature in [19], and it will be shown here for curvature derivative (which corresponds to the space curve torsion). However, a constraint can be obtained in two ways. One is when at least three views of the same point are available, in which case tangents in two views determine the tangent in a third view [15, 19, 7], curvatures in two views determine the curvature in a third view [19, 21, 7], and, as will be shown here, curvature derivatives in two views determine the curvature derivative in a third view; see Sect. 3. Another way to impose a constraint is when a *pair* of neighboring points on one curve can be found in correspondence to another pair of points on a corresponding curve in another view, as discussed above.

The main contribution of this paper is theoretical. First, we derive a relationship between curvature derivatives of projected curves and curvature derivative and torsion of the underlying space curve. Second, we show how the latter quantities can be reconstructed from two views. Third, we show how curvature derivative in two views can determine curvature derivative in a third view. Finally, we show how to relate parametrization of projected curves to each other and to the parametrization of the space curve. In the process, we give new derivations for the results of [8, 7] in a simpler way that easily generalize to higher orders.

2   Background and Notation

The multiple view formulation consists of n pinhole camera models as shown in Fig. 3. All vectors are written with respect to a common, global frame with origin O (the world coordinates). The i-th image, $i = 1, \ldots, n$, has camera center $c_i(c_i^x, c_i^y, c_i^z)$, unit focal vector $\boldsymbol{F}_i$, and focal length f_i. For simplicity, without loss of generality we assume $f_i = 1$.[2]

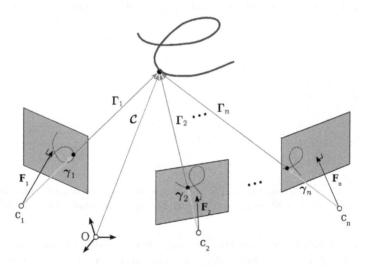

Fig. 3. The projection of a space curve in n views

A 3D space curve $\boldsymbol{C}$ is a mapping $S \mapsto \boldsymbol{C}(S)$ from $\mathbb{R}$ to $\mathbb{R}^3$, where S is an arbitrary parameter. The arc-length parameter along $\boldsymbol{C}$ is denoted by $\tilde{S}$. We define $\boldsymbol{\Gamma}_i := \boldsymbol{C} - \boldsymbol{c}_i$, namely the curve coordinates relative to a camera center. We refer to the local Frenet frame of the space curve $\boldsymbol{C}$ by tangent $\boldsymbol{T}$, normal

---

[2] Since in theory we are working in global coordinates and with intrinsic measures, the size and orientation of the retinas need only be explicitly specified when translating image coordinates to world coordinates and vice-versa in the implementation.

$\boldsymbol{N}$, binormal $\boldsymbol{B}$, and let K and τ denote its curvature and torsion, respectively. Then, by classical differential geometry [33], we have:

$$
\begin{cases}
G = \|\boldsymbol{\Gamma}'\| \\[2mm]
\boldsymbol{T} = \dfrac{\boldsymbol{\Gamma}'}{G} \qquad \boldsymbol{N} = \dfrac{\boldsymbol{T}'}{\|\boldsymbol{T}'\|} \qquad \boldsymbol{B} = \boldsymbol{T} \times \boldsymbol{N} \\[4mm]
K = \dfrac{\|\boldsymbol{T}'\|}{G} \qquad \dot{K} = \dfrac{K'}{G} \qquad \tau = \dfrac{-\boldsymbol{B}' \cdot \boldsymbol{N}}{G} \;,
\end{cases}
\tag{2.1}
$$

where v' indicates differentiation of v with respect to an arbitrary parameter throughout this paper. We use $\dot{v}$ to denote differentiation with respect to arc-length *of the curve to which v refers to*, depending on the context. The chain rule relates $\dot{v}$ and v':

$$
v' = G\dot{v} \;,
\tag{2.2}
$$

using $G = \frac{d\tilde{S}}{dS}$. The Frenet equations are given by:

$$
\begin{bmatrix} \boldsymbol{T}' \\ \boldsymbol{N}' \\ \boldsymbol{B}' \end{bmatrix} = G \begin{bmatrix} 0 & K & 0 \\ -K & 0 & \tau \\ 0 & -\tau & 0 \end{bmatrix} \begin{bmatrix} \boldsymbol{T} \\ \boldsymbol{N} \\ \boldsymbol{B} \end{bmatrix} \;.
\tag{2.3}
$$

Similarly, a 2D curve $\boldsymbol{\gamma}_i$ in image i is a mapping $s \mapsto \boldsymbol{\gamma}_i(s)$ from $\mathbb{R}$ to $\mathbb{R}^2$, where s is an arbitrary parameter and $\tilde{s}$ denotes the arc-length parameter. The curve will have speed g_i, tangent $\boldsymbol{t}_i$, normal $\boldsymbol{n}_i$, and curvature k_i. All formulas in Equations (2.1) and (2.3) apply also to $\boldsymbol{\gamma}_i$ by setting $\tau = 0$. We drop the index i on vectors related to any particular camera when the index is not necessary.

The space curve and a projected image curve are related by:

$$
\boldsymbol{\Gamma}(s) = \lambda(s)\boldsymbol{\gamma}(s) \;,
\tag{2.4}
$$

where λ is a positive scalar. Since the curve $\boldsymbol{\gamma}$ lies in the image plane with normal $\boldsymbol{F}$,

$$
(\boldsymbol{\gamma} - \boldsymbol{F}) \cdot \boldsymbol{F} = 0 \;.
\tag{2.5}
$$

Therefore,

$$
\begin{cases} \boldsymbol{\gamma} \cdot \boldsymbol{F} = 1 \\ \boldsymbol{\Gamma} \cdot \boldsymbol{F} = \lambda \;, \end{cases}
\tag{2.6}
$$

which, by substituting in (2.4), gives

$$
\boldsymbol{\gamma} = \frac{\boldsymbol{\Gamma}}{\boldsymbol{\Gamma} \cdot \boldsymbol{F}} \;.
\tag{2.7}
$$

The latter formula shows how to project points using our notation (without any change in the coordinate system). We also note that

$$
\begin{cases} \boldsymbol{\gamma}^{(i)} \cdot \boldsymbol{F} = 0 \\ \boldsymbol{\Gamma}^{(i)} \cdot \boldsymbol{F} = \lambda^{(i)} \;, \end{cases}
\tag{2.8}
$$

where $\gamma^{(i)}$ is the ith derivative of γ, for any positive integer i.

The reconstruction of a point on the space curve $\mathcal{C}$ from two corresponding image curve points $\gamma_1 = (x_1, y_1, z_1)$ and $\gamma_2 = (x_2, y_2, z_2)$ can be obtained by equating two expressions for $\mathcal{C} = \Gamma_i + c_i$, with Γ_i given by (2.4)

$$\begin{cases} \mathcal{C} = c_1 + \lambda_1 \gamma_1 \\ \mathcal{C} = c_2 + \lambda_2 \gamma_2 \end{cases}$$

thus

$$\gamma_1 \lambda_1 - \gamma_2 \lambda_2 = c_2 - c_1 \tag{2.9}$$

or, more explicitly,

$$\begin{cases} x_1 \lambda_1 - x_2 \lambda_2 = c_2^x - c_1^x \\ y_1 \lambda_1 - y_2 \lambda_2 = c_2^y - c_1^y \\ z_1 \lambda_1 - z_2 \lambda_2 = c_2^z - c_1^z \end{cases}$$

It is well-known that this system of three equations in two unknowns λ_1 and λ_2 can only be solved if the lines $c_1 \gamma_1$ and $c_2 \gamma_2$ intersect. Also note that $\gamma_1 \times \gamma_2$ is a normal to the epipolar plane, which is defined by three points c_1, c_2, and Γ.

3   Multiview Differential Geometry of Curves

We follow a *direct* route to relating the intrinsic entities between the space curve and its perspective views. The main idea is to express $\Gamma^{(i)}$ first in terms of the differential geometry attributes of $\mathcal{C}$, namely $T, N, K, \dot{K}, \tau$, and, second, using $\Gamma = \lambda \gamma$, write $\Gamma^{(i)}$ in terms of the differential geometry attributes of γ, namely $t, n, k, \dot{k}$. In equating these two expressions we relate $T, N, B, K, \dot{K}, \tau$ to $t, n, k, \dot{k}$. Our purpose is to eliminate the dependence on the parametrizations, which means that our final expressions cannot contain unknowns $g^{(i)}$, $G^{(i)}$, depth scalar λ, and its derivatives $\lambda^{(i)}$, for all i.

Lemma 1. *The following equations relate T, N, B, K, $\dot{K}$, τ, and $G^{(i)}$ to γ, t, n, k, $\dot{k}$, $g^{(i)}$, and $\lambda^{(i)}$:*

$$\begin{cases} GT = \lambda' \gamma + \lambda g t & (3.1) \\ G'T + G^2 KN = \lambda'' \gamma + (2\lambda' g + \lambda g')t + \lambda g^2 kn & (3.2) \\ (G'' - G^3 K^2)T + (3GG'K + G^3 \dot{K})N + G^3 K\tau B = \\ \lambda''' \gamma + [3\lambda'' g + 3\lambda' g' + \lambda(g'' - g^3 k^2)]t + [3\lambda' g^2 k + \lambda(3gg'k + g^3 \dot{k})]n & (3.3) \end{cases}$$

Proof. First, writing $\Gamma^{(i)}$ in the Frenet frame of Γ, we have:

$$\begin{cases} \Gamma' = GT & (3.4) \\ \Gamma'' = G'T + G^2 KN & (3.5) \\ \Gamma''' = (G'' - G^3 K^2)T + (3GG'K + G^2 K')N + G^3 K\tau B \ , & (3.6) \end{cases}$$

which, when expressed with respect to the arc-length of $\boldsymbol{\Gamma}$, i.e., $G \equiv 1$, yield:

$$\begin{cases} \dot{\boldsymbol{\Gamma}} = \boldsymbol{T} & (3.7) \\ \ddot{\boldsymbol{\Gamma}} = K\boldsymbol{N} & (3.8) \\ \dddot{\boldsymbol{\Gamma}} = -K^2\boldsymbol{T} + \dot{K}\boldsymbol{N} + K\tau\boldsymbol{B} \ . & (3.9) \end{cases}$$

Second, differentiating $\boldsymbol{\Gamma} = \lambda\boldsymbol{\gamma}$ gives:

$$\begin{cases} \boldsymbol{\Gamma}' = \lambda'\boldsymbol{\gamma} + \lambda\boldsymbol{\gamma}' & (3.10) \\ \boldsymbol{\Gamma}'' = \lambda''\boldsymbol{\gamma} + 2\lambda'\boldsymbol{\gamma}' + \lambda\boldsymbol{\gamma}'' & (3.11) \\ \boldsymbol{\Gamma}''' = \lambda'''\boldsymbol{\gamma} + 3\lambda''\boldsymbol{\gamma}' + 3\lambda'\boldsymbol{\gamma}'' + \lambda\boldsymbol{\gamma}''' \ . & (3.12) \end{cases}$$

This can be rewritten using expressions for the derivatives of $\boldsymbol{\gamma}$, i.e. $\boldsymbol{\gamma}^{(i)}$, which are obtained by the product rule of differentiation and Frenet equations:

$$\begin{cases} \boldsymbol{\gamma}' = g\boldsymbol{t} & (3.13) \\ \boldsymbol{\gamma}'' = g'\boldsymbol{t} + g^2k\boldsymbol{n} & (3.14) \\ \boldsymbol{\gamma}''' = (g'' - g^3k^2)\boldsymbol{t} + (3gg'k + g^2k')\boldsymbol{n} \ . & (3.15) \end{cases}$$

Thus, $\boldsymbol{\Gamma}^{(i)}$ can be written in terms of $\boldsymbol{\gamma}, \boldsymbol{t}, \boldsymbol{n}, k, \dot{k}, \lambda^{(i)}, g^{(i)}$:

$$\begin{cases} \boldsymbol{\Gamma}' = \lambda'\boldsymbol{\gamma} + \lambda g\boldsymbol{t} & (3.16) \\ \boldsymbol{\Gamma}'' = \lambda''\boldsymbol{\gamma} + (2\lambda'g + \lambda g')\boldsymbol{t} + \lambda g^2k\boldsymbol{n} & (3.17) \\ \boldsymbol{\Gamma}''' = \lambda'''\boldsymbol{\gamma} + [3\lambda''g + 3\lambda'g' + \lambda(g'' - g^3k^2)]\boldsymbol{t} \\ \qquad + [3\lambda'g^2k + \lambda(3gg'k + g^3\dot{k})]\boldsymbol{n} \ , & (3.18) \end{cases}$$

where we used $k' = g\dot{k}$. Equating (3.4-3.6) and (3.16-3.18) proves the lemma. $\square$

Corolary 1. *Using the arc-length $\tilde{S}$ of the space curve as the common parameter, i.e., when $G \equiv 1$, we have:*

$$\begin{cases} \boldsymbol{T} = \lambda'\boldsymbol{\gamma} + \lambda g\boldsymbol{t} & (3.19) \\ K\boldsymbol{N} = \lambda''\boldsymbol{\gamma} + (2\lambda'g + \lambda g')\boldsymbol{t} + \lambda g^2k\boldsymbol{n} & (3.20) \\ -K^2\boldsymbol{T} + \dot{K}\boldsymbol{N} + K\tau\boldsymbol{B} = \lambda'''\boldsymbol{\gamma} + [3\lambda''g + 3\lambda'g' + \lambda(g'' - g^3k^2)]\boldsymbol{t} \\ \qquad + [3\lambda'g^2k + \lambda(3gg'k + g^3\dot{k})]\boldsymbol{n} \ , & (3.21) \end{cases}$$

where the right hand side uses the notation $v' = \frac{dv}{d\tilde{S}}$ and $\dot{v} = \frac{dv}{d\tilde{s}}$.

We are now in a position to relate first-order differential attributes of the space curve $(G, \boldsymbol{T})$ with those of an image curve $(g, \boldsymbol{T})$. Note from (3.1) or (3.19) that $\boldsymbol{T}$ lies on the plane spanned by $\boldsymbol{t}$ and $\boldsymbol{\gamma}$, i.e., $\boldsymbol{T}$ is a linear combination of these vectors. An exact relationship is expressed bellow.

Theorem 2. *Given the tangent T at Γ, when T is not aligned with γ, then the corresponding tangent t and normal n at γ are determined by:*

$$t = \frac{T - (T \cdot F)\gamma}{\|T - (T \cdot F)\gamma\|} \tag{3.22}$$

$$n = t \times F \tag{3.23}$$

Proof. From Equation (3.1), we have:

$$T = \frac{1}{G}\left[\lambda'\gamma + \lambda g t\right]$$

$$= \frac{1}{G}\left[(\Gamma' \cdot F)\gamma + \lambda g t\right] \tag{3.24}$$

$$= \left(\frac{\Gamma'}{G} \cdot F\right)\gamma + \lambda\frac{g}{G} t \tag{3.25}$$

$$= (T \cdot F)\gamma + \lambda\frac{g}{G} t , \tag{3.26}$$

thus

$$\lambda\frac{g}{G} t = T - (T \cdot F)\gamma \tag{3.27}$$

and the result follows. The formula for the normal comes from the fact that it lies in the image plane, therefore being orthogonal to both t and F. □

Observe that the depth scale factor λ is not needed to find t from T. Moreover, when γ and T are aligned for a point on a segment of the curve, then Equation (3.27) still holds, implying that $g = 0$ and t is undefined, i.e., that the image curve will have stationary points and possibly corners or cusps. Stationary points are in principle not detectable from the trace of γ alone, but by the assumption of general position these do not concern us.

A quantity that is crucial in relating differential geometry along the space curve with that of the projected image curve is the ratio of speed of parametrizations $\frac{g}{G}(s)$. According to the following theorem, this quantity is intrinsic in that it does not depend on either $g(s)$ or $G(s)$ at each arbitrary s.

Theorem 3. *The ratio of speeds of the projected 2D curve g and of the 3D curve G with respect to the same parameter is an intrinsic quantity:*

$$\frac{g}{G} = \frac{\|T - (T \cdot F)\gamma\|}{\Gamma \cdot F} , \tag{3.28}$$

i.e., it does not depend on the parametrization of Γ or of γ.

Proof. Follows from (3.27). □

Corollary 4. *The speed of an image curve in terms of the arc-length of the space curve, and vice-versa, are respectively given by:*

$$g(\tilde{S}) = \frac{\|T - (T \cdot F)\gamma\|}{\Gamma \cdot F} , \qquad G(\tilde{s}) = \frac{\Gamma \cdot F}{\|T - (T \cdot F)\gamma\|} . \tag{3.29}$$

Thus the arclengths of the image and space curves can be expressed as:

$$\tilde{s}(\tilde{S}) = \int_{\tilde{S}_0}^{\tilde{S}} g(\tilde{S}) \, d\tilde{S} \ , \qquad\qquad \tilde{S}(\tilde{s}) = \int_{\tilde{s}_0}^{\tilde{s}} G(\tilde{s}) \, d\tilde{s} \ . \tag{3.30}$$

Proof. Set $g(\tilde{s}) = 1$ or $G(\tilde{S}) = 1$ in (3.28). □

Corolary 5. *Given two views of a 3D space curve the ratio of velocities in the two views at corresponding points is given by:*

$$\frac{g_1}{g_2} = \frac{\lambda_2}{\lambda_1} \frac{\|T - (T \cdot F_1)\gamma_1\|}{\|T - (T \cdot F_2)\gamma_2\|} \ . \tag{3.31}$$

Proof. Follows by dividing expressions for $\frac{g_1}{G}$ and $\frac{g_2}{G}$. □

Note from Equation (3.27) that the vector T lies on the half-plane spanned by t and γ, i.e., it is a linear combination:

$$T = at + b\gamma \ , \tag{3.32}$$

with $a \geq 0$. Thus the reconstruction of T from t requires one additional parameter since T is a unit vector. This can be provided from the tangent at the corresponding point, as shown in the next theorem.

Theorem 6. *Given tangent vectors at a pair of corresponding points, namely t_1 at γ_1 and t_2 at γ_2, the corresponding space tangent T at Γ is given by:*

$$\varepsilon T = \frac{(t_1 \times \gamma_1) \times (t_2 \times \gamma_2)}{\|(t_1 \times \gamma_1) \times (t_2 \times \gamma_2)\|} \qquad\qquad \varepsilon = \pm 1 \tag{3.33}$$

whenever t_1 and t_2 are not both in the epipolar plane. The sign of ε can be found by projecting εT onto the retinas and comparing to the orientation of t_1 and t_2 there. More explicitly, ε is such that the following inequations are satisfied:

$$\begin{cases} [\varepsilon T - (\varepsilon T \cdot F_1)\gamma_1] \cdot t_1 > 0 \\ [\varepsilon T - (\varepsilon T \cdot F_2)\gamma_2] \cdot t_2 > 0 \ . \end{cases} \tag{3.34}$$

Proof. From Equation (3.19) we have that T lies in two planes having normals $\gamma_1 \times t_1$ and $\gamma_2 \times t_2$, as illustrated in Fig. 4. Formally:

$$\begin{cases} T \cdot (\gamma_1 \times t_1) = 0 \\ T \cdot (\gamma_2 \times t_2) = 0 \ . \end{cases} \tag{3.35}$$

Thus, when the two planes are not parallel, T must be proportional to $(\gamma_1 \times t_1) \times (\gamma_2 \times t_2)$, from which the formula follows. Furthermore, when the two planes are parallel, they are equal to the epipolar plane since they will both pass through Γ, c_1 and c_2. So there would be infinitely many possible space tangents, solutions to the above system, that projects to the image tangents. □

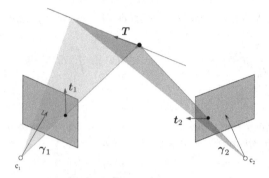

Fig. 4. 3D Tangent reconstruction from two views as the intersection of two planes

This theorem implies that *any* two tangents at corresponding points can be consistent with at least one space tangent. Similarly, curvatures of the space curve and of an image curve can be related, as shown by the next theorem.

Theorem 7. *The curvature k of a projected image curve is given by:*

$$k = \left[\frac{N - (N \cdot F)\gamma}{\lambda g^2} \cdot n \right] K \tag{3.36}$$

or

$$k = \left[\frac{N \cdot (\gamma \times t)}{\lambda g^2 \; n \cdot (\gamma \times t)} \right] K \; , \tag{3.37}$$

where $g = g(\tilde{S})$ is given by (3.29), and $\lambda = \boldsymbol{\Gamma} \cdot \boldsymbol{F}$.

Proof. From Equation (3.20), we have:

$$KN = \lambda'' \gamma + (2\lambda' g + \lambda g')t + \lambda g^2 kn \tag{3.38}$$

$$= (\ddot{\boldsymbol{\Gamma}} \cdot \boldsymbol{F})\gamma + 2(\dot{\boldsymbol{\Gamma}} \cdot \boldsymbol{F})gt + \lambda g't + \lambda g^2 kn \tag{3.39}$$

$$= K(N \cdot F)\gamma + 2(T \cdot F)gt + \lambda g't + \lambda g^2 kn \; . \tag{3.40}$$

We can isolate k by taking the dot product of the last equation with n which gives the curvature projection formula (3.36). Alternatively, taking the dot product with $\gamma \times t$ also isolates k, giving the variant (3.37). □

Theorem 8. *The normal vector and curvature of a point on a space curve with point-tangent-curvature at projections in two views (γ_1, t_1, k_1) and (γ_2, t_2, k_2) is given by solving the following system in the vector $\boldsymbol{NK}$:*

$$\begin{cases} (\gamma_1 \times t_1) \cdot \boldsymbol{NK} = n_1 \cdot (\gamma_1 \times t_1)\lambda_1 g_1^2 \, k_1 \\ (\gamma_2 \times t_2) \cdot \boldsymbol{NK} = n_2 \cdot (\gamma_2 \times t_2)\lambda_2 g_2^2 \, k_2 \\ \qquad\quad T \cdot \boldsymbol{NK} = 0 \; , \end{cases} \tag{3.41}$$

where T, g_1, and g_2 are obtained by previous derivations.

Proof. Taking the dot product of (3.40) with $\boldsymbol{\gamma} \times \boldsymbol{t}$, and applying the resulting equation for two views, we arrive at the first two equations. The third equation imposes the solution $\boldsymbol{N}K$ to be normal to $\boldsymbol{T}$.   □

Note that formulas for the projection of 3D tangent and curvatures onto 2D tangent and geodesic curvature appear in [34] and [35–pp. 73–75], but an actual image curvature was not determined there. That the curvature of the space curve is related to the curvature of the projected curve was derived in previous work [8, 19], but our proof is direct and much simpler. Moreover, our proof methodology generalizes to relating higher order derivatives such as curvature derivative and torsion, as shown below. Before we proceed, however, an explicit formula for tangential acceleration will prove useful in proofs.

Theorem 9. *The tangential acceleration of a projected curve with respect to the arc length of the space curve is given by:*

$$\frac{dg}{d\tilde{S}} = \frac{[\boldsymbol{N} - (\boldsymbol{N} \cdot \boldsymbol{F})\boldsymbol{\gamma}] \cdot \boldsymbol{t}\,K}{\lambda} - 2g\frac{\boldsymbol{T} \cdot \boldsymbol{F}}{\lambda} \ , \tag{3.42}$$

or

$$\frac{dg}{d\tilde{S}} = \frac{K\boldsymbol{N} \cdot (\boldsymbol{\gamma} \times \boldsymbol{n})}{\lambda \boldsymbol{t} \cdot (\boldsymbol{\gamma} \times \boldsymbol{n})} - 2g\frac{\boldsymbol{T} \cdot \boldsymbol{F}}{\lambda} \ . \tag{3.43}$$

Proof. By taking the dot product of Equation (3.40) with $\boldsymbol{t}$ and isolating g', we get the first formula. The second expression is obtained by instead taking the dot product with $\boldsymbol{\gamma} \times \boldsymbol{n}$.   □

Theorem 10. *The curvature derivative at a point of a projected image curve $\boldsymbol{\gamma}$ is derived from the local differential geometry of the space curve as follows:*

$$\dot{k} = \frac{(\dot{K}\boldsymbol{N} + K\tau\boldsymbol{B}) \cdot (\boldsymbol{\gamma} \times \boldsymbol{t})}{\lambda g^3 \boldsymbol{n} \cdot (\boldsymbol{\gamma} \times \boldsymbol{t})} - 3k\left(\frac{\boldsymbol{T} \cdot \boldsymbol{F}}{\lambda g} + \frac{g'}{g^2}\right) \ , \tag{3.44}$$

where by our notation $g' = \frac{dg}{d\tilde{S}}$, and $\dot{k} = \frac{dk}{d\tilde{s}}$, and $\dot{K} = \frac{dk}{d\tilde{S}}$.

Proof. Taking the scalar product of (3.21) with $\boldsymbol{\gamma} \times \boldsymbol{t}$, and using $\boldsymbol{T} \cdot (\boldsymbol{\gamma} \times \boldsymbol{t}) = 0$, we have:

$$(\dot{K}\boldsymbol{N} + K\tau\boldsymbol{B}) \cdot (\boldsymbol{\gamma} \times \boldsymbol{t}) = [3\lambda' g^2 k + \lambda(3gg'k + g^3\dot{k})]\boldsymbol{n} \cdot (\boldsymbol{\gamma} \times \boldsymbol{t}) \tag{3.45}$$

thus

$$3\lambda' g^2 k + \lambda(3gg'k + g^3\dot{k}) = \frac{(\dot{K}\boldsymbol{N} + K\tau\boldsymbol{B}) \cdot (\boldsymbol{\gamma} \times \boldsymbol{t})}{\boldsymbol{n} \cdot (\boldsymbol{\gamma} \times \boldsymbol{t})} \ . \tag{3.46}$$

After isolating $\dot{k}$, we use $\lambda' = \frac{d\lambda}{d\tilde{S}} = \dot{\boldsymbol{\Gamma}} \cdot \boldsymbol{F} = \boldsymbol{T} \cdot \boldsymbol{F}$ to get the final formula.   □

This result shows how torsion and curvature derivative of the space curve are related to curvature derivative of a projected image curve. The next theorem shows the inverse problem, namely how to reconstruct torsion and curvature derivative given a third order approximation of two image curves.

Theorem 11. *Given point, tangent, curvature, and curvature derivative measures on two perspective projections of a space curve, the torsion and curvature derivative at the corresponding point of the space curve can be obtained by first solving the following system in* $\mathbf{V}$:

$$\begin{cases} (\boldsymbol{\gamma}_1 \times \boldsymbol{t}_1) \cdot \mathbf{V} = [3g_1^2 k_1 \boldsymbol{T} \cdot \boldsymbol{F}_1 + \lambda_1(3g_1 g_1' k_1 + g_1^3 \dot{k}_1)]\boldsymbol{n}_1 \cdot (\boldsymbol{\gamma}_1 \times \boldsymbol{t}_1) \\ (\boldsymbol{\gamma}_2 \times \boldsymbol{t}_2) \cdot \mathbf{V} = [3g_2^2 k_2 \boldsymbol{T} \cdot \boldsymbol{F}_2 + \lambda_2(3g_2 g_2' k_2 + g_2^3 \dot{k}_2)]\boldsymbol{n}_2 \cdot (\boldsymbol{\gamma}_2 \times \boldsymbol{t}_2) \qquad (3.47) \\ \qquad \boldsymbol{T} \cdot \mathbf{V} = 0 \ , \end{cases}$$

with $\boldsymbol{T}$, $\boldsymbol{N}$, $\boldsymbol{B}$, K, g_i, g_i', *and* λ_i *determined from previous derivations. Then, the torsion* τ *and curvature derivative* $\dot{K}$ *of the space curve are given by solving for* $\dot{K}$ *and* τ *from* $\mathbf{V} = \dot{K}\boldsymbol{N} + K\tau\boldsymbol{B}$:

$$\begin{cases} \tau = \dfrac{\mathbf{V} \cdot \boldsymbol{B}}{K} & (3.48) \\ \dot{K} = \mathbf{V} \cdot \boldsymbol{N} \ . & (3.49) \end{cases}$$

Proof. Apply Equation (3.45) for two views, letting $\mathbf{V} := \dot{K}\boldsymbol{N} + K\tau\boldsymbol{B}$. □

References

1. Marr, D., Poggio, T.: A theory of human stereo vision. Proceedings of the Royal Society of London **B 204** (1979) 301–328
2. Grimson, W.E.L.: A Computer Implementation of a Theory of Human Stereo Vision. Royal Society of London Philosophical Transactions Series B **292** (1981) 217–253
3. Pollard, S.B., Mayhew, J.E.W., Frisby, J.P.: PMF: a stereo correspondence algorithm using a disparity gradient limit. Perception **14** (1985) 449–470
4. Medioni, G., Nevatia, R.: Segment-based stereo matching. CVGIP **31** (1985) 2–18
5. Ayache, N., Faverjon, B.: Efficient registration of stereo images by matching graph descriptions of edge segments. International Journal of Computer Vision **1** (1987) 107–131
6. Zhang, Z.: Token tracking in a cluttered scene. Image Vision Comput. **12** (1994) 110–120
7. Faugeras, O.: Three-Dimensional Computer Vision — A Geometric Viewpoint. Artificial Intelligence. MIT Press, Cambridge, MA, USA (1993)
8. Li, G., Zucker, S.W.: A differential geometrical model for contour-based stereo correspondence. In: Proc. IEEE Workshop on Variational, Geometric, and Level Set Methods in Computer Vision, Nice, France (2003)
9. Quan, L.: Conic reconstruction and correspondence from two views. IEEE Transactions on Pattern Analysis and Machine Intelligence **18** (1996) 151–160
10. Papadopoulo, T., Faugeras, O.D.: Computing structure and motion of general 3D curves from monocular sequences of perspective images. In: Proceedings of the 4th European Conference on Computer Vision, London, UK, Springer-Verlag (1996) 696–708
11. Ma, S.D., Chen, X.: Quadric reconstruction from its occluding contours. In: Proceedings of the International Conference on Pattern Recognition, Jerusalem, Israel (1994)

12. Ma, S.D., Li, L.: Ellipsoid reconstruction from three perspective views. In: Proceedings of the International Conference on Pattern Recognition, Vienna, Austria (1996) 344–348
13. Berthilsson, R., Åström, K., Heyden, A.: Reconstruction of general curves, using factorization and bundle adjustment. International Journal of Computer Vision **41** (2001) 171–182
14. Kaminski, J.Y., Shashua, A.: Multiple view geometry of general algebraic curves. International Journal of Computer Vision **56** (2004) 195–219
15. Ayache, N., Lustman, L.: Fast and reliable passive trinocular stereovision. In: 1st International Conference on Computer Vision. (1987)
16. Spetsakis, M., Aloimonos, J.Y.: A multi-frame approach to visual motion perception. Int. J. Comput. Vision **6** (1991) 245–255
17. Shashua, A.: Trilinearity in visual recognition by alignment. In: Proceedings of the third European conference on Computer vision, Secaucus, NJ, USA, Springer-Verlag (1994) 479–484
18. Hartley, R.I.: A linear method for reconstruction from lines and points. In: Proceedings of the Fifth International Conference on Computer Vision, Boston, Massachusetts, IEEE Computer Society Press (1995) 882–887
19. Robert, L., Faugeras, O.D.: Curve-based stereo: figural continuity and curvature. In: Proceedings of Computer Vision and Pattern Recognition. (1991) 57–62
20. Ohta, Y., Kanade, T.: Stereo by intra- and inter-scanline search using dynamic programming. IEEE Trans. Pattern Analysis and Machine Intelligence **7** (1985) 139–154
21. Schmid, C., Zisserman, A.: The geometry and matching of lines and curves over multiple views. International Journal of Computer Vision **40** (2000) 199–233
22. Robert, L., Deriche, R.: Dense depth map reconstruction: A minimization and regularization approach which preserves discontinuities. In: Fourth European Conference on Computer Vision, Cambridge, England, Springer Verlag (1996) 439–451
23. Kahl, F., August, J.: Multiview reconstruction of space curves. In: Proceedings of the IEEE International Conference on Computer Vision, Washington, DC, USA (2003) 1017
24. Mumford, D.: Elastica and computer vision. In: Algebraic Geometry and Its Applications, Springer-Verlag (1994) 491–506
25. Williams, L., Jacobs, D.: Stochastic completion fields: A neural model of illusory contour shape and salience. Neural Computation **9** (1997) 849–870
26. Kimia, B.B., Frankel, I., Popescu, A.M.: Euler spiral for shape completion. International Journal of Computer Vision **54** (2003) 159–182
27. Zucker, S.W.: 22. Differential Geometry from the Frenet Point of View: Boundary Detection, Stereo, Texture and Color. In: Mathematical Models of Computer Vision: The Handbook. Springer (2005) 361–376 To appear.
28. Alibhai, S., Zucker, S.: Contour-based correspondence for stereo. In: Proc. Sixth European Conf. on Computer Vision, Dublin, Ireland (2000)
29. Arnold, R., Binford, T.: Geometric constraints in stereo vision. In: Proc. SPIE. Volume 238–Image Processing for Missile Guidance., San Diego, CA (1980) 281–292
30. Sherman, D., Peleg, S.: Stereo by incremental matching of contours. IEEE Trans. on Pattern Analylis and Machine Intelligence **12** (1990) 1102–1106
31. Kong, W., Kimia, B.: On solving 2D and 3D puzzles under curve matching. In: Proceedings of the IEEE Computer Society Conference on Computer Vision and Pattern Recognition, Kauai, Hawaii, USA, IEEE Computer Society Press (2001) 583–590

32. Siddiqi, K., Kimia, B.B., Shu, C.: Geometric shock-capturing ENO schemes for subpixel interpolation, computation and curve evolution. Graphical Models and Image Processing **59** (1997) 278–301
33. do Carmo, M.P.: Differential Geometry of Curves and Surfaces. Prentice-Hall, New Jersey (1976)
34. Cipolla, R., Zisserman, A.: Qualitative surface shape from deformation of image curves. International Journal of Computer Vision **8** (1992) 53–69
35. Cipolla, R., Giblin, P.: Visual Motion of Curves and Surfaces. Cambridge University Press (1999)

Appendix: Taylor Expansion of a Space Curve

The (geometric) Taylor expansion of $\boldsymbol{\Gamma}(s)$ for an arbitrary parameter S is

$$\boldsymbol{\Gamma}(S) = \boldsymbol{\Gamma}_0 + S\,G_0\boldsymbol{T}_0 + \frac{1}{2}S^2\left[G_0'\boldsymbol{T}_0 + G_0^2 K_0\boldsymbol{N}_0\right] + \qquad (3.50)$$

$$\frac{1}{6}S^3\left[(G_0'' - G_0^3 K_0^2)\boldsymbol{T}_0 + (3G_0G_0'K_0 + G_0^3\dot{K}_0)\boldsymbol{N}_0 + G_0^3 K_0\tau_0\boldsymbol{B}_0\right] + \boldsymbol{O}(S^4)$$

where the subscript 0 indicates evaluation at $S = 0$. Therefore, where the sampling space is small enough relative to the degree of fourth and higher order variation of the space curve, we expect differential attributes at one sample to predict the corresponding attributes at the adjacent sample. For the first order geometry, we have:

$$\boldsymbol{T}(S) = \boldsymbol{T}_0 + S\boldsymbol{T}_0' + \frac{S^2}{2}\boldsymbol{T}_0'' + \boldsymbol{O}(S^3)$$

$$= \boldsymbol{T}_0 + S\,G_0 K\boldsymbol{N} + \frac{S^2}{2}\left[(G'K + G^2\dot{K})\boldsymbol{N} - G^2 K^2\boldsymbol{T} + G^2 K\tau\boldsymbol{B}\right] + \boldsymbol{O}(S^3)$$

$$(3.51)$$

Similarly, for second order geometry:

$$\begin{cases} \boldsymbol{N}(S) = \boldsymbol{N}_0 + S\,G(-K\boldsymbol{T} + \tau\boldsymbol{B}) + \boldsymbol{O}(S^2) & (3.52) \\ K(S) = K_0 + SG_0\dot{K}_0 + O(S^2) & (3.53) \\ \boldsymbol{B}(S) = \boldsymbol{T}(S) \times \boldsymbol{N}(S) + \boldsymbol{O}(S^2) & (3.54) \end{cases}$$

and for third order:

$$\tau(S) = \tau_0 + O(S) \ . \qquad (3.55)$$

Subject Index

Author Index

Lecture Notes in Computer Science

For information about Vols. 1–3693

please contact your bookseller or Springer